The Martin-Gay Student Success Program

Each Martin-Gay product is motivated by Elayn's firm belief that every student can succeed. This Student Success Program is designed to help students review and retain basic algebra concepts <u>and</u> gain the study skills necessary for success in all levels of mathematics!

Options to support a variety of classroom environments!

MyMathLab® for School

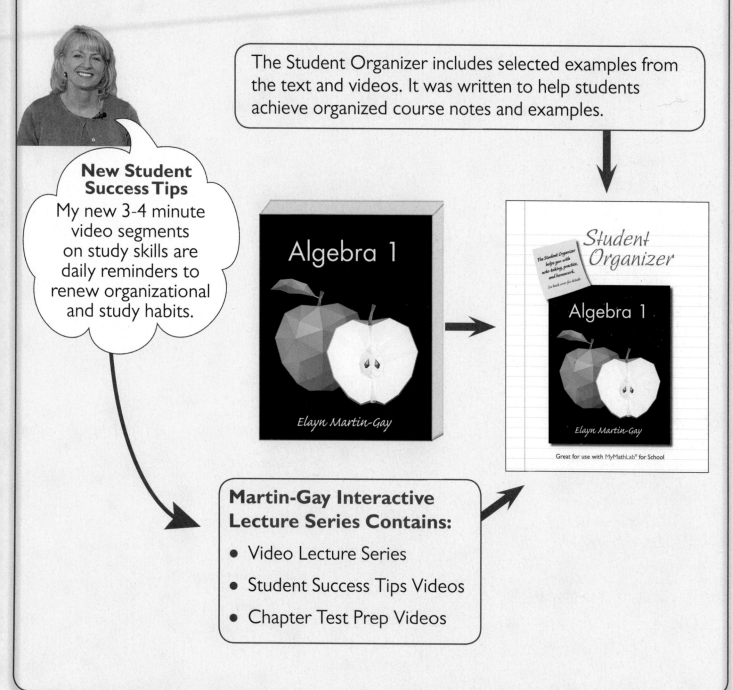

The Student Organizer includes selected examples from the text and videos. It was written to help students achieve organized course notes and examples.

New Student Success Tips
My new 3-4 minute video segments on study skills are daily reminders to renew organizational and study habits.

Algebra 1

Elayn Martin-Gay

Student Organizer

The Student Organizer helps you with note-taking, practice, and homework.

See back cover for details

Algebra 1

Elayn Martin-Gay

Great for use with MyMathLab® for School

Martin-Gay Interactive Lecture Series Contains:

- Video Lecture Series
- Student Success Tips Videos
- Chapter Test Prep Videos

Algebra 1

Elayn Martin-Gay

PEARSON

Boston   Columbus   Hoboken   Indianapolis   New York   San Francisco
Amsterdam   Cape Town   Dubai   London   Madrid   Milan   Munich   Paris   Montréal   Toronto
Delhi   Mexico City   São Paulo   Sydney   Hong Kong   Seoul   Singapore   Taipei   Tokyo

Editorial Director, Mathematics: *Christine Hoag*
Editor-in-Chief: *Michael Hirsch*
Acquisitions Editor: *Mary Beckwith*
Project Manager: *Christine Whitlock*
Project Team Lead: *Peter Silvia*
Assistant Editor: *Matthew Summers*
Editorial Assistant: *Megan Tripp*
Executive Development Editor: *Dawn Nuttall*
Program Team Lead: *Karen Wernholm*
Program Manager: *Patty Bergin*
Cover Design: *Tamara Newnam*
Program Design Lead: *Heather Scott*
Director, Course Production: *Ruth Berry*

Executive Content Manager, MathXL: *Rebecca Williams*
Senior Content Developer, TestGen: *John Flanagan*
Media Producer: *Shana Siegmund/Marielle Guiney*
Executive Marketing Manager: *Jaclyn Flynn*
Director of Marketing, Mathematics: *Roxanne McCarley*
Senior Marketing Manager: *Rachel Ross*
Marketing Assistant: *Kelly Cross*
Senior Author Support/Technology Specialist: *Joe Vetere*
Senior Procurement Specialist: *Carol Melville*
Interior Design, Production Management, Answer Art, and Composition: *Integra Software Services Pvt. Ltd.*
Text Art: *Scientific Illustrators*
Cover Image: *Natalia NK/Shutterstock*

Acknowledgments of third party content appear on pages P1–P4, which constitutes an extension of this copyright page.

Library of Congress Cataloging-in-Publication Data
Martin-Gay, K. Elayn, 1955-
   Algebra 1 / Elayn Martin-Gay, University of New Orleans.—1st edition.
     pages cm
   ISBN 0-13-409389-5 (alk. paper)
1. Mathematics—Textbooks.   2. Mathematics—Study and teaching (Secondary)   I. Title.
II. Title: Algebra one.
   QA135.6.M3655 2016
   512.9—dc23   2015004912

2 3 4 5 6 7 8 9 10—V011—19 18 17 16 15

www.pearsonschool.com

ISBN-10: 0-13-409389-5 (Student Edition)
ISBN-13: 978-0-13-409389-5

Contents

Preface

Algebra 1 was written to provide a solid foundation in algebra for students who might not have previous experience in algebra. Specific care was taken to make sure students have the most up-to-date relevant text preparation for their next mathematics course or for nonmathematical courses that require an understanding of algebraic fundamentals. I have tried to achieve this by writing a user-friendly text that is keyed to objectives and contains many worked-out examples and illustrations. As suggested by AMATYC and the NCTM Standards (plus Addenda), real-life and real-data applications, data interpretation, conceptual understanding, problem solving, writing, cooperative learning, appropriate use of technology, mental mathematics, number sense, estimation, critical thinking, and geometric concepts are emphasized and integrated throughout the book.

What's in this text?

- **The Martin-Gay Program** and MyMathLab® for School actively encourage students to use the text, video program, and Student Organizer as an integrated learning system.

- **The Student Organizer** guides students through the 3 main components of studying effectively—notetaking, practice, and homework.

  - The Organizer includes before-class preparation exercises, notetaking pages in a 2-column format for use in class, and examples paired with exercises for practice for each section. Includes an outline and questions for use with the Student Success Tip Videos.

  It is 3-hole-punched. Available in loose-leaf, notebook-ready format and in MyMathLab for School.

- **Student Success Tips Videos** are 3- to 5-minute video segments designed to be daily reminders to students to continue practicing and maintaining good organizational and study habits. They are organized in three categories and are available in MyMathLab for School and the Interactive Lecture Series. The categories are:

  1. Success Tips that apply to any course such as Time Management.
  2. Success Tips that apply to any mathematics course. One example is based on understanding that mathematics is a course that requires homework to be completed in a timely fashion.
  3. Section- or Content-specific Success Tips to help students avoid common mistakes or to better understand concepts that often prove challenging. One example of this type of tip is how to apply the order of operations to simplify an expression.

- **Interactive Lecture Series**, featuring your text author (Elayn Martin-Gay), provides students with active learning at their own pace. The videos are available in MyMathLab for School and offer the following resources and more:

  A complete lecture for each section of the text highlights key examples and exercises from the text. "Pop-ups" reinforce key terms, definitions, and concepts.

  An interface with menu navigation features allows students to quickly find and focus on the examples and exercises they need to review.

  Student Success Tips Videos.

- **The Interactive Lecture Series** also includes the following resources for test prep:

  The Chapter Test Prep Videos help students during their most teachable moment—when they are preparing for a test. This innovation provides step-by-step solutions for the exercises found in each Chapter Test. The chapter test prep videos are also available on YouTube™. The videos are captioned in English and Spanish.

- **The Martin-Gay MyMathLab** course includes extensive exercise coverage and a comprehensive video program. There are section lecture videos for every section, which students can also access at the specific objective level; Student Success Tips Videos; and watch clips at the exercise level to help students while doing homework.

Key Pedagogical Features

Chapters   Chapters are divided into Sections. Below is an overview of a Section, then an Exercise Set, then the End-of-Chapter features.

Sections   Each section begins with a list of Objectives. These objectives are also repeated at the place of discussion within the section. When applicable, under the list of objectives there is a list of new Vocabulary words. Throughout the section, each new vocabulary word is highlighted at place of definition.

Examples   Detailed, step-by-step examples are available throughout each section. Many examples reflect real life and include illustrations. Additional instructional support is provided in the annotated examples.

Practice Exercises   Throughout the text, each worked-out example has a parallel Practice exercise. These invite students to be actively involved in the learning process. Students should try each Practice exercise after finishing the corresponding example. Learning by doing will help students grasp ideas before moving on to other concepts. All answers to the Practice exercises are provided at the back of the text.

Helpful Hints   Helpful Hints contain practical advice on applying mathematical concepts. Strategically placed where students are most likely to need immediate reinforcement, Helpful Hints help students avoid common trouble areas and mistakes.

Exercise Sets   The exercise sets have been carefully written with a special focus on making sure that even- and odd-numbered exercises are paired and that they contain real-life applications and illustrations. In addition, many types of exercises were included to help students obtain a full conceptual knowledge of the section's topics. These types of exercises are labeled and include: Multiple Choice, Complete the Table, Multiple Steps, Sketch, Construction, Fill in the Blank, Complete the Proof, Proof, Coordinate Geometry, and Find the Error.

Overall, the exercises in an exercise set are written starting with less difficult ones and then increasing in difficulty. This allows students to gain confidence while working the earlier exercises. To help achieve this, the exercises at the beginning of a section are keyed to previously worked examples. If applicable, a section of Mixed Practice exercises are included. The odd answers to these exercises are found at the end of this text.

Vocabulary and Readiness Check   These questions are immediately prior to a section's exercise set. These exercises quickly check a student's understanding of new vocabulary words. Also, the readiness exercises center on a student's understanding of a concept that is necessary in order to continue to the exercise set. The odd answers to these exercises are in the back of this text.

Applications   Real-world and real-data application exercises occur in almost every exercise set and show the relevance of mathematics and geometry and help students gradually and continuously develop their problem-solving skills.

Concept Extensions   These exercises are found toward the end of every exercise set, but before the Review and Preview exercises (described below). Concept Extension exercises require students to take the concepts from that section a step further by combining them with concepts learned in previous sections or by combining several concepts from the current section.

Writing Exercises   These exercises occur in almost every exercise set and require students to provide a written response to explain concepts or justify their thinking.

Review and Preview Exercises   These exercises occur at the end of each exercise set (except in Chapter 1) and are keyed to earlier sections. They review concepts learned earlier in the text that will be needed in the next section or chapter.

Exercise Set Resource Icons   Located at the opening of each exercise set, these icons remind students of the resources available for extra practice and support:

MyMathLab® for School

See Student Resources descriptions on page xiii for details on the individual resources available.

End-of-Chapter   The following features can be found at the end of each chapter. They are meant to give students an overall view of the chapter and thus help them have an understanding of how the concepts of a chapter fit together. All answers to these features below are found at the end of this text.

Mixed Practice Exercises   In the section exercise sets, these exercises require students to determine the problem type and strategy needed to solve it just as they would need to do on a test.

Vocabulary Check   This feature provides an opportunity for students to become more familiar with the use of mathematical terms as they strengthen their verbal skills. These appear at the end of each chapter before the Chapter Review.

Chapter Review   The end of every chapter contains a comprehensive review of topics introduced in the chapter. The Chapter Review offers exercises keyed to every section in the chapter, as well as Mixed Review exercises that are not keyed to sections.

Chapter Test and Chapter Test Prep Videos   The Chapter Test is structured to include those problems that involve common student errors. The **Chapter Test Prep Videos** give students instant access to a step-by-step video solution of each exercise in the Chapter Test.

Chapter Standardized Test   After each Chapter Test, there is a standardized test. These chapter standardized tests are written to help students prepare for standardized tests in the future. They are multiple choice tests and cover the material presented in the associated chapter.

Instructor and Student Resources

INSTRUCTOR RESOURCES

Many of the teacher supplements are available electronically, at no charge, to qualified adopters on the Instructor Resource Center (IRC). To obtain IRC access, you must first register and set up a user name and password. To register, visit **PearsonSchool. com/access_request.** You will be required to complete a brief, one-time registration subject to verification of educator status. Upon verification, access information and instructions will be sent via email.

After you receive your confirmation, go to **pearsonhighered.com** and choose **Support** from the top right navigation, then select **Educator.** Enter the ISBN of your student edition in the search box. Once you locate your program select the *Resources* tab to preview a list of available online resources.

MyMathLab® for School (available for purchase; access code required)

MyMathLab for School is a text-specific, easily customizable, online course that integrates interactive multimedia instruction with textbook content. MyMathLab for School gives you the tools you need to deliver all or a portion of your course online.

MyMathLab for School features include:

- Interactive eText, including highlighting and note taking tools, and links to videos and exercises
- Rich and flexible course management, communication, and teacher support tools
- Online homework and assessment, and personalized study plans
- Complete multimedia library to enhance learning
- All teacher resources in one convenient location

For more information, visit **www.mymathlabforschool. com** or contact your Pearson Account General Manager.

Instructor's Solutions Manual (Available for download from the IRC)

TestGen® (Available for download from the IRC)

Instructor-to-Instructor Videos—available in the Instructor Resources section of the MyMathLab for School course.

MathXL® for School (access code required)

MathXL for School is a powerful online homework, tutorial, and assessment supplement that aligns to Pearson Education's textbooks in mathematics or statistics. With MathXL for School, teachers can:

- Create, edit, and assign auto-graded online homework and tests correlated at the objective level to the textbook
- Utilize automatic grading to rapidly assess student understanding
- Track both student and group performance in an online gradebook
- Prepare students for high-stakes testing, including aligning assignments to state standards, where available
- Deliver quality, effective instruction regardless of experience level

With MathXL for School, students can:

- Do their homework and receive immediate feedback
- Get self-paced assistance on problems in a variety of ways (guided solutions, step-by-step examples, video clips, animations)
- Have a large number of practice problems to choose from, helping them master a topic
- Receive personalized study plans and homework based on test results

For more information and to purchase student access codes after the first year, visit our Web site at www.mathxlforschool. com, or contact your Pearson Account General Manager.

STUDENT RESOURCES

The following resources are available for purchase and in MyMathLab for School:

Interactive Lecture Series Videos	**Student Organizer**	**Student Solutions Manual**
Provides students with active learning at their pace. The videos offer: • A complete lecture for each text section. The interface allows easy navigation to examples and exercises students need to review. • Interactive Concept Check exercises • Student Success Tips Videos • Chapter Test Prep Videos	Guides students through the 3 main components of studying effectively—notetaking, practice, and homework. • The Organizer includes before-class preparation exercises, notetaking pages in a 2-column format for use in class, and examples paired with exercises for practice for each section. Includes an outline and questions for use with the Student Success Tip Videos. It is 3-hole-punched. Available in loose-leaf, notebook-ready format and in MyMathLab.	Provides completely worked-out solutions to the odd-numbered section exercises; all exercises in the Integrated Reviews, Chapter Reviews, Chapter Tests, and Cumulative Reviews

ABOUT THE AUTHOR

Elayn Martin-Gay has taught mathematics at the University of New Orleans for more than 25 years. Her numerous teaching awards include the local University Alumni Association's Award for Excellence in Teaching, and Outstanding Developmental Educator at University of New Orleans, presented by the Louisiana Association of Developmental Educators.

Prior to writing textbooks, Elayn Martin-Gay developed an acclaimed series of lecture videos to support developmental mathematics students in their quest for success. These highly successful videos originally served as the foundation material for her texts. Today, the videos are specific to each book in the Martin-Gay series. The author has also created Chapter Test Prep Videos to help students during their most "teachable moment"—as they prepare for a test—along with Instructor-to-Instructor videos that provide teaching tips, hints, and suggestions for each developmental mathematics course, including basic mathematics, prealgebra, beginning algebra, and intermediate algebra.

Elayn is the author of 12 published textbooks as well as multimedia, interactive mathematics, all specializing in developmental mathematics courses. She has also published series in Geometry and Algebra 2. She has participated as an author across the broadest range of educational materials: textbooks, videos, tutorial software, and courseware. This provides an opportunity of various combinations for an integrated teaching and learning package offering great consistency for the student.

Review of Real Numbers

Star	Apparent Magnitude	Star	Apparent Magnitude
Arcturus	−0.04	Spica	0.98
Sirius	−1.46	Rigel	0.12
Vega	0.03	Regulus	1.35
Antares	0.96	Canopus	−0.72
Sun	−26.7	Hadar	0.61

(*Source: Norton's 2000.0: Star Atlas and Reference Handbook,* 18th ed., Longman Group, UK, 1989)

The apparent magnitude of a star is the measure of its brightness as seen by someone on Earth. The smaller the apparent magnitude, the brighter the star. Above, the apparent magnitudes of some stars are listed.

Around 150 B.C., a Greek astronomer, Hipparchus, devised a system of classifying the brightness of stars. Hipparchus's system is the basis of the apparent magnitude scale used by modern astronomers. In this chapter, we shall see how this scale is used to describe the brightness of objects such as the sun, the moon, and some planets.

1.1 TIPS FOR SUCCESS IN MATHEMATICS

OBJECTIVES

1 Get ready for this course.

2 Understand some general tips for success.

3 Understand how to use the resources provided in MyMathLab and Math XL.

4 Get help as soon as you need it.

5 Learn how to prepare for and take an exam.

6 Develop good time management.

Before reading this section, remember that your instructor is your best source for information. Please see your instructor for any additional help or information.

OBJECTIVE 1 ▶ Getting ready for this course. Now that you have decided to take this course, remember that a *positive attitude* will make all the difference in the world. Your belief that you can succeed is just as important as your commitment to this course. Make sure you are ready for this course by having the time and positive attitude that it takes to succeed.

Next, make sure you have scheduled your math course at a time that will give you the best chance for success. For example, if you are also working, you may want to check with your employer to make sure that your work hours will not conflict with your course schedule. Also, schedule your class during a time of day when you are more attentive and do your best work.

This online course is different than traditional math courses that you have taken in the past. You will work exercises and complete homework online. Because of this, it is your responsibility to keep a written notebook or journal of your work. You will need this documentation of your work when it comes to studying for a quiz, exam or test.

On the day of your first class period, double-check your schedule and allow yourself plenty of time to arrive. Make sure you bring a notebook or binder, paper, and a pencil or some other writing instrument. If you are required to have a lab manual, graph paper, calculator, or some other supply, bring these with you, also.

OBJECTIVE 2 ▶ General tips for success. Below are some general tips that will increase your chance for success in a mathematics class. Many of these tips will also help you in other courses you may be taking.

Note: Many tips have to do with the specifics of this online course and will be listed in Objective 3.

Exchange names and phone numbers with at least one other person in class. This contact person can be a great help if you miss an assignment or want to discuss math concepts or exercises that you find difficult.

Choose to attend all class periods and be on time. If possible, sit near the front of the classroom. This way, you will see and hear the presentation better. It may also be easier for you to participate in classroom activities.

Do your homework. You've probably heard the phrase "practice makes perfect" in relation to music and sports. It also applies to mathematics. You will find that the more time you spend solving math exercises, the easier the process becomes. In this online course, homework can be submitted as many times as you like. This means you can work and re-work those exercises that you struggle with until you master them. It is a good idea to work through all homework exercises twice before the submission deadline. Also, be sure to schedule enough time to complete your assignments before the due date assigned by your teacher.

Check your work. Checking work is the same for an online course as it is with a traditional course. This is why it is imperative that you work each exercise on paper before submitting the answer. If it's on paper, you can go back, check your work, and follow your steps to ensure the answer is correct, or find any mistakes and correct them. If you can't find your mistake or if you have any questions, make sure you talk to your teacher.

Learn from your mistakes and be patient with yourself. Everyone, even your instructor, makes mistakes. (That definitely includes me—Elayn Martin-Gay.) Use your errors to learn and to become a better math student. The key is finding and understanding your errors.

Was your mistake a careless one, or did you make it because you can't read your own math writing? If so, try to work more slowly or write more neatly and make a conscious effort to carefully check your work.

Did you make a mistake because you don't understand a concept? Take the time to review the concept or ask questions to better understand it.

Did you skip too many steps? Skipping steps or trying to do too many steps mentally may lead to preventable mistakes.

Know how to get help if you need it. It's always a good idea to ask for help whenever there is something that you don't understand. One great advantage about doing homework in MathXL is that there is built-in "help" whenever you need it. Should you get a wrong answer, a box will appear and offer you hints for working the exercise correctly. Again, this is why it is so important to keep a record of all your work on paper so you can go back and follow the suggestions. You will have three attempts to get each exercise correct before it is marked wrong. **Remember:** Even though you are working online, your teacher is your most valuable resource for answering questions. Having a written journal of neatly worked exercises helps your teacher identify mistakes on an exercise or about a concept in general.

Organize your class materials, including homework assignments, graded quizzes and tests, and notes from your class or lab. All of these items will be valuable references throughout your course, especially when studying for upcoming tests or your final exam. Make sure you can locate these materials when you need them. An excellent way to do this is by using the Organizer, which is reviewed in Objective 3.

Read your ebook or watch the section lecture videos before class. Your course ebook is available through MyMathLab. Use this online text just as you would a printed textbook. Read the assigned section(s), then write down any questions you may have. You will then be prepared to ask any questions in class the next day. Also, familiarizing yourself with the material before class will help you understand it much more readily when it is presented. There is also a reading assessment homework if assigned by your teacher.

Lecture videos, approximately 20 minutes in length, are available for every section of your ebook. These videos are specific to the material in the ebook and are presented by the ebook author, Elayn Martin-Gay. Watching a section video before class is another way to familiarize yourself with the material. Write down any questions you may have so that you can ask them in class. Watching a section video after class is also an excellent way to review concepts that are difficult for you.

Don't be afraid to ask questions. Teachers are not mind readers. Many times they do not know a concept is unclear until a student asks a question. You are not the only person in class with questions. Other students are normally grateful that someone has spoken up.

Turn in assignments on time. Always be aware of the schedule of assignments and due dates set by your teacher. Do not wait until the last minute to submit your work online. It is a good idea to submit your assignments 6–8 hours before the submission deadline to ensure some "cushion" time in case you have technology trouble.

When assignments are turned in online, it is extremely important for you to keep a copy of your written work. You will find it helpful to organize this work in a 3-ring binder. This way, you can refer to your written work to ask questions and to use it later to study for tests. (See the Organizer in Objective 3.)

OBJECTIVE 3 ▶ Understanding how to use the resources provided in MathXL and MyMathLab. There are many helpful resources available to you through MathXL and MyMathLab. It is important that you understand these resources and know when to use them. Let's start with the resources that are available within MathXL to help you successfully complete and master the exercises in your assigned homework. When working your homework assignments, you will find the following buttons listed on the right hand side of the screen.

- **Help Me Solve This**—Select this resource to get guided, step-by-step help for the exercise you are working. Once you have reached the correct answer (through the help feature) you must work an additional exercise of the same type before you receive credit for having worked it correctly.

- **View an Example**—Select this resource to view a correctly worked example similar to the exercise you are working on. After viewing the example, you can go back to your original exercise and complete it on your own.

- **Textbook**—Select this resource to go to the section of the ebook where you can find exercises similar to the one you are working on.

- **Video**—Select this resource to view a video clip of Elayn Martin-Gay (your ebook author) working an exercise similar to the one you need help with. **Not all exercises have an accompanying video clip. This button will not be listed if no video clip is available.

- **Ask My Instructor**—Select this resource to send an email to your teacher that will include the exercise that you are unsure of.

Let's now take a moment to go over a few of the features available in MyMathLab to help you prepare for class, review outside class, organize, improve your study skills, and succeed.

- **Ebook and Videos**—You can choose to read the ebook and/or watch the videos for every section of the text. The ebook includes worked examples, helpful hints, practice exercises, and section exercises for every text section. Read the material actively, and make a note of any questions you have so that you can then ask them in class.

  There are lecture **videos,** approximately 20 minutes in length, for every ebook section. Watch these videos to prepare for class, to review after class, or to help you catch up if you miss class. The videos are presented by your ebook author, Elayn Martin-Gay, so all material covered in the videos is consistent with the coverage in your ebook. Make a note of any questions you have after watching the videos so that you can ask your instructor. Your instructor may assign watching the videos as homework to prepare for class.

- **Organizer**—This is a special resource designed to help you prepare for class, take notes, practice exercise solving, and organize your homework and tests. The Organizer is intended to be placed in a 3-ring binder, and it is divided into the following segments for each ebook section:

  Before Class—directs you to read specific material in the ebook and answer questions.

  During Class—provides an organized, 2 column, in-class note taking format for you to write key examples and concepts presented in the lesson. In the **Class Notes/Examples** column, write down any examples (line-by-line) demonstrated by your instructor, seen as an example in MyMathLab, or in the Lecture Videos. In the **Your Own Notes** column, annotate the examples with your personal notes that you do not want to forget. Insert additional pages as needed.

  Practice—provides you with worked examples paired with matching **Your Turn** exercises for each text section. Read the **Review this Example** to make sure you understand the work. Then, complete the matched **Your Turn** exercise. **Complete the Example** exercises provide you with guided practice by completing part of the solution and asking you to fill in specific steps.

  After this page, insert your completed, written work for each exercise on your MathXL homework assignment.

  This Organizer is available in MyMathLab and in print.

OBJECTIVE 4 ▶ Getting help. If you have trouble completing assignments or understanding the mathematics, get help as soon as you need it! This tip is presented as an objective on its own because it is so important. In mathematics, usually the material presented in one section builds on your understanding of the previous section. This means that if you don't understand the concepts covered during a class period, there is a good chance that you will not understand the concepts covered during the next class period. If this happens to you, get help as soon as you can.

Where can you get help? Many suggestions have been made in the section on where to get help, and now it is up to you to do it. Try your instructor, a tutoring center, or a math lab, or you may want to form a study group with fellow classmates. If you do decide to see your instructor or go to a tutoring center, make sure that you have a neat notebook and are ready with your questions.

OBJECTIVE 5 ▶ Preparing for and taking an exam. Make sure that you allow yourself plenty of time to prepare for a test. If you think that you are a little "math anxious," it may be that you are not preparing for a test in a way that will ensure success. The way that you prepare for a test in mathematics is important. To prepare for a test,

1. Review your previous homework assignments. You may also want to rework some of them.
2. Review any notes from class and section-level quizzes you have taken. (If this is a final exam, also review chapter tests you have taken.)
3. Practice working out exercises by completing the Chapter Review found at the end of each chapter.
4. Since homework exercises are online, you may easily work new homework exercises. If you open an already submitted homework assignment, you can get new exercises by clicking "similar exercise." This will generate new exercises similar to the homework exercises you have already submitted. You can then work and rework exercises until you fully understand them. *Don't stop here!*
5. It is important that you place yourself in conditions similar to test conditions to find out how you will perform. In other words, as soon as you feel that you know the material, try taking some sample tests.

   In your ebook, there are two forms of chapter tests at the end of each chapter. One form is an open response test form and the second is a standardized test form. You can use these two tests as practice tests. Do not use your notes or any other help when completing these tests. Check your answers by using the answer section in the ebook. There are also exact video clip solutions to the open response practice test form. Finally, identify any concepts that you do not understand and consult your teacher.
6. Get a good night's sleep before the exam.
7. On the day of the actual test, allow yourself plenty of time to arrive at your exam location.

When taking your test,

1. Read the directions on the test carefully.
2. Read each problem carefully as you take the test. Make sure that you answer the question asked.
3. Pace yourself by first completing the problems you are most confident with. Then work toward the problems you are least confident with. Watch your time so you do not spend too much time on one particular problem.
4. If you have time, check your work and answers.
5. Do not turn your test in early. If you have extra time, spend it double-checking your work.

OBJECTIVE 6 ▶ Managing your time. As a student, you know the demands that classes, homework, work, and family place on your time. Some days you probably wonder how you'll ever get everything done. One key to managing your time is developing a schedule. Here are some hints for making a schedule:

1. Make a list of all of your weekly commitments for the term. Include classes, work, regular meetings, extracurricular activities, etc.

2. Next, estimate the time needed for each item on the list. Also make a note of how often you will need to do each item. Don't forget to include time estimates for reading, studying, and homework you do outside of your classes. You may want to ask your instructor for help estimating the time needed.

3. In the following exercise set, you are asked to block out a typical week on the schedule grid given. Start with items with fixed time slots like classes and work.

4. Next, include the items on your list with flexible time slots. Think carefully about how best to schedule some items such as study time.

5. Don't fill up every time slot on the schedule. Remember that you need to allow time for eating, sleeping, and relaxing! You should also allow a little extra time in case some items take longer than planned.

6. If you find that your weekly schedule is too full for you to handle, you may need to make some changes in your workload, classload, or in other areas of your life. If you work, you may want to talk to your advisor, manager or supervisor, or someone in your school's counseling center for help with such decisions.

1.1 EXERCISE SET

MyMathLab PRACTICE WATCH DOWNLOAD READ REVIEW

1. How many times is it suggested that you work through homework exercises before the submission deadline?

2. How does the "Help Me Solve This" feature work?

3. Why is it important that you write your step-by-step solutions to homework exercises and keep a hard copy of all work submitted online?

4. How many times are you allowed to submit homework online?

5. How can the lecture videos for each section help you in this course? When is the best time to use them?

6. In the homework assignments, how many attempts do you get to correct an exercise before it is marked incorrect?

7. If the "View an Example" feature is used, is it necessary to work an additional exercise before continuing the assignment?

8. How does reading the ebook section before class help you prepare for class?

9. Do all homework exercises in MathXL come with an accompanying video clip solution?

10. How can you use MathXL to contact your teacher about an exercise you don't understand?

11. When are your homework assignments due?

12. How much "cushion" time is recommended before your deadline when submitting homework online?

13. Is it still OK to ask your teacher for help even though this is an online course?

14. Name two ways you can prepare for any chapter tests.

15. If you are absent, name two ways you can review the material you missed.

16. List the resources available to help you in MyMathLab. Which of these resources do you think will be most helpful to you?

17. Are you allowed to use a calculator in this class?

18. Review objective 6 and fill in the schedule grid below.

19. Study your completed grid from Exercise 18. Decide whether you have the time necessary to successfully complete this course and any others you are registered for.

	Monday	*Tuesday*	*Wednesday*	*Thursday*	*Friday*	*Saturday*	*Sunday*
4:00 A.M.							
5:00 A.M.							
6:00 A.M.							
7:00 A.M.							
8:00 A.M.							
9:00 A.M.							
10:00 A.M.							
11:00 A.M.							
12:00 P.M.							
1:00 P.M.							
2:00 P.M.							
3:00 P.M.							
4:00 P.M.							
5:00 P.M.							
6:00 P.M.							
7:00 P.M.							
8:00 P.M.							
9:00 P.M.							
10:00 P.M.							
11:00 P.M.							
Midnight							
1:00 A.M.							
2:00 A.M.							
3:00 A.M.							

1.2 SYMBOLS AND SETS OF NUMBERS

OBJECTIVES

1 Use a number line to order numbers.

2 Translate sentences into mathematical statements.

3 Identify natural numbers, whole numbers, integers, rational numbers, irrational numbers, and real numbers.

4 Find the absolute value of a real number.

5 Use counterexamples.

OBJECTIVE 1 ▶ Using a number line to order numbers. We begin with a review of the set of natural numbers and the set of whole numbers and how we use symbols to compare these numbers. A **set** is a collection of objects, each of which is called a **member** or **element** of the set. A pair of brace symbols { } encloses the list of elements and is translated as "the set of" or "the set containing."

Natural Numbers
The set of **natural numbers** is $\{1, 2, 3, 4, 5, 6, \ldots\}$.

Whole Numbers
The set of **whole numbers** is $\{0, 1, 2, 3, 4, \ldots\}$.

The three dots (an ellipsis) at the end of the list of elements of a set means that the list continues in the same manner indefinitely.

These numbers can be pictured on a **number line.** We will use number lines often to help us visualize distance and relationships between numbers. Visualizing mathematical concepts is an important skill and tool, and later we will develop and explore other visualizing tools.

To draw a number line, first draw a line. Choose a point on the line and label it 0. To the right of 0, label any other point 1. Being careful to use the same distance as from 0 to 1, mark off equally spaced distances. Label these points 2, 3, 4, 5, and so on. Since the whole numbers continue indefinitely, it is not possible to show every whole number on this number line. The arrow at the right end of the line indicates that the pattern continues indefinitely.

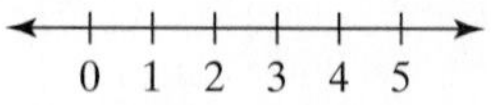

Picturing whole numbers on a number line helps us to see the order of the numbers. Symbols can be used to describe concisely in writing the order that we see.

The **equal symbol** $=$ means "is equal to."

The symbol $\neq$ means "is not equal to."

These symbols may be used to form a **mathematical statement.** The statement might be true or it might be false. The two statements below are both true.

$2 = 2$ states that "two is equal to two"

$2 \neq 6$ states that "two is not equal to six"

If two numbers are not equal, then one number is larger than the other. The symbol $>$ means "is greater than." The symbol $<$ means "is less than." For example,

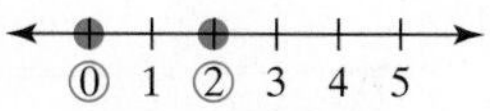

$2 > 0$ states that "two is greater than zero"

$3 < 5$ states that "three is less than five"

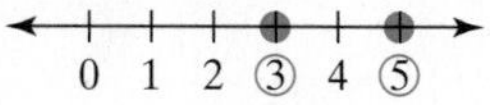

On a number line, we see that a number **to the right of** another number is **larger.** Similarly, a number **to the left of** another number is smaller. For example, 3 is to the left of 5 on a number line, which means that 3 is less than 5, or $3 < 5$. Similarly, 2 is to the right of 0 on a number line, which means 2 is greater than 0, or $2 > 0$. Since 0 is to the left of 2, we can also say that 0 is less than 2, or $0 < 2$.

The symbols $\neq$, $<$, and $>$ are called **inequality symbols.**

> ▶ Helpful Hint
>
> Notice that $2 > 0$ has exactly the same meaning as $0 < 2$. Switching the order of the numbers and reversing the "direction of the inequality symbol" does not change the meaning of the statement.
>
> $5 > 3$ has the same meaning as $3 < 5$.
>
> Also notice that, when the statement is true, the inequality arrow points to the smaller number.

EXAMPLE 1   Insert $<$, $>$, or $=$ in the space between each pair of numbers to make each statement true.

a. 2   3   **b.** 7   4   **c.** 72   27

Solution

a. $2 < 3$ since 2 is to the left of 3 on the number line.

b. $7 > 4$ since 7 is to the right of 4 on the number line.

c. $72 > 27$ since 72 is to the right of 27 on the number line.   □

PRACTICE
1   Insert $<$, $>$, or $=$ in the space between each pair of numbers to make each statement true.

a. 5   8   **b.** 6   4   **c.** 16   82

Number line figures (left margin):

$2 > 0$ or $0 < 2$

$3 < 5$

Two other symbols are used to compare numbers. The symbol $\leq$ means "is less than or equal to." The symbol $\geq$ means "is greater than or equal to." For example,

$$7 \leq 10 \text{ states that "seven is less than or equal to ten"}$$

This statement is true since $7 < 10$ is true. If either $7 < 10$ or $7 = 10$ is true, then $7 \leq 10$ is true.

$$3 \geq 3 \text{ states that "three is greater than or equal to three"}$$

This statement is true since $3 = 3$ is true. If either $3 > 3$ or $3 = 3$ is true, then $3 \geq 3$ is true.

The statement $6 \geq 10$ is false since neither $6 > 10$ nor $6 = 10$ is true. The symbols $\leq$ and $\geq$ are also called **inequality symbols.**

EXAMPLE 2   Tell whether each statement is true or false.

a. $8 \geq 8$ **b.** $8 \leq 8$ **c.** $23 \leq 0$ **d.** $23 \geq 0$

Solution

a. True, since $8 = 8$ is true.

b. True, since $8 = 8$ is true.

c. False, since neither $23 < 0$ nor $23 = 0$ is true.

d. True, since $23 > 0$ is true.   ☐

PRACTICE
2   Tell whether each statement is true or false.

a. $9 \geq 3$ **b.** $3 \geq 8$ **c.** $25 \leq 25$ **d.** $4 \leq 14$

OBJECTIVE 2 ▶ Translating sentences. Now, let's use the symbols discussed above to translate sentences into mathematical statements.

EXAMPLE 3   Translate each sentence into a mathematical statement.

a. Nine is less than or equal to eleven.

b. Eight is greater than one.

c. Three is not equal to four.

Solution

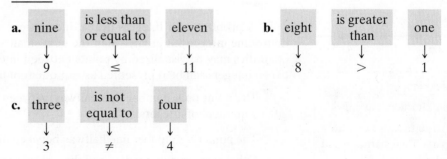

PRACTICE
3   Translate each sentence into a mathematical statement.

a. Three is less than eight.

b. Fifteen is greater than or equal to nine.

c. Six is not equal to seven.

OBJECTIVE 3 ▶ Identifying common sets of numbers. Whole numbers are not sufficient to describe many situations in the real world. For example, quantities smaller than zero must sometimes be represented, such as temperatures less than 0 degrees. We can picture numbers less than zero on a number line as follows:

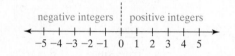

Numbers less than 0 are to the left of 0 and are labeled $-1, -2, -3$, and so on. A $-$ sign, such as the one in -1, tells us that the number is to the left of 0 on a number line. In words, -1 is read "negative one." A $+$ sign or no sign tells us that a number lies to the right of 0 on the number line. For example, 3 and $+3$ both mean positive three.

The numbers we have pictured are called the set of **integers.** Integers to the left of 0 are called **negative integers;** integers to the right of 0 are called **positive integers.** The integer **0 is neither positive nor negative.**

negative integers | positive integers

```
←—+——+——+——+——+——+——+——+——+——+——+→
 −5 −4 −3 −2 −1  0  1  2  3  4  5
```

> **Integers**
> The set of **integers** is $\{\ldots, -3, -2, -1, 0, 1, 2, 3, \ldots\}$.

Notice the ellipses (three dots) to the left and to the right of the list for the integers. This indicates that the positive integers and the negative integers continue indefinitely.

EXAMPLE 4   Use an integer to express the number in the following. "Pole of Inaccessibility, Antarctica, is the coldest location in the world, with an average annual temperature of 72 degrees below zero." (*Source: The Guinness Book of Records*)

Solution   The integer -72 represents 72 degrees below zero.   ☐

PRACTICE
4   Use an integer to express the number in the following: Fred overdrew his checking account and now owes his bank 52 dollars.

A problem with integers in real-life settings arises when quantities are smaller than some integer but greater than the next smallest integer. On a number line, these quantities may be visualized by points between integers. Some of these quantities between integers can be represented as a quotient of integers. For example,

The point on a number line halfway between 0 and 1 can be represented by $\frac{1}{2}$, a quotient of integers.

The point on a number line halfway between 0 and -1 can be represented by $-\frac{1}{2}$.

Other quotients of integers and their graphs are shown to the left.

These numbers, each of which can be represented as a quotient of integers, are examples of **rational numbers.** It's not possible to list the set of rational numbers using the notation that we have been using. For this reason, we will use a different notation.

> ▶ **Helpful Hint**
> To graph a fraction, like $\frac{3}{4}$, divide the distance from 0 to 1, into 4 equal parts. Then start at 0 and count over 3 parts.
>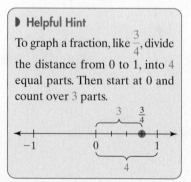

Rational Numbers

$$\left\{ \frac{a}{b} \middle| a \text{ and } b \text{ are integers and } b \neq 0 \right\}$$

We read this set as "the set of all numbers $\frac{a}{b}$ such that a and b are integers and **b is not equal to 0.**" Notice that every integer is also a rational number since each integer can be expressed as a quotient of integers. For example, the integer 5 is also a rational number since $5 = \frac{5}{1}$.

The number line also contains points that cannot be expressed as quotients of integers. These numbers are called **irrational numbers** because they cannot be represented by rational numbers. For example, $\sqrt{2}$ and π are irrational numbers.

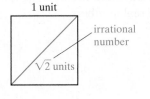

1 unit

irrational number

$\sqrt{2}$ units

Irrational Numbers

The set of **irrational numbers** is

{Nonrational numbers that correspond to points on the number line}.

That is, an irrational number is a number that cannot be expressed as a quotient of integers.

Both rational numbers and irrational numbers can be written as decimal numbers. The decimal equivalent of a rational number will either terminate or repeat in a pattern. For example, upon dividing we find that

$$\frac{3}{4} = 0.75 \text{ (decimal number terminates or ends) and}$$

$$\frac{2}{3} = 0.66666\ldots \text{ (decimal number repeats in a pattern)}$$

The decimal representation of an irrational number will neither terminate nor repeat. For example, the decimal representations of irrational numbers $\sqrt{2}$ and π are

$$\sqrt{2} = 1.414213562\ldots \text{ (decimal number does not terminate or repeat in a pattern)}$$
$$\pi = 3.141592653\ldots \text{ (decimal number does not terminate or repeat in a pattern)}$$

(For further review of decimals, see the Appendix.)

Combining the rational numbers with the irrational numbers gives the set of **real numbers.** One and only one point on a number line corresponds to each real number.

Helpful Hint

To graph a decimal, like 1.7, remember that the decimal system is base 10. Divide the distance from 1 to 2 into 10 equal parts and count over 7 parts.

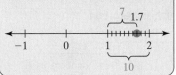

Real Numbers

The set of **real numbers** is

{All numbers that correspond to points on the number line}

Helpful Hint

From our previous definitions, we have that

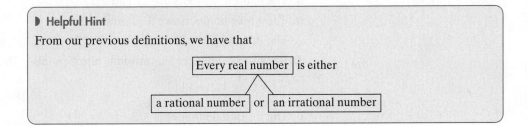

On the following number line, we see that real numbers can be positive, negative, or 0. Numbers to the left of 0 are called **negative numbers;** numbers to the right of 0 are called **positive numbers.** Positive and negative numbers are also called **signed numbers.**

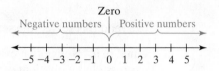

Several different sets of numbers have been discussed in this section. The following diagram shows the relationships among these sets of real numbers.

Common Sets of Numbers

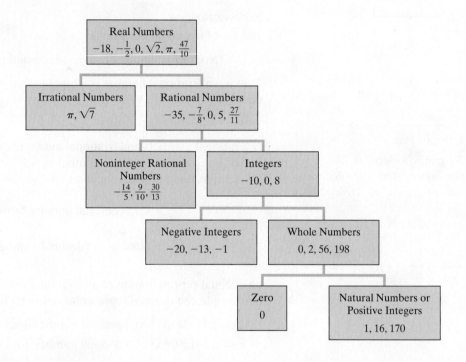

EXAMPLE 5   Given the set $\left\{-2, 0, \frac{1}{4}, -1.5, 112, -3, 11, \sqrt{2}\right\}$, list the numbers in this set that belong to the set of:

a. Natural numbers   **b.** Whole numbers

c. Integers   **d.** Rational numbers

e. Irrational numbers   **f.** Real numbers

Solution

a. The natural numbers are 11 and 112.

b. The whole numbers are 0, 11, and 112.

c. The integers are $-3, -2, 0, 11,$ and 112.

d. Recall that integers are rational numbers also. The rational numbers are $-3, -2,$ $-1.5, 0, \frac{1}{4}, 11,$ and 112.

e. The irrational number is $\sqrt{2}$.

f. The real numbers are all numbers in the given set.   □

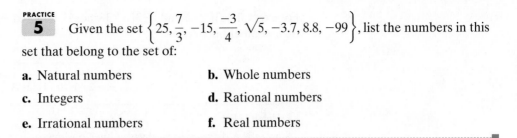

PRACTICE
5   Given the set $\left\{ 25, \dfrac{7}{3}, -15, \dfrac{-3}{4}, \sqrt{5}, -3.7, 8.8, -99 \right\}$, list the numbers in this set that belong to the set of:

a. Natural numbers   **b.** Whole numbers

c. Integers   **d.** Rational numbers

e. Irrational numbers   **f.** Real numbers

We can now extend the meaning and use of inequality symbols such as $<$ and $>$ to apply to all real numbers.

Order Property for Real Numbers

Given any two real numbers a and b, $a < b$ if a is to the left of b on a number line. Similarly, $a > b$ if a is to the right of b on a number line.

$$a < b \qquad\qquad a > b$$

EXAMPLE 6   Insert $<$, $>$, or $=$ in the appropriate space to make each statement true.

a. $-1 \quad 0$ **b.** $7 \quad \dfrac{14}{2}$ **c.** $-5 \quad -6$

Solution

a. $-1 < 0$ since -1 is to the left of 0 on a number line.

$$-1 < 0$$

b. $7 = \dfrac{14}{2}$ since $\dfrac{14}{2}$ simplifies to 7.

c. $-5 > -6$ since -5 is to the right of -6 on the number line.

$$-5 > -6$$

PRACTICE
6   Insert $<$, $>$, or $=$ in the appropriate space to make each statement true.

a. $0 \quad 3$ **b.** $15 \quad -5$ **c.** $3 \quad \dfrac{12}{4}$

OBJECTIVE 4 ▶ Finding the absolute value of a real number. A number line not only gives us a picture of the real numbers, it also helps us visualize the distance between numbers. The distance between a real number a and 0 is given a special name called the **absolute value** of a. "The absolute value of a" is written in symbols as $|a|$.

Absolute Value

The absolute value of a real number a, denoted by $|a|$, is the distance between a and 0 on a number line.

For example, $|3| = 3$ and $|-3| = 3$ since both 3 and -3 are a distance of 3 units from 0 on a number line.

> ▶ **Helpful Hint**
>
> Since $|a|$ is a distance, $|a|$ is always either positive or 0, never negative. That is, **for any real number a, $|a| \geq 0$.**

EXAMPLE 7   Find the absolute value of each number.

a. $|4|$ **b.** $|-5|$ **c.** $|0|$ **d.** $\left|-\dfrac{1}{2}\right|$ **e.** $|5.6|$

Solution

a. $|4| = 4$ since 4 is 4 units from 0 on a number line.

b. $|-5| = 5$ since -5 is 5 units from 0 on a number line.

c. $|0| = 0$ since 0 is 0 units from 0 on a number line.

d. $\left|-\dfrac{1}{2}\right| = \dfrac{1}{2}$ since $-\dfrac{1}{2}$ is $\dfrac{1}{2}$ unit from 0 on a number line.

e. $|5.6| = 5.6$ since 5.6 is 5.6 units from 0 on a number line.   □

PRACTICE
7   Find the absolute value of each number.

a. $|-8|$ **b.** $|9|$ **c.** $|-2.5|$ **d.** $\left|\dfrac{5}{11}\right|$ **e.** $|\sqrt{3}|$

EXAMPLE 8   Insert $<$, $>$, or $=$ in the appropriate space to make each statement true.

a. $|0|$ 2   **b.** $|-5|$ 5   **c.** $|-3|$ $|-2|$ **d.** $|5|$ $|6|$ **e.** $|-7|$ $|6|$

Solution

a. $|0| < 2$ since $|0| = 0$ and $0 < 2$.   **b.** $|-5| = 5$ since $5 = 5$.

c. $|-3| > |-2|$ since $3 > 2$.   **d.** $|5| < |6|$ since $5 < 6$.

e. $|-7| > |6|$ since $7 > 6$.   □

PRACTICE
8   Insert $<$, $>$, or $=$ in the appropriate space to make each statement true.

a. $|8|$ $|-8|$ **b.** $|-3|$ 0   **c.** $|-7|$ $|-11|$ **d.** $|3|$ $|2|$ **e.** $|0|$ $|-4|$

OBJECTIVE 5 ▶ **Using counterexamples.** Next, we use our knowledge of absolute value and sets of numbers to determine whether statements are true or false.

In mathematics, we can use counterexamples to prove that a statement is false. A **counterexample** is a specific example of the falsity of a statement as we see below. (To prove that a statement is true, you use previous definitions or proofs or show that it is true for every single example.)

EXAMPLE 9   Tell whether each statement is true or false. If false, give a counterexample.

a. The absolute value of a number is always a positive number.

b. 0 is whole number.

Solution

a. False. Counterexample: $|0| = 0$ and 0 is not a positive number.

b. True, by definition of whole numbers.

PRACTICE
9   Tell whether each statement is true or false. If false, give a counterexample.

a. -5 is a rational number.

b. All whole numbers are also natural numbers.

VOCABULARY & READINESS CHECK

Use the choices below to fill in each blank.

real	natural	whole	irrational	counterexample
$|b|$	inequality	integers	rational	

1. The _____ numbers are $\{0, 1, 2, 3, 4, \dots\}$.

2. The _____ numbers are $\{1, 2, 3, 4, 5, \dots\}$.

3. The symbols $\neq$, $\leq$, and $>$ are called _____ symbols.

4. The _____ are $\{\dots, -3, -2, -1, 0, 1, 2, 3, \dots\}$.

5. The _____ numbers are {all numbers that correspond to points on the number line}.

6. The _____ numbers are $\left\{ \dfrac{a}{b} \,\middle|\, a \text{ and } b \text{ are integers}, b \neq 0 \right\}$.

7. The _____ numbers are {nonrational numbers that correspond to points on the number line}.

8. The distance between a number b and 0 on a number line is _____.

9. A specific example of the falsity of a statement is called a(n) _____.

1.2 EXERCISE SET

Insert $<$, $>$, or $=$ in the appropriate space to make the statement true. See Example 1.

1. 7 _ 3   **2.** 9 _ 15

3. 6.26 _ 6.26   **4.** 2.13 _ 1.13

5. 0 _ 7   **6.** 20 _ 0

7. -2 _ -1 **8.** -4 _ -6

9. The freezing point of water is $32°$ Fahrenheit. The boiling point of water is $212°$ Fahrenheit. Write an inequality statement using $<$ or $>$ comparing the numbers 32 and 212.

10. The freezing point of water is $0°$ Celsius. The boiling point of water is $100°$ Celsius. Write an inequality statement using $<$ or $>$ comparing the numbers 0 and 100.

11. The spring 2007 tuition and fees for a Texas resident undergraduate student at University of Texas at El Paso were approximately \$2631 for a 15-credit load. At the same time the tuition and fees for a Florida resident attending University of Florida were approximately \$2456. Write an inequality statement using $<$ or $>$ comparing the numbers 2631 and 2456. (*Source:* UTEP and UF)

12. The average salary in the San Jose, California, area for a chemical engineer is \$67,841. The average salary for a database administrator in the same area is \$75,657. Write an inequality statement using $<$ or $>$ comparing the numbers 67,841 and 75,657. (*Source: The Wall Street Journal*)

Are the following statements true or false? See Example 2.

13. $11 \leq 11$ **14.** $4 \geq 7$ **15.** $10 > 11$

16. $17 > 16$ **17.** $3 + 8 \geq 3(8)$ **18.** $8 \cdot 8 \leq 8 \cdot 7$

19. $7 > 0$ **20.** $4 < 7$

△ **21.** An angle measuring $30°$ is shown and an angle measuring $45°$ is shown. Use the inequality symbol $\leq$ or $\geq$ to write a statement comparing the numbers 30 and 45.

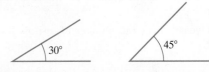

△ **22.** The sum of the measures of the angles of a triangle is 180°. The sum of the measures of the angles of a parallelogram is 360°. Use the inequality symbol ≤ or ≥ to write a statement comparing the numbers 360 and 180.

Write each sentence as a mathematical statement. See Example 3.

23. Eight is less than twelve.

24. Fifteen is greater than five.

25. Five is greater than or equal to four.

26. Negative ten is less than or equal to thirty-seven.

27. Fifteen is not equal to negative two.

28. Negative seven is not equal to seven.

Use integers to represent the values in each statement. See Example 4.

29. Driskill Mountain, in Louisiana, has an altitude of 535 feet. New Orleans, Louisiana, lies 8 feet below sea level. (*Source:* U.S. Geological Survey)

30. During a Green Bay Packers football game, the team gained 23 yards and then lost 12 yards on consecutive plays.

31. From 2005 to 2010, the population of Washington, D.C., is expected to decrease by approximately 21,350. (*Source:* U.S. Census Bureau)

32. From 2005 to 2010, the population of Alaska is expected to grow by about 33,000 people. (*Source:* U.S. Census Bureau)

33. Aaron Miller deposited $350 in his savings account. He later withdrew $126.

34. Aris Peña was deep-sea diving. During her dive, she ascended 30 feet and later descended 50 feet.

The graph below is called a bar graph. This particular graph shows the annual numbers of recreational visitors to U.S. National Parks. Each bar represents a different year, and the height of the bar represents the number of visitors (in millions) in that year.

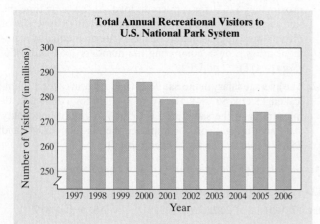

35. In which year(s) was the number of visitors the greatest?

36. What was the greatest number of visitors shown?

37. In what year(s) was the number of visitors greater than 280 million?

38. In what year(s) was the number of visitors less than 270 million?

39. Write an inequality statement comparing the number of annual visitors in 2001 and 2006.

40. Do you notice any trends shown by this bar graph?

Tell which set or sets each number belongs to: natural numbers, whole numbers, integers, rational numbers, irrational numbers, and real numbers. See Example 5.

41. 0

42. $\frac{1}{4}$

43. −2

44. $-\frac{1}{2}$

45. 6

46. 5

47. $\frac{2}{3}$

48. $\sqrt{3}$

49. $-\sqrt{5}$

50. $-1\frac{5}{9}$

Tell whether each statement is true or false. If false, give a counterexample. See Example 9.

51. Every rational number is also an integer.

52. Every negative number is also a rational number.

53. Every natural number is positive.

54. Every rational number is also a real number.

55. The absolute value of a positive number is always greater than the absolute value of a negative number.

56. The absolute value of a negative number is always a positive number.

57. Every whole number is an integer.

58. Every integer is a whole number.

59. The absolute value of every number equals itself.

60. Every whole number is positive.

Insert <, >, or = in the appropriate space to make a true statement. If necessary, graph each number on a number line. See Examples 6 through 8 and the Helpful Hints on pages 10 and 11.

61. −10   −100

62. −200   −20

63. 0.9 $\frac{3}{4}$

64. $\frac{2}{3}$ 0.5

65. $-1\frac{5}{6}$ $-1\frac{2}{3}$

66. $-1\frac{9}{10}$ $-1\frac{3}{4}$

67. −51   −50

68. $|-20|$ −200

69. $|-5|$ −4

70. 0 $|0|$

71. $|-1|$ $|1|$

72. $\left|\frac{2}{5}\right|$ $\left|-\frac{2}{5}\right|$

73. $|-2|$ $|-3|$

74. −500 $|-50|$

75. $|0|$ $|-8|$

76. $|-12|$ $\frac{24}{2}$

CONCEPT EXTENSIONS

The apparent magnitude of a star is the measure of its brightness as seen by someone on Earth. The smaller the apparent magnitude, the brighter the star. Use the apparent magnitudes in the table to answer Exercises 77 through 82.

Star	Apparent Magnitude	Star	Apparent Magnitude
Arcturus	−0.04	Spica	0.98
Sirius	−1.46	Rigel	0.12
Vega	0.03	Regulus	1.35
Antares	0.96	Canopus	−0.72
Sun	−26.7	Hadar	0.61

(*Source: Norton's 2000: Star Atlas and Reference Handbook,* 18th ed., Longman Group, UK, 1989)

77. The apparent magnitude of the sun is −26.7. The apparent magnitude of the star Arcturus is −0.04. Write an inequality statement comparing the numbers −0.04 and −26.7.

78. The apparent magnitude of Antares is 0.96. The apparent magnitude of Spica is 0.98. Write an inequality statement comparing the numbers 0.96 and 0.98.

79. Which is brighter, the sun or Arcturus?

80. Which is dimmer, Antares or Spica?

81. Which star listed is the brightest?

82. Which star listed is the dimmest?

Matching. *Choose the letter that correctly completes each statement.*

a) −7   **b)** 7   **c)** 0   **d)** $-\dfrac{10}{11}$

83. $|0| = $ ___   **84.** $|-7| = $ ___

85. A rational number that is not an integer is ___.

86. A negative integer is ___.

87. In your own words, explain how to find the absolute value of a number.

88. Give an example of a real-life situation that can be described with integers but not with whole numbers.

1.3 FRACTIONS

OBJECTIVES

1 Write fractions in simplest form.

2 Multiply and divide fractions.

3 Add and subtract fractions.

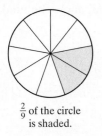

$\frac{2}{9}$ of the circle is shaded.

OBJECTIVE 1 ▶ Writing fractions in simplest form. A quotient of two numbers such as $\frac{2}{9}$ is called a **fraction.** In the fraction $\frac{2}{9}$, the top number, 2, is called the **numerator** and the bottom number, 9, is called the **denominator.**

A fraction may be used to refer to part of a whole. For example, $\frac{2}{9}$ of the circle to the left is shaded. The denominator 9 tells us how many equal parts the whole circle is divided into and the numerator 2 tells us how many equal parts are shaded.

To simplify fractions, we can factor the numerator and the denominator. In the statement $3 \cdot 5 = 15$, 3 and 5 are called **factors** and 15 is the **product.** (The raised dot symbol indicates multiplication.)

$$
\begin{array}{ccccc}
3 & \cdot & 5 & = & 15 \\
\uparrow & & \uparrow & & \uparrow \\
\text{factor} & & \text{factor} & & \text{product}
\end{array}
$$

To **factor** 15 means to write it as a product. The number 15 can be factored as $3 \cdot 5$ or as $1 \cdot 15$.

A fraction is said to be **simplified** or in **lowest terms** when the numerator and the denominator have no factors in common other than 1. For example, the fraction $\frac{5}{11}$ is in lowest terms since 5 and 11 have no common factors other than 1.

To help us simplify fractions, we write the numerator and the denominator as a product of **prime numbers.**

> **Prime Number**
>
> A prime number is a natural number, other than 1, whose only factors are 1 and itself. The first few prime numbers are
>
> $$2, 3, 5, 7, 11, 13, 17, 19, 23, 29, \text{ and so on.}$$

A natural number, other than 1, that is not a prime number is called a **composite number.** Every composite number can be written as a product of prime numbers. We call this product of prime numbers the prime factorization of the composite number.

EXAMPLE 1 Write each of the following numbers as a product of primes.

a. 40   **b.** 63

Solution

a. First, write 40 as the product of any two whole numbers, other than 1.

$$40 = 4 \cdot 10$$

Next, factor each of these numbers. Continue this process until all of the factors are prime numbers.

$$40 = 4 \quad \cdot \quad 10$$
$$= 2 \cdot 2 \cdot 2 \cdot 5$$

All the factors are now prime numbers. Then 40 written as a product of primes is

$$40 = 2 \cdot 2 \cdot 2 \cdot 5$$

b. $63 = 9 \quad \cdot \quad 7$
$$= 3 \cdot 3 \cdot 7$$

PRACTICE

1   Write each of the following numbers as a product of primes.

a. 36   **b.** 75

To use prime factors to write a fraction in lowest terms, apply the fundamental principle of fractions.

> **Fundamental Principle of Fractions**
>
> If $\dfrac{a}{b}$ is a fraction and c is a nonzero real number, then
>
> $$\frac{a \cdot c}{b \cdot c} = \frac{a}{b}$$

To understand why this is true, we use the fact that since c is not zero, then $\dfrac{c}{c} = 1$.

$$\frac{a \cdot c}{b \cdot c} = \frac{a}{b} \cdot \frac{c}{c} = \frac{a}{b} \cdot 1 = \frac{a}{b}$$

We will call this process dividing out the common factor of c.

EXAMPLE 2   Write each fraction in lowest terms.

a. $\dfrac{42}{49}$ **b.** $\dfrac{11}{27}$ **c.** $\dfrac{88}{20}$

Solution

a. Write the numerator and the denominator as products of primes; then apply the fundamental principle to the common factor 7.

$$\frac{42}{49} = \frac{2 \cdot 3 \cdot 7}{7 \cdot 7} = \frac{2 \cdot 3}{7} = \frac{6}{7}$$

b. $\dfrac{11}{27} = \dfrac{11}{3 \cdot 3 \cdot 3}$

There are no common factors other than 1, so $\dfrac{11}{27}$ is already in lowest terms.

c. $\dfrac{88}{20} = \dfrac{2 \cdot 2 \cdot 2 \cdot 11}{2 \cdot 2 \cdot 5} = \dfrac{22}{5}$ □

PRACTICE
2   Write each fraction in lowest terms.

a. $\dfrac{63}{72}$ **b.** $\dfrac{64}{12}$ **c.** $\dfrac{7}{25}$

Concept Check ☑

Explain the error in the following steps.

a. $\dfrac{15}{55} = \dfrac{1\,\cancel{5}}{5\,\cancel{5}} = \dfrac{1}{5}$ **b.** $\dfrac{6}{7} = \dfrac{5+1}{5+2} = \dfrac{1}{2}$

OBJECTIVE 2 ▶ Multiplying and dividing fractions. To multiply two fractions, multiply numerator times numerator to obtain the numerator of the product; multiply denominator times denominator to obtain the denominator of the product.

> **Multiplying Fractions**
>
> $$\frac{a}{b} \cdot \frac{c}{d} = \frac{a \cdot c}{b \cdot d}, \qquad \text{if } b \neq 0 \text{ and } d \neq 0$$

EXAMPLE 3   Multiply $\dfrac{2}{15}$ and $\dfrac{5}{13}$. Write the product in lowest terms.

Solution

$$\frac{2}{15} \cdot \frac{5}{13} = \frac{2 \cdot 5}{15 \cdot 13} \qquad \begin{array}{l}\text{Multiply numerators.}\\ \text{Multiply denominators.}\end{array}$$

Next, simplify the product by dividing the numerator and the denominator by any common factors.

$$= \frac{2 \cdot 5}{3 \cdot 5 \cdot 13}$$

$$= \frac{2}{39} \qquad\qquad\qquad\qquad □$$

PRACTICE
3   Multiply $\dfrac{3}{8}$ and $\dfrac{7}{9}$. Write the product in lowest terms.

Before dividing fractions, we first define **reciprocals.** Two fractions are reciprocals of each other if their product is 1. For example $\dfrac{2}{3}$ and $\dfrac{3}{2}$ are reciprocals since $\dfrac{2}{3} \cdot \dfrac{3}{2} = 1$. Also, the reciprocal of 5 is $\dfrac{1}{5}$ since $5 \cdot \dfrac{1}{5} = \dfrac{5}{1} \cdot \dfrac{1}{5} = 1$.

Answers to Concept Check:

answers may vary

To divide fractions, multiply the first fraction by the reciprocal of the second fraction.

> **Dividing Fractions**
>
> $$\frac{a}{b} \div \frac{c}{d} = \frac{a}{b} \cdot \frac{d}{c}, \quad \text{if } b \neq 0, d \neq 0, \text{ and } c \neq 0$$

EXAMPLE 4 Divide. Write all quotients in lowest terms.

a. $\dfrac{4}{5} \div \dfrac{5}{16}$ **b.** $\dfrac{7}{10} \div 14$ **c.** $\dfrac{3}{8} \div \dfrac{3}{10}$

Solution

a. $\dfrac{4}{5} \div \dfrac{5}{16} = \dfrac{4}{5} \cdot \dfrac{16}{5} = \dfrac{4 \cdot 16}{5 \cdot 5} = \dfrac{64}{25}$

b. $\dfrac{7}{10} \div 14 = \dfrac{7}{10} \div \dfrac{14}{1} = \dfrac{7}{10} \cdot \dfrac{1}{14} = \dfrac{7 \cdot 1}{2 \cdot 5 \cdot 2 \cdot 7} = \dfrac{1}{20}.$

c. $\dfrac{3}{8} \div \dfrac{3}{10} = \dfrac{3}{8} \cdot \dfrac{10}{3} = \dfrac{3 \cdot 2 \cdot 5}{2 \cdot 2 \cdot 2 \cdot 3} = \dfrac{5}{4}$

PRACTICE
4 Divide. Write all quotients in lowest terms.

a. $\dfrac{3}{4} \div \dfrac{4}{9}$ **b.** $\dfrac{5}{12} \div 15$ **c.** $\dfrac{7}{6} \div \dfrac{7}{15}$

OBJECTIVE 3 ▶ Adding and subtracting fractions. To add or subtract fractions with the same denominator, combine numerators and place the sum or difference over the common denominator.

> **Adding and Subtracting Fractions with the Same Denominator**
>
> $$\frac{a}{b} + \frac{c}{b} = \frac{a + c}{b}, \quad \text{if } b \neq 0$$
>
> $$\frac{a}{b} - \frac{c}{b} = \frac{a - c}{b}, \quad \text{if } b \neq 0$$

EXAMPLE 5 Add or subtract as indicated. Write each result in lowest terms.

a. $\dfrac{2}{7} + \dfrac{4}{7}$ **b.** $\dfrac{3}{10} + \dfrac{2}{10}$ **c.** $\dfrac{9}{7} - \dfrac{2}{7}$ **d.** $\dfrac{5}{3} - \dfrac{1}{3}$

Solution

a. $\dfrac{2}{7} + \dfrac{4}{7} = \dfrac{2 + 4}{7} = \dfrac{6}{7}$ **b.** $\dfrac{3}{10} + \dfrac{2}{10} = \dfrac{3 + 2}{10} = \dfrac{5}{10} = \dfrac{5}{2 \cdot 5} = \dfrac{1}{2}$

c. $\dfrac{9}{7} - \dfrac{2}{7} = \dfrac{9 - 2}{7} = \dfrac{7}{7} = 1$ **d.** $\dfrac{5}{3} - \dfrac{1}{3} = \dfrac{5 - 1}{3} = \dfrac{4}{3}$

PRACTICE
5 Add or subtract as indicated. Write each result in lowest terms.

a. $\dfrac{8}{5} - \dfrac{3}{5}$ **b.** $\dfrac{8}{5} - \dfrac{2}{5}$ **c.** $\dfrac{3}{5} + \dfrac{1}{5}$ **d.** $\dfrac{5}{12} + \dfrac{1}{12}$

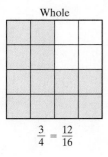

Whole

$$\frac{3}{4} = \frac{12}{16}$$

To add or subtract fractions without the same denominator, first write the fractions as **equivalent fractions** with a common denominator. Equivalent fractions are fractions that represent the same quantity. For example, $\frac{3}{4}$ and $\frac{12}{16}$ are equivalent fractions since they represent the same portion of a whole, as the diagram shows. Count the larger squares and the shaded portion is $\frac{3}{4}$. Count the smaller squares and the shaded portion is $\frac{12}{16}$. Thus, $\frac{3}{4} = \frac{12}{16}$.

We can write equivalent fractions by multiplying a given fraction by 1, as shown in the next example. Multiplying a fraction by 1 does not change the value of the fraction.

EXAMPLE 6 Write $\frac{2}{5}$ as an equivalent fraction with a denominator of 20.

Solution Since $5 \cdot 4 = 20$, multiply the fraction by $\frac{4}{4}$. Multiplying by $\frac{4}{4} = 1$ does not change the value of the fraction.

Multiply by $\frac{4}{4}$ or 1.

$$\frac{2}{5} = \frac{2}{5} \cdot \frac{4}{4} = \frac{2 \cdot 4}{5 \cdot 4} = \frac{8}{20}$$

**PRACTICE
6** Write $\frac{2}{3}$ as an equivalent fraction with a denominator of 21.

EXAMPLE 7 Add or subtract as indicated. Write each answer in lowest terms.

a. $\frac{2}{5} + \frac{1}{4}$ **b.** $\frac{1}{2} + \frac{17}{22} - \frac{2}{11}$ **c.** $3\frac{1}{6} - 1\frac{11}{12}$

Solution

a. Fractions must have a common denominator before they can be added or subtracted. Since 20 is the smallest number that both 5 and 4 divide into evenly, 20 is the **least common denominator.** Write both fractions as equivalent fractions with denominators of 20. Since

$$\frac{2}{5} \cdot \frac{4}{4} = \frac{2 \cdot 4}{5 \cdot 4} = \frac{8}{20} \quad \text{and} \quad \frac{1}{4} \cdot \frac{5}{5} = \frac{1 \cdot 5}{4 \cdot 5} = \frac{5}{20}$$

then

$$\frac{2}{5} + \frac{1}{4} = \frac{8}{20} + \frac{5}{20} = \frac{13}{20}$$

b. The least common denominator for denominators 2, 22, and 11 is 22. First, write each fraction as an equivalent fraction with a denominator of 22. Then add or subtract from left to right.

$$\frac{1}{2} = \frac{1}{2} \cdot \frac{11}{11} = \frac{11}{22}, \quad \frac{17}{22} = \frac{17}{22}, \quad \text{and} \quad \frac{2}{11} = \frac{2}{11} \cdot \frac{2}{2} = \frac{4}{22}$$

Then

$$\frac{1}{2} + \frac{17}{22} - \frac{2}{11} = \frac{11}{22} + \frac{17}{22} - \frac{4}{22} = \frac{24}{22} = \frac{12}{11}$$

c. To find $3\frac{1}{6} - 1\frac{11}{12}$, let's use a vertical format.

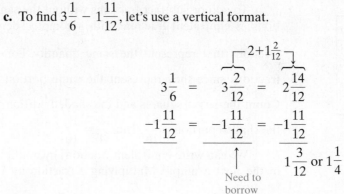

$$3\frac{1}{6} = 3\frac{2}{12} = 2\frac{14}{12}$$

$$-1\frac{11}{12} = -1\frac{11}{12} = -1\frac{11}{12}$$

$$1\frac{3}{12} \text{ or } 1\frac{1}{4}$$

Need to borrow

PRACTICE 7 Add or subtract as indicated. Write answers in lowest terms.

a. $\dfrac{5}{11} + \dfrac{1}{7}$ **b.** $9\dfrac{1}{13} - 5\dfrac{1}{2}$ **c.** $\dfrac{1}{3} + \dfrac{29}{30} - \dfrac{4}{5}$

VOCABULARY & READINESS CHECK

Use the choices below to fill in each blank. Some choices may be used more than once.

simplified	reciprocals	equivalent	denominator
product	factors	fraction	numerator

1. A quotient of two numbers, such as $\dfrac{5}{8}$, is called a _____.

2. In the fraction $\dfrac{3}{11}$, the number 3 is called the _____ and the number 11 is called the _____.

3. To factor a number means to write it as a _____.

4. A fraction is said to be _____ when the numerator and the denominator have no common factors other than 1.

5. In $7 \cdot 3 = 21$, the numbers 7 and 3 are called _____ and the number 21 is called the _____.

6. The fractions $\dfrac{2}{9}$ and $\dfrac{9}{2}$ are called _____.

7. Fractions that represent the same quantity are called _____ fractions.

Represent the shaded part of each geometric figure by a fraction

8.   **9.**   **10.**   **11.**

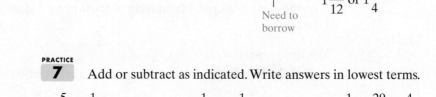

1.3 EXERCISE SET

MyMathLab *Powered by CourseCompass™ and MathXL®*   PRACTICE   WATCH   DOWNLOAD   READ   REVIEW

Write each number as a product of primes. See Example 1.

1. 33   **2.** 60   **3.** 98

4. 27   **5.** 20   **6.** 56

7. 75   **8.** 32   **9.** 45

10. 24

Write the fraction in lowest terms. See Example 2.

11. $\dfrac{2}{4}$ **12.** $\dfrac{3}{6}$ **13.** $\dfrac{10}{15}$

14. $\dfrac{15}{20}$ **15.** $\dfrac{3}{7}$ **16.** $\dfrac{5}{9}$

17. $\dfrac{18}{30}$ **18.** $\dfrac{42}{45}$

Multiply or divide as indicated. Write the answer in lowest terms. See Examples 3 and 4.

19. $\dfrac{1}{2} \cdot \dfrac{3}{4}$

20. $\dfrac{1}{8} \cdot \dfrac{3}{5}$

21. $\dfrac{2}{3} \cdot \dfrac{3}{4}$

22. $\dfrac{7}{8} \cdot \dfrac{3}{21}$

23. $\dfrac{1}{2} \div \dfrac{7}{12}$

24. $\dfrac{7}{12} \div \dfrac{1}{2}$

25. $\dfrac{3}{4} \div \dfrac{1}{20}$

26. $\dfrac{3}{5} \div \dfrac{9}{10}$

27. $\dfrac{7}{10} \cdot \dfrac{5}{21}$

28. $\dfrac{3}{35} \cdot \dfrac{10}{63}$

29. $2\dfrac{7}{9} \cdot \dfrac{1}{3}$

30. $\dfrac{1}{4} \cdot 5\dfrac{5}{6}$

The area of a plane figure is a measure of the amount of surface of the figure. Find the area of each figure below. (The area of a rectangle is the product of its length and width. The area of a triangle is $\dfrac{1}{2}$ the product of its base and height.)

△ **31.**

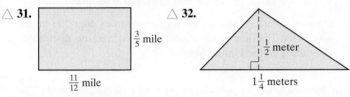

$\dfrac{3}{5}$ mile

$\dfrac{11}{12}$ mile

△ **32.**

$\dfrac{1}{2}$ meter

$1\dfrac{1}{4}$ meters

Add or subtract as indicated. Write the answer in lowest terms. See Example 5.

33. $\dfrac{4}{5} - \dfrac{1}{5}$

34. $\dfrac{6}{7} - \dfrac{1}{7}$

35. $\dfrac{4}{5} + \dfrac{1}{5}$

36. $\dfrac{6}{7} + \dfrac{1}{7}$

37. $\dfrac{17}{21} - \dfrac{10}{21}$

38. $\dfrac{18}{35} - \dfrac{11}{35}$

39. $\dfrac{23}{105} + \dfrac{4}{105}$

40. $\dfrac{13}{132} + \dfrac{35}{132}$

Write each fraction as an equivalent fraction with the given denominator. See Example 6.

41. $\dfrac{7}{10}$ with a denominator of 30

42. $\dfrac{2}{3}$ with a denominator of 9

43. $\dfrac{2}{9}$ with a denominator of 18

44. $\dfrac{8}{7}$ with a denominator of 56

45. $\dfrac{4}{5}$ with a denominator of 20

46. $\dfrac{4}{5}$ with a denominator of 25

Add or subtract as indicated. Write the answer in lowest terms. See Example 7.

47. $\dfrac{2}{3} + \dfrac{3}{7}$

48. $\dfrac{3}{4} + \dfrac{1}{6}$

49. $2\dfrac{13}{15} - 1\dfrac{1}{5}$

50. $5\dfrac{2}{9} - 3\dfrac{1}{6}$

51. $\dfrac{5}{22} - \dfrac{5}{33}$

52. $\dfrac{7}{10} - \dfrac{8}{15}$

53. $\dfrac{12}{5} - 1$

54. $2 - \dfrac{3}{8}$

Each circle below represents a whole, or 1. Use subtraction to determine the unknown part of the circle.

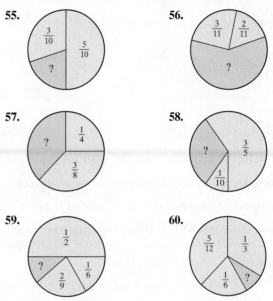

55.

$\dfrac{3}{10}$ $\dfrac{5}{10}$?

56.

$\dfrac{3}{11}$ $\dfrac{2}{11}$?

57.

? $\dfrac{1}{4}$ $\dfrac{3}{8}$

58.

? $\dfrac{3}{5}$ $\dfrac{1}{10}$

59.

$\dfrac{1}{2}$? $\dfrac{2}{9}$ $\dfrac{1}{6}$

60.

$\dfrac{5}{12}$ $\dfrac{1}{3}$ $\dfrac{1}{6}$?

MIXED PRACTICE

Perform the following operations. Write answers in lowest terms.

61. $\dfrac{10}{21} + \dfrac{5}{21}$

62. $\dfrac{11}{35} + \dfrac{3}{35}$

63. $\dfrac{10}{3} - \dfrac{5}{21}$

64. $\dfrac{11}{7} - \dfrac{3}{35}$

65. $\dfrac{2}{3} \cdot \dfrac{3}{5}$

66. $\dfrac{2}{3} \div \dfrac{3}{5}$

67. $\dfrac{3}{4} \div \dfrac{7}{12}$

68. $\dfrac{3}{4} \cdot \dfrac{7}{12}$

69. $\dfrac{5}{12} + \dfrac{4}{12}$

70. $\dfrac{2}{7} + \dfrac{4}{7}$

71. $5 + \dfrac{2}{3}$

72. $7 + \dfrac{1}{10}$

73. $\dfrac{7}{8} \div 3\dfrac{1}{4}$

74. $3 \div \dfrac{3}{4}$

75. $\dfrac{7}{18} \div \dfrac{14}{36}$

76. $4\dfrac{3}{7} \div \dfrac{31}{7}$

77. $\dfrac{23}{105} - \dfrac{2}{105}$

78. $\dfrac{57}{132} - \dfrac{13}{132}$

79. $1\dfrac{1}{2} + 3\dfrac{2}{3}$

80. $2\dfrac{3}{5} + 4\dfrac{7}{10}$

81. $\dfrac{2}{3} - \dfrac{5}{9} + \dfrac{5}{6}$

82. $\dfrac{8}{11} - \dfrac{1}{4} + \dfrac{1}{2}$

The perimeter of a plane figure is the total distance around the figure. Find the perimeter of each figure in Exercises 83 and 84.

△ **83.**

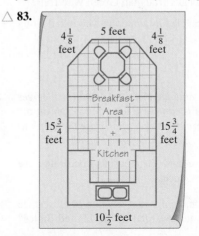

$4\dfrac{1}{8}$ feet   5 feet $4\dfrac{1}{8}$ feet

$15\dfrac{3}{4}$ feet   Breakfast Area $15\dfrac{3}{4}$ feet

Kitchen

$10\dfrac{1}{2}$ feet

△ **84.**

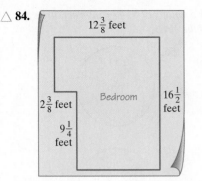

85. Yelena Isinbaeva currently holds the women's pole vault world record at $5\frac{1}{50}$ meters. The men's pole vault world record is currently held by Sergei Bubka, at $1\frac{3}{25}$ meters higher than the Women's record. What is the current men's pole vault record? (*Source: International Association of Athletics Federations*)

86. The Preakness, one of the horse races in the Triple Crown, is a $1\frac{3}{16}$-mile race. The Belmont, another of the three races, is $\frac{5}{16}$ of a mile longer than the Preakness. How long is the Belmont? (*Source: Sports Illustrated*)

87. In your own words, explain how to add two fractions with different denominators.

88. In your own words, explain how to multiply two fractions.

The following trail chart is given to visitors at the Lakeview Forest Preserve.

Trail Name	Distance (miles)
Robin Path	$3\frac{1}{2}$
Red Falls	$5\frac{1}{2}$
Green Way	$2\frac{1}{8}$
Autumn Walk	$1\frac{3}{4}$

89. How much longer is Red Falls Trail than Green Way Trail?

90. Find the total distance traveled by someone who hiked along all four trails.

CONCEPT EXTENSIONS

The breakdown of science and engineering doctorate degrees awarded in the United States is summarized in the graph on the next column, called a circle graph or a pie chart. Use the graph to answer the questions. (Source: National Science Foundation)

91. What fraction of science and engineering doctorates are awarded in the physical sciences?

92. Engineering doctorates make up what fraction of all science and engineering doctorates awarded in the United States?

Science and Engineering Doctorates Awarded, by Field of Study

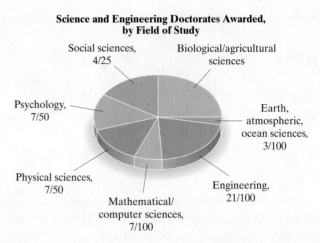

93. What fraction of all science and engineering doctorates are awarded in the biological and agricultural sciences?

94. Social sciences and psychology doctorates together make up what fraction of all science and engineering doctorates awarded in the United States?

In 2006, Gap Inc. operated a total of 3054 stores worldwide. The following chart shows the store breakdown by brand. (Source: Gap Inc.)

Gap Inc. Stores

Brand	Number of Stores
Gap (Domestic)	1335
Gap (International)	256
Banana Republic	498
Old Navy	960
Forth & Towne	5
Total	3054

95. Multiple Choice. Choose the fraction of Gap Inc. stores that are *not* Forth & Towne.

a. 5   **b.** 3049   **c.** $\frac{3049}{3054}$ **d.** $\frac{5}{3054}$

96. Multiple Choice. Choose the fraction of Gap Inc. stores that are Gap (Domestic) or Gap (International).

a. 1591   **b.** 1463   **c.** $\frac{1463}{3054}$ **d.** $\frac{1591}{3054}$

The area of a plane figure is a measure of the amount of surface of the figure. Find the area of each figure. (The area of a triangle is $\frac{1}{2}$ the product of its base and height. The area of a rectangle is the product of its length and width. Recall that area is measured in square units.)

△ **97.**   △ **98.**

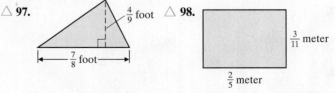

1.4 INTRODUCTION TO VARIABLE EXPRESSIONS AND EQUATIONS

OBJECTIVES

1 Define and use exponents and the order of operations.

2 Evaluate algebraic expressions, given replacement values for variables.

3 Determine whether a number is a solution of a given equation.

4 Translate phrases into expressions and sentences into equations.

OBJECTIVE 1 ▶ Using exponents and the order of operations. Frequently in algebra, products occur that contain repeated multiplication of the same factor. For example, the volume of a cube whose sides each measure 2 centimeters is $(2 \cdot 2 \cdot 2)$ cubic centimeters. We may use **exponential notation** to write such products in a more compact form. For example,

$$2 \cdot 2 \cdot 2 \quad \textit{may be written as} \quad 2^3.$$

The 2 in 2^3 is called the **base**; it is the repeated factor. The 3 in 2^3 is called the **exponent** and is the number of times the base is used as a factor. The expression 2^3 is called an **exponential expression.**

$$\text{base} \searrow 2^{\overset{\displaystyle \curvearrowleft \text{exponent}}{3}} = 2 \cdot 2 \cdot 2 = 8$$

2 is a factor 3 times

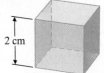

2 cm

Volume is $(2 \cdot 2 \cdot 2)$ cubic centimeters.

EXAMPLE 1 Evaluate the following:

a. 3^2 [read as "3 squared" or as "3 to the second power"]

b. 5^3 [read as "5 cubed" or as "5 to the third power"]

c. 2^4 [read as "2 to the fourth power"]

d. 7^1 **e.** $\left(\dfrac{3}{7}\right)^2$

Solution

a. $3^2 = 3 \cdot 3 = 9$ **b.** $5^3 = 5 \cdot 5 \cdot 5 = 125$

c. $2^4 = 2 \cdot 2 \cdot 2 \cdot 2 = 16$ **d.** $7^1 = 7$

e. $\left(\dfrac{3}{7}\right)^2 = \left(\dfrac{3}{7}\right)\left(\dfrac{3}{7}\right) = \dfrac{9}{49}$

PRACTICE
1 Evaluate:

a. 1^3 **b.** 5^2 **c.** $\left(\dfrac{1}{10}\right)^2$ **d.** 9^1 **e.** $\left(\dfrac{2}{5}\right)^3$

▶ **Helpful Hint**
$2^3 \neq 2 \cdot 3$ since 2^3 indicates repeated **multiplication** of the same factor.

$$2^3 = 2 \cdot 2 \cdot 2 = 8, \text{ whereas } 2 \cdot 3 = 6.$$

Using symbols for mathematical operations is a great convenience. However, the more operation symbols presented in an expression, the more careful we must be when performing the indicated operation. For example, in the expression $2 + 3 \cdot 7$, do we add first or multiply first? To eliminate confusion, **grouping symbols** are used. Examples of grouping symbols are parentheses ( ), brackets [ ], braces { }, and the fraction bar. If we wish $2 + 3 \cdot 7$ to be simplified by adding first, we enclose $2 + 3$ in parentheses.

$$(2 + 3) \cdot 7 = 5 \cdot 7 = 35$$

If we wish to multiply first, $3 \cdot 7$ may be enclosed in parentheses.

$$2 + (3 \cdot 7) = 2 + 21 = 23$$

To eliminate confusion when no grouping symbols are present, use the following agreed upon order of operations.

> **Order of Operations**
>
> Simplify expressions using the order below. If grouping symbols such as parentheses are present, simplify expressions within those first, starting with the innermost set. If fraction bars are present, simplify the numerator and the denominator separately.
>
> **1.** Evaluate exponential expressions.
>
> **2.** Perform multiplications or divisions in order from left to right.
>
> **3.** Perform additions or subtractions in order from left to right.

Now simplify $2 + 3 \cdot 7$. There are no grouping symbols and no exponents, so we multiply and then add.

$$2 + 3 \cdot 7 = 2 + 21 \quad \text{Multiply.}$$
$$= 23 \quad \text{Add.}$$

EXAMPLE 2   Simplify each expression.

a. $6 \div 3 + 5^2$ **b.** $\dfrac{2(12 + 3)}{|-15|}$ **c.** $3 \cdot 10 - 7 \div 7$ **d.** $3 \cdot 4^2$ **e.** $\dfrac{3}{2} \cdot \dfrac{1}{2} - \dfrac{1}{2}$

Solution

a. Evaluate 5^2 first.

$$6 \div 3 + 5^2 = 6 \div 3 + 25$$

Next divide, then add.

$$= 2 + 25 \quad \text{Divide.}$$
$$= 27 \quad \text{Add.}$$

b. First, simplify the numerator and the denominator separately.

$$\frac{2(12 + 3)}{|-15|} = \frac{2(15)}{15} \quad \begin{array}{l}\text{Simplify numerator and}\\ \text{denominator separately.}\end{array}$$
$$= \frac{30}{15}$$
$$= 2 \quad \text{Simplify.}$$

c. Multiply and divide from left to right. Then subtract.

$$3 \cdot 10 - 7 \div 7 = 30 - 1$$
$$= 29 \quad \text{Subtract.}$$

d. In this example, only the 4 is squared. The factor of 3 is not part of the base because no grouping symbol includes it as part of the base.

$$3 \cdot 4^2 = 3 \cdot 16 \quad \text{Evaluate the exponential expression.}$$
$$= 48 \quad \text{Multiply.}$$

e. The order of operations applies to operations with fractions in exactly the same way as it applies to operations with whole numbers.

$$\frac{3}{2} \cdot \frac{1}{2} - \frac{1}{2} = \frac{3}{4} - \frac{1}{2} \quad \text{Multiply.}$$

$$= \frac{3}{4} - \frac{2}{4} \quad \text{The least common denominator is 4.}$$

$$= \frac{1}{4} \quad \text{Subtract.} \qquad \square$$

PRACTICE
2 Simplify each expression

a. $6 + 3 \cdot 9$ **b.** $4^3 \div 8 + 3$ **c.** $\left(\frac{2}{3}\right)^2 \cdot |-8|$

d. $\dfrac{9(14 - 6)}{|-2|}$ **e.** $\dfrac{7}{4} \cdot \dfrac{1}{4} - \dfrac{1}{4}$

> **▶ Helpful Hint**
>
> Be careful when evaluating an exponential expression. In $3 \cdot 4^2$, the exponent 2 applies only to the base 4. In $(3 \cdot 4)^2$, we multiply first because of parentheses, so the exponent 2 applies to the product $3 \cdot 4$.
>
> $$3 \cdot 4^2 = 3 \cdot 16 = 48 \qquad (3 \cdot 4)^2 = (12)^2 = 144$$

Expressions that include many grouping symbols can be confusing. When simplifying these expressions, keep in mind that grouping symbols separate the expression into distinct parts. Each is then simplified separately.

EXAMPLE 3   Simplify $\dfrac{3 + |4 - 3| + 2^2}{6 - 3}$.

Solution   The fraction bar serves as a grouping symbol and separates the numerator and denominator. Simplify each separately. Also, the absolute value bars here serve as a grouping symbol. We begin in the numerator by simplifying within the absolute value bars.

$$\frac{3 + |4 - 3| + 2^2}{6 - 3} = \frac{3 + |1| + 2^2}{6 - 3} \quad \begin{array}{l}\text{Simplify the expression inside} \\ \text{the absolute value bars.}\end{array}$$

$$= \frac{3 + 1 + 2^2}{3} \quad \begin{array}{l}\text{Find the absolute value and} \\ \text{simplify the denominator.}\end{array}$$

$$= \frac{3 + 1 + 4}{3} \quad \text{Evaluate the exponential expression.}$$

$$= \frac{8}{3} \quad \text{Simplify the numerator.} \qquad \square$$

PRACTICE
3 Simplify $\dfrac{6^2 - 5}{3 + |6 - 5| \cdot 8}$

EXAMPLE 4   Simplify $3[4 + 2(10 - 1)]$.

Solution   Notice that both parentheses and brackets are used as grouping symbols. Start with the innermost set of grouping symbols.

> ▶ **Helpful Hint**
> Be sure to follow order of operations and resist the temptation to incorrectly add 4 and 2 first.

$$3[4 + 2(10 - 1)] = 3[4 + 2(9)] \quad \text{Simplify the expression in parentheses.}$$
$$= 3[4 + 18] \quad \text{Multiply.}$$
$$= 3[22] \quad \text{Add.}$$
$$= 66 \quad \text{Multiply.}$$

PRACTICE
4   Simplify $4[25 - 3(5 + 3)]$.

EXAMPLE 5   Simplify $\dfrac{8 + 2 \cdot 3}{2^2 - 1}$.

Solution

$$\frac{8 + 2 \cdot 3}{2^2 - 1} = \frac{8 + 6}{4 - 1} = \frac{14}{3}$$

PRACTICE
5   Simplify $\dfrac{36 \div 9 + 5}{5^2 - 3}$.

OBJECTIVE 2 ▶ **Evaluating algebraic expressions.**   In algebra, we use symbols, usually letters such as x, y, or z, to represent unknown numbers. A symbol that is used to represent a number is called a **variable.** An **algebraic expression** is a collection of numbers, variables, operation symbols, and grouping symbols. For example,

$$2x, \quad -3, \quad 2x + 10, \quad 5(p^2 + 1), \quad \text{and} \quad \frac{3y^2 - 6y + 1}{5}$$

are algebraic expressions. The expression $2x$ means $2 \cdot x$. Also, $5(p^2 + 1)$ means $5 \cdot (p^2 + 1)$ and $3y^2$ means $3 \cdot y^2$. If we give a specific value to a variable, we can **evaluate an algebraic expression.** To evaluate an algebraic expression means to find its numerical value once we know the values of the variables.

Algebraic expressions often occur during problem solving. For example, the expression

$$16t^2$$

gives the distance in feet (neglecting air resistance) that an object will fall in t seconds. (See Exercise 63 in this section.)

EXAMPLE 6   Evaluate each expression if $x = 3$ and $y = 2$.

a. $2x - y$ **b.** $\dfrac{3x}{2y}$ **c.** $\dfrac{x}{y} + \dfrac{y}{2}$ **d.** $x^2 - y^2$

Solution

a. Replace x with 3 and y with 2.

$$2x - y = 2(3) - 2 \quad \text{Let } x = 3 \text{ and } y = 2.$$
$$= 6 - 2 \qquad \text{Multiply.}$$
$$= 4 \qquad \text{Subtract.}$$

b. $\dfrac{3x}{2y} = \dfrac{3 \cdot 3}{2 \cdot 2} = \dfrac{9}{4}$ Let $x = 3$ and $y = 2$.

c. Replace x with 3 and y with 2. Then simplify.

$$\frac{x}{y} + \frac{y}{2} = \frac{3}{2} + \frac{2}{2} = \frac{5}{2}$$

d. Replace x with 3 and y with 2.

$$x^2 - y^2 = 3^2 - 2^2 = 9 - 4 = 5$$ □

PRACTICE
6   Evaluate each expression if $x = 2$ and $y = 5$.

a. $2x + y$ **b.** $\dfrac{4x}{3y}$ **c.** $\dfrac{3}{x} + \dfrac{x}{y}$ **d.** $x^3 + y^2$

OBJECTIVE 3 ▶ Determining whether a number is a solution of an equation. Many times a problem-solving situation is modeled by an equation. An **equation** is a mathematical statement that two expressions have equal value. The equal symbol "=" is used to equate the two expressions. For example, $3 + 2 = 5$, $7x = 35$, $\dfrac{2(x - 1)}{3} = 0$, and $I = PRT$ are all equations.

> ▶ **Helpful Hint**
> An equation contains the equal symbol "=". An algebraic expression does not.

Concept Check ☑

Which of the following are equations? Which are expressions?

a. $5x = 8$ **b.** $5x - 8$ **c.** $12y + 3x$ **d.** $12y = 3x$

When an equation contains a variable, deciding which values of the variable make an equation a true statement is called **solving** an equation for the variable. A **solution** of an equation is a value for the variable that makes the equation true. For example, 3 is a solution of the equation $x + 4 = 7$, because if x is replaced with 3 the statement is true.

$$x + 4 = 7$$
$$\downarrow$$
$$3 + 4 = 7 \quad \text{Replace } x \text{ with 3.}$$
$$7 = 7 \quad \text{True}$$

Answers to Concept Check:

equations: a, d; expressions: b, c.

Similarly, 1 is not a solution of the equation $x + 4 = 7$, because $1 + 4 = 7$ is **not** a true statement.

EXAMPLE 7   Decide whether 2 is a solution of $3x + 10 = 8x$.

Solution   Replace x with 2 and see if a true statement results.

$$3x + 10 = 8x \quad \text{Original equation}$$
$$3(2) + 10 \stackrel{?}{=} 8(2) \quad \text{Replace } x \text{ with 2.}$$
$$6 + 10 \stackrel{?}{=} 16 \quad \text{Simplify each side.}$$
$$16 = 16 \quad \text{True}$$

Since we arrived at a true statement after replacing x with 2 and simplifying both sides of the equation, 2 is a solution of the equation. □

PRACTICE
7   Decide whether 4 is a solution of $9x - 6 = 7x$.

OBJECTIVE 4 ▶ Translating phrases to expressions and sentences to equations. Now that we know how to represent an unknown number by a variable, let's practice translating phrases into algebraic expressions and sentences into equations. Oftentimes solving problems requires the ability to translate word phrases and sentences into symbols. Below is a list of some key words and phrases to help us translate.

> **▶ Helpful Hint**
> Order matters when subtracting and also dividing, so be especially careful with these translations.

Addition (+)	Subtraction (−)	Multiplication (·)	Division (÷)	Equality (=)
Sum	Difference of	Product	Quotient	Equals
Plus	Minus	Times	Divide	Gives
Added to	Subtracted from	Multiply	Into	Is/was/should be
More than	Less than	Twice	Ratio	Yields
Increased by	Decreased by	Of	Divided by	Amounts to
Total	Less			Represents/Is the same as

EXAMPLE 8   Write an algebraic expression that represents each phrase. Let the variable x represent the unknown number.

a. The sum of a number and 3
b. The product of 3 and a number
c. Twice a number
d. 10 decreased by a number
e. 5 times a number, increased by 7

Solution

a. $x + 3$ since "sum" means to add

b. $3 \cdot x$ and $3x$ are both ways to denote the product of 3 and x

c. $2 \cdot x$ or $2x$

d. $10 - x$ because "decreased by" means to subtract

e. $\underbrace{5x}_{5 \text{ times a number}} + 7$ □

PRACTICE

8   Write an algebraic expression that represents each phase. Let the variable *x* represent the unknown number.

a. Six times a number

b. A number decreased by 8

c. The product of a number and 9

d. Two times a number, plus 3

e. The sum of 7 and a number

▶ **Helpful Hint**

Make sure you understand the difference when translating phrases containing "decreased by," "subtracted from," and "less than."

Phrase	Translation	
A number decreased by 10	$x - 10$	⎫
A number subtracted from 10	$10 - x$	⎬ Notice the order.
10 less than a number	$x - 10$	⎬
A number less 10	$x - 10$	⎭

Now let's practice translating sentences into equations.

EXAMPLE 9   Write each sentence as an equation or inequality. Let *x* represent the unknown number.

a. The quotient of 15 and a number is 4.

b. Three subtracted from 12 is a number.

c. Four times a number, added to 17, is not equal to 21.

d. Triple a number is less than 48.

Solution

a. In words:

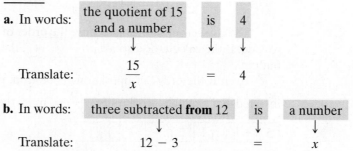

the quotient of 15 and a number	is	4
↓	↓	↓

Translate: $\dfrac{15}{x}$ $=$ 4

b. In words:

three subtracted **from** 12	is	a number
↓	↓	↓

Translate: $12 - 3$ $=$ x

Care must be taken when the operation is subtraction. The expression $3 - 12$ would be incorrect. Notice that $3 - 12 \neq 12 - 3$.

c. In words:

four times a number	added to	17	is not equal to	21
↓	↓	↓	↓	↓

Translate: $4x$ $+$ 17 $\neq$ 21

d. In words:

triple a number	is less than	48
↓	↓	↓

Translate: $3x$ $<$ 48

PRACTICE
9 Write each sentence as an equation or inequality. Let x represent the unknown number.

a. A number increased by 7 is equal to 13.

b. Two less than a number is 11.

c. Double a number, added to 9, is not equal to 25.

d. Five times 11 is greater than or equal to an unknown number.

Calculator Explorations

Exponents

To evaluate exponential expressions on a scientific calculator, find the key marked $\boxed{y^x}$ or $\boxed{\wedge}$. To evaluate, for example, 3^5, press the following keys: $\boxed{3}\ \boxed{y^x}\ \boxed{5}\ \boxed{=}$ or $\boxed{3}\ \boxed{\wedge}\ \boxed{5}\ \boxed{=}$.

$\updownarrow$ or
$\boxed{\text{ENTER}}$

The display should read $\boxed{\qquad 243}$ or $\boxed{\begin{array}{l} 3\wedge 5 \\ \qquad 243 \end{array}}$

Order of Operations

Some calculators follow the order of operations, and others do not. To see whether or not your calculator has the order of operations built in, use your calculator to find $2 + 3 \cdot 4$. To do this, press the following sequence of keys:

$\boxed{2}\ \boxed{+}\ \boxed{3}\ \boxed{\times}\ \boxed{4}\ \boxed{=}$.

$\updownarrow$ or
$\boxed{\text{ENTER}}$

The correct answer is 14 because the order of operations is to multiply before we add. If the calculator displays $\boxed{\qquad 14}$, then it has the order of operations built in.

Even if the order of operations is built in, parentheses must sometimes be inserted. For example, to simplify $\dfrac{5}{12 - 7}$, press the keys

$\boxed{5}\ \boxed{\div}\ \boxed{(}\ \boxed{1}\ \boxed{2}\ \boxed{-}\ \boxed{7}\ \boxed{)}\ \boxed{=}$.

$\updownarrow$ or
$\boxed{\text{ENTER}}$

The display should read $\boxed{\quad 1}$ or $\boxed{\begin{array}{l} 5/(12-7) \\ \qquad\qquad 1 \end{array}}$

Use a calculator to evaluate each expression.

1. 5^4

2. 7^4

3. 9^5

4. 8^6

5. $2(20 - 5)$

6. $3(14 - 7) + 21$

7. $24(862 - 455) + 89$

8. $99 + (401 + 962)$

9. $\dfrac{4623 + 129}{36 - 34}$

10. $\dfrac{956 - 452}{89 - 86}$

VOCABULARY & READINESS CHECK

Use the choices below to fill in each blank.

| add | multiply | equation | variable | base | grouping |
| subtract | divide | expression | solution | solving | exponent |

1. In the expression 5^2, the 5 is called the _____ and the 2 is called the _____ .

2. The symbols ( ), [ ], and { } are examples of _____ symbols.

3. A symbol that is used to represent a number is called a(n) _____ .

4. A collection of numbers, variables, operation symbols, and grouping symbols is called a(n) _____ .

5. A mathematical statement that two expressions are equal is called a(n) _____ .

6. A value for the variable that makes an equation a true statement is called a(n) _____ .

7. Deciding what values of a variable make an equation a true statement is called _____ the equation.

8. To simplify the expression $1 + 3 \cdot 6$, first _____ .

9. To simplify the expression $(1 + 3) \cdot 6$, first _____ .

10. To simplify the expression $(20 - 4) \cdot 2$, first _____ .

11. To simplify the expression $20 - 4 \div 2$, first _____ .

1.4 | EXERCISE SET

MyMathLab®   Powered by CourseCompass™ and MathXL®

MathXL PRACTICE · WATCH · DOWNLOAD · READ · REVIEW

Evaluate. See Example 1.

1. 3^5

2. 2^5

3. 3^3

4. 4^4

5. 1^5

6. 1^8

7. 5^1

8. 8^1

9. $\left(\dfrac{1}{5}\right)^3$

10. $\left(\dfrac{6}{11}\right)^2$

11. $\left(\dfrac{2}{3}\right)^4$

12. $\left(\dfrac{1}{2}\right)^5$

13. 7^2

14. 9^2

15. 4^2

16. 4^3

17. $(1.2)^2$

18. $(0.07)^2$

MIXED PRACTICE

Simplify each expression. See Examples 2 through 5.

19. $5 + 6 \cdot 2$

20. $8 + 5 \cdot 3$

21. $4 \cdot 8 - 6 \cdot 2$

22. $12 \cdot 5 - 3 \cdot 6$

23. $2(8 - 3)$

24. $5(6 - 2)$

25. $2 + (5 - 2) + 4^2$

26. $6 - 2 \cdot 2 + 2^5$

27. $5 \cdot 3^2$

28. $2 \cdot 5^2$

29. $\dfrac{1}{4} \cdot \dfrac{2}{3} - \dfrac{1}{6}$

30. $\dfrac{3}{4} \cdot \dfrac{1}{2} + \dfrac{2}{3}$

31. $\dfrac{6 - 4}{9 - 2}$

32. $\dfrac{8 - 5}{24 - 20}$

33. $2[5 + 2(8 - 3)]$

34. $3[4 + 3(6 - 4)]$

35. $\dfrac{19 - 3 \cdot 5}{6 - 4}$

36. $\dfrac{4 \cdot 3 + 2}{4 + 3 \cdot 2}$

37. $\dfrac{|6 - 2| + 3}{8 + 2 \cdot 5}$

38. $\dfrac{15 - |3 - 1|}{12 - 3 \cdot 2}$

39. $\dfrac{3 + 3(5 + 3)}{3^2 + 1}$

40. $\dfrac{3 + 6(8 - 5)}{4^2 + 2}$

41. $\dfrac{6 + |8 - 2| + 3^2}{18 - 3}$

42. $\dfrac{16 + |13 - 5| + 4^2}{17 - 5}$

43. Are parentheses necessary in the expression $2 + (3 \cdot 5)$? Explain your answer.

44. Are parentheses necessary in the expression $(2 + 3) \cdot 5$? Explain your answer.

Matching. *For Exercises 45 and 46, match each expression in the first column with its value in the second column.*

45. a. $(6 + 2) \cdot (5 + 3)$ — 19
b. $(6 + 2) \cdot 5 + 3$ — 22
c. $6 + 2 \cdot 5 + 3$ — 64
d. $6 + 2 \cdot (5 + 3)$ — 43

46. a. $(1 + 4) \cdot 6 - 3$ — 15
b. $1 + 4 \cdot (6 - 3)$ — 13
c. $1 + 4 \cdot 6 - 3$ — 27
d. $(1 + 4) \cdot (6 - 3)$ — 22

Evaluate each expression when $x = 1$, $y = 3$, and $z = 5$. See Example 6.

47. $3y$

48. $4x$

49. $\dfrac{z}{5x}$

50. $\dfrac{y}{2z}$

51. $3x - 2$

52. $6y - 8$

53. $|2x + 3y|$

54. $|5z - 2y|$

55. $5y^2$

56. $2z^2$

Evaluate each expression if $x = 12$, $y = 8$, and $z = 4$. See Example 6.

57. $\dfrac{x}{z} + 3y$

58. $\dfrac{y}{z} + 8x$

59. $x^2 - 3y + x$

60. $y^2 - 3x + y$

61. $\dfrac{x^2 + z}{y^2 + 2z}$

62. $\dfrac{y^2 + x}{x^2 + 3y}$

Neglecting air resistance, the expression $16t^2$ gives the distance in feet an object will fall in t seconds.

63. Complete the chart below. To evaluate $16t^2$, remember to first find t^2, then multiply by 16.

Time t (in seconds)	Distance $16t^2$ (in feet)
1	
2	
3	
4	

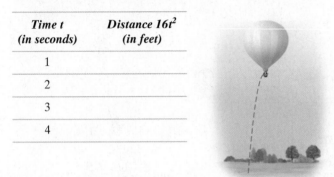

64. Does an object fall the same distance *during* each second? Why or why not? (See Exercise 63.)

Decide whether the given number is a solution of the given equation. See Example 7.

65. Is 5 a solution of $3x + 30 = 9x$?

66. Is 6 a solution of $2x + 7 = 3x$?

67. Is 0 a solution of $2x + 6 = 5x - 1$?

68. Is 2 a solution of $4x + 2 = x + 8$?

69. Is 8 a solution of $2x - 5 = 5$?

70. Is 6 a solution of $3x - 10 = 8$?

71. Is 2 a solution of $x + 6 = x + 6$?

72. Is 10 a solution of $x + 6 = x + 6$?

73. Is 0 a solution of $x = 5x + 15$?

74. Is 1 a solution of $4 = 1 - x$?

Write each phrase as an algebraic expression. Let x represent the unknown number. See Example 8.

75. Fifteen more than a number

76. One-half times a number

77. Five subtracted from a number

78. The quotient of a number and 9

79. Three times a number, increased by 22

80. The product of 8 and a number, decreased by 10

Write each sentence as an equation or inequality. Use x to represent any unknown number. See Example 9.

81. One increased by two equals the quotient of nine and three.

82. Four subtracted from eight is equal to two squared.

83. Three is not equal to four divided by two.

84. The difference of sixteen and four is greater than ten.

85. The sum of 5 and a number is 20.

86. Twice a number is 17.

87. Thirteen minus three times a number is 13.

88. Seven subtracted from a number is 0.

89. The quotient of 12 and a number is $\dfrac{1}{2}$.

90. The sum of 8 and twice a number is 42.

91. In your own words, explain the difference between an expression and an equation.

92. Determine whether each is an expression or an equation.
   a. $3x^2 - 26$
   b. $3x^2 - 26 = 1$
   c. $2x - 5 = 7x - 5$
   d. $9y + x - 8$

CONCEPT EXTENSIONS

93. Insert parentheses so that the following expression simplifies to 32.
$$20 - 4 \cdot 4 \div 2$$

94. Insert parentheses so that the following expression simplifies to 28.
$$2 \cdot 5 + 3^2$$

Solve the following.

95. The perimeter of a figure is the distance around the figure. The expression $2l + 2w$ represents the perimeter of a rectangle when l is its length and w is its width. Find the perimeter of the following rectangle by substituting 8 for l and 6 for w.

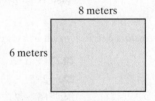

96. The expression $a + b + c$ represents the perimeter of a triangle when a, b, and c are the lengths of its sides. Find the perimeter of the following triangle.

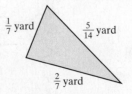

97. Multiple Choice. $2(12 \div 3 \cdot 4)$ simplifies to

    a. 32   **b.** 16   **c.** 2   **d.** 3

98. Multiple Choice. What is the perimeter of a rectangle with length 4 inches and width 3 inches?

    a. 7 inches   **b.** 14 inches   **c.** 12 inches   **d.** 24 inches

△ **99.** The area of a figure is the total enclosed surface of the figure. Area is measured in square units. The expression lw represents the area of a rectangle when l is its length and w is its width. Find the area of the following rectangular-shaped lot.

100 feet

120 feet

△ **100.** A trapezoid is a four-sided figure with exactly one pair of parallel sides. The expression $\frac{1}{2}h(B + b)$ represents its area,

when B and b are the lengths of the two parallel sides and h is the height between these sides. Find the area if $B = 15$ inches, $b = 7$ inches, and $h = 5$ inches.

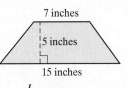

7 inches

5 inches

15 inches

101. The expression $\dfrac{I}{PT}$ represents the rate of interest being charged if a loan of P dollars for T years required I dollars in interest to be paid. Find the interest rate if a $650 loan for 3 years to buy a used IBM personal computer requires $126.75 in interest to be paid.

102. The expression $\dfrac{d}{t}$ represents the average speed r in miles per hour if a distance of d miles is traveled in t hours. Find the rate to the nearest whole number if the distance between Dallas, Texas, and Kaw City, Oklahoma, is 432 miles, and it takes Peter Callac 8.5 hours to drive the distance.

1.5 ADDING REAL NUMBERS

OBJECTIVES

1 Add real numbers with the same sign.

2 Add real numbers with unlike signs.

3 Solve problems that involve addition of real numbers.

4 Find the opposite of a number.

OBJECTIVE 1 ▶ Adding real numbers with the same sign. Real numbers can be added, subtracted, multiplied, divided, and raised to powers, just as whole numbers can. We use a number line to help picture the addition of real numbers.

EXAMPLE 1   Add: $3 + 2$

Solution   Recall that 3 and 2 are called addends. We start at 0 on a number line, and draw an arrow representing the addend 3. This arrow is three units long and points to the right since 3 is positive. From the tip of this arrow, we draw another arrow representing the addend 2. The number below the tip of this arrow is the sum, 5.

Start   End

3   2

−5 −4 −3 −2 −1 0 1 2 3 4 ⑤

$$3 + 2 = 5$$

PRACTICE
1   Add using a number line: $2 + 4$.

EXAMPLE 2   Add: $-1 + (-2)$

Solution   Here, -1 and -2 are addends. We start at 0 on a number line, and draw an arrow representing -1. This arrow is one unit long and points to the left since -1 is negative. From the tip of this arrow, we draw another arrow representing -2. The number below the tip of this arrow is the sum, -3.

End   Start

−2   −1

−5 −4 ⊖3 −2 −1 0 1 2 3 4 5

$$-1 + (-2) = -3$$

PRACTICE
2 Add using a number line: $-2 + (-3)$.

Thinking of signed numbers as money earned or lost might help make addition more meaningful. Earnings can be thought of as positive numbers. If $1 is earned and later another $3 is earned, the total amount earned is $4. In other words, $1 + 3 = 4$.

On the other hand, losses can be thought of as negative numbers. If $1 is lost and later another $3 is lost, a total of $4 is lost. In other words, $(-1) + (-3) = -4$.

Using a number line each time we add two numbers can be time consuming. Instead, we can notice patterns in the previous examples and write rules for adding signed numbers. When adding two numbers with the same sign, notice that the sign of the sum is the same as the sign of the addends.

> **Adding Two Numbers with the Same Sign**
> Add their absolute values. Use their common sign as the sign of the sum.

EXAMPLE 3 Add.

a. $-3 + (-7)$ **b.** $-1 + (-20)$ **c.** $-2 + (-10)$

Solution Notice that each time, we are adding numbers with the same sign.

a. $-3 + (-7) = -10$ ⟵ Add their absolute values: $3 + 7 = 10$.
⤷ Use their common sign.

b. $-1 + (-20) = -21$ ⟵ Add their absolute values: $1 + 20 = 21$.
⤷ Common sign.

c. $-2 + (-10) = -12$ ⟵ Add their absolute values.
⤷ Common sign.

PRACTICE
3 Add.   **a.** $-5 + (-8)$ **b.** $-31 + (-1)$

OBJECTIVE 2 ▶ Adding real numbers with unlike signs. Adding numbers whose signs are not the same can also be pictured on a number line.

EXAMPLE 4 Add: $-4 + 6$

Solution

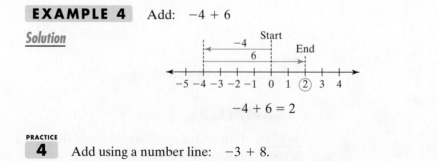

$$-4 + 6 = 2$$

PRACTICE
4 Add using a number line: $-3 + 8$.

Using temperature as an example, if the thermometer registers 4 degrees below 0 degrees and then rises 6 degrees, the new temperature is 2 degrees above 0 degrees. Thus, it is reasonable that $-4 + 6 = 2$.

Once again, we can observe a pattern: when adding two numbers with different signs, the sign of the sum is the same as the sign of the addend whose absolute value is larger.

> **Adding Two Numbers with Different Signs**
> Subtract the smaller absolute value from the larger absolute value. Use the sign of the number whose absolute value is larger as the sign of the sum.

EXAMPLE 5   Add.

a. $3 + (-7)$ **b.** $-2 + 10$ **c.** $0.2 + (-0.5)$

Solution   Notice that each time, we are adding numbers with different signs.

a. $3 + (-7) = -4$ ⟵ Subtract their absolute values: $7 - 3 = 4$.
    The negative number, -7, has the larger absolute value so the sum is negative.

b. $-2 + 10 = 8$ ⟵ Subtract their absolute values: $10 - 2 = 8$.
    The positive number, 10, has the larger absolute value so the sum is positive.

c. $0.2 + (-0.5) = -0.3$ ⟵ Subtract their absolute values: $0.5 - 0.2 = 0.3$.
    The negative number, -0.5, has the larger absolute value so the sum is negative.   ☐

PRACTICE
5   Add.

a. $15 + (-18)$ **b.** $-19 + 20$ **c.** $-0.6 + 0.4$

EXAMPLE 6   Add.

a. $-8 + (-11)$ **b.** $-5 + 35$ **c.** $0.6 + (-1.1)$

d. $-\dfrac{7}{10} + \left(-\dfrac{1}{10}\right)$ **e.** $11.4 + (-4.7)$ **f.** $-\dfrac{3}{8} + \dfrac{2}{5}$

Solution

a. $-8 + (-11) = -19$ Same sign. Add absolute values and use the common sign.

b. $-5 + 35 = 30$ Different signs. Subtract absolute values and use the sign of the number with the larger absolute value.

c. $0.6 + (-1.1) = -0.5$ Different signs.

d. $-\dfrac{7}{10} + \left(-\dfrac{1}{10}\right) = -\dfrac{8}{10} = -\dfrac{4}{5}$ Same sign.

e. $11.4 + (-4.7) = 6.7$

f. $-\dfrac{3}{8} + \dfrac{2}{5} = -\dfrac{15}{40} + \dfrac{16}{40} = \dfrac{1}{40}$ ☐

> ▶ **Helpful Hint**
> Don't forget that a common denominator is needed when adding or subtracting fractions. The common denominator here is 40.

PRACTICE
6   Add.

a. $-\dfrac{3}{5} + \left(-\dfrac{2}{5}\right)$ **b.** $3 + (-9)$

c. $2.2 + (-1.7)$ **d.** $-\dfrac{2}{7} + \dfrac{3}{10}$

EXAMPLE 7 Add.

a. $3 + (-7) + (-8)$ **b.** $[7 + (-10)] + [-2 + |-4|]$

Solution

a. Perform the additions from left to right.

$$3 + (-7) + (-8) = -4 + (-8) \quad \text{Adding numbers with different signs.}$$
$$= -12 \quad \text{Adding numbers with like signs.}$$

b. Simplify inside brackets first.

> ▶ **Helpful Hint**
> Don't forget that brackets are grouping symbols. We simplify within them first.

$$[7 + (-10)] + [-2 + |-4|] = [-3] + [-2 + 4]$$

$$= [-3] + [2]$$
$$= -1 \quad \text{Add.} \quad \square$$

PRACTICE
7 Add.

a. $8 + (-5) + (-9)$ **b.** $[-8 + 5] + [-5 + |-2|]$

OBJECTIVE 3 ▶ **Solving problems by adding real numbers.** Positive and negative numbers are often used in everyday life. Stock market returns show gains and losses as positive and negative numbers. Temperatures in cold climates often dip into the negative range, commonly referred to as "below zero" temperatures. Bank statements report deposits and withdrawals as positive and negative numbers.

EXAMPLE 8 **Finding the Gain or Loss of a Stock**

During a three-day period, a share of Fremont General Corporation stock recorded the following gains and losses:

Monday	Tuesday	Wednesday
a gain of $2	a loss of $1	a loss of $3

Find the overall gain or loss for the stock for the three days.

Solution   Gains can be represented by positive numbers. Losses can be represented by negative numbers. The overall gain or loss is the sum of the gains and losses.

In words: gain   plus   loss   plus   loss
              ↓   ↓   ↓   ↓   ↓
Translate: 2   +   (−1)   +   (−3) = −2

The overall loss is $2.   □

PRACTICE
8   During a three-day period, a share of McDonald's stock recorded the following gain and losses:

Monday	Tuesday	Wednesday
a loss of $5	a gain of $8	a loss of $2

Find the overall gain or loss for the stock for the three days.

OBJECTIVE 4 ▶ Finding the opposite of a number. To help us subtract real numbers in the next section, we first review the concept of opposites. The graphs of 4 and −4 are shown on a number line below.

Notice that 4 and −4 lie on opposite sides of 0, and each is 4 units away from 0.

This relationship between −4 and +4 is an important one. Such numbers are known as **opposites** or **additive inverses** of each other.

> **Opposites or Additive Inverses**
> Two numbers that are the same distance from 0 but lie on opposite sides of 0 are called opposites or additive inverses of each other.

Let's discover another characteristic about opposites. Notice that the sum of a number and its opposite is 0.

$$10 + (-10) = 0$$
$$-3 + 3 = 0$$
$$\frac{1}{2} + \left(-\frac{1}{2}\right) = 0$$

In general, we can write the following:

> The sum of a number a and its opposite $-a$ is 0.
> $$a + (-a) = 0$$

This is why opposites are also called additive inverses. Notice that this also means that the opposite of 0 is then 0 since $0 + 0 = 0$.

EXAMPLE 9   Find the opposite or additive inverse of each number.

a. 5   **b.** −6   **c.** $\dfrac{1}{2}$ **d.** −4.5

Solution

a. The opposite of 5 is −5. Notice that 5 and −5 are on opposite sides of 0 when plotted on a number line and are equal distances away.

b. The opposite of −6 is 6.

c. The opposite of $\dfrac{1}{2}$ is $-\dfrac{1}{2}$.

d. The opposite of −4.5 is 4.5.   ☐

PRACTICE
9   Find the opposite or additive inverse of each number.

a. $-\dfrac{5}{9}$ **b.** 8   **c.** 6.2   **d.** −3

We use the symbol "−" to represent the phrase "the opposite of" or "the additive inverse of." In general, if a is a number, we write the opposite or additive inverse of a as $-a$. We know that the opposite of -3 is 3. Notice that this translates as

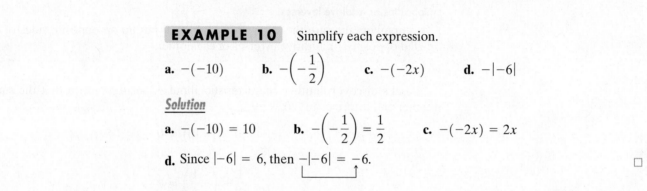

This is true in general.

> If a is a number, then $-(-a) = a$.

EXAMPLE 10   Simplify each expression.

a. $-(-10)$ **b.** $-\left(-\dfrac{1}{2}\right)$ **c.** $-(-2x)$ **d.** $-|-6|$

Solution

a. $-(-10) = 10$ **b.** $-\left(-\dfrac{1}{2}\right) = \dfrac{1}{2}$ **c.** $-(-2x) = 2x$

d. Since $|-6| = 6$, then $-|-6| = -6$.

PRACTICE
10   Simplify each expression.

a. $-|-15|$ **b.** $-\left(-\dfrac{3}{5}\right)$

c. $-(-5y)$ **d.** $-(-8)$

VOCABULARY & READINESS CHECK

Use the choices below to fill in each blank.

positive number	n	opposites
negative number	0	$-n$

1. Two numbers that are the same distance from 0 but lie on opposite sides of 0 are called _____.

2. The sum of a number and its opposite is always _____.

3. If n is a number, then $-(-n) = $ _____.

Tell whether the sum is a positive number, a negative number, or 0. Do not actually find the sum.

4. $-80 + (-127) = $ _____.

5. $-162 + 164 = $ _____.

6. $-162 + 162 = $ _____.

7. $-1.26 + (-8.3) = $ _____.

8. $-3.68 + 0.27 = $ _____.

9. $-\dfrac{2}{3} + \dfrac{2}{3} = $ _____.

1.5 | EXERCISE SET

MyMathLab
Powered by CourseCompass™ and MathXL®

MathXL PRACTICE   WATCH   DOWNLOAD   READ   REVIEW

MIXED PRACTICE

Add. See Examples 1 through 7.

1. $6 + 3$ **2.** $9 + (-12)$

3. $-6 + (-8)$ **4.** $-6 + (-14)$

5. $8 + (-7)$ **6.** $6 + (-4)$

7. $-14 + 2$ **8.** $-10 + 5$

9. $-2 + (-3)$ **10.** $-7 + (-4)$

11. $-9 + (-3)$ **12.** $7 + (-5)$

13. $-7 + 3$ **14.** $-5 + 9$

15. $10 + (-3)$ **16.** $8 + (-6)$

17. $5 + (-7)$ **18.** $3 + (-6)$

19. $-16 + 16$ **20.** $23 + (-23)$

21. $27 + (-46)$ **22.** $53 + (-37)$

23. $-18 + 49$ **24.** $-26 + 14$

25. $-33 + (-14)$ **26.** $-18 + (-26)$

27. $6.3 + (-8.4)$ **28.** $9.2 + (-11.4)$

29. $|-8| + (-16)$ **30.** $|-6| + (-61)$

31. $117 + (-79)$ **32.** $144 + (-88)$

33. $-9.6 + (-3.5)$ **34.** $-6.7 + (-7.6)$

35. $-\dfrac{3}{8} + \dfrac{5}{8}$ **36.** $-\dfrac{5}{12} + \dfrac{7}{12}$

37. $-\dfrac{7}{16} + \dfrac{1}{4}$ **38.** $-\dfrac{5}{9} + \dfrac{1}{3}$

39. $-\dfrac{7}{10} + \left(-\dfrac{3}{5}\right)$ **40.** $-\dfrac{5}{6} + \left(-\dfrac{2}{3}\right)$

41. $-15 + 9 + (-2)$ **42.** $-9 + 15 + (-5)$

43. $-21 + (-16) + (-22)$ **44.** $-18 + (-6) + (-40)$

45. $-23 + 16 + (-2)$ **46.** $-14 + (-3) + 11$

47. $|5 + (-10)|$ **48.** $|7 + (-17)|$

49. $6 + (-4) + 9$ **50.** $8 + (-2) + 7$

51. $[-17 + (-4)] + [-12 + 15]$

52. $[-2 + (-7)] + [-11 + 22]$

53. $|9 + (-12)| + |-16|$

54. $|43 + (-73)| + |-20|$

55. $-1.3 + [0.5 + (-0.3) + 0.4]$

56. $-3.7 + [0.1 + (-0.6) + 8.1]$

Solve. See Example 8.

57. The low temperature in Anoka, Minnesota, was $-15°$ last night. During the day it rose only $9°$. Find the high temperature for the day.

58. On January 2, 1943, the temperature was $-4°$ at 7:30 A.M. in Spearfish, South Dakota. Incredibly, it got $49°$ warmer in the next 2 minutes. To what temperature did it rise by 7:32?

59. The deepest canyon in the world is the Great Canyon of the Yarlung Tsangpo in Tibet. The bottom of the canyon is 17,657 feet below the surrounding terrain, called the rim. If you are standing

1230 feet above the bottom of the canyon, how far from the rim are you?

60. The lowest point in Africa is -512 feet at Lake Assal in Djibouti. If you are standing at a point 658 feet above Lake Assal, what is your elevation? (*Source:* Microsoft Encarta)

A negative net income results when a company's expenses are more than the money brought in.

61. The table below shows net incomes for Ford Motor Company's Automotive sector for the years 2004, 2005, and 2006. Find the total net income for three years.

Year	Net Income (in millions)
2004	$-\$155$
2005	$-\$3895$
2006	$-\$5200$

(*Source:* Ford Motor Company)

62. The table below shows net incomes for Continental Airlines for the years 2004, 2005, and 2006. Find the total net income for these years.

Year	Net Income (in millions)
2004	$-\$409$
2005	$-\$68$
2006	$\$343$

(*Source:* Continental Airlines)

In golf, scores that are under par for the entire round are shown as negative scores; positive scores are shown for scores that are over par, and 0 is par.

63. Paula Creamer was the winner of the 2007 LPGA SBS Open at Turtle Bay. Her scores were $-5, -2,$ and -2. What was her overall score? (*Source:* Ladies Professional Golf Association)

64. During the 2007 PGA Buick Invitational Golf Tournament, Tiger Woods won with scores of $-6, 0, -3,$ and -6. What was his overall score? (*Source:* Professional Golf Association)

Find each additive inverse or opposite. See Example 9.

65. 6

66. 4

67. -2

68. -8

69. 0

70. $-\dfrac{1}{4}$

71. $|-6|$

72. $|-11|$

73. In your own words, explain how to find the opposite of a number.

74. In your own words, explain why 0 is the only number that is its own opposite.

Simplify each of the following. See Example 10.

75. $-|-2|$

76. $-(-3)$

77. $-|0|$

78. $\left|-\dfrac{2}{3}\right|$

79. $-\left|-\dfrac{2}{3}\right|$

80. $-(-7)$

81. Explain why adding a negative number to another negative number always gives a negative sum.

82. When a positive and a negative number are added, sometimes the sum is positive, sometimes it is zero, and sometimes it is negative. Explain why and when this happens.

Decide whether the given number is a solution of the given equation.

83. Is -4 a solution of $x + 9 = 5$?

84. Is 10 a solution of $7 = -x + 3$?

85. Is -1 a solution of $y + (-3) = -7$?

86. Is -6 a solution of $1 = y + 7$?

Multiple Steps. *The following bar graph shows each month's average daily low temperature in degrees Fahrenheit for Barrow, Alaska. Use this graph to answer Exercises 87 through 92.*

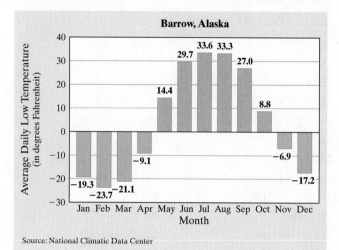

Source: National Climatic Data Center

87. For what month is the graphed temperature the highest?

88. For what month is the graphed temperature the lowest?

89. For what month is the graphed temperature positive *and* closest to 0°?

90. For what month is the graphed temperature negative *and* closest to 0°?

91. Find the average of the temperatures shown for the months of April, May, and October. (To find the average of three temperatures, find their sum and divide by 3.)

92. Find the average of the temperatures shown for the months of January, September, and October.

Fill in the Blank. *If a is a positive number and b is a negative number, fill in the blanks with the words positive or negative.*

93. $-a$ is _____.

94. $-b$ is _____.

95. $a + a$ is _____.

96. $b + b$ is _____.

1.6 SUBTRACTING REAL NUMBERS

OBJECTIVES

1 Subtract real numbers.

2 Add and subtract real numbers.

3 Evaluate algebraic expressions using real numbers.

4 Solve problems that involve subtraction of real numbers.

OBJECTIVE 1 ▶ Subtracting real numbers. Now that addition of signed numbers has been discussed, we can explore subtraction. We know that $9 - 7 = 2$. Notice that $9 + (-7) = 2$, also. This means that

$$9 - 7 = 9 + (-7)$$

Notice that the difference of 9 and 7 is the same as the sum of 9 and the opposite of 7. In general, we have the following.

Subtracting Two Real Numbers

If a and b are real numbers, then $a - b = a + (-b)$.

In other words, to find the difference of two numbers, add the first number to the opposite of the second number.

EXAMPLE 1   Subtract.

a. $-13 - 4$ **b.** $5 - (-6)$ **c.** $3 - 6$ **d.** $-1 - (-7)$

Solution

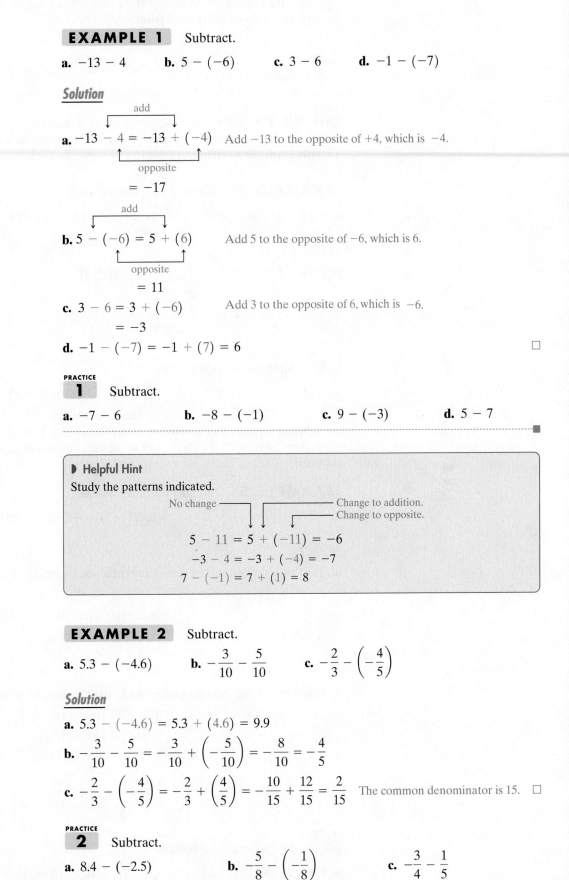

a. $\overbrace{-13 - 4}^{\text{add}} = -13 + (-4)$ Add -13 to the opposite of $+4$, which is -4.

$= -17$

b. $\overbrace{5 - (-6)}^{\text{add}} = 5 + (6)$ Add 5 to the opposite of -6, which is 6.

$= 11$

c. $3 - 6 = 3 + (-6)$ Add 3 to the opposite of 6, which is -6.

$= -3$

d. $-1 - (-7) = -1 + (7) = 6$ □

PRACTICE
1   Subtract.

a. $-7 - 6$ **b.** $-8 - (-1)$ **c.** $9 - (-3)$ **d.** $5 - 7$

▶ **Helpful Hint**

Study the patterns indicated.

No change ─────┐ ┌───── Change to addition.
                        └───── Change to opposite.

$$5 - 11 = 5 + (-11) = -6$$
$$-3 - 4 = -3 + (-4) = -7$$
$$7 - (-1) = 7 + (1) = 8$$

EXAMPLE 2   Subtract.

a. $5.3 - (-4.6)$ **b.** $-\dfrac{3}{10} - \dfrac{5}{10}$ **c.** $-\dfrac{2}{3} - \left(-\dfrac{4}{5}\right)$

Solution

a. $5.3 - (-4.6) = 5.3 + (4.6) = 9.9$

b. $-\dfrac{3}{10} - \dfrac{5}{10} = -\dfrac{3}{10} + \left(-\dfrac{5}{10}\right) = -\dfrac{8}{10} = -\dfrac{4}{5}$

c. $-\dfrac{2}{3} - \left(-\dfrac{4}{5}\right) = -\dfrac{2}{3} + \left(\dfrac{4}{5}\right) = -\dfrac{10}{15} + \dfrac{12}{15} = \dfrac{2}{15}$ The common denominator is 15.   □

PRACTICE
2   Subtract.

a. $8.4 - (-2.5)$ **b.** $-\dfrac{5}{8} - \left(-\dfrac{1}{8}\right)$ **c.** $-\dfrac{3}{4} - \dfrac{1}{5}$

EXAMPLE 3 Subtract 8 from −4.

Solution Be careful when interpreting this: The order of numbers in subtraction is important. 8 is to be subtracted **from** −4.

$$-4 - 8 = -4 + (-8) = -12 \qquad \square$$

PRACTICE
3 Subtract 5 from −2.

OBJECTIVE 2 ▶ Adding and subtracting real numbers. If an expression contains additions and subtractions, just write the subtractions as equivalent additions. Then simplify from left to right.

EXAMPLE 4 Simplify each expression.

a. $-14 - 8 + 10 - (-6)$ **b.** $1.6 - (-10.3) + (-5.6)$

Solution

a. $-14 - 8 + 10 - (-6) = -14 + (-8) + 10 + 6$
$$= -6$$

b. $1.6 - (-10.3) + (-5.6) = 1.6 + 10.3 + (-5.6)$
$$= 6.3 \qquad \square$$

PRACTICE
4 Simplify each expression.

a. $-15 - 2 - (-4) + 7$ **b.** $3.5 + (-4.1) - (-6.7)$

When an expression contains parentheses and brackets, remember the order of operations. Start with the innermost set of parentheses or brackets and work your way outward.

EXAMPLE 5 Simplify each expression.

a. $-3 + [(-2 - 5) - 2]$ **b.** $2^3 - |10| + [-6 - (-5)]$

Solution

a. Start with the innermost sets of parentheses. Rewrite $-2 - 5$ as a sum.

$$\begin{aligned}
-3 + [(-2 - 5) - 2] &= -3 + [(-2 + (-5)) - 2] \\
&= -3 + [(-7) - 2] && \text{Add: } -2 + (-5). \\
&= -3 + [-7 + (-2)] && \text{Write } -7 - 2 \text{ as a sum.} \\
&= -3 + [-9] && \text{Add.} \\
&= -12 && \text{Add.}
\end{aligned}$$

b. Start simplifying the expression inside the brackets by writing $-6 - (-5)$ as a sum.

$$\begin{aligned}
2^3 - |10| + [-6 - (-5)] &= 2^3 - |10| + [-6 + 5] \\
&= 2^3 - |10| + [-1] && \text{Add.} \\
&= 8 - 10 + (-1) && \text{Evaluate } 2^3 \text{ and } |10|. \\
&= 8 + (-10) + (-1) && \text{Write } 8 - 10 \text{ as a sum.} \\
&= -2 + (-1) && \text{Add.} \\
&= -3 && \text{Add.} \qquad \square
\end{aligned}$$

PRACTICE
5 Simplify each expression.

a. $-4 + [(-8 - 3) - 5]$ **b.** $|-13| - 3^2 + [2 - (-7)]$

OBJECTIVE 3 ▶ Evaluating algebraic expressions. Knowing how to evaluate expressions for given replacement values is helpful when checking solutions of equations and when solving problems whose unknowns satisfy given expressions. The next example illustrates this.

EXAMPLE 6 Find the value of each expression when $x = 2$ and $y = -5$.

a. $\dfrac{x - y}{12 + x}$ **b.** $x^2 - 3y$

Solution

a. Replace x with 2 and y with -5. Be sure to put parentheses around -5 to separate signs. Then simplify the resulting expression.

$$\frac{x - y}{12 + x} = \frac{2 - (-5)}{12 + 2}$$

$$= \frac{2 + 5}{14}$$

$$= \frac{7}{14} = \frac{1}{2}$$

b. Replace the x with 2 and y with -5 and simplify.

$$x^2 - 3y = 2^2 - 3(-5)$$
$$= 4 - 3(-5)$$
$$= 4 - (-15)$$
$$= 4 + 15$$
$$= 19$$

☐

PRACTICE

6 Find the value of each expression when $x = -3$ and $y = 4$.

a. $\dfrac{7 - x}{2y + x}$ **b.** $y^2 + x$

OBJECTIVE 4 ▶ Solving problems by subtracting real numbers. One use of positive and negative numbers is in recording altitudes above and below sea level, as shown in the next example.

EXAMPLE 7 **Finding the Difference in Elevations**

The lowest point on the surface of the Earth is the Dead Sea, at an elevation of 1349 feet below sea level. The highest point is Mt. Everest, at an elevation of 29,035 feet. How much of a variation in elevation is there between these two world extremes? (*Source: National Geographic Society*)

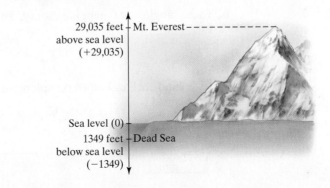

29,035 feet ─ Mt. Everest ─ ─ ─ ─ ─ ─ ─ ─
above sea level
(+29,035)

Sea level (0) ─

1349 feet ─ Dead Sea
below sea level
(−1349)

Solution To find the variation in elevation between the two heights, find the difference of the high point and the low point.

In words: | high point | minus | low point |

Translate: $29{,}035 \quad - \quad (-1349) \quad = 29{,}035 + 1349$
$$= 30{,}384 \text{ feet}$$

Thus, the variation in elevation is 30,384 feet. □

PRACTICE
7 On Tuesday morning, a bank account balance was $282. On Thursday the account balance had dropped to $-\$75$. Find the overall change in this account balance.

A knowledge of geometric concepts is needed by many professionals, such as doctors, carpenters, electronic technicians, gardeners, machinists, and pilots, just to name a few. With this in mind, we review the geometric concepts of **complementary** and **supplementary angles.**

Complementary and Supplementary Angles
Two angles are **complementary** if their sum is 90°.

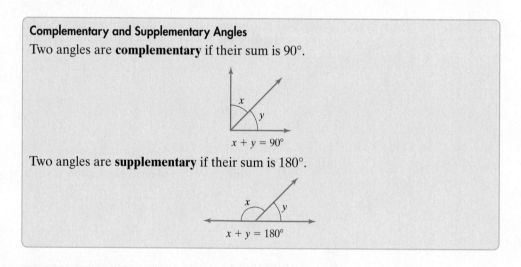

$x + y = 90°$

Two angles are **supplementary** if their sum is 180°.

$x + y = 180°$

△ **EXAMPLE 8** Find each unknown complementary or supplementary angle.

a.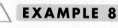

b.

Solution

a. These angles are complementary, so their sum is 90°. This means that x is $90° - 38°$.
$$x = 90° - 38° = 52°$$

b. These angles are supplementary, so their sum is 180°. This means that y is $180° - 62°$.
$$y = 180° - 62° = 118°$$ □

PRACTICE
8 Find each unknown complementary or supplementary angle.

a.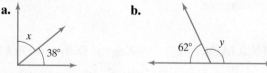

b.

VOCABULARY & READINESS CHECK

Translate each phrase. Let x represent "a number." Use the choices below to fill in each blank.

$$7 - x \qquad x - 7$$

1. 7 minus a number _____

2. 7 subtracted from a number _____

3. A number decreased by 7 _____

4. 7 less a number _____

5. A number less than 7 _____

6. A number subtracted from 7 _____

1.6 | EXERCISE SET

MIXED PRACTICE

Subtract. See Examples 1 through 5.

1. $-6 - 4$

2. $-12 - 8$

3. $4 - 9$

4. $8 - 11$

5. $16 - (-3)$

6. $12 - (-5)$

7. $\dfrac{1}{2} - \dfrac{1}{3}$

8. $\dfrac{3}{4} - \dfrac{7}{8}$

9. $-16 - (-18)$

10. $-20 - (-48)$

11. $-6 - 5$

12. $-8 - 4$

13. $7 - (-4)$

14. $3 - (-6)$

15. $-6 - (-11)$

16. $-4 - (-16)$

17. $16 - (-21)$

18. $15 - (-33)$

19. $9.7 - 16.1$

20. $8.3 - 11.2$

21. $-44 - 27$

22. $-36 - 51$

23. $-21 - (-21)$

24. $-17 - (-17)$

25. $-2.6 - (-6.7)$

26. $-6.1 - (-5.3)$

27. $-\dfrac{3}{11} - \left(-\dfrac{5}{11}\right)$

28. $-\dfrac{4}{7} - \left(-\dfrac{1}{7}\right)$

29. $-\dfrac{1}{6} - \dfrac{3}{4}$

30. $-\dfrac{1}{10} - \dfrac{7}{8}$

31. $8.3 - (-0.62)$

32. $4.3 - (-0.87)$

Perform the operation. See Example 3.

33. Subtract -5 from 8.

34. Subtract 3 from -2.

35. Subtract -1 from -6.

36. Subtract 17 from 1.

37. Subtract 8 from 7.

38. Subtract 9 from -4.

39. Decrease -8 by 15.

40. Decrease 11 by -14.

41. In your own words, explain why $5 - 8$ simplifies to a negative number.

42. Explain why $6 - 11$ is the same as $6 + (-11)$.

Simplify each expression. (Remember the order of operations.) See Examples 4 and 5.

43. $-10 - (-8) + (-4) - 20$

44. $-16 - (-3) + (-11) - 14$

45. $5 - 9 + (-4) - 8 - 8$

46. $7 - 12 + (-5) - 2 + (-2)$

47. $-6 - (2 - 11)$

48. $-9 - (3 - 8)$

49. $3^3 - 8 \cdot 9$

50. $2^3 - 6 \cdot 3$

51. $2 - 3(8 - 6)$

52. $4 - 6(7 - 3)$

53. $(3 - 6) + 4^2$

54. $(2 - 3) + 5^2$

55. $-2 + [(8 - 11) - (-2 - 9)]$

56. $-5 + [(4 - 15) - (-6) - 8]$

57. $|-3| + 2^2 + [-4 - (-6)]$

58. $|-2| + 6^2 + (-3 - 8)$

Evaluate each expression when $x = -5$, $y = 4$, and $t = 10$. See Example 6.

59. $x - y$

60. $y - x$

61. $|x| + 2t - 8y$

62. $|x + t - 7y|$

63. $\dfrac{9 - x}{y + 6}$

64. $\dfrac{15 - x}{y + 2}$

65. $y^2 - x$

66. $t^2 - x$

67. $\dfrac{|x - (-10)|}{2t}$

68. $\dfrac{|5y - x|}{6t}$

Solve. See Example 7.

69. Within 24 hours in 1916, the temperature in Browning, Montana, fell from 44 degrees to -56 degrees. How large a drop in temperature was this?

70. Much of New Orleans is below sea level. If George descends 12 feet from an elevation of 5 feet above sea level, what is his new elevation?

71. In a series of plays, the San Francisco 49ers gain 2 yards, lose 5 yards, and then lose another 20 yards. What is their total gain or loss of yardage?

72. In some card games, it is possible to have a negative score. Lavonne Schultz currently has a score of 15 points. She then loses 24 points. What is her new score?

73. Pythagoras died in the year −475 (or 475 B.C.). When was he born, if he was 94 years old when he died?

74. The Greek astronomer and mathematician Geminus died in 60 A.D. at the age of 70. When was he born?

75. A commercial jet liner hits an air pocket and drops 250 feet. After climbing 120 feet, it drops another 178 feet. What is its overall vertical change?

76. Tyson Industries stock posted a loss of 1.625 points yesterday. If it drops another 0.75 point today, find its overall change for the two days.

77. The highest point in Africa is Mt. Kilimanjaro, Tanzania, at an elevation of 19,340 feet. The lowest point is Lake Assal, Djibouti, at 512 feet below sea level. How much higher is Mt. Kilimanjaro than Lake Assal? (*Source:* National Geographic Society)

78. The airport in Bishop, California, is at an elevation of 4101 feet above sea level. The nearby Furnace Creek Airport in Death Valley, California, is at an elevation of 226 feet below sea level. How much higher in elevation is the Bishop Airport than the Furnace Creek Airport? (*Source:* National Climatic Data Center)

Find each unknown complementary or supplementary angle. See Example 8.

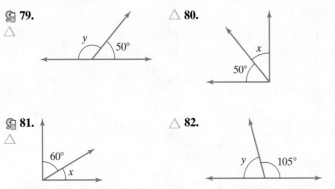

79.

y 50°

80.

x 50°

81.

60° *x*

82.

y 105°

Decide whether the given number is a solution of the given equation.

83. Is −4 a solution of $x - 9 = 5$?

84. Is 3 a solution of $x - 10 = -7$?

85. Is −2 a solution of $-x + 6 = -x - 1$?

86. Is −10 a solution of $-x - 6 = -x - 1$?

87. Is 2 a solution of $-x - 13 = -15$?

88. Is 5 a solution of $4 = 1 - x$?

CONCEPT EXTENSIONS

Multiple Steps. *Recall from the last section the bar graph that shows each month's average daily low temperature in degrees Fahrenheit for Barrow, Alaska. Use this graph to answer Exercises 89 through 91.*

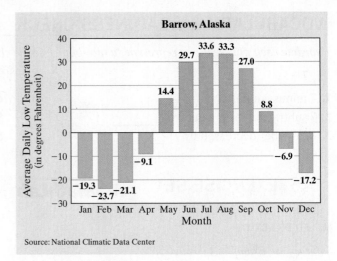

Source: National Climatic Data Center

89. Record the monthly increases and decreases in the low temperature from the previous month.

Month	*Monthly Increase or Decrease*
February	
March	
April	
May	
June	
July	
August	
September	
October	
November	
December	

90. Which month had the greatest increase in temperature?

91. Which month had the greatest decrease in temperature?

Estimation. *Without calculating, determine whether each answer is positive or negative. Then use a calculator to find the exact difference.*

92. 56,875 − 87,262

93. 4.362 − 7.0086

If a is a positive number and b is a negative number, determine whether each statement is true or false. If false, give a counterexample.

94. $a - b$ is always a positive number.

95. $b - a$ is always a negative number.

96. $|b| - |a|$ is always a positive number.

97. $|a| - |b|$ is always a positive number.

INTEGRATED REVIEW OPERATIONS ON REAL NUMBERS

Sections 1.1–1.6

Answer the following with positive, negative, or 0.

1. The opposite of a positive number is a _____ number.

2. The sum of two negative numbers is a _____ number.

3. The absolute value of a negative number is a _____ number.

4. The absolute value of zero is _____.

5. The reciprocal of a positive number is a _____ number.

6. The sum of a number and its opposite is _____.

7. The absolute value of a positive number is a _____ number.

8. The opposite of a negative number is a _____ number.

Fill in the chart:

	Number	Opposite	Absolute Value
9.	$\dfrac{1}{7}$		
10.	$-\dfrac{12}{5}$		
11.		-3	
12.		$\dfrac{9}{11}$	

Perform each indicated operation and simplify.

13. $-19 + (-23)$

14. $7 - (-3)$

15. $-15 + 17$

16. $-8 - 10$

17. $18 + (-25)$

18. $-2 + (-37)$

19. $-14 - (-12)$

20. $5 - 14$

21. $4.5 - 7.9$

22. $-8.6 - 1.2$

23. $-\dfrac{3}{4} - \dfrac{1}{7}$

24. $\dfrac{2}{3} - \dfrac{7}{8}$

25. $-9 - (-7) + 4 - 6$

26. $11 - 20 + (-3) - 12$

27. $24 - 6(14 - 11)$

28. $30 - 5(10 - 8)$

29. $(7 - 17) + 4^2$

30. $9^2 + (10 - 30)$

31. $|-9| + 3^2 + (-4 - 20)$

32. $|-4 - 5| + 5^2 + (-50)$

33. $-7 + [(1 - 2) + (-2 - 9)]$

34. $-6 + [(-3 + 7) + (4 - 15)]$

35. Subtract 5 from 1.

36. Subtract -2 from -3.

37. Subtract $-\dfrac{2}{5}$ from $\dfrac{1}{4}$.

38. Subtract $\dfrac{1}{10}$ from $-\dfrac{5}{8}$.

39. $2(19 - 17)^3 - 3(-7 + 9)^2$

40. $3(10 - 9)^2 + 6(20 - 19)^3$

Evaluate each expression when $x = -2$, $y = -1$, and $z = 9$.

41. $x - y$

42. $x + y$

43. $y + z$

44. $z - y$

45. $\dfrac{|5z - x|}{y - x}$

46. $\dfrac{|-x - y + z|}{2z}$

1.7 ADDING AND SUBTRACTING MATRICES

OBJECTIVES

1 Use matrix notation.

2 Understand what is meant by equal matrices.

3 Add and subtract matrices.

The data below show that we spend a lot of time sprucing up.

Average Number of Minutes per Day Americans Spend on Grooming

	Ages 15–19	*Ages 20–24*	*Ages 45–54*	*Ages 65+*	*Married*	*Single*
Men	37	37	34	28	31	34
Women	59	49	46	46	44	50

Source: Bureau of Labor Statistics' American Time-Use Survey

The 12 numbers inside the brackets are arranged in two rows and six columns. This rectangular array of 12 numbers, arranged in rows and columns and placed in brackets, is an example of a **matrix** (plural: **matrices**). The numbers inside the brackets are called **elements** of the matrix.

Matrices have applications in numerous fields, including the new technology of digital photography in which pictures are represented by numbers rather than film. In this section, we turn our attention to the matrix algebra of adding and subtracting and some of its applications.

OBJECTIVE 1 ▶ Use matrix notation. We have seen that an array of numbers, arranged in rows and columns and placed in brackets, is called a matrix. We can represent a matrix by a capital letter, such as A, B, or C.

A general element in matrix A is denoted by a_{ij}. This refers to the element in the ith row and jth column. For example, a_{32} is the element of A located in the third row, second column.

A matrix of **order $m \times n$** has m rows and n columns. If $m = n$, a matrix has the same number of rows as columns and is called a **square matrix.**

EXAMPLE 1   **Matrix Notation**

Let

$$A = \begin{bmatrix} 3 & 2 & 0 \\ -4 & -5 & -\frac{1}{5} \end{bmatrix}.$$

a. What is the order of A?

b. Identify a_{23} and a_{12}.

Solution

a. The matrix has 2 rows and 3 columns, so it is of order 2×3.

b. The element a_{23} is in the second row and third column. Thus, $a_{23} = -\dfrac{1}{5}$. The element a_{12} is in the first row and second column. Consequently, $a_{12} = 2$. ☐

PRACTICE

1   Let

$$A = \begin{bmatrix} 5 & -2 \\ -3 & \pi \\ 1 & 6 \end{bmatrix}.$$

a. What is the order of A?   **b.** Identify a_{12} and a_{31}.

OBJECTIVE 2 ▶ Understand what is meant by equal matrices. Two matrices are **equal** if and only if they have the same order and corresponding elements are equal.

Definition of Equality of Matrices Two matrices A and B are **equal** if and only if they have the same order $m \times n$ and the elements in the same position are equal.

For example, if $A = \begin{bmatrix} x & y + 1 \\ z & 6 \end{bmatrix}$ and $B = \begin{bmatrix} 1 & 5 \\ 3 & 6 \end{bmatrix}$, then $A = B$ if and only if $x = 1$, $y + 1 = 5$ (so $y = 4$), and $z = 3$.

OBJECTIVE 3 ▶ Add and subtract matrices. The table below shows that matrices of the same order can be added or subtracted by simply adding or subtracting corresponding elements.

Adding and Subtracting Matrices

Let A and B be matrices of order $m \times n$.

Definition	The Definition in Words	Example
Matrix Addition $A + B$	Matrices of the same order are added by adding the elements in corresponding positions.	$\begin{bmatrix} 1 & -2 \\ 3 & 5 \end{bmatrix} + \begin{bmatrix} -1 & 6 \\ 0 & 4 \end{bmatrix}$ $= \begin{bmatrix} 1 + (-1) & -2 + 6 \\ 3 + 0 & 5 + 4 \end{bmatrix} = \begin{bmatrix} 0 & 4 \\ 3 & 9 \end{bmatrix}$
Matrix Subtraction $A - B$	Matrices of the same order are subtracted by subtracting the elements in corresponding positions.	$\begin{bmatrix} 1 & -2 \\ 3 & 5 \end{bmatrix} - \begin{bmatrix} -1 & 6 \\ 0 & 4 \end{bmatrix}$ $= \begin{bmatrix} 1 - (-1) & -2 - 6 \\ 3 - 0 & 5 - 4 \end{bmatrix} = \begin{bmatrix} 2 & -8 \\ 3 & 1 \end{bmatrix}$

The sum or difference of two matrices of different orders is undefined. For example, consider the matrices

$$A = \begin{bmatrix} 0 & 3 \\ 4 & 3 \end{bmatrix} \quad \text{and} \quad B = \begin{bmatrix} 1 & 9 \\ 4 & 5 \\ 2 & 3 \end{bmatrix}.$$

The order of A is 2×2; the order of B is 3×2. These matrices are of different orders and cannot be added or subtracted.

EXAMPLE 2 **Adding and Subtracting Matrices**

Perform the indicated matrix operations:

a. $\begin{bmatrix} 0 & 5 & 3 \\ -2 & 6 & -8 \end{bmatrix} + \begin{bmatrix} -2 & 3 & 5 \\ 7 & -9 & 6 \end{bmatrix}$

b. $\begin{bmatrix} -6 & 7 \\ 2 & -3 \end{bmatrix} - \begin{bmatrix} -5 & 6 \\ 0 & -4 \end{bmatrix}.$

Solution

a. 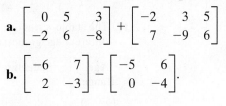 $\begin{bmatrix} 0 & 5 & 3 \\ -2 & 6 & -8 \end{bmatrix} + \begin{bmatrix} -2 & 3 & 5 \\ 7 & -9 & 6 \end{bmatrix}$

TECHNOLOGY NOTE

Graphing utilities can add and subtract matrices. Enter the matrices and name them $[A]$ and $[B]$. Then use a keystroke sequence similar to

$[A]$ $+$ $[B]$ ENTER

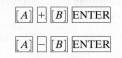 $[A]$ $-$ $[B]$ ENTER

Consult your manual and verify the results in Example 2.

$$= \begin{bmatrix} 0 + (-2) & 5 + 3 & 3 + 5 \\ -2 + 7 & 6 + (-9) & -8 + 6 \end{bmatrix}$$ Add the corresponding elements in the 2×3 matrices.

$$= \begin{bmatrix} -2 & 8 & 8 \\ 5 & -3 & -2 \end{bmatrix}$$ Simplify.

b. $\begin{bmatrix} -6 & 7 \\ 2 & -3 \end{bmatrix} - \begin{bmatrix} -5 & 6 \\ 0 & -4 \end{bmatrix}$

$$= \begin{bmatrix} -6 - (-5) & 7 - 6 \\ 2 - 0 & -3 - (-4) \end{bmatrix}$$ Subtract the corresponding elements in the 2×2 matrices.

$$= \begin{bmatrix} -1 & 1 \\ 2 & 1 \end{bmatrix}$$ Simplify. □

PRACTICE
2 Perform the indicated matrix operations:

a. $\begin{bmatrix} -4 & 3 \\ 7 & -6 \end{bmatrix} + \begin{bmatrix} 6 & -3 \\ 2 & -4 \end{bmatrix}$ **b.** $\begin{bmatrix} 5 & 4 \\ -3 & 7 \\ 0 & 1 \end{bmatrix} - \begin{bmatrix} -4 & 8 \\ 6 & 0 \\ -5 & 3 \end{bmatrix}$.

1.7 | EXERCISE SET

PRACTICE EXERCISES

In Exercises 1–4,

  a. *Give the order of each matrix.*

  b. *Identify a_{32} and a_{23}, or explain why identification is not possible.*

1. $\begin{bmatrix} 4 & -7 & 5 \\ -6 & 8 & -1 \end{bmatrix}$ **2.** $\begin{bmatrix} -6 & 4 & -1 \\ -9 & 0 & \frac{1}{2} \end{bmatrix}$

3. $\begin{bmatrix} 1 & -5 & \pi & e \\ 0 & 7 & -6 & -\pi \\ -2 & \frac{1}{2} & 11 & -\frac{1}{5} \end{bmatrix}$ **4.** $\begin{bmatrix} -4 & 1 & 3 & -5 \\ 2 & -1 & \pi & 0 \\ 1 & 0 & -e & \frac{1}{5} \end{bmatrix}$

In Exercises 5–8, find values for the variables so that the matrices in each exercise are equal.

5. $\begin{bmatrix} x \\ 4 \end{bmatrix} = \begin{bmatrix} 6 \\ y \end{bmatrix}$ **6.** $\begin{bmatrix} x \\ 7 \end{bmatrix} = \begin{bmatrix} 11 \\ y \end{bmatrix}$

7. $\begin{bmatrix} x & 2y \\ z & 9 \end{bmatrix} = \begin{bmatrix} 4 & 12 \\ 3 & 9 \end{bmatrix}$ **8.** $\begin{bmatrix} x & y+3 \\ 2z & 8 \end{bmatrix} = \begin{bmatrix} 12 & 5 \\ 6 & 8 \end{bmatrix}$

In Exercises 9–16, find the following matrices:

  a. $A + B$ **b.** $A - B$

9. $A = \begin{bmatrix} 4 & 1 \\ 3 & 2 \end{bmatrix}$, $B = \begin{bmatrix} 5 & 9 \\ 0 & 7 \end{bmatrix}$

10. $A = \begin{bmatrix} -2 & 3 \\ 0 & 1 \end{bmatrix}$, $B = \begin{bmatrix} 8 & 1 \\ 5 & 4 \end{bmatrix}$

11. $A = \begin{bmatrix} 1 & 3 \\ 3 & 4 \\ 5 & 6 \end{bmatrix}$, $B = \begin{bmatrix} 2 & -1 \\ 3 & -2 \\ 0 & 1 \end{bmatrix}$

12. $A = \begin{bmatrix} 3 & 1 & 1 \\ -1 & 2 & 5 \end{bmatrix}$, $B = \begin{bmatrix} 2 & -3 & 6 \\ -3 & 1 & -4 \end{bmatrix}$

13. $A = \begin{bmatrix} 2 \\ -4 \\ 1 \end{bmatrix}$, $B = \begin{bmatrix} -5 \\ 3 \\ -1 \end{bmatrix}$

14. $A = \begin{bmatrix} 6 & 2 & -3 \end{bmatrix}$, $B = \begin{bmatrix} 4 & -2 & 3 \end{bmatrix}$

15. $A = \begin{bmatrix} 2 & -10 & -2 \\ 14 & 12 & 10 \\ 4 & -2 & 2 \end{bmatrix}$, $B = \begin{bmatrix} 6 & 10 & -2 \\ 0 & -12 & -4 \\ -5 & 2 & -2 \end{bmatrix}$

16. $A = \begin{bmatrix} 6 & -3 & 5 \\ 6 & 0 & -2 \\ -4 & 2 & -1 \end{bmatrix}$, $B = \begin{bmatrix} -3 & 5 & 1 \\ -1 & 2 & -6 \\ 2 & 0 & 4 \end{bmatrix}$

17. The table gives an estimate of basic caloric needs for different age groups and activity levels.

Age Range	Sedentary		Moderately Active		Active	
	Men	Women	Men	Women	Men	Women
19 − 30	2400	2000	2700	2100	3000	2400
31 − 50	2200	1800	2500	2000	2900	2200
51 +	2000	1600	2300	1800	2600	2100

Source: USA Today

a. Use a 3 × 3 matrix to represent the daily caloric needs, by age and activity level, for men. Call this matrix M.

b. Use a 3 × 3 matrix to represent the daily caloric needs, by age and activity level, for women. Call this matrix W.

c. Find $M - W$. What does this matrix represent?

Multiple Steps. Use the matrix $A = \begin{bmatrix} 5 & 9 & -2.3 & 0 \\ 0 & \frac{1}{2} & -11 & -1 \end{bmatrix}$

answer each question.

18. What is the order of A?

19. Identify a_{12}.

20. Is A a square matrix?

21. What is meant by the order of a matrix? Give an example with your explanation.

22. What does a_{ij} mean?

23. What are equal matrices?

24. How are matrices added?

25. Describe how to subtract matrices.

26. Describe matrices that cannot be added or subtracted.

1.8 MULTIPLYING AND DIVIDING REAL NUMBERS

OBJECTIVES

1 Multiply and divide real numbers.

2 Evaluate algebraic expressions using real numbers.

OBJECTIVE 1 ▶ Multiplying and dividing real numbers. In this section, we discover patterns for multiplying and dividing real numbers. To discover sign rules for multiplication, recall that multiplication is repeated addition. Thus $3 \cdot 2$ means that 2 is an addend 3 times. That is,

$$2 + 2 + 2 = 3 \cdot 2$$

which equals 6. Similarly, $3 \cdot (-2)$ means -2 is an addend 3 times. That is,

$$(-2) + (-2) + (-2) = 3 \cdot (-2)$$

Since $(-2) + (-2) + (-2) = -6$, then $3 \cdot (-2) = -6$. This suggests that the product of a positive number and a negative number is a negative number.

What about the product of two negative numbers? To find out, consider the following pattern.

Factor decreases by 1 each time

$$\left.\begin{array}{l} -3 \cdot 2 = -6 \\ -3 \cdot 1 = -3 \\ -3 \cdot 0 = 0 \end{array}\right\} \text{Product increases by 3 each time.}$$

This pattern continues as

Factor decreases by 1 each time

$$\left.\begin{array}{l} -3 \cdot -1 = 3 \\ -3 \cdot -2 = 6 \end{array}\right\} \text{Product increases by 3 each time.}$$

This suggests that the product of two negative numbers is a positive number.

Multiplying Real Numbers

1. The product of two numbers with the *same* sign is a positive number.

2. The product of two numbers with *different* signs is a negative number.

EXAMPLE 1 Multiply.

a. $(-8)(4)$ **b.** $14(-1)$ **c.** $-9(-10)$

Solution

a. $-8(4) = -32$ **b.** $14(-1) = -14$ **c.** $-9(-10) = 90$ □

PRACTICE
1 Multiply.

a. $8(-5)$ **b.** $(-3)(-4)$ **c.** $(-6)(9)$

We know that every whole number multiplied by zero equals zero. This remains true for real numbers.

> **Zero as a Factor**
> If b is a real number, then $b \cdot 0 = 0$. Also, $0 \cdot b = 0$.

EXAMPLE 2 Perform the indicated operations.

a. $(7)(0)(-6)$ **b.** $(-2)(-3)(-4)$ **c.** $(-1)(5)(-9)$ **d.** $(-4)(-11) - (5)(-2)$

Solution

a. By the order of operations, we multiply from left to right. Notice that, because one of the factors is 0, the product is 0.

$$(7)(0)(-6) = 0(-6) = 0$$

b. Multiply two factors at a time, from left to right.

$$(-2)(-3)(-4) = (6)(-4) \quad \text{Multiply } (-2)(-3).$$
$$= -24$$

c. Multiply from left to right.

$$(-1)(5)(-9) = (-5)(-9) \quad \text{Multiply } (-1)(5).$$
$$= 45$$

d. Follow the rules for order of operation.

$$(-4)(-11) - (5)(-2) = 44 - (-10) \quad \text{Find each product.}$$
$$= 44 + 10 \quad \text{Add 44 to the opposite of } -10.$$
$$= 54 \quad \text{Add.} \quad □$$

PRACTICE
2 Perform the indicated operations.

a. $(-1)(-5)(-6)$ **b.** $(-3)(-2)(4)$
c. $(-4)(0)(5)$ **d.** $(-2)(-3) - (-4)(5)$

> ▶ **Helpful Hint**
> You may have noticed from the example that if we multiply:
>
> • an *even* number of negative numbers, the product is *positive*.
>
> • an *odd* number of negative numbers, the product is *negative*.

Multiplying signed decimals or fractions is carried out exactly the same way as multiplying by integers.

EXAMPLE 3   Multiply.

a. $(-1.2)(0.05)$ **b.** $\dfrac{2}{3} \cdot \left(-\dfrac{7}{10}\right)$ **c.** $\left(-\dfrac{4}{5}\right)(-20)$

Solution

a. The product of two numbers with different signs is negative.

$$(-1.2)(0.05) = -[(1.2)(0.05)]$$
$$= -0.06$$

b. $\dfrac{2}{3} \cdot \left(-\dfrac{7}{10}\right) = -\dfrac{2 \cdot 7}{3 \cdot 10} = -\dfrac{2 \cdot 7}{3 \cdot 2 \cdot 5} = -\dfrac{7}{15}$

c. $\left(-\dfrac{4}{5}\right)(-20) = \dfrac{4 \cdot 20}{5 \cdot 1} = \dfrac{4 \cdot 4 \cdot 5}{5 \cdot 1} = \dfrac{16}{1}$ or 16

PRACTICE
3   Multiply.

a. $(0.23)(-0.2)$ **b.** $\left(-\dfrac{3}{5}\right) \cdot \left(\dfrac{4}{9}\right)$ **c.** $\left(-\dfrac{7}{12}\right)(-24)$

Now that we know how to multiply positive and negative numbers, let's see how we find the values of $(-4)^2$ and -4^2, for example. Although these two expressions look similar, the difference between the two is the parentheses. In $(-4)^2$, the parentheses tell us that the base, or repeated factor, is -4. In -4^2, only 4 is the base. Thus,

$$(-4)^2 = (-4)(-4) = 16 \quad \text{The base is } -4.$$

$$-4^2 = -(4 \cdot 4) = -16 \quad \text{The base is } 4.$$

EXAMPLE 4   Evaluate.

a. $(-2)^3$ **b.** -2^3 **c.** $(-3)^2$ **d.** -3^2

Solution

a. $(-2)^3 = (-2)(-2)(-2) = -8$ The base is -2.
b. $-2^3 = -(2 \cdot 2 \cdot 2) = -8$ The base is 2.
c. $(-3)^2 = (-3)(-3) = 9$ The base is -3.
d. $-3^2 = -(3 \cdot 3) = -9$ The base is 3.

PRACTICE
4   Evaluate.

a. $(-6)^2$ **b.** -6^2 **c.** $(-4)^3$ **d.** -4^3

▶ **Helpful Hint**
Be careful when identifying the base of an exponential expression.

$(-3)^2$	-3^2
Base is -3	Base is 3
$(-3)^2 = (-3)(-3) = 9$	$-3^2 = -(3 \cdot 3) = -9$

Just as every difference of two numbers $a - b$ can be written as the sum $a + (-b)$, so too every quotient of two numbers can be written as a product. For example, the quotient $6 \div 3$ can be written as $6 \cdot \frac{1}{3}$. Recall that the pair of numbers 3 and $\frac{1}{3}$ has a special relationship. Their product is 1 and they are called reciprocals or **multiplicative inverses** of each other.

> **Reciprocals or Multiplicative Inverses**
> Two numbers whose product is 1 are called reciprocals or multiplicative inverses of each other.

Notice that **0 has no multiplicative inverse** since 0 multiplied by any number is never 1 but always 0.

EXAMPLE 5   Find the reciprocal of each number.

a. 22   **b.** $\frac{3}{16}$ **c.** -10 **d.** $-\frac{9}{13}$

Solution

a. The reciprocal of 22 is $\frac{1}{22}$ since $22 \cdot \frac{1}{22} = 1$.

b. The reciprocal of $\frac{3}{16}$ is $\frac{16}{3}$ since $\frac{3}{16} \cdot \frac{16}{3} = 1$.

c. The reciprocal of -10 is $-\frac{1}{10}$.

d. The reciprocal of $-\frac{9}{13}$ is $-\frac{13}{9}$.

PRACTICE
5   Find the reciprocal of each number.

a. $\frac{8}{3}$ **b.** 15   **c.** $-\frac{2}{7}$ **d.** -5

We may now write a quotient as an equivalent product.

> **Quotient of Two Real Numbers**
> If a and b are real numbers and b is not 0, then
> $$a \div b = \frac{a}{b} = a \cdot \frac{1}{b}$$

In other words, the quotient of two real numbers is the product of the first number and the multiplicative inverse or reciprocal of the second number.

EXAMPLE 6   Use the definition of the quotient of two numbers to divide.

a. $-18 \div 3$ **b.** $\frac{-14}{-2}$ **c.** $\frac{20}{-4}$

Solution

a. $-18 \div 3 = -18 \cdot \frac{1}{3} = -6$ **b.** $\frac{-14}{-2} = -14 \cdot -\frac{1}{2} = 7$

c. $\frac{20}{-4} = 20 \cdot -\frac{1}{4} = -5$

PRACTICE
6   Use the definition of the quotient of two numbers to divide.

a. $\dfrac{16}{-2}$ **b.** $24 \div (-6)$ **c.** $\dfrac{-35}{-7}$

Since the quotient $a \div b$ can be written as the product $a \cdot \dfrac{1}{b}$, it follows that sign patterns for dividing two real numbers are the same as sign patterns for multiplying two real numbers.

> **Multiplying and Dividing Real Numbers**
> **1.** The product or quotient of two numbers with the *same* sign is a positive number.
> **2.** The product or quotient of two numbers with *different* signs is a negative number.

EXAMPLE 7   Divide.

a. $\dfrac{-24}{-4}$ **b.** $\dfrac{-36}{3}$ **c.** $\dfrac{2}{3} \div \left(-\dfrac{5}{4}\right)$ **d.** $-\dfrac{3}{2} \div 9$

Solution

a. $\dfrac{-24}{-4} = 6$ **b.** $\dfrac{-36}{3} = -12$ **c.** $\dfrac{2}{3} \div \left(-\dfrac{5}{4}\right) = \dfrac{2}{3} \cdot \left(-\dfrac{4}{5}\right) = -\dfrac{8}{15}$

d. $-\dfrac{3}{2} \div 9 = -\dfrac{3}{2} \cdot \dfrac{1}{9} = -\dfrac{3 \cdot 1}{2 \cdot 9} = -\dfrac{3 \cdot 1}{2 \cdot 3 \cdot 3} = -\dfrac{1}{6}$ □

PRACTICE
7   Divide.

a. $\dfrac{-18}{-6}$ **b.** $\dfrac{-48}{3}$ **c.** $\dfrac{3}{5} \div \left(-\dfrac{1}{2}\right)$ **d.** $-\dfrac{4}{9} \div 8$

The definition of the quotient of two real numbers does not allow for division by 0 because 0 does not have a multiplicative inverse. There is no number we can multiply 0 by to get 1. How then do we interpret $\dfrac{3}{0}$? We say that division by 0 is not allowed or not defined and that $\dfrac{3}{0}$ does not represent a real number. The denominator of a fraction can never be 0.

Can the numerator of a fraction be 0? Can we divide 0 by a number? Yes. For example,

$$\frac{0}{3} = 0 \cdot \frac{1}{3} = 0$$

In general, the quotient of 0 and any nonzero number is 0.

> **Zero as a Divisor or Dividend**
> **1.** The quotient of any nonzero real number and 0 is undefined. In symbols, if $a \neq 0, \dfrac{a}{0}$ is **undefined.**
> **2.** The quotient of 0 and any real number except 0 is 0. In symbols, if $a \neq 0, \dfrac{0}{a} = 0$.

EXAMPLE 8 Perform the indicated operations.

a. $\dfrac{1}{0}$ **b.** $\dfrac{0}{-3}$ **c.** $\dfrac{0(-8)}{2}$

Solution

a. $\dfrac{1}{0}$ is undefined   **b.** $\dfrac{0}{-3} = 0$ **c.** $\dfrac{0(-8)}{2} = \dfrac{0}{2} = 0$ □

PRACTICE
8 Perform the indicated operations.

a. $\dfrac{0}{-2}$ **b.** $\dfrac{-4}{0}$ **c.** $\dfrac{-5}{6(0)}$

Notice that $\dfrac{12}{-2} = -6$, $-\dfrac{12}{2} = -6$, and $\dfrac{-12}{2} = -6$. This means that

$$\frac{12}{-2} = -\frac{12}{2} = \frac{-12}{2}$$

In words, a single negative sign in a fraction can be written in the denominator, in the numerator, or in front of the fraction without changing the value of the fraction. Thus,

$$\frac{1}{-7} = \frac{-1}{7} = -\frac{1}{7}$$

In general, if a and b are real numbers, $b \neq 0$, $\dfrac{a}{-b} = \dfrac{-a}{b} = -\dfrac{a}{b}$.

Examples combining basic arithmetic operations along with the principles of order of operations help us to review these concepts.

EXAMPLE 9 Simplify each expression.

a. $\dfrac{(-12)(-3) + 3}{-7 - (-2)}$ **b.** $\dfrac{2(-3)^2 - 20}{-5 + 4}$

Solution

a. First, simplify the numerator and denominator separately, then divide.

$$\frac{(-12)(-3) + 3}{-7 - (-2)} = \frac{36 + 3}{-7 + 2}$$

$$= \frac{39}{-5} \text{ or } -\frac{39}{5}$$

b. Simplify the numerator and denominator separately, then divide.

$$\frac{2(-3)^2 - 20}{-5 + 4} = \frac{2 \cdot 9 - 20}{-5 + 4} = \frac{18 - 20}{-5 + 4} = \frac{-2}{-1} = 2$$ □

PRACTICE
9 Simplify each expression.

a. $\dfrac{(-8)(-11) - 4}{-9 - (-4)}$ **b.** $\dfrac{3(-2)^3 - 9}{-6 + 3}$

OBJECTIVE 2 ▶ Evaluating algebraic expressions using real numbers. Using what we have learned about multiplying and dividing real numbers, we continue to practice evaluating algebraic expressions.

EXAMPLE 10   If $x = -2$ and $y = -4$, evaluate each expression.

a. $5x - y$ **b.** $x^4 - y^2$ **c.** $\dfrac{3x}{2y}$

Solution

a. Replace x with -2 and y with -4 and simplify.

$$5x - y = 5(-2) - (-4) = -10 - (-4) = -10 + 4 = -6$$

b. Replace x with -2 and y with -4.

$$
\begin{aligned}
x^4 - y^2 &= (-2)^4 - (-4)^2 && \text{Substitute the given values for the variables.}\\
&= 16 - (16) && \text{Evaluate exponential expressions.}\\
&= 0 && \text{Subtract.}
\end{aligned}
$$

c. Replace x with -2 and y with -4 and simplify.

$$\frac{3x}{2y} = \frac{3(-2)}{2(-4)} = \frac{-6}{-8} = \frac{3}{4}$$

PRACTICE
10   If $x = -5$ and $y = -2$, evaluate each expression.

a. $7y - x$ **b.** $x^2 - y^3$ **c.** $\dfrac{2x}{3y}$

Calculator Explorations

Entering Negative Numbers on a Scientific Calculator

To enter a negative number on a scientific calculator, find a key marked $\boxed{+/-}$. (On some calculators, this key is marked $\boxed{\text{CHS}}$ for "change sign.") To enter -8, for example, press the keys $\boxed{8}$ $\boxed{+/-}$. The display will read $\boxed{-8}$.

Entering Negative Numbers on a Graphing Calculator

To enter a negative number on a graphing calculator, find a key marked $\boxed{(-)}$. Do not confuse this key with the key $\boxed{-}$, which is used for subtraction. To enter -8, for example, press the keys $\boxed{(-)}$ $\boxed{8}$. The display will read $\boxed{-8}$.

Operations with Real Numbers

To evaluate $-2(7 - 9) - 20$ on a calculator, press the keys
$\boxed{2}\ \boxed{+/-}\ \boxed{\times}\ \boxed{(}\ \boxed{7}\ \boxed{-}\ \boxed{9}\ \boxed{)}\ \boxed{-}\ \boxed{2}\ \boxed{0}\ \boxed{=}$, or
$\boxed{(-)}\ \boxed{2}\ \boxed{(}\ \boxed{7}\ \boxed{-}\ \boxed{9}\ \boxed{)}\ \boxed{-}\ \boxed{2}\ \boxed{0}\ \boxed{\text{ENTER}}$.

The display will read $\boxed{-16}$ or $\boxed{\begin{array}{l} -2(7-9)-20 \\ \qquad\qquad\quad -16 \end{array}}$.

Use a calculator to simplify each expression.

1. $-38(26 - 27)$ **2.** $-59(-8) + 1726$

3. $134 + 25(68 - 91)$ **4.** $45(32) - 8(218)$

5. $\dfrac{-50(294)}{175 - 265}$ **6.** $\dfrac{-444 - 444.8}{-181 - 324}$

7. $9^5 - 4550$ **8.** $5^8 - 6259$

9. $(-125)^2$ (Be careful.)   **10.** -125^2 (Be careful.)

VOCABULARY & READINESS CHECK

Use the choices below to fill in each blank.

positive   0   negative   undefined

1. If n is a real number, then $n \cdot 0 =$ ___ and $0 \cdot n =$ ___ .

2. If n is a real number, but not 0, then $\dfrac{0}{n} =$ ___ and we say $\dfrac{n}{0}$ is _____ .

3. The product of two negative numbers is a _____ number.

4. The quotient of two negative numbers is a _____ number.

5. The quotient of a positive number and a negative number is a _____ number.

6. The product of a positive number and a negative number is a _____ number.

7. The reciprocal of a positive number is a _____ number.

8. The opposite of a positive number is a _____ number.

1.8 EXERCISE SET

Multiply. See Examples 1 through 3.

1. $-6(4)$ **2.** $-8(5)$

3. $2(-1)$ **4.** $7(-4)$

5. $-5(-10)$ **6.** $-6(-11)$

7. $-3 \cdot 4$ **8.** $-2 \cdot 8$

9. $-7 \cdot 0$ **10.** $-6 \cdot 0$

11. $2(-9)$ **12.** $3(-5)$

13. $-\dfrac{1}{2}\left(-\dfrac{3}{5}\right)$ **14.** $-\dfrac{1}{8}\left(-\dfrac{1}{3}\right)$

15. $-\dfrac{3}{4}\left(-\dfrac{8}{9}\right)$ **16.** $-\dfrac{5}{6}\left(-\dfrac{3}{10}\right)$

17. $5(-1.4)$ **18.** $6(-2.5)$

19. $-0.2(-0.7)$ **20.** $-0.5(-0.3)$

21. $-10(80)$ **22.** $-20(60)$

23. $4(-7)$ **24.** $5(-9)$

25. $(-5)(-5)$ **26.** $(-7)(-7)$

27. $\dfrac{2}{3}\left(-\dfrac{4}{9}\right)$ **28.** $\dfrac{2}{7}\left(-\dfrac{2}{11}\right)$

29. $-11(11)$ **30.** $-12(12)$

31. $-\dfrac{20}{25}\left(\dfrac{5}{16}\right)$ **32.** $-\dfrac{25}{36}\left(\dfrac{6}{15}\right)$

33. $(-1)(2)(-3)(-5)$ **34.** $(-2)(-3)(-4)(-2)$

Perform the indicated operations. See Example 2.

35. $(-2)(5) - (-11)(3)$ **36.** $8(-3) - 4(-5)$

37. $(-6)(-1)(-2) - (-5)$ **38.** $20 - (-4)(3)(-2)$

Decide whether each statement is true or false.

39. The product of three negative integers is negative.

40. The product of three positive integers is positive.

41. The product of four negative integers is negative.

42. The product of four positive integers is positive.

Evaluate. See Example 4.

43. $(-2)^4$ **44.** -2^4

45. -1^5 **46.** $(-1)^5$

47. $(-5)^2$ **48.** -5^2

49. -7^2 **50.** $(-7)^2$

Find each reciprocal or multiplicative inverse. See Example 5.

51. 9 **52.** 100 **53.** $\dfrac{2}{3}$

54. $\dfrac{1}{7}$ **55.** -14 **56.** -8

57. $-\dfrac{3}{11}$ **58.** $-\dfrac{6}{13}$ **59.** 0.2

60. 1.5 **61.** $\dfrac{1}{-6.3}$ **62.** $\dfrac{1}{-8.9}$

Divide. See Examples 6 through 8.

63. $\dfrac{18}{-2}$ **64.** $\dfrac{20}{-10}$ **65.** $\dfrac{-16}{-4}$

66. $\dfrac{-18}{-6}$ **67.** $\dfrac{-48}{12}$ **68.** $\dfrac{-60}{5}$

69. $\dfrac{0}{-4}$ **70.** $\dfrac{0}{-9}$ **71.** $-\dfrac{15}{3}$

72. $-\dfrac{24}{8}$ **73.** $\dfrac{5}{0}$ **74.** $\dfrac{3}{0}$

75. $\dfrac{-12}{-4}$ **76.** $\dfrac{-45}{-9}$ **77.** $\dfrac{30}{-2}$

78. $\dfrac{14}{-2}$ **79.** $\dfrac{6}{7} \div \left(-\dfrac{1}{3}\right)$ **80.** $\dfrac{4}{5} \div \left(-\dfrac{1}{2}\right)$

81. $-\dfrac{5}{9} \div \left(-\dfrac{3}{4}\right)$ **82.** $-\dfrac{1}{10} \div \left(-\dfrac{8}{11}\right)$

83. $-\dfrac{4}{9} \div \dfrac{4}{9}$ **84.** $-\dfrac{5}{12} \div \dfrac{5}{12}$

MIXED PRACTICE

Simplify. See Example 9.

85. $\dfrac{-9(-3)}{-6}$

86. $\dfrac{-6(-3)}{-4}$

87. $\dfrac{12}{9-12}$

88. $\dfrac{-15}{1-4}$

89. $\dfrac{-6^2+4}{-2}$

90. $\dfrac{3^2+4}{5}$

91. $\dfrac{8+(-4)^2}{4-12}$

92. $\dfrac{6+(-2)^2}{4-9}$

93. $\dfrac{22+(3)(-2)}{-5-2}$

94. $\dfrac{-20+(-4)(3)}{1-5}$

95. $\dfrac{-3-5^2}{2(-7)}$

96. $\dfrac{-2-4^2}{3(-6)}$

97. $\dfrac{6-2(-3)}{4-3(-2)}$

98. $\dfrac{8-3(-2)}{2-5(-4)}$

99. $\dfrac{-3-2(-9)}{-15-3(-4)}$

100. $\dfrac{-4-8(-2)}{-9-2(-3)}$

101. $\dfrac{|5-9|+|10-15|}{|2(-3)|}$

102. $\dfrac{|-3+6|+|-2+7|}{|-2\cdot2|}$

If $x=-5$ and $y=-3$, evaluate each expression. See Example 10.

103. $3x+2y$

104. $4x+5y$

105. $2x^2-y^2$

106. x^2-2y^2

107. x^3+3y

108. y^3+3x

109. $\dfrac{2x-5}{y-2}$

110. $\dfrac{2y-12}{x-4}$

111. $\dfrac{-3-y}{x-4}$

112. $\dfrac{4-2x}{y+3}$

113. At the end of 2006, Delta Airlines posted a net loss of $6203 million, which we will write as $-\$6203$ million. If this continues, what will Delta's income be after four years? (*Source:* Delta Airlines)

114. At the end of the third quarter of 2006, General Motors reported a net loss of $115 million. If this continued, what would General Motor's income be after four more quarters? (*Source:* General Motors)

Decide whether the given number is a solution of the given equation.

115. Is 7 a solution of $-5x=-35$?

116. Is -4 a solution of $2x=x-1$?

117. Is -20 a solution of $\dfrac{x}{10}=2$?

118. Is -3 a solution of $\dfrac{45}{x}=-15$?

119. Is 5 a solution of $-3x-5=-20$?

120. Is -4 a solution of $2x+4=x+8$?

CONCEPT EXTENSIONS

121. Explain why the product of an even number of negative numbers is a positive number.

122. If a and b are any real numbers, is the statement $a\cdot b=b\cdot a$ always true? Why or why not?

Complete a Table. *Use the symbols and their meaning to complete the table using $+$, $-$, or ?. The first few rows are completed for you.*

Given:
q: a negative number: $-$
r: a negative number: $-$
t: a positive number: $+$

Symbol	+	−	?
Meaning	a positive number	a negative number	not possible to determine

	Expression	Value
	$q\cdot t$	$-$
	$q+t$	?
123.	$q\cdot r$	
124.	$q\div t$	
125.	$t+r$	
126.	$t-r$	
127.	$\dfrac{q}{r\cdot t}$	
128.	$q^2\cdot r\cdot t$	
129.	$q+r$	
130.	$t(q+r)$	
131.	$r(q-t)$	
132.	$q(r-t)$	

133. Find any real numbers that are their own reciprocal.

134. Explain why 0 has no reciprocal.

Write each of the following as an expression and evaluate.

135. The sum of -2 and the quotient of -15 and 3

136. The sum of 1 and the product of -8 and -5

137. Twice the sum of -5 and -3

138. 7 subtracted from the quotient of 0 and 5

Scalar Multiplication. *It is possible to multiply a matrix, A, by a real number, such as -5. This is called scalar multiplication and we call the real number, -5, a scalar.*

To multiply a matrix A by a scalar c, we multiply each element of the matrix by c. For example,

$$-5\begin{bmatrix}3 & -2\\0 & 6\end{bmatrix}=\begin{bmatrix}-5(3) & -5(-2)\\-5(0) & -5(6)\end{bmatrix}=\begin{bmatrix}-15 & 10\\0 & -30\end{bmatrix}$$

If $A=\begin{bmatrix}4 & 3\\-1 & 6\end{bmatrix}$ and $B=\begin{bmatrix}5 & 0\\1 & -3\end{bmatrix}$, find

139. $-3A$

140. $-2B$

141. $3A+2B$

142. $5A-4B$

1.9 PROPERTIES OF REAL NUMBERS

OBJECTIVES

1 Use the commutative and associative properties.

2 Use the distributive property.

3 Use the identity and inverse properties.

OBJECTIVE 1 ▶ Using the commutative and associative properties. In this section we give names to properties of real numbers with which we are already familiar. Throughout this section, the variables a, b, and c represent real numbers.

We know that order does not matter when adding numbers. For example, we know that $7 + 5$ is the same as $5 + 7$. This property is given a special name—the **commutative property of addition.** We also know that order does not matter when multiplying numbers. For example, we know that $-5(6) = 6(-5)$. This property means that multiplication is commutative also and is called the **commutative property of multiplication.**

Commutative Properties	
Addition:	$a + b = b + a$
Multiplication:	$a \cdot b = b \cdot a$

These properties state that the *order* in which any two real numbers are added or multiplied does not change their sum or product. For example, if we let $a = 3$ and $b = 5$, then the commutative properties guarantee that

$$3 + 5 = 5 + 3 \quad \text{and} \quad 3 \cdot 5 = 5 \cdot 3$$

> **▶ Helpful Hint**
>
> Is subtraction also commutative? Try an example. Does $3 - 2 = 2 - 3$? **No!** The left side of this statement equals 1; the right side equals -1. There is no commutative property of subtraction. Similarly, there is no commutative property for division. For example, $10 \div 2$ does not equal $2 \div 10$.

EXAMPLE 1 Use a commutative property to complete each statement.

a. $x + 5 = $ _____   **b.** $3 \cdot x = $ _____

Solution

a. $x + 5 = 5 + x$ By the commutative property of addition

b. $3 \cdot x = x \cdot 3$ By the commutative property of multiplication   □

PRACTICE

1 Use a commutative property to complete each statement.

a. $x \cdot 8 = $ _____   **b.** $x + 17 = $ _____

Concept Check ☑

Which of the following pairs of actions are commutative?

a. "raking the leaves" and "bagging the leaves"
b. "putting on your left glove" and "putting on your right glove"
c. "putting on your coat" and "putting on your shirt"
d. "reading a novel" and "reading a newspaper"

Let's now discuss grouping numbers. We know that when we add three numbers, the way in which they are grouped or associated does not change their sum. For example, we know that $2 + (3 + 4) = 2 + 7 = 9$. This result is the same if we group the numbers differently. In other words, $(2 + 3) + 4 = 5 + 4 = 9$, also. Thus, $2 + (3 + 4) = (2 + 3) + 4$. This property is called the **associative property of addition.**

We also know that changing the grouping of numbers when multiplying does not change their product. For example, $2 \cdot (3 \cdot 4) = (2 \cdot 3) \cdot 4$ (check it). This is the **associative property of multiplication.**

> **Associative Properties**
> **Addition:** $(a + b) + c = a + (b + c)$
> **Multiplication:** $(a \cdot b) \cdot c = a \cdot (b \cdot c)$

These properties state that the way in which three numbers are *grouped* does not change their sum or their product.

EXAMPLE 2   Use an associative property to complete each statement.

a. $5 + (4 + 6) =$ _____

b. $(-1 \cdot 2) \cdot 5 =$ _____

Solution

a. $5 + (4 + 6) = (5 + 4) + 6$ By the associative property of addition
b. $(-1 \cdot 2) \cdot 5 = -1 \cdot (2 \cdot 5)$ By the associative property of multiplication □

PRACTICE
2   Use an associative property to complete each statement.

a. $(2 + 9) + 7 =$ _____

b. $-4 \cdot (2 \cdot 7) =$ _____

> **▶ Helpful Hint**
> Remember the difference between the commutative properties and the associative properties. The commutative properties have to do with the *order* of numbers, and the associative properties have to do with the *grouping* of numbers.

Let's now illustrate how these properties can help us simplify expressions.

EXAMPLE 3   Simplify each expression.

a. $10 + (x + 12)$ **b.** $-3(7x)$

Solution

a. $10 + (x + 12) = 10 + (12 + x)$ By the commutative property of addition
$= (10 + 12) + x$ By the associative property of addition
$= 22 + x$ Add.
b. $-3(7x) = (-3 \cdot 7)x$ By the associative property of multiplication
$= -21x$ Multiply. □

PRACTICE
3   Simplify each expression.

a. $(5 + x) + 9$ **b.** $5(-6x)$

OBJECTIVE 2 ▶ Using the distributive property. The **distributive property of multiplication over addition** is used repeatedly throughout algebra. It is useful because it allows us to write a product as a sum or a sum as a product.

We know that $7(2 + 4) = 7(6) = 42$. Compare that with $7(2) + 7(4) = 14 + 28 = 42$. Since both original expressions equal 42, they must equal each other, or

$$7(2 + 4) = 7(2) + 7(4)$$

This is an example of the distributive property. The product on the left side of the equal sign is equal to the sum on the right side. We can think of the 7 as being distributed to each number inside the parentheses.

> **Distributive Property of Multiplication Over Addition**
>
> $$a(b + c) = ab + ac$$

Since multiplication is commutative, this property can also be written as

$$(b + c)a = ba + ca$$

The distributive property can also be extended to more than two numbers inside the parentheses. For example,

$$3(x + y + z) = 3(x) + 3(y) + 3(z)$$
$$= 3x + 3y + 3z$$

Since we define subtraction in terms of addition, the distributive property is also true for subtraction. For example

$$2(x - y) = 2(x) - 2(y)$$
$$= 2x - 2y$$

EXAMPLE 4 Use the distributive property to write each expression without parentheses. Then simplify if possible.

a. $2(x + y)$ **b.** $-5(-3 + 2z)$ **c.** $5(x + 3y - z)$
d. $-1(2 - y)$ **e.** $-(3 + x - w)$ **f.** $4(3x + 7) + 10$

Solution

a. $2(x + y) = 2 \cdot x + 2 \cdot y$
$ = 2x + 2y$

b. $-5(-3 + 2z) = -5(-3) + (-5)(2z)$
$ = 15 - 10z$

c. $5(x + 3y - z) = 5(x) + 5(3y) - 5(z)$
$ = 5x + 15y - 5y$

d. $-1(2 - y) = (-1)(2) - (-1)(y)$
$ = -2 + y$

e. $-(3 + x - w) = -1(3 + x - w)$
$ = (-1)(3) + (-1)(x) - (-1)(w)$
$ = -3 - x + w$

> ▶ **Helpful Hint**
>
> Notice in part **(e)** that $-(3 + x - w)$ is first rewritten as $-1(3 + x - w)$.

f. $4(3x + 7) + 10 = 4(3x) + 4(7) + 10$ Apply the distributive property.
$ = 12x + 28 + 10$ Multiply.
$ = 12x + 38$ Add. ☐

PRACTICE
4   Use the distributive property to write each expression without parentheses. Then simplify, if possible.

a. $5(x - y)$ **b.** $-6(4 + 2t)$

c. $2(3x - 4y - z)$ **d.** $(3 - y) \cdot (-1)$

e. $-(x - 7 + 2s)$ **f.** $2(7x + 4) + 6$

We can use the distributive property in reverse to write a sum as a product.

EXAMPLE 5   Use the distributive property to write each sum as a product.

a. $8 \cdot 2 + 8 \cdot x$ **b.** $7s + 7t$

Solution

a. $8 \cdot 2 + 8 \cdot x = 8(2 + x)$ **b.** $7s + 7t = 7(s + t)$ ☐

PRACTICE
5   Use the distributive property to write each sum as a product.

a. $5 \cdot w + 5 \cdot 3$ **b.** $9w + 9z$

OBJECTIVE 3 ▶ Using the identity and inverse properties. Next, we look at the **identity properties.**

The number 0 is called the identity for addition because when 0 is added to any real number, the result is the same real number. In other words, the *identity* of the real number is not changed.

The number 1 is called the identity for multiplication because when a real number is multiplied by 1, the result is the same real number. In other words, the *identity* of the real number is not changed.

Identities for Addition and Multiplication

0 is the identity element for addition.

$$a + 0 = a \quad \text{and} \quad 0 + a = a$$

1 is the identity element for multiplication.

$$a \cdot 1 = a \quad \text{and} \quad 1 \cdot a = a$$

Notice that 0 is the *only* number that can be added to any real number with the result that the sum is the same real number. Also, 1 is the *only* number that can be multiplied by any real number with the result that the product is the same real number.

Additive inverses or **opposites** were introduced in Section 1.5. Two numbers are called additive inverses or opposites if their sum is 0. The additive inverse or opposite of 6 is -6 because $6 + (-6) = 0$. The additive inverse or opposite of -5 is 5 because $-5 + 5 = 0$.

Reciprocals or **multiplicative inverses** were introduced in Section 1.3. Two nonzero numbers are called reciprocals or multiplicative inverses if their product is 1. The reciprocal or multiplicative inverse of $\frac{2}{3}$ is $\frac{3}{2}$ because $\frac{2}{3} \cdot \frac{3}{2} = 1$. Likewise, the reciprocal of -5 is $-\frac{1}{5}$ because $-5\left(-\frac{1}{5}\right) = 1$.

Concept Check ☑

Which of the following, $1, -\dfrac{10}{3}, \dfrac{3}{10}, 0, \dfrac{10}{3}, -\dfrac{3}{10}$, is the

a. opposite of $-\dfrac{3}{10}$? **b.** reciprocal of $-\dfrac{3}{10}$?

Additive or Multiplicative Inverses

The numbers a and $-a$ are additive inverses or opposites of each other because their sum is 0; that is,

$$a + (-a) = 0$$

The numbers b and $\dfrac{1}{b}$ (for $b \neq 0$) are reciprocals or multiplicative inverses of each other because their product is 1; that is,

$$b \cdot \dfrac{1}{b} = 1$$

EXAMPLE 6 Name the property or properties illustrated by each true statement.

Solution

a. $3 \cdot y = y \cdot 3$ Commutative property of multiplication (order changed)

b. $(x + 7) + 9 = x + (7 + 9)$ Associative property of addition (grouping changed)

c. $(b + 0) + 3 = b + 3$ Identity element for addition

d. $0.2 \cdot (z \cdot 5) = 0.2 \cdot (5 \cdot z)$ Commutative property of multiplication (order changed)

e. $-2 \cdot \left(-\dfrac{1}{2}\right) = 1$ Multiplicative inverse property

f. $-2 + 2 = 0$ Additive inverse property

g. $-6 \cdot (y \cdot 2) = (-6 \cdot 2) \cdot y$ Commutative and associative properties of multiplication (order and grouping changed) ☐

PRACTICE

6 Name the property or properties illustrated by each true statement.

a. $(7 \cdot 3x) \cdot 4 = (3x \cdot 7) \cdot 4$

b. $6 + (3 + y) = (6 + 3) + y$

c. $8 + (t + 0) = 8 + t$

d. $-\dfrac{3}{4} \cdot \left(-\dfrac{4}{3}\right) = 1$

e. $(2 + x) + 5 = 5 + (2 + x)$

f. $3 + (-3) = 0$

g. $(-3b) \cdot 7 = (-3 \cdot 7) \cdot b$

Answers to Concept Check:

a. $\dfrac{3}{10}$ **b.** $-\dfrac{10}{3}$

VOCABULARY & READINESS CHECK

Word Bank. *Use the choices below to fill in each blank.*

distributive property   associative property of multiplication   commutative property of addition
opposites or additive inverses   associative property of addition
reciprocals or multiplicative inverses   commutative property of multiplication

1. $x + 5 = 5 + x$ is a true statement by the _____ .

2. $x \cdot 5 = 5 \cdot x$ is a true statement by the _____ .

3. $3(y + 6) = 3 \cdot y + 3 \cdot 6$ is true by the _____ .

4. $2 \cdot (x \cdot y) = (2 \cdot x) \cdot y$ is a true statement by the _____ .

5. $x + (7 + y) = (x + 7) + y$ is a true statement by the _____ .

6. The numbers $-\dfrac{2}{3}$ and $-\dfrac{3}{2}$ are called _____ .

7. The numbers $-\dfrac{2}{3}$ and $\dfrac{2}{3}$ are called _____ .

1.9 | EXERCISE SET

Use a commutative property to complete each statement. See Example 1.

1. $x + 16 = $ _____   **2.** $4 + y = $ _____
 3. $-4 \cdot y = $ _____ **4.** $-2 \cdot x = $ _____
5. $xy = $ ____   **6.** $ab = $ ____
 7. $2x + 13 = $ _____ **8.** $19 + 3y = $ _____

Use an associative property to complete each statement. See Example 2.

9. $(xy) \cdot z = $ _____ **10.** $3 \cdot (xy) = $ _____
11. $2 + (a + b) = $ _____ **12.** $(y + 4) + z = $ _____
13. $4 \cdot (ab) = $ _____ **14.** $(-3y) \cdot z = $ _____
15. $(a + b) + c = $ _____
16. $6 + (r + s) = $ _____

Use the commutative and associative properties to simplify each expression. See Example 3.

17. $8 + (9 + b)$ **18.** $(r + 3) + 11$
19. $4(6y)$ **20.** $2(42x)$
21. $\dfrac{1}{5}(5y)$ **22.** $\dfrac{1}{8}(8z)$
23. $(13 + a) + 13$ **24.** $7 + (x + 4)$
25. $-9(8x)$ **26.** $-3(12y)$
27. $\dfrac{3}{4}\left(\dfrac{4}{3}s\right)$ **28.** $\dfrac{2}{7}\left(\dfrac{7}{2}r\right)$

29. Write an example that shows that division is not commutative.

30. Write an example that shows that subtraction is not commutative.

Use the distributive property to write each expression without parentheses. Then simplify the result. See Example 4.

31. $4(x + y)$ **32.** $7(a + b)$

33. $9(x - 6)$ **34.** $11(y - 4)$
35. $2(3x + 5)$ **36.** $5(7 + 8y)$
37. $7(4x - 3)$ **38.** $3(8x - 1)$
39. $3(6 + x)$ **40.** $2(x + 5)$
41. $-2(y - z)$ **42.** $-3(z - y)$
43. $-7(3y + 5)$ **44.** $-5(2r + 11)$
45. $5(x + 4m + 2)$
46. $8(3y + z - 6)$
47. $-4(1 - 2m + n)$
48. $-4(4 + 2p + 5)$
49. $-(5x + 2)$
50. $-(9r + 5)$
51. $-(r - 3 - 7p)$
52. $-(q - 2 + 6r)$
53. $\dfrac{1}{2}(6x + 8)$
54. $\dfrac{1}{4}(4x - 2)$
55. $-\dfrac{1}{3}(3x - 9y)$
56. $-\dfrac{1}{5}(10a - 25b)$
57. $3(2r + 5) - 7$
58. $10(4s + 6) - 40$
59. $-9(4x + 8) + 2$
60. $-11(5x + 3) + 10$
61. $-4(4x + 5) - 5$
62. $-6(2x + 1) - 1$

Use the distributive property to write each sum as a product. See Example 5.

63. $4 \cdot 1 + 4 \cdot y$

64. $14 \cdot z + 14 \cdot 5$

65. $11x + 11y$

66. $9a + 9b$

67. $(-1) \cdot 5 + (-1) \cdot x$

68. $(-3)a + (-3)b$

69. $30a + 30b$

70. $25x + 25y$

Name the properties illustrated by each true statement. See Example 6.

71. $3 \cdot 5 = 5 \cdot 3$

72. $4(3 + 8) = 4 \cdot 3 + 4 \cdot 8$

73. $2 + (x + 5) = (2 + x) + 5$

74. $(x + 9) + 3 = (9 + x) + 3$

75. $9(3 + 7) = 9 \cdot 3 + 9 \cdot 7$

76. $1 \cdot 9 = 9$

77. $(4 \cdot y) \cdot 9 = 4 \cdot (y \cdot 9)$

78. $6 \cdot \dfrac{1}{6} = 1$

79. $0 + 6 = 6$

80. $(a + 9) + 6 = a + (9 + 6)$

81. $-4(y + 7) = -4 \cdot y + (-4) \cdot 7$

82. $(11 + r) + 8 = (r + 11) + 8$

83. $-4 \cdot (8 \cdot 3) = (8 \cdot -4) \cdot 3$

84. $r + 0 = r$

CONCEPT EXTENSIONS

Complete a Table. *Fill in the table with the opposite (additive inverse), and the reciprocal (multiplicative inverse). Assume that the value of each expression is not 0.*

	Expression	Opposite	Reciprocal
85.	8		
86.	$-\dfrac{2}{3}$		
87.	x		
88.	$4y$		
89.			$\dfrac{1}{2x}$
90.		$7x$	

Determine which pairs of actions are commutative.

91. "taking a test" and "studying for the test"

92. "putting on your shoes" and "putting on your socks"

93. "putting on your left shoe" and "putting on your right shoe"

94. "reading the sports section" and "reading the comics section"

95. Explain why 0 is called the identity element for addition.

96. Explain why 1 is called the identity element for multiplication.

EXTENSION: PROBABILITY AND ODDS

OBJECTIVES

1. Compute theoretical probability.

2. Understand and use odds.

The Hours of Sleep Americans Get on a Typical Night

Hours of Sleep	Number of Americans, in millions
4 or less	12
5	27
6	75
7	90
8	81
9	9
10 or more	6
	Total: 300

Source: Discovery Health Media

How many hours of sleep do you typically get each night? The table above indicates that 75 million out of 300 million Americans are getting six hours of sleep on a typical night. The *probability* of an American getting six hours of sleep on a typical night is $\frac{75}{300}$. This fraction can be reduced to $\frac{1}{4}$, or expressed as 0.25, or 25%. Thus, 25% of Americans get six hours of sleep each night.

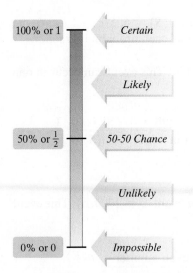

- 100% or 1 — *Certain*
- *Likely*
- 50% or $\frac{1}{2}$ — *50-50 Chance*
- *Unlikely*
- 0% or 0 — *Impossible*

Possible Values for Probabilities

We find a probability by dividing one number by another. Probabilities of events are expressed as numbers ranging from 0 to 1, or 0% to 100%. The closer the probability of a given event is to 1, the more likely it is that the event will occur. The closer the probability of a given event is to 0, the less likely it is that the event will occur.

OBJECTIVE 1 ▶ Compute theoretical probability. You toss a coin. Although it is equally likely to land either heads up, denoted by H, or tails up, denoted by T, the actual outcome is uncertain. Any occurrence for which the outcome is uncertain is called an **experiment.** Thus, tossing a coin is an example of an experiment. The set of all possible outcomes of an experiment is the **sample space** of the experiment, denoted by S. The sample space for the coin-tossing experiment is

$$S = \{H, T\}.$$

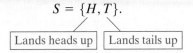

Lands heads up | Lands tails up

An **event,** denoted by E, is any subset of a sample space. For example, the subset $E = \{T\}$ is the event of landing tails up when a coin is tossed.

Theoretical probability applies to situations like this, in which the sample space only contains equally likely outcomes, all of which are known. To calculate the theoretical probability of an event, we divide the number of outcomes resulting in the event by the total number of outcomes in the sample space.

Computing Theoretical Probability

If an event E has $n(E)$ equally likely outcomes and its sample space S has $n(S)$ equally likely outcomes, the **theoretical probability** of event E, denoted by $P(E)$, is

$$P(E) = \frac{\text{number of outcomes in event } E}{\text{total number of possible outcomes}} = \frac{n(E)}{n(S)}.$$

How can we use this formula to compute the probability of a coin landing tails up? We use the following sets:

$$E = \{T\} \qquad S = \{H, T\}.$$

This is the event of landing tails up. | This is the sample space with all equally likely outcomes.

The probability of a coin landing tails up is

$$P(E) = \frac{\text{number of outcomes that result in tails up}}{\text{total number of possible outcomes}} = \frac{n(E)}{n(S)} = \frac{1}{2}.$$

Theoretical probability applies to many games of chance, including dice rolling, lotteries, card games, and roulette. We begin with rolling a die. The figure in the margin illustrates that when a die is rolled, there are six equally likely possible outcomes. The sample space can be shown as

$$S = \{1, 2, 3, 4, 5, 6\}.$$

Outcomes when a die is rolled

EXAMPLE 1 Computing Theoretical Probability

A die is rolled once. Find the probability of rolling

a. a 3. **b.** an even number. **c.** a number less than 5.

d. a number less than 10. **e.** a number greater than 6.

Solution The sample space is $S = \{1, 2, 3, 4, 5, 6\}$ with $n(S) = 6$. We will use 6, the total number of possible outcomes, in the denominator of each probability fraction.

a. The phrase "rolling a 3" describes the event $E = \{3\}$. This event can occur in one way: $n(E) = 1$.

$$P(3) = \frac{\text{number of outcomes that result in } 3}{\text{total number of possible outcomes}} = \frac{n(E)}{n(S)} = \frac{1}{6}$$

The probability of rolling a 3 is $\frac{1}{6}$.

b. The phrase "rolling an even number" describes the event $E = \{2, 4, 6\}$. This event can occur in three ways: $n(E) = 3$.

$$P(\text{even number}) = \frac{\text{number of outcomes that result in an even number}}{\text{total number of possible outcomes}} = \frac{n(E)}{n(S)} = \frac{3}{6} = \frac{1}{2}$$

The probability of rolling an even number is $\frac{1}{2}$.

c. The phrase "rolling a number less than 5" describes the event $E = \{1, 2, 3, 4\}$. This event can occur in four ways: $n(E) = 4$.

$$P(\text{less than } 5) = \frac{\text{number of outcomes that are less than } 5}{\text{total number of possible outcomes}} = \frac{n(E)}{n(S)} = \frac{4}{6} = \frac{2}{3}$$

The probability of rolling a number less than 5 is $\frac{2}{3}$.

d. The phrase "rolling a number less than 10" describes the event $E = \{1, 2, 3, 4, 5, 6\}$. This event can occur in six ways: $n(E) = 6$. Can you see that all of the possible outcomes are less than 10? This event is certain to occur.

$$P(\text{less than } 10) = \frac{\text{number of outcomes that are less than } 10}{\text{total number of possible outcomes}} = \frac{n(E)}{n(S)} = \frac{6}{6} = 1$$

The probability of any certain event is 1.

e. The phrase "rolling a number greater than 6" describes an event that cannot occur, or the empty set. Thus, $E = \varnothing$ and $n(E) = 0$.

$$P(\text{greater than } 6) = \frac{\text{number of outcomes that are greater than } 6}{\text{total number of possible outcomes}} = \frac{n(E)}{n(S)} = \frac{0}{6} = 0$$

The probability of an event that cannot occur is 0. ☐

In Example 1, there are six possible outcomes, each with a probability of $\frac{1}{6}$:

$$P(1) = \frac{1}{6} \quad P(2) = \frac{1}{6} \quad P(3) = \frac{1}{6} \quad P(4) = \frac{1}{6} \quad P(5) = \frac{1}{6} \quad P(6) = \frac{1}{6}.$$

The sum of these probabilities is 1: $\frac{1}{6} + \frac{1}{6} + \frac{1}{6} + \frac{1}{6} + \frac{1}{6} + \frac{1}{6} = 1$. In general, **the sum of the theoretical probabilities of all possible outcomes in the sample space is 1.**

PRACTICE

1 A die is rolled once. Find the probability of rolling

a. a 2.

b. a number less than 4.

c. a number greater than 7.

d. a number less than 7.

Our next example involves a standard 52-card bridge deck, illustrated in the following figure. The deck has four suits: Hearts and diamonds are red, and clubs and spades are black. Each suit has 13 different face values—A(ace), 2, 3, 4, 5, 6, 7, 8, 9, 10, J(jack), Q(queen), and K(king). Jacks, queens, and kings are called **picture cards** or **face cards.**

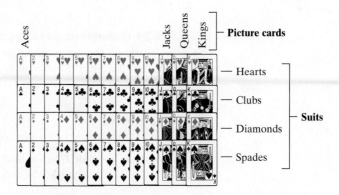

A standard 52-card bridge deck

EXAMPLE 2   Probability and a Deck of 52 Cards

You are dealt one card from a standard 52-card deck. Find the probability of being dealt

a. a king.   **b.** a heart.   **c.** the king of hearts.

Solution Because there are 52 cards in the deck, the total number of possible ways of being dealt a single card is 52. The number of outcomes in the sample space is 52: $n(S) = 52$. We use 52 as the denominator of each probability fraction.

a. Let E be the event of being dealt a king. Because there are four kings in the deck, this event can occur in four ways: $n(E) = 4$.

$$P(\text{king}) = \frac{\text{number of outcomes that result in a king}}{\text{total number of possible outcomes}} = \frac{n(E)}{n(S)} = \frac{4}{52} = \frac{1}{13}$$

The probability of being dealt a king is $\frac{1}{13}$.

b. Let E be the event of being dealt a heart. Because there are 13 hearts in the deck, this event can occur in 13 ways: $n(E) = 13$.

$$P(\text{heart}) = \frac{\text{number of outcomes that result in a heart}}{\text{total number of possible outcomes}} = \frac{n(E)}{n(S)} = \frac{13}{52} = \frac{1}{4}$$

The probability of being dealt a heart is $\frac{1}{4}$.

c. Let E be the event of being dealt the king of hearts. Because there is only one card in the deck that is the king of hearts, this event can occur in just one way: $n(E) = 1$.

$$P(\text{king of hearts}) = \frac{\text{number of outcomes that result in the king of hearts}}{\text{total number of possible outcomes}} = \frac{n(E)}{n(S)} = \frac{1}{52}$$

The probability of being dealt the king of hearts is $\frac{1}{52}$.

PRACTICE
2 You are dealt one card from a standard 52-card deck. Find the probability of being dealt

      a. an ace.   **b.** a red card.   **c.** a red king.

OBJECTIVE 2 ▶ Understand and use odds. If we know the probability of an event E, we can also speak of the *odds in favor*, or the *odds against*, the event. The following definitions link together the concepts of odds and probabilities:

Probability to Odds

If $P(E)$ is the probability of an event E occurring, then

1. The **odds in favor of E** are found by taking the probability that E will occur and dividing by the probability that E will not occur.

$$\text{Odds in favor of } E = \frac{P(E)}{P(\text{not } E)}$$

2. The **odds against E** are found by taking the probability that E will not occur and dividing by the probability that E will occur.

$$\text{Odds against } E = \frac{P(\text{not } E)}{P(E)}$$

The odds against E can also be found by reversing the ratio representing the odds in favor of E.

EXAMPLE 3 From Probability to Odds

You roll a single, six-sided die.

  a. Find the odds in favor of rolling a 2.

  b. Find the odds against rolling a 2.

Solution Let E represent the event of rolling a 2. In order to determine odds, we must first find the probability of E occurring and the probability of E not occurring. With $S = \{1, 2, 3, 4, 5, 6\}$ and $E = \{2\}$, we see that

$$P(E) = \frac{1}{6}$$

$$\text{and} \quad P(\text{not } E) = 1 - \frac{1}{6} = \frac{6}{6} - \frac{1}{6} = \frac{5}{6}.$$

Now we are ready to construct the ratios for the odds in favor of E and the odds against E.

  a. $\text{Odds in favor of } E(\text{rolling a 2}) = \dfrac{P(E)}{P(\text{not } E)} = \dfrac{\frac{1}{6}}{\frac{5}{6}} = \dfrac{1}{6} \cdot \dfrac{6}{5} = \dfrac{1}{5}$

> **▶ Helpful Hint**
> When computing odds, the denominators of two probabilities will always divide out.

The odds in favor of rolling a 2 are $\frac{1}{5}$. The ratio $\frac{1}{5}$ is usually written 1:5 and is read "1 to 5." Thus, the odds in favor of rolling a 2 are 1 to 5.

b. Now that we have the odds in favor of rolling a 2, namely $\frac{1}{5}$ or 1:5, we can find the odds against rolling a 2 by reversing this ratio. Thus,

$$\text{Odds against } E(\text{rolling a 2}) = \frac{5}{1} \quad \text{or} \quad 5:1.$$

The odds against rolling a 2 are 5 to 1.

PRACTICE
3 You are dealt one card from a 52-card deck.

  a. Find the odds in favor of getting a red queen.
  b. Find the odds against getting a red queen.

EXAMPLE 4 From Probability to Odds

The winner of a raffle will receive a new sports utility vehicle. If 500 raffle tickets were sold and you purchased ten tickets, what are the odds against your winning the car?

Solution Let E represent the event of winning the SUV. Because you purchased ten tickets and 500 tickets were sold,

$$P(E) = \frac{10}{500} = \frac{1}{50} \quad \text{and} \quad P(\text{not } E) = 1 - \frac{1}{50} = \frac{50}{50} - \frac{1}{50} = \frac{49}{50}.$$

Now we are ready to construct the ratio for the odds against E (winning the SUV).

$$\text{Odds against } E = \frac{P(\text{not } E)}{P(E)} = \frac{\frac{49}{50}}{\frac{1}{50}} = \frac{49}{50} \cdot \frac{50}{1} = \frac{49}{1}$$

The odds against winning the SUV are 49 to 1, written 49:1.

PRACTICE
4 The winner of a raffle will receive a two-year scholarship to the college of his or her choice. If 1000 raffle tickets were sold and you purchased five tickets, what are the odds against your winning the scholarship?

Now that we know how to convert from probability to odds, let's see how to convert from odds to probability. Suppose that the odds in favor of event E occurring are a to b. This means that

$$\frac{P(E)}{P(\text{not } E)} = \frac{a}{b} \quad \text{or} \quad \frac{P(E)}{1 - P(E)} = \frac{a}{b}.$$

By solving the equation on the right for $P(E)$, we obtain the following formula for converting from odds to probability:

Odds to Probability
If the odds in favor of event E are a to b, then the probability of the event is given by

$$P(E) = \frac{a}{a + b}.$$

EXAMPLE 5 From Odds to Probability

The odds in favor of a particular horse winning a race are 2 to 5. What is the probability that this horse will win the race?

Solution Because odds in favor, a to b, means a probability of $\frac{a}{a+b}$, then odds in favor, 2 to 5, means a probability of

$$\frac{2}{2+5} = \frac{2}{7}.$$

The probability that this horse will win the race is $\frac{2}{7}$.   ☐

PRACTICE
5   The odds against a particular horse winning a race are 15 to 1. Find the odds in favor of the horse winning the race and the probability of the horse winning the race.

CHAPTER 1 EXTENSION | EXERCISES

PRACTICE AND APPLICATION EXERCISES

Exercises 1–40 involve theoretical probability. Use the theoretical probability formula to solve each exercise. Express each probability as a fraction reduced to lowest terms.

In Exercises 1–10, a die is rolled. The set of equally likely outcomes is $\{1, 2, 3, 4, 5, 6\}$. Find the probability of rolling

1. a 4.
2. a 5.
3. an odd number.
4. a number greater than 3.
5. a number less than 3.
6. a number greater than 4.
7. a number less than 7.
8. a number less than 8.
9. a number greater than 7.
10. a number greater than 8.

In Exercises 11–20, you are dealt one card from a standard 52-card deck. Find the probability of being dealt

11. a queen.
12. a jack.
13. a club.
14. a diamond.
15. a picture card.
16. a card greater than 3 and less than 7.
17. the queen of spades.
18. the ace of clubs.
19. a diamond and a spade.
20. a card with a green heart.

In Exercises 21–26, a fair coin is tossed two times in succession. The set of equally likely outcomes is $\{HH, HT, TH, TT\}$. Find the probability of getting

21. two heads.
22. two tails.
23. the same outcome on each toss.
24. different outcomes on each toss.
25. a head on the second toss.
26. at least one head.

In Exercises 27–32, a single die is rolled twice. The 36 equally likely outcomes are shown as follows:

		Second Roll					
		⚀	⚁	⚂	⚃	⚄	⚅
First Roll	⚀	(1, 1)	(1, 2)	(1, 3)	(1, 4)	(1, 5)	(1, 6)
	⚁	(2, 1)	(2, 2)	(2, 3)	(2, 4)	(2, 5)	(2, 6)
	⚂	(3, 1)	(3, 2)	(3, 3)	(3, 4)	(3, 5)	(3, 6)
	⚃	(4, 1)	(4, 2)	(4, 3)	(4, 4)	(4, 5)	(4, 6)
	⚄	(5, 1)	(5, 2)	(5, 3)	(5, 4)	(5, 5)	(5, 6)
	⚅	(6, 1)	(6, 2)	(6, 3)	(6, 4)	(6, 5)	(6, 6)

Find the probability of getting

27. two even numbers.
28. two odd numbers.
29. two numbers whose sum is 5.
30. two numbers whose sum is 6.
31. two numbers whose sum exceeds 12.
32. two numbers whose sum is less than 13.

Use the spinner shown to answer Exercises 33–40. Assume that it is equally probable that the pointer will land on any one of the ten colored regions. If the pointer lands on a borderline, spin again.

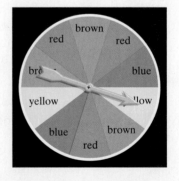

Find the probability that the spinner lands in

33. a red region.
34. a yellow region.

35. a blue region.

36. a brown region.

37. a region that is red or blue.

38. a region that is yellow or brown.

39. a region that is red and blue.

40. a region that is yellow and brown.

The table shows the educational attainment of the U.S. population, ages 25 and over, in 2004. Use the data in the table, expressed in millions, to solve Exercises 41–48.

Educational Attainment of the U.S. Population, Ages 25 and Over, in Millions

	Less Than 4 Years High School	4 Years High School Only	Some College (Less than 4 years)	4 Years College (or More)	Total
Male	14	28	22	26	90
Female	14	32	26	25	97
Total	28	60	48	51	187

Source: U.S. Census Bureau

Find the probability, expressed as a simplified fraction, that a randomly selected American, aged 25 or over,

41. has not completed four years (or more) of college.

42. has not completed four years of high school.

43. has completed four years of high school only or less than four years of college.

44. has completed less than four years of high school or four years of high school only.

45. has completed four years of high school only or is a man.

46. has completed four years of high school only or is a woman.

Find the odds in favor and the odds against a randomly selected American, aged 25 and over, with

47. four years (or more) of college.

48. less than four years of high school.

The graph shows the distribution, by branch and gender, of the 1.43 million, or 1430 thousand, active-duty personnel in the U.S. military in 2003. Numbers are given in thousands and rounded to the nearest ten thousand. Use the data to solve Exercises 49–60.

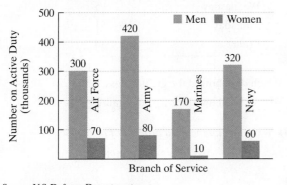

Active Duty U.S. Military Personnel

Source: U.S. Defense Department

If one person is randomly selected from the population represented in the bar graph in the previous column, find the probability, expressed as a simplified fraction, that the person

49. is not in the Army.

50. is not in the Marines.

51. is in the Navy or is a man.

52. is in the Army or is a woman.

53. is in the Air Force or the Marines.

54. is in the Army or the Navy.

Find the odds in favor and the odds against a randomly selected person from the population represented in the bar graph in the previous column being

55. in the Navy.

56. in the Army.

57. a woman in the Marines.

58. a woman in the Air Force.

59. a man.

60. a woman.

In Exercises 61–64, a single die is rolled. Find the odds

61. in favor of rolling a number greater than 2.

62. in favor of rolling a number less than 5.

63. against rolling a number greater than 2.

64. against rolling a number less than 5.

The circle graphs show the percentage of children in the United States whose parents are college graduates in one-parent households and two-parent households. Use the information shown to solve Exercises 65–66.

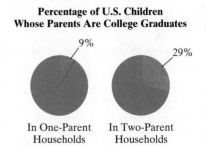

Percentage of U.S. Children Whose Parents Are College Graduates

9%
29%

In One-Parent Households   In Two-Parent Households

Source: U.S. Census Bureau

65. a. What are the odds in favor of a child in a one-parent household having a parent who is a college graduate?

b. What are the odds against a child in a one-parent household having a parent who is a college graduate?

66. a. What are the odds in favor of a child in a two-parent household having parents who are college graduates?

b. What are the odds against a child in a two-parent household having parents who are college graduates?

67. If you are given odds of 3 to 4 in favor of winning a bet, what is the probability of winning the bet?

68. If you are given odds of 3 to 7 in favor of winning a bet, what is the probability of winning the bet?

69. How is the theoretical probability of an event computed?

70. Use the definition of theoretical probability to explain why the probability of an event that cannot occur is 0.

71. Use the definition of theoretical probability to explain why the probability of an event that is certain to occur is 1.

72. Explain how to find the probability of an event not occuring. Give an example.

CHAPTER 1 VOCABULARY CHECK

Fill in each blank with one of the words or phrases listed below.

set	inequality symbols	opposites	absolute value	numerator
denominator	grouping symbols	exponent	base	reciprocals
variable	equation	solution	counterexample	matrix

1. The symbols $\neq$, $<$, and $>$ are called _____.

2. A mathematical statement that two expressions are equal is called an _____.

3. The _____ of a number is the distance between that number and 0 on the number line.

4. A symbol used to represent a number is called a _____.

5. Two numbers that are the same distance from 0 but lie on opposite sides of 0 are called _____.

6. The number in a fraction above the fraction bar is called the _____.

7. A _____ of an equation is a value for the variable that makes the equation a true statement.

8. Two numbers whose product is 1 are called _____.

9. In 2^3, the 2 is called the _____ and the 3 is called the _____.

10. The number in a fraction below the fraction bar is called the _____.

11. Parentheses and brackets are examples of _____.

12. A _____ is a collection of objects.

13. A specific example of the falsity of a statement is called a _____.

14. An array of numbers, arranged in rows and columns is called a _____.

CHAPTER 1 REVIEW

(1.2) Insert $<$, $>$, or $=$ in the appropriate space to make the following statements true.

1. 8 _____ 10

2. 7 _____ 2

3. -4 _____ -5

4. $\dfrac{12}{2}$ _____ -8

5. $|-7|$ _____ $|-8|$

6. $|-9|$ _____ -9

7. $-|-1|$ _____ -1

8. $|-14|$ _____ $-(-14)$

9. 1.2 _____ 1.02

10. $-\dfrac{3}{2}$ _____ $-\dfrac{3}{4}$

Translate each statement into symbols.

11. Four is greater than or equal to negative three.

12. Six is not equal to five.

13. 0.03 is less than 0.3.

14. New York City has 155 museums and 400 art galleries. Write an inequality comparing the numbers 155 and 400. (*Source:* Absolute Trivia.com)

Given the following sets of numbers, list the numbers in each set that also belong to the set of:

a. Natural numbers
b. Whole numbers
c. Integers
d. Rational numbers
e. Irrational numbers
f. Real numbers

15. $\left\{ -6, 0, 1, 1\dfrac{1}{2}, 3, \pi, 9.62 \right\}$

16. $\left\{ -3, -1.6, 2, 5, \dfrac{11}{2}, 15.1, \sqrt{5}, 2\pi \right\}$

The following chart shows the gains and losses in dollars of Density Oil and Gas stock for a particular week.

Day	Gain or Loss in Dollars
Monday	+1
Tuesday	−2
Wednesday	+5
Thursday	+1
Friday	−4

17. Which day showed the greatest loss?

18. Which day showed the greatest gain?

(1.3) Write the number as a product of prime factors.

19. 36

20. 120

Perform the indicated operations. Write results in lowest terms.

21. $\dfrac{8}{15} \cdot \dfrac{27}{30}$

22. $\dfrac{7}{8} \div \dfrac{21}{32}$

23. $\dfrac{7}{15} + \dfrac{5}{6}$

24. $\dfrac{3}{4} - \dfrac{3}{20}$

25. $2\dfrac{3}{4} + 6\dfrac{5}{8}$

26. $7\dfrac{1}{6} - 2\dfrac{2}{3}$

27. $5 \div \dfrac{1}{3}$

28. $2 \cdot 8\dfrac{3}{4}$

29. Determine the unknown part of the given circle.

Find the area and the perimeter of each figure.

△ **30.**

△ **31.**

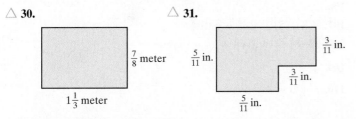

$\dfrac{7}{8}$ meter

$1\dfrac{1}{3}$ meter

$\dfrac{5}{11}$ in.

$\dfrac{3}{11}$ in.

$\dfrac{3}{11}$ in.

$\dfrac{5}{11}$ in.

△ **32.** A trim carpenter needs a piece of quarter round molding $6\dfrac{1}{8}$ feet long for a bathroom. She finds a piece $7\dfrac{1}{2}$ feet long.

How long a piece does she need to cut from the $7\dfrac{1}{2}$-foot-long molding in order to use it in the bathroom?

In December 1998, Nkem Chukwu gave birth to the world's first surviving octuplets in Houston, Texas. The following chart gives the octuplets' birthweights. The babies are listed in order of birth.

Baby's Name	Gender	Birthweight (pounds)
Ebuka	girl	$1\dfrac{1}{2}$
Chidi	girl	$1\dfrac{11}{16}$
Echerem	girl	$1\dfrac{3}{4}$
Chima	girl	$1\dfrac{5}{8}$
Odera	girl	$\dfrac{11}{16}$
Ikem	boy	$1\dfrac{1}{8}$
Jioke	boy	$1\dfrac{13}{16}$
Gorom	girl	$1\dfrac{1}{8}$

(*Source:* Texas Children's Hospital, Houston, Texas)

33. What was the total weight of the boy octuplets?

34. What was the total weight of the girl octuplets?

35. Find the combined weight of all eight octuplets.

36. Which baby weighed the most?

37. Which baby weighed the least?

38. How much more did the heaviest baby weigh than the lightest baby?

39. By March 1999, Chima weighed $5\dfrac{1}{2}$ pounds. How much weight had she gained since birth?

40. By March 1999, Ikem weighed $4\dfrac{5}{32}$ pounds. How much weight had he gained since birth?

(1.4) *Simplify each expression.*

41. 2^4

42. 5^2

43. $\left(\dfrac{2}{7}\right)^2$

44. $\left(\dfrac{3}{4}\right)^3$

45. $6 \cdot 3^2 + 2 \cdot 8$

46. $68 - 5 \cdot 2^3$

47. $3(1 + 2 \cdot 5) + 4$

48. $8 + 3(2 \cdot 6 - 1)$

49. $\dfrac{4 + |6 - 2| + 8^2}{4 + 6 \cdot 4}$

50. $5[3(2 + 5) - 5]$

Translate each word statement to symbols.

51. The difference of twenty and twelve is equal to the product of two and four.

52. The quotient of nine and two is greater than negative five.

Evaluate each expression if $x = 6$, $y = 2$, and $z = 8$.

53. $2x + 3y$

54. $x(y + 2z)$

55. $\dfrac{x}{y} + \dfrac{z}{2y}$

56. $x^2 - 3y^2$

57. The expression $180 - a - b$ represents the measure of the unknown angle of the given triangle. Replace a with 37 and b with 80 to find the measure of the unknown angle.

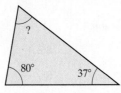

Decide whether the given number is a solution to the given equation.

58. Is $x = 3$ a solution of $7x - 3 = 18$?

59. Is $x = 1$ a solution of $3x^2 + 4 = x - 1$?

(1.5) *Find the additive inverse or the opposite.*

60. -9

61. $\dfrac{2}{3}$

62. $|-2|$

63. $-|-7|$

Find the following sums.

64. $-15 + 4$

65. $-6 + (-11)$

66. $\dfrac{1}{16} + \left(-\dfrac{1}{4}\right)$

67. $-8 + |-3|$

68. $-4.6 + (-9.3)$ **69.** $-2.8 + 6.7$

70. The lowest elevation in North America is -282 feet at Death Valley in California. If you are standing at a point 728 feet above Death Valley, what is your elevation? (*Source:* National Geographic Society)

(1.6) *Perform the indicated operations.*

71. $6 - 20$ **72.** $-3.1 - 8.4$

73. $-6 - (-11)$ **74.** $4 - 15$

75. $-21 - 16 + 3(8 - 2)$ **76.** $\dfrac{11 - (-9) + 6(8 - 2)}{2 + 3 \cdot 4}$

If $x = 3$, $y = -6$, and $z = -9$, evaluate each expression.

77. $2x^2 - y + z$ **78.** $\dfrac{y - x + 5x}{2x}$

(1.7)

79. Find values for x, y, and z so that the following matrices are equal:

$$\begin{bmatrix} x & y + 7 \\ z & 4 \end{bmatrix} = \begin{bmatrix} -5 & 13 \\ 6 & 4 \end{bmatrix}.$$

In Exercises 80–82, perform the indicated matrix operations given that A, B, C, and D are defined as follows. If an operation is not defined, state the reason.

$$A = \begin{bmatrix} 2 & -1 & 2 \\ 5 & 3 & -1 \end{bmatrix} \quad B = \begin{bmatrix} 0 & -2 \\ 3 & 2 \\ 1 & -5 \end{bmatrix}$$

$$C = \begin{bmatrix} 1 & 2 & 3 \\ -1 & 1 & 2 \\ -1 & 2 & 1 \end{bmatrix} \quad D = \begin{bmatrix} -2 & 3 & 1 \\ 3 & -2 & 4 \end{bmatrix}$$

80. $A + D$ **81.** $D - A$ **82.** $B + C$

(1.8) *Find the multiplicative inverse or reciprocal.*

83. -6 **84.** $\dfrac{3}{5}$

Simplify each expression.

85. $6(-8)$ **86.** $(-2)(-14)$

87. $\dfrac{-18}{-6}$ **88.** $\dfrac{42}{-3}$

89. $\dfrac{4(-3) + (-8)}{2 + (-2)}$ **90.** $\dfrac{3(-2)^2 - 5}{-14}$

91. $\dfrac{-6}{0}$ **92.** $\dfrac{0}{-2}$

93. $-4^2 - (-3 + 5) \div (-1) \cdot 2$

94. $-5^2 - (2 - 20) \div (-3) \cdot 3$

If $x = -5$ and $y = -2$, evaluate each expression.

95. $x^2 - y^4$ **96.** $x^2 - y^3$

97. During an LPGA Sara Lee Classic, Michelle McGann had scores of -9, -7, and $+1$ in three rounds of golf. Find her average score per round. (*Source:* Ladies Professional Golf Association)

98. During a PGA Masters Tournament, Bob Estes had scores of -1, 0, -3, and 0 in four rounds of golf. Find his average score per round. (*Source:* Professional Golf Association)

Use the matrices for Exercises 80–82 to find.

99. $2B$ **100.** $-3A + D$

(1.9) *Name the property illustrated.*

101. $-6 + 5 = 5 + (-6)$

102. $6 \cdot 1 = 6$

103. $3(8 - 5) = 3 \cdot 8 + 3 \cdot (-5)$

104. $4 + (-4) = 0$

105. $2 + (3 + 9) = (2 + 3) + 9$

106. $2 \cdot 8 = 8 \cdot 2$

107. $6(8 + 5) = 6 \cdot 8 + 6 \cdot 5$

108. $(3 \cdot 8) \cdot 4 = 3 \cdot (8 \cdot 4)$

109. $4 \cdot \dfrac{1}{4} = 1$

110. $8 + 0 = 8$

Use the distributive property to write each expression without parentheses.

111. $5(y - 2)$

112. $-3(z + y)$

113. $-(7 - x + 4z)$

114. $\dfrac{1}{2}(6z - 10)$

115. $-4(3x + 5) - 7$

116. $-8(2y + 9) - 1$

MIXED REVIEW

Insert $<$, $>$, or $=$ in the space between each pair of numbers.

117. $-|-11|$ $|11.4|$ **118.** $-1\dfrac{1}{2}$ $-2\dfrac{1}{2}$

Perform the indicated operations.

119. $-7.2 + (-8.1)$ **120.** $14 - 20$

121. $4(-20)$ **122.** $\dfrac{-20}{4}$

123. $-\dfrac{4}{5}\left(\dfrac{5}{16}\right)$ **124.** $-0.5(-0.3)$

125. $8 \div 2 \cdot 4$ **126.** $(-2)^4$

127. $\dfrac{-3 - 2(-9)}{-15 - 3(-4)}$ **128.** $5 + 2[(7 - 5)^2 + (1 - 3)]$

129. $-\dfrac{5}{8} \div \dfrac{3}{4}$ **130.** $\dfrac{-15 + (-4)^2 + |-9|}{10 - 2 \cdot 5}$

CHAPTER 1 TEST

TEST PREP VIDEO The fully worked-out solutions to any exercises you want to review are available in MyMathLab.

Translate the statement into symbols.

1. The absolute value of negative seven is greater than five.

2. The sum of nine and five is greater than or equal to four.

Simplify the expression.

3. $-13 + 8$

4. $-13 - (-2)$

5. $12 \div 4 \cdot 3 - 6 \cdot 2$

6. $(13)(-3)$

7. $(-6)(-2)$

8. $\dfrac{|-16|}{-8}$

9. $\dfrac{-8}{0}$

10. $\dfrac{|-6| + 2}{5 - 6}$

11. $\dfrac{1}{2} - \dfrac{5}{6}$

12. $-1\dfrac{1}{8} + 5\dfrac{3}{4}$

13. $(2 - 6) \div \dfrac{-2 - 6}{-3 - 1} - \dfrac{1}{2}$

14. $3(-4)^2 - 80$

15. $6[5 + 2(3 - 8) - 3]$

16. $\dfrac{-12 + 3 \cdot 8}{4}$

17. $\dfrac{(-2)(0)(-3)}{-6}$

Insert $<$, $>$, or $=$ in the appropriate space to make each of the following statements true.

18. -3 ___ -7

19. 4 ___ -8

20. 2 ___ $|-3|$

21. $|-2|$ ___ $-1 - (-3)$

22. In the state of Massachusetts, there are 2221 licensed child care centers and 10,993 licensed home-based child care providers. Write an inequality statement comparing the numbers 2221 and 10,993. (*Source:* Children's Foundation)

23. Given $\left\{ -5, -1, 0, \dfrac{1}{4}, 1, 7, 11.6, \sqrt{7}, 3\pi \right\}$, list the numbers in this set that also belong to the set of:
    a. Natural numbers
    b. Whole numbers
    c. Integers
    d. Rational numbers
    e. Irrational numbers
    f. Real numbers

If $x = 6$, $y = -2$, and $z = -3$, evaluate each expression.

24. $x^2 + y^2$

25. $x + yz$

26. $2 + 3x - y$

27. $\dfrac{y + z - 1}{x}$

Identify the property illustrated by each expression.

28. $8 + (9 + 3) = (8 + 9) + 3$

29. $6 \cdot 8 = 8 \cdot 6$

30. $-6(2 + 4) = -6 \cdot 2 + (-6) \cdot 4$

31. $\dfrac{1}{6}(6) = 1$

32. Find the opposite of -9.

33. Find the reciprocal of $-\dfrac{1}{3}$.

Gains and Losses in Yards	
First Down	5
Second Down	-10
Third Down	-2
Fourth Down	29

The New Orleans Saints were 22 yards from the goal when the following series of gains and losses occurred.

34. During which down did the greatest loss of yardage occur?

35. Was a touchdown scored?

36. The temperature at the Winter Olympics was a frigid 14 degrees below zero in the morning, but by noon it had risen 31 degrees. What was the temperature at noon?

37. United HealthCare is a health insurance provider. In 3 consecutive recent years, it had net incomes of $356 million, $460 million, and $-$166 million. What was United HealthCare's total net income for these three years? (*Source:* United HealthCare Corp.)

38. Jean Avarez decided to sell 280 shares of stock, which decreased in value by $1.50 per share yesterday. How much money did she lose?

In Exercises 39–40, let

$$B = \begin{bmatrix} 1 & -1 \\ 2 & 1 \end{bmatrix}, \text{ and } C = \begin{bmatrix} 1 & 2 \\ -1 & 3 \end{bmatrix}.$$

Carry out the indicated operations.

39. $B + C$

40. $C - B$

CHAPTER 1 STANDARDIZED TEST

Multiple Choice. *Choose the one alternative that best completes the statement or answers the question.*

Translate the statement into symbols.

1. The absolute value of negative six is greater than one.
  a. $|-6| > 1$ **b.** $|-1| > 6$
  c. $|6| > 1$ **d.** $-|6| > 1$

2. The sum of six and seven is greater than or equal to seven.
  a. $6 + 7 > 7$ **b.** $6 + 6 \le 7$
  c. $6 + 7 = 7$ **d.** $6 + 7 \ge 7$

Simplify the expression.

3. $-8 + 6$
  a. -2 **b.** -14
  c. 14 **d.** 2

4. $-11 - (-2)$
  a. -9 **b.** 9
  c. 13 **d.** -13

5. $28 \div 7 \cdot 4 - 9 \cdot 5$
  a. -29 **b.** -44
  c. -40 **d.** 35

6. $(8)(-6)$
  a. -56 **b.** -148
  c. -48 **d.** -480

7. $\dfrac{1-121}{-6}$
  a. -1 **b.** -3
  c. -2 **d.** 2

8. $\dfrac{-65}{0}$
  a. 0 **b.** 65
  c. undefined   **d.** 1

9. $\dfrac{|-6| + 5}{3 - 6}$
  a. $\dfrac{1}{3}$ **b.** $\dfrac{5}{3}$
  c. $\dfrac{11}{3}$ **d.** $-\dfrac{11}{3}$

10. $\dfrac{1}{3} - \dfrac{8}{9}$
  a. $-\dfrac{7}{9}$ **b.** $-\dfrac{5}{9}$
  c. $\dfrac{11}{9}$ **d.** $-\dfrac{5}{3}$

11. $-8\dfrac{5}{8} + 16\dfrac{13}{16}$
  a. $9\dfrac{7}{16}$ **b.** $-7\dfrac{13}{16}$
  c. $8\dfrac{3}{16}$ **d.** $24\dfrac{3}{16}$

12. $(2 - 6) \div \dfrac{-2 - 6}{-3 - 1} - \dfrac{1}{2}(2 - 10) \div \dfrac{-1 - 7}{-1 - 1} + \dfrac{1}{2}$
  a. $-\dfrac{3}{2}$ **b.** $-\dfrac{3}{4}$
  c. $-\dfrac{16}{9}$ **d.** $-\dfrac{5}{2}$

13. $3(-2)^2 - 70$
  a. 58 **b.** -82
  c. -58 **d.** -76
  e. none of these

14. $5[-4 + 5(-5 + 7)]$
  a. -10 **b.** 30
  c. 6 **d.** 10
  e. none of these

15. $\dfrac{-15 + 4(10)}{5}$
  a. -5 **b.** 11
  c. -22 **d.** 5
  e. none of these

16. $\dfrac{(-6)(0)(-8)}{-9}$
  a. $-\dfrac{16}{3}$ **b.** $\dfrac{14}{9}$
  c. 0 **d.** undefined
  e. none of these

Insert $<, >,$ *or* $=$ *to make the statement true.*

17. $-4 \underline{\hspace{2em}} -8$
  a. $=$ **b.** $>$ **c.** $<$

18. $|-4| \underline{\hspace{2em}} -2 - (-6)$
  a. $>$ **b.** $<$ **c.** $=$

Provide an appropriate response.

19. As part of a fund raiser, Maria sold 278 candy bars. Drew sold 162 candy bars. Write an inequality statement using $<$ or $>$ comparing the numbers 278 and 162.
  a. $278 < 162$ **b.** $278 > 162$

For Exercise 20 and 21, let $A = \begin{bmatrix} 5 & -7 \\ 0 & 4 \\ -2 & 1 \end{bmatrix}$ *and*

$B = \begin{bmatrix} 3 & 3 \\ -9 & 2 \\ 0 & -4 \end{bmatrix}.$

20. $A + B = $ ___?___

a. $\begin{bmatrix} 8 & -4 \\ -9 & 6 \\ -2 & -3 \end{bmatrix}$ **b.** $\begin{bmatrix} 8 & -4 \\ 0 & 6 \\ 0 & -3 \end{bmatrix}$

c. $\begin{bmatrix} 15 & -21 \\ 0 & 8 \\ 0 & -4 \end{bmatrix}$ **d.** $\begin{bmatrix} 8 & 10 \\ 9 & 6 \\ 2 & 5 \end{bmatrix}$

21. $B - A = $ ___?___

a. $\begin{bmatrix} -2 & -4 \\ -9 & -2 \\ -2 & -5 \end{bmatrix}$ **b.** $\begin{bmatrix} -2 & 10 \\ -9 & -2 \\ -2 & -5 \end{bmatrix}$

c. $\begin{bmatrix} 2 & -10 \\ 9 & 2 \\ -2 & 5 \end{bmatrix}$ **d.** $\begin{bmatrix} -2 & 10 \\ -9 & -2 \\ 2 & -5 \end{bmatrix}$

List the numbers in set B that belong to the indicated set.

22. $B = \left\{ 2, \sqrt{7}, -20, 0, \dfrac{0}{4}, 2\pi, \sqrt{4} \right\}$

Natural numbers

a. $2, 0, \dfrac{0}{9}$ **b.** $2, 0$

c. $2, 0, \sqrt{4}$ **d.** $2, \sqrt{4}$

23. $B = \left\{ 3, \sqrt{7}, -13, 0, \dfrac{0}{6}, 2\pi, \sqrt{25} \right\}$

Whole numbers

a. $3, -13, 0, \sqrt{25}, 2\pi$ **b.** $3, 0$

c. $3, 0, \dfrac{0}{6}, \sqrt{25}$ **d.** $3, -13, 0$

24. $B = \left\{ 18, \sqrt{8}, -24, 0, \dfrac{0}{9}, 2\pi, \sqrt{4} \right\}$

Integers

a. $18, 0$ **b.** $18, -24, 0, \dfrac{0}{9}, \sqrt{4}$

c. $18, -24, 0$ **d.** $18, 0, \sqrt{4}, 2\pi$

25. $B = \left\{ 20, \sqrt{5}, -17, 0, \dfrac{0}{3}, \sqrt{4}, \dfrac{-8}{0}, 2\pi, 0.46 \right\}$

Rational numbers

a. $20, -17, 0, \dfrac{0}{3}, \sqrt{4}, 0.46$ **b.** $\sqrt{5}, \sqrt{4}$

c. $\sqrt{5}, \dfrac{0}{3}, 0.46$ **d.** $20, 0, \sqrt{4}, 2\pi$

26. $B = \left\{ 4, \sqrt{8}, -20, 0, \dfrac{0}{1}, \sqrt{16}, \dfrac{-5}{0}, 2\pi, 0.22 \right\}$

Irrational numbers

a. $\sqrt{8}, \dfrac{-5}{0}, 2\pi$ **b.** $\sqrt{8}, \sqrt{16}$

c. $\sqrt{8}, \sqrt{16}, 0.22, 2\pi$ **d.** $\sqrt{8}, 2\pi$

Evaluate the expression for the given replacement values.

27. $x^2 + y^2$ $x = 4, y = -9$

a. 97   **b.** 1296

c. 26   **d.** 72

28. $3 + 8x - y$ $x = 3, y = -9$

a. 99   **b.** 42

c. 36   **d.** 20

29. $\dfrac{y + z - 4}{x}$ $x = 6, y = -10, z = 20$

a. $-\dfrac{8}{3}$ **b.** -1

c. 1 **d.** $\dfrac{8}{3}$

Identify the property illustrated by the expression.

30. $19 + (17 + 3) = (19 + 17) + 3$

   a. commutative property of addition

   b. identity element for addition

   c. distributive property

   d. associative property of addition

31. $9 \cdot 4 = 4 \cdot 9$

   a. commutative property of multiplication

   b. distributive property

   c. associative property of multiplication

   d. identity element for multiplication

32. $-2(4 + 4) = -2 \cdot 4 + (-2) \cdot 4$

   a. distributive property

   b. associative property of addition

   c. commutative property of multiplication

   d. associative property of multiplication

33. $\dfrac{1}{8}(8) = 1$

   a. multiplicative inverse property

   b. distributive property

   c. identity element for multiplication

   d. associative property of multiplication

34. Find the opposite of -12.

a. 12   **b.** 0

c. $-\dfrac{1}{12}$ **d.** -12

35. Find the reciprocal of $-\dfrac{1}{8}$.

a. 1   **b.** -8

c. 8   **d.** $\dfrac{1}{8}$

36. An NFL football team was 35 yards from the goal when the following series of gains and losses occurred.

	Gains and Losses in Yards
First Down	10
Second Down	−4
Third Down	−11
Fourth Down	18

During which down did the greatest gain of yardage occur?

a. first down **b.** second down

c. fourth down **d.** third down

37. An NFL football team was 39 yards from the goal when the following series of gains and losses occurred.

	Gains and Losses in Yards
First Down	12
Second Down	−8
Third Down	−8
Fourth Down	13

Was a touchdown scored?

a. Yes **b.** No

38. The temperature at a mountain resort was a frigid 14 degrees below zero in the morning, but by noon it had risen 29 degrees. What was the temperature at noon?

a. 43° **b.** −43°

c. 15° **d.** −15°

39. Allied Health Provider is a health insurance provider. In three consecutive recent years, it had net incomes of $337 million, $471 million, and −$200 million. What was Allied Health Provider's total net income for these three years?

a. $808 million **b.** $334 million

c. $608 million **d.** $1008 million

40. Noah Field decided to sell 390 shares of stock, which decreased in value by $3.50 per share yesterday. How much money did he lose?

a. $386.50 **b.** $2730

c. $1365 **d.** $6825

2 Solving Equations and Problem Solving

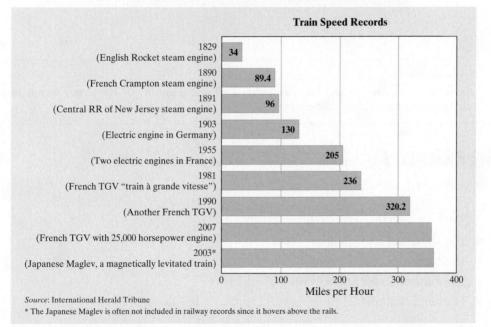

Train Speed Records

1829 (English Rocket steam engine) — 34

1890 (French Crampton steam engine) — 89.4

1891 (Central RR of New Jersey steam engine) — 96

1903 (Electric engine in Germany) — 130

1955 (Two electric engines in France) — 205

1981 (French TGV "train à grande vitesse") — 236

1990 (Another French TGV) — 320.2

2007 (French TGV with 25,000 horsepower engine)

2003* (Japanese Maglev, a magnetically levitated train)

Miles per Hour

Source: International Herald Tribune

* The Japanese Maglev is often not included in railway records since it hovers above the rails.

There is an expanding market for high-speed trains as more countries, such as China, turn to bullet trains. In April 2007, a French TGV, short for "train à grande vitesse" or "very fast train," broke the previous world speed record on rails. (The current record for overall train speed is held by a magnetically levitated train called the Maglev, from Japan. This train hovers above the rails.)

The bar graph above shows a history of train speed records. In this chapter, you will have the opportunity to calculate the speeds of the Maglev and the TGV.

2.1 SIMPLIFYING ALGEBRAIC EXPRESSIONS

OBJECTIVES

1 Identify terms, like terms, and unlike terms.

2 Combine like terms.

3 Use the distributive property to remove parentheses.

4 Write word phrases as algebraic expressions.

As we explore in this section, an expression such as $3x + 2x$ is not as simple as possible, because—even without replacing x by a value—we can perform the indicated addition.

OBJECTIVE 1 ▶ **Identifying terms, like terms, and unlike terms.** Before we practice simplifying expressions, some new language of algebra is presented. A **term** is a number or the product of a number and variables raised to powers.

Terms

$$-y, \quad 2x^3, \quad -5, \quad 3xz^2, \quad \frac{2}{y}, \quad 0.8z$$

The **numerical coefficient** (sometimes also simply called the **coefficient**) of a term is the numerical factor. The numerical coefficient of $3x$ is 3. Recall that $3x$ means $3 \cdot x$.

Term	Numerical Coefficient
$3x$	3
$\dfrac{y^3}{5}$	$\dfrac{1}{5}$ since $\dfrac{y^3}{5}$ means $\dfrac{1}{5} \cdot y^3$
$0.7ab^3c^5$	0.7
z	1
$-y$	-1
-5	-5

▶ **Helpful Hint**

The term $-y$ means $-1y$ and thus has a numerical coefficient of -1. The term z means $1z$ and thus has a numerical coefficient of 1.

EXAMPLE 1 Identify the numerical coefficient in each term.

a. $-3y$ **b.** $22z^4$ **c.** y **d.** $-x$ **e.** $\dfrac{x}{7}$

Solution

a. The numerical coefficient of $-3y$ is -3.

b. The numerical coefficient of $22z^4$ is 22.

c. The numerical coefficient of y is 1, since y is $1y$.

d. The numerical coefficient of $-x$ is -1, since $-x$ is $-1x$.

e. The numerical coefficient of $\dfrac{x}{7}$ is $\dfrac{1}{7}$, since $\dfrac{x}{7}$ means $\dfrac{1}{7} \cdot x$.

PRACTICE

1 Identify the numerical coefficients in each term.

a. t **b.** $-7x$ **c.** $-\dfrac{w}{5}$ **d.** $43x^4$ **e.** $-b$

Terms with the same variables raised to exactly the same powers are called **like terms.** Terms that aren't like terms are called **unlike terms.**

Like Terms	*Unlike Terms*	
$3x, 2x$	$5x, 5x^2$	Why? Same variable x, but different powers x and x^2
$-6x^2y, 2x^2y, 4x^2y$	$7y, 3z, 8x^2$	Why? Different variables
$2ab^2c^3, ac^3b^2$	$6abc^3, 6ab^2$	Why? Different variables and different powers

▶ **Helpful Hint**

In like terms, each variable and its exponent must match exactly, but these factors don't need to be in the same order.

$$2x^2y \text{ and } 3yx^2 \text{ are like terms.}$$

EXAMPLE 2   Determine whether the terms are like or unlike.

a. $2x, 3x^2$ **b.** $4x^2y, x^2y, -2x^2y$ **c.** $-2yz, -3zy$ **d.** $-x^4, x^4$

Solution

a. Unlike terms, since the exponents on x are not the same.

b. Like terms, since each variable and its exponent match.

c. Like terms, since $zy = yz$ by the commutative property.

d. Like terms.   □

PRACTICE
2   Determine whether the terms are like or unlike.

a. $-4xy, 5yx$ **b.** $5q, -3q^2$

c. $3ab^2, -2ab^2, 43ab^2$ **d.** $y^5, \dfrac{y^5}{2}$

OBJECTIVE 2 ▶ Combining like terms. An algebraic expression containing the sum or difference of like terms can be simplified by applying the distributive property. For example, by the distributive property, we rewrite the sum of the like terms $3x + 2x$ as

$$3x + 2x = (3 + 2)x = 5x$$

Also,

$$-y^2 + 5y^2 = (-1 + 5)y^2 = 4y^2$$

Simplifying the sum or difference of like terms is called **combining like terms.**

EXAMPLE 3   Simplify each expression by combining like terms.

a. $7x - 3x$ **b.** $10y^2 + y^2$ **c.** $8x^2 + 2x - 3x$

Solution

a. $7x - 3x = (7 - 3)x = 4x$

b. $10y^2 + y^2 = 10y^2 + 1y^2 = (10 + 1)y^2 = 11y^2$

c. $8x^2 + 2x - 3x = 8x^2 + (2 - 3)x = 8x^2 - x$ □

PRACTICE
3   Simplify each expression by combining like terms.

a. $4x^2 + 3x^2$ **b.** $-3y + y$ **c.** $5x - 3x^2 + 8x^2$

EXAMPLE 4 Simplify each expression by combining like terms.

a. $2x + 3x + 5 + 2$　　　　**b.** $-5a - 3 + a + 2$　　　　**c.** $4y - 3y^2$

d. $2.3x + 5x - 6$　　　　**e.** $-\dfrac{1}{2}b + b$

Solution　Use the distributive property to combine like terms.

a. $2x + 3x + 5 + 2 = (2 + 3)x + (5 + 2)$
$$= 5x + 7$$

b. $-5a - 3 + a + 2 = -5a + 1a + (-3 + 2)$
$$= (-5 + 1)a + (-3 + 2)$$
$$= -4a - 1$$

c. $4y - 3y^2$　These two terms cannot be combined because they are unlike terms.

d. $2.3x + 5x - 6 = (2.3 + 5)x - 6$
$$= 7.3x - 6$$

e. $-\dfrac{1}{2}b + b = -\dfrac{1}{2}b + 1b = \left(-\dfrac{1}{2} + 1\right)b = \dfrac{1}{2}b$　　　　□

PRACTICE
4　Use the distributive property to combine like terms.

a. $3y + 8y - 7 + 2$　　　　**b.** $6x - 3 - x - 3$　　　　**c.** $\dfrac{3}{4}t - t$

d. $9y + 3.2y + 10 + 3$　　　　**e.** $5z - 3z^4$

The examples above suggest the following:

> **Combining Like Terms**
>
> To **combine like terms,** add the numerical coefficients and multiply the result by the common variable factors.

OBJECTIVE 3 ▶ Using the distributive property. Simplifying expressions makes frequent use of the distributive property to also remove parentheses.

EXAMPLE 5　Find each product by using the distributive property to remove parentheses.

a. $5(x + 2)$　　　　**b.** $-2(y + 0.3z - 1)$　　　　**c.** $-(x + y - 2z + 6)$

Solution

a. $5(x + 2) = 5 \cdot x + 5 \cdot 2$　　　　Apply the distributive property.
$$= 5x + 10$$　　　　Multiply.

b. $-2(y + 0.3z - 1) = -2(y) + (-2)(0.3z) + (-2)(-1)$　　Apply the distributive property.
$$= -2y - 0.6z + 2$$　　　　Multiply.

c. $-(x + y - 2z + 6) = -1(x + y - 2z + 6)$　　　Distribute -1 over each term.
$$= -1(x) - 1(y) - 1(-2z) - 1(6)$$
$$= -x - y + 2z - 6$$　　　　□

PRACTICE
5　Find each product by using the distributive property to remove parentheses.

a. $3(2x - 7)$　　　　**b.** $-5(3x - 4z - 5)$　　　　**c.** $-(2x - y + z - 2)$

> ▶ **Helpful Hint**
>
> If a "−" sign precedes parentheses, the sign of each term inside the parentheses is changed when the distributive property is applied to remove parentheses.
>
> **Examples:**
>
> $$-(2x + 1) = -2x - 1 \qquad -(-5x + y - z) = 5x - y + z$$
> $$-(x - 2y) = -x + 2y \qquad -(-3x - 4y - 1) = 3x + 4y + 1$$

When simplifying an expression containing parentheses, we often use the distributive property in both directions—first to remove parentheses and then again to combine any like terms.

EXAMPLE 6   Simplify the following expressions.

a. $3(2x - 5) + 1$ **b.** $-2(4x + 7) - (3x - 1)$ **c.** $9 - 3(4x + 10)$

Solution

> ▶ **Helpful Hint**
>
> Don't forget to use the distributive property to multiply before adding or subtracting like terms.

a. $3(2x - 5) + 1 = 6x - 15 + 1$ Apply the distributive property.
$$= 6x - 14 \qquad\qquad\quad \text{Combine like terms.}$$

b. $-2(4x + 7) - (3x - 1) = -8x - 14 - 3x + 1$ Apply the distributive property.
$$= -11x - 13 \qquad\qquad \text{Combine like terms.}$$

c. $9 - 3(4x + 10) = 9 - 12x - 30$ Apply the distributive property.
$$= -21 - 12x \qquad\qquad \text{Combine like terms.} \qquad \square$$

PRACTICE
6   Simplify the following expressions.

a. $4(9x + 1) + 6$ **b.** $-7(2x - 1) - (6 - 3x)$ **c.** $8 - 5(6x + 5)$

EXAMPLE 7   Write the phrase below as an algebraic expression. Then simplify if possible.

"Subtract $4x - 2$ from $2x - 3$."

Solution   "Subtract $4x - 2$ **from** $2x - 3$" translates to $(2x - 3) - (4x - 2)$. Next, simplify the algebraic expression.

$$(2x - 3) - (4x - 2) = 2x - 3 - 4x + 2 \quad \text{Apply the distributive property.}$$
$$= -2x - 1 \qquad\qquad \text{Combine like terms.} \qquad \square$$

PRACTICE
7   Write the phrase below as an algebraic expression. Then simplify if possible.

"Subtract $7x - 1$ from $2x + 3$."

OBJECTIVE 4 ▶ **Writing word phrases as algebraic expressions.** Next, we practice writing word phrases as algebraic expressions.

EXAMPLE 8   Write the following phrases as algebraic expressions and simplify if possible. Let x represent the unknown number.

a. Twice a number, added to 6

b. The difference of a number and 4, divided by 7

c. Five added to 3 times the sum of a number and 1

d. The sum of twice a number, 3 times the number, and 5 times the number

Solution

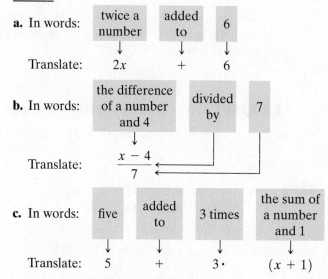

a. In words:

twice a number	added to	6
↓	↓	↓

Translate: $2x$ $+$ 6

b. In words:

| the difference of a number and 4 | divided by | 7 |

↓

Translate: $\dfrac{x - 4}{7}$

c. In words:

| five | added to | 3 times | the sum of a number and 1 |
| ↓ | ↓ | ↓ | ↓ |

Translate: 5 $+$ $3 \cdot$ $(x + 1)$

Next, we simplify this expression.

$$5 + 3(x + 1) = 5 + 3x + 3 \quad \text{Use the distributive property.}$$
$$= 8 + 3x \quad \text{Combine like terms.}$$

d. The phrase "the sum of" means that we add.

In words:

| twice a number | added to | 3 times the number | added to | 5 times the number |
| ↓ | ↓ | ↓ | ↓ | ↓ |

Translate: $2x$ $+$ $3x$ $+$ $5x$

Now let's simplify.

$$2x + 3x + 5x = 10x \quad \text{Combine like terms.}$$ □

PRACTICE
8   Write the following phrases as algebraic expressions and simplify if possible. Let x represent the unknown number.

a. Three added to double a number

b. Six subtracted from the sum of 5 and a number

c. Two times the sum of 3 and a number, increased by 4

d. The sum of a number, half the number, and 5 times the number

VOCABULARY & READINESS CHECK

Word Bank. *Use the choices below to fill in each blank. Some choices may be used more than once.*

like	numerical coefficient	term	distributive
unlike	combine like terms	expression	

1. $23y^2 + 10y - 6$ is called a(n) _____ while $23y^2$, $10y$, and -6 are each called a(n) _____.

2. To simplify $x + 4x$, we _____.

3. The term y has an understood _____ of 1.

4. The terms $7z$ and $7y$ are _____ terms and the terms $7z$ and $-z$ are _____ terms.

5. For the term $-\dfrac{1}{2}xy^2$, the number $-\dfrac{1}{2}$ is the _____.

6. $5(3x - y)$ equals $15x - 5y$ by the _____ property.

Fill in the Blank. *Fill in the blank with the numerical coefficient of each term. See Example 1.*

7. $-7y$ _____   8. $3x$ _____   9. x _____   10. $-y$ _____   11. $-\dfrac{5y}{3}$ _____   12. $-\dfrac{2}{3}z$ _____

Decision Making. *Indicate whether the following lists of terms are like or unlike. See Example 2.*

13. $5y, -y$ _____   14. $-2x^2y, 6xy$ _____   15. $2z, 3z^2$ _____   16. $b^2a, -\dfrac{7}{8}ab^2$ _____

2.1 EXERCISE SET

MyMathLab *Powered by CourseCompass™ and MathXL®*

PRACTICE   WATCH   DOWNLOAD   READ   REVIEW

Simplify each expression by combining any like terms. See Examples 3 and 4.

1. $7y + 8y$
2. $3x + 2x$
3. $8w - w + 6w$
4. $c - 7c + 2c$
5. $3b - 5 - 10b - 4$
6. $6g + 5 - 3g - 7$
7. $m - 4m + 2m - 6$
8. $a + 3a - 2 - 7a$
9. $5g - 3 - 5 - 5g$
10. $8p + 4 - 8p - 15$
11. $6.2x - 4 + x - 1.2$
12. $7.9y - 0.7 - y + 0.2$
13. $6x - 5x + x - 3 + 2x$
14. $8h + 13h - 6 + 7h - h$
15. $7x^2 + 8x^2 - 10x^2$
16. $8x^3 + x^3 - 11x^3$
17. $6x + 0.5 - 4.3x - 0.4x + 3$
18. $0.4y - 6.7 + y - 0.3 - 2.6y$
19. In your own words, explain how to combine like terms.
20. Do like terms contain the same numerical coefficients? Explain your answer.

Simplify each expression. First use the distributive property to remove any parentheses. See Examples 5 and 6.

21. $5(y - 4)$
22. $7(r - 3)$
23. $-2(x + 2)$
24. $-4(y + 6)$
25. $7(d - 3) + 10$
26. $9(z + 7) - 15$
27. $-5(2x - 3y + 6)$
28. $-2(4x - 3z - 1)$
29. $-(3x - 2y + 1)$
30. $-(y + 5z - 7)$
31. $5(x + 2) - (3x - 4)$
32. $4(2x - 3) - 2(x + 1)$

Write each of the following as an algebraic expression. Simplify if possible. See Example 7.

33. Add $6x + 7$ to $4x - 10$.
34. Add $3y - 5$ to $y + 16$.
35. Subtract $7x + 1$ from $3x - 8$.
36. Subtract $4x - 7$ from $12 + x$.
37. Subtract $5m - 6$ from $m - 9$.
38. Subtract $m - 3$ from $2m - 6$.

MIXED PRACTICE

Simplify each expression. See Examples 3 through 7.

39. $2k - k - 6$

40. $7c - 8 - c$

41. $-9x + 4x + 18 - 10x$

42. $5y - 14 + 7y - 20y$

43. $-4(3y - 4) + 12y$

44. $-3(2x + 5) - 6x$

45. $3(2x - 5) - 5(x - 4)$

46. $2(6x - 1) - (x - 7)$

47. $-2(3x - 4) + 7x - 6$

48. $8y - 2 - 3(y + 4)$

49. $5k - (3k - 10)$

50. $-11c - (4 - 2c)$

51. Subtract $6x - 1$ from $3x + 4$

52. Subtract $4 + 3y$ from $8 - 5y$

53. $3.4m - 4 - 3.4m - 7$

54. $2.8w - 0.9 - 0.5 - 2.8w$

55. $\frac{1}{3}(7y - 1) + \frac{1}{6}(4y + 7)$

56. $\frac{1}{5}(9y + 2) + \frac{1}{10}(2y - 1)$

57. $2 + 4(6x - 6)$

58. $8 + 4(3x - 4)$

59. $0.5(m + 2) + 0.4m$

60. $0.2(k + 8) - 0.1k$

61. $10 - 3(2x + 3y)$

62. $14 - 11(5m + 3n)$

63. $6(3x - 6) - 2(x + 1) - 17x$

64. $7(2x + 5) - 4(x + 2) - 20x$

65. $\frac{1}{2}(12x - 4) - (x + 5)$

66. $\frac{1}{3}(9x - 6) - (x - 2)$

Write each phrase as an algebraic expression and simplify if possible. Let x represent the unknown number. See Examples 7 and 8.

67. Twice a number, decreased by four

68. The difference of a number and two, divided by five

69. Seven added to double a number

70. Eight more than triple a number

71. Three-fourths of a number, increased by twelve

72. Eleven, increased by two-thirds of a number

73. The sum of 5 times a number and -2, added to 7 times a number

74. The sum of 3 times a number and 10, **subtracted from** 9 times a number

75. Eight times the sum of a number and six

76. Six times the difference of a number and five

77. Double a number, minus the sum of the number and ten

78. Half a number, minus the product of the number and eight

79. Seven, multiplied by the quotient of a number and six

80. The product of a number and ten, less twenty

81. The sum of 2, three times a number, -9, and four times a number

82. The sum of twice a number, -1, five times a number, and -12

83. Step Justification. The **expression** $\frac{1}{3}(6x + 9) + 2(5x)$ is correctly **simplified** below. Use the given list to justify how each expression is equivalent to the one above it. Some steps are filled in for you.

A. Distributive Property $[a(b + c) = ab + ac]$

B. Commutative Property of Addition [ordering of addition of terms]

C. Associative Property of Addition [grouping of addition of terms]

D. Commutative Property of Multiplication [ordering of multiplication of terms]

E. Associative Property of Multiplication [grouping of multiplication of terms]

F. 0 is the identity element for addition $[0 + a = a]$

G. 1 is the identity element for multiplication $[1 \cdot a = a]$

Step	Justification
$\frac{1}{3}(6x + 9) + 2(5x)$	Given expression
$= \left(\frac{1}{3} \cdot 6x + \frac{1}{3} \cdot 9\right) + (2 \cdot 5x)$	A
$= (2x + 3) + 10x$	Simplify each term.
$= (3 + 2x) + 10x$	_____
$= 3 + (2x + 10x)$	_____
$= 3 + (2 + 10)x$	_____
$= 3 + 12x$	$2 + 10 = 12$
or $12x + 3$	_____

84. Step Justification. The **expression** $\frac{2}{5}(15x) + 4(9 + x)$ is correctly simplified. Follow the same directions as for Exercise 83.

Step	Justification
$\frac{2}{5}(15x) + 4(9 + x)$	Given expression
$= \left(\frac{2}{5} \cdot 15x\right) + (4 \cdot 9 + 4 \cdot x)$	A
$= 6x + (36 + 4x)$	Simplify each term.
$= 6x + (4x + 36)$	_____
$= (6x + 4x) + 36$	_____
$= (6 + 4)x + 36$	_____
$= 10x + 36$	$6 + 4 = 10$
or $36 + 10x$	_____

REVIEW AND PREVIEW

Evaluate the following expressions for the given values. See Section 1.8.

85. If $a = 2$ and $b = -5$, find $a - b^2$.

86. If $x = -3$, find $x^3 - x^2 + 4$.

87. If $y = -5$ and $z = 0$, find $yz - y^2$.

88. If $x = -2$, find $x^3 - x^2 - x$.

CONCEPT EXTENSIONS

△ **89.** Recall that the perimeter of a figure is the total distance around the figure. Given the following rectangle, express the perimeter as an algebraic expression containing the variable x.

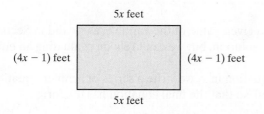

5x feet

(4x − 1) feet   (4x − 1) feet

5x feet

△ **90.** Given the following triangle, express its perimeter as an algebraic expression containing the variable x.

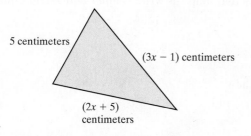

5 centimeters

(3x − 1) centimeters

(2x + 5) centimeters

Given the following two rules, determine whether each scale in Exercises 91 through 94 is balanced or not.

1 cone balances 1 cube

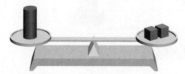

1 cylinder balances 2 cubes

91.

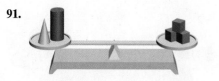

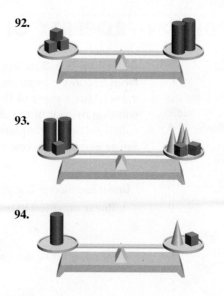

92.

93.

94.

Write each algebraic expression described.

95. Write an expression with 4 terms that simplifies to $3x - 4$.

96. Fill in the Blank. Write an expression of the form _____ (_____ + _____) whose product is $6x + 24$.

97. To convert from feet to inches, we multiply by 12. For example, the number of inches in 2 feet is $12 \cdot 2$ inches. If one board has a length of $(x + 2)$ *feet* and a second board has a length of $(3x - 1)$ *inches,* express their total length in inches as an algebraic expression.

98. The value of 7 nickels is $5 \cdot 7$ cents. Likewise, the value of x nickels is $5x$ cents. If the money box in a drink machine contains x *nickels,* $3x$ *dimes,* and $(30x - 1)$ *quarters,* express their total value in cents as an algebraic expression.

For Exercises 99 through 104, see the example below.

Example

Simplify $-3xy + 2x^2y - (2xy - 1)$.

Solution

$$-3xy + 2x^2y - (2xy - 1)$$
$$= -3xy + 2x^2y - 2xy + 1 = -5xy + 2x^2y + 1$$

Simplify each expression.

99. $5b^2c^3 + 8b^3c^2 - 7b^3c^2$

100. $4m^4p^2 + m^4p^2 - 5m^2p^4$

101. $3x - (2x^2 - 6x) + 7x^2$

102. $9y^2 - (6xy^2 - 5y^2) - 8xy^2$

103. $-(2x^2y + 3z) + 3z - 5x^2y$

104. $-(7c^3d - 8c) - 5c - 4c^3d$

2.2 THE ADDITION PROPERTY OF EQUALITY

OBJECTIVES

1 Define linear equations and use the addition property of equality to solve linear equations.

2 Write word phrases as algebraic expressions.

OBJECTIVE 1 ▶ Defining linear equations and using the addition property. Recall from Section 1.4 that an equation is a statement that two expressions have the same value. Also, a value of the variable that makes an equation a true statement is called a solution or root of the equation. The process of finding the solution of an equation is called **solving** the equation for the variable. In this section we concentrate on solving **linear equations** in one variable.

> **Linear Equation in One Variable**
>
> **A linear equation in one variable** can be written in the form
>
> $$ax + b = c$$
>
> where a, b, and c are real numbers and $a \neq 0$.

Evaluating a linear equation for a given value of the variable, as we did in Section 1.4, can tell us whether that value is a solution, but we can't rely on evaluating an equation as our method of solving it.

Instead, to solve a linear equation in x, we write a series of simpler equations, all *equivalent* to the original equation, so that the final equation has the form

$$x = \text{number} \qquad \text{or} \qquad \text{number} = x$$

Equivalent equations are equations that have the same solution. This means that the "number" above is the solution to the original equation.

The first property of equality that helps us write simpler equivalent equations is the **addition property of equality.**

> **Addition Property of Equality**
>
> If a, b, and c are real numbers, then
>
> $$a = b \qquad \text{and} \qquad a + c = b + c$$
>
> are equivalent equations.

This property guarantees that adding the same number to both sides of an equation does not change the solution of the equation. Since subtraction is defined in terms of addition, we may also **subtract the same number from both sides** without changing the solution.

A good way to picture a true equation is as a balanced scale. Since it is balanced, each side of the scale weighs the same amount.

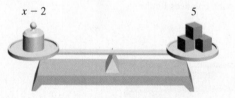

If the same weight is added to or subtracted from each side, the scale remains balanced.

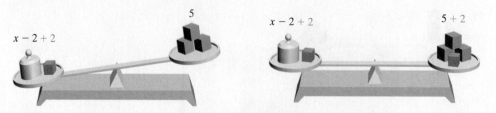

We use the addition property of equality to write equivalent equations until the variable is by itself on one side of the equation, and the equation looks like "x = number" or "number = x."

EXAMPLE 1   Solve $x - 7 = 10$ for x.

Solution   To solve for x, we want x alone on one side of the equation. To do this, we add 7 to both sides of the equation.

$$x - 7 = 10$$
$$x - 7 + 7 = 10 + 7 \quad \text{Add 7 to both sides.}$$
$$x = 17 \quad \text{Simplify.}$$

The solution of the equation $x = 17$ is obviously 17. Since we are writing equivalent equations, the solution of the equation $x - 7 = 10$ is also 17.

Check: To check, replace x with 17 in the original equation.

$$x - 7 = 10$$
$$17 - 7 \stackrel{?}{=} 10 \quad \text{Replace } x \text{ with 17 in the original equation.}$$
$$10 = 10 \quad \text{True}$$

Since the statement is true, 17 is the solution or we can say that the solution set is $\{17\}$.

□

PRACTICE
1   Solve: $x + 3 = -5$ for x.

Concept Check ☑
Use the addition property to fill in the blank so that the middle equation simplifies to the last equation.

$$x - 5 = 3$$
$$x - 5 + \underline{\quad} = 3 + \underline{\quad}$$
$$x = 8$$

EXAMPLE 2   Solve $y + 0.6 = -1.0$ for y.

Solution   To get y alone on one side of the equation, subtract 0.6 from both sides of the equation.

$$y + 0.6 = -1.0$$
$$y + 0.6 - 0.6 = -1.0 - 0.6 \quad \text{Subtract 0.6 from both sides.}$$
$$y = -1.6 \quad \text{Combine like terms.}$$

Check: To check the proposed solution, -1.6, replace y with -1.6 in the original equation.

$$y + 0.6 = -1.0$$
$$-1.6 + 0.6 \stackrel{?}{=} -1.0 \quad \text{Replace } y \text{ with } -1.6 \text{ in the original equation.}$$
$$-1.0 = -1.0 \quad \text{True}$$

The solution is -1.6 or we can say that the solution set is $\{-1.6\}$.

□

PRACTICE
2   Solve: $y - 0.3 = -2.1$ for y.

Answer to Concept Check: 5

EXAMPLE 3 Solve: $\dfrac{1}{2} = x - \dfrac{3}{4}$

Solution To get x alone, we add $\dfrac{3}{4}$ to both sides.

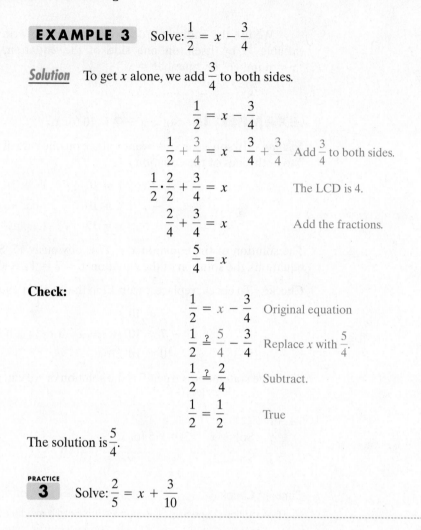

$$\dfrac{1}{2} = x - \dfrac{3}{4}$$

$$\dfrac{1}{2} + \dfrac{3}{4} = x - \dfrac{3}{4} + \dfrac{3}{4} \qquad \text{Add } \dfrac{3}{4} \text{ to both sides.}$$

$$\dfrac{1}{2} \cdot \dfrac{2}{2} + \dfrac{3}{4} = x \qquad \text{The LCD is 4.}$$

$$\dfrac{2}{4} + \dfrac{3}{4} = x \qquad \text{Add the fractions.}$$

$$\dfrac{5}{4} = x$$

Check:

$$\dfrac{1}{2} = x - \dfrac{3}{4} \qquad \text{Original equation}$$

$$\dfrac{1}{2} \overset{?}{=} \dfrac{5}{4} - \dfrac{3}{4} \qquad \text{Replace } x \text{ with } \dfrac{5}{4}.$$

$$\dfrac{1}{2} \overset{?}{=} \dfrac{2}{4} \qquad \text{Subtract.}$$

$$\dfrac{1}{2} = \dfrac{1}{2} \qquad \text{True}$$

The solution is $\dfrac{5}{4}$.

PRACTICE
3 Solve: $\dfrac{2}{5} = x + \dfrac{3}{10}$

> ▶ **Helpful Hint**
>
> We may solve an equation so that the variable is alone on *either* side of the equation. For example, $\dfrac{5}{4} = x$ is equivalent to $x = \dfrac{5}{4}$.

EXAMPLE 4 Solve $5t - 5 = 6t + 2$ for t.

Solution To solve for t, we first want all terms containing t on one side of the equation and all other terms on the other side of the equation. To do this, first subtract $5t$ from both sides of the equation.

$$5t - 5 = 6t + 2$$

$$5t - 5 - 5t = 6t + 2 - 5t \quad \text{Subtract } 5t \text{ from both sides.}$$

$$-5 = t + 2 \qquad \text{Combine like terms.}$$

Next, subtract 2 from both sides and the variable t will be isolated.

$$-5 = t + 2$$

$$-5 - 2 = t + 2 - 2 \quad \text{Subtract 2 from both sides.}$$

$$-7 = t$$

Check: Check the solution, -7, in the original equation. The solution is -7.

PRACTICE
4 Solve: $4t + 7 = 5t - 3$

Many times, it is best to simplify one or both sides of an equation before applying the addition property of equality.

EXAMPLE 5   Solve: $2x + 3x - 5 + 7 = 10x + 3 - 6x - 4$

Solution   First we simplify both sides of the equation.

$$2x + 3x - 5 + 7 = 10x + 3 - 6x - 4$$
$$5x + 2 = 4x - 1 \qquad \text{Combine like terms on each side of the equation.}$$

Next, we want all terms with a variable on one side of the equation and all numbers on the other side.

$$5x + 2 - 4x = 4x - 1 - 4x \qquad \text{Subtract } 4x \text{ from both sides.}$$
$$x + 2 = -1 \qquad \text{Combine like terms.}$$
$$x + 2 - 2 = -1 - 2 \qquad \text{Subtract 2 from both sides to get } x \text{ alone.}$$
$$x = -3 \qquad \text{Combine like terms.}$$

Check:

$$2x + 3x - 5 + 7 = 10x + 3 - 6x - 4 \qquad \text{Original equation}$$
$$2(-3) + 3(-3) - 5 + 7 \stackrel{?}{=} 10(-3) + 3 - 6(-3) - 4 \qquad \text{Replace } x \text{ with } -3.$$
$$-6 - 9 - 5 + 7 \stackrel{?}{=} -30 + 3 + 18 - 4 \qquad \text{Multiply.}$$
$$-13 = -13 \qquad \text{True}$$

The solution is -3.   □

PRACTICE
5   Solve: $8x - 5x - 3 + 9 = x + x + 3 - 7$

If an equation contains parentheses, we use the distributive property to remove them, as before. Then we combine any like terms.

EXAMPLE 6   Solve: $6(2a - 1) - (11a + 6) = 7$

Solution
$$6(2a - 1) - 1(11a + 6) = 7$$
$$6(2a) + 6(-1) - 1(11a) - 1(6) = 7 \qquad \text{Apply the distributive property.}$$
$$12a - 6 - 11a - 6 = 7 \qquad \text{Multiply.}$$
$$a - 12 = 7 \qquad \text{Combine like terms.}$$
$$a - 12 + 12 = 7 + 12 \qquad \text{Add 12 to both sides.}$$
$$a = 19 \qquad \text{Simplify.}$$

Check: Check by replacing a with 19 in the original equation.   □

PRACTICE
6   Solve: $4(2a - 3) - (7a + 4) = 2$

EXAMPLE 7   Solve: $3 - x = 7$

Solution   First we subtract 3 from both sides.

$$3 - x = 7$$
$$3 - x - 3 = 7 - 3 \qquad \text{Subtract 3 from both sides.}$$
$$-x = 4 \qquad \text{Simplify.}$$

We have not yet solved for x since x is not alone. However, this equation does say that the opposite of x is 4. If the opposite of x is 4, then x is the opposite of 4, or $x = -4$. If $-x = 4$, then $x = -4$.

Check:

$$3 - x = 7 \quad \text{Original equation}$$
$$3 - (-4) \stackrel{?}{=} 7 \quad \text{Replace } x \text{ with } -4.$$
$$3 + 4 \stackrel{?}{=} 7 \quad \text{Add.}$$
$$7 = 7 \quad \text{True}$$

The solution is -4.   □

PRACTICE
7   Solve: $12 - x = 20$

OBJECTIVE 2 ▶ Writing word phrases as algebraic expressions. Next, we practice writing word phrases as algebraic expressions.

EXAMPLE 8

a. The sum of two numbers is 8. If one number is 3, find the other number.

b. The sum of two numbers is 8. If one number is x, write an expression representing the other number.

c. An 8-foot board is cut into two pieces. If one piece is x feet, express the length of the other piece in terms of x.

Solution

a. If the sum of two numbers is 8 and one number is 3, we find the other number by subtracting 3 from 8. The other number is $8 - 3$ or 5.

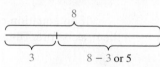

b. If the sum of two numbers is 8 and one number is x, we find the other number by subtracting x from 8. The other number is represented by $8 - x$.

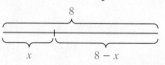

c. If an 8-foot board is cut into two pieces and one piece is x feet, we find the other length by subtracting x from 8. The other piece is $(8 - x)$ feet.

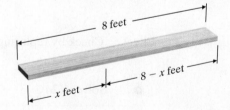

□

PRACTICE
8

a. The sum of two numbers is 9. If one number is 2, find the other number.

b. The sum of two numbers is 9. If one number is x, write an expression representing the other number.

c. A 9-foot rope is cut into two pieces. If one piece is x feet, express the length of the other piece in terms of x.

EXAMPLE 9

The Verrazano-Narrows Bridge in New York City is the longest suspension bridge in North America. The Golden Gate Bridge in San Francisco is 60 feet shorter than the Verrazano-Narrows Bridge. If the length of the Verrazano-Narrows Bridge is m feet, express the length of the Golden Gate Bridge as an algebraic expression in m. (*Source:* Survey of State Highway Engineers)

Solution   Since the Golden Gate is 60 feet shorter than the Verrazano-Narrows Bridge, we have that its length is

In words:	length of Verrazano-Narrows Bridge	minus	60
Translate:	m	$-$	60

The Golden Gate Bridge is $(m - 60)$ feet long.

PRACTICE

9   Currently, the fastest train is the Japanese Maglev. The French TGV is 3.8 mph slower than the Maglev (see the Chapter 2 opener). If the speed of the Maglev is s miles per hour, express the speed of the French TGV as an algebraic expression in s.

VOCABULARY & READINESS CHECK

Word Bank. *Use the choices below to fill in each blank. Not all choices will be used.*

addition	solving	expression	true
equivalent	equation	solution	false

1. The difference between an equation and an expression is that a(n) _____ contains an equal sign, whereas an _____ does not.

2. _____ equations are equations that have the same solution.

3. A value of the variable that makes the equation a true statement is called a(n) _____ of the equation.

4. The process of finding the solution of an equation is called _____ the equation for the variable.

5. By the _____ property of equality, $x = -2$ and $x + 10 = -2 + 10$ are equivalent equations.

6. **True or False.** The equations $x = \dfrac{1}{2}$ and $\dfrac{1}{2} = x$ are equivalent equations. _____

2.2 | EXERCISE SET

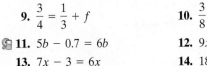

Solve each equation. Check each solution. See Examples 1 through 3.

1. $x + 7 = 10$

2. $x + 14 = 25$

3. $x - 2 = -4$

4. $y - 9 = 1$

5. $-2 = t - 5$

6. $-17 = x + 3$

7. $r - 8.6 = -8.1$

8. $t - 9.2 = -6.8$

9. $\dfrac{3}{4} = \dfrac{1}{3} + f$

10. $\dfrac{3}{8} = c + \dfrac{1}{6}$

11. $5b - 0.7 = 6b$

12. $9x + 5.5 = 10x$

13. $7x - 3 = 6x$

14. $18x - 9 = 19x$

15. In your own words, explain what is meant by the solution of an equation.

16. In your own words, explain how to check a solution of an equation.

Solve each equation. Don't forget to first simplify each side of the equation, if possible. Check each solution. See Examples 4 through 7.

17. $7x + 2x = 8x - 3$

18. $3n + 2n = 7 + 4n$

19. $\frac{5}{6}x + \frac{1}{6}x = -9$

20. $\frac{13}{11}y - \frac{2}{11}y = -3$

21. $2y + 10 = 5y - 4y$

22. $4x - 4 = 10x - 7x$

23. $-5(n - 2) = 8 - 4n$

24. $-4(z - 3) = 2 - 3z$

25. $\frac{3}{7}x + 2 = -\frac{4}{7}x - 5$

26. $\frac{1}{5}x - 1 = -\frac{4}{5}x - 13$

27. $5x - 6 = 6x - 5$

28. $2x + 7 = x - 10$

29. $8y + 2 - 6y = 3 + y - 10$

30. $4p - 11 - p = 2 + 2p - 20$

31. $-3(x - 4) = -4x$

32. $-2(x - 1) = -3x$

33. $\frac{3}{8}x - \frac{1}{6} = -\frac{5}{8}x - \frac{2}{3}$

34. $\frac{2}{5}x - \frac{1}{12} = -\frac{3}{5}x - \frac{3}{4}$

35. $2(x - 4) = x + 3$

36. $3(y + 7) = 2y - 5$

37. $3(n - 5) - (6 - 2n) = 4n$

38. $5(3 + z) - (8z + 9) = -4z$

39. $-2(x + 6) + 3(2x - 5) = 3(x - 4) + 10$

40. $-5(x + 1) + 4(2x - 3) = 2(x + 2) - 8$

MIXED PRACTICE

Solve. See Examples 1 through 7.

41. $-11 = 3 + x$

42. $-8 = 8 + z$

43. $x - \frac{2}{5} = -\frac{3}{20}$

44. $y - \frac{4}{7} = -\frac{3}{14}$

45. $3x - 6 = 2x + 5$

46. $7y + 2 = 6y + 2$

47. $13x - 9 + 2x - 5 = 12x - 1 + 2x$

48. $15x + 20 - 10x - 9 = 25x + 8 - 21x - 7$

49. $7(6 + w) = 6(2 + w)$

50. $6(5 + c) = 5(c - 4)$

51. $n + 4 = 3.6$

52. $m + 2 = 7.1$

53. $10 - (2x - 4) = 7 - 3x$

54. $15 - (6 - 7k) = 2 + 6k$

55. $\frac{1}{3} = x + \frac{2}{3}$

56. $\frac{1}{11} = y + \frac{10}{11}$

57. $-6.5 - 4x - 1.6 - 3x = -6x + 9.8$

58. $-1.4 - 7x - 3.6 - 2x = -8x + 4.4$

59. $-3\left(x - \frac{1}{4}\right) = -4x$

60. $-2\left(x - \frac{1}{7}\right) = -3x$

61. $7(m - 2) - 6(m + 1) = -20$

62. $-4(x - 1) - 5(2 - x) = -6$

63. $0.8t + 0.2(t - 0.4) = 1.75$

64. $0.6v + 0.4(0.3 + v) = 2.34$

See Examples 8 and 9.

65. Two numbers have a sum of 20. If one number is p, express the other number in terms of p.

66. Two numbers have a sum of 13. If one number is y, express the other number in terms of y.

67. A 10-foot board is cut into two pieces. If one piece is x feet long, express the other length in terms of x.

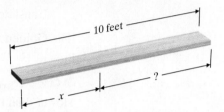

68. A 5-foot piece of string is cut into two pieces. If one piece is x feet long, express the other length in terms of x.

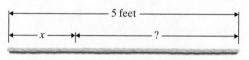

69. Two angles are *supplementary* if their sum is 180°. If one angle measures $x°$, express the measure of its supplement in terms of x.

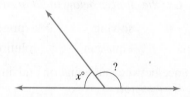

70. Two angles are *complementary* if their sum is 90°. If one angle measures $x°$, express the measure of its complement in terms of x.

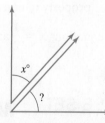

71. The length of the top of a computer desk is $1\frac{1}{2}$ feet longer than its width. If its width measures m feet, express its length as an algebraic expression in m.

72. In a mayoral election, April Catarella received 284 more votes than Charles Pecot. If Charles received n votes, how many votes did April receive?

73. The area of the Sahara Desert in Africa is 7 times the area of the Gobi Desert in Asia. If the area of the Gobi Desert is x square miles, express the area of the Sahara Desert as an algebraic expression in x.

74. The largest meteorite in the world is the Hoba West located in Namibia. Its weight is 3 times the weight of the Armanty meteorite located in Outer Mongolia. If the weight of the Armanty meteorite is y kilograms, express the weight of the Hoba West meteorite as an algebraic expression in y.

Step Justification. *The equation* $3(7x + 2) - 5(4x - 3) = 7$ *is solved correctly below. Use the given list to justify how each equation is equivalent to the one above it. Some steps are filled in for you.*

A. Distributive Property $[a(b + c) = ab + ac]$

B. Commutative Property of Addition [ordering of addition of terms]

C. Associative Property of Addition [grouping of addition of terms]

D. Commutative Property of Multiplication [ordering of multiplication of terms]

E. Associative Property of Multiplication [grouping of multiplication of terms]

F. 0 is the identity element for addition $[0 + a = a]$

G. 1 is the identity element for Multiplication $[1 \cdot a = a]$

H. Adding or subtracting the same number to/from both sides of an equation does not change its solution.

Exercise Number	Step	Justification
	$3(7x + 2) - 5(4x - 3) = 7$	Given equation.
75.	$(21x + 6) + (-20x + 15) = 7$	_____
	$[(21x + 6) + (-20x)] + 15 = 7$	C
76.	$[21x + (6 + (-20x))] + 15 = 7$	_____
77.	$[21x + ((-20x) + 6)] + 15 = 7$	_____
78.	$[(21x + (-20x)) + 6] + 15 = 7$	_____
	$[(21 + (-20))x + 6] + 15 = 7$	D
	$(1x + 6) + 15 = 7$	$21 + (-20) = 1$, and $1x$ is x.
79.	$(x + 6) + 15 = 7$	_____
	$x + (6 + 15) = 7$	C
	$x + 23 = 7$	$6 + 15 = 23$
80.	$(x + 23) - 23 = 7 - 23$	_____
81.	$x + (23 - 23) = 7 - 23$	_____
	$x + 0 = -16$	$23 - 23 = 0$
82.	$x = -16$	_____

REVIEW AND PREVIEW

Find the reciprocal or multiplicative inverse of each. See Section 1.8.

83. $\dfrac{5}{8}$ **84.** $\dfrac{7}{6}$ **85.** 2

86. 5 **87.** $-\dfrac{1}{9}$ **88.** $-\dfrac{3}{5}$

Perform each indicated operation and simplify. See Section 1.8.

89. $\dfrac{3x}{3}$ **90.** $\dfrac{-2y}{-2}$ **91.** $-5\left(-\dfrac{1}{5}y\right)$

92. $7\left(\dfrac{1}{7}r\right)$ **93.** $\dfrac{3}{5}\left(\dfrac{5}{3}x\right)$ **94.** $\dfrac{9}{2}\left(\dfrac{2}{9}x\right)$

CONCEPT EXTENSIONS

△ **95.** The sum of the angles of a triangle is 180°. If one angle of a triangle measures $x°$ and a second angle measures $(2x + 7)°$, express the measure of the third angle in terms of x. Simplify the expression.

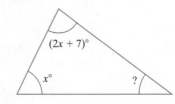

△ **96.** A quadrilateral is a four-sided figure like the one shown below whose angle sum is 360°. If one angle measures $x°$, a second angle measures $3x°$, and a third angle measures $5x°$, express the measure of the fourth angle in terms of x. Simplify the expression.

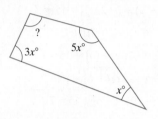

⟍ **97.** Write two terms whose sum is $-3x$.

⟍ **98.** Write four terms whose sum is $2y - 6$.

Fill in the Blank. *Use the addition property to fill in the blank so that the middle equation simplifies to the last equation. See the Concept Check in this section.*

99.
$$x - 4 = -9$$
$$x - 4 + (\ \ ) = -9 + (\ \ )$$
$$x = -5$$

100.
$$a + 9 = 15$$
$$a + 9 + (\ \ ) = 15 + (\ \ )$$
$$a = 6$$

Fill in the Blank. *Fill in the blanks with numbers of your choice so that each equation has the given solution. Note: Each blank may be replaced with a different number.*

101. ____ $+ x =$ ____ ; Solution: -3

102. $x -$ ____ $=$ ____ ; Solution: -10

103. A nurse's aide recorded the following fluid intakes for a patient on her night shift: 200 ml, 150 ml, 400 ml. If the patient's doctor requested that a total of 1000 ml of fluid be taken by the patient overnight, how much more fluid must the nurse give the patient? To solve this problem, solve the equation $200 + 150 + 400 + x = 1000$.

⟍ **104.** Let $x = 1$ and then $x = 2$ in the equation $x + 5 = x + 6$. Is either number a solution? How many solutions do you think this equation has? Explain your answer.

⟍ **105.** Let $x = 1$ and then $x = 2$ in the equation $x + 3 = x + 3$. Is either number a solution? How many solutions do you think this equation has? Explain your answer.

Use a calculator to determine whether the given value is a solution of the given equation.

▦ **106.** $1.23x - 0.06 = 2.6x - 0.1285$; $x = 0.05$

▦ **107.** $8.13 + 5.85y = 20.05y - 8.91$; $y = 1.2$

▦ **108.** $3(a + 4.6) = 5a + 2.5$; $a = 6.3$

▦ **109.** $7(z - 1.7) + 9.5 = 5(z + 3.2) - 9.2$; $z = 4.8$

2.3 THE MULTIPLICATION PROPERTY OF EQUALITY

OBJECTIVES

1. Use the multiplication property of equality to solve linear equations.

2. Use both the addition and multiplication properties of equality to solve linear equations.

3. Write word phrases as algebraic expressions.

OBJECTIVE 1 ▶ Using the multiplication property. As useful as the addition property of equality is, it cannot help us solve every type of linear equation in one variable. For example, adding or subtracting a value on both sides of the equation does not help solve

$$\frac{5}{2}x = 15.$$

Instead, we apply another important property of equality, the **multiplication property of equality.**

> **Multiplication Property of Equality**
>
> If a, b, and c are real numbers and $c \neq 0$, then
>
> $$a = b \qquad \text{and} \qquad ac = bc$$
>
> are equivalent equations.

This property guarantees that multiplying both sides of an equation by the same nonzero number does not change the solution of the equation. Since division is defined in terms of multiplication, we may also **divide both sides of the equation by the same nonzero number** without changing the solution.

EXAMPLE 1   Solve: $\frac{5}{2}x = 15$.

___Solution___   To get x alone, multiply both sides of the equation by the reciprocal of $\frac{5}{2}$, which is $\frac{2}{5}$.

$$\frac{5}{2}x = 15$$

$$\frac{2}{5} \cdot \frac{5}{2}x = \frac{2}{5} \cdot 15 \quad \text{Multiply both sides by } \frac{2}{5}.$$

$$\left(\frac{2}{5} \cdot \frac{5}{2}\right)x = \frac{2}{5} \cdot 15 \quad \text{Apply the associative property.}$$

$$1x = 6 \qquad \text{Simplify.}$$

or

$$x = 6$$

Check: Replace x with 6 in the original equation.

$$\frac{5}{2}x = 15 \quad \text{Original equation}$$

$$\frac{5}{2}(6) \stackrel{?}{=} 15 \quad \text{Replace } x \text{ with 6.}$$

$$15 = 15 \quad \text{True}$$

The solution is 6 or we say that the solution set is $\{6\}$.   □

PRACTICE
1   Solve: $\frac{4}{5}x = 16$

In the equation $\frac{5}{2}x = 15$, $\frac{5}{2}$ is the coefficient of x. When the coefficient of x is a _fraction,_ we will get x alone by multiplying by the reciprocal. When the coefficient of x is an integer or a decimal, it is usually more convenient to divide both sides by the coefficient. (Dividing by a number is, of course, the same as multiplying by the reciprocal of the number.)

EXAMPLE 2   Solve: $-3x = 33$

___Solution___   Recall that $-3x$ means $-3 \cdot x$. To get x alone, we divide both sides by the coefficient of x, that is, -3.

$$-3x = 33$$

$$\frac{-3x}{-3} = \frac{33}{-3} \quad \text{Divide both sides by } -3.$$

$$1x = -11 \quad \text{Simplify.}$$

$$x = -11$$

Check:
$$-3x = 33 \quad \text{Original equation}$$

$$-3(-11) \stackrel{?}{=} 33 \quad \text{Replace } x \text{ with } -11.$$

$$33 = 33 \quad \text{True}$$

The solution is -11, or the solution set is $\{-11\}$.   □

PRACTICE
2   Solve: $8x = -96$

EXAMPLE 3 Solve: $\dfrac{y}{7} = 20$

Solution Recall that $\dfrac{y}{7} = \dfrac{1}{7}y$. To get y alone, we multiply both sides of the equation by 7, the reciprocal of $\dfrac{1}{7}$.

$$\dfrac{y}{7} = 20$$

$$\dfrac{1}{7}y = 20$$

$$7 \cdot \dfrac{1}{7}y = 7 \cdot 20 \qquad \text{Multiply both sides by 7.}$$

$$1y = 140 \qquad \text{Simplify.}$$

$$y = 140$$

Check:
$$\dfrac{y}{7} = 20 \qquad \text{Original equation}$$

$$\dfrac{140}{7} \stackrel{?}{=} 20 \qquad \text{Replace } y \text{ with 140.}$$

$$20 = 20 \qquad \text{True}$$

The solution is 140. □

PRACTICE
3 Solve: $\dfrac{x}{5} = 13$

EXAMPLE 4 Solve: $3.1x = 4.96$

Solution
$$3.1x = 4.96$$

$$\dfrac{3.1x}{3.1} = \dfrac{4.96}{3.1} \qquad \text{Divide both sides by 3.1.}$$

$$1x = 1.6 \qquad \text{Simplify.}$$

$$x = 1.6$$

Check: Check by replacing x with 1.6 in the original equation. The solution is 1.6. □

PRACTICE
4 Solve: $2.7x = 4.05$

EXAMPLE 5 Solve: $-\dfrac{2}{3}x = -\dfrac{5}{2}$

Solution To get x alone, we multiply both sides of the equation by $-\dfrac{3}{2}$, the reciprocal of the coefficient of x.

$$-\dfrac{2}{3}x = -\dfrac{5}{2}$$

$$-\dfrac{3}{2} \cdot -\dfrac{2}{3}x = -\dfrac{3}{2} \cdot -\dfrac{5}{2} \qquad \text{Multiply both sides by } -\dfrac{3}{2}, \text{ the reciprocal of } -\dfrac{2}{3}.$$

$$x = \dfrac{15}{4} \qquad \text{Simplify.}$$

▶ **Helpful Hint**
Don't forget to multiply *both* sides by $-\dfrac{3}{2}$.

Check: Check by replacing x with $\dfrac{15}{4}$ in the original equation. The solution is $\dfrac{15}{4}$. □

PRACTICE
5 Solve: $-\dfrac{5}{3}x = \dfrac{4}{7}$

OBJECTIVE 2 ▶ Using both the addition and multiplication properties. We are now ready to combine the skills learned in the last section with the skills learned from this section to solve equations by applying more than one property.

EXAMPLE 6   Solve: $-z - 4 = 6$

Solution   First, get $-z$, the term containing the variable alone on one side. To do so, add 4 to both sides of the equation.

$$-z - 4 + 4 = 6 + 4 \quad \text{Add 4 to both sides.}$$
$$-z = 10 \quad \text{Simplify.}$$

Next, recall that $-z$ means $-1 \cdot z$. To get z alone, either multiply or divide both sides of the equation by -1. In this example, we divide.

$$-z = 10$$
$$\frac{-z}{-1} = \frac{10}{-1} \quad \text{Divide both sides by the coefficient } -1.$$
$$z = -10 \quad \text{Simplify.}$$

Check: To check, replace z with -10 in the original equation. The solution is -10.   □

Solve: $-y + 3 = -8$

Don't forget to simplify one or both sides of an equation, if possible.

EXAMPLE 7   Solve: $12a - 8a = 10 + 2a - 13 - 7$

Solution   First, simplify both sides of the equation by combining like terms.

$$12a - 8a = 10 + 2a - 13 - 7$$
$$4a = 2a - 10 \quad \text{Combine like terms.}$$

To get all terms containing a variable on one side, subtract $2a$ from both sides.

$$4a - 2a = 2a - 10 - 2a \quad \text{Subtract } 2a \text{ from both sides.}$$
$$2a = -10 \quad \text{Simplify.}$$
$$\frac{2a}{2} = \frac{-10}{2} \quad \text{Divide both sides by 2.}$$
$$a = -5 \quad \text{Simplify.}$$

Check: Check by replacing a with -5 in the original equation. The solution is -5.   □

PRACTICE
7   Solve: $6b - 11b = 18 + 2b - 6 + 9$

EXAMPLE 8   Solve: $7x - 3 = 5x + 9$

Solution   To get x alone, let's first use the addition property to get variable terms on one side of the equation and numbers on the other side. One way to get variable terms on one side is to subtract $5x$ from both sides.

$$7x - 3 = 5x + 9$$
$$7x - 3 - 5x = 5x + 9 - 5x \quad \text{Subtract } 5x \text{ from both sides.}$$
$$2x - 3 = 9 \quad \text{Simplify.}$$

Now, to get numbers on the other side, let's add 3 to both sides.

$$2x - 3 + 3 = 9 + 3 \quad \text{Add 3 to both sides.}$$
$$2x = 12 \quad \text{Simplify.}$$

Use the multiplication property to get x alone.

$$\frac{2x}{2} = \frac{12}{2} \quad \text{Divide both sides by 2.}$$
$$x = 6 \quad \text{Simplify.}$$

Check: To check, replace x with 6 in the original equation to see that a true statement results. The solution is 6. □

PRACTICE
8 Solve: $10x - 4 = 7x + 14$

If an equation has parentheses, don't forget to use the distributive property to remove them. Then combine any like terms.

EXAMPLE 9 Solve: $5(2x + 3) = -1 + 7$

Solution
$$5(2x + 3) = -1 + 7$$
$$5(2x) + 5(3) = -1 + 7 \quad \text{Apply the distributive property.}$$
$$10x + 15 = 6 \quad \text{Multiply and write } -1 + 7 \text{ as 6.}$$
$$10x + 15 - 15 = 6 - 15 \quad \text{Subtract 15 from both sides.}$$
$$10x = -9 \quad \text{Simplify.}$$
$$\frac{10x}{10} = -\frac{9}{10} \quad \text{Divide both sides by 10.}$$
$$x = -\frac{9}{10} \quad \text{Simplify.}$$

Check: To check, replace x with $-\frac{9}{10}$ in the original equation to see that a true statement results. The solution is $-\frac{9}{10}$. □

PRACTICE
9 Solve: $4(3x - 2) = -1 + 4$

OBJECTIVE 3 ▶ Writing word phrases as algebraic expressions. Next, we continue to sharpen our problem-solving skills by writing word phrases as algebraic expressions.

EXAMPLE 10 If x is the first of three consecutive integers, express the sum of the three integers in terms of x. Simplify if possible.

Solution An example of three consecutive integers is

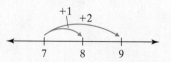

The second consecutive integer is always 1 more than the first, and the third consecutive integer is 2 more than the first. If x is the first of three consecutive integers, the three consecutive integers are

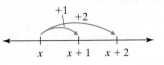

Their sum is

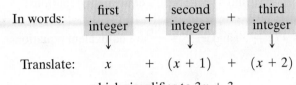

which simplifies to $3x + 3$.

PRACTICE

10 If x is the first of three consecutive *even* integers, express their sum in terms of x.

Below are examples of consecutive even and odd integers.

Consecutive Even integers:

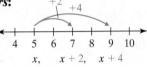

Consecutive Odd integers:

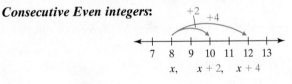

> ▶ **Helpful Hint**
>
> If x is an odd integer, then $x + 2$ is the next odd integer. This 2 simply means that odd integers are always 2 units from each other. (The same is true for even integers. They are always 2 units from each other.)
>
>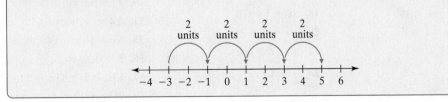

VOCABULARY & READINESS CHECK

Word Bank. *Use the choices below to fill in each blank. Not all choices will be used.*

addition   multiplication

1. By the _____ property of equality, $y = \dfrac{1}{2}$ and $5 \cdot y = 5 \cdot \dfrac{1}{2}$ are equivalent equations.

2. By the _____ property of equality, $9x = -63$ and $\dfrac{9x}{9} = \dfrac{-63}{9}$ are equivalent equations.

3. **True or False.** The equations $\dfrac{z}{4} = 10$ and $4 \cdot \dfrac{z}{4} = 10$ are equivalent equations. _____

4. **True or False.** The equations $-7x = 30$ and $\dfrac{-7x}{-7} = \dfrac{30}{7}$ are equivalent equations. _____

Solve each equation mentally.

5. $3a = 27$ **6.** $9c = 54$ **7.** $5b = 10$ **8.** $7t = 14$

2.3 EXERCISE SET

MyMathLab PRACTICE WATCH DOWNLOAD READ REVIEW

Solve each equation. Check each solution. See Examples 1 through 5.

1. $-5x = -20$ **2.** $-7x = -49$

3. $3x = 0$ **4.** $2x = 0$

5. $-x = -12$ **6.** $-y = 8$

7. $\dfrac{2}{3}x = -8$ **8.** $\dfrac{3}{4}n = -15$

9. $\dfrac{1}{6}d = \dfrac{1}{2}$ **10.** $\dfrac{1}{8}v = \dfrac{1}{4}$

11. $\dfrac{a}{2} = 1$ **12.** $\dfrac{d}{15} = 2$

13. $\dfrac{k}{-7} = 0$ **14.** $\dfrac{f}{-5} = 0$

15. $1.7x = 10.71$ **16.** $8.5y = 19.55$

Solve each equation. Check each solution. See Examples 6 and 7.

17. $2x - 4 = 16$ **18.** $3x - 1 = 26$

19. $-x + 2 = 22$ **20.** $-x + 4 = -24$

21. $6a + 3 = 3$ **22.** $8t + 5 = 5$

23. $\dfrac{x}{3} - 2 = -5$ **24.** $\dfrac{b}{4} - 1 = -7$

25. $6z - z = -2 + 2z - 1 - 6$

26. $4a + a = -1 + 3a - 1 - 2$

27. $1 = 0.4x - 0.6x - 5$ **28.** $19 = 0.4x - 0.9x - 6$

29. $\dfrac{2}{3}y - 11 = -9$ **30.** $\dfrac{3}{5}x - 14 = -8$

31. $\dfrac{3}{4}t - \dfrac{1}{2} = \dfrac{1}{3}$ **32.** $\dfrac{2}{7}z - \dfrac{1}{5} = \dfrac{1}{2}$

Solve each equation. See Examples 8 and 9.

33. $8x + 20 = 6x + 18$ **34.** $11x + 13 = 9x + 9$

35. $3(2x + 5) = -18 + 9$ **36.** $2(4x + 1) = -12 + 6$

37. $2x - 5 = 20x + 4$ **38.** $6x - 4 = -2x - 10$

39. $2 + 14 = -4(3x - 4)$ **40.** $8 + 4 = -6(5x - 2)$

41. $-6y - 3 = -5y - 7$ **42.** $-17z - 4 = -16z - 20$

43. $\dfrac{1}{2}(2x - 1) = -\dfrac{1}{7} - \dfrac{3}{7}$ **44.** $\dfrac{1}{3}(3x - 1) = -\dfrac{1}{10} - \dfrac{2}{10}$

45. $-10z - 0.5 = -20z + 1.6$ **46.** $-14y - 1.8 = -24y + 3.9$

47. $-4x + 20 = 4x - 20$ **48.** $-3x + 15 = 3x - 15$

MIXED PRACTICE

See Examples 1 through 9.

49. $42 = 7x$ **50.** $81 = 3x$

51. $4.4 = -0.8x$ **52.** $6.3 = -0.6x$

53. $6x + 10 = -20$ **54.** $10y + 15 = -5$

55. $5 - 0.3k = 5$ **56.** $2 - 0.4p = 2$

57. $13x - 5 = 11x - 11$ **58.** $20x - 20 = 16x - 40$

59. $9(3x + 1) = 4x - 5x$ **60.** $7(2x + 1) = 18x - 19x$

61. $-\dfrac{3}{7}p = -2$ **62.** $-\dfrac{4}{5}r = -5$

63. $-\dfrac{4}{3}x = 12$ **64.** $-\dfrac{10}{3}x = 30$

65. $-2x - \dfrac{1}{2} = \dfrac{7}{2}$ **66.** $-3n - \dfrac{1}{3} = \dfrac{8}{3}$

67. $10 = 2x - 1$ **68.** $12 = 3j - 4$

69. $10 - 3x - 6 - 9x = 7$ **70.** $12x + 30 + 8x - 6 = 10$

71. $z - 5z = 7z - 9 - z$ **72.** $t - 6t = -13 + t - 3t$

73. $-x - \dfrac{4}{5} = x + \dfrac{1}{2} + \dfrac{2}{5}$ **74.** $x + \dfrac{3}{7} = -x + \dfrac{1}{3} + \dfrac{4}{7}$

75. $-15 + 37 = -2(x + 5)$ **76.** $-19 + 74 = -5(x + 3)$

Write each algebraic expression described. Simplify if possible. See Example 10.

77. If x represents the first of two consecutive odd integers, express the sum of the two integers in terms of x.

78. If x is the first of four consecutive even integers, write their sum as an algebraic expression in x.

79. If x is the first of four consecutive integers, express the sum of the first integer and the third integer as an algebraic expression containing the variable x.

80. If x is the first of two consecutive integers, express the sum of 20 and the second consecutive integer as an algebraic expression containing the variable x.

81. Classrooms on one side of the science building are all numbered with consecutive even integers. If the first room on this side of the building is numbered x, write an expression in x for the sum of five classroom numbers in a row. Then simplify this expression.

82. Two sides of a quadrilateral have the same length, x, while the other two sides have the same length, both being the next consecutive odd integer. Write the sum of these lengths. Then simplify this expression.

83. Step Justification. The equation $3x + 7 = -5$ is correctly solved below. Use the given list to justify how each equation is equivalent to the one above it. Some Steps are filled in for you.

a. Distributive Property $[a(b + c) = ab + ac]$

b. Commutative Property of Addition [ordering of addition of terms]

c. Associative Property of Addition [grouping of addition of terms]

d. Commutative Property of Multiplication [ordering of multiplication of terms]

e. Associative Property of Multiplication [grouping of Multiplication of terms]

f. 0 is the identity element for addition $[0 + a = a]$

g. 1 is the identity element for multiplication $[1 \cdot a = a]$

h. Adding or subtracting the same number to/from both sides of an equation does not change its solution.

i. Multiplying or dividing the same nonzero number to/by both sides of an equation does not change its solution.

Step	Justification
$3x + 7 = -5$	Given equation
$(3x + 7) - 7 = -5 - 7$	H
$3x + (7 - 7) = -5 - 7$	_____
$3x + 0 = -12$	$7 - 7 = 0; -5 - 7 = -12$
$3x = -12$	_____
$\dfrac{3x}{3} = \dfrac{-12}{3}$	_____
$1 \cdot x = -4$	$\dfrac{3}{3} = 1; \dfrac{-12}{3} = -4$
$x = -4$	_____

84. Step Justification. The equation $5x + 1 = -9$ is correctly solved below. Follow the same directions as for Exercise 83.

Step	Justification
$5x + 1 = -9$	Given equation
$(5x + 1) - 1 = -9 - 1$	H
$5x + (1 - 1) = -9 - 1$	_____
$5x + 0 = -10$	$1 - 1 = 0; -9 - 1 = -10$
$5x = -10$	_____
$\dfrac{5x}{5} = \dfrac{-10}{5}$	_____
$1 \cdot x = -2$	$\dfrac{5}{5} = 1; \dfrac{-10}{5} = -2$
$x = -2$	_____

REVIEW AND PREVIEW

Simplify each expression. See Section 2.1.

85. $-(x - 1) + x$

86. $-(3a - 3) + 2a - 6$

Decision Making. *Insert $<$, $>$, or $=$ in the appropriate space to make each statement true. See Sections 1.2 and 1.8.*

87. $(-3)^2$ ___ -3^2 **88.** $(-2)^4$ ___ -2^4

89. $(-2)^3$ ___ -2^3 **90.** $(-4)^3$ ___ -4^3

91. $-|-6|$ ___ 6 **92.** $-|-0.7|$ ___ -0.7

CONCEPT EXTENSIONS

Fill in the Blank. *For Exercises 93–94, fill in the blank with a number so that each equation has the given solution.*

93. $6x =$ _____ ; solution: -8 **94.** _____ $x = 10$; solution: $\dfrac{1}{2}$

95. The equation $3x + 6 = 2x + 10 + x - 4$ is true for all real numbers. Substitute a few real numbers for x to see that this is so and then try solving the equation. Describe what happens.

96. The equation $6x + 2 - 2x = 4x + 1$ has no solution. Try solving this equation for x and describe what happens.

97. From the results of Exercises 95 and 96, when do you think an equation has all real numbers as its solutions?

98. From the results of Exercises 95 and 96, when do you think an equation has no solution?

99. A licensed nurse practitioner is instructed to give a patient 2100 milligrams of an antibiotic over a period of 36 hours. If the antibiotic is to be given every 4 hours starting immediately, how much antibiotic should be given in each dose? To answer this question, solve the equation $9x = 2100$.

100. Suppose you are a pharmacist and a customer asks you the following question. His child is to receive 13.5 milliliters of a nausea medicine over a period of 54 hours. If the nausea medicine is to be administered every 6 hours starting immediately, how much medicine should be given in each dose?

Solve each equation.

101. $-3.6x = 10.62$

102. $4.95y = -31.185$

103. $7x - 5.06 = -4.92$

104. $0.06y + 2.63 = 2.5562$

2.4 SOLVING LINEAR EQUATIONS

OBJECTIVES

1 Apply a general strategy for solving a linear equation.

2 Solve equations containing fractions.

3 Solve equations containing decimals.

4 Recognize identities and equations with no solution.

OBJECTIVE 1 ▶ Apply a general strategy for solving a linear equation. We now present a general strategy for solving linear equations. One new piece of strategy is a suggestion to "clear an equation of fractions" as a first step. Doing so makes the equation more manageable, since operating on integers is more convenient than operating on fractions.

> **Solving Linear Equations in One Variable**
>
> **STEP 1.** Multiply on both sides by the LCD to clear the equation of fractions if they occur.
>
> **STEP 2.** Use the distributive property to remove parentheses if they occur.
>
> **STEP 3.** Simplify each side of the equation by combining like terms.
>
> **STEP 4.** Get all variable terms on one side and all numbers on the other side by using the addition property of equality.
>
> **STEP 5.** Get the variable alone by using the multiplication property of equality.
>
> **STEP 6.** Check the solution by substituting it into the original equation.

EXAMPLE 1 Solve: $4(2x - 3) + 7 = 3x + 5$

Solution There are no fractions, so we begin with Step 2.

$$4(2x - 3) + 7 = 3x + 5$$

STEP 2. $\qquad 8x - 12 + 7 = 3x + 5$ Apply the distributive property.

STEP 3. $\qquad\qquad 8x - 5 = 3x + 5$ Combine like terms.

STEP 4. Get all variable terms on the same side of the equation by subtracting $3x$ from both sides, then adding 5 to both sides.

$$8x - 5 - 3x = 3x + 5 - 3x \quad \text{Subtract } 3x \text{ from both sides.}$$
$$5x - 5 = 5 \qquad\qquad \text{Simplify.}$$
$$5x - 5 + 5 = 5 + 5 \qquad \text{Add 5 to both sides.}$$
$$5x = 10 \qquad\qquad \text{Simplify.}$$

STEP 5. Use the multiplication property of equality to get x alone.

$$\frac{5x}{5} = \frac{10}{5} \quad \text{Divide both sides by 5.}$$
$$x = 2 \quad \text{Simplify.}$$

STEP 6. Check.

> ▶ **Helpful Hint**
>
> When checking solutions, remember to use the original written equation.

$$4(2x - 3) + 7 = 3x + 5 \quad \text{Original equation}$$
$$4[2(2) - 3] + 7 \stackrel{?}{=} 3(2) + 5 \quad \text{Replace } x \text{ with 2.}$$
$$4(4 - 3) + 7 \stackrel{?}{=} 6 + 5$$
$$4(1) + 7 \stackrel{?}{=} 11$$
$$4 + 7 \stackrel{?}{=} 11$$
$$11 = 11 \qquad \text{True}$$

The solution is 2 or the solution set is $\{2\}$.

PRACTICE
1 Solve: $2(4a - 9) + 3 = 5a - 6$

EXAMPLE 2 Solve: $8(2 - t) = -5t$

Solution First, we apply the distributive property.

$$8(2 - t) = -5t$$

STEP 2. $16 - 8t = -5t$ \qquad Use the distributive property.

STEP 4. $16 - 8t + 8t = -5t + 8t$ \quad To get variable terms on one side, add $8t$ to both sides.
$$16 = 3t \qquad\qquad \text{Combine like terms.}$$

STEP 5. $$\frac{16}{3} = \frac{3t}{3} \qquad\qquad \text{Divide both sides by 3.}$$
$$\frac{16}{3} = t \qquad\qquad \text{Simplify.}$$

STEP 6. Check.

$$8(2 - t) = -5t \qquad \text{Original equation}$$
$$8\left(2 - \frac{16}{3}\right) \stackrel{?}{=} -5\left(\frac{16}{3}\right) \quad \text{Replace } t \text{ with } \frac{16}{3}.$$
$$8\left(\frac{6}{3} - \frac{16}{3}\right) \stackrel{?}{=} -\frac{80}{3} \quad \text{The LCD is 3.}$$
$$8\left(-\frac{10}{3}\right) \stackrel{?}{=} -\frac{80}{3} \quad \text{Subtract fractions.}$$
$$-\frac{80}{3} = -\frac{80}{3} \quad \text{True}$$

The solution is $\frac{16}{3}$.

PRACTICE
2 Solve: $7(x - 3) = -6x$

OBJECTIVE 2 ▶ **Solving equations containing fractions.** If an equation contains fractions, we can clear the equation of fractions by multiplying both sides by the LCD of all denominators. By doing this, we avoid working with time-consuming fractions.

EXAMPLE 3 Solve: $\dfrac{x}{2} - 1 = \dfrac{2}{3}x - 3$

Solution We begin by clearing fractions. To do this, we multiply both sides of the equation by the LCD of 2 and 3, which is 6.

$$\frac{x}{2} - 1 = \frac{2}{3}x - 3$$

STEP 1. $6\left(\dfrac{x}{2} - 1\right) = 6\left(\dfrac{2}{3}x - 3\right)$ Multiply both sides by the LCD, 6.

STEP 2. $6\left(\dfrac{x}{2}\right) - 6(1) = 6\left(\dfrac{2}{3}x\right) - 6(3)$ Apply the distributive property.

$$3x - 6 = 4x - 18 \quad \text{Simplify.}$$

> ▶ **Helpful Hint**
> Don't forget to multiply *each* term by the LCD.

There are no longer grouping symbols and no like terms on either side of the equation, so we continue with Step 4.

$$3x - 6 = 4x - 18$$

STEP 4. $3x - 6 - 3x = 4x - 18 - 3x$ To get variable terms on one side, subtract $3x$ from both sides.

$$-6 = x - 18 \quad \text{Simplify.}$$
$$-6 + 18 = x - 18 + 18 \quad \text{Add 18 to both sides.}$$
$$12 = x \quad \text{Simplify.}$$

STEP 5. The variable is now alone, so there is no need to apply the multiplication property of equality.

STEP 6. Check.

$$\frac{x}{2} - 1 = \frac{2}{3}x - 3 \quad \text{Original equation}$$
$$\frac{12}{2} - 1 \stackrel{?}{=} \frac{2}{3}\cdot 12 - 3 \quad \text{Replace } x \text{ with 12.}$$
$$6 - 1 \stackrel{?}{=} 8 - 3 \quad \text{Simplify.}$$
$$5 = 5 \quad \text{True}$$

The solution is 12. □

PRACTICE
3 Solve: $\dfrac{3}{5}x - 2 = \dfrac{2}{3}x - 1$

EXAMPLE 4 Solve: $\dfrac{2(a + 3)}{3} = 6a + 2$

Solution We clear the equation of fractions first.

$$\frac{2(a + 3)}{3} = 6a + 2$$

STEP 1. $3\cdot\dfrac{2(a + 3)}{3} = 3(6a + 2)$ Clear the fraction by multiplying both sides by the LCD, 3.

$$2(a + 3) = 3(6a + 2)$$

STEP 2. Next, we use the distributive property and remove parentheses.

$$2a + 6 = 18a + 6 \qquad \text{Apply the distributive property.}$$

STEP 4.
$$2a + 6 - 6 = 18a + 6 - 6 \qquad \text{Subtract 6 from both sides.}$$
$$2a = 18a$$
$$2a - 18a = 18a - 18a \qquad \text{Subtract } 18a \text{ from both sides.}$$
$$-16a = 0$$

STEP 5.
$$\frac{-16a}{-16} = \frac{0}{-16} \qquad \text{Divide both sides by } -16.$$
$$a = 0 \qquad \text{Write the fraction in simplest form.}$$

STEP 6. To check, replace a with 0 in the original equation. The solution is 0.   □

PRACTICE
4 Solve: $\dfrac{4(y + 3)}{3} = 5y - 7$

OBJECTIVE 3 ▶ **Solving equations containing decimals.** When solving a problem about money, you may need to solve an equation containing decimals. If you choose, you may multiply to clear the equation of decimals.

EXAMPLE 5   Solve: $0.25x + 0.10(x - 3) = 0.05(22)$

Solution   First we clear this equation of decimals by multiplying both sides of the equation by 100. Recall that multiplying a decimal number by 100 has the effect of moving the decimal point 2 places to the right.

$$0.25x + 0.10(x - 3) = 0.05(22)$$

▶ **Helpful Hint**

By the distributive property, 0.10 is multiplied by x and -3. Thus to multiply each term here by 100, we only need to multiply 0.10 by 100.

STEP 1.
$$0.25x + 0.10(x - 3) = 0.05(22) \qquad \text{Multiply both sides by 100.}$$
$$25x + 10(x - 3) = 5(22)$$

STEP 2.
$$25x + 10x - 30 = 110 \qquad \text{Apply the distributive property.}$$

STEP 3.
$$35x - 30 = 110 \qquad \text{Combine like terms.}$$

STEP 4.
$$35x - 30 + 30 = 110 + 30 \qquad \text{Add 30 to both sides.}$$
$$35x = 140 \qquad \text{Combine like terms.}$$

STEP 5.
$$\frac{35x}{35} = \frac{140}{35} \qquad \text{Divide both sides by 35.}$$
$$x = 4$$

STEP 6. To check, replace x with 4 in the original equation. The solution is 4.   □

PRACTICE
5 Solve: $0.35x + 0.09(x + 4) = 0.03(12)$

OBJECTIVE 4 ▶ **Recognizing identities and equations with no solution.** So far, each equation that we have solved has had a single solution. However, not every equation in one variable has a single solution. Some equations have no solution, while others have an infinite number of solutions. For example,

$$x + 5 = x + 7$$

has no solution since no matter which **real number** we replace x with, the equation is false.

real number $+ 5 =$ same **real number** $+ 7$ **FALSE**

On the other hand,

$$x + 6 = x + 6$$

has infinitely many solutions since x can be replaced by any real number and the equation is always true.

$$\text{\textbf{real number}} + 6 = \text{same } \textbf{real number} + 6 \qquad \textbf{TRUE}$$

The equation $x + 6 = x + 6$ is called an **identity.** The next few examples illustrate special equations like these.

EXAMPLE 6 Solve: $-2(x - 5) + 10 = -3(x + 2) + x$

Solution

$$-2(x - 5) + 10 = -3(x + 2) + x$$
$$-2x + 10 + 10 = -3x - 6 + x \qquad \text{Apply the distributive property on both sides.}$$
$$-2x + 20 = -2x - 6 \qquad \text{Combine like terms.}$$
$$-2x + 20 + 2x = -2x - 6 + 2x \qquad \text{Add } 2x \text{ to both sides.}$$
$$20 = -6 \qquad \text{Combine like terms.}$$

The final equation contains no variable terms, and there is no value for x that makes $20 = -6$ a true equation. We conclude that there is **no solution** to this equation. In set notation, we can indicate that there is no solution with the empty set, { }, or use the empty set or null set symbol, $\varnothing$. In this chapter, we will simply write *no solution*. $\square$

PRACTICE
6 Solve: $4(x + 4) - x = 2(x + 11) + x$

EXAMPLE 7 Solve: $3(x - 4) = 3x - 12$

Solution
$$3(x - 4) = 3x - 12$$
$$3x - 12 = 3x - 12 \qquad \text{Apply the distributive property.}$$

The left side of the equation is now identical to the right side. Every real number may be substituted for x and a true statement will result. We arrive at the same conclusion if we continue.

$$3x - 12 = 3x - 12$$
$$3x - 12 + 12 = 3x - 12 + 12 \qquad \text{Add 12 to both sides.}$$
$$3x = 3x \qquad \text{Combine like terms.}$$
$$3x - 3x = 3x - 3x \qquad \text{Subtract } 3x \text{ from both sides.}$$
$$0 = 0$$

Again, one side of the equation is identical to the other side. Thus, $3(x - 4) = 3x - 12$ is an **identity** and **all real numbers** are solutions. In set notation, this is {all real numbers}. $\square$

PRACTICE
7 Solve: $12x - 18 = 9(x - 2) + 3x$

Answers to Concept Check:
a. Every real number is a solution.
b. The solution is 0.
c. There is no solution.

Concept Check ☑

Suppose you have simplified several equations and obtain the following results. What can you conclude about the solutions to the original equation?

a. $7 = 7$ **b.** $x = 0$ **c.** $7 = -4$

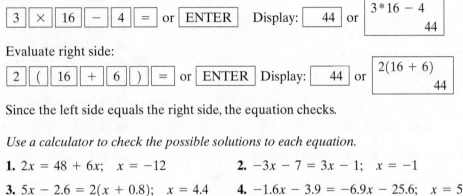

Calculator Explorations

Checking Equations

We can use a calculator to check possible solutions of equations. To do this, replace the variable by the possible solution and evaluate both sides of the equation separately.

Equation: $\quad\quad\quad 3x - 4 = 2(x + 6)$ $\quad\quad\quad\quad\quad$ *Solution:* $x = 16$

$\quad\quad\quad\quad\quad 3x - 4 = 2(x + 6)$ $\quad$ Original equation

$\quad\quad\quad 3(16) - 4 \overset{?}{=} 2(16 + 6)$ $\quad$ Replace x with 16.

Now evaluate each side with your calculator.

Evaluate left side:

$\boxed{3}$ $\boxed{\times}$ $\boxed{16}$ $\boxed{-}$ $\boxed{4}$ $\boxed{=}$ or $\boxed{\text{ENTER}}$ $\quad$ Display: $\boxed{44}$ or $\boxed{\begin{array}{r} 3*16 - 4 \\ 44 \end{array}}$

Evaluate right side:

$\boxed{2}$ $\boxed{(}$ $\boxed{16}$ $\boxed{+}$ $\boxed{6}$ $\boxed{)}$ $\boxed{=}$ or $\boxed{\text{ENTER}}$ Display: $\boxed{44}$ or $\boxed{\begin{array}{r} 2(16 + 6) \\ 44 \end{array}}$

Since the left side equals the right side, the equation checks.

Use a calculator to check the possible solutions to each equation.

1. $2x = 48 + 6x; \quad x = -12$ $\quad\quad\quad$ **2.** $-3x - 7 = 3x - 1; \quad x = -1$

3. $5x - 2.6 = 2(x + 0.8); \quad x = 4.4$ $\quad$ **4.** $-1.6x - 3.9 = -6.9x - 25.6; \quad x = 5$

5. $\dfrac{564x}{4} = 200x - 11(649); \quad x = 121$ $\quad$ **6.** $20(x - 39) = 5x - 432; \quad x = 23.2$

VOCABULARY & READINESS CHECK

Throughout algebra, it is important to be able to identify equations and expressions.

Remember,

- an equation contains an equals sign and
- an expression does not.

Among other things,

- we solve equations and
- we simplify or perform operations on expressions.

Fill in the Blank. *Identify each as an equation or an expression.*

1. $x = -7$ _____ $\quad\quad\quad$ **2.** $x - 7$ _____ $\quad\quad\quad$ **3.** $4y - 6 + 9y + 1$ _____

4. $4y - 6 = 9y + 1$ _____ $\quad\quad$ **5.** $\dfrac{1}{x} - \dfrac{x - 1}{8}$ _____ $\quad\quad$ **6.** $\dfrac{1}{x} - \dfrac{x - 1}{8} = 6$ _____

7. $0.1x + 9 = 0.2x$ _____ $\quad\quad$ **8.** $0.1x^2 + 9y - 0.2x^2$ _____

2.4 EXERCISE SET

Solve each equation. See Examples 1 and 2.

1. $-4y + 10 = -2(3y + 1)$

2. $-3x + 1 = -2(4x + 2)$

3. $15x - 8 = 10 + 9x$

4. $15x - 5 = 7 + 12x$

5. $-2(3x - 4) = 2x$

6. $-(5x - 10) = 5x$

7. $5(2x - 1) - 2(3x) = 1$

8. $3(2 - 5x) + 4(6x) = 12$

9. $-6(x - 3) - 26 = -8$

10. $-4(n - 4) - 23 = -7$

11. $8 - 2(a + 1) = 9 + a$

12. $5 - 6(2 + b) = b - 14$

13. $4x + 3 = -3 + 2x + 14$

14. $6y - 8 = -6 + 3y + 13$

15. $-2y - 10 = 5y + 18$

16. $-7n + 5 = 8n - 10$

Solve each equation. See Examples 3 through 5.

17. $\frac{2}{3}x + \frac{4}{3} = -\frac{2}{3}$

18. $\frac{4}{5}x - \frac{8}{5} = -\frac{16}{5}$

19. $\frac{3}{4}x - \frac{1}{2} = 1$

20. $\frac{2}{9}x - \frac{1}{3} = 1$

21. $0.50x + 0.15(70) = 35.5$

22. $0.40x + 0.06(30) = 9.8$

23. $\frac{2(x + 1)}{4} = 3x - 2$

24. $\frac{3(y + 3)}{5} = 2y + 6$

25. $x + \frac{7}{6} = 2x - \frac{7}{6}$

26. $\frac{5}{2}x - 1 = x + \frac{1}{4}$

27. $0.12(y - 6) + 0.06y = 0.08y - 0.7$

28. $0.60(z - 300) + 0.05z = 0.70z - 205$

Solve each equation. See Examples 6 and 7.

29. $4(3x + 2) = 12x + 8$

30. $14x + 7 = 7(2x + 1)$

31. $\frac{x}{4} + 1 = \frac{x}{4}$

32. $\frac{x}{3} - 2 = \frac{x}{3}$

33. $3x - 7 = 3(x + 1)$

34. $2(x - 5) = 2x + 10$

35. $-2(6x - 5) + 4 = -12x + 14$

36. $-5(4y - 3) + 2 = -20y + 17$

MIXED PRACTICE

Solve. See Examples 1 through 7.

37. $\frac{6(3 - z)}{5} = -z$

38. $\frac{4(5 - w)}{3} = -w$

39. $-3(2t - 5) + 2t = 5t - 4$

40. $-(4a - 7) - 5a = 10 + a$

41. $5y + 2(y - 6) = 4(y + 1) - 2$

42. $9x + 3(x - 4) = 10(x - 5) + 7$

43. $\frac{3(x - 5)}{2} = \frac{2(x + 5)}{3}$

44. $\frac{5(x - 1)}{4} = \frac{3(x + 1)}{2}$

45. $0.7x - 2.3 = 0.5$

46. $0.9x - 4.1 = 0.4$

47. $5x - 5 = 2(x + 1) + 3x - 7$

48. $3(2x - 1) + 5 = 6x + 2$

49. $4(2n + 1) = 3(6n + 3) + 1$

50. $4(4y + 2) = 2(1 + 6y) + 8$

51. $x + \frac{5}{4} = \frac{3}{4}x$

52. $\frac{7}{8}x + \frac{1}{4} = \frac{3}{4}x$

53. $\frac{x}{2} - 1 = \frac{x}{5} + 2$

54. $\frac{x}{5} - 7 = \frac{x}{3} - 5$

55. $2(x + 3) - 5 = 5x - 3(1 + x)$

56. $4(2 + x) + 1 = 7x - 3(x - 2)$

57. $0.06 - 0.01(x + 1) = -0.02(2 - x)$

58. $-0.01(5x + 4) = 0.04 - 0.01(x + 4)$

59. $\frac{9}{2} + \frac{5}{2}y = 2y - 4$

60. $3 - \frac{1}{2}x = 5x - 8$

61. $-2y - 10 = 5y + 18$

62. $7n + 5 = 10n - 10$

63. $0.6x - 0.1 = 0.5x + 0.2$

64. $0.2x - 0.1 = 0.6x - 2.1$

65. $0.02(6t - 3) = 0.12(t - 2) + 0.18$

66. $0.03(2m + 7) = 0.06(5 + m) - 0.09$

Step Justification. *The equation below is correctly solved. Use the given list to justify how each equation is equivalent to the one above it. Some steps are filled in for you.*

A. Distributive Property $[a(b + c) = ab + ac]$

B. Commutative Property of Addition [ordering of addition of terms]

C. Associative Property of Addition [grouping of addition of terms]

D. Commutative Property of Multiplication [ordering of multiplication of terms]

E. Associative Property of Multiplication [grouping of multiplication of terms]

F. 0 is the identity element for addition [$0 + a = a$]

G. 1 is the identity element for multiplication [$1 \cdot a = a$]

H. Adding or subtracting the same number to/from both sides of an equation does not change its solution.

I. Multiplying or dividing the same nonzero number to/by both sides of an equation does not change its solution.

Exercise Number	Step	Justification
	$\dfrac{25x - 8}{2} = 11x + 2$	Given equation
	$2 \cdot \dfrac{25x - 8}{2} = 2(11x + 2)$	I
	$25x - 8 = 2(11x + 2)$	$2/2 = 1$
67.	$25x - 8 = 22x + 4$	_____
68.	$(25x - 8) + 8 = (22x + 4) + 8$	_____
69.	$25x + (-8 + 8) = 22x + (4 + 8)$	_____
	$25x + 0 = 22x + 12$	$-8 + 8 = 0;\ 4 + 8 = 12$
70.	$25x = 22x + 12$	_____
71.	$25x - 22x = (22x + 12) - 22x$	_____
	$3x = (22x + 12) - 22x$	$25x - 22x = 3x$
72.	$3x = (12 + 22x) - 22x$	_____
73.	$3x = 12 + (22x - 22x)$	_____
	$3x = 12 + 0$	$22x - 22x = 0$
74.	$3x = 12$	_____
75.	$\dfrac{3x}{3} = \dfrac{12}{3}$	_____
	$1 \cdot x = 4$	$3/3 = 1;\ 12/3 = 4$
76.	$x = 4$	_____

REVIEW AND PREVIEW

Write each phrase as an algebraic expression. Use x for the unknown number. See Section 2.1.

77. The sum of -3 and twice a number

78. The difference of 8 and twice a number

79. The product of 9 and the sum of a number and 20

80. The quotient of -12 and the difference of a number and 3

See Section 2.1.

81. A plot of land is in the shape of a triangle. If one side is x meters, a second side is $(2x - 3)$ meters and a third side is $(3x - 5)$ meters, express the perimeter of the lot as a simplified expression in x.

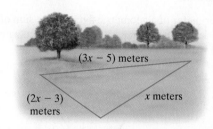

(3x − 5) meters

(2x − 3) meters

x meters

82. A portion of a board has length x feet. The other part has length $(7x - 9)$ feet. Express the total length of the board as a simplified expression in x.

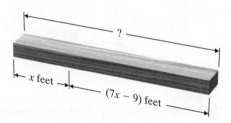

?

x feet

(7x − 9) feet

CONCEPT EXTENSIONS

Multiple Steps. *See the Concept Check in this section.*

83. a. Solve: $x + 3 = x + 3$

  b. If you simplify an equation and get $0 = 0$, what can you conclude about the solution(s) of the original equation?

  c. On your own, construct an equation for which every real number is a solution.

84. a. Solve: $x + 3 = x + 5$

  b. If you simplify an equation and get $3 = 5$, what can you conclude about the solution(s) of the original equation?

  c. On your own, construct an equation that has no solution.

Matching. *Match each equation in the first column with its solution in the second column. Items in the second column may be used more than once.*

85. $5x + 1 = 5x + 1$ **a.** all real numbers

86. $3x + 1 = 3x + 2$ **b.** no solution

87. $2x - 6x - 10 = -4x + 3 - 10$ **c.** 0

88. $x - 11x - 3 = -10x - 1 - 2$

89. $9x - 20 = 8x - 20$

90. $-x + 15 = x + 15$

91. Explain the difference between simplifying an expression and solving an equation.

92. On your own, write an expression and then an equation. Label each.

Multiple Steps. *For Exercises 93 and 94,* **a.** *Write an equation for perimeter.* **b.** *Solve the equation in part (a).* **c.** *Find the length of each side.*

△ **93.** The perimeter of a geometric figure is the sum of the lengths of its sides. The perimeter of the following pentagon (five-sided figure) is 28 centimeters.

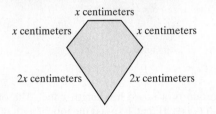

x centimeters

x centimeters   *x* centimeters

2*x* centimeters   2*x* centimeters

△ **94.** The perimeter of the following triangle is 35 meters.

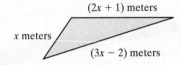

$(2x + 1)$ meters

x meters

$(3x - 2)$ meters

Fill in the Blank. *Fill in the blanks with numbers of your choice so that each equation has the given solution.* Note: *Each blank may be replaced by a different number.*

95. $x + \underline{} = 2x - \underline{}$; solution: 9

96. $-5x - \underline{} = \underline{}$; solution: 2

Solve.

🖩 **97.** $1000(7x - 10) = 50(412 + 100x)$

🖩 **98.** $1000(x + 40) = 100(16 + 7x)$

🖩 **99.** $0.035x + 5.112 = 0.010x + 5.107$

🖩 **100.** $0.127x - 2.685 = 0.027x - 2.38$

For Exercises 101 through 104, see the example below.

Example

Solve: $t(t + 4) = t^2 - 2t + 6$.

Solution
$$t(t + 4) = t^2 - 2t + 6$$
$$t^2 + 4t = t^2 - 2t + 6$$
$$t^2 + 4t - t^2 = t^2 - 2t + 6 - t^2$$
$$4t = -2t + 6$$
$$4t + 2t = -2t + 6 + 2t$$
$$6t = 6$$
$$t = 1$$

Solve each equation.

101. $x(x - 3) = x^2 + 5x + 7$

102. $t^2 - 6t = t(8 + t)$

103. $2z(z + 6) = 2z^2 + 12z - 8$

104. $y^2 - 4y + 10 = y(y - 5)$

INTEGRATED REVIEW   SOLVING LINEAR EQUATIONS

Sections 2.1–2.4

Solve. Feel free to use the steps given in Section 2.4.

1. $x - 10 = -4$ **2.** $y + 14 = -3$

3. $9y = 108$ **4.** $-3x = 78$

5. $-6x + 7 = 25$ **6.** $5y - 42 = -47$

7. $\dfrac{2}{3}x = 9$ **8.** $\dfrac{4}{5}z = 10$

9. $\dfrac{r}{-4} = -2$ **10.** $\dfrac{y}{-8} = 8$

11. $6 - 2x + 8 = 10$ **12.** $-5 - 6y + 6 = 19$

13. $2x - 7 = 2x - 27$

14. $3 + 8y = 8y - 2$

15. $-3a + 6 + 5a = 7a - 8a$

16. $4b - 8 - b = 10b - 3b$

17. $-\dfrac{2}{3}x = \dfrac{5}{9}$ **18.** $-\dfrac{3}{8}y = -\dfrac{1}{16}$

19. $10 = -6n + 16$ **20.** $-5 = -2m + 7$

21. $3(5c - 1) - 2 = 13c + 3$

22. $4(3t + 4) - 20 = 3 + 5t$

23. $\dfrac{2(z + 3)}{3} = 5 - z$ **24.** $\dfrac{3(w + 2)}{4} = 2w + 3$

25. $-2(2x - 5) = -3x + 7 - x + 3$

26. $-4(5x - 2) = -12x + 4 - 8x + 4$

27. $0.02(6t - 3) = 0.04(t - 2) + 0.02$

28. $0.03(m + 7) = 0.02(5 - m) + 0.03$

29. $-3y = \dfrac{4(y - 1)}{5}$ **30.** $-4x = \dfrac{5(1 - x)}{6}$

31. $\dfrac{5}{3}x - \dfrac{7}{3} = x$ **32.** $\dfrac{7}{5}n + \dfrac{3}{5} = -n$

33. $\dfrac{1}{10}(3x - 7) = \dfrac{3}{10}x + 5$

34. $\dfrac{1}{7}(2x - 5) = \dfrac{2}{7}x + 1$

35. $5 + 2(3x - 6) = -4(6x - 7)$

36. $3 + 5(2x - 4) = -7(5x + 2)$

2.5 AN INTRODUCTION TO PROBLEM SOLVING

OBJECTIVES

Apply the steps for problem solving as we

1 Solve problems involving direct translations.

2 Solve problems involving relationships among unknown quantities.

3 Solve problems involving consecutive integers.

OBJECTIVE 1 ▶ Solving direct translation problems. In previous sections, you practiced writing word phrases and sentences as algebraic expressions and equations to help prepare for problem solving. We now use these translations to help write equations that model a problem. The problem-solving steps given next may be helpful.

General Strategy for Problem Solving

1. **UNDERSTAND** the problem. During this step, become comfortable with the problem. Some ways of doing this are:

      Read and reread the problem.

      Choose a variable to represent the unknown.

      Construct a drawing, whenever possible.

      Propose a solution and check. Pay careful attention to how you check your proposed solution. This will help when writing an equation to model the problem.

2. **TRANSLATE** the problem into an equation.

3. **SOLVE** the equation.

4. **INTERPRET** the results: *Check* the proposed solution in the stated problem and state your conclusion.

Much of problem solving involves a direct translation from a sentence to an equation.

EXAMPLE 1   **Finding an Unknown Number**

Twice a number, added to seven, is the same as three subtracted from the number. Find the number.

Solution   Translate the sentence into an equation and solve.

In words: | twice a number | added to | seven | is the same as | three subtracted from the number |

Translate: $2x$ $+$ 7 $=$ $x - 3$

To solve, begin by subtracting x from both sides to isolate the variable term.

$$2x + 7 = x - 3$$
$$2x + 7 - x = x - 3 - x \quad \text{Subtract } x \text{ from both sides.}$$
$$x + 7 = -3 \quad \text{Combine like terms.}$$
$$x + 7 - 7 = -3 - 7 \quad \text{Subtract 7 from both sides.}$$
$$x = -10 \quad \text{Combine like terms.}$$

Check the solution in the problem as it was originally stated. To do so, replace "number" in the sentence with -10. Twice "-10" added to 7 is the same as 3 subtracted from "-10."

$$2(-10) + 7 = -10 - 3$$
$$-13 = -13$$

The unknown number is -10.   □

PRACTICE

1   Three times a number, minus 6, is the same as two times a number, plus 3. Find the number.

> ▶ **Helpful Hint**
>
> When checking solutions, go back to the original stated problem, rather than to your equation in case errors have been made in translating to an equation.

EXAMPLE 2 Finding an Unknown Number

Twice the sum of a number and 4 is the same as four times the number, decreased by 12. Find the number.

Solution

1. UNDERSTAND. Read and reread the problem. If we let

$$x = \text{the unknown number, then}$$

"the sum of a number and 4" translates to "$x + 4$" and "four times the number" translates to "$4x$."

2. TRANSLATE.

twice	sum of a number and 4	is the same as	four times the number	decreased by	12
↓	↓	↓	↓	↓	↓
2	$(x + 4)$	=	$4x$	−	12

3. SOLVE.

$$2(x + 4) = 4x - 12$$
$$2x + 8 = 4x - 12 \qquad \text{Apply the distributive property.}$$
$$2x + 8 - 4x = 4x - 12 - 4x \quad \text{Subtract } 4x \text{ from both sides.}$$
$$-2x + 8 = -12$$
$$-2x + 8 - 8 = -12 - 8 \qquad \text{Subtract 8 from both sides.}$$
$$-2x = -20$$
$$\frac{-2x}{-2} = \frac{-20}{-2} \qquad \text{Divide both sides by } -2.$$
$$x = 10$$

4. INTERPRET.

Check: Check this solution in the problem as it was originally stated. To do so, replace "number" with 10. Twice the sum of "10" and 4 is 28, which is the same as 4 times "10" decreased by 12.

State: The number is 10. ◻

PRACTICE

2 Three times a number, decreased by 4, is the same as double the difference of the number and 1.

OBJECTIVE 2 ▶ Solving problems involving relationships among unknown quantities.
The next three examples have to do with relationships among unknown quantities.

EXAMPLE 3 Finding the Length of a Board

Balsa wood sticks are commonly used for building models (for example, bridge models). A 48-inch Balsa wood stick is to be cut into two pieces so that the longer piece is 3 times the shorter. Find the length of each piece.

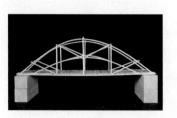

Solution

1. UNDERSTAND the problem. To do so, read and reread the problem. You may also want to propose a solution. For example, if 10 inches represents the length of the shorter piece, then $3(10) = 30$ inches is the length of the longer piece, since it is 3 times the length of the shorter piece. This guess gives a total board length of 10 inches + 30 inches = 40 inches, too short. However, the purpose of proposing a solution is not to guess correctly, but to help better understand the problem and how to model it.

Since the length of the longer piece is given in terms of the length of the shorter piece, let's let

$$x = \text{length of shorter piece, then}$$
$$3x = \text{length of longer piece}$$

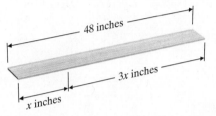

2. TRANSLATE the problem. First, we write the equation in words.

length of shorter piece	added to	length of longer piece	equals	total length of board
↓	↓	↓	↓	↓
x	$+$	$3x$	$=$	48

3. SOLVE.

$$x + 3x = 48$$
$$4x = 48 \quad \text{Combine like terms.}$$
$$\frac{4x}{4} = \frac{48}{4} \quad \text{Divide both sides by 4.}$$
$$x = 12$$

4. INTERPRET.

Check: Check the solution in the stated problem. If the shorter piece of board is 12 inches, the longer piece is $3 \cdot (12 \text{ inches}) = 36$ inches and the sum of the two pieces is 12 inches + 36 inches = 48 inches.

State: The shorter piece of Balsa wood is 12 inches and the longer piece of Balsa wood is 36 inches.   □

▶ **Helpful Hint**

Make sure that units are included in your answer, if appropriate.

PRACTICE

3   A 45-inch board is to be cut into two pieces so that the longer piece is 4 times the shorter. Find the length of each piece.

EXAMPLE 4   Finding the Number of Democratic and Republican Representatives

In a recent year, the U.S. House of Representatives had a total of 435 Democrats and Republicans. There were 31 more Democratic representatives than Republican representatives. Find the number of representatives from each party. (*Source:* Office of the Clerk of the U.S. House of Representatives)

Solution

1. UNDERSTAND. Read and reread the problem. Let's suppose that there were 200 Republican representatives. Since there were 31 more Democrats than Republicans,

there must have been $200 + 31 = 231$ Democrats. The total number of Democrats and Republicans was then $200 + 231 = 431$. This is incorrect since the total should be 435, but now we have a better understanding of the problem.

In general, if we let

$$x = \text{number of Republicans, then}$$
$$x + 31 = \text{number of Democrats}$$

2. TRANSLATE. First we write the equation in words.

Number of Republicans	added to	number of Democrats	equals	435
↓	↓	↓	↓	↓
x	$+$	$(x + 31)$	$=$	435

3. SOLVE.

$$x + (x + 31) = 435$$
$$2x + 31 = 435$$
$$2x + 31 - 31 = 435 - 31$$
$$2x = 404$$
$$\frac{2x}{2} = \frac{404}{2}$$
$$x = 202$$

4. INTERPRET.

Check: If there were 202 Republican representatives, then there were $202 + 31 = 233$ Democratic representatives. The total number of Democratic or Republican representatives is $202 + 233 = 435$. The results check.

State: There were 202 Republican and 233 Democratic representatives in Congress. □

PRACTICE
4 In a recent year, there were 6 more Democratic State Governors than Republican State Governors. Find the number of State Governors from each party. (We are only counting the 50 states.) (*Source:* National Conference of State Legislatures).

△ **EXAMPLE 5** **Finding Angle Measures**

If the two walls of the Vietnam Veterans Memorial in Washington, D.C., were connected, an isosceles triangle would be formed. The measure of the third angle is 97.5° more than the measure of either of the other two equal angles. Find the measure of the third angle. (*Source:* National Park Service)

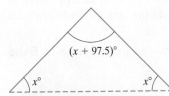

Solution

1. UNDERSTAND. Read and reread the problem. We then draw a diagram (recall that an isosceles triangle has two angles with the same measure) and let

$$x = \text{degree measure of one angle}$$
$$x = \text{degree measure of the second equal angle}$$
$$x + 97.5 = \text{degree measure of the third angle}$$

2. TRANSLATE. Recall that the sum of the measures of the angles of a triangle equals 180.

measure of first angle		measure of second angle		measure of third angle		equals		180
↓		↓		↓		↓		↓
x	$+$	x	$+$	$(x + 97.5)$		$=$		180

3. SOLVE.

$$x + x + (x + 97.5) = 180$$

$$3x + 97.5 = 180 \qquad \text{Combine like terms.}$$

$$3x + 97.5 - 97.5 = 180 - 97.5 \qquad \text{Subtract 97.5 from both sides.}$$

$$3x = 82.5$$

$$\frac{3x}{3} = \frac{82.5}{3} \qquad \text{Divide both sides by 3.}$$

$$x = 27.5$$

4. INTERPRET.

Check: If $x = 27.5$, then the measure of the third angle is $x + 97.5 = 125$. The sum of the angles is then $27.5 + 27.5 + 125 = 180$, the correct sum.

State: The third angle measures 125°.*   ☐

PRACTICE

5   The second angle of a triangle measures three times as large as the first. If the third angle measures 55° more than the first, find the measures of all three angles.

OBJECTIVE 3 ▶ Solving consecutive integer problems. The next example has to do with consecutive integers. Recall what we have learned thus far about these integers.

	Example	*General Representation*	
Consecutive Integers	11, 12, 13 ↳+1↗↳+1↗	Let x be an integer.	x, $x + 1$, $x + 2$ ↳+1↗↳+1↗
Consecutive Even Integers	38, 40, 42 ↳+2↗↳+2↗	Let x be an even integer.	x, $x + 2$, $x + 4$ ↳+2↗↳+2↗
Consecutive Odd Integers	57, 59, 61 ↳+2↗↳+2↗	Let x be an odd integer.	x, $x + 2$, $x + 4$ ↳+2↗↳+2↗

EXAMPLE 6   Some states have a single area code for the entire state. Two such states have area codes that are consecutive odd integers. If the sum of these integers is 1208, find the two area codes. (*Source:* North American Numbering Plan Administration)

Solution:

1. UNDERSTAND. Read and reread the problem. If we let

$$x = \text{the first odd integer, then}$$

$$x + 2 = \text{the next odd integer}$$

▶ **Helpful Hint**

Remember, the 2 here means that odd integers are 2 units apart, for example, the odd integers 13 and $13 + 2 = 15$.

*The two walls actually meet at an angle of 125 degrees 12 minutes. The measurement of 97.5° given in the problem is an approximation.

2. TRANSLATE.

first odd integer	the sum of	next odd integer	is	1208
↓	↓	↓	↓	↓
x	$+$	$(x + 2)$	$=$	1208

3. SOLVE.

$$x + x + 2 = 1208$$
$$2x + 2 = 1208$$
$$2x + 2 - 2 = 1208 - 2$$
$$2x = 1206$$
$$\frac{2x}{2} = \frac{1206}{2}$$
$$x = 603$$

4. INTERPRET.

Check: If $x = 603$, then the next odd integer $x + 2 = 603 + 2 = 605$. Notice their sum, $603 + 605 = 1208$, as needed.

State: The area codes are 603 and 605.

Note: New Hampshire's area code is 603 and South Dakota's area code is 605. ☐

PRACTICE
6 The sum of three-consecutive even integers is 144. Find the integers.

VOCABULARY & READINESS CHECK

Complete a Table. *Given the variable in the 1ˢᵗ column, use the phrase in the 2ⁿᵈ column to translate to an expression, then the phrase in the 3ʳᵈ column to translate to an expression.*

1.	A number: x	→	Double the number:	→	Double the number, decreased by 31:
2.	A number: x	→	Three times the number:	→	Three times the number, increased by 17:
3.	A number: x	→	The sum of the number and 5:	→	Twice the sum of the number and 5:
4.	A number: x	→	The difference of the number and 11:	→	Seven times the difference of a number and 11:
5.	A number: y	→	The difference of 20 and the number:	→	The difference of 20 and the number, divided by 3:
6.	A number: y	→	The sum of -10 and the number:	→	The sum of -10 and the number, divided by 9:

2.5 | EXERCISE SET

Write each of the following as equations. Then solve. See Examples 1 and 2.

1. The sum of twice a number, and 7, is equal to the sum of a number and 6. Find the number.

2. The difference of three times a number, and 1, is the same as twice a number. Find the number.

3. Three times a number, minus 6, is equal to two times a number, plus 8. Find the number.

4. The sum of 4 times a number, and −2, is equal to the sum of 5 times a number, and −2. Find the number.

5. Twice the difference of a number and 8 is equal to three times the sum of the number and 3. Find the number.

6. Five times the sum of a number and −1 is the same as 6 times the number. Find the number.

7. Four times the sum of −2 and a number is the same as five times the number increased by $\frac{1}{2}$. Find the number.

8. If the difference of a number and four is doubled, the result is $\frac{1}{4}$ less than the number. Find the number.

Solve. See Examples 3 through 5.

9. A 17-foot piece of string is cut into two pieces so that the longer piece is 2 feet longer than twice the shorter piece. Find the lengths of both pieces.

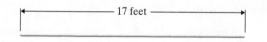

|← 17 feet →|

10. A 25-foot wire is to be cut so that the longer piece is one foot longer than 5 times the shorter piece. Find the length of each piece.

11. The largest meteorite in the world is the Hoba West located in Namibia. Its weight is 3 times the weight of the Armanty meteorite located in Outer Mongolia. If the sum of their weights is 88 tons, find the weight of each.

12. The area of the Sahara Desert is 7 times the area of the Gobi Desert. If the sum of their areas is 4,000,000 square miles, find the area of each desert.

13. The countries with the most cinema screens in the world are China and the United States. China has 5806 more cinema screens than the United States whereas the total screens for both countries is 78,994. Find the number of cinema screens for both countries. (*Source:* Film Distributor's Association)

14. The countries with the most television stations in the world are Russia and China. Russia has 4066 more television stations than China whereas the total stations for both countries is 10,546. Find the number of television stations for both countries. (*Source:* Central Intelligence Agency, *The World Factbook 2006*)

15. The flag of Equatorial Guinea contains an isosceles triangle. (Recall that an isosceles triangle contains two angles with the same measure.) If the measure of the third angle of the triangle is 30° more than twice the measure of either of the other two angles, find the measure of each angle of the triangle. (*Hint:* Recall that the sum of the measures of the angles of a triangle is 180°.)

16. Recall that the sum of the measures of the angles of a triangle is 180°. In the triangle below, angle *C* has the same measure as angle *B*, and angle *A* measures 42° less than angle *B*. Find the measure of each angle.

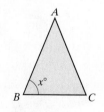

Complete a Table. *Most of the first row has been completed for you. See Example 6.*

	First Integer →	Next Integers		→	Indicated Sum
17. Three consecutive integers:	Integer: x	$x + 1$	$x + 2$		Sum of the three consecutive integers, simplified:
18. Three consecutive integers:	Integer: x				Sum of the second and third consecutive integers, simplified:
19. Three consecutive even integers:	Even integer: x				Sum of the first and third even consecutive integers, simplified:
20. Three consecutive odd integers:	Odd integer: x				Sum of the three consecutive odd integers, simplified:
21. Four consecutive integers:	Integer: x				Sum of the four consecutive integers, simplified:
22. Four consecutive integers:	Integer: x				Sum of the first and fourth consecutive integers, simplified:
23. Three consecutive odd integers:	Odd integer: x				Sum of the second and third consecutive odd integers, simplified:
24. Three consecutive even integers:	Even integer: x				Sum of the three consecutive even integers, simplified:

25. The left and right page numbers of an open book are two consecutive integers whose sum is 469. Find these page numbers.

26. The room numbers of two adjacent classrooms are two consecutive even numbers. If their sum is 654, find the classroom numbers.

27. To make an international telephone call, you need the code for the country you are calling. The codes for Belgium, France, and Spain are three consecutive integers whose sum is 99. Find the code for each country. (*Source: The World Almanac and Book of Facts, 2007*)

28. To make an international telephone call, you need the code for the country you are calling. The codes for Mali Republic, Côte d'Ivoire, and Niger are three consecutive odd integers whose sum is 675. Find the code for each country.

MIXED PRACTICE

Solve. See Examples 1 through 6.

29. A 25-inch piece of steel is cut into three pieces so that the second piece is twice as long as the first piece, and the third piece is one inch more than five times the length of the first piece. Find the lengths of the pieces.

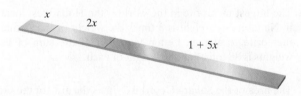

30. A 46-foot piece of rope is cut into three pieces so that the second piece is three times as long as the first piece, and the third piece is two feet more than seven times the length of the first piece. Find the lengths of the pieces.

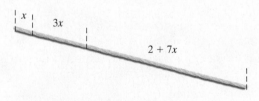

31. Five times a number, subtracted from ten, is triple the number. Find the number.

32. Nine is equal to ten subtracted from double a number. Find the number.

33. The greatest producer of diamonds in carats is Botswana. This country produces about four times the amount produced in Angola. If the total produced in both countries is 40,000,000 carats, find the amount produced in each country. (*Source: Diamond Facts 2006.*)

34. Beetles have the greatest number of different species. There are twenty times the number of beetle species as grasshopper species, and the total number of species for both is 420,000. Find the number of species for each type of insect.

 35. The measures of the angles of a triangle are 3 consecutive even integers. Find the measure of each angle.

36. A quadrilateral is a polygon with 4 sides. The sum of the measures of the 4 angles in a quadrilateral is 360°. If the measures of the angles of a quadrilateral are consecutive odd integers, find the measures.

37. For the 2006 Winter Olympics, the total number of medals won by athletes in each of the countries of Russia, Austria, Canada, and the United States are four consecutive integers whose sum is 94. Find the number of medals for each country.

38. The code to unlock a student's combination lock happens to be three consecutive odd integers whose sum is 51. Find the integers.

39. If the sum of a number and five is tripled, the result is one less than twice the number. Find the number.

40. Twice the sum of a number and six equals three times the sum of the number and four. Find the number.

41. In a recent election in Illinois for a seat in the United States House of Representatives, Jerry Weller received 20,196 more votes than opponent John Pavich. If the total number of votes was 196,554, find the number of votes for each candidate. (*Source: The Washington Post*)

42. In a recent election in New York for a seat in the United States House of Representatives, Timothy Bishop received 35,650 more votes than opponent Italo Zanzi. If the total number of votes was 158,192, find the number of votes for each candidate. (*Source: The New York Times*)

43. Two angles are supplementary if their sum is 180°. The larger angle measures eight degree more than three times the measure of a smaller angle. If x represents the measure of the smaller angle and these two angles are supplementary, find the measure of each angle.

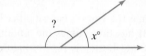

44. Two angles are complementary if their sum is 90°. The larger angle measures three degrees less than twice the measure of a smaller angle. If x represents the measure of the smaller angle and these two angles are complementary, find the measure of each angle.

45. If the quotient of a number and 4 is added to $\frac{1}{2}$, the result is $\frac{3}{4}$. Find the number.

46. If $\frac{3}{4}$ is added to three times a number, the result is $\frac{1}{2}$ subtracted from twice the number. Find the number.

47. The flag of Brazil contains a parallelogram. One angle of the parallelogram is 15° less than twice the measure of the angle next to it. Find the measure of each angle of the parallelogram. (*Hint:* Recall that opposite angles of a parallelogram have the same measure and that the sum of the measures of the angles is 360°.)

48. The sum of the measures of the angles of a parallelogram is 360°. In the parallelogram below, angles A and D have the same measure as well as angles C and B. If the measure of angle C is twice the measure of angle A, find the measure of each angle.

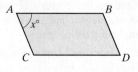

49. Currently, the two fastest trains are the Japanese Maglev and the French TGV. The sum of their fastest speeds is 718.2 miles per hour. If the speed of the Maglev is 3.8 mph faster than the speed of the TGV, find the speeds of each.

50. The Pentagon is the world's largest office building in terms of floor space. It has three times the amount of floor space as the Empire State Building. If the total floor space for these two buildings is approximately 8700 thousand square feet, find the floor space of each building.

51. One-third of a number is five-sixths. Find the number.

52. Seven-eighths of a number is one-half. Find the number.

53. The number of counties in California and the number of counties in Montana are consecutive even integers whose sum is 114. If California has more counties than Montana, how many counties does each state have? (*Source: The World Almanac and Book of Facts 2007*)

54. A student is building a bookcase with stepped shelves for her dorm room. She buys a 48-inch board and wants to cut the board into three pieces with lengths equal to three consecutive even integers. Find the three board lengths.

55. In Super Bowl XLI in Miami, Florida, the Indianapolis Colts won over the Chicago Bears with a 12-point lead. If the total of the two scores was 46, find the individual team scores. (*Source:* National Football League)

56. During the 2007 Rose Bowl, University of Southern California beat Michigan by 14 points. If their combined scores total 50, find the individual team scores. (*Source: ESPN Sports Almanac*)

57. A geodesic dome, based on the design by Buckminster Fuller, is composed of two different types of triangular panels. One of these is an isosceles triangle. In one geodesic dome, the measure of the third angle is 76.5° more than the measure of either of the two equal angles. Find the measure of the third angle. (*Source:* Buckminster Fuller Institute)

58. The measures of the angles of a particular triangle are such that the second and third angles are each four times larger than the smallest angle. Find the measures of the angles of this triangle.

59. A 40-inch board is to be cut into three pieces so that the second piece is twice as long as the first piece and the third piece is 5 times as long as the first piece. If x represents the length of the first piece, find the lengths of all three pieces.

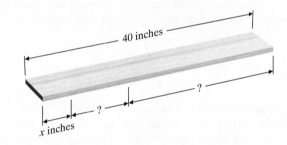

60. A 30-foot piece of siding is cut into three pieces so that the second piece is four times as long as the first piece and the third piece is five times as long as the first piece. If x represents the length of the first piece, find the lengths of all three pieces.

The graph below shows the states with the highest tourism budgets. Use the graph for Exercises 61 through 66.

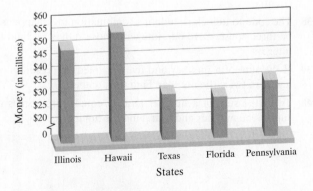

Source: Travel Industry Association

61. Which state spends the most money on tourism?

62. Which states spend between $30 and $40 million on tourism?

63. The states of Texas and Florida spend a total of $60.5 million for tourism. The state of Texas spends $1.7 million more than the state of Florida. Find the amount that each state spends on tourism.

64. The states of Hawaii and Pennsylvania spend a total of $91.1 million for tourism. The state of Hawaii spends $14.2 million less than twice the amount of money that the state of Pennsylvania spends. Find the amount that each state spends   on   tourism.

Compare the heights of the bars in the graph with your results of the exercises below. Are your answers reasonable?

65. Exercise 63

66. Exercise 64

REVIEW AND PREVIEW

Evaluate each expression for the given values. See Section 1.4.

67. $2W + 2L$; $W = 7$ and $L = 10$

68. $\frac{1}{2}Bh$; $B = 14$ and $h = 22$

69. πr^2; $r = 15$ **70.** $r \cdot t$; $r = 15$ and $t = 2$

CONCEPT EXTENSIONS

71. In your own words, explain why a solution of a word problem should be checked using the original wording of the problem and not the equation written from the wording.

72. Give an example of how you recently solved a problem using mathematics.

2.6 FORMULAS AND PROBLEM SOLVING

OBJECTIVES

1 Use formulas to solve problems.

2 Solve a formula or equation for one of its variables.

OBJECTIVE 1 ▶ Using formulas to solve problems. An equation that describes a known relationship among quantities, such as distance, time, volume, weight, and money is called a **formula.** These quantities are represented by letters and are thus variables of the formula. Here are some common formulas and their meanings.

Formulas and Their Meanings

$A = lw$
Area of a rectangle = length · width

$I = PRT$
Simple interest = principal · rate · time

$P = a + b + c$
Perimeter of a triangle = side a + side b + side c

$d = rt$
distance = rate · time

$V = lwh$
Volume of a rectangular solid = length · width · height

$F = \left(\frac{9}{5}\right)C + 32$ or $F = 1.8C + 32$

degrees Fahrenheit = $\left(\frac{9}{5}\right) \cdot$ degrees Celsius + 32

Formulas are valuable tools because they allow us to calculate measurements as long as we know certain other measurements. For example, if we know we traveled a distance of 100 miles at a rate of 40 miles per hour, we can replace the variables d and r in the formula $d = rt$ and find our time, t.

$d = rt$ Formula.

$100 = 40t$ Replace d with 100 and r with 40.

This is a linear equation in one variable, t. To solve for t, divide both sides of the equation by 40.

$$\frac{100}{40} = \frac{40t}{40} \quad \text{Divide both sides by 40.}$$

$$\frac{5}{2} = t \quad \text{Simplify.}$$

The time traveled is $\frac{5}{2}$ hours or $2\frac{1}{2}$ hours.

In this section we solve problems that can be modeled by known formulas. We use the same problem-solving steps that were introduced in the previous section. These steps have been slightly revised to include formulas.

EXAMPLE 1 Finding Time Given Rate and Distance

A glacier is a giant mass of rocks and ice that flows downhill like a river. Portage Glacier in Alaska is about 6 miles, or 31,680 *feet,* long and moves 400 *feet* per year. Icebergs are created when the front end of the glacier flows into Portage Lake. How long does it take for ice at the head (beginning) of the glacier to reach the lake?

Solution

1. UNDERSTAND. Read and reread the problem. The appropriate formula needed to solve this problem is the distance formula, $d = rt$. To become familiar with this formula, let's find the distance that ice traveling at a rate of 400 feet per year travels in 100 years. To do so, we let time t be 100 years and rate r be the given 400 feet per year, and substitute these values into the formula $d = rt$. We then have that distance $d = 400(100) = 40,000$ feet. Since we are interested in finding how long it takes ice to travel 31,680 feet, we now know that it is less than 100 years.

   Since we are using the formula $d = rt$, we let

   t = the time in years for ice to reach the lake

   r = rate or speed of ice

   d = distance from beginning of glacier to lake

2. TRANSLATE. To translate to an equation, we use the formula $d = rt$ and let distance $d = 31,680$ feet and rate $r = 400$ feet per year.

$$d = r \cdot t$$
$$31,680 = 400 \cdot t \quad \text{Let } d = 31,680 \text{ and } r = 400.$$

3. SOLVE. Solve the equation for t. To solve for t, divide both sides by 400.

$$\frac{31,680}{400} = \frac{400 \cdot t}{400} \quad \text{Divide both sides by 400.}$$

$$79.2 = t \quad \text{Simplify.}$$

4. INTERPRET.

Check: To check, substitute 79.2 for t and 400 for r in the distance formula and check to see that the distance is 31,680 feet.

State: It takes 79.2 years for the ice at the head of Portage Glacier to reach the lake. □

> ▶ **Helpful Hint**
> Don't forget to include units, if appropriate.

PRACTICE

1 The Stromboli Volcano, in Italy, began erupting in 2002, after a dormant period of over 17 years. In 2007, a vulcanologist measured the lava flow to be moving at 5 meters/second. If the path the lava followed to the sea is 580 meters long, how long does it take the lava to reach the sea? (*Source:* Thorsten Boeckel and CNN)

⚠️ **EXAMPLE 2**   **Calculating the Length of a Garden**

Charles Pecot can afford enough fencing to enclose a rectangular garden with a perimeter of 140 feet. If the width of his garden must be 30 feet, find the length.

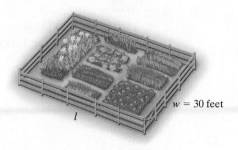

$w = 30$ feet

l

Solution

1. UNDERSTAND. Read and reread the problem. The formula needed to solve this problem is the formula for the perimeter of a rectangle, $P = 2l + 2w$. Before continuing, let's become familiar with this formula.

l = the length of the rectangular garden

w = the width of the rectangular garden

P = perimeter of the garden

2. TRANSLATE. To translate to an equation, we use the formula $P = 2l + 2w$ and let perimeter $P = 140$ feet and width $w = 30$ feet.

$$P = 2l + 2w$$
$$\downarrow \qquad\qquad \searrow$$
$$140 = 2l + 2(30) \quad \text{Let } P = 140 \text{ and } w = 30.$$

3. SOLVE.

$$140 = 2l + 2(30)$$
$$140 = 2l + 60 \qquad\qquad \text{Multiply } 2(30).$$
$$140 - 60 = 2l + 60 - 60 \qquad \text{Subtract 60 from both sides.}$$
$$80 = 2l \qquad\qquad\qquad \text{Combine like terms.}$$
$$40 = l \qquad\qquad\qquad \text{Divide both sides by 2.}$$

4. INTERPRET.

Check: Substitute 40 for l and 30 for w in the perimeter formula and check to see that the perimeter is 140 feet.

State: The length of the rectangular garden is 40 feet.   □

PRACTICE

2   Evelyn Gryk fenced in part of her back yard for a dog run. The dog run was 40 feet in length and used 98 feet of fencing. Find the width of the dog run.

EXAMPLE 3 Finding an Equivalent Temperature

The average minimum temperature for July in Shanghai, China, is 77° Fahrenheit. Find the equivalent temperature in degrees Celsius.

Solution

1. UNDERSTAND. Read and reread the problem. A formula that can be used to solve this problem is the formula for converting degrees Celsius to degrees Fahrenheit, $F = \frac{9}{5}C + 32$. Before continuing, become familiar with this formula. Using this formula, we let

$$C = \text{temperature in degrees Celsius, and}$$
$$F = \text{temperature in degrees Fahrenheit.}$$

2. TRANSLATE. To translate to an equation, we use the formula $F = \frac{9}{5}C + 32$ and let degrees Fahrenheit $F = 77$.

$$\text{Formula:} \quad F = \frac{9}{5}C + 32$$
$$\text{Substitute:} \quad 77 = \frac{9}{5}C + 32 \quad \text{Let } F = 77.$$

3. SOLVE.

$$77 = \frac{9}{5}C + 32$$
$$77 - 32 = \frac{9}{5}C + 32 - 32 \quad \text{Subtract 32 from both sides.}$$
$$45 = \frac{9}{5}C \quad \text{Combine like terms.}$$
$$\frac{5}{9} \cdot 45 = \frac{5}{9} \cdot \frac{9}{5}C \quad \text{Multiply both sides by } \frac{5}{9}.$$
$$25 = C \quad \text{Simplify.}$$

4. INTERPRET.

Check: To check, replace C with 25 and F with 77 in the formula and see that a true statement results.

State: Thus, 77° Fahrenheit is equivalent to 25° Celsius.

Note: There is a formula for directly converting degrees Fahrenheit to degrees Celsius. It is $C = \frac{5}{9}(F - 32)$, as we shall see in Example 8. □

PRACTICE
3 The average minimum temperature for July in Sydney, Australia, is 8° Celsius. Find the equivalent temperature in degrees Fahrenheit.

In the next example, we again use the formula for perimeter of a rectangle as in Example 2. In Example 2, we knew the width of the rectangle. In this example, both the length and width are unknown.

⚠ **EXAMPLE 4**   **Finding Road Sign Dimensions**

The length of a rectangular road sign is 2 feet less than three times its width. Find the dimensions if the perimeter is 28 feet.

5 feet

13 feet

Solution

1. **UNDERSTAND.** Read and reread the problem. Recall that the formula for the perimeter of a rectangle is $P = 2l + 2w$. Draw a rectangle and guess the solution. If the width of the rectangular sign is 5 feet, its length is 2 feet less than 3 times the width or 3(5 feet) − 2 feet = 13 feet. The perimeter P of the rectangle is then 2(13 feet) + 2(5 feet) = 36 feet, too much. We now know that the width is less than 5 feet.

Let

w = the width of the rectangular sign; then

$3w - 2$ = the length of the sign.

Draw a rectangle and label it with the assigned variables.

2. **TRANSLATE.**

Formula: $P = 2l + 2w$ or

Substitute: $28 = 2(3w - 2) + 2w$.

3. **SOLVE.**

$$28 = 2(3w - 2) + 2w$$
$$28 = 6w - 4 + 2w \qquad \text{Apply the distributive property.}$$
$$28 = 8w - 4$$
$$28 + 4 = 8w - 4 + 4 \qquad \text{Add 4 to both sides.}$$
$$32 = 8w$$
$$\frac{32}{8} = \frac{8w}{8} \qquad \text{Divide both sides by 8.}$$
$$4 = w$$

4. **INTERPRET.**

Check: If the width of the sign is 4 feet, the length of the sign is 3(4 feet) − 2 feet = 10 feet. This gives a perimeter of $P = 2(4 \text{ feet}) + 2(10 \text{ feet}) = 28$ feet, the correct perimeter.

State: The width of the sign is 4 feet and the length of the sign is 10 feet.   □

PRACTICE

4   The new street signs along Route 114 have a length that is 3 inches more than 5 times the width. Find the dimensions of the signs if the perimeter of the signs is 66 inches.

OBJECTIVE 2 ▶ **Solving a formula for one of its variables.** We say that the formula $F = \frac{9}{5}C + 32$ is solved for F because F is alone on one side of the equation and the other side of the equation contains no F's. Suppose that we need to convert many Fahrenheit temperatures to equivalent degrees Celsius. In this case, it is easier to perform this task by solving the formula $F = \frac{9}{5}C + 32$ for C. (See Example 8.) For this reason, it is important to be able to solve an equation for any one of its specified variables. For example, the formula $d = rt$ is solved for d in terms of r and t. We can also solve $d = rt$ for t in terms of d and r. To solve for t, divide both sides of the equation by r.

$$d = rt$$
$$\frac{d}{r} = \frac{rt}{r} \quad \text{Divide both sides by } r.$$
$$\frac{d}{r} = t \quad \text{Simplify.}$$

To solve a formula or an equation for a specified variable, we use the same steps as for solving a linear equation. These steps are listed next.

Solving Equations for a Specified Variable

STEP 1. Multiply on both sides to clear the equation of fractions if they occur.

STEP 2. Use the distributive property to remove parentheses if they occur.

STEP 3. Simplify each side of the equation by combining like terms.

STEP 4. Get all terms containing the specified variable on one side and all other terms on the other side by using the addition property of equality.

STEP 5. Get the specified variable alone by using the multiplication property of equality.

△ **EXAMPLE 5** Solve $V = lwh$ for l.

Solution This formula is used to find the volume of a box. To solve for l, divide both sides by wh.

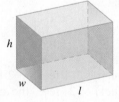

$$V = lwh$$
$$\frac{V}{wh} = \frac{lwh}{wh} \quad \text{Divide both sides by } wh.$$
$$\frac{V}{wh} = l \quad \text{Simplify.}$$

Since we have l alone on one side of the equation, we have solved for l in terms of V, w, and h. Remember that it does not matter on which side of the equation we isolate the variable. □

PRACTICE
5 Solve $I = Prt$ for r.

EXAMPLE 6 Solve $y = mx + b$ for x.

Solution The term containing the variable we are solving for, mx, is on the right side of the equation. Get mx alone by subtracting b from both sides.

$$y = mx + b$$
$$y - b = mx + b - b \quad \text{Subtract } b \text{ from both sides.}$$
$$y - b = mx \quad \text{Combine like terms.}$$

Next, solve for x by dividing both sides by m.

$$\frac{y - b}{m} = \frac{mx}{m}$$

$$\frac{y - b}{m} = x \qquad \text{Simplify.} \qquad \square$$

PRACTICE
6   Solve $H = 5as + 10a$ for s.

Concept Check ☑

Solve:

a. ⬤ = ▢ − ▢ for ▢   **b.** ⬤ = ▢ · ▲ − ▢ for ▢

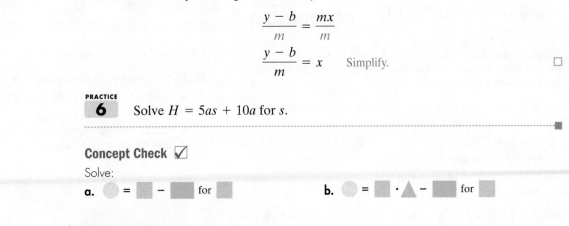

EXAMPLE 7   Solve $P = 2l + 2w$ for w.

Solution   This formula relates the perimeter of a rectangle to its length and width. Find the term containing the variable w. To get this term, $2w$, alone subtract $2l$ from both sides.

▶ **Helpful Hint**

The 2's may *not* be divided out here. Although 2 is a factor of the denominator, 2 is *not* a factor of the numerator since it is not a factor of both terms in the numerator.

$$P = 2l + 2w$$
$$P - 2l = 2l + 2w - 2l \qquad \text{Subtract } 2l \text{ from both sides.}$$
$$P - 2l = 2w \qquad \text{Combine like terms.}$$
$$\frac{P - 2l}{2} = \frac{2w}{2} \qquad \text{Divide both sides by 2.}$$
$$\frac{P - 2l}{2} = w \qquad \text{Simplify.} \qquad \square$$

PRACTICE
7   Solve $N = F + d(n - 1)$ for d.

The next example has an equation containing a fraction. We will first clear the equation of fractions and then solve for the specified variable.

EXAMPLE 8   Solve $F = \frac{9}{5}C + 32$ for C.

Solution

$$F = \frac{9}{5}C + 32$$

$$5(F) = 5\left(\frac{9}{5}C + 32\right) \qquad \text{Clear the fraction by multiplying both sides by the LCD.}$$

$$5F = 9C + 160 \qquad \text{Distribute the 5.}$$

$$5F - 160 = 9C + 160 - 160 \qquad \text{To get the term containing the variable } C \text{ alone, subtract 160 from both sides.}$$

$$5F - 160 = 9C \qquad \text{Combine like terms.}$$

$$\frac{5F - 160}{9} = \frac{9C}{9} \qquad \text{Divide both sides by 9.}$$

$$\frac{5F - 160}{9} = C \qquad \text{Simplify.}$$

Note: Another equivalent way to write this formula is $C = \frac{5}{9}(F - 32)$. $\qquad \square$

Answers to Concept Check:

a. ⬤ + ▢   **b.** $\dfrac{⬤ + ▢}{▲}$

PRACTICE
8   Solve $A = \frac{1}{2}a(b + B)$ for B.

2.6 | EXERCISE SET

PRACTICE   WATCH   DOWNLOAD   READ   REVIEW

Substitute the given values into each given formula and solve for the unknown variable. If necessary, round to one decimal place. See Examples 1 through 3.

△ **1.** $A = bh$; $A = 45, b = 15$ (Area of a parallelogram)

2. $d = rt$; $d = 195, t = 3$ (Distance formula)

△ **3.** $S = 4lw + 2wh$; $S = 102, l = 7, w = 3$ (Surface area of a special rectangular box)

△ **4.** $V = lwh$; $l = 14, w = 8, h = 3$ (Volume of a rectangular box)

△ **5.** $A = \frac{1}{2}h(B + b)$; $A = 180, B = 11, b = 7$ (Area of a trapezoid)

△ **6.** $A = \frac{1}{2}h(B + b)$; $A = 60, B = 7, b = 3$ (Area of a trapezoid)

△ **7.** $P = a + b + c$; $P = 30, a = 8, b = 10$ (Perimeter of a triangle)

△ **8.** $V = \frac{1}{3}Ah$; $V = 45, h = 5$ (Volume of a pyramid)

9. $C = 2\pi r$; $C = 15.7$ (use the approximation 3.14 or a calculator approximation for π) (Circumference of a circle)

10. $A = \pi r^2$; $r = 4.5$ (use the approximation 3.14 or a calculator approximation for π) (Area of a circle)

11. $I = PRT$; $I = 3750, P = 25,000, R = 0.05$ (Simple interest formula)

12. $I = PRT$; $I = 1,056,000, R = 0.055, T = 6$ (Simple interest formula)

13. $V = \frac{1}{3}\pi r^2 h$; $V = 565.2, r = 6$ (use a calculator approximation for π) (Volume of a cone)

14. $V = \frac{4}{3}\pi r^3$; $r = 3$ (use a calculator approximation for π) (Volume of a sphere)

Solve each formula for the specified variable. See Examples 5 through 8.

15. $f = 5gh$ for h

16. $A = \pi ab$ for b

17. $V = lwh$ for w

18. $T = mnr$ for n

19. $3x + y = 7$ for y

20. $-x + y = 13$ for y

21. $A = P + PRT$ for R

22. $A = P + PRT$ for T

23. $V = \frac{1}{3}Ah$ for A

24. $D = \frac{1}{4}fk$ for k

25. $P = a + b + c$ for a

26. $PR = x + y + z + w$ for z

27. $S = 2\pi rh + 2\pi r^2$ for h

△ **28.** $S = 4lw + 2wh$ for h

Solve. See Examples 1 through 4.

29. For the purpose of purchasing new baseboard and carpet,

  a. Find the area and perimeter of the room below (neglecting doors).

  b. Identify whether baseboard has to do with area or perimeter and the same with carpet.

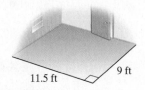

11.5 ft   9 ft

30. For the purpose of purchasing lumber for a new fence and seed to plant grass,

  a. Find the area and perimeter of the yard below.

  b. Identify whether a fence has to do with area or perimeter and the same with grass seed.

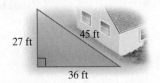

27 ft   45 ft

36 ft

31. A frame shop charges according to both the amount of framing needed to surround the picture and the amount of glass needed to cover the picture.

  a. Find the area and perimeter of the trapezoid-shaped framed picture below.

  b. Identify whether the amount of framing has to do with perimeter or area and the same with the amount of glass.

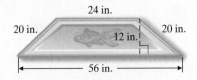

24 in.

20 in.   20 in.

12 in.

56 in.

32. A decorator is painting and placing a border completely around the parallelogram-shaped wall.

  a. Find the area and perimeter of the wall below.

  b. Identify whether the border has to do with perimeter or area and the same with paint.

11.7 ft

7 ft

9.3 ft

33. The world's largest pink ribbon, the sign of the fight against breast cancer, was erected out of pink post-it notes on a billboard in New York City in October, 2004. If the area of the rectangular billboard covered by the ribbon is approximately 3990 square feet, and the width of the billboard was approximately 57 feet, what was the height of this billboard?

△ **34.** The world's largest sign for Coca-Cola is located in Arica, Chile. The rectangular sign has a length of 400 feet and has an area of 52,400 square feet. Find the width of the sign. (*Source: Fabulous Facts about Coca-Cola, Atlanta, GA*)

35. Convert Nome, Alaska's 14°F high temperature to Celsius.

36. Convert Paris, France's low temperature of −5°C to Fahrenheit.

37. The X-30 is a "space plane" that skims the edge of space at 4000 miles per hour. Neglecting altitude, if the circumference of the Earth is approximately 25,000 miles, how long will it take for the X-30 to travel around the Earth?

38. In the United States, a notable hang glider flight was a 303-mile, $8\frac{1}{2}$ hour flight from New Mexico to Kansas. What was the average rate during this flight?

△ **39.** An architect designs a rectangular flower garden such that the width is exactly two-thirds of the length. If 260 feet of antique picket fencing are to be used to enclose the garden, find the dimensions of the garden.

x feet

△ **40.** If the length of a rectangular parking lot is 10 meters less than twice its width, and the perimeter is 400 meters, find the length of the parking lot.

x meters

△ **41.** A flower bed is in the shape of a triangle with one side twice the length of the shortest side, and the third side is 30 feet more than the length of the shortest side. Find the dimensions if the perimeter is 102 feet.

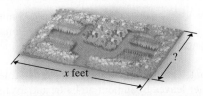

△ **42.** The perimeter of a yield sign in the shape of an isosceles triangle is 22 feet. If the shortest side is 2 feet less than the other two sides, find the length of the shortest side. (*Hint:* An isosceles triangle has two sides the same length.)

x feet   *x* feet

43. The Cat is a high-speed catamaran auto ferry that operates between Bar Harbor, Maine, and Yarmouth, Nova Scotia. The Cat can make the 138-mile trip in about $2\frac{1}{2}$ hours. Find the catamaran speed for this trip. (*Source:* Bay Ferries)

44. A family is planning their vacation to Disney World. They will drive from a small town outside New Orleans, Louisiana, to Orlando, Florida, a distance of 700 miles. They plan to average a rate of 55 mph. How long will this trip take?

△ **45.** Piranha fish require 1.5 cubic feet of water per fish to maintain a healthy environment. Find the maximum number of piranhas you could put in a tank measuring 8 feet by 3 feet by 6 feet.

6 feet

3 feet   8 feet

△ **46.** Find the maximum number of goldfish you can put in a cylindrical tank whose diameter is 8 meters and whose height is 3 meters if each goldfish needs 2 cubic meters of water.

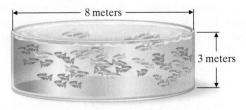

8 meters

3 meters

△ **47.** A lawn is in the shape of a trapezoid with a height of 60 feet and bases of 70 feet and 130 feet. How many whole bags of fertilizer must be purchased to cover the lawn if each bag covers 4000 square feet?

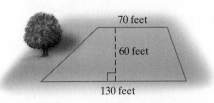

70 feet

60 feet

130 feet

△ **48.** If the area of a right-triangularly shaped sail is 20 square feet and its base is 5 feet, find the height of the sail.

△ **49.** Maria's Pizza sells one 16-inch cheese pizza or two 10-inch cheese pizzas for $9.99. Determine which size gives more pizza.

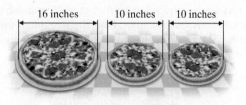

△ **50.** Find how much rope is needed to wrap around the Earth at the equator, if the radius of the Earth is 4000 miles. (*Hint:* Use 3.14 for π and the formula for circumference.)

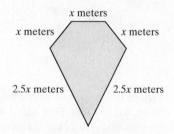

△ **51.** The perimeter of a geometric figure is the sum of the lengths of its sides. If the perimeter of the following pentagon (five-sided figure) is 48 meters, find the length of each side.

x meters

x meters x meters

2.5x meters   2.5x meters

△ **52.** The perimeter of the following triangle is 82 feet. Find the length of each side.

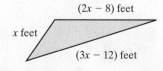

$(2x - 8)$ feet

x feet

$(3x - 12)$ feet

53. A Japanese "bullet" train set a new world record for train speed at 361 miles per hour during a manned test run on the Yamanashi Maglev Test Line in 2003. How long does it take this train to travel 72.2 miles at this speed? Give the result in hours; then convert to minutes.

54. In 1983, the Hawaiian volcano Kilauea began erupting in a series of episodes still occurring at the time of this writing. At times, the lava flows advanced at speeds of up to 0.5 kilometer per hour. In 1983 and 1984 lava flows destroyed 16 homes in the Royal Gardens subdivision, about 6 km away from the eruption site. Roughly how long did it take the lava to reach Royal Gardens? Assume that the lava traveled at its fastest rate, 0.5 kph. (*Source:* U.S. Geological Survey Hawaiian Volcano Observatory)

△ **55.** The perimeter of an equilateral triangle is 7 inches more than the perimeter of a square, and the side of the triangle is 5 inches longer than the side of the square. Find the side of the triangle. (*Hint:* An equilateral triangle has three sides the same length.)

△ **56.** A square animal pen and a pen shaped like an equilateral triangle have equal perimeters. Find the length of the sides of each pen if the sides of the triangular pen are fifteen less than twice a side of the square pen.

57. Find how long it takes a person to drive 135 miles on I-10 if she merges onto I-10 at 10 a.m. and drives nonstop with her cruise control set on 60 mph.

58. Beaumont, Texas, is about 150 miles from Toledo Bend. If Leo Miller leaves Beaumont at 4 a.m. and averages 45 mph, when should he arrive at Toledo Bend?

△ **59.** The longest runway at Los Angeles International Airport has the shape of a rectangle and an area of 1,813,500 square feet. This runway is 150 feet wide. How long is the runway? (*Source:* Los Angeles World Airports)

60. Normal room temperature is about 78°F. Convert this temperature to Celsius.

61. The highest temperature ever recorded in Europe was 122°F in Seville, Spain, in August of 1881. Convert this record high temperature to Celsius. (*Source:* National Climatic Data Center)

62. The lowest temperature ever recorded in Oceania was −10°C at the Haleakala Summit in Maui, Hawaii, in January 1961. Convert this record low temperature to Fahrenheit. (*Source:* National Climatic Data Center)

△ **63.** The CART FedEx Championship Series is an open-wheeled race car competition based in the United States. A CART car has a maximum length of 199 inches, a maximum width of 78.5 inches, and a maximum height of 33 inches. When the CART series travels to another country for a grand prix, teams must ship their cars. Find the volume of the smallest shipping crate needed to ship a CART car of maximum dimensions. (*Source:* Championship Auto Racing Teams, Inc.)

CART Racing Car

Max. height = 33 inches

Max. length = 199 inches

Max. width = 78.5 inches

64. On a road course, a CART car's speed can average up to around 105 mph. Based on this speed, how long would it take a CART driver to travel from Los Angeles to New York City, a distance of about 2810 miles by road, without stopping? Round to the nearest tenth of an hour.

65. The Hoberman Sphere is a toy ball that expands and contracts. When it is completely closed, it has a diameter of 9.5 inches. Find the volume of the Hoberman Sphere when it is completely closed. Use 3.14 for π. Round to the nearest whole cubic inch. (*Source:* Hoberman Designs, Inc.)

66. When the Hoberman Sphere (see Exercise 65) is completely expanded, its diameter is 30 inches. Find the volume of the Hoberman Sphere when it is completely expanded. Use 3.14 for π. Round to the nearest whole cubic inch. (*Source:* Hoberman Designs, Inc.)

67. The average temperature on the planet Mercury is 167°C. Convert this temperature to degrees Fahrenheit. (*Source:* National Space Science Data Center)

68. The average temperature on the planet Jupiter is −227°F. Convert this temperature to degrees Celsius. Round to the nearest degree. (*Source:* National Space Science Data Center)

REVIEW AND PREVIEW

Write the following phrases as algebraic expressions. See Section 2.1.

69. Nine divided by the sum of a number and 5

70. Half the product of a number and five

71. Three times the sum of a number and four

72. Double the sum of ten and four times a number

73. Triple the difference of a number and twelve

74. A number minus the sum of the number and six

CONCEPT EXTENSIONS

Solve. See the Concept Check in this section.

75. ■ − ● · ■ = ▲ for ●

76. ◆ · ■ + ▲ = ● for ■

77. Dry ice is a name given to solidified carbon dioxide. At −78.5° Celsius it changes directly from a solid to a gas. Convert this temperature to Fahrenheit.

78. Lightning bolts can reach a temperature of 50,000° Fahrenheit. Convert this temperature to Celsius.

79. The distance from the sun to the Earth is approximately 93,000,000 miles. If light travels at a rate of 186,000 miles per second, how long does it take light from the sun to reach us?

80. Light travels at a rate of 186,000 miles per second. If our moon is 238,860 miles from the Earth, how long does it take light from the moon to reach us? (Round to the nearest tenth of a second.)

238,860 miles

81. A glacier is a giant mass of rocks and ice that flows downhill like a river. Exit Glacier, near Seward, Alaska, moves at a rate of 20 inches a day. Find the distance in feet the glacier moves in a year. (Assume 365 days a year. Round to 2 decimal places.)

82. Flying fish do not *actually* fly, but glide. They have been known to travel a distance of 1300 feet at a rate of 20 miles per hour. How many seconds did it take to travel this distance? (*Hint:* First convert miles per hour to feet per second. Recall that 1 mile = 5280 feet. Round to the nearest tenth of a second.)

83. Stalactites join stalagmites to form columns. A column found at Natural Bridge Caverns near San Antonio, Texas, rises 15 feet and has a *diameter* of only 2 inches. Find the volume of this column in cubic inches. (*Hint:* Use the formula for volume of a cylinder and use a calculator approximation for π. Round to the nearest tenth of an inch.)

84. Find the temperature at which the Celsius measurement and Fahrenheit measurement are the same number.

85. The formula $A = bh$ is used to find the area of a parallelogram. If the base of a parallelogram is doubled and its height is doubled, how does this affect the area?

86. The formula $V = LWH$ is used to find the volume of a box. If the length of a box is doubled, the width is doubled, and the height is doubled, how does this affect the volume?

2.7 PERCENT AND PROBLEM SOLVING

OBJECTIVES

1 Solve percent equations.

2 Solve discount and mark-up problems.

3 Solve percent increase and percent decrease problems.

This section is devoted to solving problems in the categories listed. The same problem-solving steps used in previous sections are also followed in this section. They are listed below for review.

General Strategy for Problem Solving

1. UNDERSTAND the problem. During this step, become comfortable with the problem. Some ways of doing this are as follows:

   Read and reread the problem.

   Choose a variable to represent the unknown.

   Construct a drawing, whenever possible.

   Propose a solution and check. Pay careful attention to how you check your proposed solution. This will help writing an equation to model the problem.

2. TRANSLATE the problem into an equation.

3. SOLVE the equation.

4. INTERPRET the results: *Check* the proposed solution in the stated problem and *state* your conclusion.

OBJECTIVE 1 ▶ Solving percent equations. Many of today's statistics are given in terms of percent: a basketball player's free throw percent, current interest rates, stock market trends, and nutrition labeling, just to name a few. In this section, we first explore percent, percent equations, and applications involving percents. See Appendix F.2 if a further review of percents is needed.

EXAMPLE 1 The number 63 is what percent of 72?

Solution

1. UNDERSTAND. Read and reread the problem. Next, let's suppose that the percent is 80%. To check, we find 80% of 72.

$$80\% \text{ of } 72 = 0.80(72) = 57.6$$

This is close, but not 63. At this point, though, we have a better understanding of the problem, we know the correct answer is close to and greater than 80%, and we know how to check our proposed solution later.

Let x = the unknown percent.

2. TRANSLATE. Recall that "is" means "equals" and "of" signifies multiplying. Let's translate the sentence directly.

the number 63	is	what percent	of	72
↓	↓	↓	↓	↓
63	=	x	·	72

3. SOLVE.

$$63 = 72x$$
$$0.875 = x \quad \text{Divide both sides by 72.}$$
$$87.5\% = x \quad \text{Write as a percent.}$$

4. INTERPRET.

Check: Verify that 87.5% of 72 is 63.

State: The number 63 is 87.5% of 72.   □

PRACTICE
1   The number 35 is what percent of 56?

EXAMPLE 2   The number 120 is 15% of what number?

Solution

1. UNDERSTAND. Read and reread the problem.

Let x = the unknown number.

2. TRANSLATE.

the number 120	is	15%	of	what number
↓	↓	↓	↓	↓
120	=	15%	·	x

3. SOLVE.

$$120 = 0.15x \quad \text{Write 15\% as 0.15.}$$
$$800 = x \quad \text{Divide both sides by 0.15.}$$

4. INTERPRET.

Check: Check the proposed solution by finding 15% of 800 and verifying that the result is 120.

State: Thus, 120 is 15% of 800.   □

PRACTICE
2   The number 198 is 55% of what number?

The next example contains a circle graph. This particular circle graph shows percents of American travelers in certain categories. Since the circle graph represents all American travelers, the percents should add to 100%.

▶ **Helpful Hint**
The percents in a circle graph should have a sum of 100%.

EXAMPLE 3 The circle graph below shows the purpose of trips made by American travelers. Use this graph to answer the questions below.

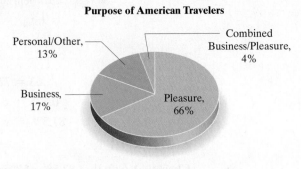

Purpose of American Travelers

Personal/Other, 13%

Combined Business/Pleasure, 4%

Business, 17%

Pleasure, 66%

Source: Travel Industry Association of America

a. What percent of trips made by American travelers are solely for the purpose of business?

b. What percent of trips made by American travelers are for the purpose of business or combined business/pleasure?

c. On an airplane flight of 253 Americans, how many of these people might we expect to be traveling solely for business?

Solution

a. From the circle graph, we see that 17% of trips made by American travelers are solely for the purpose of business.

b. From the circle graph, we know that 17% of trips are solely for business and 4% of trips are for combined business/pleasure. The sum 17% + 4% or 21% of trips made by American travelers are for the purpose of business or combined business/pleasure.

c. Since 17% of trips made by American travelers are for business, we find 17% of 253. Remember that "of" translates to "multiplication."

$$17\% \text{ of } 253 = 0.17(253) \quad \text{Replace "of" with the operation of multiplication.}$$
$$= 43.01$$

We might then expect that about 43 American travelers on the flight are traveling solely for business.   □

PRACTICE
3 Use the Example 3 circle graph to answer each question.

a. What percent of trips made by American travelers are for combined business/pleasure?

b. What percent of trips made by American travelers are for the purpose of business, pleasure, or combined business/pleasure?

c. On a flight of 325 Americans, how many of these people might we expect to be traveling for business/pleasure?

OBJECTIVE 2 ▶ Solving discount and mark-up problems. The next example has to do with discounting the price of a cell phone.

EXAMPLE 4   Cell Phones Unlimited recently reduced the price of a $140 phone by 20%. What is the discount and the new price?

Solution

1. UNDERSTAND. Read and reread the problem. Make sure you understand the meaning of the word "discount." Discount is the amount of money by which the cost of an item has been decreased. To find the discount, we simply find 20% of $140. In other words, we have the formulas,

$$\text{discount} = \text{percent} \cdot \text{original price}   \quad \text{Then}$$

$$\text{new price} = \text{original price} - \text{discount}$$

2, 3. TRANSLATE and SOLVE.

$$
\begin{aligned}
\text{discount} &= \text{percent} \cdot \text{original price} \\
&= 20\% \cdot \$140 \\
&= 0.20 \cdot \$140 \\
&= \$28
\end{aligned}
$$

Thus, the discount in price is $28.

$$
\begin{aligned}
\text{new price} &= \text{original price} - \text{discount} \\
&= \$140 - \$28 \\
&= \$112
\end{aligned}
$$

4. INTERPRET.

Check: Check your calculations in the formulas, and also see if our results are reasonable. They are.

State: The discount in price is $28 and the new price is $112.   □

PRACTICE
4   A used treadmill, originally purchased for $480, was sold at a garage sale at a discount of 85% of the original price. What was the discount and the new price?

A concept similar to discount is mark-up. What is the difference between the two? A discount is subtracted from the original price while a mark-up is added to the original price. For mark-ups,

$$\text{mark-up} = \text{percent} \cdot \text{original price}$$

$$\text{new price} = \text{original price} + \text{mark-up}$$

> ▶ **Helpful Hint**
> Discounts are subtracted from the original price while mark-ups are added.

Mark-up exercises can be found in Exercise Set 2.7.

OBJECTIVE 3 ▶ Solving percent increase and percent decrease problems. Percent increase or percent decrease is a common way to describe how some measurement has increased or decreased. For example, crime increased by 8%, teachers received a 5.5% increase in salary, or a company decreased its employees by 10%. The next example is a review of percent increase.

EXAMPLE 5 The cost of attending a public college rose from $9258 in 1996 to $12,796 in 2006. Find the percent increase, rounded to the nearest tenth of a percent. (*Source:* The College Board)

Solution

1. UNDERSTAND. Read and reread the problem. Let's guess that the percent increase is 20%. To see if this is the case, we find 20% of $9258 to find the *increase* in cost. Then we add this increase to $9258 to find the *new cost*. In other words, 20%($9258) = 0.20($9258) = $1851.60, the *increase* in cost. The new cost then would be $9258 + $1851.60 = $11,109.60, less than the actual new cost of $12,976. We now know that the increase is greater than 20% and we know how to check our proposed solution.

Let x = the percent increase.

2. TRANSLATE. First, find the **increase,** and then the **percent increase.** The increase in cost is found by

In words:　increase　=　new cost　−　old cost　or

Translate:　increase　=　$12,796　−　$9258
　　　　　　　　　　=　$3538

Next, find the percent increase. The percent increase or percent decrease is always a percent of the original number or, in this case, the old cost.

In words:　increase　is　what percent increase　of　old cost

Translate:　$3538　=　　　　x　　　·　　$9258

3. SOLVE.

$$3538 = x \cdot 9258 \qquad \text{Divide both sides by 9258.}$$
$$0.382 \approx x \qquad \text{Round to 3 decimal places.}$$
$$38.2\% \approx x \qquad \text{Write as a percent.}$$

4. INTERPRET.

Check: Check the proposed solution, as shown in Step 1.

State: The percent increase in cost is approximately 38.2%.

PRACTICE
5 The average price of a single family home in the United States rose from $198,900 in 2000 to $299,800 in 2005. Find the percent increase. Round to the nearest tenth of a percent. (*Source:* Federal Housing Finance Board)

Percent decrease is found using a similar method. First find the decrease, then determine what percent of the original or first amount is that decrease.

Read the next example carefully. For Example 5, we were asked to find percent increase. In Example 6, we are given the percent increase and asked to find the number before the increase.

EXAMPLE 6   Most of the movie screens globally project analog film, but the number of cinemas using digital is increasing. Find the number of digital screens worldwide last year if, after a 153% increase the number this year is 849. Round to the nearest whole number. (*Source:* Motion Picture Association of America)

Solution

1. UNDERSTAND. Read and reread the problem. Let's guess a solution and see how we would check our guess. If the number of digital screens worldwide last year was 400, we would see if 400 plus the increase is 849; that is,

$$400 + 153\%(400) = 400 + 1.53(400) = 2.53(400) = 1012$$

Since 1012 is too large, we know that our guess of 400 is too large. We also have a better understanding of the problem. Let

$$x = \text{number of digital screens last year}$$

2. TRANSLATE. To translate an equation, we remember that

In words:	number of digital screens last year	plus	increase	equals	number of digital screens this year
Translate:	x	$+$	$1.53x$	$=$	849

3. SOLVE.

$$2.53x = 849 \qquad \text{Add like terms.}$$
$$x = \frac{849}{2.53}$$
$$x \approx 336$$

4. INTERPRET.

Check: Recall that x represents the number of digital screens worldwide last year. If this number is approximately 336, let's see if 336 plus the increase is close to 849. (We use the word "close" since 336 is rounded.)

$$336 + 153\%(336) = 336 + 1.53(336) = 2.53(336) = 850.08$$

which is close to 849.

State: There were approximately 336 digital screens worldwide last year.   □

PRACTICE
6   In 2005, 535 new feature films were released in the United States. This was an increase of 2.8% over the number of new feature films released in 2004. Find the number of new feature films released in 2004. (*Source:* Motion Picture Association of America)

VOCABULARY & READINESS CHECK

Tell whether the percent labels in the circle graphs are correct.

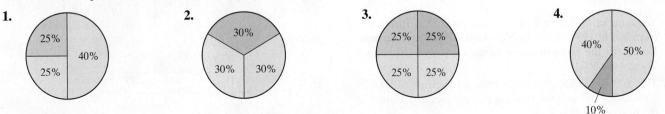

1.   25%   25%   40%

2.   30%   30%   30%

3.   25%   25%   25%   25%

4.   40%   50%   10%

2.7 EXERCISE SET

PRACTICE · WATCH · DOWNLOAD · READ · REVIEW

Find each number described. See Examples 1 and 2.

1. What number is 16% of 70?
2. What number is 88% of 1000?
3. The number 28.6 is what percent of 52?
4. The number 87.2 is what percent of 436?
5. The number 45 is 25% of what number?
6. The number 126 is 35% of what number?

The circle graph below shows the uses of U.S. corn production. Use this graph for Exercises 7 through 10. See Example 3.

U.S. Corn Production Use

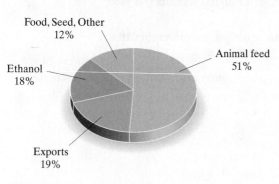

Food, Seed, Other 12%
Ethanol 18%
Animal feed 51%
Exports 19%

Source: USDA, American Farm Bureau Federation

7. What percent of corn production is used for animal feed or ethanol?
8. What percent of corn production is *not* used for exports?
9. The U.S. corn production in 2006–2007 was 10,535 million bushels. How many bushels were used to make ethanol?
10. How many bushels of the 2006–2007 corn production was used for food, seed, or other? (See Exercise 9.)

Solve. If needed, round answers to the nearest cent. See Example 4.

11. A used automobile dealership recently reduced the price of a used compact car by 8%. If the price of the car before discount was $18,500, find the discount and the new price.
12. A music store is advertising a 25%-off sale on all new releases. Find the discount and the sale price of a newly released CD that regularly sells for $12.50.
13. A birthday celebration meal is $40.50 including tax. Find the total cost if a 15% tip is added to the cost.
14. A retirement dinner for two is $65.40 including tax. Find the total cost if a 20% tip is added to the cost.

Solve. See Example 5.

15. The number of different cars sold in the United States rose from 208 in 1997 to 280 in 2007. Find the percent increase. Round to the nearest whole percent. (*Source: New York Times*, May 2007)
16. The cost of attending a private college rose from $19,000 in 2000 to $22,200 in 2006. Find the percent increase. Round to the nearest whole percent.

17. By decreasing each dimension by 1 unit, the area of a rectangle decreased from 40 square feet (on the left) to 28 square feet (on the right). Find the percent decrease in area.

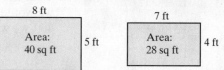

8 ft
Area: 40 sq ft
5 ft

7 ft
Area: 28 sq ft
4 ft

18. By decreasing the length of the side by one unit, the area of a square decreased from 100 square meters to 81 square meters. Find the percent decrease in area.

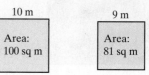

10 m
Area: 100 sq m

9 m
Area: 81 sq m

Solve. See Example 6.

19. Find the original price of a pair of shoes if the sale price is $78 after a 25% discount.
20. Find the original price of a popular pair of shoes if the increased price is $80 after a 25% increase.
21. Find last year's salary if after a 4% pay raise, this year's salary is $44,200.
22. Find last year's salary if after a 3% pay raise, this year's salary is $55,620.

MIXED PRACTICE

Solve. If needed, round money amounts to two decimal places and all other amounts to one decimal place. See Examples 1 through 6.

23. Find 23% of 20.
24. Find 140% of 86.
25. The number 40 is 80% of what number?
26. The number 56.25 is 45% of what number?
27. The number 144 is what percent of 480?
28. The number 42 is what percent of 35?

The graph shows the communities in the United States that have the highest percents of citizens that shop by catalog. Use the graph to answer Exercises 29 through 32.

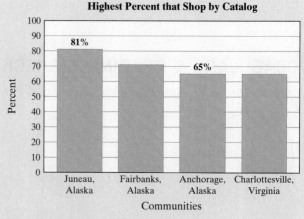

Highest Percent that Shop by Catalog

81%
65%

Juneau, Alaska · Fairbanks, Alaska · Anchorage, Alaska · Charlottesville, Virginia

Communities

Source: Polk Research

29. Estimate the percent of the population in Fairbanks, Alaska, who shops by catalog.

30 Estimate the percent of the population in Charlottesville, Virginia, who shops by catalog.

31. According to the *World Almanac*, Anchorage has a population of 275,043. How many catalog shoppers might we predict live in Anchorage? Round to the nearest whole number.

32. According to the *World Almanac*, Juneau has a population of 30,987. How many catalog shoppers might we predict live in Juneau? Round to the nearest whole number.

Complete a Table. *For Exercises 33 and 34, fill in the percent column in each table. Each table contains a worked-out example.*

33.

Ford Motor Company Model Year 2006 Vehicle Sales Worldwide		
	Thousands of Vehicles	*Percent of Total (Rounded to Nearest Percent)*
North America	3051	
Europe	1846	
Asia-Pacific-Africa	589	
South America	381	
Rest of the World	730	Example: $\frac{730}{6597} \approx 11\%$
Total	6597	
Source: Ford Motor Company		

34.

Kraft Foods North America Volume Food Produced in a year		
Food Group	*Volume (in pounds)*	*Percent (Round to Nearest Percent)*
Cheese, Meals, and Enhancers	6183	
Biscuits, Snacks, and Confectionaries	2083	Example: $\frac{2083}{13,741} \approx 15\%$
Beverages, Desserts, and Cereals	3905	
Oscar Mayer and Pizza	1570	
Total	13,741	
Source: Kraft Foods, North America		

35. Nordstrom advertised a 25%-off sale. If a London Fog coat originally sold for $256, find the decrease in price and the sale price.

36. A gasoline station decreased the price of a $0.95 cola by 15%. Find the decrease in price and the new price.

37. Iceberg lettuce is grown and shipped to stores for about 40 cents a head, and consumers purchase it for about 86 cents

a head. Find the percent increase. (*Source: Statistical Abstract of the United States*)

38. The lettuce consumption per capita in 1980 was about 25.6 pounds, and in 2005 the consumption dropped to about 22.4 pounds. Find the percent decrease. (*Source: Statistical Abstract of the United States*)

39. Smart Cards (cards with an embedded computer chip) have been growing in popularity in recent years. In 2006, about 1900 million Smart Cards were expected to be issued. This represents a 726% increase from the number of cards that were issued in 2001. How many Smart Cards were issued in 2001? Round to the nearest million. (*Source:* The Freedonia Group)

40. Fuel ethanol production is projected to be 10,800 million gallons in 2009. This represents a 44% increase from the number of gallons produced in 2007. How many millions of gallons were produced in 2007? (*Source:* Renewable Fuels Association)

41. A junior one-day admission to Hershey Park amusement park in Hershey, Pennsylvania, is $27. This price is increased by 70% for (nonsenior) adults. Find the mark-up and the adult price. (*Note:* Prices given are approximations.)

42. The price of a biology book recently increased by 10%. If this book originally cost $99.90, find the mark-up and the new price.

43. By doubling each dimension, the area of a parallelogram increased from 36 square centimeters to 144 square centimeters. Find the percent increase in area.

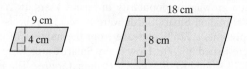

44. By doubling each dimension, the area of a triangle increased from 6 square miles to 24 square miles. Find the percent increase in area.

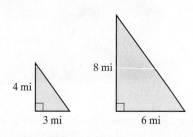

45. A company recently downsized its number of employees by 35%. If there are still 78 employees, how many employees were there prior to the layoffs?

46. The average number of children born to each U.S. woman has decreased by 44% since 1920. If this average is now 1.9, find the average in 1920. Round to the nearest tenth.

47. The number of farms in the United States was 2.19 million in 2000. By 2006, the number had dropped to 2.09 million. What was the percent of decrease? Round to the nearest tenth of a percent. (*Source:* USDA: National Agricultural Statistical Service)

48. The average size of farms in the United States was 436 acres in 2000. By 2005, the average size had increased to 444 acres. What was the percent increase? Round to the nearest tenth of a percent. (*Source:* USDA: National Agricultural Statistical Service)

49. The number of Supreme Court decisions has been decreasing in recent years. During the 2005–2006 term, 182 decisions were announced. This is a 45.7% decrease from the number of decisions announced during the 1982–1983 term. How many decisions were announced during 1982–1983? Round to the nearest whole. (*Source:* World Almanac)

50. The total number of movie screens in the United States has been increasing in recent years. In 2005, there were 37,092 indoor movie screens. This is a 4.3% increase from the number of indoor movie screens in 2000. How many movie screens were operating in 2000? Round to the nearest whole. (*Source:* National Association of Theater Owners)

51. Scoville units are used to measure the hotness of a pepper. Measuring 577 thousand Scoville units, the "Red Savina" habañero pepper was known as the hottest chili pepper. That has recently changed with the discovery of Naga Jolokia pepper from India. It measures 48% hotter than the habañero. Find the measure of the Naga Jolokia pepper. Round to the nearest thousand units.

52. At this writing, the women's world record for throwing a disc (like a heavy Frisbee) was set by Jennifer Griffin of the United States in 2000. Her throw was 138.56 meters. The men's world record was set by Christian Sandstrom of Sweden in 2002. His throw was 80.4% farther than Jennifer's. Find the distance of his throw. Round to the nearest meter. (*Source:* World Flying Disc Federation)

53. A recent survey showed that 42% of recent college graduates named flexible hours as their most desired employment benefit. In a graduating class of 860 college students, how many would you expect to rank flexible hours as their top priority in job benefits? (Round to the nearest whole.) (*Source:* JobTrak.com)

54. A recent survey showed that 64% of U.S. colleges have Internet access in their classrooms. There are approximately 9800 post-secondary institutions in the United States. How many of these would you expect to have Internet access in their classrooms? (*Source:* Market Data Retrieval, National Center for Education Statistics)

REVIEW AND PREVIEW

Place $<$, $>$, *or* $=$ *in the appropriate space to make each a true statement. See Sections 1.2, 1.3, and 1.6.*

55. -5 ___ -7

56. $\dfrac{12}{3}$ ___ 2^2

57. $|-5|$ ___ $-(-5)$

58. -3^3 ___ $(-3)^3$

59. $(-3)^2$ ___ -3^2

60. $|-2|$ ___ $-|-2|$

CONCEPT EXTENSIONS

61. Must the percents in a circle graph have a sum of 100%? Why or why not?

62. a. Can an item be marked-up by more than 100%? Why or why not?
  b. Can an item be discounted by more than 100%? Why or why not?

Standardized nutrition labels like the one below have been displayed on food items since 1994. The percent column on the right shows the percent of daily values (based on a 2000-calorie diet) shown at the bottom of the label. For example, a serving of this food contains 4 grams of total fat, where the recommended daily fat based on a 2000-calorie diet is less than 65 grams of fat. This means that $\dfrac{4}{65}$ *or approximately 6% (as shown) of your daily recommended fat is taken in by eating a serving of this food. Use this nutrition label to answer Exercises 63 through 65.*

Nutrition Facts

Serving Size   18 Crackers (31g)
Servings Per Container   About 9

Amount Per Serving

Calories 130   Calories from Fat 35

	% Daily Value*
Total Fat 4g	**6%**
Saturated Fat 0.5g	**3%**
Polyunsaturated Fat 0g	
Monounsaturated Fat 1.5g	
Cholesterol 0mg	**0%**
Sodium 230mg	*x*
Total Carbohydrate 23g	*y*
Dietary Fiber 2g	**8%**
Sugars 3g	
Protein 2g	

Vitamin A 0%	•	Vitamin C 0%	
Calcium 2%	•	Iron 6%	

* Percent Daily Values are based on a 2,000 calorie diet. Your daily values may be higher or lower depending on your calorie needs.

		Calories	2,000	2,500
Total Fat	Less than		65g	80g
Sat. Fat	Less than		20g	25g
Cholesterol	Less than		300mg	300mg
Sodium	Less than		2400mg	2400mg
Total Carbohydrate			300g	375g
Dietary Fiber			25g	30g

63. Based on a 2000-calorie diet, what percent of daily value of sodium is contained in a serving of this food? In other words, find *x* in the label. (Round to the nearest tenth of a percent.)

64. Based on a 2000-calorie diet, what percent of daily value of total carbohydrate is contained in a serving of this food? In other words, find *y* in the label. (Round to the nearest tenth of a percent.)

65. Notice on the nutrition label that one serving of this food contains 130 calories and 35 of these calories are from fat. Find the percent of calories from fat. (Round to the nearest tenth of a percent.) It is recommended that no more than 30% of calorie intake come from fat. Does this food satisfy this recommendation?

Use the nutrition label below to answer Exercises 66 through 68.

NUTRITIONAL INFORMATION PER SERVING

Serving Size: 9.8 oz.	Servings Per Container: 1
Calories 280	Polyunsaturated Fat 1g
Protein 12g	Saturated Fat 3g
Carbohydrate 45g	Cholesterol 20mg
Fat .6g	Sodium 520mg
Percent of Calories from Fat....?	Potassium 220mg

66. If fat contains approximately 9 calories per gram, find the percent of calories from fat in one serving of this food. (Round to the nearest tenth of a percent.)

67. If protein contains approximately 4 calories per gram, find the percent of calories from protein from one serving of this food. (Round to the nearest tenth of a percent.)

68. Find a food that contains more than 30% of its calories per serving from fat. Analyze the nutrition label and verify that the percents shown are correct.

2.8 MIXTURE AND DISTANCE PROBLEM SOLVING

OBJECTIVES

1 Solve mixture problems.

2 Solve distance (uniform motion) problems.

This section is devoted to solving problems in the categories listed. The same problem-solving steps used in previous sections are also followed in this section. They are listed below for review.

General Strategy for Problem Solving

1. UNDERSTAND the problem. During this step, become comfortable with the problem. Some ways of doing this are as follows:

Read and reread the problem.

Choose a variable to represent the unknown.

Construct a drawing, whenever possible.

Propose a solution and check. Pay careful attention to how you check your proposed solution. This will help writing an equation to model the problem.

2. TRANSLATE the problem into an equation.

3. SOLVE the equation.

4. INTERPRET the results: *Check* the proposed solution in the stated problem and *state* your conclusion.

OBJECTIVE 1 ▶ Solving mixture problems. Mixture problems involve two or more different quantities being combined to form a new mixture. These applications range from Dow Chemical's need to form a chemical mixture of a required strength to Planter's Peanut Company's need to find the correct mixture of peanuts and cashews, given taste and price constraints.

EXAMPLE 1 Calculating Percent for a Lab Experiment

A chemist working on his doctoral degree at Massachusetts Institute of Technology needs 12 liters of a 50% acid solution for a lab experiment. The stockroom has only 40% and 70% solutions. How much of each solution should be mixed together to form 12 liters of a 50% solution?

Solution:

1. UNDERSTAND. First, read and reread the problem a few times. Next, guess a solution. Suppose that we need 7 liters of the 40% solution. Then we need $12 - 7 = 5$ liters of the 70% solution. To see if this is indeed the solution, find the amount of pure acid in 7 liters of the 40% solution, in 5 liters of the 70% solution, and in 12 liters of a 50% solution, the required amount and strength.

number of liters	×	acid strength	=	amount of pure acid
↓		↓		↓
7 liters	×	40%	=	7(0.40) or 2.8 liters
5 liters	×	70%	=	5(0.70) or 3.5 liters
12 liters	×	50%	=	12(0.50) or 6 liters

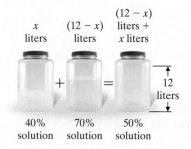

x liters $(12 - x)$ liters $(12 - x)$ liters + x liters

+   =   12 liters

40% solution   70% solution   50% solution

Since 2.8 liters + 3.5 liters = 6.3 liters and not 6, our guess is incorrect, but we have gained some valuable insight into how to model and check this problem.

Let

$$x = \text{number of liters of 40\% solution; then}$$
$$12 - x = \text{number of liters of 70\% solution.}$$

2. TRANSLATE. To help us translate to an equation, the following table summarizes the information given. Recall that the amount of acid in each solution is found by multiplying the acid strength of each solution by the number of liters.

	No. of Liters	·	Acid Strength	=	Amount of Acid
40% Solution	x		40%		$0.40x$
70% Solution	$12 - x$		70%		$0.70(12 - x)$
50% Solution Needed	12		50%		$0.50(12)$

The amount of acid in the final solution is the sum of the amounts of acid in the two beginning solutions.

In words: acid in 40% solution   +   acid in 70% solution   =   acid in 50% mixture

↓   ↓   ↓

Translate: $0.40x$ + $0.70(12 - x)$ = $0.50(12)$

3. SOLVE.

$$0.40x + 0.70(12 - x) = 0.50(12)$$

$$0.4x + 8.4 - 0.7x = 6 \qquad \text{Apply the distributive property.}$$

$$-0.3x + 8.4 = 6 \qquad \text{Combine like terms.}$$

$$-0.3x = -2.4 \qquad \text{Subtract 8.4 from both sides.}$$

$$x = 8 \qquad \text{Divide both sides by } -0.3.$$

4. INTERPRET.

Check: To check, recall how we checked our guess.

State: If 8 liters of the 40% solution are mixed with 12 − 8 or 4 liters of the 70% solution, the result is 12 liters of a 50% solution. □

PRACTICE

1 How much 20% dye solution and 50% dye solution should be mixed to obtain 6 liters of a 40% solution?

The next example has to do with finding an unknown number of a certain denomination of coin or bill. These problems are extremely useful in that they help you understand the difference between the number of coins or bills and the total value of the money.

For example, suppose there are seven $5 bills. The *number* of $5 bills is 7 and the *total value* of the money is $5(7) = $35.

Study the table below for more examples.

Denomination or Coin or Bill	Number of Coins or Bills	Value of Coins or Bills
20-dollar bills	17	$20(17) = $340
nickels	31	$0.05(31) = $1.55
quarters	x	$0.25(x) = $0.25x$

EXAMPLE 2 **Finding Numbers of Denominations**

Part of the proceeds from a local talent show was $2420 worth of $10 and $20 bills. If there were 37 more $20 bills than $10 bills, find the number of each denomination.

Solution

1. UNDERSTAND the problem. To do so, read and reread the problem. If you'd like, let's guess a solution. Suppose that there are 25 $10 bills. Since there are 37 more $20 bills, we have 25 + 37 = 62 $20 bills. The total amount of money is $10(25) + $20(62) = $1490, below the given amount of $2420. Remember that our purpose for guessing is to help us better understand the problem.

We are looking for the number of each denomination, so we let

$$x = \text{number of \$10 bills}$$

There are 37 more $20 bills, so

$$x + 37 = \text{number of \$20 bills}$$

2. TRANSLATE. To help us translate to an equation, study the table below

Denomination	Number of Bills	Value of Bills (in dollars)
$10 bills	x	$10x$
$20 bills	$x + 37$	$20(x + 37)$

Since the total value of these bills is $2420, we have

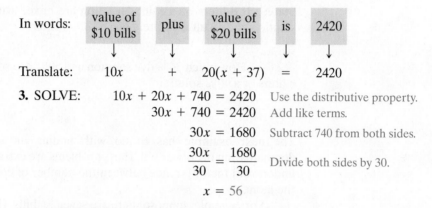

In words:

value of $10 bills	plus	value of $20 bills	is	2420

Translate: $10x$ $+$ $20(x + 37)$ $=$ 2420

3. SOLVE:

$$10x + 20x + 740 = 2420 \quad \text{Use the distributive property.}$$
$$30x + 740 = 2420 \quad \text{Add like terms.}$$
$$30x = 1680 \quad \text{Subtract 740 from both sides.}$$
$$\frac{30x}{30} = \frac{1680}{30} \quad \text{Divide both sides by 30.}$$
$$x = 56$$

4. INTERPRET the results.

Check: Since x represents the number of $10 bills, we have 56 $10 bills and $56 + 37$, or 93 $20 bills. The total amount of these bills is $\$10(56) + \$20(93) = \$2420$, the correct total.

State: There are 56 $10 bills and 93 $20 bills. □

PRACTICE

2   A stack of $5 and $20 bills was counted by the treasurer of an organization. The total value of the money was $1710, and there were 47 more $5 bills than $20 bills. Find the number of each type of bill.

OBJECTIVE 2 ▶ Solving distance problems. This example involves the distance formula, $d = r \cdot t$.

EXAMPLE 3   **Finding Time Given Rate and Distance**

Marie Antonio, a bicycling enthusiast, rode her 21-speed at an average speed of 18 miles per hour on level roads and then slowed down to an average of 10 mph on the hilly roads of the trip. If she covered a distance of 98 miles, how long did the entire trip take if traveling the level roads took the same time as traveling the hilly roads?

Solution

1. UNDERSTAND the problem. To do so, read and reread the problem. The formula $d = r \cdot t$ is needed. At this time, let's guess a solution. Suppose that she spent 2 hours traveling on the level roads. This means that she also spent 2 hours traveling on the hilly roads, since the times spent were the same. What is her total distance? Her distance on the level road is rate · time = $18(2) = 36$ miles. Her distance on the hilly roads is rate · time = $10(2) = 20$ miles. This gives a total distance of 36 miles + 20 miles = 56 miles, not the correct distance of 98 miles. Remember that the purpose of guessing a solution is not to guess correctly (although this may happen) but to help better understand the problem and how to model it with an equation. We are looking for the length of the entire trip, so we begin by letting

$$x = \text{the time spent on level roads.}$$

Because the same amount of time is spent on hilly roads, then also

$$x = \text{the time spent on hilly roads.}$$

2. TRANSLATE. To help us translate to an equation, we now summarize the information from the problem on the following chart. Fill in the rates given, the variables used to represent the times, and use the formula $d = r \cdot t$ to fill in the distance column.

	Rate	*· Time*	*= Distance*
Level	18	x	$18x$
Hilly	10	x	$10x$

We'll draw a diagram to help visualize distance.

Since the entire trip covered 98 miles, we have that

In words: total distance   =   level distance   +   hilly distance

Translate: 98   = $18x$ + $10x$

3. SOLVE.

$$98 = 28x \quad \text{Add like terms.}$$

$$\frac{98}{28} = \frac{28x}{28} \quad \text{Divide both sides by 28.}$$

$$3.5 = x$$

4. INTERPRET the results.

Check: Recall that x represents the time spent on the level portion of the trip and also the time spent on the hilly portion. If Marie rides for 3.5 hours at 18 mph, her distance is $18(3.5) = 63$ miles. If Marie rides for 3.5 hours at 10 mph, her distance is $10(3.5) = 35$ miles. The total distance is 63 miles + 35 miles = 98 miles, the required distance.

State: The time of the entire trip is then 3.5 hours + 3.5 hours or 7 hours.   □

PRACTICE
3   Sat Tranh took a short hike with his friends up Mt. Wachusett. They hiked uphill at a steady pace of 1.5 miles per hour, and downhill at a rate of 4 miles per hour. If the time to climb the mountain took an hour more than the time to hike down, how long was the entire hike?

EXAMPLE 4   **Finding Train Speeds**

The Kansas City Southern Railway operates in 10 states and Mexico. Suppose two trains leave Neosho, Missouri, at the same time. One travels north and the other travels south at a speed that is 15 miles per hour faster. In 2 hours, the trains are 230 miles apart. Find the speed of each train. Study the following table for more examples.

Solution

1. **UNDERSTAND** the problem. Read and reread the problem. Guess a solution and check. Let's let

$$x = \text{speed of train traveling north}$$

Because the train traveling south is 15 mph faster, we have

$$x + 15 = \text{speed of train traveling south}$$

2. **TRANSLATE.** Just as for Example 1, let's summarize our information on a chart. Use the formula $d = r \cdot t$ to fill in the distance column.

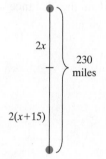

	r	$\cdot$ t =	d
North Train	x	2	$2x$
South Train	$x + 15$	2	$2(x + 15)$

Since the total distance between the trains is 230 miles, we have

In words:	north train distance	+	south train distance	=	total distance
	↓		↓		↓
Translate:	$2x$	+	$2(x + 15)$	=	230

3. **SOLVE.**

$$2x + 2x + 30 = 230 \quad \text{Use the distributive property.}$$
$$4x + 30 = 230 \quad \text{Combine like terms.}$$
$$4x = 200 \quad \text{Subtract 30 from both sides.}$$
$$\frac{4x}{4} = \frac{200}{4} \quad \text{Divide both sides by 4.}$$
$$x = 50 \quad \text{Simplify.}$$

4. **INTERPRET** the results.

Check: Recall that x is the speed of the train traveling north, or 50 mph. In 2 hours, this train travels a distance of $2(50) = 100$ miles. The speed of the train traveling south is $x + 15$ or $50 + 15 = 65$ mph. In 2 hours, this train travels $2(65) = 130$ miles. The total distance of the trains is 100 miles $+ 130$ miles $= 230$ miles, the required distance.

State: The northbound train's speed is 50 mph and the southbound train's speed is 65 mph. □

PRACTICE

4 The Kansas City Southern Railway has a station in Mexico City, Mexico. Suppose two trains leave Mexico City at the same time. One travels east and the other west at a speed that is 10 mph slower. In 1.5 hours, the trains are 171 miles apart. Find the speed of each train.

2.8 EXERCISE SET

PRACTICE WATCH DOWNLOAD READ REVIEW

Solve. For each exercise, a table is given for you to complete and use to write an equation that models the situation. See Example 1.

1. How much pure acid should be mixed with 2 gallons of a 40% acid solution in order to get a 70% acid solution?

	Number of Gallons ·	Acid Strength =	Amount of Acid
Pure Acid		100%	
40% Acid Solution			
70% Acid Solution Needed			

2. How many cubic centimeters (cc) of a 25% antibiotic solution should be added to 10 cubic centimeters of a 60% antibiotic solution in order to get a 30% antibiotic solution?

	Number of Cubic cm ·	Antibiotic Strength =	Amount of Antibiotic
25% Antibiotic Solution			
60% Antibiotic Solution			
30% Antibiotic Solution Needed			

3. Community Coffee Company wants a new flavor of Cajun coffee. How many pounds of coffee worth $7 a pound should be added to 14 pounds of coffee worth $4 a pound to get a mixture worth $5 a pound?

	Number of Pounds ·	Cost per Pound =	Value
$7 per lb Coffee			
$4 per lb Coffee			
$5 per lb Coffee Wanted			

4. Planter's Peanut Company wants to mix 20 pounds of peanuts worth $3 a pound with cashews worth $5 a pound in order to make an experimental mix worth $3.50 a pound. How many pounds of cashews should be added to the peanuts?

	Number of Pounds ·	Cost per Pound =	Value
$3 per lb Peanuts			
$5 per lb Cashews			
$3.50 per lb Mixture Wanted			

Complete the table. The first and sixth rows have been completed for you. See Example 2.

		Number of Coins or Bills	Value of Coins or Bills (in dollars)
	pennies	x	$0.01x$
5.	*dimes*	y	
6.	*quarters*	z	
7.	*nickels*	$(x + 7)$	
8.	*half-dollars*	$(20 - z)$	
	$5 bills	$9x$	$5(9x)$
9.	*$20 bills*	$4y$	
10.	*$100 bills*	$97z$	
11.	*$50 bills*	$(35 - x)$	
12.	*$10 bills*	$(15 - y)$	

13. Part of the proceeds from a garage sale was $280 worth of $5 and $10 bills. If there were 20 more $5 bills than $10 bills, find the number of each denomination.

	Number of Bills	Value of Bills
$5 bills		
$10 bills		
Total		

14. A bank teller is counting $20 and $50-dollar bills. If there are six times as many $20 bills as $50 bills and the total amount of money is $3910, find the number of each denomination.

	Number of Bills	Value of Bills
$20 bills		
$50 bills		
Total		

15. How much of an alloy that is 20% copper should be mixed with 200 ounces of an alloy that is 50% copper in order to get an alloy that is 30% copper?

16. How much water should be added to 30 gallons of a solution that is 70% antifreeze in order to get a mixture that is 60% antifreeze?

17. A new self-tanning lotion for everyday use is to be sold. First, an experimental lotion mixture is made by mixing 800 ounces of everyday moisturizing lotion worth $0.30 an ounce with self-tanning lotion worth $3 per ounce. If the experimental lotion is to cost $1.20 per ounce, how many ounces of the self-tanning lotion should be in the mixture?

18. The owner of a local chocolate shop wants to develop a new trail mix. How many pounds of chocolate-covered peanuts worth $5 a pound should be mixed with 10 pounds of granola bites worth $2 a pound to get a mixture worth $3 per pound?

Solve. See Example 3.

19. Two cars leave Richmond, at the same time after visiting the nearby Richmond International Speedway. The cars travel in opposite directions, one traveling north at 56 mph and one traveling south at 47 mph. When will the two cars be 206 miles apart?

20. Two cars leave Las Vegas, Nevada at the same time after visiting the Las Vegas Motor Speedway. The cars travel in opposite directions, one traveling northeast at 65 mph and one traveling southwest at 41 mph. When will the two cars be 530 miles apart?

Solve. See Example 4.

21. Suppose two trains leave Corpus Christi, Texas at the same time, traveling in opposite directions. One train travels 10 mph faster than the other. In 2.5 hours, the trains are 205 miles apart. Find the speed of each train.

22. Suppose two trains leave Edmonton Canada, at the same time, traveling in opposite directions. One train travels 8 mph faster than the other. In 1.5 hours, the trains are 162 miles apart. Find the speed of each train.

Solve. See Examples 3 and 4.

23. A truck and a van leave the same location at the same time and travel in opposite directions. The truck's speed is 52 mph and the van's speed is 63 mph. When will the truck and the van be 460 miles apart?

24. Two cars leave the same location at the same time and travel in opposite directions. One car's speed is 65 mph and the other car's speed is 45 mph. When will the two cars be 330 miles apart?

25. Two cars leave Pecos, Texas the same time and both travel east on Interstate 20. The first car's speed is 70 mph and the second car's speed is 58 mph. When will the cars be 30 miles apart?

26. Two cars leave Savannah, Georgia at the same time and both travel north on Interstate 95. The first car's speed is 40 mph and the second car's speed is 50 mph. When will the cars be 20 miles apart?

27. A jet plane traveling at 500 mph overtakes a propeller plane traveling at 200 mph that had a 2-hour head start. How far from the starting point are the planes?

28. How long will it take a bus traveling at 60 miles per hour to overtake a car traveling at 40 mph if the car had a 1.5-hour head start?

29. A bus traveled on a level road for 3 hours at an average speed 20 miles per hour faster than it traveled on a winding road. The time spent on the winding road was 4 hours. Find the average speed on the level road if the entire trip was 305 miles.

30. The Jones family drove to Disneyland at 50 miles per hour and returned on the same route at 40 mph. Find the distance to Disneyland if the total driving time was 7.2 hours.

31. Alan and Dave Schaferkötter leave from the same point driving in opposite directions, Alan driving at 55 miles per hour and Dave at 65 mph. Alan has a one-hour head start. How long will they be able to talk on their car phones if the phones have a 250-mile range?

32. Kathleen and Cade Williams leave simultaneously from the same point hiking in opposite directions, Kathleen walking at 4 miles per hour and Cade at 5 mph. How long can they talk on their walkie-talkies if the walkie-talkies have a 20-mile radius?

33. Two hikers are 11 miles apart and walking toward each other. They meet in 2 hours. Find the rate of each hiker if one hiker walks 1.1 mph faster than the other.

34. Nedra and Latonya Dominguez are 12 miles apart hiking toward each other. How long will it take them to meet if Nedra walks at 3 mph and Latonya walks 1 mph faster?

35. Mark Martin can row upstream at 5 mph and downstream at 11 mph. If Mark starts rowing upstream until he gets tired and then rows downstream to his starting point, how far did Mark row if the entire trip took 4 hours?

36. On a 255-mile trip, Gary Alessandrini traveled at an average speed of 70 mph, got a speeding ticket, and then traveled at 60 mph for the remainder of the trip. If the entire trip took 4.5 hours and the speeding ticket stop took 30 minutes, how long did Gary speed before getting stopped?

REVIEW AND PREVIEW

Perform the indicated operations. See Sections 1.5 and 1.6.

37. $3 + (-7)$

38. $(-2) + (-8)$

39. $\dfrac{3}{4} - \dfrac{3}{16}$

40. $-11 + 2.9$

41. $-5 - (-1)$

42. $-12 - 3$

CONCEPT EXTENSIONS

43. A stack of $20, $50, and $100 bills was retrieved as part of an FBI investigation. There were 46 more $50 bills than $100 bills. Also, the number of $20 bills was 7 times the number of $100 bills. If the total value of the money was $9550, find the number of each type of bill.

44. A man places his pocket change in a jar every day. The jar is full and his children have counted the change. The total value is $44.86. Let x represent the number of quarters and use the information below to find the number of each type of coin.

There are: 136 more dimes than quarters
8 times as many nickels as quarters
32 more than 16 times as many pennies
as quarters

To "break even" in a manufacturing business, revenue R (income) ***must equal*** *the cost C of production, or R = C.*

45. The cost C to produce x number of skateboards is given by $C = 100 + 20x$. The skateboards are sold wholesale for $24 each, so revenue R is given by $R = 24x$. Find how many skateboards the manufacturer needs to produce and sell to break even. (*Hint:* Set the expression for R equal to the expression for C, then solve for x.)

46. The revenue R from selling x number of computer boards is given by $R = 60x$, and the cost C of producing them is given by $C = 50x + 5000$. Find how many boards must be sold to break even. Find how much money is needed to produce the break-even number of boards.

47. The cost C of producing x number of paperback books is given by $C = 4.50x + 2400$. Income R from these books is given by $R = 7.50x$. Find how many books should be produced and sold to break even.

48. Find the break-even quantity for a company that makes x number of computer monitors at a cost C given by $C = 870 + 70x$ and receives revenue R given by $R = 105x$.

49. Exercises 45 through 48 involve finding the break-even point for manufacturing. Discuss what happens if a company makes and sells fewer products than the break-even point. Discuss what happens if more products than the break-even point are made and sold.

EXTENSION: INDUCTIVE AND DEDUCTIVE REASONING

OBJECTIVES

1. Understand and use inductive reasoning.

2. Understand and use deductive reasoning.

OBJECTIVE 1 ▶ Inductive reasoning. Mathematics involves the study of patterns. In everyday life, we frequently rely on patterns and routines to draw conclusions. Here is an example:

The last six times I went to the beach, the traffic was light on Wednesdays and heavy on Sundays. My conclusion is that weekdays have lighter traffic than weekends.

This type of reasoning process is referred to as *inductive reasoning*, or *induction*.

> **Inductive Reasoning**
>
> **Inductive reasoning** is the process of arriving at a general conclusion based on observations of specific examples.

Although inductive reasoning is a powerful method of drawing conclusions, we can never be absolutely certain that these conclusions are true. For this reason, the conclusions are called **conjectures, hypotheses,** or educated guesses. A strong inductive argument does not guarantee the truth of the conclusion, but rather provides strong support for the conclusion. If there is just one case for which the conjecture does not hold, then the conjecture is false. Such a case is called a **counterexample.** We studied counterexamples in Chapter 1.

Inductive reasoning is extremely important to mathematicians. Discovery in mathematics often begins with an examination of individual cases to reveal patterns about numbers.

EXAMPLE 1 Using Inductive Reasoning

Identify a pattern in each list of numbers. Then use this pattern to find the next number.

a. 3, 12, 21, 30, 39, _____

b. 3, 12, 48, 192, 768, _____

c. 3, 4, 6, 9, 13, 18, _____

d. 3, 6, 18, 36, 108, 216, _____

Solution

a. Because 3, 12, 21, 30, 39, _____ is increasing relatively slowly, let's use addition as the basis for our individual observations.

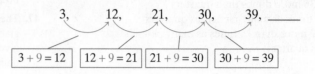

Generalizing from these observations, we conclude that each number after the first is obtained by adding 9 to the previous number. Using this pattern, the next number is 39 + 9, or 48.

b. Because 3, 12, 48, 192, 768, _____ is increasing relatively rapidly, let's use multiplication as the basis for our individual observations.

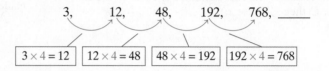

Generalizing from these observations, we conclude that each number after the first is obtained by multiplying the previous number by 4. Using this pattern, the next number is 768 × 4, or 3072.

c. Because 3, 4, 6, 9, 13, 18, _____ is increasing relatively slowly, let's use addition as the basis for our individual observations.

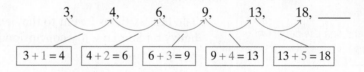

Generalizing from these observations, we conclude that each number after the first is obtained by adding a counting number to the previous number. The additions begin with 1 and continue through each successive counting number. Using this pattern, the next number is 18 + 6, or 24.

d. Because 3, 6, 18, 36, 108, 216, _____ is increasing relatively rapidly, let's use multiplication as the basis for our individual observations.

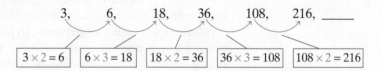

Generalizing from these observations, we conclude that each number after the first is obtained by multiplying the previous number by 2 or by 3. The multiplications begin with 2 and then alternate, multiplying by 2, then 3, then 2, then 3, and so on. Using this pattern, the next number is 216 × 3, or 648. □

PRACTICE

1 Identify a pattern in each list of numbers. Then use this pattern to find the next number.

a. 3, 9, 15, 21, 27, _____   **b.** 2, 10, 50, 250, _____

c. 3, 6, 18, 72, 144, 432, 1728, _____

d. 1, 9, 17, 3, 11, 19, 5, 13, 21, _____

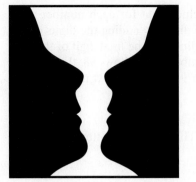

▶ **Helpful Hint**

The illusion in the margin is an ambiguous figure containing two patterns, where it is not clear which pattern should predominate. Do you see a wine goblet or two faces looking at each other? Like this ambiguous figure, some lists of numbers can display more than one pattern, particularly if only a few numbers are given. Inductive reasoning can result in more than one probable next number in a list.

> **Example:** 1, 2, 4, _____
> **Pattern:** Each number after the first is obtained by multiplying the previous number by 2. The missing number is 4×2, or 8.
> **Pattern:** Each number after the first is obtained by adding successive counting numbers, starting with 1, to the previous number. The second number is $1 + 1$, or 2. The third number is $2 + 2$, or 4. The missing number is $4 + 3$, or 7.

Inductive reasoning can also result in different patterns that produce the same probable next number in a list.

> **Example:** 1, 4, 9, 16, 25, _____
> **Pattern:** Start by adding 3 to the first number. Then add successive odd numbers, 5, 7, 9, and so on. The missing number is $25 + 11$, or 36.
> **Pattern:** Each number is obtained by squaring its position in the list: The first number is $1^2 = 1 \times 1 = 1$, the second number is $2^2 = 2 \times 2 = 4$, the third number is $3^2 = 3 \times 3 = 9$, and so on. The missing sixth number is $6^2 = 6 \times 6$, or 36.

The numbers that we found in Example 1 are probable numbers. Perhaps you found patterns other than the ones we pointed out that might have resulted in different answers.

In our next example, the patterns are a bit more complex than the additions and multiplications we encountered in Example 1.

EXAMPLE 2   Using Inductive Reasoning

Identify a pattern in each list of numbers. Then use this pattern to find the next number.

a. 1, 1, 2, 3, 5, 8, 13, 21, _____   **b.** 23, 54, 95, 146, 117, 98, _____

Solution

a. Starting with the third number in the list, let's form our observations by comparing each number with the two numbers that immediately precede it.

As this tree branches, the number of branches forms the Fibonacci sequence.

1,   1,   2,   3,   5,   8,   13,   21, _____

| preceded by 1 and 1: $1 + 1 = 2$ | preceded by 1 and 2: $1 + 2 = 3$ | preceded by 2 and 3: $2 + 3 = 5$ | preceded by 3 and 5: $3 + 5 = 8$ | preceded by 5 and 8: $5 + 8 = 13$ | preceded by 8 and 13: $8 + 13 = 21$ |

Generalizing from these observations, we conclude that the first two numbers are 1. Each number thereafter is the sum of the two preceding numbers. Using this pattern, the next number is $13 + 21$, or 34. (The numbers 1, 1, 2, 3, 5, 8, 13, 21, and 34 are the first nine terms of a sequence called the *Fibonacci sequence.*)

b. Let's use the digits that form each number as the basis for our individual observations. Focus on the sum of the digits, as well as the final digit increased by 1.

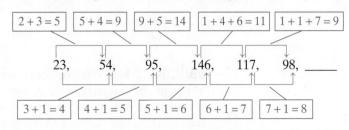

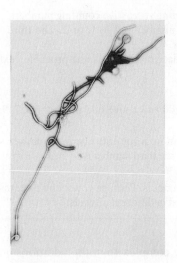

This electron microscope photograph shows the knotty shape of the Ebola virus.

Generalizing from these observations, we conclude that for each number after the first, we obtain the first digit or the first two digits by adding the digits of the previous number. We obtain the last digit by adding 1 to the final digit of the preceding number. Applying this pattern to the number that follows 98, the first two digits are 9 + 8, or 17. The last digit is 8 + 1, or 9. Thus, the next number in the list is 179. □

PRACTICE
2   Identify a pattern in each list of numbers. Then use this pattern to find the next number.

      a. 1, 3, 4, 7, 11, 18, 29, 47, _____

      b. 2, 3, 5, 9, 17, 33, 65, 129, _____

Mathematics is more than recognizing number patterns. It is about the patterns that arise in the world around us. For example, by describing patterns formed by various kinds of knots, mathematicians are helping scientists investigate the knotty shapes and patterns of viruses. One of the weapons used against viruses is based on recognizing visual patterns in the possible ways that knots can be tied.

Our next example deals with recognizing visual patterns.

EXAMPLE 3   Finding the Next Figure in a Visual Sequence

Describe two patterns in this sequence of figures. Use the patterns to draw the next figure in the sequence.

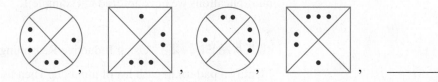

Solution The more obvious pattern is that the figures alternate between circles and squares. We conclude that the next figure will be a circle. We can identify the second pattern in the four regions containing no dots, one dot, two dots, and three dots. The dots are placed in order (no dots, one dot, two dots, three dots) in a clockwise direction. However, the entire pattern of the dots rotates counterclockwise as we follow the figures from left to right.

    This means that the next figure should be a circle with a single dot in the right-hand region, two dots in the bottom region, three dots in the left-hand region, and no dots in the top region. This figure is drawn to the right. □

PRACTICE
3   Describe two patterns in this sequence of figures. Use the patterns to draw the next figure in the sequence.

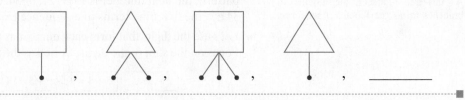

OBJECTIVE 2 ▶ Deductive reasoning. We use inductive reasoning in everyday life. Many of the conjectures that come from this kind of thinking seem highly likely, although we can never be absolutely certain that they are true. Another method of reasoning, called *deductive reasoning*, or *deduction*, can be used to prove that some conjectures are true.

> **Deductive Reasoning**
>
> **Deductive reasoning** is the process of proving a specific conclusion from one or more general statements. A conclusion that is proved true by deductive reasoning is called a **theorem**.

Deductive reasoning allows us to draw a specific conclusion from one or more general statements. Here is an example of deductive reasoning. Notice that in this situation, the general statement from which the conclusion is drawn is implied rather than directly stated.

Situation	Deductive Reasoning
One player to another in a Scrabble game: "You have to remove those five letters. You can't use TEXAS as a word."	• All proper names are prohibited in Scrabble. TEXAS is a proper name. Therefore, TEXAS is prohibited in Scrabble. — general statement — conclusion

Our next example illustrates the difference between inductive and deductive reasoning. The first part of the example involves reasoning that moves from specific examples to a general statement, illustrating inductive reasoning. The second part of the example begins with the general case rather than specific examples, and illustrates deductive reasoning.

EXAMPLE 4   Using Inductive and Deductive Reasoning

Consider the following procedure:

Select a number. Multiply the number by 6. Add 8 to the product. Divide this sum by 2. Subtract 4 from the quotient.

a. Repeat this procedure for at least four different numbers. Write a conjecture that relates the result of this process to the original number selected.

b. Represent the original number by the variable n and use deductive reasoning to prove the conjecture in part (a).

Solution

a. First, let us pick our starting numbers. We will use 4, 7, 11, and 100, but we could pick any four numbers. Next we will apply the procedure given in this example to 4, 7, 11, and 100, four individual cases.

APPLYING A PROCEDURE TO FOUR INDIVIDUAL CASES				
Select a number.	4	7	11	100
Multiply the number by 6.	$4 \times 6 = 24$	$7 \times 6 = 42$	$11 \times 6 = 66$	$100 \times 6 = 600$
Add 8 to the product.	$24 + 8 = 32$	$42 + 8 = 50$	$66 + 8 = 74$	$600 + 8 = 608$
Divide this sum by 2.	$\frac{32}{2} = 16$	$\frac{50}{2} = 25$	$\frac{74}{2} = 37$	$\frac{608}{2} = 304$
Subtract 4 from the quotient.	$16 - 4 = 12$	$25 - 4 = 21$	$37 - 4 = 33$	$304 - 4 = 300$

Because we are asked to write a conjecture that relates the result of this process to the original number selected, let us focus on the result of each case.

Original number selected	4	7	11	100
Result of the process	12	21	33	300

Do you see a pattern? Our conjecture is that the result of the process is three times the original number selected. We have used inductive reasoning.

b. Now we begin with the general case rather than specific examples. We use the variable n to represent any number.

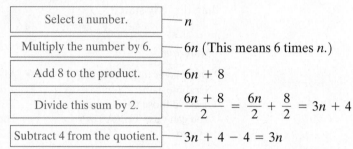

Select a number.	n
Multiply the number by 6.	$6n$ (This means 6 times n.)
Add 8 to the product.	$6n + 8$
Divide this sum by 2.	$\dfrac{6n + 8}{2} = \dfrac{6n}{2} + \dfrac{8}{2} = 3n + 4$
Subtract 4 from the quotient.	$3n + 4 - 4 = 3n$

Using the variable n to represent any number, the result is $3n$, or three times the number n. This proves that the result of the procedure is three times the original number selected for any number. We have used deductive reasoning. ☐

PRACTICE
4 Consider the following procedure:

Select a number. Multiply the number by 4. Add 6 to the product. Divide this sum by 2. Subtract 3 from the quotient.

a. Repeat this procedure for at least four different numbers. Write a conjecture that relates the result of this process to the original number selected.

b. Represent the original number by the variable n and use deductive reasoning to prove the conjecture in part (a).

CHAPTER 2 EXTENSION EXERCISES

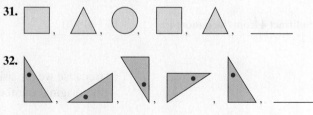

Identify a pattern in each list of numbers. Then use this pattern to find the next number. (More than one pattern might exist, so it is possible that there is more than one correct answer.)

1. 8, 12, 16, 20, 24, _____   **2.** 19, 24, 29, 34, 39, _____

3. 37, 32, 27, 22, 17, _____   **4.** 33, 29, 25, 21, 17, _____

5. 3, 9, 27, 81, 243, _____   **6.** 2, 8, 32, 128, 512, _____

7. 1, 2, 4, 8, 16, _____   **8.** 1, 5, 25, 125, _____

9. 1, 4, 1, 8, 1, 16, 1, _____   **10.** 1, 4, 1, 7, 1, 10, 1, _____

11. 4, 2, 0, −2, −4, _____   **12.** 6, 3, 0, −3, −6, _____

13. $\frac{1}{2}, \frac{1}{6}, \frac{1}{10}, \frac{1}{14}, \frac{1}{18}$, _____   **14.** $1, \frac{1}{2}, \frac{1}{3}, \frac{1}{4}, \frac{1}{5}$, _____

15. $1, \frac{1}{3}, \frac{1}{9}, \frac{1}{27}$, _____   **16.** $1, \frac{1}{2}, \frac{1}{4}, \frac{1}{8}$, _____

17. 3, 7, 12, 18, 25, 33, _____   **18.** 2, 5, 9, 14, 20, 27, _____

19. 3, 6, 11, 18, 27, 38, _____   **20.** 2, 5, 10, 17, 26, 37, _____

21. 3, 7, 10, 17, 27, 44, _____   **22.** 2, 5, 7, 12, 19, 31, _____

23. 2, 7, 12, 5, 10, 15, 8, 13, _____

24. 3, 9, 15, 5, 11, 17, 7, 13, _____

25. 3, 6, 5, 10, 9, 18, 17, 34, _____

26. 2, 6, 5, 15, 14, 42, 41, 123, _____

27. 64, −16, 4, −1, _____

28. 125, −25, 5, −1, _____

29. $(6, 2), (0, -4), \left(7\frac{1}{2}, 3\frac{1}{2}\right), (2, -2), (3, \underline{\hspace{0.3in}})$

30. $\left(\frac{2}{3}, \frac{4}{9}\right), \left(\frac{1}{5}, \frac{1}{25}\right), (7, 49), \left(-\frac{5}{6}, \frac{25}{36}\right), \left(-\frac{4}{7}, \underline{\hspace{0.3in}}\right)$

Identify a pattern in each sequence of figures. Then use the pattern to find the next figure in the sequence.

31.

32.

33.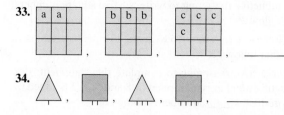

34.

, , , , _____

Exercises 35–38 describe procedures that are to be applied to numbers. In each exercise,

  a. *Repeat the procedure for four numbers of your choice. Write a conjecture that relates the result of the process to the original number selected.*

  b. *Represent the original number by the variable n and use deductive reasoning to prove the conjecture in part (a).*

35. Select a number. Multiply the number by 4. Add 8 to the product. Divide this sum by 2. Subtract 4 from the quotient.

36. Select a number. Multiply the number by 3. Add 6 to the product. Divide this sum by 3. Subtract the original selected number from the quotient.

37. Select a number. Add 5. Double the result. Subtract 4. Divide by 2. Subtract the original selected number.

38. Select a number. Add 3. Double the result. Add 4. Divide by 2. Subtract the original selected number.

In Exercises 39–44, use inductive reasoning to predict the next line in each sequence of computations. Then use a calculator or perform the arithmetic by hand to determine whether your conjecture is correct.

39.
$$1 + 2 = \frac{2 \times 3}{2}$$
$$1 + 2 + 3 = \frac{3 \times 4}{2}$$
$$1 + 2 + 3 + 4 = \frac{4 \times 5}{2}$$
$$1 + 2 + 3 + 4 + 5 = \frac{5 \times 6}{2}$$

40.
$$3 + 6 = \frac{6 \times 3}{2}$$
$$3 + 6 + 9 = \frac{9 \times 4}{2}$$
$$3 + 6 + 9 + 12 = \frac{12 \times 5}{2}$$
$$3 + 6 + 9 + 12 + 15 = \frac{15 \times 6}{2}$$

41.
$$1 + 3 = 2 \times 2$$
$$1 + 3 + 5 = 3 \times 3$$
$$1 + 3 + 5 + 7 = 4 \times 4$$
$$1 + 3 + 5 + 7 + 9 = 5 \times 5$$

42.
$$\frac{1}{1 \times 2} + \frac{1}{2 \times 3} = \frac{2}{3}$$
$$\frac{1}{1 \times 2} + \frac{1}{2 \times 3} + \frac{1}{3 \times 4} = \frac{3}{4}$$
$$\frac{1}{1 \times 2} + \frac{1}{2 \times 3} + \frac{1}{3 \times 4} + \frac{1}{4 \times 5} = \frac{4}{5}$$

43.
$$9 \times 9 + 7 = 88$$
$$98 \times 9 + 6 = 888$$
$$987 \times 9 + 5 = 8888$$
$$9876 \times 9 + 4 = 88{,}888$$

44.
$$1 \times 9 - 1 = 8$$
$$21 \times 9 - 1 = 188$$
$$321 \times 9 - 1 = 2888$$
$$4321 \times 9 - 1 = 38{,}888$$

In Exercises 45–46, use inductive reasoning to predict the next line in each sequence of computations. Then use a calculator or perform the arithmetic by hand to determine whether your conjecture is correct.

45.
$$33 \times 3367 = 111{,}111$$
$$66 \times 3367 = 222{,}222$$
$$99 \times 3367 = 333{,}333$$
$$132 \times 3367 = 444{,}444$$

46.
$$1 \times 8 + 1 = 9$$
$$12 \times 8 + 2 = 98$$
$$123 \times 8 + 3 = 987$$
$$1234 \times 8 + 4 = 9876$$
$$12{,}345 \times 8 + 5 = 98{,}765$$

47. Multiple Choice. Study the pattern in these examples:
$$a^2 \# a^4 = a^{10} \quad a^3 \# a^2 = a^7 \quad a^5 \# a^3 = a^{11}.$$

Select the equation that describes the pattern.

a. $a^x \# a^y = a^{2x+y}$

b. $a^x \# a^y = a^{x+2y}$

c. $a^x \# a^y = a^{x+y+4}$

d. $a^x \# a^y = a^{xy+2}$

48. Multiple Choice. Study the pattern in these examples:
$$a^5 * a^3 * a^2 = a^5 \quad a^3 * a^7 * a^2 = a^6 \quad a^2 * a^4 * a^8 = a^7.$$

Select the equation that describes the pattern.

a. $a^x * a^y * a^z = a^{x+y+z}$

b. $a^x * a^y * a^z = a^{\frac{xyz}{2}}$

c. $a^x * a^y * a^z = a^{\frac{x+y+z}{2}}$

d. $a^x * a^y * a^z = a^{\frac{xy}{2}+z}$

49. Multiple Choice. Study the pattern, or trend, shown by the data in the bar graph. Then select the expression that *best* describes the number of movie tickets sold, in billions, *n* years after 2002.

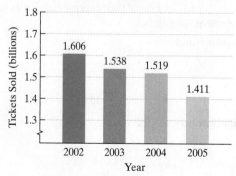

Theater Attendance: Number of Movie Tickets Sold in the United States

Source: Entertainment Weekly

a. $1.6 + 0.06n$

b. $1.6 + 1.06n$

c. $1.6 - 0.06n$

d. $1.6 - 1.06n$

50. Multiple Choice. The data displayed by the graph indicate that watching movies at home is becoming more popular. Study the pattern, or trend, shown by the data. Then select the expression that *best* describes the number of hours Americans watched prerecorded movies at home *n* years after 2004.

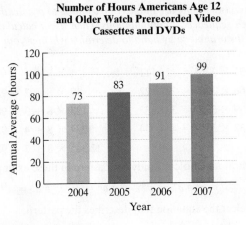

Number of Hours Americans Age 12 and Older Watch Prerecorded Video Cassettes and DVDs

Source: U.S. Census Bureau

a. $73.6 + 12.5n$

b. $73.6 + 8.6n$

c. $73.6 - 12.5n$

d. $73.6 - 8.6n$

In Exercises 51–52, identify the reasoning process, induction or deduction, in each example. Explain your answer.

51. It can be shown that

$$1 + 2 + 3 + \cdots + n = \frac{n(n + 1)}{2}.$$

I can use this formula to conclude that the sum of the first one hundred counting numbers, $1 + 2 + 3 + \cdots + 100$, is

$$\frac{100(100 + 1)}{2} = \frac{100(101)}{2} = 50(101), \text{ or } 5050.$$

52. The course policy states that work turned in late will be marked down a grade. I turned in my report a day late, so it was marked down from B to C.

53. Multiple Steps. The ancient Greeks studied **figurate numbers,** so named because of their representations as geometric arrangements of points.

Triangular Numbers

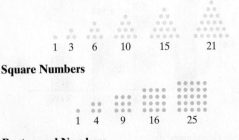

1   3   6   10   15   21

Square Numbers

1   4   9   16   25

Pentagonal Numbers

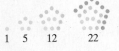

1   5   12   22

a. Use inductive reasoning to write the five triangular numbers that follow 21.

b. Use inductive reasoning to write the five square numbers that follow 25.

c. Use inductive reasoning to write the five pentagonal numbers that follow 22.

d. Use inductive reasoning to complete this statement: If a triangular number is multiplied by 8 and then 1 is added to the product, a _____ number is obtained.

54. The triangular arrangement of numbers shown below is known as **Pascal's triangle,** credited to French mathematician Blaise Pascal (1623–1662). Use inductive reasoning to find the six numbers designated by question marks.

$$
\begin{array}{ccccccccccc}
 & & & & & 1 & & & & & \\
 & & & & 1 & & 1 & & & & \\
 & & & 1 & & 2 & & 1 & & & \\
 & & 1 & & 3 & & 3 & & 1 & & \\
 & 1 & & 4 & & 6 & & 4 & & 1 & \\
? & & ? & & ? & & ? & & ? & & ?
\end{array}
$$

55. The word *induce* comes from a Latin term meaning to lead. Explain what leading has to do with inductive reasoning.

56. Describe what is meant by deductive reasoning. Give an example.

57. Give an example of a decision that you made recently in which the method of reasoning you used to reach the decision was induction. Describe your reasoning process.

CONCEPT EXTENSION

58. If $(6 - 2)^2 = 36 - 24 + 4$ and $(8 - 5)^2 = 64 - 80 + 25$, use inductive reasoning to write a compatible expression for $(11 - 7)^2$.

59. Study the first three figures. Then use inductive reasoning to determine the area of the same type of figure with a radius of 9 and a height of 10.

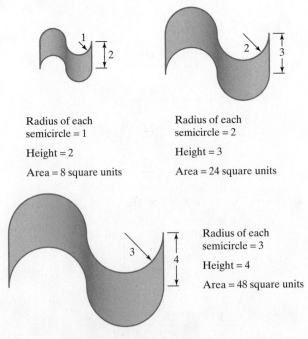

Radius of each semicircle = 1
Height = 2
Area = 8 square units

Radius of each semicircle = 2
Height = 3
Area = 24 square units

Radius of each semicircle = 3
Height = 4
Area = 48 square units

60. Write a list of numbers that has two patterns so that the next number in the list can be 15 or 20.

61. Multiple Steps. a. Repeat the following procedure with at least five people. Write a conjecture that relates the result of the procedure to each person's birthday.

> Take the number of the month of your birthday (January = 1, February = 2, ..., December = 12), multiply by 5, add 6, multiply this sum by 4, add 9, multiply this new sum by 5, and add the number of the day on which you were born. Finally, subtract 165.

   b. Let M represent the month number and let D represent the day number of any person's birthday. Use deductive reasoning to prove your conjecture in part (a).

62. Multiple Steps. a. Use a calculator to find 6×6, 66×66, 666×666, and 6666×6666.

   b. Describe a pattern in the numbers being multiplied and the resulting products.

   c. Use the pattern to write the next two multiplications and their products. Then use your calculator to verify these results.

   d. Is this process an example of inductive or deductive reasoning? Explain your answer.

63. Multiple Steps. a. Use a calculator to find 3367×3, 3367×6, 3367×9, and 3367×12.

   b. Describe a pattern in the numbers being multiplied and the resulting products.

   c. Use the pattern to write the next two multiplications and their products. Then use your calculator to verify these results.

   d. Is this process an example of inductive or deductive reasoning? Explain your answer.

CHAPTER 2 VOCABULARY CHECK

Fill in each blank with one of the words or phrases listed below.

like terms   numerical coefficient   linear inequality in one variable
equivalent equations   formula   compound inequalities
linear equation in one variable

1. Terms with the same variables raised to exactly the same powers are called _____.

2. A _____ can be written in the form $ax + b = c$.

3. Equations that have the same solution are called _____.

4. An equation that describes a known relationship among quantities is called a _____.

5. The _____ of a term is its numerical factor.

CHAPTER 2 REVIEW

(2.1) Simplify the following expressions.

1. $5x - x + 2x$

2. $0.2z - 4.6x - 7.4z$

3. $\frac{1}{2}x + 3 + \frac{7}{2}x - 5$

4. $\frac{4}{5}y + 1 + \frac{6}{5}y + 2$

5. $2(n - 4) + n - 10$

6. $3(w + 2) - (12 - w)$

7. Subtract $7x - 2$ from $x + 5$.

8. Subtract $1.4y - 3$ from $y - 0.7$.

Write each of the following as algebraic expressions.

9. Three times a number decreased by 7

10. Twice the sum of a number and 2.8 added to 3 times a number

(2.2) Solve each equation.

11. $8x + 4 = 9x$

12. $5y - 3 = 6y$

13. $\frac{2}{7}x + \frac{5}{7}x = 6$

14. $3x - 5 = 4x + 1$

15. $2x - 6 = x - 6$

16. $4(x + 3) = 3(1 + x)$

17. $6(3 + n) = 5(n - 1)$

18. $5(2 + x) - 3(3x + 2) = -5(x - 6) + 2$

Use the addition property to fill in the blank so that the middle equation simplifies to the last equation.

19. $x - 5 = 3$
     $x - 5 + \underline{\quad} = 3 + \underline{\quad}$
              $x = 8$

20. $x + 9 = -2$
     $x + 9 - \underline{\quad} = -2 - \underline{\quad}$
              $x = -11$

Choose the correct algebraic expression.

21. The sum of two numbers is 10. If one number is x, express the other number in terms of x.

   a. $x - 10$ **b.** $10 - x$
   c. $10 + x$ **d.** $10x$

22. Mandy is 5 inches taller than Melissa. If x inches represents the height of Mandy, express Melissa's height in terms of x.

   a. $x - 5$ **b.** $5 - x$
   c. $5 + x$ **d.** $5x$

△ **23.** If one angle measures $x°$, express the measure of its complement in terms of x.

    a. $(180 - x)°$ **b.** $(90 - x)°$

    c. $(x - 180)°$ **d.** $(x - 90)°$

△ **24.** If one angle measures $(x + 5)°$, express the measure of its supplement in terms of x.

    a. $(185 + x)°$

    b. $(95 + x)°$

    c. $(175 - x)°$

    d. $(x - 170)°$

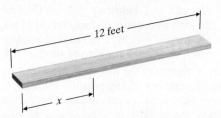

$(x + 5)°$?

(2.3) *Solve each equation.*

25. $\dfrac{3}{4}x = -9$ **26.** $\dfrac{x}{6} = \dfrac{2}{3}$

27. $-5x = 0$ **28.** $-y = 7$

29. $0.2x = 0.15$ **30.** $\dfrac{-x}{3} = 1$

31. $-3x + 1 = 19$ **32.** $5x + 25 = 20$

33. $7(x - 1) + 9 = 5x$ **34.** $7x - 6 = 5x - 3$

35. $-5x + \dfrac{3}{7} = \dfrac{10}{7}$ **36.** $5x + x = 9 + 4x - 1 + 6$

37. Write the sum of three consecutive integers as an expression in x. Let x be the first integer.

38. Write the sum of the first and fourth of four consecutive even integers. Let x be the first even integer.

(2.4) *Solve each equation.*

39. $\dfrac{5}{3}x + 4 = \dfrac{2}{3}x$ **40.** $\dfrac{7}{8}x + 1 = \dfrac{5}{8}x$

41. $-(5x + 1) = -7x + 3$ **42.** $-4(2x + 1) = -5x + 5$

43. $-6(2x - 5) = -3(9 + 4x)$

44. $3(8y - 1) = 6(5 + 4y)$

45. $\dfrac{3(2 - z)}{5} = z$ **46.** $\dfrac{4(n + 2)}{5} = -n$

47. $0.5(2n - 3) - 0.1 = 0.4(6 + 2n)$

48. $-9 - 5a = 3(6a - 1)$ **49.** $\dfrac{5(c + 1)}{6} = 2c - 3$

50. $\dfrac{2(8 - a)}{3} = 4 - 4a$

🖩 **51.** $200(70x - 3560) = -179(150x - 19{,}300)$

52. $1.72y - 0.04y = 0.42$

(2.5) *Solve each of the following.*

53. The height of the Washington Monument is 50.5 inches more than 10 times the length of a side of its square base. If the sum of these two dimensions is 7327 inches, find the height of the Washington Monument. (*Source:* National Park Service)

54. A 12-foot board is to be divided into two pieces so that one piece is twice as long as the other. If x represents the length of the shorter piece, find the length of each piece.

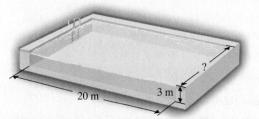

12 feet

x

55. In a recent year, Kellogg Company acquired Keebler Foods Company. After the merger, the total number of Kellogg and Keebler manufacturing plants was 53. The number of Kellogg plants was one less than twice the number of Keebler plants. How many of each type of plant were there? (*Source: Kellogg Company 2000 Annual Report*)

56. Find three consecutive integers whose sum is -114.

57. The quotient of a number and 3 is the same as the difference of the number and two. Find the number.

58. Double the sum of a number and 6 is the opposite of the number. Find the number.

(2.6) *Substitute the given values into the given formulas and solve for the unknown variable.*

59. $P = 2l + 2w$; $P = 46, l = 14$

60. $V = lwh$; $V = 192, l = 8, w = 6$

Solve each equation for the indicated variable.

61. $y = mx + b$ for m

62. $r = vst - 5$ for s

63. $2y - 5x = 7$ for x

64. $3x - 6y = -2$ for y

△ **65.** $C = \pi D$ for π

△ **66.** $C = 2\pi r$ for π

△ **67.** A swimming pool holds 900 cubic meters of water. If its length is 20 meters and its height is 3 meters, find its width.

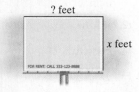

?

20 m   3 m

68. The perimeter of a rectangular billboard is 60 feet and has a length 6 feet longer than its width. Find the dimensions of the billboard.

? feet

x feet

FOR RENT: CALL 333-123-8888

69. A charity 10K race is given annually to benefit a local hospice organization. How long will it take to run/walk a 10K race (10 kilometers or 10,000 meters) if your average pace is 125 **meters** per minute? Give your time in hours and minutes.

70. On April 28, 2001, the highest temperature recorded in the United States was 104°F, which occurred in Death Valley, California. Convert this temperature to degrees Celsius. (*Source:* National Weather Service)

(2.7) *Find each of the following.*

71. The number 9 is what percent of 45?

72. The number 59.5 is what percent of 85?

73. The number 137.5 is 125% of what number?

74. The number 768 is 60% of what number?

75. The price of a small diamond ring was recently increased by 11%. If the ring originally cost $1900, find the mark-up and the new price of the ring.

76. A recent survey found that 66.9% of Americans use the Internet. If a city has a population of 76,000 how many people in that city would you expect to use the Internet? (*Source:* UCLA Center for Communication Policy)

The graph below shows the percent(s) of cell phone users who have engaged in various behaviors while driving and talking on their cell phones. Use this graph to answer Exercises 77 through 80.

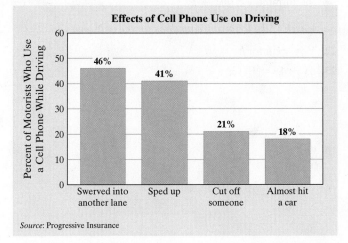

Effects of Cell Phone Use on Driving

Source: Progressive Insurance

77. What percent of motorists who use a cell phone while driving have almost hit another car?

78. What is the most common effect of cell phone use on driving?

79. If a cell-phone service has an estimated 4600 customers who use their cell phones while driving, how many of these customers would you expect to have cut someone off while driving and talking on their cell phones?

80. Do the percents in the graph have a sum of 100%? Why or why not?

(2.8) *Find each of the following.*

81. Thirty gallons of a 20% acid solution is needed for an experiment. Only 40% and 10% acid solutions are available. How much of each should be mixed to form the needed solution?

82. Forty liters of a 20% garden growth solution is needed. Only 50% and 10% solutions are available. How much of each should be mixed to form the needed solution?

83. A youth organization collected nickels and dimes for a charity drive. By the end of the 1-day drive, the youth had collected $56.35. If there were three times as many dimes as nickels, how many of each type of coin was collected?

84. A collection of dimes and quarters are retrieved from a soft drink machine. There are five times as many dimes as quarters and the total value of the coins is $27.75. Find the number of dimes and the number of quarters.

85. Two jets depart from the same location and travel in opposite directions. One jet's speed is 480mph and other jet's speed is 510 mph. When will the jets be 1485 miles apart?

86. Two cars leave the same location at the same time and travel in opposite directions. One car's speed is 60 mph and the other car's speed is 64mph. When will the two cars be 434 miles apart?

87. Two cars leave Miami, Florida at the same time and both travel north on Interstate 95. The first car's speed is 55 mph and the second car's speed is 61 mph. When will the cars be 18 miles apart?

88. Two cars leave Lincoln, Nebraska at the same time and both travel west on Interstate 80. The first car's speed is 58 mph and the second car's speed is 70 mph. When will the cars be 24 miles apart?

MIXED REVIEW

Solve each equation.

89. $6x + 2x - 1 = 5x + 11$

90. $2(3y - 4) = 6 + 7y$

91. $4(3 - a) - (6a + 9) = -12a$

92. $\dfrac{x}{3} - 2 = 5$

93. $2(y + 5) = 2y + 10$

94. $7x - 3x + 2 = 2(2x - 1)$

Solve.

95. The sum of six and twice a number is equal to seven less than the number. Find the number.

96. A 23-inch piece of string is to be cut into two pieces so that the length of the longer piece is three more than four times the shorter piece. If x represents the length of the shorter piece, find the lengths of both pieces.

Solve for the specified variable.

97. $V = \dfrac{1}{3} Ah$ for h

98. What number is 26% of 85?

99. The number 72 is 45% of what number?

100. A company recently increased their number of employees from 235 to 282. Find the percent increase.

CHAPTER 2 TEST TEST PREP VIDEO The fully worked-out solutions to any exercises you want to review are available in MyMathLab.

Simplify each of the following expressions.

1. $2y - 6 - y - 4$
2. $2.7x + 6.1 + 3.2x - 4.9$
3. $4(x - 2) - 3(2x - 6)$
4. $7 + 2(5y - 3)$

Solve each of the following equations.

5. $-\dfrac{4}{5}x = 4$
6. $4(n - 5) = -(4 - 2n)$
7. $5y - 7 + y = -(y + 3y)$
8. $4z + 1 - z = 1 + z$
9. $\dfrac{2(x + 6)}{3} = x - 5$
10. $\dfrac{1}{2} - x + \dfrac{3}{2} = x - 4$
11. $-0.3(x - 4) + x = 0.5(3 - x)$
12. $-4(a + 1) - 3a = -7(2a - 3)$
13. $-2(x - 3) = x + 5 - 3x$

Solve each of the following applications.

14. A number increased by two-thirds of the number is 35. Find the number.

△ 15. A gallon of water seal covers 200 square feet. How many gallons are needed to paint two coats of water seal on a deck that measures 20 feet by 35 feet?

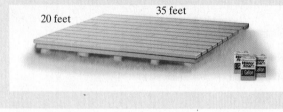

16. Some states have a single area code for the entire state. Two such states have area codes where one is double the other. If the sum of these integers is 1203, find the two area codes. (*Source:* North American Numbering Plan Administration)

17. New York State has more public libraries than any other state. It has 650 more public libraries than Indiana does. If the total number of public libraries for these state is 1504, find the number of public libraries in New York and the number in Indiana. (*Source: The World Almanac and book of facts*)

18. Part of the proceeds from a hospital fund raiser was $3750 in $10 and $20 bills. If there were 30 more $20 bills than $10 bills, find the number of each denomination.

19. Two cars leave Charlotte, North Carolina at the same time, both traveling north on Interstate 77. One car's speed is 64 mph and the other is 52 mph. When will the two cars be 15 miles apart?

20. Suppose two trains leave a city at the same time, traveling in opposite directions. One train travels 6 mph faster than the other. In 3 hours, the trains are 282 miles apart. Find the speed of each train.

21. Find the value of x if $y = -14, m = -2$, and $b = -2$ in the formula $y = mx + b$.

Solve each of the following equations for the indicated variable.

22. $V = \pi r^2 h$ for h
23. $3x - 4y = 10$ for y

CHAPTER 2 STANDARDIZED TEST

Multiple Choice. *Choose the one alternative that best completes the statement or answers the question.*

Simplify the expression.

1. $6x + 10 - 2x + 9$
   a. $23x$
   b. $8x + 19$
   c. $4x + 1$
   d. $4x + 19$
2. $1.8x + 3.8 + 5.3x - 6.5$
   a. $7.1x - 2.7$
   b. -3.2
   c. $7.1x + 2.7$
   d. $7.1x - 10.3$
3. $3(x - 3) - 4(2x - 2)$
   a. $5x - 1$
   b. $-5x - 1$
   c. $-11x + 17$
   d. $-5x - 5$

4. $7 + 4(3y - 9)$
   a. $12y - 43$
   b. $12y - 29$
   c. $12y + 63$
   d. $12y + 29$

Solve the equation.

5. $\dfrac{1}{7}x = -4$
   a. -28
   b. 3
   c. 2
   d. -1
6. $3(2n - 3) = 5(n + 3)$
   a. 6
   b. -6
   c. 9
   d. 24

7. $3y - 6 + y = -(y + 6y)$

   a. $-\dfrac{6}{11}$ **b.** $\dfrac{6}{11}$

   c. 0   **d.** no solution

8. $-7z + 2 + 5z = -3z + 7$

   a. -2 **b.** 5

   c. -7 **d.** 7

9. $\dfrac{2(x - 2)}{3} = x - 7$

   a. 3   **b.** 23

   c. 17   **d.** -17

10. $\dfrac{1}{2} - x + \dfrac{7}{2} = x - 6$

   a. -1 **b.** -5

   c. 5   **d.** 10

11. $-0.3(x - 9) + x = 0.5(9 - x)$

   a. 1.5   **b.** 1

   c. 9   **d.** 6

12. $-3(2x + 5) - 2 = -4(x + 3) + 3x$

   a. $-\dfrac{5}{7}$ **b.** 3

   c. -1 **d.** 0

13. $-3(x - 4) = x + 9 - 4x$

   a. 0   **b.** $-<b>$

   c. $<a>$ **d.** no solution

Solve.

14. A number increased by three-fourths of the number is 14. Find the number.

   a. 8   **b.** $\dfrac{14}{3}$

   c. 2   **d.** 4

15. A gallon of stain covers 200 square feet. How many gallons are needed to paint two coats of stain on a deck that measures 20 feet by 45 feet?

   a. 6 gal   **b.** 9 gal

   c. 18 gal   **d.** 5 gal

16. The Discovery Museum is building a second parking garage. The second parking garage will have double the capacity, in parking spaces, of their original parking garage. If the sum of these integers is 1896, find the capacity for both parking garages.

   a. 632 spaces, 1264 spaces

   b. 532 spaces, 1164 spaces

   c. 532 spaces, 1364 spaces

   d. 732 spaces, 1164 spaces

17. There are 22 more sophomores than juniors in an 8 AM algebra class. If there are 48 students in this class, find the number of sophomores and the number of juniors in the class.

   a. 13 sophomores; 35 juniors

   b. 70 sophomores; 26 juniors

   c. 48 sophomores; 26 juniors

   d. 35 sophomores; 13 juniors

18. Part of the proceeds from a hospital fund raiser was $2250 in $10 and $20 bills. If there are seven times as many $10 bills than $20 bills, find the number of each denomination.

   a. 25 $20 bills; 7 $10 bills

   b. 175 $20 bills; 7 $10 bills

   c. 175 $20 bills; 25 $10 bills

   d. 25 $20 bills; 175 $10 bills

19. Suppose two trains leave a city at the same time, traveling in opposite directions. One train travels 4 mph faster than the other. In 4 hours, the trains are 360 miles apart. Find the speed of each train.

   a. 43 mph; 47 mph

   b. 51 mph; 55 mph

   c. 47 mph; 51 mph

   d. 39 mph; 43 mph

20. Find the value of x if $y = -22$, $m = -3$, and $b = -1$ in the formula $y = mx + b$.

   a. $x = -7$ **b.** $x = -63$

   c. $x = 63$ **d.** $x = 7$

Solve the equation for the indicated variable.

21. $I = Prt$ *for* t

   a. $t = P - Ir$ **b.** $t = \dfrac{P - 1}{Ir}$

   c. $t = \dfrac{P - I}{1 + r}$ **d.** $t = \dfrac{I}{Pr}$

22. $5x - 7y = 13$ *for* y

   a. $y = \dfrac{5x + 13}{-7}$ **b.** $y = \dfrac{5x - 13}{7}$

   c. $y = \dfrac{5x - 13}{-7}$ **d.** $y = \dfrac{5x + 13}{7}$

3

Graphs and Functions

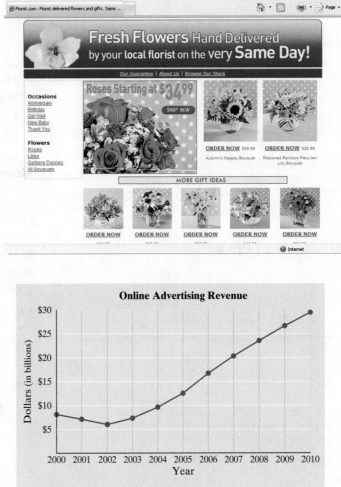

Source: PriceWaterHouse Cooper's IAB Internet Advertising Revenue Report

Online advertising is a way to promote services and products via the Internet. The broken-line graph above shows the quickly growing yearly revenue generated by online advertising.

In Chapter 3's Integrated Review, Exercise 16, you will have the opportunity to use a linear equation, generated by the years 2003–2010, to predict online advertising revenue.

3.1 READING GRAPHS AND THE RECTANGULAR COORDINATE SYSTEM

OBJECTIVES

1 Read bar and line graphs.

2 Define the rectangular coordinate system and plot ordered pairs of numbers.

3 Graph paired data to create a scatter diagram and determine correlation.

4 Determine whether an ordered pair is a solution of an equation in two variables.

5 Find the missing coordinate of an ordered pair solution, given one coordinate of the pair.

In today's world, where the exchange of information must be fast and entertaining, graphs are becoming increasingly popular. They provide a quick way of making comparisons, drawing conclusions, and approximating quantities.

OBJECTIVE 1 ▶ Reading bar and line graphs. A **bar graph** consists of a series of bars arranged vertically or horizontally. The bar graph in Example 1 shows a comparison of worldwide Internet users by country. The names of the countries are listed vertically and a bar is shown for each country. Corresponding to the length of the bar for each country is a number along a horizontal axis. These horizontal numbers are the number of Internet users in millions.

EXAMPLE 1

The following bar graph shows the estimated number of Internet users worldwide by country, as of a recent year.

a. Find the country that has the most Internet users and approximate the number of users.

b. How many more users are in the United States than in China?

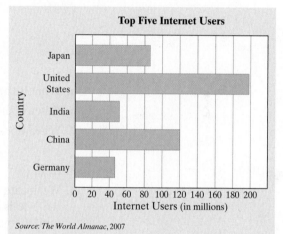

Source: *The World Almanac*, 2007

Solution

a. Since these bars are arranged horizontally, we look for the longest bar, which is the bar representing the United States. To approximate the number associated with this country, we move from the right edge of this bar vertically downward to the Internet user axis. This country has approximately 198 million Internet users.

b. The United States has approximately 198 million Internet users. China has approximately 120 million Internet users. To find how many more users are in the United States, we subtract $198 - 120 = 78$ or 78 million more Internet users.   ☐

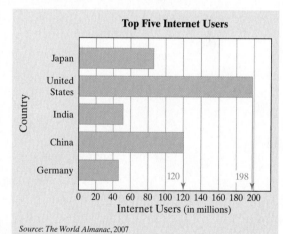

Source: *The World Almanac*, 2007

PRACTICE
1   Use the graph from Example 1 to answer the following.

a. Find the country shown with the fewest Internet users and approximate the number of users.

b. How many more users are in India than in Germany?

A **line graph** consists of a series of points connected by a line. The next graph is an example of a line graph. It is also sometimes called a **broken line graph.**

EXAMPLE 2 The line graph shows the relationship between time spent smoking a cigarette and pulse rate. Time is recorded along the horizontal axis in minutes, with 0 minutes being the moment a smoker lights a cigarette. Pulse is recorded along the vertical axis in heartbeats per minute.

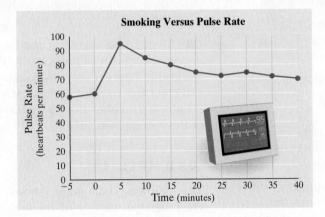

a. What is the pulse rate 15 minutes after a cigarette is lit?

b. When is the pulse rate the lowest?

c. When does the pulse rate show the greatest change?

Solution

a. We locate the number 15 along the time axis and move vertically upward until the line is reached. From this point on the line, we move horizontally to the left until the pulse rate axis is reached. Reading the number of beats per minute, we find that the pulse rate is 80 beats per minute 15 minutes after a cigarette is lit.

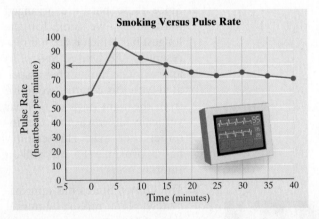

b. We find the lowest point of the line graph, which represents the lowest pulse rate. From this point, we move vertically downward to the time axis. We find that the pulse rate is the lowest at −5 minutes, which means 5 minutes *before* lighting a cigarette.

c. The pulse rate shows the greatest change during the 5 minutes between 0 and 5. Notice that the line graph is *steepest* between 0 and 5 minutes.   □

PRACTICE

2 Use the graph from Example 2 to answer the following.

a. What is the pulse rate 40 minutes after lighting a cigarette?

b. What is the pulse rate when the cigarette is being lit?

c. When is the pulse rate the highest?

OBJECTIVE 2 ▶ Defining the rectangular coordinate system and plotting ordered pairs of numbers. Notice in the previous graph that there are two numbers associated with each point of the graph. For example, we discussed earlier that 15 minutes after lighting a cigarette, the pulse rate is 80 beats per minute. If we agree to write the time first and the pulse rate second, we can say there is a point on the graph corresponding to the **ordered pair** of numbers (15, 80). A few more ordered pairs are listed alongside their corresponding points.

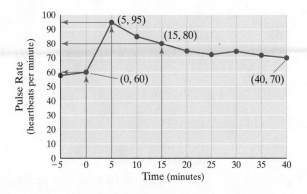

In general, we use this same ordered pair idea to describe the location of a point in a plane (such as a piece of paper). We start with a horizontal and a vertical axis. Each axis is a number line, and for the sake of consistency we construct our axes to intersect at the 0 coordinate of both. This point of intersection is called the **origin.** Notice that these two number lines or axes divide the plane into four regions called **quadrants.** The quadrants are usually numbered with Roman numerals as shown. The axes are not considered to be in any quadrant.

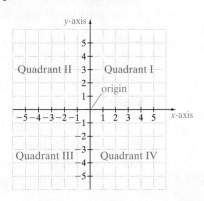

It is helpful to label axes, so we label the horizontal axis the **x-axis** and the vertical axis the **y-axis.** We call the system described above the **rectangular coordinate system.**

Just as with the pulse rate graph, we can then describe the locations of points by ordered pairs of numbers. We list the horizontal **x-axis** measurement first and the vertical **y-axis** measurement second.

To plot or graph the point corresponding to the ordered pair

$$(a, b)$$

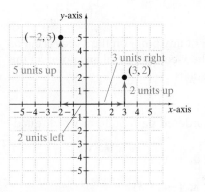

we start at the origin. We then move a units left or right (right if a is positive, left if a is negative). From there, we move b units up or down (up if b is positive, down if b is negative). For example, to plot the point corresponding to the ordered pair (3, 2), we start at the origin, move 3 units right, and from there move 2 units up. (See the figure to the left.) The x-value, 3, is called the **x-coordinate** and the y-value, 2, is called the **y-coordinate.** From now on, we will call the point with coordinates (3, 2) simply the point (3, 2). The point (−2, 5) is graphed to the left also.

Does the order in which the coordinates are listed matter? Yes! Notice that the point corresponding to the ordered pair (2, 3) is in a different location than the point corresponding to (3, 2). These two ordered pairs of numbers describe two different points of the plane.

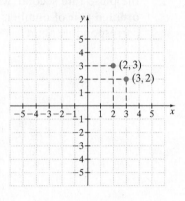

Concept Check ☑

Is the graph of the point (−5, 1) in the same location as the graph of the point (1, −5)? Explain.

> ▶ **Helpful Hint**
>
> Don't forget that **each ordered pair corresponds to exactly one point in the plane and that each point in the plane corresponds to exactly one ordered pair.**

EXAMPLE 3   On a single coordinate system, plot each ordered pair. State in which quadrant, if any, each point lies.

a. (5, 3)   **b.** (−5, 3)   **c.** (−2, −4)   **d.** (1, −2)

e. (0, 0)   **f.** (0, 2)   **g.** (−5, 0)   **h.** $\left(0, -5\frac{1}{2}\right)$

Solution

Point (5, 3) lies in quadrant I.
Point (−5, 3) lies in quadrant II.
Point (−2, −4) lies in quadrant III.
Point (1, −2) lies in quadrant IV.

Points (0, 0), (0, 2), (−5, 0), and $\left(0, -5\frac{1}{2}\right)$ lie on axes, so they are not in any quadrant.

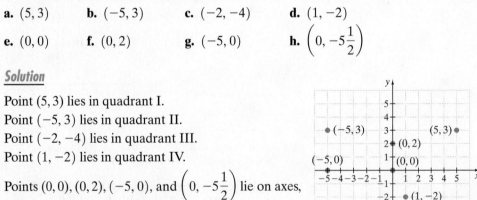

From Example 1, notice that the *y*-coordinate of any point on the *x*-axis is 0. For example, the point (−5, 0) lies on the *x*-axis. Also, the *x*-coordinate of any point on the *y*-axis is 0. For example, the point (0, 2) lies on the *y*-axis. □

PRACTICE
3   On a single coordinate system, plot each ordered pair. State in which quadrant, if any, each point lies.

a. (4, −3)   **b.** (−3, 5)   **c.** (0, 4)   **d.** (−6, 1)

e. (−2, 0)   **f.** (5, 5)   **g.** $\left(3\frac{1}{2}, 1\frac{1}{2}\right)$ **h.** (−4, −5)

Answer to Concept Check:

The graph of point (−5, 1) lies in quadrant II and the graph of point (1, −5) lies in quadrant IV. They are *not* in the same location.

Concept Check ☑

For each description of a point in the rectangular coordinate system, write an ordered pair that represents it.

a. Point A is located three units to the left of the *y*-axis and five units above the *x*-axis.

b. Point B is located six units below the origin.

OBJECTIVE 3 ▶ Graphing paired data. Data that can be represented as an ordered pair is called **paired data.** Many types of data collected from the real world are paired data. For instance, the annual measurement of a child's height can be written as an ordered pair of the form (year, height in inches) and is paired data. The graph of paired data as points in the rectangular coordinate system is called a **scatter diagram.** Scatter diagrams can be used to look for patterns and trends in paired data.

EXAMPLE 4   The table gives the annual net sales for Wal-Mart Stores for the years shown. (*Source:* Wal-Mart Stores, Inc.)

Year	Wal-Mart Net Sales (in billions of dollars)
2000	181
2001	204
2002	230
2003	256
2004	285
2005	312
2006	345

a. Write this paired data as a set of ordered pairs of the form (year, sales in billions of dollars).

b. Create a scatter diagram of the paired data.

c. What trend in the paired data does the scatter diagram show?

Solution

a. The ordered pairs are (2000, 181), (2001, 204), (2002, 230), (2003, 256), (2004, 285), (2005, 312), and (2006, 345).

b. We begin by plotting the ordered pairs. Because the *x*-coordinate in each ordered pair is a year, we label the *x*-axis "Year" and mark the horizontal axis with the years given. Then we label the *y*-axis or vertical axis "Net Sales (in billions of dollars)." In this case it is convenient to mark the vertical axis in multiples of 20. Since no net sale is less than 180, we use the notation ⌇ to skip to 180, then proceed by multiples of 20.

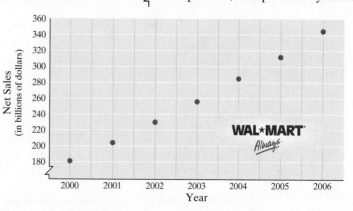

c. The scatter diagram shows that Wal-Mart net sales steadily increased over the years 2000–2006.

Answers to Concept Check:
a. $(-3, 5)$ **b.** $(0, -6)$

PRACTICE
4 The table gives the approximate annual number of wildfires (in the thousands) that have occurred in the United States for the years shown. (*Source: National Interagency Fire Center*)

Year	Wildfires (in thousands)
2000	92
2001	84
2002	73
2003	64
2004	65
2005	67
2006	96

a. Write this paired data as a set of ordered pairs of the form (year, number of wildfires in thousands).

b. Create a scatter diagram of the paired data.

A scatter diagram (or plot) like the one in Example 4 can be used to determine whether two quantities are related. If there is a clear relationship, the quantities are said to be **correlated.** The scatter plot in Example 4 shows an upward trend among the data points. **Correlation** is used to determine if there is a relationship between two variables and, if so, the strength and direction of that relationship.

Note: Establishing that one thing causes another is extremely difficult, even if there is a strong correlation between these things. For example, as the air temperature increases, there is an increase in the number of people stung by jellyfish at the beach. This does not mean that an increase in air temperature causes more people to be stung. It might mean that because it is hotter, more people go into the water. With an increased number of swimmers, more people are likely to be stung. In short, correlation is not necessarily causation.

A measure that is used to describe the strength and direction of a relationship between variables whose data points lie on or near a line is called the **correlation coefficient,** designated by r. Figures (a)–(g) below show scatter plots and correlation

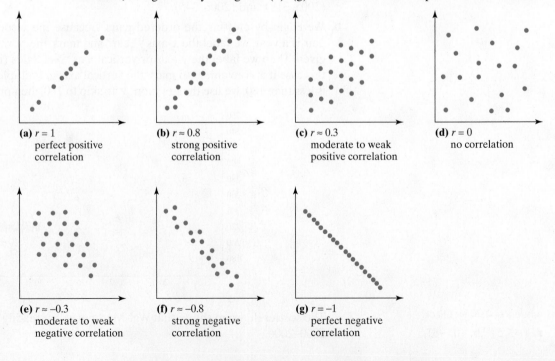

(a) $r = 1$
perfect positive
correlation

(b) $r \approx 0.8$
strong positive
correlation

(c) $r \approx 0.3$
moderate to weak
positive correlation

(d) $r = 0$
no correlation

(e) $r \approx -0.3$
moderate to weak
negative correlation

(f) $r \approx -0.8$
strong negative
correlation

(g) $r = -1$
perfect negative
correlation

coefficients. Although we will not study how the correlation coefficient r is calculated, various values of r are shown for you.

Below is the graph of Example 4 again. Notice that there is a strong positive correlation between the variables (years and net sales).

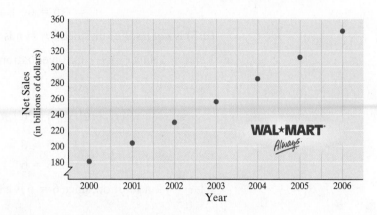

Example of a strong positive correlation.

OBJECTIVE 4 ▶ Determining whether an ordered pair is a solution. Let's see how we can use ordered pairs to record solutions of equations containing two variables. An equation in one variable such as $x + 1 = 5$ has one solution, which is 4: the number 4 is the value of the variable x that makes the equation true.

An equation in two variables, such as $2x + y = 8$, has solutions consisting of two values, one for x and one for y. For example, $x = 3$ and $y = 2$ is a solution of $2x + y = 8$ because, if x is replaced with 3 and y with 2, we get a true statement.

$$2x + y = 8$$
$$2(3) + 2 = 8$$
$$8 = 8 \quad \text{True}$$

The solution $x = 3$ and $y = 2$ can be written as $(3, 2)$, an **ordered pair** of numbers. The first number, 3, is the x-value and the second number, 2, is the y-value.

In general, an ordered pair is a **solution** of an equation in two variables if replacing the variables by the values of the ordered pair results in a true statement.

EXAMPLE 5   Determine whether each ordered pair is a solution of the equation $x - 2y = 6$.

a. $(6, 0)$ **b.** $(0, 3)$ **c.** $\left(1, -\dfrac{5}{2}\right)$

Solution

a. Let $x = 6$ and $y = 0$ in the equation $x - 2y = 6$.

$$x - 2y = 6$$
$$6 - 2(0) = 6 \quad \text{Replace } x \text{ with 6 and } y \text{ with 0.}$$
$$6 - 0 = 6 \quad \text{Simplify.}$$
$$6 = 6 \quad \text{True}$$

$(6, 0)$ is a solution, since $6 = 6$ is a true statement.

b. Let $x = 0$ and $y = 3$.

$$x - 2y = 6$$
$$0 - 2(3) = 6 \quad \text{Replace } x \text{ with 0 and } y \text{ with 3.}$$
$$0 - 6 = 6$$
$$-6 = 6 \quad \text{False}$$

$(0, 3)$ is *not* a solution, since $-6 = 6$ is a false statement.

c. Let $x = 1$ and $y = -\dfrac{5}{2}$ in the equation.

$$x - 2y = 6$$
$$1 - 2\left(-\frac{5}{2}\right) = 6 \quad \text{Replace } x \text{ with 1 and } y \text{ with } -\frac{5}{2}.$$
$$1 + 5 = 6$$
$$6 = 6 \quad \text{True}$$

$\left(1, -\dfrac{5}{2}\right)$ is a solution, since $6 = 6$ is a true statement.   □

> **PRACTICE**
> **5**   Determine whether each ordered pair is a solution of the equation $x + 3y = 6$.
>
> **a.** $(3, 1)$ **b.** $(6, 0)$ **c.** $\left(-2, \dfrac{2}{3}\right)$

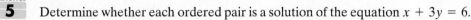

OBJECTIVE 5 ▶ Completing ordered pair solutions. If one value of an ordered pair solution of an equation is known, the other value can be determined. To find the unknown value, replace one variable in the equation by its known value. Doing so results in an equation with just one variable that can be solved for the variable using the methods of Chapter 2.

> **EXAMPLE 6**   Complete the following ordered pair solutions for the equation $3x + y = 12$.
>
> **a.** $(0, \ \ )$ **b.** $(\ \ , 6)$ **c.** $(-1, \ \ )$

Solution

a. In the ordered pair $(0, \ \ )$, the x-value is 0. Let $x = 0$ in the equation and solve for y.

$$3x + y = 12$$
$$3(0) + y = 12 \quad \text{Replace } x \text{ with 0.}$$
$$0 + y = 12$$
$$y = 12$$

The completed ordered pair is $(0, 12)$.

b. In the ordered pair $(\ \ , 6)$, the y-value is 6. Let $y = 6$ in the equation and solve for x.

$$3x + y = 12$$
$$3x + 6 = 12 \quad \text{Replace } y \text{ with 6.}$$
$$3x = 6 \quad \text{Subtract 6 from both sides.}$$
$$x = 2 \quad \text{Divide both sides by 3.}$$

The ordered pair is $(2, 6)$.

c. In the ordered pair $(-1, \ )$, the x-value is -1. Let $x = -1$ in the equation and solve for y.

$$3x + y = 12$$
$$3(-1) + y = 12 \quad \text{Replace } x \text{ with } -1.$$
$$-3 + y = 12$$
$$y = 15 \quad \text{Add 3 to both sides.}$$

The ordered pair is $(-1, 15)$. □

PRACTICE
6   Complete the following ordered pair solutions for the equation $2x - y = 8$.

a. $(0, \ )$ **b.** $(\ , 4)$ **c.** $(-3, \ )$

Solutions of equations in two variables can also be recorded in a **table of values,** as shown in the next example.

EXAMPLE 7   Complete the table for the equation $y = 3x$.

	x	y
a.	-1	
b.		0
c.		-9

Solution

a. Replace x with -1 in the equation and solve for y.

$$y = 3x$$
$$y = 3(-1) \quad \text{Let } x = -1.$$
$$y = -3$$

The ordered pair is $(-1, -3)$.

b. Replace y with 0 in the equation and solve for x.

$$y = 3x$$
$$0 = 3x \quad \text{Let } y = 0.$$
$$0 = x \quad \text{Divide both sides by 3.}$$

The ordered pair is $(0, 0)$.

c. Replace y with -9 in the equation and solve for x.

$$y = 3x$$
$$-9 = 3x \quad \text{Let } y = -9.$$
$$-3 = x \quad \text{Divide both sides by 3.}$$

x	y
-1	-3
0	0
-3	-9

The ordered pair is $(-3, -9)$. The completed table is shown to the left. □

PRACTICE
7   Complete the table for the equation $y = -4x$.

	x	y
a.	-2	
b.		-12
c.	0	

EXAMPLE 8 Complete the table for the equation

$$y = \frac{1}{2}x - 5.$$

	x	y
a.	−2	
b.	0	
c.		0

Solution

a. Let $x = -2$.

$$y = \frac{1}{2}x - 5$$
$$y = \frac{1}{2}(-2) - 5$$
$$y = -1 - 5$$
$$y = -6$$

b. Let $x = 0$.

$$y = \frac{1}{2}x - 5$$
$$y = \frac{1}{2}(0) - 5$$
$$y = 0 - 5$$
$$y = -5$$

c. Let $y = 0$.

$$y = \frac{1}{2}x - 5$$
$$0 = \frac{1}{2}x - 5 \quad \text{Now, solve for } x.$$
$$5 = \frac{1}{2}x \quad \text{Add 5.}$$
$$10 = x \quad \text{Multiply by 2.}$$

Ordered Pairs: $(-2, -6)$ $(0, -5)$ $(10, 0)$

The completed table is

x	y
−2	−6
0	−5
10	0

□

PRACTICE
8 Compute the table for the equation $y = \frac{1}{5}x - 2$.

	x	y
a.	−10	
b.	0	
c.		0

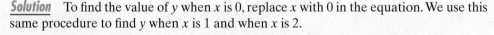

EXAMPLE 9 **Finding the Value of a Computer**

A computer was recently purchased for a small business for $2000. The business manager predicts that the computer will be used for 5 years and the value in dollars y of the computer in x years is $y = -300x + 2000$. Complete the table.

x	0	1	2	3	4	5
y						

Solution To find the value of y when x is 0, replace x with 0 in the equation. We use this same procedure to find y when x is 1 and when x is 2.

Computers for the Home

When $x = 0$,
$$y = -300x + 2000$$
$$y = -300 \cdot 0 + 2000$$
$$y = 0 + 2000$$
$$y = 2000$$

When $x = 1$,
$$y = -300x + 2000$$
$$y = -300 \cdot 1 + 2000$$
$$y = -300 + 2000$$
$$y = 1700$$

When $x = 2$,
$$y = -300x + 2000$$
$$y = -300 \cdot 2 + 2000$$
$$y = -600 + 2000$$
$$y = 1400$$

We have the ordered pairs $(0, 2000)$, $(1, 1700)$, and $(2, 1400)$. This means that in 0 years the value of the computer is $2000, in 1 year the value of the computer is $1700, and in

2 years the value is $1400. To complete the table of values, we continue the procedure for $x = 3$, $x = 4$, and $x = 5$.

When x = 3,	When x = 4,	When x = 5,
$y = -300x + 2000$	$y = -300x + 2000$	$y = -300x + 2000$
$y = -300 \cdot 3 + 2000$	$y = -300 \cdot 4 + 2000$	$y = -300 \cdot 5 + 2000$
$y = -900 + 2000$	$y = -1200 + 2000$	$y = -1500 + 2000$
$y = 1100$	$y = 800$	$y = 500$

The completed table is

x	0	1	2	3	4	5
y	2000	1700	1400	1100	800	500

PRACTICE
9   A college student purchased a used car for $12,000. The student predicted that she would need to use the car for four years and the value in dollars y of the car in x years is $y = -1800x + 12{,}000$. Complete this table.

x	0	1	2	3	4
y					

The ordered pair solutions recorded in the completed table for the example above are graphed below. Notice that the graph gives a visual picture of the decrease in value of the computer.

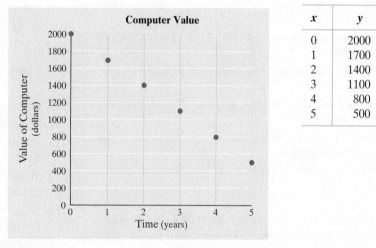

x	y
0	2000
1	1700
2	1400
3	1100
4	800
5	500

VOCABULARY & READINESS CHECK

Word Bank. *Use the choices below to fill in each blank. The exercises below all have to do with the rectangular coordinate system.*

origin	x-coordinate	x-axis	one	four
quadrants	y-coordinate	y-axis	solution	

1. The horizontal axis is called the _____.
2. The vertical axis is called the _____.
3. The intersection of the horizontal axis and the vertical axis is a point called the _____.
4. The axes divide the plane into regions, called _____. There are _____ of these regions.
5. In the ordered pair of numbers $(-2, 5)$, the number -2 is called the _____ and the number 5 is called the _____.
6. Each ordered pair of numbers corresponds to _____ point in the plane.
7. An ordered pair is a _____ of an equation in two variables if replacing the variables by the coordinates of the ordered pair results in a true statement.

3.1 EXERCISE SET

Read a Graph. *The following bar graph shows the top 10 tourist destinations and the number of tourists that visit each country per year. Use this graph to answer Exercises 1 through 6. See Example 1.*

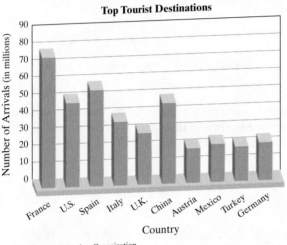

Top Tourist Destinations

Source: World Tourism Organization

1. Which country shown is the most popular tourist destination?

2. Which country shown is the least popular tourist destination?

3. Which countries shown have more than 40 million tourists per year?

4. Which countries shown have between 40 and 50 million tourists per year?

5. Estimate the number of tourists per year whose destination is the United Kingdom.

6. Estimate the number of tourists per year whose destination is Turkey.

Read a Graph. *The following line graph shows the attendance at each Super Bowl game from 2000 through 2007. Use this graph to answer Exercises 7 through 10. See Example 2.*

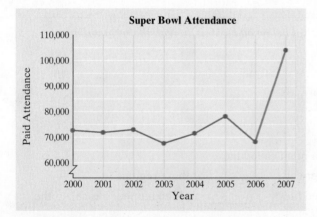

Super Bowl Attendance

7. Estimate the Super Bowl attendance in 2000.

8. Estimate the Super Bowl attendance in 2004.

9. Find the year on the graph with the greatest Super Bowl attendance and approximate that attendance.

10. Find the year on the graph with the least Super Bowl attendance and approximate that attendance.

Read a Graph. *The line graph below shows the number of students per teacher in U.S. public elementary and secondary schools. Use this graph for Exercises 11 through 16. See Example 2.*

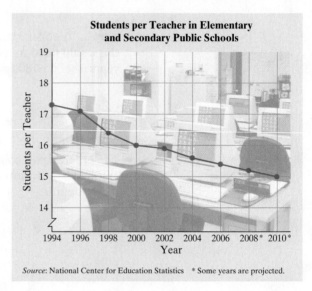

Students per Teacher in Elementary and Secondary Public Schools

Source: National Center for Education Statistics   * Some years are projected.

11. Approximate the number of students per teacher in 2002.

12. Approximate the number of students per teacher in 2010.

13. Between what years shown did the greatest decrease in number of students per teacher occur?

14. What was the first year shown that the number of students per teacher fell below 17?

15. What was the first year shown that the number of students per teacher fell below 16?

16. Discuss any trends shown by this line graph.

Plot each ordered pair. State in which quadrant or on which axis each point lies. See Example 3.

17. a. $(1, 5)$ **b.** $(-5, -2)$
  c. $(-3, 0)$ **d.** $(0, -1)$
  e. $(2, -4)$ **f.** $\left(-1, 4\frac{1}{2}\right)$

  g. $(3.7, 2.2)$ **h.** $\left(\frac{1}{2}, -3\right)$

18. a. $(2, 4)$ **b.** $(0, 2)$
  c. $(-2, 1)$ **d.** $(-3, -3)$
  e. $\left(3\frac{3}{4}, 0\right)$ **f.** $(5, -4)$

  g. $(-3.4, 4.8)$ **h.** $\left(\frac{1}{3}, -5\right)$

Read a Graph. *Find the x- and y-coordinates of each labeled point. See Example 3.*

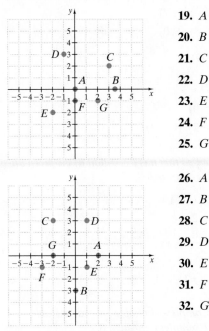

19. *A*
20. *B*
21. *C*
22. *D*
23. *E*
24. *F*
25. *G*

26. *A*
27. *B*
28. *C*
29. *D*
30. *E*
31. *F*
32. *G*

Solve. See Example 4.

33. The table shows the number of regular-season NFL football games won by the winner of the Super Bowl for the years shown. (*Source:* National Football League)

Year	Regular-Season Games Won by Super Bowl Winner
2002	12
2003	14
2004	14
2005	11
2006	12

a. Write each paired data as an ordered pair of the form (year, games won).

b. Draw a grid such as the one in Example 4 and create a scatter diagram of the paired data.

34. The table shows the average price of a gallon of regular unleaded gasoline (in dollars) for the years shown. (*Source:* Energy Information Administration)

Year	Price per Gallon of Unleaded Gasoline (in dollars)
2001	1.38
2002	1.31
2003	1.52
2004	1.81
2005	2.24
2006	2.53

a. Write each paired data as an ordered pair of the form (year, gasoline price).

b. Draw a grid such as the one in Example 4 and create a scatter diagram of the paired data.

35. The table shows the ethanol fuel production in the United States. (*Source:* Renewable Fuels Association; *some years projected)

Year	Ethanol Fuel Production (in millions of gallons)
2001	1770
2003	2800
2005	3904
2007*	7500
2009*	10,800

a. Write each paired data as an ordered pair of the form (year, millions of gallons produced)

b. Draw a grid such as the one in Example 4 and create a scatter diagram of the paired data.

c. What trend in the paired data does the scatter diagram show?

36. The table shows the enrollment in college in the United States for the years shown. (*Source:* U.S. Department of Education)

Year	Enrollment in College (in millions)
1970	8.6
1980	12.1
1990	13.8
2000	15.3
2010*	18.7

*projected

a. Write each paired data as an ordered pair of the form (year, number of institutions).

b. Draw a grid such as the one in Example 4 and create a scatter diagram of the paired data.

c. What trend in the paired data does the scatter diagram show?

37. The table shows the distance from the equator (in miles) and the average annual snowfall (in inches) for each of eight

selected U.S. cities. (*Sources:* National Climatic Data Center, Wake Forest University Albatross Project)

City	Distance from Equator (in miles)	Average Annual Snowfall (in inches)
1. Atlanta, GA	2313	2
2. Austin, TX	2085	1
3. Baltimore, MD	2711	21
4. Chicago, IL	2869	39
5. Detroit, MI	2920	42
6. Juneau, AK	4038	99
7. Miami, FL	1783	0
8. Winston-Salem, NC	2493	9

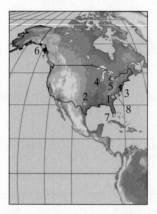

a. Write this paired data as a set of ordered pairs of the form (distance from equator, average annual snowfall).

b. Create a scatter diagram of the paired data. Be sure to label the axes appropriately.

c. What trend in the paired data does the scatter diagram show?

38. The table shows the average farm size (in acres) in the United States during the years shown. (*Source:* National Agricultural Statistics Service)

Year	Average Farm Size (in acres)
2001	438
2002	440
2003	441
2004	443
2005	445
2006	446

a. Write this paired data as a set of ordered pairs of the form (year, average farm size).

b. Create a scatter diagram of the paired data. Be sure to label the axes appropriately.

Determine whether each ordered pair is a solution of the given linear equation. See Example 5.

39. $2x + y = 7$; $(3, 1), (7, 0), (0, 7)$

40. $3x + y = 8$; $(2, 3), (0, 8), (8, 0)$

41. $x = -\frac{1}{3}y$; $(0, 0), (3, -9)$

42. $y = -\frac{1}{2}x$; $(0, 0), (4, 2)$

43. $x = 5$; $(4, 5), (5, 4), (5, 0)$

44. $y = -2$; $(-2, 2), (2, -2), (0, -2)$

Complete each ordered pair so that it is a solution of the given linear equation. See Examples 6 through 8.

45. $x - 4y = 4$; $(\quad, -2), (4, \quad)$

46. $x - 5y = -1$; $(\quad, -2), (4, \quad)$

47. $y = \frac{1}{4}x - 3$; $(-8, \quad), (\quad, 1)$

48. $y = \frac{1}{5}x - 2$; $(-10, \quad), (\quad, 1)$

Complete a Table. *Complete the table of ordered pairs for each linear equation. See Examples 6 through 8.*

49. $y = -7x$

x	y
0	
−1	
	2

50. $y = -9x$

x	y
0	0
−3	
	2

51. $y = -x + 2$

x	y
0	
	0
−3	

52. $x = -y + 4$

x	y
	0
0	
	−3

53. $y = \frac{1}{2}x$

x	y
0	
−6	
	1

54. $y = \frac{1}{3}x$

x	y
0	
−6	
	1

55. $x + 3y = 6$

x	y
0	
	0
	1

56. $2x + y = 4$

x	y
	4
2	
	2

57. $y = 2x - 12$

x	y
0	
	−2
3	

58. $y = 5x + 10$

x	y
0	
	5
0	

59. $2x + 7y = 5$

x	y
0	
	0
	1

60. $x - 6y = 3$

x	y
0	
1	
	−1

MIXED PRACTICE

Complete the table of ordered pairs for each equation. Then plot the ordered pair solutions. See Examples 1 through 7.

61. $x = -5y$

x	y
	0
	1
10	

62. $y = -3x$

x	y
0	
−2	
	9

63. $y = \dfrac{1}{3}x + 2$

x	y
0	
−3	
	0

64. $y = \dfrac{1}{2}x + 3$

x	y
0	
−4	
	0

Multiple Steps. *Solve. See Example 9.*

65. The cost in dollars y of producing x computer desks is given by $y = 80x + 5000$.

  a. Complete the table.

x	100	200	300
y			

  b. Find the number of computer desks that can be produced for $8600. (*Hint:* Find x when $y = 8600$.)

66. The hourly wage y of an employee at a certain production company is given by $y = 0.25x + 9$ where x is the number of units produced by the employee in an hour.

  a. Complete the table.

x	0	1	5	10
y				

  b. Find the number of units that an employee must produce each hour to earn an hourly wage of $12.25. (*Hint:* Find x when $y = 12.25$.)

67. The average amount of money y spent per person on recorded music from 2001 to 2005 is given by $y = -2.35x + 55.92$. In this equation, x represents the number of years after 2001. (*Source:* Veronis Suhler Stevenson)

  a. Complete the table.

x	1	3	5
y			

  b. Find the year in which the yearly average amount of money per person spent on recorded music was approximately $46. (*Hint:* Find x when $y = 46$ and round to the nearest whole number.)

68. The amount y of land operated by farms in the United States (in million acres) from 2000 through 2006 is given by $y = -2.18x + 944.68$. In the equation, x represents the number of years after 2000. (*Source:* National Agricultural Statistics Service)

  a. Complete the table.

x	2	4	6
y			

  b. Find the year in which there were approximately 933 million acres of land operated by farms. (*Hint:* Find x when $y = 933$ and round to the nearest whole number.)

Read a Graph. *The graph below shows the number of Target stores for each year. Use this graph to answer Exercises 69 through 72.*

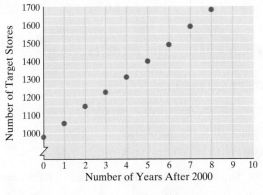

Source: Target

69. The ordered pair (4, 1308) is a point of the graph. Write a sentence describing the meaning of this ordered pair.

70. The ordered pair (6, 1488) is a point of the graph. Write a sentence describing the meaning of this ordered pair.

71. Estimate the increase in Target stores for years 1, 2, and 3.

72. Use a straightedge or ruler and this graph to predict the number of Target stores in the year 2009.

73. When is the graph of the ordered pair (a, b) the same as the graph of the ordered pair (b, a)?

74. In your own words, describe how to plot an ordered pair.

Use the scatter plots shown, labeled (a)–(f), to solve Exercises 75–80.

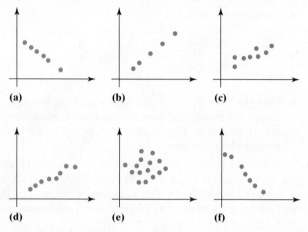

(a)   **(b)**   **(c)**

(d)   **(e)**   **(f)**

75. Which scatter plot indicates a perfect negative correlation?

76. Which scatter plot indicates a perfect positive correlation?

77. Which scatter plot best indicates no correlation?

78. Choose a scatter plot that indicates a strong positive correlation.

79. Choose a scatter plot that indicates a strong negative correlation.

80. In which scatter plot is $r = 1$?

REVIEW AND PREVIEW

Solve each equation for y. See Section 2.6.

81. $x + y = 5$

82. $x - y = 3$

83. $2x + 4y = 5$

84. $5x + 2y = 7$

85. $10x = -5y$

86. $4y = -8x$

87. $x - 3y = 6$

88. $2x - 9y = -20$

CONCEPT EXTENSIONS

True or False. *Answer each exercise with true or false.*

89. Point $(-1, 5)$ lies in quadrant IV.

90. Point $(3, 0)$ lies on the y-axis.

91. For the point $\left(-\dfrac{1}{2}, 1.5\right)$, the first value, $-\dfrac{1}{2}$, is the x-coordinate and the second value, 1.5, is the y-coordinate.

92. The ordered pair $\left(2, \dfrac{2}{3}\right)$ is a solution of $2x - 3y = 6$.

Fill in the Blank. *For Exercises 93 through 97, fill in each blank with "0," "positive," or "negative." For Exercises 98 and 99, fill in each blank with "x" or "y."*

	Point	Location
93.	(_____ , _____)	quadrant III
94.	(_____ , _____)	quadrant I
95.	(_____ , _____)	quadrant IV
96.	(_____ , _____)	quadrant II
97.	(_____ , _____)	origin
98.	(number, 0)	___-axis
99.	(0, number)	___-axis

100. Give an example of an ordered pair whose location is in (or on)

   a. quadrant I   **b.** quadrant II

   c. quadrant III   **d.** quadrant IV

   e. x-axis   **f.** y-axis

Solve. See the Concept Check in this section.

101. Is the graph of $(3, 0)$ in the same location as the graph of $(0, 3)$? Explain why or why not.

102. Give the coordinates of a point such that if the coordinates are reversed, their location is the same.

103. In general, what points can have coordinates reversed and still have the same location?

104. In your own words, describe how to plot or graph an ordered pair of numbers.

Write an ordered pair for each point described.

105. Point C is four units to the right of the y-axis and seven units below the x-axis.

106. Point D is three units to the left of the origin.

107. **Multiple Steps.** Three vertices of a rectangle are $(-2, -3)$, $(-7, -3)$, and $(-7, 6)$.

   a. Find the coordinates of the fourth vertex of a rectangle.

   b. Find the perimeter of the rectangle.

   c. Find the area of the rectangle.

108. **Multiple Steps.** Three vertices of a square are $(-4, -1)$, $(-4, 8)$, and $(5, 8)$.

   a. Find the coordinates of the fourth vertex of the square.

   b. Find the perimeter of the square.

   c. Find the area of the square.

3.2 GRAPHING LINEAR EQUATIONS

OBJECTIVES

1 Identify linear equations.

2 Graph a linear equation by finding and plotting ordered pair solutions.

OBJECTIVE 1 ▶ Identifying linear equations. In the previous section, we found that equations in two variables may have more than one solution. For example, both $(6, 0)$ and $(2, -2)$ are solutions of the equation $x - 2y = 6$. In fact, this equation has an infinite number of solutions. Other solutions include $(0, -3)$, $(4, -1)$, and $(-2, -4)$. If we graph these solutions, notice that a pattern appears.

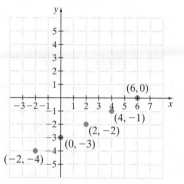

These solutions all appear to lie on the same line, which has been filled in below. It can be shown that every ordered pair solution of the equation corresponds to a point on this line, and every point on this line corresponds to an ordered pair solution. Thus, we say that this line is the **graph of the equation** $x - 2y = 6$.

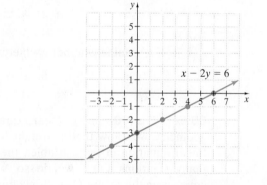

▶ **Helpful Hint**

Notice that we can only show a part of a line on a graph. The arrowheads on each end of the line remind us that the line actually extends indefinitely in both directions.

The equation $x - 2y = 6$ is called a **linear equation in two variables** and **the graph of every linear equation in two variables is a line.**

Linear Equation in Two Variables

A linear equation in two variables is an equation that can be written in the form

$$Ax + By = C$$

where A, B, and C are real numbers and A and B are not both 0. **The graph of a linear equation in two variables is a straight line.**

The form $Ax + By = C$ is called **standard form.**

▶ **Helpful Hint**

Notice in the form $Ax + By = C$, the understood exponent on both x and y is 1.

Examples of Linear Equations in Two Variables

$$2x + y = 8 \qquad -2x = 7y \qquad y = \frac{1}{3}x + 2 \qquad y = 7$$

(Standard Form)

Before we graph linear equations in two variables, let's practice identifying these equations.

EXAMPLE 1 Determine whether each equation is a linear equation in two variables.

a. $x - 1.5y = -1.6$ **b.** $y = -2x$ **c.** $x + y^2 = 9$ **d.** $x = 5$

Solution

a. This is a linear equation in two variables because it is written in the form $Ax + By = C$ with $A = 1$, $B = -1.5$, and $C = -1.6$.

b. This is a linear equation in two variables because it can be written in the form $Ax + By = C$.

$$y = -2x$$
$$2x + y = 0 \qquad \text{Add } 2x \text{ to both sides.}$$

c. This is *not* a linear equation in two variables because y is squared.

d. This is a linear equation in two variables because it can be written in the form $Ax + By = C$.

$$x = 5$$
$$x + 0y = 5 \qquad \text{Add } 0 \cdot y.$$

□

PRACTICE

1   Determine whether each equation is a linear equation in two variables.

a. $3x + 2.7y = -5.3$ **b.** $x^2 + y = 8$ **c.** $y = 12$ **d.** $5x = -3y$

OBJECTIVE 2 ▶ Graphing linear equations by plotting ordered pair solutions. From geometry, we know that a straight line is determined by just two points. Graphing a linear equation in two variables, then, requires that we find just two of its infinitely many solutions. Once we do so, we plot the solution points and draw the line connecting the points. Usually, we find a third solution as well, as a check.

EXAMPLE 2 Graph the linear equation $2x + y = 5$.

Solution   Find three ordered pair solutions of $2x + y = 5$. To do this, choose a value for one variable, x or y, and solve for the other variable. For example, let $x = 1$. Then $2x + y = 5$ becomes

$$2x + y = 5$$
$$2(1) + y = 5 \qquad \text{Replace } x \text{ with 1.}$$
$$2 + y = 5 \qquad \text{Multiply.}$$
$$y = 3 \qquad \text{Subtract 2 from both sides.}$$

Since $y = 3$ when $x = 1$, the ordered pair $(1, 3)$ is a solution of $2x + y = 5$. Next, let $x = 0$.

$$2x + y = 5$$
$$2(0) + y = 5 \qquad \text{Replace } x \text{ with 0.}$$
$$0 + y = 5$$
$$y = 5$$

The ordered pair $(0, 5)$ is a second solution.

The two solutions found so far allow us to draw the straight line that is the graph of all solutions of $2x + y = 5$. However, we find a third ordered pair as a check. Let $y = -1$.

$$2x + y = 5$$
$$2x + (-1) = 5 \quad \text{Replace } y \text{ with } -1.$$
$$2x - 1 = 5$$
$$2x = 6 \quad \text{Add 1 to both sides.}$$
$$x = 3 \quad \text{Divide both sides by 2.}$$

The third solution is $(3, -1)$. These three ordered pair solutions are listed in table form as shown. The graph of $2x + y = 5$ is the line through the three points.

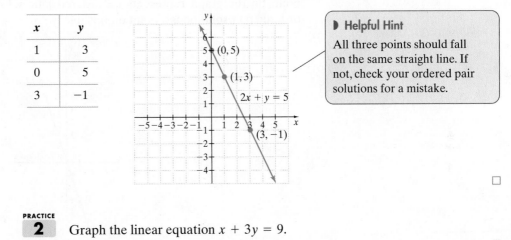

x	y
1	3
0	5
3	-1

▶ **Helpful Hint**

All three points should fall on the same straight line. If not, check your ordered pair solutions for a mistake.

PRACTICE
2 Graph the linear equation $x + 3y = 9$.

EXAMPLE 3 Graph the linear equation $-5x + 3y = 15$.

Solution Find three ordered pair solutions of $-5x + 3y = 15$.

Let $x = 0$.	**Let $y = 0$.**	**Let $x = -2$.**
$-5x + 3y = 15$	$-5x + 3y = 15$	$-5x + 3y = 15$
$-5 \cdot 0 + 3y = 15$	$-5x + 3 \cdot 0 = 15$	$-5(-2) + 3y = 15$
$0 + 3y = 15$	$-5x + 0 = 15$	$10 + 3y = 15$
$3y = 15$	$-5x = 15$	$3y = 5$
$y = 5$	$x = -3$	$y = \dfrac{5}{3}$

The ordered pairs are $(0, 5)$, $(-3, 0)$, and $\left(-2, \dfrac{5}{3}\right)$. The graph of $-5x + 3y = 15$ is the line through the three points.

x	y
0	5
-3	0
-2	$\dfrac{5}{3} = 1\dfrac{2}{3}$

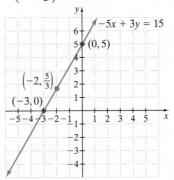

PRACTICE
3 Graph the linear equation $3x - 4y = 12$.

EXAMPLE 4   Graph the linear equation $y = 3x$.

Solution   To graph this linear equation, we find three ordered pair solutions. Since this equation is solved for y, choose three x values.

x	y
2	6
0	0
-1	-3

If $x = 2$, $y = 3 \cdot 2 = 6$.

If $x = 0$, $y = 3 \cdot 0 = 0$.

If $x = -1$, $y = 3 \cdot -1 = -3$.

Next, graph the ordered pair solutions listed in the table above and draw a line through the plotted points as shown on the next page. The line is the graph of $y = 3x$. Every point on the graph represents an ordered pair solution of the equation and every ordered pair solution is a point on this line.

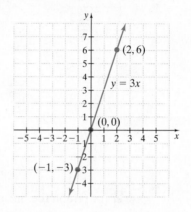

PRACTICE

4   Graph the linear equation $y = -2x$.

EXAMPLE 5   Graph the linear equation $y = -\dfrac{1}{3}x + 2$.

Solution   Find three ordered pair solutions, graph the solutions, and draw a line through the plotted solutions. To avoid fractions, choose x values that are multiples of 3 to substitute in the equation. When a multiple of 3 is multiplied by $-\dfrac{1}{3}$, the result is an integer. See the calculations shown above the table.

If $x = 6$, then $y = -\dfrac{1}{3} \cdot 6 + 2 = -2 + 2 = 0$

If $x = 0$, then $y = -\dfrac{1}{3} \cdot 0 + 2 = 0 + 2 = 2$

If $x = -3$, then $y = -\dfrac{1}{3} \cdot -3 + 2 = 1 + 2 = 3$

x	y
6	0
0	2
-3	3

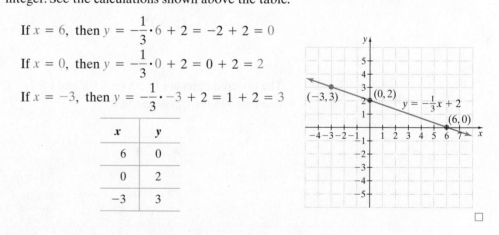

PRACTICE

5   Graph the linear equation $y = \dfrac{1}{2}x + 3$.

Let's compare the graphs in Examples 4 and 5. The graph of $y = 3x$ tilts upward (as we follow the line from left to right) and the graph of $y = -\dfrac{1}{3}x + 2$ tilts downward (as we follow the line from left to right). We will learn more about the tilt, or slope, of a line in Section 3.4.

EXAMPLE 6   Graph the linear equation $y = 3x + 6$ and compare this graph with the graph of $y = 3x$ in Example 4.

Solution   Find ordered pair solutions, graph the solutions, and draw a line through the plotted solutions. We choose x values and substitute in the equation $y = 3x + 6$.

x	y
-3	-3
0	6
1	9

If $x = -3$, then $y = 3(-3) + 6 = -3$.

If $x = 0$, then $y = 3(0) + 6 = 6$.

If $x = 1$, then $y = 3(1) + 6 = 9$.

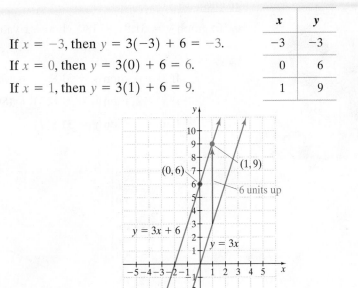

The most startling similarity is that both graphs appear to have the same upward tilt as we move from left to right. Also, the graph of $y = 3x$ crosses the y-axis at the origin, while the graph of $y = 3x + 6$ crosses the y-axis at 6. In fact, the graph of $y = 3x + 6$ is the same as the graph of $y = 3x$ moved vertically upward 6 units.   □

PRACTICE

6   Graph the linear equation $y = -2x + 3$ and compare this graph with the graph of $y = -2x$ in Practice 4.

Notice that the graph of $y = 3x + 6$ crosses the y-axis at 6. This happens because when $x = 0$, $y = 3x + 6$ becomes $y = 3 \cdot 0 + 6 = 6$. The graph contains the point $(0, 6)$, which is on the y-axis.

In general, if a linear equation in two variables is solved for y, we say that it is written in the form $y = mx + b$. The graph of this equation contains the point $(0, b)$ because when $x = 0$, $y = mx + b$ is $y = m \cdot 0 + b = b$.

> The graph of $y = mx + b$ crosses the y-axis at $(0, b)$.

We will review this again in Section 3.5.

Linear equations are often used to model real data as seen in the next example.

EXAMPLE 7 Estimating the Number of Medical Assistants

One of the occupations expected to have the most growth in the next few years is medical assistant. The number of people y (in thousands) employed as medical assistants in the United States can be estimated by the linear equation $y = 31.8x + 180$, where x is the number of years after the year 1995. (*Source:* Based on data from the Bureau of Labor Statistics)

a. Graph the equation.

b. Use the graph to predict the number of medical assistants in the year 2010.

Solution

a. To graph $y = 31.8x + 180$, choose x-values and substitute in the equation.

If $x = 0$, then $y = 31.8(0) + 180 = 180$.

If $x = 2$, then $y = 31.8(2) + 180 = 243.6$.

If $x = 7$, then $y = 31.8(7) + 180 = 402.6$.

x	y
0	180
2	243.6
7	402.6

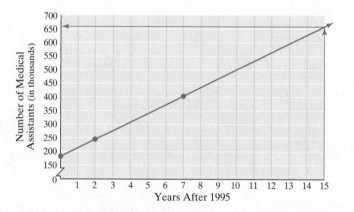

b. To use the graph to *predict* the number of medical assistants in the year 2010, we need to find the y-coordinate that corresponds to $x = 15$. (15 years after 1995 is the year 2010.) To do so, find 15 on the x-axis. Move vertically upward to the graphed line and then horizontally to the left. We approximate the number on the y-axis to be 655. Thus in the year 2010, we predict that there will be 655 thousand medical assistants. (The actual value, using 15 for x, is 657.) □

PRACTICE

7 One of the occupations expected to have the most growth in the next few years is computer software application engineers. The number of people y (in thousands) employed as computer software application engineers in the United States can be estimated by the linear equation $y = 22.2x + 371$, where x is the number of years after 2000. (*Source:* Based on data from the Bureau of Labor Statistics)

a. Graph the equation.

b. Use the graph to predict the number of computer software application engineers in the year 2015.

▶ **Helpful Hint**

Make sure you understand that models are mathematical approximations of the data for the known years. (For example, see the model in Example 7.) Any number of unknown factors can affect future years, so be cautious when using models to predict.

Graphing Calculator Explorations

In this section, we begin an optional study of graphing calculators and graphing software packages for computers. These graphers use the same point plotting technique that was introduced in this section. The advantage of this graphing technology is, of course, that graphing calculators and computers can find and plot ordered pair solutions much faster than we can. Note, however, that the features described in these boxes may not be available on all graphing calculators.

The rectangular screen where a portion of the rectangular coordinate system is displayed is called a **window.** We call it a **standard window** for graphing when both the x- and y-axes show coordinates between -10 and 10. This information is often displayed in the window menu on a graphing calculator as

$$\text{Xmin} = -10$$
$$\text{Xmax} = 10$$
$$\text{Xscl} = 1 \qquad \text{\textit{The scale on the x-axis is one unit per tick mark.}}$$
$$\text{Ymin} = -10$$
$$\text{Ymax} = 10$$
$$\text{Yscl} = 1 \qquad \text{\textit{The scale on the y-axis is one unit per tick mark.}}$$

To use a graphing calculator to graph the equation $y = 2x + 3$, press the $\boxed{\text{Y=}}$ key and enter the keystrokes $\boxed{2}$ $\boxed{x}$ $\boxed{+}$ $\boxed{3}$. The top row should now read $Y_1 = 2x + 3$. Next press the $\boxed{\text{GRAPH}}$ key, and the display should look like this:

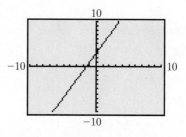

Use a standard window and graph the following linear equations. (Unless otherwise stated, use a standard window when graphing.)

1. $y = -3x + 7$ **2.** $y = -x + 5$ **3.** $y = 2.5x - 7.9$

4. $y = -1.3x + 5.2$ **5.** $y = -\dfrac{3}{10}x + \dfrac{32}{5}$ **6.** $y = \dfrac{2}{9}x - \dfrac{22}{3}$

3.2 | EXERCISE SET

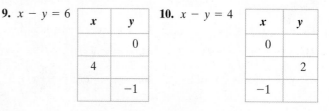

Determine whether each equation is a linear equation in two variables. See Example 1.

1. $-x = 3y + 10$

2. $y = x - 15$

3. $x = y$

4. $x = y^3$

5. $x^2 + 2y = 0$

6. $0.01x - 0.2y = 8.8$

7. $y = -1$

8. $x = 25$

For each equation, find three ordered pair solutions by completing the table. Then use the ordered pairs to graph the equation. See Examples 2 through 6.

9. $x - y = 6$

x	y
	0
4	
	-1

10. $x - y = 4$

x	y
	0
	2
-1	

11. $y = -4x$

x	y
1	
0	
-1	

12. $y = -5x$

x	y
1	
0	
-1	

13. $y = \dfrac{1}{3}x$

x	y
0	
6	
-3	

14. $y = \dfrac{1}{2}x$

x	y
0	
-4	
2	

15. $y = -4x + 3$

x	y
0	
1	
2	

16. $y = -5x + 2$

x	y
0	
1	
2	

MIXED PRACTICE

Graph each linear equation. See Examples 2 through 6.

17. $x + y = 1$

18. $x + y = 7$

19. $x - y = -2$

20. $-x + y = 6$

21. $x - 2y = 6$

22. $-x + 5y = 5$

23. $y = 6x + 3$

24. $y = -2x + 7$

25. $x = -4$

26. $y = 5$

27. $y = 3$

28. $x = -1$

29. $y = x$

30. $y = -x$

31. $x = -3y$

32. $x = -5y$

33. $x + 3y = 9$

34. $2x + y = 2$

35. $y = \dfrac{1}{2}x + 2$

36. $y = \dfrac{1}{4}x + 3$

37. $3x - 2y = 12$

38. $2x - 7y = 14$

39. $y = -3.5x + 4$

40. $y = -1.5x - 3$

Graph each pair of linear equations on the same set of axes. Discuss how the graphs are similar and how they are different. See Example 6.

41. $y = 5x; y = 5x + 4$

42. $y = 2x; y = 2x + 5$

43. $y = -2x; y = -2x - 3$

44. $y = x; y = x - 7$

45. $y = \dfrac{1}{2}x; y = \dfrac{1}{2}x + 2$

46. $y = -\dfrac{1}{4}x; y = -\dfrac{1}{4}x + 3$

Matching. *The graph of $y = 5x$ is given below as well as Figures a–d. For Exercises 47 through 50, match each equation with its graph. Hint: Recall that if an equation is written in the form $y = mx + b$, its graph crosses the y-axis at $(0, b)$.*

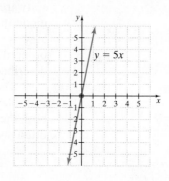

47. $y = 5x + 5$

48. $y = 5x - 4$

49. $y = 5x - 1$

50. $y = 5x + 2$

a.

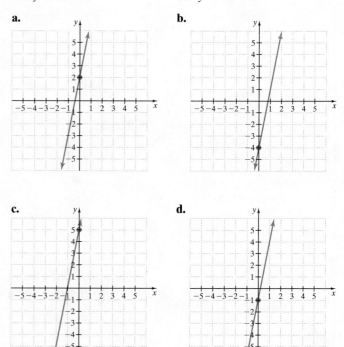

b.

c.

d.

Solve. See Example 7.

51. Multiple Steps. Snowboarding is the fastest growing snow sport, and the numbers of participants has been increasing at a steady rate. The number of people involved in snowboarding (in millions) from the years 1997 to 2005 is given by the equation $y = 0.5x + 3$, where x is the number of years after 1997. (*Source:* Based on data from the National Sporting Goods Association)

  a. Use this equation or a graph of it to complete the ordered pair (8,).

  b. Write a sentence explaining the meaning of the answer to part (a).

  c. If this trend continues, how many snowboarders will there be in 2012?

52. Multiple Steps. The revenue y (in billions of dollars) for Home Depot stores during the years 2000 through 2005 is given by the equation $y = 7x + 45$, where x is the number of years after 2000. (*Source:* Based on data from Home Depot stores)

a. Use this equation or a graph of it to complete the ordered pair (5,   ).

b. Write a sentence explaining the meaning of the answer to part (a).

c. If this trend continues, predict the revenue for Home Depot stores for the year 2015.

53. The minimum salary for a player in the NFL is determined by the league and depends on the years of experience. In a recent year, the salary of a player earning only the minimum y (in thousands of dollars) can be approximated by the equation $y = 54x + 275$, where x is the number of years experience. If this trend continues, use this equation to predict the minimum salary for an NFL player after 5 years' experience. Write your answer as a sentence. (*Source:* Based on data from the National Football League)

54. The U.S. silver production (in metric tons) from 2000 to 2004 has been steadily dropping, and can be approximated by the equation $y = -196x + 1904$ where x is the number of years after 2000. If this current trend continues, use the equation to estimate the U.S. silver production in 2009. Write your answer as a sentence. (*Source*: U.S. Geological Survey)

REVIEW AND PREVIEW

55. The coordinates of three vertices of a rectangle are $(-2, 5)$, $(4, 5)$, and $(-2, -1)$. Find the coordinates of the fourth vertex. See Section 3.1.

56. The coordinates of two vertices of a square are $(-3, -1)$ and $(2, -1)$. Find the coordinates of two pairs of points possible for the third and fourth vertices. See Section 3.1.

Solve the following equations. See Section 2.4.

57. $3(x - 2) + 5x = 6x - 16$

58. $5 + 7(x + 1) = 12 + 10x$

59. $3x + \dfrac{2}{5} = \dfrac{1}{10}$ **60.** $\dfrac{1}{6} + 2x = \dfrac{2}{3}$

CONCEPT EXTENSIONS

Write each statement as an equation in two variables. Then graph the equation.

61. The y-value is 5 more than the x-value.

62. The y-value is twice the x-value.

63. Two times the x-value, added to three times the y-value is 6.

64. Five times the x-value, added to twice the y-value is -10.

65. The perimeter of the trapezoid below is 22 centimeters. Write a linear equation in two variables for the perimeter. Find y if x is 3 cm.

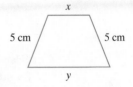

66. The perimeter of the rectangle below is 50 miles. Write a linear equation in two variables for this perimeter. Use this equation to find x when y is 20.

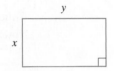

67. Explain how to find ordered pair solutions of linear equations in two variables.

68. If (a, b) is an ordered pair solution of $x + y = 5$, is (b, a) also a solution? Explain why or why not.

69. Graph the nonlinear equation $y = x^2$ by completing the table shown. Plot the ordered pairs and connect them with a smooth curve.

x	y
0	
1	
-1	
2	
-2	

70. Graph the nonlinear equation $y = |x|$ by completing the table shown. Plot the ordered pairs and connect them. This curve is "V" shaped.

$y = |x|$

x	y
0	
1	
-1	
2	
-2	

3.3 INTERCEPTS

OBJECTIVES

1 Identify intercepts of a graph.

2 Graph a linear equation by finding and plotting intercepts.

3 Identify and graph vertical and horizontal lines.

OBJECTIVE 1 ▶ Identifying intercepts. In this section, we graph linear equations in two variables by identifying intercepts. For example, the graph of $y = 4x - 8$ is shown on right. Notice that this graph crosses the y-axis at the point $(0, -8)$. This point is called the **y-intercept.** Likewise, the graph crosses the x-axis at $(2, 0)$, and this point is called the **x-intercept.**

The intercepts are $(2, 0)$ and $(0, -8)$.

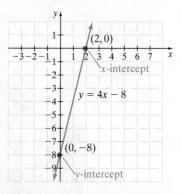

▶ **Helpful Hint**

If a graph crosses the x-axis at $(-3, 0)$ and the y-axis at $(0, 7)$, then

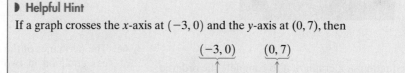

Notice that for the y-intercept, the x-value is 0 and for the x-intercept, the y-value is 0.

Note: Sometimes in mathematics, you may see just the number 7 stated as the y-intercept, and -3 stated as the x-intercept.

EXAMPLES   Identify the x- and y-intercepts.

1.

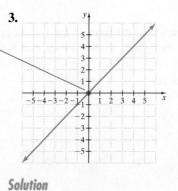

Solution

x-intercept: $(-3, 0)$

y-intercept: $(0, 2)$

2.

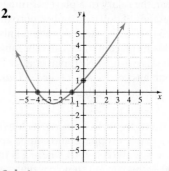

Solution

x-intercepts: $(-4, 0), (-1, 0)$

y-intercept: $(0, 1)$

▶ **Helpful Hint**

Notice that any time $(0, 0)$ is a point of a graph, then it is an x-intercept and a y-intercept.

3.

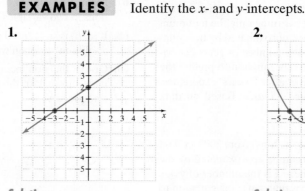

Solution

x-intercept: $(0, 0)$

y-intercept: $(0, 0)$

4.

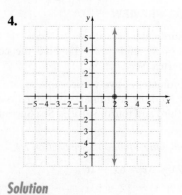

Solution

x-intercept: $(2, 0)$

y-intercept: none

5.

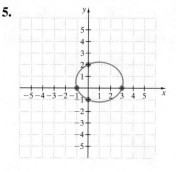

Solution

x-intercepts: $(-1, 0)$, $(3, 0)$

y-intercepts: $(0, 2)$, $(0, -1)$ □

PRACTICES

1–5   Identify the x- and y-intercepts.

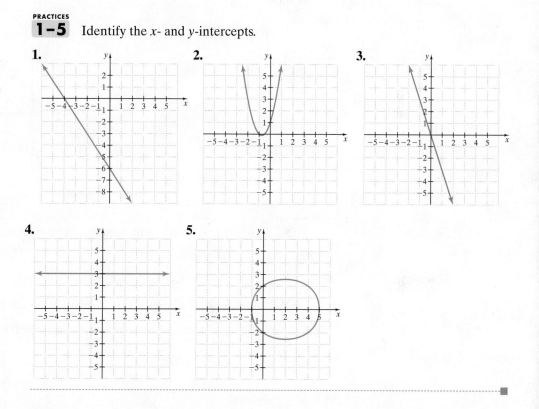

OBJECTIVE 2 ▶ Using intercepts to graph a linear equation. Given the equation of a line, intercepts are usually easy to find since one coordinate is 0.

One way to find the y-intercept of a line, given its equation, is to let $x = 0$, since a point on the y-axis has an x-coordinate of 0. To find the x-intercept of a line, let $y = 0$, since a point on the x-axis has a y-coordinate of 0.

> **Finding x- and y-intercepts**
>
> To find the x-intercept, let $y = 0$ and solve for x.
> To find the y-intercept, let $x = 0$ and solve for y.

EXAMPLE 6   Graph $x - 3y = 6$ by finding and plotting intercepts.

Solution   Let $y = 0$ to find the x-intercept and let $x = 0$ to find the y-intercept.

Let $y = 0$	Let $x = 0$
$x - 3y = 6$	$x - 3y = 6$
$x - 3(0) = 6$	$0 - 3y = 6$
$x - 0 = 6$	$-3y = 6$
$x = 6$	$y = -2$

The x-intercept is $(6, 0)$ and the y-intercept is $(0, -2)$. We find a third ordered pair solution to check our work. If we let $y = -1$, then $x = 3$. Plot the points $(6, 0)$, $(0, -2)$, and $(3, -1)$. The graph of $x - 3y = 6$ is the line drawn through these points, as shown.

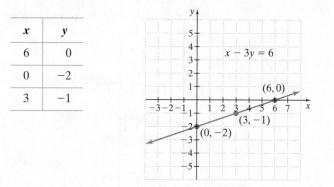

x	y
6	0
0	-2
3	-1

PRACTICE
6   Graph $x + 2y = -4$ by finding and plotting intercepts.

EXAMPLE 7   Graph $x = -2y$ by plotting intercepts.

Solution   Let $y = 0$ to find the x-intercept and $x = 0$ to find the y-intercept.

Let $y = 0$	Let $x = 0$
$x = -2y$	$x = -2y$
$x = -2(0)$	$0 = -2y$
$x = 0$	$0 = y$

Both the x-intercept and y-intercept are $(0, 0)$. In other words, when $x = 0$, then $y = 0$, which gives the ordered pair $(0, 0)$. Also, when $y = 0$, then $x = 0$, which gives the same ordered pair $(0, 0)$. This happens when the graph passes through the origin. Since two points are needed to determine a line, we must find at least one more ordered pair that satisfies $x = -2y$. Let $y = -1$ to find a second ordered pair solution and let $y = 1$ as a checkpoint.

Let $y = -1$	Let $y = 1$
$x = -2(-1)$	$x = -2(1)$
$x = 2$	$x = -2$

The ordered pairs are $(0, 0)$, $(2, -1)$, and $(-2, 1)$. Plot these points to graph $x = -2y$.

x	y
0	0
2	−1
−2	1

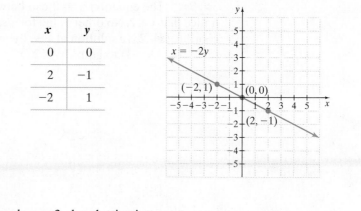

PRACTICE
7   Graph $x = 3y$ by plotting intercepts.

EXAMPLE 8   Graph $4x = 3y - 9$.

Solution   Find the x- and y-intercepts, and then choose $x = 2$ to find a third checkpoint.

Let $y = 0$ Let $x = 0$ Let $x = 2$

$4x = 3(0) - 9$ $4 \cdot 0 = 3y - 9$ $4(2) = 3y - 9$

$4x = -9$ $9 = 3y$ $8 = 3y - 9$

Solve for x.   Solve for y.   Solve for y.

$x = -\dfrac{9}{4}$ or $-2\dfrac{1}{4}$ $3 = y$ $17 = 3y$

$\dfrac{17}{3} = y$ or $y = 5\dfrac{2}{3}$

The ordered pairs are $\left(-2\dfrac{1}{4}, 0\right)$, $(0, 3)$, and $\left(2, 5\dfrac{2}{3}\right)$. The equation $4x = 3y - 9$ is graphed as follows.

x	y
$-2\dfrac{1}{4}$	0
0	3
2	$5\dfrac{2}{3}$

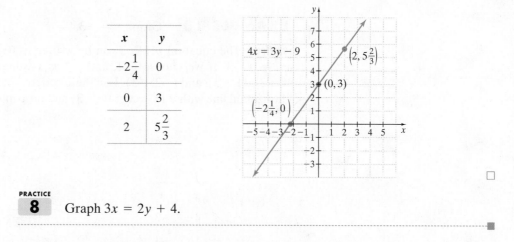

PRACTICE
8   Graph $3x = 2y + 4$.

OBJECTIVE 3 ▶ Graphing vertical and horizontal lines. The equation $x = c$, where c is a real number constant, is a linear equation in two variables because it can be written in the form $x + 0y = c$. The graph of this equation is a vertical line as shown in the next example.

EXAMPLE 9   Graph $x = 2$.

Solution   The equation $x = 2$ can be written as $x + 0y = 2$. For any y-value chosen, notice that x is 2. No other value for x satisfies $x + 0y = 2$. Any ordered pair whose x-coordinate is 2 is a solution of $x + 0y = 2$. We will use the ordered pair solutions $(2, 3)$, $(2, 0)$, and $(2, -3)$ to graph $x = 2$.

x	y
2	3
2	0
2	-3

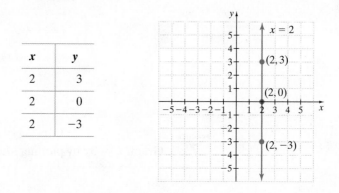

The graph is a vertical line with x-intercept $(2, 0)$. Note that this graph has no y-intercept because x is never 0. □

PRACTICE
9   Graph $y = 2$.

Vertical Lines

The graph of $x = c$, where c is a real number, is a vertical line with x-intercept $(c, 0)$.

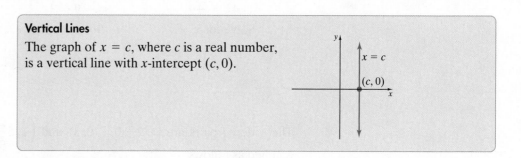

EXAMPLE 10   Graph $y = -3$.

Solution   The equation $y = -3$ can be written as $0x + y = -3$. For any x-value chosen, y is -3. If we choose 4, 1, and -2 as x-values, the ordered pair solutions are $(4, -3)$, $(1, -3)$, and $(-2, -3)$. Use these ordered pairs to graph $y = -3$. The graph is a horizontal line with y-intercept $(0, -3)$ and no x-intercept.

x	y
4	-3
1	-3
-2	-3

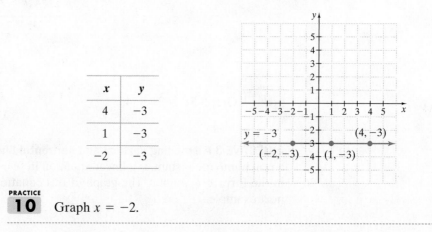

□

PRACTICE
10   Graph $x = -2$.

Horizontal Lines

The graph of $y = c$, where c is a real number, is a horizontal line with y-intercept $(0, c)$.

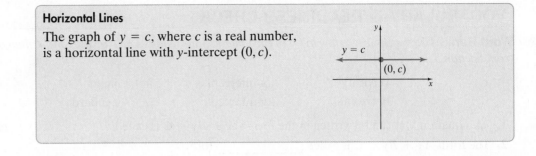

Graphing Calculator Explorations

You may have noticed that to use the $\boxed{Y=}$ key on a grapher to graph an equation, the equation must be solved for y. For example, to graph $2x + 3y = 7$, we solve this equation for y.

$$2x + 3y = 7$$
$$3y = -2x + 7 \qquad \text{Subtract } 2x \text{ from both sides.}$$
$$\frac{3y}{3} = -\frac{2x}{3} + \frac{7}{3} \qquad \text{Divide both sides by 3.}$$
$$y = -\frac{2}{3}x + \frac{7}{3} \qquad \text{Simplify.}$$

To graph $2x + 3y = 7$ or $y = -\frac{2}{3}x + \frac{7}{3}$, press the $\boxed{Y=}$ key and enter

$$Y_1 = -\frac{2}{3}x + \frac{7}{3}$$

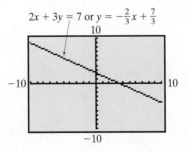

Graph each linear equation.

1. $x = 3.78y$ **2.** $-2.61y = x$ **3.** $3x + 7y = 21$

4. $-4x + 6y = 12$ **5.** $-2.2x + 6.8y = 15.5$ **6.** $5.9x - 0.8y = -10.4$

VOCABULARY & READINESS CHECK

Word Bank. *Use the choices below to fill in each blank. Some choices may be used more than once. Exercises 1 and 2 come from Section 3.2.*

x	vertical	x-intercept	linear
y	horizontal	y-intercept	standard

1. An equation that can be written in the form $Ax + By = C$ is called a _____ equation in two variables.
2. The form $Ax + By = C$ is called _____ form.
3. The graph of the equation $y = -1$ is a _____ line.
4. The graph of the equation $x = 5$ is a _____ line.
5. A point where a graph crosses the y-axis is called a(n) _____.
6. A point where a graph crosses the x-axis is called a(n) _____.
7. Given an equation of a line, to find the x-intercept (if there is one), let _____ = 0 and solve for _____.
8. Given an equation of a line, to find the y-intercept (if there is one), let _____ = 0 and solve for _____.

True or False. *Answer the following true or false.*

9. All lines have an x-intercept *and* a y-intercept.
10. The graph of $y = 4x$ contains the point $(0, 0)$.
11. The graph of $x + y = 5$ has an x-intercept of $(5, 0)$ and a y-intercept of $(0, 5)$.
12. The graph of $y = 5x$ contains the point $(5, 1)$.

3.3 | EXERCISE SET

MyMathLab Powered by CourseCompass™ and MathXL®

Math XL PRACTICE   WATCH   DOWNLOAD   READ   REVIEW

Identify the intercepts. See Examples 1 through 5.

1.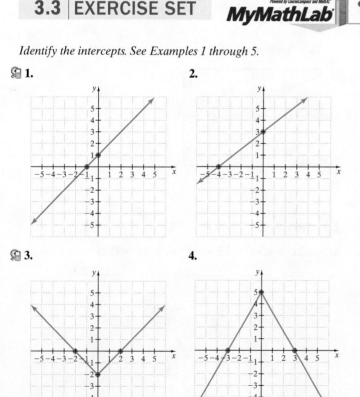

2.

5.

6.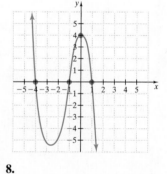

3.

4.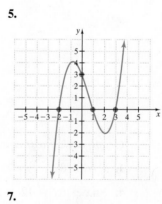

7.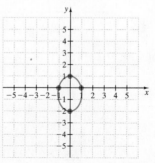

8.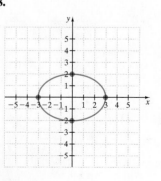

Solve. See Example 1.

9. What is the greatest number of intercepts for a line?

10. What is the least number of intercepts for a line?

11. What is the least number of intercepts for a circle?

12. What is the greatest number of intercepts for a circle?

Graph each linear equation by finding and plotting its intercepts. See Examples 6 through 8.

13. $x - y = 3$ **14.** $x - y = -4$ **15.** $x = 5y$

16. $x = 2y$ **17.** $-x + 2y = 6$ **18.** $x - 2y = -8$

19. $2x - 4y = 8$ **20.** $2x + 3y = 6$ **21.** $y = 2x$

22. $y = -2x$ **23.** $y = 3x + 6$ **24.** $y = 2x + 10$

Graph each linear equation. See Examples 9 and 10.

25. $x = -1$ **26.** $y = 5$ **27.** $y = 0$

28. $x = 0$ **29.** $y + 7 = 0$ **30.** $x - 2 = 0$

31. $x + 3 = 0$ **32.** $y - 6 = 0$

MIXED PRACTICE

Graph each linear equation. See Examples 6 through 10.

33. $x = y$ **34.** $x = -y$

35. $x + 8y = 8$ **36.** $x + 3y = 9$

37. $5 = 6x - y$ **38.** $4 = x - 3y$

39. $-x + 10y = 11$ **40.** $-x + 9y = 10$

41. $x = -4\frac{1}{2}$ **42.** $x = -1\frac{3}{4}$

43. $y = 3\frac{1}{4}$ **44.** $y = 2\frac{1}{2}$

45. $y = -\frac{2}{3}x + 1$ **46.** $y = -\frac{3}{5}x + 3$

47. $4x - 6y + 2 = 0$ **48.** $9x - 6y + 3 = 0$

Matching. *For Exercises 49 through 54, match each equation with its graph.*

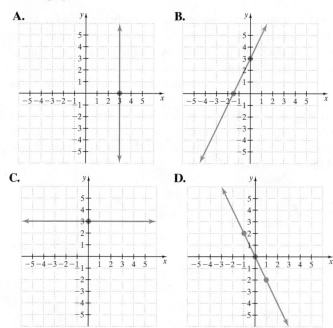

A.   **B.**

C.   **D.**

E.   **F.**

49. $y = 3$ **50.** $y = 2x + 2$

51. $x = -1$ **52.** $x = 3$

53. $y = 2x + 3$ **54.** $y = -2x$

REVIEW AND PREVIEW

Simplify. See Sections 1.3 and 1.6.

55. $\dfrac{-6 - 3}{2 - 8}$ **56.** $\dfrac{4 - 5}{-1 - 0}$

57. $\dfrac{-8 - (-2)}{-3 - (-2)}$ **58.** $\dfrac{12 - 3}{10 - 9}$

59. $\dfrac{0 - 6}{5 - 0}$ **60.** $\dfrac{2 - 2}{3 - 5}$

CONCEPT EXTENSIONS

Multiple Steps. *Solve Exercises 61–65.*

61. The revenue for the Disney Parks and Resorts y (in millions) for the years 2003–2006 can be approximated by the equation $y = 1181x + 6505$, where x represents the number of years after 2003. (*Source:* Based on data from The Walt Disney Company)

   a. Find the y-intercept of this equation.

   b. What does the y-intercept mean?

62. The average price of a digital camera y (in dollars) can be modeled by the linear equation $y = -78.1x + 491.8$ where x represents the number of years after 2000. (*Source*: NPD Techworld)

   a. Find the y-intercept of this equation.

   b. What does this y-intercept mean?

63. Since 2002, admissions at movie theaters have been in a decline. The number of people y (in billions) who go to movie theaters each year can be estimated by the equation $y = -0.075x + 1.65$, where x represents the number of years since 2002. (*Source:* Based on data from Motion Picture Association of America)

a. Find the *x*-intercept of this equation.

b. What does this *x*-intercept mean?

c. Use part (b) to comment on the limitations of using equations to model real data.

64. The price of admission to a movie theater has been steadily increasing. The price of regular admission *y* (in dollars) to a movie theater may be represented by the equation $y = 0.2x + 5.42$, where *x* is the number of years after 2000. (*Source:* Based on data from Motion Picture Association of America)

a. Find the *x*-intercept of this equation.

b. What does this *x*-intercept mean?

c. Use part (b) to comment on the limitation of using equations to model real data.

65. The production supervisor at Alexandra's Office Products finds that it takes 3 hours to manufacture a particular office chair and 6 hours to manufacture a computer desk. A total of 1200 hours is available to produce office chairs and desks of this style. The linear equation that models this situation is $3x + 6y = 1200$, where *x* represents the number of chairs produced and *y* the number of desks manufactured.

a. Complete the ordered pair solution (0,) of this equation. Describe the manufacturing situation that corresponds to this solution.

b. Complete the ordered pair solution (, 0) of this equation. Describe the manufacturing situation that corresponds to this solution.

c. Use the ordered pairs found above and graph the equation $3x + 6y = 1200$.

d. If 50 computer desks are manufactured, find the greatest number of chairs that they can make.

Two lines in the same plane that do not intersect are called **parallel lines.**

66. Draw a line parallel to the line $x = 5$ that intersects the *x*-axis at $(1, 0)$. What is the equation of this line?

67. Draw a line parallel to the line $y = -1$ that intersects the *y*-axis at $(0, -4)$. What is the equation of this line?

68. Discuss whether a vertical line ever has a *y*-intercept.

69. Explain why it is a good idea to use three points to graph a linear equation.

70. Discuss whether a horizontal line ever has an *x*-intercept.

71. Explain how to find intercepts.

3.4 SLOPE AND RATE OF CHANGE

OBJECTIVES

1 Find the slope of a line given two points of the line.

2 Find the slope of a line given its equation.

3 Find the slopes of horizontal and vertical lines.

4 Compare the slopes of parallel and perpendicular lines.

5 Slope as a rate of change.

OBJECTIVE 1 ▶ Finding the slope of a line given two points of the line. Thus far, much of this chapter has been devoted to graphing lines. You have probably noticed by now that a key feature of a line is its slant or steepness. In mathematics, the slant or steepness of a line is formally known as its **slope.** We measure the slope of a line by the ratio of vertical change to the corresponding horizontal change as we move along the line.

On the line on the next page, for example, suppose that we begin at the point $(1, 2)$ and move to the point $(4, 6)$. The vertical change is the change in *y*-coordinates: $6 - 2$ or 4 units. The corresponding horizontal change is the change in *x*-coordinates: $4 - 1 = 3$ units. The ratio of these changes is

$$\text{slope} = \frac{\text{change in } y \text{ (vertical change)}}{\text{change in } x \text{ (horizontal change)}} = \frac{4}{3}$$

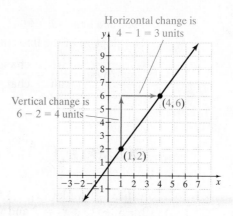

The slope of this line, then, is $\dfrac{4}{3}$. This means that for every 4 units of change in y-coordinates, there is a corresponding change of 3 units in x-coordinates.

> ▶ **Helpful Hint**
>
> It makes no difference what two points of a line are chosen to find its slope. The slope of a line is the same everywhere on the line.

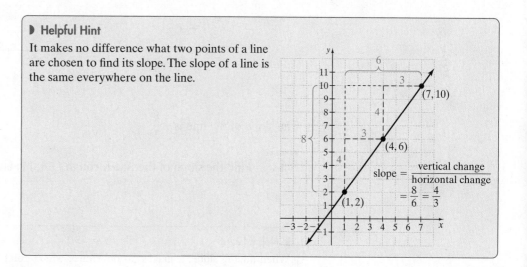

To find the slope of a line, then, choose two points of the line. Label the two x-coordinates of two points, x_1 and x_2 (read "x sub one" and "x sub two"), and label the corresponding y-coordinates y_1 and y_2.

The vertical change or **rise** between these points is the difference in the y-coordinates: $y_2 - y_1$. The horizontal change or **run** between the points is the difference of the x-coordinates: $x_2 - x_1$. The slope of the line is the ratio of $y_2 - y_1$ to $x_2 - x_1$, and we traditionally use the letter m to denote slope $m = \dfrac{y_2 - y_1}{x_2 - x_1}$.

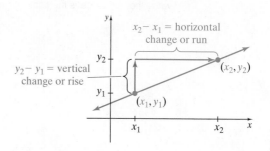

> **Slope of a Line**
> The slope m of the line containing the points (x_1, y_1) and (x_2, y_2) is given by
> $$m = \frac{\text{rise}}{\text{run}} = \frac{\text{change in } y}{\text{change in } x} = \frac{y_2 - y_1}{x_2 - x_1}, \quad \text{as long as } x_2 \neq x_1$$

EXAMPLE 1   Find the slope of the line through $(-1, 5)$ and $(2, -3)$. Graph the line.

Solution   If we let (x_1, y_1) be $(-1, 5)$, then $x_1 = -1$ and $y_1 = 5$. Also, let (x_2, y_2) be $(2, -3)$ so that $x_2 = 2$ and $y_2 = -3$. Then, by the definition of slope,

$$m = \frac{y_2 - y_1}{x_2 - x_1}$$

$$= \frac{-3 - 5}{2 - (-1)}$$

$$= \frac{-8}{3} = -\frac{8}{3}$$

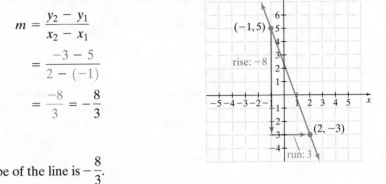

The slope of the line is $-\dfrac{8}{3}$.

PRACTICE
1   Find the slope of the line through $(-4, 11)$ and $(2, 5)$.

> ▶ **Helpful Hint**
> When finding slope, it makes no difference which point is identified as (x_1, y_1) and which is identified as (x_2, y_2). Just remember that whatever y-value is first in the numerator, its corresponding x-value is first in the denominator. Another way to calculate the slope in Example 1 is:
> $$m = \frac{y_2 - y_1}{x_2 - x_1} = \frac{5 - (-3)}{-1 - 2} = \frac{8}{-3} \quad \text{or} \quad -\frac{8}{3} \quad \leftarrow \text{Same slope as found in Example 1.}$$

Concept Check ☑

The points $(-2, -5)$, $(0, -2)$, $(4, 4)$, and $(10, 13)$ all lie on the same line. Work with a partner and verify that the slope is the same no matter which points are used to find slope.

EXAMPLE 2 Find the slope of the line through $(-1, -2)$ and $(2, 4)$. Graph the line.

Solution Let (x_1, y_1) be $(2, 4)$ and (x_2, y_2) be $(-1, -2)$.

$$m = \frac{y_2 - y_1}{x_2 - x_1}$$

$$= \frac{-2 - 4}{-1 - 2} \quad \begin{array}{l} y\text{-value} \\ \text{corresponding } x\text{-value} \end{array}$$

$$= \frac{-6}{-3} = 2$$

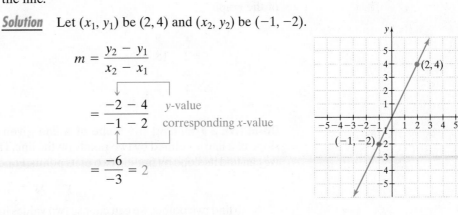

▶ **Helpful Hint**

The slope for Example 2 is the same if we let (x_1, y_1) be $(-1, -2)$ and (x_2, y_2) be $(2, 4)$.

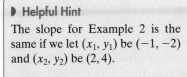

$$m = \frac{4 - (-2)}{2 - (-1)} = \frac{6}{3} = 2$$

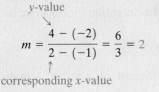

PRACTICE

2 Find the slope of the line through $(-3, -1)$ and $(3, 1)$.

Concept Check ☑

What is wrong with the following slope calculation for the points $(3, 5)$ and $(-2, 6)$?

$$m = \frac{5 - 6}{-2 - 3} = \frac{-1}{-5} = \frac{1}{5}$$

Notice that the slope of the line in Example 1 is negative, whereas the slope of the line in Example 2 is positive. Let your eye follow the line with negative slope from left to right and notice that the line "goes down." Following the line with positive slope from left to right, notice that the line "goes up." This is true in general.

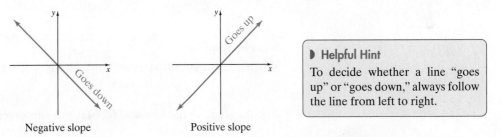

Negative slope   Positive slope

▶ **Helpful Hint**

To decide whether a line "goes up" or "goes down," always follow the line from left to right.

EXAMPLE 3 The table below contains ordered-pair solutions of a linear equation in two variables. Use this table to find the slope of the graph.

x	y
0	2
-1	7
2	-8

Solution Remember, a line has a consistent tilt, or a single slope. Any two ordered pairs will generate this same slope.

Answer to Concept Check:

The order in which the x- and y-values are used must be the same.

$$m = \frac{5 - 6}{3 - (-2)} = \frac{-1}{5} = -\frac{1}{5}$$

We will use $(0, 2)$, and $(-1, 7)$ from the table and the slope formula.

$$m = \frac{7 - 2}{-1 - 0} \quad \text{Let } (x_1, y_1) = (0, 2), \text{ and } (x_2, y_2) = (-1, 7) \text{ in the slope formula.}$$

$$= \frac{5}{-1} \text{ or } -5.$$

The slope of the line generated by the points in the table is -5.

PRACTICE
3   Follow the directions for Example 3 and use the given table to find the slope of the graph.

x	y
-2	18
0	4
1	-3

OBJECTIVE 2 ▶ Finding the slope of a line given its equation. As we have seen, the slope of a line is defined by two points on the line. Thus, if we know the equation of a line, we can find its slope by finding two of its points. For example, let's find the slope of the line

$$y = 3x + 2$$

To find two points, we can choose two values for x and substitute to find corresponding y-values. If $x = 0$, for example, $y = 3 \cdot 0 + 2$ or $y = 2$. If $x = 1$, $y = 3 \cdot 1 + 2$ or $y = 5$. This gives the ordered pairs $(0, 2)$ and $(1, 5)$. Using the definition for slope, we have

$$m = \frac{5 - 2}{1 - 0} = \frac{3}{1} = 3 \quad \text{The slope is 3.}$$

Notice that the slope, 3, is the same as the coefficient of x in the equation $y = 3x + 2$.

Also, recall from Section 3.2 that the graph of an equation of the form $y = mx + b$ has y-intercept $(0, b)$.

This means that the y-intercept of the graph of $y = 3x + 2$ is $(0, 2)$. This is true in general.

When a linear equation is written in the form $y = mx + b$, not only is $(0, b)$ the y-intercept of the line, but m is its slope. The form $y = mx + b$ is appropriately called the **slope-intercept form.**

$$\uparrow \qquad \uparrow$$
$$\text{slope} \quad y\text{-intercept}$$
$$(0, b)$$

Slope-Intercept Form

When a linear equation in two variables is written in slope-intercept form,

$$y = mx + b$$

m is the slope of the line and $(0, b)$ is the y-intercept of the line.

EXAMPLE 4   Find the slope and y-intercept of the line whose equation is $y = \frac{3}{4}x + 6$.

Solution   The equation is in slope-intercept form, $y = mx + b$.

$$y = \frac{3}{4}x + 6$$

The coefficient of x, $\frac{3}{4}$, is the slope and the constant term, 6 is the y-value of the y-intercept, $(0, 6)$.   □

PRACTICE
4   Find the slope and y-intercept of the line whose equation is $y = \frac{2}{3}x - 2$.

EXAMPLE 5 Find the slope and the y-intercept of the line whose equation is $5x + y = 2$.

Solution Write the equation in slope-intercept form by solving the equation for y.

$$5x + y = 2$$
$$y = -5x + 2 \quad \text{Subtract } 5x \text{ from both sides.}$$

The coefficient of x, -5, is the slope and the constant term, 2, is the y-value of the y-intercept, $(0, 2)$. □

PRACTICE
5 Find the slope and y-intercept of the line whose equation is $6x - y = 5$.

EXAMPLE 6 Find the slope and the y-intercept of the line whose equation is $3x - 4y = 4$.

Solution Write the equation in slope-intercept form by solving for y.

$$3x - 4y = 4$$
$$-4y = -3x + 4 \quad \text{Subtract } 3x \text{ from both sides.}$$
$$\frac{-4y}{-4} = \frac{-3x}{-4} + \frac{4}{-4} \quad \text{Divide both sides by } -4.$$
$$y = \frac{3}{4}x - 1 \quad \text{Simplify.}$$

The coefficient of x, $\dfrac{3}{4}$, is the slope, and the y-intercept is $(0, -1)$. □

PRACTICE
6 Find the slope and the y-intercept of the line whose equation is $5x + 2y = 8$.

OBJECTIVE 3 ▶ Finding slopes of horizontal and vertical lines. Recall that if a line tilts upward from left to right, its slope is positive. If a line tilts downward from left to right, its slope is negative. Let's now find the slopes of two special lines, horizontal and vertical lines.

EXAMPLE 7 Find the slope of the line $y = -1$.

Solution Recall that $y = -1$ is a horizontal line with y-intercept $(0, -1)$. To find the slope, find two ordered pair solutions of $y = -1$. Solutions of $y = -1$ must have a y-value of -1. Let's use points $(2, -1)$ and $(-3, -1)$, which are on the line.

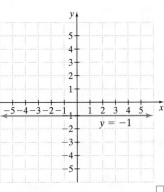

$$m = \frac{y_2 - y_1}{x_2 - x_1} = \frac{-1 - (-1)}{-3 - 2} = \frac{0}{-5} = 0$$

The slope of the line $y = -1$ is 0 and its graph is shown. □

PRACTICE
7 Find the slope of the line $y = 3$.

Any two points of a horizontal line will have the same y-values. This means that the y-values will always have a difference of 0 for all horizontal lines. Thus, **all horizontal lines have a slope 0.**

EXAMPLE 8   Find the slope of the line $x = 5$.

Solution   Recall that the graph of $x = 5$ is a vertical line with x-intercept $(5, 0)$.

To find the slope, find two ordered pair solutions of $x = 5$. Solutions of $x = 5$ must have an x-value of 5. Let's use points $(5, 0)$ and $(5, 4)$, which are on the line.

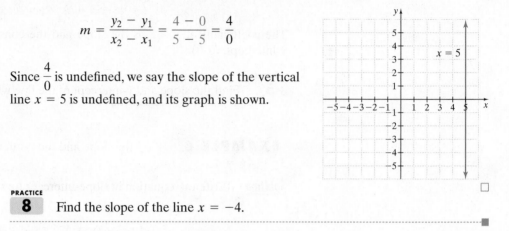

$$m = \frac{y_2 - y_1}{x_2 - x_1} = \frac{4 - 0}{5 - 5} = \frac{4}{0}$$

Since $\dfrac{4}{0}$ is undefined, we say the slope of the vertical line $x = 5$ is undefined, and its graph is shown.

PRACTICE
8   Find the slope of the line $x = -4$.

Any two points of a vertical line will have the same x-values. This means that the x-values will always have a difference of 0 for all vertical lines. Thus **all vertical lines have undefined slope.**

> ▶ **Helpful Hint**
> Slope of 0 and undefined slope are not the same. Vertical lines have undefined slope or no slope, while horizontal lines have a slope of 0.

Here is a general review of slope.

Summary of Slope

Slope m of the line through (x_1, y_1) and (x_2, y_2) is given by the equation $m = \dfrac{y_2 - y_1}{x_2 - x_1}$.

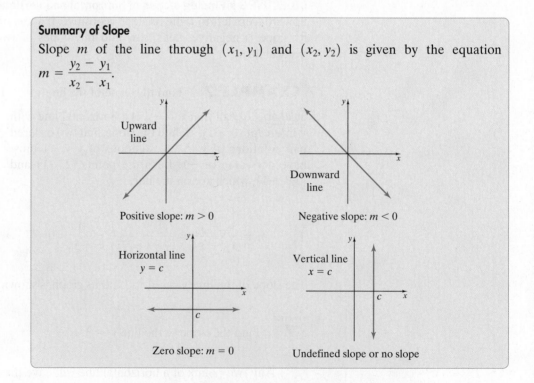

OBJECTIVE 4 ▶ Slopes of parallel and perpendicular lines. Two lines in the same plane are **parallel** if they do not intersect. Slopes of lines can help us determine whether lines are parallel. Parallel lines have the same steepness, so it follows that they have the same slope.

For example, the graphs of

$$y = -2x + 4$$

and

$$y = -2x - 3$$

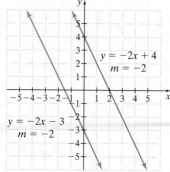

are shown. These lines have the same slope, -2. They also have different y-intercepts, so the lines are parallel. (If the y-intercepts were the same also, the lines would be the same.)

Parallel Lines

Nonvertical parallel lines have the same slope and different y-intercepts.

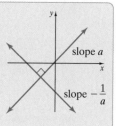

Two lines are **perpendicular** if they lie in the same plane and meet at a 90° (right) angle. How do the slopes of perpendicular lines compare? The product of the slopes of two perpendicular lines is -1.

For example, the graphs of

$$y = 4x + 1$$

and

$$y = -\frac{1}{4}x - 3$$

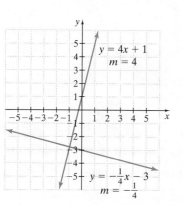

are shown. The slopes of the lines are 4 and $-\dfrac{1}{4}$. Their product is $4\left(-\dfrac{1}{4}\right) = -1$, so the lines are perpendicular.

Perpendicular Lines

If the product of the slopes of two lines is -1, then the lines are perpendicular.

(Two nonvertical lines are perpendicular if the slopes of one is the negative reciprocal of the slope of the other.)

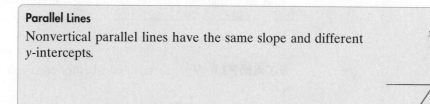

> ▶ **Helpful Hint**
>
> Here are examples of numbers that are negative (opposite) reciprocals.
>
> | *Number* | *Negative Reciprocal* | *Their Product Is* -1. |
> |:---:|:---:|:---:|
> | $\dfrac{2}{3}$ | $-\dfrac{3}{2}$ | $\dfrac{2}{3} \cdot -\dfrac{3}{2} = -\dfrac{6}{6} = -1$ |
> | -5 or $-\dfrac{5}{1}$ | $\dfrac{1}{5}$ | $-5 \cdot \dfrac{1}{5} = -\dfrac{5}{5} = -1$ |

> ▶ **Helpful Hint**
>
> Here are a few important facts about vertical and horizontal lines.
>
> • Two distinct vertical lines are parallel.
> • Two distinct horizontal lines are parallel.
> • A horizontal line and a vertical line are always perpendicular.

△ **EXAMPLE 9** Determine whether each pair of lines is parallel, perpendicular, or neither.

a. $y = -\dfrac{1}{5}x + 1$ **b.** $x + y = 3$ **c.** $3x + y = 5$

      $2x + 10y = 3$ $-x + y = 4$ $2x + 3y = 6$

Solution

a. The slope of the line $y = -\dfrac{1}{5}x + 1$ is $-\dfrac{1}{5}$. We find the slope of the second line by solving its equation for y.

$$2x + 10y = 3$$

$$10y = -2x + 3 \qquad \text{Subtract } 2x \text{ from both sides.}$$

$$y = \frac{-2}{10}x + \frac{3}{10} \qquad \text{Divide both sides by 10.}$$

$$y = -\frac{1}{5}x + \frac{3}{10} \qquad \text{Simplify.}$$

The slope of this line is $-\dfrac{1}{5}$ also. Since the lines have the same slope and different y-intercepts, they are parallel, as shown in the figure on the next page.

b. To find each slope, we solve each equation for y.

$$x + y = 3 \qquad\qquad -x + y = 4$$

$$y = -x + 3 \qquad\qquad y = x + 4$$

              ↑   ↑

The slope is -1.   The slope is 1.

The slopes are not the same, so the lines are not parallel. Next we check the product of the slopes: $(-1)(1) = -1$. Since the product is -1, the lines are perpendicular, as shown in the figure.

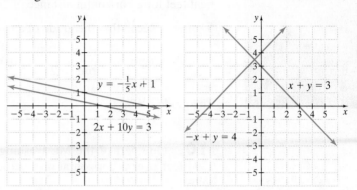

c. We solve each equation for y to find each slope. The slopes are -3 and $-\dfrac{2}{3}$. The slopes are not the same and their product is not -1. Thus, the lines are neither parallel nor perpendicular. ☐

PRACTICE

9   Determine whether each pair of lines is parallel, perpendicular, or neither.

a. $y = -5x + 1$
$x - 5y = 10$

b. $x + y = 11$
$2x + y = 11$

c. $2x + 3y = 21$
$6y = -4x - 2$

Concept Check ☑

Consider the line $-6x + 2y = 1$.

a. Write the equations of two lines parallel to this line.

b. Write the equations of two lines perpendicular to this line.

OBJECTIVE 5 ▶ Slope as a rate of change. Slope can also be interpreted as a rate of change. In other words, slope tells us how fast y is changing with respect to x. To see this, let's look at a few of the many real-world applications of slope. For example, the pitch of a roof, used by builders and architects, is its slope. The pitch of the roof on the left is $\dfrac{7}{10}\left(\dfrac{\text{rise}}{\text{run}}\right)$. This means that the roof rises vertically 7 feet for every horizontal 10 feet. The rate of change for the roof is 7 vertical feet (y) per 10 horizontal feet (x).

The grade of a road is its slope written as a percent. A 7% grade, as shown below, means that the road rises (or falls) 7 feet for every horizontal 100 feet. $\Big($ Recall that $7\% = \dfrac{7}{100}.\Big)$ Here, the slope of $\dfrac{7}{100}$ gives us the rate of change. The road rises (in our diagram) 7 vertical feet (y) for every 100 horizontal feet (x).

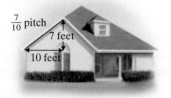

EXAMPLE 10 Finding the Grade of a Road

At one part of the road to the summit of Pikes Peak, the road rises at a rate of 15 vertical feet for a horizontal distance of 250 feet. Find the grade of the road.

Solution Recall that the grade of a road is its slope written as a percent.

$$\text{grade} = \frac{\text{rise}}{\text{run}} = \frac{15}{250} = 0.06 = 6\%$$

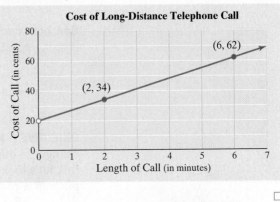

15 feet

250 feet

The grade is 6%.

PRACTICE
10 One part of the Mt. Washington (New Hampshire) cog railway rises about 1794 feet over a horizontal distance of 7176 feet. Find the grade of this part of the railway.

EXAMPLE 11 Finding the Slope of a Line

The following graph shows the cost y (in cents) of a nationwide long-distance telephone call from Texas with a certain telephone-calling plan, where x is the length of the call in minutes. Find the slope of the line and attach the proper units for the rate of change. Then write a sentence explaining the meaning of slope in this application.

Solution Use $(2, 34)$ and $(6, 62)$ to calculate slope.

$$m = \frac{62 - 34}{6 - 2} = \frac{28}{4} = \frac{7 \text{ cents}}{1 \text{ minute}}$$

This means that the rate of change of a phone call is 7 cents per 1 minute or the cost of the phone call is 7 cents per minute.

Cost of Long-Distance Telephone Call

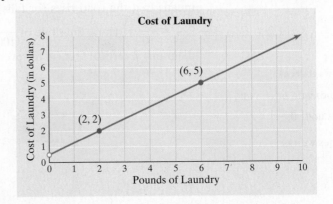

PRACTICE
11 The following graph shows the cost y (in dollars) of having laundry done at the Wash-n-Fold, where x is the number of pounds of laundry. Find the slope of the line, and attach the proper units for the rate of change.

Cost of Laundry

(6, 5)

(2, 2)

Graphing Calculator Explorations

It is possible to use a grapher to sketch the graph of more than one equation on the same set of axes. This feature can be used to confirm our findings from Section 3.2 when we learned that the graph of an equation written in the form $y = mx + b$ has a y-intercept of b. For example, graph the equations $y = \frac{2}{5}x$, $y = \frac{2}{5}x + 7$, and $y = \frac{2}{5}x - 4$ on the same set of axes. To do so, press the $\boxed{Y=}$ key and enter the equations on the first three lines.

$$Y_1 = \left(\frac{2}{5}\right)x$$

$$Y_2 = \left(\frac{2}{5}\right)x + 7$$

$$Y_3 = \left(\frac{2}{5}\right)x - 4$$

The screen should look like:

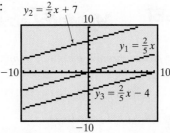

Notice that all three graphs appear to have the same positive slope. The graph of $y = \frac{2}{5}x + 7$ is the graph of $y = \frac{2}{5}x$ moved 7 units upward with a y-intercept of 7. Also, the graph of $y = \frac{2}{5}x - 4$ is the graph of $y = \frac{2}{5}x$ moved 4 units downward with a y-intercept of -4.

Graph the equations on the same set of axes. Describe the similarities and differences in their graphs.

1. $y = 3.8x$, $y = 3.8x - 3$, $y = 3.8x + 9$

2. $y = -4.9x$, $y = -4.9x + 1$, $y = -4.9x + 8$

3. $y = \frac{1}{4}x$; $y = \frac{1}{4}x + 5$, $y = \frac{1}{4}x - 8$

4. $y = -\frac{3}{4}x$, $y = -\frac{3}{4}x - 5$, $y = -\frac{3}{4}x + 6$

VOCABULARY & READINESS CHECK

Word Bank. *Use the choices below to fill in each blank. Not all choices will be used.*

m	x	0	positive	undefined
b	y	slope	negative	

1. The measure of the steepness or tilt of a line is called _____.

2. If an equation is written in the form $y = mx + b$, the value of the letter _____ is the value of the slope of the graph.

3. The slope of a horizontal line is _____.

4. The slope of a vertical line is _____.

5. If the graph of a line moves upward from left to right, the line has _____ slope.

6. If the graph of a line moves downward from left to right, the line has _____ slope.

7. Given two points of a line, slope = $\dfrac{\text{change in } \underline{}}{\text{change in } \underline{}}$.

State whether the slope of the line is positive, negative, 0, or is undefined.

8.

9.

10.

11.

Decision Making. *Decide whether a line with the given slope is upward, downward, horizontal, or vertical.*

12. $m = \dfrac{7}{6}$ _____

13. $m = -3$ _____

14. $m = 0$ _____

15. m is undefined. _____

3.4 EXERCISE SET

MyMathLab   MathXL PRACTICE   WATCH   DOWNLOAD   READ   REVIEW

Find the slope of the line that passes through the given points. See Examples 1 and 2.

1. $(-1, 5)$ and $(6, -2)$

2. $(3, 1)$ and $(2, 6)$

3. $(-4, 3)$ and $(-4, 5)$

4. $(6, -6)$ and $(6, 2)$

5. $(-2, 8)$ and $(1, 6)$

6. $(4, -3)$ and $(2, 2)$

7. $(5, 1)$ and $(-2, 1)$

8. $(0, 13)$ and $(-4, 13)$

Read a Graph. *Find the slope of each line if it exists. See Examples 1 and 2.*

9.

10.

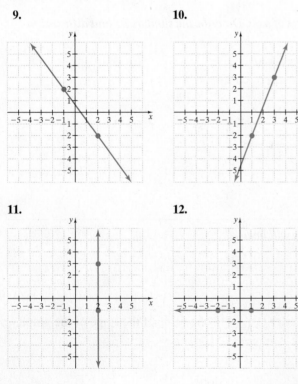

11.

12.

13.

14.

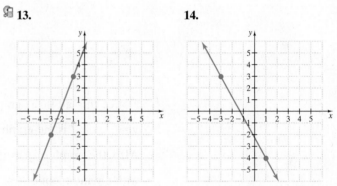

Each table contains ordered-pair solutions of a linear equation in two variables. Use each table to find the slope of each graph. See Example 3.

15.

x	y
3	0
-3	-4
0	-2

16.

x	y
4	0
-4	-6
0	-3

17.

x	y
-2	-5
1	1
-4	-9

18.

x	y
-1	1
2	4
-3	-11

Decision Making. *For each graph, determine which line has the greater slope.*

19.

20.

21.

22.

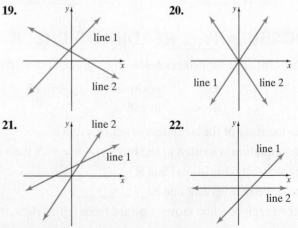

Matching. *In Exercises 23 through 28, match each line with its slope.*

A. $m = 0$ **B.** undefined slope   **C.** $m = 3$

D. $m = 1$ **E.** $m = -\dfrac{1}{2}$ **F.** $m = -\dfrac{3}{4}$

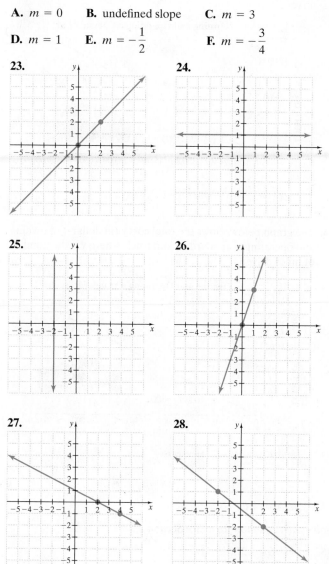

23.

24.

25.

26.

27.

28.

Find the slope of each line. See Examples 7 and 8.

29. $x = 6$ **30.** $y = 4$

31. $y = -4$ **32.** $x = 2$

33. $x = -3$ **34.** $y = -11$

35. $y = 0$ **36.** $x = 0$

MIXED PRACTICE

Find the slope of each line. See Examples 4 through 8.

37. $y = 5x - 2$ **38.** $y = -2x + 6$

39. $y = -0.3x + 2.5$ **40.** $y = -7.6x - 0.1$

41. $2x + y = 7$ **42.** $-5x + y = 10$

43. $2x - 3y = 10$ **44.** $3x - 5y = 1$

45. $x = 1$ **46.** $y = -2$

47. $x = 2y$ **48.** $x = -4y$

49. $y = -3$ **50.** $x = 5$

51. $-3x - 4y = 6$ **52.** $-4x - 7y = 9$

53. $20x - 5y = 1.2$ **54.** $24x - 3y = 5.7$

△ **Decision Making.** *Determine whether each pair of lines is parallel, perpendicular, or neither. See Example 9.*

55. $y = \dfrac{2}{9}x + 3$

$\quad\ y = -\dfrac{2}{9}x$

56. $y = \dfrac{1}{5}x + 20$

$\quad\ y = -\dfrac{1}{5}x$

57. $x - 3y = -6$

$\quad\ y = 3x - 9$

58. $y = 4x - 2$

$\quad\ 4x + y = 5$

59. $6x = 5y + 1$

$\quad\ -12x + 10y = 1$

60. $-x + 2y = -2$

$\quad\ 2x = 4y + 3$

61. $6 + 4x = 3y$

$\quad\ 3x + 4y = 8$

62. $10 + 3x = 5y$

$\quad\ 5x + 3y = 1$

The pitch of a roof is its slope. Find the pitch of each roof shown. See Example 10.

63.

6 feet

10 feet

64.

5

10

The grade of a road is its slope written as a percent. Find the grade of each road shown. See Example 10.

65.

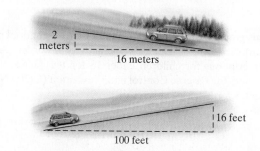

2 meters

16 meters

66.

16 feet

100 feet

67. One of Japan's superconducting "bullet" trains is researched and tested at the Yamanashi Maglev Test Line near Otsuki City. The steepest section of the track has a rise of 2580 meters for a horizontal distance of 6450 meters. What is the grade of this section of track? (*Source:* Japan Railways Central Co.)

2580 meters

6450 meters

68. Professional plumbers suggest that a sewer pipe should rise 0.25 inch for every horizontal foot. Find the recommended slope for a sewer pipe. Round to the nearest hundredth.

69. The steepest street is Baldwin Street in Dunedin, New Zealand. It has a maximum rise of 10 meters for a horizontal distance of 12.66 meters. Find the grade of this section of road. Round to the nearest whole percent. (*Source: The Guinness Book of Records*)

70. According to federal regulations, a wheelchair ramp should rise no more than 1 foot for a horizontal distance of 12 feet. Write the slope as a grade. Round to the nearest tenth of a percent.

Read a Graph. *Find the slope of each line and write the slope as a rate of change. Don't forget to attach the proper units. See Example 11.*

71. This graph approximates the number of U.S. households that have personal computers *y* (in millions) for year *x*.

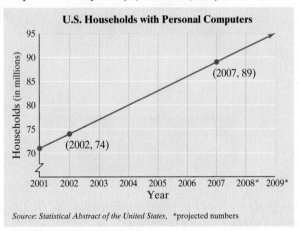

U.S. Households with Personal Computers

(2007, 89)

(2002, 74)

*Source: Statistical Abstract of the United States, *projected numbers*

72. This graph approximates the number *y* (per hundred population) of Attention Deficit Hyperactivity Disorder (ADHD) prescriptions for children under 18 for the year *x*. (*Source: Centers for Disease Control and Prevention (CDC) National Center for Health Statistics*)

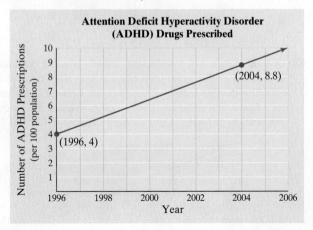

Attention Deficit Hyperactivity Disorder (ADHD) Drugs Prescribed

(2004, 8.8)

(1996, 4)

73. The graph below shows the total cost *y* (in dollars) of owning and operating a compact car where *x* is the number of miles driven.

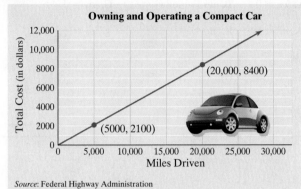

Owning and Operating a Compact Car

(20,000, 8400)

(5000, 2100)

Source: Federal Highway Administration

74. The graph below shows the total cost *y* (in dollars) of owning and operating a standard pickup truck, where *x* is the number of miles driven.

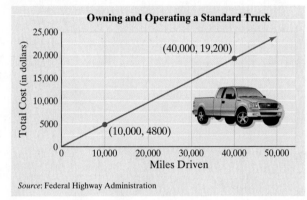

Owning and Operating a Standard Truck

(40,000, 19,200)

(10,000, 4800)

Source: Federal Highway Administration

REVIEW AND PREVIEW

Solve each equation for y. See Section 2.5.

75. $y - (-6) = 2(x - 4)$

76. $y - 7 = -9(x - 6)$

77. $y - 1 = -6(x - (-2))$

78. $y - (-3) = 4(x - (-5))$

CONCEPT EXTENSIONS

△ *Find the slope of the line that is (**a**) parallel and (**b**) perpendicular to the line through each pair of points.*

79. $(-3, -3)$ and $(0, 0)$

80. $(6, -2)$ and $(1, 4)$

81. $(-8, -4)$ and $(3, 5)$

82. $(6, -1)$ and $(-4, -10)$

Solve. See a Concept Check in this section.

83. Verify that the points $(2, 1), (0, 0), (-2, -1)$ and $(-4, -2)$ are all on the same line by computing the slope between each pair of points. (See the first Concept Check.)

84. Given the points $(2, 3)$ and $(-5, 1)$, can the slope of the line through these points be calculated by $\dfrac{1 - 3}{2 - (-5)}$? Why or why not? (See the second Concept Check.)

85. Write the equations of three lines parallel to $10x - 5y = -7$. (See the third Concept Check.)

86. Write the equations of two lines perpendicular to $10x - 5y = -7$. (See the third Concept Check.)

Read a Graph. *The following line graph shows the average fuel economy (in miles per gallon) by mid-size passenger automobiles produced during each of the model years shown. Use this graph to answer Exercises 87 through 92.*

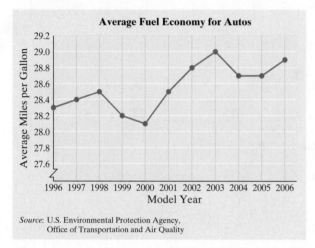

Average Fuel Economy for Autos

Source: U.S. Environmental Protection Agency, Office of Transportation and Air Quality

87. What was the average fuel economy (in miles per gallon) for automobiles produced during 2001?

88. Find the decrease in average fuel economy for automobiles between the years 2003 to 2004.

89. During which of the model years shown was average fuel economy the lowest?

What was the average fuel economy for that year?

90. During which of the model years shown was average fuel economy the highest?

What was the average fuel economy for that year?

91. What line segment has the greatest slope?

92. What line segment has the least positive slope?

Solve.

93. Find x so that the pitch of the roof is $\dfrac{1}{3}$.

94. Find x so that the pitch of the roof is $\dfrac{2}{5}$.

95. The average price of an acre of U.S. farmland was $1132 in 2001. In 2006, the price of an acre rose to approximately $1657. (*Source:* National Agricultural Statistics Service)

   a. Write two ordered pairs of the form (year, price of acre)

   b. Find the slope of the line through the two points.

   c. Write a sentence explaining the meaning of the slope as a rate of change.

96. There were approximately 14,774 kidney transplants performed in the United States in 2002. In 2006, the number of kidney transplants performed in the United States rose to 15,722. (*Source:* Organ Procurement and Transplantation Network)

   a. Write two ordered pairs of the form (year, number of kidney transplants).

   b. Find the slope of the line between the two points.

   c. Write a sentence explaining the meaning of the slope as a rate of change.

97. Show that a triangle with vertices at the points $(1, 1)$, $(-4, 4)$, and $(-3, 0)$ is a right triangle.

98. Show that the quadrilateral with vertices $(1, 3)$, $(2, 1)$, $(-4, 0)$, and $(-3, -2)$ is a parallelogram.

Find the slope of the line through the given points.

99. $(2.1, 6.7)$ and $(-8.3, 9.3)$

100. $(-3.8, 1.2)$ and $(-2.2, 4.5)$

101. $(2.3, 0.2)$ and $(7.9, 5.1)$

102. $(14.3, -10.1)$ and $(9.8, -2.9)$

103. The graph of $y = -\dfrac{1}{3}x + 2$ has a slope of $-\dfrac{1}{3}$. The graph of $y = -2x + 2$ has a slope of -2. The graph of $y = -4x + 2$ has a slope of -4. Graph all three equations on a single coordinate system. As the absolute value of the slope becomes larger, how does the steepness of the line change?

104. The graph of $y = \dfrac{1}{2}x$ has a slope of $\dfrac{1}{2}$. The graph of $y = 3x$ has a slope of 3. The graph of $y = 5x$ has a slope of 5. Graph all three equations on a single coordinate system. As slope becomes larger, how does the steepness of the line change?

INTEGRATED REVIEW SUMMARY ON SLOPE & GRAPHING LINEAR EQUATIONS

Sections 3.1–3.4

Read a Graph. *Find the slope of each line.*

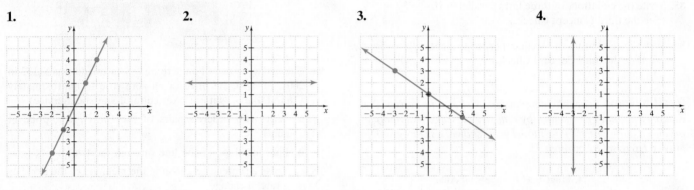

1.   2.   3.   4.

Graph each linear equation.

5. $y = -2x$

6. $x + y = 3$

7. $x = -1$

8. $y = 4$

9. $x - 2y = 6$

10. $y = 3x + 2$

11. $5x + 3y = 15$

12. $2x - 4y = 8$

Determine whether the lines through the points are parallel, perpendicular, or neither.

13. $y = -\dfrac{1}{5}x + \dfrac{1}{3}$
  $3x = -15y$

14. $x - y = \dfrac{1}{2}$
  $3x - y = \dfrac{1}{2}$

15. In the years 2002 through 2005 the number of admissions to movie theaters in the United States can be modeled by the linear equation $y = -75x + 1650$ where x is years after 2002 and y is admissions in millions. (*Source:* Motion Picture Assn. of America)

   a. Find the y-intercept of this line.

   b. Write a sentence explaining the meaning of this intercept.

   c. Find the slope of this line.

   d. Write a sentence explaining the meaning of the slope as a rate of change.

16. Online advertising is a means of promoting products and services using the Internet. The revenue (in billions of dollars) for online advertising for the years 2003 through a projected 2010 is given by $y = 3.3x - 3.1$, where x is the number of years after 2000.

   a. Use this equation to complete the ordered pair $(9, \quad)$.

   b. Write a sentence explaining the meaning of the answer to part (a).

3.5 EQUATIONS OF LINES

Recall that the form $y = mx + b$ is appropriately called the *slope-intercept form* of a linear equation.

y-intercept is $(0, b)$

slope

> **Slope-Intercept Form**
>
> When a linear equation in two variables is written in **slope-intercept form,**
>
> $$y = mx + b$$
>
> slope $(0, b)$, y-intercept
>
> then m is the slope of the line and $(0, b)$ is the y-intercept of the line.

OBJECTIVE 1 ▶ Using the slope-intercept form to write an equation. As we know from the previous section, writing an equation in slope-intercept form is a way to find the slope and y-intercept of its graph. The slope-intercept form can be used to write the equation of a line when we know its slope and y-intercept.

EXAMPLE 1   Find an equation of the line with y-intercept $(0, -3)$ and slope of $\dfrac{1}{4}$.

Solution   We are given the slope and the y-intercept. We let $m = \dfrac{1}{4}$ and $b = -3$ and write the equation in slope-intercept form, $y = mx + b$.

$$y = mx + b$$

$$y = \frac{1}{4}x + (-3) \quad \text{Let } m = \frac{1}{4} \text{ and } b = -3.$$

$$y = \frac{1}{4}x - 3 \qquad \text{Simplify.}$$

PRACTICE

1   Find an equation of the line with y-intercept $(0, 7)$ and slope of $\dfrac{1}{2}$.

OBJECTIVE 2 ▶ Using the slope-intercept form to graph an equation. We also can use the slope-intercept form of the equation of a line to graph a linear equation.

EXAMPLE 2   Use the slope-intercept form to graph the equation

$$y = \frac{3}{5}x - 2$$

Solution   Since the equation $y = \dfrac{3}{5}x - 2$ is written in slope-intercept form $y = mx + b$, the slope of its graph is $\dfrac{3}{5}$ and the y-intercept is $(0, -2)$. To graph this equation, we begin by plotting the point $(0, -2)$. From this point, we can find another point of the graph by using the slope $\dfrac{3}{5}$ and recalling that slope is $\dfrac{\text{rise}}{\text{run}}$. We start at the y-intercept and move 3 units up since the numerator of the slope is 3; then we move 5 units to the right since the denominator of the slope is 5. We stop at the point $(5, 1)$. The line through $(0, -2)$ and $(5, 1)$ is the graph of $y = \dfrac{3}{5}x - 2$.

PRACTICE

2   Graph $y = \dfrac{2}{3}x - 5$.

EXAMPLE 3 Use the slope-intercept form to graph the equation $4x + y = 1$.

<u>Solution</u> First we write the given equation in slope-intercept form.

$$4x + y = 1$$
$$y = -4x + 1$$

The graph of this equation will have slope -4 and y-intercept $(0, 1)$. To graph this line, we first plot the point $(0, 1)$. To find another point of the graph, we use the slope -4, which can be written as $\dfrac{-4}{1}\left(\dfrac{4}{-1}\text{ could also be used}\right)$. We start at the point $(0, 1)$ and move 4 units down (since the numerator of the slope is -4), and then 1 unit to the right (since the denominator of the slope is 1).

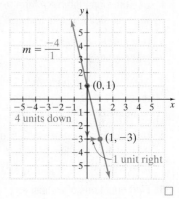

We arrive at the point $(1, -3)$. The line through $(0, 1)$ and $(1, -3)$ is the graph of $4x + y = 1$. □

> **Helpful Hint**
> In Example 3, if we interpret the slope of -4 as $\dfrac{4}{-1}$, we arrive at $(-1, 5)$ for a second point. Notice that this point is also on the line.

PRACTICE
3 Use the slope-intercept form to graph the equation $3x - y = 2$.

OBJECTIVE 3 ▶ Writing an equation given slope and a point. Thus far, we have seen that we can write an equation of a line if we know its slope and y-intercept. We can also write an equation of a line if we know its slope and any point on the line. To see how we do this, let m represent slope and (x_1, y_1) represent the point on the line. Then if (x, y) is any other point of the line, we have that

$$\dfrac{y - y_1}{x - x_1} = m$$
$$y - y_1 = m(x - x_1) \quad \text{Multiply both sides by } (x - x_1).$$
$$\underset{\text{slope}}{\uparrow}$$

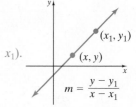

This is the *point-slope form* of the equation of a line.

Point-Slope Form of the Equation of a Line

The **point-slope form** of the equation of a line is

$$y - y_1 = m(x - x_1)$$

where m is the slope of the line and (x_1, y_1) is a point on the line.

EXAMPLE 4 Find an equation of the line with slope -2 that passes through $(-1, 5)$. Write the equation in slope-intercept form, $y = mx + b$, and in standard form, $Ax + By = C$.

<u>Solution</u> Since the slope and a point on the line are given, we use point-slope form $y - y_1 = m(x - x_1)$ to write the equation. Let $m = -2$ and $(-1, 5) = (x_1, y_1)$.

$$y - y_1 = m(x - x_1)$$
$$y - 5 = -2[x - (-1)] \quad \text{Let } m = -2 \text{ and } (x_1, y_1) = (-1, 5).$$
$$y - 5 = -2(x + 1) \quad \text{Simplify.}$$
$$y - 5 = -2x - 2 \quad \text{Use the distributive property.}$$

To write the equation in slope-intercept form, $y = mx + b$, we simply solve the equation for y. To do this, we add 5 to both sides.

$$y - 5 = -2x - 2$$
$$y = -2x + 3 \quad \text{Slope-intercept form.}$$
$$2x + y = 3 \quad \text{Add } 2x \text{ to both sides and we have standard form.} \quad \square$$

PRACTICE
4 Find an equation of the line passing through (2, 3) with slope 4. Write the equation in standard form: $Ax + By = C$.

OBJECTIVE 4 ▶ Writing an equation given two points. We can also find the equation of a line when we are given any two points of the line.

EXAMPLE 5 Find an equation of the line through $(2, 5)$ and $(-3, 4)$. Write the equation in standard form.

Solution First, use the two given points to find the slope of the line.

$$m = \frac{4 - 5}{-3 - 2} = \frac{-1}{-5} = \frac{1}{5}$$

Next we use the slope $\frac{1}{5}$ and either one of the given points to write the equation in point-slope form. We use $(2, 5)$. Let $x_1 = 2$, $y_1 = 5$, and $m = \frac{1}{5}$.

$$y - y_1 = m(x - x_1) \quad \text{Use point-slope form.}$$

$$y - 5 = \frac{1}{5}(x - 2) \quad \text{Let } x_1 = 2, y_1 = 5, \text{ and } m = \frac{1}{5}.$$

$$5(y - 5) = 5 \cdot \frac{1}{5}(x - 2) \quad \text{Multiply both sides by 5 to clear fractions.}$$

$$5y - 25 = x - 2 \quad \text{Use the distributive property and simplify.}$$
$$-x + 5y - 25 = -2 \quad \text{Subtract } x \text{ from both sides.}$$
$$-x + 5y = 23 \quad \text{Add 25 to both sides.} \quad \square$$

PRACTICE
5 Find an equation of the line through $(-1, 6)$ and $(3, 1)$. Write the equation in standard form.

▶ **Helpful Hint**
Multiply both sides of the equation $-x + 5y = 23$ by -1, and it becomes $x - 5y = -23$. Both $-x + 5y = 23$ and $x - 5y = -23$ are in standard form, and they are equations of the same line.

OBJECTIVE 5 ▶ Finding equations of vertical and horizontal lines. Recall from Section 3.3 that:

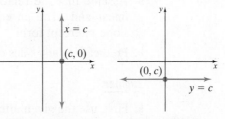

Vertical Line   Horizontal Line

EXAMPLE 6 Find an equation of the vertical line through $(-1, 5)$.

Solution The equation of a vertical line can be written in the form $x = c$, so an equation for a vertical line passing through $(-1, 5)$ is $x = -1$.

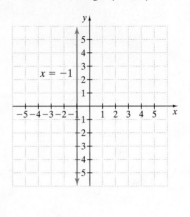

PRACTICE
6 Find an equation of the vertical line through $(3, -2)$.

EXAMPLE 7 Find an equation of the line parallel to the line $y = 5$ and passing through $(-2, -3)$.

Solution Since the graph of $y = 5$ is a horizontal line, any line parallel to it is also horizontal. The equation of a horizontal line can be written in the form $y = c$. An equation for the horizontal line passing through

$$(-2, -3) \text{ is } y = -3.$$

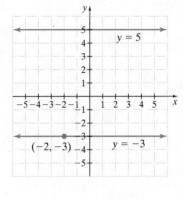

PRACTICE
7 Find an equation of the line parallel to the line $y = -2$ and passing through $(4, 3)$.

OBJECTIVE 6 ▶ Using the point-slope form to solve problems. Problems occurring in many fields can be modeled by linear equations in two variables. The next example is from the field of marketing and shows how consumer demand of a product depends on the price of the product.

EXAMPLE 8 Predicting the Sales of T-Shirts

A web-based T-shirt company has learned that by pricing a clearance-sale T-shirt at $6, sales will reach 2000 T-shirts per day. Raising the price to $8 will cause the sales to fall to 1500 T-shirts per day.

a. Assume that the relationship between sales price and number of T-shirts sold is linear and write an equation describing this relationship. Write the equation in slope-intercept form.

b. Predict the daily sales of T-shirts if the price is $7.50.

Solution

a. First, use the given information and write two ordered pairs. Ordered pairs will be in the form (sales price, number sold) so that our ordered pairs are (6, 2000) and

(8, 1500). Use the point-slope form to write an equation. To do so, we find the slope of the line that contains these points.

$$m = \frac{2000 - 1500}{6 - 8} = \frac{500}{-2} = -250$$

Next, use the slope and either one of the points to write the equation in point-slope form. We use (6, 2000).

$$y - y_1 = m(x - x_1) \qquad \text{Use point-slope form.}$$

$$y - 2000 = -250(x - 6) \qquad \text{Let } x_1 = 6, y_1 = 2000, \text{ and } m = -250.$$

$$y - 2000 = -250x + 1500 \qquad \text{Use the distributive property.}$$

$$y = -250x + 3500 \qquad \text{Write in slope-intercept form.}$$

b. To predict the sales if the price is \$7.50, we find y when $x = 7.50$.

$$y = -250x + 3500$$

$$y = -250(7.50) + 3500 \qquad \text{Let } x = 7.50.$$

$$y = -1875 + 3500$$

$$y = 1625$$

If the price is \$7.50, sales will reach 1625 T-shirts per day. □

PRACTICE

8 The new *Camelot* condos were selling at a rate of 30 per month when they were priced at \$150,000 each. Lowering the price to \$120,000 caused the sales to rise to 50 condos per month.

a. Assume that the relationship between number of condos sold and price is linear, and write an equation describing this relationship. Write the equation in slope-intercept form.

b. What should the condos be priced at if the developer wishes to sell 60 condos per month?

The preceding example may also be solved by using ordered pairs of the form (number sold, sales price).

Forms of Linear Equations	
$Ax + By = C$	**Standard form** of a linear equation. A and B are not both 0.
$y = mx + b$	**Slope-intercept form** of a linear equation. The slope is m and the y-intercept is $(0, b)$.
$y - y_1 = m(x - x_1)$	**Point-slope form** of a linear equation. The slope is m and (x_1, y_1) is a point on the line.
$y = c$	**Horizontal line** The slope is 0 and the y-intercept is $(0, c)$.
$x = c$	**Vertical line** The slope is undefined and the x-intercept is $(c, 0)$.

Parallel and Perpendicular Lines

Nonvertical parallel lines have the same slope.

The product of the slopes of two nonvertical perpendicular lines is -1.

Graphing Calculator Explorations

A grapher is a very useful tool for discovering patterns. To discover the change in the graph of a linear equation caused by a change in slope, try the following. Use a standard window and graph a linear equation in the form $y = mx + b$. Recall that the graph of such an equation will have slope m and y-intercept b.

First graph $y = x + 3$. To do so, press the $\boxed{Y=}$ key and enter $Y_1 = x + 3$. Notice that this graph has slope 1 and that the y-intercept is 3. Next, on the same set of axes, graph $y = 2x + 3$ and $y = 3x + 3$ by pressing $\boxed{Y=}$ and entering $Y_2 = 2x + 3$ and $Y_3 = 3x + 3$.

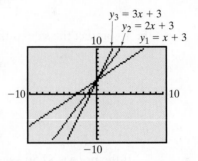

Notice the difference in the graph of each equation as the slope changes from 1 to 2 to 3. How would the graph of $y = 5x + 3$ appear? To see the change in the graph caused by a change in negative slope, try graphing $y = -x + 3$, $y = -2x + 3$, and $y = -3x + 3$ on the same set of axes.

Use a grapher to graph the following equations. For each exercise, graph the first equation and use its graph to predict the appearance of the other equations. Then graph the other equations on the same set of axes and check your prediction.

1. $y = x$; $y = 6x$, $y = -6x$

2. $y = -x$; $y = -5x$, $y = -10x$

3. $y = \dfrac{1}{2}x + 2$; $y = \dfrac{3}{4}x + 2$, $y = x + 2$

4. $y = x + 1$; $y = \dfrac{5}{4}x + 1$, $y = \dfrac{5}{2}x + 1$

5. $y = -7x + 5$; $y = 7x + 5$

6. $y = 3x - 1$; $y = -3x - 1$

VOCABULARY & READINESS CHECK

Word Bank. *Use the choices below to fill in each blank. Some choices may be used more than once and some not at all.*

b	(y_1, x_1)	point-slope	vertical	standard
m	(x_1, y_1)	slope-intercept	horizontal	

1. The form $y = mx + b$ is called _____ form. When a linear equation in two variables is written in this form, _____ is the slope of its graph and (0, _____) is its y-intercept.

2. The form $y - y_1 = m(x - x_1)$ is called _____ form. When a linear equation in two variables is written in this form, _____ is the slope of its graph and _____ is a point on the graph.

Decision Making. *For Exercises 3, 4, and 7, identify the form that the linear equation in two variables is written in. For Exercises 5 and 6, identify the appearance of the graph of the equation.*

3. $y - 7 = 4(x + 3)$; _____ form

4. $5x - 9y = 11$; _____ form

5. $y = \dfrac{1}{2}$; _____ line

6. $x = -17$; _____ line

7. $y = \dfrac{3}{4}x - \dfrac{1}{3}$; _____ form

3.5 | EXERCISE SET

MyMathLab — Powered by CourseCompass™ and MathXL® · Math XP PRACTICE · WATCH · DOWNLOAD · READ · REVIEW

Write an equation of the line with each given slope, m, and y-intercept, (0, b). See Example 1.

1. $m = 5, b = 3$

2. $m = -3, b = -3$

3. $m = -4, b = -\dfrac{1}{6}$

4. $m = 2, b = \dfrac{3}{4}$

5. $m = \dfrac{2}{3}, b = 0$

6. $m = -\dfrac{4}{5}, b = 0$

7. $m = 0, b = -8$

8. $m = 0, b = -2$

9. $m = -\dfrac{1}{5}, b = \dfrac{1}{9}$

10. $m = \dfrac{1}{2}, b = -\dfrac{1}{3}$

Use the slope-intercept form to graph each equation. See Examples 2 and 3.

11. $y = 2x + 1$

12. $y = -4x - 1$

13. $y = \dfrac{2}{3}x + 5$

14. $y = \dfrac{1}{4}x - 3$

15. $y = -5x$

16. $y = -6x$

17. $4x + y = 6$

18. $-3x + y = 2$

19. $4x - 7y = -14$

20. $3x - 4y = 4$

21. $x = \dfrac{5}{4}y$

22. $x = \dfrac{3}{2}y$

Find an equation of each line with the given slope that passes through the given point. Write the equation in the form $Ax + By = C$. See Example 4.

23. $m = 6;\quad (2, 2)$

24. $m = 4;\quad (1, 3)$

25. $m = -8;\quad (-1, -5)$

26. $m = -2;\quad (-11, -12)$

27. $m = \dfrac{3}{2};\quad (5, -6)$

28. $m = \dfrac{2}{3};\quad (-8, 9)$

29. $m = -\dfrac{1}{2};\quad (-3, 0)$

30. $m = -\dfrac{1}{5};\quad (4, 0)$

Find an equation of the line passing through each pair of points. Write the equation in the form $Ax + By = C$. See Example 5.

31. $(3, 2)$ and $(5, 6)$

32. $(6, 2)$ and $(8, 8)$

33. $(-1, 3)$ and $(-2, -5)$

34. $(-4, 0)$ and $(6, -1)$

35. $(2, 3)$ and $(-1, -1)$

36. $(7, 10)$ and $(-1, -1)$

37. $(0, 0)$ and $\left(-\dfrac{1}{8}, \dfrac{1}{13}\right)$

38. $(0, 0)$ and $\left(-\dfrac{1}{2}, \dfrac{1}{3}\right)$

Find an equation of each line. See Example 6.

39. Vertical line through $(0, 2)$

40. Horizontal line through $(1, 4)$

41. Horizontal line through $(-1, 3)$

42. Vertical line through $(-1, 3)$

43. Vertical line through $\left(-\dfrac{7}{3}, -\dfrac{2}{5}\right)$

44. Horizontal line through $\left(\dfrac{2}{7}, 0\right)$

Find an equation of each line. See Example 7.

45. Parallel to $y = 5$, through $(1, 2)$

46. Perpendicular to $y = 5$, through $(1, 2)$

47. Perpendicular to $x = -3$, through $(-2, 5)$

48. Parallel to $y = -4$, through $(0, -3)$

49. Parallel to $x = 0$, through $(6, -8)$

50. Perpendicular to $x = 7$, through $(-5, 0)$

MIXED PRACTICE

See Examples 1 through 7. Find an equation of each line described. Write each equation in slope-intercept form (solved for y), when possible.

51. With slope $-\dfrac{1}{2}$, through $\left(0, \dfrac{5}{3}\right)$

52. With slope $\dfrac{5}{7}$, through $(0, -3)$

53. Through $(10, 7)$ and $(7, 10)$

54. Through $(5, -6)$ and $(-6, 5)$

55. With undefined slope, through $\left(-\dfrac{3}{4}, 1\right)$

56. With slope 0, through $(6.7, 12.1)$

57. Slope 1, through $(-7, 9)$

58. Slope 5, through $(6, -8)$

59. Slope -5, y-intercept $(0, 7)$

60. Slope -2; y-intercept $(0, -4)$

61. Through $(6, 7)$, parallel to the x-axis

62. Through $(1, -5)$, parallel to the y-axis

63. Through $(2, 3)$ and $(0, 0)$

64. Through $(4, 7)$ and $(0, 0)$

65. Through $(-2, -3)$, perpendicular to the y-axis

66. Through $(0, 12)$, perpendicular to the x-axis

67. Slope $-\dfrac{4}{7}$, through $(-1, -2)$

68. Slope $-\dfrac{3}{5}$, through $(4, 4)$

Multiple Steps. *Solve. Assume each exercise describes a linear relationship. Write the equations in slope-intercept form. See Example 8.*

69. A rock is dropped from the top of a 400-foot cliff. After 1 second, the rock is traveling 32 feet per second. After 3 seconds, the rock is traveling 96 feet per second.

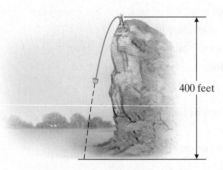

400 feet

a. Assume that the relationship between time and speed is linear and write an equation describing this relationship. Use ordered pairs of the form (time, speed).

b. Use this equation to determine the speed of the rock 4 seconds after it was dropped.

70. A Hawaiian fruit company is studying the sales of a pineapple sauce to see if this product is to be continued. At the end of its first year, profits on this product amounted to $30,000. At the end of the fourth year, profits were $66,000.

a. Assume that the relationship between years on the market and profit is linear and write an equation describing this relationship. Use ordered pairs of the form (years on the market, profit).

b. Use this equation to predict the profit at the end of 7 years.

71. In January 2007, there were 71,000 registered gasoline-electric hybrid cars in the United States. In 2004, there were only 29,000 registered gasoline-electric hybrids. (*Source:* U.S. Energy Information Administration)

a. Write an equation describing the relationship between time and number of registered gasoline-hybrid cars. Use ordered pairs of the form (years past 2004, number of cars).

b. Use this equation to predict the number of gasoline-electric hybrids in the year 2010.

72. In 2006, there were 935 thousand eating establishments in the United States. In 1996, there were 457 thousand eating establishments. (*Source:* National Restaurant Association)

a. Write an equation describing the relationship between time and number of eating establishments. Use ordered pairs of the form (years past 1996, number of eating establishments in thousands).

b. Use this equation to predict the number of eating establishments in 2010.

73. In 2006, the U.S. population per square mile of land area was 85. In 2000, the person per square mile population was 79.6.

a. Write an equation describing the relationship between year and persons per square mile. Use ordered pairs of the form (years past 2000, persons per square mile).

b. Use this equation to predict the person per square mile population in 2010.

74. In 2001, there were a total of 152 thousand apparel and accessory stores. In 2005, there were a total of 150 thousand apparel and accessory stores. (*Source:* U.S. Bureau of the Census. *County Business Patterns, annual*)

a. Write an equation describing this relationship. Use ordered pairs of the form (years past 2001, numbers of stores in thousand).

b. Use this equation to predict the number of apparel and accessory stores in 2011.

75. The birth rate in the United States in 1996 was 14.7 births per thousand population. In 2006, the birth rate was 14.14 births per thousand. (*Source:* Department of Health and Human Services, National Center for Health Statistics)

a. Write two ordered pairs of the form (years after 1996, birth rate per thousand population).

b. Assume that the relationship between years after 1996 and birth rate per thousand is linear over this period. Use the ordered pairs from part (a) to write an equation of the line relating years to birth rate.

c. Use the linear equation from part (b) to estimate the birth rate in the United States in the year 2016.

76. In 2002, crude oil production by OPEC countries was about 28.7 million barrels per day. In 2007, crude oil production had risen to about 34.5 million barrels per day. (*Source:* OPEC)

   a. Write two ordered pairs of the form (years after 2002, crude oil production) for this situation.

   b. Assume that crude oil production is linear between the years 2002 and 2007. Use the ordered pairs from part (a) to write an equation of the line relating year and crude oil production.

   c. Use the linear equation from part (b) to estimate the crude oil production by OPEC countries in 2004.

77. Better World Club is a relatively new automobile association which prides itself on its "green" philosophy. In 2003, the membership totaled 5 thousand. By 2006, there were 20 thousand members of this ecologically minded club. (*Source:* Better World Club)

   a. Write two ordered pairs of the form (years after 2003, membership in thousands)

   b. Assume that the membership is linear between the years 2003 and 2006. Use the ordered pairs from part (a) to write an equation of the line relating year and Better World membership.

   c. Use the linear equation from part (b) to predict the Better World Club membership in 2012.

78. In 2002, 9.9 million electronic bill statements were delivered and payment occurred. In 2005, that number rose to 26.9 million. (*Source:* Forrester Research)

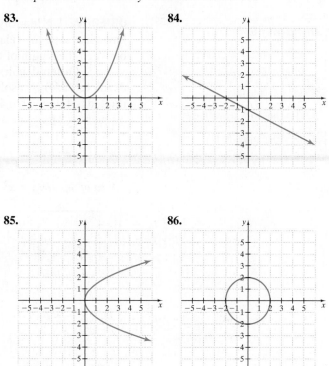

   a. Write two ordered pairs of the form (years after 2002, millions of electronic bills).

   b. Assume that this method of delivery and payment between the years 2002 and 2005 is linear. Use the ordered pairs from part (a) to write an equation of the line relating year and number of electronic bills.

   c. Use the linear equation from part (b) to predict the number of electronic bills to be delivered and paid in 2011.

REVIEW AND PREVIEW

Find the value of $x^2 - 3x + 1$ for each given value of x. See Section 1.8.

79. 2   **80.** 5   **81.** -1 **82.** -3

Read a Graph. *For each graph, determine whether any x-values correspond to two or more y-values. See Section 3.1.*

83.

84.

85.

86.

CONCEPT EXTENSIONS

87. Given the equation of a nonvertical line, explain how to find the slope without finding two points on the line.

88. Given two points on a nonvertical line, explain how to use the point-slope form to find the equation of the line.

89. Write an equation in standard form of the line that contains the point $(-1, 2)$ and is

   a. parallel to the line $y = 3x - 1$.

   b. perpendicular to the line $y = 3x - 1$.

90. Write an equation in standard form of the line that contains the point $(4, 0)$ and is

   a. parallel to the line $y = -2x + 3$.

   b. perpendicular to the line $y = -2x + 3$.

91. Write an equation in standard form of the line that contains the point $(3, -5)$ and is

   a. parallel to the line $3x + 2y = 7$.

   b. perpendicular to the line $3x + 2y = 7$.

92. Write an equation in standard form of the line that contains the point $(-2, 4)$ and is

   a. parallel to the line $x + 3y = 6$.

   b. perpendicular to the line $x + 3y = 6$.

3.6 FUNCTIONS

OBJECTIVES

1 Identify relations, domains, and ranges.

2 Identify functions.

3 Use the vertical line test.

4 Use function notation.

OBJECTIVE 1 ▶ Identifying relations, domains, and ranges. In previous sections, we have discussed the relationships between two quantities. For example, the relationship between the length of the side of a square x and its area y is described by the equation $y = x^2$. Ordered pairs can be used to write down solutions of this equation. For example, $(2, 4)$ is a solution of $y = x^2$, and this notation tells us that the x-value 2 is related to the y-value 4 for this equation. In other words, when the length of the side of a square is 2 units, its area is 4 square units.

Examples of Relationships Between Two Quantities

Area of Square: $y = x^2$	Equation of Line: $y = x + 2$	Online Advertising Revenue

Some Ordered Pairs		Some Ordered Pairs		Ordered Pairs	
x	y	x	y	Year	Billions of Dollars
2	4	−3	−1	2006	16.7
5	25	0	2	2007	20.3
7	49	2	4	2008	23.5
12	144	9	11	2009	26.6
				2010	29.4

A set of ordered pairs is called a **relation.** The set of all x-coordinates is called the **domain** of a relation, and the set of all y-coordinates is called the **range** of a relation. Equations such as $y = x^2$ are also called relations since equations in two variables define a set of ordered pair solutions.

EXAMPLE 1 Find the domain and the range of the relation $\{(0, 2), (3, 3), (-1, 0), (3, -2)\}$.

Solution The domain is the set of all x-values or $\{-1, 0, 3\}$, and the range is the set of all y-values, or $\{-2, 0, 2, 3\}$. ☐

PRACTICE
1 Find the domain and the range of the relation $\{(1, 3), (5, 0), (0, -2), (5, 4)\}$.

OBJECTIVE 2 ▶ Identifying functions. Some relations are also functions.

Function
A function is a set of ordered pairs that assigns to each x-value exactly one y-value.

EXAMPLE 2   Which of the following relations are also functions?

a. $\{(-1, 1), (2, 3), (7, 3), (8, 6)\}$ **b.** $\{(0, -2), (1, 5), (0, 3), (7, 7)\}$

Solution

a. Although the ordered pairs $(2, 3)$ and $(7, 3)$ have the same *y*-value, each *x*-value is assigned to only one *y*-value so this set of ordered pairs is a function.

b. The *x*-value 0 is assigned to two *y*-values, -2 and 3, so this set of ordered pairs is not a function.   □

PRACTICE
2   Which of the following relations are also functions?

a. $\{(4, 1), (3, -2), (8, 5), (-5, 3)\}$ **b.** $\{(1, 2), (-4, 3), (0, 8), (1, 4)\}$

Relations and functions can be described by a graph of their ordered pairs.

EXAMPLE 3   Which graph is the graph of a function?

a.   **b.**

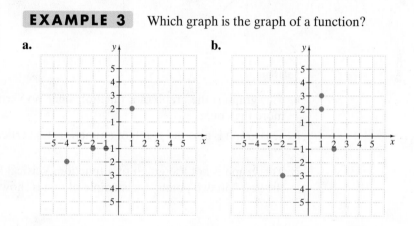

Solution

a. This is the graph of the relation $\{(-4, -2), (-2, -1)(-1, -1), (1, 2)\}$. Each *x*-coordinate has exactly one *y*-coordinate, so this is the graph of a function.

b. This is the graph of the relation $\{(-2, -3), (1, 2), (1, 3), (2, -1)\}$. The *x*-coordinate 1 is paired with two *y*-coordinates, 2 and 3, so this is not the graph of a function.   □

PRACTICE
3   Which graph is the graph of a function?

a.   **b.**

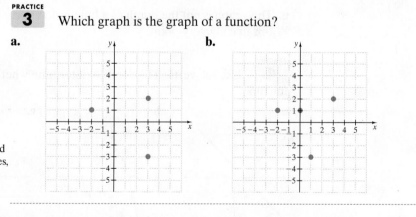

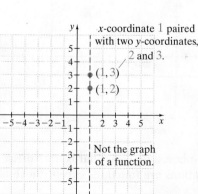

OBJECTIVE 3 ▶ Using the vertical line test. The graph in Example 3(b) was not the graph of a function because the *x*-coordinate 1 was paired with two *y*-coordinates, 2 and 3. Notice that when an *x*-coordinate is paired with more than one *y*-coordinate, a vertical line can be drawn that will intersect the graph at more than one point. We can use this fact to determine whether a relation is also a function. We call this the **vertical line test.**

> **Vertical Line Test**
>
> If a vertical line can be drawn so that it intersects a graph more than once, the graph is not the graph of a function.

This vertical line test works for all types of graphs on the rectangular coordinate system.

EXAMPLE 4 Use the vertical line test to determine whether each graph is the graph of a function.

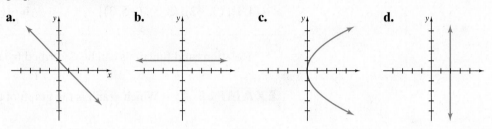

a.   b.   c.   d.

Solution

a. This graph is the graph of a function since no vertical line will intersect this graph more than once.

b. This graph is also the graph of a function; no vertical line will intersect it more than once.

c. This graph is not the graph of a function. Vertical lines can be drawn that intersect the graph in two points. An example of one is shown.

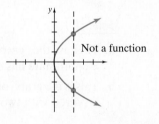

Not a function

d. This graph is not the graph of a function. A vertical line can be drawn that intersects this line at every point. □

PRACTICE

4 Use the vertical line test to determine whether each graph is the graph of a function.

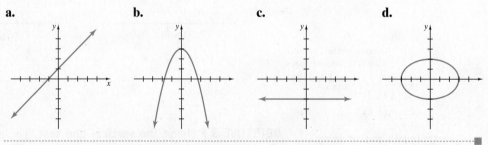

a.   b.   c.   d.

Recall that the graph of a linear equation is a line, and a line that is not vertical will pass the vertical line test. **Thus, all linear equations are functions except those of the form $x = c$, which are vertical lines.**

EXAMPLE 5 Which of the following linear equations are functions?

a. $y = x$ **b.** $y = 2x + 1$ **c.** $y = 5$ **d.** $x = -1$

Solution **a**, **b**, and **c** are functions because their graphs are nonvertical lines. **d** is not a function because its graph is a vertical line. ☐

PRACTICE
5 Which of the following linear equations are functions?

a. $y = 2x$ **b.** $y = -3x - 1$ **c.** $y = 8$ **d.** $x = 2$

Examples of functions can often be found in magazines, newspapers, books, and other printed material in the form of tables or graphs such as that in Example 6.

EXAMPLE 6 The graph shows the sunrise time for Indianapolis, Indiana, for the year. Use this graph to answer the questions.

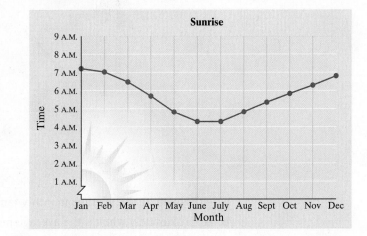

a. Approximate the time of sunrise on February 1.
b. Approximately when does the sun rise at 5 A.M.?
c. Is this the graph of a function?

Solution

a. To approximate the time of sunrise on February 1, we find the mark on the horizontal axis that corresponds to February 1. From this mark, we move vertically upward until the graph is reached. From that point on the graph, we move horizontally to the left until the vertical axis is reached. The vertical axis there reads 7 A.M.

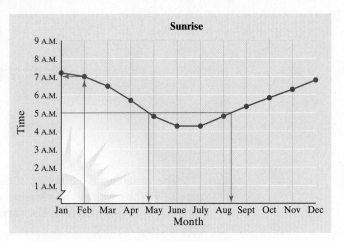

b. To approximate when the sun rises at 5 A.M., we find 5 A.M. on the time axis and move horizontally to the right. Notice that we will reach the graph twice, corresponding to two dates for which the sun rises at 5 A.M. We follow both points on the graph vertically downward until the horizontal axis is reached. The sun rises at 5 A.M. at approximately the end of the month of April and the middle of the month of August.

c. The graph is the graph of a function since it passes the vertical line test. In other words, for every day of the year in Indianapolis, there is exactly one sunrise time. ☐

PRACTICE
6 The graph shows the average monthly temperature for Chicago, Illinois, for the year. Use this graph to answer the questions.

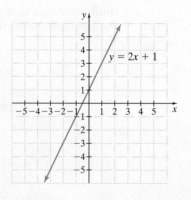

Average Monthly Temperature

*(1 is Jan., 12 is Dec.)

a. Approximate the average monthly temperature for June.

b. Approximately when is the average monthly temperature 40°?

c. Is this the graph of a function?

OBJECTIVE 4 ▶ Using function notation. The graph of the linear equation $y = 2x + 1$ passes the vertical line test, so we say that $y = 2x + 1$ is a function. In other words, $y = 2x + 1$ gives us a rule for writing ordered pairs where every x-coordinate is paired with one y-coordinate.

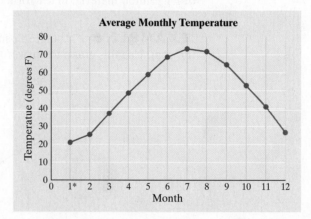

The variable y is a function of the variable x. For each value of x, there is only one value of y. Thus, we say the variable x is the **independent variable** as any value in the domain can be assigned to x. The variable y is the **dependent variable** because its value depends on x.

We often use letters such as f, g, and h to name functions. For example, the symbol $f(x)$ means *function of x* and is read "f of x." This notation is called **function notation.** The equation $y = 2x + 1$ can be written as $f(x) = 2x + 1$ using function notation, and these equations mean the same thing. In other words, $y = f(x)$.

The notation $f(1)$ means to replace x with 1 and find the resulting y or function value. Since

$$f(x) = 2x + 1$$

then

$$f(1) = 2(1) + 1 = 3$$

This means that, when $x = 1$, y or $f(x) = 3$, and we have the ordered pair $(1, 3)$. Now let's find $f(2)$, $f(0)$, and $f(-1)$.

> ▶ **Helpful Hint**
> Note that, for example, if $f(2) = 5$, the corresponding ordered pair is $(2, 5)$.

$$
\begin{array}{lll}
f(x) = 2x + 1 & f(x) = 2x + 1 & f(x) = 2x + 1 \\
f(2) = 2(2) + 1 & f(0) = 2(0) + 1 & f(-1) = 2(-1) + 1 \\
\quad = 4 + 1 & \quad = 0 + 1 & \quad = -2 + 1 \\
\quad = 5 & \quad = 1 & \quad = -1
\end{array}
$$

Ordered
Pair: $(2, 5)$ $(0, 1)$ $(-1, -1)$

> ▶ **Helpful Hint**
> Note that $f(x)$ is a special symbol in mathematics used to denote a function. The symbol $f(x)$ is read "f of x." It does **not** mean $f \cdot x$ (f times x).

EXAMPLE 7   Given $g(x) = x^2 - 3$, find the following. Then write down the corresponding ordered pairs generated.

a. $g(2)$ **b.** $g(-2)$ **c.** $g(0)$

Solution

$$
\begin{array}{lll}
\textbf{a.}\ g(x) = x^2 - 3 & \textbf{b.}\ g(x) = x^2 - 3 & \textbf{c.}\ g(x) = x^2 - 3 \\
\quad g(2) = 2^2 - 3 & \quad g(-2) = (-2)^2 - 3 & \quad g(0) = 0^2 - 3 \\
\qquad\quad = 4 - 3 & \qquad\quad = 4 - 3 & \qquad\quad = 0 - 3 \\
\qquad\quad = 1 & \qquad\quad = 1 & \qquad\quad = -3
\end{array}
$$

Ordered Pairs:	$g(2) = 1$ gives $(2, 1)$	$g(-2) = 1$ gives $(-2, 1)$	$g(0) = -3$ gives $(0, -3)$

□

PRACTICE
7   Given $h(x) = x^2 + 5$, find the following. Then write the corresponding ordered pairs generated.

a. $h(2)$ **b.** $h(-5)$ **c.** $h(0)$

We now practice finding the domain and the range of a function. The domain of our functions will be the set of all possible real numbers that x can be replaced by. The range is the set of corresponding y-values.

EXAMPLE 8 Find the domain of each function.

a. $g(x) = \dfrac{1}{x}$ **b.** $f(x) = 2x + 1$

Solution

a. Recall that we cannot divide by 0 so that the domain of $g(x)$ is the set of all real numbers except 0.

b. In this function, x can be any real number. The domain of $f(x)$ is the set of all real numbers. □

PRACTICE
8 Find the domain of each function.

a. $h(x) = 6x + 3$ **b.** $f(x) = \dfrac{1}{x^2}$

Concept Check ☑

Suppose that the value of f is -7 when the function is evaluated at 2. Write this situation in function notation.

EXAMPLE 9 Find the domain and the range of each function graphed. Use interval notation.

a.

b.

Solution

a.
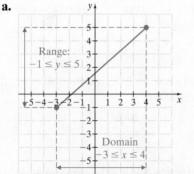

b.
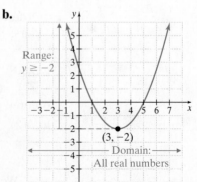

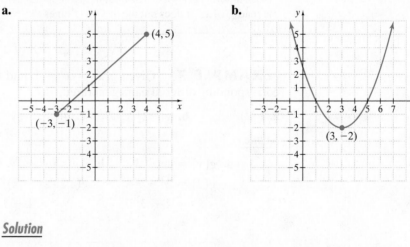

Answer to Concept Check:
$f(2) = -7$

□

PRACTICE
9 Find the domain and the range of each function graphed. Use interval notation.

a.

b.

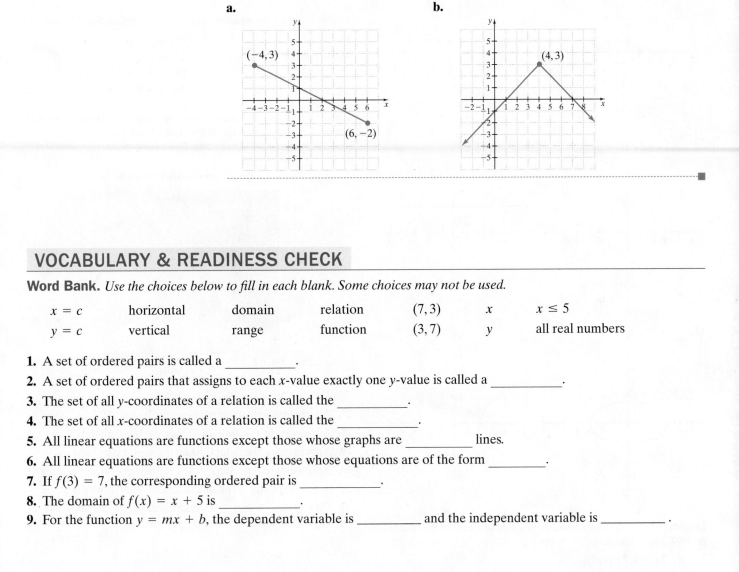

VOCABULARY & READINESS CHECK

Word Bank. *Use the choices below to fill in each blank. Some choices may not be used.*

$x = c$	horizontal	domain	relation	$(7, 3)$	x	$x \le 5$
$y = c$	vertical	range	function	$(3, 7)$	y	all real numbers

1. A set of ordered pairs is called a _____ .
2. A set of ordered pairs that assigns to each x-value exactly one y-value is called a _____ .
3. The set of all y-coordinates of a relation is called the _____ .
4. The set of all x-coordinates of a relation is called the _____ .
5. All linear equations are functions except those whose graphs are _____ lines.
6. All linear equations are functions except those whose equations are of the form _____ .
7. If $f(3) = 7$, the corresponding ordered pair is _____ .
8. The domain of $f(x) = x + 5$ is _____ .
9. For the function $y = mx + b$, the dependent variable is _____ and the independent variable is _____ .

3.6 | EXERCISE SET

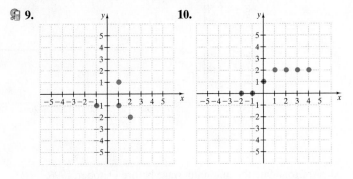

Find the domain and the range of each relation. See Example 1.

1. $\{(2, 4), (0, 0), (-7, 10), (10, -7)\}$

2. $\{(3, -6), (1, 4), (-2, -2)\}$

3. $\{(0, -2), (1, -2), (5, -2)\}$

4. $\{(5, 0), (5, -3), (5, 4), (5, 3)\}$

Determine whether each relation is also a function. See Example 2.

5. $\{(1, 1), (2, 2), (-3, -3), (0, 0)\}$

6. $\{(11, 6), (-1, -2), (0, 0), (3, -2)\}$

7. $\{(-1, 0), (-1, 6), (-1, 8)\}$

8. $\{(1, 2), (3, 2), (1, 4)\}$

MIXED PRACTICE

Read a Graph. *Determine whether each graph is the graph of a function. See Examples 3 and 4.*

9.

10.

11.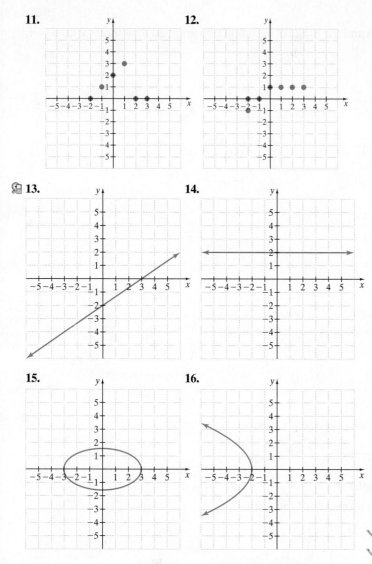

12.

13.

14.

15.

16.

Logic. *For each exercise, choose the value of x so that the relation is NOT also a function.*

17. $\{(2,3), (-1,7), (x,9)\}$

    a. -1 **b.** 1 **c.** 9 **d.** 7

18. $\{(-8,0), (x,1), (5,-3)\}$

    a. 0 **b.** -3 **c.** -5 **d.** 5

Decide whether the equation describes a function. See Example 5.

19. $y - x = 7$ **20.** $2x - 3y = 9$

21. $y = 6$ **22.** $x = 3$

23. $x = -2$ **24.** $y = -9$

25. $x = y^2$ **26.** $y = x^2 - 3$

The graph shows the sunset times for Seward, Alaska. Use this graph to answer Exercises 27 through 32. See Example 6.

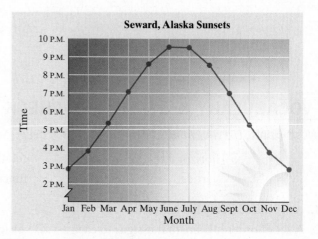

27. Approximate the time of sunset on June 1.

28. Approximate the time of sunset on November 1.

29. Approximate the date(s) when the sunset is at 3 P.M.

30. Approximate the date(s) when the sunset is at 9 P.M.

31. Is this graph the graph of a function? Why or why not?

32. Do you think a graph of sunset times for any location will always be a function? Why or why not?

This graph shows the U.S. hourly minimum wage for each year shown. Use this graph to answer Exercises 33 through 38. See Example 6.

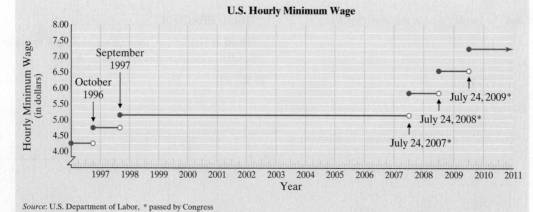

Source: U.S. Department of Labor, * passed by Congress

33. Approximate the minimum wage before October, 1996.

34. Approximate the minimum wage in 2006.

35. Approximate the year when the minimum wage will increase to over $7.00 per hour.

36. According to the graph, what hourly wage was in effect for the greatest number of years?

37. Is this graph the graph of a function? Why or why not?

38. Do you think that a similar graph of your hourly wage on January 1 of every year (whether you are working or not) will be the graph of a function? Why or why not?

Find $f(-2)$, $f(0)$, and $f(3)$ for each function. See Example 7.

39. $f(x) = 2x - 5$

40. $f(x) = 3 - 7x$

41. $f(x) = x^2 + 2$

42. $f(x) = x^2 - 4$

43. $f(x) = 3x$

44. $f(x) = -3x$

45. $f(x) = |x|$

46. $f(x) = |2 - x|$

Find $h(-1)$, $h(0)$, and $h(4)$ for each function. See Example 7.

47. $h(x) = -5x$

48. $h(x) = -3x$

49. $h(x) = 2x^2 + 3$

50. $h(x) = 3x^2$

For each given function value, write a corresponding ordered pair.

51. $f(3) = 6$,

52. $f(7) = -2$,

53. $g(0) = -\dfrac{1}{2}$

54. $g(0) = -\dfrac{7}{8}$

55. $h(-2) = 9$

56. $h(-10) = 1$

Find the domain of each function. See Example 8.

57. $f(x) = 3x - 7$

58. $g(x) = 5 - 2x$

59. $h(x) = \dfrac{1}{x + 5}$

60. $f(x) = \dfrac{1}{x - 6}$

61. $g(x) = |x + 1|$

62. $h(x) = |2x|$

Find the domain and the range of each relation graphed. See Example 9.

63.

64.

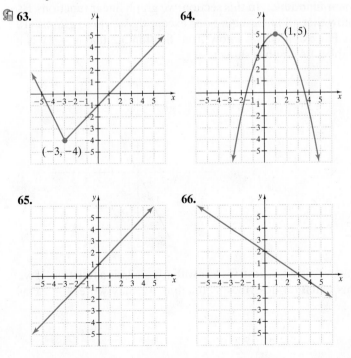

65.

66.

67.

68.

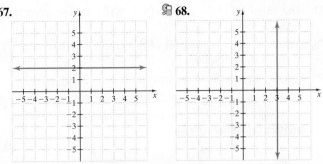

REVIEW AND PREVIEW

Find the coordinates of the point of intersection. See Section 3.1.

69.

70.

71.

72.

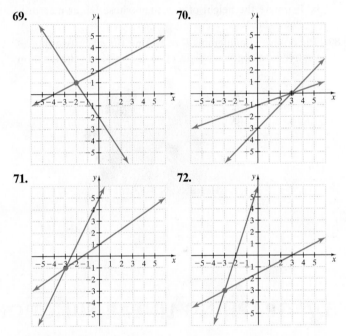

CONCEPT EXTENSIONS

Solve. See the Concept Check in this section.

73. If a function f is evaluated at -5, the value of the function is 12. Write this situation using function notation.

74. Suppose $(9, 20)$ is an ordered-pair solution for the function g. Write this situation using function notation.

The graph of the function, f, is below. Use this graph to answer Exercises 75 through 78.

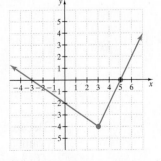

75. Write the coordinates of the lowest point of the graph.

76. Write the answer to Exercise 73 in function notation.

77. An x-intercept of this graph is $(5, 0)$. Write this using function notation.

78. Write the other x-intercept of this graph (see Exercise 77) using function notation.

79. Forensic scientists use the function

$$H(x) = 2.59x + 47.24$$

to estimate the height of a woman in centimeters given the length x of her femur bone.

    a. Estimate the height of a woman whose femur measures 46 centimeters.

    b. Estimate the height of a woman whose femur measures 39 centimeters.

80. The dosage in milligrams D of Ivermectin, a heartworm preventive for a dog who weighs x pounds, is given by the function

$$D(x) = \frac{136}{25}x$$

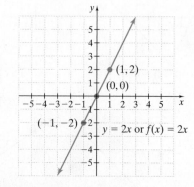

    a. Find the proper dosage for a dog that weighs 35 pounds.

    b. Find the proper dosage for a dog that weighs 70 pounds.

81. In your own words define **(a)** function; **(b)** domain; **(c)** range.

82. Explain the vertical line test and how it is used.

83. Since $y = x + 7$ is a function, rewrite the equation using function notation.

See the example below for Exercises 84 through 87.

Example

If $f(x) = x^2 + 2x + 1$, find $f(\pi)$.

Solution:

$$f(x) = x^2 + 2x + 1$$
$$f(\pi) = \pi^2 + 2\pi + 1$$

Given the following functions, find the indicated values.

84. $f(x) = 2x + 7$

    a. $f(2)$ **b.** $f(a)$

85. $g(x) = -3x + 12$

    a. $g(s)$ **b.** $g(r)$

86. $h(x) = x^2 + 7$

    a. $h(3)$ **b.** $h(a)$

87. $f(x) = x^2 - 12$

    a. $f(12)$ **b.** $f(a)$

3.7 | GRAPHING LINEAR FUNCTIONS

OBJECTIVES

1 Graph linear functions.

2 Decide whether a situation describes a linear function.

OBJECTIVE 1 ▶ Graphing linear functions. In this section, we graph linear functions. By the vertical line test, we know that all linear equations except those whose graphs are vertical lines are functions. For example, we know from Section 3.2 that $y = 2x$ is a linear equation in two variables. Its graph is shown.

x	$y = 2x$
1	2
0	0
-1	-2

Because this graph passes the vertical line test, we know that $y = 2x$ is a function. If we want to emphasize that this equation describes a function, we may write $y = 2x$ as $f(x) = 2x$.

EXAMPLE 1 Graph $g(x) = 2x + 1$. Compare this graph with the graph of $f(x) = 2x$.

Solution To graph $g(x) = 2x + 1$, find three ordered pair solutions.

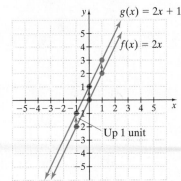

x	$f(x) = 2x$	$g(x) = 2x + 1$
0	0	1
-1	-2	-1
1	2	3

┌─ add 1 ─┐ (over the last two columns)

Notice that y-values for the graph of $g(x) = 2x + 1$ are obtained by adding 1 to each y-value of each corresponding point of the graph of $f(x) = 2x$. The graph of $g(x) = 2x + 1$ is the same as the graph of $f(x) = 2x$ shifted upward 1 unit. □

PRACTICE
1 Graph $g(x) = 4x - 3$ and $f(x) = 4x$ on the same axes.

▶ **Helpful Hint**

To graph a linear function, $f(x) = mx + b$, you may always replace the function notation with y and graph $y = mx + b$.

In general, a **linear function** is a function that can be written in the form $f(x) = mx + b$. For example, $g(x) = 2x + 1$ is in this form, with $m = 2$ and $b = 1$.

EXAMPLE 2 Graph the linear functions $f(x) = -3x$ and $g(x) = -3x - 6$ on the same set of axes.

Solution To graph $f(x)$ and $g(x)$, find ordered pair solutions.

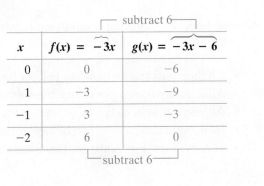
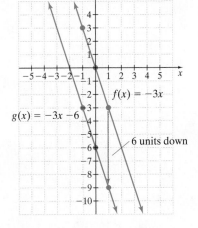

x	$f(x) = -3x$	$g(x) = -3x - 6$
0	0	-6
1	-3	-9
-1	3	-3
-2	6	0

┌─ subtract 6 ─┐ (top)
└─ subtract 6 ─┘ (bottom)

Each y-value for the graph of $g(x) = -3x - 6$ is obtained by subtracting 6 from the y-value of the corresponding point of the graph of $f(x) = -3x$. The graph of $g(x) = -3x - 6$ is the same as the graph of $f(x) = -3x$ shifted down 6 units. □

PRACTICE
2 Graph the linear functions $f(x) = -2x$ and $g(x) = -2x + 5$ on the same set of axes.

Notice that the y-intercept of the graph of $g(x) = -3x - 6$ in the preceding figure is $(0, -6)$. In general, if *a linear function is written in the form $f(x) = mx + b$ or $y = mx + b$, the y-intercept is $(0, b)$.* This is because if x is 0, then $f(x) = mx + b$ becomes $f(0) = m \cdot 0 + b = b$, and we have the ordered pair solution $(0, b)$.

Let's now see how changes in the slope of a linear function affect its graph.

EXAMPLE 3 Graph the linear functions $f(x) = 3x$ and $g(x) = 4x$ on the same set of axes.

Solution As usual, let's find three ordered-pair solutions for each graph.

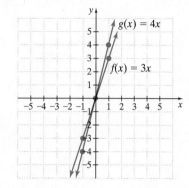

multiply by 4		
multiply by 3		

x	$f(x) = 3x$	$g(x) = 4x$
0	0	0
−1	−3	−4
1	3	4

Notice that the graph of $g(x)$ is steeper than the graph of $f(x)$. This is because the slope of $g(x)$ is a greater positive number. □

PRACTICE
3 Graph the linear functions $f(x) = -3x$ and $g(x) = -4x$ on the same set of axes.

In general, we have the following about the slope of a line:

- For a line with positive slope m, as m increases, the line becomes steeper.
- For a line with negative slope, m, as $|m|$ increases, the line becomes steeper.

Also, we have the following about linear functions:

- All lines pass the vertical line test for functions except vertical lines.
- All lines are the graphs of functions except vertical lines.
- All linear functions can be written in the form: $f(x) = mx + b$.
- Horizontal lines, $y = c$, can be written as $f(x) = c$ and are functions.
- Vertical lines, $x = c$, are not functions.

Finding x- and y-Intercepts
To find an x-intercept, let $y = 0$ or $f(x) = 0$ and solve for x.
To find a y-intercept, let $x = 0$ and solve for y.

▶ **Helpful Hint**
Any linear equation that describes a function can be written using function notation. To do so,

1. solve the equation for y and then
2. replace y with $f(x)$, as we did above.

OBJECTIVE 2 ▶ Deciding whether a situation is a linear function. Now that we have studied linear functions, let's decide whether a situation describes a linear function.

EXAMPLE 4 A manufacturing company needs to produce stainless steel rectangles with widths of two units and varying lengths. To find the area of rectangles with a width of two units and a varying length, we multiply the length by 2.

a. Use this information to complete the table.

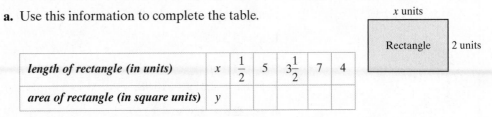

length of rectangle (in units)	x	$\frac{1}{2}$	5	$3\frac{1}{2}$	7	4
area of rectangle (in square units)	y					

b. Graph the data from part a).

c. Use parts a) or b) to decide whether the situation describes a linear function.

d. If the answer to part c) is yes, write a linear function, $f(x)$, that describes the situation.

Solution

a. To complete the table, let's multiply each given length by 2.

length of rectangle (in units)	$\frac{1}{2}$	5	$3\frac{1}{2}$	7	4
area of rectangle (in square units)	1	10	7	14	8

b. Since the length of a rectangle is a positive number, let's concentrate on quadrant I only.

c. From the table or graph, notice that as x increases by 1, for example, y increases steadily by 2. Thus, this situation describes a linear function.

d. From part a), b), or c), we have $y = 2x$. To write as a function, replace y with $f(x)$, and we have the linear function $f(x) = 2x$.

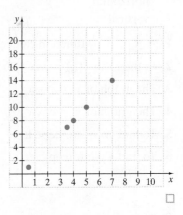

PRACTICE
4 To find the perimeter of a regular pentagon, we multiply by 5.

a. Use this information to complete the table.

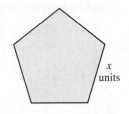

side length (in units)	x	2	$\frac{1}{2}$	5	1	7
perimeter of pentagon (in units)	y					

b. Graph the data from part a).

c. Use parts a) or b) to decide whether the situation describes a linear function.

d. If the answer to part c) is yes, write a linear function, $f(x)$, that describes the situation.

Graphing Calculator Explorations

You may have noticed by now that to use the $\boxed{Y =}$ key on a graphing calculator to graph an equation, the equation must be solved for y.

Graph each function by first solving the function for y.

1. $x = 3.5y$

2. $-2.7y = x$

3. $5.78x + 2.31y = 10.98$

4. $-7.22x + 3.89y = 12.57$

5. $y - |x| = 3.78$

6. $3y - 5x^2 = 6x - 4$

7. $y - 5.6x^2 = 7.7x + 1.5$

8. $y + 2.6|x| = -3.2$

VOCABULARY & READINESS CHECK

Word Bank. *Use the choices below to fill in each blank. Some choices may be used more than once and some not at all.*

horizontal	y	$(c, 0)$	$(b, 0)$	$(m, 0)$	linear
vertical	x	$(0, c)$	$(0, b)$	$(0, m)$	$f(x)$

1. A _____ function can be written in the form $f(x) = mx + b$.

2. In the form $f(x) = mx + b$, the y-intercept is _____.

3. The graph of $x = c$ is a _____ line with x-intercept _____.

4. The graph of $y = c$ is a _____ line with y-intercept _____.

5. To find an x-intercept, let ____ = 0 or _____ = 0 and solve for ____.

6. To find a y-intercept, let _____ = 0 and solve for ____.

3.7 | EXERCISE SET

MyMathLab *Powered by CourseCompass™ and MathXL®*   Math XL PRACTICE   WATCH   DOWNLOAD   READ   REVIEW

Graph each linear function. See Examples 1 through 3.

1. $f(x) = -2x$

2. $f(x) = 2x$

3. $f(x) = -2x + 3$

4. $f(x) = 2x + 6$

5. $f(x) = \dfrac{1}{2}x$

6. $f(x) = \dfrac{1}{3}x$

7. $f(x) = \dfrac{1}{2}x - 4$

8. $f(x) = \dfrac{1}{3}x - 2$

The graph of $f(x) = 5x$ follows. Use this graph to match each linear function with its graph in exercises 9–12. See Examples 1 through 3.

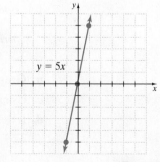

$y = 5x$

(Exercises 9–12 next page)

9. $f(x) = 5x - 3$

10. $f(x) = 5x - 2$

11. $f(x) = 5x + 1$

12. $f(x) = 5x + 3$

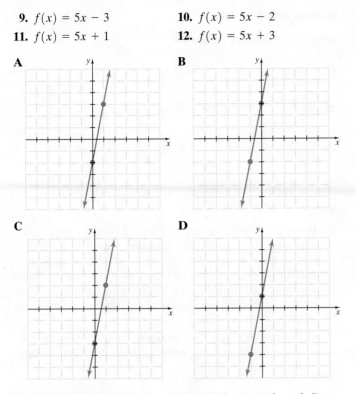

A   B

C   D

Use the graph of $f(x) = 5x$ on page 242 to match each linear function with its graph. See Examples 1 through 3.

13. $f(x) = 2x$

14. $f(x) = 6x$

15. $f(x) = -5x$

16. $f(x) = -2x$

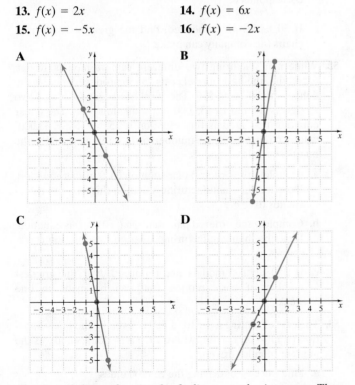

A   B

C   D

Graph each linear function by finding x- and y-intercepts. Then write each equation using function notation. See Examples 1 through 3.

17. $x - y = 3$

18. $x - y = -4$

19. $x = 5y$

20. $2x = y$

21. $-x + 2y = 6$

22. $x - 2y = -8$

23. $2x - 4y = 8$

24. $2x + 3y = 6$

25. In your own words, explain how to find x- and y-intercepts.

26. Explain why it is a good idea to use three points to graph a linear equation.

MIXED PRACTICE

Graph each linear function. See Examples 1 through 3.

27. $f(x) = \dfrac{3}{2}$

28. $g(x) = \dfrac{7}{2}$

29. $f(x) = \dfrac{3}{4}x + 2$

30. $f(x) = \dfrac{4}{3}x + 2$

31. $f(x) = x$

32. $f(x) = -x$

33. $f(x) = \dfrac{1}{2}x$

34. $f(x) = -2x$

35. $f(x) = 4x - \dfrac{1}{3}$

36. $f(x) = -3x + \dfrac{3}{4}$

37. $f(x) = 0$

38. $f(x) = 3$

Multiple Steps. *Solve. See Example 4.*

39. To find the perimeter, y, of a regular hexigon given its side length x, we multiply by 6.

  a. Use this information to complete the table.

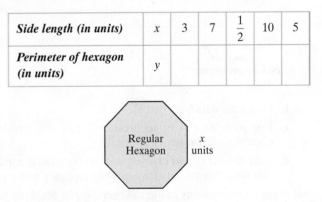

Side length (in units)	x	3	7	$\dfrac{1}{2}$	10	5
Perimeter of hexagon (in units)	y					

Regular Hexagon x units

  b. Graph the data from part a).

  c. Use parts a) and b) to decide whether the situation describes a linear function.

40. To find the perimeter of a square, y, given its side length x, we multiply by 4.

  a. Use this information to complete the table.

x units

side length (in units)	x	1	$\dfrac{1}{4}$	3	4	$5\dfrac{1}{2}$
perimeter of square (in units)	y					

  b. Graph the data from part a).

  c. Use parts a) and b) to decide whether this situation describes a linear function.

41. To find the area, y, of a square given its side length x, we square x.

a. Use this information to complete the table.

side length (in units)	x	1	3	4	7	$\frac{1}{2}$
area of square (in square units)	y					

b. Graph the data from part a).

c. Use parts a) and b) to decide whether this situation describes a linear function.

42. To find the volume of a cube, y, given its side length x, we cube x.

a. Use this information to complete the table.

side length (in units)	x	3	1	$\frac{1}{2}$	2	5
volume of cube (in cubic units)	y					

b. Graph the data from part a).

c. Use parts a) and b) to decide whether this situation describes a linear function.

43. A private charter bus company charges $2.20 per person plus $0.40 per mile.

a. Use this information to complete the table below for one person.

miles	x	0	1	10	75	60
charge per person	y					

b. Graph the data from part a).

c. Use parts a) and b) to decide whether this situation describes a linear function.

d. If the answer to part c) is yes, write an equation in x and y that describes the relationship. Then replace y with $f(x)$.

44. A car rental company charges $42 per day plus $0.30 per mile for a certain type of car.

a. Use this information to complete the table below for a one-day rental.

miles	x	0	1	10	100	101
charge for the day	y					

b. Graph the data from part a).

c. Use parts a) and b) to decide whether this situation describes a linear function.

d. If the answer to part c) is yes, write an equation in x and y that describes the relationship. If needed, solve the equation for y then replace y with $f(x)$.

REVIEW AND PREVIEW

Simplify. See Sections 1.3 and 1.6.

45. $\dfrac{-6 - 3}{2 - 8}$

46. $\dfrac{4 - 5}{-1 - 0}$

47. $\dfrac{-8 - (-2)}{-3 - (-2)}$

48. $\dfrac{12 - 3}{10 - 9}$

49. $\dfrac{0 - 6}{5 - 0}$

50. $\dfrac{2 - 2}{3 - 5}$

CONCEPT EXTENSIONS

Solve.

51. Broyhill Furniture found that it takes 2 hours to manufacture each table for one of its special dining room sets. Each chair takes 3 hours to manufacture. A total of 1500 hours is available to produce tables and chairs of this style. The linear equation that models this situation is $2x + 3y = 1500$, where x represents the number of tables produced and y the number of chairs produced.

a. Complete the ordered pair solution $(0, \ )$ of this equation. Describe the manufacturing situation this solution corresponds to.

b. Complete the ordered pair solution $(\ , 0)$ for this equation. Describe the manufacturing situation this solution corresponds to.

c. If 50 tables are produced, find the greatest number of chairs the company can make.

52. While manufacturing two different camera models, Kodak found that the basic model costs $55 to produce, whereas the deluxe model costs $75. The weekly budget for these two models is limited to $33,000 in production costs. The linear equation that models this situation is $55x + 75y = 33,000$, where x represents the number of basic models and y the number of deluxe models.

a. Complete the ordered pair solution $(0, \ )$ of this equation. Describe the manufacturing situation this solution corresponds to.

b. Complete the ordered pair solution $(\ , 0)$ of this equation. Describe the manufacturing situation this solution corresponds to.

c. If 350 deluxe models are produced, find the greatest number of basic models that can be made in one week.

53. The cost of renting a car for a day is given by the linear function $C(x) = 0.2x + 24$, where $C(x)$ is in dollars and x is the number of miles driven.

a. Find the cost of driving the car 200 miles.

b. Graph $C(x) = 0.2x + 24$.

c. How can you tell from the graph of $C(x)$ that as the number of miles driven increases, the total cost increases also?

54. The cost of renting a piece of machinery is given by the linear function $C(x) = 4x + 10$, where $C(x)$ is in dollars and x is given in hours.

   a. Find the cost of renting the piece of machinery for 8 hours.

   b. Graph $C(x) = 4x + 10$.

   c. How can you tell from the graph of $C(x)$ that as the number of hours increases, the total cost increases also?

55. The yearly cost of tuition (in-state) and required fees for attending a public two-year college full time can be estimated by the linear function $f(x) = 107.3x + 1245.62$, where x is the number of years after 2000 and $f(x)$ is the total cost. (*Source:* U.S. National Center for Education Statistics)

   a. Use this function to approximate the yearly cost of attending a two-year college in the year 2015. [*Hint:* Find $f(15)$.]

   b. Use the given function to predict in what year the yearly cost of tuition and required fees will exceed $2500. [*Hint:* Let $f(x) = 2500$, solve for x, then round your solution up to the next whole year.

   c. Use this function to approximate the yearly cost of attending a two-year college in the present year. If you attend a two-year college, is this amount greater than or less than the amount that is currently charged by the college you attend?

56. The yearly cost of tuition (in-state) and required fees for attending a public four-year college full time can be estimated by the linear function $f(x) = 291.5x + 2944.05$, where x is the number of years after 2000 and $f(x)$ is the total cost in dollars. (*Source:* U.S. National Center for Education Statistics)

   a. Use this function to approximate the yearly cost of attending a four-year college in the year 2015. [*Hint:* Find $f(15)$.]

   b. Use the given function to predict in what year the yearly cost of tuition and required fees will exceed $6000. [*Hint:* Let $f(x) = 6000$, solve for x, then round your solution up to the next whole year.]

   c. Use this function to approximate the yearly cost of attending a four-year college in the present year. If you attend a four-year college, is this amount greater than or less than the amount that is currently charged by the college you attend?

Use a graphing calculator to verify the results of each exercise.

57. Exercise 9   **58.** Exercise 10

59. Exercise 21   **60.** Exercise 22

61. The graph of $f(x)$ or $y = -4x$ is given below. Without actually graphing, describe the shape and location of

   a. $y = -4x + 2$ **b.** $y = -4x - 5$

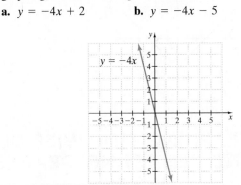

It is true that for any function $f(x)$, the graph of $f(x) + K$ is the same as the graph of $f(x)$ shifted K units up if K is positive and $|K|$ units down if K is negative. (We study this further in Section 3.8.)

The graph of $y = |x|$ is

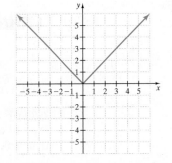

Without actually graphing, match each equation with its graph.

   a. $y = |x| - 1$

   b. $y = |x| + 1$

   c. $y = |x| - 3$

   d. $y = |x| + 3$

62.

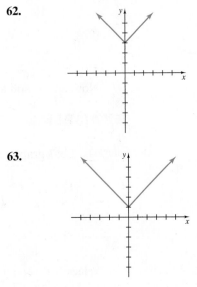

63.

(Exercises 64, 65 next page)

64.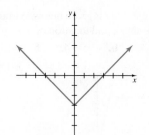

65.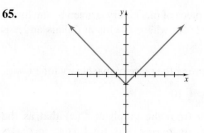

3.8 GRAPHING PIECEWISE-DEFINED FUNCTIONS AND SHIFTING AND REFLECTING GRAPHS OF FUNCTIONS

OBJECTIVES

1 Graph piecewise-defined functions.

2 Vertical and horizontal shifts.

3 Reflect graphs.

OBJECTIVE 1 ▶ Graphing piecewise-defined functions. Throughout Chapter 3, we have graphed functions. There are many special functions. In this objective, we study functions defined by two or more expressions. The expression used to complete the function varies with, and depends upon the value of x. Before we actually graph these piecewise-defined functions, let's practice finding function values.

EXAMPLE 1 Evaluate $f(2)$, $f(-6)$, and $f(0)$ for the function

$$f(x) = \begin{cases} 2x + 3 & \text{if } x \le 0 \\ -x - 1 & \text{if } x > 0 \end{cases}$$

Then write your results in ordered-pair form.

Solution Take a moment and study this function. It is a single function defined by two expressions depending on the value of x. From above, if $x \le 0$, use $f(x) = 2x + 3$. If $x > 0$, use $f(x) = -x - 1$. Thus

$f(2) = -(2) - 1$	$f(-6) = 2(-6) + 3$	$f(0) = 2(0) + 3$
$= -3$ since $2 > 0$	$= -9$ since $-6 \le 0$	$= 3$ since $0 \le 0$
$f(2) = -3$	$f(-6) = -9$	$f(0) = 3$
Ordered pairs: $(2, -3)$	$(-6, -9)$	$(0, 3)$

□

PRACTICE
1 Evaluate $f(4)$, $f(-2)$, and $f(0)$ for the function

$$f(x) = \begin{cases} -4x - 2 & \text{if } x \le 0 \\ x + 1 & \text{if } x > 0. \end{cases}$$

Now, let's graph a piecewise-defined function.

EXAMPLE 2 Graph $f(x) = \begin{cases} 2x + 3 & \text{if } x \le 0 \\ -x - 1 & \text{if } x > 0 \end{cases}$

Solution Let's graph each piece.

If $x \le 0$,
$f(x) = 2x + 3$

Values ≤ 0 $\begin{cases} \\ \\ \\ \end{cases}$

x	$f(x) = 2x + 3$
0	3 Closed circle
-1	1
-2	-1

If $x > 0$,
$f(x) = -x - 1$

Values > 0 $\begin{cases} \\ \\ \\ \end{cases}$

x	$f(x) = -x - 1$
1	-2
2	-3
3	-4

The graph of the first part of $f(x)$ listed will look like a ray with a closed-circle endpoint at $(0, 3)$. The graph of the second part of $f(x)$ listed will look like a ray with an open-circle endpoint. To find the exact location of the open-circle endpoint, use $f(x) = -x - 1$ and find $f(0)$. Since $f(0) = -0 - 1 = -1$, we graph the second table and place an open circle at $(0, -1)$.

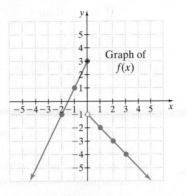

Graph of
$f(x)$

Notice that this graph is the graph of a function because it passes the vertical line test. The domain of this function is all real numbers and the range is $y \leq 3$. □

PRACTICE

2   Graph

$$f(x) = \begin{cases} -4x - 2 & \text{if } x \leq 0 \\ x + 1 & \text{if } x > 0 \end{cases}$$

OBJECTIVE 2 ▶ Vertical and horizontal shifting.

Review of Common Graphs

We now take common graphs and learn how more complicated graphs are actually formed by shifting and reflecting these common graphs. These shifts and reflections are called transformations, and it is possible to combine transformations. A knowledge of these transformations will help you simplify future graphs.

Let's begin with a review of the graphs of four common functions. Many of these functions we graphed in earlier sections.

First, **let's graph the linear function $f(x) = x$, or $y = x$.** Ordered-pair solutions of this graph consist of ordered pairs whose x- and y-values are the same.

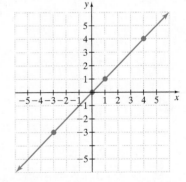

x	y or $f(x) = x$
-3	-3
0	0
1	1
4	4

Next, **let's graph the nonlinear function $f(x) = x^2$ or $y = x^2$.**

This equation is not linear because the x^2 term does not allow us to write it in the form $Ax + By = C$. Its graph is not a line. We begin by finding ordered pair solutions. Because this graph is solved for $f(x)$, or y, we choose x-values and find corresponding $f(x)$, or y-values.

If $x = -3$, then $y = (-3)^2$, or 9.

If $x = -2$, then $y = (-2)^2$, or 4.

If $x = -1$, then $y = (-1)^2$, or 1.

If $x = 0$, then $y = 0^2$, or 0.

If $x = 1$, then $y = 1^2$, or 1.

If $x = 2$, then $y = 2^2$, or 4.

If $x = 3$, then $y = 3^2$, or 9.

x	$f(x)$ or y
-3	9
-2	4
-1	1
0	0
1	1
2	4
3	9

Study the table for a moment and look for patterns. Notice that the ordered pair solution $(0, 0)$ contains the smallest y-value because any other x-value squared will give a positive result. This means that the point $(0, 0)$ will be the lowest point on the graph. Also notice that all other y-values correspond to two different x-values. For example, $3^2 = 9$ and also $(-3)^2 = 9$. This means that the graph will be a mirror image of itself across the y-axis. Connect the plotted points with a smooth curve to sketch its graph.

This curve is given a special name, a **parabola**. We will study more about parabolas in later chapters.

Next, **let's graph another nonlinear function $f(x) = |x|$ or $y = |x|$.**

This is not a linear equation since it cannot be written in the form $Ax + By = C$. Its graph is not a line. Because we do not know the shape of this graph, we find many ordered pair solutions. We will choose x-values and substitute to find corresponding y-values.

If $x = -3$, then $y = |-3|$, or 3.

If $x = -2$, then $y = |-2|$, or 2.

If $x = -1$, then $y = |-1|$, or 1.

If $x = 0$, then $y = |0|$, or 0.

If $x = 1$, then $y = |1|$, or 1.

If $x = 2$, then $y = |2|$, or 2.

If $x = 3$, then $y = |3|$, or 3.

x	y
-3	3
-2	2
-1	1
0	0
1	1
2	2
3	3

Again, study the table of values for a moment and notice any patterns.

From the plotted ordered pairs, we see that the graph of this absolute value equation is V-shaped.

Finally, a fourth common function, $f(x) = \sqrt{x}$ or $y = \sqrt{x}$. For this graph, you need to recall basic facts about square roots and use your calculator to approximate some square roots to help locate points. Recall also that the square root of a negative number is not a real number, so be careful when finding your domain.

Now **let's graph the square root function $f(x) = \sqrt{x}$, or $y = \sqrt{x}$.**

To graph, we identify the domain, evaluate the function for several values of x, plot the resulting points, and connect the points with a smooth curve. Since $\sqrt{x}$ represents the nonnegative square root of x, the domain of this function is the set of all nonnegative numbers, $\{x \mid x \geq 0\}$, or $[0, \infty)$. We have approximated $\sqrt{3}$ below to help us locate the point corresponding to $(3, \sqrt{3})$.

If $x = 0$, then $y = \sqrt{0}$, or 0.

If $x = 1$, then $y = \sqrt{1}$, or 1.

If $x = 3$, then $y = \sqrt{3}$, or 1.7.

If $x = 4$, then $y = \sqrt{4}$, or 2.

If $x = 9$, then $y = \sqrt{9}$, or 3.

x	$f(x) = \sqrt{x}$
0	0
1	1
3	$\sqrt{3} \approx 1.7$
4	2
9	3

Notice that the graph of this function passes the vertical line test, as expected.

Below is a summary of our four common graphs. Take a moment and study these graphs. Your success in the rest of this section depends on your knowledge of these graphs.

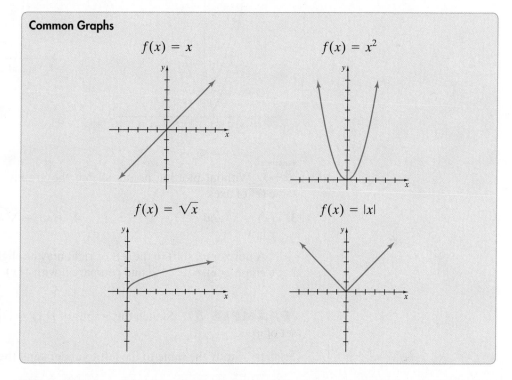

Common Graphs

$f(x) = x$

$f(x) = x^2$

$f(x) = \sqrt{x}$

$f(x) = |x|$

Your knowledge of the slope-intercept form, $f(x) = mx + b$, will help you understand simple shifting of transformations such as vertical shifts. For example, what is the difference between the graphs of $f(x) = x$ and $g(x) = x + 3$?

$f(x) = x$
slope, $m = 1$
y-intercept is $(0, 0)$

$g(x) = x + 3$
slope, $m = 1$
y-intercept is $(0, 3)$

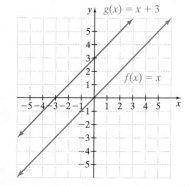

Notice that the graph of $g(x) = x + 3$ is the same as the graph of $f(x) = x$, but moved upward 3 units. This is an example of a **vertical shift** and is true for graphs in general.

Vertical Shifts (Upward and Downward)
Let k be a Positive Number

Graph of	Same As	Moved
$g(x) = f(x) + k$	$f(x)$	k units upward
$g(x) = f(x) - k$	$f(x)$	k units downward

EXAMPLES   Without plotting points, sketch the graph of each pair of functions on the same set of axes.

3. $f(x) = x^2$ and $g(x) = x^2 + 2$ **4.** $f(x) = \sqrt{x}$ and $g(x) = \sqrt{x} - 3$

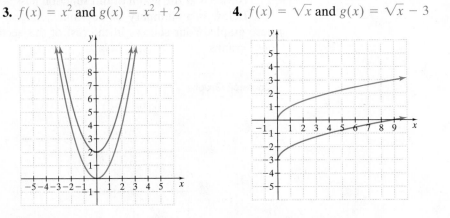

PRACTICES
3-4 Without plotting points, sketch the graphs of each pair of functions on the same set of axes.

3. $f(x) = x^2$ and $g(x) = x^2 - 3$ **4.** $f(x) = \sqrt{x}$ and $g(x) = \sqrt{x} + 1$

A horizontal shift to the left or right may be slightly more difficult to understand. Let's graph $g(x) = |x - 2|$ and compare it with $f(x) = |x|$.

EXAMPLE 5   Sketch the graphs of $f(x) = |x|$ and $g(x) = |x - 2|$ on the same set of axes.

Solution   Study the table to the left to understand the placement of both graphs.

x	$f(x) = |x|$	$g(x) = |x - 2|$
-3	3	5
-2	2	4
-1	1	3
0	0	2
1	1	1
2	2	0
3	3	1

PRACTICE
5   Sketch the graphs of $f(x) = |x|$ and $g(x) = |x - 3|$ on the same set of axes.

The graph of $g(x) = |x - 2|$ is the same as the graph of $f(x) = |x|$, but moved 2 units to the right. This is an example of a **horizontal shift** and is true for graphs in general.

Horizontal Shift (To the Left or Right)
Let h be a Positive Number

Graph of	Same as	Moved
$g(x) = f(x - h)$	$f(x)$	h units to the right
$g(x) = f(x + h)$	$f(x)$	h units to the left

> **▶ Helpful Hint**
>
> Notice that $f(x - h)$ corresponds to a shift to the right and $f(x + h)$ corresponds to a shift to the left.

Vertical and horizontal shifts can be combined.

EXAMPLE 6   Sketch the graphs of $f(x) = x^2$ and $g(x) = (x - 2)^2 + 1$ on the same set of axes.

Solution   The graph of $g(x)$ is the same as the graph of $f(x)$ shifted 2 units to the right and 1 unit up.

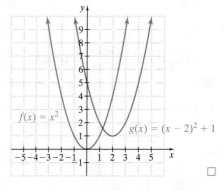

PRACTICE
6   Sketch the graphs of $f(x) = |x|$ and $g(x) = |x - 2| + 3$ on the same set of axes.

OBJECTIVE 3 ▶ Reflecting graphs.   Another type of transformation is called a **reflection.** In this section, we will study reflections (mirror images) about the x-axis only. For example, take a moment and study these two graphs. The graph of $g(x) = -x^2$ can be verified, as usual, by plotting points.

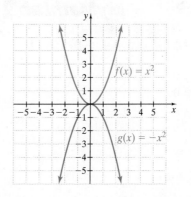

Reflection about the x-axis
The graph of $g(x) = -f(x)$ is the graph of $f(x)$ reflected about the x-axis.

EXAMPLE 7 Sketch the graph of $h(x) = -|x - 3| + 2$.

Solution The graph of $h(x) = -|x - 3| + 2$ is the same as the graph of $f(x) = |x|$ reflected about the x-axis, then moved three units to the right and two units upward.

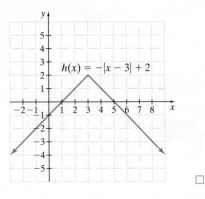

PRACTICE
7 Sketch the graph of $h(x) = -(x + 2)^2 - 1$.

There are other transformations, such as stretching that won't be covered in this section. For a review of this transformation, see the Appendix.

VOCABULARY & READINESS CHECK

Matching. *Match each equation with its graph.*

1. $y = \sqrt{x}$ **2.** $y = x^2$ **3.** $y = x$ **4.** $y = |x|$

A   **B**   **C**   **D**

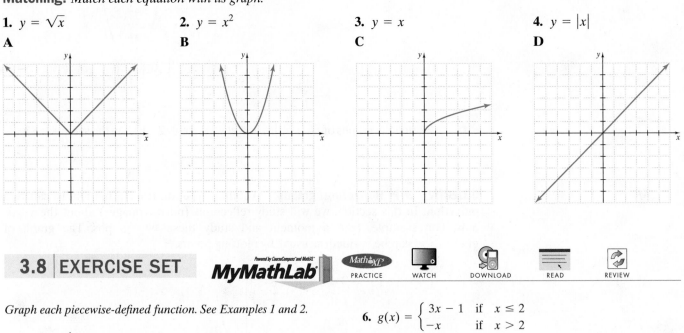

3.8 | EXERCISE SET

Graph each piecewise-defined function. See Examples 1 and 2.

1. $f(x) = \begin{cases} 2x & \text{if } x < 0 \\ x + 1 & \text{if } x \ge 0 \end{cases}$

2. $f(x) = \begin{cases} 3x & \text{if } x < 0 \\ x + 2 & \text{if } x \ge 0 \end{cases}$

3. $f(x) = \begin{cases} 4x + 5 & \text{if } x \le 0 \\ \dfrac{1}{4}x + 2 & \text{if } x > 0 \end{cases}$

4. $f(x) = \begin{cases} 5x + 4 & \text{if } x \le 0 \\ \dfrac{1}{3}x - 1 & \text{if } x > 0 \end{cases}$

5. $g(x) = \begin{cases} -x & \text{if } x \le 1 \\ 2x + 1 & \text{if } x > 1 \end{cases}$

6. $g(x) = \begin{cases} 3x - 1 & \text{if } x \le 2 \\ -x & \text{if } x > 2 \end{cases}$

7. $f(x) = \begin{cases} 5 & \text{if } x < -2 \\ 3 & \text{if } x \ge -2 \end{cases}$

8. $f(x) = \begin{cases} 4 & \text{if } x < -3 \\ -2 & \text{if } x \ge -3 \end{cases}$

MIXED PRACTICE

(Sections 3.6, 3.8) Graph each piecewise-defined function. Use the graph to determine the domain and range of the function. See Examples 1 and 2.

9. $f(x) = \begin{cases} -2x & \text{if } x \le 0 \\ 2x + 1 & \text{if } x > 0 \end{cases}$

10. $g(x) = \begin{cases} -3x & \text{if } x \le 0 \\ 3x + 2 & \text{if } x > 0 \end{cases}$

11. $h(x) = \begin{cases} 5x - 5 & \text{if } x < 2 \\ -x + 3 & \text{if } x \ge 2 \end{cases}$

12. $f(x) = \begin{cases} 4x - 4 & \text{if } x < 2 \\ -x + 1 & \text{if } x \ge 2 \end{cases}$

13. $f(x) = \begin{cases} x + 3 & \text{if } x < -1 \\ -2x + 4 & \text{if } x \ge -1 \end{cases}$

14. $h(x) = \begin{cases} x + 2 & \text{if } x < 1 \\ 2x + 1 & \text{if } x \ge 1 \end{cases}$

15. $g(x) = \begin{cases} -2 & \text{if } x \le 0 \\ -4 & \text{if } x \ge 1 \end{cases}$

16. $f(x) = \begin{cases} -1 & \text{if } x \le 0 \\ -3 & \text{if } x \ge 2 \end{cases}$

MIXED PRACTICE

Sketch the graph of function. See Examples 3 through 6.

17. $f(x) = |x| + 3$

18. $f(x) = |x| - 2$

19. $f(x) = \sqrt{x} - 2$

20. $f(x) = \sqrt{x} + 3$

21. $f(x) = |x - 4|$

22. $f(x) = |x + 3|$

23. $f(x) = \sqrt{x + 2}$

24. $f(x) = \sqrt{x - 2}$

25. $y = (x - 4)^2$

26. $y = (x + 4)^2$

27. $f(x) = x^2 + 4$

28. $f(x) = x^2 - 4$

29. $f(x) = \sqrt{x - 2} + 3$

30. $f(x) = \sqrt{x - 1} + 3$

31. $f(x) = |x - 1| + 5$

32. $f(x) = |x - 3| + 2$

33. $f(x) = \sqrt{x + 1} + 1$

34. $f(x) = \sqrt{x + 3} + 2$

35. $f(x) = |x + 3| - 1$

36. $f(x) = |x + 1| - 4$

37. $g(x) = (x - 1)^2 - 1$

38. $h(x) = (x + 2)^2 + 2$

39. $f(x) = (x + 3)^2 - 2$

40. $f(x) = (x + 2)^2 + 4$

Sketch the graph of each function. See Examples 3 through 7.

41. $f(x) = -(x - 1)^2$

42. $g(x) = -(x + 2)^2$

43. $h(x) = -\sqrt{x} + 3$

44. $f(x) = -\sqrt{x + 3}$

45. $h(x) = -|x + 2| + 3$

46. $g(x) = -|x + 1| + 1$

47. $f(x) = (x - 3) + 2$

48. $f(x) = (x - 1) + 4$

REVIEW AND PREVIEW

Match each equation with its graph. See Section 3.3.

49. $y = -1$

50. $x = -1$

51. $x = 3$

52. $y = 3$

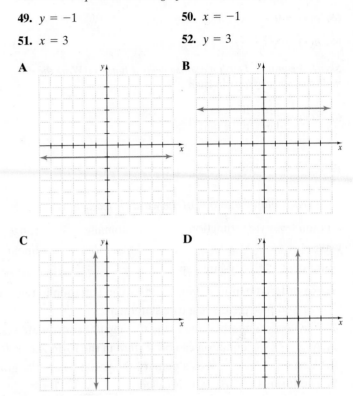

A   B

C   D

CONCEPT EXTENSIONS

53. Draw a graph whose domain is $x \le 5$ and whose range is $y \ge 2$.

54. In your own words, describe how to graph a piecewise-defined function.

55. Graph: $f(x) = \begin{cases} -\dfrac{1}{2}x & \text{if } x \le 0 \\ x + 1 & \text{if } 0 < x \le 2 \\ 2x - 1 & \text{if } x > 2 \end{cases}$

56. Graph: $f(x) = \begin{cases} -\dfrac{1}{3}x & \text{if } x \le 0 \\ x + 2 & \text{if } 0 < x \le 4 \\ 3x - 4 & \text{if } x > 4 \end{cases}$

Write the domain and range of the following exercises.

57. Exercise 29

58. Exercise 30

59. Exercise 45

60. Exercise 46

Without graphing, find the domain of each function.

61. $f(x) = 5\sqrt{x - 20} + 1$

62. $g(x) = -3\sqrt{x + 5}$

63. $h(x) = 5|x - 20| + 1$

64. $f(x) = -3|x + 5.7|$

65. $g(x) = 9 - \sqrt{x + 103}$

66. $h(x) = \sqrt{x - 17} - 3$

Sketch the graph of each piecewise-defined function. Write the domain and range of each function.

67. $f(x) = \begin{cases} |x| & \text{if} \quad x \leq 0 \\ x^2 & \text{if} \quad x > 0 \end{cases}$

68. $f(x) = \begin{cases} x^2 & \text{if} \quad x < 0 \\ \sqrt{x} & \text{if} \quad x \geq 0 \end{cases}$

69. $g(x) = \begin{cases} |x - 2| & \text{if} \quad x < 0 \\ -x^2 & \text{if} \quad x \geq 0 \end{cases}$

70. $g(x) = \begin{cases} -|x + 1| - 1 & \text{if} \quad x < -2 \\ \sqrt{x + 2} - 4 & \text{if} \quad x \geq -2 \end{cases}$

CHAPTER 3 VOCABULARY CHECK

Fill in each blank with one of the words listed below.

relation	function	domain	range	standard	slope-intercept
y-axis	x-axis	solution	linear	slope	point-slope
x-intercept	y-intercept	y	x	linear function	perpendicular

1. An ordered pair is a _____ of an equation in two variables if replacing the variables by the coordinates of the ordered pair results in a true statement.

2. The vertical number line in the rectangular coordinate system is called the _____.

3. A _____ equation can be written in the form $Ax + By = C$.

4. A(n) _____ is a point of the graph where the graph crosses the x-axis.

5. The form $Ax + By = C$ is called _____ form.

6. A(n) _____ is a point of the graph where the graph crosses the y-axis.

7. The equation $y = 7x - 5$ is written in _____ form.

8. The equation $y + 1 = 7(x - 2)$ is written in _____ form.

9. To find an x-intercept of a graph, let _____ = 0.

10. The horizontal number line in the rectangular coordinate system is called the _____.

11. To find a y-intercept of a graph, let _____ = 0.

12. The _____ of a line measures the steepness or tilt of a line.

13. A set of ordered pairs that assigns to each x-value exactly one y-value is called a _____.

14. The set of all x-coordinates of a relation is called the _____ of the relation.

15. The set of all y-coordinates of a relation is called the _____ of the relation.

16. A set of ordered pairs is called a _____.

17. Two lines are _____ if the product of their slopes is -1.

18. A _____ is a function that can be written in the form $f(x) = mx + b$.

CHAPTER 3 REVIEW

(3.1) Plot the following ordered pairs on a Cartesian coordinate system.

1. $(-7, 0)$

2. $\left(0, 4\frac{4}{5}\right)$

3. $(-2, -5)$

4. $(1, -3)$

5. $(0.7, 0.7)$

6. $(-6, 4)$

7. A local lumberyard uses quantity pricing. The table shows the price per board for different amounts of lumber purchased.

Price per Board (in dollars)	Number of Boards Purchased
8.00	1
7.50	10
6.50	25
5.00	50
2.00	100

a. Write each paired data as an ordered pair of the form (price per board, number of boards purchased).

b. Create a scatter diagram of the paired data. Be sure to label the axes appropriately.

8. The table shows the annual overnight stays in national parks (*Source*: National Park Service)

Year	Overnight Stays in National Parks (in millions)
2001	9.8
2002	15.1
2003	14.6
2004	14.0
2005	13.8
2006	13.6

  a. Write each paired data as an ordered pair of the form (year, number of overnight stays).

  b. Create a scatter diagram of the paired data. Be sure to label the axes properly.

  c. Decide whether there is a positive, negative, or no correlation relationship between the variables.

Determine whether each ordered pair is a solution of the given equation.

9. $7x - 8y = 56$; $(0, 56), (8, 0)$

10. $-2x + 5y = 10$; $(-5, 0), (1, 1)$

11. $x = 13$; $(13, 5), (13, 13)$

12. $y = 2$; $(7, 2), (2, 7)$

Complete the ordered pairs so that each is a solution of the given equation.

13. $-2 + y = 6x$; $(7, \quad)$ **14.** $y = 3x + 5$; $\left(\quad, -8\right)$

Complete the table of values for each given equation; then plot the ordered pairs. Use a single coordinate system for each exercise.

15. $9 = -3x + 4y$

x	y
	0
	3
9	

16. $y = 5$

x	y
7	
-7	
0	

17. $x = 2y$

x	y
	0
	5
	-5

18. The cost in dollars of producing x compact disk holders is given by $y = 5x + 2000$.

  a. Complete the following table.

x	y
1	
100	
1000	

  b. Find the number of compact disk holders that can be produced for $6430.

(3.2) Graph each linear equation.

19. $x - y = 1$ **20.** $x + y = 6$

21. $x - 3y = 12$ **22.** $5x - y = -8$

23. $x = 3y$ **24.** $y = -2x$

25. $2x - 3y = 6$ **26.** $4x - 3y = 12$

27. The projected U.S. long-distance revenue (in billions of dollars) from 1999 to 2004 is given by the equation, $y = 3x + 111$ where x is the number of years after 1999. Graph this equation and use it to estimate the amount of long-distance revenue in 2007. (*Source*: Giga Information Group)

(3.3) Identify the intercepts.

28.   **29.**

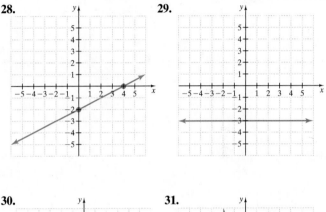

30.   **31.**

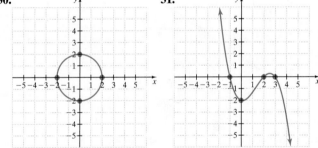

Graph each linear equation by finding its intercepts.

32. $x - 3y = 12$ **33.** $-4x + y = 8$

34. $y = -3$ **35.** $x = 5$

36. $y = -3x$ **37.** $x = 5y$

38. $x - 2 = 0$ **39.** $y + 6 = 0$

(3.4) Find the slope of each line.

40.   **41.**

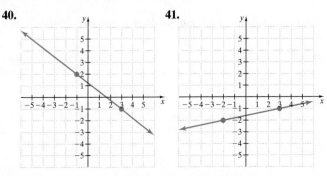

In Exercises 42 through 45, match each line with its slope.

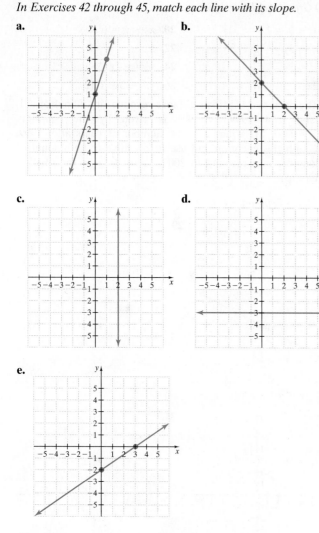

a.

b.

c.

d.

e.

42. $m = 0$

43. $m = -1$

44. undefined slope

45. $m = 3$

46. $m = \dfrac{2}{3}$

Find the slope of the line that goes through the given points.

47. $(2, 5)$ and $(6, 8)$

48. $(4, 7)$ and $(1, 2)$

49. $(1, 3)$ and $(-2, -9)$

50. $(-4, 1)$ and $(3, -6)$

Find the slope of each line.

51. $y = 3x + 7$

52. $x - 2y = 4$

53. $y = -2$

54. $x = 0$

△ *Determine whether each pair of lines is parallel, perpendicular, or neither.*

55. $x - y = -6$
  $x + y = 3$

56. $3x + y = 7$
  $-3x - y = 10$

57. $y = 4x + \dfrac{1}{2}$
  $4x + 2y = 1$

58. $x = 4$
  $y = -2$

Find the slope of each line and write the slope as a rate of change. Don't forget to attach the proper units.

59. The graph below shows the average monthly day care cost for a 3-year-old attending 8 hours a day, 5 days a week.

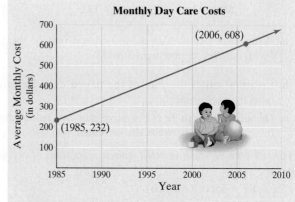

Source: U.S. Senate Joint Economic Committee Fact Sheet

60. The graph below shows the U.S. government's projected spending (in billions of dollars) on technology. (Some years projected.)

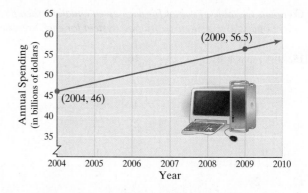

(3.5) Determine the slope and the y-intercept of the graph of each equation.

61. $3x + y = 7$

62. $x - 6y = -1$

63. $y = 2$

64. $x = -5$

Write an equation of each line in slope-intercept form.

65. slope -5; y-intercept $\dfrac{1}{2}$

66. slope $\dfrac{2}{3}$; y-intercept 6

Use the slope-intercept form to graph each equation.

67. $y = 3x - 1$

68. $y = -3x$

69. $5x - 3y = 15$

70. $-x + 2y = 8$

Match each equation with its graph.

71. $y = -4x$ **72.** $y = -2x + 1$

73. $y = 2x - 1$ **74.** $y = 2x$

a.   **b.**

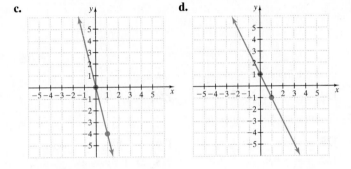

c.   **d.**

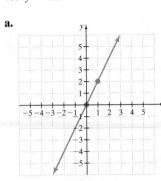
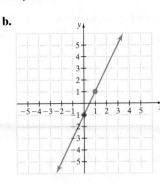

Write an equation of each line in standard form.

75. With slope -3, through $(0, -5)$

76. With slope $\dfrac{1}{2}$, through $\left(0, -\dfrac{7}{2}\right)$

77. With slope 0, through $(-2, -3)$

78. With 0 slope, through the origin

79. With slope -6, through $(2, -1)$

80. With slope 12, through $\left(\dfrac{1}{2}, 5\right)$

81. Through $(0, 6)$ and $(6, 0)$

82. Through $(0, -4)$ and $(-8, 0)$

83. Vertical line, through $(5, 7)$

84. Horizontal line, through $(-6, 8)$

85. Through $(6, 0)$, perpendicular to $y = 8$

86. Through $(10, 12)$, perpendicular to $x = -2$

(3.6) Determine which of the following are functions

87. $\{(7, 1), (7, 5), (2, 6)\}$

88. $\{(0, -1), (5, -1), (2, 2)\}$

89. $7x - 6y = 1$ **90.** $y = 7$

91. $x = 2$ **92.** $y = x^3$

93.   **94.**

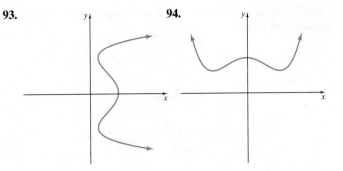

Given the following functions, find the indicated function values.

95. Given $f(x) = -2x + 6$, find

    a. $f(0)$ **b.** $f(-2)$ **c.** $f\left(\dfrac{1}{2}\right)$

96. Given $h(x) = -5 - 3x$, find

    a. $h(2)$ **b.** $h(-3)$ **c.** $h(0)$

97. Given $g(x) = x^2 + 12x$, find

    a. $g(3)$ **b.** $g(-5)$ **c.** $g(0)$

98. Given $h(x) = 6 - |x|$, find

    a. $h(-1)$ **b.** $h(1)$ **c.** $h(-4)$

Find the domain of each function.

99. $f(x) = 2x + 7$ **100.** $g(x) = \dfrac{7}{x - 2}$

Find the domain and the range of each function graphed.

101.   **102.**

103.   **104.**

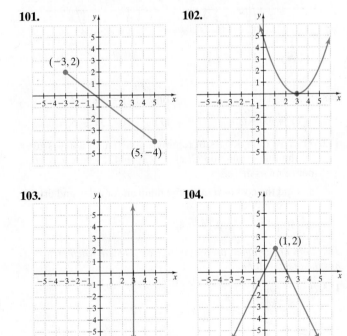

(3.7) Graph each linear function.

105. $f(x) = x$

106. $f(x) = -\dfrac{1}{3}x$

107. $g(x) = 4x - 1$

The graph of $f(x) = 3x$ is sketched below. Use this graph to match each linear function with its graph.

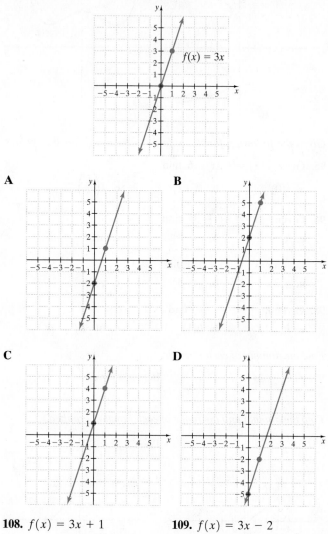

$f(x) = 3x$

A

B

C

D

108. $f(x) = 3x + 1$ **109.** $f(x) = 3x - 2$

110. $f(x) = 3x + 2$ **111.** $f(x) = 3x - 5$

112. The cost C, in dollars, of renting a minivan for a day is given by the linear function $C(x) = 0.3x + 42$, where x is number of miles driven.

   a. Find the cost of renting the minivan for a day and driving it 150 miles.

   b. Graph $C(x) = 0.3x + 42$.

Two lines are graphed on the set of axes. Decide whether l_1 or l_2 has the greater slope.

113.

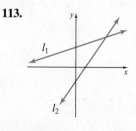

l_1

l_2

(3.8) Graph each function.

114. $f(x) = \begin{cases} -3x & \text{if} \quad x < 0 \\ x - 3 & \text{if} \quad x \geq 0 \end{cases}$

115. $g(x) = \begin{cases} -\dfrac{1}{5}x & \text{if} \quad x \leq -1 \\ -4x + 2 & \text{if} \quad x > -1 \end{cases}$

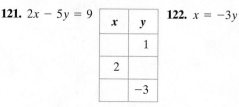

Graph each function.

116. $y = \sqrt{x} - 4$ **117.** $f(x) = \sqrt{x - 4}$

118. $g(x) = |x - 2| - 2$ **119.** $h(x) = -(x + 3)^2 - 1$

120. $f(x) = |x| + 1$

MIXED REVIEW

Complete the table of values for each given equation.

121. $2x - 5y = 9$

x	y
	1
2	
	-3

122. $x = -3y$

x	y
0	
	1
6	

Find the intercepts for each equation.

123. $2x - 3y = 6$ **124.** $-5x + y = 10$

Graph each linear equation.

125. $x - 5y = 10$ **126.** $x + y = 4$

127. $y = -4x$ **128.** $2x + 3y = -6$

129. $x = 3$ **130.** $y = -2$

Find the slope of the line that passes through each pair of points.

131. $(3, -5)$ and $(-4, 2)$ **132.** $(1, 3)$ and $(-6, -8)$

Find the slope of each line.

133.

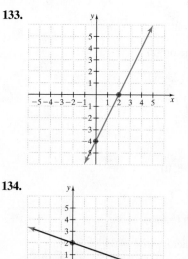

134.

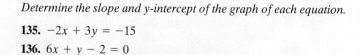

Determine the slope and y-intercept of the graph of each equation.

135. $-2x + 3y = -15$

136. $6x + y - 2 = 0$

Write an equation of the line with the given slope that passes through the given point. Write the equation in the form $Ax + By = C$.

137. $m = -5; (3, -7)$

138. $m = 3; (0, 6)$

Write an equation of the line passing through each pair of points. Write the equation in the form $Ax + By = C$.

139. $(-3, 9)$ and $(-2, 5)$

140. $(3, 1)$ and $(5, -9)$

Use the line graph to answer Exercises 141 through 144.

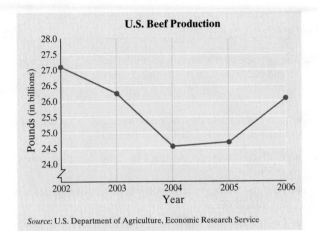

U.S. Beef Production

Source: U.S. Department of Agriculture, Economic Research Service

141. Which year shows the greatest production of beef? Estimate production for that year.

142. Which year shows the least production of beef? Estimate production for that year.

143. Which years had beef production greater then 25 billion pounds?

144. Which year shows the greatest increase in beef production?

Graph each piecewise-defined function.

145. $f(x) = \begin{cases} x - 2 & \text{if } x \le 0 \\ -\dfrac{x}{3} & \text{if } x \ge 3 \end{cases}$

146. $g(x) = \begin{cases} 4x - 3 & \text{if } x \le 1 \\ 2x & \text{if } x > 1 \end{cases}$

Graph each function.

147. $f(x) = \sqrt{x - 2}$

148. $f(x) = |x + 1| - 3$

CHAPTER 3 TEST

TEST PREP **VIDEO** 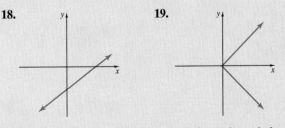 The fully worked-out solutions to any exercises you want to review are available in MyMathLab.

Graph the following.

1. $y = \dfrac{1}{2}x$

2. $2x + y = 8$

3. $5x - 7y = 10$

4. $y = -1$

5. $x - 3 = 0$

Find the slopes of the following lines.

6.   **7.**

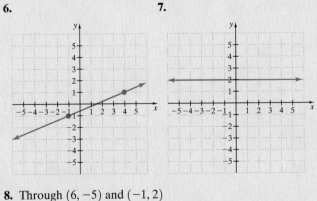

8. Through $(6, -5)$ and $(-1, 2)$

9. $-3x + y = 5$ **10.** $x = 6$

11. Determine the slope and the y-intercept of the graph of $7x - 3y = 2$.

△ **12.** Determine whether the graphs of $y = 2x - 6$ and $-4x = 2y$ are parallel lines, perpendicular lines, or neither.

Find equations of the following lines. Write the equation in standard form.

13. With slope of $-\dfrac{1}{4}$, through $(2, 2)$

14. Through the origin and $(6, -7)$

15. Through $(2, -5)$ and $(1, 3)$

△ **16.** Through $(-5, -1)$ and parallel to $x = 7$

17. With slope $\dfrac{1}{8}$ and y-intercept $(0, 12)$

Which of the following are functions?

18.   **19.**

Given the following functions, find the indicated function values.

20. $h(x) = x^3 - x$

    a. $h(-1)$ **b.** $h(0)$ **c.** $h(4)$

21. Find the domain of $y = \dfrac{1}{x+1}$.

Find the domain and the range of each function graphed.

22.

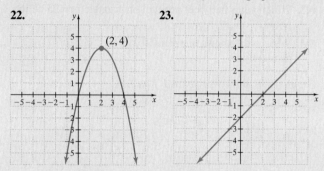

23.

24. If $f(7) = 20$, write the corresponding ordered pair.

Use the bar graph below to answer Exercises 25 and 26.

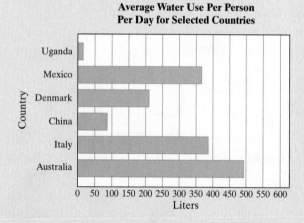

Average Water Use Per Person Per Day for Selected Countries

25. Estimate the average water use per person per day in Denmark.

26. Estimate the average water use per person per day in Australia.

Use this graph to answer Exercises 27 through 29.

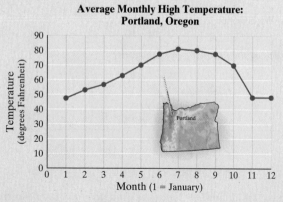

Average Monthly High Temperature: Portland, Oregon

Source: The Weather Channel Enterprises, Inc.

27. During what month is the average high temperature the greatest?

28. Approximate the average high temperature for the month of April.

29. During what month(s) is the average high temperature below 60°F?

Graph each linear function.

30. $f(x) = \dfrac{2}{3}x$

31. $f(x) = \dfrac{2}{3}x + 2$

32. The average yearly earnings for high school graduates age 18 and older is given by the linear function

$$f(x) = 1031x + 25{,}193$$

where x is the number of years since 2000 that a person graduated. (*Source:* U.S. Census Bureau)

a. Find the average earnings in 2000 for high school graduates.

b. Find the average earnings for high school graduates in the year 2007.

c. Predict the first whole year that the average earnings for high school graduates will be greater than $40,000.

d. Find and interpret the slope of this equation.

e. Find and interpret the y-intercept of this equation.

Graph each function. For Exercises 33 and 35, state the domain and the range of the function.

33. $f(x) = \begin{cases} -\dfrac{1}{2}x & \text{if } x \le 0 \\ 2x - 3 & \text{if } x > 0 \end{cases}$

34. $f(x) = (x - 4)^2$

35. $g(x) = -|x + 2| - 1$

36. $h(x) = \sqrt{x} - 1$

CHAPTER 3 STANDARDIZED TEST

Multiple Choice. *Choose the one alternative that best completes the statement or answers the question.*

Graph

1. $y = \frac{1}{2}x$

a.

b.

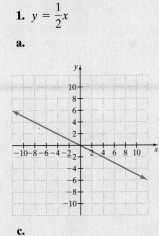
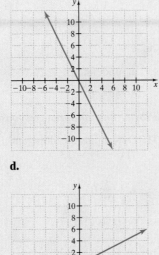

c.

d.

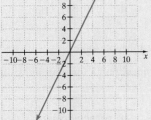

2. $f(x) = -6x + 6$

a.

b.

c.

d.

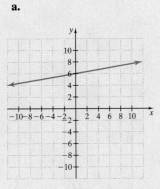
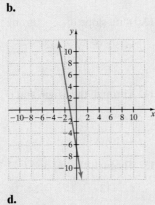
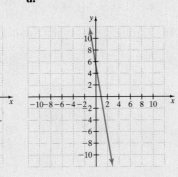

3. $3x + 4y = -16$

a.

b.

c.

d.

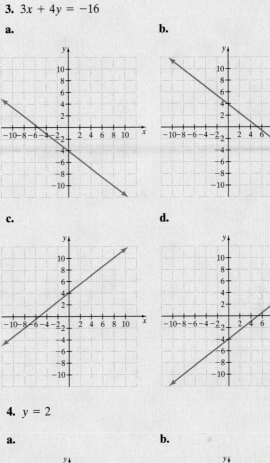

4. $y = 2$

a.

b.

c.

d.

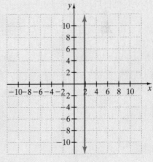
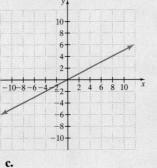
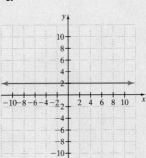
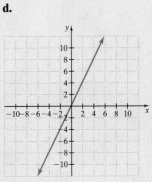

5. $x - 2 = 0$

a.

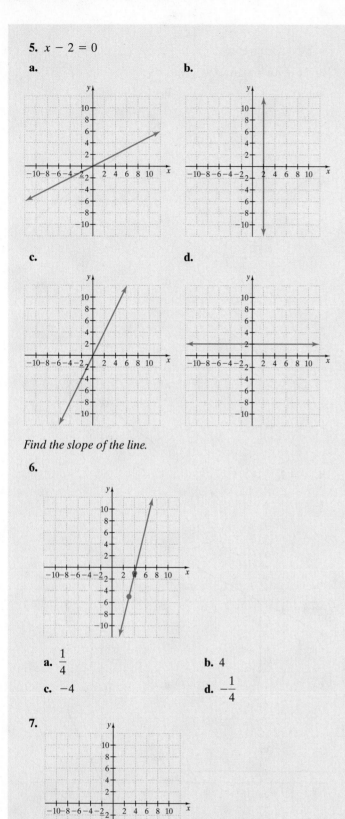

b.

c.

d.

Find the slope of the line.

6.

a. $\dfrac{1}{4}$

b. 4

c. -4

d. $-\dfrac{1}{4}$

7.

a. 0

b. -9

c. undefined slope

d. 2

8. Through $(-8, 8)$ and $(4, -1)$

   a. $-\dfrac{4}{3}$

   b. $-\dfrac{7}{4}$

   c. $\dfrac{3}{4}$

   d. $-\dfrac{3}{4}$

9. $8x + y = 6$

   a. 8

   b. $\dfrac{4}{3}$

   c. $-\dfrac{1}{8}$

   d. -8

10. $x = 1$

   a. undefined

   b. $m = -1$

   c. $m = 0$

   d. $m = 1$

Provide an appropriate response.

11. Determine the slope and the y-intercept of the graph of $11x - 3y = 33$.

   a. $-\dfrac{11}{3}; (0, 11)$

   b. $\dfrac{11}{3}; (0, -11)$

   c. $11; (0, 33)$

   d. $\dfrac{3}{11}; (0, 3)$

12. Determine whether the graphs of $4x - y = -10$ and $y = \dfrac{1}{4}x + 15$ are parallel lines, perpendicular lines, or neither.

   a. parallel

   b. perpendicular

   c. neither

Find an equation for the line. Write the equation in standard form.

13. With slope of $-\dfrac{5}{9}$, through $(2, 3)$

   a. $9x + 5y = -37$

   b. $5x - 9y = 37$

   c. $5x + 9y = 37$

   d. $5x + 9y = -37$

14. Through the origin and $(7, -5)$

   a. $-5x + 7y = 0$

   b. $5x - 7y = 0$

   c. $5x + 7y = 0$

   d. $7x + 5y = 0$

15. Through $(8, -6)$ and $(-7, 7)$

   a. $-13x + 15y = 14$

   b. $14x - 14y = 0$

   c. $-14x + 14y = 0$

   d. $13x + 15y = 14$

16. Through $(-5, 11)$ and parallel to $x = 3$

   a. $x = -5$

   b. $y = 11$

   c. $x = 11$

   d. $y = -\dfrac{11}{8}x + \dfrac{33}{8}$

17. With slope $-\dfrac{1}{6}$ and y-intercept $(0, 2)$

    a. $x + 6y = 12$ **b.** $-6x + y = 12$

    c. $x - 6y = 12$ **d.** $6x + y = 12$

Determine whether the graph is the graph of a function.

18.

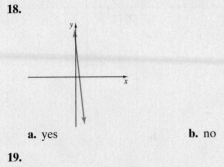

    a. yes   **b.** no

19.

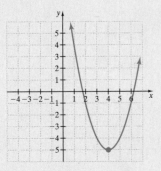

    a. yes   **b.** no

Find the indicated function values.

20. If $h(x) = x^3 - x$, find

    a. $h(-1)$ **b.** $h(0)$ **c.** $h(2)$

A. **a.** 0	**B.** **a.** -2
b. 0	**b.** 0
c. 6	**c.** 10
C. **a.** 0	**D.** **a.** -2
b. 0	**b.** 0
c. 10	**c.** 6

Find the domain.

21. $y = \dfrac{6}{x + 15}$

    a. all real numbers except -15

    b. all real numbers except 6

    c. all real numbers except 15

    d. all real numbers

Find the domain and range of the function graphed.

22.

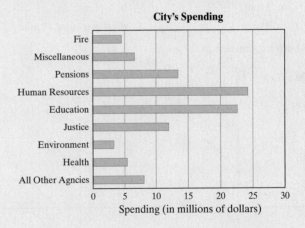

    a. domain: all real numbers; range: all real numbers

    b. domain: all real numbers; range: $y \geq -5$

    c. domain: $x \geq 4$; range: $y \geq -5$

    d. domain: all real numbers except $+4$; range: all real numbers except -5

23.

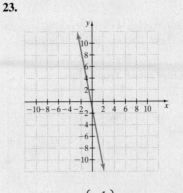

    a. domain: $\left\{-\dfrac{1}{5}\right\}$; range: all real numbers

    b. domain: $\left\{-\dfrac{1}{5}\right\}$; range: -1

    c. domain: all real numbers; range: all real numbers

    d. domain: all real numbers; range: -1

Provide an appropriate response.

24. If $f(5) = 875$, write the corresponding ordered pair.

    a. $(875, 5)$ **b.** $(0, 5)$

    c. $(5, 875)$ **d.** $(0, 875)$

The bar graph shows the expenditures of one city government in a recent year. Use the graph to answer the question.

City's Spending

Agency	Spending (in millions of dollars)
Fire	
Miscellaneous	
Pensions	
Human Resources	
Education	
Justice	
Environment	
Health	
All Other Agncies	

Spending (in millions of dollars): 0 5 10 15 20 25 30

25. Name the agency with the smallest spending and estimate this value.

    a. Justice; $12.1 million

    b. All Other Agencies; $8.2 million

    c. Environment; $3.2 million

    d. Human Resources; $24.2 million

26. Name the agency whose spending is between $3 million and $4 million and estimate its value.

   a. Fire; $4.3 million

   b. Fire; $3.2 million

   c. Environment; $3.2 million

   d. Environment; $4.3 million

The line graph shows the recorded hourly temperatures in degrees Fahrenheit at an airport. Use the graph to answer the question.

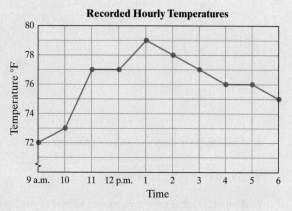

27. At what time was the temperature the highest?

   a. 5 p.m.   b. 12 p.m.

   c. 1 p.m.   d. 2 p.m.

28. What temperature was recorded at 9 a.m.?

   a. 70° F   b. 72° F

   c. 73° F   d. 74° F

29. At what time was the temperature 73°?

   a. 9 a.m.   b. 5 p.m.

   c. 10 a.m.   d. 10 a.m. and 11 a.m.

Match the function to the graph.

30. $f(x) = \begin{cases} x - 2; & x > 0 \\ x + 3; & x \le 0 \end{cases}$

   a.

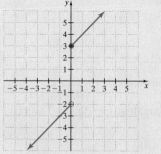

   b.

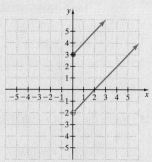

   c.

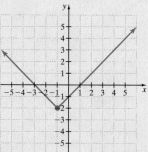

   d.

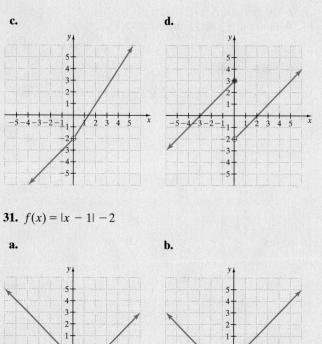

31. $f(x) = |x - 1| - 2$

   a.

   b.

   c.

   d.

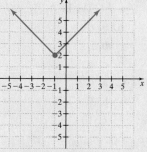
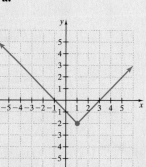

CHAPTER

4

Solving Inequalities and Absolute Value Equations and Inequalities

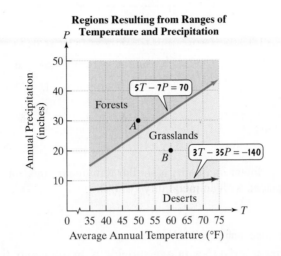

Regions Resulting from Ranges of Temperature and Precipitation

- $5T - 7P = 70$
- $3T - 35P = -140$

Forests

Grasslands

Deserts

Annual Precipitation (inches)

Average Annual Temperature (°F)

What variables affect whether regions are forests, grasslands, or deserts, and what kinds of mathematical models are used to describe the incredibly diverse land that forms the surface of our planet?

The role that temperature and precipitation play in determining whether regions are forests, grasslands, or deserts can be modeled using inequalities in two variables.

The graph above shows three kinds of regions—deserts, grasslands, and forests—that result from various ranges of temperature, T, and precipitation, P.

4.1 LINEAR INEQUALITIES AND PROBLEM SOLVING

OBJECTIVES

1 Define linear inequality in one variable and graph solution sets on a number line.

2 Solve linear inequalities.

3 Solve inequality applications.

OBJECTIVE 1 ▶ Graphing solution sets to linear inequalities. In Chapter 1, we reviewed these inequality symbols and their meanings:

$<$ means "is less than" $\qquad$ $\leq$ means "is less than or equal to"

$>$ means "is greater than" $\qquad$ $\geq$ means "is greater than or equal to"

Equations	Inequalities
$x = 3$	$x \leq 3$
$5n - 6 = 14$	$5n - 6 > 14$
$12 = 7 - 3y$	$12 \leq 7 - 3y$
$\dfrac{x}{4} - 6 = 1$	$\dfrac{x}{4} - 6 > 1$

A linear inequality is similar to a linear equation except that the equality symbol is replaced with an inequality symbol.

Linear Inequality in One Variable

A **linear inequality in one variable** is an inequality that can be written in the form

$$ax + b < c$$

where a, b, and c are real numbers and a is not 0.

This definition and all other definitions, properties, and steps in this section also hold true for the inequality symbols, $>$, $\geq$, and $\leq$.

A **solution of an inequality** is a value of the variable that makes the inequality a true statement. The solution set is the set of all solutions. For the inequality $x < 3$, replacing x with any number less than 3, that is, to the left of 3 on a number line, makes the resulting inequality true. This means that any number less than 3 is a solution of the inequality $x < 3$.

Since there are infinitely many such numbers, we cannot list all the solutions of the inequality. We *can* use set notation and write

$$\{x \mid x < 3\}.$$ Recall that this is read

$\{x$ — the set of all x

$\mid$ — such that

$x < 3$ — x is less than 3.

We can also picture the solutions on a number line. If we use open/solid-dot notation, the graph of $\{x \mid x < 3\}$ looks like the following.

Picturing the solutions of an inequality on a number line is called **graphing** the solutions or graphing the inequality, and the picture is called the **graph** of the inequality.

To graph $\{x \mid x \leq 3\}$ or simply $x \leq 3$, shade the numbers to the left of 3 and place a solid dot at 3 on the number line. The solid dot indicates that 3 **is** a solution: 3 **is** less than or equal to 3.

EXAMPLE 1   Graph $x \geq -1$.

Solution   We place a solid dot at -1 since the inequality symbol is $\geq$ and -1 is greater than or equal to -1. Then we shade to the right of -1.

$$\xleftarrow{\hspace{1em}} \overset{\bullet}{\underset{-4 \ -3 \ -2 \ -1 \ \ 0 \ \ 1 \ \ 2 \ \ 3}{\rule{0pt}{0pt}}} \xrightarrow{\hspace{1em}}$$

□

PRACTICE
1   Graph $x < 5$.

OBJECTIVE 2 ▶ **Solving linear inequalities.** When solutions of a linear inequality are not immediately obvious, they are found through a process similar to the one used to solve a linear equation. Our goal is to get the variable alone, and we use properties of inequality similar to properties of equality.

> **Addition Property of Inequality**
> If a, b, and c are real numbers, then
> $$a < b \qquad \text{and} \qquad a + c < b + c$$
> are equivalent inequalities.

This property also holds true for subtracting values, since subtraction is defined in terms of addition. In other words, adding or subtracting the same quantity from both sides of an inequality does not change the solution of the inequality.

EXAMPLE 2   Solve $x + 4 \leq -6$ for x. Graph the solutions.

Solution   To solve for x, subtract 4 from both sides of the inequality.

$$\xleftarrow{\hspace{1em}} \overset{\bullet}{\underset{-12 \ -11 \ -10 \ -9 \ -8 \ -7 \ -6}{\rule{0pt}{0pt}}} \xrightarrow{\hspace{1em}}$$

$x + 4 \leq -6$	Original inequality
$x + 4 - 4 \leq -6 - 4$	Subtract 4 from both sides.
$x \leq -10$	Simplify.

□

PRACTICE
2   Solve $x + 11 \geq 6$. Graph the solutions.

> ▶ **Helpful Hint**
> Notice that any number less than or equal to -10 is a solution to $x \leq -10$. For example, solutions include
> $$-10, \ -200, \ -11\frac{1}{2}, \ -7\pi, \ -\sqrt{130}, \ -50.3$$

An important difference between linear equations and linear inequalities is shown when we multiply or divide both sides of an inequality by a nonzero real number. For example, start with the true statement $6 < 8$ and multiply both sides by 2. As we see below, the resulting inequality is also true.

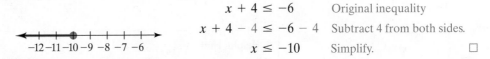

$$6 < 8 \qquad \text{True}$$
$$2(6) < 2(8) \qquad \text{Multiply both sides by 2.}$$
$$12 < 16 \qquad \text{True}$$

But if we start with the same true statement $6 < 8$ and multiply both sides by -2, the resulting inequality is not a true statement.

$$6 < 8 \qquad \text{True}$$
$$-2(6) < -2(8) \qquad \text{Multiply both sides by } -2.$$
$$-12 < -16 \qquad \text{False}$$

Notice, however, that if we reverse the direction of the inequality symbol, the resulting inequality is true.

$$-12 < -16 \qquad \text{False}$$
$$-12 > -16 \qquad \text{True}$$

This demonstrates the multiplication property of inequality.

Multiplication Property of Inequality

1. If a, b, and c are real numbers, and c is **positive,** then

$$a < b \qquad \text{and} \qquad ac < bc$$

are equivalent inequalities.

2. If a, b, and c are real numbers, and c is **negative,** then

$$a < b \qquad \text{and} \qquad ac > bc$$

are equivalent inequalities.

Because division is defined in terms of multiplication, this property also holds true when dividing both sides of an inequality by a nonzero number. If we multiply or divide both sides of an inequality by a negative number, **the direction of the inequality sign must be reversed for the inequalities to remain equivalent.**

▶ **Helpful Hint**

Whenever both sides of an inequality are multiplied or divided by a negative number, the direction of the inequality symbol **must be** reversed to form an equivalent inequality.

EXAMPLE 3 Solve $-2x \leq -4$. Graph the solutions.

Solution Remember to reverse the direction of the inequality symbol when dividing by a negative number.

▶ **Helpful Hint**

Don't forget to reverse the direction of the inequality sign.

$$-2x \leq -4$$
$$\frac{-2x}{-2} \geq \frac{-4}{-2} \qquad \text{Divide both sides by } -2 \text{ and reverse the direction of the inequality sign.}$$
$$x \geq 2 \qquad \text{Simplify.}$$

The solutions are graphed as shown.

PRACTICE

3 Solve $-5x \geq -15$. Graph the solutions.

EXAMPLE 4   Solve $2x < -4$. Graph the solutions.

Solution

$$2x < -4$$

▶ **Helpful Hint**

Do not reverse the inequality sign.

$$\frac{2x}{2} < \frac{-4}{2} \quad \text{Divide both sides by 2.}$$

Do not reverse the direction of the inequality sign.

$$x < -2 \quad \text{Simplify.}$$

The solutions are graphed as shown.

PRACTICE
4   Solve $3x > -9$. Graph the solutions.

Concept Check ☑
Fill in the blank with $<$, $>$, $\leq$, or $\geq$.

a. Since $-8 < -4$, then $3(-8)$____$3(-4)$.

b. Since $5 \geq -2$, then $\dfrac{5}{-7}$ ____ $\dfrac{-2}{-7}$.

c. If $a < b$, then $2a$ ____ $2b$.

d. If $a \geq b$, then $\dfrac{a}{-3}$ ____ $\dfrac{b}{-3}$.

The following steps may be helpful when solving inequalities. Notice that these steps are similar to the ones given in Section 2.4 for solving equations.

> **Solving Linear Inequalities in One Variable**
>
> **STEP 1.** Clear the inequality of fractions by multiplying both sides of the inequality by the lowest common denominator (LCD) of all fractions in the inequality.
>
> **STEP 2.** Remove grouping symbols such as parentheses by using the distributive property.
>
> **STEP 3.** Simplify each side of the inequality by combining like terms.
>
> **STEP 4.** Write the inequality with variable terms on one side and numbers on the other side by using the addition property of inequality.
>
> **STEP 5.** Get the variable alone by using the multiplication property of inequality.

▶ **Helpful Hint**

Don't forget that if both sides of an inequality are multiplied or divided by a negative number, the direction of the inequality sign must be reversed.

EXAMPLE 5   Solve $-4x + 7 \geq -9$. Graph the solutions.

Solution

$$-4x + 7 \geq -9$$

$$-4x + 7 - 7 \geq -9 - 7 \quad \text{Subtract 7 from both sides.}$$

$$-4x \geq -16 \quad \text{Simplify.}$$

$$\frac{-4x}{-4} \leq \frac{-16}{-4} \quad \text{Divide both sides by } -4 \text{ and reverse the direction of the inequality sign.}$$

$$x \leq 4 \quad \text{Simplify.}$$

The solutions is graphed as shown.

PRACTICE
5   Solve $45 - 7x \leq -4$. Graph the solutions.

EXAMPLE 6   Solve $2x + 7 \le x - 11$. Graph the solutions.

Solution

$$2x + 7 \le x - 11$$

$2x + 7 - x \le x - 11 - x$ Subtract x from both sides.

$x + 7 \le -11$ Combine like terms.

$x + 7 - 7 \le -11 - 7$ Subtract 7 from both sides.

$x \le -18$ Combine like terms.

The graph of the solutions is shown.

$$\xleftarrow{\quad\;+\;\;+\;\;\bullet\;\;+\;\;+\;\;+\;\;+\;}\rightarrow$$
$$\;\;-20\,{-}19\,{-}18\,{-}17\,{-}16\,{-}15\,{-}14$$

PRACTICE
6   Solve $3x + 20 \le 2x + 13$. Graph the solutions.

EXAMPLE 7   Solve $-5x + 7 < 2(x - 3)$. Graph the solutions.

Solution

$$-5x + 7 < 2(x - 3)$$

$-5x + 7 < 2x - 6$ Apply the distributive property.

$-5x + 7 - 2x < 2x - 6 - 2x$ Subtract $2x$ from both sides.

$-7x + 7 < -6$ Combine like terms.

$-7x + 7 - 7 < -6 - 7$ Subtract 7 from both sides.

$-7x < -13$ Combine like terms.

$\dfrac{-7x}{-7} > \dfrac{-13}{-7}$ Divide both sides by -7 and reverse the direction of the inequality sign.

$x > \dfrac{13}{7}$ Simplify.

The graph of the solutions is shown.

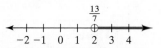

PRACTICE
7   Solve $6 - 5x > 3(x - 4)$. Graph the solutions.

EXAMPLE 8   Solve $2(x - 3) - 5 \le 3(x + 2) - 18$. Graph the solutions.

Solution

$$2(x - 3) - 5 \le 3(x + 2) - 18$$

$2x - 6 - 5 \le 3x + 6 - 18$ Apply the distributive property.

$2x - 11 \le 3x - 12$ Combine like terms.

$-x - 11 \le -12$ Subtract $3x$ from both sides.

$-x \le -1$ Add 11 to both sides.

$\dfrac{-x}{-1} \ge \dfrac{-1}{-1}$ Divide both sides by -1 and reverse the direction of the inequality sign.

$x \ge 1$ Simplify.

The graph of the solutions is shown.

$$\xleftarrow{} \overset{\bullet}{\underset{-3\ -2\ -1\ \ \ 0\ \ \ 1\ \ \ 2\ \ \ 3}{|\ \ \ |\ \ \ |\ \ \ |\ \ \ |\ \ \ |\ \ \ |}} \xrightarrow{}$$

☐

PRACTICE
8   Solve $3(x - 4) - 5 \le 5(x - 1) - 12$. Graph the solutions.

■

OBJECTIVE 3 ▶ Solving inequality applications. Problems containing words such as "at least," "at most," "between," "no more than," and "no less than" usually indicate that an inequality should be solved instead of an equation. In solving applications involving linear inequalities, use the same procedure you use to solve applications involving linear equations.

EXAMPLE 9   **Staying within Budget**

Marie Chase and Jonathan Edwards are having their wedding reception at the Gallery Reception Hall. They may spend at most $2000 for the reception. If the reception hall charges a $100 cleanup fee plus $36 per person, find the greatest number of people that they can invite and still stay within their budget.

Solution

1. UNDERSTAND. Read and reread the problem. Next, guess a solution. If 40 people attend the reception, the cost is $100 + $36(40) = $100 + $1440 = $1540. Let x = the number of people who attend the reception.

2. TRANSLATE.

In words:	cleanup fee	+	cost per person	must be less than or equal to	$2000
	↓		↓	↓	↓
Translate:	100	+	36x	≤	2000

3. SOLVE.

$$100 + 36x \le 2000$$
$$36x \le 1900 \quad \text{Subtract 100 from both sides.}$$
$$x \le 52\frac{7}{9} \quad \text{Divide both sides by 36.}$$

4. INTERPRET.

Check: Since x represents the number of people, we round down to the nearest whole, or 52. Notice that if 52 people attend, the cost is

$$\$100 + \$36(52) = \$1972. \text{ If 53 people attend, the cost is}$$
$$\$100 + \$36(53) = \$2008, \text{ which is more than the given } \$2000.$$

State: Marie Chase and Jonathan Edwards can invite at most 52 people to the reception.   ☐

PRACTICE
9   Kasonga is eager to begin his education at his local community college. He has budgeted $1500 for college this semester. His local college charges a $300 matriculation fee and costs an average of $375 for tuition, fees, and books for each three-credit course. Find the greatest number of classes Kasonga can afford to take this semester.

■

VOCABULARY & READINESS CHECK

Word Bank. *Use the choices below to fill in each blank.*

expression   inequality   equation

1. $6x - 7(x + 9)$ _____

2. $6x = 7(x + 9)$ _____

3. $6x < 7(x + 9)$ _____

4. $5y - 2 \geq -38$ _____

5. $\dfrac{9}{7} = \dfrac{x + 2}{14}$ _____

6. $\dfrac{9}{7} - \dfrac{x + 2}{14}$ _____

Decision Making. *Decide which number listed is not a solution to each given inequality.*

7. $x \geq -3$; $-3, 0, -5, \pi$ _____

8. $x < 6$; $-6, |-6|, 0, -3.2$ _____

9. $x < 4.01$; $4, -4.01, 4.1, -4.1$ _____

10. $x \geq -3$; $-4, -3, -2, -(-2)$ _____

4.1 EXERCISE SET

Graph each inequality on a number line. See Example 1.

1. $x > 2$

2. $x > -3$

3. $x \leq -1$

4. $y \leq 0$

5. $x < \dfrac{1}{2}$

6. $z < -\dfrac{2}{3}$

7. $y \geq 0$

8. $x \geq 4$

Solve each inequality. Graph the solutions. See Examples 2 through 4.

9. $2x < -6$

10. $3x > -9$

11. $-2x < -6$

12. $-3x > -9$

13. $x - 2 \geq -7$

14. $x + 4 \leq 1$

15. $-8x \leq 16$

16. $-5x < 20$

Solve each inequality. Graph the solutions. See Examples 5 and 6.

17. $3x - 5 > 2x - 8$

18. $3 - 7x \geq 10 - 8x$

19. $4x - 1 \leq 5x - 2x$

20. $7x + 3 < 9x - 3x$

Solve each inequality. Graph the solutions. See Examples 7 and 8.

21. $x - 7 < 3(x + 1)$

22. $3x + 9 \leq 5(x - 1)$

23. $-6x + 2 \geq 2(5 - x)$

24. $-7x + 4 > 3(4 - x)$

25. $4(3x - 1) \leq 5(2x - 4)$

26. $3(5x - 4) \leq 4(3x - 2)$

27. $3(x + 2) - 6 > -2(x - 3) + 14$

28. $7(x - 2) + x \leq -4(5 - x) - 12$

MIXED PRACTICE

Solve the following inequalities.

29. $-2x \leq -40$

30. $-7x > 21$

31. $-9 + x > 7$

32. $y - 4 \leq 1$

33. $3x - 7 < 6x + 2$

34. $2x - 1 \geq 4x - 5$

35. $5x - 7x \geq x + 2$

36. $4 - x < 8x + 2x$

37. $\dfrac{3}{4}x > 2$

38. $\dfrac{5}{6}x \geq -8$

39. $3(x - 5) < 2(2x - 1)$

40. $5(x + 4) < 4(2x + 3)$

41. $4(2x + 1) < 4$

42. $6(2 - x) \geq 12$

43. $-5x + 4 \geq -4(x - 1)$

44. $-6x + 2 < -3(x + 4)$

45. $-2(x - 4) - 3x < -(4x + 1) + 2x$

46. $-5(1 - x) + x \le -(6 - 2x) + 6$

47. $-3x + 6 \ge 2x + 6$

48. $-(x - 4) < 4$

49. Explain how solving a linear inequality is similar to solving a linear equation.

50. Explain how solving a linear inequality is different from solving a linear equation.

Solve. See Example 9.

51. Six more than twice a number is greater than negative fourteen. Find all numbers that make this statement true.

52. Five times a number, increased by one, is less than or equal to ten. Find all such numbers.

53. Dennis and Nancy Wood are celebrating their 30th wedding anniversary by having a reception at Tiffany Oaks reception hall. They have budgeted $3000 for their reception. If the reception hall charges a $50.00 cleanup fee plus $34 per person, find the greatest number of people that they may invite and still stay within their budget.

54. A surprise retirement party is being planned for Pratep Puri. A total of $860 has been collected for the event, which is to be held at a local reception hall. This reception hall charges a cleanup fee of $40 and $15 per person for drinks and light snacks. Find the greatest number of people that may be invited and still stay within $860.

△ 55. Find the values for x so that the perimeter of this rectangle is no greater than 100 centimeters.

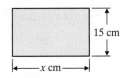

△ 56. Find the values for x so that the perimeter of this triangle is no longer than 87 inches.

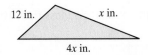

57. A financial planner has a client with $15,000 to invest. If he invests $10,000 in a certificate of deposit paying 11% annual simple interest, at what rate does the remainder of the money need to be invested so that the two investments together yield at least $1600 in yearly interest?

58. Alex earns $600 per month plus 4% of all his sales over $1000. Find the minimum sales that will allow Alex to earn at least $3000 per month.

59. Ben Holladay bowled 146 and 201 in his first two games. What must he bowl in his third game to have an average of at least 180?

60. On an NBA team the two forwards measure 6'8" and 6'6" and the two guards measure 6'0" and 5'9" tall. How tall a center should they hire if they wish to have a starting team average height of at least 6'5"?

Evaluate the following. See Section 1.4.

61. $(2)^3$

62. $(3)^3$

63. $(1)^{12}$

64. 0^5

65. $\left(\dfrac{4}{7}\right)^2$

66. $\left(\dfrac{2}{3}\right)^3$

This broken line graph shows the average annual per person expenditure on newspapers for the given years. Use this graph for Exercises 67 through 70. See Section 3.1. (Source: Veronis Suhler Stevenson)

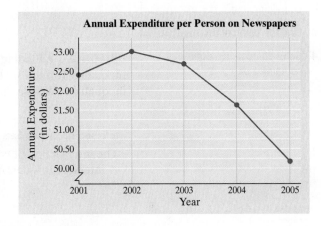

67. What was the average per person expenditure on newspapers in 2003?

68. What was the average per person expenditure on newspapers in 2005?

69. What year had the greatest drop in newspaper expenditures?

70. What years had per person newspaper expenditures over $52?

CONCEPT EXTENSIONS

For Exercises 71 through 74, see the example below.

Solve $x(x - 6) > x^2 - 5x + 6$.
Solution

$$x(x - 6) > x^2 - 5x + 6$$

$$x^2 - 6x > x^2 - 5x + 6$$

$$x^2 - 6x - x^2 > x^2 - 5x + 6 - x^2$$

$$-6x > -5x + 6$$

$$-x > 6$$

$$\frac{-x}{-1} < \frac{6}{-1}$$

$$x < -6$$

Solve each inequality.

71. $x(x + 4) > x^2 - 2x + 6$

72. $x(x - 3) \geq x^2 - 5x - 8$

73. $x^2 + 6x - 10 < x(x - 10)$

74. $x^2 - 4x + 8 < x(x + 8)$

4.2 COMPOUND INEQUALITIES

OBJECTIVES

1 Find the intersection of two sets.

2 Solve compound inequalities containing **and**.

3 Find the union of two sets.

4 Solve compound inequalities containing **or**.

Two inequalities joined by the words **and** or **or** are called **compound inequalities.**

> ### *Compound Inequalities*
>
> $$x + 3 < 8 \quad \text{and} \quad x > 2$$
> $$\frac{2x}{3} \geq 5 \quad \text{or} \quad -x + 10 < 7$$

OBJECTIVE 1 ▶ Finding the intersection of two sets. The solution set of a compound inequality formed by the word **and** is the **intersection** of the solution sets of the two inequalities. We use the symbol ∩ to represent "intersection."

> **Intersection of Two Sets**
>
> The intersection of two sets, A and B, is the set of all elements common to both sets. A intersect B is denoted by
>
> $A \cap B$
>
> A B

EXAMPLE 1   If $A = \{x \mid x$ is an even number greater than 0 and less than 10$\}$ and $B = \{3, 4, 5, 6\}$, find $A \cap B$.

Solution   Let's list the elements in set A.

$$A = \{2, 4, 6, 8\}$$

The numbers 4 and 6 are in sets A and B. The intersection is $\{4, 6\}$.   □

PRACTICE

1   If $A = \{x \mid x$ is an odd number greater than 0 and less than 10$\}$ and $B = \{1, 2, 3, 4\}$, find $A \cap B$.

OBJECTIVE 2 ▶ Solving compound inequalities containing "and." A value is a solution of a compound inequality formed by the word **and** if it is a solution of *both* inequalities. For example, the solution set of the compound inequality $x \leq 5$ and $x \geq 3$ contains all values of x that make the inequality $x \leq 5$ a true statement **and** the inequality $x \geq 3$ a true statement. The first graph shown below is the graph of $x \leq 5$, the second graph is the graph of $x \geq 3$, and the third graph shows the intersection of the two graphs. The third graph is the graph of $x \leq 5$ **and** $x \geq 3$.

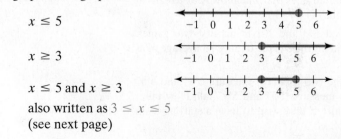

$x \leq 5$

$x \geq 3$

$x \leq 5$ and $x \geq 3$
also written as $3 \leq x \leq 5$
(see next page)

Since $x \geq 3$ is the same as $3 \leq x$, the compound inequality $3 \leq x$ and $x \leq 5$ can be written in a more compact form as $3 \leq x \leq 5$. This inequality includes all numbers that are greater than or equal to 3 and at the same time less than or equal to 5.

When possible, we will write compound inequalities in a compact form.

> ▶ **Helpful Hint**
>
> Don't forget that some compound inequalities containing "and" can be written in a more compact form.
>
> | *Compound Inequality* | *Compact Form* |
> |---|---|
> | $2 \leq x$ and $x \leq 6$ | $2 \leq x \leq 6$ |
>
> Graph:

EXAMPLE 2   Solve: $x - 7 < 2$ *and* $2x + 1 < 9$

Solution   First we solve each inequality separately.

$$x - 7 < 2 \quad and \quad 2x + 1 < 9$$
$$x < 9 \quad and \quad 2x < 8$$
$$x < 9 \quad and \quad x < 4$$

Now we can graph the two inequalities on two number lines and find their intersection. Their intersection is shown on the third number line.

$x < 9$

$x < 4$

$x < 9$ *and* $x < 4$, also written as $x < 4$

As we see from the last number line, the solutions are all numbers less than 4, written as $x < 4$. □

PRACTICE
2   Solve: $x + 3 < 8$ *and* $2x - 1 < 3$.

EXAMPLE 3   Solve: $2x \geq 0$ *and* $4x - 1 \leq -9$.

Solution   First we solve each inequality separately.

$$2x \geq 0 \quad and \quad 4x - 1 \leq -9$$
$$x \geq 0 \quad and \quad 4x \leq -8$$
$$x \geq 0 \quad and \quad x \leq -2$$

Now we can graph the two inequalities and find their intersection.

$x \geq 0$

$x \leq -2$

$x \geq 0$ *and* $x \leq -2$, which is no solution

There is no number that is greater than or equal to 0 *and* less than or equal to -2. The answer is no solution. □

PRACTICE
3   Solve: $4x \leq 0$ *and* $3x + 2 > 8$.

> ▶ Helpful Hint
> Example 3 shows that some compound inequalities have no solution. Also, some have all real numbers as solutions.

To solve a compound inequality written in a compact form, such as $2 < 4 - x < 7$, we get x alone in the "middle part." Since a compound inequality is really two inequalities in one statement, we must perform the same operations on all three parts of the inequality.

EXAMPLE 4 Solve: $2 < 4 - x < 7$

Solution To get x alone, we first subtract 4 from all three parts.

$$2 < 4 - x < 7$$
$$2 - 4 < 4 - x - 4 < 7 - 4 \quad \text{Subtract 4 from all three parts.}$$
$$-2 < -x < 3 \quad \text{Simplify.}$$
$$\frac{-2}{-1} > \frac{-x}{-1} > \frac{3}{-1} \quad \text{Divide all three parts by } -1 \text{ and reverse the inequality symbols.}$$
$$2 > x > -3$$

> ▶ Helpful Hint
> Don't forget to reverse both inequality symbols.

This is equivalent to $-3 < x < 2$.
The graph is shown.

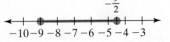

PRACTICE
4 Solve: $3 < 5 - x < 9$.

EXAMPLE 5 Solve: $-1 \leq \dfrac{2x}{3} + 5 \leq 2$.

Solution First, clear the inequality of fractions by multiplying all three parts by the LCD of 3.

$$-1 \leq \frac{2x}{3} + 5 \leq 2$$
$$3(-1) \leq 3\left(\frac{2x}{3} + 5\right) \leq 3(2) \quad \text{Multiply all three parts by the LCD of 3.}$$
$$-3 \leq 2x + 15 \leq 6 \quad \text{Use the distributive property and multiply.}$$
$$-3 - 15 \leq 2x + 15 - 15 \leq 6 - 15 \quad \text{Subtract 15 from all three parts.}$$
$$-18 \leq 2x \leq -9 \quad \text{Simplify.}$$
$$\frac{-18}{2} \leq \frac{2x}{2} \leq \frac{-9}{2} \quad \text{Divide all three parts by 2.}$$
$$-9 \leq x \leq -\frac{9}{2} \quad \text{Simplify.}$$

The graph of the solutions are shown.

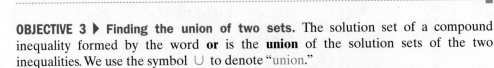

PRACTICE
5 Solve: $-4 \leq \dfrac{x}{2} - 1 \leq 3$.

OBJECTIVE 3 ▶ Finding the union of two sets. The solution set of a compound inequality formed by the word **or** is the **union** of the solution sets of the two inequalities. We use the symbol $\cup$ to denote "union."

> **Helpful Hint**
> The word "either" in this definition means "one or the other or both."

Union of Two Sets

The **union** of two sets, A and B, is the set of elements that belong to *either* of the sets. A union B is denoted by

$$A \cup B$$

EXAMPLE 6 If $A = \{x \mid x \text{ is an even number greater than 0 and less than 10}\}$ and $B = \{3, 4, 5, 6\}$. Find $A \cup B$.

Solution Recall from Example 1 that $A = \{2, 4, 6, 8\}$. The numbers that are in either set or both sets are $\{2, 3, 4, 5, 6, 8\}$. This set is the union. □

PRACTICE
6 If $A = \{x \mid x \text{ is an odd number greater than 0 and less than 10}\}$ and $B = \{2, 3, 4, 5, 6\}$. Find $A \cup B$.

OBJECTIVE 4 ▶ Solving compound inequalities containing "or." A value is a solution of a compound inequality formed by the word **or** if it is a solution of **either** inequality. For example, the solution set of the compound inequality $x \leq 1$ **or** $x \geq 3$ contains all numbers that make the inequality $x \leq 1$ a true statement **or** the inequality $x \geq 3$ a true statement.

$x \leq 1$

$x \geq 3$

$x \leq 1 \text{ or } x \geq 3$

As we see from the last number line, there is no more compact way to write the solutions. They are all numbers, x, such that $x \leq 1$ or $x \geq 3$.

EXAMPLE 7 Solve: $5x - 3 \leq 10 \text{ or } x + 1 \geq 5$.

Solution First we solve each inequality separately.

$$5x - 3 \leq 10 \quad or \quad x + 1 \geq 5$$
$$5x \leq 13 \quad or \quad x \geq 4$$
$$x \leq \frac{13}{5} \quad or \quad x \geq 4$$

Now we can graph each inequality and find their union.

$x \leq \dfrac{13}{5}$

$x \geq 4$

$x \leq \dfrac{13}{5} \text{ or } x \geq 4$

The solutions are $x \leq \dfrac{13}{5}$ or $x \geq 4$. □

PRACTICE
7 Solve: $8x + 5 \leq 8 \text{ or } x - 1 \geq 2$.

EXAMPLE 8 Solve: $-2x - 5 < -3 \text{ or } 6x < 0$.

Solution First we solve each inequality separately.

$$
\begin{array}{ccc}
-2x - 5 < -3 & or & 6x < 0 \\
-2x < 2 & or & x < 0 \\
x > -1 & or & x < 0
\end{array}
$$

Now we can graph each inequality and find their union.

$x > -1$

$x < 0$

$x > -1 \text{ or } x < 0$,
also written as all real numbers

The solutions are all real numbers.

PRACTICE
8 Solve: $-3x - 2 > -8 \text{ or } 5x > 0$.

Concept Check ☑

Which of the following is _not_ a correct way to represent all numbers between -3 and 5?

a. $-3 < x < 5$

b. $-3 < x \text{ or } x < 5$

c. $x > -3 \text{ and } x < 5$

Answer to Concept Check:
b is not correct

VOCABULARY & READINESS CHECK

Word Bank. _Use the choices below to fill in each blank. Some choices may be used more than once._

or $\cup$ $\varnothing$

and $\cap$ compound

1. Two inequalities joined by the words "and" or "or" are called _____ inequalities.

2. The word _____ means intersection.

3. The word _____ means union.

4. The symbol _____ represents intersection.

5. The symbol _____ represents union.

6. The symbol _____ is the empty set.

7. The inequality $-2 \le x < 1$ means $-2 \le x$ _____ $x < 1$.

8. $\{x \mid x < 0 \text{ and } x > 0\} =$ _____

4.2 | EXERCISE SET

MyMathLab®

PRACTICE   WATCH   DOWNLOAD   READ   REVIEW

MIXED PRACTICE

_If_ $A = \{x \mid x \text{ is an even integer}\}$, $B = \{x \mid x \text{ is an odd integer}\}$, $C = \{2, 3, 4, 5\}$, _and_ $D = \{4, 5, 6, 7\}$, _list the elements of each set. See Examples 1 and 6._

1. $C \cup D$

2. $C \cap D$

3. $A \cap D$

4. $A \cup D$

5. $A \cup B$

6. $A \cap B$

7. $B \cap D$

8. $B \cup D$

9. $B \cup C$

10. $B \cap C$

11. $A \cap C$

12. $A \cup C$

Solve each compound inequality. Graph the solutions. See Examples 2 and 3.

13. $x < 1 \text{ and } x > -3$

14. $x \le 0 \text{ and } x \ge -2$

15. $x \le -3 \text{ and } x \ge -2$

16. $x < 2 \text{ and } x > 4$

17. $x < -1$ and $x < 1$

18. $x \geq -4$ and $x > 1$

Solve each compound inequality. See Examples 2 and 3.

19. $x + 1 \geq 7$ and $3x - 1 \geq 5$

20. $x + 2 \geq 3$ and $5x - 1 \geq 9$

21. $4x + 2 \leq -10$ and $2x \leq 0$

22. $2x + 4 > 0$ and $4x > 0$

23. $-2x < -8$ and $x - 5 < 5$

24. $-7x \leq -21$ and $x - 20 \leq -15$

Solve each compound inequality. See Examples 4 and 5.

25. $5 < x - 6 < 11$

26. $-2 \leq x + 3 \leq 0$

27. $-2 \leq 3x - 5 \leq 7$

28. $1 < 4 + 2x < 7$

29. $1 \leq \dfrac{2}{3}x + 3 \leq 4$

30. $-2 < \dfrac{1}{2}x - 5 < 1$

31. $-5 \leq \dfrac{-3x + 1}{4} \leq 2$

32. $-4 \leq \dfrac{-2x + 5}{3} \leq 1$

Solve each compound inequality. Graph the solutions. See Examples 7 and 8.

33. $x < 4$ or $x < 5$

34. $x \geq -2$ or $x \leq 2$

35. $x \leq -4$ or $x \geq 1$

36. $x < 0$ or $x < 1$

37. $x > 0$ or $x < 3$

38. $x \geq -3$ or $x \leq -4$

Solve each compound inequality. See Examples 7 and 8.

39. $-2x \leq -4$ or $5x - 20 \geq 5$

40. $-5x \leq 10$ or $3x - 5 \geq 1$

41. $x + 4 < 0$ or $6x > -12$

42. $x + 9 < 0$ or $4x > -12$

43. $3(x - 1) < 12$ or $x + 7 > 10$

44. $5(x - 1) \geq -5$ or $5 - x \leq 11$

MIXED PRACTICE

Solve each compound inequality. See Examples 1 through 8.

45. $x < \dfrac{2}{3}$ and $x > -\dfrac{1}{2}$

46. $x < \dfrac{5}{7}$ and $x < 1$

47. $x < \dfrac{2}{3}$ or $x > -\dfrac{1}{2}$

48. $x < \dfrac{5}{7}$ or $x < 1$

49. $0 \leq 2x - 3 \leq 9$

50. $3 < 5x + 1 < 11$

51. $\dfrac{1}{2} < x - \dfrac{3}{4} < 2$

52. $\dfrac{2}{3} < x + \dfrac{1}{2} < 4$

53. $x + 3 \geq 3$ and $x + 3 \leq 2$

54. $2x - 1 \geq 3$ and $-x > 2$

55. $3x \geq 5$ or $-\dfrac{5}{8}x - 6 > 1$

56. $\dfrac{3}{8}x + 1 \leq 0$ or $-2x < -4$

57. $0 < \dfrac{5 - 2x}{3} < 5$

58. $-2 < \dfrac{-2x - 1}{3} < 2$

59. $-6 < 3(x - 2) \leq 8$

60. $-5 < 2(x + 4) < 8$

61. $-x + 5 > 6$ and $1 + 2x \leq -5$

62. $5x \leq 0$ and $-x + 5 < 8$

63. $3x + 2 \leq 5$ or $7x > 29$

64. $-x < 7$ or $3x + 1 < -20$

65. $5 - x > 7$ and $2x + 3 \geq 13$

66. $-2x < -6$ or $1 - x > -2$

67. $-\dfrac{1}{2} \leq \dfrac{4x - 1}{6} < \dfrac{5}{6}$

68. $-\dfrac{1}{2} \leq \dfrac{3x - 1}{10} < \dfrac{1}{2}$

69. $\dfrac{1}{15} < \dfrac{8 - 3x}{15} < \dfrac{4}{5}$

70. $-\dfrac{1}{4} < \dfrac{6 - x}{12} < -\dfrac{1}{6}$

71. $0.3 < 0.2x - 0.9 < 1.5$

72. $-0.7 \leq 0.4x + 0.8 < 0.5$

REVIEW AND PREVIEW

Evaluate the following. See Sections 1.2, 1.5, and 1.6.

73. $|-7| - |19|$

74. $|-7 - 19|$

75. $-(-6) - |-10|$

76. $|-4| - (-4) + |-20|$

Find by inspection all values for x that make each equation true.

77. $|x| = 7$

78. $|x| = 5$

79. $|x| = 0$

80. $|x| = -2$

CONCEPT EXTENSIONS

Read a Graph. *Use the graph to answer Exercises 81 and 82.*

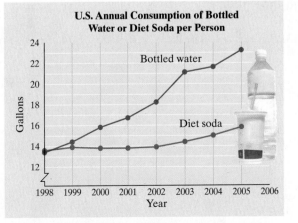

81. For what years was the consumption of bottled water greater than 20 gallons per person *and* the consumption of diet soda greater than 14 gallons per person?

82. For what years was the consumption of bottled water less than 15 gallons per person *or* the consumption of diet soda greater than 14 gallons per person?

The formula for converting Fahrenheit temperatures to Celsius temperatures is $C = \dfrac{5}{9}(F - 32)$. Use this formula for Exercises 83 and 84.

83. During a recent year, the temperatures in Chicago ranged from $-29°$ to $35°C$. Use a compound inequality to convert these temperatures to Fahrenheit temperatures.

84. In Oslo, the average temperature ranges from $-10°$ to $18°$ Celsius. Use a compound inequality to convert these temperatures to the Fahrenheit scale.

Solve.

85. Christian D'Angelo has scores of 68, 65, 75, and 78 on his algebra tests. Use a compound inequality to find the scores he can make on his final exam to receive a C in the course. The final exam counts as two tests, and a C is received if the final course average is from 70 to 79.

86. Wendy Wood has scores of 80, 90, 82, and 75 on her chemistry tests. Use a compound inequality to find the range of scores she can make on her final exam to receive a B in the course. The final exam counts as two tests, and a B is received if the final course average is from 80 to 89.

*Solve each compound inequality for x. See the example below. To solve $x - 6 < 3x < 2x + 5$, notice that this inequality contains a variable not only in the middle, but also on the left and the right. When this occurs, we solve by rewriting the inequality using the word **and**.*

$$x - 6 < 3x \quad \text{and} \quad 3x < 2x + 5$$
$$-6 < 2x \quad \text{and} \quad x < 5$$
$$-3 < x$$
$$x > -3 \quad \text{and} \quad x < 5$$

$x > -3$

$x < 5$

$-3 < x < 5$

87. $2x - 3 < 3x + 1 < 4x - 5$

88. $x + 3 < 2x + 1 < 4x + 6$

89. $-3(x - 2) \le 3 - 2x \le 10 - 3x$

90. $7x - 1 \le 7 + 5x \le 3(1 + 2x)$

91. $5x - 8 < 2(2 + x) < -2(1 + 2x)$

92. $1 + 2x < 3(2 + x) < 1 + 4x$

INTEGRATED REVIEW LINEAR AND COMPOUND INEQUALITIES

Sections 4.1– 4.2

Solve each inequality.

1. $-4x < 20$

2. $\dfrac{3x}{4} \ge 2$

3. $5x + 3 \ge 2 + 4x$

4. $-4x \le \dfrac{2}{5}$

5. $-3x \ge \dfrac{1}{2}$

6. $\dfrac{-5x + 11}{2} \le 7$

7. $12x + 14 < 11x - 2$

8. $2(x - 3) > 70$

9. $8(x + 3) < 7(x + 5) + x$

10. $5 \le 2x - 1 < 9$

11. $2x + 7 < -11 \text{ or } -3x - 2 < 13$

12. $5 - 2x \ge 9 \text{ and } 5x + 3 > -17$

13. $3x - 2 > -8 \text{ or } 2x + 1 < 9$

14. $5x + 1 \ge 4x - 2 \text{ and } 2x - 3 > 5$

4.3 ABSOLUTE VALUE EQUATIONS

OBJECTIVE 1 ▶ Solving absolute equations. In Chapter 1, we defined the absolute value of a number as its distance from 0 on a number line.

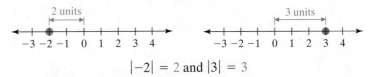

$$|-2| = 2 \text{ and } |3| = 3$$

In this section, we concentrate on solving equations containing the absolute value of a variable or a variable expression. Examples of absolute value equations are

$$|x| = 3 \qquad -5 = |2y + 7| \qquad |z - 6.7| = |3z + 1.2|$$

Since distance and absolute value are so closely related, absolute value equations and inequalities (see Section 4.4) are extremely useful in solving distance-type problems, such as calculating the possible error in a measurement.

For the absolute value equation $|x| = 3$, its solution set will contain all numbers whose distance from 0 is 3 units. Two numbers are 3 units away from 0 on the number line: 3 and -3.

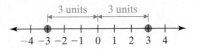

Thus, the solution set of the equation $|x| = 3$ is $\{3, -3\}$. This suggests the following:

Solving Equations of the Form $|X| = a$

If a is a positive number, then $|X| = a$ is equivalent to $X = a$ or $X = -a$.

EXAMPLE 1   Solve: $|p| = 2$.

Solution   Since 2 is positive, $|p| = 2$ is equivalent to $p = 2$ or $p = -2$.

To check, let $p = 2$ and then $p = -2$ in the original equation.

$|p| = 2$	Original equation	$|p| = 2$	Original equation
$|2| = 2$	Let $p = 2$.	$|-2| = 2$	Let $p = -2$.
$2 = 2$	True	$2 = 2$	True

The solutions are 2 and -2 or the solution set is $\{2, -2\}$.   □

PRACTICE

1   Solve: $|q| = 7$.

If the expression inside the absolute value bars is more complicated than a single variable, we can still apply the absolute value property.

▶ **Helpful Hint**

For the equation $|X| = a$ in the box above, X can be a single variable or a variable expression.

EXAMPLE 2 Solve: $|5w + 3| = 7$.

Solution Here the expression inside the absolute value bars is $5w + 3$. If we think of the expression $5w + 3$ as X in the absolute value property, we see that $|X| = 7$ is equivalent to

$$X = 7 \quad \text{or} \quad X = -7$$

Then substitute $5w + 3$ for X, and we have

$$5w + 3 = 7 \quad \text{or} \quad 5w + 3 = -7$$

Solve these two equations for w.

$$5w + 3 = 7 \quad \text{or} \quad 5w + 3 = -7$$
$$5w = 4 \quad \text{or} \quad 5w = -10$$
$$w = \frac{4}{5} \quad \text{or} \quad w = -2$$

Check: To check, let $w = -2$ and then $w = \frac{4}{5}$ in the original equation.

Let $w = -2$

$$|5(-2) + 3| = 7$$
$$|-10 + 3| = 7$$
$$|-7| = 7$$
$$7 = 7 \quad \text{True}$$

Let $w = \frac{4}{5}$

$$\left|5\left(\frac{4}{5}\right) + 3\right| = 7$$
$$|4 + 3| = 7$$
$$|7| = 7$$
$$7 = 7 \quad \text{True}$$

Both solutions check, and the solutions are -2 and $\frac{4}{5}$. □

PRACTICE
2 Solve: $|2x - 3| = 5$.

EXAMPLE 3 Solve: $\left|\dfrac{x}{2} - 1\right| = 11$.

Solution $\left|\dfrac{x}{2} - 1\right| = 11$ is equivalent to

$$\frac{x}{2} - 1 = 11 \quad \text{or} \quad \frac{x}{2} - 1 = -11$$
$$2\left(\frac{x}{2} - 1\right) = 2(11) \quad \text{or} \quad 2\left(\frac{x}{2} - 1\right) = 2(-11) \quad \text{Clear fractions.}$$
$$x - 2 = 22 \quad \text{or} \quad x - 2 = -22 \quad \text{Apply the distributive property.}$$
$$x = 24 \quad \text{or} \quad x = -20$$

The solutions are 24 and -20. □

PRACTICE
3 Solve: $\left|\dfrac{x}{5} + 1\right| = 15$.

To apply the absolute value rule, first make sure that the absolute value expression is isolated.

▶ **Helpful Hint**

If the equation has a single absolute value expression containing variables, isolate the absolute value expression first.

EXAMPLE 4   Solve: $|2x| + 5 = 7$.

Solution   We want the absolute value expression alone on one side of the equation, so begin by subtracting 5 from both sides. Then apply the absolute value property.

$$|2x| + 5 = 7$$
$$|2x| = 2 \qquad \text{Subtract 5 from both sides.}$$
$$2x = 2 \quad \text{or} \quad 2x = -2$$
$$x = 1 \quad \text{or} \quad x = -1$$

The solutions are -1 and 1.   □

PRACTICE
4   Solve: $|3x| + 8 = 14$.

EXAMPLE 5   Solve: $|y| = 0$.

Solution   We are looking for all numbers whose distance from 0 is zero units. The only number is 0. The solution is 0.   □

PRACTICE
5   Solve: $|z| = 0$.

The next two examples illustrate a special case for absolute value equations. This special case occurs when an isolated absolute value is equal to a negative number.

EXAMPLE 6   Solve: $2|x| + 25 = 23$.

Solution   First, isolate the absolute value.

$$2|x| + 25 = 23$$
$$2|x| = -2 \quad \text{Subtract 25 from both sides.}$$
$$|x| = -1 \quad \text{Divide both sides by 2.}$$

The absolute value of a number is never negative, so this equation has no solution.   □

PRACTICE
6   Solve: $3|z| + 9 = 7$.

EXAMPLE 7   Solve: $\left|\dfrac{3x + 1}{2}\right| = -2$.

Solution   Again, the absolute value of any expression is never negative, so no solution exists. This equation has no solution.   □

PRACTICE
7   Solve: $\left|\dfrac{5x + 3}{4}\right| = -8$.

Given two absolute value expressions, we might ask, when are the absolute values of two expressions equal? To see the answer, notice that

$$|2| = |2|, \quad |-2| = |-2|, \quad |-2| = |2|, \quad \text{and} \quad |2| = |-2|$$

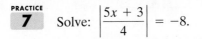
$$\underbrace{}_{\text{same}} \quad \underbrace{}_{\text{same}} \quad \underbrace{}_{\text{opposites}} \quad \underbrace{}_{\text{opposites}}$$

Two absolute value expressions are equal when the expressions inside the absolute value bars are equal to or are opposites of each other.

EXAMPLE 8   Solve: $|3x + 2| = |5x - 8|$.

Solution   This equation is true if the expressions inside the absolute value bars are equal to or are opposites of each other.

$$3x + 2 = 5x - 8 \quad \text{or} \quad 3x + 2 = -(5x - 8)$$

Next, solve each equation.

$$
\begin{aligned}
3x + 2 &= 5x - 8 \quad &\text{or} \quad 3x + 2 &= -5x + 8 \\
-2x + 2 &= -8 \quad &\text{or} \quad 8x + 2 &= 8 \\
-2x &= -10 \quad &\text{or} \quad 8x &= 6 \\
x &= 5 \quad &\text{or} \quad x &= \frac{3}{4}
\end{aligned}
$$

The solutions are $\frac{3}{4}$ and 5.

PRACTICE
8   Solve: $|2x + 4| = |3x - 1|$.

EXAMPLE 9   Solve: $|x - 3| = |5 - x|$.

Solution

$$
\begin{aligned}
x - 3 &= 5 - x \quad &\text{or} \quad x - 3 &= -(5 - x) \\
2x - 3 &= 5 \quad &\text{or} \quad x - 3 &= -5 + x \\
2x &= 8 \quad &\text{or} \quad x - 3 - x &= -5 + x - x \\
x &= 4 \quad &\text{or} \quad -3 &= -5 \quad \text{False}
\end{aligned}
$$

Recall from Section 2.1 that when an equation simplifies to a false statement, the equation has no solution. Thus, the only solution for the original absolute value equation is 4.

PRACTICE
9   Solve: $|x - 2| = |8 - x|$.

Concept Check ☑

True or false? Absolute value equations always have two solutions. Explain your answer.

The following box summarizes the methods shown for solving absolute value equations.

Absolute Value Equations

$|X| = a$ $\begin{cases} \text{If } a \text{ is positive, then solve } X = a \text{ or } X = -a. \\ \text{If } a \text{ is } 0, \text{ solve } X = 0. \\ \text{If } a \text{ is negative, the equation } |X| = a \text{ has no solution.} \end{cases}$

$|X| = |Y|$ Solve $X = Y$ or $X = -Y$.

Answer to Concept Check:
false; answers may vary

VOCABULARY & READINESS CHECK

Matching. *Match each absolute value equation with an equivalent statement.*

1. $|x - 2| = 5$

2. $|x - 2| = 0$

3. $|x - 2| = |x + 3|$

4. $|x + 3| = 5$

5. $|x + 3| = -5$

A. $x - 2 = 0$

B. $x - 2 = x + 3$ or $x - 2 = -(x + 3)$

C. $x - 2 = 5$ or $x - 2 = -5$

D. $\varnothing$

E. $x + 3 = 5$ or $x + 3 = -5$

4.3 | EXERCISE SET

Solve each absolute value equation. See Examples 1 through 7.

1. $|x| = 7$

2. $|y| = 15$

3. $|3x| = 12.6$

4. $|6n| = 12.6$

5. $|2x - 5| = 9$

6. $|6 + 2n| = 4$

7. $\left|\dfrac{x}{2} - 3\right| = 1$

8. $\left|\dfrac{n}{3} + 2\right| = 4$

9. $|z| + 4 = 9$

10. $|x| + 1 = 3$

11. $|3x| + 5 = 14$

12. $|2x| - 6 = 4$

13. $|2x| = 0$

14. $|7z| = 0$

15. $|4n + 1| + 10 = 4$

16. $|3z - 2| + 8 = 1$

17. $|5x - 1| = 0$

18. $|3y + 2| = 0$

19. Write an absolute value equation representing all numbers x whose distance from 0 is 5 units.

20. Write an absolute value equation representing all numbers x whose distance from 0 is 2 units.

Solve. See Examples 8 and 9.

21. $|5x - 7| = |3x + 11|$

22. $|9y + 1| = |6y + 4|$

23. $|z + 8| = |z - 3|$

24. $|2x - 5| = |2x + 5|$

25. Describe how solving an absolute value equation such as $|2x - 1| = 3$ is similar to solving an absolute value equation such as $|2x - 1| = |x - 5|$.

26. Describe how solving an absolute value equation such as $|2x - 1| = 3$ is different from solving an absolute value equation such as $|2x - 1| = |x - 5|$.

MIXED PRACTICE

Solve each absolute value equation. See Examples 1 through 9.

27. $|x| = 4$

28. $|x| = 1$

29. $|y| = 0$

30. $|y| = 8$

31. $|z| = -2$

32. $|y| = -9$

33. $|7 - 3x| = 7$

34. $|4m + 5| = 5$

35. $|6x| - 1 = 11$

36. $|7z| + 1 = 22$

37. $|4p| = -8$

38. $|5m| = -10$

39. $|x - 3| + 3 = 7$

40. $|x + 4| - 4 = 1$

41. $\left|\dfrac{z}{4} + 5\right| = -7$

42. $\left|\dfrac{c}{5} - 1\right| = -2$

43. $|9v - 3| = -8$

44. $|1 - 3b| = -7$

45. $|8n + 1| = 0$

46. $|5x - 2| = 0$

47. $|1 + 6c| - 7 = -3$

48. $|2 + 3m| - 9 = -7$

49. $|5x + 1| = 11$

50. $|8 - 6c| = 1$

51. $|4x - 2| = |-10|$

52. $|3x + 5| = |-4|$

53. $|5x + 1| = |4x - 7|$

54. $|3 + 6n| = |4n + 11|$

55. $|6 + 2x| = -|-7|$

56. $|4 - 5y| = -|-3|$

57. $|2x - 6| = |10 - 2x|$

58. $|4n + 5| = |4n + 3|$

59. $\left|\dfrac{2x - 5}{3}\right| = 7$

60. $\left|\dfrac{1 + 3n}{4}\right| = 4$

61. $2 + |5n| = 17$

62. $8 + |4m| = 24$

63. $\left|\dfrac{2x - 1}{3}\right| = |-5|$

64. $\left|\dfrac{5x + 2}{2}\right| = |-6|$

65. $|2y - 3| = |9 - 4y|$

66. $|5z - 1| = |7 - z|$

67. $\left|\dfrac{3n + 2}{8}\right| = |-1|$

68. $\left|\dfrac{2r - 6}{5}\right| = |-2|$

69. $|x + 4| = |7 - x|$

70. $|8 - y| = |y + 2|$

71. $\left|\dfrac{8c - 7}{3}\right| = -|-5|$

72. $\left|\dfrac{5d + 1}{6}\right| = -|-9|$

73. Explain why some absolute value equations have two solutions.

74. Explain why some absolute value equations have one solution.

REVIEW AND PREVIEW

Read a Graph. *The circle graph shows the U.S. Cheese consumption for 2005. Use this graph to answer Exercises 75–77. See Section 2.7.* (*Source:* National Agriculture Statistics Service, USDA)

U.S. Cheese Consumption

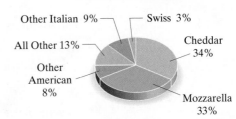

Other Italian 9%   Swiss 3%
All Other 13%   Cheddar 34%
Other American 8%   Mozzarella 33%

75. What percent of cheese consumption came from chedder cheese?

76. A circle contains 360°. Find the number of degrees in the 3% sector for swiss cheese.

77. If a family consumed 120 pounds of cheese in 2005, find the amount of mozzarella we might expect they consumed.

List five integer solutions of each inequality. See Section 1.2.

78. $|x| \leq 3$

79. $|x| \geq -2$

80. $|y| > -10$

81. $|y| < 0$

CONCEPT EXTENSIONS

82. Write an absolute value equation representing all numbers x whose distance from 1 is 5 units.

83. Write an absolute value equation representing all numbers x whose distance from 7 is 2 units.

Write each as an equivalent absolute value.

84. $x = 6$ or $x = -6$

85. $2x - 1 = 4$ or $2x - 1 = -4$

86. $x - 2 = 3x - 4$ or $x - 2 = -(3x - 4)$

87. For what value(s) of c will an absolute value equation of the form $|ax + b| = c$ have

  a. one solution?

  b. no solution?

  c. two solutions?

4.4 ABSOLUTE VALUE INEQUALITIES

OBJECTIVE 1 ▶ Solving absolute value inequalities of the form $|x| < a$. The solution set of an absolute value inequality such as $|x| < 2$ contains all numbers whose distance from 0 is less than 2 units, as shown below.

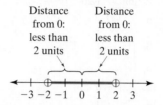

The solutions are $-2 < x < 2$.

EXAMPLE 1 Solve: $|x| \le 3$.

Solution The solution set of this inequality contains all numbers whose distance from 0 is less than or equal to 3. Thus 3, -3, and all numbers between 3 and -3 are in the solution set.

The solutions are $-3 \le x \le 3$. □

PRACTICE
1 Solve: $|x| < 2$ and graph the solutions.

In general, we have the following.

Solving Absolute Value Inequalities of the Form $|X| < a$
If a is a positive number, then $|X| < a$ is equivalent to $-a < X < a$.

This property also holds true for the inequality symbol $\le$.

EXAMPLE 2 Solve for m: $|m - 6| < 2$.

Solution Replace X with $m - 6$ and a with 2 in the preceding property, and we see that

$$|m - 6| < 2 \quad \text{is equivalent to} \quad -2 < m - 6 < 2$$

Solve this compound inequality for m by adding 6 to all three parts.

$$-2 < m - 6 < 2$$
$$-2 + 6 < m - 6 + 6 < 2 + 6 \quad \text{Add 6 to all three parts.}$$
$$4 < m < 8 \quad \text{Simplify.}$$

The graph is shown.

□

PRACTICE
2 Solve for b: $|b + 1| < 3$. Graph the solutions.

> ▶ Helpful Hint
> Before using an absolute value inequality property, isolate the absolute value expression on one side of the inequality.

EXAMPLE 3   Solve for x: $|5x + 1| + 1 \le 10$.

Solution   First, isolate the absolute value expression by subtracting 1 from both sides.

$$|5x + 1| + 1 \le 10$$

$$|5x + 1| \le 10 - 1 \quad \text{Subtract 1 from both sides.}$$

$$|5x + 1| \le 9 \quad\quad\quad \text{Simplify.}$$

Since 9 is positive, we apply the absolute value property for $|X| \le a$.

$$-9 \le 5x + 1 \le 9$$

$$-9 - 1 \le 5x + 1 - 1 \le 9 - 1 \quad \text{Subtract 1 from all three parts.}$$

$$-10 \le 5x \le 8 \quad\quad\quad\quad\quad \text{Simplify.}$$

$$-2 \le x \le \frac{8}{5} \quad\quad\quad\quad\quad \text{Divide all three parts by 5.}$$

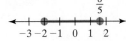

The solutions are $-2, \dfrac{8}{5}$, and all numbers between these two. The graph is shown above.   □

PRACTICE
3   Solve for x: $|3x - 2| + 5 \le 9$. Graph the solutions.

EXAMPLE 4   Solve for x: $\left|2x - \dfrac{1}{10}\right| < -13$.

Solution   The absolute value of a number is always nonnegative and can never be less than -13. Thus, this absolute value inequality has no solution.   □

PRACTICE
4   Solve for x: $\left|3x + \dfrac{5}{8}\right| < -4$.

OBJECTIVE 2 ▶ Solving absolute value inequalities of the form $|x| > a$. Let us now solve an absolute value inequality of the form $|X| > a$, such as $|x| \ge 3$. The solution set contains all numbers whose distance from 0 is 3 or more units. Thus the graph of the solution set contains 3 and all points to the right of 3 on the number line or -3 and all points to the left of -3 on the number line.

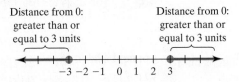

The solutions are $x \leq -3$ or $x \geq 3$. In general, we have the following.

> **Solving Absolute Value Inequalities of the Form $|X| > a$**
>
> If a is a positive number, then $|X| > a$ is equivalent to $X < -a$ or $X > a$.

This property also holds true for the inequality symbol $\geq$.

EXAMPLE 5 Solve for y: $|y - 3| > 7$.

Solution Since 7 is positive, we apply the property for $|X| > a$.

$$|y - 3| > 7 \text{ is equivalent to } y - 3 < -7 \text{ or } y - 3 > 7$$

Next, solve the compound inequality.

$$
\begin{array}{llll}
y - 3 < -7 & \text{or} & y - 3 > 7 & \\
y - 3 + 3 < -7 + 3 & \text{or} & y - 3 + 3 > 7 + 3 & \text{Add 3 to both sides.} \\
y < -4 & \text{or} & y > 10 & \text{Simplify.}
\end{array}
$$

The solutions are all numbers x such that $y < -4$ or $y > 10$. The graph is shown.

$$-6\ -4\ -2\ \ 0\ \ 2\ \ 4\ \ 6\ \ 8\ \ 10\ \ 12$$

□

PRACTICE
5 Solve for y: $|y + 4| \geq 6$.

Examples 6 and 8 illustrate special cases of absolute value inequalities. These special cases occur when an isolated absolute value expression is less than, less than or equal to, greater than, or greater than or equal to a negative number or 0.

EXAMPLE 6 Solve: $|2x + 9| + 5 > 3$.

Solution First isolate the absolute value expression by subtracting 5 from both sides.

$$
\begin{array}{ll}
|2x + 9| + 5 > 3 & \\
|2x + 9| + 5 - 5 > 3 - 5 & \text{Subtract 5 from both sides.} \\
|2x + 9| > -2 & \text{Simplify.}
\end{array}
$$

The absolute value of any number is always nonnegative and thus is always greater than -2. This inequality and the original inequality are true for all values of x. The solutions are all real numbers. The graph is shown.

$$-3\ -2\ -1\ \ 0\ \ 1\ \ 2\ \ 3\ \ 4$$

□

PRACTICE
6 Solve: $|4x + 3| + 5 > 3$. Graph the solutions.

Concept Check ☑

Without taking any solution steps, how do you know that the absolute value inequality $|3x - 2| > -9$ has a solution? What is its solution?

EXAMPLE 7   Solve: $\left|\dfrac{x}{3} - 1\right| - 7 \geq -5$.

Solution   First, isolate the absolute value expression by adding 7 to both sides.

$$\left|\frac{x}{3} - 1\right| - 7 \geq -5$$

$$\left|\frac{x}{3} - 1\right| - 7 + 7 \geq -5 + 7 \quad \text{Add 7 to both sides.}$$

$$\left|\frac{x}{3} - 1\right| \geq 2 \qquad \text{Simplify.}$$

Next, write the absolute value inequality as an equivalent compound inequality and solve.

$$\frac{x}{3} - 1 \leq -2 \qquad \text{or} \qquad \frac{x}{3} - 1 \geq 2$$

$$3\left(\frac{x}{3} - 1\right) \leq 3\,(-2) \qquad \text{or} \qquad 3\left(\frac{x}{3} - 1\right) \geq 3(2) \quad \text{Clear the inequalities of fractions.}$$

$$x - 3 \leq -6 \qquad \text{or} \qquad x - 3 \geq 6 \qquad \text{Apply the distributive property.}$$

$$x \leq -3 \qquad \text{or} \qquad x \geq 9 \qquad \text{Add 3 to both sides.}$$

The solutions are $x \leq -3$ or $x \geq 9$, and the graph is shown.

PRACTICE
7   Solve: $\left|\dfrac{x}{2} - 3\right| - 5 > -2$. Graph the solutions.

EXAMPLE 8   Solve for x: $\left|\dfrac{2(x + 1)}{3}\right| \leq 0$.

Solution   Recall that "$\leq$" means "less than or equal to." The absolute value of any expression will never be less than 0, but it may be equal to 0. Thus, to solve $\left|\dfrac{2(x + 1)}{3}\right| \leq 0$ we solve $\left|\dfrac{2(x + 1)}{3}\right| = 0$

$$\frac{2(x + 1)}{3} = 0$$

$$3\left[\frac{2(x + 1)}{3}\right] = 3(0) \quad \text{Clear the equation of fractions.}$$

$$2x + 2 = 0 \qquad \text{Apply the distributive property.}$$

$$2x = -2 \qquad \text{Subtract 2 from both sides.}$$

$$x = -1 \qquad \text{Divide both sides by 2.}$$

The solutions is -1.

PRACTICE
8   Solve for x: $\left|\dfrac{3(x - 2)}{5}\right| \leq 0$.

The following box summarizes the types of absolute value equations and inequalities.

Solving Absolute Value Equations and Inequalities with $a > 0$

Algebraic Solution	Solution Graph
$|X| = a$ is equivalent to $X = a$ or $X = -a$.	
$|X| < a$ is equivalent to $-a < X < a$.	
$|X| > a$ is equivalent to $X < -a$ or $X > a$.	

VOCABULARY & READINESS CHECK

Matching. *Match each absolute value statement with an equivalent statement.*

1. $|2x + 1| = 3$

2. $|2x + 1| \le 3$

3. $|2x + 1| < 3$

4. $|2x + 1| \ge 3$

5. $|2x + 1| > 3$

A. $2x + 1 > 3$ or $2x + 1 < -3$

B. $2x + 1 \ge 3$ or $2x + 1 \le -3$

C. $-3 < 2x + 1 < 3$

D. $2x + 1 = 3$ or $2x + 1 = -3$

E. $-3 \le 2x + 1 \le 3$

4.4 | EXERCISE SET

Solve each inequality. Then graph the solutions. See Examples 1 through 4.

1. $|x| \le 4$

2. $|x| < 6$

3. $|x - 3| < 2$

4. $|y - 7| \le 5$

5. $|x + 3| < 2$

6. $|x + 4| < 6$

7. $|2x + 7| \le 13$

8. $|5x - 3| \le 18$

9. $|x| + 7 \le 12$

10. $|x| + 6 \le 7$

11. $|3x - 1| < -5$

12. $|8x - 3| < -2$

13. $|x - 6| - 7 \le -1$

14. $|z + 2| - 7 < -3$

Solve each inequality. Graph the solutions. See Examples 5 through 7.

15. $|x| > 3$

16. $|y| \ge 4$

17. $|x + 10| \ge 14$

18. $|x - 9| \ge 2$

19. $|x| + 2 > 6$

20. $|x| - 1 > 3$

21. $|5x| > -4$

22. $|4x - 11| > -1$

23. $|6x - 8| + 3 > 7$

24. $|10 + 3x| + 1 > 2$

Solve each inequality. Graph the solutions. See Example 8.

25. $|x| \le 0$

26. $|x| \ge 0$

27. $|8x + 3| > 0$

28. $|5x - 6| < 0$

MIXED PRACTICE

Solve each inequality. Graph the solutions. See Examples 1 through 8.

29. $|x| \le 2$

30. $|z| < 8$

31. $|y| > 1$

32. $|x| \ge 10$

33. $|x - 3| < 8$

34. $|-3 + x| \le 10$

35. $|0.6x - 3| > 0.6$

36. $|1 + 0.3x| \ge 0.1$

37. $5 + |x| \le 2$

38. $8 + |x| < 1$

39. $|x| > -4$

40. $|x| \le -7$

41. $|2x - 7| \le 11$

42. $|5x + 2| < 8$

43. $|x + 5| + 2 \ge 8$

44. $|-1 + x| - 6 > 2$

45. $|x| > 0$

46. $|x| < 0$

47. $9 + |x| > 7$

48. $5 + |x| \ge 4$

49. $6 + |4x - 1| \le 9$

50. $-3 + |5x - 2| \le 4$

51. $\left|\frac{2}{3}x + 1\right| > 1$

52. $\left|\frac{3}{4}x - 1\right| \ge 2$

53. $|5x + 3| < -6$

54. $|4 + 9x| \ge -6$

55. $\left|\frac{8x - 3}{4}\right| \le 0$

56. $\left|\frac{5x + 6}{2}\right| \le 0$

57. $|1 + 3x| + 4 < 5$

58. $|7x - 3| - 1 \le 10$

59. $\left|\frac{x + 6}{3}\right| > 2$

60. $\left|\frac{7 + x}{2}\right| \ge 4$

61. $-15 + |2x - 7| \le -6$

62. $-9 + |3 + 4x| < -4$

63. $\left|2x + \dfrac{3}{4}\right| - 7 \le -2$

64. $\left|\dfrac{3}{5} + 4x\right| - 6 < -1$

MIXED PRACTICE

Solve each equation or inequality for x. (Sections 4.3, 4.4)

65. $|2x - 3| < 7$

66. $|2x - 3| > 7$

67. $|2x - 3| = 7$

68. $|5 - 6x| = 29$

69. $|x - 5| \ge 12$

70. $|x + 4| \ge 20$

71. $|9 + 4x| = 0$

72. $|9 + 4x| \ge 0$

73. $|2x + 1| + 4 < 7$

74. $8 + |5x - 3| \ge 11$

75. $|3x - 5| + 4 = 5$

76. $|5x - 3| + 2 = 4$

77. $|x + 11| = -1$

78. $|4x - 4| = -3$

79. $\left|\dfrac{2x - 1}{3}\right| = 6$

80. $\left|\dfrac{6 - x}{4}\right| = 5$

81. $\left|\dfrac{3x - 5}{6}\right| > 5$

82. $\left|\dfrac{4x - 7}{5}\right| < 2$

REVIEW AND PREVIEW

Recall the formula:

$$\text{Probability of an event} = \dfrac{\text{number of ways that the event can occur}}{\text{number of possible outcomes}}$$

Find the probability of rolling each number on a single toss of a die. (Recall that a die is a cube with each of its six sides containing 1, 2, 3, 4, 5, and 6 black dots, respectively.) See Chapter 1 Extension.

83. $P(\text{rolling a } 2)$

84. $P(\text{rolling a } 5)$

85. $P(\text{rolling a } 7)$

86. $P(\text{rolling a } 0)$

87. $P(\text{rolling a 1 or 3})$

88. $P(\text{rolling a 1, 2, 3, 4, 5, or 6})$

Consider the equation $3x - 4y = 12$. For each value of x or y given, find the corresponding value of the other variable that makes the statement true. See Section 3.1.

89. If $x = 2$, find y

90. If $y = -1$, find x

91. If $y = -3$, find x

92. If $x = 4$, find y

CONCEPT EXTENSIONS

93. Write an absolute value inequality representing all numbers x whose distance from 0 is less than 7 units.

94. Write an absolute value inequality representing all numbers x whose distance from 0 is greater than 4 units.

95. Write $-5 \le x \le 5$ as an equivalent inequality containing an absolute value.

96. Write $x > 1$ or $x < -1$ as an equivalent inequality containing an absolute value.

97. Describe how solving $|x - 3| = 5$ is different from solving $|x - 3| < 5$.

98. Describe how solving $|x + 4| = 0$ is similar to solving $|x + 4| \le 0$.

The expression $|x_T - x|$ is defined to be the absolute error in x, where x_T is the true value of a quantity and x is the measured value or value as stored in a computer.

99. If the true value of a quantity is 3.5 and the absolute error must be less than 0.05, find the acceptable measured values.

100. If the true value of a quantity is 0.2 and the approximate value stored in a computer is $\dfrac{51}{256}$, find the absolute error.

4.5 GRAPHING LINEAR INEQUALITIES

OBJECTIVE

1 Graph a linear inequality in two variables.

Recall that a linear equation in two variables is an equation that can be written in the form $Ax + By = C$ where A, B, and C are real numbers and A and B are not both 0. The definition of a linear inequality is the same except that the equal sign is replaced with an inequality sign.

A **linear inequality in two variables** is an inequality that can be written in one of the forms:

$$Ax + By < C \qquad Ax + By \le C$$
$$Ax + By > C \qquad Ax + By \ge C$$

where A, B, and C are real numbers and A and B are not both 0. Just as for linear equations in x and y, an ordered pair is a **solution** of an inequality in x and y if replacing the variables by coordinates of the ordered pair results in a true statement.

OBJECTIVE 1 ▶ Graphing linear inequalities in two variables. The linear equation $x - y = 1$ is graphed next. Recall that all points on the line correspond to ordered pairs that satisfy the equation $x - y = 1$.

Notice the line defined by $x - y = 1$ divides the rectangular coordinate system plane into 2 sides. All points on one side of the line satisfy the inequality $x - y < 1$ and all points on the other side satisfy the inequality $x - y > 1$. The graph below shows a few examples of this.

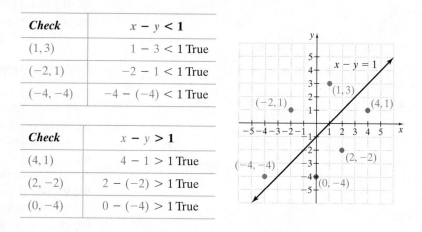

Check	$x - y < 1$
$(1, 3)$	$1 - 3 < 1$ True
$(-2, 1)$	$-2 - 1 < 1$ True
$(-4, -4)$	$-4 - (-4) < 1$ True

Check	$x - y > 1$
$(4, 1)$	$4 - 1 > 1$ True
$(2, -2)$	$2 - (-2) > 1$ True
$(0, -4)$	$0 - (-4) > 1$ True

The graph of $x - y < 1$ is the region shaded blue and the graph of $x - y > 1$ is the region shaded red below.

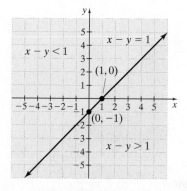

The region to the left of the line and the region to the right of the line are called **half-planes.** Every line divides the plane (similar to a sheet of paper extending indefinitely in all directions) into two half-planes; the line is called the **boundary.**

Recall that the inequality $x - y \le 1$ means

$$x - y = 1 \quad \text{or} \quad x - y < 1$$

Thus, the graph of $x - y \le 1$ is the half-plane $x - y < 1$ along with the boundary line $x - y = 1$.

> **Graphing a Linear Inequality in Two Variables**
>
> **STEP 1.** Graph the boundary line found by replacing the inequality sign with an equal sign. If the inequality sign is $>$ or $<$, graph a dashed boundary line (indicating that the points on the line are not solutions of the inequality). If the inequality sign is $\geq$ or $\leq$, graph a solid boundary line (indicating that the points on the line are solutions of the inequality).
>
> **STEP 2.** Choose a point, *not* on the boundary line, as a test point. Substitute the coordinates of this test point into the *original* inequality.
>
> **STEP 3.** If a true statement is obtained in Step 2, shade the half-plane that contains the test point. If a false statement is obtained, shade the half-plane that does not contain the test point.

EXAMPLE 1   Graph: $x + y < 7$

Solution

STEP 1. First we graph the boundary line by graphing the equation $x + y = 7$. We graph this boundary as a dashed line because the inequality sign is $<$, and thus the points on the line are not solutions of the inequality $x + y < 7$.

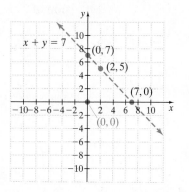

STEP 2. Next, choose a test point, being careful not to choose a point on the boundary line. We choose $(0, 0)$. Substitute the coordinates of $(0, 0)$ into $x + y < 7$.

$$x + y < 7 \quad \text{Original inequality}$$
$$0 + 0 \overset{?}{<} 7 \quad \text{Replace } x \text{ with } 0 \text{ and } y \text{ with } 0.$$
$$0 < 7 \quad \text{True}$$

STEP 3. Since the result is a true statement, $(0, 0)$ is a solution of $x + y < 7$, and every point in the same half-plane as $(0, 0)$ is also a solution. To indicate this, shade the entire half-plane containing $(0, 0)$, as shown.

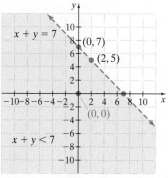

PRACTICE

1   Graph: $x + y > 5$

Concept Check

Determine whether $(0, 0)$ is included in the graph of

a. $y \geq 2x + 3$ **b.** $x < 7$ **c.** $2x - 3y < 6$

EXAMPLE 2   Graph: $2x - y \geq 3$

Solution

STEP 1. We graph the boundary line by graphing $2x - y = 3$. We draw this line as a solid line because the inequality sign is $\geq$, and thus the points on the line are solutions of $2x - y \geq 3$.

STEP 2. Once again, $(0, 0)$ is a convenient test point since it is not on the boundary line. We substitute 0 for x and 0 for y into the original inequality.

$$2x - y \geq 3$$
$$2(0) - 0 \geq 3 \quad \text{Let } x = 0 \text{ and } y = 0.$$
$$0 \geq 3 \quad \text{False}$$

STEP 3. Since the statement is false, no point in the half-plane containing $(0, 0)$ is a solution. Therefore, we shade the half-plane that does not contain $(0, 0)$. Every point in the shaded half-plane and every point on the boundary line is a solution of $2x - y \geq 3$.

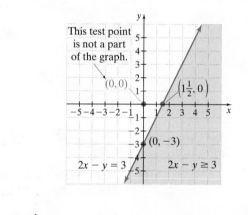

PRACTICE

2   Graph: $3x - y \geq 4$

> ▶ **Helpful Hint**
>
> When graphing an inequality, make sure the test point is substituted into the **original inequality.** For Example 2, we substituted the test point $(0, 0)$ into the **original inequality** $2x - y \geq 3$, *not* $2x - y = 3$.

EXAMPLE 3   Graph: $x > 2y$

Solution

STEP 1. We find the boundary line by graphing $x = 2y$. The boundary line is a dashed line since the inequality symbol is $>$.

STEP 2. We cannot use $(0, 0)$ as a test point because it is a point on the boundary line. We choose instead $(0, 2)$.

$$x > 2y$$
$$0 > 2(2) \quad \text{Let } x = 0 \text{ and } y = 2.$$
$$0 > 4 \quad \text{False}$$

Answers to Concept Check:

a. no   **b.** yes   **c.** yes

STEP 3. Since the statement is false, we shade the half-plane that does not contain the test point $(0, 2)$, as shown.

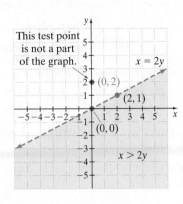

PRACTICE
3 Graph: $x > 3y$

EXAMPLE 4 Graph: $5x + 4y \leq 20$

Solution We graph the solid boundary line $5x + 4y = 20$ and choose $(0, 0)$ as the test point.

$$5x + 4y \leq 20$$
$$5(0) + 4(0) \overset{?}{\leq} 20 \quad \text{Let } x = 0 \text{ and } y = 0.$$
$$0 \leq 20 \quad \text{True}$$

We shade the half-plane that contains $(0, 0)$, as shown.

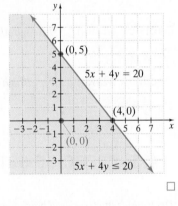

PRACTICE
4 Graph: $3x + 4y \geq 12$

EXAMPLE 5 Graph: $y > 3$

Solution We graph the dashed boundary line $y = 3$ and choose $(0, 0)$ as the test point. (Recall that the graph of $y = 3$ is a horizontal line with y-intercept 3.)

$$y > 3$$
$$0 \overset{?}{>} 3 \quad \text{Let } y = 0.$$
$$0 > 3 \quad \text{False}$$

We shade the half-plane that does not contain $(0, 0)$, as shown.

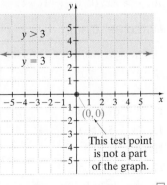

PRACTICE
5 Graph: $x > 3$

VOCABULARY & READINESS CHECK

Word Bank. *Use the choices below to fill in each blank. Some choices may be used more than once, and some not at all.*

true	$x < 3$	$y < 3$	half-planes	yes
false	$x \leq 3$	$y \leq 3$	linear inequality in two variables	no

1. The statement $5x - 6y < 7$ is an example of a(n) _____.
2. A boundary line divides a plane into two regions called _____.
3. True or false: The graph of $5x - 6y < 7$ includes its corresponding boundary line. _____
4. True or false: When graphing a linear inequality, to determine which side of the boundary line to shade, choose a point *not* on the boundary line. _____
5. True or false: The boundary line for the inequality $5x - 6y < 7$ is the graph of $5x - 6y = 7$. _____
6. The graph of _____ is

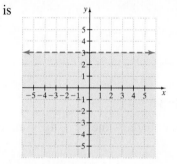

Decision Making. *State whether the graph of each inequality includes its corresponding boundary line.*

7. $y \geq x + 4$ 8. $x - y > -7$ 9. $y \geq x$ 10. $x > 0$

Decision Making. *Decide whether (0, 0) is a solution of each given inequality.*

11. $x + y > -5$ 12. $2x + 3y < 10$ 13. $x - y \leq -1$ 14. $\frac{2}{3}x + \frac{5}{6}y > 4$

4.5 EXERCISE SET

Determine which ordered pairs given are solutions of the linear inequality in two variables. See Example 1.

1. $x - y > 3$; $(2, -1), (5, 1)$
2. $y - x < -2$; $(2, 1), (5, -1)$
3. $3x - 5y \leq -4$; $(-1, -1), (4, 0)$
4. $2x + y \geq 10$; $(-1, -4), (5, 0)$
5. $x < -y$; $(0, 2), (-5, 1)$
6. $y > 3x$; $(0, 0), (-1, -4)$

MIXED PRACTICE

Graph each inequality. See Examples 2 through 5.

7. $x + y \leq 1$ 8. $x + y \geq -2$
9. $2x + y > -4$ 10. $x + 3y \leq 3$
11. $x + 6y \leq -6$ 12. $7x + y > -14$
13. $2x + 5y > -10$ 14. $5x + 2y \leq 10$
15. $x + 2y \leq 3$ 16. $2x + 3y > -5$
17. $2x + 7y > 5$ 18. $3x + 5y \leq -2$
19. $x - 2y \geq 3$ 20. $4x + y \leq 2$
21. $5x + y < 3$ 22. $x + 2y > -7$
23. $4x + y < 8$ 24. $9x + 2y \geq -9$

25. $y \geq 2x$ 26. $x < 5y$ 27. $x \geq 0$
28. $y \leq 0$ 29. $y \leq -3$ 30. $x > -\frac{2}{3}$
31. $2x - 7y > 0$ 32. $5x + 2y \leq 0$ 33. $3x - 7y \geq 0$
34. $-2x - 9y > 0$ 35. $x > y$ 36. $x \leq -y$
37. $x - y \leq 6$ 38. $x - y > 10$ 39. $-\frac{1}{4}y + \frac{1}{3}x > 1$
40. $\frac{1}{2}x - \frac{1}{3}y \leq -1$ 41. $-x < 0.4y$ 42. $0.3x \geq 0.1y$

Matching. *In Exercises 43 through 48, match each inequality with its graph.*

a. $x > 2$ b. $y < 2$ c. $y < 2x$
d. $y \leq -3x$ e. $2x + 3y < 6$ f. $3x + 2y > 6$

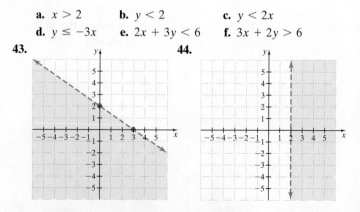

43.

44.

45.

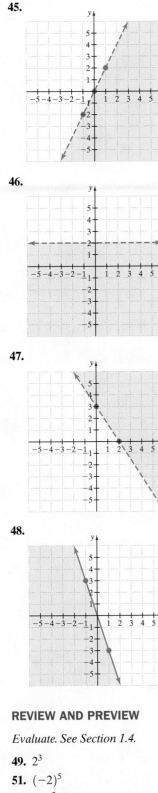

46.

47.

48.

REVIEW AND PREVIEW

Evaluate. See Section 1.4.

49. 2^3 **50.** 3^4

51. $(-2)^5$ **52.** -2^5

53. $3 \cdot 4^2$ **54.** $4 \cdot 3^3$

Evaluate each expression for the given replacement value. See Section 1.4.

55. x^2 if x is -5 **56.** x^3 if x is -5

57. $2x^3$ if x is -1 **58.** $3x^2$ if x is -1

CONCEPT EXTENSIONS

Decision Making. *For Exercises 59–62, determine whether* $(1, 1)$ *is included in each graph. See the Concept Check in this section.*

59. $3x + 4y < 8$ **60.** $y > 5x$

61. $y \geq -\dfrac{1}{2}x$ **62.** $x > 3$

63. Write an inequality whose solutions are all pairs of numbers x and y whose sum is at least 13. Graph the inequality.

64. Write an inequality whose solutions are all the pairs of numbers x and y whose sum is at most -4. Graph the inequality.

65. Explain why a point on the boundary line should not be chosen as the test point.

66. Describe the graph of a linear inequality.

67. The price for a taxi cab in a small city is \$2.50 per mile, x, while traveling, and \$.25 every minute, y, while waiting. If you have \$20 to spend on a cab ride, the inequality

$$2.5x + 0.25y \leq 20$$

represents your situation. Graph this inequality in the first quadrant only.

68. A word processor charges \$22 per hour, x, for typing a first draft, and \$15 per hour, y, for making changes and typing a second draft. If you need a document typed and have \$100, the inequality

$$22x + 15y \leq 100$$

represents your situation. Graph the inequality in the first quadrant only.

69. In Exercises 67 and 68, why were you instructed to graph each inequality in the first quadrant only?

70. **Multiple Steps.** Scott Sambracci and Sara Thygeson are planning their wedding. They have calculated that they want the cost of their wedding ceremony x plus the cost of their reception y to be no more than \$5000.

   a. Write an inequality describing this relationship.

   b. Graph this inequality.

   c. Why should we be interested in only quadrant I of this graph?

71. **Multiple Steps.** It's the end of the budgeting period for Dennis Fernandes and he has \$500 left in his budget for car rental expenses. He plans to spend this budget on a sales trip throughout southern Texas. He will rent a car that costs \$30 per day and \$0.15 per mile and he can spend no more than \$500.

   a. Write an inequality describing this situation. Let $x =$ number of days and let $y =$ number of miles.

   b. Graph this inequality.

   c. Why should we be interested in only quadrant I of this graph?

CHAPTER 4 VOCABULARY CHECK

Fill in each blank with one of the words or phrases listed below.

linear inequality in one variable	compound inequality
absolute value	union
linear equation in one variable	intersection

1. The statement "$x < 5$ or $x > 7$" is called a(n) _____ .
2. The _____ of two sets is the set of all elements common to both sets.
3. The _____ of two sets is the set of all elements that belong to either of the sets.
4. A number's distance from 0 is called its _____ .
5. The statement $5x - 0.2 < 7$ is an example of a(n) _____ .
6. The statement $5x - 0.2 = 7$ is an example of a(n) _____ .

CHAPTER 4 REVIEW

(4.1) Solve and graph the solutions of each of the following inequalities.

1. $x > 0$

2. $x \le -2$

3. $-3x > 12$

4. $-2x \ge -20$

5. $x + 4 \ge 6x - 16$

6. $5x - 7 > 8x + 5$

7. $4(2x - 5) \le 5x - 1$

8. $-2(x - 5) > 2(3x - 2)$

9. Tina earns \$175 per week plus a 5% commission on all her sales. Find the minimum amount of sales to ensure that she earns at least \$300 per week.

10. Ellen Catarella shot rounds of 76, 82, and 79 golfing. What must she shoot on her next round so that her average will be below 80?

(4.2) Solve each inequality.

11. $1 \le 4x - 7 \le 3$

12. $-2 \le 8 + 5x < -1$

13. $-3 < 4(2x - 1) < 12$

14. $-6 < x - (3 - 4x) < -3$

15. $\dfrac{1}{6} < \dfrac{4x - 3}{3} \le \dfrac{4}{5}$

16. $x \le 2$ and $x > -5$

17. $3x - 5 > 6$ or $-x < -5$

(4.3) Solve each absolute value equation.

18. $|x - 7| = 9$

19. $|8 - x| = 3$

20. $|2x + 9| = 9$

21. $|-3x + 4| = 7$

22. $|3x - 2| + 6 = 10$

23. $5 + |6x + 1| = 5$

24. $-5 = |4x - 3|$

25. $|5 - 6x| + 8 = 3$

26. $-8 = |x - 3| - 10$

27. $\left| \dfrac{3x - 7}{4} \right| = 2$

28. $|6x + 1| = |15 + 4x|$

(4.4) Solve each absolute value inequality. Graph the solutions.

29. $|5x - 1| < 9$

30. $|6 + 4x| \ge 10$

31. $|3x| - 8 > 1$

32. $9 + |5x| < 24$

33. $|6x - 5| \le -1$

34. $\left| 3x + \dfrac{2}{5} \right| \ge 4$

35. $\left| \dfrac{x}{3} + 6 \right| - 8 > -5$

36. $\left| \dfrac{4(x - 1)}{7} \right| + 10 < 2$

(4.5) Graph each inequality.

37. $5x + 4y < 20$

38. $x + 3y > 4$

39. $y \ge -7$

40. $y \le -4$

41. $-x \le y$

42. $x \ge -y$

MIXED REVIEW

Solve each inequality. Graph the solutions.

43. $4x - 7 > 3x + 2$

44. $-5x < 20$

45. $-3(1 + 2x) + x \geq -(3 - x)$

Solve.

46. $0 \leq \dfrac{2(3x + 4)}{5} \leq 3$

47. $x \leq 2$ or $x > -5$

48. $-2x \leq 6$ and $-2x + 3 < -7$

49. $|7x| - 26 = -5$

50. $\left| \dfrac{9 - 2x}{5} \right| = -3$

51. $|x - 3| = |7 + 2x|$

52. $|6x - 5| \geq -1$

53. $\left| \dfrac{4x - 3}{5} \right| < 1$

Graph each inequality.

54. $x + y > -2$　　　　**55.** $x + 6y < 6$

CHAPTER 4 TEST TEST PREP VIDEO

The fully worked-out solutions to any exercises you want to review are available in MyMathLab.

Solve and graph each of the following inequalities.

1. $3x - 5 \geq 7x + 3$

2. $x + 6 > 4x - 6$

3. $\dfrac{2(5x + 1)}{3} > 2$

Solve each equation or inequality.

4. $|6x - 5| - 3 = -2$

5. $|8 - 2t| = -6$

6. $|2x - 3| = |4x + 5|$

7. $|x - 5| = |x + 2|$

8. $|3x + 1| > 5$

9. $|x - 5| - .4 < -2$

10. $x \geq 5$ and $x \geq 4$

11. $x \geq 5$ or $x \geq 4$

12. $-1 \leq \dfrac{2x - 5}{3} < 2$

13. $6x + 1 > 5x + 4$ or $1 - x > -4$

Graph each inequality.

14. $x - y \geq -2$

15. $y > -4x$

16. $2x - 3y > -6$

CHAPTER 4 STANDARDIZED TEST

Multiple Choice. *Choose the one alternative that best completes the statement or answers the question.*

Solve the equation.

1. $|8x + 6| + 9 = 14$

　　a. $\dfrac{1}{8}, \dfrac{11}{8}$　　　**b.** $-\dfrac{1}{8}, -\dfrac{11}{8}$

　　c. no solution　**d.** $-\dfrac{1}{6}, -\dfrac{11}{6}$

2. $|8x + 3| + 14 = 8$

　　a. $\dfrac{3}{8}, -\dfrac{9}{8}$　　**b.** $-\dfrac{3}{8}, \dfrac{9}{8}$　　**c.** $1, -3$　　**d.** no solution

3. $|-7x + 8| = |7 - 5x|$

　　a. $\dfrac{1}{2}, -\dfrac{5}{4}$　　**b.** $\dfrac{1}{2}$　　　**c.** $\dfrac{1}{2}, \dfrac{5}{4}$　　**d.** no solution

4. $|x + 2| = |4 - x|$

　　a. no solution　　**b.** 1　　**c.** -1　　**d.** 2

Solve the inequality.

5. $3x - 5 \geq 2x - 2$

　　a. $x > -7$　　**b.** $x \leq 3$　　**c.** $x \geq 3$　　**d.** $x > 3$

6. $x + 4 > 9x - 4$

　　a. $x > -1$　　**b.** $x < 1$　　**c.** $x > 1$　　**d.** $x < -1$

Solve the inequality and graph the solutions.

7. $-1 < 2x + 1 < 10$

a. $-1 < x < \dfrac{9}{2}$

b. $-\dfrac{9}{2} < x < 1$

c. $x < \dfrac{9}{2}$

d. $x > -1$

8. $\dfrac{3(2x + 1)}{5} > 3$

a. $x > -2$

b. $x < 2$

c. $x < -2$

d. $x > 2$

Solve the inequality.

9. $|2k + 3| \geq 2$

a. $k \leq -\dfrac{5}{2}$ or $k \geq -\dfrac{1}{2}$

b. $-\dfrac{5}{2} < k < -\dfrac{1}{2}$

c. $k \geq -\dfrac{1}{2}$

d. $-\dfrac{5}{2} \leq k \leq -\dfrac{1}{2}$

10. $|x - 8| + 5 \leq 14$

a. $-1 < x < 17$ **b.** $-1 \leq x \leq 14$

c. no solution   **d.** $-1 \leq x \leq 17$

11. $x \leq 2$ and $x \leq -3$

a. $-3 \leq x \leq 2$ **b.** $x \geq -3$

c. $x \leq -3$ or $x \geq 2$ **d.** $x \leq -3$

12. $x < 3$ or $x < 8$

a. $x < 8$ **b.** $x > 3$

c. $3 < x < 8$ **d.** $x < 3$ or $x > 8$

13. $0 \leq \dfrac{2x + 3}{2} < 3$

a. $-\dfrac{3}{2} < x < \dfrac{3}{2}$ **b.** $-\dfrac{3}{2} \leq x < \dfrac{3}{2}$

c. $-\dfrac{3}{2} < x \leq \dfrac{3}{2}$ **d.** none of these

14. $-3x + 1 \geq 7$ or $4x + 3 \geq -13$

a. $x \geq -4$ **b.** $x \geq -2$

c. all real numbers   **d.** $-4 \leq x \leq -2$

Solving Systems of Linear Equations and Inequalities

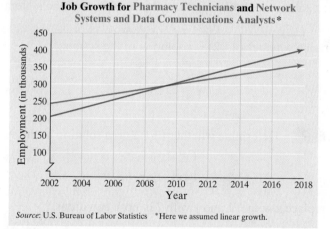

Job Growth for Pharmacy Technicians and Network Systems and Data Communications Analysts*

Source: U.S. Bureau of Labor Statistics   *Here we assumed linear growth.

Many of the occupations predicted to have the largest percent increase in number of jobs are in the fields of medicine and computer science. For example, from 2004 to 2014, the job growth predicted for pharmacy technicians is 28.6%, and for network systems and data communication analysts it is 54.5%. Although the demand for both jobs is growing, these jobs are growing at different rates. In this chapter, we will predict when these occupations might have the same number of jobs.

Job Title	Job Description	Employment (in thousands)	
		2004	2014
Pharmacy technician	Prepare medications under the direction of a pharmacist	258	332
Network systems and data communications analyst	Analyze, design, test, and evaluate network systems, Internet, intranet, and other data communication systems	231	357

5.1 SOLVING SYSTEMS OF LINEAR EQUATIONS BY GRAPHING

OBJECTIVES

1 Determine if an ordered pair is a solution of a system of equations in two variables.

2 Solve a system of linear equations by graphing.

3 Without graphing, determine the number of solutions of a system.

OBJECTIVE 1 ▶ Deciding whether an ordered pair is a solution. A **system of linear equations** consists of two or more linear equations. In this section, we focus on solving systems of linear equations containing two equations in two variables. Examples of such linear systems are

$$\begin{cases} 3x - 3y = 0 \\ x = 2y \end{cases} \quad \begin{cases} x - y = 0 \\ 2x + y = 10 \end{cases} \quad \begin{cases} y = 7x - 1 \\ y = 4 \end{cases}$$

A **solution** of a system of two equations in two variables is an ordered pair of numbers that is a solution of both equations in the system.

EXAMPLE 1 Determine whether $(12, 6)$ is a solution of the system

$$\begin{cases} 2x - 3y = 6 \\ x = 2y \end{cases}$$

Solution To determine whether $(12, 6)$ is a solution of the system, we replace x with 12 and y with 6 in both equations.

$2x - 3y = 6$ First equation	$x = 2y$ Second equation
$2(12) - 3(6) \stackrel{?}{=} 6$ Let $x = 12$ and $y = 6$.	$12 \stackrel{?}{=} 2(6)$ Let $x = 12$ and $y = 6$.
$24 - 18 \stackrel{?}{=} 6$ Simplify.	$12 = 12$ True
$6 = 6$ True	

Since $(12, 6)$ is a solution of both equations, it is a solution of the system. □

PRACTICE
1 Determine whether $(4, 12)$ is a solution of the system.

$$\begin{cases} 4x - y = 2 \\ y = 3x \end{cases}$$

EXAMPLE 2 Determine whether $(-1, 2)$ is a solution of the system

$$\begin{cases} x + 2y = 3 \\ 4x - y = 6 \end{cases}$$

Solution We replace x with -1 and y with 2 in both equations.

$x + 2y = 3$ First equation	$4x - y = 6$ Second equation
$-1 + 2(2) \stackrel{?}{=} 3$ Let $x = -1$ and $y = 2$.	$4(-1) - 2 \stackrel{?}{=} 6$ Let $x = -1$ and $y = 2$.
$-1 + 4 \stackrel{?}{=} 3$ Simplify.	$-4 - 2 \stackrel{?}{=} 6$ Simplify.
$3 = 3$ True	$-6 = 6$ False

$(-1, 2)$ is not a solution of the second equation, $4x - y = 6$, so it is not a solution of the system. □

PRACTICE
2 Determine whether $(-4, 1)$ is a solution of the system.

$$\begin{cases} x - 3y = -7 \\ 2x + 9y = 1 \end{cases}$$

OBJECTIVE 2 ▶ Solving systems of equations by graphing. Since a solution of a system of two equations in two variables is a solution common to both equations, it is also a point common to the graphs of both equations. Let's practice finding solutions of both equations in a system—that is, solutions of a system—by graphing and identifying points of intersection.

EXAMPLE 3   Solve the system of equations by graphing.

$$\begin{cases} -x + 3y = 10 \\ x + y = 2 \end{cases}$$

Solution   On a single set of axes, graph each linear equation.

$-x + 3y = 10$

x	y
0	$\frac{10}{3}$
-4	2
2	4

$x + y = 2$

x	y
0	2
2	0
1	1

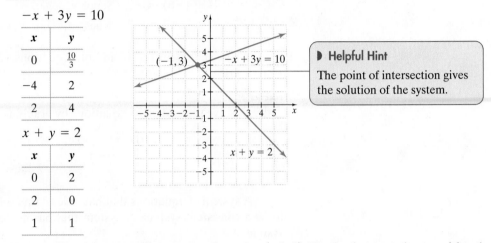

▶ **Helpful Hint**

The point of intersection gives the solution of the system.

The two lines appear to intersect at the point $(-1, 3)$. To check, we replace x with -1 and y with 3 in both equations.

$-x + 3y = 10$ First equation $x + y = 2$ Second equation

$-(-1) + 3(3) \stackrel{?}{=} 10$ Let $x = -1$ and $y = 3$. $-1 + 3 \stackrel{?}{=} 2$ Let $x = -1$ and $y = 3$.

$1 + 9 \stackrel{?}{=} 10$ Simplify. $2 = 2$ True

$10 = 10$ True

$(-1, 3)$ checks, so it is the solution of the system.   □

PRACTICE
3   Solve the system of equations by graphing:

$$\begin{cases} x - y = 3 \\ x + 2y = 18 \end{cases}$$

▶ **Helpful Hint**

Neatly drawn graphs can help when you are estimating the solution of a system of linear equations by graphing.

In the example above, notice that the two lines intersected in a point. This means that the system has 1 solution.

EXAMPLE 4   Solve the system of equations by graphing.

$$\begin{cases} 2x + 3y = -2 \\ x = 2 \end{cases}$$

Solution   We graph each linear equation on a single set of axes.

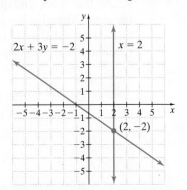

The two lines appear to intersect at the point $(2, -2)$. To determine whether $(2, -2)$ is the solution, we replace x with 2 and y with -2 in both equations.

$2x + 3y = -2$	First equation	$x = 2$	Second equation
$2(2) + 3(-2) \overset{?}{=} -2$	Let $x = 2$ and $y = -2$.	$2 \overset{?}{=} 2$	Let $x = 2$.
$4 + (-6) \overset{?}{=} -2$	Simplify.	$2 = 2$	True
$-2 = -2$	True		

Since a true statement results in both equations, $(2, -2)$ is the solution of the system.

□

PRACTICE
4   Solve the system of equations by graphing.

$$\begin{cases} -4x + 3y = -3 \\ y = -5 \end{cases}$$

A system of equations that has at least one solution as in Examples 3 and 4 is said to be a **consistent system**. A system that has no solution is said to be an **inconsistent system**.

EXAMPLE 5   Solve the following system of equations by graphing.

$$\begin{cases} 2x + y = 7 \\ 2y = -4x \end{cases}$$

Solution   Graph the two lines in the system.

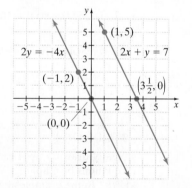

The lines **appear** to be parallel. To confirm this, write both equations in slope-intercept form by solving each equation for y.

$2x + y = 7$	First equation	$2y = -4x$	Second equation
$y = -2x + 7$	Subtract $2x$ from both sides.	$\dfrac{2y}{2} = \dfrac{-4x}{2}$	Divide both sides by 2.
		$y = -2x$	

Recall that when an equation is written in slope-intercept form, the coefficient of x is the slope. Since both equations have the same slope, -2, but different y-intercepts, the lines are parallel and have no points in common. Thus, there is no solution of the system and the system is inconsistent.

□

PRACTICE
5   Solve the system of equations by graphing.

$$\begin{cases} 3y = 9x \\ 6x - 2y = 12 \end{cases}$$

In Examples 3, 4, and 5, the graphs of the two linear equations of each system are different. When this happens, we call these equations **independent equations.** If the graphs of the two equations in a system are identical, we call the equations **dependent equations.**

EXAMPLE 6   Solve the system of equations by graphing.

$$\begin{cases} x - y = 3 \\ -x + y = -3 \end{cases}$$

Solution   Graph each line.

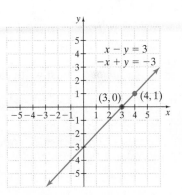

These graphs **appear** to be identical. To confirm this, write each equation in slope-intercept form.

$x - y = 3$	First equation	$-x + y = -3$	Second equation
$-y = -x + 3$	Subtract x from both sides.	$y = x - 3$	Add x to both sides.

$\dfrac{-y}{-1} = \dfrac{-x}{-1} + \dfrac{3}{-1}$ Divide both sides by -1.

$y = x - 3$

The equations are identical and so must be their graphs. The lines have an infinite number of points in common. Thus, there is an infinite number of solutions of the system and this is a consistent system. The equations are dependent equations.   □

PRACTICE
6   Solve the system of equations by graphing.

$$\begin{cases} x - y = 4 \\ -2x + 2y = -8 \end{cases}$$

As we have seen, three different situations can occur when graphing the two lines associated with the equations in a linear system:

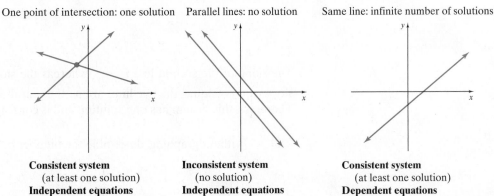

One point of intersection: one solution	Parallel lines: no solution	Same line: infinite number of solutions
Consistent system (at least one solution) **Independent equations** (graphs of equations differ)	**Inconsistent system** (no solution) **Independent equations** (graphs of equations differ)	**Consistent system** (at least one solution) **Dependent equations** (graphs of equations identical)

OBJECTIVE 3 ▶ **Finding the number of solutions of a system without graphing.** You may have suspected by now that graphing alone is not an accurate way to solve a system of linear equations. For example, a solution of $\left(\frac{1}{2}, \frac{2}{9}\right)$ is unlikely to be read correctly from a graph. The next two sections present two accurate methods of solving these systems. In the meantime, we can decide how many solutions a system has by writing each equation in the slope-intercept form.

EXAMPLE 7   Without graphing, determine the number of solutions of the system.

$$\begin{cases} \dfrac{1}{2}x - y = 2 \\ x = 2y + 5 \end{cases}$$

Solution   First write each equation in slope-intercept form.

$\dfrac{1}{2}x - y = 2$	First equation	$x = 2y + 5$	Second equation
$\dfrac{1}{2}x = y + 2$	Add y to both sides.	$x - 5 = 2y$	Subtract 5 from both sides.
$\dfrac{1}{2}x - 2 = y$	Subtract 2 from both sides.	$\dfrac{x}{2} - \dfrac{5}{2} = \dfrac{2y}{2}$	Divide both sides by 2.
		$\dfrac{1}{2}x - \dfrac{5}{2} = y$	Simplify.

The slope of each line is $\dfrac{1}{2}$, but they have different y-intercepts. This tells us that the lines representing these equations are parallel. Since the lines are parallel, the system has no solution and is inconsistent. ☐

PRACTICE
7   Without graphing, determine the number of solutions of the system.

$$\begin{cases} 5x + 4y = 6 \\ x - y = 3 \end{cases}$$

EXAMPLE 8   Without graphing, determine the number of solutions of the system.

$$\begin{cases} 3x - y = 4 \\ x + 2y = 8 \end{cases}$$

Solution   Once again, the slope-intercept form helps determine how many solutions this system has.

$3x - y = 4$	First equation	$x + 2y = 8$	Second equation
$3x = y + 4$	Add y to both sides.	$x = -2y + 8$	Subtract $2y$ from both sides.
$3x - 4 = y$	Subtract 4 from both sides.	$x - 8 = -2y$	Subtract 8 from both sides.
		$\dfrac{x}{-2} - \dfrac{8}{-2} = \dfrac{-2y}{-2}$	Divide both sides by -2.
		$-\dfrac{1}{2}x + 4 = y$	Simplify.

The slope of the second line is $-\dfrac{1}{2}$, whereas the slope of the first line is 3. Since the slopes are not equal, the two lines are neither parallel nor identical and must intersect. Therefore, this system has one solution and is consistent. ☐

PRACTICE
8   Without graphing, determine the number of solutions of the system.

$$\begin{cases} -\dfrac{2}{3}x + y = 6 \\ 3y = 2x + 5 \end{cases}$$

Graphing Calculator Explorations

A graphing calculator may be used to approximate solutions of systems of equations. For example, to approximate the solution of the system

$$\begin{cases} y = -3.14x - 1.35 \\ y = 4.88x + 5.25, \end{cases}$$

first graph each equation on the same set of axes. Then use the intersect feature of your calculator to approximate the point of intersection.

The approximate point of intersection is $(-0.82, 1.23)$.

Solve each system of equations. Approximate the solutions to two decimal places.

1. $\begin{cases} y = -2.68x + 1.21 \\ y = 5.22x - 1.68 \end{cases}$

2. $\begin{cases} y = 4.25x + 3.89 \\ y = -1.88x + 3.21 \end{cases}$

3. $\begin{cases} 4.3x - 2.9y = 5.6 \\ 8.1x + 7.6y = -14.1 \end{cases}$

4. $\begin{cases} -3.6x - 8.6y = 10 \\ -4.5x + 9.6y = -7.7 \end{cases}$

VOCABULARY & READINESS CHECK

Word Bank. *Fill in each blank with one of the words or phrases listed below.*

system of linear equations   solution   consistent

dependent   inconsistent   independent

1. In a system of linear equations in two variables, if the graphs of the equations are the same, the equations are _____ equations.

2. Two or more linear equations are called a _____.

3. A system of equations that has at least one solution is called a(n) _____ system.

4. A _____ of a system of two equations in two variables is an ordered pair of numbers that is a solution of both equations in the system.

5. A system of equations that has no solution is called a(n) _____ system.

6. In a system of linear equations in two variables, if the graphs of the equations are different, the equations are _____ equations.

Read a Graph. *Each rectangular coordinate system shows the graph of the equations in a system of equations. Use each graph to determine the number of solutions for each associated system. If the system has only one solution, give its coordinates.*

7.   8.   9.   10.

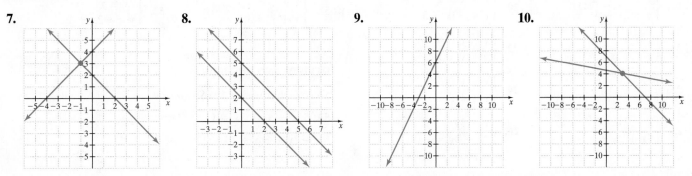

5.1 EXERCISE SET

PRACTICE WATCH DOWNLOAD READ REVIEW

Determine whether each ordered pair is a solution of the system of linear equations. See Examples 1 and 2.

1. $\begin{cases} x + y = 8 \\ 3x + 2y = 21 \end{cases}$
  a. $(2, 4)$
  b. $(5, 3)$

2. $\begin{cases} 2x + y = 5 \\ x + 3y = 5 \end{cases}$
  a. $(5, 0)$
  b. $(2, 1)$

3. $\begin{cases} 3x - y = 5 \\ x + 2y = 11 \end{cases}$
  a. $(3, 4)$
  b. $(0, -5)$

4. $\begin{cases} 2x - 3y = 8 \\ x - 2y = 6 \end{cases}$
  a. $(-2, -4)$
  b. $(7, 2)$

5. $\begin{cases} 2y = 4x + 6 \\ 2x - y = -3 \end{cases}$
  a. $(-3, -3)$
  b. $(0, 3)$

6. $\begin{cases} x + 5y = -4 \\ -2x = 10y + 8 \end{cases}$
  a. $(-4, 0)$
  b. $(6, -2)$

7. $\begin{cases} -2 = x - 7y \\ 6x - y = 13 \end{cases}$
  a. $(-2, 0)$
  b. $\left(\dfrac{1}{2}, \dfrac{5}{14}\right)$

8. $\begin{cases} 4x = 1 - y \\ x - 3y = -8 \end{cases}$
  a. $(0, 1)$
  b. $\left(\dfrac{1}{6}, \dfrac{1}{3}\right)$

MIXED PRACTICE

Solve each system of linear equations by graphing. See Examples 3 through 6.

9. $\begin{cases} x + y = 4 \\ x - y = 2 \end{cases}$

10. $\begin{cases} x + y = 3 \\ x - y = 5 \end{cases}$

11. $\begin{cases} x + y = 6 \\ -x + y = -6 \end{cases}$

12. $\begin{cases} x + y = 1 \\ -x + y = -3 \end{cases}$

13. $\begin{cases} y = 2x \\ 3x - y = -2 \end{cases}$

14. $\begin{cases} y = -3x \\ 2x - y = -5 \end{cases}$

15. $\begin{cases} y = x + 1 \\ y = 2x - 1 \end{cases}$

16. $\begin{cases} y = 3x - 4 \\ y = x + 2 \end{cases}$

17. $\begin{cases} 2x + y = 0 \\ 3x + y = 1 \end{cases}$

18. $\begin{cases} 2x + y = 1 \\ 3x + y = 0 \end{cases}$

19. $\begin{cases} y = -x - 1 \\ y = 2x + 5 \end{cases}$

20. $\begin{cases} y = x - 1 \\ y = -3x - 5 \end{cases}$

21. $\begin{cases} x + y = 5 \\ x + y = 6 \end{cases}$

22. $\begin{cases} x - y = 4 \\ x - y = 1 \end{cases}$

23. $\begin{cases} 2x - y = 6 \\ y = 2 \end{cases}$

24. $\begin{cases} x + y = 5 \\ x = 4 \end{cases}$

25. $\begin{cases} x - 2y = 2 \\ 3x + 2y = -2 \end{cases}$

26. $\begin{cases} x + 3y = 7 \\ 2x - 3y = -4 \end{cases}$

27. $\begin{cases} 2x + y = 4 \\ 6x = -3y + 6 \end{cases}$

28. $\begin{cases} y + 2x = 3 \\ 4x = 2 - 2y \end{cases}$

29. $\begin{cases} y - 3x = -2 \\ 6x - 2y = 4 \end{cases}$

30. $\begin{cases} x - 2y = -6 \\ -2x + 4y = 12 \end{cases}$

31. $\begin{cases} x = 3 \\ y = -1 \end{cases}$

32. $\begin{cases} x = -5 \\ y = 3 \end{cases}$

33. $\begin{cases} y = x - 2 \\ y = 2x + 3 \end{cases}$

34. $\begin{cases} y = x + 5 \\ y = -2x - 4 \end{cases}$

35. $\begin{cases} 2x - 3y = -2 \\ -3x + 5y = 5 \end{cases}$

36. $\begin{cases} 4x - y = 7 \\ 2x - 3y = -9 \end{cases}$

37. $\begin{cases} 6x - y = 4 \\ \dfrac{1}{2}y = -2 + 3x \end{cases}$

38. $\begin{cases} 3x - y = 6 \\ \dfrac{1}{3}y = -2 + x \end{cases}$

Multiple Steps. *Without graphing, decide.*

a. Are the graphs of the equations identical lines, parallel lines, or lines intersecting at a single point?

b. How many solutions does the system have? See Examples 7 and 8.

39. $\begin{cases} 4x + y = 24 \\ x + 2y = 2 \end{cases}$

40. $\begin{cases} 3x + y = 1 \\ 3x + 2y = 6 \end{cases}$

41. $\begin{cases} 2x + y = 0 \\ 2y = 6 - 4x \end{cases}$

42. $\begin{cases} 3x + y = 0 \\ 2y = -6x \end{cases}$

43. $\begin{cases} 8x - y = 6 \\ \dfrac{1}{2}y = -3 + 4x \end{cases}$

44. $\begin{cases} 3x - y = 2 \\ \dfrac{1}{3}y = -2 + 3x \end{cases}$

45. $\begin{cases} x = 5 \\ y = -2 \end{cases}$

46. $\begin{cases} y = 3 \\ x = -4 \end{cases}$

47. $\begin{cases} 3y - 2x = 3 \\ x + 2y = 9 \end{cases}$

48. $\begin{cases} 2y = x + 2 \\ y + 2x = 3 \end{cases}$

49. $\begin{cases} 6y + 4x = 6 \\ 3y - 3 = -2x \end{cases}$

50. $\begin{cases} 8y + 6x = 4 \\ 4y - 2 = 3x \end{cases}$

51. $\begin{cases} x + y = 4 \\ x + y = 3 \end{cases}$

52. $\begin{cases} 2x + y = 0 \\ y = -2x + 1 \end{cases}$

REVIEW AND PREVIEW

Solve each equation. See Section 2.4.

53. $5(x - 3) + 3x = 1$

54. $-2x + 3(x + 6) = 17$

55. $4\left(\dfrac{y+1}{2}\right) + 3y = 0$

56. $-y + 12\left(\dfrac{y-1}{4}\right) = 3$

57. $8a - 2(3a - 1) = 6$

58. $3z - (4z - 2) = 9$

CONCEPT EXTENSIONS

59. Draw a graph of two linear equations whose associated system has the solution $(-1, 4)$.

60. Draw a graph of two linear equations whose associated system has the solution $(3, -2)$.

61. Draw a graph of two linear equations whose associated system has no solution.

62. Draw a graph of two linear equations whose associated system has an infinite number of solutions.

63. Explain how to use a graph to determine the number of solutions of a system.

64. The ordered pair $(-2, 3)$ is a solution of all three independent equations:

$$x + y = 1$$
$$2x - y = -7$$
$$x + 3y = 7$$

Describe the graph of all three equations on the same axes.

Read a Graph. *The double line graph below shows the number of pounds of fish and shellfish consumed per person in the United States for the years shown. Use the graph for Exercises 65 and 66.* (*Source: Economic Research Service, U.S. Department of Agriculture*)

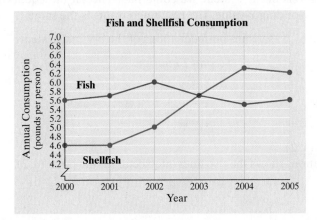

65. In what year(s) was the pounds per person of fish greater than the pounds per person of shellfish?

66. In what year(s) was the pounds per person of shellfish greater than or equal to the pounds per person of fish?

Read a Graph. *The double line graph below shows the annual number of Toyota cars and General Motors cars sold in the United States for the years shown. Use this graph to answer Exercises 67–70.* (*Sources:* Toyota Corporation, General Motors Corporation)

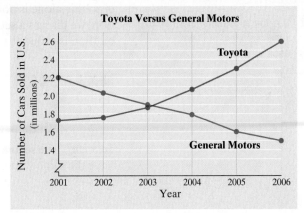

67. In what year(s) was the number of Toyota cars sold in the United States less than the number of GM cars sold in the United States?

68. In what year(s) was the number of GM cars sold in the United States less than the number of Toyota cars sold in the United States?

69. Describe any trends you see in this graph.

70. Approximate how many more cars Toyota sold in the United States than GM in 2005.

71. Construct a system of two linear equations that has $(1, 3)$ as a solution.

72. Construct a system of two linear equations that has $(0, 7)$ as a solution.

73. **Multiple Steps.** Below are two tables of values for two linear equations. Using the tables,

    a. find a solution of the corresponding system.

    b. graph several ordered pairs from each table and sketch the two lines.

    c. Does your graph confirm the solution from part a?

x	y	x	y
1	3	1	6
2	5	2	7
3	7	3	8
4	9	4	9
5	11	5	10

74. Explain how writing each equation in a linear system in slope-intercept form helps determine the number of solutions of a system.

75. Is it possible for a system of two linear equations in two variables to be inconsistent, but with dependent equations? Why or why not?

5.2 SOLVING SYSTEMS OF LINEAR EQUATIONS BY SUBSTITUTION

OBJECTIVE

1 Use the substitution method to solve a system of linear equations.

OBJECTIVE 1 ▶ Using the substitution method. As we stated in the preceding section, graphing alone is not an accurate way to solve a system of linear equations. In this section, we discuss a second, more accurate method for solving systems of equations. This method is called the **substitution method** and is introduced in the next example.

EXAMPLE 1 Solve the system:

$$\begin{cases} 2x + y = 10 & \text{First equation} \\ x = y + 2 & \text{Second equation} \end{cases}$$

Solution The second equation in this system is $x = y + 2$. This tells us that x and $y + 2$ have the same value. This means that we may substitute $y + 2$ for x in the first equation.

$$2x + y = 10 \quad \text{First equation}$$

$$2\,(y + 2) + y = 10 \quad \text{Substitute } y + 2 \text{ for } x \text{ since } x = y + 2.$$

Notice that this equation now has one variable, y. Let's now solve this equation for y.

> ▶ **Helpful Hint**
> Don't forget the distributive property.

$$2(y + 2) + y = 10$$
$$2y + 4 + y = 10 \quad \text{Use the distributive property.}$$
$$3y + 4 = 10 \quad \text{Combine like terms.}$$
$$3y = 6 \quad \text{Subtract 4 from both sides.}$$
$$y = 2 \quad \text{Divide both sides by 3.}$$

Now we know that the y-value of the ordered pair solution of the system is 2. To find the corresponding x-value, we replace y with 2 in the equation $x = y + 2$ and solve for x.

$$x = y + 2$$
$$x = 2 + 2 \quad \text{Let } y = 2.$$
$$x = 4$$

The solution of the system is the ordered pair $(4, 2)$. Since an ordered pair solution must satisfy both linear equations in the system, we could have chosen the equation $2x + y = 10$ to find the corresponding x-value. The resulting x-value is the same.

Check: We check to see that $(4, 2)$ satisfies both equations of the original system.

First Equation	*Second Equation*
$2x + y = 10$	$x = y + 2$
$2(4) + 2 \overset{?}{=} 10$	$4 \overset{?}{=} 2 + 2 \quad$ Let $x = 4$ and $y = 2$.
$10 = 10 \quad$ True	$4 = 4 \quad$ True

The solution of the system is $(4, 2)$.

A graph of the two equations shows the two lines intersecting at the point $(4, 2)$.

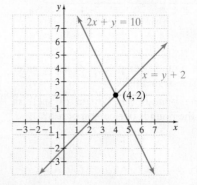

□

PRACTICE
1   Solve the system:

$$\begin{cases} 2x - y = 9 \\ x = y + 1 \end{cases}$$

EXAMPLE 2   Solve the system:

$$\begin{cases} 5x - y = -2 \\ y = 3x \end{cases}$$

Solution   The second equation is solved for y in terms of x. We substitute $3x$ for y in the first equation.

$$5x - y = -2 \quad \text{First equation}$$

$$5x - (3x) = -2 \quad \text{Substitute } 3x \text{ for } y.$$

Now we solve for x.

$$5x - 3x = -2$$
$$2x = -2 \quad \text{Combine like terms.}$$
$$x = -1 \quad \text{Divide both sides by 2.}$$

The x-value of the ordered pair solution is -1. To find the corresponding y-value, we replace x with -1 in the second equation $y = 3x$.

$$y = 3x \qquad \text{Second equation}$$
$$y = 3(-1) \quad \text{Let } x = -1.$$
$$y = -3$$

Check to see that the solution of the system is $(-1, -3)$.   □

PRACTICE
2   Solve the system:

$$\begin{cases} 7x - y = -15 \\ y = 2x \end{cases}$$

To solve a system of equations by substitution, we first need an equation solved for one of its variables, as in Examples 1 and 2. If neither equation in a system is solved for x or y, this will be our first step.

EXAMPLE 3   Solve the system:

$$\begin{cases} x + 2y = 7 \\ 2x + 2y = 13 \end{cases}$$

Solution   We choose one of the equations and solve for x or y. We will solve the first equation for x by subtracting $2y$ from both sides.

$$x + 2y = 7 \qquad \text{First equation}$$
$$x = 7 - 2y \quad \text{Subtract } 2y \text{ from both sides.}$$

Since $x = 7 - 2y$, we now substitute $7 - 2y$ for x in the second equation and solve for y.

$$2x + 2y = 13 \qquad \text{Second equation}$$
$$2(7 - 2y) + 2y = 13 \quad \text{Let } x = 7 - 2y.$$

$$14 - 4y + 2y = 13 \quad \text{Use the distributive property.}$$
$$14 - 2y = 13 \quad \text{Simplify.}$$
$$-2y = -1 \quad \text{Subtract 14 from both sides.}$$
$$y = \frac{1}{2} \quad \text{Divide both sides by } -2.$$

> ▶ **Helpful Hint**
> Don't forget to insert parentheses when substituting $7 - 2y$ for x.

To find x, we let $y = \dfrac{1}{2}$ in the equation $x = 7 - 2y$.

$$x = 7 - 2y$$
$$x = 7 - 2\left(\dfrac{1}{2}\right) \quad \text{Let } y = \dfrac{1}{2}.$$
$$x = 7 - 1$$
$$x = 6$$

> **▶ Helpful Hint**
>
> To find x, any equation in two variables equivalent to the original equations of the system may be used. We used this equation since it is solved for x.

The solution is $\left(6, \dfrac{1}{2}\right)$. Check the solution in both equations of the original system. □

PRACTICE
3   Solve the system:

$$\begin{cases} x + 3y = 6 \\ 2x + 3y = 10 \end{cases}$$

The following steps may be used to solve a system of equations by the substitution method.

> **Solving a System of Two Linear Equations by the Substitution Method**
> **STEP 1.** Solve one of the equations for one of its variables.
> **STEP 2.** Substitute the expression for the variable found in Step 1 into the other equation.
> **STEP 3.** Solve the equation from Step 2 to find the value of one variable.
> **STEP 4.** Substitute the value found in Step 3 in any equation containing both variables to find the value of the other variable.
> **STEP 5.** Check the proposed solution in the original system.

Concept Check ☑

As you solve the system $\begin{cases} 2x + y = -5 \\ x - y = 5 \end{cases}$ you find that $y = -5$. Is this the solution of the system?

EXAMPLE 4   Solve the system:

$$\begin{cases} 7x - 3y = -14 \\ -3x + y = 6 \end{cases}$$

Solution   To avoid introducing fractions, we will solve the second equation for y.

$$-3x + y = 6 \qquad \text{Second equation}$$
$$y = 3x + 6$$

Next, substitute $3x + 6$ for y in the first equation.

$$7x - 3y = -14 \quad \text{First equation}$$
$$7x - 3(3x + 6) = -14 \quad \text{Let } y = 3x + 6.$$
$$7x - 9x - 18 = -14 \quad \text{Use the distributive property.}$$
$$-2x - 18 = -14 \quad \text{Simplify.}$$
$$-2x = 4 \quad \text{Add 18 to both sides.}$$
$$x = -2 \quad \text{Divide both sides by } -2.$$

Answer to Concept Check:

No, the solution will be an ordered pair.

To find the corresponding *y*-value, substitute -2 for x in the equation $y = 3x + 6$. Then $y = 3(-2) + 6$ or $y = 0$. The solution of the system is $(-2, 0)$. Check this solution in both equations of the system. □

PRACTICE

4 Solve the system:

$$\begin{cases} 5x + 3y = -9 \\ -2x + y = 8 \end{cases}$$

▶ **Helpful Hint**

When solving a system of equations by the substitution method, begin by solving an equation for one of its variables. If possible, solve for a variable that has a coefficient of 1 or -1. This way, we avoid working with time-consuming fractions.

EXAMPLE 5 Solve the system:

$$\begin{cases} \dfrac{1}{2}x - y = 3 \\ x = 6 + 2y \end{cases}$$

Solution The second equation is already solved for x in terms of y. Thus we substitute $6 + 2y$ for x in the first equation and solve for y.

$$\frac{1}{2}x - y = 3 \quad \text{First equation}$$

$$\frac{1}{2}(6 + 2y) - y = 3 \quad \text{Let } x = 6 + 2y.$$

$$3 + y - y = 3 \quad \text{Use the distributive property.}$$

$$3 = 3 \quad \text{Simplify.}$$

Arriving at a true statement such as $3 = 3$ indicates that the two linear equations in the original system are equivalent. This means that their graphs are identical and there are an infinite number of solutions of the system. Any solution of one equation is also a solution of the other.

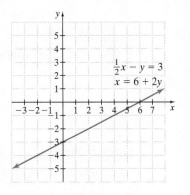

□

PRACTICE

5 Solve the system:

$$\begin{cases} \dfrac{1}{4}x - y = 2 \\ x = 4y + 8 \end{cases}$$

EXAMPLE 6 Use substitution to solve the system.

$$\begin{cases} 6x + 12y = 5 \\ -4x - 8y = 0 \end{cases}$$

Solution Choose the second equation and solve for y.

$$-4x - 8y = 0 \qquad \text{Second equation}$$

$$-8y = 4x \qquad \text{Add } 4x \text{ to both sides.}$$

$$\frac{-8y}{-8} = \frac{4x}{-8} \qquad \text{Divide both sides by } -8.$$

$$y = -\frac{1}{2}x \qquad \text{Simplify.}$$

Now replace y with $-\frac{1}{2}x$ in the first equation.

$$6x + 12y = 5 \qquad \text{First equation}$$

$$6x + 12\left(-\frac{1}{2}x\right) = 5 \qquad \text{Let } y = -\frac{1}{2}x.$$

$$6x + (-6x) = 5 \qquad \text{Simplify.}$$

$$0 = 5 \qquad \text{Combine like terms.}$$

The false statement $0 = 5$ indicates that this system has no solution and is inconsistent. The graph of the linear equations in the system is a pair of parallel lines.

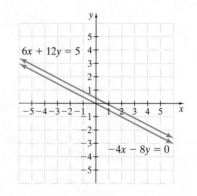

PRACTICE

6 Use substitution to solve the system.

$$\begin{cases} 4x - 3y = 12 \\ -8x + 6y = -30 \end{cases}$$

Concept Check ☑

Describe how the graphs of the equations in a system appear if the system has

a. no solution

b. one solution

c. an infinite number of solutions

Answers to Concept Check:

a. parallel lines
b. intersect at one point
c. identical graphs

VOCABULARY & READINESS CHECK

Give the solution of each system. If the system has no solution or an infinite number of solutions, say so. If the system has one solution, find it.

1. $\begin{cases} y = 4x \\ -3x + y = 1 \end{cases}$

When solving, you obtain $x = 1$

2. $\begin{cases} 4x - y = 17 \\ -8x + 2y = 0 \end{cases}$

When solving, you obtain $0 = 34$

3. $\begin{cases} 4x - y = 17 \\ -8x + 2y = -34 \end{cases}$

When solving, you obtain $0 = 0$

4. $\begin{cases} 5x + 2y = 25 \\ x = y + 5 \end{cases}$

When solving, you obtain $y = 0$

5. $\begin{cases} x + y = 0 \\ 7x - 7y = 0 \end{cases}$

When solving, you obtain $x = 0$

6. $\begin{cases} y = -2x + 5 \\ 4x + 2y = 10 \end{cases}$

When solving, you obtain $0 = 0$

5.2 | EXERCISE SET

MyMathLab   PRACTICE   WATCH   DOWNLOAD   READ   REVIEW

Solve each system of equations by the substitution method. See Examples 1 and 2.

1. $\begin{cases} x + y = 3 \\ x = 2y \end{cases}$

2. $\begin{cases} x + y = 20 \\ x = 3y \end{cases}$

3. $\begin{cases} x + y = 6 \\ y = -3x \end{cases}$

4. $\begin{cases} x + y = 6 \\ y = -4x \end{cases}$

5. $\begin{cases} y = 3x + 1 \\ 4y - 8x = 12 \end{cases}$

6. $\begin{cases} y = 2x + 3 \\ 5y - 7x = 18 \end{cases}$

7. $\begin{cases} y = 2x + 9 \\ y = 7x + 10 \end{cases}$

8. $\begin{cases} y = 5x - 3 \\ y = 8x + 4 \end{cases}$

MIXED PRACTICE

Solve each system of equations by the substitution method. See Examples 1 through 6.

9. $\begin{cases} 3x - 4y = 10 \\ y = x - 3 \end{cases}$

10. $\begin{cases} 4x - 3y = 10 \\ y = x - 5 \end{cases}$

11. $\begin{cases} x + 2y = 6 \\ 2x + 3y = 8 \end{cases}$

12. $\begin{cases} x + 3y = -5 \\ 2x + 2y = 6 \end{cases}$

13. $\begin{cases} 3x + 2y = 16 \\ x = 3y - 2 \end{cases}$

14. $\begin{cases} 2x + 3y = 18 \\ x = 2y - 5 \end{cases}$

15. $\begin{cases} 2x - 5y = 1 \\ 3x + y = -7 \end{cases}$

16. $\begin{cases} 3y - x = 6 \\ 4x + 12y = 0 \end{cases}$

17. $\begin{cases} 4x + 2y = 5 \\ -2x = y + 4 \end{cases}$

18. $\begin{cases} 2y = x + 2 \\ 6x - 12y = 0 \end{cases}$

19. $\begin{cases} 4x + y = 11 \\ 2x + 5y = 1 \end{cases}$

20. $\begin{cases} 3x + y = -14 \\ 4x + 3y = -22 \end{cases}$

21. $\begin{cases} x + 2y + 5 = -4 + 5y - x \\ \quad 2x + x = y + 4 \end{cases}$

(*Hint:* First simplify each equation.)

22. $\begin{cases} 5x + 4y - 2 = -6 + 7y - 3x \\ \quad 3x + 4x = y + 3 \end{cases}$

(*Hint:* See Exercise 21.)

23. $\begin{cases} 6x - 3y = 5 \\ x + 2y = 0 \end{cases}$

24. $\begin{cases} 10x - 5y = -21 \\ x + 3y = 0 \end{cases}$

25. $\begin{cases} 3x - y = 1 \\ 2x - 3y = 10 \end{cases}$

26. $\begin{cases} 2x - y = -7 \\ 4x - 3y = -11 \end{cases}$

27. $\begin{cases} -x + 2y = 10 \\ -2x + 3y = 18 \end{cases}$

28. $\begin{cases} -x + 3y = 18 \\ -3x + 2y = 19 \end{cases}$

29. $\begin{cases} 5x + 10y = 20 \\ 2x + 6y = 10 \end{cases}$

30. $\begin{cases} 6x + 3y = 12 \\ 9x + 6y = 15 \end{cases}$

31. $\begin{cases} 3x + 6y = 9 \\ 4x + 8y = 16 \end{cases}$

32. $\begin{cases} 2x + 4y = 6 \\ 5x + 10y = 16 \end{cases}$

33. $\begin{cases} \dfrac{1}{3}x - y = 2 \\ x - 3y = 6 \end{cases}$

34. $\begin{cases} \dfrac{1}{4}x - 2y = 1 \\ x - 8y = 4 \end{cases}$

35. $\begin{cases} x = \dfrac{3}{4}y - 1 \\ 8x - 5y = -6 \end{cases}$

36. $\begin{cases} x = \dfrac{5}{6}y - 2 \\ 12x - 5y = -9 \end{cases}$

Solve each system by the substitution method. First simplify each equation by combining like terms.

37. $\begin{cases} -5y + 6y = 3x + 2(x - 5) - 3x + 5 \\ 4(x + y) - x + y = -12 \end{cases}$

38. $\begin{cases} 5x + 2y - 4x - 2y = 2(2y + 6) - 7 \\ 3(2x - y) - 4x = 1 + 9 \end{cases}$

REVIEW AND PREVIEW

Write equivalent equations by multiplying both sides of the given equation by the given nonzero number. See Section 2.3.

39. $3x + 2y = 6$ by -2

40. $-x + y = 10$ by 5

41. $-4x + y = 3$ by 3

42. $5a - 7b = -4$ by -4

Add the binomials. See Section 2.1.

43. $\begin{array}{r} 3n + 6m \\ \underline{2n - 6m} \end{array}$ **44.** $\begin{array}{r} -2x + 5y \\ \underline{2x + 11y} \end{array}$ **45.** $\begin{array}{r} -5a - 7b \\ \underline{5a - 8b} \end{array}$ **46.** $\begin{array}{r} 9q + p \\ \underline{-9q - p} \end{array}$

CONCEPT EXTENSIONS

47. Explain how to identify a system with no solution when using the substitution method.

48. Occasionally, when using the substitution method, we obtain the equation $0 = 0$. Explain how this result indicates that the graphs of the equations in the system are identical.

Solve. See a Concept Check in this section.

49. As you solve the system $\begin{cases} 3x - y = -6 \\ -3x + 2y = 7 \end{cases}$, you find that $y = 1$. Is this the solution to the system?

50. As you solve the system $\begin{cases} x = 5y \\ y = 2x \end{cases}$, you find that $x = 0$ and $y = 0$. What is the solution to this system?

51. Decision Making. To avoid fractions, which of the equations below would you use if solving for y? Explain why.

  a. $\frac{1}{2}x - 4y = \frac{3}{4}$ **b.** $8x - 5y = 13$
  c. $7x - y = 19$

52. Decision Making. Give the number of solutions for a system if the graphs of the equations in the system are

  a. lines intersecting in one point

  b. parallel lines

  c. same line

53. Multiple Steps. The number of men and women receiving bachelor's degrees each year has been steadily increasing. For the years 1970 through the projection of 2014, the number of men receiving degrees (in thousands) is given by the equation $y = 3.9x + 443$, and for women, the equation is $y = 14.2x + 314$ where x is the number of years after 1970. (*Source:* National Center for Education Statistics)

  a. Use the substitution method to solve this system of equations. (Round your final results to the nearest whole numbers.)

b. Explain the meaning of your answer to part (a).

c. Sketch a graph of the system of equations. Write a sentence describing the trends for men and women receiving bachelor degrees.

54. Multiple Steps. The number of Adult Contemporary Music radio stations in the United States from 2000 to 2006 is given by the equation $y = -6.17x + 719$, where x is the number of years after 2000. The number of Spanish radio stations is given by $y = 33.9x + 534$ for the same time period. (*Source:* M Street Corporation)

  a. Use the substitution method to solve this system of equations. (Round your numbers to the nearest tenth.)

  b. Explain the meaning of your answer to part (a).

  c. Sketch a graph of the system of equations. Write a sentence describing the trends in the popularity of these two types of music format.

Solve each system by substitution. When necessary, round answers to the nearest hundredth.

55. $\begin{cases} y = 5.1x + 14.56 \\ y = -2x - 3.9 \end{cases}$

56. $\begin{cases} y = 3.1x - 16.35 \\ y = -9.7x + 28.45 \end{cases}$

57. $\begin{cases} 3x + 2y = 14.05 \\ 5x + y = 18.5 \end{cases}$

58. $\begin{cases} x + y = -15.2 \\ -2x + 5y = -19.3 \end{cases}$

5.3 SOLVING SYSTEMS OF LINEAR EQUATIONS BY ADDITION

OBJECTIVE

1 Use the addition method to solve a system of linear equations.

OBJECTIVE 1 ▶ Using the addition method. We have seen that substitution is an accurate way to solve a linear system. Another method for solving a system of equations accurately is the **addition** or **elimination method.** The addition method is based on the addition property of equality: adding equal quantities to both sides of an equation does not change the solution of the equation. In symbols,

$$\text{if } A = B \text{ and } C = D, \text{ then } A + C = B + D.$$

EXAMPLE 1   Solve the system:

$$\begin{cases} x + y = 7 \\ x - y = 5 \end{cases}$$

Solution   Since the left side of each equation is equal to the right side, we add equal quantities by adding the left sides of the equations together and the right sides of the equations together. This adding eliminates the variable y and gives us an equation in one variable, x. We can then solve for x.

$x + y = 7$	First equation
$\underline{x - y = 5}$	Second equation
$2x \qquad = 12$	Add the equations.
$x = 6$	Divide both sides by **2**.

> **Helpful Hint**
>
> Our goal when solving a system of equations by the addition method is to eliminate a variable when adding the equations.

The x-value of the solution is 6. To find the corresponding y-value, let $x = 6$ in either equation of the system. We will use the first equation.

$x + y = 7$	First equation
$6 + y = 7$	Let $x = 6$.
$y = 7 - 6$	Solve for y.
$y = 1$	Simplify.

Check: The solution is $(6, 1)$. Check this in both equations.

First Equation	**_Second Equation_**
$x + y = 7$	$x - y = 5$
$6 + 1 \stackrel{?}{=} 7$	$6 - 1 \stackrel{?}{=} 5$ Let $x = 6$ and $y = 1$.
$7 = 7$ True	$5 = 5$ True

Thus, the solution of the system is $(6, 1)$ and the graphs of the two equations intersect at the point $(6, 1)$ as shown next.

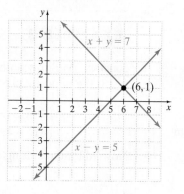

PRACTICE
1   Solve the system: $\begin{cases} x - y = 2 \\ x + y = 8 \end{cases}$

EXAMPLE 2 Solve the system: $\begin{cases} -2x + y = 2 \\ -x + 3y = -4 \end{cases}$

Solution If we simply add the two equations, the result is still an equation in two variables. However, our goal is to eliminate one of the variables. Notice what happens if we multiply *both sides* of the first equation by -3, which we are allowed to do by the multiplication property of equality. The system

$$\begin{cases} -3(-2x + y) = -3(2) \\ -x + 3y = -4 \end{cases} \quad \text{simplifies to} \quad \begin{cases} 6x - 3y = -6 \\ -x + 3y = -4 \end{cases}$$

Now add the resulting equations and the y-variable is eliminated.

$$\begin{array}{rl} 6x - 3y &= -6 \\ -x + 3y &= -4 \\ \hline 5x &= -10 \quad \text{Add.} \\ x &= -2 \quad \text{Divide both sides by 5.} \end{array}$$

To find the corresponding y-value, let $x = -2$ in any of the preceding equations containing both variables. We use the first equation of the original system.

$$\begin{array}{rl} -2x + y = 2 & \text{First equation} \\ -2(-2) + y = 2 & \text{Let } x = -2. \\ 4 + y = 2 & \\ y = -2 & \text{Subtract 4 from both sides.} \end{array}$$

The solution is $(-2, -2)$. Check this ordered pair in both equations of the original system. □

PRACTICE
2 Solve the system: $\begin{cases} x - 2y = 11 \\ 3x - y = 13 \end{cases}$

In Example 2, the decision to multiply the first equation by -3 was no accident. **To eliminate a variable** when adding two equations, **the coefficient of the variable in one equation must be the opposite of its coefficient in the other equation.**

> ▶ **Helpful Hint**
>
> Be sure to multiply *both sides* of an equation by a chosen number when solving by the addition method. A common mistake is to multiply only the side containing the variables.

EXAMPLE 3 Solve the system: $\begin{cases} 2x - y = 7 \\ 8x - 4y = 1 \end{cases}$

Solution Multiply both sides of the first equation by -4 and the resulting coefficient of x is -8, the opposite of 8, the coefficient of x in the second equation. The system becomes

> ▶ **Helpful Hint**
>
> Don't forget to multiply both sides by -4.

$$\begin{cases} -4(2x - y) = -4(7) \\ 8x - 4y = 1 \end{cases} \quad \text{simplifies to} \quad \begin{cases} -8x + 4y = -28 \\ 8x - 4y = 1 \end{cases}$$

Now add the resulting equations.

$$\begin{array}{rl} -8x + 4y &= -28 \\ 8x - 4y &= 1 \\ \hline 0 &= -27 \quad \begin{array}{l}\text{Add the equations.}\\ \text{False}\end{array} \end{array}$$

When we add the equations, both variables are eliminated and we have $0 = -27$, a false statement. This means that the system has no solution. The graphs of these equations are parallel lines. □

PRACTICE
3 Solve the system: $\begin{cases} x - 3y = 5 \\ 2x - 6y = -3 \end{cases}$

EXAMPLE 4 Solve the system: $\begin{cases} 3x - 2y = 2 \\ -9x + 6y = -6 \end{cases}$

Solution First we multiply both sides of the first equation by 3, then we add the resulting equations.

$\begin{cases} 3(3x - 2y) = 3(2) \\ -9x + 6y = -6 \end{cases}$ simplifies to $\begin{cases} 9x - 6y = 6 \\ \underline{-9x + 6y = -6} \\ 0 = 0 \end{cases}$ Add the equations.
True

Both variables are eliminated and we have $0 = 0$, a true statement. Whenever you eliminate a variable and get the equation $0 = 0$, the system has an infinite number of solutions. The graphs of these equations are identical. □

PRACTICE
4 Solve the system: $\begin{cases} 4x - 3y = 5 \\ -8x + 6y = -10 \end{cases}$

Concept Check ☑

Suppose you are solving the system

$$\begin{cases} 3x + 8y = -5 \\ 2x - 4y = 3 \end{cases}$$

You decide to use the addition method and begin by multiplying both sides of the first equation by -2. In which of the following was the multiplication performed correctly? Explain.

a. $-6x - 16y = -5$ **b.** $-6x - 16y = 10$

EXAMPLE 5 Solve the system: $\begin{cases} 3x + 4y = 13 \\ 5x - 9y = 6 \end{cases}$

Solution We can eliminate the variable y by multiplying the first equation by 9 and the second equation by 4.

$\begin{cases} 9(3x + 4y) = 9(13) \\ 4(5x - 9y) = 4(6) \end{cases}$ simplifies to $\begin{cases} 27x + 36y = 117 \\ \underline{20x - 36y = 24} \\ 47x = 141 \\ x = 3 \end{cases}$ Add the equations.
Divide both sides by 47.

To find the corresponding y-value, we let $x = 3$ in any equation in this example containing two variables. Doing so in any of these equations will give $y = 1$. The solution to this system is $(3, 1)$. Check to see that $(3, 1)$ satisfies each equation in the original system. □

PRACTICE
5 Solve the system: $\begin{cases} 4x + 3y = 14 \\ 3x - 2y = 2 \end{cases}$

If we had decided to eliminate x instead of y in Example 5, the first equation could have been multiplied by 5 and the second by -3. Try solving the original system this way to check that the solution is $(3, 1)$.

The following steps summarize how to solve a system of linear equations by the addition method.

Solving a System of Two Linear Equations by the Addition Method

STEP 1. Rewrite each equation in standard form $Ax + By = C$.

STEP 2. If necessary, multiply one or both equations by a nonzero number so that the coefficients of a chosen variable in the system are opposites.

STEP 3. Add the equations.

STEP 4. Find the value of one variable by solving the resulting equation from Step 3.

STEP 5. Find the value of the second variable by substituting the value found in Step 4 into either of the original equations.

STEP 6. Check the proposed solution in the original system.

Concept Check ☑

Suppose you are solving the system

$$\begin{cases} -4x + 7y = 6 \\ x + 2y = 5 \end{cases}$$

by the addition method.

a. What step(s) should you take if you wish to eliminate x when adding the equations?

b. What step(s) should you take if you wish to eliminate y when adding the equations?

EXAMPLE 6 Solve the system:

$$\begin{cases} -x - \dfrac{y}{2} = \dfrac{5}{2} \\ -\dfrac{x}{2} + \dfrac{y}{4} = 0 \end{cases}$$

Solution We begin by clearing each equation of fractions. To do so, we multiply both sides of the first equation by the LCD 2 and both sides of the second equation by the LCD 4. Then the system

$$\begin{cases} 2\left(-x - \dfrac{y}{2}\right) = 2\left(\dfrac{5}{2}\right) \\ 4\left(-\dfrac{x}{2} + \dfrac{y}{4}\right) = 4(0) \end{cases} \quad \text{simplifies to} \quad \begin{cases} -2x - y = 5 \\ -2x + y = 0 \end{cases}$$

Now we add the resulting equations in the simplified system.

$$\begin{array}{r} -2x - y = 5 \\ \underline{-2x + y = 0} \\ -4x = 5 \end{array} \qquad \text{Add the equations.}$$

$$x = -\dfrac{5}{4}$$

To find y, we could replace x with $-\dfrac{5}{4}$ in one of the equations with two variables.

Instead, let's go back to the simplified system and multiply by appropriate factors to eliminate the variable x and solve for y. To do this, we multiply the first equation in the simplified system by -1. Then the system

$$\begin{cases} -1(-2x - y) = -1(5) \\ -2x + y = 0 \end{cases} \quad \text{simplifies to} \quad \begin{cases} 2x + y = -5 \\ \underline{-2x + y = 0} \end{cases}$$

$$2y = -5 \quad \text{Add.}$$

$$y = -\frac{5}{2} \quad \text{Solve for } y.$$

Check the ordered pair $\left(-\dfrac{5}{4}, -\dfrac{5}{2}\right)$ in both equations of the original system. The solution is $\left(-\dfrac{5}{4}, -\dfrac{5}{2}\right)$.

PRACTICE
6 Solve the system: $\begin{cases} -2x + \dfrac{3y}{2} = 5 \\ -\dfrac{x}{2} - \dfrac{y}{4} = \dfrac{1}{2} \end{cases}$

5.3 EXERCISE SET

Solve each system of equations by the addition method. See Example 1.

1. $\begin{cases} 3x + y = 5 \\ 6x - y = 4 \end{cases}$

2. $\begin{cases} 4x + y = 13 \\ 2x - y = 5 \end{cases}$

3. $\begin{cases} x - 2y = 8 \\ -x + 5y = -17 \end{cases}$

4. $\begin{cases} x - 2y = -11 \\ -x + 5y = 23 \end{cases}$

Solve each system of equations by the addition method. If a system contains fractions or decimals, you may want to first clear each equation of fractions or decimals. See Examples 2 through 6.

5. $\begin{cases} 3x + y = -11 \\ 6x - 2y = -2 \end{cases}$

6. $\begin{cases} 4x + y = -13 \\ 6x - 3y = -15 \end{cases}$

7. $\begin{cases} 3x + 2y = 11 \\ 5x - 2y = 29 \end{cases}$

8. $\begin{cases} 4x + 2y = 2 \\ 3x - 2y = 12 \end{cases}$

9. $\begin{cases} x + 5y = 18 \\ 3x + 2y = -11 \end{cases}$

10. $\begin{cases} x + 4y = 14 \\ 5x + 3y = 2 \end{cases}$

11. $\begin{cases} x + y = 6 \\ x - y = 6 \end{cases}$

12. $\begin{cases} x - y = 1 \\ -x + 2y = 0 \end{cases}$

13. $\begin{cases} 2x + 3y = 0 \\ 4x + 6y = 3 \end{cases}$

14. $\begin{cases} 3x + y = 4 \\ 9x + 3y = 6 \end{cases}$

15. $\begin{cases} -x + 5y = -1 \\ 3x - 15y = 3 \end{cases}$

16. $\begin{cases} 2x + y = 6 \\ 4x + 2y = 12 \end{cases}$

17. $\begin{cases} 3x - 2y = 7 \\ 5x + 4y = 8 \end{cases}$

18. $\begin{cases} 6x - 5y = 25 \\ 4x + 15y = 13 \end{cases}$

19. $\begin{cases} 8x = -11y - 16 \\ 2x + 3y = -4 \end{cases}$

20. $\begin{cases} 10x + 3y = -12 \\ 5x = -4y - 16 \end{cases}$

21. $\begin{cases} 4x - 3y = 7 \\ 7x + 5y = 2 \end{cases}$

22. $\begin{cases} -2x + 3y = 10 \\ 3x + 4y = 2 \end{cases}$

23. $\begin{cases} 4x - 6y = 8 \\ 6x - 9y = 12 \end{cases}$

24. $\begin{cases} 9x - 3y = 12 \\ 12x - 4y = 18 \end{cases}$

25. $\begin{cases} 2x - 5y = 4 \\ 3x - 2y = 4 \end{cases}$

26. $\begin{cases} 6x - 5y = 7 \\ 4x - 6y = 7 \end{cases}$

27. $\begin{cases} \dfrac{x}{3} + \dfrac{y}{6} = 1 \\ \dfrac{x}{2} - \dfrac{y}{4} = 0 \end{cases}$

28. $\begin{cases} \dfrac{x}{2} + \dfrac{y}{8} = 3 \\ x - \dfrac{y}{4} = 0 \end{cases}$

29. $\begin{cases} \dfrac{10}{3}x + 4y = -4 \\ 5x + 6y = -6 \end{cases}$

30. $\begin{cases} \dfrac{3}{2}x + 4y = 1 \\ 9x + 24y = 5 \end{cases}$

31. $\begin{cases} x - \dfrac{y}{3} = -1 \\ -\dfrac{x}{2} + \dfrac{y}{8} = \dfrac{1}{4} \end{cases}$

32. $\begin{cases} 2x - \dfrac{3y}{4} = -3 \\ x + \dfrac{y}{9} = \dfrac{13}{3} \end{cases}$

33. $-4(x + 2) = 3y$
$2x - 2y = 3$

34. $-9(x + 3) = 8y$
$3x - 3y = 8$

35. $\begin{cases} \dfrac{x}{3} - y = 2 \\ -\dfrac{x}{2} + \dfrac{3y}{2} = -3 \end{cases}$

36. $\begin{cases} \dfrac{x}{2} + \dfrac{y}{4} = 1 \\ -\dfrac{x}{4} - \dfrac{y}{8} = 1 \end{cases}$

37. $\begin{cases} \dfrac{3}{5}x - y = -\dfrac{4}{5} \\ 3x + \dfrac{y}{2} = -\dfrac{9}{5} \end{cases}$

38. $\begin{cases} 3x + \dfrac{7}{2}y = \dfrac{3}{4} \\ -\dfrac{x}{2} + \dfrac{5}{3}y = -\dfrac{5}{4} \end{cases}$

39. $\begin{cases} 3.5x + 2.5y = 17 \\ -1.5x - 7.5y = -33 \end{cases}$

40. $\begin{cases} -2.5x - 6.5y = 47 \\ 0.5x - 4.5y = 37 \end{cases}$

41. $\begin{cases} 0.02x + 0.04y = 0.09 \\ -0.1x + 0.3y = 0.8 \end{cases}$

42. $\begin{cases} 0.04x - 0.05y = 0.105 \\ 0.2x - 0.6y = 1.05 \end{cases}$

MIXED PRACTICE

Solve each system by either the addition method or the substitution method.

43. $\begin{cases} 2x - 3y = -11 \\ y = 4x - 3 \end{cases}$

44. $\begin{cases} 4x - 5y = 6 \\ y = 3x - 10 \end{cases}$

45. $\begin{cases} x + 2y = 1 \\ 3x + 4y = -1 \end{cases}$

46. $\begin{cases} x + 3y = 5 \\ 5x + 6y = -2 \end{cases}$

47. $\begin{cases} 2y = x + 6 \\ 3x - 2y = -6 \end{cases}$

48. $\begin{cases} 3y = x + 14 \\ 2x - 3y = -16 \end{cases}$

49. $\begin{cases} y = 2x - 3 \\ y = 5x - 18 \end{cases}$

50. $\begin{cases} y = 6x - 5 \\ y = 4x - 11 \end{cases}$

51. $\begin{cases} x + \dfrac{1}{6}y = \dfrac{1}{2} \\ 3x + 2y = 3 \end{cases}$

52. $\begin{cases} x + \dfrac{1}{3}y = \dfrac{5}{12} \\ 8x + 3y = 4 \end{cases}$

53. $\begin{cases} \dfrac{x + 2}{2} = \dfrac{y + 11}{3} \\ \dfrac{x}{2} = \dfrac{2y + 16}{6} \end{cases}$

54. $\begin{cases} \dfrac{x + 5}{2} = \dfrac{y + 14}{4} \\ \dfrac{x}{3} = \dfrac{2y + 2}{6} \end{cases}$

55. $\begin{cases} 2x + 3y = 14 \\ 3x - 4y = -69.1 \end{cases}$

56. $\begin{cases} 5x - 2y = -19.8 \\ -3x + 5y = -3.7 \end{cases}$

REVIEW AND PREVIEW

Rewrite the following sentences using mathematical symbols. Do not solve the equations. See Sections 2.4 and 2.5.

57. Twice a number, added to 6, is 3 less than the number.

58. The sum of three consecutive integers is 66.

59. Three times a number, subtracted from 20, is 2.

60. Twice the sum of 8 and a number is the difference of the number and 20.

61. The product of 4 and the sum of a number and 6 is twice the number.

62. The quotient of twice a number and 7 is subtracted from the reciprocal of the number.

CONCEPT EXTENSIONS

Solve. See a Concept Check in this section.

63. To solve this system by the addition method and eliminate the variable y,

$$\begin{cases} 4x + 2y = -7 \\ 3x - y = -12 \end{cases}$$

by what value would you multiply the second equation? What do you get when you complete the multiplication?

Given the system of linear equations $\begin{cases} 3x - y = -8 \\ 5x + 3y = 2 \end{cases}$

64. Use the addition method and
   a. Solve the system by eliminating x.
   b. Solve the system by eliminating y.

65. **Decision Making.** Suppose you are solving the system

$$\begin{cases} 3x + 8y = -5 \\ 2x - 4y = 3. \end{cases}$$

You decide to use the addition method by multiplying both sides of the second equation by 2. In which of the following was the multiplication performed correctly? Explain.
   a. $4x - 8y = 3$
   b. $4x - 8y = 6$

66. **Decision Making.** Suppose you are solving the system

$$\begin{cases} -2x - y = 0 \\ -2x + 3y = 6. \end{cases}$$

You decide to use the addition method by multiplying both sides of the first equation by 3, then adding the resulting equation to the second equation. Which of the following is the correct sum? Explain.
   a. $-8x = 6$
   b. $-8x = 9$

67. When solving a system of equations by the addition method, how do we know when the system has no solution?

68. Explain why the addition method might be preferred over the substitution method for solving the system $\begin{cases} 2x - 3y = 5 \\ 5x + 2y = 6. \end{cases}$

69. Use the system of linear equations below to answer the questions.

$$\begin{cases} x + y = 5 \\ 3x + 3y = b \end{cases}$$

   a. Find the value of b so that the system has an infinite number of solutions.
   b. Find a value of b so that there are no solutions to the system.

70. Use the system of linear equations below to answer the questions.

$$\begin{cases} x + y = 4 \\ 2x + by = 8 \end{cases}$$

a. Find the value of b so that the system has an infinite number of solutions.

b. Find a value of b so that the system has a single solution.

Solve each system by the addition method.

71. $\begin{cases} 1.2x + 3.4y = 27.6 \\ 7.2x - 1.7y = -46.56 \end{cases}$ **72.** $\begin{cases} 5.1x - 2.4y = 3.15 \\ -15.3x + 1.2y = 27.75 \end{cases}$

73. Multiple Steps. Two occupations predicted to greatly increase in number of jobs are pharmacy technicians and network systems and data communication analysts. The number of pharmacy technician jobs predicted for 2004 through 2014 can be approximated by $7.4x - y = -258$. The number of network and data analyst jobs for the same years can be approximated by $12.6x - y = -231$. For both equations, x is the number of years since 2004 and y is the number of jobs in thousands.

a. Use the addition method to solve this system of equations:

$$\begin{cases} 7.4x - y = -258 \\ 12.6x - y = -231 \end{cases}$$

(Round answer to the nearest whole number.)

b. Use your result from part (a) and estimate the year in which the number of both jobs is equal.

c. Use your result from part (a) and estimate the number of pharmacy technician jobs (or the number of analyst jobs since they should be equal).

74. Multiple Steps. In recent years, the number of Americans (in millions) who have skateboarded at least once in a year has been increasing, while the number of Americans who have in-line roller skated has been decreasing. The number of skateboarders (people who have skateboarded at least once a year) from 1996 to 2006 is given by $-0.7x + y = 4.6$ and the number of in-line roller skaters can be given by the equation $1.3x + y = 26.9$. For both equations, x is the number of years after 1996. (*Source:* National Sporting Goods Association)

a. Use the addition method to solve this system of equations:

$$\begin{cases} -0.7x + y = 4.6 \\ 1.3x + y = 26.9 \end{cases}$$

(Round to the nearest whole number. Because of rounding, the y-value of your ordered pair solution may vary.)

b. Use your result from part (a) and estimate the year in which the number of skate boarders equals the number of in-line skaters.

c. Use your result from part (a) and estimate the number of skateboarders (or the number of in-line skaters since they should be equal).

INTEGRATED REVIEW   SOLVING SYSTEMS OF EQUATIONS

Sections 5.1–5.3

Solve each system by either the addition method or the substitution method.

1. $\begin{cases} 2x - 3y = -11 \\ y = 4x - 3 \end{cases}$

2. $\begin{cases} 4x - 5y = 6 \\ y = 3x - 10 \end{cases}$

3. $\begin{cases} x + y = 3 \\ x - y = 7 \end{cases}$

4. $\begin{cases} x - y = 20 \\ x + y = -8 \end{cases}$

5. $\begin{cases} x + 2y = 1 \\ 3x + 4y = -1 \end{cases}$

6. $\begin{cases} x + 3y = 5 \\ 5x + 6y = -2 \end{cases}$

7. $\begin{cases} y = x + 3 \\ 3x - 2y = -6 \end{cases}$

8. $\begin{cases} y = -2x \\ 2x - 3y = -16 \end{cases}$

9. $\begin{cases} y = 2x - 3 \\ y = 5x - 18 \end{cases}$

10. $\begin{cases} y = 6x - 5 \\ y = 4x - 11 \end{cases}$

11. $\begin{cases} x + \dfrac{1}{6}y = \dfrac{1}{2} \\ 3x + 2y = 3 \end{cases}$

12. $\begin{cases} x + \dfrac{1}{3}y = \dfrac{5}{12} \\ 8x + 3y = 4 \end{cases}$

13. $\begin{cases} x - 5y = 1 \\ -2x + 10y = 3 \end{cases}$ **14.** $\begin{cases} -x + 2y = 3 \\ 3x - 6y = -9 \end{cases}$ **15.** $\begin{cases} 0.2x - 0.3y = -0.95 \\ 0.4x + 0.1y = 0.55 \end{cases}$ **16.** $\begin{cases} 0.08x - 0.04y = -0.11 \\ 0.02x - 0.06y = -0.09 \end{cases}$

17. $\begin{cases} x = 3y - 7 \\ 2x - 6y = -14 \end{cases}$ **18.** $\begin{cases} y = \dfrac{x}{2} - 3 \\ 2x - 4y = 0 \end{cases}$ **19.** $\begin{cases} 2x + 5y = -1 \\ 3x - 4y = 33 \end{cases}$ **20.** $\begin{cases} 7x - 3y = 2 \\ 6x + 5y = -21 \end{cases}$

21. Which method, substitution or addition, would you prefer to use to solve the system below? Explain your reasoning.
$$\begin{cases} 3x + 2y = -2 \\ y = -2x \end{cases}$$

22. Which method, substitution or addition, would you prefer to use to solve the system below? Explain your reasoning.
$$\begin{cases} 3x - 2y = -3 \\ 6x + 2y = 12 \end{cases}$$

5.4 SYSTEMS OF LINEAR EQUATIONS AND PROBLEM SOLVING

OBJECTIVE

1 Use a system of equations to solve problems.

OBJECTIVE 1 ▶ Using a system of equations for problem solving. Many of the word problems solved earlier using one-variable equations can also be solved using two equations in **two** variables. We use the same problem-solving steps that have been used throughout this text. The only difference is that two variables are assigned to represent the two unknown quantities and that the stated problem is translated into **two** equations.

Problem-Solving Steps

1. UNDERSTAND the problem. During this step, become comfortable with the problem. Some ways of doing this are to

   Read and reread the problem.

   Choose two variables to represent the two unknowns.

   Construct a drawing, if possible.

   Propose a solution and check. Pay careful attention to how you check your proposed solution. This will help when writing equations to model the problem.

2. TRANSLATE the problem into two equations.

3. SOLVE the system of equations.

4. INTERPRET the results: **Check** the proposed solution in the stated problem and **state** your conclusion.

EXAMPLE 1   **Finding Unknown Numbers**

Find two numbers whose sum is 37 and whose difference is 21.

Solution

1. UNDERSTAND. Read and reread the problem. Suppose that one number is 20. If their sum is 37, the other number is 17 because $20 + 17 = 37$. Is their difference 21? No; $20 - 17 = 3$. Our proposed solution is incorrect, but we now have a better understanding of the problem.

   Since we are looking for two numbers, we let

   x = first number

   y = second number

2. TRANSLATE. Since we have assigned two variables to this problem, we translate our problem into two equations.

In words: two numbers whose sum   is   37

Translate: $x + y$ =   37

In words: two numbers whose difference   is   21

Translate: $x - y$ =   21

3. SOLVE. Now we solve the system

$$\begin{cases} x + y = 37 \\ x - y = 21 \end{cases}$$

Notice that the coefficients of the variable y are opposites. Let's then solve by the addition method and begin by adding the equations.

$$\begin{aligned} x + y &= 37 \\ \underline{x - y} &= \underline{21} \\ 2x \quad\; &= 58 \end{aligned}$$ Add the equations.

$$x = \frac{58}{2} = 29$$ Divide both sides by 2.

Now we let $x = 29$ in the first equation to find y.

$$x + y = 37$$ First equation
$$29 + y = 37$$
$$y = 8$$ Subtract 29 from both sides.

4. INTERPRET. The solution of the system is $(29, 8)$.

Check: Notice that the sum of 29 and 8 is $29 + 8 = 37$, the required sum. Their difference is $29 - 8 = 21$, the required difference.

State: The numbers are 29 and 8. □

PRACTICE

1 Find two numbers whose sum is 30 and whose difference is 6.

EXAMPLE 2   **Solving a Problem about Prices**

The Cirque du Soleil show Corteo is performing locally. Matinee admission for 4 adults and 2 children is $374, while admission for 2 adults and 3 children is $285.

a. What is the price of an adult's ticket?

b. What is the price of a child's ticket?

c. Suppose that a special rate of $1000 is offered for groups of 20 persons. Should a group of 4 adults and 16 children use the group rate? Why or why not?

Solution

1. UNDERSTAND. Read and reread the problem and guess a solution. Let's suppose that the price of an adult's ticket is $50 and the price of a child's ticket is $40. To check our proposed solution, let's see if admission for 4 adults and 2 children is $374.

Admission for 4 adults is 4($50) or $200 and admission for 2 children is 2($40) or $80. This gives a total admission of $200 + $80 = $280, not the required $374. Again though, we have accomplished the purpose of this process. We have a better understanding of the problem. To continue, we let

A = the price of an adult's ticket and

C = the price of a child's ticket

2. TRANSLATE. We translate the problem into two equations using both variables.

In words:	admission for 4 adults	and	admission for 2 children	is	$374
	↓	↓	↓	↓	↓
Translate:	$4A$	+	$2C$	=	374

In words:	admission for 2 adults	and	admission for 3 children	is	$285
	↓	↓	↓	↓	↓
Translate:	$2A$	+	$3C$	=	285

3. SOLVE. We solve the system.

$$\begin{cases} 4A + 2C = 374 \\ 2A + 3C = 285 \end{cases}$$

Since both equations are written in standard form, we solve by the addition method. First we multiply the second equation by -2 so that when we add the equations we eliminate the variable A. Then the system

$$\begin{cases} 4A + 2C = 374 \\ -2(2A + 3C) = -2(285) \end{cases}$$ simplifies to $$\begin{cases} 4A + 2C = 374 \\ -4A - 6C = -570 \end{cases}$$

$$\begin{aligned} -4C &= -196 \quad \text{Add the equations.} \\ C &= 49 \quad \text{Divide by } -4. \end{aligned}$$

or $49, the children's ticket price.

To find A, we replace C with 49 in the first equation.

$$\begin{aligned} 4A + 2C &= 374 \quad &\text{First equation} \\ 4A + 2(49) &= 374 \quad &\text{Let } C = 49. \\ 4A + 98 &= 374 \\ 4A &= 276 \\ A &= 69 \end{aligned}$$

or $69, the adult's ticket price.

4. INTERPRET.

Check: Notice that 4 adults and 2 children will pay $4($69) + 2($49) = $276 + $98 = 374, the required amount. Also, the price for 2 adults and 3 children is $2($69) + 3($49) = $138 + $147 = 285, the required amount.

State: Answer the three original questions.

a. Since $A = 69$, the price of an adult's ticket is $69.

b. Since $C = 49$, the price of a child's ticket is $49.

c. The regular admission price for 4 adults and 16 children is

$$\begin{aligned} 4($69) + 16($49) &= $276 + $784 \\ &= $1060 \end{aligned}$$

This is $60 more than the special group rate of $1000, so they should request the group rate. □

2   It is considered a premium game when the Red Sox or the Yankees come to Texas to play the Rangers. Admission for one of these games for three adults and three children under 14 is $75, while admission for two adults and 4 children is $62. (*Source: MLB.com,* Texas Rangers)

a. What is the price of an adult admission at Ameriquest Park?

b. What is the price of a child's admission?

c. Suppose that a special rate of $200 is offered for groups of 20 persons. Should a group of 5 adults and 15 children use the group rate? Why or why not?

EXAMPLE 3   **Finding Rates**

As part of an exercise program, Albert and Louis started walking each morning. They live 15 miles away from each other and decided to meet one day by walking toward one another. After 2 hours they meet. If Louis walks one mile per hour faster than Albert, find both walking speeds.

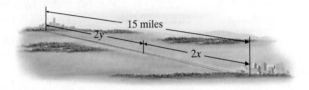

Solution

1. UNDERSTAND. Read and reread the problem. Let's propose a solution and use the formula $d = r \cdot t$ to check. Suppose that Louis's rate is 4 miles per hour. Since Louis's rate is 1 mile per hour faster, Albert's rate is 3 miles per hour. To check, see if they can walk a total of 15 miles in 2 hours. Louis's distance is rate $\cdot$ time = $4(2)$ = 8 miles and Albert's distance is rate time = $3(2)$ = 6 miles. Their total distance is 8 miles + 6 miles = 14 miles, not the required 15 miles. Now that we have a better understanding of the problem, let's model it with a system of equations.

First, we let

x = Albert's rate in miles per hour

y = Louis's rate in miles per hour

Now we use the facts stated in the problem and the formula $d = rt$ to fill in the following chart.

	r	$\cdot$ t	$=$ d
Albert	x	2	$2x$
Louis	y	2	$2y$

2. TRANSLATE. We translate the problem into two equations using both variables.

In words:	Albert's distance	$+$	Louis's distance	$=$	15
Translate:	$2x$	$+$	$2y$	$=$	15

In words:	Louis's rate	is	1 mile per hour faster than Albert's
Translate:	y	$=$	$x + 1$

3. SOLVE. The system of equations we are solving is

$$\begin{cases} 2x + 2y = 15 \\ y = x + 1 \end{cases}$$

Let's use substitution to solve the system since the second equation is solved for y.

$$2x + 2y = 15 \qquad \text{First equation}$$

$$2x + 2(x + 1) = 15 \qquad \text{Replace } y \text{ with } x + 1.$$
$$2x + 2x + 2 = 15$$
$$4x = 13$$
$$x = 3.25 \qquad \text{Divide both sides by 4 and write the result as a decimal.}$$
$$y = x + 1 = 3.25 + 1 = 4.25$$

4. INTERPRET. Albert's proposed rate is 3.25 miles per hour and Louis's proposed rate is 4.25 miles per hour.

Check: Use the formula $d = rt$ and find that in 2 hours, Albert's distance is $(3.25)(2)$ miles or 6.5 miles. In 2 hours, Louis's distance is $(4.25)(2)$ miles or 8.5 miles. The total distance walked is 6.5 miles $+$ 8.5 miles or 15 miles, the given distance.

State: Albert walks at a rate of 3.25 miles per hour and Louis walks at a rate of 4.25 miles per hour. □

PRACTICE

3 Two hikers on a straight trail are 22 miles apart and walking toward each other. After 4 hours they meet. If one hiker is a nature lover and walks 2 miles per hour slower than the other hiker, find both walking speeds.

EXAMPLE 4 **Finding Amounts of Solutions**

Eric Daly, a chemistry teaching assistant, needs 10 liters of a 20% saline solution (salt water) for his 2 p.m. laboratory class. Unfortunately, the only mixtures on hand are a 5% saline solution and a 25% saline solution. How much of each solution should he mix to produce the 20% solution?

Solution

1. UNDERSTAND. Read and reread the problem. Suppose that we need 4 liters of the 5% solution. Then we need $10 - 4 = 6$ liters of the 25% solution. To see if this gives us 10 liters of a 20% saline solution, let's find the amount of pure salt in each solution.

	concentration rate	$\times$	amount of solution	$=$	amount of pure salt
5% solution:	0.05	$\times$	4 liters	$=$	0.2 liters
25% solution:	0.25	$\times$	6 liters	$=$	1.5 liters
20% solution:	0.20	$\times$	10 liters	$=$	2 liters

Since 0.2 liters $+$ 1.5 liters $=$ 1.7 liters, not 2 liters, our proposed solution is incorrect. But we have gained some insight into how to model and check this problem. We let

x = number of liters of 5% solution

y = number of liters of 25% solution

5% saline solution 25% saline solution 20% saline solution

Now we use a table to organize the given data.

	Concentration Rate	Liters of Solution	Liters of Pure Salt
First Solution	5%	x	$0.05x$
Second Solution	25%	y	$0.25y$
Mixture Needed	20%	10	$(0.20)(10)$

2. TRANSLATE. We translate into two equations using both variables.

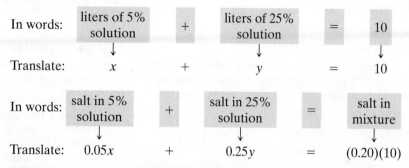

In words: liters of 5% solution $+$ liters of 25% solution $=$ 10

Translate: x $+$ y $=$ 10

In words: salt in 5% solution $+$ salt in 25% solution $=$ salt in mixture

Translate: $0.05x$ $+$ $0.25y$ $=$ $(0.20)(10)$

3. SOLVE. Here we solve the system

$$\begin{cases} x + y = 10 \\ 0.05x + 0.25y = 2 \end{cases}$$

To solve by the addition method, we first multiply the first equation by -25 and the second equation by 100. Then the system

$$\begin{cases} -25(x + y) = -25(10) \\ 100(0.05x + 0.25y) = 100(2) \end{cases} \quad \begin{matrix} \text{simplifies} \\ \text{to} \end{matrix} \quad \begin{cases} -25x - 25y = -250 \\ \underline{5x + 25y = 200} \end{cases}$$

$$-20x = -50 \quad \text{Add.}$$
$$x = 2.5 \quad \text{Divide by } -20.$$

To find y, we let $x = 2.5$ in the first equation of the original system.

$$x + y = 10$$
$$2.5 + y = 10 \quad \text{Let } x = 2.5.$$
$$y = 7.5$$

4. INTERPRET. Thus, we propose that Eric needs to mix 2.5 liters of 5% saline solution with 7.5 liters of 25% saline solution.

Check: Notice that $2.5 + 7.5 = 10$, the required number of liters. Also, the sum of the liters of salt in the two solutions equals the liters of salt in the required mixture:

$$0.05(2.5) + 0.25(7.5) = 0.20(10)$$
$$0.125 + 1.875 = 2$$

State: Eric needs 2.5 liters of the 5% saline solution and 7.5 liters of the 25% solution.

$\square$

PRACTICE
4   Jemima Juarez owns the Sola Café in southern California. She is known for her interesting coffee blends. To create a new blend, she has decided to use Hawaiian Kona and Jamaica Blue Mountain coffee. To test her new blend, she intends to create 20 pounds of the mix. If the Hawaiian Kona costs \$20 per pound and the Jamaica Blue Mountain costs \$28 per pound, how much of each coffee type should she use to create a new blend that costs \$22 per pound?

Concept Check ☑

Suppose you mix an amount of a 30% acid solution with an amount of a 50% acid solution. Which of the following acid strengths would be possible for the resulting acid mixture?

a. 22%   **b.** 44%   **c.** 63%

5.4 EXERCISE SET

PRACTICE WATCH DOWNLOAD READ REVIEW

Decision Making. *Without actually solving each problem, choose each correct solution by deciding which choice satisfies the given conditions.*

△ **1.** The length of a rectangle is 3 feet longer than the width. The perimeter is 30 feet. Find the dimensions of the rectangle.

  a. length = 8 feet; width = 5 feet

  b. length = 8 feet; width = 7 feet

  c. length = 9 feet; width = 6 feet

△ **2.** An isosceles triangle, a triangle with two sides of equal length, has a perimeter of 20 inches. Each of the equal sides is one inch longer than the third side. Find the lengths of the three sides.

  a. 6 inches, 6 inches, and 7 inches

  b. 7 inches, 7 inches, and 6 inches

  c. 6 inches, 7 inches, and 8 inches

3. Two computer disks and three notebooks cost $17. However, five computer disks and four notebooks cost $32. Find the price of each.

  a. notebook = $4; computer disk = $3

  b. notebook = $3; computer disk = $4

  c. notebook = $5; computer disk = $2

4. Two music CDs and four music cassette tapes cost a total of $40. However, three music CDs and five cassette tapes cost $55. Find the price of each.

  a. CD = $12; cassette = $4 **b.** CD = $15; cassette = $2

  c. CD = $10; cassette = $5

5. Kesha has a total of 100 coins, all of which are either dimes or quarters. The total value of the coins is $13.00. Find the number of each type of coin.

  a. 80 dimes; 20 quarters   **b.** 20 dimes; 44 quarters

  c. 60 dimes; 40 quarters

6. Samuel has 28 gallons of saline solution available in two large containers at his pharmacy. One container holds three times as much as the other container. Find the capacity of each container.

  a. 15 gallons; 5 gallons   **b.** 20 gallons; 8 gallons

  c. 21 gallons; 7 gallons

Write a system of equations in x and y describing each situation. Do not solve the system. See Example 1.

7. A smaller number and a larger number add up to 15 and have a difference of 7. (Let *x* be the larger number.)

8. The total of two numbers is 16. The first number plus 2 more than 3 times the second equals 18. (Let *x* be the first number.)

9. Keiko has a total of $6500, which she has invested in two accounts. The larger account is $800 greater than the smaller account. (Let *x* be the amount of money in the larger account.)

10. Dominique has four times as much money in his savings account as in his checking account. The total amount is $2300. (Let *x* be the amount of money in his checking account.)

MIXED PRACTICE

Solve. See Examples 1 through 4.

11. Two numbers total 83 and have a difference of 17. Find the two numbers.

12. The sum of two numbers is 76 and their difference is 52. Find the two numbers.

13. A first number plus twice a second number is 8. Twice the first number, plus the second totals 25. Find the numbers.

14. One number is 4 more than twice the second number. Their total is 25. Find the numbers.

15. The highest scorer during the WNBA 2006 regular season was Diana Taurasi of the Phoenix Mercury. Over the season, Taurasi scored 116 more points than Seimone Augustus of the Minnesota Lynx. Together, Taurasi and Augustus scored 1604 points during the 2006 regular season. How many points did each player score over the course of the season? (*Source:* Women's National Basketball Association)

16. During the 2006 regular MLB season, Ryan Howard of the Philadelphia Phillies hit the most home runs of any player in the major leagues. Over the course of the season, he hit 4 more home runs than David Ortiz of the Boston Red Sox. Together, these batting giants hit 112 home runs. How many home runs did each player hit? (*Source:* Major League Baseball)

17. Ann Marie Jones has been pricing Amtrak train fares for a group trip to New York. Three adults and four children must pay $159. Two adults and three children must pay $112. Find the price of an adult's ticket, and find the price of a child's ticket.

18. Last month, Jerry Papa purchased five DVDs and two CDs at Wall-to-Wall Sound for $65. This month he bought three DVDs and four CDs for $81. Find the price of each DVD, and find the price of each CD.

19. Johnston and Betsy Waring have a jar containing 80 coins, all of which are either quarters or nickels. The total value of the coins is $14.60. How many of each type of coin do they have?

20. Sarah and Keith Robinson purchased 40 stamps, a mixture of 39¢ and 24¢ stamps. Find the number of each type of stamp if they spent $14.85.

21. Davie and Judi Mihaly own 50 shares of Apple stock and 60 shares of Microsoft stock. At the close of the markets on March 9, 2007, their stock portfolio was worth $6035.90. The closing price of the Microsoft stock was $60.68 less than the closing price of Apple stock on that day. What was the price of each stock on March 9, 2007? (*Source:* New York Stock Exchange)

22. Pho Lin has investments in EBay and Amazon stock. On March 9, 2007, EBay stock closed at $30.82 per share and Amazon stock closed at $38.84 per share. Pho's stock portfolio was worth $2866.60 at the end of the day. If Pho owns 20 more shares of Amazon stock than EBay stock, how many of each type of stock does she own?

23. Twice last month, Judy Carter rented a car from Enterprise in Fresno, California, and traveled around the Southwest on business. Enterprise rents its cars for a daily fee, plus an additional charge per mile driven. Judy recalls that her first trip lasted 4 days, she drove 450 miles, and the rental cost her $240.50. On her second business trip she drove 200 miles in 3 days, and paid $146.00 for the rental. Find the daily fee and the mileage charge.

24. Joan Gundersen rented a car from Hertz, which rents its cars for a daily fee plus an additional charge per mile driven. Joan recalls that a car rented for 5 days and driven for 300 miles cost her $178, while a car rented for 4 days and driven for 500 miles cost $197. Find the daily fee, and find the mileage charge.

25. Pratap Puri rowed 18 miles down the Delaware River in 2 hours, but the return trip took him $4\frac{1}{2}$ hours. Find the rate Pratap can row in still water, and find the rate of the current.
Let x = rate Pratap can row in still water and
y = rate of the current

d	=	r	·	t
Downstream		$x + y$		
Upstream		$x - y$		

26. The Jonathan Schultz family took a canoe 10 miles down the Allegheny River in $1\frac{1}{4}$ hours. After lunch it took them 4 hours to return. Find the rate of the current.
Let x = rate the family can row in still water and
y = rate of the current

d	=	r	·	t
Downstream		$x + y$		
Upstream		$x - y$		

27. Dave and Sandy Hartranft are frequent flyers with Delta Airlines. They often fly from Philadelphia to Chicago, a distance of 780 miles. On one particular trip they fly into the wind, and the flight takes 2 hours. The return trip, with the wind behind them, only takes $1\frac{1}{2}$ hours. If the wind speed is the same on each trip, find the speed of the wind and find the speed of the plane in still air.

28. With a strong wind behind it, a United Airlines jet flies 2400 miles from Los Angeles to Orlando in $4\frac{3}{4}$ hours. The return trip takes 6 hours, as the plane flies into the wind. If the wind speed is the same on each trip, find the speed of the plane in still air, and find the wind speed to the nearest tenth of a mile per hour.

29. Jim Williamson began a 96-mile bicycle trip to build up stamina for a triathlete competition. Unfortunately, his bicycle chain broke, so he finished the trip walking. The whole trip took 6 hours. If Jim walks at a rate of 4 miles per hour and rides at 20 miles per hour, find the amount of time he spent on the bicycle.

30. In Canada, eastbound and westbound trains travel along the same track, with sidings to pull onto to avoid accidents. Two trains are now 150 miles apart, with the westbound train traveling twice as fast as the eastbound train. A warning must be issued to pull one train onto a siding or else the trains will crash in $1\frac{1}{4}$ hours. Find the speed of the eastbound train and the speed of the westbound train.

31. Doreen Schmidt is a chemist with Gemco Pharmaceutical. She needs to prepare 12 ounces of a 9% hydrochloric acid solution. Find the amount of a 4% solution and the amount of a 12% solution she should mix to get this solution.

Concentration Rate	Ounces of Solution	Ounces of Pure Acid
0.04	x	$0.04x$
0.12	y	?
0.09	12	?

32. Elise Everly is preparing 15 liters of a 25% saline solution. Elise has two other saline solutions with strengths of 40% and

10%. Find the amount of 40% solution and the amount of 10% solution she should mix to get 15 liters of a 25% solution.

Concentration Rate	Liters of Solution	Liters of Pure Salt
0.40	x	$0.40x$
0.10	y	?
0.25	15	?

33. Wayne Osby blends coffee for a local coffee café. He needs to prepare 200 pounds of blended coffee beans selling for $3.95 per pound. He intends to do this by blending together a high-quality bean costing $4.95 per pound and a cheaper bean costing $2.65 per pound. To the nearest pound, find how much high-quality coffee bean and how much cheaper coffee bean he should blend.

34. Macadamia nuts cost an astounding $16.50 per pound, but research by an independent firm says that mixed nuts sell better if macadamias are included. The standard mix costs $9.25 per pound. Find how many pounds of macadamias and how many pounds of the standard mix should be combined to produce 40 pounds that will cost $10 per pound. Find the amounts to the nearest tenth of a pound.

35. Recall that two angles are complementary if the sum of their measures is 90°. Find the measures of two complementary angles if one angle is twice the other.

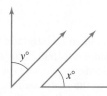

36. Recall that two angles are supplementary if the sum of their measures is 180°. Find the measures of two supplementary angles if one angle is 20° more than four times the other.

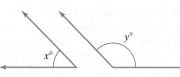

37. Find the measures of two complementary angles if one angle is 10° more than three times the other.

38. Find the measures of two supplementary angles if one angle is 18° more than twice the other.

39. Kathi and Robert Hawn had a pottery stand at the annual Skippack Craft Fair. They sold some of their pottery at the original price of $9.50 each, but later decreased the price of each by $2. If they sold all 90 pieces and took in $721, find how many they sold at the original price and how many they sold at the reduced price.

40. A charity fund-raiser consisted of a spaghetti supper where a total of 387 people were fed. They charged $6.80 for adults and half-price for children. If they took in $2444.60, find how many adults and how many children attended the supper.

41. The Santa Fe National Historic Trail is approximately 1200 miles between Old Franklin, Missouri, and Santa Fe, New Mexico. Suppose that a group of hikers start from each town and walk the trail toward each other. They meet after a total hiking time of 240 hours. If one group travels $\frac{1}{2}$ mile per hour slower than the other group, find the rate of each group. (*Source:* National Park Service)

42. California 1 South is a historic highway that stretches 123 miles along the coast from Monterey to Morro Bay. Suppose that two antique cars start driving this highway, one from each town. They meet after 3 hours. Find the rate of each car if one car travels 1 mile per hour faster than the other car. (*Source:* National Geographic)

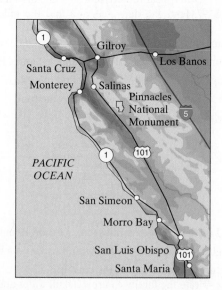

43. A 30% solution of fertilizer is to be mixed with a 60% solution of fertilizer in order to get 150 gallons of a 50% solution. How many gallons of the 30% solution and 60% solution should be mixed?

44. A 10% acid solution is to be mixed with a 50% acid solution in order to get 120 ounces of a 20% acid solution. How many ounces of the 10% solution and 50% solution should be mixed?

45. Traffic signs are regulated by the *Manual on Uniform Traffic Control Devices* (MUTCD). According to this manual, if the sign below is placed on a freeway, its perimeter must be 144 inches. Also, its length is 12 inches longer than its width. Find the dimensions of this sign.

46. According to the MUTCD (see Exercise 45), this sign must have a perimeter of 60 inches. Also, its length must be 6 inches longer than its width. Find the dimensions of this sign.

REVIEW AND PREVIEW

Solve each linear inequality. See Section 4.1.

47. $-3x < -9$

48. $2x - 7 \le 5x + 11$

49. $4(2x - 1) \ge 0$

50. $\dfrac{2}{3}x < \dfrac{1}{3}$

CONCEPT EXTENSIONS

Solve. See the Concept Check in the section.

51. Multiple Choice. Suppose you mix an amount of candy costing $0.49 a pound with candy costing $0.65 a pound. Which of the following costs per pound could result?

a. $0.58   **b.** $0.72   **c.** $0.29

52. Multiple Choice. Suppose you mix a 50% acid solution with pure acid (100%). Which of the following acid strengths are possible for the resulting acid mixture?

a. 25%   **b.** 150%   **c.** 62%   **d.** 90%

△ **53.** Dale and Sharon Mahnke have decided to fence off a garden plot behind their house, using their house as the "fence" along one side of the garden. The length (which runs parallel to the house) is 3 feet less than twice the width. Find the dimensions if 33 feet of fencing is used along the three sides requiring it.

△ **54.** Judy McElroy plans to erect 152 feet of fencing around her rectangular horse pasture. A river bank serves as one side length of the rectangle. If each width is 4 feet longer than half the length, find the dimensions.

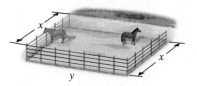

55. Multiple Steps. The percent of viewers who watch nightly network news can be approximated by the equation $y = 0.82x + 17.2$, where x is the years of age over 18 of the viewer. The percent of viewers who watch cable TV news is approximated by the equation $y = 0.33x + 30.5$ where x is also the years of age over 18 of the viewer. (*Source:* The Pew Research Center for The People & The Press)

a. Solve the system of equations: $\begin{cases} y = 0.82x + 17.2 \\ y = 0.33x + 30.5 \end{cases}$

Round x and y to the nearest tenth.

b. Explain what the point of intersection means in terms of the context of the exercise.

c. Look at the slopes of both equations of the system. What type of news attracts older viewers more? What type of news attracts younger viewers more?

56. In the triangle below, the measure of angle x is 6 times the measure of angle y. Find the measure of x and y by writing a system of two equations in two unknowns and solving the system.

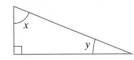

5.5 SYSTEMS OF LINEAR INEQUALITIES

OBJECTIVE 1 ▶ Solving systems of linear inequalities. In Section 4.5, we graphed linear inequalities in two variables. Just as two linear equations make a system of linear equations, two linear inequalities make a **system of linear inequalities.** Systems of inequalities are very important in a process called linear programming. Many businesses use linear programming to find the most profitable way to use limited resources such as employees, machines, or buildings.

A **solution of a system of linear inequalities** is an ordered pair that satisfies each inequality in the system. The set of all such ordered pairs is the solution set of the system. Graphing this set gives us a picture of the solution set. We can graph a system of inequalities by graphing each inequality in the system and identifying the region of overlap.

EXAMPLE 1 Graph the solution of the system: $\begin{cases} 3x \geq y \\ x + 2y \leq 8 \end{cases}$

Solution We begin by graphing each inequality on the same set of axes. The graph of the solution of the system is the region contained in the graphs of both inequalities. It is their intersection.

First, graph $3x \geq y$. The boundary line is the graph of $3x = y$. Sketch a solid boundary line since the inequality $3x \geq y$ means $3x > y$ or $3x = y$. The test point $(1, 0)$ satisfies the inequality, so shade the half-plane that includes $(1, 0)$.

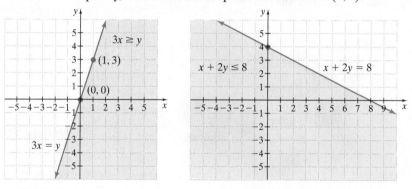

Next, sketch a solid boundary line $x + 2y = 8$ on the same set of axes. The test point $(0, 0)$ satisfies the inequality $x + 2y \leq 8$, so shade the half-plane that includes $(0, 0)$. (For clarity, the graph of $x + 2y \leq 8$ is shown on a separate set of axes.)

An ordered pair solution of the system must satisfy both inequalities. These solutions are points that lie in both shaded regions. The solution of the system is the purple shaded region as seen below. This solution includes parts of both boundary lines.

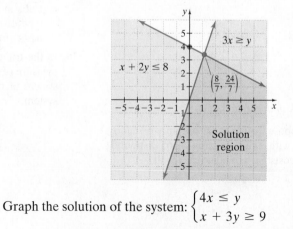

PRACTICE
1 Graph the solution of the system: $\begin{cases} 4x \leq y \\ x + 3y \geq 9 \end{cases}$

In linear programming, it is sometimes necessary to find the coordinates of the **corner point:** the point at which the two boundary lines intersect. To find the point of intersection, solve the related linear system

$$\begin{cases} 3x = y \\ x + 2y = 8 \end{cases}$$

by the substitution method or the addition method. The lines intersect at $\left(\dfrac{8}{7}, \dfrac{24}{7}\right)$, the corner point of the graph.

Graphing the Solution of a System of Linear Inequalities

STEP 1. Graph each inequality in the system on the same set of axes.

STEP 2. The solutions of the system are the points common to the graphs of all the inequalities in the system.

EXAMPLE 2   Graph the solution of the system: $\begin{cases} x - y < 2 \\ x + 2y > -1 \end{cases}$

Solution   Graph both inequalities on the same set of axes. Both boundary lines are dashed lines since the inequality symbols are $<$ and $>$. The solution of the system is the region shown by the purple shading. In this example, the boundary lines are not a part of the solution.

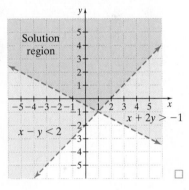

PRACTICE
2   Graph the solution of the system: $\begin{cases} x - y > 4 \\ x + 3y < -4 \end{cases}$

EXAMPLE 3   Graph the solution of the system: $\begin{cases} -3x + 4y < 12 \\ x \geq 2 \end{cases}$

Solution   Graph both inequalities on the same set of axes.

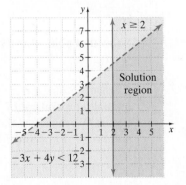

The solution of the system is the purple shaded region, including a portion of the line $x = 2$.

PRACTICE
3   Graph the solution of the system: $\begin{cases} y \leq 6 \\ -2x + 5y > 10 \end{cases}$

OBJECTIVE 2 ▶ Modeling with systems of linear inequalities. Just as two or more linear equations make up a system of linear equations, two or more linear inequalities make up a **system of linear inequalities.** A **solution of a system of linear inequalities** in two variables is an ordered pair that satisfies each inequality in the system.

EXAMPLE 4 Forests, Grasslands, Deserts, and Systems of Inequalities

Temperature and precipitation affect whether or not trees and forests can grow. At certain levels of precipitation and temperature, only grasslands and deserts will exist. The graph below shows three kinds of regions—deserts, grasslands, and forests—that result from various ranges of temperature, T, and precipitation, P.

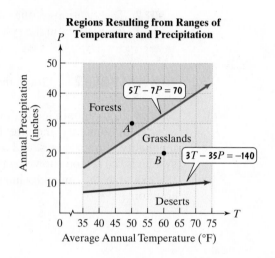

Regions Resulting from Ranges of Temperature and Precipitation

Source: A. Miller and J. Thompson, *Elements of Meteorology*

Systems of inequalities can be used to model where forests, grasslands, and deserts occur. Because these regions occur when the average annual temperature, T, is 35°F or greater, each system contains the inequality $T \geq 35$.

Forests occur if	Grasslands occur if	Deserts occur if
$T \geq 35$	$T \geq 35$	$T \geq 35$
$5T - 7P < 70.$	$5T - 7P \geq 70$	$3T - 35P > -140.$
	$3T - 35P \leq -140.$	

Show that point A is a solution of the system of inequalities that models where forests occur.

Solution Point A has coordinates $(50, 30)$. This means that if a region has an average annual temperature of 50°F and an average annual precipitation of 30 inches, a forest occurs. We can show that $(50, 30)$ satisfies the system of inequalities for forests by substituting 50 for T and 30 for P in each inequality in the system.

$$T \geq 35 \qquad\qquad\qquad 5T - 7P < 70$$
$$50 \geq 35, \quad \text{true} \qquad\qquad 5 \cdot 50 - 7 \cdot 30 \overset{?}{<} 70$$
$$250 - 210 \overset{?}{<} 70$$
$$40 < 70, \quad \text{true}$$

The coordinates (50, 30) make each inequality true. Thus, (50, 30) satisfies the system for forests.

PRACTICE

4 Show that point B in the Example 4 graph is a solution of the system of inequalities that models where grasslands occur.

5.5 EXERCISE SET

MyMathLab®

PRACTICE · WATCH · DOWNLOAD · READ · REVIEW

MIXED PRACTICE

Graph the solution of each system of linear inequalities. See Examples 1 through 3.

1. $\begin{cases} y \geq x + 1 \\ y \geq 3 - x \end{cases}$

2. $\begin{cases} y \geq x - 3 \\ y \geq -1 - x \end{cases}$

3. $\begin{cases} y < 3x - 4 \\ y \leq x + 2 \end{cases}$

4. $\begin{cases} y \leq 2x + 1 \\ y > x + 2 \end{cases}$

5. $\begin{cases} y \leq -2x - 2 \\ y \geq x + 4 \end{cases}$

6. $\begin{cases} y \leq 2x + 4 \\ y \geq -x - 5 \end{cases}$

7. $\begin{cases} y \geq -x + 2 \\ y \leq 2x + 5 \end{cases}$

8. $\begin{cases} y \geq x - 5 \\ y \leq -3x + 3 \end{cases}$

9. $\begin{cases} x \geq 3y \\ x + 3y \leq 6 \end{cases}$

10. $\begin{cases} -2x < y \\ x + 2y < 3 \end{cases}$

11. $\begin{cases} y + 2x \geq 0 \\ 5x - 3y \leq 12 \end{cases}$

12. $\begin{cases} y + 2x \leq 0 \\ 5x + 3y \geq -2 \end{cases}$

13. $\begin{cases} 3x - 4y \geq -6 \\ 2x + y \leq 7 \end{cases}$

14. $\begin{cases} 4x - y \geq -2 \\ 2x + 3y \leq -8 \end{cases}$

15. $\begin{cases} x \leq 2 \\ y \geq -3 \end{cases}$

16. $\begin{cases} x \geq -3 \\ y \geq -2 \end{cases}$

17. $\begin{cases} y \geq 1 \\ x < -3 \end{cases}$

18. $\begin{cases} y > 2 \\ x \geq -1 \end{cases}$

19. $\begin{cases} 2x + 3y < -8 \\ x \geq -4 \end{cases}$

20. $\begin{cases} 3x + 2y \leq 6 \\ x < 2 \end{cases}$

21. $\begin{cases} 2x - 5y \leq 9 \\ y \leq -3 \end{cases}$

22. $\begin{cases} 2x + 5y \leq -10 \\ y \geq 1 \end{cases}$

23. $\begin{cases} y \geq \dfrac{1}{2}x + 2 \\ y \leq \dfrac{1}{2}x - 3 \end{cases}$

24. $\begin{cases} y \geq \dfrac{-3}{2}x + 3 \\ y < \dfrac{-3}{2}x + 6 \end{cases}$

REVIEW AND PREVIEW

Find the square of each expression. For example, the square of 7 is 7^2 or 49. The square of 5x is $(5x)^2$ or $25x^2$. See Section 1.4.

25. 4

26. 3

27. $6x$

28. $11y$

29. $10y^3$

30. $8x^5$

In Exercises 31–34, systems of inequalities will be used to model three of the target heart rate ranges shown in the bar graph. We begin with the target heart rate range for cardiovascular conditioning, modeled by the following system of inequalities:

$$10 \leq a \leq 70 \quad \text{Heart rate ranges apply to ages 10 through 70, inclusive.}$$

$$H \geq 0.7(220 - a) \quad \text{Target heart rate range is greater than or equal to 70\% of maximum heart rate}$$

$$H \leq 0.8(220 - a). \quad \text{and less than or equal to 80\% of maximum heart rate.}$$

The graph of this system is shown in the figure. Use the graph to solve Exercises 31–32.

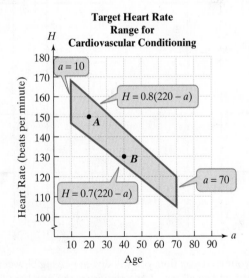

31. a. What are the coordinates of point A and what does this mean in terms of age and heart rate?

  b. Show that point A is a solution of the system of inequalities.

32. a. What are the coordinates of point B and what does this mean in terms of age and heart rate?

b. Show that point B is a solution of the system of inequalities.

33. Describe the location of the solution region of the system.

$$\begin{cases} x < 0 \\ y < 0 \end{cases}$$

34. Describe the location of the solution region of the system.

$$\begin{cases} x < 0 \\ y > 0 \end{cases}$$

CONCEPT EXTENSIONS

Matching. *For each system of inequalities, choose the corresponding graph.*

35. $\begin{cases} y < 5 \\ x > 3 \end{cases}$ **36.** $\begin{cases} y > 5 \\ x < 3 \end{cases}$

37. $\begin{cases} y \leq 5 \\ x < 3 \end{cases}$ **38.** $\begin{cases} y > 5 \\ x \geq 3 \end{cases}$

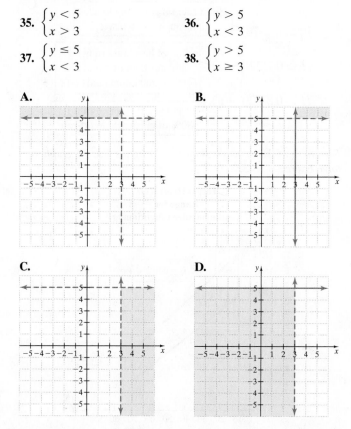

A.   **B.**

C.   **D.**

39. On your next vacation, you will divide lodging between large resorts and small inns. Let x represent the number of nights spent in large resorts. Let y represent the number of nights spent in small inns.

a. Write a system of inequalities that models the following conditions:

You want to stay at least 5 nights. At least one night should be spent at a large resort. Large resorts average \$200 per night and small inns average \$100 per night. Your budget permits no more than \$700 for lodging.

b. Graph the solution set of the system of inequalities in part (a).

c. Based on your graph in part (b), how many nights could you spend at a large resort and still stay within your budget?

40. a. An elevator can hold no more than 2000 pounds. If children average 80 pounds and adults average 160 pounds, write a system of inequalities that models when the elevator holding x children and y adults is overloaded.

b. Graph the solution set of the system of inequalities in part (a).

41. Explain how to decide which region to shade to show the solution region of the following system.

$$\begin{cases} x \geq 3 \\ y \geq -2 \end{cases}$$

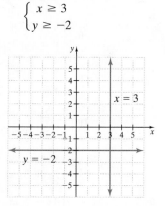

42. Describe the location of the solution region of the system

$$\begin{cases} x > 0 \\ y > 0. \end{cases}$$

43. Graph the solution of $\begin{cases} 2x - y \leq 6 \\ x \geq 3 \\ y > 2 \end{cases}$

44. Graph the solution of $\begin{cases} x + y < 5 \\ y < 2x \\ x \geq 0 \\ y \geq 0 \end{cases}$

5.6 FREQUENCY DISTRIBUTIONS, HISTOGRAMS, AND STEM-AND-LEAF PLOTS

Numerical information, such as the information about the top three TV shows of the twentieth century, shown in the table below is called **data.** The word **statistics** is often used when referring to data. However, statistics has a second meaning: Statistics is also a method for collecting, organizing, analyzing, and interpreting data, as well as drawing conclusions based on the data. This methodology divides statistics into two main areas. **Descriptive statistics** is concerned with collecting, organizing, summarizing, and presenting data. **Inferential statistics** has to do with making generalizations about and drawing conclusions from the data collected.

TV Programs with The Greatest U.S. Audience Viewing Percentage of the Twentieth Century

Program	Total Households	Viewing Percentage
1. *M*A*S*H* Feb. 28, 1983	50,150,000	60.2%
2. *Dallas* Nov. 21, 1980	41,470,000	53.3%
3. *Roots Part 8* Jan. 30, 1977	36,380,000	51.1%

Source: Nielsen Media Research

OBJECTIVE 1 ▶ Frequency distributions. After data have been collected from a sample of the population, the next task facing the statistician is to present the data in a condensed and manageable form. In this way, the data can be more easily interpreted.

Suppose, for example, that researchers are interested in determining the age at which adolescent males show the greatest rate of physical growth. A random sample of 35 ten-year-old boys is measured for height and then remeasured each year until they reach 18. The age of maximum yearly growth for each subject is as follows:

12, 14, 13, 14, 16, 14, 14, 17, 13, 10, 13, 18, 12, 15, 14, 15, 15, 14, 14, 13, 15, 16, 15, 12, 13, 16, 11, 15, 12, 13, 12, 11, 13, 14, 14.

A piece of data is called a **data item.** This list of data has 35 data items. Some of the data items are identical. Two of the data items are 11 and 11. Thus, we can say that the **data value** 11 occurs twice. Similarly, because five of the data items are 12, 12, 12, 12, and 12, the data value 12 occurs five times.

Collected data can be presented using a **frequency distribution.** Such a distribution consists of two columns. The data values are listed in one column. Numerical data are generally listed from smallest to largest. The adjacent column is labeled **frequency** and indicates the number of times each value occurs.

A Frequency Distribution for a boy's age of Maximum Yearly Growth

Age of Maximum Growth	Number of Boys (Frequency)
10	1
11	2
12	5
13	7
14	9
15	6
16	3
17	1
18	1
Total:	$n = 35$

35 is the sum of the frequencies.

EXAMPLE 1   Constructing a Frequency Distribution

Construct a frequency distribution for the data of the age of maximum yearly growth for 35 boys:

12, 14, 13, 14, 16, 14, 14, 17, 13, 10, 13, 18, 12, 15, 14, 15, 15, 14, 14, 13, 15, 16, 15, 12, 13, 16, 11, 15, 12, 13, 12, 11, 13, 14, 14.

Solution   It is difficult to determine trends in the data above in its current format. Perhaps we can make sense of the data by organizing it into a frequency distribution. Let us create two columns. One lists all possible data values, from smallest (10) to largest (18). The other column indicates the number of times the value occurs in the sample. The frequency distribution is shown in the table.

The frequency distribution indicates that one subject had maximum growth at age 10, two at age 11, five at age 12, seven at age 13, and so on. The maximum growth for most of the subjects occurred between the ages of 12 and 15. Nine boys experienced maximum growth at age 14, more than at any other age within the sample. The sum of the frequencies, 35, is equal to the original number of data items.

The trend shown by the frequency distribution in the table indicates that the number of boys who attain their maximum yearly growth at a given age increases until age 14 and decreases after that. This trend is not evident in the data in its original format. □

PRACTICE

1 Construct a frequency distribution for the data showing final course grades for students in a precalculus course, listed alphabetically by student name in a grade book:

F, A, B, B, C, C, B, C, A, A, C, C, D, C, B, D, C, C, B, C.

A frequency distribution that lists all possible data items can be quite cumbersome when there are many such items. For example, consider the following data items. These are statistics test scores for a class of 40 students.

82	47	75	64	57	82	63	93
76	68	84	54	88	77	79	80
94	92	94	80	94	66	81	67
75	73	66	87	76	45	43	56
57	74	50	78	71	84	59	76

It's difficult to determine how well the group did when the grades are displayed like this. Because there are so many data items, one way to organize these data so that the results are more meaningful is to arrange the grades into groups, or **classes**, based on something that interests us. Many grading systems assign an A to grades in the 90–100 class, B to grades in the 80–89 class, C to grades in the 70–79 class, and so on. These classes provide one way to organize the data.

Looking at the 40 statistics test scores, we see that they range from a low of 43 to a high of 94. We can use classes that run from 40 through 49, 50 through 59, 60 through 69, and so on up to 90 through 99, to organize the scores. In Example 2, we go through the data and tally each item into the appropriate class. This method for organizing data is called a **grouped frequency distribution.**

EXAMPLE 2 Constructing a Grouped Frequency Distribution

Use the classes 40–49, 50–59, 60–69, 70–79, 80–89, and 90–99 to construct a grouped frequency distribution for the 40 test scores on the previous page.

Solution We use the 40 given scores and tally the number of scores in each class.

Test Scores (Class)	Tally	Number of Students (Frequency)
40–49	|||	3
50–59	⫫⫫⫫		6
60–69	⫫⫫⫫		6
70–79	⫫⫫⫫ ⫫⫫⫫		11
80–89	⫫⫫⫫ ||||	9
90–99	⫫⫫⫫	5

The second score in the list, 47, is shown as the first tally in this row.

The first score in the list, 82, is shown as the first tally in this row.

Class	Frequency
40–49	3
50–59	6
60–69	6
70–79	11
80–89	9
90–99	5
Total:	$n = 40$

40, the sum of the frequencies, is the number of data items.

Omitting the tally column results in the grouped frequency distribution in the table to the right on page 340. The distribution shows that the greatest frequency of students scored in the 70–79 class. The number of students decreases in classes that contain successively lower and higher scores. The sum of the frequencies, 40, is equal to the original number of data items.

□

PRACTICE
2 Use the classes in the table for Example 2 to construct a grouped frequency distribution for the following 37 exam scores:

73	58	68	75	94	79	96	79
87	83	89	52	99	97	89	58
95	77	75	81	75	73	73	62
69	76	77	71	50	57	41	98
77	71	69	90	75.			

The leftmost number in each class of a grouped frequency distribution is called the **lower class limit**. For example, in the Example 2 table, the lower limit of the first class is 40 and the lower limit of the third class is 60. The rightmost number in each class is called the **upper class limit**. In this table, 49 and 69 are the upper limits for the first and third classes, respectively. Notice that if we take the difference between any two consecutive lower class limits, we get the same number:

$$50 - 40 = 10, \ 60 - 50 = 10, \ 70 - 60 = 10, \ 80 - 70 = 10, \ 90 - 80 = 10.$$

The number 10 is called the **class width.**

When setting up class limits, each class, with the possible exception of the first or last, should have the same width. Because each data item must fall into exactly one class, it is sometimes helpful to vary the width of the first or last class to allow for items that fall far above or below most of the data.

OBJECTIVE 2 ▶ Histograms and frequency polygons. Take a second look at the frequency distribution for the age of a boy's maximum yearly growth, repeated in the margin. A bar graph with bars that touch can be used to visually display the data. Such a graph is called a **histogram.** The histogram below was constructed using the frequency distribution in the margin table. A series of rectangles whose heights represent the frequencies are placed next to each other. For example, the height of the bar for the data value 10, is 1. This corresponds to the frequency for 10 given in the table. The higher the bar, the more frequent the age. The break along the horizontal axis, symbolized by ∿, eliminates listing the ages 1 through 9.

(repeated) A Frequency Distribution for a boy's age of Maximum Yearly Growth

Age of Maximum Growth	Number of Boys (Frequency)
10	1
11	2
12	5
13	7
14	9
15	6
16	3
17	1
18	1
Total: $n = 35$	

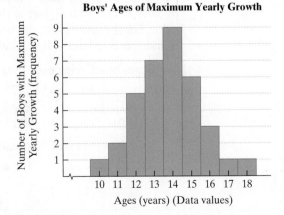

A histogram for a boy's age of maximum yearly growth

A line graph called a **frequency polygon** can also be used to visually convey the information shown on the previous page. The axes are labeled just like those in a histogram. Thus, the horizontal axis shows data values and the vertical axis shows frequencies. Once a histogram has been constructed, it's fairly easy to draw a frequency polygon. The figure to the left below shows a histogram with a dot at the top of each rectangle at its midpoint. Connect each of these midpoints with a straight line. To complete the frequency polygon at both ends, the lines should be drawn down to touch the horizontal axis. The completed frequency polygon is shown below to the right.

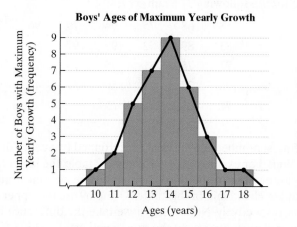

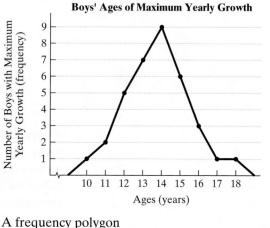

A histogram with a superimposed frequency polygon

A frequency polygon

OBJECTIVE 3 ▶ Stem-and-leaf plots. A unique way of displaying data uses a tool called a **stem-and-leaf plot.** Example 5 illustrates how we sort the data, revealing the same visual impression created by a histogram.

EXAMPLE 3   Constructing a Stem-and-Leaf Plot

Use the data showing statistics test scores for 40 students to construct a stem-and-leaf plot:

82	47	75	64	57	82	63	93
76	68	84	54	88	77	79	80
94	92	94	80	94	66	81	67
75	73	66	87	76	45	43	56
57	74	50	78	71	84	59	76.

Solution   The plot is constructed by separating each data item into two parts. The first part is the *stem*. The **stem** consists of the tens digit. For example, the stem for the score of 82 is 8. The second part is the *leaf*. The **leaf** consists of the units digit for a given value. For the score of 82, the leaf is 2. The possible stems for the 40 scores are 4, 5, 6, 7, 8, and 9, entered in the left column of the plot.

Begin by entering each data item in the first row:

82   47   75   64   57   82   63   93.

Entering 8**2**:		Adding 4**7**:		Adding 7**5**:		Adding 6**4**:	
Stems	**Leaves**	**Stems**	**Leaves**	**Stems**	**Leaves**	**Stems**	**Leaves**
4		4	**7**	4	7	4	7
5		5		5		5	
6		6		6		6	**4**
7		7		7	**5**	7	5
8	**2**	8	2	8	2	8	2
9		9		9		9	

Adding 5**7**:		Adding 8**2**:		Adding 6**3**:		Adding 9**3**:	
Stems	**Leaves**	**Stems**	**Leaves**	**Stems**	**Leaves**	**Stems**	**Leaves**
4	7	4	7	4	7	4	7
5	**7**	5	7	5	7	5	7
6	4	6	4	6	4**3**	6	4 3
7	5	7	5	7	5	7	5
8	2	8	2**2**	8	2 2	8	2 2
9		9		9		9	**3**

We continue in this manner and enter all the data items. The figure below shows the completed stem-and-leaf plot. If you turn the page so that the left margin is on the bottom and facing you, the visual impression created by the enclosed leaves is the same as that created by a histogram. An advantage over the histogram is that the stem-and-leaf plot preserves exact data items. The enclosed leaves extend farthest to the right when the stem is 7. This shows that the greatest frequency of students scored in the 70s.   □

Tens digit   Units digit

Stems	**Leaves**
4	7 5 3
5	7 4 6 7 0 9
6	4 3 8 6 7 6
7	5 6 7 9 5 3 6 4 8 1 6
8	2 2 4 8 0 0 1 7 4
9	3 4 2 4 4

A stem-and-leaf plot displaying 40 test scores

PRACTICE
3   Construct a stem-and-leaf plot for the data in Practice 2.

OBJECTIVE 4 ▶ Deceptions in visual displays of data. Graphs can be used to distort the underlying data, making it difficult for the viewer to learn the truth. One potential source of misunderstanding is the scale on the vertical axis used to draw the graph. This scale is important because it lets a researcher "inflate" or "deflate" a trend. For example, both graphs below present identical data for the percentage of people in the United States living below the poverty level from 2000 through 2004. The graph on the left stretches the scale on the vertical axis to create an overall impression of a poverty rate increasing rapidly over time. The graph on the right compresses the scale on the vertical axis to create an impression of a poverty rate that is slowly increasing, and beginning to level off, over time.

Percentage of People in the United States Living below the Poverty Level, 2000-2004

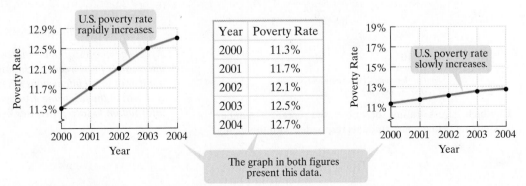

Year	Poverty Rate
2000	11.3%
2001	11.7%
2002	12.1%
2003	12.5%
2004	12.7%

The graph in both figures present this data.

Source: U.S. Census Bureau

Things to Watch for in Visual Displays of Data

1. Is there a title that explains what is being displayed?

2. Are numbers lined up with tick marks on the vertical axis that clearly indicate the scale? Has the scale been varied to create a more or less dramatic impression than shown by the actual data?

3. Do too many design and cosmetic effects draw attention from or distort the data?

4. Has the wrong impression been created about how the data are changing because equally spaced time intervals are not used on the horizontal axis?

5. Are bar sizes scaled proportionately in terms of the data they represent?

6. Is there a source that indicates where the data in the display came from? Do the data come from an entire population or a sample? Was a random sample used and, if so, are there possible differences between what is displayed in the graph and what is occurring in the entire population? Who is presenting the visual display, and does that person have a special case to make for or against the trend shown by the graph?

5.6 | EXERCISE SET

MyMathLab® PRACTICE WATCH DOWNLOAD READ REVIEW

A questionnaire was given to students in an introductory statistics class during the first week of the course. One question asked, "How stressed have you been in the last $2\frac{1}{2}$ weeks, on a scale of 0 to 10, with 0 being not at all stressed and 10 being as stressed as possible?" The students' responses are shown in the frequency distribution. Use this frequency distribution to solve Exercises 1–4.

Stress Rating	Frequency
0	2
1	1
2	3
3	12
4	16
5	18
6	13
7	31
8	26
9	15
10	14

Source: *Journal of Personality and Social Psychology*, 69, 1102–1112

1. Which stress rating describes the greatest number of students? How many students responded with this rating?

2. Which stress rating describes the least number of students? How many responded with this rating?

3. How many students were involved in this study?

4. How many students had a stress rating of 8 or more?

5. A random sample of 30 college students is selected. Each student is asked how much time he or she spent on homework during the previous week. The following times (in hours) are obtained:

16, 24, 18, 21, 18, 16, 18, 17, 15, 21, 19, 17, 17, 16, 19, 18, 15, 15, 20, 17, 15, 17, 24, 19, 16, 20, 16, 19, 18, 17.

Construct a frequency distribution for the data.

6. A random sample of 30 male college students is selected. Each student is asked his height (to the nearest inch). The heights are as follows:

72, 70, 68, 72, 71, 71, 71, 69, 73, 71, 73, 75, 66, 67, 75, 74, 73, 71, 72, 67, 72, 68, 67, 71, 73, 71, 72, 70, 73, 70.

Construct a frequency distribution for the data.

A college professor had students keep a diary of their social interactions for a week. Excluding family and work situations, the number of social interactions of ten minutes or longer over the week is shown in the following grouped frequency distribution. Use this information to solve Exercises 7–14 on the next page.

Number of Social Interactions	Frequency
0–4	12
5–9	16
10–14	16
15–19	16
20–24	10
25–29	11
30–34	4
35–39	3
40–44	3
45–49	3

Source: Society for Personality and Social Psychology

7. Identify the lower class limit for each class.

8. Identify the upper class limit for each class.

9. What is the class width?

10. How many students were involved in this study?

11. How many students had at least 30 social interactions for the week?

12. How many students had at most 14 social interactions for the week?

13. Among the classes with the greatest frequency, which class has the least number of social interactions?

14. Among the classes with the smallest frequency, which class has the least number of social interactions?

15. As of 2007, the following are the ages, in chronological order, at which U.S. presidents were inaugurated:

57, 61, 57, 57, 58, 57, 61, 54, 68, 51, 49, 64, 50, 48, 65, 52, 56, 46, 54, 49, 50, 47, 55, 55, 54, 42, 51, 56, 55, 51, 54, 51, 60, 62, 43, 55, 56, 61, 52, 69, 64, 46, 54.

Source: Time Almanac

Construct a grouped frequency distribution for the data. Use 41–45 for the first class and use the same width for each subsequent class.

16. The IQ scores of 70 students enrolled in a liberal arts course at a college are as follows:

102, 100, 103, 86, 120, 117, 111, 101, 93, 97, 99, 95, 95, 104, 104, 105, 106, 109, 109, 89, 94, 95, 99, 99, 103, 104, 105, 109, 110, 114, 124, 123, 118, 117, 116, 110, 114, 114, 96, 99, 103, 103, 104, 107, 107, 110, 111, 112, 113, 117, 115, 116, 100, 104, 102, 94, 93, 93, 96, 96, 111, 116, 107, 109, 105, 106, 97, 106, 107, 108.

Construct a grouped frequency distribution for the data. Use 85–89 for the first class and use the same width for each subsequent class.

17. Construct a histogram and a frequency polygon for the data involving stress ratings in Exercises 1–4.

18. Construct a histogram and a frequency polygon for the data in Exercise 5.

19. Construct a histogram and a frequency polygon for the data in Exercise 6.

20. **Decision Making.** The histogram shows the distribution of starting salaries (rounded to the nearest thousand dollars) for college graduates based on a random sample of recent graduates.

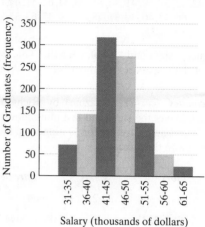

Starting Salaries of Recent College Graduates

Which one of the following is true according to the graph?

a. The graph is based on a sample of approximately 500 recent college graduates.

b. More college graduates had starting salaries in the $51,000–$55,000 range than in the $36,000–$40,000 range.

c. If the sample is truly representative, then for a group of 400 college graduates, we can expect about 28 of them to have starting salaries in the $31,000–$35,000 range.

d. The percentage of starting salaries falling above those shown by any rectangular bar is equal to the percentage of starting salaries falling below that bar.

21. **Decision Making.** The frequency polygon shows a distribution of IQ scores. Which one of the following is true based upon the graph?

a. The graph is based on a sample of approximately 50 people.

b. More people had an IQ score of 100 than any other IQ score, and as the deviation from 100 increases or decreases, the scores fall off in a symmetrical manner.

c. More people had an IQ score of 110 than a score of 90.

d. The percentage of scores above any IQ score is equal to the percentage of scores below that score.

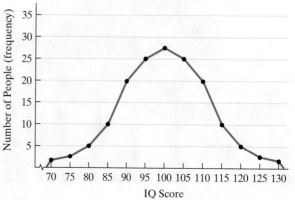

Distribution of IQ Scores

22. Construct a stem-and-leaf plot for the data in Exercise 15 showing the ages at which U.S. presidents were inaugurated.

23. A random sample of 40 college professors is selected from all professors at a university. The following list gives their ages:

63, 48, 42, 42, 38, 59, 41, 44, 45, 28, 54, 62, 51, 44, 63, 66, 59, 46, 51, 28, 37, 66, 42, 40, 30, 31, 48, 32, 29, 42, 63, 37, 36, 47, 25, 34, 49, 30, 35, 50.

Construct a stem-and-leaf plot for the data. What does the shape of the display reveal about the ages of the professors?

24. In "Ages of Oscar-Winning Best Actors and Actresses" (*Mathematics Teacher* magazine) by Richard Brown and Gretchen Davis, the stem-and-leaf plots shown compare the ages of actors and actresses for 30 winners of the Oscar at the time they won the award.

Actors	Stems	Actresses
	2	146667
98753221	3	00113344455778
88776543322100	4	11129
6651	5	
210	6	011
6	7	4
	8	0

a. What is the age of the youngest actor to win an Oscar?

b. What is the age difference between the oldest and the youngest actress to win an Oscar?

c. What is the oldest age shared by two actors to win an Oscar?

d. What differences do you observe between the two stem-and-leaf plots? What explanations can you offer for these differences?

In Exercises 25–26, describe what is misleading in each visual display of data.

25.

World Population, in Billions

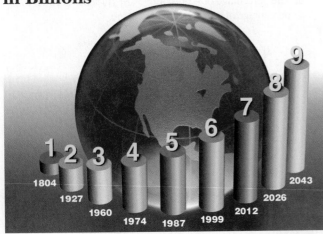

Source: U.S. Census Bureau

26.

Book Title Output in the United States

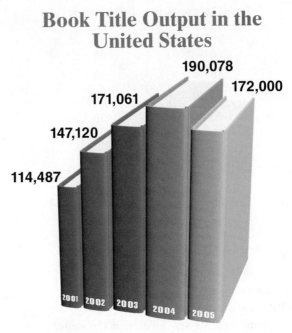

Source: R. R. Bowker

27. What is a frequency distribution?

28. What is a histogram?

29. What is a frequency polygon?

30. Describe how to construct a frequency polygon from a histogram.

31. Describe how to construct a stem-and-leaf plot from a set of data.

32. Describe two ways that graphs can be misleading.

33. Construct a grouped frequency distribution for the following data, showing the length, in miles, of the 25 longest rivers in the United States. Use five classes that have the same width.

2540	2340	1980	1900	1900
1460	1450	1420	1310	1290
1280	1240	1040	990	926
906	886	862	800	774
743	724	692	659	649

Source: U.S. Department of the Interior

34. Each group member should find one example of a graph that presents data with integrity and one example of a graph that is misleading. Use newspapers, magazines, the Internet, books, and so forth. Once graphs have been collected, each member should share his or her graphs with the entire group. Be sure to explain why one graph depicts data in a forthright manner and how the other graph misleads the viewer.

5.7 MEAN, MEDIAN, AND MODE

OBJECTIVE 1 ▸ Calculating mean, median, and mode. It is sometimes desirable to be able to describe a set of data, or a set of numbers, by a single "middle" number. Three such **measures of central tendency** are the mean, the median, and the mode.

The most common measure of central tendency is the mean (sometimes called the arithmetic mean or the average). The **mean** of a set of data items, denoted by $\overline{x}$, is the sum of the items divided by the number of items.

EXAMPLE 1   Seven students in a psychology class conducted an experiment on mazes. Each student was given a pencil and asked to successfully complete the same maze. The timed results are below.

Student	Ann	Thanh	Carlos	Jesse	Melinda	Ramzi	Dayni
Time (Seconds)	13.2	11.8	10.7	16.2	15.9	13.8	18.5

a. Who completed the maze in the shortest time? Who completed the maze in the longest time?
b. Find the mean.
c. How many students took longer than the mean time? How many students took shorter than the mean time?

Solution

a. Carlos completed the maze in 10.7 seconds, the shortest time. Dayni completed the maze in 18.5 seconds, the longest time.
b. To find the mean, $\overline{x}$, find the sum of the data items and divide by 7, the number of items.

$$\overline{x} = \frac{13.2 + 11.8 + 10.7 + 16.2 + 15.9 + 13.8 + 18.5}{7} = \frac{100.1}{7} = 14.3$$

c. Three students, Jesse, Melinda, and Dayni, had times longer than the mean time. Four students, Ann, Thanh, Carlos, and Ramzi, had times shorter than the mean time. □

PRACTICE
1   Find the mean for the data: 42, 37, 45, 12, 45, 17

Two other measures of central tendency are the median and the mode.

The **median** of an ordered set of numbers is the middle number. If the number of items is even, the median is the mean of the two middle numbers. The **mode** of a set of numbers is the number that occurs most often. It is possible for a data set to have no mode or more than one mode.

EXAMPLE 2   Find the median and the mode of the following list of numbers. These numbers were high temperatures for fourteen consecutive days in a city in Montana.

76, 80, 85, 86, 89, 87, 82, 77, 76, 79, 82, 89, 89, 92

Solution

First, write the numbers in order.

76, 76, 77, 79, 80, 82, 82, 85, 86, 87, 89, 89, 89, 92

two
middle numbers

mode

Since there are an even number of items, the median is the mean of the two middle numbers.

$$\text{median} = \frac{82 + 85}{2} = 83.5$$

The mode is 89, since 89 occurs most often.

PRACTICE
2 Find the median and the mode for the data set: 42, 37, 45, 12, 45, 17

5.7 EXERCISE SET

For each of the following data sets, find the mean, the median, and the mode. If necessary, round the mean to one decimal place.

1. 21, 28, 16, 42, 38

2. 42, 35, 36, 40, 50

3. 7.6, 8.2, 8.2, 9.6, 5.7, 9.1

4. 4.9, 7.1, 6.8, 6.8, 5.3, 4.9

5. 0.2, 0.3, 0.5, 0.6, 0.6, 0.9, 0.2, 0.7, 1.1

6. 0.6, 0.6, 0.8, 0.4, 0.5, 0.3, 0.7, 0.8, 0.1

7. 231, 543, 601, 293, 588, 109, 334, 268

8. 451, 356, 478, 776, 892, 500, 467, 780

Eight tall buildings in the United States are listed below. Use this table for Exercises 9 through 12.

Building	Height (feet)
Sears Tower, Chicago, IL	1454
Empire State, New York, NY	1250
Amoco, Chicago, IL	1136
John Hancock Center, Chicago, IL	1127
First Interstate World Center, Los Angeles, CA	1107
Chrysler, New York, NY	1046
NationsBank Tower, Atlanta, GA	1023
Texas Commerce Tower, Houston, TX	1002

9. Find the mean height for the five tallest buildings.
10. Find the median height for the five tallest buildings.
11. Find the median height for the eight tallest buildings.
12. Find the mean height for the eight tallest buildings.

During an experiment, the following times (in seconds) were recorded: 7.8, 6.9, 7.5, 4.7, 6.9, 7.0.

13. Find the mean. Round to the nearest tenth.
14. Find the median.
15. Find the mode.

In a mathematics class, the following test scores were recorded for a student: 86, 95, 91, 74, 77, 85.

16. Find the mean. Round to the nearest hundredth.
17. Find the median.
18. Find the mode.

The following pulse rates were recorded for a group of fifteen students: 78, 80, 66, 68, 71, 64, 82, 71, 70, 65, 70, 75, 77, 86, 72.

19. Find the mean.
20. Find the median.
21. Find the mode.
22. How many rates were higher than the mean?
23. How many rates were lower than the mean?
24. Have each student in your algebra class take his/her pulse rate. Record the data and find the mean, the median, and the mode.

Find the missing numbers in each list of numbers. (These numbers are not necessarily in numerical order.)

25. __, __, 16, 18, __
The mode is 21.   The mean is 20.
26. __, __, __, __, 40
The mode is 35.   The median is 37.   The mean is 38.

EXTENSION: BOX-AND-WHISKER PLOTS

OBJECTIVES

1 Draw a box-and-whisker plot.

2 Interpret a box-and-whisker plot.

OBJECTIVE 1 ▶ Drawing box-and-whisker plots. A **box-and-whisker plot** is a way to visually display data. To fully understand this plot, let's construct one. First, let's define some terms.

Second Quartile (Q_2) = median of all numbers

First Quartile (Q_1) = median of numbers less than Q_2

Third Quartile (Q_3) = median of numbers greater than Q_2

EXAMPLE 1 Given the data set below:

$$10, 3, 20, 17, 17, 9, 8, 19, 10, 14, 13, 7, 13$$

a. Find Q_2, Q_1, and Q_3.

b. Draw a box-and-whisker plot.

Solution A box-and-whisker plot is based on medians (middle number), so let's begin by writing the data in numerical order.

$$3, 7, 8, 9, 10, 10, 13, 13, 14, 17, 17, 19, 20$$

a. To find Q_2, Q_1, and Q_3, we use the definitions above and find medians,

Second quartile (Q_2) = 13

$$3, 7, 8, 9, 10, 10, 13, 13, 14, 17, 17, 19, 20$$

First quartile (Q_1)   Third quartile (Q_3)

$$= \frac{8 + 9}{2} = 8.5 \qquad = \frac{17 + 17}{2} = 17$$

b. On a number line, draw a vertical line above the main median (Q_2), 13.

Next, draw similar vertical lines for Q_1, 8.5, and Q_3, 17. Draw a **box** using these vertical lines. The **whiskers** extend to the least data value, 3, and the greatest data value, 20.

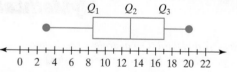

This is a box-and-whisker plot. ☐

PRACTICE
1 Given the data set below:

$$14, 11, 15, 5, 17, 2, 5, 7, 13$$

a. Find Q_2, Q_1, and Q_3.

b. Draw a box-and-whisker plot.

▶ **Helpful Hint**

Box-and-whisker plots can be drawn horizontally (as in Example 1) or vertically.

OBJECTIVE 2 ▶ Interpreting a box-and-whisker plot. The box-and-whisker plot from Example 1 is below. Let's discuss the information this plot gives us.

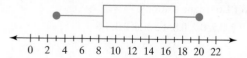

- The greatest value is 20 and the least is 3, so the range is 20 − 3, or 17.
- The median of the data (Q_2) is 13.
- The three medians (Q_1, Q_2, Q_3) separate the data into four parts.
  - One quarter of the data numbers are less than 8.5 (Q_1).
  - One quarter of the data numbers are between 8.5 (Q_1) and 13 (Q_2).

- One quarter of the data numbers are between 13 (Q_2) and 17 (Q_3).
- One quarter of the data numbers are greater than 17 (Q_3).

EXAMPLE 2   The box-and-whisker plot shows the number of hours worked per day for 99 randomly chosen individuals surveyed.

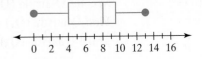

a. Find the range of the data.

b. What is the median number of hours worked?

Solution

a. The range is the greatest number minus the least number, or

$$13 - 0 = 13 \text{ hours}$$

b. The median number of hours is 8 hours.

PRACTICE
2   Use the box-and-whisker plot for Example 2 to answer the questions.

a. Explain the meaning of the least point, 0.

b. Do more people surveyed work 0−4 hours per day or 4−8.5 hours per day?

CHAPTER 5 EXTENSION | EXERCISE SET

Find the second (Q_2), first (Q_1), and third (Q_3) quartiles of each data set. (Do not forget to first place the numbers in numerical order.)

1. 5, 2, 7, 11, 1, 10, 9, 3

2. 11, 4, 6, 1, 10, 12, 8, 3

3. 8.6, 13.7, 1.3, 4.6, 11.9, 7.4, 5.2

4. 9.9, 2.0, 9.7, 3.9, 9.6, 5.8, 8.1

Draw a box-and-whisker plot of the data. (Do not forget to first place the data numbers in numerical order.)

5. 13, 9, 6, 1, 2, 5, 12, 1, 8, 4

6. 11, 11, 2, 4, 6, 9, 7, 7, 0, 3

7. 54, 82, 87, 93, 89, 83, 60, 95, 43

8. 86, 30, 75, 79, 60, 90, 29, 82, 44

9. Longest known glaciers in the world, in miles: (*Source:* Top 10 of Everything.) 249, 99, 84, 76, 62, 80, 70, 62, 118, 75, 85

10. *Longest caves in the world, in miles: (*Source:* Top 10 of Everything) 110, 140, 367, 96, 134, 122, 98, 125, 102, 121

11. Daily rainfall in lower Louisiana stations:

2.1, 1.8, 1.3, 0.9, 0.7, 0.3, 0.2, 0.2, 0.8, 1.3, 1.6, 2.3, 1.8

12. Lengths of plant growth in experiment (in inches):

6.1, 7.5, 5.6, 3.5, 2.7, 4.7, 7.9, 5.7, 3.1, 3.5, 7.7, 6.5, 4.9

For exercises 13–17, use the box-and-whisker plot showing the number of hours of high-school students driving on a school day.

13. Find the range of driving time.

14. Do more students drive 0.5−1.5 hours per day or 0−0.5 hours?

15. Find the median driving time.

16. Explain what is happening at 0 hours.

17. Do more students drive 0−1.5 hours per day or 1.5−2.7 hours?

For Exercises 13–17

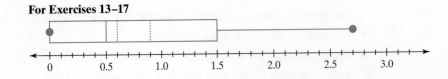

*The longest cave is Mammoth Cave System in Kentucky, USA

CHAPTER 5 VOCABULARY CHECK

Fill in each blank with one of the words or phrases listed below.

system of linear equations   solution   consistent   independent

dependent   inconsistent   substitution   addition

system of linear inequalities

1. In a system of linear equations in two variables, if the graphs of the equations are the same, the equations are _____ equations.
2. Two or more linear equations are called a _____ .
3. A system of equations that has at least one solution is called a(n) _____ system.
4. A _____ of a system of two equations in two variables is an ordered pair of numbers that is a solution of both equations in the system.
5. Two algebraic methods for solving systems of equations are _____ and _____ .
6. A system of equations that has no solution is called a(n) _____ system.
7. In a system of linear equations in two variables, if the graphs of the equations are different, the equations are _____ equations.
8. Two or more linear inequalities are called a _____ .

CHAPTER 5 REVIEW

(5.1) Determine whether any of the following ordered pairs satisfy the system of linear equations.

1. $\begin{cases} 2x - 3y = 12 \\ 3x + 4y = 1 \end{cases}$

    a. $(12, 4)$ **b.** $(3, -2)$ **c.** $(-3, 6)$

2. $\begin{cases} 4x + y = 0 \\ -8x - 5y = 9 \end{cases}$

    a. $\left(\dfrac{3}{4}, -3 \right)$ **b.** $(-2, 8)$ **c.** $\left(\dfrac{1}{2}, -2 \right)$

3. $\begin{cases} 5x - 6y = 18 \\ 2y - x = -4 \end{cases}$

    a. $(-6, -8)$ **b.** $\left(3, \dfrac{5}{2} \right)$ **c.** $\left(3, -\dfrac{1}{2} \right)$

4. $\begin{cases} 2x + 3y = 1 \\ 3y - x = 4 \end{cases}$

    a. $(2, 2)$ **b.** $(-1, 1)$ **c.** $(2, -1)$

Solve each system of equations by graphing.

5. $\begin{cases} x + y = 5 \\ x - y = 1 \end{cases}$ 6. $\begin{cases} x + y = 3 \\ x - y = -1 \end{cases}$

7. $\begin{cases} x = 5 \\ y = -1 \end{cases}$ 8. $\begin{cases} x = -3 \\ y = 2 \end{cases}$

9. $\begin{cases} 2x + y = 5 \\ x = -3y \end{cases}$ 10. $\begin{cases} 3x + y = -2 \\ y = -5x \end{cases}$

11. $\begin{cases} y = 3x \\ -6x + 2y = 6 \end{cases}$ 12. $\begin{cases} x - 2y = 2 \\ -2x + 4y = -4 \end{cases}$

(5.2) Solve each system of equations by the substitution method.

13. $\begin{cases} y = 2x + 6 \\ 3x - 2y = -11 \end{cases}$ 14. $\begin{cases} y = 3x - 7 \\ 2x - 3y = 7 \end{cases}$

15. $\begin{cases} x + 3y = -3 \\ 2x + y = 4 \end{cases}$ 16. $\begin{cases} 3x + y = 11 \\ x + 2y = 12 \end{cases}$

17. $\begin{cases} 4y = 2x + 6 \\ x - 2y = -3 \end{cases}$ 18. $\begin{cases} 9x = 6y + 3 \\ 6x - 4y = 2 \end{cases}$

19. $\begin{cases} x + y = 6 \\ y = -x - 4 \end{cases}$ 20. $\begin{cases} -3x + y = 6 \\ y = 3x + 2 \end{cases}$

(5.3) Solve each system of equations by the addition method.

21. $\begin{cases} 2x + 3y = -6 \\ x - 3y = -12 \end{cases}$ 22. $\begin{cases} 4x + y = 15 \\ -4x + 3y = -19 \end{cases}$

23. $\begin{cases} 2x - 3y = -15 \\ x + 4y = 31 \end{cases}$ 24. $\begin{cases} x - 5y = -22 \\ 4x + 3y = 4 \end{cases}$

25. $\begin{cases} 2x - 6y = -1 \\ -x + 3y = \dfrac{1}{2} \end{cases}$ 26. $\begin{cases} 0.6x - 0.3y = -1.5 \\ 0.04x - 0.02y = -0.1 \end{cases}$

27.
$$\begin{cases} \dfrac{3}{4}x + \dfrac{2}{3}y = 2 \\ x + \dfrac{y}{3} = 6 \end{cases}$$

28.
$$\begin{cases} 10x + 2y = 0 \\ 3x + 5y = 33 \end{cases}$$

(5.4) *Solve each problem by writing and solving a system of linear equations.*

29. The sum of two numbers is 16. Three times the larger number decreased by the smaller number is 72. Find the two numbers.

30. The Forrest Theater can seat a total of 360 people. They take in $15,150 when every seat is sold. If orchestra section tickets cost $45 and balcony tickets cost $35, find the number of seats in the orchestra section and the number of seats in the balcony.

31. A riverboat can head 340 miles upriver in 19 hours, but the return trip takes only 14 hours. Find the current of the river and find the speed of the riverboat in still water to the nearest tenth of a mile.

d =		r	$\cdot$	t
Upriver	340	$x - y$		19
Downriver	340	$x + y$		14

32. Find the amount of a 6% acid solution and the amount of a 14% acid solution Pat Mayfield should combine to prepare 50 cc (cubic centimeters) of a 12% solution.

33. A deli charges $3.80 for a breakfast of three eggs and four strips of bacon. The charge is $2.75 for two eggs and three strips of bacon. Find the cost of each egg and the cost of each strip of bacon.

34. An exercise enthusiast alternates between jogging and walking. He traveled 15 miles during the past 3 hours. He jogs at a rate of 7.5 miles per hour and walks at a rate of 4 miles per hour. Find how much time, to the nearest hundredth of an hour, he actually spent jogging and how much time he spent walking.

(5.5) *Graph the solutions of the following systems of linear inequalities.*

35.
$$\begin{cases} y \geq 2x - 3 \\ y \leq -2x + 1 \end{cases}$$

36.
$$\begin{cases} y \leq -3x - 3 \\ y \leq 2x + 7 \end{cases}$$

37.
$$\begin{cases} -3x + 2y > -1 \\ y < -2 \end{cases}$$

38.
$$\begin{cases} -2x + 3y > -7 \\ x \geq -2 \end{cases}$$

(5.6) *A random sample of ten college students is selected and each student is asked how much time he or she spent on homework during the previous weekend. The following times, in hours, are obtained:*

$$8, 10, 9, 7, 9, 8, 7, 6, 8, 7.$$

Use these data items to solve Exercises 39–41.

39. Construct a frequency distribution for the data.

40. Construct a histogram for the data.

41. Construct a frequency polygon for the data.

The 50 grades on a physiology test are shown. Use the data to solve Exercises 42–43.

44	24	54	81	18
34	39	63	67	60
72	36	91	47	75
57	74	87	49	86
59	14	26	41	90
13	29	13	31	68
63	35	29	70	22
95	17	50	42	27
73	11	42	31	69
56	40	31	45	51

42. Construct a grouped frequency distribution for the data. Use 0–39 for the first class, 40–49 for the second class, and make each subsequent class width the same as the second class.

43. Construct a stem-and-leaf plot for the data.

44. Describe what is misleading about the size of the barrels in the following visual display.

Average Daily Price per Barrel of Oil

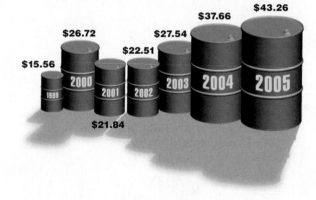

Source: U.S. Department of Energy

(5.7) *Find the mean, median, and mode for each group of data items.*

45. 28, 34, 16, 22, 28

46. 312, 783, 219, 312, 426, 219

MIXED REVIEW

Solve each system of equations by graphing.

47.
$$\begin{cases} x - 2y = 1 \\ 2x + 3y = -12 \end{cases}$$

48.
$$\begin{cases} 3x - y = -4 \\ 6x - 2y = -8 \end{cases}$$

Solve each system of equations.

49. $\begin{cases} x + 4y = 11 \\ 5x - 9y = -3 \end{cases}$ **50.** $\begin{cases} x + 9y = 16 \\ 3x - 8y = 13 \end{cases}$

51. $\begin{cases} y = -2x \\ 4x + 7y = -15 \end{cases}$ **52.** $\begin{cases} 3y = 2x + 15 \\ -2x + 3y = 21 \end{cases}$

53. $\begin{cases} 3x - y = 4 \\ 4y = 12x - 16 \end{cases}$ **54.** $\begin{cases} x + y = 19 \\ x - y = -3 \end{cases}$

55. $\begin{cases} x - 3y = -11 \\ 4x + 5y = -10 \end{cases}$ **56.** $\begin{cases} -x - 15y = 44 \\ 2x + 3y = 20 \end{cases}$

57. $\begin{cases} 2x + y = 3 \\ 6x + 3y = 9 \end{cases}$ **58.** $\begin{cases} -3x + y = 5 \\ -3x + y = -2 \end{cases}$

Solve each problem by writing and solving a system of linear equations.

59. The sum of two numbers is 12. Three times the smaller number increased by the larger number is 20. Find the numbers.

60. The difference of two numbers is −18. Twice the smaller decreased by the larger is −23. Find the two numbers.

61. Emma Hodges has a jar containing 65 coins, all of which are either nickels or dimes. The total value of the coins is $5.30. How many of each type does she have?

62. Sarah and Owen Hebert purchased 26 stamps, a mixture of 13¢ and 22¢ stamps. Find the number of each type of stamp if they spent $4.19.

CHAPTER 5 TEST TEST PREP VIDEO

The fully worked-out solutions to any exercises you want to review are available in MyMathLab.

Answer each question true or false.

1. A system of two linear equations in two variables can have exactly two solutions.

2. Although $(1, 4)$ is not a solution of $x + 2y = 6$, it can still be a solution of the system $\begin{cases} x + 2y = 6 \\ x + y = 5 \end{cases}$

3. If the two equations in a system of linear equations are added and the result is $3 = 0$, the system has no solution.

4. If the two equations in a system of linear equations are added and the result is $3x = 0$, the system has no solution.

Is the ordered pair a solution of the given linear system?

5. $\begin{cases} 2x - 3y = 5 \\ 6x + y = 1 \end{cases}; (1, -1)$

6. $\begin{cases} 4x - 3y = 24 \\ 4x + 5y = -8 \end{cases}; (3, -4)$

Solve each system by graphing.

7. $\begin{cases} x - y = 2 \\ 3x - y = -2 \end{cases}$

8. $\begin{cases} y = -3x \\ 3x + y = 6 \end{cases}$

Solve each system by the substitution method.

9. $\begin{cases} 3x - 2y = -14 \\ y = x + 5 \end{cases}$

10. $\begin{cases} \frac{1}{2}x + 2y = -\frac{15}{4} \\ 4x = -y \end{cases}$

Solve each system by the addition method.

11. $\begin{cases} x + y = 28 \\ x - y = 12 \end{cases}$

12. $\begin{cases} 4x - 6y = 7 \\ -2x + 3y = 0 \end{cases}$

Solve each system using the substitution method or the addition method.

13. $\begin{cases} 3x + y = 7 \\ 4x + 3y = 1 \end{cases}$

14. $\begin{cases} 3(2x + y) = 4x + 20 \\ x - 2y = 3 \end{cases}$

15. $\begin{cases} \dfrac{x - 3}{2} = \dfrac{2 - y}{4} \\ \dfrac{7 - 2x}{3} = \dfrac{y}{2} \end{cases}$

16. $\begin{cases} 8x - 4y = 12 \\ y = 2x - 3 \end{cases}$

17. $\begin{cases} 0.01x - 0.06y = -0.23 \\ 0.2x + 0.4y = 0.2 \end{cases}$

18. $\begin{cases} x - \dfrac{2}{3}y = 3 \\ -2x + 3y = 10 \end{cases}$

Solve each problem by writing and using a system of linear equations.

19. Two numbers have a sum of 124 and a difference of 32. Find the numbers.

20. Find the amount of a 12% saline solution a lab assistant should add to 80 cc (cubic centimeters) of a 22% saline solution in order to have a 16% solution.

21. Although the number of farms in the United States is still decreasing, small farms are making a comeback. Texas and Missouri are the states with the most number of farms. Texas has 116 thousand more farms than Missouri and the total number of farms for these two states is 336 thousand. Find the number of farms for each state.

22. Two hikers start at opposite ends of the St. Tammany Trails and walk toward each other. The trail is 36 miles long and they meet in 4 hours. If one hiker is twice as fast as the other, find both hiking speeds.

Graph the solutions of the following systems of linear inequalities.

23. $\begin{cases} y + 2x \leq 4 \\ y \geq 2 \end{cases}$

24. $\begin{cases} 2y - x \geq 1 \\ x + y \geq -4 \end{cases}$

Use these scores on a ten-point quiz to solve Exercises 25–27.

$$8, 5, 3, 6, 5, 10, 6, 9, 4, 5, 7, 9, 7, 4, 8, 8$$

25. Construct a frequency distribution for the data.

26. Construct a histogram for the data.

27. Construct a frequency polygon for the data.

Use the 30 test scores listed below to solve Exercises 28–29.

79	51	67	50	78
62	89	83	73	80
88	48	60	71	79
89	63	55	93	71
41	81	46	50	61
59	50	90	75	61

28. Construct a grouped frequency distribution for the data. Use 40–49 for the first class and use the same width for each subsequent class.

29. Construct a stem-and-leaf display for the data.

Use the six data items listed below to solve Exercises 30–32.

$$3, 6, 2, 1, 7, 3$$

30. Find the mean.

31. Find the median.

32. Find the mode.

Use the frequency distribution shown to solve Exercises 33–35.

Score x	Frequency f
1	3
2	5
3	2
4	2

33. Find the mean.

34. Find the median.

35. Find the mode.

CHAPTER 5 STANDARDIZED TEST

Multiple Choice. *Choose the one alternative that best completes the statement or answers the question.*

Answer true or false.

1. A system of two linear equations in two variables can have exactly one solution.
   a. False   **b.** True

2. Although $(9, 4)$ is not a solution of $x + 2y = 2$, it can still be a solution of the system $\begin{cases} x + 2y = 2 \\ x + y = 9 \end{cases}$.
   a. False   **b.** True

3. If the two equations in a system of linear equations are added and the result is $4 = 0$, the system has no solution.
   a. True   **b.** False

4. If the two equations in a system of linear equations are added and the result is $2x = 0$, the system has no solution.
   a. False   **b.** True

Is the ordered pair a solution of the linear system?

5. $\begin{cases} 3x - 4y = 18 \\ 5x + y = 1 \end{cases}; (2, -3)$
   a. No   **b.** Yes

6. $\begin{cases} 4x - 4y = 24 \\ 5x + 4y = -11 \end{cases}; (3, -3)$
   a. Yes   **b.** No

Solve the system by graphing.

7. $\begin{cases} x - y = 1 \\ 3x - y = -1 \end{cases}$

   a. $(-2, 1)$ **b.** $(0, -2)$
   c. $(-1, -2)$ **d.** $(-2, -1)$

8. $\begin{cases} y = -5x \\ 5x + y = 9 \end{cases}$

   a. $(5, 9)$ **b.** no solution
   c. $(0, 0)$ **d.** infinite number of solutions

Solve the system of equations by the substitution method.

9. $\begin{cases} 4x - 3y = -11 \\ y = x + 3 \end{cases}$

   a. $(0, 3)$ **b.** $(1, 2)$
   c. $(-4, -3)$ **d.** $(-2, 1)$

10. $\begin{cases} \frac{1}{2}x + 3y = -\frac{47}{4} \\ 8x = -y \end{cases}$

   a. $\left[\frac{1}{4}, -2\right]$ **b.** $(0, 0)$
   c. $(2, 4)$ **d.** $\left[\frac{1}{2}, -4\right]$

Solve the system of equations by the addition method.

11. $\begin{cases} x + y = 25 \\ x - y = 5 \end{cases}$

   a. No solution   **b.** $\left[\frac{25}{2}, \frac{5}{2}\right]$
   c. $(15, 10)$ **d.** $(10, 15)$

12. $\begin{cases} 6x - 9y = 15 \\ -2x + 3y = 1 \end{cases}$

   a. $(3, -2)$ **b.** $(16, 14)$
   c. No solution   **d.** Infinite number of solutions

Solve the system by the substitution or the addition method.

13. $\begin{cases} 3x + y = 12 \\ 4x + 3y = 11 \end{cases}$

   a. $(5, -3)$ **b.** $(12, 3)$
   c. $(3, 5)$ **d.** $(15, -4)$

14. $\begin{cases} 3(2x + y) = 3x + 27 \\ x - 2y = 0 \end{cases}$

   a. $(4, 2)$ **b.** $(6, 3)$
   c. No solution   **d.** $(-3, 6)$

15. $\begin{cases} \frac{x + 1}{2} = \frac{1 - y}{4} \\ \frac{-2 - 3x}{5} = \frac{y}{3} \end{cases}$

   a. $\left[\frac{1}{2}, 3\right]$ **b.** $(1, -3)$
   c. $(-6, 9)$ **d.** $(-1, -1)$

16. $\begin{cases} 4x - 2y = 6 \\ y = 2x - 3 \end{cases}$

   a. no solution   **b.** $\left[\frac{3}{2}, 0\right]$
   c. $(2, 3)$ **d.** infinite number of solutions

17. $\begin{cases} 0.02x - 0.06y = -0.24 \\ 0.2x + 0.3y = -0.6 \end{cases}$

   a. $(-6, 2)$ **b.** infinite number of solutions
   c. $(10, -1.24)$ **d.** $(0.06, -0.02)$

18. $\begin{cases} x - \frac{19}{81}y = 2 \\ -3x + 2y = 8 \end{cases}$

   a. $(2, -3)$ **b.** $\left[\frac{98}{15}, \frac{44}{5}\right]$
   c. $\left[\frac{68}{15}, \frac{54}{5}\right]$ **d.** $\left[-\frac{19}{81}, 1\right]$

Solve the problem by writing and using a system of linear equations.

19. Two numbers have a sum of 129 and a difference of 37. Find the numbers.

   a. $83, 46$ **b.** $73, 56$
   c. $166, -37$ **d.** $86, 49$

20. Find the amount of a 14% saline solution a lab assistant should add to 80 cc (cubic centimeters) of a 24% saline solution in order to have a 18% solution.

   a. 120 cc   **b.** 10 cc
   c. 20 cc   **d.** 170 cc

21. A national wildlife refuge in Michigan has 106 thousand more trees than a national wildlife refuge in Ohio. The total number of trees for both is 336 thousand. Find the number of trees for each.

   a. Ohio: 65 thousand trees
   Michigan: 171 thousand trees

   b. Ohio: 115 thousand trees
   Michigan: 221 thousand trees

   c. Ohio: 106 thousand trees
   Michigan: 230 thousand trees

   d. Ohio: 106 thousand trees
   Michigan: 212 thousand trees

22. Two bikers start at opposite ends of a trail and bike toward each other. The trail is 132 miles long and they meet in 4 hours. If one biker is twice as fast as the other, find both biking speeds.

   a. 66 mph, 132 mph   **b.** 11 mph, 22 mph
   c. 9 mph, 18 mph   **d.** 4 mph, 8 mph

Graph the solution of the system of linear inequalities.

23. $\begin{cases} 2x + y \le 4 \\ y \le 1 \end{cases}$

a.

b.

c.

d.

24. $\begin{cases} x + 2y \le 2 \\ x + y \ge 0 \end{cases}$

a.

b.

c.

d.

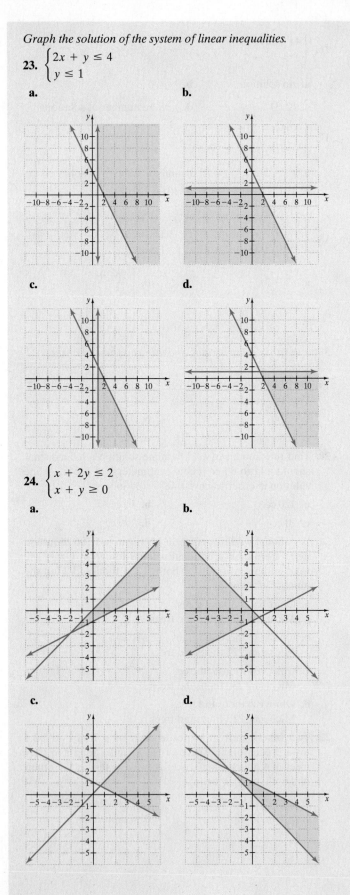

A sample of 15 high school students is selected. Each is asked to choose a whole number from 1 to 5. The result is below:

$$3, 3, 1, 2, 3, 5, 3, 4, 5, 3, 1, 3, 4, 4, 3$$

25. Construct a frequency distribution for the data.

a.

Number	Frequency
1	2
2	1
3	7
4	3
5	2

b.

Number	Frequency
1	2
2	2
3	6
4	3
5	2

c.

Number	Frequency
2	1
1	2
7	3
3	4
2	5

d.

Number	Frequency
1	1
2	2
3	3
4	4
5	5

26. Construct a histogram for the data.

a.   **b.**

c.   **d.**

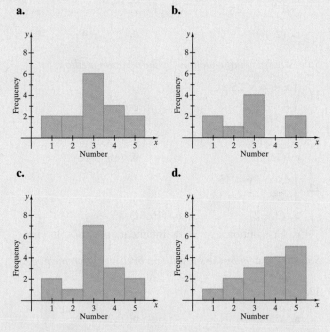

27. The ages of 12 swimmers who participated in a swim meet are as follows:

$$40, 50, 59, 43, 51, 41, 58, 49, 46, 53, 41, 49$$

Construct a grouped frequency distribution for the data. Use the classes $38-47, 48-57, 58-67$.

a.

Age	Number of Swimmers
38–47	6
48–57	4
58–67	2

b.

Age	Number of Swimmers
38–47	2
48–57	5
58–67	5

c.	Age	Number of Swimmers
	38–47	5
	48–57	5
	58–67	2

d.	Age	Number of Swimmers
	38–47	5
	48–57	2
	58–67	5

Find the mean for the group of data items. Round to the nearest hundredth, if necessary.

28. 9, 4, 6, 8, 10, 1, 12, 6

  a. 7   **b.** 7.14

  c. 6.25   **d.** 8

Find the median for the group of data items.

29. 10, 9, 4, 0, 1, 1, 1, 0, 0

  a. 4   **b.** 5

  c. 0   **d.** 1

Find the mode for the group of data items. If there is no mode, so state.

30. 97, 97, 94, 44, 74, 97

  a. no mode   **b.** 97

  c. 44   **d.** 94

CHAPTER

6 Exponents and Polynomials

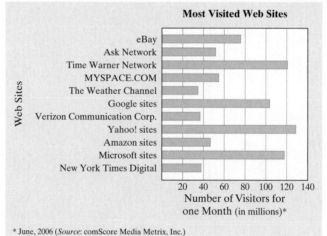

A popular use of the Internet is the World Wide Web. The World Wide Web was invented in 1989–1990 as an environment originally by which scientists could share information. It has grown into a medium containing text, graphics, audio, animation, and video. In this chapter, you will have the opportunity to estimate the number of visitors to the most popular Web sites.

6.1 EXPONENTS

OBJECTIVES

1 Evaluate exponential expressions.

2 Use the product rule for exponents.

3 Use the power rule for exponents.

4 Use the power rules for products and quotients.

5 Use the quotient rule for exponents, and define a number raised to the 0 power.

6 Decide which rule(s) to use to simplify an expression.

OBJECTIVE 1 ▶ Evaluating exponential expressions. As we reviewed in Section 1.4, an exponent is a shorthand notation for repeated factors. For example, $2 \cdot 2 \cdot 2 \cdot 2 \cdot 2$ can be written as 2^5. The expression 2^5 is called an **exponential expression.** It is also called the fifth **power** of 2, or we say that 2 is **raised** to the fifth power.

$$5^6 = \underbrace{5 \cdot 5 \cdot 5 \cdot 5 \cdot 5 \cdot 5}_{6 \text{ factors; each factor is } 5} \qquad \text{and} \qquad (-3)^4 = \underbrace{(-3) \cdot (-3) \cdot (-3) \cdot (-3)}_{4 \text{ factors; each factor is } -3}$$

The **base** of an exponential expression is the repeated factor. The **exponent** is the number of times that the base is used as a factor.

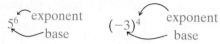

EXAMPLE 1   Evaluate each expression.

a. 2^3 **b.** 3^1 **c.** $(-4)^2$ **d.** -4^2 **e.** $\left(\dfrac{1}{2}\right)^4$ **f.** $(0.5)^3$ **g.** $4 \cdot 3^2$

Solution

a. $2^3 = 2 \cdot 2 \cdot 2 = 8$

b. To raise 3 to the first power means to use 3 as a factor only once. Therefore, $3^1 = 3$. Also, when no exponent is shown, the exponent is assumed to be 1.

c. $(-4)^2 = (-4)(-4) = 16$ **d.** $-4^2 = -(4 \cdot 4) = -16$

e. $\left(\dfrac{1}{2}\right)^4 = \dfrac{1}{2} \cdot \dfrac{1}{2} \cdot \dfrac{1}{2} \cdot \dfrac{1}{2} = \dfrac{1}{16}$ **f.** $(0.5)^3 = (0.5)(0.5)(0.5) = 0.125$

g. $4 \cdot 3^2 = 4 \cdot 9 = 36$

PRACTICE

1   Evaluate each expression.

a. 3^3 **b.** 4^1 **c.** $(-8)^2$ **d.** -8^2

e. $\left(\dfrac{3}{4}\right)^3$ **f.** $(0.3)^4$ **g.** $3 \cdot 5^2$

Notice how similar -4^2 is to $(-4)^2$ in the example above. The difference between the two is the parentheses. In $(-4)^2$, the parentheses tell us that the base, or repeated factor, is -4. In -4^2, only 4 is the base.

▶ **Helpful Hint**

Be careful when identifying the base of an exponential expression. Pay close attention to the use of parentheses.

$(-3)^2$	-3^2	$2 \cdot 3^2$
The base is -3.	The base is 3.	The base is 3.
$(-3)^2 = (-3)(-3) = 9$	$-3^2 = -(3 \cdot 3) = -9$	$2 \cdot 3^2 = 2 \cdot 3 \cdot 3 = 18$

An exponent has the same meaning whether the base is a number or a variable. If x is a real number and n is a positive integer, then x^n is the product of n factors, each of which is x.

$$x^n = \underbrace{x \cdot x \cdot x \cdot x \cdot x \cdot \ldots \cdot x}_{n \text{ factors of } x}$$

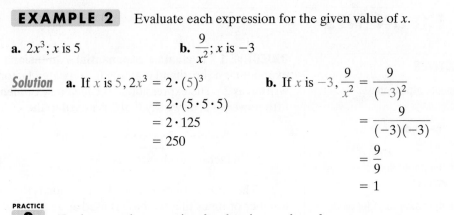

EXAMPLE 2 Evaluate each expression for the given value of x.

a. $2x^3$; x is 5 **b.** $\dfrac{9}{x^2}$; x is -3

Solution **a.** If x is 5, $2x^3 = 2 \cdot (5)^3$ **b.** If x is -3, $\dfrac{9}{x^2} = \dfrac{9}{(-3)^2}$

$$= 2 \cdot (5 \cdot 5 \cdot 5)$$
$$= 2 \cdot 125$$
$$= 250$$

$$= \dfrac{9}{(-3)(-3)}$$
$$= \dfrac{9}{9}$$
$$= 1 \qquad \square$$

PRACTICE

2 Evaluate each expression for the given value of x.

a. $3x^4$; x is 3 **b.** $\dfrac{6}{x^2}$; x is -4

OBJECTIVE 2 ▸ **Using the product rule.** Exponential expressions can be multiplied, divided, added, subtracted, and themselves raised to powers. By our definition of an exponent,

$$5^4 \cdot 5^3 = \underbrace{(5 \cdot 5 \cdot 5 \cdot 5)}_{\text{4 factors of 5}} \cdot \underbrace{(5 \cdot 5 \cdot 5)}_{\text{3 factors of 5}}$$
$$= \underbrace{5 \cdot 5 \cdot 5 \cdot 5 \cdot 5 \cdot 5 \cdot 5}_{\text{7 factors of 5}}$$
$$= 5^7$$

Also,

$$x^2 \cdot x^3 = (x \cdot x) \cdot (x \cdot x \cdot x)$$
$$= x \cdot x \cdot x \cdot x \cdot x$$
$$= x^5$$

In both cases, notice that the result is exactly the same if the exponents are added.

$$5^4 \cdot 5^3 = 5^{4+3} = 5^7 \qquad \text{and} \qquad x^2 \cdot x^3 = x^{2+3} = x^5$$

This suggests the following rule.

> **Product Rule for Exponents**
>
> If m and n are positive integers and a is a real number, then
>
> $$a^m \cdot a^n = a^{m+n} \leftarrow \text{Add exponents.}$$
> $$\uparrow\!\!\!\text{—— Keep common base.}$$

For example, $3^5 \cdot 3^7 = 3^{5+7} = 3^{12} \leftarrow$ Add exponents.
$\qquad\qquad\qquad$ —— Keep common base.

In other words, to multiply two exponential expressions with a **common base,** keep the base and add the exponents. We call this simplifying the exponential expression.

EXAMPLE 3 Use the product rule to simplify.

a. $4^2 \cdot 4^5$ **b.** $x^4 \cdot x^6$ **c.** $y^3 \cdot y$ ▣ **d.** $y^3 \cdot y^2 \cdot y^7$ ▣ **e.** $(-5)^7 \cdot (-5)^8$ **f.** $a^2 \cdot b^2$

Solution

a. $4^2 \cdot 4^5 = 4^{2+5} = 4^7 \leftarrow$ Add exponents.
$\qquad\qquad\qquad$ —— Keep common base.

b. $x^4 \cdot x^6 = x^{4+6} = x^{10}$

c. $y^3 \cdot y = y^3 \cdot y^1$

$= y^{3+1}$

$= y^4$

▶ **Helpful Hint**
Don't forget that if no exponent is written, it is assumed to be 1.

d. $y^3 \cdot y^2 \cdot y^7 = y^{3+2+7} = y^{12}$

e. $(-5)^7 \cdot (-5)^8 = (-5)^{7+8} = (-5)^{15}$

f. $a^2 \cdot b^2$ Cannot be simplified because a and b are different bases.

PRACTICE
3 Use the product rule to simplify.

a. $3^4 \cdot 3^6$ **b.** $y^3 \cdot y^2$

c. $z \cdot z^4$ **d.** $x^3 \cdot x^2 \cdot x^6$

e. $(-2)^5 \cdot (-2)^3$ **f.** $b^3 \cdot t^5$

Concept Check ✓

Where possible, use the product rule to simplify the expression.

a. $z^2 \cdot z^{14}$ **b.** $x^2 \cdot y^{14}$ **c.** $9^8 \cdot 9^3$ **d.** $9^8 \cdot 2^7$

EXAMPLE 4 Use the product rule to simplify $(2x^2)(-3x^5)$.

Solution Recall that $2x^2$ means $2 \cdot x^2$ and $-3x^5$ means $-3 \cdot x^5$.

$$(2x^2)(-3x^5) = 2 \cdot x^2 \cdot -3 \cdot x^5 \quad \text{Remove parentheses.}$$

$$= 2 \cdot -3 \cdot x^2 \cdot x^5 \quad \text{Group factors with common bases.}$$

$$= -6x^7 \quad \text{Simplify.}$$

PRACTICE
4 Use the product rule to simplify $(-5y^3)(-3y^4)$.

EXAMPLE 5 Simplify.

a. $(x^2y)(x^3y^2)$ **b.** $(-a^7b^4)(3ab^9)$

Solution

a. $(x^2y)(x^3y^2) = (x^2 \cdot x^3) \cdot (y^1 \cdot y^2)$ Group like bases and write y as y^1.

$= x^5 \cdot y^3$ or x^5y^3 Multiply.

b. $(-a^7b^4)(3ab^9) = (-1 \cdot 3) \cdot (a^7 \cdot a^1) \cdot (b^4 \cdot b^9)$

$= -3a^8b^{13}$

PRACTICE
5 Simplify.

a. $(y^7z^3)(y^5z)$ **b.** $(-m^4n^4)(7mn^{10})$

▶ **Helpful Hint**

These examples will remind you of the difference between adding and multiplying terms.

Addition

$$5x^3 + 3x^3 = (5 + 3)x^3 = 8x^3 \quad \text{By the distributive property.}$$

$$7x + 4x^2 = 7x + 4x^2 \quad \text{Cannot be combined.}$$

Multiplication

$$(5x^3)(3x^3) = 5 \cdot 3 \cdot x^3 \cdot x^3 = 15x^{3+3} = 15x^6 \quad \text{By the product rule.}$$

$$(7x)(4x^2) = 7 \cdot 4 \cdot x \cdot x^2 = 28x^{1+2} = 28x^3 \quad \text{By the product rule.}$$

Answers to Concept Check:

a. z^{16} **b.** cannot be simplified

c. 9^{11} **d.** cannot be simplified

OBJECTIVE 3 ▶ Using the power rule. Exponential expressions can themselves be raised to powers. Let's try to discover a rule that simplifies an expression like $(x^2)^3$. By definition,

$$(x^2)^3 = \underbrace{(x^2)(x^2)(x^2)}_{3 \text{ factors of } x^2}$$

which can be simplified by the product rule for exponents.

$$(x^2)^3 = (x^2)(x^2)(x^2) = x^{2+2+2} = x^6$$

Notice that the result is exactly the same if we multiply the exponents.

$$(x^2)^3 = x^{2 \cdot 3} = x^6$$

The following property states this result.

> **Power Rule for Exponents**
> If m and n are positive integers and a is a real number, then
> $$(a^m)^n = a^{mn} \leftarrow \text{Multiply exponents.}$$
> $\uparrow$ Keep common base.

For example, $(7^2)^5 = 7^{2 \cdot 5} = 7^{10}$ ← Multiply exponents.
$\qquad$ Keep common base.

To raise a power to a power, keep the base and multiply the exponents.

EXAMPLE 6 Use the power rule to simplify.

a. $(x^2)^5$ $\qquad$ **b.** $(y^8)^2$ $\qquad$ **c.** $[(-5)^3]^7$

Solution $\quad$ **a.** $(x^2)^5 = x^{2 \cdot 5} = x^{10}$ $\qquad$ **b.** $(y^8)^2 = y^{8 \cdot 2} = y^{16}$ $\qquad$ **c.** $[(-5)^3]^7 = (-5)^{21}$

$\square$

PRACTICE
6 $\quad$ Use the power rule to simplify.

a. $(x^4)^3$ $\qquad$ **b.** $(z^3)^7$ $\qquad$ **c.** $[(-2)^3]^5$

> **▶ Helpful Hint**
> Take a moment to make sure that you understand when to apply the product rule and when to apply the power rule.
>
> | *Product Rule → Add Exponents* | *Power Rule → Multiply Exponents* |
> |---|---|
> | $x^5 \cdot x^7 = x^{5+7} = x^{12}$ | $(x^5)^7 = x^{5 \cdot 7} = x^{35}$ |
> | $y^6 \cdot y^2 = y^{6+2} = y^8$ | $(y^6)^2 = y^{6 \cdot 2} = y^{12}$ |

OBJECTIVE 4 ▶ Using the power rules for products and quotients. When the base of an exponential expression is a product, the definition of x^n still applies. To simplify $(xy)^3$, for example,

$$(xy)^3 = (xy)(xy)(xy) \qquad (xy)^3 \text{ means 3 factors of } (xy).$$
$$= x \cdot x \cdot x \cdot y \cdot y \cdot y \qquad \text{Group factors with common bases.}$$
$$= x^3 y^3 \qquad \text{Simplify.}$$

Notice that to simplify the expression $(xy)^3$, we raise each factor within the parentheses to a power of 3.

$$(xy)^3 = x^3 y^3$$

In general, we have the following rule.

> **Power of a Product Rule**
>
> If n is a positive integer and a and b are real numbers, then
>
> $$(ab)^n = a^n b^n$$

For example, $(3x)^5 = 3^5 x^5$.

In other words, to raise a product to a power, we raise each factor to the power.

EXAMPLE 7   Simplify each expression.

a. $(st)^4$ **b.** $(2a)^3$ **c.** $\left(\dfrac{1}{3}mn^3\right)^2$ **d.** $(-5x^2 y^3 z)^2$

Solution

a. $(st)^4 = s^4 \cdot t^4 = s^4 t^4$ Use the power of a product rule.

b. $(2a)^3 = 2^3 \cdot a^3 = 8a^3$ Use the power of a product rule.

c. $\left(\dfrac{1}{3}mn^3\right)^2 = \left(\dfrac{1}{3}\right)^2 \cdot (m)^2 \cdot (n^3)^2 = \dfrac{1}{9}m^2 n^6$ Use the power of a product rule.

d. $(-5x^2 y^3 z)^2 = (-5)^2 \cdot (x^2)^2 \cdot (y^3)^2 \cdot (z^1)^2$ Use the power rule for exponents.

$\qquad\qquad = 25x^4 y^6 z^2$ $\qquad\qquad\qquad\qquad\qquad\qquad$ □

PRACTICE
7   Simplify each expression.

a. $(pr)^5$ **b.** $(6b)^2$ **c.** $\left(\dfrac{1}{4}x^2 y\right)^3$ **d.** $(-3a^3 b^4 c)^4$

Let's see what happens when we raise a quotient to a power. To simplify $\left(\dfrac{x}{y}\right)^3$, for example,

$$\left(\frac{x}{y}\right)^3 = \left(\frac{x}{y}\right)\left(\frac{x}{y}\right)\left(\frac{x}{y}\right) \quad \left(\frac{x}{y}\right)^3 \text{ means 3 factors of } \left(\frac{x}{y}\right)$$

$$= \frac{x \cdot x \cdot x}{y \cdot y \cdot y} \qquad\qquad \text{Multiply fractions.}$$

$$= \frac{x^3}{y^3} \qquad\qquad\qquad \text{Simplify.}$$

Notice that to simplify the expression $\left(\dfrac{x}{y}\right)^3$, we raise both the numerator and the denominator to a power of 3.

$$\left(\frac{x}{y}\right)^3 = \frac{x^3}{y^3}$$

In general, we have the following.

> **Power of a Quotient Rule**
>
> If n is a positive integer and a and c are real numbers, then
>
> $$\left(\frac{a}{c}\right)^n = \frac{a^n}{c^n}, \quad c \neq 0$$

For example, $\left(\dfrac{y}{7}\right)^4 = \dfrac{y^4}{7^4}$.

In other words, to raise a quotient to a power, we raise both the numerator and the denominator to the power.

EXAMPLE 8 Simplify each expression.

a. $\left(\dfrac{m}{n}\right)^7$ **b.** $\left(\dfrac{x^3}{3y^5}\right)^4$

<u>*Solution*</u>

a. $\left(\dfrac{m}{n}\right)^7 = \dfrac{m^7}{n^7}, n \neq 0$ Use the power of a quotient rule.

b. $\left(\dfrac{x^3}{3y^5}\right)^4 = \dfrac{(x^3)^4}{3^4 \cdot (y^5)^4}, y \neq 0$ Use the power of a product or quotient rule.

$= \dfrac{x^{12}}{81y^{20}}$ Use the power rule for exponents.   ☐

PRACTICE
8 Simplify each expression.

a. $\left(\dfrac{x}{y^2}\right)^5$ **b.** $\left(\dfrac{2a^4}{b^3}\right)^5$

OBJECTIVE 5 ▶ Using the quotient rule and defining the zero exponent. Another pattern for simplifying exponential expressions involves quotients.

To simplify an expression like $\dfrac{x^5}{x^3}$, in which the numerator and the denominator have a common base, we can apply the fundamental principle of fractions and divide the numerator and the denominator by the common base factors. Assume for the remainder of this section that denominators are not 0.

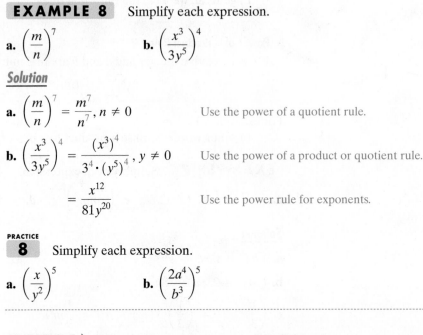

Notice that the result is exactly the same if we subtract exponents of the common bases.

$$\dfrac{x^5}{x^3} = x^{5-3} = x^2$$

The quotient rule for exponents states this result in a general way.

> **Quotient Rule for Exponents**
>
> If m and n are positive integers and a is a real number, then
>
> $$\dfrac{a^m}{a^n} = a^{m-n}$$
>
> as long as a is not 0.

For example, $\dfrac{x^6}{x^2} = x^{6-2} = x^4$.

In other words, to divide one exponential expression by another with a common base, keep the base and subtract exponents.

EXAMPLE 9   Simplify each quotient.

a. $\dfrac{x^5}{x^2}$ **b.** $\dfrac{4^7}{4^3}$ **c.** $\dfrac{(-3)^5}{(-3)^2}$ **d.** $\dfrac{s^2}{t^3}$ **e.** $\dfrac{2x^5y^2}{xy}$

Solution

a. $\dfrac{x^5}{x^2} = x^{5-2} = x^3$ Use the quotient rule.

b. $\dfrac{4^7}{4^3} = 4^{7-3} = 4^4 = 256$ Use the quotient rule.

c. $\dfrac{(-3)^5}{(-3)^2} = (-3)^3 = -27$

d. $\dfrac{s^2}{t^3}$ Cannot be simplified because s and t are different bases.

e. Begin by grouping common bases.

$$\frac{2x^5y^2}{xy} = 2 \cdot \frac{x^5}{x^1} \cdot \frac{y^2}{y^1}$$

$$= 2 \cdot (x^{5-1}) \cdot (y^{2-1}) \qquad \text{Use the quotient rule.}$$

$$= 2x^4y^1 \quad \text{or} \quad 2x^4y$$

PRACTICE
9   Simplify each quotient.

a. $\dfrac{z^8}{z^4}$ **b.** $\dfrac{(-5)^5}{(-5)^3}$ **c.** $\dfrac{8^8}{8^6}$ **d.** $\dfrac{q^5}{t^2}$ **e.** $\dfrac{6x^3y^7}{xy^5}$

Concept Check ☑

Suppose you are simplifying each expression. Tell whether you would *add* the exponents, *subtract* the exponents, *multiply* the exponents, *divide* the exponents, or *none of these*.

a. $(x^{63})^{21}$ **b.** $\dfrac{y^{15}}{y^3}$ **c.** $z^{16} + z^8$ **d.** $w^{45} \cdot w^9$

Let's now give meaning to an expression such as x^0. To do so, we will simplify $\dfrac{x^3}{x^3}$ in two ways and compare the results.

$$\frac{x^3}{x^3} = x^{3-3} = x^0 \qquad \text{Apply the quotient rule.}$$

$$\frac{x^3}{x^3} = \frac{x \cdot x \cdot x}{x \cdot x \cdot x} = 1 \quad \text{Apply the fundamental principle for fractions.}$$

Since $\dfrac{x^3}{x^3} = x^0$ and $\dfrac{x^3}{x^3} = 1$, we define that $x^0 = 1$ as long as x is not 0.

> **Zero Exponent**
> $a^0 = 1$, as long as a is not 0.

Answers to Concept Check:
a. multiply   **b.** subtract
c. none of these   **d.** add

In other words, any base raised to the 0 power is 1, as long as the base is not 0.

EXAMPLE 10 Simplify each expression.

a. 3^0 **b.** $(ab)^0$ **c.** $(-5)^0$ **d.** -5^0 **e.** $\left(\dfrac{3}{100}\right)^0$

Solution

a. $3^0 = 1$

b. Assume that neither a nor b is zero.

$$(ab)^0 = a^0 \cdot b^0 = 1 \cdot 1 = 1$$

c. $(-5)^0 = 1$

d. $-5^0 = -1 \cdot 5^0 = -1 \cdot 1 = -1$

e. $\left(\dfrac{3}{100}\right)^0 = 1$

$\square$

PRACTICE
10 Simplify the following expressions.

a. -3^0 **b.** $(-3)^0$ **c.** 8^0 **d.** $(0.2)^0$ **e.** $(xz)^0$

OBJECTIVE 6 ▸ Deciding which rule to use. Let's practice deciding which rule(s) to use to simplify. We will continue this discussion with more examples in Section 6.5.

EXAMPLE 11 Simplify each expression.

a. $\left(\dfrac{st}{2}\right)^4$ **b.** $(9y^5z^7)^2$ **c.** $\left(\dfrac{-5x^2}{y^3}\right)^2$

Solution

a. This is a quotient raised to a power, so we use the power of a quotient rule.

$$\left(\frac{st}{2}\right)^4 = \frac{s^4t^4}{2^4} = \frac{s^4t^4}{16}$$

b. This is a product raised to a power, so we use the power of a product rule.

$$(9y^5z^7)^2 = 9^2(y^5)^2(z^7)^2 = 81y^{10}z^{14}$$

c. Use the power of a product or quotient rule; then use the power rule for exponents.

$$\left(\frac{-5x^2}{y^3}\right)^2 = \frac{(-5)^2(x^2)^2}{(y^3)^2} = \frac{25x^4}{y^6}$$

$\square$

PRACTICE
11 Simplify each expression.

a. $\left(\dfrac{5}{xz}\right)^3$ **b.** $(2z^8x^5)^4$ **c.** $\left(\dfrac{-3x^3}{y^4}\right)^3$

VOCABULARY & READINESS CHECK

Word Bank. *Use the choices below to fill in each blank. Some choices may be used more than once.*

0	base	add
1	exponent	multiply

1. Repeated multiplication of the same factor can be written using a(n) _____.
2. In 5^2, the 2 is called the _____ and the 5 is called the _____.
3. To simplify $x^2 \cdot x^7$, keep the base and _____ the exponents.
4. To simplify $(x^3)^6$, keep the base and _____ the exponents.
5. The understood exponent on the term y is _____.
6. If $x^\square = 1$, the exponent is _____.

State the bases and the exponents for each of the following expressions.

7. 3^2
8. $(-3)^6$
9. -4^2
10. $5 \cdot 3^4$
11. $5x^2$
12. $(5x)^2$

6.1 | EXERCISE SET

Evaluate each expression. See Example 1.

1. 7^2
2. -3^2
3. $(-5)^1$
4. $(-3)^2$
5. -2^4
6. -4^3
7. $(-2)^4$
8. $(-4)^3$
9. $(0.1)^5$
10. $(0.2)^5$
11. $\left(\dfrac{1}{3}\right)^4$
12. $\left(-\dfrac{1}{9}\right)^2$
13. $7 \cdot 2^5$
14. $9 \cdot 1^7$
15. $-2 \cdot 5^3$
16. $-4 \cdot 3^3$
17. Explain why $(-5)^4 = 625$, while $-5^4 = -625$.
18. Explain why $5 \cdot 4^2 = 80$, while $(5 \cdot 4)^2 = 400$.

Evaluate each expression given the replacement values for x. See Example 2.

19. x^2; $x = -2$
20. x^3; $x = -2$
21. $5x^3$; $x = 3$
22. $4x^2$; $x = -1$
23. $2xy^2$; $x = 3$ and $y = 5$
24. $-4x^2y^3$; $x = 2$ and $y = -1$
25. $\dfrac{2z^4}{5}$; $z = -2$
26. $\dfrac{10}{3y^3}$; $y = 5$

Use the product rule to simplify each expression. Write the results using exponents. See Examples 3 through 5.

27. $x^2 \cdot x^5$
28. $y^2 \cdot y$
29. $(-3)^3 \cdot (-3)^9$
30. $(-5)^7 \cdot (-5)^6$
31. $(5y^4)(3y)$
32. $(-2z^3)(-2z^2)$
33. $(x^9y)(x^{10}y^5)$
34. $(a^2b)(a^{13}b^{17})$
35. $(-8mn^6)(9m^2n^2)$
36. $(-7a^3b^3)(7a^{19}b)$
37. $(4z^{10})(-6z^7)(z^3)$
38. $(12x^5)(-x^6)(x^4)$
39. The rectangle below has width $4x^2$ feet and length $5x^3$ feet. Find its area as an expression in x. ($A = l \cdot w$)

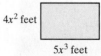

$4x^2$ feet

$5x^3$ feet

40. The parallelogram below has base length $9y^7$ meters and height $2y^{10}$ meters. Find its area as an expression in y. ($A = b \cdot h$)

$2y^{10}$ meters

$9y^7$ meters

MIXED PRACTICE

Use the power rule and the power of a product or quotient rule to simplify each expression. See Examples 6 through 8.

41. $(x^9)^4$
42. $(y^7)^5$

43. $(pq)^8$

44. $(ab)^6$

45. $(2a^5)^3$

46. $(4x^6)^2$

47. $(x^2y^3)^5$

48. $(a^4b)^7$

49. $(-7a^2b^5c)^2$

50. $(-3x^7yz^2)^3$

51. $\left(\dfrac{r}{s}\right)^9$

52. $\left(\dfrac{q}{t}\right)^{11}$

53. $\left(\dfrac{mp}{n}\right)^5$

54. $\left(\dfrac{xy}{7}\right)^2$

55. $\left(\dfrac{-2xz}{y^5}\right)^2$

56. $\left(\dfrac{xy^4}{-3z^3}\right)^3$

△ **57.** The square shown has sides of length $8z^5$ decimeters. Find its area. $(A = s^2)$

$8z^5$
decimeters

△ **58.** Given the circle below with radius $5y$ centimeters, find its area. Do not approximate π. $(A = \pi r^2)$

$5y$ cm

△ **59.** The vault below is in the shape of a cube. If each side is $3y^4$ feet, find its volume. $(V = s^3)$

$3y^4$ feet

$3y^4$ feet

$3y^4$ feet

△ **60.** The silo shown is in the shape of a cylinder. If its radius is $4x$ meters and its height is $5x^3$ meters, find its volume. Do not approximate π. $(V = \pi r^2 h)$

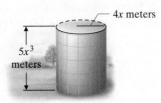

$4x$ meters

$5x^3$
meters

Use the quotient rule and simplify each expression. See Example 9.

61. $\dfrac{x^3}{x}$

62. $\dfrac{y^{10}}{y^9}$

63. $\dfrac{(-4)^6}{(-4)^3}$

64. $\dfrac{(-6)^{13}}{(-6)^{11}}$

65. $\dfrac{p^7q^{20}}{pq^{15}}$

66. $\dfrac{x^8y^6}{xy^5}$

67. $\dfrac{7x^2y^6}{14x^2y^3}$

68. $\dfrac{9a^4b^7}{27ab^2}$

Simplify each expression. See Example 10.

69. 7^0

70. 23^0

71. $(2x)^0$

72. $(4y)^0$

73. $-7x^0$

74. $-2x^0$

75. $5^0 + y^0$

76. $-3^0 + 4^0$

MIXED PRACTICE

Simplify each expression. See Examples 1 through 10.

77. -9^2

78. $(-9)^2$

79. $\left(\dfrac{1}{4}\right)^3$

80. $\left(\dfrac{2}{3}\right)^3$

81. $\left(\dfrac{9}{qr}\right)^2$

82. $\left(\dfrac{pt}{3}\right)^3$

83. a^2a^3a

84. $x^2x^{15}x$

85. $(2x^3)(-8x^4)$

86. $(3y^4)(-5y)$

87. $(a^7b^{12})(a^4b^8)$

88. $(y^2z^2)(y^{15}z^{13})$

89. $(-2mn^6)(-13m^8n)$

90. $(-3s^5t)(-7st^{10})$

91. $(z^4)^{10}$

92. $(t^5)^{11}$

93. $(-6xyz^3)^2$

94. $(-3xy^2a^3)^3$

95. $\dfrac{3x^5}{x^4}$

96. $\dfrac{5x^9}{x^3}$

97. $(9xy)^2$

98. $(2ab)^5$

99. $2^0 + 2^5$

100. $7^2 - 7^0$

101. $\left(\dfrac{3y^5}{6x^4}\right)^3$

102. $\left(\dfrac{2ab}{6yz}\right)^4$

103. $\dfrac{2x^3y^2z}{xyz}$

104. $\dfrac{x^{12}y^{13}}{x^5y^7}$

REVIEW AND PREVIEW

Simplify each expression by combining any like terms. Use the distributive property to remove any parentheses. See Section 2.1.

105. $y - 10 + y$

106. $-6z + 20 - 3z$

107. $7x + 2 - 8x - 6$

108. $10y - 14 - y - 14$

109. $2(x - 5) + 3(5 - x)$

110. $-3(w + 7) + 5(w + 1)$

CONCEPT EXTENSIONS

Matching. *See the Concept Checks in this section. For Exercises 111 through 114, match the expression with the operation needed to simplify each. A letter may be used more than once and a letter may not be used at all.*

111. $(x^{14})^{23}$

112. $x^{14} \cdot x^{23}$

113. $x^{14} + x^{23}$

114. $\dfrac{x^{35}}{x^{17}}$

a. Add the exponents

b. Subtract the exponents

c. Multiply the exponents

d. Divide the exponents

e. None of these

Decision Making. *Fill in the boxes so that each statement is true. (More than one answer is possible for each exercise.)*

115. $x^{\square} \cdot x^{\square} = x^{12}$

116. $(x^{\square})^{\square} = x^{20}$

117. $\dfrac{y^{\square}}{y^{\square}} = y^7$

118. $(y^{\square})^{\square} \cdot (y^{\square})^{\square} = y^{30}$

△ **119.** The formula $V = x^3$ can be used to find the volume V of a cube with side length x. Find the volume of a cube with side length 7 meters. (Volume is measured in cubic units.)

△ **120.** The formula $S = 6x^2$ can be used to find the surface area S of a cube with side length x. Find the surface area of a cube with side length 5 meters. (Surface area is measured in square units.)

△ **121.** To find the amount of water that a swimming pool in the shape of a cube can hold, do we use the formula for volume of the cube or surface area of the cube? (See Exercises 119 and 120.)

△ **122.** To find the amount of material needed to cover an ottoman in the shape of a cube, do we use the formula for volume of the cube or surface area of the cube? (See Exercises 119 and 120.)

123. In your own words, explain why $5^0 = 1$.

124. In your own words, explain when $(-3)^n$ is positive and when it is negative.

Simplify each expression. Assume that variables represent positive integers.

125. $x^{5a}x^{4a}$

126. $b^{9a}b^{4a}$

127. $(a^b)^5$

128. $(2a^{4b})^4$

129. $\dfrac{x^{9a}}{x^{4a}}$

130. $\dfrac{y^{15b}}{y^{6b}}$

131. Suppose you borrow money for 6 months. If the interest rate is compounded monthly, the formula $A = P\left(1 + \dfrac{r}{12}\right)^6$ gives the total amount A to be repaid at the end of 6 months. For a loan of $P = \$1000$ and interest rate of 9% ($r = 0.09$), how much money will you need to pay off the loan?

132. On January 1, 2007, the Federal Reserve discount rate was set at $5\frac{1}{4}$%. (*Source:* Federal Reserve Board) The discount rate is the interest rate at which banks can borrow money from the Federal Reserve System. Suppose a bank needs to borrow money from the Federal Reserve System for 3 months. If the interest is compounded monthly, the formula $A = P\left(1 + \dfrac{r}{12}\right)^3$ gives the total amount A to be repaid at the end of 3 months. For a loan of $P = \$500,000$ and interest rate of $r = 0.0525$, how much money will the bank repay to the Federal Reserve at the end of 3 months? Round to the nearest dollar.

6.2 ADDING AND SUBTRACTING POLYNOMIALS

OBJECTIVES

1 Define polynomial, monomial, binomial, trinomial, and degree.

2 Find the value of a polynomial given replacement values for the variables.

3 Simplify a polynomial by combining like terms.

4 Add and subtract polynomials.

OBJECTIVE 1 ▶ Defining polynomial, monomial, binomial, trinomial, and degree. In this section, we introduce a special algebraic expression called a polynomial. Let's first review some definitions presented in Section 2.1.

Recall that a term is a number or the product of a number and variables raised to powers. The terms of the expression $4x^2 + 3x$ are $4x^2$ and $3x$. The terms of the expression $9x^4 - 7x - 1$ are $9x^4$, $-7x$, and -1.

Expression	Terms
$4x^2 + 3x$	$4x^2, 3x$
$9x^4 - 7x - 1$	$9x^4, -7x, -1$
$7y^3$	$7y^3$
5	5

The **numerical coefficient** of a term, or simply the **coefficient,** is the numerical factor of each term. If no numerical factor appears in the term, then the coefficient is understood to be 1. If the term is a number only, it is called a **constant** term or simply a constant.

Term	Coefficient
x^5	1
$3x^2$	3
$-4x$	-4
$-x^2y$	-1
3 (constant)	3

Polynomial

A **polynomial in x** is a finite sum of terms of the form ax^n, where a is a real number and n is a whole number.

For example,

$$x^5 - 3x^3 + 2x^2 - 5x + 1$$

is a polynomial. Notice that this polynomial is written in **descending powers** of x because the powers of x decrease from left to right. (Recall that the term 1 can be thought of as $1x^0$.)

On the other hand,

$$x^{-5} + 2x - 3$$

is **not** a polynomial because it contains an exponent, -5, that is not a whole number. (We study negative exponents in Section 6.5 of this chapter.)

Some polynomials are given special names.

Types of Polynomials

A **monomial** is a polynomial with exactly one term.

A **binomial** is a polynomial with exactly two terms.

A **trinomial** is a polynomial with exactly three terms.

The following are examples of monomials, binomials, and trinomials. Each of these examples is also a polynomial.

POLYNOMIALS

Monomials	Binomials	Trinomials	None of These
ax^2	$x + y$	$x^2 + 4xy + y^2$	$5x^3 - 6x^2 + 3x - 6$
$-3z$	$3p + 2$	$x^5 + 7x^2 - x$	$-y^5 + y^4 - 3y^3 - y^2 + y$
4	$4x^2 - 7$	$-q^4 + q^3 - 2q$	$x^6 + x^4 - x^3 + 1$

Each term of a polynomial has a **degree.**

Degree of a Term

The degree of a term is the sum of the exponents on the variables contained in the term.

EXAMPLE 1   Find the degree of each term.

a. $-3x^2$ **b.** $5x^3yz$ **c.** 2

Solution

a. The exponent on x is 2, so the degree of the term is 2.

b. $5x^3yz$ can be written as $5x^3y^1z^1$. The degree of the term is the sum of its exponents, so the degree is $3 + 1 + 1$ or 5.

c. The constant, 2, can be written as $2x^0$ (since $x^0 = 1$). The degree of 2 or $2x^0$ is 0.   □

PRACTICE

1   Find the degree of each term.

a. $5y^3$ **b.** $-3a^2b^5c$ **c.** 8

From the preceding, we can say that **the degree of a constant is 0.**
     Each polynomial also has a degree.

> **Degree of a Polynomial**
> The degree of a polynomial is the greatest degree of any term of the polynomial.

EXAMPLE 2   Find the degree of each polynomial and tell whether the polynomial is a monomial, binomial, trinomial, or none of these.

a. $-2t^2 + 3t + 6$ **b.** $15x - 10$ **c.** $7x + 3x^3 + 2x^2 - 1$

Solution

a. The degree of the trinomial $-2t^2 + 3t + 6$ is 2, the greatest degree of any of its terms.

b. The degree of the binomial $15x - 10$ or $15x^1 - 10$ is 1.

c. The degree of the polynomial $7x + 3x^3 + 2x^2 - 1$ is 3.   □

PRACTICE

2   Find the degree of each polynomial and tell whether the polynomial is a monomial, binomial, trinomial, or none of these.

a. $5b^2 - 3b + 7$ **b.** $7t + 3$
c. $5x^2 + 3x - 6x^3 + 4$

EXAMPLE 3 Complete the table for the polynomial

$$7x^2y - 6xy + x^2 - 3y + 7$$

Use the table to give the degree of the polynomial.

Solution

Term	Numerical Coefficient	Degree of Term
$7x^2y$	7	3
$-6xy$	-6	2
x^2	1	2
$-3y$	-3	1
7	7	0

The degree of the polynomial is 3. ←

PRACTICE
3 Complete the table for the polynomial $-3x^3y^2 + 4xy^2 - y^2 + 3x - 2$.

Term	Numerical Coefficient	Degree of Term
$-3x^3y^2$		
$4xy^2$		
$-y^2$		
$3x$		
-2		

OBJECTIVE 2 ▶ Evaluating polynomials. Polynomials have different values depending on replacement values for the variables.

EXAMPLE 4 Find the value of the polynomial $3x^2 - 2x + 1$ when $x = -2$.

Solution Replace x with -2 and simplify.

$$\begin{aligned}
3x^2 - 2x + 1 &= 3(-2)^2 - 2(-2) + 1 \\
&= 3(4) + 4 + 1 \\
&= 12 + 4 + 1 \\
&= 17
\end{aligned}$$

PRACTICE
4 Find the value of the polynomial $2x^2 - 5x + 3$ when $x = -3$.

Many physical phenomena can be modeled by polynomials.

EXAMPLE 5 **Finding the Height of a Dropped Object**

The Swiss Re Building, in London, is a unique building. Londoners often refer to it as the "pickle building." The building is 592.1 feet tall. An object is dropped from the highest point of this building. Neglecting air resistance, the height in feet of the object above ground at time t seconds is given by the polynomial $-16t^2 + 592.1$. Find the height of the object when $t = 1$ second, and when $t = 6$ seconds.

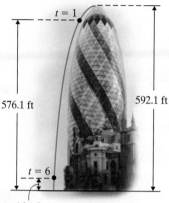

$t = 1$

576.1 ft   592.1 ft

$t = 6$

16.1 ft

Solution To find each height, we evaluate the polynomial when $t = 1$ and when $t = 6$.

$$-16t^2 + 592.1 = -16(1)^2 + 592.1 \quad \text{Replace } t \text{ with 1.}$$
$$= -16(1) + 592.1$$
$$= -16 + 592.1$$
$$= 576.1$$

The height of the object at 1 second is 576.1 feet.

$$-16t^2 + 592.1 = -16(6)^2 + 592.1 \quad \text{Replace } t \text{ with 6.}$$
$$= -16(36) + 592.1$$
$$= -576 + 592.1 = 16.1$$

The height of the object at 6 seconds is 16.1 feet.

PRACTICE
5   The cliff divers of Acapulco dive 130 feet into La Quebrada several times a day for the entertainment of the tourists. If a tourist is standing near the diving platform and drops his camera off the cliff, the height of the camera above the water at time t seconds is given by the polynomial $-16t^2 + 130$. Find the height of the camera when $t = 1$ second and when $t = 2$ seconds.

OBJECTIVE 3 ▶ Simplifying polynomials by combining like terms. Polynomials with like terms can be simplified by combining the like terms. Recall that like terms are terms that contain exactly the same variables raised to exactly the same powers.

Like Terms	Unlike Terms
$5x^2, -7x^2$	$3x, 3y$
$y, 2y$	$-2x^2, -5x$
$\frac{1}{2}a^2b, -a^2b$	$6st^2, 4s^2t$

Only like terms can be combined. We combine like terms by applying the distributive property.

EXAMPLE 6   Simplify each polynomial by combining any like terms.

a. $-3x + 7x$

b. $x + 3x^2$

c. $11x^2 + 5 + 2x^2 - 7$

d. $\frac{2}{5}x^4 + \frac{2}{3}x^3 - x^2 + \frac{1}{10}x^4 - \frac{1}{6}x^3$

Solution

a. $-3x + 7x = (-3 + 7)x = 4x$

b. $x + 3x^2$

These terms cannot be combined because x and $3x^2$ are not like terms.

c. $11x^2 + 5 + 2x^2 - 7 = 11x^2 + 2x^2 + 5 - 7$
$$= 13x^2 - 2 \qquad \text{Combine like terms.}$$

d. $\dfrac{2}{5}x^4 + \dfrac{2}{3}x^3 - x^2 + \dfrac{1}{10}x^4 - \dfrac{1}{6}x^3$

$$= \left(\dfrac{2}{5} + \dfrac{1}{10}\right)x^4 + \left(\dfrac{2}{3} - \dfrac{1}{6}\right)x^3 - x^2$$

$$= \left(\dfrac{4}{10} + \dfrac{1}{10}\right)x^4 + \left(\dfrac{4}{6} - \dfrac{1}{6}\right)x^3 - x^2$$

$$= \dfrac{5}{10}x^4 + \dfrac{3}{6}x^3 - x^2$$

$$= \dfrac{1}{2}x^4 + \dfrac{1}{2}x^3 - x^2$$

PRACTICE
6 Simplify each polynomial by combining any like terms.

a. $-4y + 2y$ **b.** $z + 5z^3$

c. $7a^2 - 5 - 3a^2 - 7$ **d.** $\dfrac{3}{8}x^3 - x^2 + \dfrac{5}{6}x^4 + \dfrac{1}{12}x^3 - \dfrac{1}{2}x^4$

Concept Check ✓

When combining like terms in the expression, $5x - 8x^2 - 8x$, which of the following is the proper result?

a. $-11x^2$ **b.** $-8x^2 - 3x$ **c.** $-11x$ **d.** $-11x^4$

EXAMPLE 7 Combine like terms to simplify.

$$-9x^2 + 3xy - 5y^2 + 7yx$$

Solution $-9x^2 + 3xy - 5y^2 + 7yx = -9x^2 + (3 + 7)xy - 5y^2$

$$= -9x^2 + 10xy - 5y^2$$

> ▶ **Helpful Hint**
>
> This term can be written as $7yx$ or $7xy$.

PRACTICE
7 Combine like terms to simplify: $9xy - 3x^2 - 4yx + 5y^2$.

△ **EXAMPLE 8** Write a polynomial that describes the total area of the squares and rectangles shown below. Then simplify the polynomial.

Solution

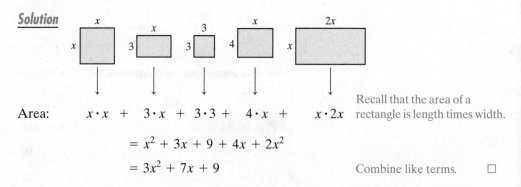

Area: $\quad x \cdot x \quad + \quad 3 \cdot x \quad + \quad 3 \cdot 3 + \quad 4 \cdot x \quad + \quad x \cdot 2x \quad$ Recall that the area of a rectangle is length times width.

$$= x^2 + 3x + 9 + 4x + 2x^2$$

$$= 3x^2 + 7x + 9 \qquad \text{Combine like terms.}$$

PRACTICE
8 Write a polynomial that describes the total area of the squares and rectangles shown below. Then simplify the polynomial.

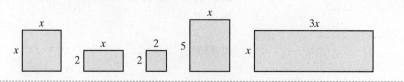

OBJECTIVE 4 ▶ Adding and subtracting polynomials. We now practice adding and subtracting polynomials.

> **Adding Polynomials**
> To add polynomials, combine all like terms.

EXAMPLE 9   Add $(-2x^2 + 5x - 1)$ and $(-2x^2 + x + 3)$.

Solution

$$
\begin{aligned}
(-2x^2 + 5x - 1) + (-2x^2 + x + 3) &= -2x^2 + 5x - 1 - 2x^2 + x + 3 \\
&= (-2x^2 - 2x^2) + (5x + 1x) + (-1 + 3) \\
&= -4x^2 + 6x + 2 \qquad \square
\end{aligned}
$$

PRACTICE
9   Add. $(-3x^2 - 4x + 9)$ and $(2x^2 - 2x)$.

EXAMPLE 10   Add: $(4x^3 - 6x^2 + 2x + 7) + (5x^2 - 2x)$.

Solution

$$
\begin{aligned}
(4x^3 - 6x^2 + 2x + 7) + (5x^2 - 2x) &= 4x^3 - 6x^2 + 2x + 7 + 5x^2 - 2x \\
&= 4x^3 + (-6x^2 + 5x^2) + (2x - 2x) + 7 \\
&= 4x^3 - x^2 + 7 \qquad \square
\end{aligned}
$$

PRACTICE
10   Add. $(-3x^3 + 7x^2 + 3x - 4) + (3x^2 - 9x)$.

Polynomials can be added vertically if we line up like terms underneath one another.

EXAMPLE 11   Add $(7y^3 - 2y^2 + 7)$ and $(6y^2 + 1)$ using the vertical format.

Solution   Vertically line up like terms and add.

$$
\begin{array}{r}
7y^3 - 2y^2 + 7 \\
6y^2 + 1 \\
\hline
7y^3 + 4y^2 + 8
\end{array} \qquad \square
$$

PRACTICE
11   Add $(5z^3 + 3z^2 + 4z)$ and $(5z^2 + 4z)$ using the vertical format.

To subtract one polynomial from another, recall the definition of subtraction. To subtract a number, we add its opposite: $a - b = a + (-b)$. To subtract a polynomial, we also add its opposite. Just as $-b$ is the opposite of b, $-(x^2 + 5)$ is the opposite of $(x^2 + 5)$.

EXAMPLE 12   Subtract: $(5x - 3) - (2x - 11)$.

Solution   From the definition of subtraction, we have

$$
\begin{aligned}
(5x - 3) - (2x - 11) &= (5x - 3) + [-(2x - 11)] \quad \text{Add the opposite.} \\
&= (5x - 3) + (-2x + 11) \quad \text{Apply the distributive property.} \\
&= (5x - 2x) + (-3 + 11) \\
&= 3x + 8 \qquad \square
\end{aligned}
$$

PRACTICE
12   Subtract: $(8x - 7) - (3x - 6)$.

> **Subtracting Polynomials**
> To subtract two polynomials, change the signs of the terms of the polynomial being subtracted and then add.

EXAMPLE 13 Subtract: $(2x^3 + 8x^2 - 6x) - (2x^3 - x^2 + 1)$.

Solution First, change the sign of each term of the second polynomial and then add.

> ▶ **Helpful Hint**
> Notice the sign of each term is changed.

$$(2x^3 + 8x^2 - 6x) - (2x^3 - x^2 + 1) = (2x^3 + 8x^2 - 6x) + (-2x^3 + x^2 - 1)$$
$$= 2x^3 - 2x^3 + 8x^2 + x^2 - 6x - 1$$
$$= 9x^2 - 6x - 1 \quad \text{Combine like terms.} \qquad \square$$

PRACTICE
13 Subtract: $(3x^3 - 5x^2 + 4x) - (x^3 - x^2 + 6)$.

EXAMPLE 14 Subtract $(5y^2 + 2y - 6)$ from $(-3y^2 - 2y + 11)$ using the vertical format.

Solution Arrange the polynomials in vertical format, lining up like terms.

$$
\begin{array}{r}
-3y^2 - 2y + 11 \\
-(5y^2 + 2y - 6) \\
\end{array}
\qquad
\begin{array}{r}
-3y^2 - 2y + 11 \\
-5y^2 - 2y + 6 \\
\hline
-8y^2 - 4y + 17 \\
\end{array}
\qquad \square
$$

PRACTICE
14 Subtract $(6z^2 + 3z - 7)$ from $(-2z^2 - 8z + 5)$ using the vertical format.

EXAMPLE 15 Subtract $(5z - 7)$ from the sum of $(8z + 11)$ and $(9z - 2)$.

Solution Notice that $(5z - 7)$ is to be subtracted **from** a sum. The translation is

$$[(8z + 11) + (9z - 2)] - (5z - 7)$$
$$= 8z + 11 + 9z - 2 - 5z + 7 \qquad \text{Remove grouping symbols.}$$
$$= 8z + 9z - 5z + 11 - 2 + 7 \qquad \text{Group like terms.}$$
$$= 12z + 16 \qquad \text{Combine like terms.} \qquad \square$$

PRACTICE
15 Subtract $(3x + 5)$ from the sum of $(8x - 11)$ and $(2x + 5)$.

EXAMPLE 16 Add or subtract as indicated.

a. $(3x^2 - 6xy + 5y^2) + (-2x^2 + 8xy - y^2)$
b. $(9a^2b^2 + 6ab - 3ab^2) - (5b^2a + 2ab - 3 - 9b^2)$

Solution

a. $(3x^2 - 6xy + 5y^2) + (-2x^2 + 8xy - y^2)$

$$= 3x^2 - 6xy + 5y^2 - 2x^2 + 8xy - y^2$$
$$= x^2 + 2xy + 4y^2 \quad \text{Combine like terms.}$$

b. $(9a^2b^2 + 6ab - 3ab^2) - (5b^2a + 2ab - 3 - 9b^2)$ Change the sign of each term

$= 9a^2b^2 + 6ab - 3ab^2 - 5b^2a - 2ab + 3 + 9b^2$ of the polynomial being subtracted.

$= 9a^2b^2 + 4ab - 8ab^2 + 3 + 9b^2$ Combine like terms.   □

PRACTICE

16   Add or subtract as indicated.

a. $(3a^2 - 4ab + 7b^2) + (-8a^2 + 3ab - b^2)$

b. $(5x^2y^2 - 6xy - 4xy^2) - (2x^2y^2 + 4xy - 5 + 6y^2)$

Answers to Concept Check:

a. $3y$ **b.** $2y^2$ **c.** $-3y$ **d.** $2y^2$
e. cannot be simplified

Concept Check ✓

If possible, simplify each expression by performing the indicated operation.

a. $2y + y$ **b.** $2y \cdot y$ **c.** $-2y - y$ **d.** $(-2y)(-y)$ **e.** $2x + y$

VOCABULARY & READINESS CHECK

Word Bank. *Use the choices below to fill in each blank. Not all choices will be used.*

least	monomial	trinomial	coefficient
greatest	binomial	constant	

1. A(n) _____ is a polynomial with exactly 2 terms.

2. A(n) _____ is a polynomial with exactly one term.

3. A(n) _____ is a polynomial with exactly three terms.

4. The numerical factor of a term is called the _____.

5. A number term is also called a _____.

6. The degree of a polynomial is the _____ degree of any term of the polynomial.

Simplify by combining like terms if possible.

7. $-9y - 5y$

8. $6m^5 + 7m^5$

9. $x + 6x$

10. $7z - z$

11. $5m^2 + 2m$

12. $8p^3 + 3p^2$

6.2 | **EXERCISE SET**   MyMathLab   MathXL PRACTICE   WATCH   DOWNLOAD   READ   REVIEW

Find the degree of each of the following polynomials and determine whether it is a monomial, binomial, trinomial, or none of these. See Examples 1 through 3.

1. $x + 2$

2. $-6y + y^2 + 4$

3. $9m^3 - 5m^2 + 4m - 8$

4. $5a^2 + 3a^3 - 4a^4$

5. $12x^4y - x^2y^2 - 12x^2y^4$

6. $7r^2s^2 + 2r - 3s^5$

7. $3zx - 5x^2$

8. $5y + 2$

In the second column, write the degree of the polynomial in the first column. See Examples 1 through 3.

Polynomial	Degree
9. $3xy^2 - 4$	
10. $8x^2y^2$	
11. $5a^2 - 2a + 1$	
12. $4z^6 + 3z^2$	

Find the value of each polynomial when **(a)** $x = 0$ *and* **(b)** $x = -1$*. See Examples 4 and 5.*

13. $x + 6$

14. $2x - 10$

15. $x^2 - 5x - 2$

16. $x^2 - 4$

17. $x^3 - 15$

18. $-2x^3 + 3x^2 - 6$

The CN Tower in Toronto, Ontario, is 1821 feet tall and is the world's tallest self-supporting structure. An object is dropped from the Skypod of the Tower which is at 1150 feet. Neglecting air resistance, the height of the object at time t seconds is given by the polynomial $-16t^2 + 1150$. Find the height of the object at the given times.

1150 ft

19. $t = 1$ second

20. $t = 7$ seconds

21. $t = 3$ seconds

22. $t = 6$ seconds

Simplify each of the following by combining like terms. See Examples 6 and 7.

23. $14x^2 + 9x^2$

24. $18x^3 - 4x^3$

25. $15x^2 - 3x^2 - y$

26. $12k^3 - 9k^3 + 11$

27. $8s - 5s + 4s$

28. $5y + 7y - 6y$

29. $0.1y^2 - 1.2y^2 + 6.7 - 1.9$

30. $7.6y + 3.2y^2 - 8y - 2.5y^2$

31. $\dfrac{2}{5}x^2 - \dfrac{1}{3}x^3 + x^2 - \dfrac{1}{4}x^3 + 6$

32. $\dfrac{1}{6}x^4 - \dfrac{1}{7}x^2 + 5 - \dfrac{1}{2}x^4 - \dfrac{3}{7}x^2 + \dfrac{1}{3}$

33. $6a^2 - 4ab + 7b^2 - a^2 - 5ab + 9b^2$

34. $x^2y + xy - y + 10x^2y - 2y + xy$

Perform the indicated operations. See Examples 9 through 13.

35. $(3x + 7) + (9x + 5)$

36. $(3x^2 + 7) + (3x^2 + 9)$

37. $(-7x + 5) + (-3x^2 + 7x + 5)$

38. $(3x - 8) + (4x^2 - 3x + 3)$

39. $(2x^2 + 5) - (3x^2 - 9)$

40. $(5x^2 + 4) - (-2y^2 + 4)$

41. $3x - (5x - 9)$

42. $4 - (-y - 4)$

43. $(2x^2 + 3x - 9) - (-4x + 7)$

44. $(-7x^2 + 4x + 7) - (-8x + 2)$

Perform the indicated operations. See Examples 11, 14, and 15.

45. $\begin{array}{r} 3t^2 + 4 \\ +5t^2 - 8 \\ \hline \end{array}$

46. $\begin{array}{r} 7x^3 + 3 \\ +2x^3 + 1 \\ \hline \end{array}$

47. $\begin{array}{r} 4z^2 - 8z + 3 \\ -(6z^2 + 8z - 3) \\ \hline \end{array}$

48. $\begin{array}{r} 5u^5 - 4u^2 + 3u - 7 \\ -(3u^5 + 6u^2 - 8u + 2) \\ \hline \end{array}$

49. $\begin{array}{r} 5x^3 - 4x^2 + 6x - 2 \\ -(3x^3 - 2x^2 - x - 4) \\ \hline \end{array}$

50. $\begin{array}{r} 7a^2 - 9a + 6 \\ -(11a^2 - 4a + 2) \\ \hline \end{array}$

51. Subtract $(19x^2 + 5)$ from $(81x^2 + 10)$.

52. Subtract $(2x + xy)$ from $(3x - 9xy)$.

53. Subtract $(2x + 2)$ from the sum of $(8x + 1)$ and $(6x + 3)$.

54. Subtract $(-12x - 3)$ from the sum of $(-5x - 7)$ and $(12x + 3)$.

MIXED PRACTICE

Perform the indicated operations.

55. $(-3y^2 - 4y) + (2y^2 + y - 1)$

56. $(7x^2 + 2x - 9) + (-3x^2 + 5)$

57. $(5x + 8) - (-2x^2 - 6x + 8)$

58. $(-6y^2 + 3y - 4) - (9y^2 - 3y)$

59. $(-8x^4 + 7x) + (-8x^4 + x + 9)$

60. $(6y^5 - 6y^3 + 4) + (-2y^5 - 8y^3 - 7)$

61. $(3x^2 + 5x - 8) + (5x^2 + 9x + 12) - (x^2 - 14)$

62. $(-a^2 + 1) - (a^2 - 3) + (5a^2 - 6a + 7)$

63. Subtract $4x$ from $7x - 3$.

64. Subtract y from $y^2 - 4y + 1$.

65. Subtract $(5x + 7)$ from $(7x^2 + 3x + 9)$.

66. Subtract $(5y^2 + 8y + 2)$ from $(7y^2 + 9y - 8)$.

67. Subtract $(4y^2 - 6y - 3)$ from the sum of $(8y^2 + 7)$ and $(6y + 9)$.

68. Subtract $(5y + 7x^2)$ from the sum of $(8y - x)$ and $(3 + 8x^2)$.

69. Subtract $(-2x^2 + 4x - 12)$ from the sum of $(-x^2 - 2x)$ and $(5x^2 + x + 9)$.

70. Subtract $(4x^2 - 2x + 2)$ from the sum of $(x^2 + 7x + 1)$ and $(7x + 5)$.

Find the area of each figure. Write a polynomial that describes the total area of the rectangles and squares shown in Exercises 71–72. Then simplify the polynomial. See Example 8.

△ **71.**

△ **72.**

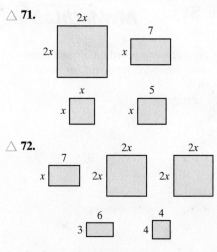

Recall that the perimeter of a figure such as the ones shown in Exercises 73 through 76 is the sum of the lengths of its sides. Find the perimeter of each polynomial.

△ **73.**   △ **74.**

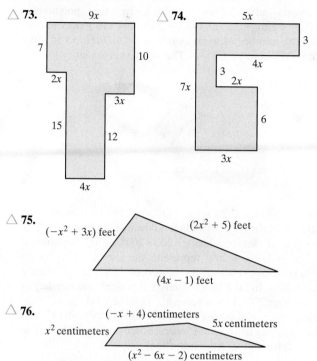

△ **75.**

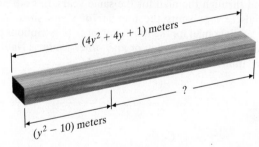

$(-x^2 + 3x)$ feet $(2x^2 + 5)$ feet

$(4x - 1)$ feet

△ **76.**

$(-x + 4)$ centimeters

x^2 centimeters $5x$ centimeters

$(x^2 - 6x - 2)$ centimeters

△ **77.** A wooden beam is $(4y^2 + 4y + 1)$ meters long. If a piece $(y^2 - 10)$ meters is cut, express the length of the remaining piece of beam as a polynomial in y.

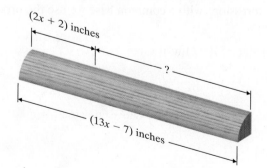

$(4y^2 + 4y + 1)$ meters

?

$(y^2 - 10)$ meters

△ **78.** A piece of quarter-round molding is $(13x - 7)$ inches long. If a piece $(2x + 2)$ inches is removed, express the length of the remaining piece of molding as a polynomial in x.

$(2x + 2)$ inches

?

$(13x - 7)$ inches

Add or subtract as indicated. See Example 16.

79. $(9a + 6b - 5) + (-11a - 7b + 6)$

80. $(3x - 2 + 6y) + (7x - 2 - y)$

81. $(4x^2 + y^2 + 3) - (x^2 + y^2 - 2)$

82. $(7a^2 - 3b^2 + 10) - (-2a^2 + b^2 - 12)$

83. $(x^2 + 2xy - y^2) + (5x^2 - 4xy + 20y^2)$

84. $(a^2 - ab + 4b^2) + (6a^2 + 8ab - b^2)$

85. $(11r^2s + 16rs - 3 - 2r^2s^2) - (3sr^2 + 5 - 9r^2s^2)$

86. $(3x^2y - 6xy + x^2y^2 - 5) - (11x^2y^2 - 1 + 5yx^2)$

Simplify each polynomial by combining like terms.

87. $7.75x + 9.16x^2 - 1.27 - 14.58x^2 - 18.34$

88. $1.85x^2 - 3.76x + 9.25x^2 + 10.76 - 4.21x$

Perform each indicated operation.

89. $[(7.9y^4 - 6.8y^3 + 3.3y) + (6.1y^3 - 5)] - (4.2y^4 + 1.1y - 1)$

90. $[(1.2x^2 - 3x + 9.1) - (7.8x^2 - 3.1 + 8)] + (1.2x - 6)$

REVIEW AND PREVIEW

Multiply. See Section 6.1.

91. $3x(2x)$ **92.** $-7x(x)$

93. $(12x^3)(-x^5)$ **94.** $6r^3(7r^{10})$

95. $10x^2(20xy^2)$ **96.** $-z^2y(11zy)$

CONCEPT EXTENSIONS

97. Describe how to find the degree of a term.

98. Describe how to find the degree of a polynomial.

99. Explain why xyz is a monomial while $x + y + z$ is a trinomial.

100. Explain why the degree of the term $5y^3$ is 3 and the degree of the polynomial $2y + y + 2y$ is 1.

Matching. *Match each expression on the left with its simplification on the right. Not all letters on the right must be used and a letter may be used more than once.*

101. $10y - 6y^2 - y$ **a.** $3y$

102. $5x + 5x$ **b.** $9y - 6y^2$
                              c. $10x$
103. $(5x - 3) + (5x - 3)$ **d.** $25x^2$

104. $(15x - 3) - (5x - 3)$ **e.** $10x - 6$
                              f. none of these

Simplify each expression by performing the indicated operation. Explain how you arrived at each answer. See the Concept Check in this section.

105. a. $z + 3z$ **106. a.** $x + x$
     b. $z \cdot 3z$ **b.** $x \cdot x$
     c. $-z - 3z$ **c.** $-x - x$
     d. $(-z)(-3z)$ **d.** $(-x)(-x)$

Decision Making. *Fill in the boxes so that the terms in each expression can be combined. Then simplify. Each exercise has more than one solution.*

107. $7x^{\square} + 2x^{\square}$

108. $(3y^2)^{\square} + (4y^3)^{\square}$

Write a polynomial that describes the surface area of each figure. (Recall that the surface area of a solid is the sum of the areas of the faces or sides of the solid.)

△ **109.**

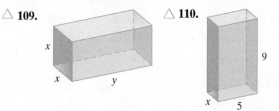

△ **110.**

111. The average tuition, fees, and room and board rates charged per year for full-time students in degree-granting two year public colleges is approximated by the polynomial $6.4x^2 + 37.9x + 2856.8$ for the years 1984 through 2006. (*Source:* National Center for Education Statistics & The College Board) Use this model to predict what the costs will

be for a student at a public two-year institution in 2010. ($x = 26$). Round to the nearest dollar.

112. The number of wireless telephone subscribers (in millions) x years after 1990 is given by the polynomial $0.74x^2 + 2.6x + 3.2$ for 1990 to 2005. Use this model to predict the number of wireless telephone subscribers in 2010 ($x = 20$). (*Source:* CTIA—The Wireless Association)

113. The polynomial $2.13x^2 + 21.89x + 1190$ represents the sale of electricity (in billion kilowatt-hours) in the U.S. residential sector during 2000–2005. The polynomial $8.71x^2 - 1.46x + 2095$ represents the sale of electricity (in billion kilowatt-hours) in all other U.S. sectors during 2000–2005. In both polynomials, x represents the number of years after 2000. Find a polynomial for the total sales of electricity (in billion kilowatt hours) to all sectors in the United States during this period. (*Source:* Based on data from the Energy Information Administration)

114. The polynomial $-3.5x^2 + 33.3x + 392$ represents the number of prescriptions (in millions) purchased from a supermarket for the years 2000–2005. The polynomial $19x + 141$ represents the number of prescriptions (in millions) purchased through the mail for the same years. In both polynomials, x represents the number of years since 2000. Find a polynomial for the total number of prescriptions purchased from a supermarket or mail order. (*Source:* National Association of Chain Drug Stores)

6.3 MULTIPLYING POLYNOMIALS

OBJECTIVES

1 Use the distributive property to multiply polynomials.

2 Multiply polynomials vertically.

OBJECTIVE 1 ▶ Using the distributive property to multiply polynomials. To multiply polynomials, we apply our knowledge of the rules and definitions of exponents.

Recall from Section 6.1 that to multiply two monomials such as $(-5x^3)$ and $(-2x^4)$, we use the associative and commutative properties and regroup. Remember, also, that to multiply exponential expressions with a common base we use the product rule for exponents and add exponents.

$$(-5x^3)(-2x^4) = (-5)(-2)(x^3)(x^4) = 10x^7$$

EXAMPLES Multiply.

1. $6x \cdot 4x = (6 \cdot 4)(x \cdot x)$ Use the commutative and associative properties.

     $= 24x^2$ Multiply.

2. $-7x^2 \cdot 0.2x^5 = (-7 \cdot 0.2)(x^2 \cdot x^5)$

     $= -1.4x^7$

3. $\left(-\dfrac{1}{3}x^5\right)\left(-\dfrac{2}{9}x\right) = \left(-\dfrac{1}{3} \cdot -\dfrac{2}{9}\right) \cdot \left(x^5 \cdot x\right)$

     $= \dfrac{2}{27}x^6$

□

PRACTICES

1–3 Multiply.

1. $5y \cdot 2y$ **2.** $(5z^3) \cdot (-0.4z^5)$ **3.** $\left(-\dfrac{1}{9}b^6\right)\left(-\dfrac{7}{8}b^3\right)$

Concept Check ☑

Simplify.

a. $3x \cdot 2x$ **b.** $3x + 2x$

To multiply polynomials that are not monomials, use the distributive property.

EXAMPLE 4   Use the distributive property to find each product.

a. $5x(2x^3 + 6)$ **b.** $-3x^2(5x^2 + 6x - 1)$

Solution

a. $5x(2x^3 + 6) = 5x(2x^3) + 5x(6)$ Use the distributive property.

$\qquad\qquad\qquad = 10x^4 + 30x$ Multiply.

b. $-3x^2(5x^2 + 6x - 1)$

$\quad = (-3x^2)(5x^2) + (-3x^2)(6x) + (-3x^2)(-1)$ Use the distributive property.

$\quad = -15x^4 - 18x^3 + 3x^2$ Multiply.   □

PRACTICE

4   Use the distributive property to find each product.

a. $3x(5x^5 + 5)$ **b.** $-5x^3(2x^2 - 9x + 2)$

We also use the distributive property to multiply two binomials. To multiply $(x + 3)$ by $(x + 1)$, distribute the factor $(x + 3)$ first.

$$
\begin{aligned}
(x + 3)(x + 1) &= x(x + 1) + 3(x + 1) &&\text{Distribute } (x + 3). \\
&= x(x) + x(1) + 3(x) + 3(1) &&\text{Apply distributive property a second time.} \\
&= x^2 + x + 3x + 3 &&\text{Multiply.} \\
&= x^2 + 4x + 3 &&\text{Combine like terms.}
\end{aligned}
$$

This idea can be expanded so that we can multiply any two polynomials.

> **To Multiply Two Polynomials**
> Multiply each term of the first polynomial by each term of the second polynomial, and then combine like terms.

Answers to Concept Check:

a. $6x^2$ **b.** $5x$

EXAMPLE 5   Multiply $(3x + 2)(2x - 5)$.

Solution   Multiply each term of the first binomial by each term of the second.

$$
\begin{aligned}
(3x + 2)(2x - 5) &= 3x(2x) + 3x(-5) + 2(2x) + 2(-5) \\
&= 6x^2 - 15x + 4x - 10 && \text{Multiply.} \\
&= 6x^2 - 11x - 10 && \text{Combine like terms.} \quad \square
\end{aligned}
$$

PRACTICE
5   Multiply $(5x - 2)(2x + 3)$

EXAMPLE 6   Multiply $(2x - y)^2$.

Solution   Recall that $a^2 = a \cdot a$, so $(2x - y)^2 = (2x - y)(2x - y)$. Multiply each term of the first polynomial by each term of the second.

$$
\begin{aligned}
(2x - y)(2x - y) &= 2x(2x) + 2x(-y) + (-y)(2x) + (-y)(-y) \\
&= 4x^2 - 2xy - 2xy + y^2 && \text{Multiply.} \\
&= 4x^2 - 4xy + y^2 && \text{Combine like terms.} \quad \square
\end{aligned}
$$

PRACTICE
6   Multiply $(5x - 3y)^2$

Concept Check ☑

Square where indicated. Simplify if possible.

a. $(4a)^2 + (3b)^2$ **b.** $(4a + 3b)^2$

EXAMPLE 7   Multiply $(t + 2)$ by $(3t^2 - 4t + 2)$.

Solution   Multiply each term of the first polynomial by each term of the second.

$$
\begin{aligned}
(t + 2)(3t^2 - 4t + 2) &= t(3t^2) + t(-4t) + t(2) + 2(3t^2) + 2(-4t) + 2(2) \\
&= 3t^3 - 4t^2 + 2t + 6t^2 - 8t + 4 \\
&= 3t^3 + 2t^2 - 6t + 4 && \text{Combine like terms.} \quad \square
\end{aligned}
$$

PRACTICE
7   Multiply $(y + 4)$ by $(2y^2 - 3y + 5)$

EXAMPLE 8   Multiply $(3a + b)^3$.

Solution   Write $(3a + b)^3$ as $(3a + b)(3a + b)(3a + b)$.

$$
\begin{aligned}
(3a + b)(3a + b)(3a + b) &= (9a^2 + 3ab + 3ab + b^2)(3a + b) \\
&= (9a^2 + 6ab + b^2)(3a + b) \\
&= (9a^2 + 6ab + b^2)3a + (9a^2 + 6ab + b^2)b \\
&= 27a^3 + 18a^2b + 3ab^2 + 9a^2b + 6ab^2 + b^3 \\
&= 27a^3 + 27a^2b + 9ab^2 + b^3 \quad \square
\end{aligned}
$$

PRACTICE
8   Multiply $(s + 2t)^3$

Answers to Concept Check:
a. $16a^2 + 9b^2$
b. $16a^2 + 24ab + 9b^2$

OBJECTIVE 2 ▶ Multiplying polynomials vertically. Another convenient method for multiplying polynomials is to use a vertical format similar to the format used to multiply real numbers. We demonstrate this method by multiplying $(3y^2 - 4y + 1)$ by $(y + 2)$.

EXAMPLE 9   Multiply $(3y^2 - 4y + 1)(y + 2)$. Use a vertical format.

Solution

$$
\begin{array}{r}
3y^2 - 4y + 1 \\
\times \quad\quad\ y + 2 \\
\hline
6y^2 - 8y + 2 \\
3y^3 - 4y^2 + \ y \quad\quad\ \\
\hline
3y^3 + 2y^2 - 7y + 2
\end{array}
$$

1st, Multiply $3y^2 - 4y + 1$ by 2.
2nd, Multiply $3y^2 - 4y + 1$ by y.
Line up like terms.
3rd, Combine like terms.

▶ **Helpful Hint**
Make sure like terms are lined up.

Thus, $(y + 2)(3y^2 - 4y + 1) = 3y^3 + 2y^2 - 7y + 2$.   □

PRACTICE
9   Multiply $(5x^2 - 3x + 5)(x - 4)$

When multiplying vertically, be careful if a power is missing, you may want to leave space in the partial products and take care that like terms are lined up.

EXAMPLE 10   Multiply $(2x^3 - 3x + 4)(x^2 + 1)$. Use a vertical format.

Solution

$$
\begin{array}{r}
2x^3 - 3x + 4 \\
\times \quad\quad\ x^2 + 1 \\
\hline
2x^3 \quad\quad\ - 3x + 4 \\
2x^5 - 3x^3 + 4x^2 \quad\quad\quad\quad \\
\hline
2x^5 - x^3 + 4x^2 - 3x + 4
\end{array}
$$

Leave space for missing powers of x.
← Line up like terms.
Combine like terms.   □

PRACTICE
10   Multiply $(x^3 - 2x^2 + 1)(x^2 + 2)$.

EXAMPLE 11   Find the product of $(2x^2 - 3x + 4)$ and $(x^2 + 5x - 2)$ using a vertical format.

Solution   First, we arrange the polynomials in a vertical format. Then we multiply each term of the second polynomial by each term of the first polynomial.

$$
\begin{array}{r}
2x^2 - \ 3x + 4 \\
x^2 + \ 5x - 2 \\
\hline
-4x^2 + \ 6x - 8 \\
10x^3 - 15x^2 + 20x \quad\quad\quad \\
2x^4 - \ 3x^3 + \ 4x^2 \quad\quad\quad\quad\quad\quad \\
\hline
2x^4 + \ 7x^3 - 15x^2 + 26x - 8
\end{array}
$$

Multiply $2x^2 - 3x + 4$ by -2.
Multiply $2x^2 - 3x + 4$ by $5x$.
Multiply $2x^2 - 3x + 4$ by x^2.
Combine like terms.   □

PRACTICE
11   Find the product of $(5x^2 + 2x - 2)$ and $(x^2 - x + 3)$ using a vertical format.

VOCABULARY & READINESS CHECK

Word Bank. *Fill in each blank with the correct choice.*

1. The expression $5x(3x + 2)$ equals $5x \cdot 3x + 5x \cdot 2$ by the _____ property.
   a. commutative   **b.** associative   **c.** distributive

2. The expression $(x + 4)(7x - 1)$ equals $x(7x - 1) + 4(7x - 1)$ by the _____ property.
   a. commutative   **b.** associative   **c.** distributive

3. The expression $(5y - 1)^2$ equals _____ .
   a. $2(5y - 1)$ **b.** $(5y - 1)(5y + 1)$ **c.** $(5y - 1)(5y - 1)$

4. The expression $9x \cdot 3x$ equals _____ .
   a. $27x$ **b.** $27x^2$ **c.** $12x$ **d.** $12x^2$

Perform the indicated operation, if possible.

5. $x^3 \cdot x^5$ **6.** $x^2 \cdot x^6$ **7.** $x^3 + x^5$ **8.** $x^2 + x^6$

9. $x^7 \cdot x^7$ **10.** $x^{11} \cdot x^{11}$ **11.** $x^7 + x^7$ **12.** $x^{11} + x^{11}$

6.3 EXERCISE SET

MyMathLab®   PRACTICE   WATCH   DOWNLOAD   READ   REVIEW

Multiply. See Examples 1 through 3.

1. $-4n^3 \cdot 7n^7$ **2.** $9t^6(-3t^5)$

3. $(-3.1x^3)(4x^9)$ **4.** $(-5.2x^4)(3x^4)$

5. $\left(-\dfrac{1}{3}y^2\right)\left(\dfrac{2}{5}y\right)$ **6.** $\left(-\dfrac{3}{4}y^7\right)\left(\dfrac{1}{7}y^4\right)$

7. $(2x)(-3x^2)(4x^5)$ **8.** $(x)(5x^4)(-6x^7)$

Multiply. See Example 4.

9. $3x(2x + 5)$ **10.** $2x(6x + 3)$

11. $-2a(a + 4)$ **12.** $-3a(2a + 7)$

13. $3x(2x^2 - 3x + 4)$

14. $4x(5x^2 - 6x - 10)$

15. $-2a^2(3a^2 - 2a + 3)$

16. $-4b^2(3b^3 - 12b^2 - 6)$

17. $-y(4x^3 - 7x^2y + xy^2 + 3y^3)$

18. $-x(6y^3 - 5xy^2 + x^2y - 5x^3)$

19. $\dfrac{1}{2}x^2(8x^2 - 6x + 1)$

20. $\dfrac{1}{3}y^2(9y^2 - 6y + 1)$

Multiply. See Examples 5 and 6.

21. $(x + 4)(x + 3)$

22. $(x + 2)(x + 9)$

23. $(a + 7)(a - 2)$

24. $(y - 10)(y + 11)$

25. $\left(x + \dfrac{2}{3}\right)\left(x - \dfrac{1}{3}\right)$

26. $\left(x + \dfrac{3}{5}\right)\left(x - \dfrac{2}{5}\right)$

27. $(3x^2 + 1)(4x^2 + 7)$

28. $(5x^2 + 2)(6x^2 + 2)$

29. $(2y - 4)^2$

30. $(6x - 7)^2$

31. $(4x - 3)(3x - 5)$

32. $(8x - 3)(2x - 4)$

33. $(3x^2 + 1)^2$

34. $(x^2 + 4)^2$

35. Multiple Steps. Perform the indicated operations.
   a. $(3x + 5) + (3x + 7)$
   b. $(3x + 5)(3x + 7)$
   c. Explain the difference between the two expressions.

36. Multiple Steps. Perform the indicated operations.
   a. $9x^2(-10x^2)$
   b. $9x^2 - 10x^2$
   c. Explain the difference between the two expressions.

Multiply. See Example 7.

37. $(x - 2)(x^2 - 3x + 7)$

38. $(x + 3)(x^2 + 5x - 8)$

39. $(x + 5)(x^3 - 3x + 4)$

40. $(a + 2)(a^3 - 3a^2 + 7)$
41. $(2a - 3)(5a^2 - 6a + 4)$
42. $(3 + b)(2 - 5b - 3b^2)$

Multiply. See Example 8.

43. $(x + 2)^3$
44. $(y - 1)^3$
45. $(2y - 3)^3$
46. $(3x + 4)^3$

Multiply vertically. See Examples 9 through 11.

47. $(2x - 11)(6x + 1)$
48. $(4x - 7)(5x + 1)$
49. $(5x + 1)(2x^2 + 4x - 1)$
50. $(4x - 5)(8x^2 + 2x - 4)$
51. $(x^2 + 5x - 7)(2x^2 - 7x - 9)$
52. $(3x^2 - x + 2)(x^2 + 2x + 1)$

MIXED PRACTICE

Multiply. See Examples 1 through 11.

53. $-1.2y(-7y^6)$
54. $-4.2x(-2x^5)$
55. $-3x(x^2 + 2x - 8)$
56. $-5x(x^2 - 3x + 10)$
57. $(x + 19)(2x + 1)$
58. $(3y + 4)(y + 11)$
59. $\left(x + \frac{1}{7}\right)\left(x - \frac{3}{7}\right)$
60. $\left(m + \frac{2}{9}\right)\left(m - \frac{1}{9}\right)$
61. $(3y + 5)^2$
62. $(7y + 2)^2$
63. $(a + 4)(a^2 - 6a + 6)$
64. $(t + 3)(t^2 - 5t + 5)$
65. $(2x - 5)^3$
66. $(3y - 1)^3$
67. $(4x + 5)(8x^2 + 2x - 4)$
68. $(5x + 4)(x^2 - x + 4)$
69. $(3x^2 + 2x - 4)(2x^2 - 4x + 3)$
70. $(a^2 + 3a - 2)(2a^2 - 5a - 1)$

Express as the product of polynomials. Then multiply.

71. Find the area of the rectangle.

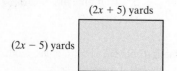

(2x + 5) yards
(2x − 5) yards

72. Find the area of the square field.

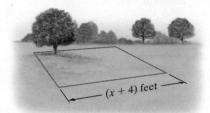

(x + 4) feet

73. Find the area of the triangle.

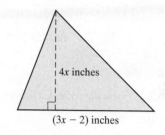

4x inches
(3x − 2) inches

74. Find the volume of the cube.

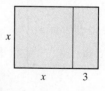

(y − 1) meters

REVIEW AND PREVIEW

Perform the indicated operation. See Section 6.1.

75. $(5x)^2$ 76. $(4p)^2$
77. $(-3y^3)^2$ 78. $(-7m^2)^2$

CONCEPT EXTENSIONS

79. The area of the larger rectangle below is $x(x + 3)$. Find another expression for this area by finding the sum of the areas of the two smaller rectangles.

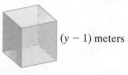

x
x   3

80. Write an expression for the area of the larger rectangle below in two different ways.

x
1   2x

81. The area of the figure below is $(x + 2)(x + 3)$. Find another expression for this area by finding the sum of the areas of the four smaller rectangles.

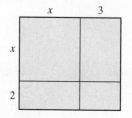

x   3
x
2

△ **82.** Write an expression for the area of the figure in two different ways.

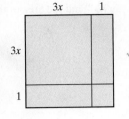

Simplify.

See the Concept Checks in this section.

83. $5a + 6a$

84. $5a \cdot 6a$

Square where indicated. Simplify if possible.

85. $(5x)^2 + (2y)^2$

86. $(5x + 2y)^2$

MIXED PRACTICE

See Sections 6.2, 6.3. Perform the indicated operations.

87. $(3x - 1) + (10x - 6)$

88. $(2x - 1) + (10x - 7)$

89. $(3x - 1)(10x - 6)$

90. $(2x - 1)(10x - 7)$

91. $(3x - 1) - (10x - 6)$

92. $(2x - 1) - (10x - 7)$

93. Multiple Steps. Multiply each of the following polynomials.

    a. $(a + b)(a - b)$

    b. $(2x + 3y)(2x - 3y)$

    c. $(4x + 7)(4x - 7)$

    d. Can you make a general statement about all products of the form $(x + y)(x - y)$?

94. Multiple Steps. Evaluate each of the following.

    a. $(2 + 3)^2; 2^2 + 3^2$

    b. $(8 + 10)^2; 8^2 + 10^2$

    Does $(a + b)^2 = a^2 + b^2$ no matter what the values of a and b are? Why or why not?

△ **95.** Write a polynomial that describes the area of the shaded region. (Find the area of the larger square minus the area of the smaller square.)

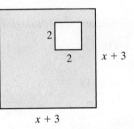

△ **96.** Write a polynomial that describes the area of the shaded region. (See Exercise 95.)

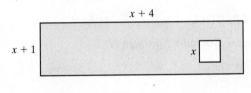

6.4 SPECIAL PRODUCTS

OBJECTIVES

1. Multiply two binomials using the FOIL method.

2. Square a binomial.

3. Multiply the sum and difference of two terms.

OBJECTIVE 1 ▶ Using the FOIL method. In this section, we multiply binomials using special products. First, a special order for multiplying binomials called the FOIL order or method is introduced. This method is demonstrated by multiplying $(3x + 1)$ by $(2x + 5)$.

The FOIL Method

F stands for the product of the **First** terms. $(3x + 1)(2x + 5)$

$$(3x)(2x) = 6x^2 \quad \mathbf{F}$$

O stands for the product of the **Outer** terms. $(3x + 1)(2x + 5)$

$$(3x)(5) = 15x \quad \mathbf{O}$$

I stands for the product of the **Inner** terms. $(3x + 1)(2x + 5)$

$$(1)(2x) = 2x \quad \mathbf{I}$$

L stands for the product of the **Last** terms. $(3x + 1)(3x + 5)$

$$(1)(5) = 5 \quad \mathbf{L}$$

$$\quad\quad\quad\quad\quad\quad \mathbf{F} \quad\quad \mathbf{O} \quad\quad \mathbf{I} \quad\, \mathbf{L}$$
$$(3x + 1)(2x + 5) = 6x^2 + 15x + 2x + 5$$
$$= 6x^2 + 17x + 5 \quad \text{Combine like terms.}$$

Answer to Concept Check:
Multiply and simplify:
$3x(2x + 5) + 1(2x + 5)$

Concept Check ☑

Multiply $(3x + 1)(2x + 5)$ using methods from the last section. Show that the product is still $6x^2 + 17x + 5$.

EXAMPLE 1   Multiply $(x - 3)(x + 4)$ by the FOIL method.

Solution

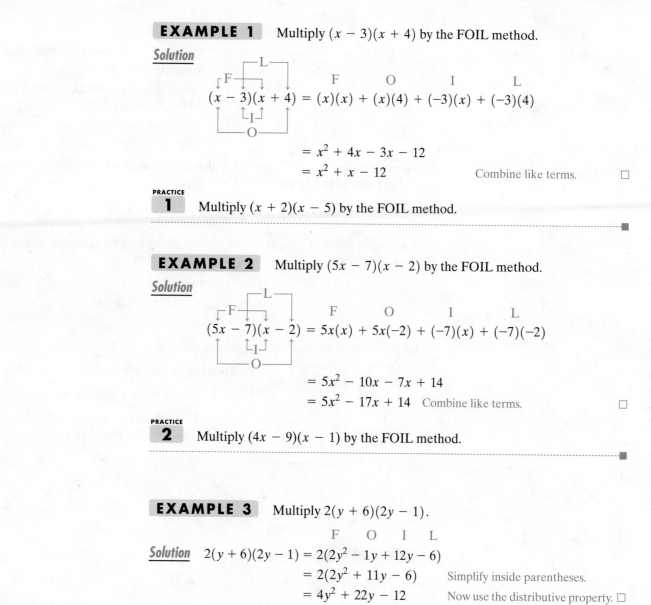

$$(x - 3)(x + 4) = (x)(x) + (x)(4) + (-3)(x) + (-3)(4)$$

$$= x^2 + 4x - 3x - 12$$

$$= x^2 + x - 12 \qquad \text{Combine like terms.} \qquad \square$$

PRACTICE
1   Multiply $(x + 2)(x - 5)$ by the FOIL method.

EXAMPLE 2   Multiply $(5x - 7)(x - 2)$ by the FOIL method.

Solution

$$(5x - 7)(x - 2) = 5x(x) + 5x(-2) + (-7)(x) + (-7)(-2)$$

$$= 5x^2 - 10x - 7x + 14$$

$$= 5x^2 - 17x + 14 \quad \text{Combine like terms.} \qquad \square$$

PRACTICE
2   Multiply $(4x - 9)(x - 1)$ by the FOIL method.

EXAMPLE 3   Multiply $2(y + 6)(2y - 1)$.

Solution $2(y + 6)(2y - 1) = 2(2y^2 - 1y + 12y - 6)$

$$= 2(2y^2 + 11y - 6) \qquad \text{Simplify inside parentheses.}$$

$$= 4y^2 + 22y - 12 \qquad \text{Now use the distributive property.} \quad \square$$

PRACTICE
3   Multiply $3(x + 5)(3x - 1)$.

OBJECTIVE 2 ▶ Squaring binomials. Now, try squaring a binomial using the FOIL method.

EXAMPLE 4   Multiply $(3y + 1)^2$.

Solution $(3y + 1)^2 = (3y + 1)(3y + 1)$

$$= (3y)(3y) + (3y)(1) + 1(3y) + 1(1)$$

$$= 9y^2 + 3y + 3y + 1$$

$$= 9y^2 + 6y + 1 \qquad \qquad \square$$

PRACTICE
4   Multiply $(4x - 1)^2$.

Notice the pattern that appears in Example 4.

$$(3y + 1)^2 = 9y^2 + 6y + 1$$

$9y^2$ is the first term of the binomial squared. $(3y)^2 = 9y^2$.

$6y$ is 2 times the product of both terms of the binomial. $(2)(3y)(1) = 6y$.

1 is the second term of the binomial squared. $(1)^2 = 1$.

This pattern leads to the following, which can be used when squaring a binomial. We call these **special products**.

> **Squaring a Binomial**
>
> A binomial squared is equal to the square of the first term plus or minus twice the product of both terms plus the square of the second term.
>
> $$(a + b)^2 = a^2 + 2ab + b^2$$
> $$(a - b)^2 = a^2 - 2ab + b^2$$

This product can be visualized geometrically.

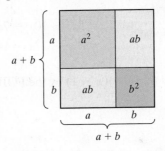

The area of the large square is side · side.

$$\text{Area} = (a + b)(a + b) = (a + b)^2$$

The area of the large square is also the sum of the areas of the smaller rectangles.

$$\text{Area} = a^2 + ab + ab + b^2 = a^2 + 2ab + b^2$$

Thus, $(a + b)^2 = a^2 + 2ab + b^2$.

EXAMPLE 5 Use a special product to square each binomial.

a. $(t + 2)^2$ **b.** $(p - q)^2$ **c.** $(2x + 5)^2$ **d.** $(x^2 - 7y)^2$

Solution

	first term squared	plus or minus	twice the product of the terms	plus	second term squared

a. $(t + 2)^2 = t^2 + 2(t)(2) + 2^2 = t^2 + 4t + 4$

b. $(p - q)^2 = p^2 - 2(p)(q) + q^2 = p^2 - 2pq + q^2$

c. $(2x + 5)^2 = (2x)^2 + 2(2x)(5) + 5^2 = 4x^2 + 20x + 25$

d. $(x^2 - 7y)^2 = (x^2)^2 - 2(x^2)(7y) + (7y^2) = x^4 - 14x^2y + 49y^2$ □

PRACTICE
5 Use a special product to square each binomial.

a. $(b + 3)^2$ **b.** $(x - y)^2$
c. $(3y + 2)^2$ **d.** $(a^2 - 5b)^2$

▶ **Helpful Hint**

Notice that

$$(a + b)^2 \neq a^2 + b^2 \quad \text{The middle term } 2ab \text{ is missing.}$$
$$(a + b)^2 = (a + b)(a + b) = a^2 + 2ab + b^2$$

Likewise,

$$(a - b)^2 \neq a^2 - b^2$$
$$(a - b)^2 = (a - b)(a - b) = a^2 - 2ab + b^2$$

OBJECTIVE 3 ▶ **Multiplying the sum and difference of two terms.** Another special product is the product of the sum and difference of the same two terms, such as $(x + y)(x - y)$. Finding this product by the FOIL method, we see a pattern emerge.

$$(x + y)(x - y) = x^2 - xy + xy - y^2$$

$$= x^2 - y^2$$

Notice that the middle two terms subtract out. This is because the **O**uter product is the opposite of the **I**nner product. Only the **difference of squares** remains.

Multiplying the Sum and Difference of Two Terms

The product of the sum and difference of two terms is the square of the first term minus the square of the second term.

$$(a + b)(a - b) = a^2 - b^2$$

EXAMPLE 6   Use a special product to multiply.

a. $4(x + 4)(x - 4)$ **b.** $(6t + 7)(6t - 7)$ **c.** $\left(x - \dfrac{1}{4}\right)\left(x + \dfrac{1}{4}\right)$

d. $(2p - q)(2p + q)$ **e.** $(3x^2 - 5y)(3x^2 + 5y)$

Solution

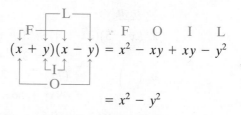

a. $4(x + 4)(x - 4) = 4(x^2 - 4^2) = 4(x^2 - 16) = 4x^2 - 64$

b. $(6t + 7)(6t - 7) = (6t)^2 - 7^2 = 36t^2 - 49$

c. $\left(x - \dfrac{1}{4}\right)\left(x + \dfrac{1}{4}\right) = x^2 - \left(\dfrac{1}{4}\right)^2 = x^2 - \dfrac{1}{16}$

d. $(2p - q)(2p + q) = (2p)^2 - q^2 = 4p^2 - q^2$

e. $(3x^2 - 5y)(3x^2 + 5y) = (3x^2)^2 - (5y)^2 = 9x^4 - 25y^2$

PRACTICE

6   Use a special product to multiply.

a. $3(x + 5)(x - 5)$ **b.** $(4b - 3)(4b + 3)$

c. $\left(x + \dfrac{2}{3}\right)\left(x - \dfrac{2}{3}\right)$ **d.** $(5s + t)(5s - t)$

e. $(2y - 3z^2)(2y + 3z^2)$

Concept Check ☑️

Match each expression on the left to the equivalent expression or expressions in the list below.

1. $(a + b)^2$ **2.** $(a + b)(a - b)$

    a. $(a + b)(a + b)$ **b.** $a^2 - b^2$ **c.** $a^2 + b^2$ **d.** $a^2 - 2ab + b^2$ **e.** $a^2 + 2ab + b^2$

Let's now practice multiplying polynomials in general. If possible, use a special product.

EXAMPLE 7   Use a special product to multiply, if possible.

a. $(x - 5)(3x + 4)$ **b.** $(7x + 4)^2$ **c.** $(y - 0.6)(y + 0.6)$

d. $(y^4 + 2)(3y^2 - 1)$ **e.** $(a - 3)(a^2 + 2a - 1)$

Solution

a. $(x - 5)(3x + 4) = 3x^2 + 4x - 15x - 20$ FOIL.

                            $= 3x^2 - 11x - 20$

b. $(7x + 4)^2 = (7x)^2 + 2(7x)(4) + 4^2$ Squaring a binomial.

                  $= 49x^2 + 56x + 16$

c. $(y - 0.6)(y + 0.6) = y^2 - (0.6)^2 = y^2 - 0.36$ Multiplying the sum and difference of 2 terms.

d. $(y^4 + 2)(3y^2 - 1) = 3y^6 - y^4 + 6y^2 - 2$ FOIL.

e. I've inserted this product as a reminder that since it is not a binomial times a binomial, the FOIL order may not be used.

$$
\begin{aligned}
(a - 3)(a^2 + 2a - 1) &= a(a^2 + 2a - 1) - 3(a^2 + 2a - 1) \\
&= a^3 + 2a^2 - a - 3a^2 - 6a + 3 \\
&= a^3 - a^2 - 7a + 3
\end{aligned}
$$

Multiplying each term of the binomial by each term of the trinomial.   ☐

PRACTICE
7   Use a special product to multiply, if possible.

a. $(4x + 3)(x - 6)$ **b.** $(7b - 2)^2$

c. $(x + 0.4)(x - 0.4)$ **d.** $(x^2 - 3)(3x^4 + 2)$

e. $(x + 1)(x^2 + 5x - 2)$

> **▶ Helpful Hint**
>
> - When multiplying two binomials, you may always use the FOIL order or method.
> - When multiplying any two polynomials, you may always use the distributive property to find the product.

Answers to Concept Check:
1. a or e   **2.** b

VOCABULARY & READINESS CHECK

True or False. *Answer each exercise true or false.*

1. $(x + 4)^2 = x^2 + 16$ **2.** For $(x + 6)(2x - 1)$ the product of the first terms is $2x^2$.

3. $(x + 4)(x - 4) = x^2 + 16$ **4.** The product $(x - 1)(x^3 + 3x - 1)$ is a polynomial of degree 5.

6.4 EXERCISE SET

Multiply using the FOIL method. See Examples 1 through 3.

1. $(x + 3)(x + 4)$

2. $(x + 5)(x - 1)$

3. $(x - 5)(x + 10)$

4. $(y - 12)(y + 4)$

5. $(5x - 6)(x + 2)$

6. $(3y - 5)(2y - 7)$

7. $(y - 6)(4y - 1)$

8. $(2x - 9)(x - 11)$

9. $(2x + 5)(3x - 1)$

10. $(6x + 2)(x - 2)$

Multiply. See Examples 4 and 5.

11. $(x - 2)^2$ **12.** $(x + 7)^2$

13. $(2x - 1)^2$ **14.** $(7x - 3)^2$

15. $(3a - 5)^2$ **16.** $(5a + 2)^2$

17. $(5x + 9)^2$ **18.** $(6s - 2)^2$

19. Using your own words, explain how to square a binomial such as $(a + b)^2$.

20. Explain how to find the product of two binomials using the FOIL method.

Multiply. See Example 6.

21. $(a - 7)(a + 7)$ **22.** $(b + 3)(b - 3)$

23. $(3x - 1)(3x + 1)$ **24.** $(4x - 5)(4x + 5)$

25. $\left(3x - \dfrac{1}{2}\right)\left(3x + \dfrac{1}{2}\right)$

26. $\left(10x + \dfrac{2}{7}\right)\left(10x - \dfrac{2}{7}\right)$

27. $(9x + y)(9x - y)$

28. $(2x - y)(2x + y)$

29. $(2x + 0.1)(2x - 0.1)$

30. $(5x - 1.3)(5x + 1.3)$

MIXED PRACTICE

Multiply. See Example 7.

31. $(a + 5)(a + 4)$

32. $(a - 5)(a - 7)$

33. $(a + 7)^2$

34. $(b - 2)^2$

35. $(4a + 1)(3a - 1)$

36. $(6a + 7)(6a + 5)$

37. $(x + 2)(x - 2)$

38. $(x - 10)(x + 10)$

39. $(3a + 1)^2$

40. $(4a - 2)^2$

41. $(x^2 + y)(4x - y^4)$

42. $(x^3 - 2)(5x + y)$

43. $(x + 3)(x^2 - 6x + 1)$

44. $(x - 2)(x^2 - 4x + 2)$

45. $(2a - 3)^2$

46. $(5b - 4x)^2$

47. $(5x - 6z)(5x + 6z)$

48. $(11x - 7y)(11x + 7y)$

49. $(x^5 - 3)(x^5 - 5)$

50. $(a^4 + 5)(a^4 + 6)$

51. $\left(x - \dfrac{1}{3}\right)\left(x + \dfrac{1}{3}\right)$

52. $\left(3x + \dfrac{1}{5}\right)\left(3x - \dfrac{1}{5}\right)$

53. $(a^3 + 11)(a^4 - 3)$

54. $(x^5 + 5)(x^2 - 8)$

55. $3(x - 2)^2$

56. $2(3b + 7)^2$

57. $(3b + 7)(2b - 5)$

58. $(3y - 13)(y - 3)$

59. $(7p - 8)(7p + 8)$

60. $(3s - 4)(3s + 4)$

61. $\left(\dfrac{1}{3}a^2 - 7\right)\left(\dfrac{1}{3}a^2 + 7\right)$

62. $\left(\dfrac{2}{3}a - b^2\right)\left(\dfrac{2}{3}a - b^2\right)$

63. $5x^2(3x^2 - x + 2)$

64. $4x^3(2x^2 + 5x - 1)$

65. $(2r - 3s)(2r + 3s)$

66. $(6r - 2x)(6r + 2x)$

67. $(3x - 7y)^2$

68. $(4s - 2y)^2$

69. $(4x + 5)(4x - 5)$

70. $(3x + 5)(3x - 5)$

71. $(8x + 4)^2$

72. $(3x + 2)^2$

73. $\left(a - \dfrac{1}{2}y\right)\left(a + \dfrac{1}{2}y\right)$

74. $\left(\dfrac{a}{2} + 4y\right)\left(\dfrac{a}{2} - 4y\right)$

75. $\left(\dfrac{1}{5}x - y\right)\left(\dfrac{1}{5}x + y\right)$

76. $\left(\dfrac{y}{6} - 8\right)\left(\dfrac{y}{6} + 8\right)$

77. $(a + 1)(3a^2 - a + 1)$

78. $(b + 3)(2b^2 + b - 3)$

Express each as a product of polynomials in x. Then multiply and simplify.

△ **79.** Find the area of the square rug shown if its side is $(2x + 1)$ feet.

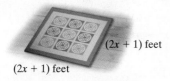

(2x + 1) feet

(2x + 1) feet

△ **80.** Find the area of the rectangular canvas if its length is $(3x - 2)$ inches and its width is $(x - 4)$ inches.

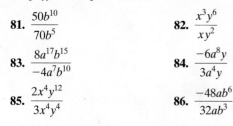

(x − 4) inches

(3x − 2) inches

REVIEW AND PREVIEW

Simplify each expression. See Section 6.1.

81. $\dfrac{50b^{10}}{70b^5}$

82. $\dfrac{x^3y^6}{xy^2}$

83. $\dfrac{8a^{17}b^{15}}{-4a^7b^{10}}$

84. $\dfrac{-6a^8y}{3a^4y}$

85. $\dfrac{2x^4y^{12}}{3x^4y^4}$

86. $\dfrac{-48ab^6}{32ab^3}$

Find the slope of each line. See Section 3.4.

87.

88.

89.

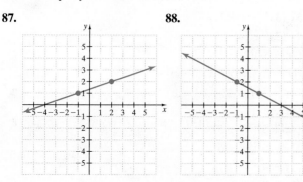

90.

CONCEPT EXTENSIONS

Matching. *Match each expression on the left to the equivalent expression on the right. See the Concept Check in this section.*

91. $(a - b)^2$

92. $(a - b)(a + b)$

93. $(a + b)^2$

94. $(a + b)^2(a - b)^2$

a. $a^2 - b^2$

b. $a^2 + b^2$

c. $a^2 - 2ab + b^2$

d. $a^2 + 2ab + b^2$

e. none of these

Decision Making. *Fill in the squares so that a true statement forms.*

95. $(x^{\square} + 7)(x^{\square} + 3) = x^4 + 10x^2 + 21$

96. $(5x^{\square} - 2)^2 = 25x^6 - 20x^3 + 4$

Find the area of each shaded region.

△ **97.**

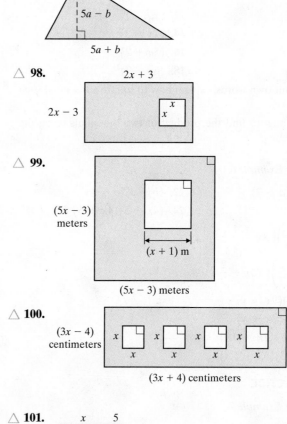

5a − b

5a + b

△ **98.**

2x + 3

2x − 3

x
x

△ **99.**

(5x − 3) meters

(x + 1) m

(5x − 3) meters

△ **100.**

(3x − 4) centimeters

x x x x

x x x x

(3x + 4) centimeters

△ **101.**

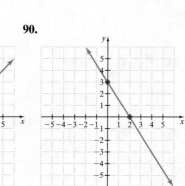

x   5

x

5

△ **102.**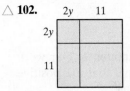

103. In your own words, describe the different methods that can be used to find the product: $(2x - 5)(3x + 1)$.

104. In your own words, describe the different methods that can be used to find the product: $(5x + 1)^2$.

Find each product. For example,

$$[(a + b) - 2][(a + b) + 2] = (a + b)^2 - 2^2$$
$$= a^2 + 2ab + b^2 - 4$$

105. $[(x + y) - 3][(x + y) + 3]$

106. $[(a + c) - 5][(a + c) + 5]$

107. $[(a - 3) + b][(a - 3) - b]$

108. $[(x - 2) + y][(x - 2) - y]$

INTEGRATED REVIEW EXPONENTS AND OPERATIONS ON POLYNOMIALS

Sections 6.1–6.4

Perform the indicated operations and simplify.

1. $(5x^2)(7x^3)$

2. $(4y^2)(8y^7)$

3. -4^2

4. $(-4)^2$

5. $(x - 5)(2x + 1)$

6. $(3x - 2)(x + 5)$

7. $(x - 5) + (2x + 1)$

8. $(3x - 2) + (x + 5)$

9. $\dfrac{7x^9y^{12}}{x^3y^{10}}$

10. $\dfrac{20a^2b^8}{14a^2b^2}$

11. $(12m^7n^6)^2$

12. $(4y^9z^{10})^3$

13. $3(4y - 3)(4y + 3)$

14. $2(7x - 1)(7x + 1)$

15. $(x^7y^5)^9$

16. $(3^1x^9)^3$

17. $(7x^2 - 2x + 3) - (5x^2 + 9)$

18. $(10x^2 + 7x - 9) - (4x^2 - 6x + 2)$

19. $0.7y^2 - 1.2 + 1.8y^2 - 6y + 1$

20. $7.8x^2 - 6.8x + 3.3 + 0.6x^2 - 9$

21. $(x + 4y)^2$

22. $(y - 9z)^2$

23. $(x + 4y) + (x + 4y)$

24. $(y - 9z) + (y - 9z)$

25. $7x^2 - 6xy + 4(y^2 - xy)$

26. $5a^2 - 3ab + 6(b^2 - a^2)$

27. $(x - 3)(x^2 + 5x - 1)$

28. $(x + 1)(x^2 - 3x - 2)$

29. $(2x^3 - 7)(3x^2 + 10)$

30. $(5x^3 - 1)(4x^4 + 5)$

31. $(2x - 7)(x^2 - 6x + 1)$

32. $(5x - 1)(x^2 + 2x - 3)$

Perform exercises and simplify, if possible.

33. $5x^3 + 5y^3$

34. $(5x^3)(5y^3)$

35. $(5x^3)^3$

36. $\dfrac{5x^3}{5y^3}$

37. $x + x$

38. $x \cdot x$

6.5 NEGATIVE EXPONENTS AND SCIENTIFIC NOTATION

OBJECTIVE 1 ▶ Simplifying expressions containing negative exponents. Our work with exponential expressions so far has been limited to exponents that are positive integers or 0. Here we expand to give meaning to an expression like x^{-3}.

Suppose that we wish to simplify the expression $\dfrac{x^2}{x^5}$. If we use the quotient rule for exponents, we subtract exponents:

$$\frac{x^2}{x^5} = x^{2-5} = x^{-3}, \quad x \neq 0$$

But what does x^{-3} mean? Let's simplify $\dfrac{x^2}{x^5}$ using the definition of x^n.

$$\frac{x^2}{x^5} = \frac{x \cdot x}{x \cdot x \cdot x \cdot x \cdot x}$$

$$= \frac{x \cdot x}{x \cdot x \cdot x \cdot x \cdot x} \qquad \text{Divide numerator and denominator by common factors by applying the fundamental principle for fractions.}$$

$$= \frac{1}{x^3}$$

If the quotient rule is to hold true for negative exponents, then x^{-3} must equal $\dfrac{1}{x^3}$. From this example, we state the definition for negative exponents.

Negative Exponents

If a is a real number other than 0 and n is an integer, then

$$a^{-n} = \frac{1}{a^n}$$

For example, $x^{-3} = \dfrac{1}{x^3}$.

In other words, another way to write a^{-n} is to take its reciprocal and change the sign of its exponent.

EXAMPLE 1 Simplify by writing each expression with positive exponents only.

a. 3^{-2} **b.** $2x^{-3}$ **c.** $2^{-1} + 4^{-1}$ **d.** $(-2)^{-4}$ **e.** $\dfrac{1}{y^{-4}}$ **f.** $\dfrac{1}{7^{-2}}$

Solution

a. $3^{-2} = \dfrac{1}{3^2} = \dfrac{1}{9}$ Use the definition of negative exponents.

b. $2x^{-3} = 2 \cdot \dfrac{1}{x^3} = \dfrac{2}{x^3}$ Use the definition of negative exponents.

c. $2^{-1} + 4^{-1} = \dfrac{1}{2} + \dfrac{1}{4} = \dfrac{2}{4} + \dfrac{1}{4} = \dfrac{3}{4}$

d. $(-2)^{-4} = \dfrac{1}{(-2)^4} = \dfrac{1}{(-2)(-2)(-2)(-2)} = \dfrac{1}{16}$

e. $\dfrac{1}{y^{-4}} = \dfrac{1}{\dfrac{1}{y^4}} = y^4$ **f.** $\dfrac{1}{7^{-2}} = \dfrac{1}{\dfrac{1}{7^2}} = \dfrac{7^2}{1}$ or 49

▶ **Helpful Hint**

Don't forget that since there are no parentheses, only x is the base for the exponent -3.

PRACTICE
1 Simplify by writing each expression with positive exponents only.

a. 5^{-3}

b. $3y^{-4}$

c. $3^{-1} + 2^{-1}$

d. $(-5)^{-2}$

e. $\dfrac{1}{x^{-5}}$

f. $\dfrac{1}{4^{-3}}$

> **Helpful Hint**
>
> A negative exponent *does not affect* the sign of its base.
>
> Remember: Another way to write a^{-n} is to take its reciprocal and change the sign of its exponent: $a^{-n} = \dfrac{1}{a^n}$. For example,
>
> $$x^{-2} = \dfrac{1}{x^2}, \qquad 2^{-3} = \dfrac{1}{2^3} \ \text{ or } \ \dfrac{1}{8}$$
>
> $$\dfrac{1}{y^{-4}} = \dfrac{1}{\dfrac{1}{y^4}} = y^4, \qquad \dfrac{1}{5^{-2}} = 5^2 \ \text{ or } \ 25$$

From the preceding Helpful Hint, we know that $x^{-2} = \dfrac{1}{x^2}$ and $\dfrac{1}{y^{-4}} = y^4$. We can use this to include another statement in our definition of negative exponents.

> **Negative Exponents**
> If a is a real number other than 0 and n is an integer, then
>
> $$a^{-n} = \dfrac{1}{a^n} \quad \text{and} \quad \dfrac{1}{a^{-n}} = a^n$$

EXAMPLE 2 Simplify each expression. Write results using positive exponents only.

a. $\dfrac{1}{x^{-3}}$

b. $\dfrac{1}{3^{-4}}$

c. $\dfrac{p^{-4}}{q^{-9}}$

d. $\dfrac{5^{-3}}{2^{-5}}$

Solution

a. $\dfrac{1}{x^{-3}} = \dfrac{x^3}{1} = x^3$ **b.** $\dfrac{1}{3^{-4}} = \dfrac{3^4}{1} = 81$ **c.** $\dfrac{p^{-4}}{q^{-9}} = \dfrac{q^9}{p^4}$ **d.** $\dfrac{5^{-3}}{2^{-5}} = \dfrac{2^5}{5^3} = \dfrac{32}{125}$ ☐

PRACTICE
2 Simplify each expression. Write results using positive exponents only.

a. $\dfrac{1}{s^{-5}}$

b. $\dfrac{1}{2^{-3}}$

c. $\dfrac{x^{-7}}{y^{-5}}$

d. $\dfrac{4^{-3}}{3^{-2}}$

EXAMPLE 3 Simplify each expression. Write answers with positive exponents.

a. $\dfrac{y}{y^{-2}}$

b. $\dfrac{3}{x^{-4}}$

c. $\dfrac{x^{-5}}{x^7}$

Solution

a. $\dfrac{y}{y^{-2}} = \dfrac{y^1}{y^{-2}} = y^{1-(-2)} = y^3$ Remember that $\dfrac{a^m}{a^n} = a^{m-n}$.

b. $\dfrac{3}{x^{-4}} = 3 \cdot \dfrac{1}{x^{-4}} = 3 \cdot x^4$ or $3x^4$

c. $\dfrac{x^{-5}}{x^7} = x^{-5-7} = x^{-12} = \dfrac{1}{x^{12}}$

PRACTICE

3   Simplify each expression. Write answers with positive exponents.

a. $\dfrac{x^{-3}}{x^2}$ **b.** $\dfrac{5}{y^{-7}}$ **c.** $\dfrac{z}{z^{-4}}$

OBJECTIVE 2 ▶ Simplifying exponential expressions. All the previously stated rules for exponents apply for negative exponents also. Here is a summary of the rules and definitions for exponents.

Summary of Exponent Rules

If m and n are integers and a, b, and c are real numbers, then:

Product rule for exponents: $a^m \cdot a^n = a^{m+n}$

Power rule for exponents: $(a^m)^n = a^{m \cdot n}$

Power of a product: $(ab)^n = a^n b^n$

Power of a quotient: $\left(\dfrac{a}{c}\right)^n = \dfrac{a^n}{c^n}, \quad c \neq 0$

Quotient rule for exponents: $\dfrac{a^m}{a^n} = a^{m-n}, \quad a \neq 0$

Zero exponent: $a^0 = 1, \quad a \neq 0$

Negative exponent: $a^{-n} = \dfrac{1}{a^n}, \quad a \neq 0$

EXAMPLE 4   Simplify the following expressions. Write each result using positive exponents only.

a. $\left(\dfrac{2}{3}\right)^{-3}$ **b.** $\dfrac{(x^3)^4 x}{x^7}$ **c.** $\left(\dfrac{3a^2}{b}\right)^{-3}$ **d.** $\dfrac{4^{-1}x^{-3}y}{4^{-3}x^2y^{-6}}$ **e.** $(y^{-3}z^6)^{-6}$ **f.** $\left(\dfrac{-2x^3y}{xy^{-1}}\right)^3$

Solution

a. $\left(\dfrac{2}{3}\right)^{-3} = \dfrac{2^{-3}}{3^{-3}} = \dfrac{3^3}{2^3} = \dfrac{27}{8}$

b. $\dfrac{(x^3)^4 x}{x^7} = \dfrac{x^{12} \cdot x}{x^7} = \dfrac{x^{12+1}}{x^7} = \dfrac{x^{13}}{x^7} = x^{13-7} = x^6$ Use the power rule.

c. $\left(\dfrac{3a^2}{b}\right)^{-3} = \dfrac{3^{-3}(a^2)^{-3}}{b^{-3}}$ Raise each factor in the numerator and the denominator to the -3 power.

$= \dfrac{3^{-3}a^{-6}}{b^{-3}}$ Use the power rule.

$= \dfrac{b^3}{3^3 a^6}$ Use the negative exponent rule.

$= \dfrac{b^3}{27a^6}$ Write 3^3 as 27.

d. $\dfrac{4^{-1}x^{-3}y}{4^{-3}x^2y^{-6}} = 4^{-1-(-3)}x^{-3-2}y^{1-(-6)} = 4^2x^{-5}y^7 = \dfrac{4^2y^7}{x^5} = \dfrac{16y^7}{x^5}$

e. $(y^{-3}z^6)^{-6} = y^{18} \cdot z^{-36} = \dfrac{y^{18}}{z^{36}}$

f. $\left(\dfrac{-2x^3y}{xy^{-1}}\right)^3 = \dfrac{(-2)^3x^9y^3}{x^3y^{-3}} = \dfrac{-8x^9y^3}{x^3y^{-3}} = -8x^{9-3}y^{3-(-3)} = -8x^6y^6$ ☐

PRACTICE
4   Simplify the following expression. Write each result using positive exponents only.

a. $\left(\dfrac{3}{4}\right)^{-2}$

b. $\dfrac{x^2(x^5)^3}{x^7}$

c. $\left(\dfrac{5p^8}{q}\right)^{-2}$

d. $\dfrac{6^{-2}x^{-4}y^{-7}}{6^{-3}x^3y^{-9}}$

e. $(a^4b^{-3})^{-5}$

f. $\left(\dfrac{-3x^4y}{x^2y^{-2}}\right)^3$

OBJECTIVE 3 ▶ Writing numbers in scientific notation. Both very large and very small numbers frequently occur in many fields of science. For example, the distance between the sun and the dwarf planet Pluto is approximately 5,906,000,000 kilometers, and the mass of a proton is approximately 0.00000000000000000000000165 gram. It can be tedious to write these numbers in this standard decimal notation, so **scientific notation** is used as a convenient shorthand for expressing very large and very small numbers.

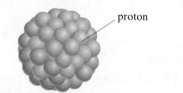

proton

Mass of proton is approximately
0.000 000 000 000 000 000 000 001 65 gram

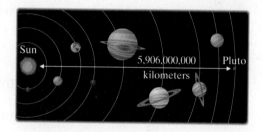

Sun

5,906,000,000
kilometers

Pluto

Scientific Notation

A positive number is written in scientific notation if it is written as the product of a number a, where $1 \le a < 10$, and an integer power r of 10:

$$a \times 10^r$$

The numbers below are written in scientific notation. The $\times$ sign for multiplication is used as part of the notation.

2.03×10^2	7.362×10^7	5.906×10^9 (Distance between the sun and Pluto)
1×10^{-3}	8.1×10^{-5}	1.65×10^{-24} (Mass of a proton)

The following steps are useful when writing numbers in scientific notation.

To Write a Number in Scientific Notation

STEP 1. Move the decimal point in the original number to the left or right so that the new number has a value between 1 and 10.

STEP 2. Count the number of decimal places the decimal point is moved in Step 1. If the original number is 10 or greater, the count is positive. If the original number is less than 1, the count is negative.

STEP 3. Multiply the new number in Step 1 by 10 raised to an exponent equal to the count found in Step 2.

EXAMPLE 5 Write each number in scientific notation.

a. 367,000,000   **b.** 0.000003   **c.** 20,520,000,000   **d.** 0.00085

Solution

a. STEP 1. Move the decimal point until the number is between 1 and 10.
367,000,000.
       8 places

    STEP 2. The decimal point is moved 8 places, and the original number is 10 or greater, so the count is positive 8.

    STEP 3. $367,000,000 = 3.67 \times 10^8$.

b. STEP 1. Move the decimal point until the number is between 1 and 10.
0.000003
    6 places

    STEP 2. The decimal point is moved 6 places, and the original number is less than 1, so the count is -6.

    STEP 3. $0.000003 = 3.0 \times 10^{-6}$

c. $20,520,000,000 = 2.052 \times 10^{10}$

d. $0.00085 = 8.5 \times 10^{-4}$ □

PRACTICE
5 Write each number in scientific notation.

a. 0.000007   **b.** 20,700,000   **c.** 0.0043   **d.** 812,000,000

OBJECTIVE 4 ▶ Converting numbers to standard form. A number written in scientific notation can be rewritten in standard form. For example, to write 8.63×10^3 in standard form, recall that $10^3 = 1000$.

$$8.63 \times 10^3 = 8.63(1000) = 8630$$

Notice that the exponent on the 10 is positive 3, and we moved the decimal point 3 places to the right.

To write 7.29×10^{-3} in standard form, recall that $10^{-3} = \dfrac{1}{10^3} = \dfrac{1}{1000}$.

$$7.29 \times 10^{-3} = 7.29\left(\frac{1}{1000}\right) = \frac{7.29}{1000} = 0.00729$$

The exponent on the 10 is negative 3, and we moved the decimal to the left 3 places.

In general, **to write a scientific notation number in standard form,** move the decimal point the same number of places as the exponent on 10. If the exponent is positive, move the decimal point to the right; if the exponent is negative, move the decimal point to the left.

EXAMPLE 6 Write each number in standard notation, without exponents.

a. 1.02×10^5 **b.** 7.358×10^{-3} **c.** 8.4×10^7 **d.** 3.007×10^{-5}

Solution

a. Move the decimal point 5 places to the right.

$$1.02 \times 10^5 = 102,000.$$

b. Move the decimal point 3 places to the left.

$$7.358 \times 10^{-3} = 0.007358$$

c. $8.4 \times 10^7 = 84{,}000{,}000.$ 7 places to the right

d. $3.007 \times 10^{-5} = 0.00003007$ 5 places to the left

$\square$

PRACTICE
6   Write each number in standard notation, without exponents.

a. 3.67×10^{-4} **b.** 8.954×10^6 **c.** 2.009×10^{-5} **d.** 4.054×10^3

Concept Check ☑

Which number in each pair is larger?

a. 7.8×10^3 or 2.1×10^5 **b.** 9.2×10^{-2} or 2.7×10^4 **c.** 5.6×10^{-4} or 6.3×10^{-5}

Performing operations on numbers written in scientific notation makes use of the rules and definitions for exponents.

EXAMPLE 7   Perform each indicated operation. Write each result in standard decimal notation.

a. $(8 \times 10^{-6})(7 \times 10^3)$ **b.** $\dfrac{12 \times 10^2}{6 \times 10^{-3}}$

Solution

a. $(8 \times 10^{-6})(7 \times 10^3) = (8 \cdot 7) \times (10^{-6} \cdot 10^3)$

$$= 56 \times 10^{-3}$$
$$= 0.056$$

b. $\dfrac{12 \times 10^2}{6 \times 10^{-3}} = \dfrac{12}{6} \times 10^{2-(-3)} = 2 \times 10^5 = 200{,}000$

$\square$

PRACTICE
7   Perform each indicated operation. Write each result in standard decimal notation.

a. $(5 \times 10^{-4})(8 \times 10^6)$ **b.** $\dfrac{64 \times 10^3}{32 \times 10^{-7}}$

Answers to Concept Check:
a. 2.1×10^5 **b.** 2.7×10^4
c. 5.6×10^{-4}

Calculator Explorations 🖩

Scientific Notation

To enter a number written in scientific notation on a scientific calculator, locate the scientific notation key, which may be marked $\boxed{\text{EE}}$ or $\boxed{\text{EXP}}$. To enter 3.1×10^7, press $\boxed{3.1}$ $\boxed{\text{EE}}$ $\boxed{7}$. The display should read $\boxed{3.1 \quad 07}$.

Enter each number written in scientific notation on your calculator.

1. 5.31×10^3 **2.** -4.8×10^{14}
3. 6.6×10^{-9} **4.** -9.9811×10^{-2}

Multiply each of the following on your calculator. Notice the form of the result.
5. $3{,}000{,}000 \times 5{,}000{,}000$ **6.** $230{,}000 \times 1000$

Multiply each of the following on your calculator. Write the product in scientific notation.
7. $(3.26 \times 10^6)(2.5 \times 10^{13})$ **8.** $(8.76 \times 10^{-4})(1.237 \times 10^9)$

VOCABULARY & READINESS CHECK

Multiple Choice. *Fill in each blank with the correct choice.*

1. The expression x^{-3} equals _____.

   a. $-x^3$ **b.** $\dfrac{1}{x^3}$ **c.** $\dfrac{-1}{x^3}$ **d.** $\dfrac{1}{x^{-3}}$

2. The expression 5^{-4} equals _____.

   a. -20 **b.** -625 **c.** $\dfrac{1}{20}$ **d.** $\dfrac{1}{625}$

3. The number 3.021×10^{-3} is written in _____.

   a. standard form   **b.** expanded form
   c. scientific notation

4. The number 0.0261 is written in _____.

   a. standard form   **b.** expanded form
   c. scientific notation

Write each expression using positive exponents only.

5. $5x^{-2}$ **6.** $3x^{-3}$ **7.** $\dfrac{1}{y^{-6}}$ **8.** $\dfrac{1}{x^{-3}}$ **9.** $\dfrac{4}{y^{-3}}$ **10.** $\dfrac{16}{y^{-7}}$

6.5 | EXERCISE SET

MyMathLab®   PRACTICE   WATCH   DOWNLOAD   READ   REVIEW

Simplify each expression. Write each result using positive exponents only. See Examples 1 through 3.

1. 4^{-3} **2.** 6^{-2} **3.** $(-2)^{-4}$

4. $(-3)^{-5}$ **5.** $7x^{-3}$ **6.** $(7x)^{-3}$

7. $\left(\dfrac{1}{2}\right)^{-5}$ **8.** $\left(\dfrac{1}{8}\right)^{-2}$ **9.** $\left(-\dfrac{1}{4}\right)^{-3}$

10. $\left(-\dfrac{1}{8}\right)^{-2}$ **11.** $3^{-1} + 2^{-1}$ **12.** $4^{-1} + 4^{-2}$

13. $\dfrac{1}{p^{-3}}$ **14.** $\dfrac{1}{q^{-5}}$ **15.** $\dfrac{p^{-5}}{q^{-4}}$

16. $\dfrac{r^{-5}}{s^{-2}}$ **17.** $\dfrac{x^{-2}}{x}$ **18.** $\dfrac{y}{y^{-3}}$

19. $\dfrac{z^{-4}}{z^{-7}}$ **20.** $\dfrac{x^{-4}}{x^{-1}}$ **21.** $3^{-2} + 3^{-1}$

22. $4^{-2} - 4^{-3}$ **23.** $\dfrac{-1}{p^{-4}}$ **24.** $\dfrac{-1}{y^{-6}}$

25. $-2^0 - 3^0$ **26.** $5^0 + (-5)^0$

MIXED PRACTICE

Simplify each expression. Write each result using positive exponents only. See Examples 1 through 4.

27. $\dfrac{x^2 x^5}{x^3}$ **28.** $\dfrac{y^4 y^5}{y^6}$ **29.** $\dfrac{p^2 p}{p^{-1}}$

30. $\dfrac{y^3 y}{y^{-2}}$ **31.** $\dfrac{(m^5)^4 m}{m^{10}}$ **32.** $\dfrac{(x^2)^8 x}{x^9}$

33. $\dfrac{r}{r^{-3} r^{-2}}$ **34.** $\dfrac{p}{p^{-3} q^{-5}}$ **35.** $(x^5 y^3)^{-3}$

36. $(z^5 x^5)^{-3}$ **37.** $\dfrac{(x^2)^3}{x^{10}}$ **38.** $\dfrac{(y^4)^2}{y^{12}}$

39. $\dfrac{(a^5)^2}{(a^3)^4}$ **40.** $\dfrac{(x^2)^5}{(x^4)^3}$ **41.** $\dfrac{8k^4}{2k}$

42. $\dfrac{27r^4}{3r^6}$ **43.** $\dfrac{-6m^4}{-2m^3}$ **44.** $\dfrac{15a^4}{-15a^5}$

45. $\dfrac{-24a^6 b}{6ab^2}$ **46.** $\dfrac{-5x^4 y^5}{15x^4 y^2}$

47. $(-2x^3 y^{-4})(3x^{-1}y)$ **48.** $(-5a^4 b^{-7})(-a^{-4} b^3)$

49. $(a^{-5} b^2)^{-6}$ **50.** $(4^{-1} x^5)^{-2}$

51. $\left(\dfrac{x^{-2} y^4}{x^3 y^7}\right)^2$ **52.** $\left(\dfrac{a^5 b}{a^7 b^{-2}}\right)^{-3}$

53. $\dfrac{4^2 z^{-3}}{4^3 z^{-5}}$ **54.** $\dfrac{3^{-1} x^4}{3^3 x^{-7}}$

55. $\dfrac{2^{-3} x^{-4}}{2^2 x}$ **56.** $\dfrac{5^{-1} z^7}{5^{-2} z^9}$

57. $\dfrac{7ab^{-4}}{7^{-1} a^{-3} b^2}$ **58.** $\dfrac{6^{-5} x^{-1} y^2}{6^{-2} x^{-4} y^4}$

59. $\left(\dfrac{a^{-5} b}{ab^3}\right)^{-4}$ **60.** $\left(\dfrac{r^{-2} s^{-3}}{r^{-4} s^{-3}}\right)^{-3}$

61. $\dfrac{(xy^3)^5}{(xy)^{-4}}$ **62.** $\dfrac{(rs)^{-3}}{(r^2 s^3)^2}$

63. $\dfrac{(-2xy^{-3})^{-3}}{(xy^{-1})^{-1}}$ **64.** $\dfrac{(-3x^2 y^2)^{-2}}{(xyz)^{-2}}$

65. $\dfrac{6x^2 y^3}{-7xy^5}$ **66.** $\dfrac{-8xa^2 b}{-5xa^5 b}$

67. $\dfrac{(a^4 b^{-7})^{-5}}{(5a^2 b^{-1})^{-2}}$ **68.** $\dfrac{(a^6 b^{-2})^4}{(4a^{-3} b^{-3})^3}$

Write each number in scientific notation. See Example 5.

69. 78,000   **70.** 9,300,000,000

71. 0.00000167   **72.** 0.00000017

73. 0.00635   **74.** 0.00194

75. 1,160,000   **76.** 700,000

77. More than 2,000,000,000 pencils are manufactured in the United States annually. Write this number in scientific notation (*Source*: AbsoluteTrivia.com)

78. The temperature at the interior of the Earth is 20,000,000 degrees Celsius. Write 20,000,000 in scientific notation.

79. The Cassini-Huygens Space Mission to Saturn was launched October 15, 1997, with a goal of reaching and orbiting Saturn and its moons. When the Cassini spacecraft disconnected the Huygens probe, which landed on the surface of the moon Titan on January 14, 2005, it was approximately 1,212,000,000 km from earth. Write 1,212,000,000 in scientific notation. (*Source:* Jet Propulsion Laboratory, California Institute of Technology)

80. At this writing, the world's largest optical telescopes are the twin Keck Telescopes located near the summit of Mauna Kea in Hawaii. The elevation of the Keck Telescopes is about 13,600 feet above sea level. Write 13,600 in scientific notation. (*Source:* W.M. Keck Observatory)

Write each number in standard notation. See Example 6.

81. 8.673×10^{-10}

82. 9.056×10^{-4}

83. 3.3×10^{-2}

84. 4.8×10^{-6}

85. 2.032×10^{4}

86. 9.07×10^{10}

87. Each second, the Sun converts 7.0×10^{8} tons of hydrogen into helium and energy in the form of gamma rays. Write this number in standard notation. (*Source:* Students for the Exploration and Development of Space)

88. In chemistry, Avogadro's number is the number of atoms in one mole of an element. Avogadro's number is $6.02214199 \times 10^{23}$. Write this number in standard notation. (*Source:* National Institute of Standards and Technology)

89. The distance light travels in 1 year is 9.460×10^{12} kilometers. Write this number in standard notation.

90. The population of the world is 6.067×10^{9}. Write this number in standard notation. (*Source:* U.S. Bureau of the Census)

MIXED PRACTICE

Read a Graph. *See Examples 5 and 6. Below are some interesting facts about the Internet. If a number is written in standard form, write it in scientific notation. If a number is written in scientific notation, write it in standard form.*

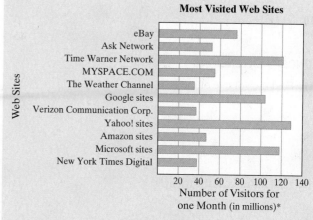

Most Visited Web Sites

* June, 2006 (*Source:* comScore Media Metrix, Inc.)

The bar graph above shows the most visited Web sites on the computer.

91. Estimate the length of the longest bar. Then write the number in scientific notation.

92. Estimate the length of the shortest bar. Then write the number in scientific notation.

93. The total number of Internet users exceeds 1,000,000,000. (*Source: Computer Industry, Almanac*)

94. In a recent year, the retail sales generated by the Internet was 1.08×10^{11} dollars. (*Source:* U.S. Census Bureau)

95. An estimated 5.7×10^{7} American adults read online weblogs (blogs). (*Source:* PEW Internet & American Life Project)

96. Junk e-mail (SPAM) costs consumers and businesses an estimated $23,000,000,000.

Evaluate each expression using exponential rules. Write each result in standard notation. See Example 7.

97. $(1.2 \times 10^{-3})(3 \times 10^{-2})$

98. $(2.5 \times 10^{6})(2 \times 10^{-6})$

99. $(4 \times 10^{-10})(7 \times 10^{-9})$

100. $(5 \times 10^{6})(4 \times 10^{-8})$

101. $\dfrac{8 \times 10^{-1}}{16 \times 10^{5}}$

102. $\dfrac{25 \times 10^{-4}}{5 \times 10^{-9}}$

103. $\dfrac{1.4 \times 10^{-2}}{7 \times 10^{-8}}$

104. $\dfrac{0.4 \times 10^{5}}{0.2 \times 10^{11}}$

REVIEW AND PREVIEW

Simplify the following. See Section 6.1.

105. $\dfrac{5x^{7}}{3x^{4}}$

106. $\dfrac{27y^{14}}{3y^{7}}$

107. $\dfrac{15z^4 y^3}{21zy}$

108. $\dfrac{18a^7 b^{17}}{30a^7 b}$

Use the distributive property and multiply. See Sections 6.3 and 6.5.

109. $\dfrac{1}{y}(5y^2 - 6y + 5)$

110. $\dfrac{2}{x}(3x^5 + x^4 - 2)$

CONCEPT EXTENSIONS

△ **111.** Find the volume of the cube.

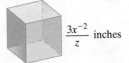

$\dfrac{3x^{-2}}{z}$ inches

△ **112.** Find the area of the triangle.

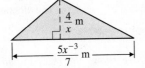

$\dfrac{4}{x}$ m

$\dfrac{5x^{-3}}{7}$ m

Simplify.

113. $(2a^3)^3 a^4 + a^5 a^8$

114. $(2a^3)^3 a^{-3} + a^{11} a^{-5}$

Decision Making. *Fill in the boxes so that each statement is true. (More than one answer is possible for these exercises.)*

115. $x^{\square} = \dfrac{1}{x^5}$

116. $7^{\square} = \dfrac{1}{49}$

117. $z^{\square} \cdot z^{\square} = z^{-10}$

118. $(x^{\square})^{\square} = x^{-15}$

119. Decision Making. Which is larger? See the Concept Check in this section.

a. 9.7×10^{-2} or 1.3×10^1

b. 8.6×10^5 or 4.4×10^7

c. 6.1×10^{-2} or 5.6×10^{-4}

120. It was stated earlier that for an integer n,

$$x^{-n} = \frac{1}{x^n}, \quad x \neq 0$$

Explain why x may not equal 0.

121. True or False. Determine whether each statement is true or false.

a. $5^{-1} < 5^{-2}$

b. $\left(\dfrac{1}{5}\right)^{-1} < \left(\dfrac{1}{5}\right)^{-2}$

c. $a^{-1} < a^{-2}$ for all nonzero numbers.

Simplify each expression. Assume that variables represent positive integers.

122. $a^{-4m} \cdot a^{5m}$

123. $(x^{-3s})^3$

124. $(3y^{2z})^3$

125. $a^{4m+1} \cdot a^4$

Simplify each expression. Write each result in standard notation.

126. $(2.63 \times 10^{12})(-1.5 \times 10^{-10})$

127. $(6.785 \times 10^{-4})(4.68 \times 10^{10})$

Light travels at a rate of 1.86×10^5 miles per second. Use this information and the distance formula $d = r \cdot t$ to answer Exercises 128 and 129.

128. If the distance from the moon to the Earth is 238,857 miles, find how long it takes the reflected light of the moon to reach the Earth. (Round to the nearest tenth of a second.)

129. If the distance from the sun to the Earth is 93,000,000 miles, find how long it takes the light of the sun to reach the Earth. (Round to the nearest tenth of a second.)

6.6 GRAPHING EXPONENTIAL FUNCTIONS AND USING THE COMPOUND INTEREST FORMULA

OBJECTIVES

1 Graph exponential functions.

2 Graph transformations of exponential functions.

3 Use the compound interest formula.

OBJECTIVE 1 ▶ Graphing exponential functions. In earlier sections, we gave meaning to exponential expressions such as 2^x, where x is an integer. For example,

$$2^3 = 2 \cdot 2 \cdot 2 \qquad \text{Three factors; each factor is 2}$$

When x is any real number (for example, the irrational number $\sqrt{3}$), what meaning can we give to $2^{\sqrt{3}}$? (We study radicals such as $\sqrt{3}$ further in Chapter 9.)

It is beyond the scope of this book to give precise meaning to 2^x if x is irrational. We can confirm your intuition and say that $2^{\sqrt{3}}$ is a real number. Using a calculator, it is true that $2^{\sqrt{3}} \approx 3.321997$. In fact, as long as the base b is positive, b^x is a real number for all real numbers x. Also, the rules of exponents apply whether x is rational or irrational, as long as b is positive. In this section, we are interested in functions of the form $f(x) = b^x$, where $b > 0$. A function of this form is called an **exponential function.**

We state all of the above so that it is clear that the graph of $f(x) = b^x$ is a smooth curve whose domain is all real numbers.

> **Exponential Function**
> A function of the form
> $$f(x) = b^x$$
> is called an **exponential function** if $b > 0$, b is not 1, and x is a real number.

Next, we practice graphing exponential functions.

EXAMPLE 1 Graph the exponential functions defined by $f(x) = 2^x$ and $g(x) = 3^x$ on the same set of axes.

Solution Graph each function by plotting points. Set up a table of values for each of the two functions.

If each set of points is plotted and connected with a smooth curve, the following graphs result.

$f(x) = 2^x$	x	0	1	2	3	−1	−2
	$f(x)$	1	2	4	8	$\frac{1}{2}$	$\frac{1}{4}$

$g(x) = 3^x$	x	0	1	2	3	−1	−2
	$g(x)$	1	3	9	27	$\frac{1}{3}$	$\frac{1}{9}$

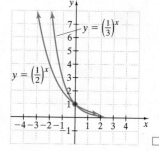

PRACTICE

1 Graph the exponential functions defined by $f(x) = 2^x$ and $g(x) = 7^x$ on the same set of axes.

A number of things should be noted about the two graphs of exponential functions in Example 1. First, the graphs show that $f(x) = 2^x$ and $g(x) = 3^x$ are functions since each graph passes the vertical line test. The y-intercept of each graph is $(0, 1)$, but neither graph has an x-intercept. From the graph, we can also see that the domain of each function is all real numbers and that the range is $y > 0$. We can also see that as x-values are increasing, y-values are increasing also.

EXAMPLE 2 Graph the exponential functions $y = \left(\frac{1}{2}\right)^x$ and $y = \left(\frac{1}{3}\right)^x$ on the same set of axes.

Solution As before, plot points and connect them with a smooth curve.

$y = \left(\frac{1}{2}\right)^x$	x	0	1	2	3	−1	−2
	y	1	$\frac{1}{2}$	$\frac{1}{4}$	$\frac{1}{8}$	2	4

$y = \left(\frac{1}{3}\right)^x$	x	0	1	2	3	−1	−2
	y	1	$\frac{1}{3}$	$\frac{1}{9}$	$\frac{1}{27}$	3	9

PRACTICE

2 Graph the exponential functions $f(x) = \left(\frac{1}{3}\right)^x$ and $g(x) = \left(\frac{1}{5}\right)^x$ on the same set of axes.

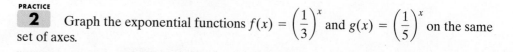

Each function in Example 2 again is a function. The y-intercept of both is $(0, 1)$. The domain is the set of all real numbers, and the range is $y > 0$.

Notice the difference between the graphs of Example 1 and the graphs of Example 2. An exponential function is always increasing if the base is greater than 1.

When the base is between 0 and 1, the graph is always decreasing. The following figures summarize these characteristics of exponential functions.

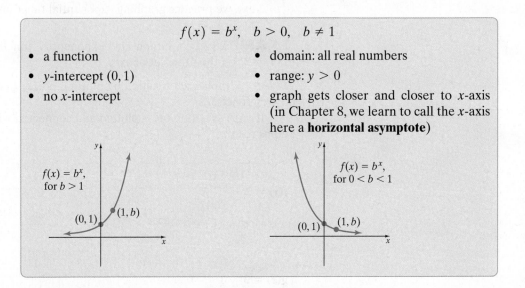

$$f(x) = b^x, \quad b > 0, \quad b \neq 1$$

- a function
- y-intercept $(0, 1)$
- no x-intercept

- domain: all real numbers
- range: $y > 0$
- graph gets closer and closer to x-axis (in Chapter 8, we learn to call the x-axis here a **horizontal asymptote**)

$f(x) = b^x$, for $b > 1$

$f(x) = b^x$, for $0 < b < 1$

EXAMPLE 3   Graph the exponential function $f(x) = 3^{x+2}$.

Solution   As before, we find and plot a few ordered pair solutions. Then we connect the points with a smooth curve.

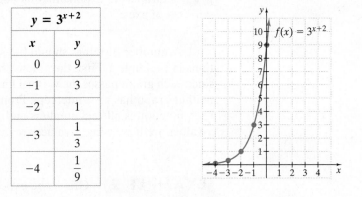

$y = 3^{x+2}$	
x	y
0	9
-1	3
-2	1
-3	$\frac{1}{3}$
-4	$\frac{1}{9}$

$f(x) = 3^{x+2}$

Notice that the graph once again approaches the x-axis—this x-axis is a horizontal asymptote.

PRACTICE
3   Graph the exponential function $f(x) = 2^{x+3}$.

Concept Check ✓

Which functions are exponential functions?

a. $f(x) = x^3$
b. $g(x) = \left(\dfrac{2}{3}\right)^x$
c. $h(x) = 5^{x-2}$
d. $w(x) = (2x)^2$

Answer to Concept Check:
b, c

The shifting and reflecting properties of graphs that we learned in Section 3.8 apply to all functions, including exponential ones. We review these below.

OBJECTIVE 2 ▶ Transformations of exponential functions. The graphs of exponential functions can be translated vertically or horizontally, and reflected. These transformations are summarized below.

Transformations Involving Exponential Functions

In each case, c represents a positive real number.

Transformation	Equation	Description
Vertical translation	$g(x) = b^x + c$	• Shifts the graph of $f(x) = b^x$ upward c units.
	$g(x) = b^x - c$	• Shifts the graph of $f(x) = b^x$ downward c units.
Horizontal translation	$g(x) = b^{x+c}$	• Shifts the graph of $f(x) = b^x$ to the left c units.
	$g(x) = b^{x-c}$	• Shifts the graph of $f(x) = b^x$ to the right c units.
Reflection	$g(x) = -b^x$	• Reflects the graph of $f(x) = b^x$ about the x-axis.

EXAMPLE 4   Transformations Involving Exponential Functions

Use the graph of $f(x) = 3^x$ to obtain the graph of $g(x) = 3^{x+1}$.

Solution   The graph of $g(x) = 3^{x+1}$ is the graph of $f(x) = 3^x$ shifted 1 unit to the left.

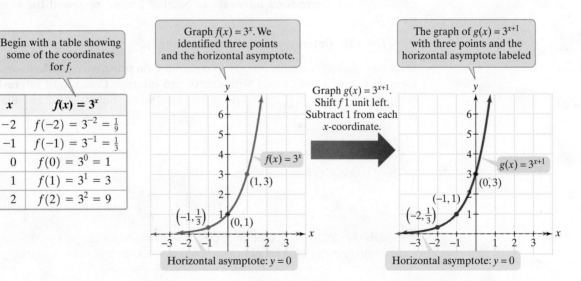

Begin with a table showing some of the coordinates for f.

x	$f(x) = 3^x$
-2	$f(-2) = 3^{-2} = \frac{1}{9}$
-1	$f(-1) = 3^{-1} = \frac{1}{3}$
0	$f(0) = 3^0 = 1$
1	$f(1) = 3^1 = 3$
2	$f(2) = 3^2 = 9$

Graph $f(x) = 3^x$. We identified three points and the horizontal asymptote.

Graph $g(x) = 3^{x+1}$. Shift f 1 unit left. Subtract 1 from each x-coordinate.

The graph of $g(x) = 3^{x+1}$ with three points and the horizontal asymptote labeled

PRACTICE
4   Use the graph of $f(x) = 3^x$ to obtain the graph of $g(x) = 3^{x-1}$.

If an exponential function is translated upward or downward, the horizontal asymptote is shifted by the amount of the vertical shift.

EXAMPLE 5 Transformations Involving Exponential Functions

Use the graph of $f(x) = 2^x$ to obtain the graph of $g(x) = 2^x - 3$.

Solution The graph of $g(x) = 2^x - 3$ is the graph of $f(x) = 2^x$ shifted down 3 units.

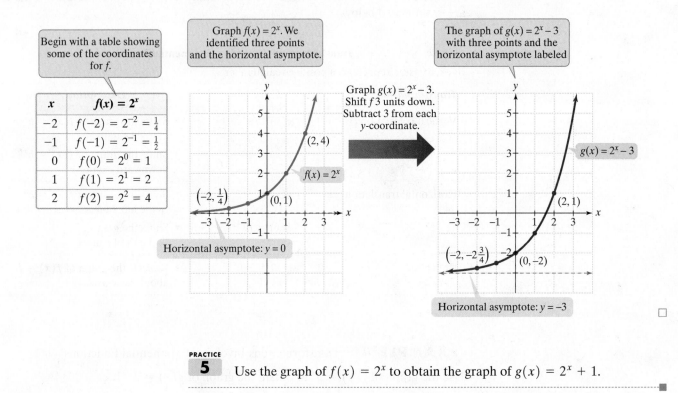

Begin with a table showing some of the coordinates for f.

x	$f(x) = 2^x$
-2	$f(-2) = 2^{-2} = \frac{1}{4}$
-1	$f(-1) = 2^{-1} = \frac{1}{2}$
0	$f(0) = 2^0 = 1$
1	$f(1) = 2^1 = 2$
2	$f(2) = 2^2 = 4$

Graph $f(x) = 2^x$. We identified three points and the horizontal asymptote.

Graph $g(x) = 2^x - 3$. Shift f 3 units down. Subtract 3 from each y-coordinate.

The graph of $g(x) = 2^x - 3$ with three points and the horizontal asymptote labeled

PRACTICE
5   Use the graph of $f(x) = 2^x$ to obtain the graph of $g(x) = 2^x + 1$.

OBJECTIVE 3 ▶ Compound interest. In Section 2.6, we reviewed the simple interest formula.

$$I = PRT \text{ (interest = principal} \cdot \text{rate} \cdot \text{time)}$$

With this interest formula, interest is computed on principal only. A more widely-used formula is one having to do with compound interest. **Compound interest** is interest computed not only on principal (original investment), but on any accumulated interest also.

Compound Interest Formula

The exponential function defined by

$$A = P\left(1 + \frac{r}{n}\right)^{nt}$$

models the dollars A accrued (or owed) after P dollars are invested (or loaned) at an annual rate of interest r compounded n times each year for t years.

EXAMPLE 6 Using the Compound Interest Formula

Find the amount owed at the end of 5 years if $1600 is loaned at a rate of 9% compounded monthly.

Solution We use the formula $A = P\left(1 + \dfrac{r}{n}\right)^{nt}$, with the following values.

$$P = \$1600 \text{ (the amount of the loan)}$$
$$r = 9\% = 0.09 \text{ (the annual rate of interest)}$$
$$n = 12 \text{ (the number of times interest is compounded each year)}$$
$$t = 5 \text{ (the duration of the loan, in years)}$$

$$A = P\left(1 + \frac{r}{n}\right)^{nt} \quad \text{Compound interest formula}$$

$$= 1600\left(1 + \frac{0.09}{12}\right)^{12(5)} \quad \text{Substitute known values.}$$

$$= 1600(1.0075)^{60}$$

To approximate A, use the $\boxed{y^x}$ or $\boxed{\wedge}$ key on your calculator.

$$\boxed{2505.0896}$$

Thus, the amount A owed is approximately $2505.09.

PRACTICE
6   Find the amount owed at the end of 4 years if $3000 is loaned at a rate of 7% compounded semiannually (twice a year).

VOCABULARY & READINESS CHECK

1. Multiple Choice. A function such as $f(x) = 2^x$ is a(n) _____ function.

   A. linear   **B.** quadratic   **C.** exponential

Fill in the Blank. *Answer the questions about the graph of $y = 2^x$, shown to the right.*

2. Is there an x-intercept? _____ If so, name the coordinates. _____
3. Is there a y-intercept? _____ If so, name the coordinates. _____
4. The domain of this function is _____.
5. The range of this function is _____.

6.6 EXERCISE SET

MyMathLab   PRACTICE   WATCH   DOWNLOAD   READ   REVIEW

Graph each exponential function. See Examples 1 through 3.

1. $y = 4^x$

2. $y = 5^x$

3. $y = 2^x + 1$

4. $y = 3^x - 1$

5. $y = \left(\frac{1}{4}\right)^x$

6. $y = \left(\frac{1}{5}\right)^x$

7. $y = \left(\frac{1}{2}\right)^x - 2$

8. $y = \left(\frac{1}{3}\right)^x + 2$

9. $y = -2^x$

10. $y = -3^x$

11. $y = -\left(\frac{1}{4}\right)^x$

12. $y = -\left(\frac{1}{5}\right)^x$

13. $f(x) = 2^{x+1}$

14. $f(x) = 3^{x-1}$

15. $f(x) = 4^{x-2}$

16. $f(x) = 2^{x+3}$

17. $g(x) = \left(\frac{3}{2}\right)^x$

18. $g(x) = \left(\frac{4}{3}\right)^x$

19. $f(x) = (0.6)^x$

20. $f(x) = (0.8)^x$

Match each exponential equation with its graph below or on page 408. See Examples 1 through 3.

21. $f(x) = \left(\frac{1}{2}\right)^x$

22. $f(x) = \left(\frac{1}{4}\right)^x$

23. $f(x) = 2^x$

24. $f(x) = 3^x$

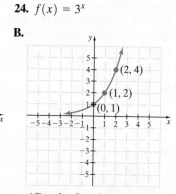

A.

B.

(Graphs C and D page 408)

C. 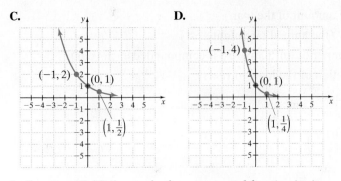   **D.**

In Exercises 25–30, the graph of an exponential function is given. Select the function for each graph from the following options:

$$f(x) = 3^x, g(x) = 3^{x-1}, h(x) = 3^x - 1,$$
$$F(x) = -3^x, G(x) = 3^{-x}, H(x) = -3^{-x}.$$

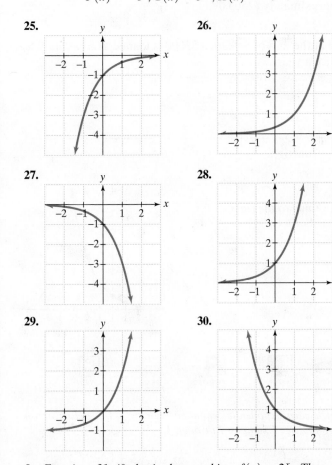

25.

26.

27.

28.

29.

30.

In Exercises 31–40, begin by graphing $f(x) = 2^x$. Then use transformations of this graph to graph the given function. Be sure to graph and give equations of the asymptotes. Use the graphs to determine each function's domain and range. If applicable, use a graphing utility to confirm your hand-drawn graphs.

31. $g(x) = 2^{x+1}$

32. $g(x) = 2^{x+2}$

33. $g(x) = 2^x - 1$

34. $g(x) = 2^x + 2$

35. $h(x) = 2^{x+1} - 1$

36. $h(x) = 2^{x+2} - 1$

37. $g(x) = -2^x$

38. $g(x) = 2^{-x}$

39. $g(x) = 2 \cdot 2^x$

40. $g(x) = \frac{1}{2} \cdot 2^x$

(*Hint:* The graph of $g(x)$ is a vertical stretch of the graph of $f(x)$.)

(*Hint:* The graph of $g(x)$ is a vertical shrink of the graph of $f(x)$.)

In Exercises 41–46, graph functions f and g in the same rectangular coordinate system. Graph and give equations of all asymptotes. If applicable, use a graphing utility to confirm your hand-drawn graphs.

41. $f(x) = 3^x$ and $g(x) = 3^{-x}$

42. $f(x) = 3^x$ and $g(x) = -3^x$

43. $f(x) = 3^x$ and $g(x) = \frac{1}{3} \cdot 3^x$ (See hint for **40.**)

44. $f(x) = 3^x$ and $g(x) = 3 \cdot 3^x$ (See hint for **39.**)

45. $f(x) = \left(\frac{1}{2}\right)^x$ and $g(x) = \left(\frac{1}{2}\right)^{x-1} + 1$

46. $f(x) = \left(\frac{1}{2}\right)^x$ and $g(x) = \left(\frac{1}{2}\right)^{x-1} + 2$

Use the compound interest formula $A = P\left(1 + \dfrac{r}{n}\right)^{nt}$ to solve Exercises 47–50. Round answers to the nearest cent.

47. Find the accumulated value of an investment of $10,000 for 5 years at an interest rate of 5.5% if the money is **a.** compounded semiannually; **b.** compounded quarterly; **c.** compounded monthly.

48. Find the accumulated value of an investment of $5000 for 10 years at an interest rate of 6.5% if the money is **a.** compounded semiannually; **b.** compounded quarterly; **c.** compounded monthly.

49. Suppose that you have $12,000 to invest. Which investment yields the greater return over 3 years: 7% compounded monthly or 6.85% compounded yearly?

50. Suppose that you have $6000 to invest. Which investment yields the greater return over 4 years: 8.25% compounded quarterly or 8.3% compounded semiannually?

REVIEW AND PREVIEW

Solve each equation. See Section 2.1.

51. $5x - 2 = 18$

52. $3x - 7 = 11$

53. $3x - 4 = 3(x + 1)$

54. $2 - 6x = 6(1 - x)$

By inspection, find the value for x that makes each statement true. See Section 6.1.

55. $2^x = 8$

56. $3^x = 9$

57. $5^x = \dfrac{1}{5}$

58. $4^x = 1$

CONCEPT EXTENSIONS

59. Graph $y = 2^x$ and $x = 2^y$ in the same rectangular coordinate system.

60. Graph $y = 3^x$ and $x = 3^y$ in the same rectangular coordinate system.

In Exercises 61–64, give the equation of each exponential function whose graph is shown.

61.   **62.**

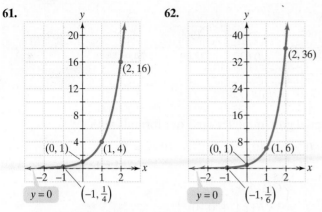

CONCEPT EXTENSIONS

63. Explain why the graph of an exponential function $y = b^x$ contains the point $(1, b)$.

64. Explain why an exponential function $y = b^x$ has a y-intercept of $(0, 1)$.

Graph.

65. $y = |3^x|$ **66.** $y = \left| \left(\dfrac{1}{3} \right)^x \right|$

67. $y = 3^{|x|}$ **68.** $y = \left(\dfrac{1}{3} \right)^{|x|}$

6.7 EXPONENTIAL GROWTH AND DECAY FUNCTIONS

OBJECTIVES

1 Model exponential growth.

2 Model exponential decay.

Now that we can graph exponential functions, let's learn about exponential growth and exponential decay.

A quantity that grows or decays by the same percent at regular time periods is said to have **exponential growth** or **exponential decay.** There are many real-life examples of exponential growth and decay, such as population, bacteria, viruses, and radioactive substances, just to name a few.

Recall the graphs of exponential functions.

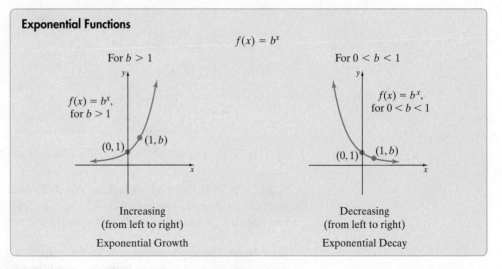

OBJECTIVE 1 ▶ Modeling exponential growth. We begin with exponential growth, as described below.

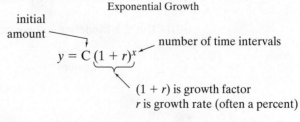

EXAMPLE 1   In 1995, let's suppose a town named Jackson had a population of 15,500 and was consistently increasing by 10% per year. If this yearly increase continues, predict the city's population in 2015. (Round to the nearest whole.)

Solution Let's begin to understand by calculating the city's population each year:

Time Interval	x = 1	x = 2	3	4	5	
Year	1996	1997	1998	1999	2000	and so on ...
Population	17,050	18,755	20,631	22,694	24,963	

$\underbrace{15,500 + 0.10(15,500)}$ $\underbrace{17,050 + 0.10(17,050)}$

This is an example of exponential growth, so let's use our formula with

$$C = 15,500; r = 0.10, x = 2015 - 1995 = 20$$

Then,

$$y = C(1 + r)^x$$
$$= 15,500(1 + 0.10)^{20}$$
$$= 15,500(1.1)^{20}$$
$$\approx 104,276$$

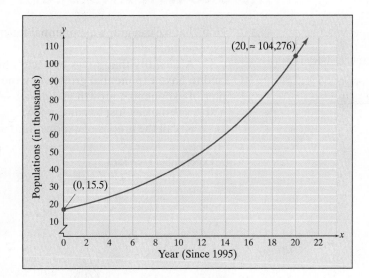

In 2015, we predict the population of Jackson to be 104,276. □

PRACTICE

1 In 2000, the town of Jackson (from Example 1) had a population of 25,000 and started consistently increasing by 12% per year. If this yearly increase continues, predict the city's population in 2015. Round to the nearest whole.

Note: The exponential growth formula, $y = C(1 + r)^x$ should remind you of the compound interest formula from the previous section, $A = P(1 + \frac{r}{n})^{nt}$. In fact, if the number of compoundings per year, n, is 1, the interest formula becomes $A = P(1 + r)^t$, which is the exponential growth formula written with different variables.

OBJECTIVE 2 ▶ Modeling exponential decay. Now lets study exponential decay.

initial
amount

Exponential Decay

$$y = C\underbrace{(1 - r)}^{x} \longleftarrow \text{number of time intervals}$$

$(1 - r)$ is decay factor
r is decay rate (often a percent)

EXAMPLE 2 A large golf country club holds a singles tournament each year. At the start of the tournament for a particular year there are 512 players. After each round, half the players are eliminated. How many players remain after 6 rounds?

Solution This is an example of exponential decay.

Let's begin to understand by calculating the number of players after a few rounds.

Round (same as interval)	1	2	3	4	and so on ...
Players	256	128	64	32	

$512 - 0.50(512)$ $256 - 0.50(256)$

Here, $C = 512$; $r = \frac{1}{2}$ or $50\% = 0.50$; $x = 6$

Thus,

$$y = 512(1 - 0.50)^6$$
$$= 512(0.50)^6$$
$$= 8$$

After 6 rounds, there are 8 players remaining.

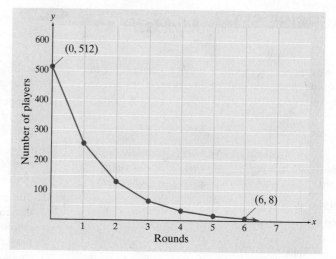

PRACTICE

2   A tournament with 800 persons is played so that after each round, the number of players decreases by 30%. Find the number of players after round 9. Round your answer to the nearest whole.

The **half-life** of a substance is the amount of time it takes for half of the substance to decay.

EXAMPLE 3   A form of DDT pesticide (banned in 1972) has a half-life of approximately 15 years. If a storage unit had 400 pounds of DDT, find how much DDT is remaining after 72 years. Round to the nearest tenth.

Solution   Here, we need to be careful because each time interval is 15 years, the half-life.

Time interval	1	2	3	4	5	and so on
Years passed	15	2·15 = 30	45	60	75	
Pounds of DDT	200	100	50	25	12.5	

From the table we see that after 72 years, between 4 and 5 intervals, there should be between 12.5 and 25 pounds of DDT remaining.

Let's calculate x, the number of time intervals.

$$x = \frac{72(\text{years})}{15(\text{half-life})} = 4.8$$

Now, using our exponential decay formula and the definition of half-life, for each time interval x, the decay rate r is $\frac{1}{2}$ or 50% or 0.50.

$$y = 400(1 - 0.50)^{4.8} \text{—time intervals for 72 years}$$

original amount   decay rate

$$y = 400(0.50)^{4.8}$$

$$y \approx 14.4$$

In 72 years, 14.4 pounds of DDT remains.

PRACTICE
3 Use the information from Example 3 and calculate how much of a 500 gram sample of DDT will remain after 51 years. Round to the nearest tenth.

6.7 EXERCISE SET

Practice using the exponential growth formula by completing the table below. Round final amounts to the nearest whole. See Example 1.

	Original amount	Growth rate per year	Number of years, x	Final amount after x years of growth
1.	305	5%	8	
2.	402	7%	5	
3.	2000	11%	41	
4.	1000	47%	19	
5.	17	29%	28	
6.	29	61%	12	

Practice using the exponential decay formula by completing the table below. Round final amounts to the nearest whole. See Example 2.

	Original amount	Decay rate per year	Number of years, x	Final amount after x years of decay
7.	305	5%	8	
8.	402	7%	5	
9.	10,000	12%	15	
10.	15,000	16%	11	
11.	207,000	32%	25	
12.	325,000	29%	31	

Solve. Unless noted otherwise, round answers to the nearest whole. See Examples 1 and 2.

13. Suppose a city with population 500,000 has been growing at a rate of 3% per year. If this rate continues, find the population of this city in 12 years.

14. Suppose a city with population 320,000 has been growing at a rate of 4% per year. If this rate continues, find the population of this city in 20 years.

15. The number of employees for a certain company has been decreasing each year by 5%. If the company currently has 640 employees and this rate continues, find the number of employees in 10 years.

16. The number of students attending summer school at a local community college has been decreasing each year by 7%. If 984 students currently attend summer school and this rate continues, find the number of students attending summer school in 5 years.

Practice using the exponential decay formula with half-lifes by completing the table below.
The first row has been completed for you. See Example 3.

	Original amount	Half-life (in years)	Number of years	Time intervals, $x\left(\frac{years}{half\text{-}life}\right)$ rounded to tenths if needed	Final amount after x time intervals (rounded to tenths)	Is your final amount reasonable?
	60	8	10	$\frac{10}{8} = 1.25$	25.2	yes
17. a.	40	7	14			
b.	40	7	11			
18. a.	200	12	36			
b.	200	12	40			
19.	21	152	500			
20.	35	119	500			

Solve. Round answers to the nearest tenth.

21. A form of nickel has a half-life of 96 years. How much of a 30 gram sample is left after 250 years?

22. A form of uranium has a half-life of 72 years. How much of a 100 gram sample is left after 500 years?

23. An item is on sale for 40% off its original price. If it is then marked down an additional 60%, does this mean the item is free? Discuss why or why not.

24. Uranium U-232 has a half-life of 72 years. What eventually happens to a 10 gram sample? Does it ever completely decay and disappear? Discuss why or why not.

6.8 DIVIDING POLYNOMIALS

OBJECTIVES

1 Divide a polynomial by a monomial.

2 Use long division to divide a polynomial by another polynomial.

OBJECTIVE 1 ▶ Dividing by a monomial. Now that we know how to add, subtract, and multiply polynomials, we practice dividing polynomials.

To divide a polynomial by a monomial, recall addition of fractions. Fractions that have a common denominator are added by adding the numerators:

$$\frac{a}{c} + \frac{b}{c} = \frac{a + b}{c}$$

If we read this equation from right to left and let a, b, and c be monomials, $c \neq 0$, we have the following:

Dividing a Polynomial By a Monomial

Divide each term of the polynomial by the monomial.

$$\frac{a + b}{c} = \frac{a}{c} + \frac{b}{c}, \quad c \neq 0$$

Throughout this section, we assume that denominators are not 0.

EXAMPLE 1   Divide $6m^2 + 2m$ by $2m$.

Solution   We begin by writing the quotient in fraction form. Then we divide each term of the polynomial $6m^2 + 2m$ by the monomial $2m$.

$$\frac{6m^2 + 2m}{2m} = \frac{6m^2}{2m} + \frac{2m}{2m}$$

$$= 3m + 1 \qquad \text{Simplify.}$$

Check: We know that if $\dfrac{6m^2 + 2m}{2m} = 3m + 1$, then $2m \cdot (3m + 1)$ must equal $6m^2 + 2m$. Thus, to check, we multiply.

$$2m(3m + 1) = 2m(3m) + 2m(1) = 6m^2 + 2m$$

The quotient $3m + 1$ checks.   □

PRACTICE
1   Divide $8t^3 + 4t^2$ by $4t^2$

EXAMPLE 2   Divide $\dfrac{9x^5 - 12x^2 + 3x}{3x^2}$.

Solution $\dfrac{9x^5 - 12x^2 + 3x}{3x^2} = \dfrac{9x^5}{3x^2} - \dfrac{12x^2}{3x^2} + \dfrac{3x}{3x^2}$ Divide each term by $3x^2$.

$$= 3x^3 - 4 + \frac{1}{x} \qquad \text{Simplify.}$$

Notice that the quotient is not a polynomial because of the term $\dfrac{1}{x}$. This expression is called a rational expression—we will study rational expressions further in Chapter 8. Although the quotient of two polynomials is not always a polynomial, we may still check by multiplying.

Check: $3x^2\left(3x^3 - 4 + \dfrac{1}{x}\right) = 3x^2(3x^3) - 3x^2(4) + 3x^2\left(\dfrac{1}{x}\right)$

$$= 9x^5 - 12x^2 + 3x \qquad\qquad □$$

PRACTICE
2   Divide $\dfrac{16x^6 + 20x^3 - 12x}{4x^2}$.

EXAMPLE 3   Divide $\dfrac{8x^2y^2 - 16xy + 2x}{4xy}$.

Solution $\dfrac{8x^2y^2 - 16xy + 2x}{4xy} = \dfrac{8x^2y^2}{4xy} - \dfrac{16xy}{4xy} + \dfrac{2x}{4xy}$ Divide each term by $4xy$.

$$= 2xy - 4 + \frac{1}{2y} \qquad \text{Simplify.}$$

Check: $4xy\left(2xy - 4 + \dfrac{1}{2y}\right) = 4xy(2xy) - 4xy(4) + 4xy\left(\dfrac{1}{2y}\right)$

$$= 8x^2y^2 - 16xy + 2x$$

☐

PRACTICE
3   Divide $\dfrac{15x^4y^4 - 10xy + y}{5xy}$.

Concept Check ☑

In which of the following is $\dfrac{x + 5}{5}$ simplified correctly?

a. $\dfrac{x}{5} + 1$ **b.** x **c.** $x + 1$

OBJECTIVE 2 ▶ **Using long division to divide by a polynomial.** To divide a polynomial by a polynomial other than a monomial, we use a process known as long division. Polynomial long division is similar to number long division, so we review long division by dividing 13 into 3660.

▶ **Helpful Hint**
Recall that 3660 is called the dividend.

$$
\begin{array}{r}
281 \\
13\overline{\smash{)}3660} \\
26 \\
\hline
106 \\
104 \\
\hline
20 \\
13 \\
\hline
7
\end{array}
$$

$2 \cdot 13 = 26$
Subtract and bring down the next digit in the dividend.
$8 \cdot 13 = 104$
Subtract and bring down the next digit in the dividend.
$1 \cdot 13 = 13$
Subtract. There are no more digits to bring down, so the remainder is 7.

The quotient is 281 R 7, which can be written as $281\dfrac{7 \leftarrow \text{remainder}}{13 \leftarrow \text{divisor}}$

Recall that division can be checked by multiplication. To check a division problem such as this one, we see that

$$13 \cdot 281 + 7 = 3660$$

Now we demonstrate long division of polynomials.

EXAMPLE 4   Divide $x^2 + 7x + 12$ by $x + 3$ using long division.

Solution

To subtract, change the signs of these terms and add.

$$
\begin{array}{r}
x \\
x + 3\overline{\smash{)}x^2 + 7x + 12} \\
x^2 + 3x\downarrow \\
\hline
4x + 12
\end{array}
$$

How many times does x divide x^2? $\dfrac{x^2}{x} = x$.
Multiply: $x(x + 3)$.
Subtract and bring down the next term.

Now we repeat this process.

To subtract, change the signs of these terms and add.

$$
\begin{array}{r}
x + 4 \\
x + 3\overline{\smash{)}x^2 + 7x + 12} \\
x^2 + 3x \\
\hline
4x + 12 \\
4x + 12 \\
\hline
0
\end{array}
$$

How many times does x divide $4x$? $\dfrac{4x}{x} = 4$.

Multiply: $4(x + 3)$.
Subtract. The remainder is 0.

The quotient is $x + 4$.

Check: We check by multiplying.

divisor	·	quotient	+	remainder	=	dividend

or

$$(x + 3) \quad \cdot \quad (x + 4) \quad + \quad 0 \quad = \quad x^2 + 7x + 12$$

The quotient checks. ▫

PRACTICE
4 Divide $x^2 + 5x + 6$ by $x + 2$ using long division.

EXAMPLE 5 Divide $6x^2 + 10x - 5$ by $3x - 1$ using long division.

Solution

$$
\begin{array}{r}
2x + 4 \\
3x - 1 \overline{)6x^2 + 10x - 5} \\
\underline{6x^2 - 2x} \\
12x - 5 \\
\underline{12x - 4} \\
-1
\end{array}
$$

$\dfrac{6x^2}{3x} = 2x$, so $2x$ is a term of the quotient.

Multiply $2x(3x - 1)$.

Subtract and bring down the next term.

$\dfrac{12x}{3x} = 4$, multiply $4(3x - 1)$

Subtract. The remainder is -1.

Thus $(6x^2 + 10x - 5)$ divided by $(3x - 1)$ is $(2x + 4)$ with a remainder of -1. This can be written as

$$\frac{6x^2 + 10x - 5}{3x - 1} = 2x + 4 + \frac{-1}{3x - 1} \quad \begin{array}{l} \leftarrow \text{remainder} \\ \leftarrow \text{divisor} \end{array}$$

Check: To check, we multiply $(3x - 1)(2x + 4)$. Then we add the remainder, -1, to this product.

$$(3x - 1)(2x + 4) + (-1) = (6x^2 + 12x - 2x - 4) - 1$$
$$= 6x^2 + 10x - 5$$

The quotient checks. ▫

PRACTICE
5 Divide $4x^2 + 8x - 7$ by $2x + 1$ using long division.

In Example 5, the degree of the divisor, $3x - 1$, is 1 and the degree of the remainder, -1, is 0. The division process is continued until the degree of the remainder polynomial is less than the degree of the divisor polynomial.

EXAMPLE 6 Divide $\dfrac{4x^2 + 7 + 8x^3}{2x + 3}$.

Solution Before we begin the division process, we rewrite

$$4x^2 + 7 + 8x^3 \quad \text{as} \quad 8x^3 + 4x^2 + 0x + 7$$

Notice that we have written the polynomial in descending order and have represented the missing x term by $0x$.

$$
\begin{array}{r}
4x^2 - 4x + 6 \\
2x + 3 \overline{)\, 8x^3 + 4x^2 + 0x + 7} \\
\underline{-8x^3 \mp 12x^2} \\
-8x^2 + 0x \\
\underline{\mp 8x^2 \mp 12x} \\
12x + 7 \\
\underline{-12x \mp 18} \\
-11 \quad \text{Remainder}
\end{array}
$$

Thus, $\dfrac{4x^2 + 7 + 8x^3}{2x + 3} = 4x^2 - 4x + 6 + \dfrac{-11}{2x + 3}$.

PRACTICE
6   Divide $\dfrac{11x - 3 + 9x^3}{3x + 2}$.

EXAMPLE 7   Divide $\dfrac{2x^4 - x^3 + 3x^2 + x - 1}{x^2 + 1}$.

Solution   Before dividing, rewrite the divisor polynomial

$$x^2 + 1 \quad \text{as} \quad x^2 + 0x + 1$$

The $0x$ term represents the missing x^1 term in the divisor.

$$
\begin{array}{r}
2x^2 - x + 1 \\
x^2 + 0x + 1 \overline{)\, 2x^4 - x^3 + 3x^2 + x - 1} \\
\underline{2x^4 \mp 0x^3 \mp 2x^2} \\
-x^3 + x^2 + x \\
\underline{\mp x^3 \mp 0x^2 \mp x} \\
x^2 + 2x - 1 \\
\underline{-x^2 \mp 0x \mp 1} \\
2x - 1 \quad \text{Remainder}
\end{array}
$$

Thus, $\dfrac{2x^4 - x^3 + 3x^2 + x - 1}{x^2 + 1} = 2x^2 - x + 1 + \dfrac{2x - 2}{x^2 + 1}$.

PRACTICE
7   Divide $\dfrac{3x^4 - 2x^3 - 3x^2 + x + 4}{x^2 + 2}$.

VOCABULARY & READINESS CHECK

Word Bank. *Use the choices below to fill in each blank. Choices may be used more than once.*

   dividend   divisor   quotient

1. In $6\overline{)18}^{\,3}$, the 18 is the _____, the 3 is the _____ and the 6 is the _____.

2. In $x + 1\overline{)x^2 + 3x + 2}^{\,x + 2}$, the $x + 1$ is the _____, the $x^2 + 3x + 2$ is the _____ and the $x + 2$ is the _____.

Simplify each expression mentally.

3. $\dfrac{a^6}{a^4}$ **4.** $\dfrac{p^8}{p^3}$ **5.** $\dfrac{y^2}{y}$ **6.** $\dfrac{a^3}{a}$

6.8 | EXERCISE SET

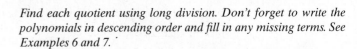

Perform each division. See Examples 1 through 3.

1. $\dfrac{12x^4 + 3x^2}{x}$

2. $\dfrac{15x^2 - 9x^5}{x}$

3. $\dfrac{20x^3 - 30x^2 + 5x + 5}{5}$

4. $\dfrac{8x^3 - 4x^2 + 6x + 2}{2}$

5. $\dfrac{15p^3 + 18p^2}{3p}$

6. $\dfrac{14m^2 - 27m^3}{7m}$

7. $\dfrac{-9x^4 + 18x^5}{6x^5}$

8. $\dfrac{6x^5 + 3x^4}{3x^4}$

9. $\dfrac{-9x^5 + 3x^4 - 12}{3x^3}$

10. $\dfrac{6a^2 - 4a + 12}{-2a^2}$

11. $\dfrac{4x^4 - 6x^3 + 7}{-4x^4}$

12. $\dfrac{-12a^3 + 36a - 15}{3a}$

Find each quotient using long division. See Examples 4 and 5.

13. $\dfrac{x^2 + 4x + 3}{x + 3}$

14. $\dfrac{x^2 + 7x + 10}{x + 5}$

15. $\dfrac{2x^2 + 13x + 15}{x + 5}$

16. $\dfrac{3x^2 + 8x + 4}{x + 2}$

17. $\dfrac{2x^2 - 7x + 3}{x - 4}$

18. $\dfrac{3x^2 - x - 4}{x - 1}$

19. $\dfrac{9a^3 - 3a^2 - 3a + 4}{3a + 2}$

20. $\dfrac{4x^3 + 12x^2 + x - 14}{2x + 3}$

21. $\dfrac{8x^2 + 10x + 1}{2x + 1}$

22. $\dfrac{3x^2 + 17x + 7}{3x + 2}$

23. $\dfrac{2x^3 + 2x^2 - 17x + 8}{x - 2}$

24. $\dfrac{4x^3 + 11x^2 - 8x - 10}{x + 3}$

Find each quotient using long division. Don't forget to write the polynomials in descending order and fill in any missing terms. See Examples 6 and 7.

25. $\dfrac{x^2 - 36}{x - 6}$

26. $\dfrac{a^2 - 49}{a - 7}$

27. $\dfrac{x^3 - 27}{x - 3}$

28. $\dfrac{x^3 + 64}{x + 4}$

29. $\dfrac{1 - 3x^2}{x + 2}$

30. $\dfrac{7 - 5x^2}{x + 3}$

31. $\dfrac{-4b + 4b^2 - 5}{2b - 1}$

32. $\dfrac{-3y + 2y^2 - 15}{2y + 5}$

MIXED PRACTICE

Divide. If the divisor contains 2 or more terms, use long division. See Examples 1 through 7.

33. $\dfrac{a^2b^2 - ab^3}{ab}$

34. $\dfrac{m^3n^2 - mn^4}{mn}$

35. $\dfrac{8x^2 + 6x - 27}{2x - 3}$

36. $\dfrac{18w^2 + 18w - 8}{3w + 4}$

37. $\dfrac{2x^2y + 8x^2y^2 - xy^2}{2xy}$

38. $\dfrac{11x^3y^3 - 33xy + x^2y^2}{11xy}$

39. $\dfrac{2b^3 + 9b^2 + 6b - 4}{b + 4}$

40. $\dfrac{2x^3 + 3x^2 - 3x + 4}{x + 2}$

41. $\dfrac{5x^2 + 28x - 10}{x + 6}$

42. $\dfrac{2x^2 + x - 15}{x + 3}$

43. $\dfrac{10x^3 - 24x^2 - 10x}{10x}$

44. $\dfrac{2x^3 + 12x^2 + 16}{4x^2}$

45. $\dfrac{6x^2 + 17x - 4}{x + 3}$

46. $\dfrac{2x^2 - 9x + 15}{x - 6}$

47. $\dfrac{30x^2 - 17x + 2}{5x - 2}$

48. $\dfrac{4x^2 - 13x - 12}{4x + 3}$

49. $\dfrac{3x^4 - 9x^3 + 12}{-3x}$

50. $\dfrac{8y^6 - 3y^2 - 4y}{4y}$

51. $\dfrac{x^3 + 6x^2 + 18x + 27}{x + 3}$

52. $\dfrac{x^3 - 8x^2 + 32x - 64}{x - 4}$

53. $\dfrac{y^3 + 3y^2 + 4}{y - 2}$

54. $\dfrac{3x^3 + 11x + 12}{x + 4}$

55. $\dfrac{5 - 6x^2}{x - 2}$

56. $\dfrac{3 - 7x^2}{x - 3}$

Divide.

57. $\dfrac{x^5 + x^2}{x^2 + x}$

58. $\dfrac{x^6 - x^4}{x^3 + 1}$

REVIEW AND PREVIEW

Multiply each expression. See Section 6.3.

59. $2a(a^2 + 1)$

60. $-4a(3a^2 - 4)$

61. $2x(x^2 + 7x - 5)$

62. $4y(y^2 - 8y - 4)$

63. $-3xy(xy^2 + 7x^2y + 8)$

64. $-9xy(4xyz + 7xy^2z + 2)$

65. $9ab(ab^2c + 4bc - 8)$

66. $-7sr(6s^2r + 9sr^2 + 9rs + 8)$

Use the bar graph below to answer Exercises 67 through 70. See Section 3.1.

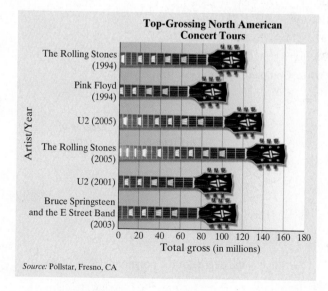

Top-Grossing North American Concert Tours

Source: Pollstar, Fresno, CA

67. Which artist has grossed the most money on one tour?

68. Estimate the amount of money made by the 2005 concert tour of The Rolling Stones.

69. Estimate the amount of money made by the 2005 concert tour of U2.

70. Which artist shown has grossed the least amount of money on a tour?

CONCEPT EXTENSIONS

△ **71.** The perimeter of a square is $(12x^3 + 4x - 16)$ feet. Find the length of its side.

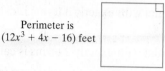

Perimeter is $(12x^3 + 4x - 16)$ feet

△ **72.** The volume of the swimming pool shown is $(36x^5 - 12x^3 + 6x^2)$ cubic feet. If its height is $2x$ feet and its width is $3x$ feet, find its length.

3x feet

2x feet

73. **Multiple Choice.** In which of the following is $\dfrac{a + 7}{7}$ simplified correctly? See the Concept Check in this section.

  a. $a + 1$ **b.** a **c.** $\dfrac{a}{7} + 1$

74. Explain how to check a polynomial long division result when the remainder is 0.

75. Explain how to check a polynomial long division result when the remainder is not 0.

△ **76.** The area of the following parallelogram is $(10x^2 + 31x + 15)$ square meters. If its base is $(5x + 3)$ meters, find its height.

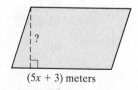

?

$(5x + 3)$ meters

△ **77.** The area of the top of the Ping-Pong table is $(49x^2 + 70x - 200)$ square inches. If its length is $(7x + 20)$ inches, find its width.

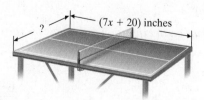

? $(7x + 20)$ inches

78. $(18x^{10a} - 12x^{8a} + 14x^{5a} - 2x^{3a}) \div 2x^{3a}$

79. $(25y^{11b} + 5y^{6b} - 20y^{3b} + 100y^b) \div 5y^b$

CHAPTER 6 VOCABULARY CHECK

Fill in each blank with one of the words or phrases listed below.

term	coefficient	monomial	binomial	trinomial	exponential
polynomials	degree of a term	degree of a polynomial	half-life	FOIL	

1. A _____ is a number or the product of numbers and variables raised to powers.
2. The _____ method may be used when multiplying two binomials.
3. A polynomial with exactly 3 terms is called a _____.
4. The _____ is the greatest degree of any term of the polynomial.
5. A polynomial with exactly 2 terms is called a _____.
6. The _____ of a term is its numerical factor.
7. The _____ is the sum of the exponents on the variables in the term.
8. A polynomial with exactly 1 term is called a _____.
9. Monomials, binomials, and trinomials are all examples of _____.
10. A function of the form $f(x) = b^x$ with $b > 0$, $b \neq 1$, and x a real number is called a(n)_____ function.
11. _____ is the amount of time it takes for half of the amount of a substance to decay.

CHAPTER 6 REVIEW

(6.1) State the base and the exponent for each expression.

1. 7^9
2. $(-5)^4$
3. -5^4
4. x^6

Evaluate each expression.

5. 8^3
6. $(-6)^2$
7. -6^2
8. $-4^3 - 4^0$
9. $(3b)^0$
10. $\dfrac{8b}{8b}$

Simplify each expression.

11. $y^2 \cdot y^7$
12. $x^9 \cdot x^5$
13. $(2x^5)(-3x^6)$
14. $(-5y^3)(4y^4)$
15. $(x^4)^2$
16. $(y^3)^5$
17. $(3y^6)^4$
18. $(2x^3)^3$
19. $\dfrac{x^9}{x^4}$
20. $\dfrac{z^{12}}{z^5}$
21. $\dfrac{a^5 b^4}{ab}$
22. $\dfrac{x^4 y^6}{xy}$
23. $\dfrac{12xy^6}{3x^4 y^{10}}$
24. $\dfrac{2x^7 y^8}{8xy^2}$
25. $5a^7(2a^4)^3$
26. $(2x)^2(9x)$
27. $(-5a)^0 + 7^0 + 8^0$
28. $8x^0 + 9^0$

Simplify the given expression and choose the correct result.

29. $\left(\dfrac{3x^4}{4y}\right)^3$

   a. $\dfrac{27x^{64}}{64y^3}$
   b. $\dfrac{27x^{12}}{64y^3}$
   c. $\dfrac{9x^{12}}{12y^3}$
   d. $\dfrac{3x^{12}}{4y^3}$

30. $\left(\dfrac{5a^6}{b^3}\right)^2$

   a. $\dfrac{10a^{12}}{b^6}$
   b. $\dfrac{25a^{36}}{b^9}$
   c. $\dfrac{25a^{12}}{b^6}$
   d. $25a^{12}b^6$

(6.2) Find the degree of each term.

31. $-5x^4 y^3$
32. $10x^3 y^2 z$
33. $35a^5 bc^2$
34. $95xyz$

Find the degree of each polynomial.

35. $y^5 + 7x - 8x^4$
36. $9y^2 + 30y + 25$
37. $-14x^2 y - 28x^2 y^3 - 42x^2 y^2$
38. $6x^2 y^2 z^2 + 5x^2 y^3 - 12xyz$

39. a. Complete the table for the polynomial
      $x^2 y^2 + 5x^2 - 7y^2 + 11xy - 1$.

Term	Numerical Coefficient	Degree of Term
$x^2 y^2$		
$5x^2$		
$-7y^2$		
$11xy$		
-1		

   b. What is the degree of the polynomial?

△ **40.** The surface area of a box with a square base and a height of 5 units is given by the polynomial $2x^2 + 20x$. Fill in the table below by evaluating $2x^2 + 20x$ for the given values of x.

x	1	3	5.1	10
$2x^2 + 20x$				

Combine like terms in each expression.

41. $7a^2 - 4a^2 - a^2$

42. $9y + y - 14y$

43. $6a^2 + 4a + 9a^2$

44. $21x^2 + 3x + x^2 + 6$

45. $4a^2b - 3b^2 - 8q^2 - 10a^2b + 7q^2$

46. $2s^{14} + 3s^{13} + 12s^{12} - s^{10}$

Add or subtract as indicated.

47. $(3x^2 + 2x + 6) + (5x^2 + x)$

48. $(2x^5 + 3x^4 + 4x^3 + 5x^2) + (4x^2 + 7x + 6)$

49. $(-5y^2 + 3) - (2y^2 + 4)$

50. $(3x^2 - 7xy + 7y^2) - (4x^2 - xy + 9y^2)$

51. Add $(-9x^2 + 6x + 2)$ and $(4x^2 - x - 1)$.

52. Subtract $(3x - y)$ from $(7x - 14y)$.

53. Subtract $(4x^2 + 8x - 7)$ from the sum of $(x^2 + 7x + 9)$ and $(x^2 + 4)$.

54. With the ownership of computers growing rapidly, the market for new software is also increasing. The revenue for software publishers (in millions of dollars) in the United States from 2001 to 2006 can be represented by the polynomial $754x^2 - 228x + 80{,}134$ where x is the number of years since 2001. Use this model to predict the revenues from software sales in 2009. (*Source:* Software & Information Industry Association)

(6.3) *Multiply each expression.*

55. $4(2a + 7)$

56. $9(6a - 3)$

57. $-7x(x^2 + 5)$

58. $-8y(4y^2 - 6)$

59. $(3a^3 - 4a + 1)(-2a)$

60. $(6b^3 - 4b + 2)(7b)$

61. $(2x + 2)(x - 7)$

62. $(2x - 5)(3x + 2)$

63. $(x - 9)^2$

64. $(x - 12)^2$

65. $(4a - 1)(a + 7)$

66. $(6a - 1)(7a + 3)$

67. $(5x + 2)^2$

68. $(3x + 5)^2$

69. $(x + 7)(x^3 + 4x - 5)$

70. $(x + 2)(x^5 + x + 1)$

71. $(x^2 + 2x + 4)(x^2 + 2x - 4)$

72. $(x^3 + 4x + 4)(x^3 + 4x - 4)$

73. $(x + 7)^3$

74. $(2x - 5)^3$

(6.4) *Use special products to multiply each of the following.*

75. $(x + 7)^2$

76. $(x - 5)^2$

77. $(3x - 7)^2$

78. $(4x + 2)^2$

79. $(5x - 9)^2$

80. $(5x + 1)(5x - 1)$

81. $(7x + 4)(7x - 4)$

82. $(a + 2b)(a - 2b)$

83. $(2x - 6)(2x + 6)$

84. $(4a^2 - 2b)(4a^2 + 2b)$

Express each as a product of polynomials in x. Then multiply and simplify.

△ **85.** Find the area of the square if its side is $(3x - 1)$ meters.

$(3x - 1)$ meters

△ **86.** Find the area of the rectangle.

$(x - 1)$ miles

$(5x + 2)$ miles

(6.5) *Simplify each expression.*

87. 7^{-2} **88.** -7^{-2} **89.** $2x^{-4}$ **90.** $(2x)^{-4}$

91. $\left(\dfrac{1}{5}\right)^{-3}$ **92.** $\left(\dfrac{-2}{3}\right)^{-2}$

93. $2^0 + 2^{-4}$ **94.** $6^{-1} - 7^{-1}$

Simplify each expression. Write each answer using positive exponents only.

95. $\dfrac{x^5}{x^{-3}}$ **96.** $\dfrac{z^4}{z^{-4}}$

97. $\dfrac{r^{-3}}{r^{-4}}$ **98.** $\dfrac{y^{-2}}{y^{-5}}$

99. $\left(\dfrac{bc^{-2}}{bc^{-3}}\right)^4$ **100.** $\left(\dfrac{x^{-3}y^{-4}}{x^{-2}y^{-5}}\right)^{-3}$

101. $\dfrac{x^{-4}y^{-6}}{x^2y^7}$ **102.** $\dfrac{a^5b^{-5}}{a^{-5}b^5}$

103. $a^{6m}a^{5m}$ **104.** $\dfrac{(x^{5+h})^3}{x^5}$

105. $(3xy^{2z})^3$ **106.** $a^{m+2}a^{m+3}$

Write each number in scientific notation.

107. 0.00027   **108.** 0.8868

109. 80,800,000   **110.** 868,000

111. Google.com is an Internet search engine that handles 91,000,000 searches every day. Write 91,000,000 in scientific notation. (*Source:* Google, Inc.)

112. The approximate diameter of the Milky Way galaxy is 150,000 light years. Write this number in scientific notation. (*Source:* NASA IMAGE/POETRY Education and Public Outreach Program)

150,000 light years

Write each number in standard form.

113. 8.67×10^5 **114.** 3.86×10^{-3}

115. 8.6×10^{-4} **116.** 8.936×10^5

117. The volume of the planet Jupiter is 1.43128×10^{15} cubic kilometers. Write this number in standard notation. (*Source:* National Space Science Data Center)

118. An angstrom is a unit of measure, equal to 1×10^{-10} meter, used for measuring wavelengths or the diameters of atoms. Write this number in standard notation. (*Source:* National Institute of Standards and Technology)

Simplify. Express each result in standard form.

119. $(8 \times 10^4)(2 \times 10^{-7})$

120. $\dfrac{8 \times 10^4}{2 \times 10^{-7}}$

(6.6) For Exercises 121–124, the graph of an exponential function is given. Choose the function for each graph from the following options:

$$f(x) = 4^x, \quad g(x) = 4^{-x},$$
$$h(x) = -4^{-x}, \quad r(x) = -4^{-x} + 3.$$

121.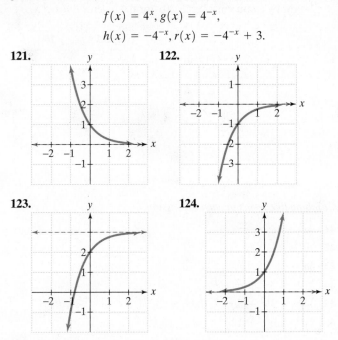

122.

123.

124.

In Exercises 125–128, graph f and g in the same rectangular coordinate system. Use transformations of the graph of f to obtain the graph of g. Graph and give equations of all asymptotes. Use the graphs to determine each function's domain and range.

125. $f(x) = 2^x$ and $g(x) = 2^{x-1}$

126. $f(x) = 3^x$ and $g(x) = 3^x - 1$

127. $f(x) = 3^x$ and $g(x) = -3^x$

128. $f(x) = \left(\frac{1}{2}\right)^x$ and $g(x) = \left(\frac{1}{2}\right)^{-x}$

Use the compound interest formulas to solve Exercises 129–130.

129. Suppose that you have $5000 to invest. Which investment yields the greater return over 5 years: 5.5% compounded semiannually or 5.25% compounded monthly?

130. Suppose that you have $14,000 to invest. Which investment yields the greater return over 10 years: 7% compounded monthly or 6.85% compounded daily?

(6.7) Solve. Round each answer to the nearest whole.

131. The city of Henderson, Nevada has been growing at a rate of 4.8% per year since the year 2000. If the population of Henderson was 179,087 in 2000 and this rate continues, predict the city's population in 2020.

132. The city of Raleigh, North Carolina has been growing at a rate of 3.9% per year since the year 2000. If the population of Raleigh was 287,370 in 2000 and this rate continues, predict the city's population in 2018.

133. A summer camp tournament starts with 1024 players. After each round, half the players are eliminated. How many players remain after 7 rounds?

134. The bear population in a certain national park is decreasing by 11% each year. If this rate continues, and there is currently an estimated bear population of 1280, find the bear population in 6 years.

(6.8) *Divide.*

135. $\dfrac{x^2 + 21x + 49}{7x^2}$

136. $\dfrac{5a^3b - 15ab^2 + 20ab}{-5ab}$

137. $(a^2 - a + 4) \div (a - 2)$

138. $(4x^2 + 20x + 7) \div (x + 5)$

139. $\dfrac{a^3 + a^2 + 2a + 6}{a - 2}$

140. $\dfrac{9b^3 - 18b^2 + 8b - 1}{3b - 2}$

141. $\dfrac{4x^4 - 4x^3 + x^2 + 4x - 3}{2x - 1}$

142. $\dfrac{-10x^2 - x^3 - 21x + 18}{x - 6}$

△ **143.** The area of the rectangle below is $(15x^3 - 3x^2 + 60)$ square feet. If its length is $3x^2$ feet, find its width.

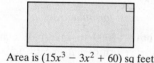

Area is $(15x^3 - 3x^2 + 60)$ sq feet

△ **144.** The perimeter of the equilateral triangle below is $(21a^3b^6 + 3a - 3)$ units. Find the length of a side.

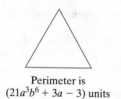

Perimeter is
$(21a^3b^6 + 3a - 3)$ units

MIXED REVIEW

Evaluate.

145. $\left(-\dfrac{1}{2}\right)^3$

Simplify each expression. Write each answer using positive exponents only.

146. $(4xy^2)(x^3y^5)$

147. $\dfrac{18x^9}{27x^3}$

148. $\left(\dfrac{3a^4}{b^2}\right)^3$

149. $(2x^{-4}y^3)^{-4}$

150. $\dfrac{a^{-3}b^6}{9^{-1}a^{-5}b^{-2}}$

Perform the indicated operations and simplify.

151. $(6x + 2) + (5x - 7)$

152. $(-y^2 - 4) + (3y^2 - 6)$

153. $(8y^2 - 3y + 1) - (3y^2 + 2)$

154. $(5x^2 + 2x - 6) - (-x - 4)$

155. $4x(7x^2 + 3)$

156. $(2x + 5)(3x - 2)$

157. $(x - 3)(x^2 + 4x - 6)$

158. $(7x - 2)(4x - 9)$

Use special products to multiply.

159. $(5x + 4)^2$

160. $(6x + 3)(6x - 3)$

Divide.

161. $\dfrac{8a^4 - 2a^3 + 4a - 5}{2a^3}$

162. $\dfrac{x^2 + 2x + 10}{x + 5}$

163. $\dfrac{4x^3 + 8x^2 - 11x + 4}{2x - 3}$

CHAPTER 6 TEST TEST PREP VIDEO

The fully worked-out solutions to any exercises you want to review are available in MyMathLab.

Evaluate each expression.

1. 2^5 **2.** $(-3)^4$ **3.** -3^4 **4.** 4^{-3}

Simplify each exponential expression. Write the result using only positive exponents.

5. $(3x^2)(-5x^9)$ **6.** $\dfrac{y^7}{y^2}$

7. $\dfrac{r^{-8}}{r^{-3}}$ **8.** $\left(\dfrac{x^2y^3}{x^3y^{-4}}\right)^2$

9. $\dfrac{6^2x^{-4}y^{-1}}{6^3x^{-3}y^7}$

Express each number in scientific notation.

10. 563,000 **11.** 0.0000863

Write each number in standard form.

12. 1.5×10^{-3} **13.** 6.23×10^4

14. Simplify. Write the answer in standard form.

$$(1.2 \times 10^5)(3 \times 10^{-7})$$

15. a. Complete the table for the polynomial
$4xy^2 + 7xyz + x^3y - 2$.

Term	Numerical Coefficient	Degree of Term
$4xy^2$		
$7xyz$		
x^3y		
-2		

b. What is the degree of the polynomial?

16. Simplify by combining like terms.

$$5x^2 + 4xy - 7x^2 + 11 + 8xy$$

Perform each indicated operation.

17. $(8x^3 + 7x^2 + 4x - 7) + (8x^3 - 7x - 6)$

18. $5x^3 + x^2 + 5x - 2 - (8x^3 - 4x^2 + x - 7)$

19. Subtract $(4x + 2)$ from the sum of $(8x^2 + 7x + 5)$ and $(x^3 - 8)$.

Multiply.

20. $(3x + 7)(x^2 + 5x + 2)$

21. $3x^2(2x^2 - 3x + 7)$

22. $(x + 7)(3x - 5)$

23. $\left(3x - \dfrac{1}{5}\right)\left(3x + \dfrac{1}{5}\right)$

24. $(4x - 2)^2$

25. $(8x + 3)^2$

26. $(x^2 - 9b)(x^2 + 9b)$

27. The height of the Bank of China in Hong Kong is 1001 feet. Neglecting air resistance, the height of an object dropped from

this building at time t seconds is given by the polynomial $-16t^2 + 1001$. Find the height of the object at the given times below.

t	0 seconds	1 second	3 seconds	5 seconds
$-16t^2 + 1001$				

△ **28.** Find the area of the top of the table. Express the area as a product, then multiply and simplify.

$(2x - 3)$ inches $(2x + 3)$ inches

Divide.

29. $\dfrac{4x^2 + 24xy - 7x}{8xy}$

30. $(x^2 + 7x + 10) \div (x + 5)$

31. $\dfrac{27x^3 - 8}{3x + 2}$

32. Graph $f(x) = 2^x$ and $g(x) = 2^{x+1}$ in the same rectangular coordinate system.

Use the compound interest formula to solve Exercise 33.

33. Suppose you have $3000 to invest. Which investment yields the greater return over 10 years: 6.5% compounded semiannually or 6% compounded monthly? How much more (to the nearest dollar) is yielded by the better investment?

Solve. Round answers to the nearest whole.

34. Suppose a city with population of 150,000 has been decreasing at a rate of 2% per year. If this rate continues, predict the population of the city in 20 years.

35. The wolf population in one geographic area is increasing at a rate of 12% per year. If the estimated population in this area is now 60 wolves, predict the number of wolves present in this area in 10 years.

CHAPTER 6 STANDARDIZED TEST

Multiple Choice. *Choose the one alternative that best completes the statement or answers the question.*

Evaluate the expression.

1. 6^2
  a. -36 **b.** 36
  c. 12 **d.** -12

2. $(-4)^3$
  a. -12 **b.** 12
  c. -64 **d.** 64

3. -6^4
  a. -1296 **b.** 1296
  c. -24 **d.** 24

4. 3^{-2}
  a. $\dfrac{1}{6}$ **b.** 9
  c. -9 **d.** $\dfrac{1}{9}$

Simplify the exponential expression. Write the result using only positive exponents.

5. $(2x^6)(-3x^7)$

    a. $6x^{13}$ **b.** $-6x^{42}$

    c. $-6x^{13}$ **d.** $6x^{42}$

6. $\dfrac{y^{13}}{y^3}$

    a. y^{16} **b.** $\dfrac{1}{y^{10}}$

    c. y^4 **d.** y^{10}

7. $\dfrac{r^{-9}}{r^{-4}}$

    a. r^5 **b.** $\dfrac{1}{r^5}$

    c. r^{13} **d.** $\dfrac{1}{r^{13}}$

Simplify the expression. Write the result using positive exponents only.

8. $\left(\dfrac{x^4 y^2}{x^5 y^{-4}}\right)^2$

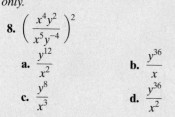

    a. $\dfrac{y^{12}}{x^2}$ **b.** $\dfrac{y^{36}}{x}$

    c. $\dfrac{y^8}{x^3}$ **d.** $\dfrac{y^{36}}{x^2}$

Simplify the exponential expression. Write the result using only positive exponents.

9. $\dfrac{5^5 x^{-1} y^2}{5^8 x^{-4} y^4}$

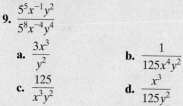

    a. $\dfrac{3x^3}{y^2}$ **b.** $\dfrac{1}{125 x^4 y^2}$

    c. $\dfrac{125}{x^3 y^2}$ **d.** $\dfrac{x^3}{125 y^2}$

Express the number in scientific notation.

10. 150,000

    a. 1.5×10^{-4} **b.** 1.5×10^{-5}

    c. 1.5×10^{5} **d.** 1.5×10^{4}

11. 0.000029316

    a. 2.9316×10^{-4} **b.** 2.9316×10^{5}

    c. 2.9316×10^{-5} **d.** 2.9316×10^{4}

Write the number in standard form.

12. 5.21×10^{-4}

    a. 0.000521   **b.** 0.00521

    c. $-521{,}000$ **d.** 0.0000521

13. 7.58×10^{7}

    a. 7,580,000   **b.** 758,000,000

    c. 75,800,000   **d.** 530.6

Simplify. Write the answer in standard form.

14. $(6.1 \times 10^{-3})(5 \times 10^{-2})$

    a. 0.0000035   **b.** 0.0035

    c. 0.00035   **d.** 0.000035

Complete the table for the polynomial and answer the question.

15. $8xy^2 - 7x^5 y^7 z + 8x^3 y - 3$

Term	Numerical Coefficient	Degree of Term
$8xy^2$		
$-7x^5 y^7 z$		
$8x^3 y$		
-3		

What is the degree of the polynomial?

a.

Term	Numerical Coefficient	Degree of Term
$8xy^2$	16	3
$-7x^5 y^7 z$	-14	13
$8x^3 y$	16	4
-3	-6	1

The degree of the polynomial is 13.

b.

Term	Numerical Coefficient	Degree of Term
$8xy^2$	-8	3
$-7x^5 y^7 z$	7	13
$8x^3 y$	-8	4
-3	3	0

The degree of the polynomial is 3.

c.

Term	Numerical Coefficient	Degree of Term
$8xy^2$	8	2
$-7x^5 y^7 z$	7	12
$8x^3 y$	8	3
-3	-3	0

The degree of the polynomial is 12.

d.

Term	Numerical Coefficient	Degree of Term
$8xy^2$	8	3
$-7x^5 y^7 z$	-7	13
$8x^3 y$	8	4
-3	-3	0

The degree of the polynomial is 13.

Simplify by combining like terms.

16. $4x^2 + 3xy - 9x^2 + 12 + 3xy$
  a. $-5x^2 + 6xy + 12$ **b.** $-5x^2 - 6xy + 12$
  c. $6x^2 + 6xy - 12$ **d.** $6x^2 + 6xy + 12$

Perform the indicated operation.

17. $(-5x^3 - 5x^2 + 9x - 7) + (-8x^3 + 9x - 7)$
  a. $-13x^3 + 18x - 14$ **b.** $-13x^3 - 5x^2 + 18x - 14$
  c. $-8x^3 + 4x^2 + 2x - 7$ **d.** $-13x^3 + 4x^2 - 7x - 7$

18. $(6x^3 - 4x^2 - 4x + 5) - (8x^3 - 8x^2 + 8x + 9)$
  a. $-2x^3 - 12x^2 + 4x + 14$ **b.** $14x^3 - 12x^2 + 4x - 4$
  c. $14x^3 - 12x^2 + 4x + 14$ **d.** $-2x^3 + 4x^2 - 12x - 4$

19. Subtract $(3x + 3)$ from the sum of $(9x^2 + 9x + 1)$ and $(x^3 - 4)$.
  a. $x^3 - 9x^2 - 6x - 6$ **b.** $x^3 + 9x^2 + 6x - 6$
  c. $-x^3 - 9x^2 - 6x + 6$ **d.** $x^3 - 9x^2 - 6x + 6$

Multiply.

20. $(9x - 1)(x^2 - 5x + 1)$
  a. $9x^3 + 46x^2 - 14x + 1$ **b.** $9x^3 - 44x^2 + 4x - 1$
  c. $9x^3 - 46x^2 + 14x - 1$ **d.** $9x^3 - 45x^2 + 9x + 1$

21. $3x^2(4x^2 + 6x + 1)$
  a. $7x^4 + 9x + 4$ **b.** $12x^4 + 18x^2 + 3$
  c. $12x^4 + 18x + 3$ **d.** $12x^4 + 18x^3 + 3x^2$

22. $(x + 1)(-2x + 12)$
  a. $-2x^2 + 10x + 12$ **b.** $-2x^2 + 8x + 12$
  c. $-2x^2 + 10x + 10$ **d.** $-2x^2 + 12x + 10$

23. $\left(11x + \dfrac{5}{6}\right)\left(11x - \dfrac{5}{6}\right)$
  a. $121x^2 - \dfrac{25}{36}$ **b.** $121x^2 - \dfrac{5}{3}$
  c. $121x^2 + \dfrac{55}{3}x - \dfrac{25}{36}$ **d.** $121x^2 - \dfrac{55}{3}x - \dfrac{25}{36}$

24. $(3x - 8)^2$
  a. $3x^2 + 64$ **b.** $9x^2 - 48x + 64$
  c. $3x^2 - 48x + 64$ **d.** $9x^2 + 64$

25. $(7x + 2)^2$
  a. $49x^2 + 28x + 4$ **b.** $49x^2 + 4$
  c. $7x^2 + 4$ **d.** $7x^2 + 28x + 4$

26. $(x^2 - 8b)(x^2 + 8b)$
  a. $x^2 - 64b^2$ **b.** $x^4 - 64b^2$
  c. $x^4 + 16x^2b + 64b^2$ **d.** $x^4 - 16x^2b + 64b^2$

Solve.

27. The height of a new building in China will be 924 feet. Neglecting air resistance, the height of an object dropped from this building at time t seconds would be given by the polynomial $-16t^2 + 924$. Find the height of the object at time $t = 3$ seconds.
  a. 780 ft   **b.** 876 ft
  c. 1068 ft   **d.** 828 ft

28. Find the area of the top of the table. Express the area as a product, then multiply and simplify.

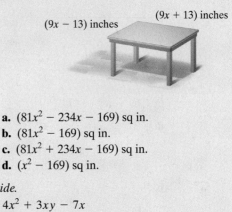

$(9x - 13)$ inches $(9x + 13)$ inches

  a. $(81x^2 - 234x - 169)$ sq in.
  b. $(81x^2 - 169)$ sq in.
  c. $(81x^2 + 234x - 169)$ sq in.
  d. $(x^2 - 169)$ sq in.

Divide.

29. $\dfrac{4x^2 + 3xy - 7x}{12xy}$
  a. $\dfrac{1}{3y} + \dfrac{1}{4} - \dfrac{7x}{12y}$ **b.** $\dfrac{x}{3y} + \dfrac{1}{4y} - \dfrac{7}{12}$
  c. $\dfrac{x}{3y} + \dfrac{1}{4} - \dfrac{7}{12y}$ **d.** $\dfrac{x}{3y} + 4 - \dfrac{7}{12y}$

30. $(x^2 + 9x + 14) \div (x + 7)$
  a. $x - 7$ **b.** $x^3 - 7$
  c. $x^2 + 2$ **d.** $x + 2$

31. $\dfrac{8x^3 + 1}{2x - 1}$
  a. $4x^2 + 2x + 1$
  b. $4x^2 + 2x + 1 + \dfrac{1}{2x - 1}$
  c. $4x^2 - 2x + 1$
  d. $4x^2 + 2x + 1 + \dfrac{2}{2x - 1}$

Graph the function.

32. Use the graph of $f(x) = 2^x$ to obtain the graph of $g(x) = 2^{x+1} + 1$.

a.

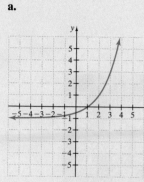

b.

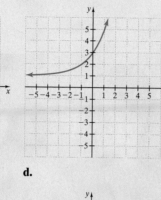

c.

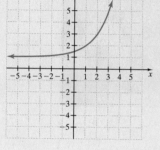

d.

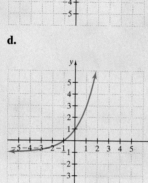

Use the compound interest formula $A = P\left(1 + \dfrac{r}{n}\right)^{nt}$ *to solve.*

33. Suppose that you have $9000 to invest. Which investment yields the greater return over 8 years: 7.5% compounded monthly or 7.6% compounded semiannually?

   a. $9000 invested at 7.6% compounded semiannually over 8 years yields the greater return.

   b. $9000 invested at 7.5% compounded monthly over 8 years yields the greater return.

   c. Both investment plans yield the same return.

34. Suppose an amount of 400 units has been decreasing at a rate of 3% per year. If this rate continues, how many units are present in 15 years? Round to the nearest whole unit.

   a. 180   **b.** 253

   c. 20   **d.** 380

35. A city with population 238,000 has been growing at a rate of 5% per year. If this rate continues, find the population of this city in 5 years. Round to the nearest whole.

   a. 238,000   **b.** 249,900

   c. 297,500   **d.** 303,755

7

Factoring Polynomials

76% of Undergraduate College Students Have Credit Cards— When Do These Students Obtain a Card?

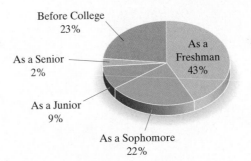

Before College 23%

As a Senior 2%

As a Junior 9%

As a Sophomore 22%

As a Freshman 43%

According to the Nellie May Corporation, 56% of final year undergraduate students carry four or more credit cards with an average balance of $2864. The circle graph above shows when students with credit cards obtained a card.

American Consumer Credit Counseling (ACCC) released the following guidelines to help protect college students from the lasting effects of credit card debt.

- Pay at least the minimum payment on all bills before the due date.
- Keep a budget. Record all income and record all outgoings for at least two months so you know where your money is going.
- Avoid borrowing money to pay off other creditors.
- Only carry as much cash as your weekly budget allows.

In this chapter, you will have the opportunity to calculate percents of students with credit cards during selected years.

7.1 THE GREATEST COMMON FACTOR AND FACTORING BY GROUPING

OBJECTIVES

1 Find the greatest common factor of a list of integers.

2 Find the greatest common factor of a list of terms.

3 Factor out the greatest common factor from a polynomial.

4 Factor a polynomial by grouping.

In the product $2 \cdot 3 = 6$, the numbers 2 and 3 are called **factors** of 6 and $2 \cdot 3$ is a **factored form** of 6. This is true of polynomials also. Since $(x + 2)(x + 3) = x^2 + 5x + 6$, then $(x + 2)$ and $(x + 3)$ are factors of $x^2 + 5x + 6$, and $(x + 2)(x + 3)$ is a factored form of the polynomial.

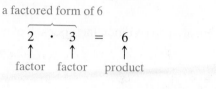

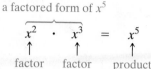

a factored form of $x^2 + 5x + 6$

$$(x + 2)(x + 3) = x^2 + 5x + 6$$

factor   factor   product

Do you see that factoring is the reverse process of multiplying?

$$x^2 + 5x + 6 = (x + 2)(x + 3)$$

factoring

multiplying

Concept Check ☑

Multiply: $2(x - 4)$

What do you think the result of factoring $2x - 8$ would be? Why?

The first step in factoring a polynomial is to see whether the terms of the polynomial have a common factor. If there is one, we can write the polynomial as a product by **factoring out** the common factor. We will usually factor out the **greatest common factor (GCF).**

OBJECTIVE 1 ▶ Finding the greatest common factor of a list of integers. The GCF of a list of integers is the largest integer that is a factor of all the integers in the list. For example, the GCF of 12 and 20 is 4 because 4 is the largest integer that is a factor of both 12 and 20. With large integers, the GCF may not be easily found by inspection. When this happens, use the following steps.

> **Finding the GCF of a List of Integers**
>
> **STEP 1.** Write each number as a product of prime numbers.
>
> **STEP 2.** Identify the common prime factors.
>
> **STEP 3.** The product of all common prime factors found in Step 2 is the greatest common factor. If there are no common prime factors, the greatest common factor is 1.

Answers to Concept Check:
$2x - 8$; The result would be $2(x - 4)$ because factoring is the reverse process of multiplying.

Recall from Section 1.3 that a prime number is a whole number other than 1, whose only factors are 1 and itself.

EXAMPLE 1 Find the GCF of each list of numbers.

a. 28 and 40   **b.** 55 and 21   **c.** 15, 18, and 66

Solution

a. Write each number as a product of primes.

$$28 = 2 \cdot 2 \cdot 7 = 2^2 \cdot 7$$
$$40 = 2 \cdot 2 \cdot 2 \cdot 5 = 2^3 \cdot 5$$

There are two common factors, each of which is 2, so the GCF is

$$\text{GCF} = 2 \cdot 2 = 4$$

b. $55 = 5 \cdot 11$
$21 = 3 \cdot 7$

There are no common prime factors; thus, the GCF is 1.

c. $15 = 3 \cdot 5$
$18 = 2 \cdot 3 \cdot 3 = 2 \cdot 3^2$
$66 = 2 \cdot 3 \cdot 11$

The only prime factor common to all three numbers is 3, so the GCF is

$$\text{GCF} = 3$$ □

PRACTICE
1 Find the GCF of each list of numbers.

a. 36 and 42   **b.** 35 and 44   **c.** 12, 16, and 40

OBJECTIVE 2 ▶ Finding the greatest common factor of a list of terms. The greatest common factor of a list of variables raised to powers is found in a similar way. For example, the GCF of x^2, x^3, and x^5 is x^2 because each term contains a factor of x^2 and no higher power of x is a factor of each term.

$$x^2 = x \cdot x$$
$$x^3 = x \cdot x \cdot x$$
$$x^5 = x \cdot x \cdot x \cdot x \cdot x$$

There are two common factors, each of which is x, so the GCF $= x \cdot x$ or x^2.

From this example, we see that **the GCF of a list of common variables raised to powers is the variable raised to the smallest exponent in the list.**

EXAMPLE 2 Find the GCF of each list of terms.

a. x^3, x^7, and x^5 **b.** y, y^4, and y^7

Solution

a. The GCF is x^3, since 3 is the smallest exponent to which x is raised.
b. The GCF is y^1 or y, since 1 is the smallest exponent on y.   □

PRACTICE
2 Find the GCF of each list of terms.

a. y^7, y^4, and y^6 **b.** x, x^4, and x^2

In general, the **greatest common factor (GCF) of a list of terms** is the product of the GCF of the numerical coefficients and the GCF of the variable factors.

EXAMPLE 3   Find the GCF of each list of terms.

a. $6x^2$, $10x^3$, and $-8x$ b. $-18y^2$, $-63y^3$, and $27y^4$ c. a^3b^2, a^5b, and a^6b^2

Solution

a. $6x^2 = 2 \cdot 3 \cdot x^2$
$10x^3 = 2 \cdot 5 \cdot x^3$
$-8x = -1 \cdot 2 \cdot 2 \cdot 2 \cdot x^1$ $\Bigg\}\rightarrow$ The GCF of x^2, x^3, and x^1 is x^1 or x.
$\text{GCF} = 2 \cdot x^1$ or $2x$

b. $-18y^2 = -1 \cdot 2 \cdot 3 \cdot 3 \cdot y^2$
$-63y^3 = -1 \cdot 3 \cdot 3 \cdot 7 \cdot y^3$ $\Bigg\}\rightarrow$ The GCF of y^2, y^3, and y^4 is y^2.
$27y^4 = 3 \cdot 3 \cdot 3 \cdot y^4$
$\text{GCF} = 3 \cdot 3 \cdot y^2$ or $9y^2$

c. The GCF of a^3, a^5, and a^6 is a^3.
   The GCF of b^2, b, and b^2 is b. Thus,
   the GCF of a^3b^2, a^5b, and a^6b^2 is a^3b.   □

> ▶ **Helpful Hint**
>
> Remember that the GCF of a list of terms contains the smallest exponent on each common variable.
>
> Smallest exponent on x.
>
> The GCF of x^5y^6, x^2y^7 and x^3y^4 is x^2y^4.
>
> Smallest exponent on y.

PRACTICE
3   Find the GCF of each list of terms.

a. $5y^4$, $15y^2$, and $-20y^3$ b. $4x^2$, x^3, and $3x^8$ c. a^4b^2, a^3b^5, and a^2b^3

OBJECTIVE 3 ▶ Factoring out the greatest common factor. The first step in factoring a polynomial is to find the GCF of its terms. Once we do so, we can write the polynomial as a product by **factoring out** the GCF.

The polynomial $8x + 14$, for example, contains two terms: $8x$ and 14. The GCF of these terms is 2. We factor out 2 from each term by writing each term as a product of 2 and the term's remaining factors.

$$8x + 14 = 2 \cdot 4x + 2 \cdot 7$$

Using the distributive property, we can write

$$8x + 14 = 2 \cdot 4x + 2 \cdot 7$$
$$= 2(4x + 7)$$

Thus, a factored form of $8x + 14$ is $2(4x + 7)$. We can check by multiplying:

$$2(4x + 7) = 2 \cdot 4x + 2 \cdot 7 = 8x + 14.$$

> ▶ **Helpful Hint**
>
> A factored form of $8x + 14$ is *not*
>
> $$2 \cdot 4x + 2 \cdot 7$$
>
> Although the *terms* have been factored (written as a product), the *polynomial $8x + 14$ has not been factored* (written as a product). A factored form of $8x + 14$ is the *product* $2(4x + 7)$.

Concept Check ☑

Which of the following is/are factored form(s) of $7t + 21$?

a. 7   b. $7 \cdot t + 7 \cdot 3$ c. $7(t + 3)$ d. $7(t + 21)$

EXAMPLE 4   Factor each polynomial by factoring out the GCF.

a. $6t + 18$ **b.** $y^5 - y^7$

Solution

a. The GCF of terms $6t$ and 18 is 6.

$$6t + 18 = 6 \cdot t + 6 \cdot 3$$
$$= 6(t + 3) \qquad \text{Apply the distributive property.}$$

Our work can be checked by multiplying 6 and $(t + 3)$.

$$6(t + 3) = 6 \cdot t + 6 \cdot 3 = 6t + 18, \text{ the original polynomial.}$$

b. The GCF of y^5 and y^7 is y^5. Thus,

$$y^5 - y^7 = y^5(1) - y^5(y^2)$$
$$= y^5(1 - y^2)$$

> ▶ **Helpful Hint**
> Don't forget the 1.

PRACTICE
4   Factor each polynomial by factoring out the GCF.

a. $4t + 12$ **b.** $y^8 + y^4$

EXAMPLE 5   Factor: $-9a^5 + 18a^2 - 3a$

Solution

$$-9a^5 + 18a^2 - 3a = (3a)(-3a^4) + (3a)(6a) + (3a)(-1)$$
$$= 3a(-3a^4 + 6a - 1)$$

> ▶ **Helpful Hint**
> Don't forget the -1.

PRACTICE
5   Factor $-8b^6 + 16b^4 - 8b^2$.

In Example 5 we could have chosen to factor out a $-3a$ instead of $3a$. If we factor out a $-3a$, we have

$$-9a^5 + 18a^2 - 3a = (-3a)(3a^4) + (-3a)(-6a) + (-3a)(1)$$
$$= -3a(3a^4 - 6a + 1)$$

> ▶ **Helpful Hint**
> Notice the changes in signs when factoring out $-3a$.

EXAMPLES   Factor.

6. $6a^4 - 12a = 6a(a^3 - 2)$

7. $\dfrac{3}{7}x^4 + \dfrac{1}{7}x^3 - \dfrac{5}{7}x^2 = \dfrac{1}{7}x^2(3x^2 + x - 5)$

8. $15p^2q^4 + 20p^3q^5 + 5p^3q^3 = 5p^2q^3(3q + 4pq^2 + p)$

PRACTICES
6–8   Factor.

6. $5x^4 - 20x$ **7.** $\dfrac{5}{9}z^5 + \dfrac{1}{9}z^4 - \dfrac{2}{9}z^3$ **8.** $8a^2b^4 - 20a^3b^3 + 12ab^3$

EXAMPLE 9 Factor: $5(x + 3) + y(x + 3)$

Solution The binomial $(x + 3)$ is the greatest common factor. Use the distributive property to factor out $(x + 3)$.

$$5(x + 3) + y(x + 3) = (x + 3)(5 + y) \qquad \square$$

PRACTICE
9 Factor $8(y - 2) + x(y - 2)$.

EXAMPLE 10 Factor: $3m^2n(a + b) - (a + b)$

Solution The greatest common factor is $(a + b)$.

$$3m^2n(a + b) - 1(a + b) = (a + b)(3m^2n - 1) \qquad \square$$

PRACTICE
10 Factor $7xy^3(p + q) - (p + q)$

OBJECTIVE 4 ▶ Factoring by grouping. Once the GCF is factored out, we can often continue to factor the polynomial, using a variety of techniques. We discuss here a technique for factoring polynomials called **grouping.**

EXAMPLE 11 Factor $xy + 2x + 3y + 6$ by grouping. Check by multiplying.

Solution The GCF of the first two terms is x, and the GCF of the last two terms is 3.

$$xy + 2x + 3y + 6 = (xy + 2x) + (3y + 6) \qquad \text{Group terms.}$$
$$= \underline{x(y + 2) + 3(y + 2)} \qquad \text{Factor out GCF from each grouping.}$$

> ▶ **Helpful Hint**
>
> Notice that this form, $x(y + 2) + 3(y + 2)$, is *not* a factored form of the original polynomial. It is a sum, not a product.

Next we factor out the common binomial factor, $(y + 2)$.

$$x(y + 2) + 3(y + 2) = (y + 2)(x + 3)$$

Now the result is a factored form because it is a product. We were able to write the polynomial as a product because of the common binomial factor, $(y + 2)$, that appeared. If this does not happen, try rearranging the terms of the original polynomial.

Check: Multiply $(y + 2)$ by $(x + 3)$.

$$(y + 2)(x + 3) = xy + 2x + 3y + 6,$$

the original polynomial.

Thus, the factored form of $xy + 2x + 3y + 6$ is the product $(y + 2)(x + 3)$. $\qquad \square$

PRACTICE
11 Factor $xy + 3y + 4x + 12$ by grouping. Check by multiplying.

You may want to try these steps when factoring by grouping.

To Factor a Four-Term Polynomial by Grouping

STEP 1. Group the terms in two groups of two terms so that each group has a common factor.

STEP 2. Factor out the GCF from each group.

STEP 3. If there is now a common binomial factor in the groups, factor it out.

STEP 4. If not, rearrange the terms and try these steps again.

EXAMPLES Factor by grouping.

12. $3x^2 + 4xy - 3x - 4y$

$= (3x^2 + 4xy) + (-3x - 4y)$

$= x(3x + 4y) - 1(3x + 4y)$ Factor each group. A -1 is factored from the second pair of terms so that there is a common factor, $(3x + 4y)$.

$= (3x + 4y)(x - 1)$ Factor out the common factor, $(3x + 4y)$.

13. $2a^2 + 5ab + 2a + 5b$

$= (2a^2 + 5ab) + (2a + 5b)$ Factor each group. An understood 1 is written before $(2a + 5b)$ to help remember that $(2a + 5b)$ is $1(2a + 5b)$.

$= a(2a + 5b) + 1(2a + 5b)$

$= (2a + 5b)(a + 1)$ Factor out the common factor, $(2a + 5b)$. □

> ▶ **Helpful Hint**
> Notice the factor of 1 is written when $(2a + 5b)$ is factored out.

PRACTICES
12–13

12. Factor $2xy + 3y^2 - 2x - 3y$ by grouping.

13. Factor $7a^3 + 5a^2 + 7a + 5$ by grouping.

EXAMPLES Factor by grouping.

14. $3xy + 2 - 3x - 2y$

Notice that the first two terms have no common factor other than 1. However, if we rearrange these terms, a grouping emerges that does lead to a common factor.

$3xy + 2 - 3x - 2y$

$= (3xy - 3x) + (-2y + 2)$

$= 3x(y - 1) - 2(y - 1)$ Factor -2 from the second group so that there is a common factor $(y - 1)$.

$= (y - 1)(3x - 2)$ Factor out the common factor, $(y - 1)$.

15. $5x - 10 + x^3 - x^2 = 5(x - 2) + x^2(x - 1)$

There is no common binomial factor that can now be factored out. No matter how we rearrange the terms, no grouping will lead to a common factor. Thus, this polynomial is not factorable by grouping. □

PRACTICES
14–15

14. Factor $4xy + 15 - 12x - 5y$ by grouping.

15. Factor $9y - 18 + y^3 - 4y^2$.

> ▶ **Helpful Hint**
>
> One more reminder: When **factoring** a polynomial, make sure the polynomial is written as a **product.** For example, it is true that
>
> $$3x^2 + 4xy - 3x - 4y = \underbrace{x(3x + 4y) - 1(3x + 4y),}_{\text{but is not a \textbf{factored form}}}$$
>
> since it is a **sum (difference),** not a **product.** A factored form of $3x^2 + 4xy - 3x - 4y$ is the product $(3x + 4y)(x - 1)$.

Factoring out a greatest common factor first makes factoring by any method easier, as we see in the next example.

EXAMPLE 16   Factor: $4ax - 4ab - 2bx + 2b^2$

Solution   First, factor out the common factor 2 from all four terms.

$$4ax - 4ab - 2bx + 2b^2$$
$$= 2(2ax - 2ab - bx + b^2) \quad \text{Factor out 2 from all four terms.}$$
$$= 2[2a(x - b) - b(x - b)] \quad \text{Factor each pair of terms. A "}-b\text{" is factored from the}$$
$$\text{second pair so that there is a common factor, } x - b.$$
$$= 2(x - b)(2a - b) \quad \text{Factor out the common binomial.} \qquad \square$$

▶ **Helpful Hint**

Throughout this chapter, we will be factoring polynomials. Even when the instructions do not so state, it is always a good idea to check your answers by multiplying.

PRACTICE 16   Factor $3xy - 3ay - 6ax + 6a^2$

VOCABULARY & READINESS CHECK

Word Bank. *Use the choices below to fill in each blank. Some choices may be used more than once and some may not be used at all.*

greatest common factor   factors   factoring   true   false   least   greatest

1. Since $5 \cdot 4 = 20$, the numbers 5 and 4 are called _____ of 20.
2. The _____ of a list of integers is the largest integer that is a factor of all the integers in the list.
3. The greatest common factor of a list of common variables raised to powers is the variable raised to the _____ exponent in the list.
4. The process of writing a polynomial as a product is called _____.
5. True or false: A factored form of $7x + 21 + xy + 3y$ is $7(x + 3) + y(x + 3)$. _____
6. True or false: A factored form of $3x^3 + 6x + x^2 + 2$ is $3x(x^2 + 2)$. _____

Write the prime factorization of the following integers.

7. 14   **8.** 15

Write the GCF of the following pairs of integers.

9. 18, 3   **10.** 7, 35   **11.** 20, 15   **12.** 6, 15

7.1 EXERCISE SET

Find the GCF for each list. See Examples 1 through 3.

1. 32, 36
2. 36, 90
3. 18, 42, 84
4. 30, 75, 135
5. 24, 14, 21
6. 15, 25, 27
7. y^2, y^4, y^7
8. x^3, x^2, x^5
9. z^7, z^9, z^{11}
10. y^8, y^{10}, y^{12}
11. $x^{10}y^2, xy^2, x^3y^3$
12. p^7q, p^8q^2, p^9q^3
13. $14x, 21$
14. $20y, 15$
15. $12y^4, 20y^3$
16. $32x^5, 18x^2$
17. $-10x^2, 15x^3$
18. $-21x^3, 14x$
19. $12x^3, -6x^4, 3x^5$
20. $15y^2, 5y^7, -20y^3$
21. $-18x^2y, 9x^3y^3, 36x^3y$
22. $7x^3y^3, -21x^2y^2, 14xy^4$
23. $20a^6b^2c^8, 50a^7b$
24. $40x^7y^2z, 64x^9y$

Factor out the GCF from each polynomial. See Examples 4 through 10.

25. $3a + 6$
26. $18a + 12$
27. $30x - 15$
28. $42x - 7$
29. $x^3 + 5x^2$
30. $y^5 + 6y^4$
31. $6y^4 + 2y^3$
32. $5x^2 + 10x^6$
33. $4x - 8y + 4$
34. $7x + 21y - 7$
35. $6x^3 - 9x^2 + 12x$
36. $12x^3 + 16x^2 - 8x$
37. $a^7b^6 - a^3b^2 + a^2b^5 - a^2b^2$
38. $x^9y^6 + x^3y^5 - x^4y^3 + x^3y^3$
39. $8x^5 + 16x^4 - 20x^3 + 12$
40. $9y^6 - 27y^4 + 18y^2 + 6$

41. $\frac{1}{3}x^4 + \frac{2}{3}x^3 - \frac{4}{3}x^5 + \frac{1}{3}x$

42. $\frac{2}{5}y^7 - \frac{4}{5}y^5 + \frac{3}{5}y^2 - \frac{2}{5}y$

43. $y(x^2 + 2) + 3(x^2 + 2)$

44. $x(y^2 + 1) - 3(y^2 + 1)$

45. $z(y + 4) - 3(y + 4)$

46. $8(x + 2) - y(x + 2)$

47. $r(z^2 - 6) + (z^2 - 6)$

48. $q(b^3 - 5) + (b^3 - 5)$

Factor a negative number or a GCF with a negative coefficient from each polynomial. See Example 5.

49. $-2x - 14$

50. $-7y - 21$

51. $-2x^5 + x^7$

52. $-5y^3 + y^6$

53. $-6a^4 + 9a^3 - 3a^2$

54. $-5m^6 + 10m^5 - 5m^3$

Factor each four-term polynomial by grouping. See Examples 11 through 16.

55. $x^3 + 2x^2 + 5x + 10$

56. $x^3 + 4x^2 + 3x + 12$

57. $5x + 15 + xy + 3y$

58. $xy + y + 2x + 2$

59. $6x^3 - 4x^2 + 15x - 10$

60. $16x^3 - 28x^2 + 12x - 21$

61. $5m^3 + 6mn + 5m^2 + 6n$

62. $8w^2 + 7wv + 8w + 7v$

63. $2y - 8 + xy - 4x$

64. $6x - 42 + xy - 7y$

65. $2x^3 - x^2 + 8x - 4$

66. $2x^3 - x^2 - 10x + 5$

67. $4x^2 - 8xy - 3x + 6y$

68. $5xy - 15x - 6y + 18$

69. $5q^2 - 4pq - 5q + 4p$

70. $6m^2 - 5mn - 6m + 5n$

71. $2x^4 + 5x^3 + 2x^2 + 5x$

72. $4y^4 + y^2 + 20y^3 + 5y$

73. $12x^2y - 42x^2 - 4y + 14$

74. $90 + 15y^2 - 18x - 3xy^2$

MIXED PRACTICE

Factor. See Examples 4 through 16.

75. $32xy - 18x^2$

76. $10xy - 15x^2$

77. $y(x + 2) - 3(x + 2)$

78. $z(y - 4) + 3(y - 4)$

79. $14x^3y + 7x^2y - 7xy$

80. $5x^3y - 15x^2y + 10xy$

81. $28x^3 - 7x^2 + 12x - 3$

82. $15x^3 + 5x^2 - 6x - 2$

83. $-40x^8y^6 - 16x^9y^5$

84. $-21x^3y - 49x^2y^2$

85. $6a^2 + 9ab^2 + 6ab + 9b^3$

86. $16x^2 + 4xy^2 + 8xy + 2y^3$

REVIEW AND PREVIEW

Multiply. See Section 6.3.

87. $(x + 2)(x + 5)$

88. $(y + 3)(y + 6)$

89. $(b + 1)(b - 4)$

90. $(x - 5)(x + 10)$

Complete a Table. *Fill in the table by finding two numbers that have the given product and sum. The first column is filled in for you.*

		91.	92.	93.	94.	95.	96.
Two Numbers	4, 7						
Their Product	28	12	20	8	16	−10	−24
Their Sum	11	8	9	−9	−10	3	−5

CONCEPT EXTENSIONS

See the Concept Checks in this section.

97. **Multiple Choice.** Which of the following is/are factored form(s) of $8a - 24$?
   a. $8 \cdot a - 24$ b. $8(a - 3)$
   c. $4(2a - 12)$ d. $8 \cdot a - 2 \cdot 12$

Decision Making. *For Exercises 98–101, decide which of the following expressions are factored.*

98. $(a + 6)(a + 2)$ 99. $(x + 5)(x + y)$

100. $5(2y + z) - b(2y + z)$ 101. $3x(a + 2b) + 2(a + 2b)$

102. Construct a binomial whose greatest common factor is $5a^3$. (*Hint:* Multiply $5a^3$ by a binomial whose terms contain no common factor other than 1. $5a^3(\square + \square)$.)

103. Construct a trinomial whose greatest common factor is $2x^2$. See the hint for Exercise 102.

104. Explain how you can tell whether a polynomial is written in factored form.

105. Construct a four-term polynomial that can be factored by grouping.

106. **Multiple Steps.** The number (in millions) of single digital downloads annually in the United States each year during 2003–2005 can be modeled by the polynomial $45x^2 + 95x$, where x is the number of years since 2003. (*Source:* Recording Industry Association of America)

   a. Find the number of single digital downloads in 2005. To do so, let $x = 2$ and evaluate $45x^2 + 95x$.

b. Use this expression to predict the number of single digital downloads in 2009.

c. Factor the polynomial $45x^2 + 95x$.

107. Multiple Steps. The number (in thousands) of students who graduated from U.S. high schools each year during 2003–2005 can be modeled by $-8x^2 + 50x + 3020$, where x is the number of years since 2003. (*Source:* National Center for Education Statistics)

   a. Find the number of students who graduated from U.S. high schools in 2005. To do so, let $x = 2$ and evaluate $-8x^2 + 50x + 3020$.

   b. Use this expression to predict the number of students who graduated from U.S. high schools in 2007.

   c. Factor the polynomial $-8x^2 + 50x + 3020$.

Write an expression for the area of each shaded region. Then write the expression as a factored polynomial.

△ **108.**

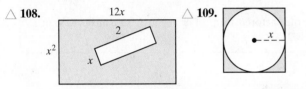

△ **109.**

Write an expression for the length of each rectangle. (**Hint:** *Factor the area binomial and recall that Area = width · length.*)

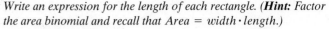

△ **110.**

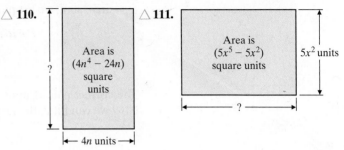

△ **111.**

Factor each polynomial by grouping.

112. $x^{2n} + 2x^n + 3x^n + 6$
   (**Hint:** Don't forget that $x^{2n} = x^n \cdot x^n$.)

113. $x^{2n} + 6x^n + 10x^n + 60$

114. $3x^{2n} + 21x^n - 5x^n - 35$

115. $12x^{2n} - 10x^n - 30x^n + 25$

7.2 FACTORING TRINOMIALS OF THE FORM $x^2 + bx + c$

OBJECTIVES

1 Factor trinomials of the form $x^2 + bx + c$.

2 Factor out the greatest common factor and then factor a trinomial of the form $x^2 + bx + c$.

OBJECTIVE 1 ▶ Factoring trinomials of the form $x^2 + bx + c$. In this section, we factor trinomials of the form $x^2 + bx + c$, such as

$$x^2 + 4x + 3, \quad x^2 - 8x + 15, \quad x^2 + 4x - 12, \quad r^2 - r - 42$$

Notice that for these trinomials, the coefficient of the squared variable is 1.

   Recall that factoring means to write as a product and that factoring and multiplying are reverse processes. Using the FOIL method of multiplying binomials, we have that

$$\overset{\text{F} \quad \text{O} \quad \text{I} \quad \text{L}}{(x + 3)(x + 1) = x^2 + 1x + 3x + 3}$$
$$= x^2 + 4x + 3$$

Thus, a factored form of $x^2 + 4x + 3$ is $(x + 3)(x + 1)$.

   Notice that the product of the first terms of the binomials is $x \cdot x = x^2$, the first term of the trinomial. Also, the product of the last two terms of the binomials is $3 \cdot 1 = 3$, the third term of the trinomial. The sum of these same terms is $3 + 1 = 4$, the coefficient of the middle term, x, of the trinomial.

The product of these numbers is 3.

$$x^2 + 4x + 3 = (x + 3)(x + 1)$$

The sum of these numbers is 4.

   Many trinomials, such as the one above, factor into two binomials. To factor $x^2 + 7x + 10$, let's assume that it factors into two binomials and begin by writing two pairs of parentheses. The first term of the trinomial is x^2, so we use x and x as the first terms of the binomial factors.

$$x^2 + 7x + 10 = (x + \square)(x + \square)$$

To determine the last term of each binomial factor, we look for two integers whose product is 10 and whose sum is 7. Since our numbers must have a positive product and a positive sum, we list pairs of positive integer factors of 10 only.

Positive Factors of 10	*Sum of Factors*
1, 10	$1 + 10 = 11$
2, 5	$2 + 5 = 7$

The correct pair of numbers is 2 and 5 because their product is 10 and their sum is 7. Now we can fill in the last terms of the binomial factors.

$$x^2 + 7x + 10 = (x + 2)(x + 5)$$

Check: To see if we have factored correctly, multiply.

$$(x + 2)(x + 5) = x^2 + 5x + 2x + 10$$
$$= x^2 + 7x + 10 \qquad \text{Combine like terms.}$$

> ▶ **Helpful Hint**
> Since multiplication is commutative, the factored form of $x^2 + 7x + 10$ can be written as either $(x + 2)(x + 5)$ or $(x + 5)(x + 2)$.

Factoring a Trinomial of the Form $x^2 + bx + c$

The factored form of $x^2 + bx + c$ is

The product of these numbers is c.

$$x^2 + bx + c = (x + \square)(x + \square)$$

The sum of these numbers is b.

EXAMPLE 1   Factor: $x^2 + 7x + 12$

Solution   We begin by writing the first terms of the binomial factors.

$$(x + \square)(x + \square)$$

Next we look for two numbers whose product is 12 and whose sum is 7. Since our numbers must have a positive product and a positive sum, we look at pairs of positive factors of 12 only.

Positive Factors of 12	*Sum of Factors*
1, 12	13
2, 6	8
3, 4	7

Correct sum, so the numbers are 3 and 4.

Thus, $x^2 + 7x + 12 = (x + 3)(x + 4)$

Check: $(x + 3)(x + 4) = x^2 + 4x + 3x + 12 = x^2 + 7x + 12.$ □

PRACTICE
1   Factor $x^2 + 5x + 6$.

EXAMPLE 2   Factor: $x^2 - 12x + 35$

Solution   Again, we begin by writing the first terms of the binomials.

$$(x + \square)(x + \square)$$

Now we look for two numbers whose product is 35 and whose sum is -12. Since our numbers must have a positive product and a negative sum, we look at pairs of negative factors of 35 only.

Negative Factors of 35	Sum of Factors
$-1, -35$	-36
$-5, -7$	-12

Correct sum, so the numbers are -5 and -7.

Thus, $x^2 - 12x + 35 = (x - 5)(x - 7)$

Check: To check, multiply $(x - 5)(x - 7)$.

PRACTICE
2   Factor $x^2 - 17x + 70$.

EXAMPLE 3   Factor: $x^2 + 4x - 12$

Solution $x^2 + 4x - 12 = (x + \square)(x + \square)$

We look for two numbers whose product is -12 and whose sum is 4. Since our numbers must have a negative product, we look at pairs of factors with opposite signs.

Factors of -12	Sum of Factors
$-1, 12$	11
$1, -12$	-11
$-2, 6$	4
$2, -6$	-4
$-3, 4$	1
$3, -4$	-1

Correct sum, so the numbers are -2 and 6.

Thus, $x^2 + 4x - 12 = (x - 2)(x + 6)$

PRACTICE
3   Factor $x^2 + 5x - 14$.

EXAMPLE 4   Factor: $r^2 - r - 42$

Solution   Because the variable in this trinomial is r, the first term of each binomial factor is r.

$$r^2 - r - 42 = (r + \square)(r + \square)$$

Now we look for two numbers whose product is -42 and whose sum is -1, the numerical coefficient of r. The numbers are 6 and -7. Therefore,

$$r^2 - r - 42 = (r + 6)(r - 7)$$

PRACTICE
4   Factor $p^2 - 2p - 63$.

EXAMPLE 5 Factor: $a^2 + 2a + 10$

Solution Look for two numbers whose product is 10 and whose sum is 2. Neither 1 and 10 nor 2 and 5 give the required sum, 2. We conclude that $a^2 + 2a + 10$ is not factorable with integers. A polynomial such as $a^2 + 2a + 10$ is called a **prime polynomial.** □

PRACTICE
5 Factor $b^2 + 5b + 1$.

EXAMPLE 6 Factor: $x^2 + 7xy + 6y^2$

Solution $$x^2 + 7xy + 6y^2 = (x + \square)(x + \square)$$

Recall that the middle term $7xy$ is the same as $7yx$. Thus, we can see that $7y$ is the "coefficient" of x. We then look for two terms whose product is $6y^2$ and whose sum is $7y$. The terms are $6y$ and $1y$ or $6y$ and y because $6y \cdot y = 6y^2$ and $6y + y = 7y$. Therefore,

$$x^2 + 7xy + 6y^2 = (x + 6y)(x + y)$$ □

PRACTICE
6 Factor $x^2 + 7xy + 12y^2$.

EXAMPLE 7 Factor: $x^4 + 5x^2 + 6$

Solution As usual, we begin by writing the first terms of the binomials. Since the greatest power of x in this polynomial is x^4, we write

$$(x^2 + \square)(x^2 + \square) \quad \text{since } x^2 \cdot x^2 = x^4$$

Now we look for two factors of 6 whose sum is 5. The numbers are 2 and 3. Thus,

$$x^4 + 5x^2 + 6 = (x^2 + 2)(x^2 + 3)$$ □

PRACTICE
7 Factor $x^4 + 13x^2 + 12$.

If the terms of a polynomial are not written in descending powers of the variable, you may want to do so before factoring.

EXAMPLE 8 Factor: $40 - 13t + t^2$

Solution First, we rearrange terms so that the trinomial is written in descending powers of t.

$$40 - 13t + t^2 = t^2 - 13t + 40$$

Next, try to factor.

$$t^2 - 13t + 40 = (t + \square)(t + \square)$$

Now we look for two factors of 40 whose sum is -13. The numbers are -8 and -5. Thus,

$$t^2 - 13t + 40 = (t - 8)(t - 5)$$ □

PRACTICE
8 Factor $48 - 14x + x^2$.

The following sign patterns may be useful when factoring trinomials.

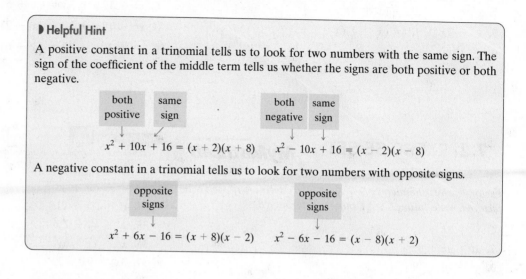

▶ **Helpful Hint**

A positive constant in a trinomial tells us to look for two numbers with the same sign. The sign of the coefficient of the middle term tells us whether the signs are both positive or both negative.

both positive   same sign   both negative   same sign

$x^2 + 10x + 16 = (x + 2)(x + 8)$ $x^2 - 10x + 16 = (x - 2)(x - 8)$

A negative constant in a trinomial tells us to look for two numbers with opposite signs.

opposite signs   opposite signs

$x^2 + 6x - 16 = (x + 8)(x - 2)$ $x^2 - 6x - 16 = (x - 8)(x + 2)$

OBJECTIVE 2 ▶ Factoring out the greatest common factor. Remember that the first step in factoring any polynomial is to factor out the greatest common factor (if there is one other than 1 or −1).

EXAMPLE 9   Factor: $3m^2 - 24m - 60$

Solution   First we factor out the greatest common factor, 3, from each term.

$$3m^2 - 24m - 60 = 3(m^2 - 8m - 20)$$

Now we factor $m^2 - 8m - 20$ by looking for two factors of −20 whose sum is −8. The factors are −10 and 2. Therefore, the complete factored form is

$$3m^2 - 24m - 60 = 3(m + 2)(m - 10) \qquad \square$$

▶ **Helpful Hint**

Remember to write the common factor 3 as part of the factored form.

PRACTICE
9   Factor $4x^2 - 24x + 36$.

EXAMPLE 10   Factor: $2x^4 - 26x^3 + 84x^2$

Solution

$$2x^4 - 26x^3 + 84x^2 = 2x^2(x^2 - 13x + 42) \qquad \text{Factor out common factor, } 2x^2.$$
$$= 2x^2(x - 6)(x - 7) \qquad \text{Factor } x^2 - 13x + 42. \qquad \square$$

PRACTICE
10   Factor $3y^4 - 18y^3 - 21y^2$.

VOCABULARY & READINESS CHECK

True or False. *Fill in each blank with "true or false."*

1. To factor $x^2 + 7x + 6$, we look for two numbers whose product is 6 and whose sum is 7. _____

2. We can write the factorization $(y + 2)(y + 4)$ also as $(y + 4)(y + 2)$. _____

3. The factorization $(4x - 12)(x - 5)$ is completely factored. _____

4. The factorization $(x + 2y)(x + y)$ may also be written as $(x + 2y)^2$. _____

Complete each factored form.

5. $x^2 + 9x + 20 = (x + 4)(x \quad)$

6. $x^2 + 12x + 35 = (x + 5)(x \quad)$

7. $x^2 - 7x + 12 = (x - 4)(x \quad)$

8. $x^2 - 13x + 22 = (x - 2)(x \quad)$

9. $x^2 + 4x + 4 = (x + 2)(x \quad)$

10. $x^2 + 10x + 24 = (x + 6)(x \quad)$

7.2 EXERCISE SET

MyMathLab · PRACTICE · WATCH · DOWNLOAD · READ · REVIEW

Factor each trinomial completely. If a polynomial can't be factored, write "prime." See Examples 1 through 8.

1. $x^2 + 7x + 6$

2. $x^2 + 6x + 8$

3. $y^2 - 10y + 9$

4. $y^2 - 12y + 11$

5. $x^2 - 6x + 9$

6. $x^2 - 10x + 25$

7. $x^2 - 3x - 18$

8. $x^2 - x - 30$

9. $x^2 + 3x - 70$

10. $x^2 + 4x - 32$

11. $x^2 + 5x + 2$

12. $x^2 - 7x + 5$

13. $x^2 + 8xy + 15y^2$

14. $x^2 + 6xy + 8y^2$

15. $a^4 - 2a^2 - 15$

16. $y^4 - 3y^2 - 70$

17. $13 + 14m + m^2$

18. $17 + 18n + n^2$

19. $10t - 24 + t^2$

20. $6q - 27 + q^2$

21. $a^2 - 10ab + 16b^2$

22. $a^2 - 9ab + 18b^2$

MIXED PRACTICE

Factor each trinomial completely. Some of these trinomials contain a greatest common factor (other than 1). Don't forget to factor out the GCF first. See Examples 1 through 10.

23. $2z^2 + 20z + 32$

24. $3x^2 + 30x + 63$

25. $2x^3 - 18x^2 + 40x$

26. $3x^3 - 12x^2 - 36x$

27. $x^2 - 3xy - 4y^2$

28. $x^2 - 4xy - 77y^2$

29. $x^2 + 15x + 36$

30. $x^2 + 19x + 60$

31. $x^2 - x - 2$

32. $x^2 - 5x - 14$

33. $r^2 - 16r + 48$

34. $r^2 - 10r + 21$

35. $x^2 + xy - 2y^2$

36. $x^2 - xy - 6y^2$

37. $3x^2 + 9x - 30$

38. $4x^2 - 4x - 48$

39. $3x^2 - 60x + 108$

40. $2x^2 - 24x + 70$

41. $x^2 - 18x - 144$

42. $x^2 + x - 42$

43. $r^2 - 3r + 6$

44. $x^2 + 4x - 10$

45. $x^2 - 8x + 15$

46. $x^2 - 9x + 14$

47. $6x^3 + 54x^2 + 120x$

48. $3x^3 + 3x^2 - 126x$

49. $4x^2y + 4xy - 12y$

50. $3x^2y - 9xy + 45y$

51. $x^2 - 4x - 21$

52. $x^2 - 4x - 32$

53. $x^2 + 7xy + 10y^2$

54. $x^2 - 3xy - 4y^2$

55. $64 + 24t + 2t^2$

56. $50 + 20t + 2t^2$

57. $x^3 - 2x^2 - 24x$

58. $x^3 - 3x^2 - 28x$

59. $2t^5 - 14t^4 + 24t^3$

60. $3x^6 + 30x^5 + 72x^4$

61. $5x^3y - 25x^2y^2 - 120xy^3$

62. $7a^3b - 35a^2b^2 + 42ab^3$

63. $162 - 45m + 3m^2$

64. $48 - 20n + 2n^2$

65. $-x^2 + 12x - 11$ (Factor out -1 first.)

66. $-x^2 + 8x - 7$ (Factor out -1 first.)

67. $\frac{1}{2}y^2 - \frac{9}{2}y - 11$ (Factor out $\frac{1}{2}$ first.)

68. $\frac{1}{3}y^2 - \frac{5}{3}y - 8$ (Factor out $\frac{1}{3}$ first.)

69. $x^3y^2 + x^2y - 20x$

70. $a^2b^3 + ab^2 - 30b$

REVIEW AND PREVIEW

Multiply. See Section 6.4.

71. $(2x + 1)(x + 5)$

72. $(3x + 2)(x + 4)$

73. $(5y - 4)(3y - 1)$

74. $(4z - 7)(7z - 1)$

75. $(a + 3b)(9a - 4b)$

76. $(y - 5x)(6y + 5x)$

CONCEPT EXTENSIONS

77. Write a polynomial that factors as $(x - 3)(x + 8)$.

78. Fill in the Blank. To factor $x^2 + 13x + 42$, think of two numbers whose _____ is 42 and whose _____ is 13.

Complete each sentence in your own words.

79. If $x^2 + bx + c$ is factorable and c is negative, then the signs of the last-term factors of the binomials are opposite because ....

80. If $x^2 + bx + c$ is factorable and c is positive, then the signs of the last-term factors of the binomials are the same because ....

Remember that perimeter means distance around. Write the perimeter of each rectangle as a simplified polynomial. Then factor the polynomial.

△ **81.**

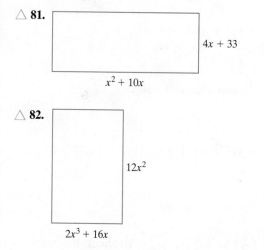

$4x + 33$

$x^2 + 10x$

△ **82.**

$12x^2$

$2x^3 + 16x$

83. An object is thrown upward from the top of an 80-foot building with an initial velocity of 64 feet per second. The height of the object after t seconds is given by $-16t^2 + 64t + 80$. Factor this polynomial.

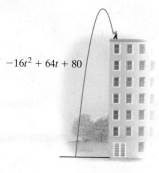

$-16t^2 + 64t + 80$

Factor each trinomial completely.

84. $x^2 + x + \dfrac{1}{4}$

85. $x^2 + \dfrac{1}{2}x + \dfrac{1}{16}$

86. $y^2(x + 1) - 2y(x + 1) - 15(x + 1)$

87. $z^2(x + 1) - 3z(x + 1) - 70(x + 1)$

Factor each trinomial. (**Hint:** *Notice that $x^{2n} + 4x^n + 3$ factors as $(x^n + 1)(x^n + 3)$.* **Remember:** $x^n \cdot x^n = x^{n+n}$ *or* x^{2n}.)

88. $x^{2n} + 5x^n + 6$

89. $x^{2n} + 8x^n - 20$

Find a positive value of c so that each trinomial is factorable.

90. $x^2 + 6x + c$

91. $t^2 + 8t + c$

92. $y^2 - 4y + c$

93. $n^2 - 16n + c$

Find a positive value of b so that each trinomial is factorable.

94. $x^2 + bx + 15$

95. $y^2 + by + 20$

96. $m^2 + bm - 27$

97. $x^2 + bx - 14$

7.3 FACTORING TRINOMIALS OF THE FORM $ax^2 + bx + c$ AND PERFECT SQUARE TRINOMIALS

OBJECTIVES

1 Factor trinomials of the form $ax^2 + bx + c$, where $a \neq 1$.

2 Factor out a GCF before factoring a trinomial of the form $ax^2 + bx + c$.

3 Factor perfect square trinomials.

OBJECTIVE 1 ▶ Factoring trinomials of the form $ax^2 + bx + c$. In this section, we factor trinomials of the form $ax^2 + bx + c$, such as

$$3x^2 + 11x + 6, \qquad 8x^2 - 22x + 5, \qquad \text{and} \qquad 2x^2 + 13x - 7$$

Notice that the coefficient of the squared variable in these trinomials is a number other than 1. We will factor these trinomials using a trial-and-check method based on our work in the last section.

To begin, let's review the relationship between the numerical coefficients of the trinomial and the numerical coefficients of its factored form. For example, since

$$(2x + 1)(x + 6) = 2x^2 + 13x + 6,$$

a factored form of $2x^2 + 13x + 6$ is $(2x + 1)(x + 6)$

Notice that $2x$ and x are factors of $2x^2$, the first term of the trinomial. Also, 6 and 1 are factors of 6, the last term of the trinomial, as shown:

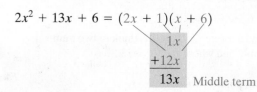

Also notice that $13x$, the middle term, is the sum of the following products:

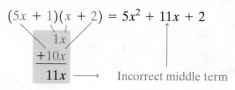

Let's use this pattern to factor $5x^2 + 7x + 2$. First, we find factors of $5x^2$. Since all numerical coefficients in this trinomial are positive, we will use factors with positive numerical coefficients only. Thus, the factors of $5x^2$ are $5x$ and x. Let's try these factors as first terms of the binomials. Thus far, we have

$$5x^2 + 7x + 2 = (5x + \square)(x + \square)$$

Next, we need to find positive factors of 2. Positive factors of 2 are 1 and 2. Now we try possible combinations of these factors as second terms of the binomials until we obtain a middle term of $7x$.

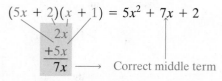

Let's try switching factors 2 and 1.

$$(5x + 2)(x + 1) = 5x^2 + 7x + 2$$

Thus the factored form of $5x^2 + 7x + 2$ is $(5x + 2)(x + 1)$. To check, we multiply $(5x + 2)$ and $(x + 1)$. The product is $5x^2 + 7x + 2$.

EXAMPLE 1 Factor: $3x^2 + 11x + 6$

Solution Since all numerical coefficients are positive, we use factors with positive numerical coefficients. We first find factors of $3x^2$.

Factors of $3x^2$: $3x^2 = 3x \cdot x$

If factorable, the trinomial will be of the form

$$3x^2 + 11x + 6 = (3x + \square)(x + \square)$$

Next we factor 6.

Factors of 6: $6 = 1 \cdot 6$, $6 = 2 \cdot 3$

Now we try combinations of factors of 6 until a middle term of $11x$ is obtained. Let's try 1 and 6 first.

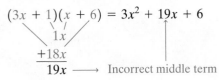

$$(3x + 1)(x + 6) = 3x^2 + 19x + 6$$

$$\begin{array}{l} 1x \\ +18x \\ \hline 19x \end{array} \longrightarrow \text{Incorrect middle term}$$

Now let's next try 6 and 1.

$$(3x + 6)(x + 1)$$

Before multiplying, notice that the terms of the factor $3x + 6$ have a common factor of 3. The terms of the original trinomial $3x^2 + 11x + 6$ have no common factor other than 1, so the terms of its factors will also contain no common factor other than 1. This means that $(3x + 6)(x + 1)$ is not a factored form.

Next let's try 2 and 3 as last terms.

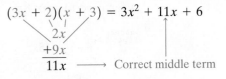

$$(3x + 2)(x + 3) = 3x^2 + 11x + 6$$

$$\begin{array}{l} 2x \\ +9x \\ \hline 11x \end{array} \longrightarrow \text{Correct middle term}$$

Thus a factored form of $3x^2 + 11x + 6$ is $(3x + 2)(x + 3)$.   □

PRACTICE

1   Factor: $2x^2 + 11x + 15$.

> **▶ Helpful Hint**
>
> If the terms of a trinomial have no common factor (other than 1), then the terms of neither of its binomial factors will contain a common factor (other than 1).

Concept Check ☑

Do the terms of $3x^2 + 29x + 18$ have a common factor? Without multiplying, decide which of the following factored forms could not be a factored form of $3x^2 + 29x + 18$.

a. $(3x + 18)(x + 1)$ **b.** $(3x + 2)(x + 9)$

c. $(3x + 6)(x + 3)$ **d.** $(3x + 9)(x + 2)$

EXAMPLE 2   Factor: $8x^2 - 22x + 5$

Solution   Factors of $8x^2$: $8x^2 = 8x \cdot x$, $8x^2 = 4x \cdot 2x$

We'll try $8x$ and x.

$$8x^2 - 22x + 5 = (8x + \square)(x + \square)$$

Since the middle term, $-22x$, has a negative numerical coefficient, we factor 5 into negative factors.

$$\text{Factors of 5:}   \quad 5 = -1 \cdot -5$$

Let's try -1 and -5.

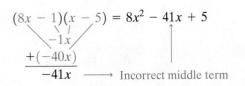

$$(8x - 1)(x - 5) = 8x^2 - 41x + 5$$

$$\begin{array}{l} -1x \\ +(-40x) \\ \hline -41x \end{array} \longrightarrow \text{Incorrect middle term}$$

Now let's try -5 and -1.

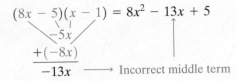

Don't give up yet! We can still try other factors of $8x^2$. Let's try $4x$ and $2x$ with -1 and -5.

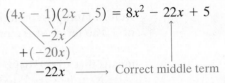

A factored form of $8x^2 - 22x + 5$ is $(4x - 1)(2x - 5)$. □

PRACTICE
2   Factor: $15x^2 - 22x + 8$.

EXAMPLE 3   Factor: $2x^2 + 13x - 7$

Solution   Factors of $2x^2$: $2x^2 = 2x \cdot x$

$$\text{Factors of } -7: \quad -7 = -1 \cdot 7, \qquad -7 = 1 \cdot -7$$

We try possible combinations of these factors:

$$(2x + 1)(x - 7) = 2x^2 - 13x - 7 \quad \text{Incorrect middle term}$$
$$(2x - 1)(x + 7) = 2x^2 + 13x - 7 \quad \text{Correct middle term}$$

A factored form of $2x^2 + 13x - 7$ is $(2x - 1)(x + 7)$. □

PRACTICE
3   Factor: $4x^2 + 11x - 3$.

EXAMPLE 4   Factor: $10x^2 - 13xy - 3y^2$

Solution   Factors of $10x^2$: $10x^2 = 10x \cdot x, \quad 10x^2 = 2x \cdot 5x$

$$\text{Factors of } -3y^2: \quad -3y^2 = -3y \cdot y, \quad -3y^2 = 3y \cdot -y$$

We try some combinations of these factors:

$$
\begin{array}{cc}
& \text{Correct} \quad\quad \text{Correct} \\
& \downarrow \quad\quad\quad\quad \downarrow
\end{array}
$$
$$(10x - 3y)(x + y) = 10x^2 + 7xy - 3y^2$$
$$(x + 3y)(10x - y) = 10x^2 + 29xy - 3y^2$$
$$(5x + 3y)(2x - y) = 10x^2 + xy - 3y^2$$
$$(2x - 3y)(5x + y) = 10x^2 - 13xy - 3y^2 \quad \text{Correct middle term}$$

A factored form of $10x^2 - 13xy - 3y^2$ is $(2x - 3y)(5x + y)$. □

PRACTICE
4   Factor: $21x^2 + 11xy - 2y^2$.

EXAMPLE 5 Factor: $3x^4 - 5x^2 - 8$

<u>**Solution**</u> Factors of $3x^4$: $3x^4 = 3x^2 \cdot x^2$
Factors of -8: $-8 = -2 \cdot 4, 2 \cdot -4, -1 \cdot 8, 1 \cdot -8$

Try combinations of these factors:

$$
\begin{array}{ccc}
 & \text{Correct} & \text{Correct} \\
 & \downarrow & \downarrow \\
(3x^2 - 2)(x^2 + 4) & = & 3x^4 + 10x^2 - 8 \\
(3x^2 + 4)(x^2 - 2) & = & 3x^4 - 2x^2 - 8 \\
(3x^2 + 8)(x^2 - 1) & = & 3x^4 + 5x^2 - 8 \\
(3x^2 - 8)(x^2 + 1) & = & 3x^4 - 5x^2 - 8
\end{array}
$$

Incorrect sign on middle term, so switch signs in binomial factors. Correct middle term.

A factored form of $3x^4 - 5x^2 - 8$ is $(3x^2 - 8)(x^2 + 1)$. □

PRACTICE

5 Factor: $2x^4 - 5x^2 - 7$.

> **Helpful Hint**
>
> Study the last two lines of Example 5. If a factoring attempt gives you a middle term whose numerical coefficient is the opposite of the desired numerical coefficient, try switching the signs of the last terms in the binomials.
>
> Switched signs
> $(3x^2 + 8)(x^2 - 1) = 3x^4 + 5x^2 - 8$ Middle term: $+5x$
> $(3x^2 - 8)(x^2 + 1) = 3x^4 - 5x^2 - 8$ Middle term: $-5x$

OBJECTIVE 2 ▶ Factoring out the greatest common factor. Don't forget that the first step in factoring any polynomial is to look for a common factor to factor out.

EXAMPLE 6 Factor: $24x^4 + 40x^3 + 6x^2$

<u>**Solution**</u> Notice that all three terms have a common factor of $2x^2$. Thus we factor out $2x^2$ first.

$$24x^4 + 40x^3 + 6x^2 = 2x^2(12x^2 + 20x + 3)$$

Next we factor $12x^2 + 20x + 3$.

Factors of $12x^2$: $12x^2 = 4x \cdot 3x$, $12x^2 = 12x \cdot x$, $12x^2 = 6x \cdot 2x$

Since all terms in the trinomial have positive numerical coefficients, we factor 3 using positive factors only.

Factors of 3: $3 = 1 \cdot 3$

We try some combinations of the factors.

$$
\begin{array}{l}
2x^2(4x + 3)(3x + 1) = 2x^2(12x^2 + 13x + 3) \\
2x^2(12x + 1)(x + 3) = 2x^2(12x^2 + 37x + 3) \\
2x^2(2x + 3)(6x + 1) = 2x^2(12x^2 + 20x + 3)
\end{array}
$$

Correct middle term

A factored form of $24x^4 + 40x^3 + 6x^2$ is $2x^2(2x + 3)(6x + 1)$. □

> **Helpful Hint**
>
> Don't forget to include the common factor in the factored form.

PRACTICE

6 Factor: $3x^3 + 17x^2 + 10x$

When the term containing the squared variable has a negative coefficient, you may want to first factor out a common factor of -1.

EXAMPLE 7 Factor: $-6x^2 - 13x + 5$

Solution We begin by factoring out a common factor of -1.

$$-6x^2 - 13x + 5 = -1(6x^2 + 13x - 5) \quad \text{Factor out } -1.$$
$$= -1(3x - 1)(2x + 5) \quad \text{Factor } 6x^2 + 13x - 5. \quad \square$$

PRACTICE
7 Factor: $-8x^2 + 2x + 3$

OBJECTIVE 3 ▶ Factoring perfect square trinomials. A trinomial that is the square of a binomial is called a **perfect square trinomial.** For example,

$$(x + 3)^2 = (x + 3)(x + 3)$$
$$= x^2 + 6x + 9$$

Thus $x^2 + 6x + 9$ is a perfect square trinomial.

In Chapter 6, we discovered special product formulas for squaring binomials.

$$(a + b)^2 = a^2 + 2ab + b^2 \quad \text{and} \quad (a - b)^2 = a^2 - 2ab + b^2$$

Because multiplication and factoring are reverse processes, we can now use these special products to help us factor perfect square trinomials. If we reverse these equations, we have the following.

Factoring Perfect Square Trinomials

$$a^2 + 2ab + b^2 = (a + b)^2$$
$$a^2 - 2ab + b^2 = (a - b)^2$$

▶ **Helpful Hint**

Notice that for both given forms of a perfect square trinomial, the last term is positive. This is because the last term is a square.

To use these equations to help us factor, we must first be able to recognize a perfect square trinomial. A trinomial is a perfect square when

1. two terms, a^2 and b^2, are squares and
2. another term is $2 \cdot a \cdot b$ or $-2 \cdot a \cdot b$. That is, this term is twice the product of a and b, or its opposite.

When a trinomial fits this description, its factored form is $(a + b)^2$.

EXAMPLE 8 Factor: $x^2 + 12x + 36$

Solution First, is this a perfect square trinomial?

$$x^2 + 12x + 36$$

1. $x^2 = (x)^2$ and $36 = 6^2$.
2. Is $2 \cdot x \cdot 6$ the middle term? Yes, $2 \cdot x \cdot 6 = 12x$.

Thus, $x^2 + 12x + 36$ factors as $(x + 6)^2$. $\quad \square$

PRACTICE
8 Factor: $x^2 + 14x + 49$

EXAMPLE 9   Factor: $25x^2 + 25xy + 4y^2$

Solution   Is this a perfect square trinomial?

$$25x^2 + 25xy + 4y^2$$

1. $25x^2 = (5x)^2$ and $4y^2 = (2y)^2$.

2. Is $2 \cdot 5x \cdot 2y$ the middle term? **No**, $2 \cdot 5x \cdot 2y = 20xy$, **not** $25xy$.

Therefore, $25x^2 + 25xy + 4y^2$ is not a perfect square trinomial. It is factorable, though. Using earlier techniques, we find that $25x^2 + 25xy + 4y^2$ factors as $(5x + 4y)(5x + y)$.

> **▶ Helpful Hint**
> A perfect square trinomial can also be factored by other methods.

PRACTICE
9   Factor $4x^2 + 20xy + 9y^2$.

EXAMPLE 10   Factor: $4m^4 - 4m^2 + 1$

Solution   Is this a perfect square trinomial?

$$4m^4 - 4m^2 + 1$$

1. $4m^4 = (2m^2)^2$ and $1 = 1^2$.

2. Is $2 \cdot 2m^2 \cdot 1$ the middle term? Yes, $2 \cdot 2m^2 \cdot 1 = 4m^2$, the opposite of the middle term.

Thus, $4m^4 - 4m^2 + 1$ factors as $(2m^2 - 1)^2$.

PRACTICE
10   Factor $36n^4 - 12n^2 + 1$.

EXAMPLE 11   Factor: $162x^3 - 144x^2 + 32x$

Solution   Don't forget to first look for a common factor. There is a greatest common factor of $2x$ in this trinomial.

$$\begin{aligned}
162x^3 - 144x^2 + 32x &= 2x(81x^2 - 72x + 16) \\
&= 2x[(9x)^2 - 2 \cdot 9x \cdot 4 + 4^2] \\
&= 2x(9x - 4)^2
\end{aligned}$$

PRACTICE
11   Factor $12x^3 - 84x^2 + 147x$.

VOCABULARY & READINESS CHECK

Word Bank. *Use the choices below to fill in each blank. Some choices will be used more than once and some not used at all.*

$5y^2$	$(x + 5y)^2$	true	perfect square trinomial
$(5y)^2$	$(x - 5y)^2$	false	perfect square binomial

1. A(n) _____ is a trinomial that is the square of a binomial.

2. The term $25y^2$ written as a square is _____.

3. The expression $x^2 + 10xy + 25y^2$ is called a(n)_____.

4. The factorization $(x + 5y)(x + 5y)$ may also be written as _____.

True or False. *Answer 5 and 6 with true or false.*

5. The factorization $(x - 5y)(x + 5y)$ may also be written as $(x - 5y)^2$. _____

6. The greatest common factor of $10x^3 - 45x^2 + 20x$ is $5x$. _____

Write each number or term as a square. For example, 16 written as a square is 4^2.

7. 64   **8.** 9   **9.** $121a^2$ **10.** $81b^2$ **11.** $36p^4$ **12.** $4q^4$

7.3 | EXERCISE SET

PRACTICE   WATCH   DOWNLOAD   READ   REVIEW

Complete each factored form. See Examples 1 through 5, and 8 through 10.

1. $5x^2 + 22x + 8 = (5x + 2)(\quad)$

2. $2y^2 + 27y + 25 = (2y + 25)(\quad)$

3. $50x^2 + 15x - 2 = (5x + 2)(\quad)$

4. $6y^2 + 11y - 10 = (2y + 5)(\quad)$

5. $25x^2 - 20x + 4 = (5x - 2)(\quad)$

6. $4y^2 - 20y + 25 = (2y - 5)(\quad)$

Factor completely. See Examples 1 through 5.

7. $2x^2 + 13x + 15$

8. $3x^2 + 8x + 4$

9. $8y^2 - 17y + 9$

10. $21x^2 - 31x + 10$

11. $2x^2 - 9x - 5$

12. $36r^2 - 5r - 24$

13. $20r^2 + 27r - 8$

14. $3x^2 + 20x - 63$

15. $10x^2 + 31x + 3$

16. $12x^2 + 17x + 5$

17. $2m^2 + 17m + 10$

18. $3n^2 + 20n + 5$

19. $6x^2 - 13xy + 5y^2$

20. $8x^2 - 14xy + 3y^2$

21. $15m^2 - 16m - 15$

22. $25n^2 - 5n - 6$

Factor completely. See Examples 1 through 7.

23. $12x^3 + 11x^2 + 2x$

24. $8a^3 + 14a^2 + 3a$

25. $21b^2 - 48b - 45$

26. $12x^2 - 14x - 10$

27. $7z + 12z^2 - 12$

28. $16t + 15t^2 - 15$

29. $6x^2y^2 - 2xy^2 - 60y^2$

30. $8x^2y + 34xy - 84y$

31. $4x^2 - 8x - 21$

32. $6x^2 - 11x - 10$

33. $-x^2 + 2x + 24$

34. $-x^2 + 4x + 21$

35. $4x^3 - 9x^2 - 9x$

36. $6x^3 - 31x^2 + 5x$

37. $24x^2 - 58x + 9$

38. $36x^2 + 55x - 14$

Factor each perfect square trinomial completely. See Examples 8 through 11.

39. $x^2 + 22x + 121$

40. $x^2 + 18x + 81$

41. $x^2 - 16x + 64$

42. $x^2 - 12x + 36$

43. $16a^2 - 24a + 9$

44. $25x^2 - 20x + 4$

45. $x^4 + 4x^2 + 4$

46. $m^4 + 10m^2 + 25$

47. $2n^2 - 28n + 98$

48. $3y^2 - 6y + 3$

49. $16y^2 + 40y + 25$

50. $9y^2 + 48y + 64$

MIXED PRACTICE

Factor each trinomial completely. See Examples 1 through 11 and Section 7.2.

51. $2x^2 - 7x - 99$

52. $2x^2 + 7x - 72$

53. $24x^2 + 41x + 12$

54. $24x^2 - 49x + 15$

55. $3a^2 + 10ab + 3b^2$

56. $2a^2 + 11ab + 5b^2$

57. $-9x + 20 + x^2$

58. $-7x + 12 + x^2$

59. $p^2 + 12pq + 36q^2$

60. $m^2 + 20mn + 100n^2$

61. $x^2y^2 - 10xy + 25$

62. $x^2y^2 - 14xy + 49$

63. $40a^2b + 9ab - 9b$

64. $24y^2x + 7yx - 5x$

65. $30x^3 + 38x^2 + 12x$

66. $6x^3 - 28x^2 + 16x$

67. $6y^3 - 8y^2 - 30y$

68. $12x^3 - 34x^2 + 24x$

69. $10x^4 + 25x^3y - 15x^2y^2$

70. $42x^4 - 99x^3y - 15x^2y^2$

71. $-14x^2 + 39x - 10$

72. $-15x^2 + 26x - 8$

73. $16p^4 - 40p^3 + 25p^2$

74. $9q^4 - 42q^3 + 49q^2$

75. $x + 3x^2 - 2$

76. $y + 8y^2 - 9$

77. $8x^2 + 6xy - 27y^2$

78. $54a^2 + 39ab - 8b^2$

79. $1 + 6x^2 + x^4$

80. $1 + 16x^2 + x^4$

81. $9x^2 - 24xy + 16y^2$

82. $25x^2 - 60xy + 36y^2$

83. $18x^2 - 9x - 14$

84. $42a^2 - 43a + 6$

85. $-27t + 7t^2 - 4$

86. $-3t + 4t^2 - 7$

87. $49p^2 - 7p - 2$

88. $3r^2 + 10r - 8$

89. $m^3 + 18m^2 + 81m$

90. $y^3 + 12y^2 + 36y$

91. $5x^2y^2 + 20xy + 1$

92. $3a^2b^2 + 12ab + 1$

93. $6a^5 + 37a^3b^2 + 6ab^4$

94. $5m^5 + 26m^3h^2 + 5mh^4$

REVIEW AND PREVIEW

Multiply the following. See Section 6.4.

95. $(x - 2)(x + 2)$

96. $(y^2 + 3)(y^2 - 3)$

97. $(a + 3)(a^2 - 3a + 9)$

98. $(z - 2)(z^2 + 2z + 4)$

Read a Graph. *As of 2006, approximately 80% of U.S. households have access to the Internet. The following graph shows the percent of households having Internet access grouped according to household income. See Section 3.1.*

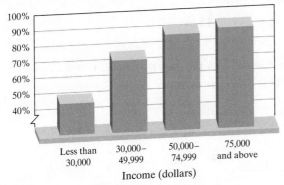

Income (dollars)

Source: Pew Internet Research

99. Which range of household income corresponds to the highest percent of households having access to the Internet?

100. Which range of household income corresponds to the greatest increase in percent of households having access to the Internet?

101. Describe any trend you see.

102. Why don't the percents shown in the graph add to 100%?

CONCEPT EXTENSIONS

See the Concept Check in this section.

103. Do the terms of $4x^2 + 19x + 12$ have a common factor (other than 1)?

104. Decision Making. Without multiplying, decide which of the following factored forms is not a factored form of $4x^2 + 19x + 12$.

  a. $(2x + 4)(2x + 3)$ **b.** $(4x + 4)(x + 3)$

  c. $(4x + 3)(x + 4)$ **d.** $(2x + 2)(2x + 6)$

105. Describe a perfect square trinomial.

106. Write the perfect square trinomial that factors as $(x + 3y)^2$.

Write the perimeter of each figure as a simplified polynomial. Then factor the polynomial.

107.

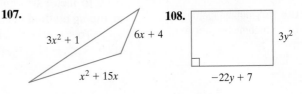

$3x^2 + 1$ $6x + 4$

$x^2 + 15x$

108.

$3y^2$

$-22y + 7$

Factor each trinomial completely.

109. $4x^2 + 2x + \dfrac{1}{4}$

110. $27x^2 + 2x - \dfrac{1}{9}$

111. $4x^2(y - 1)^2 + 10x(y - 1)^2 + 25(y - 1)^2$

112. $3x^2(a + 3)^3 - 10x(a + 3)^3 + 25(a + 3)^3$

113. Fill in the Blank. Fill in the blank so that $x^2 + $ _____ $x + 16$ is a perfect square trinomial.

114. Fill in the Blank. Fill in the blank so that $9x^2 + $ _____ $x + 25$ is a perfect square trinomial.

The area of the largest square in the figure is $(a + b)^2$. Use this figure to answer Exercises 115 and 116.

         a b

a

b

△ **115.** Write the area of the largest square as the sum of the areas of the smaller squares and rectangles.

△ **116.** What factoring formula from this section is visually represented by this square?

Find a positive value of b so that each trinomial is factorable.

117. $3x^2 + bx - 5$ **118.** $2y^2 + by + 3$

Find a positive value of c so that each trinomial is factorable.

119. $5x^2 + 7x + c$ **120.** $11y^2 - 40y + c$

Factor completely. Don't forget to first factor out the greatest common factor.

121. $-12x^3y^2 + 3x^2y^2 + 15xy^2$

122. $-12r^3x^2 + 38r^2x^2 + 14rx^2$

123. $4x^2(y - 1)^2 + 20x(y - 1)^2 + 25(y - 1)^2$

124. $3x^2(a + 3)^3 - 28x(a + 3)^3 + 25(a + 3)^3$

Factor.

125. $3x^{2n} + 17x^n + 10$

126. $2x^{2n} + 5x^n - 12$

127. In your own words, describe the steps you will use to factor a trinomial.

7.4 FACTORING TRINOMIALS OF THE FORM $ax^2 + bx + c$ BY GROUPING

OBJECTIVE 1 ▶ Using the grouping method. There is an alternative method that can be used to factor trinomials of the form $ax^2 + bx + c, a \neq 1$. This method is called the **grouping method** because it uses factoring by grouping as we learned in Section 7.1.

To see how this method works, recall from Section 7.1 that to factor a trinomial such as $x^2 + 11x + 30$, we find two numbers such that

$$\text{Product is 30}$$
$$\downarrow$$
$$x^2 + 11x + 30$$
$$\downarrow$$
$$\text{Sum is 11.}$$

To factor a trinomial such as $2x^2 + 11x + 12$ by grouping, we use an extension of the method in Section 7.1. Here we look for two numbers such that

$$\text{Product is } 2 \cdot 12 = 24$$
$$\downarrow$$
$$2x^2 + 11x + 12$$
$$\downarrow$$
$$\text{Sum is 11.}$$

This time, we use the two numbers to write

$$2x^2 + 11x + 12 \text{ as}$$
$$= 2x^2 + \Box x + \Box x + 12$$

Then we factor by grouping. Since we want a positive product, 24, and a positive sum, 11, we consider pairs of positive factors of 24 only.

Factors of 24	Sum of Factors	
1, 24	25	
2, 12	14	
3, 8	11	Correct sum

The factors are 3 and 8. Now we use these factors to write the middle term $11x$ as $3x + 8x$ (or $8x + 3x$). We replace $11x$ with $3x + 8x$ in the original trinomial and then we can factor by grouping.

$$
\begin{aligned}
2x^2 + 11x + 12 &= 2x^2 + 3x + 8x + 12 \\
&= (2x^2 + 3x) + (8x + 12) \quad \text{Group the terms.} \\
&= x(2x + 3) + 4(2x + 3) \quad \text{Factor each group.} \\
&= (2x + 3)(x + 4) \quad \text{Factor out } (2x + 3).
\end{aligned}
$$

In general, we have the following procedure.

To Factor Trinomials by Grouping

STEP 1. Factor out a greatest common factor, if there is one other than 1.

STEP 2. For the resulting trinomial $ax^2 + bx + c$, find two numbers whose product is $a \cdot c$ and whose sum is b.

STEP 3. Write the middle term, bx, using the factors found in Step 2.

STEP 4. Factor by grouping.

EXAMPLE 1   Factor $3x^2 + 31x + 10$ by grouping.

Solution

STEP 1. The terms of this trinomial contain no greatest common factor other than 1 (or −1).

STEP 2. In $3x^2 + 31x + 10$, $a = 3$, $b = 31$, and $c = 10$.

Let's find two numbers whose product is $a \cdot c$ or $3(10) = 30$ and whose sum is b or 31. The numbers are 1 and 30.

Factors of 30	Sum of factors
5, 6	11
3, 10	13
2, 15	17
1, 30	31 Correct sum

STEP 3. Write $31x$ as $1x + 30x$ so that $3x^2 + 31x + 10 = 3x^2 + 1x + 30x + 10$.

STEP 4. Factor by grouping.

$$3x^2 + 1x + 30x + 10 = x(3x + 1) + 10(3x + 1)$$
$$= (3x + 1)(x + 10) \qquad \square$$

PRACTICE
1   Factor $5x^2 + 61x + 12$ by grouping.

EXAMPLE 2   Factor $8x^2 - 14x + 5$ by grouping.

Solution

STEP 1. The terms of this trinomial contain no greatest common factor other than 1.

STEP 2. This trinomial is of the form $ax^2 + bx + c$ with $a = 8$, $b = -14$, and $c = 5$. Find two numbers whose product is $a \cdot c$ or $8 \cdot 5 = 40$, and whose sum is b or −14.

The numbers are −4 and −10.

STEP 3. Write $-14x$ as $-4x - 10x$ so that

$$8x^2 - 14x + 5 = 8x^2 - 4x - 10x + 5$$

Factors of 40	Sum of Factors
−40, −1	−41
−20, −2	−22
−10, −4	−14

Correct sum

STEP 4. Factor by grouping.

$$8x^2 - 4x - 10x + 5 = 4x(2x - 1) - 5(2x - 1)$$
$$= (2x - 1)(4x - 5) \qquad \square$$

PRACTICE
2   Factor $12x^2 - 19x + 5$ by grouping.

EXAMPLE 3   Factor $6x^2 - 2x - 20$ by grouping.

Solution

STEP 1. First factor out the greatest common factor, 2.

$$6x^2 - 2x - 20 = 2(3x^2 - x - 10)$$

STEP 2. Next notice that $a = 3$, $b = -1$, and $c = -10$ in the resulting trinomial. Find two numbers whose product is $a \cdot c$ or $3(-10) = -30$ and whose sum is b, −1. The numbers are −6 and 5.

STEP 3. $3x^2 - x - 10 = 3x^2 - 6x + 5x - 10$

STEP 4. $3x^2 - 6x + 5x - 10 = 3x(x - 2) + 5(x - 2)$

$= (x - 2)(3x + 5)$

The factored form of $6x^2 - 2x - 20 = 2(x - 2)(3x + 5)$.

⌐Don't forget to include the common factor of 2.

□

PRACTICE
3   Factor $30x^2 - 14x - 4$ by grouping.

EXAMPLE 4   Factor $18y^4 + 21y^3 - 60y^2$ by grouping.

Solution

STEP 1. First factor out the greatest common factor, $3y^2$.

$$18y^4 + 21y^3 - 60y^2 = 3y^2(6y^2 + 7y - 20)$$

STEP 2. Notice that $a = 6, b = 7$, and $c = -20$ in the resulting trinomial. Find two numbers whose product is $a \cdot c$ or $6(-20) = -120$ and whose sum is 7. It may help to factor -120 as a product of primes and -1.

$$-120 = 2 \cdot 2 \cdot 2 \cdot 3 \cdot 5 \cdot (-1)$$

Then choose pairings of factors until you have two pairings whose sum is 7.

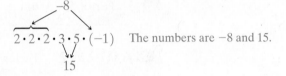

$2 \cdot 2 \cdot 2 \cdot 3 \cdot 5 \cdot (-1)$ The numbers are -8 and 15.

STEP 3. $6y^2 + 7y - 20 = 6y^2 - 8y + 15y - 20$

STEP 4. $6y^2 - 8y + 15y - 20 = 2y(3y - 4) + 5(3y - 4)$

$= (3y - 4)(2y + 5)$

The factored form of $18y^4 + 21y^3 - 60y^2$ is $3y^2(3y - 4)(2y + 5)$

⌐Don't forget to include the common factor of $3y^2$.

□

PRACTICE
4   Factor $40m^4 + 5m^3 - 35m^2$ by grouping.

EXAMPLE 5   Factor $4x^2 + 20x + 25$ by grouping.

Solution

STEP 1. The terms of this trinomial contain no greatest common factor other than 1 (or -1).

STEP 2. In $4x^2 + 20x + 25$, $a = 4, b = 20$, and $c = 25$. Find two numbers whose product is $a \cdot c$ or $4 \cdot 25 = 100$ and whose sum is 20. The numbers are 10 and 10.

STEP 3. Write $20x$ as $10x + 10x$ so that

$$4x^2 + 20x + 25 = 4x^2 + 10x + 10x + 25$$

STEP 4. Factor by grouping.

$$4x^2 + 10x + 10x + 25 = 2x(2x + 5) + 5(2x + 5)$$

$$= (2x + 5)(2x + 5)$$

The factored form of $4x^2 + 20x + 25$ is $(2x + 5)(2x + 5)$ or $(2x + 5)^2$ □

PRACTICE
5 Factor $16x^2 + 24x + 9$ by grouping.

A trinomial that is the square of a binomial, such as the trinomial in Example 5, is called a **perfect square trinomial.** From Chapter 6, there are special product formulas we can use to help us recognize and factor these trinomials. To study these formulas further, see Section 7.3, Objective 3. **Remember:** A perfect square trinomial, such as the one in Example 5, may be factored by special product formulas or by other methods of factoring trinomials, such as by grouping.

7.4 | EXERCISE SET

MyMathLab® PRACTICE WATCH DOWNLOAD READ REVIEW

Factor each polynomial by grouping. Notice that Step 3 has already been done in these exercises. See Examples 1 through 5.

1. $x^2 + 3x + 2x + 6$

2. $x^2 + 5x + 3x + 15$

3. $y^2 + 8y - 2y - 16$

4. $z^2 + 10z - 7z - 70$

5. $8x^2 - 5x - 24x + 15$

6. $4x^2 - 9x - 32x + 72$

7. $5x^4 - 3x^2 + 25x^2 - 15$

8. $2y^4 - 10y^2 + 7y^2 - 35$

MIXED PRACTICE

Factor each trinomial by grouping. Exercises 9–12 are broken into parts to help you get started. See Examples 1 through 5.

9. Multiple Steps. $6x^2 + 11x + 3$

  a. Find two numbers whose product is $6 \cdot 3 = 18$ and whose sum is 11.

  b. Write $11x$ using the factors from part (a).

  c. Factor by grouping.

10. Multiple Steps. $8x^2 + 14x + 3$

  a. Find two numbers whose product is $8 \cdot 3 = 24$ and whose sum is 14.

  b. Write $14x$ using the factors from part (a).

  c. Factor by grouping.

11. Multiple Steps. $15x^2 - 23x + 4$

  a. Find two numbers whose product is $15 \cdot 4 = 60$ and whose sum is -23.

  b. Write $-23x$ using the factors from part (a).

  c. Factor by grouping.

12. Multiple Steps. $6x^2 - 13x + 5$

  a. Find two numbers whose product is $6 \cdot 5 = 30$ and whose sum is -13.

  b. Write $-13x$ using the factors from part (a).

  c. Factor by grouping.

13. $21y^2 + 17y + 2$

14. $15x^2 + 11x + 2$

15. $7x^2 - 4x - 11$

16. $8x^2 - x - 9$

17. $10x^2 - 9x + 2$

18. $30x^2 - 23x + 3$

19. $2x^2 - 7x + 5$

20. $2x^2 - 7x + 3$

21. $12x + 4x^2 + 9$

22. $20x + 25x^2 + 4$

23. $4x^2 - 8x - 21$

24. $6x^2 - 11x - 10$

25. $10x^2 - 23x + 12$

26. $21x^2 - 13x + 2$

27. $2x^3 + 13x^2 + 15x$

28. $3x^3 + 8x^2 + 4x$

29. $16y^2 - 34y + 18$

30. $4y^2 - 2y - 12$

31. $-13x + 6 + 6x^2$

32. $-25x + 12 + 12x^2$

33. $54a^2 - 9a - 30$

34. $30a^2 + 38a - 20$

35. $20a^3 + 37a^2 + 8a$

36. $10a^3 + 17a^2 + 3a$

37. $12x^3 - 27x^2 - 27x$

38. $30x^3 - 155x^2 + 25x$

39. $3x^2y + 4xy^2 + y^3$

40. $6r^2t + 7rt^2 + t^3$

41. $20z^2 + 7z + 1$

42. $36z^2 + 6z + 1$

43. $5x^2 + 50xy + 125y^2$

44. $3x^2 + 42xy + 147y^2$

45. $24a^2 - 6ab - 30b^2$

46. $30a^2 + 5ab - 25b^2$

47. $15p^4 + 31p^3q + 2p^2q^2$

48. $20s^4 + 61s^3t + 3s^2t^2$

49. $162a^4 - 72a^2 + 8$

50. $32n^4 - 112n^2 + 98$

51. $35 + 12x + x^2$

52. $33 + 14x + x^2$

53. $6 - 11x + 5x^2$

54. $5 - 12x + 7x^2$

REVIEW AND PREVIEW

Multiply. See Sections 6.3 and 6.4.

55. $(x - 2)(x + 2)$

56. $(y - 5)(y + 5)$

57. $(y + 4)(y + 4)$

58. $(x + 7)(x + 7)$

59. $(9z + 5)(9z - 5)$

60. $(8y + 9)(8y - 9)$

61. $(x - 3)(x^2 + 3x + 9)$

62. $(2z - 1)(4z^2 + 2z + 1)$

CONCEPT EXTENSIONS

Write the perimeter of each figure as a simplified polynomial. Then factor the polynomial.

63.

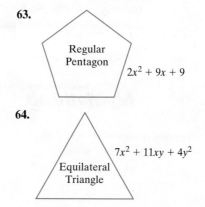

Regular Pentagon $2x^2 + 9x + 9$

64.

Equilateral Triangle $7x^2 + 11xy + 4y^2$

Factor each polynomial by grouping.

65. $x^{2n} + 2x^n + 3x^n + 6$

(**Hint:** Don't forget that $x^{2n} = x^n \cdot x^n$.)

66. $x^{2n} + 6x^n + 10x^n + 60$

67. $3x^{2n} + 16x^n - 35$

68. $12x^{2n} - 40x^n + 25$

69. In your own words, explain how to factor a trinomial by grouping.

7.5 FACTORING BINOMIALS

OBJECTIVES

1 Factor the difference of two squares.

2 Factor the sum or difference of two cubes.

OBJECTIVE 1 ▶ Factoring the difference of two squares. When learning to multiply binomials in Chapter 6, we studied a special product, the product of the sum and difference of two terms, a and b:

$$(a + b)(a - b) = a^2 - b^2$$

For example, the product of $x + 3$ and $x - 3$ is

$$(x + 3)(x - 3) = x^2 - 9$$

The binomial $x^2 - 9$ is called a **difference of squares.** In this section, we use the pattern for the product of a sum and difference to factor the binomial difference of squares.

Factoring the Difference of Two Squares
$$a^2 - b^2 = (a + b)(a - b)$$

▶ Helpful Hint

Since multiplication is commutative, remember that the order of factors does not matter. In other words,

$$a^2 - b^2 = (a + b)(a - b) \text{ or } (a - b)(a + b)$$

EXAMPLE 1   Factor: $x^2 - 25$

Solution $x^2 - 25$ is the difference of two squares since $x^2 - 25 = x^2 - 5^2$. Therefore,

$$x^2 - 25 = x^2 - 5^2 = (x + 5)(x - 5)$$

Multiply to check.   □

PRACTICE
1   Factor $x^2 - 81$.

EXAMPLE 2   Factor each difference of squares.

a. $4x^2 - 1$ **b.** $25a^2 - 9b^2$ **c.** $y^2 - \dfrac{4}{9}$

Solution

a. $4x^2 - 1 = (2x)^2 - 1^2 = (2x + 1)(2x - 1)$
b. $25a^2 - 9b^2 = (5a)^2 - (3b)^2 = (5a + 3b)(5a - 3b)$

c. $y^2 - \dfrac{4}{9} = y^2 - \left(\dfrac{2}{3}\right)^2 = \left(y + \dfrac{2}{3}\right)\left(y - \dfrac{2}{3}\right)$ □

PRACTICE
2   Factor each difference of squares.

a. $9x^2 - 1$ **b.** $36a^2 - 49b^2$ **c.** $p^2 - \dfrac{25}{36}$

EXAMPLE 3   Factor: $x^4 - y^6$

Solution   This is a difference of squares since $x^4 = (x^2)^2$ and $y^6 = (y^3)^2$. Thus,
$$x^4 - y^6 = (x^2)^2 - (y^3)^2 = (x^2 + y^3)(x^2 - y^3)$$ □

PRACTICE
3   Factor $p^4 - q^{10}$.

EXAMPLE 4   Factor each binomial.

a. $y^4 - 16$ **b.** $x^2 + 4$

Solution

a. $y^4 - 16 = (y^2)^2 - 4^2$

$= (y^2 + 4)\underbrace{(y^2 - 4)}.$ Factor the difference of two squares.
This binomial can be factored further since it is the difference of two squares.

$= (y^2 + 4)(y + 2)(y - 2)$ Factor the difference of two squares.

b. $x^2 + 4$

Note that the binomial $x^2 + 4$ is the _sum_ of two squares since we can write $x^2 + 4$ as $x^2 + 2^2$. We might try to factor using $(x + 2)(x + 2)$ or $(x - 2)(x - 2)$. But when we multiply to check, we find that neither factoring is correct.

$$(x + 2)(x + 2) = x^2 + 4x + 4$$
$$(x - 2)(x - 2) = x^2 - 4x + 4$$

In both cases, the product is a trinomial, not the required binomial. In fact, $x^2 + 4$ is a prime polynomial.   □

PRACTICE
4   Factor each binomial.

a. $z^4 - 81$ **b.** $m^2 + 49$

> ▶ **Helpful Hint**
>
> When factoring, don't forget:
>
> - See whether the terms have a greatest common factor (GCF) (other than 1) that can be factored out.
> - Other than a GCF, the **sum** of two squares cannot be factored using real numbers.
> - Factor completely. Always check to see whether any factors can be factored further.

EXAMPLES   Factor each difference of two squares.

5. $4x^3 - 49x = x(4x^2 - 49)$ Factor out the common factor, x.

$= x[(2x)^2 - 7^2]$

$= x(2x + 7)(2x - 7)$ Factor the difference of two squares.

6. $162x^4 - 2 = 2(81x^4 - 1)$ Factor out the common factor, 2.

$= 2(9x^2 + 1)(9x^2 - 1)$ Factor the difference of two squares.

$= 2(9x^2 + 1)(3x + 1)(3x - 1)$ Factor the difference of two squares.   □

PRACTICES
5–6   Factor each difference of two squares.

5. $36y^3 - 25y$ **6.** $80y^4 - 5$

EXAMPLE 7   Factor: $-49x^2 + 16$

Solution   Factor as is, or, if you like, rearrange terms.

Factor as is: $-49x^2 + 16 = -1(49x^2 - 16)$ Factor out -1.

$\qquad\qquad\qquad\qquad = -1(7x + 4)(7x - 4)$ Factor the difference of two squares.

Rewrite binomial: $-49x^2 + 16 = 16 - 49x^2 = 4^2 - (7x)^2$

$\qquad\qquad\qquad\qquad\qquad\qquad = (4 + 7x)(4 - 7x)$

Both factorizations are correct and are equal. To see this, factor -1 from $(4 - 7x)$ in the second factorization.   □

PRACTICE
7   Factor: $-9x^2 + 100$

OBJECTIVE 2 ▶ Factoring the sum or difference of two cubes.   Although the sum of two squares usually does not factor, the sum or difference of two cubes can be factored and reveals factoring patterns. The pattern for the sum of cubes is illustrated by multiplying the binomial $x + y$ and the trinomial $x^2 - xy + y^2$.

$$
\begin{array}{r}
x^2 - xy + y^2 \\
x + y \\
\hline
x^2y - xy^2 + y^3 \\
x^3 - x^2y + xy^2 \\
\hline
x^3 \qquad\qquad\qquad + y^3
\end{array}
$$

Thus, $(x + y)(x^2 - xy + y^2) = x^3 + y^3$ Sum of cubes

The pattern for the difference of two cubes is illustrated by multiplying the binomial $x - y$ by the trinomial $x^2 + xy + y^2$. The result is

$$(x - y)(x^2 + xy + y^2) = x^3 - y^3 \quad \text{Difference of cubes}$$

> **Factoring the Sum or Difference of Two Cubes**
> $$a^3 + b^3 = (a + b)(a^2 - ab + b^2)$$
> $$a^3 - b^3 = (a - b)(a^2 + ab + b^2)$$

Recall that "factor" means "to write as a product." Above are patterns for writing sums and differences as products.

EXAMPLE 8   Factor: $x^3 + 8$

Solution   First, write the binomial in the form $a^3 + b^3$.

$$x^3 + 8 = x^3 + 2^3 \quad \text{Write in the form } a^3 + b^3.$$

If we replace a with x and b with 2 in the formula above, we have

$$x^3 + 2^3 = (x + 2)[x^2 - (x)(2) + 2^2]$$
$$= (x + 2)(x^2 - 2x + 4) \qquad □$$

PRACTICE
8   Factor $x^3 + 64$.

▶ **Helpful Hint**

When factoring sums or differences of cubes, notice the sign patterns.

$$x^3 + y^3 = (x + y)(x^2 - xy + y^2)$$

same sign

opposite signs   always positive

$$x^3 - y^3 = (x - y)(x^2 + xy + y^2)$$

same sign

opposite signs   always positive

EXAMPLE 9 Factor: $y^3 - 27$

Solution $y^3 - 27 = y^3 - 3^3$ Write in the form $a^3 - b^3$.

$\qquad\qquad = (y - 3)[y^2 + (y)(3) + 3^2]$

$\qquad\qquad = (y - 3)(y^2 + 3y + 9)$ □

PRACTICE
9 Factor $x^3 - 125$.

EXAMPLE 10   Factor: $64x^3 + 1$

Solution $64x^3 + 1 = (4x)^3 + 1^3$

$\qquad\qquad\qquad = (4x + 1)[(4x)^2 - (4x)(1) + 1^2]$

$\qquad\qquad\qquad = (4x + 1)(16x^2 - 4x + 1)$ □

PRACTICE
10 Factor $27y^3 + 1$.

EXAMPLE 11   Factor: $54a^3 - 16b^3$

Solution   Remember to factor out common factors first before using other factoring methods.

$$54a^3 - 16b^3 = 2(27a^3 - 8b^3)$$ Factor out the GCF 2.

$\qquad\qquad\qquad = 2[(3a)^3 - (2b)^3]$ Difference of two cubes

$\qquad\qquad\qquad = 2(3a - 2b)[(3a)^2 + (3a)(2b) + (2b)^2]$

$\qquad\qquad\qquad = 2(3a - 2b)(9a^2 + 6ab + 4b^2)$ □

PRACTICE
11 Factor $32x^3 - 500y^3$.

Calculator Explorations

Graphing

A graphing calculator is a convenient tool for evaluating an expression at a given replacement value. For example, let's evaluate $x^2 - 6x$ when $x = 2$. To do so, store the value 2 in the variable x and then enter and evaluate the algebraic expression.

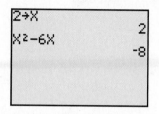

The value of $x^2 - 6x$ when $x = 2$ is -8. You may want to use this method for evaluating expressions as you explore the following.

We can use a graphing calculator to explore factoring patterns numerically. Use your calculator to evaluate $x^2 - 2x + 1$, $x^2 - 2x - 1$, and $(x - 1)^2$ for each value of x given in the table. What do you observe?

	$x^2 - 2x + 1$	$x^2 - 2x - 1$	$(x - 1)^2$
$x = 5$			
$x = -3$			
$x = 2.7$			
$x = -12.1$			
$x = 0$			

Notice in each case that $x^2 - 2x - 1 \neq (x - 1)^2$. Because for each x in the table the value of $x^2 - 2x + 1$ and the value of $(x - 1)^2$ are the same, we might guess that $x^2 - 2x + 1 = (x - 1)^2$. We can verify our guess algebraically with multiplication:

$$(x - 1)(x - 1) = x^2 - x - x + 1 = x^2 - 2x + 1$$

VOCABULARY & READINESS CHECK

Word Bank. *Use the choices below to fill in each blank. Some choices may be used more than once and some choices may not be used at all.*

   true   difference of two squares   sum of two cubes
   false   difference of two cubes

1. The expression $x^3 - 27$ is called a(n) _____.

2. The expression $x^2 - 49$ is called a(n) _____.

3. The expression $z^3 + 1$ is called a(n) _____.

4. True or false: The binomial $y^2 + 9$ factors as $(y + 3)^2$. _____

Write each number or term as a square.

5. 64   **6.** 100   **7.** $49x^2$ **8.** $25y^4$

Write each number or term as a cube.

9. 64   **10.** 1   **11.** $8y^3$ **12.** x^6

7.5 | EXERCISE SET

MyMathLab®   PRACTICE   WATCH   DOWNLOAD   READ   REVIEW

Factor each binomial completely. See Examples 1 through 7.

1. $x^2 - 4$

2. $x^2 - 36$

3. $81p^2 - 1$

4. $49m^2 - 1$

5. $25y^2 - 9$

6. $49a^2 - 16$

7. $121m^2 - 100n^2$

8. $169a^2 - 49b^2$

9. $x^2y^2 - 1$

10. $a^2b^2 - 16$

11. $x^2 - \dfrac{1}{4}$

12. $y^2 - \dfrac{1}{16}$

13. $-4r^2 + 1$

14. $-9t^2 + 1$

15. $16r^2 + 1$

16. $49y^2 + 1$

17. $-36 + x^2$

18. $-1 + y^2$

19. $m^4 - 1$

20. $n^4 - 16$

21. $m^4 - n^{18}$

22. $n^4 - r^6$

Factor the sum or difference of two cubes. See Examples 8 through 11.

23. $x^3 + 125$

24. $p^3 + 1$

25. $8a^3 - 1$

26. $27y^3 - 1$

27. $m^3 + 27n^3$

28. $y^3 + 64z^3$

29. $5k^3 + 40$

30. $6r^3 + 162$

31. $x^3y^3 - 64$

32. $a^3b^3 - 8$

33. $250r^3 - 128t^3$

34. $24x^3 - 81y^3$

MIXED PRACTICE

Factor each binomial completely. See Examples 1 through 11.

35. $r^2 - 64$

36. $q^2 - 121$

37. $x^2 - 169y^2$

38. $x^2 - 225y^2$

39. $27 - t^3$

40. $125 - r^3$

41. $18r^2 - 8$

42. $32t^2 - 50$

43. $9xy^2 - 4x$

44. $36x^2y - 25y$

45. $8m^3 + 64$

46. $2x^3 + 54$

47. $xy^3 - 9xyz^2$

48. $x^3y - 4xy^3$

49. $36x^2 - 64y^2$

50. $225a^2 - 81b^2$

51. $144 - 81x^2$

52. $12x^2 - 27$

53. $x^3y^3 - z^6$

54. $a^3b^3 - c^9$

55. $49 - \dfrac{9}{25}m^2$

56. $100 - \dfrac{4}{81}n^2$

57. $t^3 + 343$

58. $s^3 + 216$

59. $n^3 + 49n$

60. $y^3 + 64y$

61. $x^6 - 81x^2$

62. $n^9 - n^5$

63. $64p^3q - 81pq^3$

64. $100x^3y - 49xy^3$

65. $27x^2y^3 + xy^2$

66. $8x^3y^3 + x^3y$

67. $125a^4 - 64ab^3$

68. $64m^4 - 27mn^3$

69. $16x^4 - 64x^2$

70. $25y^4 - 100y^2$

REVIEW AND PREVIEW

Solve each equation. See Section 2.3.

71. $x - 6 = 0$

72. $y + 5 = 0$

73. $2m + 4 = 0$

74. $3x - 9 = 0$

75. $5z - 1 = 0$

76. $4a + 2 = 0$

Multiple Steps. *Solve. See Section 7.1. The percent of undergraduate college students who have credit cards each year from 2000 through 2006 can be approximately modeled by the polynomial* $-1.2x^2 + 4x + 80$, *where x is the number of years since 2000.*

77. Find the percent of college students who had credit cards in 2003.

78. Find the percent of college students who had credit cards in 2006.

79. Write a factored form of $-1.2x^2 + 4x + 80$ by factoring -4 from the terms of this polynomial.

80. Use your answers to Exercises 77 and 78 to write down any trends.

CONCEPT EXTENSIONS

Factor each expression completely.

81. $(x + 2)^2 - y^2$

82. $(y - 6)^2 - z^2$

83. $a^2(b - 4) - 16(b - 4)$

84. $m^2(n + 8) - 9(n + 8)$

85. $(x^2 + 6x + 9) - 4y^2$ (***Hint:*** Factor the trinomial in parentheses first.)

86. $(x^2 + 2x + 1) - 36y^2$

87. $x^{2n} - 100$

88. $x^{2n} - 81$

89. What binomial multiplied by $(x - 6)$ gives the difference of two squares?

90. What binomial multiplied by $(5 + y)$ gives the difference of two squares?

91. In your own words, explain how to tell whether a binomial is a difference of squares. Then explain how to factor a difference of squares.

92. In your own words, explain how to tell whether a binomial is a sum of cubes. Then explain how to factor a sum of cubes.

93. An object is dropped from the top of Pittsburgh's USX Tower, which is 841 feet tall. (*Source: World Almanac* research) The height of the object after t seconds is given by the expression $841 - 16t^2$.

a. Find the height of the object after 2 seconds.

b. Find the height of the object after 5 seconds.

c. To the nearest whole second, estimate when the object hits the ground.

d. Factor $841 - 16t^2$.

841 feet

94. A worker on the top of the Aetna Life Building in San Francisco accidentally drops a bolt. The Aetna Life Building is 529 feet tall. (*Source: World Almanac* research) The height of the bolt after t seconds is given by the expression $529 - 16t^2$.

a. Find the height of the bolt after 1 second.

b. Find the height of the bolt after 4 seconds.

c. To the nearest whole second, estimate when the bolt hits the ground.

d. Factor $529 - 16t^2$.

95. The world's second tallest building is the Taipei 101 in Taipei, Taiwan, at a height of 1671 feet. (*Source:* Council on Tall Buildings and Urban Habitat) Suppose a worker is suspended 71 feet below the top of the pinnacle atop the building, at a height of 1600 feet above the ground. If the worker accidentally drops a bolt, the height of the bolt after t seconds is given by the expression $1600 - 16t^2$. (Note: In January 2010, the Burj Dubai is officially the tallest building at 2684 feet.)

a. Find the height of the bolt after 3 seconds.

b. Find the height of the bolt after 7 seconds.

c. To the nearest whole second, estimate when the bolt hits the ground.

d. Factor $1600 - 16t^2$.

96. A performer with the Moscow Circus is planning a stunt involving a free fall from the top of the Moscow State University building, which is 784 feet tall. (*Source:* Council on Tall

Buildings and Urban Habitat) Neglecting air resistance, the performer's height above gigantic cushions positioned at ground level after t seconds is given by the expression $784 - 16t^2$.

a. Find the performer's height after 2 seconds.

b. Find the performer's height after 5 seconds.

c. To the nearest whole second, estimate when the performer reaches the cushions positioned at ground level.

d. Factor $784 - 16t^2$.

INTEGRATED REVIEW CHOOSING A FACTORING STRATEGY

Sections 7.1–7.5

The following steps may be helpful when factoring polynomials.

Factoring a Polynomial

STEP 1. Are there any common factors? If so, factor out the GCF.

STEP 2. How many terms are in the polynomial?

    a. If there are **two** terms, decide if one of the following can be applied.

        i. Difference of two squares: $a^2 - b^2 = (a + b)(a - b)$.

        ii. Difference of two cubes: $a^3 - b^3 = (a - b)(a^2 + ab + b^2)$.

        iii. Sum of two cubes: $a^3 + b^3 = (a + b)(a^2 - ab + b^2)$.

    b. If there are **three** terms, try one of the following.

        i. Perfect square trinomial: $a^2 + 2ab + b^2 = (a + b)^2$
                                    $a^2 - 2ab + b^2 = (a - b)^2$.

        ii. If not a perfect square trinomial, factor using the methods presented in Sections 7.2 through 7.4.

    c. If there are **four** or more terms, try factoring by grouping.

STEP 3. See if any factors in the factored polynomial can be factored further.

STEP 4. Check by multiplying.

Study the next five examples to help you use the steps above.

EXAMPLE 1 Factor $10t^2 - 17t + 3$.

Solution

STEP 1. The terms of this polynomial have no common factor (other than 1).

STEP 2. There are three terms, so this polynomial is a trinomial. This trinomial is not a perfect square trinomial, so factor using methods from earlier sections.

$$\text{Factors of } 10t^2: \quad 10t^2 = 2t \cdot 5t, \qquad 10t^2 = t \cdot 10t$$

Since the middle term, $-17t$, has a negative numerical coefficient, find negative factors of 3.

$$\text{Factors of 3:} \quad 3 = -1 \cdot -3$$

Try different combinations of these factors. The correct combination is

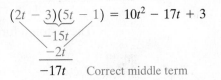

$$\underbrace{(2t - \underline{3})(5t - 1)}_{} = 10t^2 - 17t + 3$$

$$-15t$$
$$-2t$$
$$\overline{-17t} \quad \text{Correct middle term}$$

STEP 3. No factor can be factored further, so we have factored completely.

STEP 4. To check, multiply $2t - 3$ and $5t - 1$.

$$(2t - 3)(5t - 1) = 10t^2 - 2t - 15t + 3 = 10t^2 - 17t + 3$$

The factored form of $10t^2 - 17t + 3$ is $(2t - 3)(5t - 1)$.   □

PRACTICE
1   Factor $6x^2 - 11x + 3$.

EXAMPLE 2   Factor $2x^3 + 3x^2 - 2x - 3$.

Solution

STEP 1. There are no factors common to all terms.

STEP 2. Try factoring by grouping since this polynomial has four terms.

$$2x^3 + 3x^2 - 2x - 3 = x^2(2x + 3) - 1(2x + 3) \quad \text{Factor out the greatest}$$
common factor for each
pair of terms.
$$= (2x + 3)(x^2 - 1) \quad \text{Factor out } 2x + 3.$$

STEP 3. The binomial $x^2 - 1$ can be factored further. It is the difference of two squares.

$$= (2x + 3)(x + 1)(x - 1) \quad \text{Factor } x^2 - 1 \text{ as a difference}$$
of squares.

STEP 4. Check by finding the product of the three binomials. The polynomial factored completely is $(2x + 3)(x + 1)(x - 1)$.   □

PRACTICE
2   Factor $3x^3 + x^2 - 12x - 4$.

EXAMPLE 3   Factor $12m^2 - 3n^2$.

Solution

STEP 1. The terms of this binomial contain a greatest common factor of 3.

$$12m^2 - 3n^2 = 3(4m^2 - n^2) \quad \text{Factor out the greatest common factor.}$$

STEP 2. The binomial $4m^2 - n^2$ is a difference of squares.

$$= 3(2m + n)(2m - n) \quad \text{Factor the difference of squares.}$$

STEP 3. No factor can be factored further.

STEP 4. We check by multiplying.

$$3(2m + n)(2m - n) = 3(4m^2 - n^2) = 12m^2 - 3n^2$$

The factored form of $12m^2 - 3n^2$ is $3(2m + n)(2m - n)$. □

PRACTICE
3   Factor $27x^2 - 3y^2$.

EXAMPLE 4   Factor $x^3 + 27y^3$.

Solution

STEP 1.   The terms of this binomial contain no common factor (other than 1).

STEP 2.   This binomial is the sum of two cubes.

$$x^3 + 27y^3 = (x)^3 + (3y)^3$$
$$= (x + 3y)[x^2 - x(3y) + (3y)^2]$$
$$= (x + 3y)(x^2 - 3xy + 9y^2)$$

STEP 3.   No factor can be factored further.

STEP 4.   We check by multiplying.

$$(x + 3y)(x^2 - 3xy + 9y^2) = x(x^2 - 3xy + 9y^2) + 3y(x^2 - 3xy + 9y^2)$$
$$= x^3 - 3x^2y + 9xy^2 + 3x^2y - 9xy^2 + 27y^3$$
$$= x^3 + 27y^3$$

Thus, $x^3 + 27y^3$ factored completely is $(x + 3y)(x^2 - 3xy + 9y^2)$. □

PRACTICE
4   Factor $8a^3 + b^3$.

EXAMPLE 5   Factor $30a^2b^3 + 55a^2b^2 - 35a^2b$.

Solution

STEP 1. $30a^2b^3 + 55a^2b^2 - 35a^2b = 5a^2b(6b^2 + 11b - 7)$ Factor out the GCF.

STEP 2. $= 5a^2b(2b - 1)(3b + 7)$ Factor the resulting trinomial.

STEP 3.   No factor can be factored further.

STEP 4.   Check by multiplying.
The trinomial factored completely is $5a^2b(2b - 1)(3b + 7)$. □

PRACTICE
5   Factor $60x^3y^2 - 66x^2y^2 - 36xy^2$.

INTEGRATED REVIEW   EXERCISE SET

Factor the following completely.

1. $x^2 + 2xy + y^2$

2. $x^2 - 2xy + y^2$

3. $a^2 + 11a - 12$

4. $a^2 - 11a + 10$

5. $a^2 - a - 6$

6. $a^2 - 2a + 1$

7. $x^2 + 2x + 1$

8. $x^2 + x - 2$

9. $x^2 + 4x + 3$

10. $x^2 + x - 6$

11. $x^2 + 7x + 12$

12. $x^2 + x - 12$

13. $x^2 + 3x - 4$

14. $x^2 - 7x + 10$

15. $x^2 + 2x - 15$

16. $x^2 + 11x + 30$

17. $x^2 - x - 30$

18. $x^2 + 11x + 24$

19. $2x^2 - 98$

20. $3x^2 - 75$

21. $x^2 + 3x + xy + 3y$

22. $3y - 21 + xy - 7x$

23. $x^2 + 6x - 16$

24. $x^2 - 3x - 28$

25. $4x^3 + 20x^2 - 56x$

26. $6x^3 - 6x^2 - 120x$

27. $12x^2 + 34x + 24$

28. $8a^2 + 6ab - 5b^2$

29. $4a^2 - b^2$

30. $28 - 13x - 6x^2$

31. $20 - 3x - 2x^2$

32. $x^2 - 2x + 4$

33. $a^2 + a - 3$

34. $6y^2 + y - 15$

35. $4x^2 - x - 5$

36. $x^2y - y^3$

37. $4t^2 + 36$

38. $x^2 + x + xy + y$

39. $ax + 2x + a + 2$

40. $18x^3 - 63x^2 + 9x$

41. $12a^3 - 24a^2 + 4a$

42. $x^2 + 14x - 32$

43. $x^2 - 14x - 48$

44. $16a^2 - 56ab + 49b^2$

45. $25p^2 - 70pq + 49q^2$

46. $7x^2 + 24xy + 9y^2$

47. $125 - 8y^3$

48. $64x^3 + 27$

49. $-x^2 - x + 30$

50. $-x^2 + 6x - 8$

51. $14 + 5x - x^2$

52. $3 - 2x - x^2$

53. $3x^4y + 6x^3y - 72x^2y$

54. $2x^3y + 8x^2y^2 - 10xy^3$

55. $5x^3y^2 - 40x^2y^3 + 35xy^4$

56. $4x^4y - 8x^3y - 60x^2y$

57. $12x^3y + 243xy$

58. $6x^3y^2 + 8xy^2$

59. $4 - x^2$

60. $9 - y^2$

61. $3rs - s + 12r - 4$

62. $x^3 - 2x^2 + 3x - 6$

63. $4x^2 - 8xy - 3x + 6y$

64. $4x^2 - 2xy - 7yz + 14xz$

65. $6x^2 + 18xy + 12y^2$

66. $12x^2 + 46xy - 8y^2$

67. $xy^2 - 4x + 3y^2 - 12$

68. $x^2y^2 - 9x^2 + 3y^2 - 27$

69. $5(x + y) + x(x + y)$

70. $7(x - y) + y(x - y)$

71. $14t^2 - 9t + 1$

72. $3t^2 - 5t + 1$

73. $3x^2 + 2x - 5$

74. $7x^2 + 19x - 6$

75. $x^2 + 9xy - 36y^2$

76. $3x^2 + 10xy - 8y^2$

77. $1 - 8ab - 20a^2b^2$

78. $1 - 7ab - 60a^2b^2$

79. $9 - 10x^2 + x^4$

80. $36 - 13x^2 + x^4$

81. $x^4 - 14x^2 - 32$

82. $x^4 - 22x^2 - 75$

83. $x^2 - 23x + 120$

84. $y^2 + 22y + 96$

85. $6x^3 - 28x^2 + 16x$

86. $6y^3 - 8y^2 - 30y$

87. $27x^3 - 125y^3$

88. $216y^3 - z^3$

89. $x^3y^3 + 8z^3$

90. $27a^3b^3 + 8$

91. $2xy - 72x^3y$

92. $2x^3 - 18x$

93. $x^3 + 6x^2 - 4x - 24$

94. $x^3 - 2x^2 - 36x + 72$

95. $6a^3 + 10a^2$

96. $4n^2 - 6n$

97. $a^2(a + 2) + 2(a + 2)$

98. $a - b + x(a - b)$

99. $x^3 - 28 + 7x^2 - 4x$

100. $a^3 - 45 - 9a + 5a^2$

CONCEPT EXTENSIONS

Factor.

101. $(x - y)^2 - z^2$

102. $(x + 2y)^2 - 9$

103. $81 - (5x + 1)^2$

104. $b^2 - (4a + c)^2$

105. Explain why it makes good sense to factor out the GCF first, before using other methods of factoring.

106. The sum of two squares usually does not factor. Is the sum of two squares $9x^2 + 81y^2$ factorable?

107. Which of the following are equivalent to $(x + 10)(x - 7)$?

    a. $(x - 7)(x + 10)$ **b.** $-1(x + 10)(x - 7)$

    c. $-1(x + 10)(7 - x)$ **d.** $-1(-x - 10)(7 - x)$

7.6 SOLVING QUADRATIC EQUATIONS BY FACTORING

OBJECTIVES

1 Solve quadratic equations by factoring.

2 Solve equations with degree greater than 2 by factoring.

3 Find the *x*-intercepts of the graph of a quadratic equation in two variables.

144 feet

In this section, we introduce a new type of equation—the **quadratic equation.**

> **Quadratic Equation**
>
> A quadratic equation is one that can be written in the form
>
> $$ax^2 + bx + c = 0$$
>
> where a, b, and c are real numbers and $a \neq 0$.

Some examples of quadratic equations are shown below.

$$x^2 - 9x - 22 = 0 \qquad 4x^2 - 28 = -49 \qquad x(2x - 7) = 4$$

The form $ax^2 + bx + c = 0$ is called the **standard form** of a quadratic equation. The quadratic equation $x^2 - 9x - 22 = 0$ is the only equation above that is in standard form.

Quadratic equations model many real-life situations. For example, let's suppose we want to know how long before a person diving from a 144-foot cliff reaches the ocean. The answer to this question is found by solving the quadratic equation $-16t^2 + 144 = 0$. (See Example 1 in Section 7.7.)

OBJECTIVE 1 ▶ Solving quadratic equations by factoring. Some quadratic equations can be solved by making use of factoring and the **zero factor property.**

> **Zero Factor Property**
>
> If a and b are real numbers and if $ab = 0$, then $a = 0$ or $b = 0$.

This property states that if the product of two numbers is 0 then at least one of the numbers must be 0.

> ▶ **Helpful Hint**
>
> The solutions of equations are also called the **roots**.

EXAMPLE 1 Solve: $(x - 3)(x + 1) = 0$.

Solution If this equation is to be a true statement, then either the factor $x - 3$ must be 0 or the factor $x + 1$ must be 0. In other words, either

$$x - 3 = 0 \qquad \text{or} \qquad x + 1 = 0$$

If we solve these two linear equations, we have

$$x = 3 \qquad \text{or} \qquad x = -1$$

Thus, 3 and -1 are both solutions of the equation $(x - 3)(x + 1) = 0$. To check, we replace x with 3 in the original equation. Then we replace x with -1 in the original equation.

Check: Let $x = 3$.

$$(x - 3)(x + 1) = 0$$
$$(3 - 3)(3 + 1) \stackrel{?}{=} 0 \quad \text{Replace } x \text{ with 3.}$$
$$0(4) = 0 \quad \text{True}$$

Let $x = -1$.

$$(x - 3)(x + 1) = 0$$
$$(-1 - 3)(-1 + 1) \stackrel{?}{=} 0 \quad \text{Replace } x \text{ with } -1.$$
$$(-4)(0) = 0 \quad \text{True}$$

The solutions are 3 and -1, or we say that the solution set is $\{-1, 3\}$. ☐

PRACTICE

 Solve: $(x + 4)(x - 5) = 0$.

▶ **Helpful Hint**

The zero factor property says that *if a product is 0, then a factor is 0.*

If $a \cdot b = 0$, then $a = 0$ or $b = 0$.
If $x(x + 5) = 0$, then $x = 0$ or $x + 5 = 0$.
If $(x + 7)(2x - 3) = 0$, then $x + 7 = 0$ or $2x - 3 = 0$.

Use this property only when the product is 0. For example, if $a \cdot b = 8$, we do not know the value of a or b. The values may be $a = 2$, $b = 4$ or $a = 8$, $b = 1$, or any other two numbers whose product is 8.

EXAMPLE 2 Solve: $x(5x - 2) = 0$

Solution
$$x(5x - 2) = 0$$
$$x = 0 \quad \text{or} \quad 5x - 2 = 0 \quad \text{Use the zero factor property.}$$
$$5x = 2$$
$$x = \frac{2}{5}$$

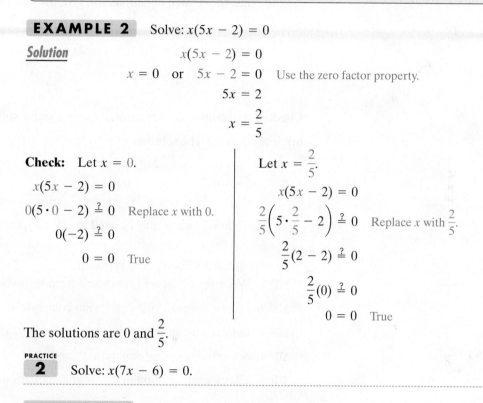

Check: Let $x = 0$.

$$x(5x - 2) = 0$$
$$0(5 \cdot 0 - 2) \overset{?}{=} 0 \quad \text{Replace } x \text{ with 0.}$$
$$0(-2) \overset{?}{=} 0$$
$$0 = 0 \quad \text{True}$$

Let $x = \frac{2}{5}$.

$$x(5x - 2) = 0$$
$$\frac{2}{5}\left(5 \cdot \frac{2}{5} - 2\right) \overset{?}{=} 0 \quad \text{Replace } x \text{ with } \frac{2}{5}.$$
$$\frac{2}{5}(2 - 2) \overset{?}{=} 0$$
$$\frac{2}{5}(0) \overset{?}{=} 0$$
$$0 = 0 \quad \text{True}$$

The solutions are 0 and $\frac{2}{5}$.

PRACTICE
2 Solve: $x(7x - 6) = 0$.

EXAMPLE 3 Solve: $x^2 - 9x - 22 = 0$

Solution One side of the equation is 0. However, to use the zero factor property, one side of the equation must be 0 *and* the other side must be written as a product (must be factored). Thus, we must first factor this polynomial.

$$x^2 - 9x - 22 = 0$$
$$(x - 11)(x + 2) = 0 \quad \text{Factor.}$$

Now we can apply the zero factor property.

$$x - 11 = 0 \quad \text{or} \quad x + 2 = 0$$
$$x = 11 \qquad \qquad x = -2$$

Check: Let $x = 11$.

$$x^2 - 9x - 22 = 0$$
$$11^2 - 9 \cdot 11 - 22 \overset{?}{=} 0$$
$$121 - 99 - 22 \overset{?}{=} 0$$
$$22 - 22 \overset{?}{=} 0$$
$$0 = 0 \quad \text{True}$$

Let $x = -2$.

$$x^2 - 9x - 22 = 0$$
$$(-2)^2 - 9(-2) - 22 \overset{?}{=} 0$$
$$4 + 18 - 22 \overset{?}{=} 0$$
$$22 - 22 \overset{?}{=} 0$$
$$0 = 0 \quad \text{True}$$

The solutions are 11 and -2.

PRACTICE
3 Solve: $x^2 - 8x - 48 = 0$.

EXAMPLE 4 Solve: $4x^2 - 28x = -49$

Solution First we rewrite the equation in standard form so that one side is 0. Then we factor the polynomial.

$$4x^2 - 28x = -49$$
$$4x^2 - 28x + 49 = 0 \qquad \text{Write in standard form by adding 49 to both sides.}$$
$$(2x - 7)(2x - 7) = 0 \qquad \text{Factor.}$$

Next we use the zero factor property and set each factor equal to 0. Since the factors are the same, the related equations will give the same solution.

$$2x - 7 = 0 \quad \text{or} \quad 2x - 7 = 0 \qquad \text{Set each factor equal to 0.}$$
$$2x = 7 \qquad\qquad 2x = 7 \qquad \text{Solve.}$$
$$x = \frac{7}{2} \qquad\qquad x = \frac{7}{2}$$

Check: Although $\frac{7}{2}$ occurs twice, there is a single solution. Check this solution in the original equation. The solution is $\frac{7}{2}$. ☐

PRACTICE
4 Solve: $9x^2 - 24x = -16$.

The following steps may be used to solve a quadratic equation by factoring.

> **To Solve Quadratic Equations by Factoring**
>
> **STEP 1.** Write the equation in standard form so that one side of the equation is 0.
>
> **STEP 2.** Factor the quadratic expression completely.
>
> **STEP 3.** Set each factor containing a variable equal to 0.
>
> **STEP 4.** Solve the resulting equations.
>
> **STEP 5.** Check each solution in the original equation.

Since it is not always possible to factor a quadratic polynomial, not all quadratic equations can be solved by factoring. Other methods of solving quadratic equations are presented in Chapter 10.

EXAMPLE 5 Solve: $x(2x - 7) = 4$

Solution First we write the equation in standard form; then we factor.

$$x(2x - 7) = 4$$
$$2x^2 - 7x = 4 \qquad\qquad \text{Multiply.}$$
$$2x^2 - 7x - 4 = 0 \qquad\qquad \text{Write in standard form.}$$
$$(2x + 1)(x - 4) = 0 \qquad\qquad \text{Factor.}$$
$$2x + 1 = 0 \quad \text{or} \quad x - 4 = 0 \qquad \text{Set each factor equal to zero.}$$
$$2x = -1 \qquad\qquad x = 4 \qquad \text{Solve.}$$
$$x = -\frac{1}{2}$$

Check the solutions in the original equation. The solutions are $-\frac{1}{2}$ and 4. ☐

PRACTICE
5 Solve: $x(3x + 7) = 6$.

▶ **Helpful Hint**

To solve the equation $x(2x - 7) = 4$, do **not** set each factor equal to 4. Remember that to apply the zero factor property, one side of the equation must be 0 and the other side of the equation must be in factored form.

Concept Check ☑

Explain the error and solve the equation correctly.

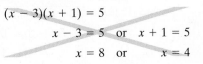

$$(x - 3)(x + 1) = 5$$
$$x - 3 = 5 \quad \text{or} \quad x + 1 = 5$$
$$x = 8 \quad \text{or} \quad x = 4$$

EXAMPLE 6   Solve: $-2x^2 - 4x + 30 = 0$.

Solution   The equation is in standard form so we begin by factoring out a common factor of -2.

$$-2x^2 - 4x + 30 = 0$$
$$-2(x^2 + 2x - 15) = 0 \quad \text{Factor out } -2.$$
$$-2(x + 5)(x - 3) = 0 \quad \text{Factor the quadratic.}$$

Next, set each factor **containing a variable** equal to 0.

$$x + 5 = 0 \quad \text{or} \quad x - 3 = 0 \quad \text{Set each factor containing a variable equal to 0.}$$
$$x = -5 \quad \text{or} \quad x = 3 \quad \text{Solve.}$$

Note: The factor -2 is a constant term containing no variables and can never equal 0. The solutions are -5 and 3.   □

PRACTICE
6   Solve: $-3x^2 - 6x + 72 = 0$.

OBJECTIVE 2 ▶ **Solving equations with degree greater than two by factoring.** Some equations involving polynomials of degree higher than 2 may also be solved by factoring and then applying the zero factor property.

EXAMPLE 7   Solve: $3x^3 - 12x = 0$.

Solution   Factor the left side of the equation. Begin by factoring out the common factor of $3x$.

$$3x^3 - 12x = 0$$
$$3x(x^2 - 4) = 0 \quad \text{Factor out the GCF } 3x.$$
$$3x(x + 2)(x - 2) = 0 \quad \text{Factor } x^2 - 4, \text{ a difference of squares.}$$

$$3x = 0 \quad \text{or} \quad x + 2 = 0 \quad \text{or} \quad x - 2 = 0 \quad \text{Set each factor equal to 0.}$$
$$x = 0 \quad \text{or} \quad x = -2 \quad \text{or} \quad x = 2 \quad \text{Solve.}$$

Thus, the equation $3x^3 - 12x = 0$ has three solutions: $0, -2,$ and 2. To check, replace x with each solution in the original equation.

Let x = 0.	*Let x = −2.*	*Let x = 2.*
$3(0)^3 - 12(0) \stackrel{?}{=} 0$	$3(-2)^3 - 12(-2) \stackrel{?}{=} 0$	$3(2)^3 - 12(2) \stackrel{?}{=} 0$
$0 = 0$	$3(-8) + 24 \stackrel{?}{=} 0$	$3(8) - 24 \stackrel{?}{=} 0$
	$0 = 0$	$0 = 0$

Substituting $0, -2,$ or 2 into the original equation results each time in a true equation. The solutions are $0, -2,$ and 2.   □

Answer to Concept Check:

To use the zero factor property, one side of the equation must be 0, not 5. Correctly, $(x - 3)(x + 1) = 5$, $x^2 - 2x - 3 = 5$, $x^2 - 2x - 8 = 0$, $(x - 4)(x + 2) = 0$, $x - 4 = 0$ or $x + 2 = 0$, $x = 4$ or $x = -2$.

PRACTICE
7   Solve: $7x^3 - 63x = 0$.

EXAMPLE 8   Solve: $(5x - 1)(2x^2 + 15x + 18) = 0$.

Solution

$$(5x - 1)(2x^2 + 15x + 18) = 0$$
$$(5x - 1)(2x + 3)(x + 6) = 0 \quad \text{Factor the trinomial.}$$
$$5x - 1 = 0 \quad \text{or} \quad 2x + 3 = 0 \quad \text{or} \quad x + 6 = 0 \quad \text{Set each factor equal to 0.}$$
$$5x = 1 \quad \text{or} \quad 2x = -3 \quad \text{or} \quad x = -6 \quad \text{Solve.}$$
$$x = \frac{1}{5} \quad \text{or} \quad x = -\frac{3}{2}$$

The solutions are $\frac{1}{5}, -\frac{3}{2}$, and -6. Check by replacing x with each solution in the original equation. The solutions are $-6, -\frac{3}{2}$, and $\frac{1}{5}$. ☐

PRACTICE
8   Solve: $(3x - 2)(2x^2 - 13x + 15) = 0$.

EXAMPLE 9   Solve: $2x^3 - 4x^2 - 30x = 0$.

Solution   Begin by factoring out the GCF $2x$.

$$2x^3 - 4x^2 - 30x = 0$$
$$2x(x^2 - 2x - 15) = 0 \quad \text{Factor out the GCF } 2x.$$
$$2x(x - 5)(x + 3) = 0 \quad \text{Factor the quadratic.}$$
$$2x = 0 \quad \text{or} \quad x - 5 = 0 \quad \text{or} \quad x + 3 = 0 \quad \begin{array}{l}\text{Set each factor containing a}\\\text{variable equal to 0.}\end{array}$$
$$x = 0 \quad \text{or} \quad x = 5 \quad \text{or} \quad x = -3 \quad \text{Solve.}$$

Check by replacing x with each solution in the cubic equation. The solutions are $-3, 0$, and 5. ☐

PRACTICE
9   Solve: $5x^3 + 5x^2 - 30x = 0$.

OBJECTIVE 3 ▶ Finding x-intercepts of the graph of a quadratic equation. In Chapter 3, we graphed linear equations in two variables, such as $y = 5x - 6$. Recall that to find the x-intercept of the graph of a linear equation, let $y = 0$ and solve for x. This is also how to find the x-intercepts of the graph of a **quadratic equation in two variables,** such as $y = x^2 - 5x + 4$.

EXAMPLE 10   Find the x-intercepts of the graph of $y = x^2 - 5x + 4$.

Solution   Let $y = 0$ and solve for x.

$$y = x^2 - 5x + 4$$
$$0 = x^2 - 5x + 4 \quad \text{Let } y = 0.$$
$$0 = (x - 1)(x - 4) \quad \text{Factor.}$$
$$x - 1 = 0 \quad \text{or} \quad x - 4 = 0 \quad \text{Set each factor equal to 0.}$$
$$x = 1 \quad \text{or} \quad x = 4 \quad \text{Solve.}$$

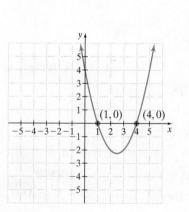

The x-intercepts of the graph of $y = x^2 - 5x + 4$ are $(1, 0)$ and $(4, 0)$.
The graph of $y = x^2 - 5x + 4$ is shown in the margin. ☐

PRACTICE
10   Find the x-intercepts of the graph of $y = x^2 - 6x + 8$.

In general, a quadratic equation in two variables is one that can be written in the form $y = ax^2 + bx + c$ where $a \neq 0$. The graph of such an equation is called a **parabola** and will open up or down depending on the sign of a.

Notice that the x-intercepts of the graph of $y = ax^2 + bx + c$ are the real number solutions of $0 = ax^2 + bx + c$. Also, the real number solutions of $0 = ax^2 + bx + c$ are the x-intercepts of the graph of $y = ax^2 + bx + c$. We study more about graphs of quadratic equations in two variables in Chapter 10.

Graph of $y = ax^2 + bx + c$
x-intercepts are solutions of $0 = ax^2 + bx + c$

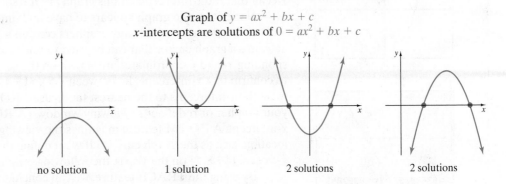

| no solution | 1 solution | 2 solutions | 2 solutions |

From the above and Example 10, since the x-intercepts of $y = x^2 - 5x + 4$ are $(1, 0)$ and $(4, 0)$, the solutions of the related equation $0 = x^2 - 5x + 4$ are 1 and 4.

$y = x^2 - 5x + 4$	x-intercepts: $(1, 0), (4, 0)$
$0 = x^2 - 5x + 4$	solutions: $1, 4$

We have already seen the relationship between factors of a quadratic expression and solutions (roots) of the related equation. Now let's review these relationships and include x-intercepts.

Factors of $ax^2 + bx + c$	*Solutions of* $ax^2 + bx + c = 0$	*x-intercepts of* $y = ax^2 + bx + c$

For a quadratic polynomial $ax^2 + bx + c$, if one of the statements below is true for a real number, k, then all three are true.

- $(x - k)$ is a factor of the expression $ax^2 + bx + c$.
- k is a solution (root) of the equation $ax^2 + bx + c = 0$.
- $(k, 0)$ is an x-intercept of the graph of $y = ax^2 + bx + c$.

> **▶ Helpful Hint**
>
> The values 5 and 1 to the right are also called the **zeros** of the function $f(x) = x^2 - 6x + 5$ since these are the values of x such that y or $f(x) = 0$.

For example, let's consider the quadratic expression
$$x^2 - 6x + 5.$$

- $(x - 5)$ and $(x - 1)$ are factors of the expression $x^2 - 6x + 5$.
- 5 and 1 are solutions of the equation $x^2 - 6x + 5 = 0$.
- $(5, 0)$ and $(1, 0)$ are x-intercepts of $y = x^2 - 6x + 5$.

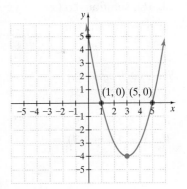

Graphing Calculator Explorations

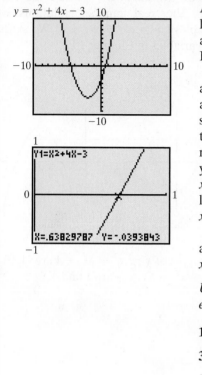

$y = x^2 + 4x - 3$

A grapher may be used to find solutions of a quadratic equation whether the related quadratic polynomial is factorable or not. For example, let's use a grapher to approximate the solutions of $0 = x^2 + 4x - 3$. To do so, graph $y_1 = x^2 + 4x - 3$. Recall that the x-intercepts of this graph are the solutions of $0 = x^2 + 4x - 3$.

Notice that the graph appears to have an x-intercept between -5 and -4 and one between 0 and 1. Many graphers contain a TRACE feature. This feature activates a graph cursor that can be used to *trace* along a graph while the corresponding x- and y-coordinates are shown on the screen. Use the TRACE feature to confirm that x-intercepts lie between -5 and -4 and also 0 and 1. To approximate the x-intercepts to the nearest tenth, use a ROOT or a ZOOM feature on your grapher or redefine the viewing window. (A ROOT feature calculates the x-intercept. A ZOOM feature magnifies the viewing window around a specific location such as the graph cursor.) If we redefine the window to $[0, 1]$ on the x-axis and $[-1, 1]$ on the y-axis, the following graph is generated.

By using the TRACE feature, we can conclude that one x-intercept is approximately 0.6 to the nearest tenth. By repeating these steps for the other x-intercept, we find that it is approximately -4.6.

Use a grapher to approximate the real number solutions to the nearest tenth. If an equation has no real number solution, state so.

1. $3x^2 - 4x - 6 = 0$

2. $x^2 - x - 9 = 0$

3. $2x^2 + x + 2 = 0$

4. $-4x^2 - 5x - 4 = 0$

5. $-x^2 + x + 5 = 0$

6. $10x^2 + 6x - 3 = 0$

VOCABULARY & READINESS CHECK

Word Bank. *Use the choices below to fill in each blank. Not all choices will be used.*

$-3, 5$	$a = 0$ or $b = 0$	0	linear
$3, -5$	quadratic	1	

1. An equation that can be written in the form $ax^2 + bx + c = 0$, (with $a \neq 0$), is called a(n) _____ equation.

2. If the product of two numbers is 0, then at least one of the numbers must be _____.

3. The solutions to $(x - 3)(x + 5) = 0$ are _____.

4. If $a \cdot b = 0$, then _____.

Solve each equation by inspection.

5. $(a - 3)(a - 7) = 0$

6. $(a - 5)(a - 2) = 0$

7. $(x + 8)(x + 6) = 0$

8. $(x + 2)(x + 3) = 0$

9. $(x + 1)(x - 3) = 0$

10. $(x - 1)(x + 2) = 0$

7.6 EXERCISE SET

Solve each equation. See Examples 1 and 2.

1. $(x - 2)(x + 1) = 0$

2. $(x + 4)(x - 10) = 0$

3. $(x + 9)(x + 17) = 0$

4. $(x + 11)(x + 1) = 0$

5. $x(x + 6) = 0$

6. $x(x - 7) = 0$

7. $3x(x - 8) = 0$

8. $2x(x + 12) = 0$

9. $(2x + 3)(4x - 5) = 0$

10. $(3x - 2)(5x + 1) = 0$

11. $(2x - 7)(7x + 2) = 0$

12. $(9x + 1)(4x - 3) = 0$

13. $\left(x - \dfrac{1}{2}\right)\left(x + \dfrac{1}{3}\right) = 0$

14. $\left(x + \dfrac{2}{9}\right)\left(x - \dfrac{1}{4}\right) = 0$

15. $(x + 0.2)(x + 1.5) = 0$

16. $(x + 1.7)(x + 2.3) = 0$

17. Write a quadratic equation that has two solutions, 6 and -1. Leave the polynomial in the equation in factored form.

18. Write a quadratic equation that has two solutions, 0 and -2. Leave the polynomial in the equation in factored form.

Solve. See Examples 3 through 6.

19. $x^2 - 13x + 36 = 0$

20. $x^2 + 2x - 63 = 0$

21. $x^2 + 2x - 8 = 0$

22. $x^2 - 5x + 6 = 0$

23. $x^2 - 7x = 0$

24. $x^2 - 3x = 0$

25. $x^2 - 4x = 32$

26. $x^2 - 5x = 24$

27. $x^2 = 16$

28. $x^2 = 9$

29. $(x + 4)(x - 9) = 4x$

30. $(x + 3)(x + 8) = x$

31. $x(3x - 1) = 14$

32. $x(4x - 11) = 3$

33. $-3x^2 + 75 = 0$

34. $-2y^2 + 72 = 0$

35. $24x^2 + 44x = 8$

36. $6x^2 + 57x = 30$

Solve each equation. See Examples 7 through 9.

37. $x^3 - 12x^2 + 32x = 0$

38. $x^3 - 14x^2 + 49x = 0$

39. $(4x - 3)(16x^2 - 24x + 9) = 0$

40. $(2x + 5)(4x^2 + 20x + 25) = 0$

41. $4x^3 - x = 0$

42. $4y^3 - 36y = 0$

43. $32x^3 - 4x^2 - 6x = 0$

44. $15x^3 + 24x^2 - 63x = 0$

MIXED PRACTICE

Solve each equation. See Examples 1 through 9. (A few exercises are linear equations.)

45. $(x + 3)(x - 2) = 0$

46. $(x - 6)(x + 7) = 0$

47. $x^2 + 20x = 0$

48. $x^2 + 15x = 0$

49. $4(x - 7) = 6$

50. $5(3 - 4x) = 9$

51. $4y^2 - 1 = 0$

52. $4y^2 - 81 = 0$

53. $(2x + 3)(2x^2 - 5x - 3) = 0$

54. $(2x - 9)(x^2 + 5x - 36) = 0$

55. $x^2 - 15 = -2x$

56. $x^2 - 26 = -11x$

57. $30x^2 - 11x - 30 = 0$

58. $12x^2 + 7x - 12 = 0$

59. $5x^2 - 6x - 8 = 0$

60. $9x^2 + 7x = 2$

61. $6y^2 - 22y - 40 = 0$

62. $3x^2 - 6x - 9 = 0$

63. $(y - 2)(y + 3) = 6$

64. $(y - 5)(y - 2) = 28$

65. $3x^3 + 19x^2 - 72x = 0$

66. $36x^3 + x^2 - 21x = 0$

67. $x^2 + 14x + 49 = 0$

68. $x^2 + 22x + 121 = 0$

69. $12y = 8y^2$

70. $9y = 6y^2$

71. $7x^3 - 7x = 0$

72. $3x^3 - 27x = 0$

73. $3x^2 + 8x - 11 = 13 - 6x$

74. $2x^2 + 12x - 1 = 4 + 3x$

75. $3x^2 - 20x = -4x^2 - 7x - 6$

76. $4x^2 - 20x = -5x^2 - 6x - 5$

Find the x-intercepts of the graph of each equation. See Example 10.

77. $y = (3x + 4)(x - 1)$

78. $y = (5x - 3)(x - 4)$

79. $y = x^2 - 3x - 10$

80. $y = x^2 + 7x + 6$

81. $y = 2x^2 + 11x - 6$

82. $y = 4x^2 + 11x + 6$

Matching. *For Exercises 83 through 88, match each equation with its graph. See Example 10.*

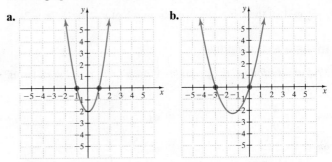

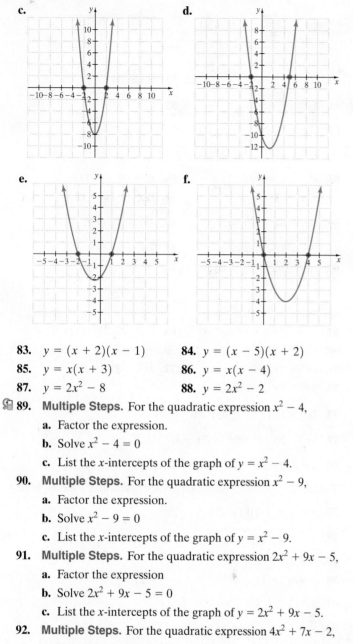

c.

d.

e.

f.

83. $y = (x + 2)(x - 1)$

84. $y = (x - 5)(x + 2)$

85. $y = x(x + 3)$

86. $y = x(x - 4)$

87. $y = 2x^2 - 8$

88. $y = 2x^2 - 2$

89. Multiple Steps. For the quadratic expression $x^2 - 4$,

  a. Factor the expression.

  b. Solve $x^2 - 4 = 0$

  c. List the x-intercepts of the graph of $y = x^2 - 4$.

90. Multiple Steps. For the quadratic expression $x^2 - 9$,

  a. Factor the expression.

  b. Solve $x^2 - 9 = 0$

  c. List the x-intercepts of the graph of $y = x^2 - 9$.

91. Multiple Steps. For the quadratic expression $2x^2 + 9x - 5$,

  a. Factor the expression

  b. Solve $2x^2 + 9x - 5 = 0$

  c. List the x-intercepts of the graph of $y = 2x^2 + 9x - 5$.

92. Multiple Steps. For the quadratic expression $4x^2 + 7x - 2$,

  a. Factor the expression.

  b. Solve $4x^2 + 7x - 2 = 0$

  c. List the x-intercepts of the graph of $y = 4x^2 + 7x - 2$.

REVIEW AND PREVIEW

Perform the following operations. Write all results in lowest terms. See Section 1.3.

93. $\dfrac{3}{5} + \dfrac{4}{9}$

94. $\dfrac{2}{3} + \dfrac{3}{7}$

95. $\dfrac{7}{10} - \dfrac{5}{12}$

96. $\dfrac{5}{9} - \dfrac{5}{12}$

97. $\dfrac{7}{8} \div \dfrac{7}{15}$

98. $\dfrac{5}{12} - \dfrac{3}{10}$

99. $\dfrac{4}{5} \cdot \dfrac{7}{8}$

100. $\dfrac{3}{7} \cdot \dfrac{12}{17}$

CONCEPT EXTENSIONS

For Exercises 101 and 102, see the Concept Check in this section.

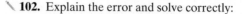

101. Explain the error and solve correctly:

$$x(x - 2) = 8$$
$$x = 8 \quad \text{or} \quad x - 2 = 8$$
$$x = 10$$

102. Explain the error and solve correctly:

$$(x - 4)(x + 2) = 0$$
$$x = -4 \quad \text{or} \quad x = 2$$

103. Write a quadratic equation in standard form that has two solutions, 5 and 7.

104. Write an equation that has three solutions, 0, 1, and 2.

105. Multiple Steps. A compass is accidentally thrown upward and out of an air balloon at a height of 300 feet. The height, y, of the compass at time x in seconds is given by the equation

$$y = -16x^2 + 20x + 300$$

300 ft

  a. Find the height of the compass at the given times by filling in the table below.

time, x	0	1	2	3	4	5	6
height, y							

  b. Use the table to determine when the compass strikes the ground.

  c. Use the table to approximate the maximum height of the compass.

  d. Plot the points (x, y) on a rectangular coordinate system and connect them with a smooth curve. Explain your results.

106. Multiple Steps. A rocket is fired upward from the ground with an initial velocity of 100 feet per second. The height, y, of the rocket at any time x is given by the equation

$$y = -16x^2 + 100x$$

b. Use the table to approximate when the rocket strikes the ground to the nearest second.

c. Use the table to approximate the maximum height of the rocket.

d. Plot the points (x, y) on a rectangular coordinate system and connect them with a smooth curve. Explain your results.

Solve each equation. First, multiply the binomial.

To solve $(x - 6)(2x - 3) = (x + 2)(x + 9)$, see below.

$$(x - 6)(2x - 3) = (x + 2)(x + 9)$$
$$2x^2 - 15x + 18 = x^2 + 11x + 18$$
$$x^2 - 26x = 0$$
$$x(x - 26) = 0$$
$$x = 0 \quad \text{or} \quad x - 26 = 0$$
$$x = 26$$

a. Find the height of the rocket at the given times by filling in the table below.

time, x	0	1	2	3	4	5	6	7
height, y								

107. $(x - 3)(3x + 4) = (x + 2)(x - 6)$

108. $(2x - 3)(x + 6) = (x - 9)(x + 2)$

109. $(2x - 3)(x + 8) = (x - 6)(x + 4)$

110. $(x + 6)(x - 6) = (2x - 9)(x + 4)$

7.7   QUADRATIC EQUATIONS AND PROBLEM SOLVING

OBJECTIVE

1   Solve problems that can be modeled by quadratic equations.

OBJECTIVE 1 ▶ Solving problems modeled by quadratic equations. Some problems may be modeled by quadratic equations. To solve these problems, we use the same problem-solving steps that were introduced in Section 2.5. When solving these problems, keep in mind that a solution of an equation that models a problem may not be a solution to the problem. For example, a person's age or the length of a rectangle is always a positive number. Discard solutions that do not make sense as solutions of the problem.

EXAMPLE 1   **Finding Free-Fall Time**

Since the 1940s, one of the top tourist attractions in Acapulco, Mexico is watching the cliff divers off the La Quebrada. The divers' platform is about 144 feet above the sea. These divers must time their descent just right, since they land in the crashing Pacific, in an inlet that is at most $9\frac{1}{2}$ feet deep. Neglecting air resistance, the height h in feet of a cliff diver above the ocean after t seconds is given by the quadratic equation $h = -16t^2 + 144$.

Find out how long it takes the diver to reach the ocean.

Solution

1. UNDERSTAND. Read and reread the problem. Then draw a picture of the problem.

   The equation $h = -16t^2 + 144$ models the height of the falling diver at time t. Familiarize yourself with this equation by find the height of the diver at time $t = 1$ second and $t = 2$ seconds.

   When $t = 1$ second, the height of the diver is $h = -16(1)^2 + 144 = 128$ feet.
   When $t = 2$ seconds, the height of the diver is $h = -16(2)^2 + 144 = 80$ feet.

2. TRANSLATE. To find out how long it takes the diver to reach the ocean, we want to know the value of t for which $h = 0$.

$$0 = -16t^2 + 144$$
$$0 = -16(t^2 - 9) \qquad \text{Factor out } -16.$$
$$0 = -16(t - 3)(t + 3) \qquad \text{Factor completely.}$$
$$t - 3 = 0 \quad \text{or} \quad t + 3 = 0 \qquad \text{Set each factor containing a variable equal to 0.}$$
$$t = 3 \quad \text{or} \qquad t = -3 \qquad \text{Solve.}$$

3. INTERPRET. Since the time t cannot be negative, the proposed solution is 3 seconds.

Check: Verify that the height of the diver when t is 3 seconds is 0.

$$\text{When } t = 3 \text{ seconds, } h = -16(3)^2 + 144 = -144 + 144 = 0.$$

State: It takes the diver 3 seconds to reach the ocean. □

PRACTICE
1 Cliff divers also frequent the falls at Waimea Falls Park in Oahu, Hawaii. One of the popular diving spots is 64 feet high. Neglecting air resistance, the height of a diver above the pool after t seconds is $h = -16t^2 + 64$. Find how long it takes a diver to reach the pool.

EXAMPLE 2 **Finding an Unknown Number**

The square of a number plus three times the number is 70. Find the number.

Solution

1. UNDERSTAND. Read and reread the problem. Suppose that the number is 5. The square of 5 is 5^2 or 25. Three times 5 is 15. Then $25 + 15 = 40$, not 70, so the number must be greater than 5. Remember, the purpose of proposing a number, such as 5, is to better understand the problem. Now that we do, we will let $x =$ the number.

2. TRANSLATE.

the square of a number	plus	three times the number	is	70
↓	↓	↓	↓	↓
x^2	$+$	$3x$	$=$	70

3. SOLVE.

$$x^2 + 3x = 70$$
$$x^2 + 3x - 70 = 0 \qquad \text{Subtract 70 from both sides.}$$
$$(x + 10)(x - 7) = 0 \qquad \text{Factor.}$$
$$x + 10 = 0 \quad \text{or} \quad x - 7 = 0 \qquad \text{Set each factor equal to 0.}$$
$$x = -10 \qquad\qquad x = 7 \qquad \text{Solve.}$$

4. INTERPRET.

Check: The square of -10 is $(-10)^2$, or 100. Three times -10 is $3(-10)$ or -30. Then $100 + (-30) = 70$, the correct sum, so -10 checks.

The square of 7 is 7^2 or 49. Three times 7 is $3(7)$, or 21. Then $49 + 21 = 70$, the correct sum, so 7 checks.

State: There are two numbers. They are -10 and 7. □

PRACTICE
2 The square of a number minus eight times the number is equal to forty-eight. Find the number.

⚠️ **EXAMPLE 3**   **Finding the Dimensions of a Sail**

The height of a triangular sail is 2 meters less than twice the length of the base. If the sail has an area of 30 square meters, find the length of its base and the height.

Solution

1. UNDERSTAND. Read and reread the problem. Since we are finding the length of the base and the height, we let

$$x = \text{the length of the base}$$

and since the height is 2 meters less than twice the base,

$$2x - 2 = \text{the height}$$

An illustration is shown to the right.

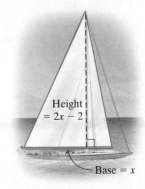

Height = $2x - 2$

Base = x

2. TRANSLATE. We are given that the area of the triangle is 30 square meters, so we use the formula for area of a triangle.

area of triangle	=	$\frac{1}{2}$	·	base	·	height
↓		↓		↓		↓
30	=	$\frac{1}{2}$	·	x	·	$(2x - 2)$

3. SOLVE. Now we solve the quadratic equation.

$$30 = \frac{1}{2}x(2x - 2)$$

$$30 = x^2 - x \qquad \text{Multiply.}$$

$$x^2 - x - 30 = 0 \qquad \text{Write in standard form.}$$

$$(x - 6)(x + 5) = 0 \qquad \text{Factor.}$$

$$x - 6 = 0 \quad \text{or} \quad x + 5 = 0 \qquad \text{Set each factor equal to 0.}$$

$$x = 6 \qquad\qquad x = -5$$

4. INTERPRET. Since x represents the length of the base, we discard the solution -5. The base of a triangle cannot be negative. The base is then 6 meters and the height is $2(6) - 2 = 10$ meters.

Check: To check this problem, we recall that $\frac{1}{2}$base · height = area, or

$$\frac{1}{2}(6)(10) = 30 \quad \text{The required area}$$

State: The base of the triangular sail is 6 meters and the height is 10 meters. □

PRACTICE
3   An engineering team from Georgia Tech earned second place in a recent flight competition, with their triangular shaped paper hang glider. The base of their prize—winning entry was 1 foot less than three times the height. If the area of the triangular glider wing was 210 square feet, find the dimensions of the wing. (*Source: The Technique* [Georgia Tech's newspaper], April 18, 2003)

The next examples make use of the **Pythagorean theorem** and consecutive integers. Before we review this theorem, recall that a **right triangle** is a triangle that contains a 90° or right angle. The **hypotenuse** of a right triangle is the side opposite the right angle and is the longest side of the triangle. The **legs** of a right triangle are the other sides of the triangle.

Pythagorean Theorem

In a right triangle, the sum of the squares of the lengths of the two legs is equal to the square of the length of the hypotenuse.

$$(\text{leg})^2 + (\text{leg})^2 = (\text{hypotenuse})^2 \qquad \text{or} \qquad a^2 + b^2 = c^2$$

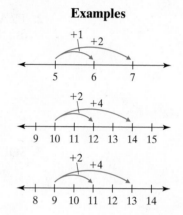

> ▶ **Helpful Hint**
>
> If you use this formula, don't forget that c represents the length of the hypotenuse.

Study the following diagrams for a review of consecutive integers.

Examples

If x is the first integer, then consecutive integers are
$x, x + 1, x + 2, \ldots$

If x is the first even integer, then consecutive even integers are
$x, x + 2, x + 4, \ldots$

If x is the first odd integer, then consecutive odd integers are
$x, x + 2, x + 4, \ldots$

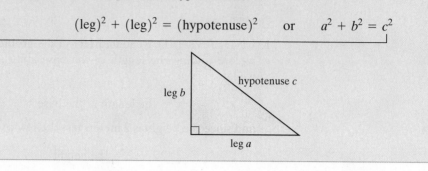

EXAMPLE 4   **Finding Consecutive Even Integers**

Find two consecutive even integers whose product is 34 more than their sum.

Solution

1. **UNDERSTAND.** Read and reread the problem. Let's just choose two consecutive even integers to help us better understand the problem. Let's choose 10 and 12. Their product is $10(12) = 120$ and their sum is $10 + 12 = 22$. The product is $120 - 22$, or 98 greater than the sum. Thus our guess is incorrect, but we have a better understanding of this example.

   Let's let x and $x + 2$ be the consecutive even integers.

2. **TRANSLATE.**

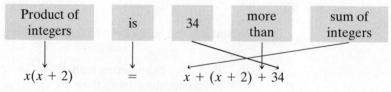

3. **SOLVE.** Now we solve the equation.

$$
\begin{aligned}
x(x + 2) &= x + (x + 2) + 34 \\
x^2 + 2x &= x + x + 2 + 34 && \text{Multiply.} \\
x^2 + 2x &= 2x + 36 && \text{Combine like terms.} \\
x^2 - 36 &= 0 && \text{Write in standard form.} \\
(x + 6)(x - 6) &= 0 && \text{Factor.} \\
x + 6 = 0 \quad \text{or} \quad x - 6 &= 0 && \text{Set each factor equal to 0.} \\
x = -6 \qquad\qquad x &= 6 && \text{Solve.}
\end{aligned}
$$

4. INTERPRET. If $x = -6$, then $x + 2 = -6 + 2$, or -4.
       If $x = 6$, then $x + 2 = 6 + 2$, or 8.

Check: $-6, -4$ $6, 8$

$$-6(-4) \stackrel{?}{=} -6 + (-4) + 34 \qquad\qquad 6(8) \stackrel{?}{=} 6 + 8 + 34$$
$$24 \stackrel{?}{=} -10 + 34 \qquad\qquad\qquad 48 \stackrel{?}{=} 14 + 34$$
$$24 = 24 \qquad\qquad \text{True} \qquad\qquad 48 = 48 \qquad\qquad \text{True}$$

State: The two consecutive even integers are -6 and -4 or 6 and 8.   □

PRACTICE
4   Find two consecutive integers whose product is 41 more than their sum.

△ **EXAMPLE 5**   **Finding the Dimensions of a Triangle**

Find the lengths of the sides of a right triangle if the lengths can be expressed as three consecutive even integers.

Solution

1. UNDERSTAND. Read and reread the problem. Let's suppose that the length of one leg of the right triangle is 4 units. Then the other leg is the next even integer, or 6 units, and the hypotenuse of the triangle is the next even integer, or 8 units. Remember that the hypotenuse is the longest side. Let's see if a triangle with sides of these lengths forms a right triangle. To do this, we check to see whether the Pythagorean theorem holds true.

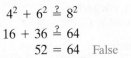

$$4^2 + 6^2 \stackrel{?}{=} 8^2$$
$$16 + 36 \stackrel{?}{=} 64$$
$$52 = 64 \quad \text{False}$$

Our proposed numbers do not check, but we now have a better understanding of the problem.

We let x, $x + 2$, and $x + 4$ be three consecutive even integers. Since these integers represent lengths of the sides of a right triangle, we have the following.

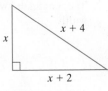

$$x = \text{one leg}$$
$$x + 2 = \text{other leg}$$
$$x + 4 = \text{hypotenuse (longest side)}$$

2. TRANSLATE. By the Pythagorean theorem, we have that

$$(\text{leg})^2 + (\text{leg})^2 = (\text{hypotenuse})^2$$
$$(x)^2 + (x + 2)^2 = (x + 4)^2$$

3. SOLVE. Now we solve the equation.

$$x^2 + (x + 2)^2 = (x + 4)^2$$
$$x^2 + x^2 + 4x + 4 = x^2 + 8x + 16 \qquad \text{Multiply.}$$
$$2x^2 + 4x + 4 = x^2 + 8x + 16 \qquad \text{Combine like terms.}$$
$$x^2 - 4x - 12 = 0 \qquad \text{Write in standard form.}$$
$$(x - 6)(x + 2) = 0 \qquad \text{Factor.}$$
$$x - 6 = 0 \quad \text{or} \quad x + 2 = 0 \qquad \text{Set each factor equal to 0.}$$
$$x = 6 \qquad\qquad x = -2$$

4. INTERPRET. We discard $x = -2$ since length cannot be negative. If $x = 6$, then $x + 2 = 8$ and $x + 4 = 10$.

Check: Verify that

$$(\text{leg})^2 + (\text{leg})^2 = (\text{hypotenuse})^2$$
$$6^2 + 8^2 \overset{?}{=} 10^2$$
$$36 + 64 \overset{?}{=} 100$$
$$100 = 100 \qquad \text{True}$$

State: The sides of the right triangle have lengths 6 units, 8 units, and 10 units.

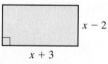

PRACTICE

5 Find the dimensions of a right triangle where the second leg is 1 unit less than double the first leg, and the hypotenuse is 1 unit more than double the length of the first leg.

7.7 | EXERCISE SET

MIXED PRACTICE

See Examples 1 through 5 for all exercises. For Exercises 1 through 6, represent each given condition using a single variable, x.

△ **1.** The length and width of a rectangle whose length is 4 centimeters more than its width

△ **2.** The length and width of a rectangle whose length is twice its width

3. Two consecutive odd integers

4. Two consecutive even integers

△ **5.** The base and height of a triangle whose height is one more than four times its base

△ **6.** The base and height of a trapezoid whose base is three less than five times its height

base

Use the information given to find the dimensions of each figure.

△ **7.** The *area* of the square is 121 square units. Find the length of its sides.

△ **8.** The *area* of the rectangle is 84 square inches. Find its length and width.

$x - 2$

$x + 3$

△ **9.** The *perimeter* of the quadrilateral is 120 centimeters. Find the lengths of the sides.

$x + 5$

$x^2 - 3x$

$x + 3$

$3x - 8$

△ **10.** The *perimeter* of the triangle is 85 feet. Find the lengths of its sides.

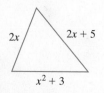

△ **11.** The *area* of the parallelogram is 96 square miles. Find its base and height.

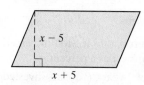

△ **12.** The *area* of the circle is 25π square kilometers. Find its radius.

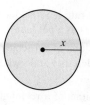

Solve.

🔎 **13.** An object is thrown upward from the top of an 80-foot building with an initial velocity of 64 feet per second. The height h of the object after t seconds is given by the quadratic equation $h = -16t^2 + 64t + 80$. When will the object hit the ground?

14. A hang glider pilot accidentally drops her compass from the top of a 400-foot cliff. The height h of the compass after t seconds is given by the quadratic equation $h = -16t^2 + 400$. When will the compass hit the ground?

△ **15.** The length of a rectangle is 7 centimeters less than twice its width. Its area is 30 square centimeters. Find the dimensions of the rectangle.

△ **16.** The length of a rectangle is 9 inches more than its width. Its area is 112 square inches. Find the dimensions of the rectangle.

The equation $D = \frac{1}{2}n(n - 3)$ gives the number of diagonals D for a polygon with n sides. For example, a polygon with 6 sides has $D = \frac{1}{2} \cdot 6(6 - 3)$ or $D = 9$ diagonals. (See if you can count all 9 diagonals. Some are shown in the figure.) Use this equation, $D = \frac{1}{2}n(n - 3)$, for Exercises 17 through 20.

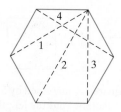

△ **17.** Find the number of diagonals for a polygon that has 12 sides.

△ **18.** Find the number of diagonals for a polygon that has 15 sides.

△ **19.** Find the number of sides n for a polygon that has 35 diagonals.

△ **20.** Find the number of sides n for a polygon that has 14 diagonals.

Solve.

21. The sum of a number and its square is 132. Find the number(s).

🔎 **22.** The sum of a number and its square is 182. Find the number(s).

23. The product of two consecutive room numbers is 210. Find the room numbers.

🔎 **24.** The product of two consecutive page numbers is 420. Find the page numbers.

25. A ladder is leaning against a building so that the distance from the ground to the top of the ladder is one foot less than the length of the ladder. Find the length of the ladder if the distance from the bottom of the ladder to the building is 5 feet.

26. Use the given figure to find the length of the guy wire.

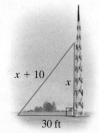

△ **27.** If the sides of a square are increased by 3 inches, the area becomes 64 square inches. Find the length of the sides of the original square.

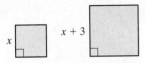

△ **28.** If the sides of a square are increased by 5 meters, the area becomes 100 square meters. Find the length of the sides of the original square.

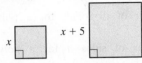

△ **29.** One leg of a right triangle is 4 millimeters longer than the smaller leg and the hypotenuse is 8 millimeters longer than the smaller leg. Find the lengths of the sides of the triangle.

△ **30.** One leg of a right triangle is 9 centimeters longer than the other leg and the hypotenuse is 45 centimeters. Find the lengths of the legs of the triangle.

△ **31.** The length of the base of a triangle is twice its height. If the area of the triangle is 100 square kilometers, find the height.

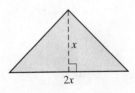

△ **32.** The height of a triangle is 2 millimeters less than the base. If the area is 60 square millimeters, find the base.

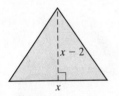

△ **33.** Find the length of the shorter leg of a right triangle if the longer leg is 12 feet more than the shorter leg and the hypotenuse is 12 feet less than twice the shorter leg.

△ **34.** Find the length of the shorter leg of a right triangle if the longer leg is 10 miles more than the shorter leg and the hypotenuse is 10 miles less than twice the shorter leg.

35. An object is dropped from 39 feet below the tip of the pinnacle atop one of the 1483-foot-tall Petronas Twin Towers in Kuala Lumpur, Malaysia. (*Source:* Council on Tall Buildings and Urban Habitat) The height h of the object after t seconds is given by the equation $h = -16t^2 + 1444$. Find how many seconds pass before the object reaches the ground.

36. An object is dropped from the top of 311 South Wacker Drive, a 961-foot-tall office building in Chicago. (*Source:* Council on Tall Buildings and Urban Habitat) The height h of the object after t seconds is given by the equation $h = -16t^2 + 961$. Find how many seconds pass before the object reaches the ground.

37. At the end of 2 years, P dollars invested at an interest rate r compounded annually increases to an amount, A dollars, given by

$$A = P(1 + r)^2$$

Find the interest rate if $100 increased to $144 in 2 years. Write your answer as a percent.

38. At the end of 2 years, P dollars invested at an interest rate r compounded annually increases to an amount, A dollars, given by

$$A = P(1 + r)^2$$

Find the interest rate if $2000 increased to $2420 in 2 years. Write your answer as a percent.

△ **39.** Find the dimensions of a rectangle whose width is 7 miles less than its length and whose area is 120 square miles.

△ **40.** Find the dimensions of a rectangle whose width is 2 inches less than half its length and whose area is 160 square inches.

41. If the cost, C, for manufacturing x units of a certain product is given by $C = x^2 - 15x + 50$, find the number of units manufactured at a cost of $9500.

42. If a switchboard handles n telephones, the number C of telephone connections it can make simultaneously is given by the equation $C = \dfrac{n(n-1)}{2}$. Find how many telephones are handled by a switchboard making 120 telephone connections simultaneously.

REVIEW AND PREVIEW

The following double line graph shows a comparison of the number of farms in the United States and the size of the average farm. Use this graph to answer Exercises 43–49. See Section 3.1.

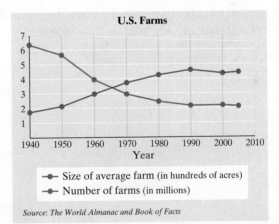

U.S. Farms

— Size of average farm (in hundreds of acres)
— Number of farms (in millions)

Source: The World Almanac and Book of Facts

△ **43.** Approximate the size of the average farm in 1940.

△ **44.** Approximate the size of the average farm in 2005.

45. Approximate the number of farms in 1940.

46. Approximate the number of farms in 2005.

47. Approximate the year that the colored lines in this graph intersect.

48. In your own words, explain the meaning of the point of intersection in the graph.

49. Describe the trends shown in this graph and speculate as to why these trends have occurred.

Write each fraction in simplest form. See Section 1.3.

50. $\dfrac{20}{35}$ **51.** $\dfrac{24}{32}$

52. $\dfrac{27}{18}$ **53.** $\dfrac{15}{27}$

54. $\dfrac{14}{42}$ **55.** $\dfrac{45}{50}$

CONCEPT EXTENSIONS

△ **56.** Two boats travel at right angles to each other after leaving the same dock at the same time. One hour later the boats are 17 miles apart. If one boat travels 7 miles per hour faster than the other boat, find the rate of each boat.

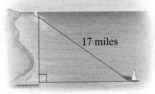

△ **57.** The side of a square equals the width of a rectangle. The length of the rectangle is 6 meters longer than its width. The sum of the areas of the square and the rectangle is 176 square meters. Find the side of the square.

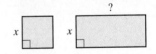

58. The sum of two numbers is 20, and the sum of their squares is 218. Find the numbers.

59. The sum of two numbers is 25, and the sum of their squares is 325. Find the numbers.

△ **60.** According to the International America's Cup Class (IACC) rule, a sailboat competing in the America's Cup match must have a 110-foot-tall mast and a combined mainsail and jib sail area of 3000 square feet. (*Source:* America's Cup Organizing Committee) A design for an IACC-class sailboat calls for the mainsail to be 60% of the combined sail area. If the

height of the triangular mainsail is 28 feet more than twice the length of the boom, find the length of the boom and the height of the mainsail.

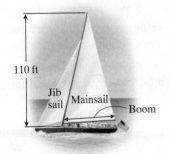

△ **61.** A rectangular pool is surrounded by a walk 4 meters wide. The pool is 6 meters longer than its width. If the total area of the pool and walk is 576 square meters more than the area of the pool, find the dimensions of the pool.

△ **62.** A rectangular garden is surrounded by a walk of uniform width. The area of the garden is 180 square yards. If the dimensions of the garden plus the walk are 16 yards by 24 yards, find the width of the walk.

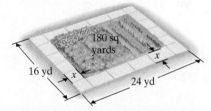

63. Write down two numbers whose sum is 10. Square each number and find the sum of the squares. Use this work to write a word problem like Exercise 59. Then give the word problem to a classmate to solve.

CHAPTER 7   VOCABULARY CHECK

Fill in each blank with one of the words or phrases listed below. Not all choices will be used.

factoring	quadratic equation	perfect square trinomial	0
greatest common factor	root	sum of two cubes	1
difference of two cubes	difference of two squares	$(x - k)$	k

1. An equation that can be written in the form $ax^2 + bx + c = 0$ (with a not 0) is called a _____.

2. _____ is the process of writing an expression as a product.

3. The _____ of a list of terms is the product of all common factors.

4. A trinomial that is the square of some binomial is called a _____.

5. The expression $a^2 - b^2$ is called a(n) _____.

6. The expression $a^3 - b^3$ is called a(n) _____.

7. The expression $a^3 + b^3$ is called a(n) _____.

8. By the zero factor property, if the product of two numbers is 0, then at least one of the numbers must be ____.

9. A solution of an equation such as $y = ax^2 + bx + c$ is called a _____.

10. If $(x - k)$ is a factor of an equation, then _____ is a solution.

CHAPTER 7 REVIEW

(7.1) *Complete the factoring.*

1. $6x^2 - 15x = 3x(\quad)$

2. $2x^3y - 6x^2y^2 - 8xy^3 = 2xy(\quad)$

Factor the GCF from each polynomial.

3. $20x^2 + 12x$

4. $6x^2y^2 - 3xy^3$

5. $-8x^3y + 6x^2y^2$

6. $3x(2x + 3) - 5(2x + 3)$

7. $5x(x + 1) - (x + 1)$

Factor.

8. $3x^2 - 3x + 2x - 2$

9. $6x^2 + 10x - 3x - 5$

10. $3a^2 + 9ab + 3b^2 + ab$

(7.2) *Factor each trinomial.*

11. $x^2 + 6x + 8$

12. $x^2 - 11x + 24$

13. $x^2 + x + 2$

14. $x^2 - 5x - 6$

15. $x^2 + 2x - 8$

16. $x^2 + 4xy - 12y^2$

17. $x^2 + 8xy + 15y^2$

18. $3x^2y + 6xy^2 + 3y^3$

19. $72 - 18x - 2x^2$

20. $32 + 12x - 4x^2$

(7.3) *or* **(7.4)** *Factor each trinomial.*

21. $2x^2 + 11x - 6$

22. $4x^2 - 7x + 4$

23. $4x^2 + 4x - 3$

24. $6x^2 + 5xy - 4y^2$

25. $6x^2 - 25xy + 4y^2$

26. $18x^2 - 60x + 50$

27. $2x^2 - 23xy - 39y^2$

28. $4x^2 - 28xy + 49y^2$

29. $18x^2 - 9xy - 20y^2$

30. $36x^3y + 24x^2y^2 - 45xy^3$

(7.5) *Factor each binomial.*

31. $4x^2 - 9$

32. $9t^2 - 25s^2$

33. $16x^2 + y^2$

34. $x^3 - 8y^3$

35. $8x^3 + 27$

36. $2x^3 + 8x$

37. $54 - 2x^3y^3$

38. $9x^2 - 4y^2$

39. $16x^4 - 1$

40. $x^4 + 16$

(7.6) *Solve the following equations.*

41. $(x + 6)(x - 2) = 0$

42. $3x(x + 1)(7x - 2) = 0$

43. $4(5x + 1)(x + 3) = 0$

44. $x^2 + 8x + 7 = 0$

45. $x^2 - 2x - 24 = 0$

46. $x^2 + 10x = -25$

47. $x(x - 10) = -16$

48. $(3x - 1)(9x^2 + 3x + 1) = 0$

49. $56x^2 - 5x - 6 = 0$

50. $20x^2 - 7x - 6 = 0$

51. $5(3x + 2) = 4$

52. $6x^2 - 3x + 8 = 0$

53. $12 - 5t = -3$

54. $5x^3 + 20x^2 + 20x = 0$

55. $4t^3 - 5t^2 - 21t = 0$

56. Write a quadratic equation that has the two solutions 4 and 5.

(7.7) Use the given information to choose the correct dimensions.

△ **57.** The perimeter of a rectangle is 24 inches. The length is twice the width. Find the dimensions of the rectangle.

   a. 5 inches by 7 inches

   b. 5 inches by 10 inches

   c. 4 inches by 8 inches

   d. 2 inches by 10 inches

△ **58.** The area of a rectangle is 80 meters. The length is one more than three times the width. Find the dimensions of the rectangle.

   a. 8 meters by 10 meters

   b. 4 meters by 13 meters

   c. 4 meters by 20 meters

   d. 5 meters by 16 meters

Use the given information to find the dimensions of each figure.

△ **59.** The *area* of the square is 81 square units. Find the length of a side.

△ **60.** The *perimeter* of the quadrilateral is 47 units. Find the lengths of the sides.

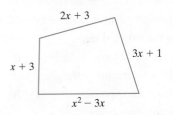

△ **61.** A flag for a local organization is in the shape of a rectangle whose length is 15 inches less than twice its width. If the area of the flag is 500 square inches, find its dimensions.

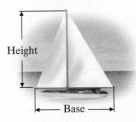

△ **62.** The base of a triangular sail is four times its height. If the area of the triangle is 162 square yards, find the base.

63. Find two consecutive positive integers whose product is 380.

64. Multiple Steps. A rocket is fired from the ground with an initial velocity of 440 feet per second. Its height h after t seconds is given by the equation

$$h = -16t^2 + 440t$$

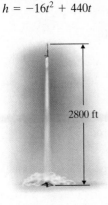

   a. Find how many seconds pass before the rocket reaches a height of 2800 feet. Explain why two answers are obtained.

   b. Find how many seconds pass before the rocket reaches the ground again.

65. An object is dropped from the top of the 625-foot-tall Waldorf-Astoria Hotel on Park Avenue in New York City. (*Source: World Almanac* research) The height h of the object after t seconds is given by the equation $h = -16t^2 + 625$. Find how many seconds pass before the object reaches the ground.

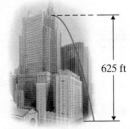

△ **66.** An architect's squaring instrument is in the shape of a right triangle. Find the length of the long leg of the right triangle if the hypotenuse is 8 centimeters longer than the long leg and the short leg is 8 centimeters shorter than the long leg.

MIXED REVIEW

Factor completely.

67. $7x - 63$

68. $11x(4x - 3) - 6(4x - 3)$

69. $m^2 - \dfrac{4}{25}$

70. $3x^3 - 4x^2 + 6x - 8$

71. $xy + 2x - y - 2$

72. $2x^2 + 2x - 24$

73. $3x^3 - 30x^2 + 27x$

74. $4x^2 - 81$

75. $2x^2 - 18$

76. $16x^2 - 24x + 9$

77. $5x^2 + 20x + 20$

78. $2x^2 + 5x - 12$

79. $4x^2y - 6xy^2$

80. $8x^2 - 15x - x^3$

81. $125x^3 + 27$

82. $24x^2 - 3x - 18$

83. $(x + 7)^2 - y^2$

84. $x^2(x + 3) - 4(x + 3)$

85. $54a^3b - 2b$

86. **Fill in the Blank.** To factor $x^2 + 2x - 48$, think of two numbers whose product is _____ and whose sum is _____.

87. What is the first step to factoring $3x^2 + 15x + 30$?

Write the perimeter of each figure as a simplified polynomial. Then factor each polynomial.

△ **88.**

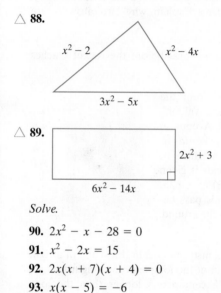

$x^2 - 2$ $x^2 - 4x$ $3x^2 - 5x$

△ **89.**

$2x^2 + 3$

$6x^2 - 14x$

Solve.

90. $2x^2 - x - 28 = 0$

91. $x^2 - 2x = 15$

92. $2x(x + 7)(x + 4) = 0$

93. $x(x - 5) = -6$

94. $x^2 = 16x$

Solve.

95. The perimeter of the following triangle is 48 inches. Find the lengths of its sides.

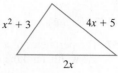

$x^2 + 3$ $4x + 5$ $2x$

96. The width of a rectangle is 4 inches less than its length. Its area is 12 square inches. Find the dimensions of the rectangle.

97. A 6-foot-tall person drops an object from the top of the Westin Peachtree Plaza in Atlanta, Georgia. The Westin building is 723 feet tall. (*Source: World Almanac* research) The height h of the object after t seconds is given by the equation $h = -16t^2 + 729$. Find how many seconds pass before the object reaches the ground.

723 ft

Write an expression for the area of the shaded region. Then write the expression as a factored polynomial.

△ **98.**

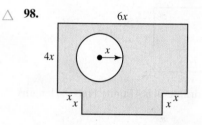

$6x$ $4x$ x x x x x

99. For the quadratic expression $x^2 - 5x - 14$,
   a. Factor the expression.
   b. Solve the equation $x^2 - 5x - 14 = 0$
   c. List the x-intercepts of the graph of $y = x^2 - 5x - 14$

100. For the quadratic expression $x^2 - 7x - 30$,
   a. Factor the expression.
   b. Solve the equation $x^2 - 7x - 30 = 0$.
   c. List the x-intercepts of the graph of $y = x^2 - 7x - 30$.

CHAPTER 7 TEST

TEST PREP **VIDEO**

The fully worked-out solutions to any exercises you want to review are available in MyMathLab.

Factor each polynomial completely. If a polynomial cannot be factored, write "prime."

1. $x^2 + 11x + 28$

2. $49 - m^2$

3. $y^2 + 22y + 121$

4. $4(a + 3) - y(a + 3)$

5. $x^2 + 4$

6. $y^2 - 8y - 48$

7. $x^2 + x - 10$

8. $9x^3 + 39x^2 + 12x$

9. $3a^2 + 3ab - 7a - 7b$

10. $3x^2 - 5x + 2$

11. $x^2 + 14xy + 24y^2$

12. $180 - 5x^2$

13. $6t^2 - t - 5$

14. $xy^2 - 7y^2 - 4x + 28$

15. $x - x^5$

16. $-xy^3 - x^3y$

17. $64x^3 - 1$

18. $8y^3 - 64$

Solve each equation.

19. $(x - 3)(x + 9) = 0$

20. $x^2 + 5x = 14$

21. $x(x + 6) = 7$

22. $3x(2x - 3)(3x + 4) = 0$

23. $5t^3 - 45t = 0$

24. $t^2 - 2t - 15 = 0$

25. $6x^2 = 15x$

Solve each problem.

△ **26.** A deck for a home is in the shape of a triangle. The length of the base of the triangle is 9 feet longer than its altitude. If the area of the triangle is 68 square feet, find the length of the base.

27. The sum of two numbers is 17 and the sum of their squares is 145. Find the numbers.

28. An object is dropped from the top of the Woolworth Building on Broadway in New York City. The height h of the object after t seconds is given by the equation

$$h = -16t^2 + 784$$

Find how many seconds pass before the object reaches the ground.

29. Find the lengths of the sides of a right triangle if the hypotenuse is 10 centimeters longer than the shorter leg and 5 centimeters longer than the longer leg.

30. For the quadratic expression $3x^2 - 22x + 7$,

   a. Factor the expression.

   b. Solve the equation $3x^2 - 22x + 7 = 0$.

   c. List the x-intercepts of the graph of $y = 3x^2 - 22x + 7$.

CHAPTER 7 STANDARDIZED TEST

Multiple Choice. *Choose the one alternative that best completes the statement or answers the question.*

Factor the polynomial completely. If the polynomial cannot be factored, write "prime."

1. $x^2 + 10x + 24$

   a. prime   **b.** $(x - 6)(x + 1)$

   c. $(x + 6)(x + 4)$ **d.** $(x - 6)(x + 4)$

2. $9 - m^2$

   a. $(3 - m)^2$ **b.** $(3 - m)(3 + m)$

   c. prime   **d.** $(3 + m)^2$

3. $y^2 + 16y + 64$

   a. $(y - 8)^2$ **b.** $(y + 8)(y - 8)$

   c. $(y + 8)^2$ **d.** prime

4. $12(a + 11) - y(a + 11)$

   a. $(a + 11)(12 - y)$ **b.** prime

   c. $(a - 11)(y - 12)$ **d.** $(a + 11)(12 + y)$

5. $x^2 + 9$

   a. prime   **b.** $(x - 3)^2$

   c. $(x + 3)^2$ **d.** $(x + 3)(x - 3)$

6. $y^2 - 5y - 50$

   a. $(y + 10)(y - 5)$ **b.** prime

   c. $(y - 10)(y + 5)$ **d.** $(y - 50)(y + 1)$

7. $x^2 - x - 48$

   a. $(x - 6)(x + 8)$ **b.** $(x + 6)(x - 8)$

   c. $(x - 48)(x + 1)$ **d.** prime

8. $6x^3 - 60x^2 + 96x$

   a. $x(6x + 8)(x + 2)$ **b.** $6x(x + 8)(x + 2)$

   c. $6x(x - 8)(x - 2)$ **d.** $x(x + 8)(6x + 12)$

9. $2a^2 + 2ab - 7a - 7b$

   a. $(2a + 7)(a - b)$ **b.** $(2a - 7)(a + b)$

   c. $(2a + 7)(a + b)$ **d.** $(2a - 7)(a - b)$

10. $5x^2 - 46x + 48$

   a. $(5x - 6)(x - 8)$ **b.** $5(x - 6)(x - 8)$

   c. $(5x - 6)(5x + 8)$ **d.** $(5x + 8)(x - 6)$

11. $x^2 + 2xy - 15y^2$

   a. $(x - 5y)(x + y)$ **b.** $(x - 5y)(x + 3y)$

   c. prime   **d.** $(x + 5y)(x - 3y)$

12. $20 - 5x^2$

   a. $5(x + 2)(x - 2)$ **b.** $5(2 + x)(2 - x)$

   c. $5(x - 2)^2$ **d.** prime

13. $6t^2 + t - 5$

   a. $(6t + 5)(t - 1)$ **b.** $(6t - 5)(t + 1)$

   c. $(6t - 1)(t + 5)$ **d.** $(6t + 1)(t - 5)$

14. $xy^2 + 4y^2 - 25x - 100$

    a. $(x - 4)(y + 5)(y - 5)$ **b.** $(x + 4)(y - 5)^2$

    c. $(x + 4)(y + 5)(y - 5)$ **d.** $(x + 4)(y^2 - 25)$

15. $x - x^5$

    a. $x(x^2 + 1)^2$ **b.** prime

    c. $x(1 + x^2)(1 - x)(1 + x)$ **d.** $x(x^2 - 1)^2$

16. $-rs^8 - r^8s$

    a. $-rs(s^7 + r^7)$ **b.** $-rs(r - s)(r^6 + rs + s^6)$

    c. $-rs(r - s)(r - s)$ **d.** $-rs(r + s)(r^6 - rs + s^6)$

17. $125x^3 - 1$

    a. $(5x + 1)(25x^2 - 5x + 1)$ **b.** $(5x - 1)(25x^2 + 1)$

    c. $(5x - 1)(25x^2 + 5x + 1)$ **d.** $(125x - 1)(x^2 + 5x + 1)$

18. $3x^3 - 81$

    a. $3(x - 3)(x^2 - 3x + 9)$ **b.** $3(x + 3)(x^2 - 3x + 9)$

    c. $3(x - 9)(x^2 + 9x + 27)$ **d.** $3(x - 3)(x^2 + 3x + 9)$

Solve the equation.

19. $(x - 5)(x + 9) = 0$

    a. $5, -9$ **b.** $5, 9$ **c.** $5, -5, 9, -9$ **d.** $-5, 9$

20. $x^2 + 4x = 12$

    a. $6, -2$ **b.** $-6, 2$ **c.** $6, 2$ **d.** $-6, 1$

21. $x(x - 4) = 12$

    a. $-2, 6$ **b.** $0, 4$ **c.** $2, 6$ **d.** $2, -6$

22. $3x(3x - 5)(6x + 5) = 0$

    a. $0, -\dfrac{5}{3}, \dfrac{5}{6}$ **b.** $0, \dfrac{2}{5}, -\dfrac{6}{5}$

    c. $\dfrac{5}{3}, -\dfrac{5}{6}$ **d.** $0, \dfrac{5}{3}, -\dfrac{5}{6}$

23. $16t^3 - 16t = 0$

    a. $-1, 1$ **b.** $-1, 1, 0$ **c.** 1 **d.** 0

24. $t^2 + 6t - 55 = 0$

    a. $-11, 5$ **b.** $-11, 1$ **c.** $11, 5$ **d.** $11, -5$

25. $11x^2 = 6x$

    a. $0, \dfrac{11}{6}$ **b.** $-\dfrac{11}{6}, 0$ **c.** $-\dfrac{6}{11}, 0$ **d.** $0, \dfrac{6}{11}$

Solve.

26. A triangular piece of glass is being cut so that the height of the triangle is 4 inches shorter than twice the base. If the area of the triangle is 120 square inches, how long is the height of the triangle?

    a. 12 in.   **b.** 22 in.   **c.** 20 in.   **d.** 24 in.

27. The sum of two numbers is 15 and the sum of their squares is 125. Find the numbers.

    a. 11 and 4   **b.** 10 and 5

    c. 12 and 3   **d.** 9 and 6

28. A window washer accidentally drops a bucket from the top of a 64-foot building. The height h of the bucket after t seconds is given by $h = -16t^2 + 64$. When will the bucket hit the ground?

    a. 32 sec   **b.** 2 sec   **c.** 4 sec   **d.** -2 sec

29. One leg of a right triangle is 21 inches longer than the smaller leg, and the hypotenuse is 24 inches longer than the smaller leg. Find the lengths of the sides of the triangle.

    a. 12 in., 33 in., 36 in.   **b.** 15 in., 36 in., 39 in.

    c. 14 in., 35 in., 40 in.   **d.** 16 in., 37 in., 40 in.

30. The expression $2x^2 + x - 15$ factors as $(2x - 5)(x + 3)$. Use this information to list the x-intercepts of the graph of $y = 2x^2 + x - 15$.

    a. $(3, 0), \left(-\dfrac{5}{2}, 0\right)$ **b.** $(-3, 0), \left(\dfrac{5}{2}, 0\right)$

    c. $(3, 0), \left(\dfrac{5}{2}, 0\right)$ **d.** $(-3, 0), (5, 0)$

Rational Expressions

Cephalic Index for Dogs		
Value	**Scientific Term**	**Meaning**
<80 or <75	*dolichocephalic*	"long-headed"
	mesocephalic	"medium-headed"
>80	*brachycephalic*	"short-headed"

Cephalic index is used by anthropologists on animal skulls to categorize animals such as dogs and cats. In this chapter, you will have the opportunity to calculate this index for a human skull.

$$\text{Cephalic Index Formula: } C = \frac{100\,W}{L}$$

where W is width of the skull and L is length of the skull.

A **brachycephalic** skull is relatively broad and short, as in the Pug.
A **mesocephalic** skull is of intermediate length and width, as in the Cocker Spaniel.
A **dolichocephalic** skull is relatively long, as in the Afghan Hound.

8.1 SIMPLIFYING RATIONAL EXPRESSIONS

OBJECTIVES

1 Find the value of a rational expression given a replacement number.

2 Identify values for which a rational expression is undefined.

3 Simplify or write rational expressions in lowest terms.

4 Write equivalent rational expressions of the form $-\dfrac{a}{b} = \dfrac{-a}{b} = \dfrac{a}{-b}$.

OBJECTIVE 1 ▶ Evaluating rational expressions. As we reviewed in Chapter 1, a rational number is a number that can be written as a quotient of integers. A **rational expression** is also a quotient; it is a quotient of polynomials.

> **Rational Expression**
>
> A rational expression is an expression that can be written in the form $\dfrac{P}{Q}$, where P and Q are polynomials and $Q \neq 0$.

Rational Expressions

$$\frac{2}{3} \qquad \frac{3y^3}{8} \qquad \frac{-4p}{p^3 + 2p + 1} \qquad \frac{5x^2 - 3x + 2}{3x + 7}$$

Rational expressions have different values depending on what value replaces the variable. Next, we review the standard order of operations by finding values of rational expressions for given replacement values of the variable.

EXAMPLE 1 Find the value of $\dfrac{x + 4}{2x - 3}$ for the given replacement values.

a. $x = 5$ **b.** $x = -2$

Solution

a. Replace each x in the expression with 5 and then simplify.

$$\frac{x + 4}{2x - 3} = \frac{5 + 4}{2(5) - 3} = \frac{9}{10 - 3} = \frac{9}{7}$$

b. Replace each x in the expression with -2 and then simplify.

$$\frac{x + 4}{2x - 3} = \frac{-2 + 4}{2(-2) - 3} = \frac{2}{-7} \quad \text{or} \quad -\frac{2}{7} \qquad \square$$

PRACTICE

1 Find the value of $\dfrac{x + 6}{3x - 2}$ for the given replacement values.

a. $x = 3$ **b.** $x = -3$

In the example above, we wrote $\dfrac{2}{-7}$ as $-\dfrac{2}{7}$. For a negative fraction such as $\dfrac{2}{-7}$, recall from Section 1.8 that

$$\frac{2}{-7} = \frac{-2}{7} = -\frac{2}{7}$$

In general, for any fraction,

$$\frac{-a}{b} = \frac{a}{-b} = -\frac{a}{b}, \qquad b \neq 0$$

This is also true for rational expressions. For example,

$$\underbrace{\frac{-(x + 2)}{x}}_{\uparrow} = \frac{x + 2}{-x} = -\frac{x + 2}{x}$$

Notice the parentheses.

▶ Helpful Hint

Do you recall why division by 0 is not defined? Remember, for example, that $\frac{8}{4} = 2$ because $2 \cdot 4 = 8$. Thus, if $\frac{8}{0} = a\ number$, then *the number* $\cdot 0 = 8$.

There is no number that when multiplied by 0 equals 8; thus $\frac{8}{0}$ is undefined. This is true in general for fractions and rational expressions.

OBJECTIVE 2 ▶ Identifying when a rational expression is undefined. In the definition of rational expression (first "box" in this section), notice that we wrote $Q \neq 0$ for the denominator Q. This is because the denominator of a rational expression must not equal 0 since division by 0 is not defined. (See the margin Helpful Hint.) This means we must be careful when replacing the variable in a rational expression by a number. For example, suppose we replace x with 5 in the rational expression $\frac{3 + x}{x - 5}$. The expression becomes

$$\frac{3 + x}{x - 5} = \frac{3 + 5}{5 - 5} = \frac{8}{0}$$

But division by 0 is undefined. Therefore, in this rational expression we can allow x to be any real number *except* 5. **A rational expression is undefined for values that make the denominator 0.** Thus, to find values for which a rational expression is undefined, find values for which the denominator is 0.

EXAMPLE 2 Are there any values for x for which each rational expression is undefined?

a. $\dfrac{x}{x - 3}$ **b.** $\dfrac{x^2 + 2}{3x^2 - 5x + 2}$ **c.** $\dfrac{x^3 - 6x^2 - 10x}{3}$ **d.** $\dfrac{2}{x^2 + 1}$

Solution To find values for which a rational expression is undefined, find values that make the *denominator* 0.

a. The denominator of $\dfrac{x}{x - 3}$ is 0 when $x - 3 = 0$ or when $x = 3$. Thus, when $x = 3$, the expression $\dfrac{x}{x - 3}$ is undefined.

b. Set the denominator equal to zero.

$$3x^2 - 5x + 2 = 0$$
$$(3x - 2)(x - 1) = 0 \qquad \text{Factor.}$$
$$3x - 2 = 0 \quad \text{or} \quad x - 1 = 0 \qquad \text{Set each factor equal to zero.}$$
$$3x = 2 \quad \text{or} \quad x = 1 \qquad \text{Solve.}$$
$$x = \frac{2}{3}$$

Thus, when $x = \dfrac{2}{3}$ or $x = 1$, the denominator $3x^2 - 5x + 2$ is 0. So the rational expression $\dfrac{x^2 + 2}{3x^2 - 5x + 2}$ is undefined when $x = \dfrac{2}{3}$ or when $x = 1$.

c. The denominator of $\dfrac{x^3 - 6x^2 - 10x}{3}$ is never 0, so there are no values of x for which this expression is undefined.

d. No matter which real number x is replaced by, the denominator $x^2 + 1$ does not equal 0, so there are no real numbers for which this expression is undefined. □

PRACTICE

2 Are there any values of x for which each rational expression is undefined?

a. $\dfrac{x}{x + 6}$ **b.** $\dfrac{x^4 - 3x^2 + 7x}{7}$ **c.** $\dfrac{x^2 - 5}{x^2 + 6x + 8}$ **d.** $\dfrac{3}{x^4 + 5}$

Note: Unless otherwise stated, we will now assume that variables in rational expressions are only replaced by values for which the expressions are defined.

OBJECTIVE 3 ▶ Simplifying rational expressions. A fraction is said to be written in lowest terms or simplest form when the numerator and denominator have no common factors other than 1 (or -1). For example, the fraction $\dfrac{7}{10}$ is in lowest terms since the numerator and denominator have no common factors other than 1 (or -1).

The process of writing a rational expression in lowest terms or simplest form is called **simplifying** a rational expression.

Simplifying a rational expression is similar to simplifying a fraction. Recall that to simplify a fraction, we essentially "remove factors of 1." Our ability to do this comes from these facts:

- Any nonzero number over itself simplifies to 1 $\left(\dfrac{5}{5} = 1, \dfrac{-7.26}{-7.26} = 1, \text{ or } \dfrac{c}{c} = 1 \text{ as long as } c \text{ is not } 0\right)$, and

- The product of any number and 1 is that number $\left(19 \cdot 1 = 19, -8.9 \cdot 1 = -8.9, \dfrac{a}{b} \cdot 1 = \dfrac{a}{b}\right)$.

In other words, we have the following:

Simplify: $\dfrac{15}{20}$

$$\dfrac{15}{20} = \dfrac{3 \cdot 5}{2 \cdot 2 \cdot 5}$$ Factor the numerator and the denominator.

$$= \dfrac{3 \cdot 5}{2 \cdot 2 \cdot 5}$$ Look for common factors.

$$= \dfrac{3}{2 \cdot 2} \cdot \dfrac{5}{5}$$ Common factors in the numerator and denominator form factors of 1.

$$= \dfrac{3}{2 \cdot 2} \cdot 1$$ Write $\dfrac{5}{5}$ as 1.

$$= \dfrac{3}{2 \cdot 2} = \dfrac{3}{4}$$ Multiply to remove a factor of 1.

$$\dfrac{a \cdot c}{b \cdot c} = \dfrac{a}{b} \cdot \dfrac{c}{c} = \dfrac{a}{b}$$

Since $\dfrac{a}{b} \cdot 1 = \dfrac{a}{b}$

Before we use the same technique to simplify a rational expression, remember that as long as the denominator is not 0, $\dfrac{a^3 b}{a^3 b} = 1$, $\dfrac{x + 3}{x + 3} = 1$, and $\dfrac{7x^2 + 5x - 100}{7x^2 + 5x - 100} = 1$.

Simplify: $\dfrac{x^2 - 9}{x^2 + x - 6}$

$$\dfrac{x^2 - 9}{x^2 + x - 6} = \dfrac{(x - 3)(x + 3)}{(x - 2)(x + 3)}$$ Factor the numerator and the denominator.

$$= \dfrac{(x - 3)(x + 3)}{(x - 2)(x + 3)}$$ Look for common factors.

$$= \dfrac{x - 3}{x - 2} \cdot \dfrac{x + 3}{x + 3}$$

$$= \dfrac{x - 3}{x - 2} \cdot 1$$ Write $\dfrac{x + 3}{x + 3}$ as 1.

$$= \dfrac{x - 3}{x - 2}$$ Multiply to remove a factor of 1.

Just as for numerical fractions, we can use a shortcut notation. Remember that as long as exact factors in both the numerator and denominator are divided out, we are "removing a factor of 1." We will use the following notation to show this:

$$\dfrac{x^2 - 9}{x^2 + x - 6} = \dfrac{(x - 3)(x + 3)}{(x - 2)(x + 3)}$$ A factor of 1 is identified by the shading.

$$= \dfrac{x - 3}{x - 2}$$ Remove a factor of 1.

Thus, the rational expression $\dfrac{x^2 - 9}{x^2 + x - 6}$ has the same value as the rational expression $\dfrac{x - 3}{x - 2}$ for all values of x except 2 and -3. (Remember that when x is 2, the denominator of both rational expressions is 0 and when x is -3, the original rational expression has a denominator of 0.)

As we simplify rational expressions, we will assume that the simplified rational expression is equal to the original rational expression for all real numbers except those for which either denominator is 0. The following steps may be used to simplify rational expressions.

> **To Simplify a Rational Expression**
> **STEP 1.** Completely factor the numerator and denominator.
> **STEP 2.** Divide out factors common to the numerator and denominator. (This is the same as "removing a factor of 1.")

EXAMPLE 3   Simplify: $\dfrac{5x - 5}{x^3 - x^2}$

Solution   To begin, we factor the numerator and denominator if possible. Then we look for common factors.

$$\frac{5x - 5}{x^3 - x^2} = \frac{5\,(x - 1)}{x^2\,(x - 1)} = \frac{5}{x^2}$$

PRACTICE
3   Simplify: $\dfrac{x^6 - x^5}{6x - 6}$

EXAMPLE 4   Simplify: $\dfrac{x^2 + 8x + 7}{x^2 - 4x - 5}$

Solution   We factor the numerator and denominator and then look for common factors.

$$\frac{x^2 + 8x + 7}{x^2 - 4x - 5} = \frac{(x + 7)\,(x + 1)}{(x - 5)\,(x + 1)} = \frac{x + 7}{x - 5}$$

PRACTICE
4   Simplify: $\dfrac{x^2 + 5x + 4}{x^2 + 2x - 8}$

EXAMPLE 5   Simplify: $\dfrac{x^2 + 4x + 4}{x^2 + 2x}$

Solution   We factor the numerator and denominator and then look for common factors.

$$\frac{x^2 + 4x + 4}{x^2 + 2x} = \frac{(x + 2)\,(x + 2)}{x\,(x + 2)} = \frac{x + 2}{x}$$

PRACTICE
5   Simplify: $\dfrac{x^3 + 9x^2}{x^2 + 18x + 81}$

> ▶ **Helpful Hint**
> When simplifying a rational expression, we look for **common *factors*, not common *terms*.**
>
>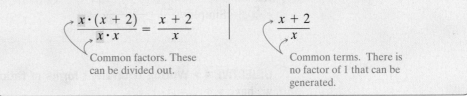
>
> $\dfrac{x \cdot (x + 2)}{x \cdot x} = \dfrac{x + 2}{x}$ $\dfrac{x + 2}{x}$
>
> Common factors. These   Common terms. There is
> can be divided out.   no factor of 1 that can be
>   generated.

Concept Check ☑

Recall that we can only remove *factors* of 1. Which of the following are *not* true? Explain why.

a. $\dfrac{3 - 1}{3 + 5}$ simplifies to $-\dfrac{1}{5}$?   **b.** $\dfrac{2x + 10}{2}$ simplifies to $x + 5$?

c. $\dfrac{37}{72}$ simplifies to $\dfrac{3}{2}$?   **d.** $\dfrac{2x + 3}{2}$ simplifies to $x + 3$?

EXAMPLE 6 Simplify: $\dfrac{x + 9}{x^2 - 81}$

Solution We factor and then divide out common factors.

$$\frac{x + 9}{x^2 - 81} = \frac{x + 9}{(x + 9)(x - 9)} = \frac{1}{x - 9}$$

PRACTICE
6 Simplify: $\dfrac{x - 7}{x^2 - 49}$

EXAMPLE 7 Simplify each rational expression.

a. $\dfrac{x + y}{y + x}$ **b.** $\dfrac{x - y}{y - x}$

Solution

a. The expression $\dfrac{x + y}{y + x}$ can be simplified by using the commutative property of addition to rewrite the denominator $y + x$ as $x + y$.

$$\frac{x + y}{y + x} = \frac{x + y}{x + y} = 1$$

b. The expression $\dfrac{x - y}{y - x}$ can be simplified by recognizing that $y - x$ and $x - y$ are opposites. In other words, $y - x = -1(x - y)$. We proceed as follows:

$$\frac{x - y}{y - x} = \frac{1 \cdot (x - y)}{-1 \cdot (x - y)} = \frac{1}{-1} = -1$$

PRACTICE
7 Simplify each rational expression.

a. $\dfrac{s - t}{t - s}$ **b.** $\dfrac{2c + d}{d + 2c}$

EXAMPLE 8 Simplify: $\dfrac{4 - x^2}{3x^2 - 5x - 2}$

Solution

$$\frac{4 - x^2}{3x^2 - 5x - 2} = \frac{(2 - x)(2 + x)}{(x - 2)(3x + 1)} \qquad \text{Factor.}$$

$$= \frac{(-1)(x - 2)(2 + x)}{(x - 2)(3x + 1)} \qquad \text{Write } 2 - x \text{ as } -1(x - 2).$$

$$= \frac{(-1)(2 + x)}{3x + 1} \quad \text{or} \quad \frac{-2 - x}{3x + 1} \qquad \text{Simplify.}$$

PRACTICE
8 Simplify: $\dfrac{2x^2 - 5x - 12}{16 - x^2}$

OBJECTIVE 4 ▶ Writing equivalent forms of rational expressions. From Example 7a, we have $y + x = x + y$. _____ $y + x$ and $x + y$ are equivalent.

From Example 7b, we have $y - x = -1(x - y)$. _____ $y - x$ and $x - y$ are opposites.

Thus, $\dfrac{x + y}{y + x} = \dfrac{x + y}{x + y} = 1$ and $\dfrac{x - y}{y - x} = \dfrac{x - y}{-1(x - y)} = \dfrac{1}{-1} = -1$.

When performing operations on rational expressions, equivalent forms of answers often result. For this reason, it is very important to be able to recognize equivalent answers.

EXAMPLE 9 List some equivalent forms of $-\dfrac{5x-1}{x+9}$.

Solution To do so, recall that $-\dfrac{a}{b} = \dfrac{-a}{b} = \dfrac{a}{-b}$. Thus

$$-\frac{5x-1}{x+9} = \frac{-(5x-1)}{x+9} = \frac{-5x+1}{x+9} \quad \text{or} \quad \frac{1-5x}{x+9}$$

Also,

$$-\frac{5x-1}{x+9} = \frac{5x-1}{-(x+9)} = \frac{5x-1}{-x-9} \quad \text{or} \quad \frac{5x-1}{-9-x}$$

Thus $-\dfrac{5x-1}{x+9} = \dfrac{-(5x-1)}{x+9} = \dfrac{-5x+1}{x+9} = \dfrac{5x-1}{-(x+9)} = \dfrac{5x-1}{-x-9}$ ☐

PRACTICE 9 List some equivalent forms of $-\dfrac{x+3}{6x-11}$.

> ▶ **Helpful Hint**
>
> Remember, a negative sign in front of a fraction or rational expression may be moved to the numerator or the denominator, but *not* both.

Keep in mind that many rational expressions may look different, but in fact be equivalent.

VOCABULARY & READINESS CHECK

Word Bank. *Use the choices below to fill in each blank. Not all choices will be used.*

-1	0	simplifying	$\dfrac{-a}{-b}$	$\dfrac{-a}{b}$	$\dfrac{a}{-b}$
1	2	rational expression			

1. A _____ is an expression that can be written in the form $\dfrac{P}{Q}$ where P and Q are polynomials and $Q \neq 0$.

2. The expression $\dfrac{x+3}{3+x}$ simplifies to _____.

3. The expression $\dfrac{x-3}{3-x}$ simplifies to _____.

4. A rational expression is undefined for values that make the denominator _____.

5. The expression $\dfrac{7x}{x-2}$ is undefined for $x =$ _____.

6. The process of writing a rational expression in lowest terms is called _____.

7. For a rational expression, $-\dfrac{a}{b} =$ _____ $=$ _____.

Decision Making. *Decide which rational expression can be simplified. (Do not actually simplify.)*

8. $\dfrac{x}{x+7}$ 9. $\dfrac{3+x}{x+3}$ 10. $\dfrac{5-x}{x-5}$ 11. $\dfrac{x+2}{x+8}$

8.1 EXERCISE SET

MyMathLab®   Math XL   PRACTICE   WATCH   DOWNLOAD   READ   REVIEW

Find the value of the following expressions when $x = 2$, $y = -2$, and $z = -5$. See Example 1.

1. $\dfrac{x+5}{x+2}$

2. $\dfrac{x+8}{x+1}$

3. $\dfrac{4z-1}{z-2}$

4. $\dfrac{7y-1}{y-1}$

5. $\dfrac{y^3}{y^2-1}$

6. $\dfrac{z}{z^2-5}$

7. $\dfrac{x^2+8x+2}{x^2-x-6}$

8. $\dfrac{x+5}{x^2+4x-8}$

Find any numbers for which each rational expression is undefined. See Example 2.

9. $\dfrac{7}{2x}$

10. $\dfrac{3}{5x}$

11. $\dfrac{x+3}{x+2}$

12. $\dfrac{5x+1}{x-9}$

13. $\dfrac{x-4}{2x-5}$

14. $\dfrac{x+1}{5x-2}$

15. $\dfrac{x^2-5x-2}{4}$

16. $\dfrac{9y^5+y^3}{9}$

17. $\dfrac{3x^2+9}{x^2-5x-6}$

18. $\dfrac{11x^2+1}{x^2-5x-14}$

19. $\dfrac{9x^3+4}{x^2+36}$

20. $\dfrac{19x^3+2}{x^2+4}$

21. $\dfrac{x}{3x^2+13x+14}$

22. $\dfrac{x}{2x^2+15x+27}$

Study Example 9. Then list four equivalent forms for each rational expression.

23. $-\dfrac{x-10}{x+8}$

24. $-\dfrac{x+11}{x-4}$

25. $-\dfrac{5y-3}{y-12}$

26. $-\dfrac{8y-1}{y-15}$

Simplify each expression. See Examples 3 through 8.

27. $\dfrac{x+7}{7+x}$

28. $\dfrac{y+9}{9+y}$

29. $\dfrac{x-7}{7-x}$

30. $\dfrac{y-9}{9-y}$

31. $\dfrac{2}{8x+16}$

32. $\dfrac{3}{9x+6}$

33. $\dfrac{x-2}{x^2-4}$

34. $\dfrac{x+5}{x^2-25}$

35. $\dfrac{2x-10}{3x-30}$

36. $\dfrac{3x-9}{4x-16}$

37. $\dfrac{-5a-5b}{a+b}$

38. $\dfrac{-4x-4y}{x+y}$

39. $\dfrac{7x+35}{x^2+5x}$

40. $\dfrac{9x+99}{x^2+11x}$

41. $\dfrac{x+5}{x^2-4x-45}$

42. $\dfrac{x-3}{x^2-6x+9}$

43. $\dfrac{5x^2+11x+2}{x+2}$

44. $\dfrac{12x^2+4x-1}{2x+1}$

45. $\dfrac{x^3+7x^2}{x^2+5x-14}$

46. $\dfrac{x^4-10x^3}{x^2-17x+70}$

47. $\dfrac{14x^2-21x}{2x-3}$

48. $\dfrac{4x^2+24x}{x+6}$

49. $\dfrac{x^2+7x+10}{x^2-3x-10}$

50. $\dfrac{2x^2+7x-4}{x^2+3x-4}$

51. $\dfrac{3x^2+7x+2}{3x^2+13x+4}$

52. $\dfrac{4x^2-4x+1}{2x^2+9x-5}$

53. $\dfrac{2x^2-8}{4x-8}$

54. $\dfrac{5x^2-500}{35x+350}$

55. $\dfrac{4-x^2}{x-2}$

56. $\dfrac{49-y^2}{y-7}$

57. $\dfrac{x^2-1}{x^2-2x+1}$

58. $\dfrac{x^2-16}{x^2-8x+16}$

59. $\dfrac{m^2-6m+9}{m^2-m-6}$

60. $\dfrac{m^2-4m+4}{m^2+m-6}$

61. $\dfrac{11x^2-22x^3}{6x-12x^2}$

62. $\dfrac{24y^2-8y^3}{15y-5y^2}$

Simplify. These expressions contain 4-term polynomials and sums and differences of cubes.

63. $\dfrac{x^2+xy+2x+2y}{x+2}$

64. $\dfrac{ab+ac+b^2+bc}{b+c}$

65. $\dfrac{5x+15-xy-3y}{2x+6}$

66. $\dfrac{xy-6x+2y-12}{y^2-6y}$

67. $\dfrac{x^3+8}{x+2}$

68. $\dfrac{x^3+64}{x+4}$

69. $\dfrac{x^3-1}{1-x}$

70. $\dfrac{3-x}{x^3-27}$

71. $\dfrac{2xy+5x-2y-5}{3xy+4x-3y-4}$

72. $\dfrac{2xy+2x-3y-3}{2xy+4x-3y-6}$

MIXED PRACTICE

Decision Making. *Simplify each expression. Then determine whether the given answer is correct. See Examples 3 through 9.*

73. $\dfrac{9-x^2}{x-3}$; Answer: $-3-x$

74. $\dfrac{100-x^2}{x-10}$; Answer: $-10-x$

75. $\dfrac{7-34x-5x^2}{25x^2-1}$; Answer: $\dfrac{x+7}{-5x-1}$

76. $\dfrac{2-15x-8x^2}{64x^2-1}$; Answer: $\dfrac{x+2}{-8x-1}$

REVIEW AND PREVIEW

Perform each indicated operation. See Section 1.3.

77. $\dfrac{1}{3}\cdot\dfrac{9}{11}$

78. $\dfrac{5}{27}\cdot\dfrac{2}{5}$

79. $\dfrac{1}{3}\div\dfrac{1}{4}$

80. $\dfrac{7}{8}\div\dfrac{1}{2}$

81. $\dfrac{13}{20}\div\dfrac{2}{9}$

82. $\dfrac{8}{15}\div\dfrac{5}{8}$

CONCEPT EXTENSIONS

Decision Making. *Which of the following are incorrect and why? See the Concept Check in this section.*

83. $\dfrac{5a-15}{5}$ simplifies to $a-3$?

84. $\dfrac{7m-9}{7}$ simplifies to $m-9$?

85. $\dfrac{1+2}{1+3}$ simplifies to $\dfrac{2}{3}$?

86. $\dfrac{46}{54}$ simplifies to $\dfrac{6}{5}$?

87. Explain how to write a fraction in lowest terms.

88. Explain how to write a rational expression in lowest terms.

89. Explain why the denominator of a fraction or a rational expression must not equal 0.

90. Does $\dfrac{(x - 3)(x + 3)}{x - 3}$ have the same value as $x + 3$ for all real numbers? Explain why or why not.

91. Multiple Steps. The total revenue R from the sale of a popular music compact disc is approximately given by the equation

$$R = \frac{150x^2}{x^2 + 3}$$

where x is the number of years since the CD has been released and revenue R is in millions of dollars.
- **a.** Find the total revenue generated by the end of the first year.
- **b.** Find the total revenue generated by the end of the second year.
- **c.** Find the total revenue generated in the second year only.

92. Multiple Steps. For a certain model fax machine, the manufacturing cost C per machine is given by the equation

$$C = \frac{250x + 10,000}{x}$$

where x is the number of fax machines manufactured and cost C is in dollars per machine.
- **a.** Find the cost per fax machine when manufacturing 100 fax machines.
- **b.** Find the cost per fax machine when manufacturing 1000 fax machines.
- **c.** Does the cost per machine decrease or increase when more machines are manufactured? Explain why this is so.

Solve.

93. The dose of medicine prescribed for a child depends on the child's age A in years and the adult dose D for the medication. Young's Rule is a formula used by pediatricians that gives a child's dose C as

$$C = \frac{DA}{A + 12}$$

Suppose that an 8-year-old child needs medication, and the normal adult dose is 1000 mg. What size dose should the child receive?

94. Calculating body-mass index is a way to gauge whether a person should lose weight. Doctors recommend that body-mass index values fall between 18.5 and 25. The formula for body-mass index B is

$$B = \frac{703w}{h^2}$$

where w is weight in pounds and h is height in inches. Should a 148-pound person who is 5 feet 6 inches tall lose weight?

95. Anthropologists and forensic scientists use a measure called the cephalic index to help classify skulls. The cephalic index of a skull with width W and length L from front to back is given by the formula

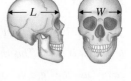

$$C = \frac{100W}{L}$$

A long skull has an index value less than 75, a medium skull has an index value between 75 and 85, and a broad skull has an index value over 85. Find the cephalic index of a skull that is 5 inches wide and 6.4 inches long. Classify the skull.

96. During a storm, water treatment engineers monitor how quickly rain is falling. If too much rain comes too fast, there is a danger of sewers backing up. A formula that gives the rainfall intensity i in millimeters per hour for a certain strength storm in eastern Virginia is

$$i = \frac{5840}{t + 29}$$

where t is the duration of the storm in minutes. What rainfall intensity should engineers expect for a storm of this strength in eastern Virginia that lasts for 80 minutes? Round your answer to one decimal place.

97. To calculate a quarterback's rating in football, you may use the formula $\left[\dfrac{20C + 0.5A + Y + 80T - 100I}{A}\right]\left(\dfrac{25}{6}\right)$, where C = the number of completed passes, A = the number of attempted passes, Y = total yards thrown for passes, T = the number of touchdown passes, and I = the number of interceptions. For the 2006 season, Peyton Manning, of the Indianapolis Colts, had final season totals of 557 attempts, 362 completions, 4397 yards, 31 touchdown passes, and 9 interceptions. Calculate Manning's quarterback rating for the 2006 season. Round the answer to the nearest tenth. (*Source:* The NFL)

98. A baseball player's slugging percent S can be calculated by the following formula: $S = \dfrac{h + d + 2t + 3r}{b}$, where h = number of hits, d = number of doubles, t = number of triples, r = number of home runs, and b = number at bats. During the 2006 season, David Ortiz of the Boston Red Sox had 558 at bats, 160 hits, 29 doubles, 2 triples, and 54 home runs. Calculate Ortiz's 2006 slugging percent. Round to the nearest tenth of a percent. (*Source:* Major League Baseball)

99. A company's gross profit margin P can be computed with the formula $P = \dfrac{R - C}{R}$, where R = the company's revenue and C = cost of goods sold. For fiscal year 2006, consumer electronics retailer Best Buy had revenues of $30.8 billion and cost of goods sold of $23.1 billion. What was Best Buy's gross profit margin in 2006? Express the answer as a percent, rounded to the nearest tenth of a percent. (*Source:* Best Buy Company, Inc.)

How does the graph of $y = \dfrac{x^2 - 9}{x - 3}$ *compare to the graph of* $y = x + 3$? *Recall that* $\dfrac{x^2 - 9}{x - 3} = \dfrac{(x + 3)(x - 3)}{x - 3} = x + 3$ *as long as x is not 3. This means that the graph of* $y = \dfrac{x^2 - 9}{x - 3}$ *is the same as the graph of* $y = x + 3$ *with* $x \neq 3$*. To graph* $y = \dfrac{x^2 - 9}{x - 3}$*, then, graph the linear equation* $y = x + 3$ *and place an open dot on the graph at 3. This open dot or interruption of the line at 3 means* $x \neq 3$.

100. Graph $y = \dfrac{x^2 - 25}{x + 5}$.

101. Graph $y = \dfrac{x^2 - 16}{x - 4}$.

102. Graph $y = \dfrac{x^2 + x - 12}{x + 4}$.

103. Graph $y = \dfrac{x^2 - 6x + 8}{x - 2}$.

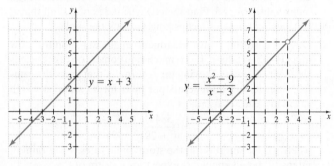

8.2 MULTIPLYING AND DIVIDING RATIONAL EXPRESSIONS

OBJECTIVES

1 Multiply rational expressions.

2 Divide rational expressions.

3 Multiply or divide rational expressions.

OBJECTIVE 1 ▶ Multiplying rational expressions. Just as simplifying rational expressions is similar to simplifying number fractions, multiplying and dividing rational expressions is similar to multiplying and dividing number fractions.

Fractions	*Rational Expressions*
Multiply: $\dfrac{3}{5} \cdot \dfrac{10}{11}$	Multiply: $\dfrac{x - 3}{x + 5} \cdot \dfrac{2x + 10}{x^2 - 9}$

Multiply numerators and then multiply denominators.

$$\frac{3}{5} \cdot \frac{10}{11} = \frac{3 \cdot 10}{5 \cdot 11} \qquad \frac{x - 3}{x + 5} \cdot \frac{2x + 10}{x^2 - 9} = \frac{(x - 3) \cdot (2x + 10)}{(x + 5) \cdot (x^2 - 9)}$$

Simplify by factoring numerators and denominators.

$$= \frac{3 \cdot 2 \cdot 5}{5 \cdot 11} \qquad = \frac{(x - 3) \cdot 2 (x + 5)}{(x + 5)(x + 3)(x - 3)}$$

Apply the fundamental principle.

$$= \frac{3 \cdot 2}{11} \quad \text{or} \quad \frac{6}{11} \qquad = \frac{2}{x + 3}$$

Multiplying Rational Expressions

If $\dfrac{P}{Q}$ and $\dfrac{R}{S}$ are rational expressions, then

$$\frac{P}{Q} \cdot \frac{R}{S} = \frac{PR}{QS}$$

To multiply rational expressions, multiply the numerators and then multiply the denominators.

Note: Recall that for Sections 8.1 through 8.4, we assume variables in rational expressions have only those replacement values for which the expressions are defined.

EXAMPLE 1   Multiply.

a. $\dfrac{25x}{2} \cdot \dfrac{1}{y^3}$ **b.** $\dfrac{-7x^2}{5y} \cdot \dfrac{3y^5}{14x^2}$

Solution   To multiply rational expressions, multiply the numerators and then multiply the denominators of both expressions. Then simplify if possible.

a. $\dfrac{25x}{2} \cdot \dfrac{1}{y^3} = \dfrac{25x \cdot 1}{2 \cdot y^3} = \dfrac{25x}{2y^3}$

The expression $\dfrac{25x}{2y^3}$ is in simplest form.

b. $\dfrac{-7x^2}{5y} \cdot \dfrac{3y^5}{14x^2} = \dfrac{-7x^2 \cdot 3y^5}{5y \cdot 14x^2}$ Multiply.

The expression $\dfrac{-7x^2 \cdot 3y^5}{5y \cdot 14x^2}$ is not in simplest form, so we factor the numerator and the denominator and divide out common factors.

$$= \dfrac{-1 \cdot 7 \cdot 3 \cdot x^2 \cdot y \cdot y^4}{5 \cdot 2 \cdot 7 \cdot x^2 \cdot y}$$

$$= -\dfrac{3y^4}{10}$$ □

PRACTICE
1   Multiply.

a. $\dfrac{4a}{5} \cdot \dfrac{3}{b^2}$ **b.** $\dfrac{-3p^4}{q^2} \cdot \dfrac{2q^3}{9p^4}$

When multiplying rational expressions, it is usually best to factor each numerator and denominator. This will help us when we divide out common factors to write the product in lowest terms.

EXAMPLE 2   Multiply: $\dfrac{x^2 + x}{3x} \cdot \dfrac{6}{5x + 5}$

Solution $\dfrac{x^2 + x}{3x} \cdot \dfrac{6}{5x + 5} = \dfrac{x(x + 1)}{3x} \cdot \dfrac{2 \cdot 3}{5(x + 1)}$ Factor numerators and denominators.

$$= \dfrac{x(x + 1) \cdot 2 \cdot 3}{3x \cdot 5 (x + 1)}$$ Multiply.

$$= \dfrac{2}{5}$$ Simplify by dividing out common factors.   □

PRACTICE
2   Multiply: $\dfrac{x^2 - x}{5x} \cdot \dfrac{15}{x^2 - 1}$.

The following steps may be used to multiply rational expressions.

Multiplying Rational Expressions

STEP 1. Completely factor numerators and denominators.

STEP 2. Multiply numerators and multiply denominators.

STEP 3. Simplify or write the product in lowest terms by dividing out common factors.

Concept Check ☑

Which of the following is a true statement?

a. $\dfrac{1}{3} \cdot \dfrac{1}{2} = \dfrac{1}{5}$ **b.** $\dfrac{2}{x} \cdot \dfrac{5}{x} = \dfrac{10}{x}$ **c.** $\dfrac{3}{x} \cdot \dfrac{1}{2} = \dfrac{3}{2x}$ **d.** $\dfrac{x}{7} \cdot \dfrac{x+5}{4} = \dfrac{2x+5}{28}$

EXAMPLE 3   Multiply: $\dfrac{3x+3}{5x-5x^2} \cdot \dfrac{2x^2+x-3}{4x^2-9}$

Solution

$$\dfrac{3x+3}{5x-5x^2} \cdot \dfrac{2x^2+x-3}{4x^2-9} = \dfrac{3(x+1)}{5x(1-x)} \cdot \dfrac{(2x+3)(x-1)}{(2x-3)(2x+3)} \quad \text{Factor.}$$

$$= \dfrac{3(x+1)(2x+3)(x-1)}{5x(1-x)(2x-3)(2x+3)} \quad \text{Multiply.}$$

$$= \dfrac{3(x+1)(x-1)}{5x(1-x)(2x-3)} \quad \text{Divide out common factors.}$$

Next, recall that $x-1$ and $1-x$ are opposites so that $x-1 = -1(1-x)$.

$$= \dfrac{3(x+1)(-1)(1-x)}{5x(1-x)(2x-3)} \quad \text{Write } x-1 \text{ as } -1(1-x).$$

$$= \dfrac{-3(x+1)}{5x(2x-3)} \quad \text{or} \quad -\dfrac{3(x+1)}{5x(2x-3)} \quad \text{Divide out common factors.} \qquad \square$$

PRACTICE
3   Multiply: $\dfrac{6-3x}{6x+6x^2} \cdot \dfrac{3x^2-2x-5}{x^2-4}$.

OBJECTIVE 2 ▶ Dividing rational expressions. We can divide by a rational expression in the same way we divide by a fraction. To divide by a fraction, multiply by its reciprocal.

▶ **Helpful Hint**

Don't forget how to find reciprocals. The reciprocal of $\dfrac{a}{b}$ is $\dfrac{b}{a}$, $a \neq 0, b \neq 0$.

For example, to divide $\dfrac{3}{2}$ by $\dfrac{7}{8}$, multiply $\dfrac{3}{2}$ by $\dfrac{8}{7}$.

$$\dfrac{3}{2} \div \dfrac{7}{8} = \dfrac{3}{2} \cdot \dfrac{8}{7} = \dfrac{3 \cdot 4 \cdot 2}{2 \cdot 7} = \dfrac{12}{7}$$

Dividing Rational Expressions

If $\dfrac{P}{Q}$ and $\dfrac{R}{S}$ are rational expressions and $\dfrac{R}{S}$ is not 0, then

$$\dfrac{P}{Q} \div \dfrac{R}{S} = \dfrac{P}{Q} \cdot \dfrac{S}{R} = \dfrac{PS}{QR}$$

To divide two rational expressions, multiply the first rational expression by the reciprocal of the second rational expression.

Answer to Concept Check: c

EXAMPLE 4 Divide: $\dfrac{3x^3y^7}{40} \div \dfrac{4x^3}{y^2}$

Solution

$$\dfrac{3x^3y^7}{40} \div \dfrac{4x^3}{y^2} = \dfrac{3x^3y^7}{40} \cdot \dfrac{y^2}{4x^3}$$ Multiply by the reciprocal of $\dfrac{4x^3}{y^2}$.

$$= \dfrac{3x^3y^9}{160x^3}$$

$$= \dfrac{3y^9}{160}$$ Simplify. □

PRACTICE
4 Divide: $\dfrac{5a^3b^2}{24} \div \dfrac{10a^5}{6}$.

EXAMPLE 5 Divide: $\dfrac{(x-1)(x+2)}{10}$ by $\dfrac{2x+4}{5}$.

Solution

$$\dfrac{(x-1)(x+2)}{10} \div \dfrac{2x+4}{5} = \dfrac{(x-1)(x+2)}{10} \cdot \dfrac{5}{2x+4}$$ Multiply by the reciprocal of $\dfrac{2x+4}{5}$.

$$= \dfrac{(x-1)(x+2)\cdot 5}{5\cdot 2\cdot 2\cdot(x+2)}$$ Factor and multiply.

$$= \dfrac{x-1}{4}$$ Simplify. □

PRACTICE
5 Divide $\dfrac{(3x+1)(x-5)}{3}$ by $\dfrac{4x-20}{9}$.

The following may be used to divide by a rational expression.

Dividing by a Rational Expression
Multiply by its reciprocal.

EXAMPLE 6 Divide: $\dfrac{6x+2}{x^2-1} \div \dfrac{3x^2+x}{x-1}$

Solution

$$\dfrac{6x+2}{x^2-1} \div \dfrac{3x^2+x}{x-1} = \dfrac{6x+2}{x^2-1} \cdot \dfrac{x-1}{3x^2+x}$$ Multiply by the reciprocal.

$$= \dfrac{2(3x+1)(x-1)}{(x+1)(x-1)\cdot x(3x+1)}$$ Factor and multiply.

$$= \dfrac{2}{x(x+1)}$$ Simplify. □

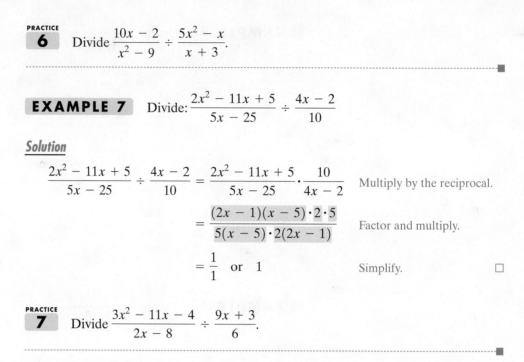

PRACTICE
6 Divide $\dfrac{10x - 2}{x^2 - 9} \div \dfrac{5x^2 - x}{x + 3}$.

EXAMPLE 7 Divide: $\dfrac{2x^2 - 11x + 5}{5x - 25} \div \dfrac{4x - 2}{10}$

Solution

$$\dfrac{2x^2 - 11x + 5}{5x - 25} \div \dfrac{4x - 2}{10} = \dfrac{2x^2 - 11x + 5}{5x - 25} \cdot \dfrac{10}{4x - 2} \qquad \text{Multiply by the reciprocal.}$$

$$= \dfrac{(2x - 1)(x - 5) \cdot 2 \cdot 5}{5(x - 5) \cdot 2(2x - 1)} \qquad \text{Factor and multiply.}$$

$$= \dfrac{1}{1} \quad \text{or} \quad 1 \qquad \text{Simplify.} \qquad \square$$

PRACTICE
7 Divide $\dfrac{3x^2 - 11x - 4}{2x - 8} \div \dfrac{9x + 3}{6}$.

OBJECTIVE 3 ▶ Multiplying or dividing rational expressions. Let's make sure that we understand the difference between multiplying and dividing rational expressions.

Rational Expressions	
Multiplication	Multiply the numerators and multiply the denominators.
Division	Multiply by the reciprocal of the divisor.

EXAMPLE 8 Multiply or divide as indicated.

a. $\dfrac{x - 4}{5} \cdot \dfrac{x}{x - 4}$ **b.** $\dfrac{x - 4}{5} \div \dfrac{x}{x - 4}$ **c.** $\dfrac{x^2 - 4}{2x + 6} \cdot \dfrac{x^2 + 4x + 3}{2 - x}$

Solution

a. $\dfrac{x - 4}{5} \cdot \dfrac{x}{x - 4} = \dfrac{(x - 4) \cdot x}{5 \cdot (x - 4)} = \dfrac{x}{5}$

b. $\dfrac{x - 4}{5} \div \dfrac{x}{x - 4} = \dfrac{x - 4}{5} \cdot \dfrac{x - 4}{x} = \dfrac{(x - 4)^2}{5x}$

c. $\dfrac{x^2 - 4}{2x + 6} \cdot \dfrac{x^2 + 4x + 3}{2 - x} = \dfrac{(x - 2)(x + 2) \cdot (x + 1)(x + 3)}{2(x + 3) \cdot (2 - x)}$ Factor and multiply.

$$= \dfrac{(x - 2)(x + 2) \cdot (x + 1)(x + 3)}{2(x + 3) \cdot (2 - x)}$$

$$= \dfrac{-1(x + 2)(x + 1)}{2} \qquad \text{Divide out common factors. Recall that}$$
$$\phantom{= \dfrac{-1(x + 2)(x + 1)}{2}} \qquad \dfrac{x - 2}{2 - x} = -1.$$

$$= -\dfrac{(x + 2)(x + 1)}{2} \qquad \square$$

PRACTICE
8 Multiply or divide as indicated.

a. $\dfrac{y+9}{8x} \cdot \dfrac{y+9}{2x}$ **b.** $\dfrac{y+9}{8x} \div \dfrac{y+9}{2}$ **c.** $\dfrac{35x - 7x^2}{x^2 - 25} \cdot \dfrac{x^2 + 3x - 10}{x^2 + 4x}$

VOCABULARY & READINESS CHECK

Word Bank. *Use one of the choices below to fill in the blank.*

opposites   reciprocals

1. The expressions $\dfrac{x}{2y}$ and $\dfrac{2y}{x}$ are called _____ .

Multiply or divide as indicated.

2. $\dfrac{a}{b} \cdot \dfrac{c}{d} = $ _____

3. $\dfrac{a}{b} \div \dfrac{c}{d} = $ _____

4. $\dfrac{x}{7} \cdot \dfrac{x}{6} = $ _____

5. $\dfrac{x}{7} \div \dfrac{x}{6} = $ _____

8.2 | EXERCISE SET

Find each product and simplify if possible. See Examples 1 through 3.

1. $\dfrac{3x}{y^2} \cdot \dfrac{7y}{4x}$

2. $\dfrac{9x^2}{y} \cdot \dfrac{4y}{3x^3}$

3. $\dfrac{8x}{2} \cdot \dfrac{x^5}{4x^2}$

4. $\dfrac{6x^2}{10x^3} \cdot \dfrac{5x}{12}$

5. $-\dfrac{5a^2b}{30a^2b^2} \cdot b^3$

6. $-\dfrac{9x^3y^2}{18xy^5} \cdot y^3$

7. $\dfrac{x}{2x-14} \cdot \dfrac{x^2 - 7x}{5}$

8. $\dfrac{4x - 24}{20x} \cdot \dfrac{5}{x-6}$

9. $\dfrac{6x + 6}{5} \cdot \dfrac{10}{36x + 36}$

10. $\dfrac{x^2 + x}{8} \cdot \dfrac{16}{x+1}$

11. $\dfrac{(m+n)^2}{m-n} \cdot \dfrac{m}{m^2 + mn}$

12. $\dfrac{(m-n)^2}{m+n} \cdot \dfrac{m}{m^2 - mn}$

13. $\dfrac{x^2 - 25}{x^2 - 3x - 10} \cdot \dfrac{x+2}{x}$

14. $\dfrac{a^2 - 4a + 4}{a^2 - 4} \cdot \dfrac{a+3}{a-2}$

15. $\dfrac{x^2 + 6x + 8}{x^2 + x - 20} \cdot \dfrac{x^2 + 2x - 15}{x^2 + 8x + 16}$

16. $\dfrac{x^2 + 9x + 20}{x^2 - 15x + 44} \cdot \dfrac{x^2 - 11x + 28}{x^2 + 12x + 35}$

Find each quotient and simplify. See Examples 4 through 7.

17. $\dfrac{5x^7}{2x^5} \div \dfrac{15x}{4x^3}$

18. $\dfrac{9y^4}{6y} \div \dfrac{y^2}{3}$

19. $\dfrac{8x^2}{y^3} \div \dfrac{4x^2y^3}{6}$

20. $\dfrac{7a^2b}{3ab^2} \div \dfrac{21a^2b^2}{14ab}$

21. $\dfrac{(x-6)(x+4)}{4x} \div \dfrac{2x - 12}{8x^2}$

22. $\dfrac{(x+3)^2}{5} \div \dfrac{5x + 15}{25}$

23. $\dfrac{3x^2}{x^2 - 1} \div \dfrac{x^5}{(x+1)^2}$

24. $\dfrac{9x^5}{a^2 - b^2} \div \dfrac{27x^2}{3b - 3a}$

25. $\dfrac{m^2 - n^2}{m+n} \div \dfrac{m}{m^2 + nm}$

26. $\dfrac{(m-n)^2}{m+n} \div \dfrac{m^2-mn}{m}$

27. $\dfrac{x+2}{7-x} \div \dfrac{x^2-5x+6}{x^2-9x+14}$

28. $\dfrac{x-3}{2-x} \div \dfrac{x^2+3x-18}{x^2+2x-8}$

29. $\dfrac{x^2+7x+10}{x-1} \div \dfrac{x^2+2x-15}{x-1}$

30. $\dfrac{x+1}{(x+1)(2x+3)} \div \dfrac{20x+100}{2x+3}$

MIXED PRACTICE

Multiply or divide as indicated. See Examples 1 through 8.

31. $\dfrac{5x-10}{12} \div \dfrac{4x-8}{8}$

32. $\dfrac{6x+6}{5} \div \dfrac{9x+9}{10}$

33. $\dfrac{x^2+5x}{8} \cdot \dfrac{9}{3x+15}$

34. $\dfrac{3x^2+12x}{6} \cdot \dfrac{9}{2x+8}$

35. $\dfrac{7}{6p^2+q} \div \dfrac{14}{18p^2+3q}$

36. $\dfrac{3x+6}{20} \div \dfrac{4x+8}{8}$

37. $\dfrac{3x+4y}{x^2+4xy+4y^2} \cdot \dfrac{x+2y}{2}$

38. $\dfrac{x^2-y^2}{3x^2+3xy} \cdot \dfrac{3x^2+6x}{3x^2-2xy-y^2}$

39. $\dfrac{(x+2)^2}{x-2} \div \dfrac{x^2-4}{2x-4}$

40. $\dfrac{x+3}{x^2-9} \div \dfrac{5x+15}{(x-3)^2}$

41. $\dfrac{x^2-4}{24x} \div \dfrac{2-x}{6xy}$

42. $\dfrac{3y}{3-x} \div \dfrac{12xy}{x^2-9}$

43. $\dfrac{a^2+7a+12}{a^2+5a+6} \cdot \dfrac{a^2+8a+15}{a^2+5a+4}$

44. $\dfrac{b^2+2b-3}{b^2+b-2} \cdot \dfrac{b^2-4}{b^2+6b+8}$

45. $\dfrac{5x-20}{3x^2+x} \cdot \dfrac{3x^2+13x+4}{x^2-16}$

46. $\dfrac{9x+18}{4x^2-3x} \cdot \dfrac{4x^2-11x+6}{x^2-4}$

47. $\dfrac{8n^2-18}{2n^2-5n+3} \div \dfrac{6n^2+7n-3}{n^2-9n+8}$

48. $\dfrac{36n^2-64}{3n^2+10n+8} \div \dfrac{3n^2-13n+12}{n^2-5n-14}$

49. Find the quotient of $\dfrac{x^2-9}{2x}$ and $\dfrac{x+3}{8x^4}$.

50. Find the quotient of $\dfrac{4x^2+4x+1}{4x+2}$ and $\dfrac{4x+2}{16}$.

Multiply or divide as indicated. Some of these expressions contain 4-term polynomials and sums and differences of cubes. See Examples 1 through 8.

51. $\dfrac{a^2+ac+ba+bc}{a-b} \div \dfrac{a+c}{a+b}$

52. $\dfrac{x^2+2x-xy-2y}{x^2-y^2} \div \dfrac{2x+4}{x+y}$

53. $\dfrac{3x^2+8x+5}{x^2+8x+7} \cdot \dfrac{x+7}{x^2+4}$

54. $\dfrac{16x^2+2x}{16x^2+10x+1} \cdot \dfrac{1}{4x^2+2x}$

55. $\dfrac{x^3+8}{x^2-2x+4} \cdot \dfrac{4}{x^2-4}$

56. $\dfrac{9y}{3y-3} \cdot \dfrac{y^3-1}{y^3+y^2+y}$

57. $\dfrac{a^2-ab}{6a^2+6ab} \div \dfrac{a^3-b^3}{a^2-b^2}$

58. $\dfrac{x^3+27y^3}{6x} \div \dfrac{x^2-9y^2}{x^2-3xy}$

REVIEW AND PREVIEW

Perform each indicated operation. See Section 1.3.

59. $\dfrac{1}{5} + \dfrac{4}{5}$

60. $\dfrac{3}{15} + \dfrac{6}{15}$

61. $\dfrac{9}{9} - \dfrac{19}{9}$

62. $\dfrac{4}{3} - \dfrac{8}{3}$

63. $\dfrac{6}{5} + \left(\dfrac{1}{5} - \dfrac{8}{5}\right)$

64. $-\dfrac{3}{2} + \left(\dfrac{1}{2} - \dfrac{3}{2}\right)$

Graph each linear equation. See Section 3.2.

65. $x - 2y = 6$

66. $5x - y = 10$

CONCEPT EXTENSIONS

True or False. *Identify each statement as true or false. If false, correct the multiplication. See the Concept Check in this section.*

67. $\dfrac{4}{a} \cdot \dfrac{1}{b} = \dfrac{4}{ab}$

68. $\dfrac{2}{3} \cdot \dfrac{2}{4} = \dfrac{2}{7}$

69. $\dfrac{x}{5} \cdot \dfrac{x+3}{4} = \dfrac{2x+3}{20}$

70. $\dfrac{7}{a} \cdot \dfrac{3}{a} = \dfrac{21}{a}$

△ **71.** Find the area of the rectangle.

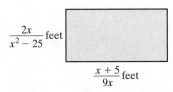

$\dfrac{2x}{x^2 - 25}$ feet

$\dfrac{x + 5}{9x}$ feet

△ **72.** Find the area of the square.

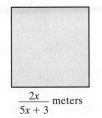

$\dfrac{2x}{5x + 3}$ meters

Multiply or divide as indicated.

73. $\left(\dfrac{x^2 - y^2}{x^2 + y^2} \div \dfrac{x^2 - y^2}{3x} \right) \cdot \dfrac{x^2 + y^2}{6}$

74. $\left(\dfrac{x^2 - 9}{x^2 - 1} \cdot \dfrac{x^2 + 2x + 1}{2x^2 + 9x + 9} \right) \div \dfrac{2x + 3}{1 - x}$

75. $\left(\dfrac{2a + b}{b^2} \cdot \dfrac{3a^2 - 2ab}{ab + 2b^2} \right) \div \dfrac{a^2 - 3ab + 2b^2}{5ab - 10b^2}$

76. $\left(\dfrac{x^2 y^2 - xy}{4x - 4y} \div \dfrac{3y - 3x}{8x - 8y} \right) \cdot \dfrac{y - x}{8}$

77. In your own words, explain how you multiply rational expressions.

78. Explain how dividing rational expressions is similar to dividing rational numbers.

8.3　ADDING AND SUBTRACTING RATIONAL EXPRESSIONS WITH COMMON DENOMINATORS AND LEAST COMMON DENOMINATOR

OBJECTIVES

1 Add and subtract rational expressions with the same denominator.

2 Find the least common denominator of a list of rational expressions.

3 Write a rational expression as an equivalent expression whose denominator is given.

OBJECTIVE 1 ▶ Adding and subtracting rational expressions with the same denominator. Like multiplication and division, addition and subtraction of rational expressions is similar to addition and subtraction of rational numbers. In this section, we add and subtract rational expressions with a common (or the same) denominator.

Add: $\dfrac{6}{5} + \dfrac{2}{5}$

Add: $\dfrac{9}{x + 2} + \dfrac{3}{x + 2}$

Add the numerators and place the sum over the common denominator.

$\dfrac{6}{5} + \dfrac{2}{5} = \dfrac{6 + 2}{5}$

$\quad = \dfrac{8}{5}$　Simplify.

$\dfrac{9}{x + 2} + \dfrac{3}{x + 2} = \dfrac{9 + 3}{x + 2}$

$\quad = \dfrac{12}{x + 2}$　Simplify.

Adding and Subtracting Rational Expressions with Common Denominators

If $\dfrac{P}{R}$ and $\dfrac{Q}{R}$ are rational expressions, then

$$\frac{P}{R} + \frac{Q}{R} = \frac{P + Q}{R} \qquad \text{and} \qquad \frac{P}{R} - \frac{Q}{R} = \frac{P - Q}{R}$$

To add or subtract rational expressions, add or subtract numerators and place the sum or difference over the common denominator.

EXAMPLE 1 Add: $\dfrac{5m}{2n} + \dfrac{m}{2n}$

Solution $\dfrac{5m}{2n} + \dfrac{m}{2n} = \dfrac{5m + m}{2n}$ Add the numerators.

$\qquad\qquad\qquad = \dfrac{6m}{2n}$ Simplify the numerator by combining like terms.

$\qquad\qquad\qquad = \dfrac{3m}{n}$ Simplify by applying the fundamental principle.   □

PRACTICE 1   Add: $\dfrac{7a}{4b} + \dfrac{a}{4b}$.

EXAMPLE 2 Subtract: $\dfrac{2y}{2y - 7} - \dfrac{7}{2y - 7}$

Solution $\dfrac{2y}{2y - 7} - \dfrac{7}{2y - 7} = \dfrac{2y - 7}{2y - 7}$ Subtract the numerators.

$\qquad\qquad\qquad\qquad\qquad = \dfrac{1}{1}$ or 1   Simplify.   □

PRACTICE 2   Subtract: $\dfrac{3x}{3x - 2} - \dfrac{2}{3x - 2}$.

EXAMPLE 3 Subtract: $\dfrac{3x^2 + 2x}{x - 1} - \dfrac{10x - 5}{x - 1}$.

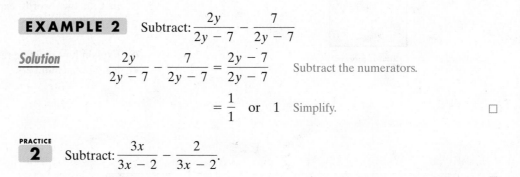

Solution $\dfrac{3x^2 + 2x}{x - 1} - \dfrac{10x - 5}{x - 1} = \dfrac{(3x^2 + 2x) - (10x - 5)}{x - 1}$ Subtract the numerators Notice the parentheses.

$\qquad\qquad\qquad\qquad\qquad = \dfrac{3x^2 + 2x - 10x + 5}{x - 1}$ Use the distributive property.

$\qquad\qquad\qquad\qquad\qquad = \dfrac{3x^2 - 8x + 5}{x - 1}$ Combine like terms.

$\qquad\qquad\qquad\qquad\qquad = \dfrac{(x - 1)(3x - 5)}{x - 1}$ Factor.

$\qquad\qquad\qquad\qquad\qquad = 3x - 5$ Simplify.   □

> **Helpful Hint**
> Parentheses are inserted so that the entire numerator, $10x - 5$, is subtracted.

PRACTICE 3   Subtract: $\dfrac{4x^2 + 15x}{x + 3} - \dfrac{8x + 15}{x + 3}$

> **Helpful Hint**
> Notice how the numerator $10x - 5$ has been subtracted in Example 3.
>
> This − sign applies to the entire numerator of $10x - 5$.
>
> So parentheses are inserted here to indicate this.
>
>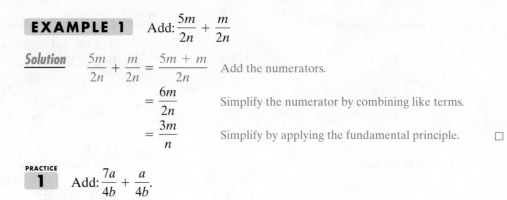
>
> $$\dfrac{3x^2 + 2x}{x - 1} - \dfrac{10x - 5}{x - 1} = \dfrac{3x^2 + 2x - (10x - 5)}{x - 1}$$

OBJECTIVE 2 ▶ Finding the least common denominator. To add and subtract fractions with **unlike** denominators, first find a least common denominator (LCD), and then write all fractions as equivalent fractions with the LCD.

For example, suppose we add $\frac{8}{3}$ and $\frac{2}{5}$. The LCD of denominators 3 and 5 is 15, since 15 is the least common multiple (LCM) of 3 and 5. That is, 15 is the smallest number that both 3 and 5 divide into evenly.

Next, rewrite each fraction so that its denominator is 15.

$$\frac{8}{3} + \frac{2}{5} = \frac{8(5)}{3(5)} + \frac{2(3)}{5(3)} = \frac{40}{15} + \frac{6}{15} = \frac{40 + 6}{15} = \frac{46}{15}$$

We are multiplying by 1.

To add or subtract rational expressions with unlike denominators, we also first find an LCD and then write all rational expressions as equivalent expressions with the LCD. The **least common denominator (LCD) of a list of rational expressions** is a polynomial of least degree whose factors include all the factors of the denominators in the list.

Finding the Least Common Denominator (LCD)

STEP 1. Factor each denominator completely.

STEP 2. The least common denominator (LCD) is the product of all unique factors found in Step 1, each raised to a power equal to the greatest number of times that the factor appears in any one factored denominator.

EXAMPLE 4   Find the LCD for each pair.

a. $\frac{1}{8}, \frac{3}{22}$ **b.** $\frac{7}{5x}, \frac{6}{15x^2}$

Solution

a. Start by finding the prime factorization of each denominator.

$$8 = 2 \cdot 2 \cdot 2 = 2^3 \quad \text{and}$$
$$22 = 2 \cdot 11$$

Next, write the product of all the unique factors, each raised to a power equal to the greatest number of times that the factor appears in any denominator.

The greatest number of times that the factor 2 appears is 3.

The greatest number of times that the factor 11 appears is 1.

$$\text{LCD} = 2^3 \cdot 11^1 = 8 \cdot 11 = 88$$

b. Factor each denominator.

$$5x = 5 \cdot x \quad \text{and}$$
$$15x^2 = 3 \cdot 5 \cdot x^2$$

The greatest number of times that the factor 5 appears is 1.

The greatest number of times that the factor 3 appears is 1.

The greatest number of times that the factor x appears is 2.

$$\text{LCD} = 3^1 \cdot 5^1 \cdot x^2 = 15x^2 \qquad \qquad \square$$

PRACTICE

4   Find the LCD for each pair.

a. $\frac{3}{14}, \frac{5}{21}$ **b.** $\frac{4}{9y}, \frac{11}{15y^3}$

EXAMPLE 5 Find the LCD of

a. $\dfrac{7x}{x + 2}$ and $\dfrac{5x^2}{x - 2}$ **b.** $\dfrac{3}{x}$ and $\dfrac{6}{x + 4}$

Solution

a. The denominators $x + 2$ and $x - 2$ are completely factored already. The factor $x + 2$ appears once and the factor $x - 2$ appears once.

$$\text{LCD} = (x + 2)(x - 2)$$

b. The denominators x and $x + 4$ cannot be factored further. The factor x appears once and the factor $x + 4$ appears once.

$$\text{LCD} = x(x + 4)$$

PRACTICE
5 Find the LCD of

a. $\dfrac{16}{y - 5}$ and $\dfrac{3y^3}{y - 4}$ **b.** $\dfrac{8}{a}$ and $\dfrac{5}{a + 2}$

EXAMPLE 6 Find the LCD of $\dfrac{6m^2}{3m + 15}$ and $\dfrac{2}{(m + 5)^2}$.

Solution We factor each denominator.

$$3m + 15 = 3(m + 5)$$

$$(m + 5)^2 = (m + 5)^2 \quad \text{This denominator is already factored.}$$

The greatest number of times that the factor 3 appears is 1.

The greatest number of times that the factor $m + 5$ appears *in any one denominator* is 2.

$$\text{LCD} = 3(m + 5)^2$$

PRACTICE
6 Find the LCD of $\dfrac{2x^3}{(2x - 1)^2}$ and $\dfrac{5x}{6x - 3}$.

Concept Check ☑

Choose the correct LCD of $\dfrac{x}{(x + 1)^2}$ and $\dfrac{5}{x + 1}$.

a. $x + 1$ **b.** $(x + 1)^2$ **c.** $(x + 1)^3$ **d.** $5x(x + 1)^2$

EXAMPLE 7 Find the LCD of $\dfrac{t - 10}{t^2 - t - 6}$ and $\dfrac{t + 5}{t^2 + 3t + 2}$.

Solution Start by factoring each denominator.

$$t^2 - t - 6 = (t - 3)(t + 2)$$

$$t^2 + 3t + 2 = (t + 1)(t + 2)$$

$$\text{LCD} = (t - 3)(t + 2)(t + 1)$$

PRACTICE
7 Find the LCD of $\dfrac{x - 5}{x^2 + 5x + 4}$ and $\dfrac{x + 8}{x^2 - 16}$.

EXAMPLE 8   Find the LCD of $\dfrac{2}{x-2}$ and $\dfrac{10}{2-x}$.

Solution   The denominators $x-2$ and $2-x$ are opposites. That is, $2-x = -1(x-2)$. Use $x-2$ or $2-x$ as the LCD.

$$\text{LCD} = x - 2 \quad \text{or} \quad \text{LCD} = 2 - x \qquad \square$$

PRACTICE
8   Find the LCD of $\dfrac{5}{3-x}$ and $\dfrac{4}{x-3}$.

OBJECTIVE 3 ▶ **Writing equivalent rational expressions.** Next we practice writing a rational expression as an equivalent rational expression with a given denominator. To do this, we multiply by a form of 1. Recall that multiplying an expression by 1 produces an equivalent expression. In other words,

$$\frac{P}{Q} = \frac{P}{Q} \cdot 1 = \frac{P}{Q} \cdot \frac{R}{R} = \frac{PR}{QR}.$$

EXAMPLE 9   Write each rational expression as an equivalent rational expression with the given denominator.

a. $\dfrac{4b}{9a} = \dfrac{}{27a^2 b}$ **b.** $\dfrac{7x}{2x+5} = \dfrac{}{6x+15}$

Solution

a. We can ask ourselves: "What do we multiply $9a$ by to get $27a^2 b$?" The answer is $3ab$, since $9a(3ab) = 27a^2 b$. So we multiply by 1 in the form of $\dfrac{3ab}{3ab}$.

$$\frac{4b}{9a} = \frac{4b}{9a} \cdot 1 = \frac{4b}{9a} \cdot \frac{3ab}{3ab}$$

$$= \frac{4b(3ab)}{9a(3ab)} = \frac{12ab^2}{27a^2 b}$$

b. First, factor the denominator on the right.

$$\frac{7x}{2x+5} = \frac{}{3(2x+5)}$$

To obtain the denominator on the right from the denominator on the left, we multiply by 1 in the form of $\dfrac{3}{3}$.

$$\frac{7x}{2x+5} = \frac{7x}{2x+5} \cdot \frac{3}{3} = \frac{7x \cdot 3}{(2x+5) \cdot 3} = \frac{21x}{3(2x+5)} \text{ or } \frac{21x}{6x+15} \qquad \square$$

PRACTICE
9   Write each rational expression as an equivalent fraction with the given denominator.

a. $\dfrac{3x}{5y} = \dfrac{}{35xy^2}$ **b.** $\dfrac{9x}{4x+7} = \dfrac{}{8x+14}$

EXAMPLE 10   Write the rational expression as an equivalent rational expression with the given denominator.

$$\frac{5}{x^2-4} = \frac{}{(x-2)(x+2)(x-4)}$$

Solution   First, factor the denominator $x^2 - 4$ as $(x - 2)(x + 2)$.

If we multiply the original denominator $(x - 2)(x + 2)$ by $x - 4$, the result is the new denominator $(x + 2)(x - 2)(x - 4)$. Thus, we multiply by 1 in the form of $\dfrac{x - 4}{x - 4}$.

$$\frac{5}{\underbrace{x^2 - 4}_{\substack{\text{Factored} \\ \text{denominator}}}} = \frac{5}{(x - 2)(x + 2)} = \frac{5}{(x - 2)(x + 2)} \cdot \frac{x - 4}{x - 4}$$

$$= \frac{5(x - 4)}{(x - 2)(x + 2)(x - 4)}$$

$$= \frac{5x - 20}{(x - 2)(x + 2)(x - 4)}$$

PRACTICE
10   Write the rational expression as an equivalent rational expression with the given denominator.

$$\frac{3}{x^2 - 2x - 15} = \frac{}{(x - 2)(x + 3)(x - 5)}$$

VOCABULARY & READINESS CHECK

Word Bank. *Use the choices below to fill in each blank. Not all choices will be used.*

$$\frac{9}{22} \qquad \frac{5}{22} \qquad \frac{9}{11} \qquad \frac{5}{11} \qquad \frac{ac}{b} \qquad \frac{a - c}{b} \qquad \frac{a + c}{b} \qquad \frac{5 - 6 + x}{x} \qquad \frac{5 - (6 + x)}{x}$$

1. $\dfrac{7}{11} + \dfrac{2}{11} =$ _____

2. $\dfrac{7}{11} - \dfrac{2}{11} =$ _____

3. $\dfrac{a}{b} + \dfrac{c}{b} =$ _____

4. $\dfrac{a}{b} - \dfrac{c}{b} =$ _____

5. $\dfrac{5}{x} - \dfrac{6 + x}{x} =$ _____

8.3 | EXERCISE SET

MyMathLab *Powered by CourseCompass™ and MathXL®*   MathXL PRACTICE   WATCH   DOWNLOAD   READ   REVIEW

Add or subtract as indicated. Simplify the result if possible. See Examples 1 through 3.

1. $\dfrac{a + 1}{13} + \dfrac{8}{13}$

2. $\dfrac{x + 1}{7} + \dfrac{6}{7}$

3. $\dfrac{4m}{3n} + \dfrac{5m}{3n}$

4. $\dfrac{3p}{2q} + \dfrac{11p}{2q}$

5. $\dfrac{4m}{m - 6} - \dfrac{24}{m - 6}$

6. $\dfrac{8y}{y - 2} - \dfrac{16}{y - 2}$

7. $\dfrac{9}{3 + y} + \dfrac{y + 1}{3 + y}$

8. $\dfrac{9}{y + 9} + \dfrac{y - 5}{y + 9}$

9. $\dfrac{5x^2 + 4x}{x - 1} - \dfrac{6x + 3}{x - 1}$

10. $\dfrac{x^2 + 9x}{x + 7} - \dfrac{4x + 14}{x + 7}$

11. $\dfrac{4a}{a^2 + 2a - 15} - \dfrac{12}{a^2 + 2a - 15}$

12. $\dfrac{3y}{y^2 + 3y - 10} - \dfrac{6}{y^2 + 3y - 10}$

13. $\dfrac{2x + 3}{x^2 - x - 30} - \dfrac{x - 2}{x^2 - x - 30}$

14. $\dfrac{3x - 1}{x^2 + 5x - 6} - \dfrac{2x - 7}{x^2 + 5x - 6}$

15. $\dfrac{2x + 1}{x - 3} + \dfrac{3x + 6}{x - 3}$

16. $\dfrac{4p - 3}{2p + 7} + \dfrac{3p + 8}{2p + 7}$

17. $\dfrac{2x^2}{x - 5} - \dfrac{25 + x^2}{x - 5}$

18. $\dfrac{6x^2}{2x - 5} - \dfrac{25 + 2x^2}{2x - 5}$

19. $\dfrac{5x + 4}{x - 1} - \dfrac{2x + 7}{x - 1}$

20. $\dfrac{7x + 1}{x - 4} - \dfrac{2x + 21}{x - 4}$

Find the LCD for each list of rational expressions. See Examples 4 through 8.

21. $\dfrac{19}{2x}$, $\dfrac{5}{4x^3}$

22. $\dfrac{17x}{4y^5}$, $\dfrac{2}{8y}$

23. $\dfrac{9}{8x}$, $\dfrac{3}{2x+4}$

24. $\dfrac{1}{6y}$, $\dfrac{3x}{4y+12}$

25. $\dfrac{2}{x+3}$, $\dfrac{5}{x-2}$

26. $\dfrac{-6}{x-1}$, $\dfrac{4}{x+5}$

27. $\dfrac{x}{x+6}$, $\dfrac{10}{3x+18}$

28. $\dfrac{12}{x+5}$, $\dfrac{x}{4x+20}$

29. $\dfrac{8x^2}{(x-6)^2}$, $\dfrac{13x}{5x-30}$

30. $\dfrac{9x^2}{7x-14}$, $\dfrac{6x}{(x-2)^2}$

31. $\dfrac{1}{3x+3}$, $\dfrac{8}{2x^2+4x+2}$

32. $\dfrac{19x+5}{4x-12}$, $\dfrac{3}{2x^2-12x+18}$

33. $\dfrac{5}{x-8}$, $\dfrac{3}{8-x}$

34. $\dfrac{2x+5}{3x-7}$, $\dfrac{5}{7-3x}$

35. $\dfrac{5x+1}{x^2+3x-4}$, $\dfrac{3x}{x^2+2x-3}$

36. $\dfrac{4}{x^2+4x+3}$, $\dfrac{4x-2}{x^2+10x+21}$

37. $\dfrac{2x}{3x^2+4x+1}$, $\dfrac{7}{2x^2-x-1}$

38. $\dfrac{3x}{4x^2+5x+1}$, $\dfrac{5}{3x^2-2x-1}$

39. $\dfrac{1}{x^2-16}$, $\dfrac{x+6}{2x^3-8x^2}$

40. $\dfrac{5}{x^2-25}$, $\dfrac{x+9}{3x^3-15x^2}$

Rewrite each rational expression as an equivalent rational expression with the given denominator. See Examples 9 and 10.

41. $\dfrac{3}{2x}=\dfrac{}{4x^2}$

42. $\dfrac{3}{9y^5}=\dfrac{}{72y^9}$

43. $\dfrac{6}{3a}=\dfrac{}{12ab^2}$

44. $\dfrac{5}{4y^2x}=\dfrac{}{32y^3x^2}$

45. $\dfrac{9}{2x+6}=\dfrac{}{2y(x+3)}$

46. $\dfrac{4x+1}{3x+6}=\dfrac{}{3y(x+2)}$

47. $\dfrac{9a+2}{5a+10}=\dfrac{}{5b(a+2)}$

48. $\dfrac{5+y}{2x^2+10}=\dfrac{}{4(x^2+5)}$

49. $\dfrac{x}{x^3+6x^2+8x}=\dfrac{}{x(x+4)(x+2)(x+1)}$

50. $\dfrac{5x}{x^3+2x^2-3x}=\dfrac{}{x(x-1)(x-5)(x+3)}$

51. $\dfrac{9y-1}{15x^2-30}=\dfrac{}{30x^2-60}$

52. $\dfrac{6m-5}{3x^2-9}=\dfrac{}{12x^2-36}$

MIXED PRACTICE

Perform the indicated operations.

53. $\dfrac{5x}{7}+\dfrac{9x}{7}$

54. $\dfrac{5x}{7}\cdot\dfrac{9x}{7}$

55. $\dfrac{x+3}{4}\div\dfrac{2x-1}{4}$

56. $\dfrac{x+3}{4}-\dfrac{2x-1}{4}$

57. $\dfrac{x^2}{x-6}-\dfrac{5x+6}{x-6}$

58. $\dfrac{x^2+5x}{x^2-25}\cdot\dfrac{3x-15}{x^2}$

59. $\dfrac{-2x}{x^3-8x}+\dfrac{3x}{x^3-8x}$

60. $\dfrac{-2x}{x^3-8x}\div\dfrac{3x}{x^3-8x}$

61. $\dfrac{12x-6}{x^2+3x}\cdot\dfrac{4x^2+13x+3}{4x^2-1}$

62. $\dfrac{x^3+7x^2}{3x^3-x^2}\div\dfrac{5x^2+36x+7}{9x^2-1}$

REVIEW AND PREVIEW

Perform each indicated operation. See Section 1.3.

63. $\dfrac{2}{3}+\dfrac{5}{7}$

64. $\dfrac{9}{10}-\dfrac{3}{5}$

65. $\dfrac{2}{6}-\dfrac{3}{4}$

66. $\dfrac{11}{15}+\dfrac{5}{9}$

67. $\dfrac{1}{12}+\dfrac{3}{20}$

68. $\dfrac{7}{30}+\dfrac{3}{18}$

CONCEPT EXTENSIONS

69. Multiple Choice. Choose the correct LCD of $\dfrac{11a^3}{4a-20}$ and $\dfrac{15a^3}{(a-5)^2}$. See the Concept Check in this section.

   a. $4a(a-5)(a+5)$ **b.** $a-5$

   c. $(a-5)^2$ **d.** $4(a-5)^2$

   e. $(4a-20)(a-5)^2$

70. An algebra student approaches you with a problem. He's tried to subtract two rational expressions, but his result does not match the book's. Check to see if the student has made an error. If so, correct his work shown below.

$$\dfrac{2x-6}{x-5}-\dfrac{x+4}{x-5}$$
$$=\dfrac{2x-6-x+4}{x-5}$$
$$=\dfrac{x-2}{x-5}$$

Multiple Choice. *Select the correct result.*

71. $\dfrac{3}{x} + \dfrac{y}{x} =$

   a. $\dfrac{3+y}{x^2}$ **b.** $\dfrac{3+y}{2x}$ **c.** $\dfrac{3+y}{x}$

72. $\dfrac{3}{x} - \dfrac{y}{x} =$

   a. $\dfrac{3-y}{x^2}$ **b.** $\dfrac{3-y}{2x}$ **c.** $\dfrac{3-y}{x}$

73. $\dfrac{3}{x} \cdot \dfrac{y}{x} =$

   a. $\dfrac{3y}{x}$ **b.** $\dfrac{3y}{x^2}$ **c.** $3y$

74. $\dfrac{3}{x} \div \dfrac{y}{x} =$

   a. $\dfrac{3}{y}$ **b.** $\dfrac{y}{3}$ **c.** $\dfrac{3}{x^2 y}$

Write each rational expression as an equivalent expression with a denominator of $x - 2$.

75. $\dfrac{5}{2-x}$ **76.** $\dfrac{8y}{2-x}$

77. $-\dfrac{7+x}{2-x}$ **78.** $\dfrac{x-3}{-(x-2)}$

△ **79.** A square has a side of length $\dfrac{5}{x-2}$ meters. Express its perimeter as a rational expression.

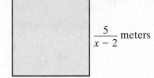

$\dfrac{5}{x-2}$ meters

△ **80.** A trapezoid has sides of the indicated lengths. Find its perimeter.

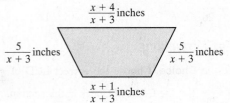

$\dfrac{x+4}{x+3}$ inches

$\dfrac{5}{x+3}$ inches $\dfrac{5}{x+3}$ inches

$\dfrac{x+1}{x+3}$ inches

81. Write two rational expressions with the same denominator whose sum is $\dfrac{5}{3x-1}$.

82. Write two rational expressions with the same denominator whose difference is $\dfrac{x-7}{x^2+1}$.

83. The planet Mercury revolves around the sun in 88 Earth days. It takes Jupiter 4332 Earth days to make one revolution around the sun. (*Source:* National Space Science Data Center) If the two planets are aligned as shown in the figure, how long will it take for them to align again?

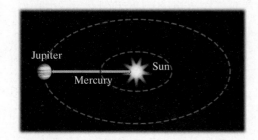

84. You are throwing a barbecue and you want to make sure that you purchase the same number of hot dogs as hot dog buns. Hot dogs come 8 to a package and hot dog buns come 12 to a package. What is the least number of each type of package you should buy?

85. Write some instructions to help a friend who is having difficulty finding the LCD of two rational expressions.

86. Explain why the LCD of the rational expressions $\dfrac{7}{x+1}$ and $\dfrac{9x}{(x+1)^2}$ is $(x+1)^2$ and not $(x+1)^3$.

87. In your own words, describe how to add or subtract two rational expressions with the same denominators.

88. Explain the similarities between subtracting $\dfrac{3}{8}$ from $\dfrac{7}{8}$ and subtracting $\dfrac{6}{x+3}$ from $\dfrac{9}{x+3}$.

8.4 ADDING AND SUBTRACTING RATIONAL EXPRESSIONS WITH UNLIKE DENOMINATORS

OBJECTIVE

1 Add and subtract rational expressions with unlike denominators.

OBJECTIVE 1 ▶ Adding and subtracting rational expressions with unlike denominators. In the previous section, we practiced all the skills we need to add and subtract rational expressions with unlike or different denominators. We add or subtract rational expressions the same way as we add or subtract fractions. You may want to use the steps below.

Adding or Subtracting Rational Expressions with Unlike Denominators

STEP 1. Find the LCD of the rational expressions.

STEP 2. Rewrite each rational expression as an equivalent expression whose denominator is the LCD found in Step 1.

STEP 3. Add or subtract numerators and write the sum or difference over the common denominator.

STEP 4. Simplify or write the rational expression in simplest form.

EXAMPLE 1   Perform each indicated operation.

a. $\dfrac{a}{4} - \dfrac{2a}{8}$ **b.** $\dfrac{3}{10x^2} + \dfrac{7}{25x}$

Solution

a. First, we must find the LCD. Since $4 = 2^2$ and $8 = 2^3$, the LCD $= 2^3 = 8$. Next we write each fraction as an equivalent fraction with the denominator 8, then we subtract.

$$\frac{a}{4} - \frac{2a}{8} = \frac{a(2)}{4(2)} - \frac{2a}{8} = \frac{2a}{8} - \frac{2a}{8} = \frac{2a - 2a}{8} = \frac{0}{8} = 0$$

Multiplying the numerator and denominator by 2 is the same as multiplying by $\dfrac{2}{2}$ or 1.

b. Since $10x^2 = 2 \cdot 5 \cdot x \cdot x$ and $25x = 5 \cdot 5 \cdot x$, the LCD $= 2 \cdot 5^2 \cdot x^2 = 50x^2$. We write each fraction as an equivalent fraction with a denominator of $50x^2$.

$$\frac{3}{10x^2} + \frac{7}{25x} = \frac{3(5)}{10x^2(5)} + \frac{7(2x)}{25x(2x)}$$

$$= \frac{15}{50x^2} + \frac{14x}{50x^2}$$

$$= \frac{15 + 14x}{50x^2} \qquad \text{Add numerators. Write the sum over the common denominator.} \quad \square$$

PRACTICE

1   Perform each indicated operation.

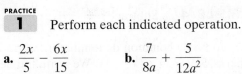

a. $\dfrac{2x}{5} - \dfrac{6x}{15}$ **b.** $\dfrac{7}{8a} + \dfrac{5}{12a^2}$

EXAMPLE 2 Subtract: $\dfrac{6x}{x^2 - 4} - \dfrac{3}{x + 2}$

Solution Since $x^2 - 4 = (x + 2)(x - 2)$, the LCD $= (x - 2)(x + 2)$. We write equivalent expressions with the LCD as denominators.

$$\frac{6x}{x^2 - 4} - \frac{3}{x + 2} = \frac{6x}{(x - 2)(x + 2)} - \frac{3(x - 2)}{(x + 2)(x - 2)}$$

$$= \frac{6x - 3(x - 2)}{(x + 2)(x - 2)} \qquad \text{Subtract numerators. Write the difference over the common denominator.}$$

$$= \frac{6x - 3x + 6}{(x + 2)(x - 2)} \qquad \text{Apply the distributive property in the numerator.}$$

$$= \frac{3x + 6}{(x + 2)(x - 2)} \qquad \text{Combine like terms in the numerator.}$$

Next we factor the numerator to see if this rational expression can be simplified.

$$= \frac{3(x + 2)}{(x + 2)(x - 2)} \qquad \text{Factor.}$$

$$= \frac{3}{x - 2} \qquad \text{Divide out common factors to simplify.} \qquad \square$$

PRACTICE
2 Subtract: $\dfrac{12x}{x^2 - 25} - \dfrac{6}{x + 5}$

EXAMPLE 3 Add: $\dfrac{2}{3t} + \dfrac{5}{t + 1}$

Solution The LCD is $3t(t + 1)$. We write each rational expression as an equivalent rational expression with a denominator of $3t(t + 1)$.

$$\frac{2}{3t} + \frac{5}{t + 1} = \frac{2(t + 1)}{3t(t + 1)} + \frac{5(3t)}{(t + 1)(3t)}$$

$$= \frac{2(t + 1) + 5(3t)}{3t(t + 1)} \qquad \text{Add numerators. Write the sum over the common denominator.}$$

$$= \frac{2t + 2 + 15t}{3t(t + 1)} \qquad \text{Apply the distributive property in the numerator.}$$

$$= \frac{17t + 2}{3t(t + 1)} \qquad \text{Combine like terms in the numerator.} \qquad \square$$

PRACTICE
3 Add: $\dfrac{3}{5y} + \dfrac{2}{y + 1}$

EXAMPLE 4 Subtract: $\dfrac{7}{x - 3} - \dfrac{9}{3 - x}$

Solution To find a common denominator, we notice that $x - 3$ and $3 - x$ are opposites. That is, $3 - x = -(x - 3)$. We write the denominator $3 - x$ as $-(x - 3)$ and simplify.

$$\frac{7}{x - 3} - \frac{9}{3 - x} = \frac{7}{x - 3} - \frac{9}{-(x - 3)}$$

$$= \frac{7}{x - 3} - \frac{-9}{x - 3} \qquad \text{Apply } \frac{a}{-b} = \frac{-a}{b}.$$

$$= \frac{7 - (-9)}{x - 3} \qquad \text{Subtract numerators. Write the difference over the common denominator.}$$

$$= \frac{16}{x - 3} \qquad\qquad\qquad\qquad\qquad\qquad\square$$

PRACTICE
4   Subtract: $\dfrac{6}{x - 5} - \dfrac{7}{5 - x}$

EXAMPLE 5   Add: $1 + \dfrac{m}{m + 1}$

Solution   Recall that 1 is the same as $\dfrac{1}{1}$. The LCD of $\dfrac{1}{1}$ and $\dfrac{m}{m + 1}$ is $m + 1$.

$$1 + \frac{m}{m + 1} = \frac{1}{1} + \frac{m}{m + 1} \qquad \text{Write 1 as } \frac{1}{1}.$$

$$= \frac{1(m + 1)}{1(m + 1)} + \frac{m}{m + 1} \qquad \text{Multiply both the numerator and the denominator of } \frac{1}{1} \text{ by } m + 1.$$

$$= \frac{m + 1 + m}{m + 1} \qquad \text{Add numerators. Write the sum over the common denominator.}$$

$$= \frac{2m + 1}{m + 1} \qquad \text{Combine like terms in the numerator.} \quad \square$$

PRACTICE
5   Add: $2 + \dfrac{b}{b + 3}$

EXAMPLE 6   Subtract: $\dfrac{3}{2x^2 + x} - \dfrac{2x}{6x + 3}$

Solution   First, we factor the denominators.

$$\frac{3}{2x^2 + x} - \frac{2x}{6x + 3} = \frac{3}{x(2x + 1)} - \frac{2x}{3(2x + 1)}$$

The LCD is $3x(2x + 1)$. We write equivalent expressions with denominators of $3x(2x + 1)$.

$$= \frac{3(3)}{x(2x + 1)(3)} - \frac{2x(x)}{3(2x + 1)(x)}$$

$$= \frac{9 - 2x^2}{3x(2x + 1)} \qquad \text{Subtract numerators. Write the difference over the common denominator.} \quad \square$$

PRACTICE
6   Subtract: $\dfrac{5}{2x^2 + 3x} - \dfrac{3x}{4x + 6}$

EXAMPLE 7 Add: $\dfrac{2x}{x^2 + 2x + 1} + \dfrac{x}{x^2 - 1}$

Solution First we factor the denominators.

$$\dfrac{2x}{x^2 + 2x + 1} + \dfrac{x}{x^2 - 1} = \dfrac{2x}{(x + 1)(x + 1)} + \dfrac{x}{(x + 1)(x - 1)}$$

Now we write the rational expressions as equivalent expressions with denominators of $(x + 1)(x + 1)(x - 1)$, the LCD.

$$= \dfrac{2x(x - 1)}{(x + 1)(x + 1)(x - 1)} + \dfrac{x(x + 1)}{(x + 1)(x - 1)(x + 1)}$$

$$= \dfrac{2x(x - 1) + x(x + 1)}{(x + 1)^2(x - 1)} \qquad \text{Add numerators. Write the sum over the common denominator.}$$

$$= \dfrac{2x^2 - 2x + x^2 + x}{(x + 1)^2(x - 1)} \qquad \text{Apply the distributive property in the numerator.}$$

$$= \dfrac{3x^2 - x}{(x + 1)^2(x - 1)} \qquad \text{or} \qquad \dfrac{x(3x - 1)}{(x + 1)^2(x - 1)}$$

PRACTICE
7 Add: $\dfrac{2x}{x^2 + 7x + 12} + \dfrac{3x}{x^2 - 9}$

The numerator was factored as a last step to see if the rational expression could be simplified further. Since there are no factors common to the numerator and the denominator, we can't simplify further.

VOCABULARY & READINESS CHECK

Matching. *Match each exercise with the first step needed to perform the operation. Do not actually perform the operation.*

1. $\dfrac{3}{4} - \dfrac{y}{4}$ **2.** $\dfrac{2}{a} \cdot \dfrac{3}{(a + 6)}$ **3.** $\dfrac{x + 1}{x} \div \dfrac{x - 1}{x}$ **4.** $\dfrac{9}{x - 2} - \dfrac{x}{x + 2}$

  a. Multiply the first rational expression by the reciprocal of the second rational expression.
  b. Find the LCD. Write each expression as an equivalent expression with the LCD as denominator.
  c. Multiply numerators, then multiply denominators.
  d. Subtract numerators. Place the difference over a common denominator.

8.4 EXERCISE SET

MyMathLab   PRACTICE   WATCH   DOWNLOAD   READ   REVIEW

MIXED PRACTICE

Perform each indicated operation. Simplify if possible. See Examples 1 through 7.

1. $\dfrac{4}{2x} + \dfrac{9}{3x}$

2. $\dfrac{15}{7a} + \dfrac{8}{6a}$

3. $\dfrac{15a}{b} - \dfrac{6b}{5}$

4. $\dfrac{4c}{d} - \dfrac{8d}{5}$

5. $\dfrac{3}{x} + \dfrac{5}{2x^2}$

6. $\dfrac{14}{3x^2} + \dfrac{6}{x}$

7. $\dfrac{6}{x + 1} + \dfrac{10}{2x + 2}$

8. $\dfrac{8}{x + 4} - \dfrac{3}{3x + 12}$

9. $\dfrac{3}{x + 2} - \dfrac{2x}{x^2 - 4}$

10. $\dfrac{5}{x - 4} + \dfrac{4x}{x^2 - 16}$

11. $\dfrac{3}{4x} + \dfrac{8}{x - 2}$

12. $\dfrac{5}{y^2} - \dfrac{y}{2y + 1}$

13. $\dfrac{6}{x - 3} + \dfrac{8}{3 - x}$

14. $\dfrac{15}{y - 4} + \dfrac{20}{4 - y}$

15. $\dfrac{9}{x-3} + \dfrac{9}{3-x}$

16. $\dfrac{5}{a-7} + \dfrac{5}{7-a}$

17. $\dfrac{-8}{x^2-1} - \dfrac{7}{1-x^2}$

18. $\dfrac{-9}{25x^2-1} + \dfrac{7}{1-25x^2}$

19. $\dfrac{5}{x} + 2$

20. $\dfrac{7}{x^2} - 5x$

21. $\dfrac{5}{x-2} + 6$

22. $\dfrac{6y}{y+5} + 1$

23. $\dfrac{y+2}{y+3} - 2$

24. $\dfrac{7}{2x-3} - 3$

25. $\dfrac{-x+2}{x} - \dfrac{x-6}{4x}$

26. $\dfrac{-y+1}{y} - \dfrac{2y-5}{3y}$

27. $\dfrac{5x}{x+2} - \dfrac{3x-4}{x+2}$

28. $\dfrac{7x}{x-3} - \dfrac{4x+9}{x-3}$

29. $\dfrac{3x^4}{7} - \dfrac{4x^2}{21}$

30. $\dfrac{5x}{6} + \dfrac{11x^2}{2}$

31. $\dfrac{1}{x+3} - \dfrac{1}{(x+3)^2}$

32. $\dfrac{5x}{(x-2)^2} - \dfrac{3}{x-2}$

33. $\dfrac{4}{5b} + \dfrac{1}{b-1}$

34. $\dfrac{1}{y+5} + \dfrac{2}{3y}$

35. $\dfrac{2}{m} + 1$

36. $\dfrac{6}{x} - 1$

37. $\dfrac{2x}{x-7} - \dfrac{x}{x-2}$

38. $\dfrac{9x}{x-10} - \dfrac{x}{x-3}$

39. $\dfrac{6}{1-2x} - \dfrac{4}{2x-1}$

40. $\dfrac{10}{3n-4} - \dfrac{5}{4-3n}$

41. $\dfrac{7}{(x+1)(x-1)} + \dfrac{8}{(x+1)^2}$

42. $\dfrac{5}{(x+1)(x+5)} - \dfrac{2}{(x+5)^2}$

43. $\dfrac{x}{x^2-1} - \dfrac{2}{x^2-2x+1}$

44. $\dfrac{x}{x^2-4} - \dfrac{5}{x^2-4x+4}$

45. $\dfrac{3a}{2a+6} - \dfrac{a-1}{a+3}$

46. $\dfrac{1}{x+y} - \dfrac{y}{x^2-y^2}$

47. $\dfrac{y-1}{2y+3} + \dfrac{3}{(2y+3)^2}$

48. $\dfrac{x-6}{5x+1} + \dfrac{6}{(5x+1)^2}$

49. $\dfrac{5}{2-x} + \dfrac{x}{2x-4}$

50. $\dfrac{-1}{a-2} + \dfrac{4}{4-2a}$

51. $\dfrac{15}{x^2+6x+9} + \dfrac{2}{x+3}$

52. $\dfrac{2}{x^2+4x+4} + \dfrac{1}{x+2}$

53. $\dfrac{13}{x^2-5x+6} - \dfrac{5}{x-3}$

54. $\dfrac{-7}{y^2-3y+2} - \dfrac{2}{y-1}$

55. $\dfrac{70}{m^2-100} + \dfrac{7}{2(m+10)}$

56. $\dfrac{27}{y^2-81} + \dfrac{3}{2(y+9)}$

57. $\dfrac{x+8}{x^2-5x-6} + \dfrac{x+1}{x^2-4x-5}$

58. $\dfrac{x+4}{x^2+12x+20} + \dfrac{x+1}{x^2+8x-20}$

59. $\dfrac{5}{4n^2-12n+8} - \dfrac{3}{3n^2-6n}$

60. $\dfrac{6}{5y^2-25y+30} - \dfrac{2}{4y^2-8y}$

MIXED PRACTICE

Perform the indicated operations. Addition, subtraction, multiplication, and division of rational expressions are included here.

61. $\dfrac{15x}{x+8} \cdot \dfrac{2x+16}{3x}$

62. $\dfrac{9z+5}{15} \cdot \dfrac{5z}{81z^2-25}$

63. $\dfrac{8x+7}{3x+5} - \dfrac{2x-3}{3x+5}$

64. $\dfrac{2z^2}{4z-1} - \dfrac{z-2z^2}{4z-1}$

65. $\dfrac{5a+10}{18} \div \dfrac{a^2-4}{10a}$

66. $\dfrac{9}{x^2-1} \div \dfrac{12}{3x+3}$

67. $\dfrac{5}{x^2-3x+2} + \dfrac{1}{x-2}$

68. $\dfrac{4}{2x^2+5x-3} + \dfrac{2}{x+3}$

REVIEW AND PREVIEW

Solve the following linear and quadratic equations. See Sections 2.4 and 7.6.

69. $3x+5=7$

70. $5x-1=8$

71. $2x^2-x-1=0$

72. $4x^2-9=0$

73. $4(x+6)+3=-3$

74. $2(3x+1)+15=-7$

CONCEPT EXTENSIONS

Perform each indicated operation.

75. $\dfrac{3}{x} - \dfrac{2x}{x^2-1} + \dfrac{5}{x+1}$

76. $\dfrac{5}{x-2} + \dfrac{7x}{x^2-4} - \dfrac{11}{x}$

77. $\dfrac{5}{x^2-4} + \dfrac{2}{x^2-4x+4} - \dfrac{3}{x^2-x-6}$

78. $\dfrac{8}{x^2+6x+5} - \dfrac{3x}{x^2+4x-5} + \dfrac{2}{x^2-1}$

79. $\dfrac{9}{x^2+9x+14} - \dfrac{3x}{x^2+10x+21} + \dfrac{x+4}{x^2+5x+6}$

80. $\dfrac{x+10}{x^2-3x-4} - \dfrac{8}{x^2+6x+5} - \dfrac{9}{x^2+x-20}$

81. A board of length $\dfrac{3}{x+4}$ inches was cut into two pieces. If one piece is $\dfrac{1}{x-4}$ inches, express the length of the other piece as a rational expression.

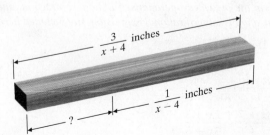

82. The length of a rectangle is $\dfrac{3}{y-5}$ feet, while its width is $\dfrac{2}{y}$ feet. Find its perimeter and then find its area.

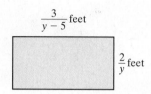

83. In ice hockey, penalty killing percentage is a statistic calculated as $1 - \dfrac{G}{P}$, where G = opponent's power play goals and P = opponent's power play opportunities. Simplify this expression.

84. The dose of medicine prescribed for a child depends on the child's age A in years and the adult dose D for the medication. Two expressions that give a child's dose are Young's Rule, $\dfrac{DA}{A+12}$, and Cowling's Rule, $\dfrac{D(A+1)}{24}$. Find an expression for the difference in the doses given by these expressions.

85. Explain when the LCD of the rational expressions in a sum is the product of the denominators.

86. Explain when the LCD is the same as one of the denominators of a rational expression to be added or subtracted.

87. Two angles are said to be complementary if the sum of their measures is 90°. If one angle measures $\dfrac{40}{x}$ degrees, find the measure of its complement.

88. Two angles are said to be supplementary if the sum of their measures is 180°. If one angle measures $\dfrac{x+2}{x}$ degrees, find the measure of its supplement.

89. In your own words, explain how to add two rational expressions with different denominators.

90. In your own words, explain how to subtract two rational expressions with different denominators.

8.5 SOLVING EQUATIONS CONTAINING RATIONAL EXPRESSIONS

OBJECTIVE 1 ▶ Solving equations containing rational expressions. In Chapter 2, we solved equations containing fractions. In this section, we continue the work we began in Chapter 2 by solving equations containing rational expressions.

Examples of Equations Containing Rational Expressions

$$\frac{x}{2} + \frac{8}{3} = \frac{1}{6} \quad \text{and} \quad \frac{4x}{x^2 + x - 30} + \frac{2}{x - 5} = \frac{1}{x + 6}$$

To solve equations such as these, use the multiplication property of equality to clear the equation of fractions by multiplying both sides of the equation by the LCD.

EXAMPLE 1   Solve: $\frac{x}{2} + \frac{8}{3} = \frac{1}{6}$

Solution   The LCD of denominators 2, 3, and 6 is 6, so we multiply both sides of the equation by 6.

$$6\left(\frac{x}{2} + \frac{8}{3}\right) = 6\left(\frac{1}{6}\right)$$

$$6\left(\frac{x}{2}\right) + 6\left(\frac{8}{3}\right) = 6\left(\frac{1}{6}\right) \quad \text{Use the distributive property.}$$

$$3 \cdot x + 16 = 1 \quad \text{Multiply and simplify.}$$

$$3x = -15 \quad \text{Subtract 16 from both sides.}$$

$$x = -5 \quad \text{Divide both sides by 3.}$$

> **Helpful Hint**
> Make sure that *each* term is multiplied by the LCD, 6.

Check: To check, we replace x with -5 in the original equation.

$$\frac{x}{2} + \frac{8}{3} = \frac{1}{6}$$

$$\frac{-5}{2} + \frac{8}{3} \overset{?}{=} \frac{1}{6} \quad \text{Replace } x \text{ with } -5.$$

$$\frac{1}{6} = \frac{1}{6} \quad \text{True}$$

This number checks, so the solution is -5.   □

**PRACTICE
1**   Solve: $\frac{x}{3} + \frac{4}{5} = \frac{2}{15}$

EXAMPLE 2   Solve: $\frac{t - 4}{2} - \frac{t - 3}{9} = \frac{5}{18}$

Solution   The LCD of denominators 2, 9, and 18 is 18, so we multiply both sides of the equation by 18.

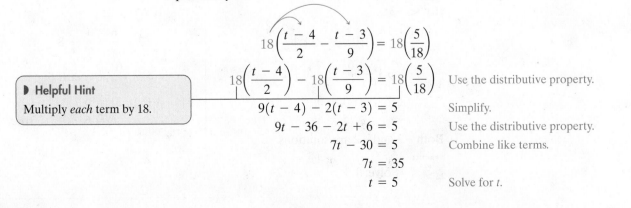

$$18\left(\frac{t - 4}{2} - \frac{t - 3}{9}\right) = 18\left(\frac{5}{18}\right)$$

$$18\left(\frac{t - 4}{2}\right) - 18\left(\frac{t - 3}{9}\right) = 18\left(\frac{5}{18}\right) \quad \text{Use the distributive property.}$$

$$9(t - 4) - 2(t - 3) = 5 \quad \text{Simplify.}$$

$$9t - 36 - 2t + 6 = 5 \quad \text{Use the distributive property.}$$

$$7t - 30 = 5 \quad \text{Combine like terms.}$$

$$7t = 35$$

$$t = 5 \quad \text{Solve for } t.$$

> **Helpful Hint**
> Multiply *each* term by 18.

Check:

$$\frac{t-4}{2} - \frac{t-3}{9} = \frac{5}{18}$$

$$\frac{5-4}{2} - \frac{5-3}{9} \overset{?}{=} \frac{5}{18} \qquad \text{Replace } t \text{ with 5.}$$

$$\frac{1}{2} - \frac{2}{9} \overset{?}{=} \frac{5}{18} \qquad \text{Simplify.}$$

$$\frac{5}{18} = \frac{5}{18} \qquad \text{True}$$

The solution is 5.

PRACTICE
2   Solve: $\dfrac{x+4}{4} - \dfrac{x-3}{3} = \dfrac{11}{12}$

Recall from Section 8.1 that a rational expression is defined for all real numbers except those that make the denominator of the expression 0. This means that if an equation contains *rational expressions with variables in the denominator,* we must be certain that the proposed solution does not make the denominator 0. If replacing the variable with the proposed solution makes the denominator 0, the rational expression is undefined and this proposed solution must be rejected.

EXAMPLE 3   Solve: $3 - \dfrac{6}{x} = x + 8$

Solution   In this equation, 0 cannot be a solution because if x is 0, the rational expression $\dfrac{6}{x}$ is undefined. The LCD is x, so we multiply both sides of the equation by x.

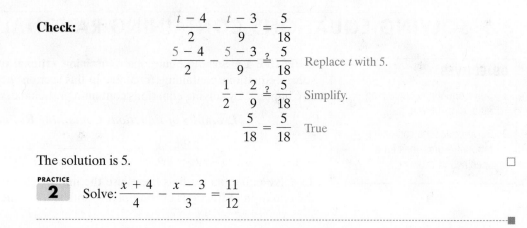

$$x\left(3 - \frac{6}{x}\right) = x(x+8)$$

> ▶ **Helpful Hint**
> Multiply *each* term by x.

$$x(3) - x\left(\frac{6}{x}\right) = x \cdot x + x \cdot 8 \qquad \text{Use the distributive property.}$$

$$3x - 6 = x^2 + 8x \qquad \text{Simplify.}$$

Now we write the quadratic equation in standard form and solve for x.

$$0 = x^2 + 5x + 6$$

$$0 = (x+3)(x+2) \qquad \text{Factor.}$$

$$x + 3 = 0 \quad \text{or} \quad x + 2 = 0 \qquad \text{Set each factor equal to 0 and solve.}$$

$$x = -3 \qquad\qquad x = -2$$

Notice that neither -3 nor -2 makes the denominator in the original equation equal to 0.

Check: To check these solutions, we replace x in the original equation by -3, and then by -2.

If $x = -3$:

$$3 - \frac{6}{} = x + 8$$

$$3 - \frac{6}{-3} \overset{?}{=} -3 + 8$$

$$3 - (-2) \overset{?}{=} 5$$

$$5 = 5 \qquad \text{True}$$

If $x = -2$:

$$3 - \frac{6}{x} = x + 8$$

$$3 - \frac{6}{-2} \overset{?}{=} -2 + 8$$

$$3 - (-3) \overset{?}{=} 6$$

$$6 = 6 \qquad \text{True}$$

Both -3 and -2 are solutions.

PRACTICE
3   Solve: $8 + \dfrac{7}{x} = x + 2$

The following steps may be used to solve an equation containing rational expressions.

Solving an Equation Containing Rational Expressions

STEP 1. Multiply both sides of the equation by the LCD of all rational expressions in the equation.

STEP 2. Remove any grouping symbols and solve the resulting equation.

STEP 3. Check the solution in the original equation.

EXAMPLE 4   Solve: $\dfrac{4x}{x^2 + x - 30} + \dfrac{2}{x - 5} = \dfrac{1}{x + 6}$

Solution

The denominator $x^2 + x - 30$ factors as $(x + 6)(x - 5)$. The LCD is then $(x + 6)(x - 5)$, so we multiply both sides of the equation by this LCD.

$$(x + 6)(x - 5)\left(\frac{4x}{x^2 + x - 30} + \frac{2}{x - 5}\right) = (x + 6)(x - 5)\left(\frac{1}{x + 6}\right) \quad \text{Multiply by the LCD.}$$

$$(x + 6)(x - 5)\cdot\frac{4x}{x^2 + x - 30} + (x + 6)(x - 5)\cdot\frac{2}{x - 5} \quad \text{Apply the distributive property.}$$

$$= (x + 6)(x - 5)\cdot\frac{1}{x + 6}$$

$$4x + 2(x + 6) = x - 5 \quad \text{Simplify.}$$

$$4x + 2x + 12 = x - 5 \quad \text{Apply the distributive property.}$$

$$6x + 12 = x - 5 \quad \text{Combine like terms.}$$

$$5x = -17$$

$$x = -\frac{17}{5} \quad \text{Divide both sides by 5.}$$

Check: Check by replacing x with $-\dfrac{17}{5}$ in the original equation. The solution is $-\dfrac{17}{5}$.

□

PRACTICE
4   Solve: $\dfrac{6x}{x^2 - 5x - 14} - \dfrac{3}{x + 2} = \dfrac{1}{x - 7}$

EXAMPLE 5   Solve: $\dfrac{2x}{x - 4} = \dfrac{8}{x - 4} + 1$

Solution   Multiply both sides by the LCD, $x - 4$.

$$(x - 4)\left(\frac{2x}{x - 4}\right) = (x - 4)\left(\frac{8}{x - 4} + 1\right) \quad \begin{array}{l}\text{Multiply by the LCD.}\\ \text{Notice that 4 cannot be a}\\ \text{solution.}\end{array}$$

$$(x - 4)\cdot\frac{2x}{x - 4} = (x - 4)\cdot\frac{8}{x - 4} + (x - 4)\cdot 1 \quad \text{Use the distributive property.}$$

$$2x = 8 + (x - 4) \quad \text{Simplify.}$$

$$2x = 4 + x$$

$$x = 4$$

Notice that 4 makes the denominator 0 in the original equation. Therefore, 4 is *not* a solution.

This equation has *no solution*.

□

PRACTICE
5   Solve: $\dfrac{7}{x - 2} = \dfrac{3}{x - 2} + 4$

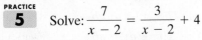

▶ **Helpful Hint**

As we can see from Example 5, it is important to check the proposed solution(s) in the *original* equation.

Concept Check ☑

When can we clear fractions by multiplying through by the LCD?

a. When adding or subtracting rational expressions
b. When solving an equation containing rational expressions
c. Both of these
d. Neither of these

EXAMPLE 6 Solve: $x + \dfrac{14}{x - 2} = \dfrac{7x}{x - 2} + 1$

Solution Notice the denominators in this equation. We can see that 2 can't be a solution. The LCD is $x - 2$, so we multiply both sides of the equation by $x - 2$.

$$(x - 2)\left(x + \frac{14}{x - 2}\right) = (x - 2)\left(\frac{7x}{x - 2} + 1\right)$$

$$(x - 2)(x) + (x - 2)\left(\frac{14}{x - 2}\right) = (x - 2)\left(\frac{7x}{x - 2}\right) + (x - 2)(1)$$

$x^2 - 2x + 14 = 7x + x - 2$	Simplify.
$x^2 - 2x + 14 = 8x - 2$	Combine like terms.
$x^2 - 10x + 16 = 0$	Write the quadratic equation in standard form.
$(x - 8)(x - 2) = 0$	Factor.
$x - 8 = 0$ or $x - 2 = 0$	Set each factor equal to 0.
$x = 8$ $x = 2$	Solve.

As we have already noted, 2 can't be a solution of the original equation. So we need only replace x with 8 in the original equation. We find that 8 is a solution; the only solution is 8. □

PRACTICE
6 Solve: $x + \dfrac{x}{x - 5} = \dfrac{5}{x - 5} - 7$

OBJECTIVE 2 ▶ **Solving equations for a specified variable.** The last example in this section is an equation containing several variables, and we are directed to solve for one of the variables. The steps used in the preceding examples can be applied to solve equations for a specified variable as well.

EXAMPLE 7 Solve: $\dfrac{1}{a} + \dfrac{1}{b} = \dfrac{1}{x}$ for x.

Solution (This type of equation often models a work problem, as we shall see in Section 8.6.) The LCD is abx, so we multiply both sides by abx.

$$abx\left(\frac{1}{a} + \frac{1}{b}\right) = abx\left(\frac{1}{x}\right)$$

$$abx\left(\frac{1}{a}\right) + abx\left(\frac{1}{b}\right) = abx \cdot \frac{1}{x}$$

$bx + ax = ab$	Simplify.
$x(b + a) = ab$	Factor out x from each term on the left side.

$$\frac{x(b + a)}{b + a} = \frac{ab}{b + a} \qquad \text{Divide both sides by } b + a.$$

$$x = \frac{ab}{b + a} \qquad \text{Simplify.}$$

This equation is now solved for x.

PRACTICE 7 Solve: $\frac{1}{a} + \frac{1}{b} = \frac{1}{x}$ for b

---

Graphing Calculator Explorations

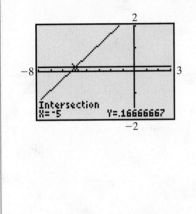

A graphing calculator may be used to check solutions of equations containing rational expressions. For example, to check the solution of Example 1, $\frac{x}{2} + \frac{8}{3} = \frac{1}{6}$, graph $y_1 = \frac{x}{2} + \frac{8}{3}$ and $y_2 = \frac{1}{6}$.

Use TRACE and ZOOM, or use INTERSECT, to find the point of intersection. The point of intersection has an x-value of -5, so the solution of the equation is -5.

Use a graphing calculator to check the examples of this section.

1. Example 2   **2.** Example 3

3. Example 5   **4.** Example 6

8.5 | EXERCISE SET

MyMathLab | Math XP PRACTICE | WATCH | DOWNLOAD | READ | REVIEW

Solve each equation and check each solution. See Examples 1 through 3.

1. $\frac{x}{5} + 3 = 9$

2. $\frac{x}{5} - 2 = 9$

3. $\frac{x}{2} + \frac{5x}{4} = \frac{x}{12}$

4. $\frac{x}{6} + \frac{4x}{3} = \frac{x}{18}$

5. $2 - \frac{8}{x} = 6$

6. $5 + \frac{4}{x} = 1$

7. $2 + \frac{10}{x} = x + 5$

8. $6 + \frac{5}{y} = y - \frac{2}{y}$

9. $\frac{a}{5} = \frac{a - 3}{2}$

10. $\frac{b}{5} = \frac{b + 2}{6}$

11. $\frac{x - 3}{5} + \frac{x - 2}{2} = \frac{1}{2}$

12. $\frac{a + 5}{4} + \frac{a + 5}{2} = \frac{a}{8}$

Solve each equation and check each proposed solution. See Examples 4 through 6.

13. $\frac{3}{2a - 5} = -1$

14. $\frac{6}{4 - 3x} = -3$

15. $\frac{4y}{y - 4} + 5 = \frac{5y}{y - 4}$

16. $\frac{2a}{a + 2} - 5 = \frac{7a}{a + 2}$

17. $2 + \frac{3}{a - 3} = \frac{a}{a - 3}$

18. $\frac{2y}{y - 2} - \frac{4}{y - 2} = 4$

19. $\frac{1}{x + 3} + \frac{6}{x^2 - 9} = 1$

20. $\frac{1}{x + 2} + \frac{4}{x^2 - 4} = 1$

21. $\frac{2y}{y + 4} + \frac{4}{y + 4} = 3$

22. $\frac{5y}{y + 1} - \frac{3}{y + 1} = 4$

23. $\frac{2x}{x + 2} - 2 = \frac{x - 8}{x - 2}$

24. $\frac{4y}{y - 3} - 3 = \frac{3y - 1}{y + 3}$

MIXED PRACTICE

Solve each equation. See Examples 1 through 6.

25. $\frac{2}{y} + \frac{1}{2} = \frac{5}{2y}$

26. $\frac{6}{3y} + \frac{3}{y} = 1$

27. $\frac{a}{a - 6} = \frac{-2}{a - 1}$

28. $\frac{5}{x - 6} = \frac{x}{x - 2}$

29. $\frac{11}{2x} + \frac{2}{3} = \frac{7}{2x}$

30. $\frac{5}{3} - \frac{3}{2x} = \frac{3}{2}$

31. $\frac{2}{x - 2} + 1 = \frac{x}{x + 2}$

32. $1 + \frac{3}{x + 1} = \frac{x}{x - 1}$

33. $\frac{x + 1}{3} - \frac{x - 1}{6} = \frac{1}{6}$

34. $\frac{3x}{5} - \frac{x - 6}{3} = -\frac{2}{5}$

35. $\dfrac{t}{t-4} = \dfrac{t+4}{6}$

36. $\dfrac{15}{x+4} = \dfrac{x-4}{x}$

37. $\dfrac{y}{2y+2} + \dfrac{2y-16}{4y+4} = \dfrac{2y-3}{y+1}$

38. $\dfrac{1}{x+2} = \dfrac{4}{x^2-4} - \dfrac{1}{x-2}$

39. $\dfrac{4r-4}{r^2+5r-14} + \dfrac{2}{r+7} = \dfrac{1}{r-2}$

40. $\dfrac{3}{x+3} = \dfrac{12x+19}{x^2+7x+12} - \dfrac{5}{x+4}$

41. $\dfrac{x+1}{x+3} = \dfrac{x^2-11x}{x^2+x-6} - \dfrac{x-3}{x-2}$

42. $\dfrac{2t+3}{t-1} - \dfrac{2}{t+3} = \dfrac{5-6t}{t^2+2t-3}$

Solve each equation for the indicated variable. See Example 7.

43. $R = \dfrac{E}{I}$ for I (Electronics: resistance of a circuit)

44. $T = \dfrac{V}{Q}$ for Q (Water purification: settling time)

45. $T = \dfrac{2U}{B+E}$ for B (Merchandising: stock turnover rate)

46. $i = \dfrac{A}{t+B}$ for t (Hydrology: rainfall intensity)

47. $B = \dfrac{705w}{h^2}$ for w (Health: body-mass index)

48. $\dfrac{A}{W} = L$ for W (Geometry: area of a rectangle)

49. $N = R + \dfrac{V}{G}$ for G (Urban forestry: tree plantings per year)

50. $C = \dfrac{D(A+1)}{24}$ for A (Medicine: Cowling's Rule for child's dose)

51. $\dfrac{C}{\pi r} = 2$ for r (Geometry: circumference of a circle)

52. $W = \dfrac{CE^2}{2}$ for C (Electronics: energy stored in a capacitor)

53. $\dfrac{1}{y} + \dfrac{1}{3} = \dfrac{1}{x}$ for x

54. $\dfrac{1}{5} + \dfrac{2}{y} = \dfrac{1}{x}$ for x

REVIEW AND PREVIEW

Write each phrase as an expression. See Section 1.8.

55. The reciprocal of x

56. The reciprocal of $x+1$

57. The reciprocal of x, added to the reciprocal of 2

58. The reciprocal of x, subtracted from the reciprocal of 5

Answer each question.

59. If a tank is filled in 3 hours, what fractional part of the tank is filled in 1 hour?

60. If a strip of beach is cleaned in 4 hours, what fractional part of the beach is cleaned in 1 hour?

Identify the x- and y-intercepts. See Section 3.3.

61.   **62.**

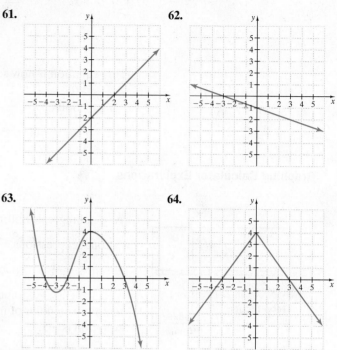

63.   **64.**

CONCEPT EXTENSIONS

65. Explain the difference between solving an equation such as $\dfrac{x}{2} + \dfrac{3}{4} = \dfrac{x}{4}$ for x and performing an operation such as adding $\dfrac{x}{2} + \dfrac{3}{4}$.

66. When solving an equation such as $\dfrac{y}{4} = \dfrac{y}{2} - \dfrac{1}{4}$, we may multiply all terms by 4. When subtracting two rational expressions such as $\dfrac{y}{2} - \dfrac{1}{4}$, we may not. Explain why.

Decision Making. *Determine whether each of the following is an equation or an expression. If it is an equation, then solve it for its variable. If it is an expression, perform the indicated operation.*

67. $\dfrac{1}{x} + \dfrac{5}{9}$

68. $\dfrac{1}{x} + \dfrac{5}{9} = \dfrac{2}{3}$

69. $\dfrac{5}{x-1} - \dfrac{2}{x} = \dfrac{5}{x(x-1)}$

70. $\dfrac{5}{x-1} - \dfrac{2}{x}$

Recall that two angles are supplementary if the sum of their measures is 180°. Find the measures of the following supplementary angles.

71.   **72.**

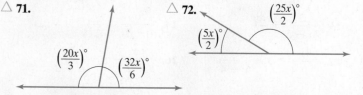

Recall that two angles are complementary if the sum of their measures is 90°. Find the measures of the following complementary angles.

△ **73.**

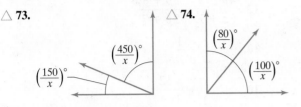

△ **74.**

Solve each equation.

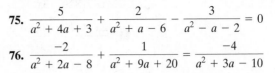

75. $\dfrac{5}{a^2 + 4a + 3} + \dfrac{2}{a^2 + a - 6} - \dfrac{3}{a^2 - a - 2} = 0$

76. $\dfrac{-2}{a^2 + 2a - 8} + \dfrac{1}{a^2 + 9a + 20} = \dfrac{-4}{a^2 + 3a - 10}$

INTEGRATED REVIEW SUMMARY ON RATIONAL EXPRESSIONS

Sections 8.1–8.5

It is important to know the difference between performing operations with rational expressions and solving an equation containing rational expressions. Study the examples below.

PERFORMING OPERATIONS WITH RATIONAL EXPRESSIONS

Adding: $\dfrac{1}{x} + \dfrac{1}{x + 5} = \dfrac{1 \cdot (x + 5)}{x(x + 5)} + \dfrac{1 \cdot x}{x(x + 5)} = \dfrac{x + 5 + x}{x(x + 5)} = \dfrac{2x + 5}{x(x + 5)}$

Subtracting: $\dfrac{3}{x} - \dfrac{5}{x^2 y} = \dfrac{3 \cdot xy}{x \cdot xy} - \dfrac{5}{x^2 y} = \dfrac{3xy - 5}{x^2 y}$

Multiplying: $\dfrac{2}{x} \cdot \dfrac{5}{x - 1} = \dfrac{2 \cdot 5}{x(x - 1)} = \dfrac{10}{x(x - 1)}$

Dividing: $\dfrac{4}{2x + 1} \div \dfrac{x - 3}{x} = \dfrac{4}{2x + 1} \cdot \dfrac{x}{x - 3} = \dfrac{4x}{(2x + 1)(x - 3)}$

SOLVING AN EQUATION CONTAINING RATIONAL EXPRESSIONS

To solve an equation containing rational expressions, we clear the equation of fractions by multiplying both sides by the LCD.

$$\dfrac{3}{x} - \dfrac{5}{x - 1} = \dfrac{1}{x(x - 1)}$$ Note that x can't be 0 or 1.

$$x(x - 1)\left(\dfrac{3}{x}\right) - x(x - 1)\left(\dfrac{5}{x - 1}\right) = x(x - 1) \cdot \dfrac{1}{x(x - 1)}$$ Multiply both sides by the LCD.

$$3(x - 1) - 5x = 1$$ Simplify.

$$3x - 3 - 5x = 1$$ Use the distributive property.

$$-2x - 3 = 1$$ Combine like terms.

$$-2x = 4$$ Add 3 to both sides.

$$x = -2$$ Divide both sides by -2.

Determine whether each of the following is an equation or an expression. If it is an equation, solve it for its variable. If it is an expression, perform the indicated operation.

1. $\dfrac{1}{x} + \dfrac{2}{3}$

2. $\dfrac{3}{a} + \dfrac{5}{6}$

3. $\dfrac{1}{x} + \dfrac{2}{3} = \dfrac{3}{x}$

4. $\dfrac{3}{a} + \dfrac{5}{6} = 1$

5. $\dfrac{2}{x - 1} - \dfrac{1}{x}$

6. $\dfrac{4}{x - 3} - \dfrac{1}{x}$

7. $\dfrac{2}{x + 1} - \dfrac{1}{x} = 1$

8. $\dfrac{4}{x - 3} - \dfrac{1}{x} = \dfrac{6}{x(x - 3)}$

9. $\dfrac{15x}{x+8} \cdot \dfrac{2x+16}{3x}$

10. $\dfrac{9z+5}{15} \cdot \dfrac{5z}{81z^2-25}$

11. $\dfrac{2x+1}{x-3} + \dfrac{3x+6}{x-3}$

12. $\dfrac{4p-3}{2p+7} + \dfrac{3p+8}{2p+7}$

13. $\dfrac{x+5}{7} = \dfrac{8}{2}$

14. $\dfrac{1}{2} = \dfrac{x-1}{8}$

15. $\dfrac{5a+10}{18} \div \dfrac{a^2-4}{10a}$

16. $\dfrac{9}{x^2-1} + \dfrac{12}{3x+3}$

17. $\dfrac{x+2}{3x-1} + \dfrac{5}{(3x-1)^2}$

18. $\dfrac{4}{(2x-5)^2} + \dfrac{x+1}{2x-5}$

19. $\dfrac{x-7}{x} - \dfrac{x+2}{5x}$

20. $\dfrac{9}{x^2-4} + \dfrac{2}{x+2} = \dfrac{-1}{x-2}$

21. $\dfrac{3}{x+3} = \dfrac{5}{x^2-9} - \dfrac{2}{x-3}$

22. $\dfrac{10x-9}{x} - \dfrac{x-4}{3x}$

8.6 PROPORTION AND PROBLEM SOLVING WITH RATIONAL EQUATIONS

OBJECTIVES

1 Solve proportions.

2 Use proportions to solve problems.

3 Solve problems about numbers.

4 Solve problems about work.

5 Solve problems about distance.

OBJECTIVE 1 ▶ Solving proportions. A **ratio** is the quotient of two numbers or two quantities. For example, the ratio of 2 to 5 can be written as $\dfrac{2}{5}$, the quotient of 2 and 5.

If two ratios are equal, we say the ratios are **in proportion** to each other. A **proportion** is a mathematical statement that two ratios are equal.

For example, the equation $\dfrac{1}{2} = \dfrac{4}{8}$ is a proportion, as is $\dfrac{x}{5} = \dfrac{8}{10}$, because both sides of the equations are ratios. When we want to emphasize the equation as a proportion, we

read the proportion $\dfrac{1}{2} = \dfrac{4}{8}$ as "one is to two as four is to eight"

In a proportion, cross products are equal. To understand cross products, let's start with the proportion

$$\frac{a}{b} = \frac{c}{d}$$

and multiply both sides by the LCD, bd.

$$bd\left(\frac{a}{b}\right) = bd\left(\frac{c}{d}\right) \quad \text{Multiply both sides by the LCD, } bd.$$
$$\underbrace{ad}_{} = \underbrace{bc}_{} \quad \text{Simplify.}$$

Cross product   Cross product

Notice why ad and bc are called cross products.

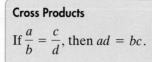

ad bc

$$\frac{a}{b} = \frac{c}{d}$$

Cross Products

If $\dfrac{a}{b} = \dfrac{c}{d}$, then $ad = bc$.

For example, if

$$\frac{1}{2} = \frac{4}{8}, \quad \text{then} \quad 1 \cdot 8 = 2 \cdot 4 \quad \text{or}$$
$$8 = 8$$

Notice that a proportion contains four numbers (or expressions). If any three numbers are known, we can solve and find the fourth number.

EXAMPLE 1   Solve for x: $\dfrac{45}{x} = \dfrac{5}{7}$

**Solution**   This is an equation with rational expressions, and also a proportion. Below are two ways to solve.

Since this is a rational equation, we can use the methods of the previous section.

$$\frac{45}{x} = \frac{5}{7}$$

$7x \cdot \dfrac{45}{x} = 7x \cdot \dfrac{5}{7}$ Multiply both sides by LCD $7x$.

$7 \cdot 45 = x \cdot 5$ Divide out common factors.

$315 = 5x$ Multiply.

$\dfrac{315}{5} = \dfrac{5x}{5}$ Divide both sides by 5.

$63 = x$ Simplify.

Since this is also a proportion, we may set cross products equal.

$$\frac{45}{x} = \frac{5}{7}$$

$45 \cdot 7 = x \cdot 5$ Set cross products equal.

$315 = 5x$ Multiply.

$\dfrac{315}{5} = \dfrac{5x}{5}$ Divide both sides by 5.

$63 = x$ Simplify.

Check: Both methods give us a solution of 63. To check, substitute 63 for x in the original proportion. The solution is 63.   □

PRACTICE
1   Solve for x: $\dfrac{36}{x} = \dfrac{4}{11}$

In this section, if the rational equation is a proportion, we will use cross products to solve.

EXAMPLE 2   Solve for x: $\dfrac{x - 5}{3} = \dfrac{x + 2}{5}$

**Solution**

$$\frac{x - 5}{3} = \frac{x + 2}{5}$$

$5(x - 5) = 3(x + 2)$ Set cross products equal.

$5x - 25 = 3x + 6$ Multiply.

$5x = 3x + 31$ Add 25 to both sides.

$2x = 31$ Subtract $3x$ from both sides.

$\dfrac{2x}{2} = \dfrac{31}{2}$ Divide both sides by 2.

$x = \dfrac{31}{2}$

Check: Verify that $\dfrac{31}{2}$ is the solution.   □

PRACTICE
2   Solve for x: $\dfrac{3x + 2}{9} = \dfrac{x - 1}{2}$

OBJECTIVE 2 ▶ **Using proportions to solve problems.** Proportions can be used to model and solve many real-life problems. When using proportions in this way, it is important to judge whether the solution is reasonable. Doing so helps us to decide if the proportion has been formed correctly. We use the same problem-solving steps that were introduced in Section 2.4.

EXAMPLE 3 Calculating the Cost of Recordable Compact Discs

Three boxes of CD-Rs (recordable compact discs) cost $37.47. How much should 5 boxes cost?

Solution

1. UNDERSTAND. Read and reread the problem. We know that the cost of 5 boxes is more than the cost of 3 boxes, or $37.47, and less than the cost of 6 boxes, which is double the cost of 3 boxes, or 2($37.47) = $74.94. Let's suppose that 5 boxes cost $60.00. To check, we see if 3 boxes is to 5 boxes as the *price* of 3 boxes is to the *price* of 5 boxes. In other words, we see if

$$\frac{3 \text{ boxes}}{5 \text{ boxes}} = \frac{\text{price of 3 boxes}}{\text{price of 5 boxes}}$$

or

$$\frac{3}{5} = \frac{37.47}{60.00}$$

$3(60.00) = 5(37.47)$ Set cross products equal.

or

$180.00 = 187.35$ Not a true statement.

Thus, $60 is not correct, but we now have a better understanding of the problem.

Let x = price of 5 boxes of CD-Rs.

2. TRANSLATE.

$$\frac{3 \text{ boxes}}{5 \text{ boxes}} = \frac{\text{price of 3 boxes}}{\text{price of 5 boxes}}$$

$$\frac{3}{5} = \frac{37.47}{x}$$

3. SOLVE.

$$\frac{3}{5} = \frac{37.47}{x}$$

$3x = 5(37.47)$ Set cross products equal.

$3x = 187.35$

$x = 62.45$ Divide both sides by **3**.

4. INTERPRET.

Check: Verify that 3 boxes is to 5 boxes as $37.47 is to $62.45. Also, notice that our solution is a reasonable one as discussed in Step 1.

State: Five boxes of CD-Rs cost $62.45.   □

PRACTICE
3   Four 2-liter bottles of Diet Pepsi cost $5.16. How much will seven 2-liter bottles cost?

> ▶ **Helpful Hint**
>
> The proportion $\dfrac{5 \text{ boxes}}{3 \text{ boxes}} = \dfrac{\text{price of 5 boxes}}{\text{price of 3 boxes}}$ could also have been used to solve Example 3.
> Notice that the cross products are the same.

Similar triangles have the same shape but not necessarily the same size. In similar triangles, the measures of corresponding angles are equal, and corresponding sides are in proportion.

If triangle ABC and triangle XYZ shown are similar, then we know that the measure of angle A = the measure of angle X, the measure of angle B = the measure of angle Y, and the measure of angle C = the measure of angle Z. We also know that corresponding sides are in proportion: $\dfrac{a}{x} = \dfrac{b}{y} = \dfrac{c}{z}$.

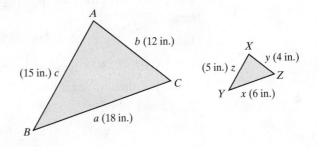

In this section, we will position similar triangles so that they have the same orientation.

To show that corresponding sides are in proportion for the triangles above, we write the ratios of the corresponding sides.

$$\frac{a}{x} = \frac{18}{6} = 3 \qquad \frac{b}{y} = \frac{12}{4} = 3 \qquad \frac{c}{z} = \frac{15}{5} = 3$$

△ **EXAMPLE 4** **Finding the Length of a Side of a Triangle**

If the following two triangles are similar, find the missing length x.

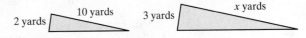

Solution

1. UNDERSTAND. Read the problem and study the figure.

2. TRANSLATE. Since the triangles are similar, their corresponding sides are in proportion and we have

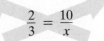

$$\frac{2}{3} = \frac{10}{x}$$

3. SOLVE. To solve, we multiply both sides by the LCD, $3x$, or cross multiply.

$$2x = 30$$
$$x = 15 \quad \text{Divide both sides by 2.}$$

4. INTERPRET.

Check: To check, replace x with 15 in the original proportion and see that a true statement results.

State: The missing length is 15 yards. ☐

PRACTICE
4 If the following two triangles are similar, find x.

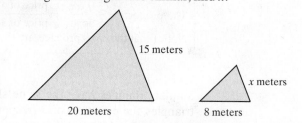

15 meters

x meters

20 meters

8 meters

OBJECTIVE 3 ▶ Solving problems about numbers. Let's continue to solve problems. The remaining problems are all modeled by rational equations.

EXAMPLE 5 Finding an Unknown Number

The quotient of a number and 6, minus $\frac{5}{3}$, is the quotient of the number and 2. Find the number.

Solution

1. UNDERSTAND. Read and reread the problem. Suppose that the unknown number is 2, then we see if the quotient of 2 and 6, or $\frac{2}{6}$, minus $\frac{5}{3}$ is equal to the quotient of 2 and 2, or $\frac{2}{2}$.

$$\frac{2}{6} - \frac{5}{3} = \frac{1}{3} - \frac{5}{3} = -\frac{4}{3}, \text{ not } \frac{2}{2}$$

Don't forget that the purpose of a proposed solution is to better understand the problem.

Let x = the unknown number.

2. TRANSLATE.

In words:	the quotient of x and 6	minus	$\frac{5}{3}$	is	the quotient of x and 2
Translate:	$\frac{x}{6}$	$-$	$\frac{5}{3}$	$=$	$\frac{x}{2}$

3. SOLVE. Here, we solve the equation $\frac{x}{6} - \frac{5}{3} = \frac{x}{2}$. We begin by multiplying both sides of the equation by the LCD, 6.

$$6\left(\frac{x}{6} - \frac{5}{3}\right) = 6\left(\frac{x}{2}\right)$$

$$6\left(\frac{x}{6}\right) - 6\left(\frac{5}{3}\right) = 6\left(\frac{x}{2}\right) \qquad \text{Apply the distributive property.}$$

$$x - 10 = 3x \qquad \text{Simplify.}$$

$$-10 = 2x \qquad \text{Subtract } x \text{ from both sides.}$$

$$\frac{-10}{2} = \frac{2x}{2} \qquad \text{Divide both sides by 2.}$$

$$-5 = x \qquad \text{Simplify.}$$

4. INTERPRET.

Check: To check, we verify that "the quotient of -5 and 6 minus $\frac{5}{3}$ is the quotient of -5 and 2," or $-\frac{5}{6} - \frac{5}{3} = -\frac{5}{2}$.

State: The unknown number is -5.

PRACTICE
5   The quotient of a number and 5, minus $\frac{3}{2}$, is the quotient of the number and 10.

OBJECTIVE 4 ▶ Solving problems about work. The next example is often called a work problem. Work problems usually involve people or machines doing a certain task.

EXAMPLE 6   **Finding Work Rates**

Sam Waterton and Frank Schaffer work in a plant that manufactures automobiles. Sam can complete a quality control tour of the plant in 3 hours while his assistant, Frank, needs 7 hours to complete the same job. The regional manager is coming to inspect the plant facilities, so both Sam and Frank are directed to complete a quality control tour together. How long will this take?

Solution

1. UNDERSTAND. Read and reread the problem. The key idea here is the relationship between the **time** (hours) it takes to complete the job and the **part of the job** completed in 1 unit of time (hour). For example, if the **time** it takes Sam to complete the job is 3 hours, the **part of the job** he can complete in 1 hour is $\frac{1}{3}$. Similarly, Frank can complete $\frac{1}{7}$ of the job in 1 hour.

   Let x = the **time** in hours it takes Sam and Frank to complete the job together. Then $\frac{1}{x}$ = the **part of the job** they complete in 1 hour.

	Hours to Complete Total Job	*Part of Job Completed in 1 Hour*
Sam	3	$\frac{1}{3}$
Frank	7	$\frac{1}{7}$
Together	x	$\frac{1}{x}$

2. TRANSLATE.

In words:	part of job Sam completed in 1 hour	added to	part of job Frank completed in 1 hour	is equal to	part of job they completed together in 1 hour
	↓	↓	↓	↓	↓
Translate:	$\frac{1}{3}$	$+$	$\frac{1}{7}$	$=$	$\frac{1}{x}$

3. SOLVE. Here, we solve the equation $\frac{1}{3} + \frac{1}{7} = \frac{1}{x}$. We begin by multiplying both sides of the equation by the LCD, $21x$.

$$21x\left(\frac{1}{3}\right) + 21x\left(\frac{1}{7}\right) = 21x\left(\frac{1}{x}\right)$$

$$7x + 3x = 21 \qquad \text{Simplify.}$$

$$10x = 21$$

$$x = \frac{21}{10} \quad \text{or} \quad 2\frac{1}{10} \text{ hours}$$

4. INTERPRET.

Check: Our proposed solution is $2\frac{1}{10}$ hours. This proposed solution is reasonable since $2\frac{1}{10}$ hours is more than half of Sam's time and less than half of Frank's time. Check this solution in the originally *stated* problem.

State: Sam and Frank can complete the quality control tour in $2\frac{1}{10}$ hours. ☐

PRACTICE

6 Cindy Liu and Mary Beckwith own a landscaping company. Cindy can complete a certain garden planting in 3 hours, while Mary takes 4 hours to complete the same Job. If both of them work together, how long will it take to plant the garden?

Concept Check ☑

Solve $E = mc^2$

a. for m.
b. for c^2.

OBJECTIVE 5 ▶ Solving problems about distance. Next we look at a problem solved by the distance formula,

$$d = r \cdot t$$

> **EXAMPLE 7** **Finding Speeds of Vehicles**

A car travels 180 miles in the same time that a truck travels 120 miles. If the car's speed is 20 miles per hour faster than the truck's, find the car's speed and the truck's speed.

Solution

1. UNDERSTAND. Read and reread the problem. Suppose that the truck's speed is 45 miles per hour. Then the car's speed is 20 miles per hour more, or 65 miles per hour.

We are given that the car travels 180 miles in the same time that the truck travels 120 miles. To find the time it takes the car to travel 180 miles, remember that since $d = rt$, we know that $\dfrac{d}{r} = t$.

Car's Time **Truck's Time**

$$t = \frac{d}{r} = \frac{180}{65} = 2\frac{50}{65} = 2\frac{10}{13}\text{ hours} \qquad t = \frac{d}{r} = \frac{120}{45} = 2\frac{30}{45} = 2\frac{2}{3}\text{ hours}$$

Since the times are not the same, our proposed solution is not correct. But we have a better understanding of the problem.

Let $x = $ the speed of the truck.

Since the car's speed is 20 miles per hour faster than the truck's, then

$$x + 20 = \text{the speed of the car}$$

Use the formula $d = r \cdot t$ or **distance** = **rate** $\cdot$ **time**. Prepare a chart to organize the information in the problem.

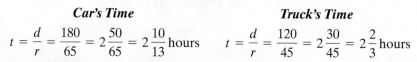

> **Helpful Hint**
>
> If $d = r \cdot t$,
>
> then $t = \dfrac{d}{r}$ }
>
> or $time = \dfrac{distance}{rate}$. }

	Distance	=	Rate	·	Time
Truck	120		x		$\begin{cases}120 \leftarrow \text{distance}\\ \overline{x} \leftarrow \text{rate}\end{cases}$
Car	180		$x + 20$		$\begin{cases}180 \leftarrow \text{distance}\\ \overline{x + 20} \leftarrow \text{rate}\end{cases}$

Answers to Concept Check:

a. $m = \dfrac{E}{c^2}$ **b.** $c^2 = \dfrac{E}{m}$

2. TRANSLATE. Since the car and the truck traveled the same amount of time, we have that

In words: | car's time | = | truck's time |

Translate: $$\frac{180}{x + 20} = \frac{120}{x}$$

3. SOLVE. We begin by multiplying both sides of the equation by the LCD, $x(x + 20)$, or cross multiplying.

$$\frac{180}{x + 20} = \frac{120}{x}$$

$$180x = 120(x + 20)$$

$180x = 120x + 2400$ Use the distributive property.

$60x = 2400$ Subtract $120x$ from both sides.

$x = 40$ Divide both sides by 60.

4. INTERPRET. The speed of the truck is 40 miles per hour. The speed of the car must then be $x + 20$ or 60 miles per hour.

Check: Find the time it takes the car to travel 180 miles and the time it takes the truck to travel 120 miles.

| **Car's Time** | **Truck's Time** |

$$t = \frac{d}{r} = \frac{180}{60} = 3 \text{ hours} \qquad t = \frac{d}{r} = \frac{120}{40} = 3 \text{ hours}$$

Since both travel the same amount of time, the proposed solution is correct.

State: The car's speed is 60 miles per hour and the truck's speed is 40 miles per hour.

□

PRACTICE
7   A bus travels 180 miles in the same time that a car travels 240 miles. If the car's speed is 15 mph faster than the speed of the bus, find the speed of the car and the speed of the bus.

VOCABULARY & READINESS CHECK

Multiple Choice. *Without solving algebraically, select the best choice for each exercise.*

1. One person can complete a job in 7 hours. A second person can complete the same job in 5 hours. How long will it take them to complete the job if they work together?

   a. more than 7 hours
   b. between 5 and 7 hours
   c. less than 5 hours

2. One inlet pipe can fill a pond in 30 hours. A second inlet pipe can fill the same pond in 25 hours. How long before the pond is filled if both inlet pipes are on?

   a. less than 25 hours
   b. between 25 and 30 hours
   c. more than 30 hours

8.6 | EXERCISE SET

Solve each proportion. See Examples 1 and 2.

1. $\dfrac{2}{3} = \dfrac{x}{6}$

2. $\dfrac{x}{2} = \dfrac{16}{6}$

3. $\dfrac{x}{10} = \dfrac{5}{9}$

4. $\dfrac{9}{4x} = \dfrac{6}{2}$

5. $\dfrac{x + 1}{2x + 3} = \dfrac{2}{3}$

6. $\dfrac{x + 1}{x + 2} = \dfrac{5}{3}$

7. $\dfrac{9}{5} = \dfrac{12}{3x + 2}$

8. $\dfrac{6}{11} = \dfrac{27}{3x - 2}$

Solve. See Example 3.

9. The ratio of the weight of an object on Earth to the weight of the same object on Pluto is 100 to 3. If an elephant weighs 4100 pounds on Earth, find the elephant's weight on Pluto.

10. If a 170-pound person weighs approximately 65 pounds on Mars, about how much does a 9000-pound satellite weigh? Round your answer to the nearest pound.

11. There are 110 calories per 28.8 grams of Frosted Flakes cereal. Find how many calories are in 43.2 grams of this cereal.

12. On an architect's blueprint, 1 inch corresponds to 4 feet. Find the length of a wall represented by a line that is $3\frac{7}{8}$ inches long on the blueprint.

Find the unknown length x or y in the following pairs of similar triangles. See Example 4.

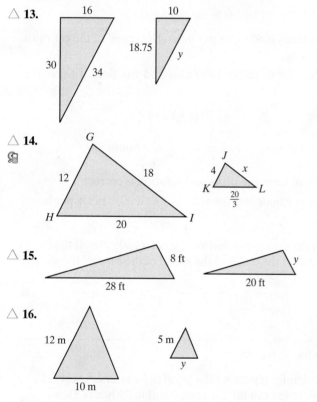

13.

14.

15.

16.

Solve the following. See Example 5.

17. Three times the reciprocal of a number equals 9 times the reciprocal of 6. Find the number.

18. Twelve divided by the sum of x and 2 equals the quotient of 4 and the difference of x and 2. Find x.

19. If twice a number added to 3 is divided by the number plus 1, the result is three halves. Find the number.

20. A number added to the product of 6 and the reciprocal of the number equals -5. Find the number.

See Example 6.

21. Smith Engineering found that an experienced surveyor surveys a roadbed in 4 hours. An apprentice surveyor needs 5 hours to survey the same stretch of road. If the two work together, find how long it takes them to complete the job.

22. An experienced bricklayer constructs a small wall in 3 hours. The apprentice completes the job in 6 hours. Find how long it takes if they work together.

23. In 2 minutes, a conveyor belt moves 300 pounds of recyclable aluminum from the delivery truck to a storage area. A smaller belt moves the same quantity of cans the same distance in 6 minutes. If both belts are used, find how long it takes to move the cans to the storage area.

24. Find how long it takes the conveyor belts described in Exercise 23 to move 1200 pounds of cans. (*Hint:* Think of 1200 pounds as four 300-pound jobs.)

See Example 7.

25. A jogger begins her workout by jogging to the park, a distance of 12 miles. She then jogs home at the same speed but along a different route. This return trip is 18 miles and her time is one hour longer. Find her jogging speed. Complete the accompanying chart and use it to find her jogging speed.

	Distance	=	Rate	·	Time
Trip to Park	12				
Return Trip	18				

26. A boat can travel 9 miles upstream in the same amount of time it takes to travel 11 miles downstream. If the current of the river is 3 miles per hour, complete the chart below and use it to find the speed of the boat in still water.

	Distance	=	Rate	·	Time
Upstream	9		$r - 3$		
Downstream	11		$r + 3$		

27. A cyclist rode the first 20-mile portion of his workout at a constant speed. For the 16-mile cooldown portion of his workout, he reduced his speed by 2 miles per hour. Each portion of the workout took the same time. Find the cyclist's speed during the first portion and find his speed during the cooldown portion.

28. A semi-truck travels 300 miles through the flatland in the same amount of time that it travels 180 miles through mountains. The rate of the truck is 20 miles per hour slower in the mountains than in the flatland. Find both the flatland rate and mountain rate.

MIXED PRACTICE

Solve the following. See Examples 1 through 7. (Note: *Some exercises can be modeled by equations without rational expressions.*)

29. A human factors expert recommends that there be at least 9 square feet of floor space in a college classroom for every student in the class. Find the minimum floor space that 40 students need.

30. Due to space problems at a local university, a 20-foot by 12-foot conference room is converted into a classroom. Find the maximum number of students the room can accommodate. (See Exercise 29.)

31. One-fourth equals the quotient of a number and 8. Find the number.

32. Four times a number added to 5 is divided by 6. The result is $\frac{7}{2}$. Find the number.

33. Marcus and Tony work for Lombardo's Pipe and Concrete. Mr. Lombardo is preparing an estimate for a customer. He knows that Marcus lays a slab of concrete in 6 hours. Tony lays the same size slab in 4 hours. If both work on the job and the cost of labor is $45.00 per hour, decide what the labor estimate should be.

34. Mr. Dodson can paint his house by himself in 4 days. His son needs an additional day to complete the job if he works by himself. If they work together, find how long it takes to paint the house.

35. A pilot can travel 400 miles with the wind in the same amount of time as 336 miles against the wind. Find the speed of the wind if the pilot's speed in still air is 230 miles per hour.

36. A fisherman on Pearl River rows 9 miles downstream in the same amount of time he rows 3 miles upstream. If the current is 6 miles per hour, find how long it takes him to cover the 12 miles.

37. Find the unknown length y.

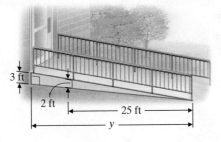

△ 38. Find the unknown length y.

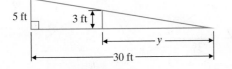

39. Ken Hall, a tailback, holds the high school sports record for total yards rushed in a season. In 1953, he rushed for 4045 total yards in 12 games. Find his average rushing yards per game. Round your answer to the nearest whole yard.

40. To estimate the number of people in Jackson, population 50,000, who have no health insurance, 250 people were polled. Of those polled, 39 had no insurance. How many people in the city might we expect to be uninsured?

41. Two divided by the difference of a number and 3 minus 4 divided by a number plus 3, equals 8 times the reciprocal of the difference of the number squared and 9. What is the number?

42. If 15 times the reciprocal of a number is added to the ratio of 9 times a number minus 7 and the number plus 2, the result is 9. What is the number?

43. A pilot flies 630 miles with a tail wind of 35 miles per hour. Against the wind, he flies only 455 miles in the same amount of time. Find the rate of the plane in still air.

44. A marketing manager travels 1080 miles in a corporate jet and then an additional 240 miles by car. If the car ride takes one hour longer than the jet ride takes, and if the rate of the jet is 6 times the rate of the car, find the time the manager travels by jet and find the time the manager travels by car.

45. To mix weed killer with water correctly, it is necessary to mix 8 teaspoons of weed killer with 2 gallons of water. Find how many gallons of water are needed to mix with the entire box if it contains 36 teaspoons of weed killer.

46. The directions for a certain bug spray concentrate is to mix 3 ounces of concentrate with 2 gallons of water. How many ounces of concentrate are needed to mix with 5 gallons of water?

47. A boater travels 16 miles per hour on the water on a still day. During one particular windy day, he finds that he travels 48 miles with the wind behind him in the same amount of time that he travels 16 miles into the wind. Find the rate of the wind.

Let x be the rate of the wind.

	r	$\times$	t	$=$	d
with wind	$16 + x$				48
into wind	$16 - x$				16

48. The current on a portion of the Mississippi River is 3 miles per hour. A barge can go 6 miles upstream in the same amount of time it takes to go 10 miles downstream. Find the speed of the boat in still water.

Let x be the speed of the boat in still water.

	r	$\times$	t	$=$	d
upstream	$x - 3$				6
downstream	$x + 3$				10

49. The best selling two-seater sports car is the Mazda Miata. A driver of this car took a day-trip around the California coastline driving at two different speeds. He drove 70 miles at a slower speed and 300 miles at a speed 40 miles per hour faster. If the time spent during the faster speed was twice that spent at a slower speed, find the two speeds during the trip. (*Source: Guinness World Records*)

50. Currently, the Toyota Corolla is the most produced car in the world. Suppose that during a drive test of two Corollas, one car travels 224 miles in the same time that the second car travels 175 miles. If the speed of one car is 14 miles per hour faster than the speed of the second car, find the speed of both cars. (*Source: Guinness World Records*)

51. One custodian cleans a suite of offices in 3 hours. When a second worker is asked to join the regular custodian, the job takes only $1\frac{1}{2}$ hours. How long does it take the second worker to do the same job alone?

52. One person proofreads a copy for a small newspaper in 4 hours. If a second proofreader is also employed, the job can be done in $2\frac{1}{2}$ hours. How long does it take for the second proofreader to do the same job alone?

△ 53. An architect is completing the plans for a triangular deck. Use the diagram below to find the missing dimension.

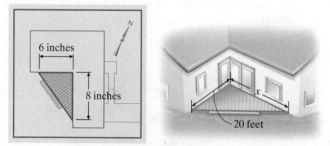

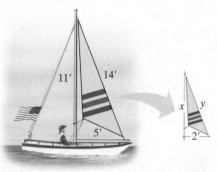

△ 54. A student wishes to make a small model of a triangular mainsail in order to study the effects of wind on the sail. The smaller model will be the same shape as a regular-size sailboat's mainsail. Use the following diagram to find the missing dimensions.

55. The manufacturers of cans of salted mixed nuts state that the ratio of peanuts to other nuts is 3 to 2. If 324 peanuts are in a can, find how many other nuts should also be in the can.

56. There are 1280 calories in a 14-ounce portion of Eagle Brand Milk. Find how many calories are in 2 ounces of Eagle Brand Milk.

57. A pilot can fly an MD-11 2160 miles with the wind in the same time as she can fly 1920 miles against the wind. If the speed of the wind is 30 mph, find the speed of the plane in still air. (*Source*: Air Transport Association of America)

58. A pilot can fly a DC-10 1365 miles against the wind in the same time as he can fly 1575 miles with the wind. If the speed of the plane in still air is 490 miles per hour, find the speed of the wind. (*Source*: Air Transport Association of America)

59. One pipe fills a storage pool in 20 hours. A second pipe fills the same pool in 15 hours. When a third pipe is added and all three are used to fill the pool, it takes only 6 hours. Find how long it takes the third pipe to do the job.

60. One pump fills a tank 2 times as fast as another pump. If the pumps work together, they fill the tank in 18 minutes. How long does it take for each pump to fill the tank?

61. A car travels 280 miles in the same time that a motorcycle travels 240 miles. If the car's speed is 10 miles per hour more than the motorcycle's, find the speed of the car and the speed of the motorcycle.

62. A walker travels 3.6 miles in the same time that a jogger travels 6 miles. If the walker's speed is 2 miles per hour less than the jogger's, find the speed of the walker and the speed of the jogger.

63. In 6 hours, an experienced cook prepares enough pies to supply a local restaurant's daily order. Another cook prepares the same number of pies in 7 hours. Together with a third cook, they prepare the pies in 2 hours. Find how long it takes the third cook to prepare the pies alone.

64. It takes 9 hours for pump A to fill a tank alone. Pump B takes 15 hours to fill the same tank alone. If pumps A, B, and C are used, the tank fills in 5 hours. How long does it take pump C to fill the tank alone?

65. One pump fills a tank 3 times as fast as another pump. If the pumps work together, they fill the tank in 21 minutes. How long does it take for each pump to fill the tank?

66. Mrs. Smith balances the company books in 8 hours. It takes her assistant 12 hours to do the same job. If they work together, find how long it takes them to balance the books.

Given that the following pairs of triangles are similar, find each missing length.

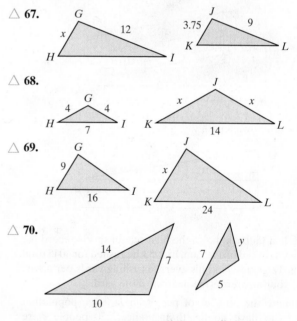

△ 67.

△ 68.

△ 69.

△ 70.

REVIEW AND PREVIEW

Find the slope of the line through each pair of points. Use the slope to determine whether the line is vertical, horizontal, or moves upward or downward from left to right. See Section 3.4.

71. $(-2, 5), (4, -3)$

72. $(0, 4), (2, 10)$

73. $(-3, -6), (1, 5)$

74. $(-2, 7), (3, -2)$

75. $(3, 7), (3, -2)$

76. $(0, -4), (2, -4)$

CONCEPT EXTENSIONS

Read a Graph. *The following bar graph shows the capacity of the United States to generate electricity from the wind in the years shown. Use this graph for Exercises 77 and 78.*

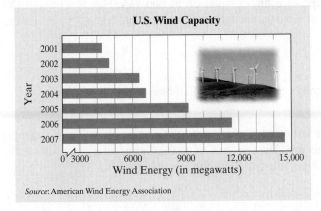

U.S. Wind Capacity

Year (vertical axis): 2001, 2002, 2003, 2004, 2005, 2006, 2007

Wind Energy (in megawatts): 0, 3000, 6000, 9000, 12,000, 15,000

Source: American Wind Energy Association

77. Find the approximate increase in megawatt capacity during the 2-year period from 2001 to 2003.

78. Find the approximate increase in megawatt capacity during the 2-year period from 2004 to 2006.

In general, 1000 megawatts will serve the average electricity needs of 560,000 people. Use this fact and the preceding graph to answer Exercises 79 and 80.

79. In 2007, the number of megawatts that were generated from wind would serve the electricity needs of how many people? (Round to the nearest ten-thousand.)

80. How many megawatts of electricity are needed to serve the city or town in which you live?

81. Person A can complete a job in 5 hours, and person B can complete the same job in 3 hours. Without solving algebraically, discuss reasonable and unreasonable answers for how long it would take them to complete the job together.

82. For which of the following equations can we immediately use cross products to solve for x?

  a. $\dfrac{2-x}{5} = \dfrac{1+x}{3}$ **b.** $\dfrac{2}{5} - x = \dfrac{1+x}{3}$

83. For what value of x is $\dfrac{x}{x-1}$ in proportion to $\dfrac{x+1}{x}$? Explain your result.

84. If x is 10, is $\dfrac{2}{x}$ in proportion to $\dfrac{x}{50}$? Explain why or why not.

One of the great algebraists of ancient times was a man named Diophantus. Little is known of his life other than that he lived and worked in Alexandria. Some historians believe he lived during the first century of the Christian era, about the time of Nero. The only clue to his personal life is the following epigram found in a collection called the Palatine Anthology.

God granted him youth for a sixth of his life and added a twelfth part to this. He clothed his cheeks in down. He lit him the light of wedlock after a seventh part and five years after his marriage, He granted him a son. Alas, lateborn wretched child. After attaining the measure of half his father's life, cruel fate overtook him, thus leaving Diophantus during the last four years of his life only such consolation as the science of numbers. How old was Diophantus at his death?*

We are looking for Diophantus' age when he died, so let x represent that age. If we sum the parts of his life, we should get the total age.

Parts of his life $\begin{cases} \dfrac{1}{6}x + \dfrac{1}{12}x \text{ is the time of his youth.} \\[2mm] \dfrac{1}{7}x \text{ is the time between his youth and when he married.} \\[2mm] 5 \text{ years is the time between his marriage and the birth of his son.} \\[2mm] \dfrac{1}{2}x \text{ is the time Diophantus had with his son.} \\[2mm] 4 \text{ years is the time between his son's death and his own.} \end{cases}$

The sum of these parts should equal Diophantus' age when he died.

$$\frac{1}{6}\cdot x + \frac{1}{12}\cdot x + \frac{1}{7}\cdot x + 5 + \frac{1}{2}\cdot x + 4 = x$$

85. Solve the epigram.

86. How old was Diophantus when his son was born? How old was the son when he died?

87. Solve the following epigram:

I was four when my mother packed my lunch and sent me off to school. Half my life was spent in school and another sixth was spent on a farm. Alas, hard times befell me. My crops and cattle fared poorly and my land was sold. I returned to school for 3 years and have spent one tenth of my life teaching. How old am I?

88. Write an epigram describing your life. Be sure that none of the time periods in your epigram overlap.

89. A hyena spots a giraffe 0.5 mile away and begins running toward it. The giraffe starts running away from the hyena just as the hyena begins running toward it. A hyena can run at a speed of 40 mph and a giraffe can run at 32 mph. How long will it take for the hyena to overtake the giraffe? (*Source: World Almanac* and *Book of Facts*)

H $\longmapsto$ 0.5 mile $\longrightarrow$ G

*From *The Nature and Growth of Modern Mathematics*, Edna Kramer, 1970, Fawcett Premier Books, Vol. 1, pages 107–108.

8.7 VARIATION AND PROBLEM SOLVING

OBJECTIVES

1 Solve problems involving direct variation.

2 Solve problems involving inverse variation.

3 Other types of direct and inverse variation.

4 Variation and problem solving.

In Chapter 3, we studied linear equations in two variables. Recall that such an equation can be written in the form $Ax + By = C$, where A and B are not both 0.

Also recall that the graph of a linear equation in two variables is a line. In this section, we begin by looking at a particular family of linear equations—those that can be written in the form

$$y = kx,$$

where k is a constant. This family of equations is called *direct variation*.

OBJECTIVE 1 ▶ Solving direct variation problems. Let's suppose that you are earning $7.25 per hour at a part-time job. The amount of money you earn depends on the number of hours you work. This is illustrated by the following table:

Hours Worked	0	1	2	3	4
Money Earned (before deductions)	0	7.25	14.50	21.75	29.00

and so on

In general, to calculate your earnings (before deductions) multiply the constant $7.25 by the number of hours you work. If we let y represent the amount of money earned and x represent the number of hours worked, we get the direct variation equation

$$y = 7.25 \cdot x$$

earnings = $7.25 · hours worked

Notice that in this direct variation equation, as the number of hours increases, the pay increases as well.

Direct Variation

y varies directly as x, or **y is directly proportional to x,** if there is a nonzero constant k such that

$$y = kx$$

The number k is called the **constant of variation** or the **constant of proportionality.**

In our direct variation example: $y = 7.25x$, the constant of variation is 7.25.

Let's use the previous table to graph $y = 7.25x$. We begin our graph at the ordered-pair solution $(0, 0)$. Why? We assume that the least amount of hours worked is 0. If 0 hours are worked, then the pay is $0.

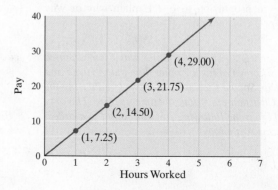

As illustrated in this graph, a direct variation equation $y = kx$ is linear. Also notice that $y = 7.25x$ is a function since its graph passes the vertical line test.

EXAMPLE 1   Write a direct variation equation of the form $y = kx$ that satisfies the ordered pairs in the table below.

x	2	9	1.5	−1
y	6	27	4.5	−3

Solution   We are given that there is a direct variation relationship between x and y. This means that

$$y = kx$$

By studying the given values, you may be able to mentally calculate k. If not, to find k, we simply substitute one given ordered pair into this equation and solve for k. We'll use the given pair $(2, 6)$.

$$y = kx$$
$$6 = k \cdot 2$$
$$\frac{6}{2} = \frac{k \cdot 2}{2}$$
$$3 = k \qquad \text{Solve for } k.$$

Since $k = 3$, we have the equation $y = 3x$.

To check, see that each given y is 3 times the given x.   □

PRACTICE

1   Write a direct variation of the form $y = kx$ that satisfies the ordered pairs in the table below.

x	2	8	−4	1.3
y	10	40	−20	6.5

Let's try another type of direct variation example.

EXAMPLE 2   Suppose that y varies directly as x. If y is 17 when x is 34, find the constant of variation and the direct variation equation. Then find y when x is 12.

Solution   Let's use the same method as in Example 1 to find x. Since we are told that y varies directly as x, we know the relationship is of the form

$$y = kx$$

Let $y = 17$ and $x = 34$ and solve for k.

$$17 = k \cdot 34$$
$$\frac{17}{34} = \frac{k \cdot 34}{34}$$
$$\frac{1}{2} = k \qquad \text{Solve for } k.$$

Thus, the constant of variation is $\frac{1}{2}$ and the equation is $y = \frac{1}{2}x$.

To find y when $x = 12$, use $y = \dfrac{1}{2}x$ and replace x with 12.

$$y = \frac{1}{2}x$$

$$y = \frac{1}{2} \cdot 12 \quad \text{Replace } x \text{ with 12.}$$

$$y = 6$$

Thus, when x is 12, y is 6. □

PRACTICE
2 If y varies directly as x and y is 12 when x is 48, find the constant of variation and the direct variation equation. Then find y when x is 20.

Let's review a few facts about linear equations of the form $y = kx$.

Direct Variation: $y = kx$

- There is a direct variation relationship between x and y.
- The graph is a line.
- The line will always go through the origin $(0, 0)$. Why?
  Let $x = 0$. Then $y = k \cdot 0$ or $y = 0$.
- The slope of the graph of $y = kx$ is k, the constant of variation. Why? Remember that the slope of an equation of the form $y = mx + b$ is m, the coefficient of x.
- The equation $y = kx$ describes a function. Each x has a unique y and its graph passes the vertical line test.

EXAMPLE 3 The line is the graph of a direct variation equation. Find the constant of variation and the direct variation equation.

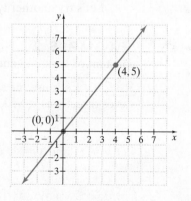

Solution Recall that k, the constant of variation is the same as the slope of the line. Thus, to find k, we use the slope formula and find slope.

Using the given points $(0, 0)$, and $(4, 5)$, we have

$$\text{slope} = \frac{5 - 0}{4 - 0} = \frac{5}{4}.$$

Thus, $k = \dfrac{5}{4}$ and the variation equation is $y = \dfrac{5}{4}x$.

PRACTICE
3 Find the constant of variation and the direct variation equation for the line below.

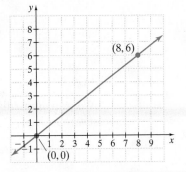

OBJECTIVE 2 ▶ Solving inverse variation problems. In this section, we will introduce another type of variation, called inverse variation.

Let's suppose you need to drive a distance of 40 miles. You know that the faster you drive the distance, the sooner you arrive at your destination. Recall that there is a mathematical relationship between distance, rate, and time. It is $d = r \cdot t$. In our example, distance is a constant 40 miles, so we have $40 = r \cdot t$ or $t = \dfrac{40}{r}$.

For example, if you drive 10 mph, the time to drive the 40 miles is

$$t = \frac{40}{r} = \frac{40}{10} = 4 \text{ hours}$$

If you drive 20 mph, the time is

$$t = \frac{40}{r} = \frac{40}{20} = 2 \text{ hours}$$

Again, notice that as speed increases, time decreases. Below are some ordered-pair solutions of $t = \dfrac{40}{r}$ and its graph.

Rate (mph)	r	5	10	20	40	60	80
Time (hr)	t	8	4	2	1	$\dfrac{2}{3}$	$\dfrac{1}{2}$

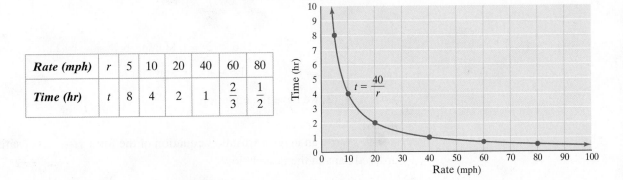

Notice that the graph of this variation is not a line, but it passes the vertical line test so $t = \dfrac{40}{r}$ does describe a function. This is an example of inverse variation.

> **Inverse Variation**
>
> **y varies inversely as x,** or **y is inversely proportional to x,** if there is a nonzero constant k such that
>
> $$y = \frac{k}{x}$$
>
> The number k is called the **constant of variation** or the **constant of proportionality.**

In our inverse variation example, $t = \frac{40}{r}$ or $y = \frac{40}{x}$, the constant of variation is 40.

We can immediately see differences and similarities in direct variation and inverse variation.

Direct variation	$y = kx$	linear equation	both
Inverse variation	$y = \dfrac{k}{x}$	rational equation	functions

Remember that $y = \frac{k}{x}$ is a rational equation and not a linear equation. Also notice that because x is in the denominator, x can be any value except 0.

We can still derive an inverse variation equation from a table of values.

EXAMPLE 4 Write an inverse variation equation of the form $y = \frac{k}{x}$ that satisfies the ordered pairs in the table below.

x	2	4	$\frac{1}{2}$
y	6	3	24

Solution Since there is an inverse variation relationship between x and y, we know that $y = \frac{k}{x}$. To find k, choose one given ordered pair and substitute the values into the equation. We'll use $(2, 6)$.

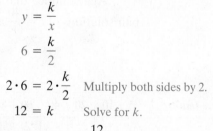

$$y = \frac{k}{x}$$
$$6 = \frac{k}{2}$$
$$2 \cdot 6 = 2 \cdot \frac{k}{2} \quad \text{Multiply both sides by 2.}$$
$$12 = k \quad \text{Solve for } k.$$

Since $k = 12$, we have the equation $y = \frac{12}{x}$. $\qquad\square$

PRACTICE

4 Write an inverse variation equation of the form $y = \frac{k}{x}$ that satisfies the ordered pairs in the table below.

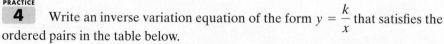

x	2	-1	$\frac{1}{3}$
y	4	-8	24

> **Helpful Hint**
> Multiply both sides of the inverse variation relationship equation $y = \dfrac{k}{x}$ by x (as long as x is not 0), and we have $xy = k$. This means that if y varies inversely as x, their product is always the constant of variation k. For an example of this, check the table from Example 4.
>
>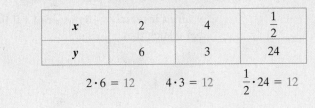
>
> | x | 2 | 4 | $\dfrac{1}{2}$ |
> |---|---|---|---|
> | y | 6 | 3 | 24 |
>
> $$2 \cdot 6 = 12 \qquad 4 \cdot 3 = 12 \qquad \frac{1}{2} \cdot 24 = 12$$

EXAMPLE 5 Suppose that y varies inversely as x. If $y = 0.02$ when $x = 75$, find the constant of variation and the inverse variation equation. Then find y when x is 30.

Solution Since y varies inversely as x, the constant of variation may be found by simply finding the product of the given x and y.

$$k = xy = 75(0.02) = 1.5$$

To check, we will use the inverse variation equation

$$y = \frac{k}{x}.$$

Let $y = 0.02$ and $x = 75$ and solve for k.

$$0.02 = \frac{k}{75}$$

$$75(0.02) = 75 \cdot \frac{k}{75} \qquad \text{Multiply both sides by 75.}$$

$$1.5 = k \qquad \text{Solve for } k.$$

Thus, the constant of variation is 1.5 and the equation is $y = \dfrac{1.5}{x}$.

To find y when $x = 30$ use $y = \dfrac{1.5}{x}$ and replace x with 30.

$$y = \frac{1.5}{x}$$

$$y = \frac{1.5}{30} \qquad \text{Replace } x \text{ with 30.}$$

$$y = 0.05$$

Thus, when x is 30, y is 0.05. □

PRACTICE

5 If y varies inversely as x and y is 0.05 when x is 42, find the constant of variation and the inverse variation equation. Then find y when x is 70.

OBJECTIVE 3 ▶ Solving other types of direct and inverse variation problems. It is possible for y to vary directly or inversely as powers of x.

Direct and Inverse Variation as *n*th Powers of *x*

y **varies directly as a power of *x*** if there is a nonzero constant *k* and a natural number *n* such that

$$y = kx^n$$

y **varies inversely as a power of *x*** if there is a nonzero constant *k* and a natural number *n* such that

$$y = \frac{k}{x^n}$$

EXAMPLE 6   The surface area of a cube *A* varies directly as the square of a length of its side *s*. If *A* is 54 when *s* is 3, find *A* when $s = 4.2$.

Solution   Since the surface area *A* varies directly as the square of side *s*, we have

$$A = ks^2.$$

To find *k*, let $A = 54$ and $s = 3$.

$$A = k \cdot s^2$$
$$54 = k \cdot 3^2 \quad \text{Let } A = 54 \text{ and } s = 3.$$
$$54 = 9k \quad\quad 3^2 = 9.$$
$$6 = k \quad\quad\quad \text{Divide by 9.}$$

The formula for surface area of a cube is then

$$A = 6s^2 \text{ where } s \text{ is the length of a side.}$$

To find the surface area when $s = 4.2$, substitute.

$$A = 6s^2$$
$$A = 6 \cdot (4.2)^2$$
$$A = 105.84$$

The surface area of a cube whose side measures 4.2 units is 105.84 square units.   □

PRACTICE
6   The area of an isosceles right triangle *A* varies directly as the square of one of its legs *x*. If *A* is 32 when *x* is 8, find *A* when $x = 3.6$.

OBJECTIVE 4 ▶ Solving applications of variation. There are many real-life applications of direct and inverse variation.

EXAMPLE 7   The weight of a body *w* varies inversely with the square of its distance from the center of Earth *d*. If a person weighs 160 pounds on the surface of Earth, what is the person's weight 200 miles above the surface? (Assume that the radius of Earth is 4000 miles.)

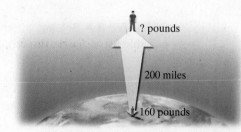

Solution

1. UNDERSTAND. Make sure you read and reread the problem.

2. TRANSLATE. Since we are told that weight w varies inversely with the square of its distance from the center of Earth, d, we have

$$w = \frac{k}{d^2}.$$

3. SOLVE. To solve the problem, we first find k. To do so, use the fact that the person weighs 160 pounds on Earth's surface, which is a distance of 4000 miles from Earth's center.

$$w = \frac{k}{d^2}$$

$$160 = \frac{k}{(4000)^2}$$

$$2,560,000,000 = k$$

Thus, we have $w = \dfrac{2,560,000,000}{d^2}$

Since we want to know the person's weight 200 miles above the Earth's surface, we let $d = 4200$ and find w.

$$w = \frac{2,560,000,000}{d^2}$$

$$w = \frac{2,560,000,000}{(4200)^2} \qquad \text{A person 200 miles above the Earth's surface is 4200 miles from the Earth's center.}$$

$$w \approx 145 \qquad \text{Simplify.}$$

4. INTERPRET.

Check: Your answer is reasonable since the farther a person is from Earth, the less the person weighs.

State: Thus, 200 miles above the surface of the Earth, a 160-pound person weighs approximately 145 pounds. □

PRACTICE

7   Robert Boyle investigated the relationship between volume of a gas and its pressure. He developed Boyle's law, which states that the volume of a gas varies inversely with pressure if the temperature is held constant. If 50 ml of oxygen is at a pressure of 20 atmospheres, what will the volume of the oxygen be at a pressure of 40 atmospheres?

VOCABULARY & READINESS CHECK

Decision Making. *State whether each equation represents direct or inverse variation.*

1. $y = \dfrac{k}{x}$, where k is a constant. _____

2. $y = kx$, where k is a constant. _____

3. $y = 5x$ _____

4. $y = \dfrac{5}{x}$ _____

5. $y = \dfrac{7}{x^2}$ _____

6. $y = 6.5x^4$ _____

7. $y = \dfrac{11}{x}$ _____

8. $y = 18x$ _____

9. $y = 12x^2$ _____

10. $y = \dfrac{20}{x^3}$ _____

8.7 | EXERCISE SET

Write a direct variation equation, $y = kx$, that satisfies the ordered pairs in each table. See Example 1.

1.

x	0	6	10
y	0	3	5

2.

x	0	2	-1	3
y	0	14	-7	21

3.

x	-2	2	4	5
y	-12	12	24	30

4.

x	3	9	-2	12
y	1	3	$-\dfrac{2}{3}$	4

Write a direct variation equation, $y = kx$, that describes each graph. See Example 3.

5. **6.**

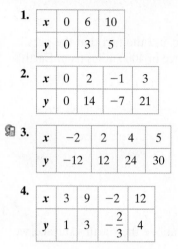

7. **8.**

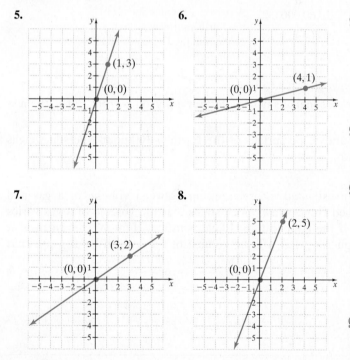

Write an inverse variation equation, $y = \dfrac{k}{x}$, that satisfies the ordered pairs in each table. See Example 4.

9.

x	1	-7	3.5	-2
y	7	-1	2	-3.5

10.

x	2	-11	4	-4
y	11	-2	5.5	-5.5

11.

x	10	$\dfrac{1}{2}$	$-\dfrac{3}{2}$
y	0.05	1	$-\dfrac{1}{3}$

12.

x	4	$\dfrac{1}{5}$	-8
y	0.1	2	-0.05

MIXED PRACTICE

Write an equation to describe each variation. Use k for the constant of proportionality. See Examples 1 through 6.

13. y varies directly as x

14. a varies directly as b

15. h varies inversely as t

16. s varies inversely as t

17. z varies directly as x^2

18. p varies inversely as x^2

19. y varies inversely as z^3

20. x varies directly as y^4

21. x varies inversely as $\sqrt{y}$

22. y varies directly as d^2

Solve. See Examples 2, 5, and 6.

23. y varies directly as x. If $y = 20$ when $x = 5$, find y when x is 10.

24. y varies directly as x. If $y = 27$ when $x = 3$, find y when x is 2.

25. y varies inversely as x. If $y = 5$ when $x = 60$, find y when x is 100.

26. y varies inversely as x. If $y = 200$ when $x = 5$, find y when x is 4.

27. z varies directly as x^2. If $z = 96$ when $x = 4$, find z when $x = 3$.

28. s varies directly as t^3. If $s = 270$ when $t = 3$, find s when $x = 1$.

29. a varies inversely as b^3. If $a = \dfrac{3}{2}$ when $b = 2$, find a when b is 3.

30. p varies inversely as q^2. If $p = \dfrac{5}{16}$ when $q = 8$, find p when $q = \dfrac{1}{2}$.

Solve. See Examples 1 through 7.

31. Your paycheck (before deductions) varies directly as the number of hours you work. If your paycheck is \$112.50 for 18 hours, find your pay for 10 hours.

32. If your paycheck (before deductions) is $244.50 for 30 hours, find your pay for 34 hours. See Exercise 31.

33. The cost of manufacturing a certain type of headphone varies inversely as the number of headphones increases. If 5000 headphones can be manufactured for $9.00 each, find the cost (per headphone) to manufacture 7500 headphones.

34. The cost of manufacturing a certain composition notebook varies inversely as the number of notebooks increases. If 10,000 notebooks can be manufactured for $0.50 each, find the cost to manufacture 18,000 notebooks.

35. The distance a spring stretches varies directly with the weight attached to the spring. If a 60-pound weight stretches the spring 4 inches, find the distance that an 80-pound weight stretches the spring.

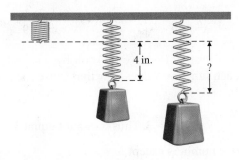

36. If a 30-pound weight stretches a spring 10 inches, find the distance a 20-pound weight stretches the spring. (See Exercise 35.)

37. The weight of an object varies inversely as the square of its distance from the *center* of the Earth. If a person weighs 180 pounds on Earth's surface, what is his weight 10 miles above the surface of the Earth? (Assume that the Earth's radius is 4000 miles.)

38. For a constant distance, the rate of travel varies inversely as the time traveled. If a family travels 55 mph and arrives at a destination in 4 hours, how long will the return trip take traveling at 60 mph?

39. The distance d that an object falls is directly proportional to the square of the time of the fall, t. A person who is parachuting for the first time is told to wait 10 seconds before opening the parachute. If the person falls 64 feet in 2 seconds, find how far he falls in 10 seconds.

40. The distance needed for a car to stop, d is directly proportional to the square of its rate of travel, r. Under certain driving conditions, a car traveling 60 mph needs 300 feet to stop. With these same driving conditions, how long does it take a car to stop if the car is traveling 30 mph when the brakes are applied?

REVIEW AND PREVIEW

Simplify. Follow the circled steps in the order shown. See Section 1.3.

41. $\dfrac{\left.\dfrac{3}{4}+\dfrac{1}{4}\right\}}{\left.\dfrac{3}{8}+\dfrac{13}{8}\right\}}$; ①Add. ③Divide. ②Add.

42. $\dfrac{\left.\dfrac{9}{5}+\dfrac{6}{5}\right\}}{\left.\dfrac{17}{6}+\dfrac{7}{6}\right\}}$; ① Add. ③ Divide. ② Add.

43. $\dfrac{\left.\dfrac{2}{5}+\dfrac{1}{5}\right\}}{\left.\dfrac{7}{10}+\dfrac{7}{10}\right\}}$; ①Add. ③Divide. ②Add.

44. $\dfrac{\left.\dfrac{1}{4}+\dfrac{5}{4}\right\}}{\left.\dfrac{3}{8}+\dfrac{7}{8}\right\}}$; ①Add. ③Divide. ②Add.

CONCEPT EXTENSIONS

45. Suppose that y varies directly as x. If x is tripled, what is the effect on y?

46. Suppose that y varies directly as x^2. If x is tripled, what is the effect on y?

47. The period, P, of a pendulum (the time of one complete back and forth swing) varies directly with the square root of its length, l. If the length of the pendulum is quadrupled, what is the effect on the period, P?

48. For a constant distance, the rate of travel r varies inversely with the time traveled, t. If a car traveling 100 mph completes a test track in 6 minutes, find the rate needed to complete the same test track in 4 minutes. (***Hint:*** Convert minutes to hours.)

8.8 GRAPHING RATIONAL FUNCTIONS BY TRANSFORMATIONS

OBJECTIVES

1 Find domains of rational functions.

2 Graph $f(x) = \dfrac{1}{x}$ and $f(x) = \dfrac{1}{x^2}$.

3 Graph transformations of rational functions.

Throughout this chapter, we have studied rational expressions. In this section, we extend our study of rational expressions to rational functions.

OBJECTIVE 1 ▶ **Finding domains of rational functions. Rational functions** are quotients of polynomial functions. This means that rational functions can be expressed as

$$f(x) = \frac{p(x)}{q(x)}.$$

where p and q are polynomial functions and $q(x) \neq 0$. The **domain** of a rational function consists of all real numbers except the x-values that make the denominator zero. For example, the domain of the rational function

$$f(x) = \frac{x^2 + 7x + 9}{x(x-2)(x+5)}$$

This is $p(x)$.

This is $q(x)$.

consists of all real numbers except 0, 2, and –5.

EXAMPLE 1   Finding the Domain of a Rational Function

Find the domain of each rational function:

a. $f(x) = \dfrac{x^2 - 9}{x - 3}$ **b.** $g(x) = \dfrac{x}{x^2 - 9}$ **c.** $h(x) = \dfrac{x + 3}{x^2 + 9}.$

Solution   Rational functions contain division. Because division by 0 is undefined, we must exclude from the domain of each function values of x that cause the polynomial function in the denominator to be 0.

a. The denominator of $f(x) = \dfrac{x^2 - 9}{x - 3}$ is 0 if $x = 3$. Thus, x cannot equal 3.

The domain of f consists of all real numbers except 3.

b. The denominator of $g(x) = \dfrac{x}{x^2 - 9}$ is 0 if $x = -3$ or $x = 3$. Thus, the domain

of g consists of all real numbers except -3 and 3.

c. No real numbers cause the denominator of $h(x) = \dfrac{x + 3}{x^2 + 9}$ to equal 0. The domain of h consists of all real numbers.

▶ **Helpful Hint**

Because the domain of a rational function is the set of all real numbers except those for which the denominator is 0, you can identify such numbers by setting the denominator equal to 0 and solving for x. Exclude the resulting real values of x from the domain.

PRACTICE

1   Find the domain of each rational function:

a. $f(x) = \dfrac{x^2 - 25}{x - 5}$ **b.** $g(x) = \dfrac{x}{x^2 - 25}$ **c.** $h(x) = \dfrac{x + 5}{x^2 + 25}.$

OBJECTIVE 2 ▶ Graphing $f(x) = \dfrac{1}{x}$ **and** $f(x) = \dfrac{1}{x^2}$. Let's graph the most basic of rational functions, the reciprocal function $f(x) = \dfrac{1}{x}$. To do so, we find as many ordered-pair solutions as needed in order to find patterns to help us graph this function.

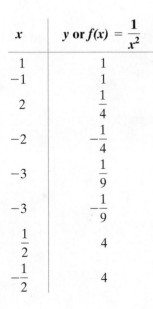

x's ≥ 1				
x	1	2	3	6
$f(x) = \dfrac{1}{x}$	1	$\dfrac{1}{2}$	$\dfrac{1}{3}$	$\dfrac{1}{6}$

x's ≤ −1				
x	−1	−2	−3	−6
$f(x) = \dfrac{1}{x}$	−1	$-\dfrac{1}{2}$	$-\dfrac{1}{3}$	$-\dfrac{1}{6}$

x's between 0 and 1			
x	$\dfrac{1}{5}$	$\dfrac{1}{2}$	$\dfrac{3}{4}$
$f(x) = \dfrac{1}{x}$	5	2	$\dfrac{4}{3}$

x's between −1 and 0			
x	$-\dfrac{3}{4}$	$-\dfrac{1}{2}$	$-\dfrac{1}{5}$
$f(x) = \dfrac{1}{x}$	$-\dfrac{4}{3}$	−2	−5

The graph of $f(x) = \dfrac{1}{x}$ is shown in the margin.

Notice the vertical and horizontal dashed lines marked asymptotes. **Asymptotes** are lines that the graph approaches.

Another basic rational function is $f(x) = \dfrac{1}{x^2}$. The graph of this function, with y-axis symmetry and positive function values, is shown below. Like the reciprocal function, $f(x) = \dfrac{1}{x^2}$ the graph has a break and is composed of two distinct branches. Study the ordered-pair solutions in the vertical table to the left and find and plot more as needed.

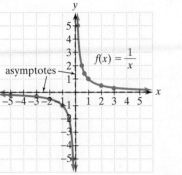

x	y or $f(x) = \dfrac{1}{x^2}$
1	1
−1	1
2	$\dfrac{1}{4}$
−2	$-\dfrac{1}{4}$
−3	$\dfrac{1}{9}$
−3	$-\dfrac{1}{9}$
$\dfrac{1}{2}$	4
$-\dfrac{1}{2}$	4

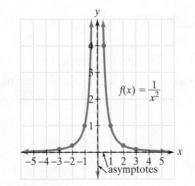

OBJECTIVE 3 ▶ Graphing Transformations of Rational Functions. We will now use the basic graphs of $f(x) = \dfrac{1}{x}$ and $f(x) = \dfrac{1}{x^2}$ and the same transformations we learned in Chapter 3 to graph the two types shown in the boxes on the next page.

To graph $f(x) = \dfrac{a}{x-h} + k$,

- Draw a dashed vertical asymptote at $x = h$
- Draw a dashed horizontal asymptote at $y = k$
- Find as many ordered-pair solutions as needed, then sketch two branches as shown in red.
- The graph passes the vertical line test since it is the graph of a function.

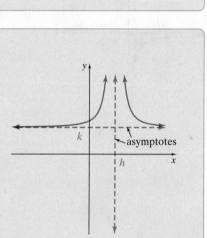

To graph $f(x) = \dfrac{a}{(x-h)^2} + k$,

- Draw a vertical asymptote at $x = h$.
- Draw a horizontal asymptote at $y = k$.
- Find as many ordered-pair solutions as needed, then sketch two branches as shown in red.
- The graph passes the vertical line test since it is the graph of a function.

EXAMPLE 2 Using Transformations to Graph a Rational Function

Use the graph of $f(x) = \dfrac{1}{x^2}$ to graph $g(x) = \dfrac{1}{(x-2)^2} + 1$.

Solution Compare the given $g(x)$ to $f(x) = \dfrac{a}{(x-h)^2} + k$. We see that h is 2 and k is 1.

- Draw a dashed vertical asymptote at $x = 2$.
- Draw a dashed horizontal asymptote at $y = 1$.
- A few ordered-pair solutions are shown along with the graph of $g(x)$. ☐

The graph of $g(x) = \dfrac{1}{(x-2)^2} + 1$ showing two points and the asymptotes

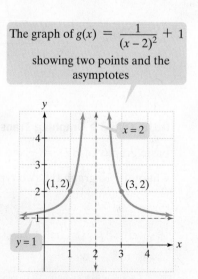

PRACTICE
2   Use the graph of $f(x) = \dfrac{1}{x^2}$ to graph $g(x) = \dfrac{1}{(x-1)^2} + 2$.

EXAMPLE 3   Use the graph of $f(x) = \dfrac{1}{x}$ to graph $g(x) = \dfrac{1}{x+1} - 2$.

Solution   Compare the given $g(x)$ to $f(x) = \dfrac{a}{x-h} + k$.

Since $g(x) = \dfrac{1}{x - (-1)} + (-2)$, we have that h is –1 and k is –2.

- Draw a dashed vertical asymptote at $x = -1$.
- Draw a dashed horizontal asymptote at $y = -2$.
- A few ordered-pair solutions are shown along with the graph of $g(x)$.

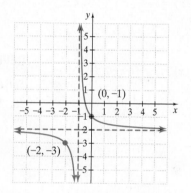

PRACTICE
3   Use the graph of $f(x) = \dfrac{1}{x}$ to graph $g(x) = \dfrac{1}{(x+2)} - 1$.

TECHNOLOGY NOTE

The graph of the rational function $f(x) = \dfrac{x}{x^2 - 9}$, is graphed below in a $[-5, 5, 1]$ by $[-4, 4, 1]$ viewing rectangle. The graph is shown in connected mode and in dot mode. In connected mode, the graphing utility plots many points and connects the points with curves. In dot mode, the utility plots the same points, but does not connect them.

Connected Mode

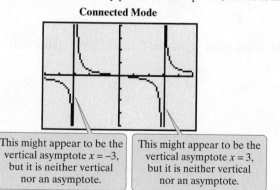

This might appear to be the vertical asymptote $x = -3$, but it is neither vertical nor an asymptote.

This might appear to be the vertical asymptote $x = 3$, but it is neither vertical nor an asymptote.

Dot Mode

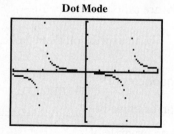

The steep lines in connected mode that are "almost" the vertical asymptotes $x = -3$ and $x = 3$ are not part of the graph and do not represent the vertical asymptotes. The graphing utility has incorrectly connected the last point to the left of $x = -3$ with the first point to the right of $x = -3$. It has also incorrectly connected the last point to the left of $x = 3$ with the first point to the right of $x = 3$. The effect is to create two near-vertical segments that look like asymptotes. This erroneous effect does not appear using dot mode.

8.8 EXERCISE SET

Find the domain of each rational function. See Example 1.

1. $f(x) = \dfrac{5x}{x-4}$

2. $f(x) = \dfrac{7x}{x-8}$

3. $g(x) = \dfrac{3x^2}{(x-5)(x+4)}$

4. $g(x) = \dfrac{2x^2}{(x-2)(x+6)}$

5. $h(x) = \dfrac{x+7}{x^2-49}$

6. $h(x) = \dfrac{x+8}{x^2-64}$

7. $f(x) = \dfrac{x+7}{x^2+49}$

8. $f(x) = \dfrac{x+8}{x^2+64}$

Use transformations of $f(x) = \dfrac{1}{x}$ or $f(x) = \dfrac{1}{x^2}$ to graph each rational function. See Examples 2 and 3.

9. $g(x) = \dfrac{1}{x-1}$

10. $g(x) = \dfrac{1}{x-2}$

11. $h(x) = \dfrac{1}{x} + 2$

12. $h(x) = \dfrac{1}{x} + 1$

13. $g(x) = \dfrac{1}{x+1} - 2$

14. $g(x) = \dfrac{1}{x+2} - 2$

15. $g(x) = \dfrac{1}{(x+2)^2}$

16. $g(x) = \dfrac{1}{(x+1)^2}$

17. $h(x) = \dfrac{1}{x^2} - 4$

18. $h(x) = \dfrac{1}{x^2} - 3$

19. $h(x) = \dfrac{1}{(x-3)^2} + 1$

20. $h(x) = \dfrac{1}{(x-3)^2} + 2$

21. What is a rational function?

22. Use a graphing utility to verify any five of your hand-drawn graphs in Exercises 9–20.

23. Use a graphing utility to graph $y = \dfrac{1}{x^2}$, $y = \dfrac{1}{x^4}$, and $y = \dfrac{1}{x^6}$ in the same viewing rectangle. For even values of n, how does changing n affect the graph of $y = \dfrac{1}{x^n}$?

24. Use a graphing utility to graph $y = \dfrac{1}{x}$, $y = \dfrac{1}{x^3}$, and $\dfrac{1}{x^5}$ in the same viewing rectangle. For odd values of n, how does changing n affect the graph of $y = \dfrac{1}{x^n}$?

REVIEW AND PREVIEW

Solve. See Section 7.6.

25. $2x^2 + x = 15$

26. $2x^2 - 5x = 7$

27. $x^3 + x^2 = 4x + 4$

28. $x^3 + 5x^2 = x + 5$

CHAPTER 8 VOCABULARY CHECK

Fill in each blank with one of the words or phrases listed below.

rational expression	direct variation	inverse variation	polynomial
cross products	ratio	proportion	

1. A _____ is the quotient of two numbers.

2. $\dfrac{x}{2} = \dfrac{7}{16}$ is an example of a _____ .

3. If $\dfrac{a}{b} = \dfrac{c}{d}$, then ad and bc are called _____ .

4. A _____ is an expression that can be written in the form $\dfrac{P}{Q}$, where P and Q are polynomials and Q is not 0.

5. Rational functions are quotients of _____ functions.

6. The equation $y = \dfrac{k}{x}$ is an example of _____ .

7. The equation $y = kx$ is an example of _____ .

CHAPTER 8 REVIEW

(8.1) *Find any real number for which each rational expression is undefined.*

1. $\dfrac{x + 5}{x^2 - 4}$

2. $\dfrac{5x + 9}{4x^2 - 4x - 15}$

Find the value of each rational expression when $x = 5$, $y = 7$, *and* $z = -2$.

3. $\dfrac{2 - z}{z + 5}$

4. $\dfrac{x^2 + xy - y^2}{x + y}$

Simplify each rational expression.

5. $\dfrac{2x + 6}{x^2 + 3x}$

6. $\dfrac{3x - 12}{x^2 - 4x}$

7. $\dfrac{x + 2}{x^2 - 3x - 10}$

8. $\dfrac{x + 4}{x^2 + 5x + 4}$

9. $\dfrac{x^3 - 4x}{x^2 + 3x + 2}$

10. $\dfrac{5x^2 - 125}{x^2 + 2x - 15}$

11. $\dfrac{x^2 - x - 6}{x^2 - 3x - 10}$

12. $\dfrac{x^2 - 2x}{x^2 + 2x - 8}$

Simplify each expression. This section contains four-term polynomials and sums and differences of two cubes.

13. $\dfrac{x^2 + xa + xb + ab}{x^2 - xc + bx - bc}$

14. $\dfrac{x^2 + 5x - 2x - 10}{x^2 - 3x - 2x + 6}$

15. $\dfrac{4 - x}{x^3 - 64}$

16. $\dfrac{x^2 - 4}{x^3 + 8}$

(8.2) *Perform each indicated operation and simplify.*

17. $\dfrac{15x^3y^2}{z} \cdot \dfrac{z}{5xy^3}$

18. $\dfrac{-y^3}{8} \cdot \dfrac{9x^2}{y^3}$

19. $\dfrac{x^2 - 9}{x^2 - 4} \cdot \dfrac{x - 2}{x + 3}$

20. $\dfrac{2x + 5}{x - 6} \cdot \dfrac{2x}{-x + 6}$

21. $\dfrac{x^2 - 5x - 24}{x^2 - x - 12} \div \dfrac{x^2 - 10x + 16}{x^2 + x - 6}$

22. $\dfrac{4x + 4y}{xy^2} \div \dfrac{3x + 3y}{x^2y}$

23. $\dfrac{x^2 + x - 42}{x - 3} \cdot \dfrac{(x - 3)^2}{x + 7}$

24. $\dfrac{2a + 2b}{3} \cdot \dfrac{a - b}{a^2 - b^2}$

25. $\dfrac{2x^2 - 9x + 9}{8x - 12} \div \dfrac{x^2 - 3x}{2x}$

26. $\dfrac{x^2 - y^2}{x^2 + xy} \div \dfrac{3x^2 - 2xy - y^2}{3x^2 + 6x}$

27. $\dfrac{x - y}{4} \div \dfrac{y^2 - 2y - xy + 2x}{16x + 24}$

28. $\dfrac{5 + x}{7} \div \dfrac{xy + 5y - 3x - 15}{7y - 35}$

(8.3) *Perform each indicated operation and simplify.*

29. $\dfrac{x}{x^2 + 9x + 14} + \dfrac{7}{x^2 + 9x + 14}$

30. $\dfrac{x}{x^2 + 2x - 15} + \dfrac{5}{x^2 + 2x - 15}$

31. $\dfrac{4x - 5}{3x^2} - \dfrac{2x + 5}{3x^2}$

32. $\dfrac{9x + 7}{6x^2} - \dfrac{3x + 4}{6x^2}$

Find the LCD of each pair of rational expressions.

33. $\dfrac{x + 4}{2x}, \dfrac{3}{7x}$

34. $\dfrac{x - 2}{x^2 - 5x - 24}, \dfrac{3}{x^2 + 11x + 24}$

Rewrite each rational expression as an equivalent expression whose denominator is the given polynomial.

35. $\dfrac{5}{7x} = \dfrac{}{14x^3y}$

36. $\dfrac{9}{4y} = \dfrac{}{16y^3x}$

37. $\dfrac{x + 2}{x^2 + 11x + 18} = \dfrac{}{(x + 2)(x - 5)(x + 9)}$

38. $\dfrac{3x - 5}{x^2 + 4x + 4} = \dfrac{}{(x + 2)^2(x + 3)}$

(8.4) *Perform each indicated operation and simplify.*

39. $\dfrac{4}{5x^2} - \dfrac{6}{y}$

40. $\dfrac{2}{x - 3} - \dfrac{4}{x - 1}$

41. $\dfrac{4}{x + 3} - 2$

42. $\dfrac{3}{x^2 + 2x - 8} + \dfrac{2}{x^2 - 3x + 2}$

43. $\dfrac{2x - 5}{6x + 9} - \dfrac{4}{2x^2 + 3x}$

44. $\dfrac{x - 1}{x^2 - 2x + 1} - \dfrac{x + 1}{x - 1}$

Find the perimeter and the area of each figure.

△ **45.**

△ **46.**

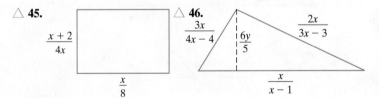

(8.5) *Solve each equation.*

47. $\dfrac{n}{10} = 9 - \dfrac{n}{5}$

48. $\dfrac{2}{x + 1} - \dfrac{1}{x - 2} = -\dfrac{1}{2}$

49. $\dfrac{y}{2y + 2} + \dfrac{2y - 16}{4y + 4} = \dfrac{y - 3}{y + 1}$

50. $\dfrac{2}{x - 3} - \dfrac{4}{x + 3} = \dfrac{8}{x^2 - 9}$

51. $\dfrac{x - 3}{x + 1} - \dfrac{x - 6}{x + 5} = 0$

52. $x + 5 = \dfrac{6}{x}$

Solve the equation for the indicated variable.

53. $\dfrac{4A}{5b} = x^2$, for b

54. $\dfrac{x}{7} + \dfrac{y}{8} = 10$, for y

(8.6) Solve each proportion.

55. $\dfrac{x}{2} = \dfrac{12}{4}$

56. $\dfrac{20}{1} = \dfrac{x}{25}$

57. $\dfrac{2}{x - 1} = \dfrac{3}{x + 3}$

58. $\dfrac{4}{y - 3} = \dfrac{2}{y - 3}$

Solve.

59. A machine can process 300 parts in 20 minutes. Find how many parts can be processed in 45 minutes.

60. As his consulting fee, Mr. Visconti charges $90.00 per day. Find how much he charges for 3 hours of consulting. Assume an 8-hour work day.

61. Five times the reciprocal of a number equals the sum of $\dfrac{3}{2}$ the reciprocal of the number and $\dfrac{7}{6}$. What is the number?

62. The reciprocal of a number equals the reciprocal of the difference of 4 and the number. Find the number.

63. A car travels 90 miles in the same time that a car traveling 10 miles per hour slower travels 60 miles. Find the speed of each car.

64. The current in a bayou near Lafayette, Louisiana, is 4 miles per hour. A paddle boat travels 48 miles upstream in the same amount of time it takes to travel 72 miles downstream. Find the speed of the boat in still water.

65. When Mark and Maria manicure Mr. Stergeon's lawn, it takes them 5 hours. If Mark works alone, it takes 7 hours. Find how long it takes Maria alone.

66. It takes pipe A 20 days to fill a fish pond. Pipe B takes 15 days. Find how long it takes both pipes together to fill the pond.

Given that the pairs of triangles are similar, find each missing length x.

△ **67.**

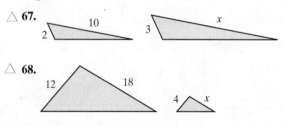

△ **68.**

(8.7) Solve.

69. y varies directly as x. If $y = 40$ when $x = 4$, find y when x is 11.

70. y varies inversely as x. If $y = 4$ when $x = 6$, find y when x is 48.

71. y varies inversely as x^3. If $y = 12.5$ when $x = 2$, find y when x is 3.

72. y varies directly as x^2. If $y = 175$ when $x = 5$, find y when $x = 10$.

73. The cost of manufacturing a certain medicine varies inversely as the amount of medicine manufactured increases. If 3000 milliliters can be manufactured for $6600, find the cost to manufacture 5000 milliliters.

74. The distance a spring stretches varies directly with the weight attached to the spring. If a 150-pound weight stretches the spring 8 inches, find the distance that a 90-pound weight stretches the spring.

(8.8) Use transformations of $f(x) = \dfrac{1}{x}$ or $f(x) = \dfrac{1}{x^2}$ to graph each rational functions.

75. $g(x) = \dfrac{1}{(x + 2)^2} - 1$

76. $f(x) = \dfrac{1}{(x - 3)^2} + 2$

77. $h(x) = \dfrac{1}{x - 1} + 3$

78. $f(x) = \dfrac{1}{x + 3} + 1$

MIXED REVIEW

Simplify each rational expression.

79. $\dfrac{4x + 12}{8x^2 + 24x}$

80. $\dfrac{x^3 - 6x^2 + 9x}{x^2 + 4x - 21}$

Perform the indicated operations and simplify.

81. $\dfrac{x^2 + 9x + 20}{x^2 - 25} \cdot \dfrac{x^2 - 9x + 20}{x^2 + 8x + 16}$

82. $\dfrac{x^2 - x - 72}{x^2 - x - 30} \div \dfrac{x^2 + 6x - 27}{x^2 - 9x + 18}$

83. $\dfrac{x}{x^2 - 36} + \dfrac{6}{x^2 - 36}$

84. $\dfrac{5x - 1}{4x} - \dfrac{3x - 2}{4x}$

85. $\dfrac{4}{3x^2 + 8x - 3} + \dfrac{2}{3x^2 - 7x + 2}$

86. $\dfrac{3x}{x^2 + 9x + 14} - \dfrac{6x}{x^2 + 4x - 21}$

Solve.

87. $\dfrac{4}{a - 1} + 2 = \dfrac{3}{a - 1}$

88. $\dfrac{x}{x + 3} + 4 = \dfrac{x}{x + 3}$

Solve.

89. The quotient of twice a number and three, minus one-sixth is the quotient of the number and two. Find the number.

90. Mr. Crocker can paint his house by himself in three days. His son will need an additional day to complete the job if he works alone. If they work together, find how long it takes to paint the house.

Given that the following pairs of triangles are similar, find each missing length.

91.

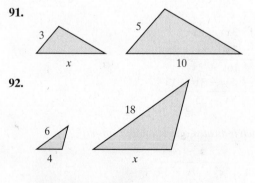

92.

CHAPTER 8 TEST

TEST PREP VIDEO The fully worked-out solutions to any exercises you want to review are available in MyMathLab.

1. Find any real numbers for which the following expression is undefined.

$$\frac{x + 5}{x^2 + 4x + 3}$$

2. For a certain computer desk, the average cost C (in dollars) per desk manufactured is

$$C = \frac{100x + 3000}{x}$$

where x is the number of desks manufactured.

 a. Find the average cost per desk when manufacturing 200 computer desks.
 b. Find the average cost per desk when manufacturing 1000 computer desks.

Simplify each rational expression.

3. $\dfrac{3x - 6}{5x - 10}$

4. $\dfrac{x + 6}{x^2 + 12x + 36}$

5. $\dfrac{x + 3}{x^3 + 27}$

6. $\dfrac{2m^3 - 2m^2 - 12m}{m^2 - 5m + 6}$

7. $\dfrac{ay + 3a + 2y + 6}{ay + 3a + 5y + 15}$

8. $\dfrac{y - x}{x^2 - y^2}$

Perform the indicated operation and simplify if possible.

9. $\dfrac{3}{x - 1} \cdot (5x - 5)$

10. $\dfrac{y^2 - 5y + 6}{2y + 4} \cdot \dfrac{y + 2}{2y - 6}$

11. $\dfrac{15x}{2x + 5} - \dfrac{6 - 4x}{2x + 5}$

12. $\dfrac{5a}{a^2 - a - 6} - \dfrac{2}{a - 3}$

13. $\dfrac{6}{x^2 - 1} + \dfrac{3}{x + 1}$

14. $\dfrac{x^2 - 9}{x^2 - 3x} \div \dfrac{xy + 5x + 3y + 15}{2x + 10}$

15. $\dfrac{x + 2}{x^2 + 11x + 18} + \dfrac{5}{x^2 - 3x - 10}$

Solve each equation.

16. $\dfrac{4}{y} - \dfrac{5}{3} = \dfrac{-1}{5}$

17. $\dfrac{5}{y + 1} = \dfrac{4}{y + 2}$

18. $\dfrac{a}{a - 3} = \dfrac{3}{a - 3} - \dfrac{3}{2}$

19. $x - \dfrac{14}{x - 1} = 4 - \dfrac{2x}{x - 1}$

20. $\dfrac{10}{x^2 - 25} = \dfrac{3}{x + 5} + \dfrac{1}{x - 5}$

Find the domain of each rational function and graph the function.

21. $f(x) = \dfrac{1}{(x + 3)^2}$

22. $f(x) = \dfrac{1}{x - 1} + 2$

23. y varies directly as x. If $y = 10$ when $x = 15$, find y when x is 42.

24. y varies inversely as x^2. If $y = 8$ when $x = 5$, find y when x is 15.

25. In a sample of 85 fluorescent bulbs, 3 were found to be defective. At this rate, how many defective bulbs should be found in 510 bulbs?

26. One number plus five times its reciprocal is equal to six. Find the number.

27. A pleasure boat traveling down the Red River takes the same time to go 14 miles upstream as it takes to go 16 miles downstream. If the current of the river is 2 miles per hour, find the speed of the boat in still water.

28. An inlet pipe can fill a tank in 12 hours. A second pipe can fill the tank in 15 hours. If both pipes are used, find how long it takes to fill the tank.

△ 29. Given that the two triangles are similar, find x.

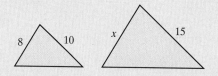

CHAPTER 8 STANDARDIZED TEST

Multiple Choice. *Choose the one alternative that best completes the statement or answers the question.*

Provide an appropriate response.

1. Find any real numbers for which the following expression is undefined.

$$\frac{x + 3}{x^2 + 7x - 144}$$

  a. $x = -16, x = 9$ **b.** $x = -3$

  c. $x = -3, x = -16, x = 9$ **d.** $x = -9, x = 16$

2. For a certain computer desk, the manufacturing cost C per desk (in dollars) is

$$C = \frac{300x + 7000}{x}$$

where x is the number of desks manufactured.

  a. Find the average cost per desk when manufacturing 200 desks.

  b. Find the average cost per desk when manufacturing 1000 desks.

    a. a. $335   **b. a.** $265
          b. $307   **b.** $293

    c. a. $65   **d. a.** $370
          b. $37   **b.** $335

Simplify the rational expression.

3. $\dfrac{4x - 16}{3x - 12}$

  a. $-\dfrac{4}{3}$ **b.** $\dfrac{4}{3}$

  c. -4 **d.** 4

4. $\dfrac{4x + 2}{20x^2 + 22x + 6}$

  a. $\dfrac{4x}{5x + 3}$ **b.** $\dfrac{4x + 2}{20x^2 + 22x + 6}$

  c. $\dfrac{1}{5x + 3}$ **d.** $\dfrac{4x + 5}{5x + 22}$

5. $\dfrac{x + 3}{x^3 + 27}$

  a. $\dfrac{1}{x^2 - 9}$ **b.** $\dfrac{1}{x^2 + 3x + 9}$

  c. $\dfrac{1}{x^2 - 3x + 9}$ **d.** $\dfrac{1}{x - 3}$

6. $\dfrac{3m^3 - 3m^2 - 36m}{m^2 - 7m + 12}$

  a. $\dfrac{3m(m - 4)(m + 3)}{(m + 4)(m - 3)}$ **b.** $3m$

  c. $\dfrac{3m(m + 4)}{(m - 4)}$ **d.** $\dfrac{3m(m + 3)}{(m - 3)}$

7. $\dfrac{ay + 2a + 2y + 4}{ay + 2a + 3y + 6}$

  a. $\dfrac{a + 2}{a + 3}$ **b.** $\dfrac{(a + 2)(y + 2)}{(a + 3)(y - 2)}$

  c. $\dfrac{2y + 4}{3y + 6}$ **d.** $\dfrac{(a + 2)(y - 2)}{(a + 3)(y + 2)}$

8. $\dfrac{n - m}{m^2 - n^2}$

  a. $-\dfrac{1}{m + n}$ **b.** $\dfrac{1}{n - m}$

  c. $\dfrac{1}{m + n}$ **d.** $\dfrac{1}{m - n}$

Perform the indicated operation and simplify if possible.

9. $\dfrac{6}{x + 1} \cdot (3x + 3)$

  a. 18   **b.** 15

  c. 6   **d.** 3

10. $\dfrac{y^2 - 6y + 8}{3y + 6} \cdot \dfrac{y + 2}{3y - 12}$

  a. $\dfrac{y - 2}{9}$ **b.** $\dfrac{y - 4}{9}$

  c. $\dfrac{(y - 2)(y - 4)}{9(y + 4)}$ **d.** $\dfrac{y + 2}{9}$

11. $\dfrac{2x}{x - 5} - \dfrac{x + 2}{x - 5}$

  a. $\dfrac{x + 2}{x - 5}$ **b.** $\dfrac{x - 2}{x - 5}$

  c. $\dfrac{3x - 2}{x - 5}$ **d.** $\dfrac{3x + 2}{x - 5}$

12. $\dfrac{7a}{a^2 - 3a - 10} - \dfrac{3}{a + 2}$

  a. $\dfrac{4a + 15}{(a + 5)(a + 2)}$ **b.** $\dfrac{4a - 15}{(a + 5)(a + 2)}$

  c. $\dfrac{4a + 15}{(a - 5)(a + 2)}$ **d.** $\dfrac{4a - 15}{(a - 5)(a + 2)}$

13. $\dfrac{4}{x^2 - 1} + \dfrac{2}{x + 1}$

  a. $\dfrac{2}{x + 1}$ **b.** $\dfrac{2(x + 3)}{x^2 - 1}$

  c. $\dfrac{2}{x - 1}$ **d.** $\dfrac{2}{x^2 - 1}$

14. $\dfrac{x^2 - 9}{x^2 + 3x} \div \dfrac{x^2 + 7x + 1}{3x - 15}$

  a. $\dfrac{(x + 3)(x^2 + 7x + 1)}{3x(x - 5)}$ **b.** $\dfrac{(x - 3)(x^2 + 7x + 1)}{3x(x - 5)}$

  c. $\dfrac{3(x - 3)(x - 5)}{x(x^2 + 7x + 1)}$ **d.** $\dfrac{3(x + 3)(x - 5)}{x(x^2 + 7x + 1)}$

15. $\dfrac{x-3}{x^2+12x+32} + \dfrac{5x+8}{x^2+6x+8}$

  a. $6x+5$ **b.** $\dfrac{6x+5}{2x^2+18x+40}$

  c. $\dfrac{6x^2+47x+58}{(x+4)(x+8)(x+2)}$ **d.** $\dfrac{6x^2+47x+58}{(x-4)(x-8)(x-2)}$

Solve the equation.

16. $\dfrac{5}{y} + 4 = 6$

  a. $-\dfrac{5}{2}$ **b.** $-\dfrac{1}{2}$

  c. $\dfrac{5}{2}$ **d.** 1

17. $\dfrac{3}{y-1} = \dfrac{2}{y+1}$

  a. -2 **b.** -5

  c. $-\dfrac{2}{5}$ **d.** 5

18. $\dfrac{5}{a-5} = \dfrac{a}{a-5} + 6$

  a. 5 **b.** -5

  c. no solution   **d.** $5, -5$

19. $x - \dfrac{19}{x-1} = 4 - \dfrac{3x}{x-1}$

  a. $-5, -3$ **b.** $3, 5$

  c. $-5, 3$ **d.** $-3, 5$

20. $\dfrac{2}{x^2-25} = \dfrac{-1}{x+5} - \dfrac{3}{x-5}$

  a. 12 **b.** no solution

  c. -3 **d.** 3

Graph the rational function.

21. $f(x) = \dfrac{1}{x+2} - 1$

a.   **b.**

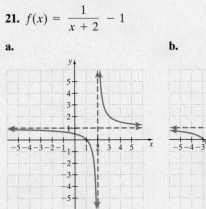
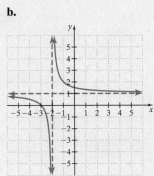

c.   **d.**

22. $f(x) = \dfrac{1}{(x-1)^2}$

a.   **b.**

c.   **d.**

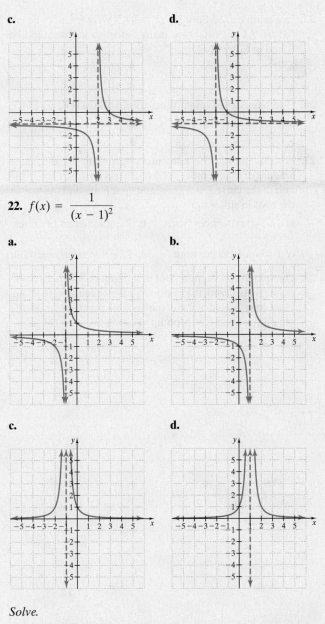

Solve.

23. y varies directly as x. If $y = 140$ when $x = 10$, find y when $x = 12$.

  a. 144 **b.** 196

  c. 168 **d.** 100

24. y varies inversely as x^2. If $y = 2$ when $x = 24$, find y when $x = 4$.

  a. 32 **b.** 6

  c. 24 **d.** 72

25. In a sample of 85 fluorescent bulbs, 4 were found to be defective. At this rate, how many defective bulbs should be found in 510 bulbs?

    a. 23   **b.** 25

    c. 26   **d.** 24

26. One number plus eight times its reciprocal is equal to six.

    a. 2 or 4   **d.** −4 or 2

    c. −2 or 4   **d.** −4 or −2

27. A boat moves 10 kilometers upstream in the same amount of time it moves 18 kilometers downstream. If the rate of the current is 6 kilometers per hour, find the rate of the boat in still water.

    a. 21 kilometers per hour   **b.** $7\frac{1}{2}$ kilometers per hour

    c. 6 kilometers per hour   **d.** $22\frac{1}{2}$ kilometers per hour

28. One pump can drain a pool in 9 minutes. When a second pump is also used, the pool only takes 3 minutes to drain. How long would it take the second pump to drain the pool if it were the only pump in use?

a. 21 min   **b.** $2\frac{1}{4}$ min

c. $\frac{2}{9}$ min   **d.** $4\frac{1}{2}$ min

Given that the pair of triangles are similar, find x.

29.

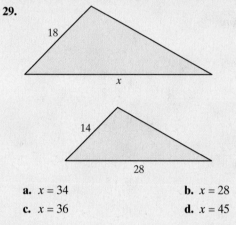

a. $x = 34$ **b.** $x = 28$

c. $x = 36$ **d.** $x = 45$

Roots, Radicals, and Trigonometric Ratios

When we think of pendulums, we often think of grandfather clocks. In fact, pendulums can be used to provide accurate timekeeping. But, did you know that pendulums can also be used to demonstrate that the earth rotates on its axis?

In 1851, French physicist Léon Foucault developed a special pendulum in an experiment to demonstrate that the Earth rotated on its axis. He connected his tall pendulum, capable of running for many hours, to the roof of the Paris Observatory. The pendulum's bob was able to swing back and forth in one plane, but not to twist in other directions. So, when the pendulum bob appeared to move in a circle over time, he demonstrated that it was not the pendulum but the building that moved. And since the building was firmly attached to the earth, it must be the earth rotating which created the apparent circular motion of the bob. In this chapter, roots are used to explore the time it takes Foucault's pendulum to complete one swing of its bob.

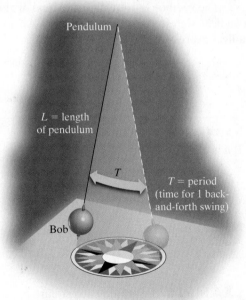

Pendulum

L = length of pendulum

T

T = period (time for 1 back-and-forth swing)

Bob

9.1 INTRODUCTION TO RADICALS AND RADICAL FUNCTIONS

OBJECTIVE 1 ▶ Finding square roots. In this section, we define finding the **root** of a number by its reverse operation, raising a number to a power. We begin with squares and square roots.

The *square* of 5 is $5^2 = 25$.

The *square* of -5 is $(-5)^2 = 25$.

The *square* of $\frac{1}{2}$ is $\left(\frac{1}{2}\right)^2 = \frac{1}{4}$.

The reverse operation of squaring a number is finding the **square root** of a number. For example,

A *square root* of 25 is 5, because $5^2 = 25$.

A *square root* of 25 is also -5, because $(-5)^2 = 25$.

A *square root* of $\frac{1}{4}$ is $\frac{1}{2}$, because $\left(\frac{1}{2}\right)^2 = \frac{1}{4}$.

> **In general, a number b is a square root of a number a if $b^2 = a$.**

Notice that both 5 and -5 are square roots of 25. The symbol $\sqrt{}$ is used to denote the **positive** or **principal square root** of a number. For example,

$$\sqrt{25} = 5 \text{ since } 5^2 = 25 \text{ and } 5 \text{ is positive}.$$

The symbol $-\sqrt{}$ is used to denote the **negative square root.** For example,

$$-\sqrt{25} = -5$$

The symbol $\sqrt{}$ is called a **radical** or **radical sign.** The expression within or under a radical sign is called the **radicand.** An expression containing a radical is called a **radical expression.**

$$\overset{\text{radical sign}}{\sqrt{a}}_{\text{radicand}}$$

> **Square Root**
>
> If a is a positive number, then
>
> $\sqrt{a}$ is the **positive square root** of a and
>
> $-\sqrt{a}$ is the **negative square root** of a.
>
> $$\sqrt{a} = b \quad \text{only if} \quad b^2 = a \text{ and } b > 0$$
>
> Also, $\sqrt{0} = 0$.

EXAMPLE 1 Find each square root.

a. $\sqrt{36}$ **b.** $-\sqrt{16}$ **c.** $\sqrt{\dfrac{9}{100}}$ **d.** $\sqrt{0}$ **e.** $\sqrt{0.64}$

Solution

a. $\sqrt{36} = 6$, because $6^2 = 36$ and 6 is positive.

b. $-\sqrt{16} = -4$. The negative sign in front of the radical indicates the negative square root of 16.

c. $\sqrt{\dfrac{9}{100}} = \dfrac{3}{10}$ because $\left(\dfrac{3}{10}\right)^2 = \dfrac{9}{100}$ and $\dfrac{3}{10}$ is positive.

d. $\sqrt{0} = 0$ because $0^2 = 0$.

e. $\sqrt{0.64} = 0.8$, because $(0.8)^2 = 0.64$ and 0.8 is positive.

PRACTICE
1   Find each square root.

a. $\sqrt{\dfrac{4}{81}}$ **b.** $-\sqrt{25}$ **c.** $\sqrt{144}$ **d.** $\sqrt{0.49}$ **e.** $-\sqrt{1}$

Is the square root of a negative number a real number? For example, is $\sqrt{-4}$ a real number? To answer this question, we ask ourselves, is there a real number whose square is -4? Since there is no real number whose square is -4, we say that $\sqrt{-4}$ is not a real number. In general,

> A square root of a negative number is not a real number.

We will discuss numbers such as $\sqrt{-4}$ in Chapter 10.

OBJECTIVE 2 ▶ Finding cube roots. We can find roots other than square roots. For example, since $2^3 = 8$, we call 2 the **cube root** of 8. In symbols, we write

$$\sqrt[3]{8} = 2 \qquad \text{The number 3 is called the } \textbf{index.}$$

Also,

$$\sqrt[3]{27} = 3 \qquad \text{Since } 3^3 = 27$$
$$\sqrt[3]{-64} = -4 \qquad \text{Since } (-4)^3 = -64$$

Notice that unlike the square root of a negative number, the cube root of a negative number is a real number. This is so because while we cannot find a real number whose **square** is negative, we **can** find a real number whose **cube** is negative. In fact, the cube of a negative number is a negative number. Therefore, the cube root of a negative number is a negative number.

EXAMPLE 2   Find each cube root.

a. $\sqrt[3]{1}$ **b.** $\sqrt[3]{-27}$ **c.** $\sqrt[3]{\dfrac{1}{125}}$

Solution

a. $\sqrt[3]{1} = 1$ because $1^3 = 1$.

b. $\sqrt[3]{-27} = -3$ because $(-3)^3 = -27$.

c. $\sqrt[3]{\dfrac{1}{125}} = \dfrac{1}{5}$ because $\left(\dfrac{1}{5}\right)^3 = \dfrac{1}{125}$.

PRACTICE
2   Find each cube root.

a. $\sqrt[3]{0}$ **b.** $\sqrt[3]{-64}$ **c.** $\sqrt[3]{\dfrac{1}{8}}$

OBJECTIVE 3 ▶ Finding *n*th roots. Just as we can raise a real number to powers other than 2 or 3, we can find roots other than square roots and cube roots. In fact, we can take the *n*th root of a number where *n* is any natural number. An ***n*th root** of a number *a* is a number whose *n*th power is *a*. The natural number *n* is called the **index.**

In symbols, the nth root of a is written as $\sqrt[n]{a}$. The index 2 is usually omitted for square roots.

> ▶ **Helpful Hint**
>
> If the index is even, such as $\sqrt{}$, $\sqrt[4]{}$, $\sqrt[6]{}$, and so on, the radicand must be nonnegative for the root to be a real number. For example,
>
> $$\sqrt[4]{16} = 2 \text{ but } \sqrt[4]{-16} \text{ is not a real number}$$
> $$\sqrt[6]{64} = 2 \text{ but } \sqrt[6]{-64} \text{ is not a real number}$$

Concept Check ☑

Which of the following is a real number?

a. $\sqrt{-64}$ **b.** $\sqrt[4]{-64}$ **c.** $\sqrt[5]{-64}$ **d.** $\sqrt[6]{-64}$

EXAMPLE 3   Find each root.

a. $\sqrt[4]{16}$ 🔲 **b.** $\sqrt[5]{-32}$ **c.** $-\sqrt[3]{8}$ 🔲 **d.** $\sqrt[4]{-81}$

Solution

a. $\sqrt[4]{16} = 2$ because $2^4 = 16$ and 2 is positive.

b. $\sqrt[5]{-32} = -2$ because $(-2)^5 = -32$.

c. $-\sqrt[3]{8} = -2$ since $\sqrt[3]{8} = 2$.

d. $\sqrt[4]{-81}$ is not a real number since the index 4 is even and the radicand -81 is negative.

□

PRACTICE
3   Find each root.

a. $\sqrt[4]{81}$ **b.** $\sqrt[5]{100{,}000}$ **c.** $\sqrt[6]{-64}$ **d.** $\sqrt[3]{-125}$

OBJECTIVE 4 ▶ Approximating square roots. Recall that numbers such as $1, 4, 9, 25,$ and $\frac{4}{25}$ are called **perfect squares**, since $1^2 = 1, 2^2 = 4, 3^2 = 9, 5^2 = 25,$ and $\left(\frac{2}{5}\right)^2 = \frac{4}{25}$.

Square roots of perfect square radicands simplify to rational numbers. What happens when we try to simplify a root such as $\sqrt{3}$? Since 3 is not a perfect square, $\sqrt{3}$ is not a rational number. It cannot be written as a quotient of integers. It is called an **irrational number** and we can find a decimal **approximation** of it. To find decimal approximations, use a calculator or an appendix. (For calculator help, see the box at the end of this section.)

EXAMPLE 4   Use a calculator or an appendix to approximate $\sqrt{3}$ to three decimal places.

Solution   We may use an appendix or a calculator to approximate $\sqrt{3}$. To use a calculator, find the square root key $\boxed{\sqrt{}}$.

$$\sqrt{3} \approx 1.732050808$$

To three decimal places, $\sqrt{3} \approx 1.732$.

□

PRACTICE
4   Use a calculator or an appendix to approximate $\sqrt{17}$ to three decimal places.

OBJECTIVE 5 ▶ Simplifying radicals containing variables. Radicals can also contain variables. To simplify radicals containing variables, special care must be taken. To see how we simplify $\sqrt{x^2}$, let's look at a few examples in this form.

If $x = 3$, we have $\sqrt{3^2} = \sqrt{9} = 3$, or x.
If x is 5, we have $\sqrt{5^2} = \sqrt{25} = 5$, or x.

From these two examples, you may think that $\sqrt{x^2}$ simplifies to x. Let's now look at an example where x is a negative number. If $x = -3$, we have $\sqrt{(-3)^2} = \sqrt{9} = 3$, not -3, our original x. To make sure that $\sqrt{x^2}$ simplifies to a nonnegative number, we have the following.

For any real number a,
$$\sqrt{a^2} = |a|.$$

Thus,
$$\sqrt{x^2} = |x|,$$
$$\sqrt{(-8)^2} = |-8| = 8$$
$$\sqrt{(7y)^2} = |7y|, \quad \text{and so on.}$$

To avoid this, for the rest of the chapter we assume that **if a variable appears in the radicand of a radical expression, it represents positive numbers only.** Then

$\sqrt{x^2} = |x| = x$ since x is a positive number.
$\sqrt{y^2} = y$ Because $(y)^2 = y^2$
$\sqrt{x^8} = x^4$ Because $(x^4)^2 = x^8$
$\sqrt{9x^2} = 3x$ Because $(3x)^2 = 9x^2$
$\sqrt[3]{8z^{12}} = 2z^4$ Because $(2z^4)^3 = 8z^{12}$

EXAMPLE 5 Simplify each expression. Assume that all variables represent positive numbers.

a. $\sqrt{z^2}$ **b.** $\sqrt{x^6}$ **c.** $\sqrt[3]{27y^6}$ **d.** $\sqrt{16x^{16}}$ **e.** $\sqrt{\dfrac{x^4}{25}}$ **f.** $\sqrt[3]{-125a^{12}b^{15}}$

Solution

a. $\sqrt{z^2} = z$ because $(z)^2 = z^2$.
b. $\sqrt{x^6} = x^3$ because $(x^3)^2 = x^6$.
c. $\sqrt[3]{27y^6} = 3y^2$ because $(3y^2)^3 = 27y^6$.
d. $\sqrt{16x^{16}} = 4x^8$ because $(4x^8)^2 = 16x^{16}$.
e. $\sqrt{\dfrac{x^4}{25}} = \dfrac{x^2}{5}$ because $\left(\dfrac{x^2}{5}\right)^2 = \dfrac{x^4}{25}$.
f. $\sqrt[3]{-125a^{12}b^{15}} = -5a^4b^5$ because $(-5a^4b^5)^3 = -125a^{12}b^{15}$.   □

PRACTICE
5 Simplify each expression. Assume that all variables represent positive numbers.

a. $\sqrt{x^{10}}$ **b.** $\sqrt{y^{14}}$ **c.** $\sqrt[3]{125z^9}$ **d.** $\sqrt{49x^2}$ **e.** $\sqrt{\dfrac{z^4}{36}}$ **f.** $\sqrt[3]{-8a^6b^{12}}$

OBJECTIVE 6 ▶ Graphing square and cube root functions. Recall that an equation in x and y describes a function if each x-value is paired with exactly one y-value. With this in mind, does the equation

$$y = \sqrt{x}$$

describe a function? First, notice that replacement values for x must be nonnegative real numbers, since $\sqrt{x}$ is not a real number if $x < 0$. The notation $\sqrt{x}$ denotes the principal square root of x, so for every nonnegative number x, there is exactly one number, $\sqrt{x}$. Therefore, $y = \sqrt{x}$ describes a function, and we may write it as

$$f(x) = \sqrt{x}.$$

In general, radical functions are functions of the form

$$f(x) = \sqrt[n]{x}.$$

Recall that the domain of a function in x is the set of all possible replacement values of x. This means that if n is even, the domain is all nonnegative numbers, or $x \geq 0$. If n is odd, the domain is the set of all real numbers. Keep this in mind as we find function values.

EXAMPLE 6 If $f(x) = \sqrt{x - 4}$ and $g(x) = \sqrt[3]{x + 2}$, find each function value.

a. $f(8)$ **b.** $f(6)$ **c.** $g(-1)$ **d.** $g(1)$

Solution

a. $f(8) = \sqrt{8 - 4} = \sqrt{4} = 2$ **b.** $f(6) = \sqrt{6 - 4} = \sqrt{2}$

c. $g(-1) = \sqrt[3]{-1 + 2} = \sqrt[3]{1} = 1$ **d.** $g(1) = \sqrt[3]{1 + 2} = \sqrt[3]{3}$ □

PRACTICE
6 If $f(x) = \sqrt{x + 5}$ and $g(x) = \sqrt[3]{x - 3}$, find each function value.

a. $f(11)$ **b.** $f(-1)$ **c.** $g(11)$ **d.** $g(-5)$

▶ **Helpful Hint**

Notice that for the function $f(x) = \sqrt{x - 4}$, the domain includes all real numbers that make the radicand ≥ 0. To see what numbers these are, solve $x - 4 \geq 0$ and find that $x \geq 4$. The domain is $x \geq 4$.

     The domain of the cube root function $g(x) = \sqrt[3]{x + 2}$ is all real numbers.

EXAMPLE 7 Graph the square root function $f(x) = \sqrt{x}$.

Solution To graph, we identify the domain, evaluate the function for several values of x, plot the resulting points, and connect the points with a smooth curve. Since $\sqrt{x}$ represents the nonnegative square root of x, the domain of this function is all nonnegative numbers, $x \geq 0$. We have approximated $\sqrt{3}$ below to help us locate the point corresponding to $(3, \sqrt{3})$.

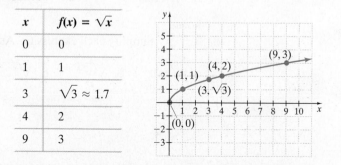

x	$f(x) = \sqrt{x}$
0	0
1	1
3	$\sqrt{3} \approx 1.7$
4	2
9	3

Notice that the graph of this function passes the vertical line test, as expected. ☐

PRACTICE
7 Graph the square root function $h(x) = \sqrt{x} + 2$.

The equation $f(x) = \sqrt[3]{x}$ also describes a function. Here x may be any real number, so the domain of this function is all real numbers. A few function values are given next.

$$f(0) = \sqrt[3]{0} = 0$$
$$f(1) = \sqrt[3]{1} = 1$$
$$f(-1) = \sqrt[3]{-1} = -1$$
$$\left.\begin{array}{l} f(6) = \sqrt[3]{6} \\ f(-6) = \sqrt[3]{-6} \end{array}\right\}$$ Here, there is no rational number whose cube is 6. Thus, the radicals do not simplify to rational numbers.
$$f(8) = \sqrt[3]{8} = 2$$
$$f(-8) = \sqrt[3]{-8} = -2$$

EXAMPLE 8 Graph the function $f(x) = \sqrt[3]{x}$.

Solution To graph, we identify the domain, plot points, and connect the points with a smooth curve. The domain of this function is the set of all real numbers. The table comes from the function values obtained earlier. We have approximated $\sqrt[3]{6}$ and $\sqrt[3]{-6}$ for graphing purposes.

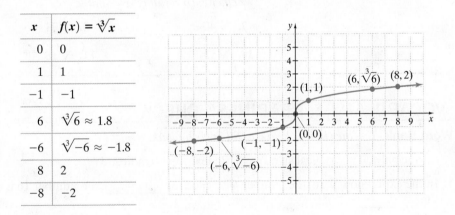

x	$f(x) = \sqrt[3]{x}$
0	0
1	1
−1	−1
6	$\sqrt[3]{6} \approx 1.8$
−6	$\sqrt[3]{-6} \approx -1.8$
8	2
−8	−2

The graph of this function passes the vertical line test, as expected. ☐

PRACTICE
8 Graph the function $f(x) = \sqrt[3]{x} - 4$.

Calculator Explorations

To simplify or approximate square roots using a calculator, locate the key marked $\boxed{\sqrt{}}$. To simplify $\sqrt{25}$ using a scientific calculator, press $\boxed{25}$ $\boxed{\sqrt{}}$. The display should read $\boxed{5}$. To simplify $\sqrt{25}$ using a graphing calculator, press $\boxed{\sqrt{}}$ $\boxed{25}$ $\boxed{\text{ENTER}}$.

To approximate $\sqrt{30}$, press $\boxed{30}$ $\boxed{\sqrt{}}$ (or $\boxed{\sqrt{}}$ $\boxed{30}$ $\boxed{\text{ENTER}}$). The display should read $\boxed{5.4772256}$. This is an approximation for $\sqrt{30}$. A three-decimal-place approximation is

$$\sqrt{30} \approx 5.477$$

Is this answer reasonable? Since 30 is between perfect squares 25 and 36, $\sqrt{30}$ is between $\sqrt{25} = 5$ and $\sqrt{36} = 6$. The calculator result is then reasonable since 5.4772256 is between 5 and 6.

Use a calculator to approximate each expression to three decimal places. Decide whether each result is reasonable.

1. $\sqrt{7}$ **2.** $\sqrt{14}$ **3.** $\sqrt{11}$

4. $\sqrt{200}$ **5.** $\sqrt{82}$ **6.** $\sqrt{46}$

Many scientific calculators have a key, such as $\boxed{\sqrt[x]{y}}$, that can be used to approximate roots other than square roots. To approximate these roots using a graphing calculator, look under the $\boxed{\text{MATH}}$ menu or consult your manual.

Use a calculator to approximate each expression to three decimal places. Decide whether each result is reasonable.

7. $\sqrt[3]{40}$ **8.** $\sqrt[3]{71}$ **9.** $\sqrt[4]{20}$

10. $\sqrt[4]{15}$ **11.** $\sqrt[5]{18}$ **12.** $\sqrt[6]{2}$

VOCABULARY & READINESS CHECK

Word Bank. *Use the choices below to fill in each blank.*

    principal   radical sign   index   radicand

1. In the expression $\sqrt[4]{16}$, the number 4 is called the _____, the number 16 is called the _____ and $\sqrt{}$ called the _____.

2. The symbol $\sqrt{}$ is used to denote the positive, or _____, square root.

True or False. *Answer each exercise true or false.*

3. $\sqrt{-16}$ simplifies to a real number.

4. $\sqrt{64} = 8$ while $\sqrt[3]{64} = 4$.

5. The number 9 has two square roots.

6. $\sqrt{0} = 0$ and $\sqrt{1} = 1$.

7. If x is a positive number, $\sqrt{x^{10}} = x^5$.

8. If x is a positive number, $\sqrt{x^{16}} = x^4$.

Fill in the Blank.

9. The domain of the function $f(x) = \sqrt{x}$ is _____.

10. The domain of the function $f(x) = \sqrt[3]{x}$ is _____.

11. If $f(16) = 4$, the corresponding ordered pair is _____.

12. If $g(-8) = -2$, the corresponding ordered pair is _____.

9.1 | EXERCISE SET

Find each square root. See Example 1.

1. $\sqrt{16}$

2. $\sqrt{64}$

3. $\sqrt{\dfrac{1}{25}}$

4. $\sqrt{\dfrac{1}{64}}$

5. $-\sqrt{100}$

6. $-\sqrt{36}$

7. $\sqrt{-4}$

8. $\sqrt{-25}$

9. $-\sqrt{121}$

10. $-\sqrt{49}$

11. $\sqrt{\dfrac{9}{25}}$

12. $\sqrt{\dfrac{4}{81}}$

13. $\sqrt{900}$

14. $\sqrt{400}$

15. $\sqrt{144}$

16. $\sqrt{169}$

17. $\sqrt{\dfrac{1}{100}}$

18. $\sqrt{\dfrac{1}{121}}$

19. $\sqrt{0.25}$

20. $\sqrt{0.49}$

Find each cube root. See Example 2.

21. $\sqrt[3]{125}$

22. $\sqrt[3]{64}$

23. $\sqrt[3]{-64}$

24. $\sqrt[3]{-27}$

25. $-\sqrt[3]{8}$

26. $-\sqrt[3]{27}$

27. $\sqrt[3]{\dfrac{1}{8}}$

28. $\sqrt[3]{\dfrac{1}{64}}$

29. $\sqrt[3]{-125}$

30. $\sqrt[3]{-1}$

MIXED PRACTICE

Find each root. See Examples 1 through 3.

31. $\sqrt[5]{32}$

32. $\sqrt[4]{81}$

33. $\sqrt{81}$

34. $\sqrt{49}$

35. $\sqrt[4]{-16}$

36. $\sqrt{-9}$

37. $\sqrt[3]{-\dfrac{27}{64}}$

38. $\sqrt[3]{-\dfrac{8}{27}}$

39. $-\sqrt[4]{625}$

40. $-\sqrt[5]{32}$

41. $\sqrt[6]{1}$

42. $\sqrt[5]{1}$

Approximate each square root to three decimal places. See Example 4.

43. $\sqrt{7}$

44. $\sqrt{10}$

45. $\sqrt{37}$

46. $\sqrt{27}$

47. $\sqrt{136}$

48. $\sqrt{8}$

49. A standard baseball diamond is a square with 90-foot sides connecting the bases. The distance from home plate to second base is $90 \cdot \sqrt{2}$ feet. Approximate $\sqrt{2}$ to two decimal places and use your result to approximate the distance $90 \cdot \sqrt{2}$ feet.

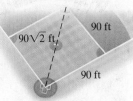

50. The roof of the warehouse shown needs to be shingled. The total area of the roof is exactly $240 \cdot \sqrt{41}$ square feet. Approximate $\sqrt{41}$ to two decimal places and use your result to approximate the area $240 \cdot \sqrt{41}$ square feet. Approximate this area to the nearest whole number.

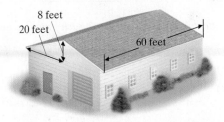

Find each root. Assume that all variables represent positive numbers. See Example 5.

51. $\sqrt{x^4}$

52. $\sqrt{y^{10}}$

53. $\sqrt{9x^8}$

54. $\sqrt{36x^{12}}$

55. $\sqrt{81x^2}$

56. $\sqrt{100z^4}$

57. $\sqrt{\dfrac{x^6}{36}}$

58. $\sqrt{\dfrac{y^8}{49}}$

59. $\sqrt{\dfrac{25y^2}{9}}$

60. $\sqrt{\dfrac{4x^2}{81}}$

61. $\sqrt{16a^6b^4}$

62. $\sqrt{4m^{14}n^2}$

63. $\sqrt[3]{a^6b^{18}}$

64. $\sqrt[3]{x^{12}y^{18}}$

65. $\sqrt[3]{-8x^3y^{27}}$

66. $\sqrt[3]{-27a^6b^{30}}$

If $f(x) = \sqrt{2x + 3}$ and $g(x) = \sqrt[3]{x - 8}$, find the following function values. See Example 6.

67. $f(0)$

68. $g(0)$

69. $g(7)$

70. $f(-1)$

71. $g(-19)$

72. $f(3)$

73. $f(2)$

74. $g(1)$

Identify the domain and then graph each function. See Example 7.

75. $f(x) = \sqrt{x} + 2$

76. $f(x) = \sqrt{x} - 2$

77. $f(x) = \sqrt{x - 3}$; use the following table.

x	$f(x)$
3	
4	
7	
12	

78. $f(x) = \sqrt{x + 1}$; use the following table.

x	$f(x)$
-1	
0	
3	
8	

Identify the domain and then graph each function. See Example 8.

79. $f(x) = \sqrt[3]{x} + 1$

80. $f(x) = \sqrt[3]{x} - 2$

81. $g(x) = \sqrt[3]{x - 1}$; use the following table.

x	$g(x)$
1	
2	
0	
9	
-7	

82. $g(x) = \sqrt[3]{x + 1}$; use the following table.

x	$g(x)$
-1	
0	
-2	
7	
-9	

REVIEW AND PREVIEW

Write each integer as a product of two integers such that one of the factors is a perfect square. For example, we can write $18 = 9 \cdot 2$, where 9 is a perfect square.

83. 50   **84.** 8

85. 32   **86.** 75

87. 28   **88.** 44

89. 27   **90.** 90

CONCEPT EXTENSIONS

Decision Making. *See the Concept Check in this section.*

91. Which of the following is a real number?

   a. $\sqrt[7]{-1}$ **b.** $\sqrt[3]{-125}$ **c.** $\sqrt[6]{-128}$ **d.** $\sqrt[8]{-1}$

92. **a.** $\sqrt{-1}$ **b.** $\sqrt[3]{-1}$ **c.** $\sqrt[4]{-1}$ **d.** $\sqrt[5]{-1}$

The length of a side of a square in given by the expression $\sqrt{A}$, where A is the square's area. Use this expression for Exercises 93 through 96. Be sure to attach the appropriate units.

△ **93.** The area of a square is 49 square miles. Find the length of a side of the square.

Square

$\sqrt{A}$

△ **94.** The area of a square is $\dfrac{1}{81}$ square meters. Find the length of a side of the square.

△ **95.** Sony makes the current smallest mini disc player. It is in the shape of a square with area of 9.0601 square inches. Find the length of a side. (*Source:* SONY)

△ **96.** A parking lot is in the shape of a square with area 2500 square yards. Find the length of a side.

97. Simplify $\sqrt{\sqrt{81}}$.

98. Simplify $\sqrt[3]{\sqrt[3]{1}}$.

99. Simplify $\sqrt{\sqrt{10{,}000}}$.

100. Simplify $\sqrt{\sqrt{1{,}600{,}000{,}000}}$.

101. The formula for calculating the period (one back and forth swing) of a pendulum is $T = 2\pi\sqrt{\dfrac{L}{g}}$, where T is time of the period of the swing, L is the length of the pendulum, and g is the acceleration of gravity. At the California Academy of Sciences, one can see a Foucault's pendulum with a length = 30 ft, and g = 32 ft/sec². Using π = 3.14, find the period of this pendulum. (Round to the nearest tenth of a second.)

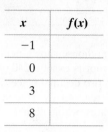

102. If the amount of gold discovered by humankind could be assembled in one place, it would make a cube with a volume of 195,112 cubic feet. Each side of the cube would be $\sqrt[3]{195{,}112}$ feet long. How long would one side of the cube be? (*Source: Reader's Digest*)

103. Explain why the square root of a negative number is not a real number.

104. Explain why the cube root of a negative number is a real number.

Recall from this section that $\sqrt{a^2} = |a|$ for any real number a. Simplify the following given that x represents any real number.

105. $\sqrt{x^2}$

106. $\sqrt{4x^2}$

107. $\sqrt{(x + 2)^2}$

108. $\sqrt{x^2 + 6x + 9}$ (**Hint:** First factor $x^2 + 6x + 9$.)

9.2 SIMPLIFYING RADICALS

OBJECTIVES

1 Use the product rule to simplify square roots.

2 Use the quotient rule to simplify square roots.

3 Simplify radicals containing variables.

4 Simplify higher roots.

OBJECTIVE 1 ▶ Simplifying radicals using the product rule. A square root is simplified when the radicand contains no perfect square factors (other than 1). For example, $\sqrt{20}$ is not simplified because $\sqrt{20} = \sqrt{4 \cdot 5}$ and 4 is a perfect square.

To begin simplifying square roots, we notice the following pattern.

$$\sqrt{9 \cdot 16} = \sqrt{144} = 12$$
$$\sqrt{9} \cdot \sqrt{16} = 3 \cdot 4 = 12$$

Since both expressions simplify to 12, we can write

$$\sqrt{9 \cdot 16} = \sqrt{9} \cdot \sqrt{16}$$

This suggests the following product rule for square roots.

> **Product Rule for Square Roots**
> If $\sqrt{a}$ and $\sqrt{b}$ are real numbers, then
> $$\sqrt{a \cdot b} = \sqrt{a} \cdot \sqrt{b}$$

In other words, the square root of a product is equal to the product of the square roots.

To simplify $\sqrt{20}$, for example, we factor 20 so that one of its factors is a perfect square factor.

$$\sqrt{20} = \sqrt{4 \cdot 5} \qquad \text{Factor 20.}$$
$$= \sqrt{4} \cdot \sqrt{5} \qquad \text{Use the product rule.}$$
$$= 2\sqrt{5} \qquad \text{Write } \sqrt{4} \text{ as 2.}$$

The notation $2\sqrt{5}$ means $2 \cdot \sqrt{5}$. Since the radicand 5 has no perfect square factor other than 1 then $2\sqrt{5}$ is in simplest form.

> ▶ **Helpful Hint**
> A radical expression in simplest form does *not mean* a decimal approximation. The simplest form of a radical expression is an exact form and may still contain a radical.
>
> $$\sqrt{20} = 2\sqrt{5} \qquad\qquad \sqrt{20} \approx 4.47$$
> $\qquad\quad$ exact $\qquad\qquad\qquad$ decimal approximation

EXAMPLE 1 Simplify.

a. $\sqrt{54}$ **b.** $\sqrt{12}$ **c.** $\sqrt{200}$ **d.** $\sqrt{35}$

Solution

a. Try to factor 54 so that at least one of the factors is a perfect square. Since 9 is a perfect square and $54 = 9 \cdot 6$,

$$
\begin{aligned}
\sqrt{54} &= \sqrt{9 \cdot 6} && \text{Factor 54 so that one factor is a perfect square.} \\
&= \sqrt{9} \cdot \sqrt{6} && \text{Apply the product rule.} \\
&= 3\sqrt{6} && \text{Write } \sqrt{9} \text{ as 3.}
\end{aligned}
$$

b.
$$
\begin{aligned}
\sqrt{12} &= \sqrt{4 \cdot 3} && \text{Factor 12 so that one factor is a perfect square.} \\
&= \sqrt{4} \cdot \sqrt{3} && \text{Apply the product rule.} \\
&= 2\sqrt{3} && \text{Write } \sqrt{4} \text{ as 2.}
\end{aligned}
$$

c.
$$
\begin{aligned}
\sqrt{200} &= \sqrt{100 \cdot 2} && \text{Factor 200 so that one factor is a perfect square.} \\
&= \sqrt{100} \cdot \sqrt{2} && \text{Apply the product rule.} \\
&= 10\sqrt{2} && \text{Write } \sqrt{100} \text{ as 10.}
\end{aligned}
$$

d. The radicand 35 contains no perfect square factors other than 1. Thus $\sqrt{35}$ is in simplest form. □

PRACTICE
1 Simplify.

a. $\sqrt{24}$ **b.** $\sqrt{60}$ **c.** $\sqrt{42}$ **d.** $\sqrt{300}$

In Example 1, part **(c)**, 100 is the largest perfect square factor of 200. What happens if we don't use the largest perfect square factor? Although using the largest perfect square factor saves time, the result is the same no matter what perfect square factor is used. For example, it is also true that $200 = 4 \cdot 50$. Then

$$
\begin{aligned}
\sqrt{200} &= \sqrt{4} \cdot \sqrt{50} \\
&= 2 \cdot \sqrt{50}
\end{aligned}
$$

Since $\sqrt{50}$ is not in simplest form, we continue.

$$
\begin{aligned}
\sqrt{200} &= 2 \cdot \sqrt{50} \\
&= 2 \cdot \sqrt{25 \cdot 2} \\
&= 2 \cdot \sqrt{25} \cdot \sqrt{2} \\
&= 2 \cdot 5 \cdot \sqrt{2} \\
&= 10\sqrt{2}
\end{aligned}
$$

EXAMPLE 2 Simplify $3\sqrt{8}$.

Solution Remember that $3\sqrt{8}$ means $3 \cdot \sqrt{8}$.

$$
\begin{aligned}
3 \cdot \sqrt{8} &= 3 \cdot \sqrt{4 \cdot 2} && \text{Factor 8 so that one factor is a perfect square.} \\
&= 3 \cdot \sqrt{4} \cdot \sqrt{2} && \text{Use the product rule.} \\
&= 3 \cdot 2 \cdot \sqrt{2} && \text{Write } \sqrt{4} \text{ as 2.} \\
&= 6 \cdot \sqrt{2} \text{ or } 6\sqrt{2} && \text{Write } 3 \cdot 2 \text{ as 6.}
\end{aligned}
$$
□

PRACTICE
2 Simplify $5\sqrt{40}$.

OBJECTIVE 2 ▶ **Simplifying radicals using the quotient rule.** Next, let's examine the square root of a quotient.

$$\sqrt{\frac{16}{4}} = \sqrt{4} = 2$$

Also,

$$\frac{\sqrt{16}}{\sqrt{4}} = \frac{4}{2} = 2$$

Since both expressions equal 2, we can write

$$\sqrt{\frac{16}{4}} = \frac{\sqrt{16}}{\sqrt{4}}$$

This suggests the following quotient rule.

Quotient Rule for Square Roots

If $\sqrt{a}$ and $\sqrt{b}$ are real numbers and $b \neq 0$, then

$$\sqrt{\frac{a}{b}} = \frac{\sqrt{a}}{\sqrt{b}}$$

In other words, the square root of a quotient is equal to the quotient of the square roots.

EXAMPLE 3   Simplify.

a. $\sqrt{\dfrac{25}{36}}$ **b.** $\sqrt{\dfrac{3}{64}}$ **c.** $\sqrt{\dfrac{40}{81}}$

Use the quotient rule.

Solution

a. $\sqrt{\dfrac{25}{36}} = \dfrac{\sqrt{25}}{\sqrt{36}} = \dfrac{5}{6}$

b. $\sqrt{\dfrac{3}{64}} = \dfrac{\sqrt{3}}{\sqrt{64}} = \dfrac{\sqrt{3}}{8}$

c. $\sqrt{\dfrac{40}{81}} = \dfrac{\sqrt{40}}{\sqrt{81}}$ Use the quotient rule.

$\phantom{\textbf{c.} \sqrt{\dfrac{40}{81}}} = \dfrac{\sqrt{4} \cdot \sqrt{10}}{9}$ Apply the product rule and write $\sqrt{81}$ as 9.

$\phantom{\textbf{c.} \sqrt{\dfrac{40}{81}}} = \dfrac{2\sqrt{10}}{9}$ Write $\sqrt{4}$ as 2.   □

PRACTICE
3   Simplify.

a. $\sqrt{\dfrac{5}{49}}$ **b.** $\sqrt{\dfrac{9}{100}}$ **c.** $\sqrt{\dfrac{18}{25}}$

OBJECTIVE 3 ▶ Simplifying radicals containing variables. Recall that $\sqrt{x^6} = x^3$ because $(x^3)^2 = x^6$. If an odd exponent occurs, we write the exponential expression so that one factor is the greatest even power contained in the expression. Then we use the product rule to simplify.

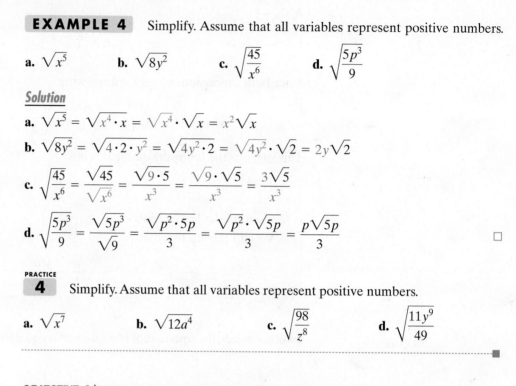

EXAMPLE 4 Simplify. Assume that all variables represent positive numbers.

a. $\sqrt{x^5}$ b. $\sqrt{8y^2}$ c. $\sqrt{\dfrac{45}{x^6}}$ d. $\sqrt{\dfrac{5p^3}{9}}$

Solution

a. $\sqrt{x^5} = \sqrt{x^4 \cdot x} = \sqrt{x^4} \cdot \sqrt{x} = x^2\sqrt{x}$

b. $\sqrt{8y^2} = \sqrt{4 \cdot 2 \cdot y^2} = \sqrt{4y^2 \cdot 2} = \sqrt{4y^2} \cdot \sqrt{2} = 2y\sqrt{2}$

c. $\sqrt{\dfrac{45}{x^6}} = \dfrac{\sqrt{45}}{\sqrt{x^6}} = \dfrac{\sqrt{9 \cdot 5}}{x^3} = \dfrac{\sqrt{9} \cdot \sqrt{5}}{x^3} = \dfrac{3\sqrt{5}}{x^3}$

d. $\sqrt{\dfrac{5p^3}{9}} = \dfrac{\sqrt{5p^3}}{\sqrt{9}} = \dfrac{\sqrt{p^2 \cdot 5p}}{3} = \dfrac{\sqrt{p^2} \cdot \sqrt{5p}}{3} = \dfrac{p\sqrt{5p}}{3}$ □

PRACTICE
4 Simplify. Assume that all variables represent positive numbers.

a. $\sqrt{x^7}$ b. $\sqrt{12a^4}$ c. $\sqrt{\dfrac{98}{z^8}}$ d. $\sqrt{\dfrac{11y^9}{49}}$

OBJECTIVE 4 ▶ Simplifying higher roots. The product and quotient rules also apply to roots other than square roots. In general, we have the following product and quotient rules for radicals.

Product Rule for Radicals

If $\sqrt[n]{a}$ and $\sqrt[n]{b}$ are real numbers, then

$$\sqrt[n]{a \cdot b} = \sqrt[n]{a} \cdot \sqrt[n]{b}$$

Quotient Rule for Radicals

If $\sqrt[n]{a}$ and $\sqrt[n]{b}$ are real numbers and $b \neq 0$, then

$$\sqrt[n]{\dfrac{a}{b}} = \dfrac{\sqrt[n]{a}}{\sqrt[n]{b}}$$

To simplify cube roots, look for perfect cube factors of the radicand. For example, 8 is a perfect cube, since $2^3 = 8$.

To simplify $\sqrt[3]{48}$, factor 48 as $8 \cdot 6$.

$$\sqrt[3]{48} = \sqrt[3]{8 \cdot 6} \qquad \text{Factor 48.}$$
$$= \sqrt[3]{8} \cdot \sqrt[3]{6} \qquad \text{Apply the product rule.}$$
$$= 2\sqrt[3]{6} \qquad \text{Write } \sqrt[3]{8} \text{ as 2.}$$

$2\sqrt[3]{6}$ is in simplest form since the radicand 6 contains no perfect cube factors other than 1.

EXAMPLE 5 Simplify.

a. $\sqrt[3]{54}$ **b.** $\sqrt[3]{18}$ **c.** $\sqrt[3]{\dfrac{7}{8}}$ **d.** $\sqrt[3]{\dfrac{40}{27}}$

Solution

a. $\sqrt[3]{54} = \sqrt[3]{27 \cdot 2} = \sqrt[3]{27} \cdot \sqrt[3]{2} = 3\sqrt[3]{2}$

b. The number 18 contains no perfect cube factors, so $\sqrt[3]{18}$ cannot be simplified further.

c. $\sqrt[3]{\dfrac{7}{8}} = \dfrac{\sqrt[3]{7}}{\sqrt[3]{8}} = \dfrac{\sqrt[3]{7}}{2}$

d. $\sqrt[3]{\dfrac{40}{27}} = \dfrac{\sqrt[3]{40}}{\sqrt[3]{27}} = \dfrac{\sqrt[3]{8 \cdot 5}}{3} = \dfrac{\sqrt[3]{8} \cdot \sqrt[3]{5}}{3} = \dfrac{2\sqrt[3]{5}}{3}$ ☐

PRACTICE
5 Simplify.

a. $\sqrt[3]{24}$ **b.** $\sqrt[3]{38}$ **c.** $\sqrt[3]{\dfrac{5}{27}}$ **d.** $\sqrt[3]{\dfrac{15}{64}}$

To simplify fourth roots, look for perfect fourth powers of the radicand. For example, 16 is a perfect fourth power since $2^4 = 16$.

To simplify $\sqrt[4]{32}$, factor 32 as $16 \cdot 2$.

$$\sqrt[4]{32} = \sqrt[4]{16 \cdot 2} \qquad \text{Factor 32.}$$
$$= \sqrt[4]{16} \cdot \sqrt[4]{2} \qquad \text{Apply the product rule.}$$
$$= 2\sqrt[4]{2} \qquad \text{Write } \sqrt[4]{16} \text{ as 2.}$$

EXAMPLE 6 Simplify.

a. $\sqrt[4]{243}$ **b.** $\sqrt[4]{\dfrac{3}{16}}$ **c.** $\sqrt[5]{64}$

Solution

a. $\sqrt[4]{243} = \sqrt[4]{81 \cdot 3} = \sqrt[4]{81} \cdot \sqrt[4]{3} = 3\sqrt[4]{3}$ **b.** $\sqrt[4]{\dfrac{3}{16}} = \dfrac{\sqrt[4]{3}}{\sqrt[4]{16}} = \dfrac{\sqrt[4]{3}}{2}$

c. $\sqrt[5]{64} = \sqrt[5]{32 \cdot 2} = \sqrt[5]{32} \cdot \sqrt[5]{2} = 2\sqrt[5]{2}$ ☐

PRACTICE
6 Simplify.

a. $\sqrt[4]{32}$ **b.** $\sqrt[4]{\dfrac{5}{81}}$ **c.** $\sqrt[5]{96}$

VOCABULARY & READINESS CHECK

Word Bank. *Use the choices below to fill in the blanks. Not all choices will be used.*

$a \cdot b \qquad \dfrac{a}{b} \qquad \dfrac{\sqrt{a}}{\sqrt{b}} \qquad \sqrt{a} \cdot \sqrt{b}$

1. If $\sqrt{a}$ and $\sqrt{b}$ are real numbers, then $\sqrt{a \cdot b} = $ _____ .

2. If $\sqrt{a}$ and $\sqrt{b}$ are real numbers, then $\sqrt{\dfrac{a}{b}} = $ _____ .

Fill in the Blank. *For Exercises 3 and 4, fill in the blanks using the example:* $\sqrt{4 \cdot 9} = \sqrt{4} \cdot \sqrt{9} = \underline{2} \cdot \underline{3} = \underline{6}$.

3. $\sqrt{16 \cdot 25} = \sqrt{\rule{1.2em}{0.1pt}} \cdot \sqrt{\rule{1.2em}{0.1pt}} = \underline{\hspace{1.5em}} \cdot \underline{\hspace{1.5em}} = \underline{\hspace{1.5em}}$ **4.** $\sqrt{36 \cdot 3} = \sqrt{\rule{1.2em}{0.1pt}} \cdot \sqrt{\rule{1.2em}{0.1pt}} = \underline{\hspace{1.5em}} \cdot \sqrt{\rule{1.2em}{0.1pt}} = \underline{\hspace{2em}}$

9.2 EXERCISE SET

Use the product rule to simplify each radical. See Examples 1 and 2.

1. $\sqrt{20}$

2. $\sqrt{44}$

3. $\sqrt{50}$

4. $\sqrt{28}$

5. $\sqrt{33}$

6. $\sqrt{21}$

7. $\sqrt{98}$

8. $\sqrt{125}$

9. $\sqrt{60}$

10. $\sqrt{90}$

11. $\sqrt{180}$

12. $\sqrt{150}$

13. $\sqrt{52}$

14. $\sqrt{75}$

15. $3\sqrt{25}$

16. $9\sqrt{36}$

17. $7\sqrt{63}$

18. $11\sqrt{99}$

19. $-5\sqrt{27}$

20. $-6\sqrt{75}$

Use the quotient rule and the product rule to simplify each radical. See Example 3.

21. $\sqrt{\dfrac{8}{25}}$

22. $\sqrt{\dfrac{63}{16}}$

23. $\sqrt{\dfrac{27}{121}}$

24. $\sqrt{\dfrac{24}{169}}$

25. $\sqrt{\dfrac{9}{4}}$

26. $\sqrt{\dfrac{100}{49}}$

27. $\sqrt{\dfrac{125}{9}}$

28. $\sqrt{\dfrac{27}{100}}$

29. $\sqrt{\dfrac{11}{36}}$

30. $\sqrt{\dfrac{30}{49}}$

31. $-\sqrt{\dfrac{27}{144}}$

32. $-\sqrt{\dfrac{84}{121}}$

Simplify each radical. Assume that all variables represent positive numbers. See Example 4.

33. $\sqrt{x^7}$

34. $\sqrt{y^3}$

35. $\sqrt{x^{13}}$

36. $\sqrt{y^{17}}$

37. $\sqrt{36a^3}$

38. $\sqrt{81b^5}$

39. $\sqrt{96x^4}$

40. $\sqrt{40y^{10}}$

41. $\sqrt{\dfrac{12}{m^2}}$

42. $\sqrt{\dfrac{63}{p^2}}$

43. $\sqrt{\dfrac{9x}{y^{10}}}$

44. $\sqrt{\dfrac{6y^2}{z^{16}}}$

45. $\sqrt{\dfrac{88}{x^{12}}}$

46. $\sqrt{\dfrac{500}{y^{22}}}$

MIXED PRACTICE

Simplify each radical. See Examples 1 through 4.

47. $8\sqrt{4}$

48. $6\sqrt{49}$

49. $\sqrt{\dfrac{36}{121}}$

50. $\sqrt{\dfrac{25}{144}}$

51. $\sqrt{175}$

52. $\sqrt{700}$

53. $\sqrt{\dfrac{20}{9}}$

54. $\sqrt{\dfrac{45}{64}}$

55. $\sqrt{24m^7}$

56. $\sqrt{50n^{13}}$

57. $\sqrt{\dfrac{23y^3}{4x^6}}$

58. $\sqrt{\dfrac{41x^5}{9y^8}}$

Simplify each radical. See Example 5.

59. $\sqrt[3]{24}$

60. $\sqrt[3]{81}$

61. $\sqrt[3]{250}$

62. $\sqrt[3]{56}$

63. $\sqrt[3]{\dfrac{5}{64}}$

64. $\sqrt[3]{\dfrac{32}{125}}$

65. $\sqrt[3]{\dfrac{23}{8}}$

66. $\sqrt[3]{\dfrac{37}{27}}$

67. $\sqrt[3]{\dfrac{15}{64}}$

68. $\sqrt[3]{\dfrac{4}{27}}$

69. $\sqrt[3]{80}$

70. $\sqrt[3]{108}$

Simplify. See Example 6.

71. $\sqrt[4]{48}$

72. $\sqrt[4]{405}$

73. $\sqrt[4]{\dfrac{8}{81}}$

74. $\sqrt[4]{\dfrac{25}{256}}$

75. $\sqrt[5]{96}$

76. $\sqrt[5]{128}$

77. $\sqrt[5]{\dfrac{5}{32}}$

78. $\sqrt[5]{\dfrac{16}{243}}$

Simplify.

△ **79.** If a cube is to have a volume of 80 cubic inches, then each side must be $\sqrt[3]{80}$ inches long. Simplify the radical representing the side length.

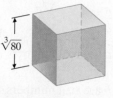

$\sqrt[3]{80}$

△ **80.** Jeannie Boswell is swimming across a 40-foot-wide river, trying to head straight across to the opposite shore. However, the current is strong enough to move her downstream 100 feet by the time she reaches land. (See the figure.) Because of the current, the actual distance she swam is $\sqrt{11,600}$ feet. Simplify this radical.

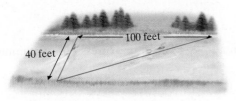

REVIEW AND PREVIEW

Perform the following operations. See Sections 6.2 and 6.3.

81. $6x + 8x$

82. $(6x)(8x)$

83. $(2x + 3)(x - 5)$

84. $(2x + 3) + (x - 5)$

85. $9y^2 - 9y^2$

86. $(9y^2)(-8y^2)$

CONCEPT EXTENSIONS

Simplify each radical. Assume that all variables represent positive numbers.

87. $\sqrt{x^6 y^3}$

88. $\sqrt{a^{13} b^{14}}$

89. $\sqrt{98 x^5 y^4}$

90. $\sqrt{27 x^8 y^{11}}$

91. $\sqrt[3]{-8x^6}$

92. $\sqrt[3]{27 x^{12}}$

93. By using replacement values for a and b, show that $\sqrt{a^2 + b^2}$ does not equal $a + b$.

94. By using replacement values for a and b, show that $\sqrt{a + b}$ does not equal $\sqrt{a} + \sqrt{b}$.

The length of a side of a cube is given by the expression $\sqrt{\dfrac{A}{6}}$ units where A square units is the cube's surface area. Use this expression for Exercises 95 through 98. Be sure to attach the appropriate units.

95. The surface area of a cube is 120 square inches. Find the exact length of a side of the cube.

96. The surface area of a cube is 594 square feet. Find the exact length of a side of the cube.

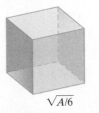

$\sqrt{A/6}$

97. A Guinness World record was set in December 2004, when an electrical engineering student from Johannesburg, South Africa, solved 42 Rubik's cubes in one hour, the most ever in that time. Rubik's cube, named after its inventor, Erno Rubik, was first imagined by him in 1974, and by 1980 was a worldwide phenomenon. These cubes have remained unchanged in size, and a standard Rubik's cube has a surface area of 30.375 square inches. Find the length of one side of a Rubik's cube. (*Source: Guinness Book of World Records*)

98. The Borg spaceship on *Star Trek: The Next Generation* is in the shape of a cube. Suppose a model of this ship has a surface area of 121 square inches. Find the length of a side of the ship.

The cost C in dollars per day to operate a small delivery service is given by $C = 100 \sqrt[3]{n} + 700$, where n is the number of deliveries per day.

99. Find the cost if the number of deliveries is 1000.

100. Approximate the cost if the number of deliveries is 500.

The Mosteller formula for calculating body surface area is $B = \sqrt{\dfrac{hw}{3600}}$, where B is an individual's body surface area in square meters, h is the individual's height in centimeters, and w is the individual's weight in kilograms. Use this formula in Exercises 101 and 102. Round answers to the nearest tenth.

101. Find the body surface area of a person who is 169 cm tall and weighs 64 kilograms.

102. Approximate the body surface area of a person who is 183 cm tall and weighs 85 kilograms.

9.3 ADDING AND SUBTRACTING RADICALS

OBJECTIVES

1 Add or subtract like radicals.

2 Simplify radical expressions, and then add or subtract any like radicals.

OBJECTIVE 1 ▶ Adding and subtracting like radicals. To combine like terms, we use the distributive property.

$$5x + 3x = (5 + 3)x = 8x$$

The distributive property can also be applied to expressions containing radicals. For example,

$$5\sqrt{2} + 3\sqrt{2} = (5 + 3)\sqrt{2} = 8\sqrt{2}$$

Also,

$$9\sqrt{5} - 6\sqrt{5} = (9 - 6)\sqrt{5} = 3\sqrt{5}$$

Radical terms $5\sqrt{2}$ and $3\sqrt{2}$ are **like radicals,** as are $9\sqrt{5}$ and $6\sqrt{5}$.

> **Like Radicals**
>
> Like radicals are radical expressions that have the same index and the same radicand.

From the examples above, we can see that **only like radicals can be combined** in this way. For example, the expression $2\sqrt{3} + 3\sqrt{2}$ cannot be simplified further since the radicals are not like radicals. Also, the expression $4\sqrt{7} + 4\sqrt[3]{7}$ cannot be simplified further because the radicals are not like radicals since the indices are different.

EXAMPLE 1 Simplify by combining like radical terms.

a. $4\sqrt{5} + 3\sqrt{5}$ **b.** $\sqrt{10} - 6\sqrt{10}$ **c.** $\sqrt[3]{7} + \sqrt[3]{7} - 4\sqrt[3]{5}$ **d.** $2\sqrt{6} + 2\sqrt[3]{6}$

Solution

a. $4\sqrt{5} + 3\sqrt{5} = (4 + 3)\sqrt{5} = 7\sqrt{5}$

b. $\sqrt{10} - 6\sqrt{10} = 1\sqrt{10} - 6\sqrt{10} = (1 - 6)\sqrt{10} = -5\sqrt{10}$

c. $\sqrt[3]{7} + \sqrt[3]{7} - 4\sqrt[3]{5} = 1\sqrt[3]{7} + 1\sqrt[3]{7} - 4\sqrt[3]{5} = (1 + 1)\sqrt[3]{7} - 4\sqrt[3]{5} = 2\sqrt[3]{7} - 4\sqrt[3]{5}$

This expression cannot be simplified further since the radicands are not the same.

d. $2\sqrt{6} + 2\sqrt[3]{6}$ cannot be simplified further since the indices are not the same. □

PRACTICE

1 Simplify by combining like radical terms.

a. $3\sqrt{2} + 5\sqrt{2}$ **b.** $\sqrt{6} - 8\sqrt{6}$

c. $6\sqrt[4]{5} - 2\sqrt[4]{5} + 11\sqrt[4]{7}$ **d.** $4\sqrt{13} - 5\sqrt[3]{13}$

Concept Check ☑

Which is true?

a. $2 + 3\sqrt{5} = 5\sqrt{5}$ **b.** $2\sqrt{3} + 2\sqrt{7} = 2\sqrt{10}$ **c.** $\sqrt{3} + \sqrt{5} = \sqrt{8}$

d. $\sqrt{3} + \sqrt{3} = 3$ **e.** None of the above is true.

Answer to Concept Check:

e (a, b, and c are not true since each left side cannot be simplified further. For d, $\sqrt{3} + \sqrt{3} = 2\sqrt{3}$.)

OBJECTIVE 2 ▶ Simplifying radicals, then adding or subtracting. At first glance, it appears that the expression $\sqrt{50} + \sqrt{8}$ cannot be simplified further because the radicands are different. However, the product rule can be used to simplify each radical, and then further simplification might be possible.

EXAMPLE 2 Add or subtract by first simplifying each radical.

a. $\sqrt{50} + \sqrt{8}$ **b.** $7\sqrt{12} - \sqrt{75}$ **c.** $\sqrt{25} - \sqrt{27} - 2\sqrt{18} - \sqrt{16}$

Solution

a. First simplify each radical.

$$
\begin{aligned}
\sqrt{50} + \sqrt{8} &= \sqrt{25 \cdot 2} + \sqrt{4 \cdot 2} && \text{Factor radicands.} \\
&= \sqrt{25} \cdot \sqrt{2} + \sqrt{4} \cdot \sqrt{2} && \text{Apply the product rule.} \\
&= 5\sqrt{2} + 2\sqrt{2} && \text{Simplify } \sqrt{25} \text{ and } \sqrt{4}. \\
&= 7\sqrt{2} && \text{Add like radicals.}
\end{aligned}
$$

b.
$$
\begin{aligned}
7\sqrt{12} - \sqrt{75} &= 7\sqrt{4 \cdot 3} - \sqrt{25 \cdot 3} && \text{Factor radicands.} \\
&= 7\sqrt{4} \cdot \sqrt{3} - \sqrt{25} \cdot \sqrt{3} && \text{Apply the product rule.} \\
&= 7 \cdot 2\sqrt{3} - 5\sqrt{3} && \text{Simplify } \sqrt{4} \text{ and } \sqrt{25}. \\
&= 14\sqrt{3} - 5\sqrt{3} && \text{Multiply.} \\
&= 9\sqrt{3} && \text{Subtract like radicals.}
\end{aligned}
$$

c.
$$
\begin{aligned}
&\sqrt{25} - \sqrt{27} - 2\sqrt{18} - \sqrt{16} \\
&= 5 - \sqrt{9 \cdot 3} - 2\sqrt{9 \cdot 2} - 4 && \text{Factor radicands.} \\
&= 5 - \sqrt{9} \cdot \sqrt{3} - 2\sqrt{9} \cdot \sqrt{2} - 4 && \text{Apply the product rule.} \\
&= 5 - 3\sqrt{3} - 2 \cdot 3\sqrt{2} - 4 && \text{Simplify.} \\
&= 1 - 3\sqrt{3} - 6\sqrt{2} && \text{Write } 5 - 4 \text{ as } 1 \text{ and } 2 \cdot 3 \text{ as } 6. \quad \square
\end{aligned}
$$

PRACTICE
2 Add or subtract by first simplifying each radical.

a. $\sqrt{45} + \sqrt{20}$ **b.** $\sqrt{36} + 3\sqrt{24} - \sqrt{40} - \sqrt{150}$
c. $\sqrt{98} - 5\sqrt{8}$

If radical expressions contain variables, we proceed in a similar way. Simplify radicals using the product and quotient rules. Then add or subtract any like radicals.

EXAMPLE 3 Simplify $2\sqrt{x^2} - \sqrt{25x^5} + \sqrt{x^5}$. Assume variables represent positive numbers.

Solution $2\sqrt{x^2} - \sqrt{25x^5} + \sqrt{x^5}$

$$
\begin{aligned}
&= 2x - \sqrt{25x^4 \cdot x} + \sqrt{x^4 \cdot x} && \text{Factor radicands so that one factor is a perfect square. Simplify } \sqrt{x^2}. \\
&= 2x - \sqrt{25x^4} \cdot \sqrt{x} + \sqrt{x^4} \cdot \sqrt{x} && \text{Use the product rule.} \\
&= 2x - 5x^2\sqrt{x} + x^2\sqrt{x} && \text{Write } \sqrt{25x^4} \text{ as } 5x^2 \text{ and } \sqrt{x^4} \text{ as } x^2. \\
&= 2x - 4x^2\sqrt{x} && \text{Add like radicals.} \quad \square
\end{aligned}
$$

PRACTICE
3 Simplify $\sqrt{x^3} - 8x\sqrt{x} + 3\sqrt{x^2}$. Assume variables represent positive numbers.

EXAMPLE 4 Simplify the radical expression: $5\sqrt[3]{16x^3} - \sqrt[3]{54x^3}$

Solution $5\sqrt[3]{16x^3} - \sqrt[3]{54x^3}$

$$
\begin{aligned}
&= 5\sqrt[3]{8x^3 \cdot 2} - \sqrt[3]{27x^3 \cdot 2} && \text{Factor radicands so that one factor is a perfect cube.} \\
&= 5 \cdot \sqrt[3]{8x^3} \cdot \sqrt[3]{2} - \sqrt[3]{27x^3} \cdot \sqrt[3]{2} && \text{Use the product rule.}
\end{aligned}
$$

$$= 5 \cdot 2x \cdot \sqrt[3]{2} - 3x \cdot \sqrt[3]{2}$$

Write $\sqrt[3]{8x^3}$ as $2x$ and $\sqrt[3]{27x^3}$ as $3x$.

$$= 10x\sqrt[3]{2} - 3x\sqrt[3]{2}$$

Write $5 \cdot 2x$ as $10x$.

$$= 7x\sqrt[3]{2}$$

Subtract like radicands. ☐

PRACTICE
4   Simplify the radical expression: $4\sqrt[3]{81x^6} - \sqrt[3]{24x^6}$

VOCABULARY & READINESS CHECK

Fill in the Blank.

1. Radicals that have the same index and same radicand are called _____.

2. The expressions $7\sqrt[3]{2x}$ and $-\sqrt[3]{2x}$ are called _____.

3. $11\sqrt{2} + 6\sqrt{2} =$ _____.
   a. $66\sqrt{2}$ **b.** $17\sqrt{2}$ **c.** $17\sqrt{4}$

4. $\sqrt{5}$ is the same as _____.
   a. $0\sqrt{5}$ **b.** $1\sqrt{5}$ **c.** $5\sqrt{5}$

5. $\sqrt{5} + \sqrt{5} =$ _____
   a. $\sqrt{10}$ **b.** 5   **c.** $2\sqrt{5}$

6. $9\sqrt{7} - \sqrt{7} =$ _____
   a. $8\sqrt{7}$ **b.** 9   **c.** 0

9.3 | EXERCISE SET

MyMathLab *Powered by CourseCompass™ and MathXL®*

PRACTICE   WATCH   DOWNLOAD   READ   REVIEW

Simplify each expression by combining like radicals where possible. See Example 1.

1. $4\sqrt{3} - 8\sqrt{3}$

2. $2\sqrt{5} - 9\sqrt{5}$

3. $3\sqrt{6} + 8\sqrt{6} - 2\sqrt{6} - 5$

4. $12\sqrt{2} - 3\sqrt{2} + 8\sqrt{2} + 10$

5. $\sqrt{11} + \sqrt{11} + 11$

6. $\sqrt{13} + 13 + \sqrt{13}$

7. $6\sqrt{5} - 5\sqrt{5} + \sqrt{2}$

8. $4\sqrt{3} + \sqrt{5} - 3\sqrt{3}$

9. $\sqrt[3]{15} + \sqrt[3]{15} - 4\sqrt[3]{15}$

10. $\sqrt[3]{49} - 8\sqrt[3]{49} + \sqrt[3]{49}$

11. $2\sqrt[3]{3} + 5\sqrt[3]{3} - \sqrt{3}$

12. $8\sqrt[3]{5} + 2\sqrt[3]{5} + \sqrt{5}$

13. $2\sqrt[3]{2} - 7\sqrt[3]{2} - 6$

14. $5\sqrt[3]{9} + 2 - 11\sqrt[3]{9}$

MIXED PRACTICE

Add or subtract by first simplifying each radical and then combining any like radical terms. Assume that all variables represent positive real numbers. See Examples 2 and 3.

15. $\sqrt{12} + \sqrt{27}$

16. $\sqrt{50} + \sqrt{18}$

17. $\sqrt{45} + 3\sqrt{20}$

18. $\sqrt{28} + \sqrt{63}$

19. $2\sqrt{54} - \sqrt{20} + \sqrt{45} - \sqrt{24}$

20. $2\sqrt{8} - \sqrt{128} + \sqrt{48} + \sqrt{18}$

21. $4x - 3\sqrt{x^2} + \sqrt{x}$

22. $x - 6\sqrt{x^2} + 2\sqrt{x}$

23. $\sqrt{25x} + \sqrt{36x} - 11\sqrt{x}$

24. $3\sqrt{x^3} - x\sqrt{4x}$

25. $\sqrt{16x} - \sqrt{x^3}$

26. $\sqrt{8x^3} - \sqrt{x^2}$

27. $12\sqrt{5} - \sqrt{5} - 4\sqrt{5}$

28. $7\sqrt{3} + 2\sqrt{3} - 13\sqrt{3}$

29. $\sqrt{5} + \sqrt[3]{5}$

30. $\sqrt{5} + \sqrt{5}$

31. $4 + 8\sqrt{2} - 9$

32. $6 - 2\sqrt{3} - \sqrt{3}$

33. $8 - \sqrt{2} - 5\sqrt{2}$

34. $\sqrt{75} + \sqrt{48}$

35. $5\sqrt{32} - \sqrt{72}$

36. $2\sqrt{80} - \sqrt{45}$

37. $\sqrt{8} + \sqrt{9} + \sqrt{18} + \sqrt{81}$

38. $\sqrt{6} + \sqrt{16} + \sqrt{24} + \sqrt{25}$

39. $\sqrt{\dfrac{5}{9}} + \sqrt{\dfrac{5}{81}}$

40. $\sqrt{\dfrac{3}{64}} + \sqrt{\dfrac{3}{16}}$

41. $\sqrt{\dfrac{3}{4}} - \sqrt{\dfrac{3}{64}}$

42. $\sqrt{\dfrac{7}{25}} - \sqrt{\dfrac{7}{100}}$

43. $2\sqrt{45} - 2\sqrt{20}$

44. $5\sqrt{18} + 2\sqrt{32}$

45. $\sqrt{35} - \sqrt{140}$

46. $\sqrt{6} - \sqrt{600}$

47. $5\sqrt{2x} + \sqrt{98x}$

48. $3\sqrt{9x} + 2\sqrt{x}$

49. $5\sqrt{x} + 4\sqrt{4x} - 13\sqrt{x}$

50. $\sqrt{9x} + \sqrt{81x} - 11\sqrt{x}$

51. $\sqrt{3x^3} + 3x\sqrt{x}$

52. $x\sqrt{4x} + \sqrt{9x^3}$

Add or subtract by first simplifying each radical and then combining any like radical terms. Assume that all variables represent positive real numbers. See Example 4.

53. $\sqrt[3]{81} + \sqrt[3]{24}$

54. $\sqrt[3]{32} - \sqrt[3]{4}$

55. $4\sqrt[3]{9} - \sqrt[3]{243}$

56. $7\sqrt[3]{6} - \sqrt[3]{48}$

57. $2\sqrt[3]{8} + 2\sqrt[3]{16}$

58. $3\sqrt[3]{27} + 3\sqrt[3]{81}$

59. $\sqrt[3]{8} + \sqrt[3]{54} - 5$

60. $\sqrt[3]{64} + \sqrt[3]{14} - 9$

61. $\sqrt{32x^2} + \sqrt[3]{32} + \sqrt{4x^2}$

62. $\sqrt{18x^2} + \sqrt[3]{24} + \sqrt{2x^2}$

63. $\sqrt{40x} + \sqrt[3]{40} - 2\sqrt{10x} - \sqrt[3]{5}$

64. $\sqrt{72x^2} + \sqrt[3]{54} - x\sqrt{50} - 3\sqrt[3]{2}$

REVIEW AND PREVIEW

Square each binomial. See Section 6.4.

65. $(x + 6)^2$

66. $(3x + 2)^2$

67. $(2x - 1)^2$

68. $(x - 5)^2$

Solve each system of linear equations. See Section 5.2.

69. $\begin{cases} x = 2y \\ x + 5y = 14 \end{cases}$

70. $\begin{cases} y = -5x \\ x + y = 16 \end{cases}$

CONCEPT EXTENSIONS

71. In your own words, describe like radicals.

72. In the expression $\sqrt{5} + 2 - 3\sqrt{5}$, explain why 2 and -3 cannot be combined.

73. Find the perimeter of the rectangular picture frame.

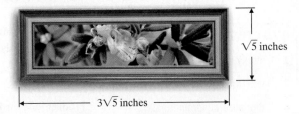

$\sqrt{5}$ inches

$3\sqrt{5}$ inches

74. Find the perimeter of the plot of land.

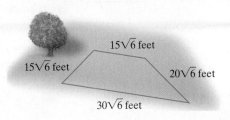

$15\sqrt{6}$ feet

$15\sqrt{6}$ feet

$20\sqrt{6}$ feet

$30\sqrt{6}$ feet

75. An 8-foot-long water trough is to be made of wood. Each of the two triangular end pieces has an area of $\dfrac{3\sqrt{27}}{4}$ square feet. The two side panels are both rectangular. In simplest radical form, find the total area of the wood needed.

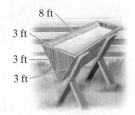

8 ft

3 ft

3 ft

3 ft

76. Eight wooden braces are to be attached along the diagonals of the vertical sides of a storage bin. Each of four of these diagonals has a length of $\sqrt{52}$ feet, while each of the other four has a length of $\sqrt{80}$ feet. In simplest radical form, find the total length of the wood needed for these braces.

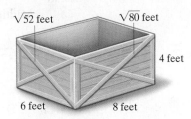

$\sqrt{52}$ feet

$\sqrt{80}$ feet

4 feet

6 feet

8 feet

Simplify.

77. $\sqrt{\dfrac{x^3}{16}} - x\sqrt{\dfrac{9x}{25}} + \dfrac{\sqrt{81x^3}}{2}$

78. $7\sqrt{x^{11}y^7} - x^2y\sqrt{25x^7y^5} + \sqrt{8x^8y^2}$

9.4 | MULTIPLYING AND DIVIDING RADICALS

OBJECTIVES

1 Multiply radicals.

2 Divide radicals.

3 Rationalize denominators.

4 Rationalize using conjugates.

OBJECTIVE 1 ▶ Multiplying radicals. In Section 9.2 we used the product and quotient rules for radicals to help us simplify radicals. In this section, we use these rules to simplify products and quotients of radicals.

> **Product Rule for Radicals**
>
> If $\sqrt[n]{a}$ and $\sqrt[n]{b}$ are real numbers, then
>
> $$\sqrt[n]{a} \cdot \sqrt[n]{b} = \sqrt[n]{a \cdot b}$$

This property says that the product of the nth roots of two numbers is the nth root of the product of the two numbers. For example,

$$\sqrt{3} \cdot \sqrt{2} = \sqrt{3 \cdot 2} = \sqrt{6} \quad \text{Also,} \quad \sqrt[3]{5} \cdot \sqrt[3]{7} = \sqrt[3]{5 \cdot 7} = \sqrt[3]{35}$$

EXAMPLE 1 Multiply. Then simplify if possible.

a. $\sqrt{7} \cdot \sqrt{3}$ **b.** $\sqrt{3} \cdot \sqrt{3}$ **c.** $\sqrt{3} \cdot \sqrt{15}$ **d.** $2\sqrt{3} \cdot 5\sqrt{2}$ **e.** $\sqrt{2x^3} \cdot \sqrt{6x}$

Solution

a. $\sqrt{7} \cdot \sqrt{3} = \sqrt{7 \cdot 3} = \sqrt{21}$

b. $\sqrt{3} \cdot \sqrt{3} = \sqrt{3 \cdot 3} = \sqrt{9} = 3$

c. $\sqrt{3} \cdot \sqrt{15} = \sqrt{45}$. Next, simplify $\sqrt{45}$.

$\qquad \sqrt{45} = \sqrt{9 \cdot 5} = \sqrt{9} \cdot \sqrt{5} = 3\sqrt{5}$

d. $2\sqrt{3} \cdot 5\sqrt{2} = 2 \cdot 5\sqrt{3 \cdot 2} = 10\sqrt{6}$

e. $\sqrt{2x^3} \cdot \sqrt{6x} = \sqrt{2x^3 \cdot 6x}$ Use the product rule.

$\qquad\qquad\quad = \sqrt{12x^4}$ Multiply.

$\qquad\qquad\quad = \sqrt{4x^4 \cdot 3}$ Write $12x^4$ so that one factor is a perfect square.

$\qquad\qquad\quad = \sqrt{4x^4} \cdot \sqrt{3}$ Use the product rule.

$\qquad\qquad\quad = 2x^2\sqrt{3}$ Simplify.   □

PRACTICE

1 Multiply. Then simplify if possible.

a. $\sqrt{11} \cdot \sqrt{7}$ **b.** $9\sqrt{10} \cdot 8\sqrt{3}$ **c.** $\sqrt{5} \cdot \sqrt{10}$

d. $\sqrt{17} \cdot \sqrt{17}$ **e.** $\sqrt{15y} \cdot \sqrt{5y^3}$

From Example 1b, we found that

$$\sqrt{3} \cdot \sqrt{3} = 3 \quad \text{or} \quad \left(\sqrt{3}\right)^2 = 3$$

This is true in general.

> If a is a positive number,
>
> $$\sqrt{a} \cdot \sqrt{a} = a \quad \text{or} \quad \left(\sqrt{a}\right)^2 = a$$

Concept Check ☑

Identify the true statement(s).

a. $\sqrt{7} \cdot \sqrt{7} = 7$ **b.** $\sqrt{2} \cdot \sqrt{3} = 6$

c. $\left(\sqrt{131}\right)^2 = 131$ **d.** $\sqrt{5x} \cdot \sqrt{5x} = 5x$ (Here x is a positive number.)

Answer to Concept Check:
a, c, d

EXAMPLE 2 Find $\left(3\sqrt{2}\right)^2$.

Solution $\left(3\sqrt{2}\right)^2 = 3^2 \cdot \left(\sqrt{2}\right)^2 = 9 \cdot 2 = 18$ $\qquad\square$

PRACTICE
2 Find $\left(2\sqrt{7}\right)^2$.

EXAMPLE 3 Multiply $\sqrt[3]{4} \cdot \sqrt[3]{18}$. Then simplify if possible.

Solution $\sqrt[3]{4} \cdot \sqrt[3]{18} = \sqrt[3]{4 \cdot 18} = \sqrt[3]{4 \cdot 2 \cdot 9} = \sqrt[3]{8 \cdot 9} = \sqrt[3]{8} \cdot \sqrt[3]{9} = 2\sqrt[3]{9}$ $\qquad\square$

PRACTICE
3 Multiply $\sqrt[3]{10} \cdot \sqrt[3]{50}$. Then simplify if possible.

When multiplying radical expressions containing more than one term, use the same techniques we use to multiply other algebraic expressions with more than one term.

EXAMPLE 4 Multiply. Then simplify if possible.

a. $\sqrt{5}\left(\sqrt{5} - \sqrt{2}\right)$ $\qquad$ **b.** $\sqrt{3x}\left(\sqrt{x} - 5\sqrt{3}\right)$
c. $\left(\sqrt{x} + \sqrt{2}\right)\left(\sqrt{3} - \sqrt{2}\right)$

Solution

a. Using the distributive property, we have

$$\sqrt{5}\left(\sqrt{5} - \sqrt{2}\right) = \sqrt{5} \cdot \sqrt{5} - \sqrt{5} \cdot \sqrt{2}$$

$$= 5 - \sqrt{10} \qquad \text{Since } \sqrt{5} \cdot \sqrt{5} = 5 \text{ and } \sqrt{5} \cdot \sqrt{2} = \sqrt{10}$$

b. $\sqrt{3x}\left(\sqrt{x} - 5\sqrt{3}\right) = \sqrt{3x} \cdot \sqrt{x} - \sqrt{3x} \cdot 5\sqrt{3}$ $\qquad$ Use the distributive property.

$$= \sqrt{3x \cdot x} - 5\sqrt{3x \cdot 3} \qquad \text{Use the product rule.}$$

$$= \sqrt{3 \cdot x^2} - 5\sqrt{9 \cdot x} \qquad \begin{array}{l}\text{Factor each radicand so that one}\\\text{factor is a perfect square.}\end{array}$$

$$= \sqrt{3} \cdot \sqrt{x^2} - 5 \cdot \sqrt{9} \cdot \sqrt{x} \qquad \text{Use the product rule.}$$

$$= x\sqrt{3} - 5 \cdot 3 \cdot \sqrt{x} \qquad \text{Simplify.}$$

$$= x\sqrt{3} - 15\sqrt{x} \qquad \text{Simplify.}$$

c. Use the FOIL method of multiplication.

$$\qquad\qquad\qquad\qquad\quad \overset{\text{F}}{} \qquad \overset{\text{O}}{} \qquad \overset{\text{I}}{} \qquad \overset{\text{L}}{}$$

$$\left(\sqrt{x} + \sqrt{2}\right)\left(\sqrt{3} - \sqrt{2}\right) = \sqrt{x} \cdot \sqrt{3} - \sqrt{x} \cdot \sqrt{2} + \sqrt{2} \cdot \sqrt{3} - \sqrt{2} \cdot \sqrt{2}$$

$$= \sqrt{3x} - \sqrt{2x} + \sqrt{6} - \sqrt{4} \qquad \text{Apply the product rule.}$$

$$= \sqrt{3x} - \sqrt{2x} + \sqrt{6} - 2 \qquad \text{Simplify.} \qquad\square$$

PRACTICE
4 Multiply. Then simplify if possible.

a. $\sqrt{3}\left(\sqrt{3} - \sqrt{5}\right)$ $\qquad\qquad$ **b.** $\sqrt{2z}\left(\sqrt{z} + 7\sqrt{2}\right)$
c. $\left(\sqrt{x} - \sqrt{7}\right)\left(\sqrt{x} + \sqrt{2}\right)$

The special product formulas can be used to multiply expressions containing radicals.

EXAMPLE 5   Multiply. Then simplify if possible.

a. $\left(\sqrt{5} - 7\right)\left(\sqrt{5} + 7\right)$ **b.** $\left(\sqrt{7x} + 2\right)^2$

Solution

a. Recall from Chapter 5 that $(a - b)(a + b) = a^2 - b^2$. Then

$$
\begin{aligned}
\left(\sqrt{5} - 7\right)\left(\sqrt{5} + 7\right) &= \left(\sqrt{5}\right)^2 - 7^2 \\
&= 5 - 49 \\
&= -44
\end{aligned}
$$

b. Recall that $(a + b)^2 = a^2 + 2ab + b^2$. Then

$$
\begin{aligned}
\left(\sqrt{7x} + 2\right)^2 &= \left(\sqrt{7x}\right)^2 + 2\left(\sqrt{7x}\right)(2) + (2)^2 \\
&= 7x + 4\sqrt{7x} + 4
\end{aligned}
$$

PRACTICE
5   Multiply. Then simplify if possible.

a. $\left(\sqrt{7} + 4\right)\left(\sqrt{7} - 4\right)$ **b.** $\left(\sqrt{3x} - 5\right)^2$

OBJECTIVE 2 ▶ Dividing radicals. To simplify quotients of radical expressions, we use the quotient rule.

> **Quotient Rule for Radicals**
> If $\sqrt[n]{a}$ and $\sqrt[n]{b}$ are real numbers and $b \neq 0$, then
> $$\frac{\sqrt[n]{a}}{\sqrt[n]{b}} = \sqrt[n]{\frac{a}{b}}, \text{ providing } b \neq 0$$

EXAMPLE 6   Divide. Then simplify if possible.

a. $\dfrac{\sqrt{14}}{\sqrt{2}}$ **b.** $\dfrac{\sqrt{100}}{\sqrt{5}}$ **c.** $\dfrac{\sqrt{12x^3}}{\sqrt{3x}}$

Solution   Use the quotient rule and then simplify the resulting radicand.

a. $\dfrac{\sqrt{14}}{\sqrt{2}} = \sqrt{\dfrac{14}{2}} = \sqrt{7}$

b. $\dfrac{\sqrt{100}}{\sqrt{5}} = \sqrt{\dfrac{100}{5}} = \sqrt{20} = \sqrt{4 \cdot 5} = \sqrt{4} \cdot \sqrt{5} = 2\sqrt{5}$

c. $\dfrac{\sqrt{12x^3}}{\sqrt{3x}} = \sqrt{\dfrac{12x^3}{3x}} = \sqrt{4x^2} = 2x$

PRACTICE
6   Divide. Then simplify if possible.

a. $\dfrac{\sqrt{21}}{\sqrt{7}}$ **b.** $\dfrac{\sqrt{48}}{\sqrt{6}}$ **c.** $\dfrac{\sqrt{45y^5}}{\sqrt{5y}}$

EXAMPLE 7   Divide $\dfrac{\sqrt[3]{32}}{\sqrt[3]{4}}$. Then simplify if possible.

Solution $\dfrac{\sqrt[3]{32}}{\sqrt[3]{4}} = \sqrt[3]{\dfrac{32}{4}} = \sqrt[3]{8} = 2$ □

PRACTICE 7   Divide $\dfrac{\sqrt[3]{625}}{\sqrt[3]{5}}$. Then simplify if possible.

OBJECTIVE 3 ▶ Rationalizing denominators. It is sometimes easier to work with radical expressions if the denominator does not contain a radical. To rewrite the expression so that the denominator does not contain a radical expression, we use the fact that we can multiply the numerator and the denominator of a fraction by the same nonzero number without changing the value of the expression. This is the same as multiplying the fraction by 1. For example, to get rid of the radical in the denominator of $\dfrac{\sqrt{5}}{\sqrt{2}}$, we multiply by 1 in the form of $\dfrac{\sqrt{2}}{\sqrt{2}}$. Then

$$\frac{\sqrt{5}}{\sqrt{2}} = \frac{\sqrt{5}}{\sqrt{2}} \cdot 1 = \frac{\sqrt{5}}{\sqrt{2}} \cdot \frac{\sqrt{2}}{\sqrt{2}} = \frac{\sqrt{5} \cdot \sqrt{2}}{\sqrt{2} \cdot \sqrt{2}} = \frac{\sqrt{10}}{2}$$

This process is called **rationalizing** the denominator.

EXAMPLE 8   Rationalize each denominator.

a. $\dfrac{2}{\sqrt{7}}$ **b.** $\dfrac{\sqrt{5}}{\sqrt{12}}$ **c.** $\sqrt{\dfrac{1}{18x}}$

Solution

a. To rewrite $\dfrac{2}{\sqrt{7}}$ so that there is no radical in the denominator, we multiply by 1 in the form of $\dfrac{\sqrt{7}}{\sqrt{7}}$.

$$\frac{2}{\sqrt{7}} = \frac{2}{\sqrt{7}} \cdot \frac{\sqrt{7}}{\sqrt{7}} = \frac{2 \cdot \sqrt{7}}{\sqrt{7} \cdot \sqrt{7}} = \frac{2\sqrt{7}}{7}$$

b. We can multiply by $\dfrac{\sqrt{12}}{\sqrt{12}}$, but see what happens if we simplify first.

$$\frac{\sqrt{5}}{\sqrt{12}} = \frac{\sqrt{5}}{\sqrt{4 \cdot 3}} = \frac{\sqrt{5}}{2\sqrt{3}}$$

To rationalize the denominator now, we multiply by $\dfrac{\sqrt{3}}{\sqrt{3}}$.

$$\frac{\sqrt{5}}{2\sqrt{3}} = \frac{\sqrt{5}}{2\sqrt{3}} \cdot \frac{\sqrt{3}}{\sqrt{3}} = \frac{\sqrt{5} \cdot \sqrt{3}}{2\sqrt{3} \cdot \sqrt{3}} = \frac{\sqrt{15}}{2 \cdot 3} = \frac{\sqrt{15}}{6}$$

c. First we simplify.

$$\sqrt{\frac{1}{18x}} = \frac{\sqrt{1}}{\sqrt{18x}} = \frac{1}{\sqrt{9} \cdot \sqrt{2x}} = \frac{1}{3\sqrt{2x}}$$

Now to rationalize the denominator, we multiply by $\dfrac{\sqrt{2x}}{\sqrt{2x}}$.

$$\frac{1}{3\sqrt{2x}} = \frac{1}{3\sqrt{2x}} \cdot \frac{\sqrt{2x}}{\sqrt{2x}} = \frac{1 \cdot \sqrt{2x}}{3\sqrt{2x} \cdot \sqrt{2x}} = \frac{\sqrt{2x}}{3 \cdot 2x} = \frac{\sqrt{2x}}{6x}$$ □

PRACTICE
8 Rationalize each denominator.

a. $\dfrac{4}{\sqrt{5}}$　　　　**b.** $\dfrac{\sqrt{3}}{\sqrt{18}}$　　　　**c.** $\sqrt{\dfrac{3}{14x}}$

As a general rule, simplify a radical expression first and then rationalize the denominator.

EXAMPLE 9 Rationalize each denominator.

a. $\dfrac{5}{\sqrt[3]{4}}$　**b.** $\dfrac{\sqrt[3]{7}}{\sqrt[3]{3}}$

Solution

a. Since the denominator contains a cube root, we multiply the numerator and the denominator by a factor that gives the **cube root of a perfect cube** in the denominator. Recall that $\sqrt[3]{8} = 2$ and that the denominator $\sqrt[3]{4}$ multiplied by $\sqrt[3]{2}$ is $\sqrt[3]{4 \cdot 2}$ or $\sqrt[3]{8}$.

$$\frac{5}{\sqrt[3]{4}} = \frac{5 \cdot \sqrt[3]{2}}{\sqrt[3]{4} \cdot \sqrt[3]{2}} = \frac{5\sqrt[3]{2}}{\sqrt[3]{8}} = \frac{5\sqrt[3]{2}}{2}$$

b. Recall that $\sqrt[3]{27} = 3$. Multiply the denominator $\sqrt[3]{3}$ by $\sqrt[3]{9}$ and the result is $\sqrt[3]{3 \cdot 9}$ or $\sqrt[3]{27}$.

$$\frac{\sqrt[3]{7}}{\sqrt[3]{3}} = \frac{\sqrt[3]{7} \cdot \sqrt[3]{9}}{\sqrt[3]{3} \cdot \sqrt[3]{9}} = \frac{\sqrt[3]{63}}{\sqrt[3]{27}} = \frac{\sqrt[3]{63}}{3}$$ □

PRACTICE
9 Rationalize each denominator.

a. $\dfrac{3}{\sqrt[3]{25}}$　　　　**b.** $\dfrac{\sqrt[3]{6}}{\sqrt[3]{5}}$

OBJECTIVE 4 ▶ Rationalizing denominators using conjugates. To rationalize a denominator that is a sum, such as the denominator in

$$\frac{2}{4 + \sqrt{3}}$$

we multiply the numerator and the denominator by $4 - \sqrt{3}$. The expressions $4 + \sqrt{3}$ and $4 - \sqrt{3}$ are called **conjugates** of each other. When a radical expression such as $4 + \sqrt{3}$ is multiplied by its conjugate $4 - \sqrt{3}$, the product simplifies to an expression that contains no radicals.

$$(a + b)(a - b) = a^2 - b^2$$
$$\left(4 + \sqrt{3}\right)\left(4 - \sqrt{3}\right) = 4^2 - \left(\sqrt{3}\right)^2 = 16 - 3 = 13$$

Then

$$\frac{2}{4 + \sqrt{3}} = \frac{2(4 - \sqrt{3})}{(4 + \sqrt{3})(4 - \sqrt{3})} = \frac{2(4 - \sqrt{3})}{13}$$

EXAMPLE 10 Rationalize each denominator and simplify.

a. $\dfrac{2}{1 + \sqrt{3}}$ **b.** $\dfrac{\sqrt{5} + 4}{\sqrt{5} - 1}$ **c.** $\dfrac{3}{1 + \sqrt{x}}$

Solution

a. Multiply the numerator and the denominator of this fraction by the conjugate of $1 + \sqrt{3}$, that is, by $1 - \sqrt{3}$.

$$\frac{2}{1 + \sqrt{3}} = \frac{2(1 - \sqrt{3})}{(1 + \sqrt{3})(1 - \sqrt{3})}$$

$$= \frac{2(1 - \sqrt{3})}{1^2 - (\sqrt{3})^2}$$

> ▶ **Helpful Hint**
> Don't forget that $(\sqrt{3})^2 = 3$.

$$= \frac{2(1 - \sqrt{3})}{1 - 3}$$

$$= \frac{2(1 - \sqrt{3})}{-2}$$

$$= -\frac{2(1 - \sqrt{3})}{2} \quad \frac{a}{-b} = -\frac{a}{b}$$

$$= -1(1 - \sqrt{3}) \quad \text{Simplify.}$$

$$= -1 + \sqrt{3} \quad \text{Multiply.}$$

b. $\dfrac{\sqrt{5} + 4}{\sqrt{5} - 1} = \dfrac{(\sqrt{5} + 4)(\sqrt{5} + 1)}{(\sqrt{5} - 1)(\sqrt{5} + 1)}$ Multiply the numerator and denominator by $\sqrt{5} + 1$, the conjugate of $\sqrt{5} - 1$.

$$= \frac{5 + \sqrt{5} + 4\sqrt{5} + 4}{5 - 1} \quad \text{Multiply.}$$

$$= \frac{9 + 5\sqrt{5}}{4} \quad \text{Simplify.}$$

c. $\dfrac{3}{1 + \sqrt{x}} = \dfrac{3(1 - \sqrt{x})}{(1 + \sqrt{x})(1 - \sqrt{x})}$ Multiply the numerator and denominator by $1 - \sqrt{x}$, the conjugate of $1 + \sqrt{x}$.

$$= \frac{3(1 - \sqrt{x})}{1 - x}$$

□

PRACTICE
10 Rationalize each denominator and simplify.

a. $\dfrac{4}{1 + \sqrt{5}}$ **b.** $\dfrac{\sqrt{3} + 2}{\sqrt{3} - 1}$ **c.** $\dfrac{8}{5 - \sqrt{x}}$

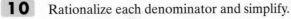

EXAMPLE 11 Simplify $\dfrac{12 - \sqrt{18}}{9}$.

**Solution** First simplify $\sqrt{18}$.

$$\frac{12 - \sqrt{18}}{9} = \frac{12 - \sqrt{9 \cdot 2}}{9} = \frac{12 - 3\sqrt{2}}{9}$$

Next, factor out a common factor of 3 from the terms in the numerator and the denominator and simplify.

$$\frac{12 - 3\sqrt{2}}{9} = \frac{3(4 - \sqrt{2})}{3 \cdot 3} = \frac{4 - \sqrt{2}}{3}$$

PRACTICE
11 Simplify $\dfrac{14 - \sqrt{28}}{6}$.

VOCABULARY & READINESS CHECK

Fill in the Blank.

1. $\sqrt{7} \cdot \sqrt{3} =$ _____

2. $\sqrt{10} \cdot \sqrt{10} =$ _____

3. $\dfrac{\sqrt{15}}{\sqrt{3}} =$ _____

4. The process of eliminating the radical in the denominator of a radical expression is called

_____ .

5. The conjugate of $2 + \sqrt{3}$ is _____ .

9.4 | EXERCISE SET

MyMathLab MathXL PRACTICE WATCH DOWNLOAD READ REVIEW

Multiply and simplify. Assume that all variables represent positive real numbers. See Examples 1, 2, 4, and 5.

1. $\sqrt{8} \cdot \sqrt{2}$

2. $\sqrt{3} \cdot \sqrt{12}$

3. $\sqrt{10} \cdot \sqrt{5}$

4. $\sqrt{2} \cdot \sqrt{14}$

5. $\left(\sqrt{6}\right)^2$

6. $\left(\sqrt{10}\right)^2$

7. $\sqrt{2x} \cdot \sqrt{2x}$

8. $\sqrt{5y} \cdot \sqrt{5y}$

9. $\left(2\sqrt{5}\right)^2$

10. $\left(3\sqrt{10}\right)^2$

11. $\left(6\sqrt{x}\right)^2$

12. $\left(8\sqrt{y}\right)^2$

13. $\sqrt{3x^5} \cdot \sqrt{6x}$

14. $\sqrt{21y^7} \cdot \sqrt{3y}$

15. $\sqrt{2xy^2} \cdot \sqrt{8xy}$

16. $\sqrt{18x^2y^2} \cdot \sqrt{2x^2y}$

17. $\sqrt{6}\left(\sqrt{5} + \sqrt{7}\right)$

18. $\sqrt{10}\left(\sqrt{3} - \sqrt{7}\right)$

19. $\sqrt{10}\left(\sqrt{2} + \sqrt{5}\right)$

20. $\sqrt{6}\left(\sqrt{3} + \sqrt{2}\right)$

21. $\sqrt{7y}\left(\sqrt{y} - 2\sqrt{7}\right)$

22. $\sqrt{5b}\left(2\sqrt{b} + \sqrt{5}\right)$

23. $\left(\sqrt{3} + 6\right)\left(\sqrt{3} - 6\right)$

24. $\left(\sqrt{5} + 2\right)\left(\sqrt{5} - 2\right)$

25. $\left(\sqrt{3} + \sqrt{5}\right)\left(\sqrt{2} - \sqrt{5}\right)$

26. $\left(\sqrt{7} + \sqrt{5}\right)\left(\sqrt{2} - \sqrt{5}\right)$

27. $\left(2\sqrt{11} + 1\right)\left(\sqrt{11} - 6\right)$

28. $\left(5\sqrt{3} + 2\right)\left(\sqrt{3} - 1\right)$

29. $(\sqrt{x} + 6)(\sqrt{x} - 6)$

30. $(\sqrt{y} + 5)(\sqrt{y} - 5)$

31. $(\sqrt{x} - 7)^2$

32. $(\sqrt{x} + 4)^2$

33. $\left(\sqrt{6y} + 1\right)^2$

34. $\left(\sqrt{3y} - 2\right)^2$

Divide and simplify. Assume that all variables represent positive real numbers. See Example 6.

35. $\dfrac{\sqrt{32}}{\sqrt{2}}$

36. $\dfrac{\sqrt{40}}{\sqrt{10}}$

37. $\dfrac{\sqrt{21}}{\sqrt{3}}$

38. $\dfrac{\sqrt{55}}{\sqrt{5}}$

39. $\dfrac{\sqrt{90}}{\sqrt{5}}$

40. $\dfrac{\sqrt{96}}{\sqrt{8}}$

41. $\dfrac{\sqrt{75y^5}}{\sqrt{3y}}$

42. $\dfrac{\sqrt{24x^7}}{\sqrt{6x}}$

43. $\dfrac{\sqrt{150}}{\sqrt{2}}$

44. $\dfrac{\sqrt{120}}{\sqrt{3}}$

45. $\dfrac{\sqrt{72y^5}}{\sqrt{3y^3}}$

46. $\dfrac{\sqrt{54x^3}}{\sqrt{2x}}$

47. $\dfrac{\sqrt{24x^3y^4}}{\sqrt{2xy}}$

48. $\dfrac{\sqrt{96x^5y^3}}{\sqrt{3x^2y}}$

Rationalize each denominator and simplify. Assume that all variables represent positive real numbers. See Example 8.

49. $\dfrac{\sqrt{3}}{\sqrt{5}}$

50. $\dfrac{\sqrt{2}}{\sqrt{3}}$

51. $\dfrac{7}{\sqrt{2}}$

52. $\dfrac{8}{\sqrt{11}}$

53. $\dfrac{1}{\sqrt{6y}}$

54. $\dfrac{1}{\sqrt{10z}}$

55. $\sqrt{\dfrac{3}{x}}$

56. $\sqrt{\dfrac{5}{x}}$

57. $\sqrt{\dfrac{1}{8}}$

58. $\sqrt{\dfrac{1}{27}}$

59. $\sqrt{\dfrac{2}{15}}$

60. $\sqrt{\dfrac{11}{14}}$

61. $\dfrac{8y}{\sqrt{5}}$

62. $\dfrac{7x}{\sqrt{2}}$

63. $\sqrt{\dfrac{y}{12x}}$

64. $\sqrt{\dfrac{x}{20y}}$

Rationalize each denominator and simplify. Assume that all variables represent positive real numbers. See Example 10.

65. $\dfrac{3}{\sqrt{2}+1}$

66. $\dfrac{6}{\sqrt{5}+2}$

67. $\dfrac{\sqrt{5}+1}{\sqrt{6}-\sqrt{5}}$

68. $\dfrac{\sqrt{3}+1}{\sqrt{3}-\sqrt{2}}$

69. $\dfrac{3}{\sqrt{x}-4}$

70. $\dfrac{4}{\sqrt{x}-1}$

MIXED PRACTICE

Rationalize each denominator and simplify.

71. $\sqrt{\dfrac{3}{20}}$

72. $\sqrt{\dfrac{3}{50}}$

73. $\dfrac{4}{2-\sqrt{5}}$

74. $\dfrac{2}{1-\sqrt{2}}$

75. $\dfrac{3x}{\sqrt{2x}}$

76. $\dfrac{5y}{\sqrt{3y}}$

77. $\dfrac{5}{2+\sqrt{x}}$

78. $\dfrac{9}{3+\sqrt{x}}$

Simplify the following. See Example 11.

79. $\dfrac{6+2\sqrt{3}}{2}$

80. $\dfrac{9+6\sqrt{2}}{3}$

81. $\dfrac{18-12\sqrt{5}}{6}$

82. $\dfrac{8-20\sqrt{3}}{4}$

83. $\dfrac{15\sqrt{3}+5}{5}$

84. $\dfrac{8+16\sqrt{2}}{8}$

Multiply or divide as indicated. See Examples 3 and 7.

85. $\sqrt[3]{12}\cdot\sqrt[3]{4}$

86. $\sqrt[3]{9}\cdot\sqrt[3]{6}$

87. $2\sqrt[3]{5}\cdot6\sqrt[3]{2}$

88. $8\sqrt[3]{4}\cdot7\sqrt[3]{7}$

89. $\sqrt[3]{15}\cdot\sqrt[3]{25}$

90. $\sqrt[3]{4}\cdot\sqrt[3]{4}$

91. $\dfrac{\sqrt[3]{54}}{\sqrt[3]{2}}$

92. $\dfrac{\sqrt[3]{80}}{\sqrt[3]{10}}$

93. $\dfrac{\sqrt[3]{120}}{\sqrt[3]{5}}$

94. $\dfrac{\sqrt[3]{270}}{\sqrt[3]{5}}$

Rationalize each denominator. See Example 9.

95. $\sqrt[3]{\dfrac{5}{4}}$

96. $\sqrt[3]{\dfrac{7}{9}}$

97. $\dfrac{6}{\sqrt[3]{2}}$

98. $\dfrac{3}{\sqrt[3]{5}}$

99. $\sqrt[3]{\dfrac{1}{9}}$

100. $\sqrt[3]{\dfrac{8}{11}}$

101. $\sqrt[3]{\dfrac{2}{9}}$

102. $\sqrt[3]{\dfrac{3}{4}}$

REVIEW AND PREVIEW

Solve each equation. See Sections 2.4 and 6.3.

103. $x+5=7^2$

104. $2y-1=3^2$

105. $4z^2+6z-12=(2z)^2$

106. $16x^2+x+9=(4x)^2$

107. $9x^2+5x+4=(3x+1)^2$

108. $x^2+3x+4=(x+2)^2$

CONCEPT EXTENSIONS

△ **109.** Find the area of a rectangle whose length is $13\sqrt{2}$ meters and width is $5\sqrt{6}$ meters.

$5\sqrt{6}$

$13\sqrt{2}$

△ **110.** Find the volume of a cube whose length is $\sqrt{3}$ feet, width is $\sqrt{2}$ feet, and height is $\sqrt{2}$ feet.

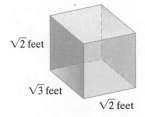

$\sqrt{2}$ feet

$\sqrt{3}$ feet

$\sqrt{2}$ feet

△ **111.** If a circle has area A, then the formula for the radius r of the circle is

$$r=\sqrt{\dfrac{A}{\pi}}$$

Simplify this expression by rationalizing the denominator.

△ **112.** If a round ball has volume V, then the formula for the radius r of the ball is

$$r = \sqrt[3]{\frac{3V}{4\pi}}$$

Simplify this expression by rationalizing the denominator.

True or False. *Identify each statement as true or false. See the Concept Check in this section.*

113. $\sqrt{5} \cdot \sqrt{5} = 5$

114. $\sqrt{5} \cdot \sqrt{3} = 15$

115. $\sqrt{3x} \cdot \sqrt{3x} = 2\sqrt{3x}$

116. $\sqrt{3x} + \sqrt{3x} = 2\sqrt{3x}$

117. $\sqrt{11} + \sqrt{2} = \sqrt{13}$

118. $\sqrt{11} \cdot \sqrt{2} = \sqrt{22}$

119. When rationalizing the denominator of $\dfrac{\sqrt{2}}{\sqrt{3}}$, explain why both the numerator and the denominator must be multiplied by $\sqrt{3}$.

120. In your own words, explain why $\sqrt{6} + \sqrt{2}$ cannot be simplified further, but $\sqrt{6} \cdot \sqrt{2}$ can be.

121. When rationalizing the denominator of $\dfrac{\sqrt[3]{2}}{\sqrt[3]{3}}$, explain why both the numerator and the denominator must be multiplied by $\sqrt[3]{9}$.

122. When rationalizing the denominator of $\dfrac{5}{1 + \sqrt{2}}$, explain why multiplying by $\dfrac{\sqrt{2}}{\sqrt{2}}$ will not accomplish this, but multiplying by $\dfrac{1 - \sqrt{2}}{1 - \sqrt{2}}$ will.

It is often more convenient to work with a radical expression whose numerator is rationalized. Rationalize the numerator of each expression by multiplying the numerator and denominator by the conjugate of the numerator.

123. $\dfrac{\sqrt{3} + 1}{\sqrt{2} - 1}$

124. $\dfrac{\sqrt{2} - 2}{2 - \sqrt{3}}$

INTEGRATED REVIEW SIMPLIFYING RADICALS

Sections 9.1–9.4

Simplify. Assume that all variables represent positive numbers.

1. $\sqrt{36}$ **2.** $\sqrt{48}$ **3.** $\sqrt{x^4}$ **4.** $\sqrt{y^7}$

5. $\sqrt{16x^2}$ **6.** $\sqrt{18x^{11}}$ **7.** $\sqrt[3]{8}$ **8.** $\sqrt[4]{81}$

9. $\sqrt[3]{-27}$ **10.** $\sqrt{-4}$ **11.** $\sqrt{\dfrac{11}{9}}$ **12.** $\sqrt[3]{\dfrac{7}{64}}$

13. $-\sqrt{16}$ **14.** $-\sqrt{25}$ **15.** $\sqrt{\dfrac{9}{49}}$ **16.** $\sqrt{\dfrac{1}{64}}$

17. $\sqrt{a^8b^2}$ **18.** $\sqrt{x^{10}y^{20}}$ **19.** $\sqrt{25m^6}$ **20.** $\sqrt{9n^{16}}$

Add or subtract as indicated.

21. $5\sqrt{7} + \sqrt{7}$ **22.** $\sqrt{50} - \sqrt{8}$

23. $5\sqrt{2} - 5\sqrt{3}$ **24.** $2\sqrt{x} + \sqrt{25x} - \sqrt{36x} + 3x$

Multiply and simplify if possible.

25. $\sqrt{2} \cdot \sqrt{15}$ **26.** $\sqrt{3} \cdot \sqrt{3}$ **27.** $\left(2\sqrt{7}\right)^2$

28. $\left(3\sqrt{5}\right)^2$ **29.** $\sqrt{3}\left(\sqrt{11} + 1\right)$ **30.** $\sqrt{6}\left(\sqrt{3} - 2\right)$

31. $\sqrt{8y} \cdot \sqrt{2y}$ **32.** $\sqrt{15x^2} \cdot \sqrt{3x^2}$ **33.** $\left(\sqrt{x} - 5\right)\left(\sqrt{x} + 2\right)$

34. $\left(3 + \sqrt{2}\right)^2$

Divide and simplify if possible.

35. $\dfrac{\sqrt{8}}{\sqrt{2}}$ **36.** $\dfrac{\sqrt{45}}{\sqrt{15}}$ **37.** $\dfrac{\sqrt{24x^5}}{\sqrt{2x}}$ **38.** $\dfrac{\sqrt{75a^4b^5}}{\sqrt{5ab}}$

Rationalize each denominator.

39. $\sqrt{\dfrac{1}{6}}$ **40.** $\dfrac{x}{\sqrt{20}}$ **41.** $\dfrac{4}{\sqrt{6}+1}$ **42.** $\dfrac{\sqrt{2}+1}{\sqrt{x}-5}$

9.5 SOLVING EQUATIONS CONTAINING RADICALS

OBJECTIVES

1 Solve radical equations by using the squaring property of equality once.

2 Solve radical equations by using the squaring property of equality twice.

OBJECTIVE 1 ▶ Using the squaring property once. In this section, we solve **radical equations** such as

$$\sqrt{x+3} = 5 \quad \text{and} \quad \sqrt{2x+1} = \sqrt{3x}$$

Radical equations contain variables in the radicand. To solve these equations, we rely on the following squaring property.

> **The Squaring Property of Equality**
> If $a = b$, then $a^2 = b^2$.

Unfortunately, this squaring property does not guarantee that all solutions of the new equation are solutions of the original equation. For example, if we square both sides of the equation

$$x = 2$$

we have

$$x^2 = 4$$

This new equation has two solutions, 2 and -2, while the original equation $x = 2$ has only one solution. Thus, squaring both sides of the original equation resulted in an equation that has an **extraneous solution** that isn't a solution of the original equation. For this reason, we must **always check proposed solutions of radical equations in the original equation.** If a proposed solution does not work, we call that value an **extraneous solution.**

EXAMPLE 1   Solve: $\sqrt{x+3} = 5$

Solution   To solve this radical equation, we use the squaring property of equality and square both sides of the equation.

$$\sqrt{x+3} = 5$$
$$\left(\sqrt{x+3}\right)^2 = 5^2 \quad \text{Square both sides.}$$
$$x + 3 = 25 \quad \text{Simplify.}$$
$$x = 22 \quad \text{Subtract 3 from both sides.}$$

Check: We replace x with 22 in the original equation.

> ▶ **Helpful Hint**
> Don't forget to check the proposed solutions of radical equations in the original equation.

$$\sqrt{x+3} = 5 \quad \text{Original equation}$$
$$\sqrt{22+3} \stackrel{?}{=} 5 \quad \text{Let } x = 22.$$
$$\sqrt{25} \stackrel{?}{=} 5$$
$$5 = 5 \quad \text{True}$$

Since a true statement results, 22 is the solution.   □

PRACTICE
1   Solve: $\sqrt{x-5} = 2$

EXAMPLE 2 Solve: $\sqrt{x} + 6 = 4$

Solution First we set the radical by itself on one side of the equation. Then we square both sides.

$$\sqrt{x} + 6 = 4$$

$$\sqrt{x} = -2 \quad \text{Subtract 6 from both sides to get the radical by itself.}$$

Recall that $\sqrt{x}$ is the principal or nonnegative square root of x so that $\sqrt{x}$ cannot equal -2 and thus this equation has no solution. We arrive at the same conclusion if we continue by applying the squaring property.

$$\sqrt{x} = -2$$

$$\left(\sqrt{x}\right)^2 = (-2)^2 \quad \text{Square both sides.}$$

$$x = 4 \quad \text{Simplify.}$$

Check: We replace x with 4 in the original equation.

$$\sqrt{x} + 6 = 4 \quad \text{Original equation}$$

$$\sqrt{4} + 6 \stackrel{?}{=} 4 \quad \text{Let } x = 4.$$

$$2 + 6 = 4 \quad \text{False}$$

Since 4 *does not* satisfy the original equation, this equation has no solution. □

PRACTICE
2 Solve: $\sqrt{x} + 5 = 3$

Example 2 makes it very clear that we *must* check proposed solutions in the original equation to determine if they are truly solutions. Remember, if a proposed solution is not an actual solution, we say that the value is an **extraneous solution.**

The following steps can be used to solve radical equations containing square roots.

Solving a Radical Equation Containing Square Roots

STEP 1. Arrange terms so that one radical is by itself on one side of the equation. That is, isolate a radical.

STEP 2. Square both sides of the equation.

STEP 3. Simplify both sides of the equation.

STEP 4. If the equation still contains a radical term, repeat steps 1 through 3.

STEP 5. Solve the equation.

STEP 6. Check all solutions in the original equation for extraneous solutions.

EXAMPLE 3 Solve: $\sqrt{x} = \sqrt{5x - 2}$

Solution Each of the radicals is already isolated, since each is by itself on one side of the equation. So we begin solving by squaring both sides.

$$\sqrt{x} = \sqrt{5x - 2} \quad \text{Original equation}$$

$$\left(\sqrt{x}\right)^2 = \left(\sqrt{5x - 2}\right)^2 \quad \text{Square both sides.}$$

$$x = 5x - 2 \quad \text{Simplify.}$$

$$-4x = -2 \quad \text{Subtract } 5x \text{ from both sides.}$$

$$x = \frac{-2}{-4} = \frac{1}{2} \quad \text{Divide both sides by } -4 \text{ and simplify.}$$

Check: We replace x with $\frac{1}{2}$ in the original equation.

$$\sqrt{x} = \sqrt{5x - 2} \qquad \text{Original equation}$$

$$\sqrt{\frac{1}{2}} \overset{?}{=} \sqrt{5 \cdot \frac{1}{2} - 2} \qquad \text{Let } x = \frac{1}{2}.$$

$$\sqrt{\frac{1}{2}} \overset{?}{=} \sqrt{\frac{5}{2} - 2} \qquad \text{Multiply.}$$

$$\sqrt{\frac{1}{2}} \overset{?}{=} \sqrt{\frac{5}{2} - \frac{4}{2}} \qquad \text{Write 2 as } \frac{4}{2}.$$

$$\sqrt{\frac{1}{2}} = \sqrt{\frac{1}{2}} \qquad \text{True}$$

This statement is true, so the solution is $\frac{1}{2}$. □

PRACTICE
3 Solve: $\sqrt{7x - 4} = \sqrt{x}$

EXAMPLE 4 Solve: $\sqrt{4y^2 + 5y - 15} = 2y$

Solution The radical is already isolated, so we start by squaring both sides.

$$\sqrt{4y^2 + 5y - 15} = 2y$$

$$\left(\sqrt{4y^2 + 5y - 15}\right)^2 = (2y)^2 \qquad \text{Square both sides.}$$

$$4y^2 + 5y - 15 = 4y^2 \qquad \text{Simplify.}$$

$$5y - 15 = 0 \qquad \text{Subtract } 4y^2 \text{ from both sides.}$$

$$5y = 15 \qquad \text{Add 15 to both sides.}$$

$$y = 3 \qquad \text{Divide both sides by 5.}$$

Check: We replace y with 3 in the original equation.

$$\sqrt{4y^2 + 5y - 15} = 2y \qquad \text{Original equation}$$

$$\sqrt{4 \cdot 3^2 + 5 \cdot 3 - 15} \overset{?}{=} 2 \cdot 3 \qquad \text{Let } y = 3.$$

$$\sqrt{4 \cdot 9 + 15 - 15} \overset{?}{=} 6 \qquad \text{Simplify.}$$

$$\sqrt{36} \overset{?}{=} 6$$

$$6 = 6 \qquad \text{True}$$

This statement is true, so the solution is 3. □

PRACTICE
4 Solve: $\sqrt{16y^2 + 4y - 28} = 4y$

EXAMPLE 5 Solve: $\sqrt{x + 3} - x = -3$

Solution First we isolate the radical by adding x to both sides. Then we square both sides.

$$\sqrt{x + 3} - x = -3$$

$$\sqrt{x + 3} = x - 3 \qquad \text{Add } x \text{ to both sides.}$$

$$\left(\sqrt{x + 3}\right)^2 = (x - 3)^2 \qquad \text{Square both sides.}$$

$$x + 3 = \underbrace{x^2 - 6x + 9}$$

▶ **Helpful Hint**
Don't forget that $(x - 3)^2 = (x - 3)(x - 3) = x^2 - 6x + 9$.

To solve the resulting quadratic equation, we write the equation in standard form by subtracting x and 3 from both sides.

$$3 = x^2 - 7x + 9 \qquad \text{Subtract } x \text{ from both sides.}$$
$$0 = x^2 - 7x + 6 \qquad \text{Subtract 3 from both sides.}$$
$$0 = (x - 6)(x - 1) \qquad \text{Factor.}$$
$$0 = x - 6 \quad \text{or} \quad 0 = x - 1 \qquad \text{Set each factor equal to zero.}$$
$$6 = x \qquad\qquad 1 = x \qquad \text{Solve for } x.$$

Check: We replace x with 6 and then x with 1 in the original equation.

Let $x = 6$.

$$\sqrt{x + 3} - x = -3$$
$$\sqrt{6 + 3} - 6 \overset{?}{=} -3$$
$$\sqrt{9} - 6 \overset{?}{=} -3$$
$$3 - 6 \overset{?}{=} -3$$
$$-3 = -3 \quad \text{True}$$

Let $x = 1$.

$$\sqrt{x + 3} - x = -3$$
$$\sqrt{1 + 3} - 1 \overset{?}{=} -3$$
$$\sqrt{4} - 1 \overset{?}{=} -3$$
$$2 - 1 \overset{?}{=} -3$$
$$1 = -3 \quad \text{False}$$

Since replacing x with 1 resulted in a false statement, 1 is an extraneous solution. The only solution is 6. □

PRACTICE
5   Solve: $\sqrt{x + 15} - x = -5$

OBJECTIVE 2 ▶ Using the squaring property twice. If a radical equation contains two radicals, we may need to use the squaring property twice.

EXAMPLE 6   Solve: $\sqrt{x - 4} = \sqrt{x} - 2$

Solution

$$\sqrt{x - 4} = \sqrt{x} - 2$$
$$\left(\sqrt{x - 4}\right)^2 = \left(\sqrt{x} - 2\right)^2 \qquad \text{Square both sides.}$$
$$x - 4 = \underbrace{x - 4\sqrt{x} + 4}$$
$$-8 = -4\sqrt{x}$$
$$2 = \sqrt{x} \qquad \text{Divide both sides by } -4.$$
$$4 = x \qquad \text{Square both sides again.}$$

▶ **Helpful Hint**

$$\left(\sqrt{x} - 2\right)^2 = \left(\sqrt{x} - 2\right)\left(\sqrt{x} - 2\right)$$
$$= \sqrt{x} \cdot \sqrt{x} - 2\sqrt{x} - 2\sqrt{x} + 4$$
$$= x - 4\sqrt{x} + 4$$

Check the proposed solution in the original equation. The solution is 4. □

PRACTICE
6   Solve: $\sqrt{x - 4} = \sqrt{x - 16}$

9.5 | EXERCISE SET

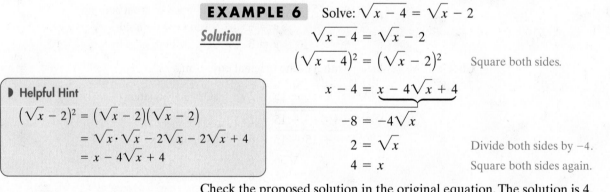

Solve each equation. See Examples 1 through 3.

1. $\sqrt{x} = 9$

2. $\sqrt{x} = 4$

3. $\sqrt{x + 5} = 2$

4. $\sqrt{x + 12} = 3$

5. $\sqrt{x} - 2 = 5$

6. $4\sqrt{x} - 7 = 5$

7. $3\sqrt{x} + 5 = 2$

8. $3\sqrt{x} + 8 = 5$

9. $\sqrt{x} = \sqrt{3x - 8}$

10. $\sqrt{x} = \sqrt{4x - 3}$

11. $\sqrt{4x - 3} = \sqrt{x + 3}$

12. $\sqrt{5x - 4} = \sqrt{x + 8}$

Solve each equation. See Examples 4 and 5.

13. $\sqrt{9x^2 + 2x - 4} = 3x$

14. $\sqrt{4x^2 + 3x - 9} = 2x$

15. $\sqrt{x} = x - 6$

16. $\sqrt{x} = x - 2$

17. $\sqrt{x + 7} = x + 5$

18. $\sqrt{x + 5} = x - 1$

19. $\sqrt{3x + 7} - x = 3$

20. $x = \sqrt{4x - 7} + 1$

21. $\sqrt{16x^2 + 2x + 2} = 4x$

22. $\sqrt{4x^2 + 3x + 2} = 2x$

23. $\sqrt{2x^2 + 6x + 9} = 3$

24. $\sqrt{3x^2 + 6x + 4} = 2$

Solve each equation. See Example 6.

25. $\sqrt{x - 7} = \sqrt{x} - 1$

26. $\sqrt{x - 8} = \sqrt{x} - 2$

27. $\sqrt{x} + 2 = \sqrt{x + 24}$

28. $\sqrt{x} + 5 = \sqrt{x + 55}$

29. $\sqrt{x + 8} = \sqrt{x} + 2$

30. $\sqrt{x} + 1 = \sqrt{x + 15}$

MIXED PRACTICE

Solve each equation. See Examples 1 through 6.

31. $\sqrt{2x + 6} = 4$

32. $\sqrt{3x + 7} = 5$

33. $\sqrt{x + 6} + 1 = 3$

34. $\sqrt{x + 5} + 2 = 5$

35. $\sqrt{x + 6} + 5 = 3$

36. $\sqrt{2x - 1} + 7 = 1$

37. $\sqrt{16x^2 - 3x + 6} = 4x$

38. $\sqrt{9x^2 - 2x + 8} = 3x$

39. $-\sqrt{x} = -6$

40. $-\sqrt{y} = -8$

41. $\sqrt{x + 9} = \sqrt{x} - 3$

42. $\sqrt{x} - 6 = \sqrt{x + 36}$

43. $\sqrt{2x + 1} + 3 = 5$

44. $\sqrt{3x - 1} + 1 = 4$

45. $\sqrt{x} + 3 = 7$

46. $\sqrt{x} + 5 = 10$

47. $\sqrt{4x} = \sqrt{2x + 6}$

48. $\sqrt{5x + 6} = \sqrt{8x}$

49. $\sqrt{2x + 1} = x - 7$

50. $\sqrt{2x + 5} = x - 5$

51. $x = \sqrt{2x - 2} + 1$

52. $\sqrt{2x - 4} + 2 = x$

53. $\sqrt{1 - 8x} - x = 4$

54. $\sqrt{2x + 5} - 1 = x$

REVIEW AND PREVIEW

Translate each sentence into an equation and then solve. See Section 2.5.

55. If 8 is subtracted from the product of 3 and x, the result is 19. Find x.

56. If 3 more than x is subtracted from twice x, the result is 11. Find x.

57. The length of a rectangle is twice the width. The perimeter is 24 inches. Find the length.

58. The length of a rectangle is 2 inches longer than the width. The perimeter is 24 inches. Find the length.

CONCEPT EXTENSIONS

Solve each equation.

59. $\sqrt{x - 3} + 3 = \sqrt{3x + 4}$

60. $\sqrt{2x + 3} = \sqrt{x - 2} + 2$

61. Explain why proposed solutions of radical equations must be checked in the original equation.

62. Is 8 a solution of the equation $\sqrt{x - 4} - 5 = \sqrt{x + 1}$? Explain why or why not.

63. **Multiple Steps.** The formula $b = \sqrt{\dfrac{V}{2}}$ can be used to determine the length b of a side of the base of a square-based pyramid with height 6 units and volume V cubic units.

a. Find the length of the side of the base that produces a pyramid with each volume. (Round to the nearest tenth of a unit.)

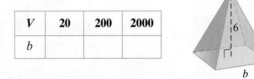

V	20	200	2000
b			

b. Notice in the table that volume V has been increased by a factor of 10 each time. Does the corresponding length b of a side increase by a factor of 10 each time also?

64. **Multiple Steps.** The formula $r = \sqrt{\dfrac{V}{2\pi}}$ can be used to determine the radius r of a cylinder with height 2 units and volume V cubic units.

a. Find the radius needed to manufacture a cylinder with each volume. (Round to the nearest tenth of a unit.)

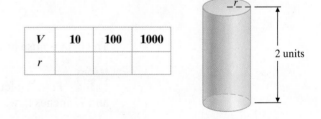

V	10	100	1000
r			

b. Notice in the table that volume V has been increased by a factor of 10 each time. Does the corresponding radius increase by a factor of 10 each time also?

Graphing calculators can be used to solve equations. To solve $\sqrt{x - 2} = x - 5$, for example, graph $y_1 = \sqrt{x - 2}$ and $y_2 = x - 5$ on the same set of axes. Use the Trace and Zoom features or an Intersect feature to find the point of intersection of the graphs. The x-value of the point is the solution of the equation. Use a graphing calculator to solve the equations below. Approximate solutions to the nearest hundredth.

65. $\sqrt{x - 2} = x - 5$

66. $\sqrt{x + 1} = 2x - 3$

67. $-\sqrt{x + 4} = 5x - 6$

68. $-\sqrt{x + 5} = -7x + 1$

9.6 RADICAL EQUATIONS AND PROBLEM SOLVING

OBJECTIVES

1 Use the Pythagorean formula to solve problems.

2 Use the converse of the Pythagorean theorem.

3 Use the distance formula.

4 Use the midpoint formula.

5 Solve problems using formulas containing radicals.

OBJECTIVE 1 ▶ Using the Pythagorean formula. Applications of radicals can be found in geometry, finance, science, and other areas of technology. Our first application involves the Pythagorean theorem, giving a formula that relates the lengths of the three sides of a right triangle. We first studied the Pythagorean theorem in Chapter 7 and we review it here.

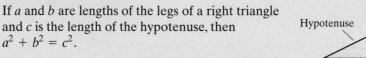

The Pythagorean Theorem

If a and b are lengths of the legs of a right triangle and c is the length of the hypotenuse, then $a^2 + b^2 = c^2$.

That is, the square of the length of the hypotenuse is equal to the sum of the squares of the lengths of the legs.

△ **EXAMPLE 1** Find the length of the hypotenuse of a right triangle whose legs are 6 inches and 8 inches long.

Solution Because this is a right triangle, we use the Pythagorean theorem. We let $a = 6$ inches and $b = 8$ inches. Length c must be the length of the hypotenuse.

$$a^2 + b^2 = c^2 \quad \text{Use the Pythagorean theorem.}$$
$$6^2 + 8^2 = c^2 \quad \text{Substitute the lengths of the legs.}$$
$$36 + 64 = c^2 \quad \text{Simplify.}$$
$$100 = c^2$$

Since c represents a length, we know that c is positive and is the principal square root of 100.

$$100 = c^2$$
$$\sqrt{100} = c \quad \text{Use the definition of principal square root.}$$
$$10 = c \quad \text{Simplify.}$$

The hypotenuse has a length of 10 inches. □

PRACTICE

1 Find the length of the hypotenuse of a right triangle whose legs are 5 inches and 12 inches long.

EXAMPLE 2 Find the length of the leg of the right triangle shown. Give the exact length and a two-decimal-place approximation.

Solution We let $a = 2$ meters and b be the unknown length of the other leg. The hypotenuse is $c = 5$ meters.

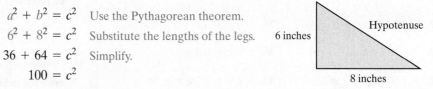

$$a^2 + b^2 = c^2 \quad \text{Use the Pythagorean theorem.}$$
$$2^2 + b^2 = 5^2 \quad \text{Let } a = 2 \text{ and } c = 5.$$
$$4 + b^2 = 25$$
$$b^2 = 21$$
$$b = \sqrt{21} \approx 4.58 \text{ meters}$$

The length of the leg is exactly $\sqrt{21}$ meters or approximately 4.58 meters. □

2   Find the length of the leg of the right triangle shown. Give the exact length and a two-decimal-place approximation.

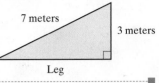

7 meters

3 meters

Leg

EXAMPLE 3   Finding a Distance

A surveyor must determine the distance across a lake at points P and Q as shown in the figure. To do this, she finds a third point R perpendicular to line PQ. If the length of $\overline{PR}$ is 320 feet and the length of $\overline{QR}$ is 240 feet, what is the distance across the lake? Approximate this distance to the nearest whole foot.

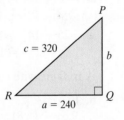

P

320 feet

R 240 feet Q

Solution

1. **UNDERSTAND.** Read and reread the problem. We will set up the problem using the Pythagorean theorem. By creating a line perpendicular to line PQ, the surveyor deliberately constructed a right triangle. The hypotenuse, $\overline{PR}$, has a length of 320 feet, so we let $c = 320$ in the Pythagorean theorem. The side $\overline{QR}$ is one of the legs, so we let $a = 240$ and $b =$ the unknown length.

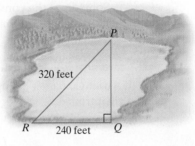

P

$c = 320$

b

R $a = 240$ Q

2. **TRANSLATE.**

$$a^2 + b^2 = c^2 \quad \text{Use the Pythagorean theorem.}$$
$$240^2 + b^2 = 320^2 \quad \text{Let } a = 240 \text{ and } c = 320.$$

3. **SOLVE.**

$$57{,}600 + b^2 = 102{,}400$$
$$b^2 = 44{,}800 \quad \text{Subtract 57,600 from both sides.}$$
$$b = \sqrt{44{,}800} \quad \text{Use the definition of principal square root.}$$

4. **INTERPRET.**

Check: See that $240^2 + \left(\sqrt{44{,}800}\right)^2 = 320^2$.

State: The distance across the lake is **exactly** $\sqrt{44{,}800}$ feet. The surveyor can now use a calculator to find that $\sqrt{44{,}800}$ feet is **approximately** 211.6601 feet, so the distance across the lake is roughly 212 feet.   □

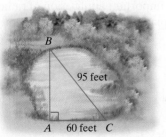

B

95 feet

A 60 feet C

3   Find the length of a bridge, to the nearest whole foot, to be constructed from point A to point B across Little Marsh. Use the distances shown in the diagram.

OBJECTIVE 2 ▶ Using the converse of the Pythagorean theorem. It is sometimes important to know whether a right triangle is formed, without the knowledge of the angle measures. For example, carpenters use the fact that if a triangle has side lengths of 3 units, 4 units, and 5 units, then it is a right triangle.

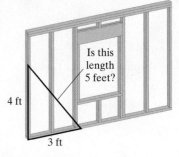

If the diagonal length between side marks of 3 and 4 feet, as shown, is 5 feet, the wall is "square." If not, adjustments are made.

The Pythagorean theorem, stated earlier in this section, states that if we have a right triangle, then $a^2 + b^2 = c^2$.

We call such a statement an "If p, then q" statement.

The **converse** of this statement is "If q, then p."

Sometimes the converse is true, sometimes it is false. In this case, the converse of the Pythagorean theorem is true and is stated below.

Converse of Pythagorean Theorem

If a triangle has side lengths a, b, and c units so that $a^2 + b^2 = c^2$, then the triangle is a right triangle.

EXAMPLE 4 Determine whether a triangle with the given side lengths is a right triangle.

a. 5, 12, 13   **b.** 3.1, 4.1, 5

Solution Let c be the longest length each time, the possible hypotenuse. The other two lengths are a and b, in any order.

a. Is $5^2 + 12^2 = 13^2$ True or false?

$$5^2 + 12^2 \stackrel{?}{=} 13^2$$
$$25 + 144 \stackrel{?}{=} 169$$
$$169 = 169 \quad \text{True.}$$

A triangle with side lengths 5, 12, and 13 units is a right triangle.

b. Is $3.1^2 + 4.1^2 = 5.1^2$?

$$9.61 + 16.81 \stackrel{?}{=} 26.01$$
$$26.42 \stackrel{?}{=} 26.01 \quad \text{False.}$$

A triangle with side lengths 3.1, 4.1, and 5.1 is *not* a right triangle.   ☐

PRACTICE

4 Determine whether a triangle with the given side lengths is a right triangle.

a. 6, 11, 13   **b.** 0.3, 0.4, 0.5

OBJECTIVE 3 ▶ Using the distance formula. A second important application of radicals is in finding the distance between two points in the plane. By using the Pythagorean theorem, the following formula can be derived.

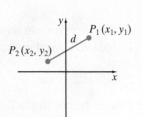

Distance Formula

The distance d between two points with coordinates (x_1, y_1) and (x_2, y_2) is given by

$$d = \sqrt{(x_2 - x_1)^2 + (y_2 - y_1)^2}$$

EXAMPLE 5   Find the distance between $(-1, 9)$ and $(-3, -5)$.

Solution   Use the distance formula with $(x_1, y_1) = (-1, 9)$ and $(x_2, y_2) = (-3, -5)$.

$$d = \sqrt{(x_2 - x_1)^2 + (y_2 - y_1)^2}$$ The distance formula.

$$= \sqrt{[-3 - (-1)]^2 + (-5 - 9)^2}$$ Substitute known values.

$$= \sqrt{(-2)^2 + (-14)^2}$$ Simplify.

$$= \sqrt{4 + 196}$$

$$= \sqrt{200} = 10\sqrt{2}$$ Simplify the radical.

The distance is **exactly** $10\sqrt{2}$ units or **approximately** 14.1 units.

PRACTICE
5   Find the distance between $(-2, 5)$ and $(-4, -7)$.

OBJECTIVE 4 ▶ Using the midpoint formula. The **midpoint** of a line segment is the **point** located exactly halfway between the two endpoints of the line segment. On the graph to the left, the point M is the midpoint of line segment PQ. Thus, the distance between M and P equals the distance between M and Q.

Note: We usually need no knowledge of roots to calculate the midpoint of a line segment. We review midpoint here only because it is often confused with the distance between two points.

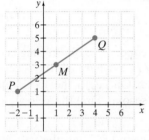

The x-coordinate of M is at half the distance between the x-coordinates of P and Q, and the y-coordinate of M is at half the distance between the y-coordinates of P and Q. That is, the x-coordinate of M is the average of the x-coordinates of P and Q; the y-coordinate of M is the average of the y-coordinates of P and Q.

Midpoint Formula

The midpoint of the line segment whose endpoints are (x_1, y_1) and (x_2, y_2) is the point with coordinates

$$\left(\frac{x_1 + x_2}{2}, \frac{y_1 + y_2}{2} \right)$$

EXAMPLE 6   Find the midpoint of the line segment that joins points $P(-3, 3)$ and $Q(1, 0)$.

Solution   Use the midpoint formula. It makes no difference which point we call (x_1, y_1) or which point we call (x_2, y_2). Let $(x_1, y_1) = (-3, 3)$ and $(x_2, y_2) = (1, 0)$.

$$\text{midpoint} = \left(\frac{x_1 + x_2}{2}, \frac{y_1 + y_2}{2} \right)$$

$$= \left(\frac{-3 + 1}{2}, \frac{3 + 0}{2} \right)$$

$$= \left(\frac{-2}{2}, \frac{3}{2} \right)$$

$$= \left(-1, \frac{3}{2} \right)$$

The midpoint of the segment is $\left(-1, \dfrac{3}{2}\right)$. □

PRACTICE
6 Find the midpoint of the line segment that joins points $P(5, -2)$ and $Q(8, -6)$.

▶ **Helpful Hint**

The distance between two points is a distance. The midpoint of a line segment is the point halfway between the endpoints of the segment.

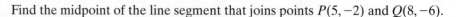

distance—measured in units

midpoint—it is a point

OBJECTIVE 5 ▶ **Using formulas containing radicals.** The Pythagorean theorem is an extremely important result in mathematics and should be memorized. But there are other applications involving formulas containing radicals that are not quite as well known, such as the velocity formula used in the next example.

EXAMPLE 7 Determining Velocity

A formula used to determine the velocity v, in feet per second, of an object (neglecting air resistance) after it has fallen a certain height is $v = \sqrt{2gh}$, where g is the acceleration due to gravity, and h is the height the object has fallen. On Earth, the acceleration g due to gravity is approximately 32 feet per second per second. Find the velocity of a person after falling 5 feet.

Solution We are told that $g = 32$ feet per second per second. To find the velocity v when $h = 5$ feet, we use the velocity formula.

$$
\begin{aligned}
v &= \sqrt{2gh} &&\text{Use the velocity formula.} \\
&= \sqrt{2 \cdot 32 \cdot 5} &&\text{Substitute known values.} \\
&= \sqrt{320} \\
&= 8\sqrt{5} &&\text{Simplify the radicand.}
\end{aligned}
$$

The velocity of the person after falling 5 feet is **exactly** $8\sqrt{5}$ feet per second, or **approximately** 17.9 feet per second. □

PRACTICE
7 Use the formula in Example 5 to find the velocity of an object after it has fallen 12 feet.

VOCABULARY & READINESS CHECK

Word Bank. *Use the choices below to fill in each blank. Some choices may be used more than once.*

distance   midpoint   point

1. The _____ of a line segment is a _____ exactly halfway between the two endpoints of the line segment.

2. The _____ formula is $d = \sqrt{(x_2 - x_1)^2 + (y_2 - y_1)^2}$.

3. The _____ formula is $\left(\dfrac{x_1 + x_2}{2}, \dfrac{y_1 + y_2}{2}\right)$.

9.6 | EXERCISE SET

Use the Pythagorean theorem to find the unknown side of each right triangle. See Examples 1 and 2.

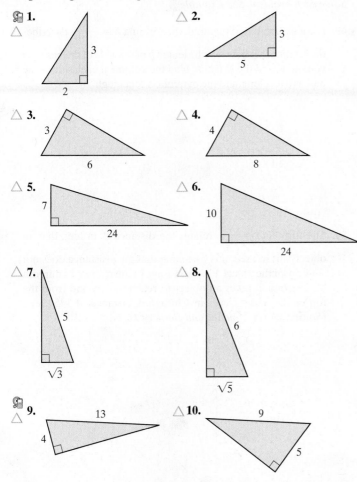

1.

3

2

2.

3

5

3.

3

6

4.

4

8

5.

7

24

6.

10

24

7.

5

$\sqrt{3}$

8.

6

$\sqrt{5}$

9.

13

4

10.

9

5

Find the length of the unknown side of each right triangle with sides a, b, and c, where c is the hypotenuse. See Examples 1 and 2.

11. $a = 4, b = 5$

12. $a = 2, b = 7$

13. $b = 2, c = 6$

14. $b = 1, c = 5$

15. $a = \sqrt{10}, c = 10$

16. $a = \sqrt{7}, c = \sqrt{35}$

Solve. See Examples 3 and 7.

17. Evan and Noah Saacks want to determine the distance at certain points across a pond on their property. They are able to measure the distances shown on the following diagram. Find how wide the pond is to the nearest tenth of a foot.

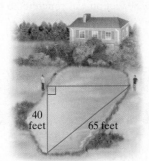

40 feet

65 feet

18. Use the formula from Example 7 and find the velocity of an object after it has fallen 20 feet.

20 feet

19. A wire is used to anchor a 20-foot-high pole. One end of the wire is attached to the top of the pole. The other end is fastened to a stake five feet away from the bottom of the pole. Find the length of the wire, to the nearest tenth of a foot.

20 feet

5 feet

20. Jim Spivey needs to connect two underground pipelines, which are offset by 3 feet, as pictured in the diagram. Neglecting the joints needed to join the pipes, find the length of the shortest possible connecting pipe rounded to the nearest hundredth of a foot.

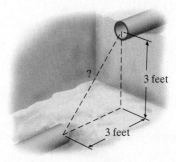

?

3 feet

3 feet

21. Robert Weisman needs to attach a diagonal brace to a rectangular frame in order to make it structurally sound. If the framework is 6 feet by 10 feet, find how long the brace needs to be to the nearest tenth of a foot.

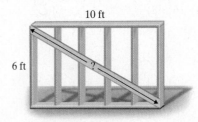

10 ft

6 ft

?

△ **22.** Elizabeth Kaster is flying a kite. She let out 80 feet of string and attached the string to a stake in the ground. The kite is now directly above her brother Mike, who is 32 feet away from Elizabeth. Find the height of the kite to the nearest foot.

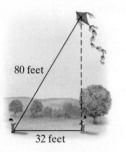

80 feet

32 feet

Determine whether a triangle with the given side lengths is a right triangle. See Example 4.

23. $0.6, 0.8, 1$

24. $0.5, 1.2, 1.3$

25. $9, 10, 13.5$

26. $8, 9, 12$

27. $2, 7, \sqrt{53}$

28. $3, 5, \sqrt{34}$

Use the distance formula to find the distance between the points given. See Example 5.

29. $(3, 6), (5, 11)$

30. $(2, 3), (9, 7)$

31. $(-3, 1), (5, -2)$

32. $(-2, 6), (3, -2)$

33. $(3, -2), (1, -8)$

34. $(-5, 8), (-2, 2)$

35. $\left(\frac{1}{2}, 2\right), (2, -1)$

36. $\left(\frac{1}{3}, 1\right), (1, -1)$

37. $(3, -2), (5, 7)$

38. $(-2, -3), (-1, 4)$

Find the midpoint of the line segment whose endpoints are given. See Example 6.

39. $(6, -8), (2, 4)$

40. $(3, 9), (7, 11)$

41. $(-2, -1), (-8, 6)$

42. $(-3, -4), (6, -8)$

43. $(7, 3), (-1, -3)$

44. $(-2, 5), (-1, 6)$

45. $\left(\frac{1}{2}, \frac{3}{8}\right), \left(-\frac{3}{2}, \frac{5}{8}\right)$

46. $\left(-\frac{2}{5}, \frac{7}{15}\right), \left(-\frac{2}{5}, -\frac{4}{15}\right)$

47 $(4.6, -3.5), (7.8, -9.8)$

48. $(-4.6, 2.1), (-6.7, 1.9)$

Solve each problem. See Example 7.

△ **49.** For a square-based pyramid, the formula $b = \sqrt{\dfrac{3V}{h}}$ describes the relationship between the length b of one side of the base, the volume V, and the height h. Find the volume if each side of the base is 6 feet long, and the pyramid is 2 feet high.

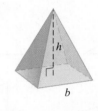

h

b

50. The formula $t = \dfrac{\sqrt{d}}{4}$ relates the distance d, in feet, that an object falls in t seconds, assuming that air resistance does not slow down the object. Find how long, to the nearest hundredth of a second, it takes an object to reach the ground from the top of the Sears Tower in Chicago, a distance of 1450 feet. (*Source: World Almanac and Book of Facts*)

d

51. Police use the formula $s = \sqrt{30fd}$ to estimate the speed s of a car in miles per hour. In this formula, d represents the distance the car skidded in feet and f represents the coefficient of friction. The value of f depends on the type of road surface, and for wet concrete f is 0.35. Find how fast a car was moving if it skidded 280 feet on wet concrete, to the nearest mile per hour.

d

52. The coefficient of friction of a certain dry road is 0.95. Use the formula in Exercise 35 to find how far a car will skid on this dry road if it is traveling at a rate of 60 mph. Round the length to the nearest foot.

53. The formula $v = \sqrt{2.5r}$ can be used to estimate the maximum safe velocity, v, in miles per hour, at which a car can travel if it is driven along a curved road with a **radius of curvature,** r, in feet. To the nearest whole number, find the maximum safe speed if a cloverleaf exit on an expressway has a radius of curvature of 300 feet.

54. Use the formula from Exercise 53 to find the radius of curvature if the safe velocity is 30 mph.

55. The maximum distance d in kilometers that you can see from a height of h meters is given by $d = 3.5\sqrt{h}$. Find how far you can see from the top of the Texas Commerce Tower in Houston, a height of 305.4 meters. Round to the nearest tenth of a kilometer. (*Source: World Almanac and Book of Facts*)

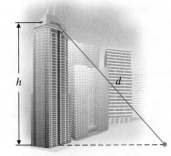

56. Use the formula from Exercise 55 to determine how high above the ground you need to be to see 40 kilometers. Round to the nearest tenth of a meter.

REVIEW AND PREVIEW

Simplify using rules for exponents. See Section 6.1.

57. 2^5

58. $(-3)^3$

59. $\left(-\dfrac{1}{5}\right)^2$

60. $\left(\dfrac{2}{7}\right)^3$

61. $x^2 \cdot x^3$

62. $x^4 \cdot x^2$

63. $y^3 \cdot y$

64. $x \cdot x^7$

CONCEPT EXTENSIONS

For each triangle, find the length of y, then x.

65.

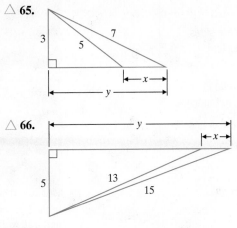

66.

Solve.

67. Mike and Sandra Hallahan leave the seashore at the same time. Mike drives northward at a rate of 30 miles per hour, while Sandra drives west at 60 mph. Find how far apart they are after 3 hours to the nearest mile.

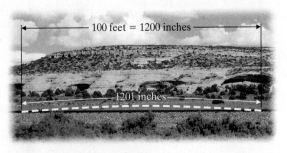

68. Railroad tracks are invariably made up of relatively short sections of rail connected by expansion joints. To see why this construction is necessary, consider a single rail 100 feet long (or 1200 inches). On an extremely hot day, suppose it expands 1 inch in the hot sun to a new length of 1201 inches. Theoretically, the track would bow upward as pictured.

Let us approximate the bulge in the railroad this way. Calculate the height h of the bulge.

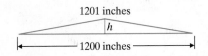

69. Based on the results of Exercise 68, explain why railroads use short sections of rail connected by expansion joints.

9.7 RIGHT TRIANGLE TRIGONOMETRY

OBJECTIVES

1 Use the lengths of the sides of a right triangle to find trigonometric ratios.

2 Use trigonometric ratios to find missing parts of right triangles.

3 Use trigonometric ratios to solve applied problems.

In the last century, Ang Rita Sherpa climbed Mount Everest ten times, all without the use of bottled oxygen.

Mountain climbers have forever been fascinated by reaching the top of Mount Everest, sometimes with tragic results. The mountain, on Asia's Tibet-Nepal border, is Earth's highest, peaking at an incredible 29,035 feet. The heights of mountains can be found using **trigonometry**. The word *trigonometry* means *measurement of triangles*. Trigonometry is used in navigation, building, and engineering. Today, trigonometry is used to study the structure of DNA, the master molecule that determines how we grow from a single cell to a complex, fully developed adult.

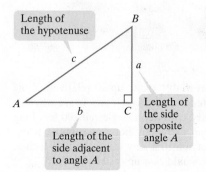

Naming a right triangle's sides from the point of view of an acute angle

OBJECTIVE 1 ▶ **Ratios in right triangles.** The right triangle forms the basis of trigonometry. If either acute angle of a right triangle stays the same size, the shape of the triangle does not change even if it is made larger or smaller. Because of properties of similar triangles, this means that the ratios of certain lengths stay the same regardless of the right triangle's size. These ratios have special names and are defined in terms of the **side opposite** an acute angle, the **side adjacent** to the acute angle, and the **hypotenuse.** In the right triangle shown, the length of the hypotenuse, the side opposite the 90° angle, is represented by c. The length of the side opposite angle A is represented by a. The length of the side adjacent to angle A is represented by b.

The three fundamental trigonometric ratios, **sine** (abbreviated sin), **cosine** (abbreviated cos), and **tangent** (abbreviated tan), are defined as ratios of the lengths of the sides of a right triangle. In the box that follows, when a side of a triangle is mentioned, we are referring to the *length* of that side.

Trigonometric Ratios

Let A represent an acute angle of a right triangle, with right angle C, shown in the margin. For angle A, the trigonometric ratios are defined as follows:

$$\boxed{\text{sine of } A} \quad \sin A = \frac{\text{side opposite angle } A}{\text{hypotenuse}} = \frac{a}{c}$$

$$\boxed{\text{cosine of } A} \quad \cos A = \frac{\text{side adjacent to angle } A}{\text{hypotenuse}} = \frac{b}{c}$$

$$\boxed{\text{tangent of } A} \quad \tan A = \frac{\text{side opposite angle } A}{\text{side adjacent to angle } A} = \frac{a}{b}.$$

> ▶ **Helpful Hint**
>
> The word
>
>   SOHCAHTOA (pronounced: so-cah-tow-ah)
>
> is a way to remember the definitions of the three trigonometric ratios.
>
>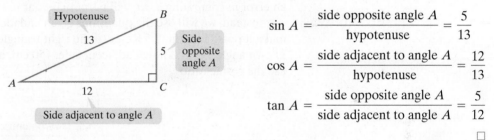
>
> "<u>S</u>ome <u>O</u>ld <u>H</u>og <u>C</u>ame <u>A</u>round <u>H</u>ere and <u>T</u>ook <u>O</u>ur <u>A</u>pples."

EXAMPLE 1   Becoming Familiar with the Trigonometric Ratios

Find the sine, cosine, and tangent of A in the triangle shown.

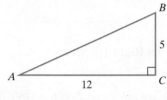

Solution   We begin by finding the measure of the hypotenuse c using the Pythagorean Theorem.

$$c^2 = a^2 + b^2 = 5^2 + 12^2 = 25 + 144 = 169$$
$$c = \sqrt{169} = 13$$

Now, we apply the definitions of the trigonometric ratios.

$$\sin A = \frac{\text{side opposite angle } A}{\text{hypotenuse}} = \frac{5}{13}$$

$$\cos A = \frac{\text{side adjacent to angle } A}{\text{hypotenuse}} = \frac{12}{13}$$

$$\tan A = \frac{\text{side opposite angle } A}{\text{side adjacent to angle } A} = \frac{5}{12}$$

PRACTICE

1   Find the sine, cosine, and tangent of A in the figure shown.

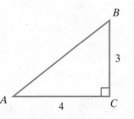

OBJECTIVE 2 ▶ Finding missing parts of right triangles. A scientific or graphing calculator in the degree mode will give you decimal approximations for the trigonometric ratios of any angle. For example, to find an approximation for tan 37°, the tangent of 37°, a keystroke sequence similar to one of the following can be used:

Many Scientific Calculators: 37 TAN

Many Graphing Calculators: TAN 37 ENTER .

The tangent of 37°, rounded to four decimal places, is 0.7536.

If we are given the length of one side and the measure of an acute angle of a right triangle, we can use trigonometry to solve for the length of either of the other two sides. Example 2 illustrates how this is done.

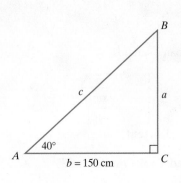

A   40°

b = 150 cm   C

EXAMPLE 2   Finding a Missing Leg of a Right Triangle

Find a in the right triangle shown in the margin.

Solution   We need to identify a trigonometric ratio that will make it possible to find a. Because we have a known angle, 40°, an unknown opposite side, a, and a known adjacent side, 150 cm, we use the tangent ratio.

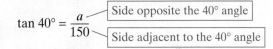

$$\tan 40° = \frac{a}{150}$$

⟶ Side opposite the 40° angle
⟶ Side adjacent to the 40° angle

Now we solve for a by multiplying both sides by 150.

$$a = 150 \tan 40° \approx 126$$

The tangent ratio reveals that a is approximately 126 centimeters. ☐

PRACTICE
2   In the triangle for Example 2, let $m \angle A = 62°$ and $b = 140$ cm. Find a to the nearest centimeter.

EXAMPLE 3   Finding a Missing Hypotenuse of a Right Triangle

Find c in the right triangle used in Example 2.

Solution   In Example 2, we found a: $a \approx 126$. Because we are given that $b = 150$, it is possible to find c using the Pythagorean Theorem: $c^2 = a^2 + b^2$. However, if we made an error in computing a, we will perpetuate our mistake using this approach.

Instead, we will use the quantities given and identify a trigonometric ratio that will make it possible to find c. Refer to the right triangle in the margin. Because we have a known angle, 40°, a known adjacent side, 150 cm, and an unknown hypotenuse, c, we use the cosine ratio.

$$\cos 40° = \frac{150}{c}$$

⟶ Side adjacent to the 40° angle
⟶ Hypotenuse

$c \cos 40° = 150$	Multiply both sides by c.
$c = \dfrac{150}{\cos 40°}$	Divide both sides by $\cos 40°$.
$c \approx 196$	Use a calculator.

The cosine ratio reveals that the hypotenuse is approximately 196 centimeters. ☐

PRACTICE
3   In the triangle for Example 2, let $m \angle A = 62°$ and $b = 140$ cm. Find c to the nearest centimeter.

OBJECTIVE 3 ▶ Applications of the trigonometric ratios. Trigonometry was first developed to measure heights and distances that are inconvenient or impossible to measure. These applications often involve the angle made with an imaginary horizontal line. As shown in the figure that follows, an angle formed by a horizontal line and the line of sight to an object that is above the horizontal line is called the **angle of elevation.** The angle formed by a horizontal line and the line of sight to an object that is below the horizontal line is called the **angle of depression.** Transits and sextants are instruments used to measure such angles.

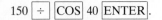

TECHNOLOGY NOTE

Here is the keystroke sequence for 150 tan 40°:

MANY SCIENTIFIC CALCULATORS

150 ☒ 40 TAN =

MANY GRAPHING CALCULATORS

150 TAN 40 ENTER.

TECHNOLOGY NOTE

Here is the keystroke sequence for $\dfrac{150}{\cos 40°}$:

MANY SCIENTIFIC CALCULATORS

150 ÷ 40 COS =

MANY GRAPHING CALCULATORS

150 ÷ COS 40 ENTER.

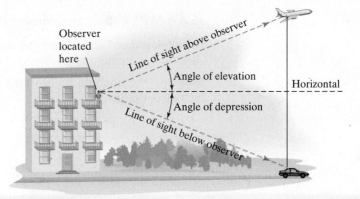

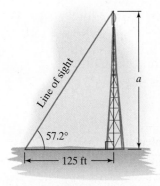

Determining height without using
direct measurement

EXAMPLE 4   Problem Solving Using an Angle of Elevation

From a point on level ground 125 feet from the base of a tower, the angle of elevation to the top of the tower is 57.2°. Approximate the height of the tower to the nearest foot.

Solution   A sketch is shown in the margin, where a represents the height of the tower. In the right triangle, we have a known angle, an unknown opposite side, and a known adjacent side. Therefore, we use the tangent ratio.

$$\tan 57.2° = \frac{a}{125}$$

- Side opposite the 57.2° angle
- Side adjacent to the 57.2° angle

We solve for a by multiplying both sides of this equation by 125:

$$a = 125 \tan 57.2° \approx 194.$$

The tower is approximately 194 feet high.   □

PRACTICE
4   From a point on level ground 80 feet from the base of the Eiffel Tower, the angle of elevation is 85.4°. Approximate the height of the Eiffel Tower to the nearest foot.

If the measures of two sides of a right triangle are known, the measures of the two acute angles can be found using the **inverse trigonometric keys** on a calculator. For example, suppose that $\sin A = 0.866$. We can find the measure of angle A by using the _inverse sine_ key, usually labeled $\boxed{\text{SIN}^{-1}}$. The key $\boxed{\text{SIN}^{-1}}$ is not a button you will actually press; it is the secondary function for the button labeled $\boxed{\text{SIN}}$.

Many Scientific Calculators:

.866 $\boxed{\text{2nd}}$ $\boxed{\text{SIN}}$

Pressing $\boxed{\text{2nd}}$ $\boxed{\text{SIN}}$ accesses the inverse sine key, $\boxed{\text{SIN}^{-1}}$.

Many Graphing Calculators:

$\boxed{\text{2nd}}$ $\boxed{\text{SIN}}$ .866 $\boxed{\text{ENTER}}$

The display should show approximately 59.99°, which can be rounded to 60°. Thus, if $\sin A = 0.866$, then $m\angle A \approx 60°$.

EXAMPLE 5 Determining the Angle of Elevation

A building that is 21 meters tall casts a shadow 25 meters long. Find the angle of elevation of the sun.

Solution The situation is illustrated below. We are asked to find $m\angle A$. We begin with the tangent ratio.

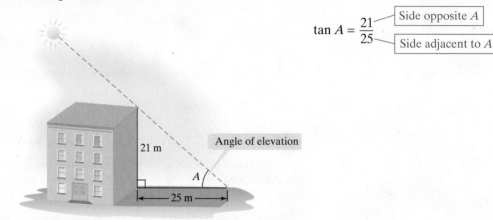

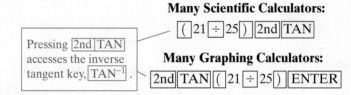

We use the **inverse tangent** key, $\boxed{\text{TAN}^{-1}}$, to find A.

Many Scientific Calculators:

$$\boxed{(}\ 21\ \boxed{\div}\ 25\ \boxed{)}\ \boxed{\text{2nd}}\ \boxed{\text{TAN}}$$

Pressing $\boxed{\text{2nd}}\ \boxed{\text{TAN}}$ accesses the inverse tangent key, $\boxed{\text{TAN}^{-1}}$.

Many Graphing Calculators:

$$\boxed{\text{2nd}}\ \boxed{\text{TAN}}\ \boxed{(}\ 21\ \boxed{\div}\ 25\ \boxed{)}\ \boxed{\text{ENTER}}$$

The display should show approximately 40. Thus, the angle of elevation of the sun is approximately 40°. □

PRACTICE
5 A flagpole that is 14 meters tall casts a shadow 10 meters long. Find the angle of elevation of the sun to the nearest degree.

9.7 | EXERCISE SET

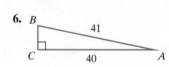

In Exercises 1–8, use the given right triangles to find ratios, in reduced form, for sin A, cos A, and tan A.

1.

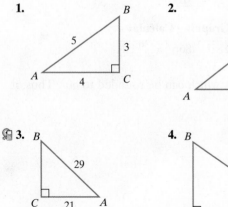

2.

3.

4.

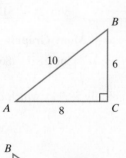

5.

6.

7.

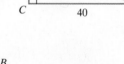

8.

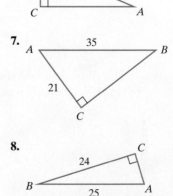

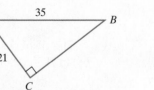

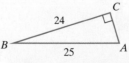

In Exercises 9–18, find the measure of the side of the right triangle whose length is designated by a lowercase letter. Round answers to the nearest whole number.

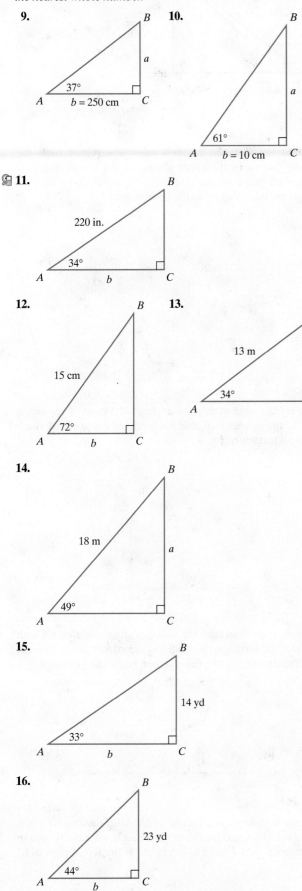

9.

B
a
37°
A *b* = 250 cm *C*

10.

B
a
61°
A *b* = 10 cm *C*

11.

B
220 in.
34°
A *b* *C*

12.

B
15 cm
72°
A *b* *C*

13.

B
13 m
a
34°
A *C*

14.

B
18 m
a
49°
A *C*

15.

B
14 yd
33°
A *b* *C*

16.

B
23 yd
44°
A *b* *C*

17.

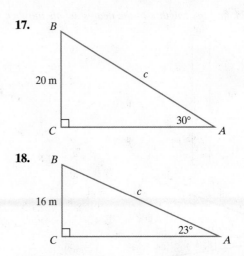

B
20 m
c
30°
C *A*

18.

B
16 m
c
23°
C *A*

In Exercises 19–22, find the measures of the parts of the right triangle that are not given. Round all answers to the nearest whole number.

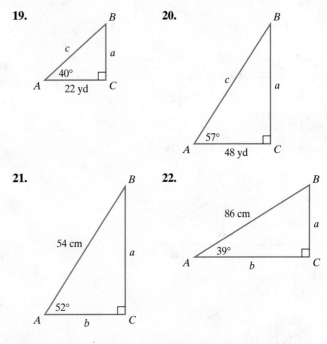

19.

B
c
a
40°
A 22 yd *C*

20.

B
c
a
57°
A 48 yd *C*

21.

B
54 cm
a
52°
A *b* *C*

22.

B
86 cm
a
39°
A *b* *C*

In Exercises 23–26, use the inverse trigonometric keys on a calculator to find the measure of angle *A*, rounded to the nearest whole degree.

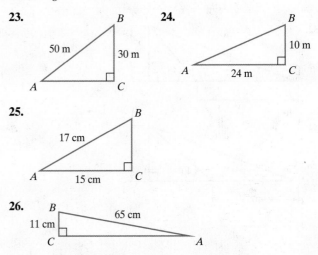

23.

B
50 m
30 m
A *C*

24.

B
10 m
A 24 m *C*

25.

B
17 cm
A 15 cm *C*

26.

B
65 cm
11 cm
C *A*

In Exercises 27–34, find the length x to the nearest whole number.

27.

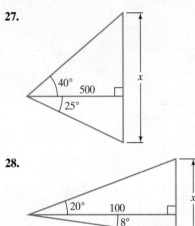

28.

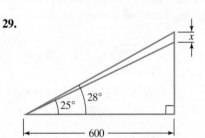

29.

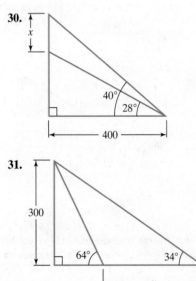

30.

31.

32.

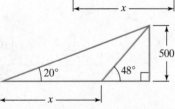

33.

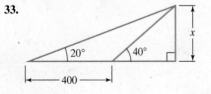

34.

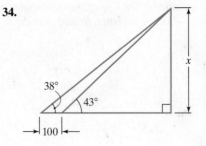

Solve.

35. To find the distance across a lake, a surveyor took the measurements in the figure shown at the top of the next page. Use these measurements to determine how far it is across the lake. Round to the nearest yard.

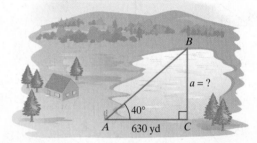

36. At a certain time of day, the angle of elevation of the sun is 40°. To the nearest foot, find the height of a tree whose shadow is 35 feet long.

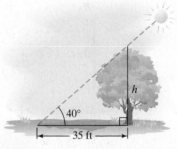

37. A plane rises from take-off and flies at an angle of 10° with the horizontal runway. When it has gained 500 feet in altitude, find the distance, to the nearest foot, the plane has flown.

38. A road is inclined at an angle of 5°. After driving 5000 feet along this road, find the driver's increase in altitude. Round to the nearest foot. (Refer to the figure at the top of page 611.)

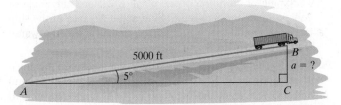

5000 ft

5°

B

a = ?

A   *C*

39. The tallest television transmitting tower in the world is in North Dakota. From a point on level ground 5280 feet (one mile) from the base of the tower, the angle of elevation to the top of the tower is 21.3°. Approximate the height of the tower to the nearest foot.

40. From a point on level ground 30 yards from the base of a building, the angle of elevation to the top of the building is 38.7°. Approximate the height of the building to the nearest foot.

41. The Statue of Liberty is approximately 305 feet tall. If the angle of elevation of a ship to the top of the statue is 23.7°, how far, to the nearest foot, is the ship from the statue's base?

42. A 200-foot cliff drops vertically into the ocean. If the angle of elevation of a ship to the top of the cliff is 22.3°, how far off shore, to the nearest foot, is the ship?

43. A tower that is 125 feet tall casts a shadow 172 feet long. Find the angle of elevation of the sun to the nearest degree.

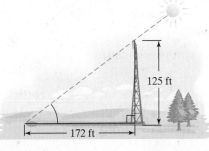

125 ft

172 ft

44. The Washington Monument is 555 feet high. If you stand one quarter of a mile, or 1320 feet, from the base of the monument and look to the top, find the angle of elevation to the nearest degree.

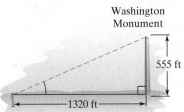

Washington
Monument

555 ft

1320 ft

45. A helicopter hovers 1000 feet above a small island. The figure shows that the angle of depression from the helicopter to point *P* is 36°. How far off the coast, to the nearest foot, is the island?

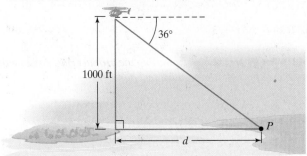

36°

1000 ft

P

d

46. A police helicopter is flying at 800 feet. A stolen car is sighted at an angle of depression of 72°. Find the distance of the stolen car, to the nearest foot, from a point directly below the helicopter.

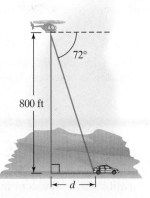

72°

800 ft

d

47. A wheelchair ramp is to be built beside the steps to the campus library. Find the angle of elevation of the 23-foot ramp, to the nearest tenth of a degree, if its final height is 6 feet.

48. A kite flies at a height of 30 feet when 65 feet of string is out. If the string is in a straight line, find the angle that it makes with the ground. Round to the nearest tenth of a degree.

49. If you are given the lengths of the sides of a right triangle, describe how to find the sine of either acute angle.

50. If the measure of one of the acute angles and the hypotenuse of a right triangle are known, describe how to find the measure of the remaining parts of the triangle.

51. Describe what is meant by an angle of elevation and an angle of depression.

52. Give an example of an applied problem that can be solved using one or more trigonometric ratios. Be as specific as possible.

53. Use a calculator to find each of the following: sin 32° and cos 58°; sin 17° and cos 73°; sin 50° and cos 40°; sin 88° and cos 2°. Describe what you observe. Based on your observations, what do you think the *co* in *cosine* stands for?

54. Stonehenge, the famous "stone circle" in England, was built between 2750 B.C. and 1300 B.C. using solid stone blocks weighing over 99,000 pounds each. It required 550 people to pull a single stone up a ramp inclined at a 9° angle. Describe how right triangle trigonometry can be used to determine the distance the 550 workers had to drag a stone in order to raise it to a height of 30 feet.

Decision Making

55. Explain why the sine or cosine of an acute angle cannot be greater than or equal to 1.

56. Describe what happens to the tangent of an angle as the measure of the angle gets close to 90°. What happens at 90°?

Solve.

57. From the top of a 250-foot lighthouse, a plane is sighted overhead and a ship is observed directly below the plane.

The angle of elevation of the plane is 22° and the angle of depression of the ship is 35°. Find **a.** the distance of the ship from the lighthouse; **b.** the plane's height above the water. Round to the nearest foot.

58. Sighting the top of a building, a surveyor measured the angle of elevation to be 22°. The transit is 5 feet above the ground and 300 feet from the building. Find the building's height. Round to the nearest foot.

CHAPTER 9 VOCABULARY CHECK

Fill in each blank with one of the words or phrases listed below.

index   rationalizing the denominator   principal square root   radicand $\left(\dfrac{x_1 + x_2}{2}, \dfrac{y_1 + y_2}{2}\right)$

conjugate   radical   like radicals   hypotenuse   trigonometry

$$a^2 + b^2 = c^2 \qquad \sqrt{(x_2 - x_1)^2 - (y_2 - y_1)^3}$$

1. The expressions $5\sqrt{x}$ and $7\sqrt{x}$ are examples of _____.

2. In the expression $\sqrt[3]{45}$ the number 3 is the _____, the number 45 is the _____, and $\sqrt{}$ is called the _____ sign.

3. The _____ of $(a + b)$ is $(a - b)$.

4. The _____ of 25 is 5.

5. The process of eliminating the radical in the denominator of a radical expression is called

_____.

6. The word _____ means measurement of triangles.

7. The sine of angle A is the quotient of the length of the side opposite angle A and the _____.

8. The distance formula is _____.

9. The midpoint formula is _____.

10. The Pythagorean formula is _____.

CHAPTER 9 REVIEW

(9.1) Find the root.

1. $\sqrt{81}$

2. $-\sqrt{49}$

3. $\sqrt[3]{27}$

4. $\sqrt[4]{16}$

5. $\sqrt[4]{\dfrac{16}{81}}$

6. $\sqrt[3]{-\dfrac{27}{64}}$

7. Which radical(s) is not a real number?

   a. $\sqrt{4}$ **b.** $-\sqrt{4}$ **c.** $\sqrt{-4}$ **d.** $\sqrt[3]{-4}$

8. Which radical(s) is not a real number?

   a. $\sqrt{-5}$ **b.** $\sqrt[3]{-5}$ **c.** $\sqrt[4]{-5}$ **d.** $\sqrt[5]{-5}$

Find the following roots. Assume that variables represent positive numbers only.

9. $\sqrt{x^{12}}$

10. $\sqrt{x^8}$

11. $\sqrt{9x^6}$

12. $\sqrt{25x^4}$

13. $\sqrt{\dfrac{16}{y^{10}}}$

14. $\sqrt{\dfrac{y^{12}}{49}}$

Identify the domain and then graph each function.

15. $g(x) = \sqrt[3]{x - 3}$; use the accompanying table.

x	-5	2	3	4	11
$g(x)$					

16. $f(x) = \sqrt{x} + 3$

(9.2) Simplify each expression using the product rule. Assume that variables represent nonnegative real numbers.

17. $\sqrt{54}$

18. $\sqrt{88}$

19. $\sqrt{150x^3}$

20. $\sqrt{92y^5}$

21. $\sqrt[3]{54}$

22. $\sqrt[3]{88}$

23. $\sqrt[4]{48}$

24. $\sqrt[4]{162}$

Simplify each expression using the quotient rule. Assume that variables represent positive real numbers.

25. $\sqrt{\dfrac{18}{25}}$

26. $\sqrt{\dfrac{75}{64}}$

27. $\sqrt{\dfrac{45y^2}{4x^4}}$

28. $\sqrt{\dfrac{20x^5}{9x^2}}$

29. $\sqrt[4]{\dfrac{9}{16}}$

30. $\sqrt[3]{\dfrac{40}{27}}$

31. $\sqrt[3]{\dfrac{3}{8}}$

32. $\sqrt[4]{\dfrac{5}{81}}$

(9.3) *Add or subtract by combining like radicals.*

33. $3\sqrt[3]{2} + 2\sqrt[3]{3} - 4\sqrt[3]{2}$

34. $5\sqrt{2} + 2\sqrt[3]{2} - 8\sqrt{2}$

35. $\sqrt{6} + 2\sqrt[3]{6} - 4\sqrt[3]{6} + 5\sqrt{6}$

36. $3\sqrt{5} - \sqrt[3]{5} - 2\sqrt{5} + 3\sqrt[3]{5}$

Add or subtract by simplifying each radical and then combining like terms. Assume that variables represent nonnegative real numbers.

37. $\sqrt{28x} + \sqrt{63x} + \sqrt[3]{56}$

38. $\sqrt{75y} + \sqrt{48y} - \sqrt[4]{16}$

39. $\sqrt{\dfrac{5}{9}} - \sqrt{\dfrac{5}{36}}$

40. $\sqrt{\dfrac{11}{25}} + \sqrt{\dfrac{11}{16}}$

41. $2\sqrt[3]{125} - 5\sqrt[3]{8}$

42. $3\sqrt[3]{16} - 2\sqrt[3]{2}$

(9.4) *Find the product and simplify if possible.*

43. $3\sqrt{10} \cdot 2\sqrt{5}$

44. $2\sqrt[3]{4} \cdot 5\sqrt[3]{6}$

45. $\sqrt{3}\left(2\sqrt{6} - 3\sqrt{12}\right)$

46. $4\sqrt{5}\left(2\sqrt{10} - 5\sqrt{5}\right)$

47. $\left(\sqrt{3} + 2\right)\left(\sqrt{6} - 5\right)$

48. $\left(2\sqrt{5} + 1\right)\left(4\sqrt{5} - 3\right)$

49. $\left(\sqrt{x} - 2\right)^2$

50. $\left(\sqrt{y} + 4\right)^2$

Divide and simplify if possible. Assume that all variables represent positive numbers.

51. $\dfrac{\sqrt{27}}{\sqrt{3}}$

52. $\dfrac{\sqrt{20}}{\sqrt{5}}$

53. $\dfrac{\sqrt{160}}{\sqrt{8}}$

54. $\dfrac{\sqrt{96}}{\sqrt{3}}$

55. $\dfrac{\sqrt{30x^6}}{\sqrt{2x^3}}$

56. $\dfrac{\sqrt{54x^5y^2}}{\sqrt{3xy^2}}$

Rationalize each denominator and simplify.

57. $\dfrac{\sqrt{2}}{\sqrt{11}}$

58. $\dfrac{\sqrt{3}}{\sqrt{13}}$

59. $\sqrt{\dfrac{5}{6}}$

60. $\sqrt{\dfrac{7}{10}}$

61. $\dfrac{1}{\sqrt{5x}}$

62. $\dfrac{5}{\sqrt{3y}}$

63. $\sqrt{\dfrac{3}{x}}$

64. $\sqrt{\dfrac{6}{y}}$

65. $\dfrac{3}{\sqrt{5} - 2}$

66. $\dfrac{8}{\sqrt{10} - 3}$

67. $\dfrac{\sqrt{2} + 1}{\sqrt{3} - 1}$

68. $\dfrac{\sqrt{3} - 2}{\sqrt{5} + 2}$

69. $\dfrac{10}{\sqrt{x} + 5}$

70. $\dfrac{8}{\sqrt{x} - 1}$

71. $\sqrt[3]{\dfrac{7}{9}}$

72. $\sqrt[3]{\dfrac{3}{4}}$

73. $\sqrt[3]{\dfrac{3}{2}}$

74. $\sqrt[3]{\dfrac{5}{4}}$

(9.5) *Solve each radical equations.*

75. $\sqrt{2x} = 6$

76. $\sqrt{x + 3} = 4$

77. $\sqrt{x + 3} = 8$

78. $\sqrt{x + 8} = 3$

79. $\sqrt{2x + 1} = x - 7$

80. $\sqrt{3x + 1} = x - 1$

81. $\sqrt{x + 3} = \sqrt{x + 15}$

82. $\sqrt{x - 5} = \sqrt{x - 1}$

(9.6) *Use the Pythagorean theorem to find the length of each unknown side. Give an exact answer and a two-decimal-place approximation.*

△ **83.**

△ **84.**

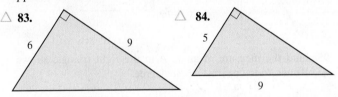

Solve. Give an exact answer and a two-decimal-place approximation.

△ **85.** Romeo is standing 20 feet away from the wall below Juliet's balcony during a school play. Juliet is on the balcony, 12 feet above the ground. Find how far apart Romeo and Juliet are.

△ **86.** The diagonal of a rectangle is 10 inches long. If the width of the rectangle is 5 inches, find the length of the rectangle.

Use the distance formula to find the distance between the points. Then use the midpoint formula to find the midpoint of the line segment whose endpoints are the two given points.

87. $(6, -2)$ and $(-3, 5)$

88. $(2, 8)$ and $(-6, 10)$

Use the formula $r = \sqrt{\dfrac{S}{4\pi}}$, where r = the radius of a sphere and S = the surface area of the sphere, for Exercises 89 and 90.

89. Find the radius of a sphere to the nearest tenth of an inch if the area is 72 square inches.

△ **90.** Find the exact surface area of a sphere if its radius is 6 inches. (Do not approximate π.)

(9.7)

91. Use the right triangle shown to find ratios, in reduced form, for sin *A*, cos *A*, and tan *A*.

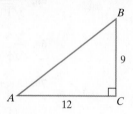

In Exercises 92–94, find the measure of the side of the right triangle whose length is designated by a lowercase letter. Round answers to the nearest whole number.

92.

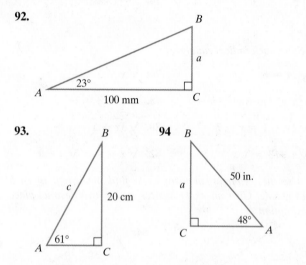

93.   **94.**

95. Find the measure of angle *A* in the right triangle shown. Round to the nearest whole degree.

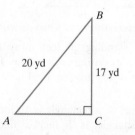

96. A hiker climbs for a half mile (2640 feet) up a slope whose inclination is 17°. How many feet of altitude, to the nearest foot, does the hiker gain?

97. To find the distance across a lake, a surveyor took the measurements in the figure shown. What is the distance across the lake? Round to the nearest meter.

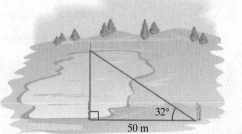

98. When a six-foot pole casts a four-foot shadow, what is the angle of elevation of the sun? Round to the nearest whole degree.

MIXED REVIEW

Find each root. Assume all variables represent positive numbers.

99. $\sqrt{144}$

100. $-\sqrt[3]{64}$

101. $\sqrt{16x^{16}}$

102. $\sqrt{4x^{24}}$

Simplify each expression. Assume all variables represent positive numbers.

103. $\sqrt{18x^7}$

104. $\sqrt{48y^6}$

105. $\sqrt{\dfrac{y^4}{81}}$

106. $\sqrt{\dfrac{x^9}{9}}$

Add or subtract by simplifying and then combining like terms. Assume all variables represent positive numbers.

107. $\sqrt{12} + \sqrt{75}$

108. $\sqrt{63} + \sqrt{28} - \sqrt[3]{27}$

109. $\sqrt{\dfrac{3}{16}} - \sqrt{\dfrac{3}{4}}$

110. $\sqrt{45x^3} + x\sqrt{20x} - \sqrt{5x^3}$

Multiply and simplify if possible. Assume all variables represent positive numbers.

111. $\sqrt{7} \cdot \sqrt{14}$

112. $\sqrt{3}\left(\sqrt{9} - \sqrt{2}\right)$

113. $\left(\sqrt{2} + 4\right)\left(\sqrt{5} - 1\right)$

114. $\left(\sqrt{x} + 3\right)^2$

Divide and simplify if possible. Assume all variables represent positive numbers.

115. $\dfrac{\sqrt{120}}{\sqrt{5}}$

116. $\dfrac{\sqrt{60x^9}}{\sqrt{15x^7}}$

Rationalize each denominator and simplify.

117. $\sqrt{\dfrac{2}{7}}$

118. $\dfrac{3}{\sqrt{2x}}$

119. $\dfrac{3}{\sqrt{x} - 6}$

120. $\dfrac{\sqrt{7} - 5}{\sqrt{5} + 3}$

Solve each radical equation.

121. $\sqrt{4x} = 2$

122. $\sqrt{x - 4} = 3$

123. $\sqrt{4x + 8} + 6 = x$

124. $\sqrt{x - 8} = \sqrt{x} - 2$

125. Use the Pythagorean theorem to find the length of the unknown side. Give an exact answer and a two-decimal-place approximation.

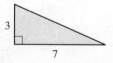

126. The diagonal of a rectangle is 6 inches long. If the width of the rectangle is 2 inches, find the length of the rectangle.

127. The Apple (computer) store on Fifth Avenue in New York City, which opened in 2006, features a distinctive glass cube. If the glass surface area of this cube (which includes only the four walls and the roof) is 5120 square feet, find the length of a side of the cube.

CHAPTER 9 TEST  The fully worked-out solutions to any exercises you want to review are available in MyMathLab.

Simplify the following. Indicate if the expression is not a real number.

1. $\sqrt{\dfrac{9}{25}}$

2. $\sqrt[3]{-125}$

3. $\sqrt[4]{-81}$

4. Identify the domain of $g(x)$. Then complete the accompanying table and graph $g(x)$.

$$g(x) = \sqrt{x+2}$$

x	-2	-1	2	7
$g(x)$				

Simplify each radical expression. Assume that variables represent positive numbers only.

5. $\sqrt{54}$

6. $\sqrt{92}$

7. $\sqrt{3x^6}$

8. $\sqrt{8x^4y^7}$

9. $\sqrt{9x^9}$

10. $\sqrt[3]{8}$

11. $\sqrt[3]{40}$

12. $\sqrt{x^{10}}$

13. $\sqrt{y^7}$

14. $\sqrt{\dfrac{5}{16}}$

15. $\sqrt{\dfrac{y^3}{25}}$

16. $\sqrt[3]{\dfrac{2}{27}}$

17. $3\sqrt{8x}$

Perform each indicated operation. Assume that all variables represent positive numbers.

18. $\sqrt{13} + \sqrt{13} - 4\sqrt{13}$

19. $\sqrt{12} - 2\sqrt{75}$

20. $\sqrt{2x^2} + \sqrt[3]{54} - x\sqrt{18}$

21. $\sqrt{\dfrac{3}{4}} + \sqrt{\dfrac{3}{25}}$

22. $\sqrt{7} \cdot \sqrt{14}$

23. $\sqrt{2}(\sqrt{6} - \sqrt{5})$

24. $(\sqrt{x} + 2)(\sqrt{x} - 3)$

25. $\dfrac{\sqrt{50}}{\sqrt{10}}$

26. $\dfrac{\sqrt{40x^4}}{\sqrt{2x}}$

Rationalize the denominator.

27. $\sqrt{\dfrac{2}{3}}$

28. $\sqrt[3]{\dfrac{5}{9}}$

29. $\sqrt{\dfrac{5}{12x^2}}$

30. $\dfrac{2\sqrt{3}}{\sqrt{3} - 3}$

Solve each of the following radical equations.

31. $\sqrt{x} + 8 = 11$

32. $\sqrt{3x - 6} = \sqrt{x + 4}$

33. $\sqrt{2x - 2} = x - 5$

△ **34.** Find the length of the unknown leg of a right triangle if the other leg is 8 inches long and the hypotenuse is 12 inches long.

35. Find the distance between $(-3, 6)$ and $(-2, 8)$.

36. Find the midpoint of the line segment whose endpoints are $\left(-\dfrac{2}{3}, -\dfrac{1}{5}\right)$ and $\left(-\dfrac{1}{3}, \dfrac{4}{5}\right)$.

37. Determine whether triangle with sides of lengths $2, 5$, and $\sqrt{29}$ units in a right triangle.

38. Find $\sin A$, $\cos A$, and $\tan A$.

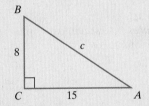

39. At a certain time of day, the angle of elevation of the sun is $34°$. If a building casts a shadow measuring 104 feet, find the height of the building to the nearest foot.

CHAPTER 9 STANDARDIZED TEST

Multiple Choice. *Choose the one alternative that best completes the statement or answers the question.*

Simplify the following. Indicate if the expression is not a real number.

1. $\sqrt{\dfrac{16}{49}}$

a. $\dfrac{4}{49}$

b. $\dfrac{8}{49}$

c. $\dfrac{4}{7}$

d. $\dfrac{8}{7}$

2. $\sqrt[3]{-27}$

a. 3

b. -9

c. -3

d. 9

3. $\sqrt[4]{-81}$

a. -3

b. not real number

c. -9

d. 3

Identify the domain of f(x). Then complete the accompanying table and graph f(x).

4. $f(x) = \sqrt{x} + 3$

x	$f(x)$
-3	
-2	
1	

a. $x \geq 0$

b. $x \geq 3$

c. $x \geq 0$

d. $x \geq -3$

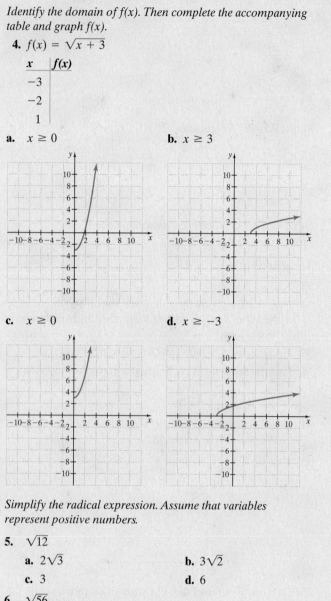

Simplify the radical expression. Assume that variables represent positive numbers.

5. $\sqrt{12}$

  a. $2\sqrt{3}$ **b.** $3\sqrt{2}$

  c. 3 **d.** 6

6. $\sqrt{56}$

  a. $4\sqrt{14}$ **b.** 28

  c. $2\sqrt{14}$ **d.** $14\sqrt{2}$

7. $\sqrt{7x^{10}}$

  a. $x^5\sqrt{7}$ **b.** $7\sqrt{x^5}$

  c. $7x^5$ **d.** $x^{10}\sqrt{7}$

8. $\sqrt{18x^4y^5}$

  a. $3x^2y^2\sqrt{2y}$ **b.** $9x^4y^4\sqrt{2y}$

  c. $3x^2y^2\sqrt{2xy}$ **d.** $9x^2y^2\sqrt{2y}$

9. $\sqrt{49x^{13}}$

  a. $7x^6x$ **b.** $7x^6\sqrt{x}$

  c. $49x^6\sqrt{x}$ **d.** $7x\sqrt{x^{11}}$

10. $\sqrt[3]{8}$

  a. 4 **b.** 2

  c. ± 2 **d.** 3

11. $\sqrt[3]{16}$

  a. $4\sqrt[3]{2}$ **b.** $2\sqrt[3]{4}$

  c. 4 **d.** $2\sqrt[3]{2}$

12. $\sqrt{z^{10}}$

  a. $2z$ **b.** z^{20}

  c. z^5 **d.** $5\sqrt{z}$

13. $\sqrt{y^{15}}$

  a. $y^{14}\sqrt{y}$ **b.** $\sqrt{y^{15}}$

  c. $y\sqrt{y^{13}}$ **d.** $y^7\sqrt{y}$

14. $\sqrt{\dfrac{17}{16}}$

  a. $\dfrac{17}{4}$ **b.** $\dfrac{\sqrt{17}}{4}$

  c. $\sqrt{\dfrac{17}{16}}$ **d.** $\dfrac{\sqrt{17}}{16}$

15. $\sqrt{\dfrac{x^{15}}{49}}$

  a. $\dfrac{x\sqrt{x^{13}}}{7}$ **b.** $\dfrac{x^7\sqrt{x}}{49}$

  c. $\dfrac{x^7x}{7}$ **d.** $\dfrac{x^7\sqrt{x}}{7}$

16. $\sqrt[3]{\dfrac{15}{64}}$

  a. $\dfrac{\sqrt[3]{15}}{4}$ **b.** $\dfrac{\sqrt[3]{15}}{4\sqrt{4}}$

  c. $\dfrac{15}{4}$ **d.** $\dfrac{\sqrt[3]{15}}{64}$

17. $2\sqrt{18y}$

  a. $3y\sqrt{2}$ **b.** $6y\sqrt{2}$

  c. $18\sqrt{2y}$ **d.** $6\sqrt{2y}$

Perform the indicated operation. Assume that variables represent positive numbers.

18. $3\sqrt{13} + \sqrt{13} - 6\sqrt{13}$

  a. $-3\sqrt{39}$ **b.** $-2\sqrt{13}$

  c. $-3\sqrt{13}$ **d.** $-2\sqrt{39}$

19. $\sqrt{75} - 2\sqrt{48}$

  a. $-7\sqrt{3}$ **b.** $-3\sqrt{3}$

  c. $5\sqrt{3} - 2\sqrt{48}$ **d.** $9\sqrt{3}$

20. $\sqrt{6x^2} - \sqrt[3]{108} - x\sqrt{96}$

  a. $-3x\sqrt{6} - 27\sqrt[3]{4}$

  b. $x^2\sqrt{6} - 27\sqrt[3]{4} - 4x\sqrt{6}$

  c. $-3x\sqrt{6} - 3\sqrt[3]{4}$

  d. $x^2\sqrt{6} - 3\sqrt[3]{4} - 4x\sqrt{6}$

21. $\sqrt{\dfrac{5}{16}} + \sqrt{\dfrac{5}{49}}$

  a. $\dfrac{11\sqrt{5}}{28}$ **b.** $\dfrac{65\sqrt{5}}{784}$

  c. $\dfrac{55}{28}$ **d.** $\dfrac{11\sqrt{10}}{28}$

22. $\sqrt{7} \cdot \sqrt{21}$

  a. 21 **b.** 7

  c. $\sqrt{147}$ **d.** $7\sqrt{3}$

23. $\sqrt{6}(\sqrt{30} - \sqrt{7})$

  a. $36\sqrt{5} - \sqrt{42}$ **b.** $6\sqrt{5} - 6\sqrt{7}$

  c. $6\sqrt{5} - \sqrt{42}$ **d.** $6\sqrt{5} - \sqrt{7}$

24. $(\sqrt{x} - 8)(\sqrt{x} + 6)$

  a. $x + 2\sqrt{x} + 48$ **b.** $2x - 48$

  c. $x^2 - 2x - 48$ **d.** $x - 2\sqrt{x} - 48$

25. $\dfrac{\sqrt{30}}{\sqrt{6}}$

  a. $\dfrac{5}{\sqrt{6}}$ **b.** $\sqrt{5}$

  c. $\dfrac{\sqrt{5}}{6}$ **d.** 5

26. $\dfrac{\sqrt{48x^6}}{\sqrt{2x}}$

  a. $2x^2\sqrt{6x}$ **b.** $6x^4\sqrt{2x}$

  c. $2x^4\sqrt{6x}$ **d.** $4x^2\sqrt{6x}$

Rationalize the denominator.

27. $\sqrt{\dfrac{3}{5}}$

  a. $\sqrt{15}$ **b.** $\dfrac{\sqrt{15}}{25}$

  c. $\dfrac{\sqrt{3}}{5}$ **d.** $\dfrac{\sqrt{15}}{5}$

28. $\sqrt[3]{\dfrac{3}{16}}$

  a. $\dfrac{\sqrt[3]{12}}{16}$ **b.** $\dfrac{\sqrt[3]{48}}{4}$

  c. $\dfrac{\sqrt[3]{12}}{4}$ **d.** $\dfrac{\sqrt[3]{3}}{4}$

29. $\sqrt{\dfrac{3}{448x^2}}$

  a. $\dfrac{\sqrt{21}}{56x^2}$ **b.** $\dfrac{\sqrt{3}}{8x}$

  c. $\dfrac{\sqrt{21}}{56x}$ **d.** $\dfrac{\sqrt{21}}{392x}$

30. $\dfrac{9\sqrt{10}}{\sqrt{10} - 10}$

  a. $-1 - \sqrt{10}$ **b.** $-1 + \sqrt{10}$

  c. $\dfrac{-10 + \sqrt{10}}{10}$ **d.** $-\dfrac{10 + \sqrt{10}}{10}$

Solve the radical equation.

31. $\sqrt{x} + 2 = 10$

  a. $2\sqrt{2}$ **b.** 8

  c. 64 **d.** 144

32. $\sqrt{12x - 9} = \sqrt{x + 10}$

  a. $\dfrac{1}{11}$ **b.** $\dfrac{1}{13}$

  c. $\dfrac{19}{11}$ **d.** $\dfrac{19}{12}$

33. $\sqrt{2x - 3} = x - 3$

  a. $6, 2$ **b.** no solution

  c. 3 **d.** 6

Solve.

34. Find the length of the hypotenuse of a right triangle if the legs are 14 and 6 inches long.

  a. $2\sqrt{58}$ in.   **b.** 80 in.

  c. $2\sqrt{21}$ in.   **d.** 116 in.

35. Find the distance between $(7, 2)$ and $(-2, -2)$.

  a. $\sqrt{65}$ **b.** $\sqrt{97}$

  c. 36 **d.** 97

Solve the problem.

36. Find the midpoint of the line segment whose endpoints are $(-2, 3), (6, -6)$.

  a. $(4, -3)$ **b.** $\left(-4, \dfrac{9}{2}\right)$

  c. $\left(2, -\dfrac{3}{2}\right)$ **d.** $(-8, 9)$

37. Determine whether a triangle with sides of lengths 3, 7, and $\sqrt{21}$ units is a right triangle.

  a. yes   **b.** no

Solve the problem.

38. At a certain time of day, the angle of elevation of the sun is 64°. To the nearest foot, find the height of a pole whose shadow at that time is 13 feet long.

  a. 6 feet   **b.** 27 feet

  c. 28 feet   **d.** 30 feet

10 Quadratic Equations

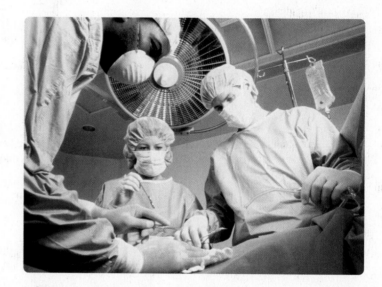

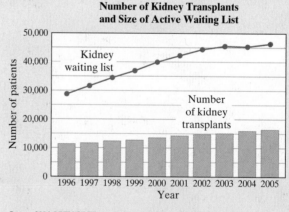

Number of Kidney Transplants and Size of Active Waiting List

Source: 2006 OPTN/SRTR Annual Report, Additional Analyses.

There are currently over 90,000 people living in the United States with a functioning kidney transplant, and that number is increasing every year. The bars on the graph above show the yearly number of kidney transplants performed, and the broken line shows the number of patients waiting for a kidney transplant. Physicians use these data to help plan for the future. In this chapter, we will use a formula called the quadratic formula to predict the number of kidney transplants and the number of patients on the waiting list at a future date.

10.1 SOLVING QUADRATIC EQUATIONS BY THE SQUARE ROOT PROPERTY

OBJECTIVES

1 Use the square root property to solve quadratic equations.

2 Solve problems modeled by quadratic equations.

OBJECTIVE 1 ▶ Using the square root property. Recall that a quadratic equation is an equation that can be written in the form

$$ax^2 + bx + c = 0$$

where a, b, and c are real numbers and $a \neq 0$.

To solve quadratic equations by factoring, use the **zero factor property:** If the product of two numbers is zero, then at least one of the two numbers is zero. For example, to solve $x^2 - 4 = 0$, we first factor the left side of the equation and then set each factor equal to 0.

$$x^2 - 4 = 0$$
$$(x + 2)(x - 2) = 0 \quad \text{Factor.}$$
$$x + 2 = 0 \quad \text{or} \quad x - 2 = 0 \quad \text{Apply the zero factor theorem.}$$
$$x = -2 \quad \text{or} \quad x = 2 \quad \text{Solve each equation.}$$

The solutions are -2 and 2.

Now let's solve $x^2 - 4 = 0$ another way. First, add 4 to both sides of the equation.

$$x^2 - 4 = 0$$
$$x^2 = 4 \quad \text{Add 4 both sides.}$$

Now we see that the value for x must be a number whose square is 4. Therefore $x = \sqrt{4} = 2$ or $x = -\sqrt{4} = -2$. This reasoning is an example of the square root property.

Square Root Property

If $x^2 = a$ for $a \geq 0$, then

$$x = \sqrt{a} \quad \text{or} \quad x = -\sqrt{a}$$

EXAMPLE 1   Use the square root property to solve $x^2 - 9 = 0$.

Solution   First we solve for x^2 by adding 9 to both sides.

$$x^2 - 9 = 0$$
$$x^2 = 9 \quad \text{Add 9 to both sides.}$$

Next we use the square root property.

$$x = \sqrt{9} \quad \text{or} \quad x = -\sqrt{9}$$
$$x = 3 \qquad\qquad x = -3$$

Check:

$x^2 - 9 = 0$ Original equation	$x^2 - 9 = 0$ Original equation
$3^2 - 9 \stackrel{?}{=} 0$ Let $x = 3$.	$(-3)^2 - 9 \stackrel{?}{=} 0$ Let $x = -3$.
$0 = 0$ True	$0 = 0$ True

The solutions are 3 and -3.

PRACTICE

1   Use the square root property to solve $x^2 - 16 = 0$.

EXAMPLE 2 Use the square root property to solve $2x^2 = 7$.

Solution First we solve for x^2 by dividing both sides by 2. Then we use the square root property.

$$2x^2 = 7$$

$$x^2 = \frac{7}{2} \qquad \text{Divide both sides by 2.}$$

$$x = \sqrt{\frac{7}{2}} \quad \text{or} \quad x = -\sqrt{\frac{7}{2}} \qquad \text{Use the square root property.}$$

If the denominators are rationalized, we have

$$x = \frac{\sqrt{7} \cdot \sqrt{2}}{\sqrt{2} \cdot \sqrt{2}} \quad \text{or} \quad x = -\frac{\sqrt{7} \cdot \sqrt{2}}{\sqrt{2} \cdot \sqrt{2}} \qquad \text{Rationalize the denominator.}$$

$$x = \frac{\sqrt{14}}{2} \qquad\qquad x = -\frac{\sqrt{14}}{2} \qquad \text{Simplify.}$$

Remember to check both solutions in the original equation. The solutions are $\dfrac{\sqrt{14}}{2}$ and $-\dfrac{\sqrt{14}}{2}$. ☐

PRACTICE
2 Use the square root property to solve $5x^2 = 13$.

EXAMPLE 3 Use the square root property to solve $(x - 3)^2 = 16$.

Solution Instead of x^2, here we have $(x - 3)^2$. But the square root property can still be used.

$$(x - 3)^2 = 16$$

$$x - 3 = \sqrt{16} \quad \text{or} \quad x - 3 = -\sqrt{16} \qquad \text{Use the square root property.}$$

$$x - 3 = 4 \qquad\qquad x - 3 = -4 \qquad \text{Write } \sqrt{16} \text{ as 4 and } -\sqrt{16} \text{ as } -4.$$

$$x = 7 \qquad\qquad\quad x = -1 \qquad \text{Solve.}$$

Check:

$$(x - 3)^2 = 16 \quad \text{Original equation} \qquad\qquad (x - 3)^2 = 16 \quad \text{Original equation}$$

$$(7 - 3)^2 \stackrel{?}{=} 16 \quad \text{Let } x = 7. \qquad\qquad\quad (-1 - 3)^2 \stackrel{?}{=} 16 \quad \text{Let } x = -1.$$

$$4^2 \stackrel{?}{=} 16 \quad \text{Simplify.} \qquad\qquad\qquad\quad (-4)^2 \stackrel{?}{=} 16 \quad \text{Simplify.}$$

$$16 = 16 \quad \text{True} \qquad\qquad\qquad\qquad\quad 16 = 16 \quad \text{True}$$

Both 7 and -1 are solutions. ☐

PRACTICE
3 Use the square root property to solve $(x - 5)^2 = 36$.

EXAMPLE 4 Use the square root property to solve $(x + 1)^2 = 8$.

Solution $(x + 1)^2 = 8$

$$x + 1 = \sqrt{8} \quad \text{or} \quad x + 1 = -\sqrt{8} \qquad \text{Use the square root property.}$$

$$x + 1 = 2\sqrt{2} \qquad\qquad x + 1 = -2\sqrt{2} \qquad \text{Simplify the radical.}$$

$$x = -1 + 2\sqrt{2} \qquad\quad x = -1 - 2\sqrt{2} \qquad \text{Solve for } x.$$

Check both solutions in the original equation. The solutions are $-1 + 2\sqrt{2}$ and $-1 - 2\sqrt{2}$. This can be written compactly as $-1 \pm 2\sqrt{2}$. The notation $\pm$ is read as "plus or minus." ☐

▶ **Helpful Hint**

read "plus or minus"
↓

The notation $-1 \pm \sqrt{5}$, for example, is just a shorthand notation for both $-1 + \sqrt{5}$ and $-1 - \sqrt{5}$.

PRACTICE
4 Use the square root property to solve $(x + 2)^2 = 12$.

EXAMPLE 5   Use the square root property to solve $(x - 1)^2 = -2$.

Solution   This equation has no real solution because the square root of -2 is not a real number.   □

PRACTICE
5   Use the square root property to solve $(x - 8)^2 = -5$.

EXAMPLE 6   Use the square root property to solve $(5x - 2)^2 = 10$.

Solution $(5x - 2)^2 = 10$

$$5x - 2 = \sqrt{10} \quad \text{or} \quad 5x - 2 = -\sqrt{10} \qquad \text{Use the square root property.}$$
$$5x = 2 + \sqrt{10} \qquad\qquad 5x = 2 - \sqrt{10} \qquad \text{Add 2 to both sides.}$$
$$x = \frac{2 + \sqrt{10}}{5} \qquad\qquad x = \frac{2 - \sqrt{10}}{5} \qquad \text{Divide both sides by 5.}$$

Check both solutions in the original equation. The solutions are $\dfrac{2 + \sqrt{10}}{5}$ and $\dfrac{2 - \sqrt{10}}{5}$, which can be written as $\dfrac{2 \pm \sqrt{10}}{5}$.   □

PRACTICE
6   Use the square root property to solve $(3x - 5)^2 = 17$.

▶ Helpful Hint

For some applications and graphing purposes, decimal approximations of exact solutions to quadratic equations may be desired.

Exact Solutions from Example 6		Decimal Approximations
$\dfrac{2 + \sqrt{10}}{5}$	$\approx$	1.032
$\dfrac{2 - \sqrt{10}}{5}$	$\approx$	-0.232

OBJECTIVE 2 ▶ Solving problems modeled by quadratic equations. Many real-world applications are modeled by quadratic equations.

EXAMPLE 7   **Finding the Length of Time of a Dive**

The record for the highest dive into a lake was made by Harry Froboess of Switzerland. In 1936 he dove 394 feet from the airship Hindenburg into Lake Constance. To the nearest tenth of a second, how long did his dive take? (_Source: The Guiness Book of Records_)

Solution

1. **UNDERSTAND.** To approximate the time of the dive, we use the formula $h = 16t^2$ *
   where t is time in seconds and h is the distance in feet, traveled by a free-falling body or object. For example, to find the distance traveled in 1 second, or 3 seconds, we let $t = 1$ and then $t = 3$.

$$\text{If } t = 1, h = 16(1)^2 = 16 \cdot 1 = 16 \text{ feet}$$
$$\text{If } t = 3, h = 16(3)^2 = 16 \cdot 9 = 144 \text{ feet}$$

Since a body travels 144 feet in 3 seconds, we now know the dive of 394 feet lasted longer than 3 seconds.

*The formula $h = 16t^2$ does not take into account air resistance.

2. TRANSLATE. Use the formula $h = 16t^2$, let the distance $h = 394$, and we have the equation $394 = 16t^2$.

3. SOLVE. To solve $394 = 16t^2$ for t, we will use the square root property.

$$394 = 16t^2$$

$$\frac{394}{16} = t^2 \qquad \text{Divide both sides by 16.}$$

$$24.625 = t^2 \qquad \text{Simplify.}$$

$$\sqrt{24.625} = t \quad \text{or} \quad -\sqrt{24.625} = t \qquad \text{Use the square root property.}$$

$$5.0 \approx t \quad \text{or} \qquad\quad -5.0 \approx t \qquad \text{Approximate.}$$

4. INTERPRET.

Check: We reject the solution -5.0 since the length of the dive is not a negative number.

State: The dive lasted approximately 5 seconds. $\qquad\qquad \square$

PRACTICE

7 On August 16, 1960, as part of an Air Force research program, Air Force Captain Joseph W. Kittinger, Jr. stepped off a platform lifted to 102,800 feet above the New Mexico desert by a hot air balloon. As part of the research, Captain Kittinger free fell for 84,700 feet before opening his parachute. To the nearest tenth of a second, how long did Captain Kittinger free fall before he opened his chute? (*Source: PBS, Nova*)

10.1 EXERCISE SET

MyMathLab | MathXL PRACTICE | WATCH | DOWNLOAD | READ | REVIEW

Use the square root property to solve each quadratic equation. See Examples 1, 2, and 5.

1. $x^2 = 64$

2. $x^2 = 121$

3. $x^2 = 21$

4. $x^2 = 22$

5. $x^2 = \dfrac{1}{25}$

6. $x^2 = \dfrac{1}{16}$

7. $x^2 = -4$

8. $x^2 = -25$

9. $3x^2 = 13$

10. $5x^2 = 2$

11. $7x^2 = 4$

12. $2x^2 = 9$

13. $x^2 - 2 = 0$

14. $x^2 - 15 = 0$

15. $2x^2 - 10 = 0$

16. $7x^2 - 21 = 0$

17. Explain why the equation $x^2 = -9$ has no real solution.

18. Explain why the equation $x^2 = 9$ has two solutions.

Use the square root property to solve each quadratic equation. See Examples 3 through 6.

19. $(x - 5)^2 = 49$

20. $(x + 2)^2 = 25$

21. $(x + 2)^2 = 7$

22. $(x - 7)^2 = 2$

23. $\left(m - \dfrac{1}{2}\right)^2 = \dfrac{1}{4}$

24. $\left(m + \dfrac{1}{3}\right)^2 = \dfrac{1}{9}$

25. $(p + 2)^2 = 10$

26. $(p - 7)^2 = 13$

27. $(3y + 2)^2 = 100$

28. $(4y - 3)^2 = 81$

29. $(z - 4)^2 = -9$

30. $(z + 7)^2 = -20$

31. $(2x - 11)^2 = 50$

32. $(3x - 17)^2 = 28$

33. $(3x - 7)^2 = 32$

34. $(5x - 11)^2 = 54$

35. $(2p - 5)^2 = 121$

36. $(3p - 1)^2 = 4$

MIXED PRACTICE

Use the square root property to solve. See Examples 3 through 6.

37. $x^2 - 2 = 0$

38. $x^2 - 15 = 0$

39. $(x + 6)^2 = 24$

40. $(x + 5)^2 = 20$

41. $\dfrac{1}{2}n^2 = 5$

42. $\dfrac{1}{5}y^2 = 2$

43. $(4x - 1)^2 = 5$

44. $(7x - 2)^2 = 11$

45. $3z^2 = 36$

46. $3z^2 = 24$

47. $(8 - 3x)^2 - 45 = 0$

48. $(10 - 9x)^2 - 75 = 0$

The formula for area of a square is $A = s^2$ where s is the length of a side. Use this formula for Exercises 49 through 52. For each exercise, give an exact answer and a two-decimal-place approximation.

△ **49.** If the area of a square is 20 square inches, find the length of a side.

△ **50.** If the area of a square is 32 square meters, find the length of a side.

△ **51.** The "Water Cube" National Swimming Center was constructed in Beijing for the 2008 Summer Olympics. Its square base has an area of 31,329 sq meters. Find the length of a side of this building. (*Source:* ARUP East Asia)

△ **52.** The Washington Monument has a square base whose area is approximately 3039 square feet. Find the length of a side. (*Source: The World Almanac*)

Solve. See Example 7. For Exercises 53 through 58, use the formula from $h = 16t^2$ and round answers to the nearest tenth of a second. (Recall that this formula does not take into account any air resistance.)

53. If a sandblaster drops his goggles from a bridge 400 feet from the water below, find how long it takes for the goggles to hit the water.

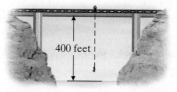

400 feet

54. In 1988, Eddie Turner saved Frank Fanan, who became unconscious after an injury while jumping out of an airplane. Fanan fell 11,136 feet before Turner pulled his ripcord. Determine the time of Fanan's unconscious free-fall.

55. The highest regularly performed dives are made by professional divers from La Quebrada, in Acapulco, Mexico. The performer dives head first from a height of 115 feet (into 12 feet of water). Determine the time of a dive. (*Source: The Guinness Book of Records*)

56. In 1962, Vesna Vulovic, a flight attendant from Yugoslavia, survived a fall from 33,300 feet when the DC-9 airplane in which she was traveling blew up. She fell still strapped into her flight attendant's seat in the tail section of the plane. To the nearest tenth of a second, determine the time it took her to reach the ground. (*Source: Aviation Security*)

57. In March 2007, the Hualapai Indian Tribe allowed the Grand Canyon Skywalk to be built over the rim of the Grand Canyon on its tribal land. The skywalk extends 70 feet beyond the canyon's edge and is 4000 feet above the canyon floor. Determine the time, to the nearest tenth of a second, it would take an object, dropped off the skywalk, to land at the bottom of the Grand Canyon. (*Source: Boston Globe; 03/21/07*)

△ **58.** In 1997, stuntman Stig Gunther of Denmark jumped from a height of 343 feet off a crane onto an airbag. Determine the time of Gunther's stunt fall. (*Source: Guinness Book of World Records*)

△ **59.** The area of a circle is found by the equation $A = \pi r^2$. If the area A of a certain circle is 36π square inches, find its radius r.

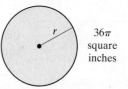

r 36π square inches

60. If the area of the circle below is 10π square units, find its exact radius. (See Exercise 59.)

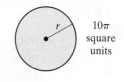

r 10π square units

REVIEW AND PREVIEW

Factor each perfect square trinomial. See Section 7.3.

61. $x^2 + 6x + 9$ **62.** $y^2 + 10y + 25$

63. $x^2 - 4x + 4$ **64.** $x^2 - 20x + 100$

CONCEPT EXTENSIONS

Solve each quadratic equation by first factoring the perfect square trinomial on the left side. Then apply the square root property.

65. $x^2 + 4x + 4 = 16$ **66.** $z^2 - 6z + 9 = 25$

67. $x^2 + 14x + 49 = 31$ **68.** $y^2 - 10y + 25 = 11$

For Exercises 69 through 72, solve each quadratic equation by using the square root property. If necessary, use a calculator and round each solution to the nearest hundredth.

69. $x^2 = 1.78$ **70.** $(x - 1.37)^2 = 5.71$

71. The number y of CVS stores open for business from 2003 through 2006 is given by the equation $y = -120(x - 4)^2 + 6200$, where $x = 0$ represents the year 2003. Assume that this trend continues and find the year after 2006 in which there will be 6080 stores open. (*Hint*: Replace y with 6080 and solve for x.) (*Source*: Based on Data from CVS Corporation)

72. U.S. soybean production y (in billion bushels) from 2004 through 2006 is given by the equation $y = 0.09(x - 1)^2 + 3.06$, where $x = 0$ represents the year 2004. Assume that this trend continues and find the year in which there will be

4.5 billion bushels. (*Hint*: Replace y with 4.5 and solve for x.) (*Source*: Based on Data from U.S. Department of Agriculture)

73. The number of cattle y (in thousands) on farms in Kansas from 2003 through 2006 is approximated by the equation $y = 75x^2 + 6400$, where $x = 0$ represents the year 2003. Assume that this trend continues and find the year in which there are 7600 cattle. (*Hint*: Replace y with 7600 and solve for x.) (*Source*: Based on Data from U.S. Department of Agriculture)

10.2 SOLVING QUADRATIC EQUATIONS BY COMPLETING THE SQUARE

OBJECTIVES

1 Write perfect square trinomials.

2 Solve quadratic equations of the form $x^2 + bx + c = 0$ by completing the square.

3 Solve quadratic equations of the form $ax^2 + bx + c = 0$ by completing the square.

OBJECTIVE 1 ▶ Writing perfect square trinomials. In the last section, we used the square root property to solve equations such as

$$(x + 1)^2 = 8 \quad \text{and} \quad (5x - 2)^2 = 3$$

Notice that one side of each equation is a quantity squared and that the other side is a constant. To solve

$$x^2 + 2x = 4$$

notice that if we add 1 to both sides of the equation, the left side is a perfect square trinomial that can be factored.

$$x^2 + 2x + 1 = 4 + 1 \quad \text{Add 1 to both sides.}$$
$$(x + 1)^2 = 5 \quad \text{Factor.}$$

Now we can solve this equation as we did in the previous section by using the square root property.

$$x + 1 = \sqrt{5} \quad \text{or} \quad x + 1 = -\sqrt{5} \quad \text{Use the square root property.}$$
$$x = -1 + \sqrt{5} \qquad x = -1 - \sqrt{5} \quad \text{Solve.}$$

The solutions are $-1 \pm \sqrt{5}$.

Adding a number to $x^2 + 2x$ to form a perfect square trinomial is called **completing the square** on $x^2 + 2x$.

In general, we have the following.

Completing the Square
To complete the square on $x^2 + bx$, add $\left(\dfrac{b}{2}\right)^2$. To find $\left(\dfrac{b}{2}\right)^2$, **find half the coefficient of x, then square the result.**

EXAMPLE 1   Complete the square for each expression and then factor the resulting perfect square trinomial.

a. $x^2 + 10x$ **b.** $m^2 - 6m$ **c.** $x^2 + x$

Solution

a. The coefficient of the x-term is 10. Half of 10 is 5, and $5^2 = 25$. Add 25.

$$x^2 + 10x + 25 = (x + 5)^2$$

b. Half the coefficient of m is -3, and $(-3)^2$ is 9. Add 9.

$$m^2 - 6m + 9 = (m - 3)^2$$

c. Half the coefficient of x is $\dfrac{1}{2}$ and $\left(\dfrac{1}{2}\right)^2 = \dfrac{1}{4}$. Add $\dfrac{1}{4}$.

$$x^2 + x + \frac{1}{4} = \left(x + \frac{1}{2}\right)^2$$
□

PRACTICE
1   Complete the square for each expression and then factor the resulting perfect square trinomial.

a. $z^2 + 8z$ **b.** $x^2 - 12x$ **c.** $b^2 + 5b$

OBJECTIVE 2 ▶ Completing the square to solve $x^2 + bx + c = 0$. By completing the square, a quadratic equation can be solved using the square root property.

EXAMPLE 2   Solve $x^2 + 6x + 3 = 0$ by completing the square.

Solution   First we get the variable terms alone by subtracting 3 from both sides of the equation.

$$x^2 + 6x + 3 = 0$$
$$x^2 + 6x = -3 \quad \text{Subtract 3 from both sides.}$$

Next we find half the coefficient of the x-term, then square it. Add this result to **both sides** of the equation. This will make the left side a perfect square trinomial. The coefficient of x is 6, and half of 6 is 3. So we add 3^2 or 9 to both sides.

$$x^2 + 6x + 9 = -3 + 9 \qquad \text{Complete the square.}$$
$$(x + 3)^2 = 6 \qquad \text{Factor the trinomial } x^2 + 6x + 9.$$
$$x + 3 = \sqrt{6} \quad \text{or} \quad x + 3 = -\sqrt{6} \qquad \text{Use the square root property.}$$
$$x = -3 + \sqrt{6} \qquad x = -3 - \sqrt{6} \quad \text{Subtract 3 from both sides.}$$

Check by substituting $-3 + \sqrt{6}$ and $-3 - \sqrt{6}$ in the original equation. The solutions are $-3 \pm \sqrt{6}$.
□

PRACTICE
2   Solve $x^2 + 2x - 5 = 0$ by completing the square.

> ▶ **Helpful Hint**
> Remember, when solving an equation by completing the square, add the number that completes the square to **both sides of the equation.**

EXAMPLE 3 Solve $x^2 - 10x = -14$ by completing the square.

Solution The variable terms are already alone on one side of the equation. The coefficient of x is -10. Half of -10 is -5, and $(-5)^2 = 25$. So we add 25 to both sides.

> ▶ **Helpful Hint**
> Add 25 to *both* sides of the equation.

$$x^2 - 10x = -14$$
$$x^2 - 10x + 25 = -14 + 25$$
$$(x - 5)^2 = 11 \qquad \text{Factor the trinomial and simplify } -14 + 25.$$
$$x - 5 = \sqrt{11} \quad \text{or} \quad x - 5 = -\sqrt{11} \qquad \text{Use the square root property.}$$
$$x = 5 + \sqrt{11} \qquad x = 5 - \sqrt{11} \qquad \text{Add 5 to both sides.}$$

The solutions are $5 \pm \sqrt{11}$.

PRACTICE
3 Solve $x^2 - 8x = -8$ by completing the square.

OBJECTIVE 3 ▶ **Completing the square to solve $ax^2 + bx + c = 0$.** The method of completing the square can be used to solve *any* quadratic equation whether the coefficient of the squared variable is 1 or not. When the coefficient of the squared variable is not 1, we first divide both sides of the equation by the coefficient of the squared variable so that the new coefficient is 1. Then we complete the square.

EXAMPLE 4 Solve $4x^2 - 8x - 5 = 0$ by completing the square.

Solution $4x^2 - 8x - 5 = 0$

$$x^2 - 2x - \frac{5}{4} = 0 \qquad \text{Divide both sides by 4.}$$

$$x^2 - 2x = \frac{5}{4} \qquad \text{Get the variable terms alone on one side of the equation.}$$

The coefficient of x is -2. Half of -2 is -1, and $(-1)^2 = 1$. So we add 1 to both sides.

$$x^2 - 2x + 1 = \frac{5}{4} + 1$$

$$(x - 1)^2 = \frac{9}{4} \qquad\qquad\qquad \text{Factor } x^2 - 2x + 1 \text{ and simplify } \frac{5}{4} + 1.$$

$$x - 1 = \sqrt{\frac{9}{4}} \quad \text{or} \quad x - 1 = -\sqrt{\frac{9}{4}} \qquad \text{Use the square root property.}$$

$$x = 1 + \frac{3}{2} \qquad\qquad x = 1 - \frac{3}{2} \qquad \text{Add 1 to both sides and simplify the radical.}$$

$$x = \frac{5}{2} \qquad\qquad\quad x = -\frac{1}{2} \qquad \text{Simplify.}$$

Both $\frac{5}{2}$ and $-\frac{1}{2}$ are solutions.

PRACTICE
4 Solve $9x^2 - 36x - 13 = 0$ by completing the square.

The following steps may be used to solve a quadratic equation in x by completing the square.

Solving a Quadratic Equation in x by Completing the Square

STEP 1. If the coefficient of x^2 is 1, go to Step 2. If not, divide both sides of the equation by the coefficient of x^2.

STEP 2. Get all terms with variables on one side of the equation and constants on the other side.

STEP 3. Find half the coefficient of x and then square the result. Add this number to both sides of the equation.

STEP 4. Factor the resulting perfect square trinomial.

STEP 5. Use the square root property to solve the equation.

EXAMPLE 5   Solve $2x^2 + 6x = -7$ by completing the square.

Solution   The coefficient of x^2 is not 1. We divide both sides by 2, the coefficient of x^2.

$$2x^2 + 6x = -7$$

$$x^2 + 3x = -\frac{7}{2} \qquad \text{Divide both sides by 2.}$$

$$x^2 + 3x + \frac{9}{4} = -\frac{7}{2} + \frac{9}{4} \quad \text{Add } \left(\frac{3}{2}\right)^2 \text{ or } \frac{9}{4} \text{ to both sides.}$$

$$\left(x + \frac{3}{2}\right)^2 = -\frac{5}{4} \qquad \text{Factor the left side and simplify the right.}$$

There is no real solution to this equation since the square root of a negative number is not a real number.   □

PRACTICE
5   Solve $2x^2 + 12x = -20$ by completing the square.

EXAMPLE 6   Solve $2x^2 = 10x + 1$ by completing the square.

Solution   First we divide both sides of the equation by 2, the coefficient of x^2.

$$2x^2 = 10x + 1$$

$$x^2 = 5x + \frac{1}{2} \qquad \text{Divide both sides by 2.}$$

Next we get the variable terms alone by subtracting $5x$ from both sides.

$$x^2 - 5x = \frac{1}{2}$$

$$x^2 - 5x + \frac{25}{4} = \frac{1}{2} + \frac{25}{4} \qquad\qquad\qquad \text{Add } \left(-\frac{5}{2}\right)^2 \text{ or } \frac{25}{4} \text{ to both sides.}$$

$$\left(x - \frac{5}{2}\right)^2 = \frac{27}{4} \qquad\qquad\qquad\qquad \text{Factor the left side and simplify the right side.}$$

$$x - \frac{5}{2} = \sqrt{\frac{27}{4}} \quad \text{or} \quad x - \frac{5}{2} = -\sqrt{\frac{27}{4}} \qquad \text{Use the square root property.}$$

$$x - \frac{5}{2} = \frac{3\sqrt{3}}{2} \qquad\qquad x - \frac{5}{2} = -\frac{3\sqrt{3}}{2} \qquad \text{Simplify.}$$

$$x = \frac{5}{2} + \frac{3\sqrt{3}}{2} \qquad\qquad x = \frac{5}{2} - \frac{3\sqrt{3}}{2}$$

The solutions are $\dfrac{5 \pm 3\sqrt{3}}{2}$.

PRACTICE

6 Solve $2x^2 = 6x - 3$ by completing the square.

VOCABULARY & READINESS CHECK

Word Bank. *Use the choices below to fill in each blank. Not all choices will be used, and these exercises come from Sections 10.1 and 10.2.*

$\sqrt{a}$	linear equation	zero	$\left(\dfrac{b}{2}\right)^2$	$\dfrac{b}{2}$	6
$\pm\sqrt{a}$	quadratic equation	one	completing the square	9	3

1. By the zero factor property, if the product of two numbers is zero, then at least one of these two numbers must be _____.
2. If a is a positive number, and if $x^2 = a$, then $x =$ _____.
3. An equation that can be written in the form $ax^2 + bx + c = 0$ where a, b, and c are real numbers and a is not zero is called a(n) _____.
4. The process of solving a quadratic equation by writing it in the form $(x + a)^2 = c$ is called _____.
5. To complete the square on $x^2 + 6x$, add _____.
6. To complete the square on $x^2 + bx$, add _____.

Fill in the Blank. *Fill in the blank with the number needed to make each expression a perfect square trinomial. See Example 1.*

7. $p^2 + 8p +$ _____
8. $p^2 + 6p +$ _____
9. $x^2 + 20x +$ _____
10. $x^2 + 18x +$ _____
11. $y^2 + 14y +$ _____
12. $y^2 + 2y +$ _____

10.2 EXERCISE SET

MyMathLab   Math XL PRACTICE   WATCH   DOWNLOAD   READ   REVIEW

Complete the square for each expression and then factor the resulting perfect square trinomial. See Example 1.

1. $x^2 + 4x$
2. $x^2 + 6x$
3. $k^2 - 12k$
4. $k^2 - 16k$
5. $x^2 - 3x$
6. $x^2 - 5x$
7. $m^2 - m$
8. $y^2 + y$

Solve each quadratic equation by completing the square. See Examples 2 and 3.

9. $x^2 + 8x = -12$
10. $x^2 - 10x = -24$
11. $x^2 + 2x - 7 = 0$
12. $z^2 + 6z - 9 = 0$
13. $x^2 - 6x = 0$
14. $y^2 + 4y = 0$

15. $z^2 + 5z = 7$

16. $x^2 - 7x = 5$

17. $x^2 - 2x - 1 = 0$

18. $x^2 - 4x + 2 = 0$

19. $y^2 + 5y + 4 = 0$

20. $y^2 - 5y + 6 = 0$

Solve each quadratic equation by completing the square. See Examples 4 through 6.

21. $3x^2 - 6x = 24$

22. $2x^2 + 18x = -40$

23. $5x^2 + 10x + 6 = 0$

24. $3x^2 - 12x + 14 = 0$

25. $2x^2 = 6x + 5$

26. $4x^2 = -20x + 3$

27. $2y^2 + 8y + 5 = 0$

28. $4z^2 - 8z + 1 = 0$

MIXED PRACTICE

Solve each quadratic equation by completing the square. See Examples 1 through 6.

29. $x^2 + 6x - 25 = 0$

30. $x^2 - 6x + 7 = 0$

31. $x^2 - 3x - 3 = 0$

32. $x^2 - 9x + 3 = 0$

33. $2y^2 - 3y + 1 = 0$

34. $2y^2 - y - 1 = 0$

35. $x(x + 3) = 18$

36. $x(x - 3) = 18$

37. $3z^2 + 6z + 4 = 0$

38. $2y^2 + 8y + 9 = 0$

39. $4x^2 + 16x = 48$

40. $6x^2 - 30x = -36$

REVIEW AND PREVIEW

Simplify each expression. See Section 9.3.

41. $\dfrac{3}{4} - \sqrt{\dfrac{25}{16}}$

42. $\dfrac{3}{5} + \sqrt{\dfrac{16}{25}}$

43. $\dfrac{1}{2} - \sqrt{\dfrac{9}{4}}$

44. $\dfrac{9}{10} - \sqrt{\dfrac{49}{100}}$

Simplify each expression. See Section 9.4.

45. $\dfrac{6 + 4\sqrt{5}}{2}$

46. $\dfrac{10 - 20\sqrt{3}}{2}$

47. $\dfrac{3 - 9\sqrt{2}}{6}$

48. $\dfrac{12 - 8\sqrt{7}}{16}$

CONCEPT EXTENSIONS

49. In your own words, describe a perfect square trinomial.

50. Describe how to find the number to add to $x^2 - 7x$ to make a perfect square trinomial.

51. **Multiple Steps.** Write your own quadratic equation to be solved by completing the square. Write it in the form

perfect square trinomial = a number that is not a perfect square

$$x^2 + 6x + 9 = 11$$

For example,

  a. Solve $x^2 + 6x + 9 = 11$.

  b. Write and solve your quadratic equation by completing the square.

52. **Multiple Steps.** Follow the directions of Exercise 51, except write your equation in the form

perfect square trinomial = negative number

Solve your quadratic equation by completing the square.

53. Find a value of k that will make $x^2 + kx + 16$ a perfect square trinomial.

54. Find a value of k that will make $x^2 + kx + 25$ a perfect square trinomial.

55. Retail sales y (in millions of dollars) for bookstores in the United States from 2003 through 2005 can be represented by the equation $y = 250x^2 - 750x + 7800$. In this equation x is the number of years after 2002. Assume that this trend continues and predict the years after 2002 in which the retail sales for U.S. bookstores will be $8800 million. (*Source: Based on data from the Statistical Abstract of the United States*)

56. The average price of gold y (in dollars per ounce) from 2000 through 2006 is given by the equation $y = 10x^2 - 6x + 280$. Assume that this trend continues and find the year after 2000 in which the price of gold will be $1036 per ounce. (*Source: Based on data from U.S. Geological survey, Minerals Information*)

Recall that a graphing calculator may be used to solve an equation. For example, to solve $x^2 + 8x = -12$ (Exercise 1), graph

$$y_1 = x^2 + 8x \quad \text{(left side of equation) and}$$
$$y_2 = -12 \quad \text{(right side of equation)}$$

The x-coordinate of the point of intersection of the graphs is the solution. Use a graphing calculator and solve each equation. Round solutions to the nearest hundredth.

57. Exercise 9

58. Exercise 10

59. Exercise 25

60. Exercise 26

10.3 SOLVING QUADRATIC EQUATIONS BY THE QUADRATIC FORMULA

OBJECTIVE 1 ▶ Using the quadratic formula. We can use the technique of completing the square to develop a formula to find solutions of any quadratic equation. We develop and use the **quadratic formula** in this section.

Recall that a quadratic equation in **standard form** is

$$ax^2 + bx + c = 0, \quad a \neq 0$$

To develop the quadratic formula, let's complete the square for this quadratic equation in standard form.

First we divide both sides of the equation by the coefficient of x^2 and then get the variable terms alone on one side of the equation.

$$x^2 + \frac{b}{a}x + \frac{c}{a} = 0 \qquad \text{Divide by } a; \text{ recall that } a \text{ cannot be 0.}$$

$$x^2 + \frac{b}{a}x = -\frac{c}{a} \qquad \text{Get the variable terms alone on one side of the equation.}$$

The coefficient of x is $\frac{b}{a}$. Half of $\frac{b}{a}$ is $\frac{b}{2a}$ and $\left(\frac{b}{2a}\right)^2 = \frac{b^2}{4a^2}$. So we add $\frac{b^2}{4a^2}$ to both sides of the equation.

$$x^2 + \frac{b}{a}x + \frac{b^2}{4a^2} = -\frac{c}{a} + \frac{b^2}{4a^2} \qquad \text{Add } \frac{b^2}{4a^2} \text{ to both sides.}$$

$$\left(x + \frac{b}{2a}\right)^2 = -\frac{c}{a} + \frac{b^2}{4a^2} \qquad \text{Factor the left side.}$$

$$\left(x + \frac{b}{2a}\right)^2 = -\frac{4ac}{4a^2} + \frac{b^2}{4a^2} \qquad \text{Multiply } -\frac{c}{a} \text{ by } \frac{4a}{4a} \text{ so that both terms on the right side have a common denominator.}$$

$$\left(x + \frac{b}{2a}\right)^2 = \frac{b^2 - 4ac}{4a^2} \qquad \text{Simplify the right side.}$$

Now we use the square root property.

$$x + \frac{b}{2a} = \sqrt{\frac{b^2 - 4ac}{4a^2}} \quad \text{or} \quad x + \frac{b}{2a} = -\sqrt{\frac{b^2 - 4ac}{4a^2}} \qquad \text{Use the square root property.}$$

$$x + \frac{b}{2a} = \frac{\sqrt{b^2 - 4ac}}{2a} \qquad x + \frac{b}{2a} = -\frac{\sqrt{b^2 - 4ac}}{2a} \qquad \text{Simplify the radical.}$$

$$x = -\frac{b}{2a} + \frac{\sqrt{b^2 - 4ac}}{2a} \qquad x = -\frac{b}{2a} - \frac{\sqrt{b^2 - 4ac}}{2a} \qquad \text{Subtract } \frac{b}{2a} \text{ from both sides.}$$

$$x = \frac{-b + \sqrt{b^2 - 4ac}}{2a} \qquad x = \frac{-b - \sqrt{b^2 - 4ac}}{2a} \qquad \text{Simplify.}$$

The solutions are $\dfrac{-b \pm \sqrt{b^2 - 4ac}}{2a}$. This final equation is called the **quadratic formula** and gives the solutions of any quadratic equation.

Quadratic Formula

If a, b, and c are real numbers and $a \neq 0$, a quadratic equation written in the form $ax^2 + bx + c = 0$ has solutions

$$x = \frac{-b \pm \sqrt{b^2 - 4ac}}{2a}$$

> ▶ **Helpful Hint**
>
> Don't forget that to correctly identify a, b, and c in the quadratic formula, you should write the equation in standard form.
>
> **Quadratic Equations in Standard Form**
>
> | | |
> |---|---|
> | $5x^2 - 6x + 2 = 0$ | $a = 5, b = -6, c = 2$ |
> | $4y^2 - 9 = 0$ | $a = 4, b = 0, c = -9$ |
> | $x^2 + x = 0$ | $a = 1, b = 1, c = 0$ |
> | $\sqrt{2}x^2 + \sqrt{5}x + \sqrt{3} = 0$ | $a = \sqrt{2}, b = \sqrt{5}, c = \sqrt{3}$ |

EXAMPLE 1 Solve $3x^2 + x - 3 = 0$ using the quadratic formula.

Solution This equation is in standard form with $a = 3$, $b = 1$, and $c = -3$. By the quadratic formula, we have

$$x = \frac{-b \pm \sqrt{b^2 - 4ac}}{2a}$$

$$x = \frac{-1 \pm \sqrt{1^2 - 4 \cdot 3 \cdot (-3)}}{2 \cdot 3} \quad \text{Let } a = 3, b = 1, \text{ and } c = -3.$$

$$= \frac{-1 \pm \sqrt{1 + 36}}{6} \quad \text{Simplify.}$$

$$= \frac{-1 \pm \sqrt{37}}{6}$$

Check both solutions in the original equation. The solutions are $\dfrac{-1 + \sqrt{37}}{6}$ and $\dfrac{-1 - \sqrt{37}}{6}$. ☐

PRACTICE
1 Solve $5x^2 + x - 2 = 0$ using the quadratic formula.

EXAMPLE 2 Solve $2x^2 - 9x = 5$ using the quadratic formula.

Solution First we write the equation in standard form by subtracting 5 from both sides.

$$2x^2 - 9x = 5$$
$$2x^2 - 9x - 5 = 0$$

Next we note that $a = 2$, $b = -9$, and $c = -5$. We substitute these values into the quadratic formula.

> ▶ **Helpful Hint**
>
> Notice that the fraction bar is under the entire numerator of $-b \pm \sqrt{b^2 - 4ac}$.

$$x = \frac{-b \pm \sqrt{b^2 - 4ac}}{2a}$$

$$x = \frac{-(-9) \pm \sqrt{(-9)^2 - 4 \cdot 2 \cdot (-5)}}{2 \cdot 2} \quad \text{Substitute in the formula.}$$

$$= \frac{9 \pm \sqrt{81 + 40}}{4} \quad \text{Simplify.}$$

$$= \frac{9 \pm \sqrt{121}}{4} = \frac{9 \pm 11}{4}$$

Then,

$$x = \frac{9 - 11}{4} = -\frac{1}{2} \quad \text{or} \quad x = \frac{9 + 11}{4} = 5$$

Check $-\dfrac{1}{2}$ and 5 in the original equation. Both $-\dfrac{1}{2}$ and 5 are solutions. ☐

PRACTICE
2 Solve $3x^2 + 2x = 8$ using the quadratic formula.

The following steps may be useful when solving a quadratic equation by the quadratic formula.

> **Solving a Quadratic Equation by the Quadratic Formula**
> **STEP 1.** Write the quadratic equation in standard form: $ax^2 + bx + c = 0$.
> **STEP 2.** If necessary, clear the equation of fractions to simplify calculations.
> **STEP 3.** Identify a, b, and c.
> **STEP 4.** Replace a, b, and c in the quadratic formula with the identified values, and simplify.

Concept Check ☑

For the quadratic equation $2x^2 - 5 = 7x$, if $a = 2$ and $c = -5$ in the quadratic formula, the value of b is which of the following?

a. $\dfrac{7}{2}$ **b.** 7   **c.** -5 **d.** -7

EXAMPLE 3   Solve $7x^2 = 1$ using the quadratic formula.

Solution   First we write the equation in standard form by subtracting 1 from both sides.

$$7x^2 = 1$$
$$7x^2 - 1 = 0$$

> ▶ **Helpful Hint**
> $7x^2 - 1 = 0$ can be written as $7x^2 + 0x - 1 = 0$. This form helps you see that $b = 0$.

Next we replace a, b, and c with the identified values: $a = 7$, $b = 0$ and $c = -1$.

$$x = \frac{0 \pm \sqrt{0^2 - 4 \cdot 7 \cdot (-1)}}{2 \cdot 7} \qquad \text{Substitute in the formula.}$$

$$= \frac{\pm \sqrt{28}}{14} \qquad \text{Simplify.}$$

$$= \frac{\pm 2\sqrt{7}}{14}$$

$$= \pm \frac{\sqrt{7}}{7}$$

The solutions are $\dfrac{\sqrt{7}}{7}$ and $-\dfrac{\sqrt{7}}{7}$.

PRACTICE
3   Solve $3x^2 = 5$ using the quadratic formula.

Notice that the equation in Example 3, $7x^2 = 1$, could have been easily solved by dividing both sides by 7 and then using the square root property. We solved the equation by the quadratic formula to show that this formula can be used to solve any quadratic equation.

Answer to Concept Check: d

EXAMPLE 4   Solve $x^2 = -x - 1$ using the quadratic formula.

Solution   First we write the equation in standard form.

$$x^2 + x + 1 = 0$$

Next we replace a, b, and c in the quadratic formula with $a = 1$, $b = 1$, and $c = 1$.

$$x = \frac{-1 \pm \sqrt{1^2 - 4 \cdot 1 \cdot 1}}{2 \cdot 1} \qquad \text{Substitute in the formula.}$$

$$= \frac{-1 \pm \sqrt{-3}}{2} \qquad \text{Simplify.}$$

There is no real number solution because $\sqrt{-3}$ is not a real number.   □

PRACTICE
4   Solve $x^2 = 3x - 4$ using the quadratic formula.

EXAMPLE 5   Solve $\frac{1}{2}x^2 - x = 2$ by using the quadratic formula.

Solution   We write the equation in standard form and then clear the equation of fractions by multiplying both sides by the LCD, 2.

$$\frac{1}{2}x^2 - x = 2$$

$$\frac{1}{2}x^2 - x - 2 = 0 \quad \text{Write in standard form.}$$

$$x^2 - 2x - 4 = 0 \quad \text{Multiply both sides by 2.}$$

Here, $a = 1$, $b = -2$, and $c = -4$, so we substitute these values into the quadratic formula.

$$x = \frac{-(-2) \pm \sqrt{(-2)^2 - 4 \cdot 1 \cdot (-4)}}{2 \cdot 1}$$

$$= \frac{2 \pm \sqrt{20}}{2} = \frac{2 \pm 2\sqrt{5}}{2} \qquad \text{Simplify.}$$

$$= \frac{2\,(1 \pm \sqrt{5})}{2} = 1 \pm \sqrt{5} \qquad \text{Factor and simplify.}$$

The solutions are $1 - \sqrt{5}$ and $1 + \sqrt{5}$.   □

PRACTICE
5   Solve $\frac{1}{5}x^2 - x = 1$ using the quadratic formula.

Notice that in Example 5, although we cleared the equation of fractions, the coefficients $a = \frac{1}{2}$, $b = -1$, and $c = -2$ will give the same results.

> ▶ **Helpful Hint**
> When simplifying an expression such as
>
> $$\frac{3 \pm 6\sqrt{2}}{6}$$
>
> first factor out a common factor from the terms of the numerator and then simplify.
>
> $$\frac{3 \pm 6\sqrt{2}}{6} = \frac{3(1 \pm 2\sqrt{2})}{2 \cdot 3} = \frac{1 \pm 2\sqrt{2}}{2}$$

OBJECTIVE 2 ▶ Approximate solutions to quadratic equations. Sometimes approximate solutions for quadratic equations are appropriate.

EXAMPLE 6 Approximate the exact solutions of the quadratic equation in Example 1. Round the approximations to the nearest tenth.

Solution From Example 1, we have exact solutions $\dfrac{-1 \pm \sqrt{37}}{6}$. Thus,

$$\frac{-1 + \sqrt{37}}{6} \approx 0.847127088 \approx 0.8 \text{ to the nearest tenth.}$$

$$\frac{-1 - \sqrt{37}}{6} \approx -1.180460422 \approx -1.2 \text{ to the nearest tenth.}$$

Thus approximate solutions to the quadratic equation in Example 1 are 0.8 and −1.2. □

PRACTICE 6 Approximate the exact solutions of the quadratic equation in Practice 1. Round the approximations to the nearest tenth.

OBJECTIVE 3 ▶ Using the discriminant. In the quadratic formula, $x = \dfrac{-b \pm \sqrt{b^2 - 4ac}}{2a}$, the radicand $b^2 - 4ac$ is called the **discriminant** because, by knowing its value, we can **discriminate** among the possible number and type of solutions of a quadratic equation. Possible values of the discriminant and their meanings are summarized next.

Discriminant

The following table corresponds the discriminant $b^2 - 4ac$ of a quadratic equation of the form $ax^2 + bx + c = 0$ with the number of solutions of the equation.

$b^2 - 4ac$	*Number of Solutions*
Positive	Two distinct real solutions
Zero	One real solution
Negative	No real solution*

*In this case, the quadratic equation will have two complex (but not real) solutions.

EXAMPLE 7 Use the discriminant to determine the number of solutions of $3x^2 + x - 3 = 0$.

Solution In $3x^2 + x - 3 = 0$, $a = 3$, $b = 1$, and $c = -3$. Then

$$b^2 - 4ac = (1)^2 - 4(3)(-3) = 1 + 36 = 37$$

Since the discriminant is 37, a positive number, this equation has two distinct real solutions.

We solved this equation in Example 1 of this section, and the solutions are

$$\frac{-1 + \sqrt{37}}{6} \text{ and } \frac{-1 - \sqrt{37}}{6}, \text{ two distinct real solutions.} \qquad \square$$

PRACTICE
7 Use the discriminant to determine the number of solutions of $5x^2 + x - 2 = 0$.

EXAMPLE 8 Use the discriminant to determine the number of solutions of each quadratic equation.

a. $x^2 - 6x + 9 = 0$ **b.** $5x^2 + 4 = 0$

Solution

a. In $x^2 - 6x + 9 = 0$, $a = 1$, $b = -6$, and $c = 9$.

$$b^2 - 4ac = (-6)^2 - 4(1)(9) = 36 - 36 = 0$$

Since the discriminant is 0, this equation has one real solution.

b. In $5x^2 + 4 = 0$, $a = 5$, $b = 0$, and $c = 4$.

$$b^2 - 4ac = 0^2 - 4(5)(4) = 0 - 80 = -80$$

Since the discriminant is -80, a negative number, this equation has no real solution. $\square$

PRACTICE
8 Use the discriminant to determine the number of solutions of each quadratic equation.

a. $x^2 - 10x + 35 = 0$ **b.** $5x^2 + 3x = 0$

VOCABULARY & READINESS CHECK

Fill in the Blank.

1. The quadratic formula is _____ .

Identify the values of a, b, and c in each quadratic equation.

2. $5x^2 - 7x + 1 = 0$; $a = \underline{\ \ }$, $b = \underline{\ \ \ }$, $c = \underline{\ \ }$

3. $x^2 + 3x - 7 = 0$; $a = \underline{\ \ }$, $b = \underline{\ \ }$, $c = \underline{\ \ \ }$

4. $x^2 - 6 = 0$; $a = \underline{\ \ }$, $b = \underline{\ \ }$, $c = \underline{\ \ \ }$

5. $x^2 + x - 1 = 0$; $a = \underline{\ \ }$, $b = \underline{\ \ }$, $c = \underline{\ \ \ }$

6. $9x^2 - 4 = 0$; $a = \underline{\ \ }$, $b = \underline{\ \ }$, $c = \underline{\ \ \ }$

10.3 EXERCISE SET

Simplify the following.

1. $\dfrac{-1 \pm \sqrt{1^2 - 4(1)(-2)}}{2(1)}$

2. $\dfrac{-(-5) \pm \sqrt{(-5)^2 - 4(2)(3)}}{2(2)}$

3. $\dfrac{-5 \pm \sqrt{5^2 - 4(1)(2)}}{2(1)}$

4. $\dfrac{-7 \pm \sqrt{7^2 - 4(2)(1)}}{2(2)}$

5. $\dfrac{-(-4) \pm \sqrt{(-4)^2 - 4(2)(1)}}{2(2)}$

6. $\dfrac{-6 \pm \sqrt{6^2 - 4(3)(1)}}{2(3)}$

Use the quadratic formula to solve each quadratic equation. See Examples 1 through 4.

7. $x^2 - 3x + 2 = 0$

8. $x^2 - 5x - 6 = 0$

9. $3k^2 + 7k + 1 = 0$

10. $7k^2 + 3k - 1 = 0$

11. $49x^2 - 4 = 0$

12. $25x^2 - 15 = 0$

13. $5z^2 - 4z + 3 = 0$

14. $3z^2 + 2z + 1 = 0$

15. $y^2 = 7y + 30$

16. $y^2 = 5y + 36$

17. $2x^2 = 10$

18. $5x^2 = 15$

19. $m^2 - 12 = m$

20. $m^2 - 14 = 5m$

21. $3 - x^2 = 4x$

22. $10 - x^2 = 2x$

23. $2a^2 - 7a + 3 = 0$

24. $3a^2 - 7a + 2 = 0$

25. $x^2 - 5x - 2 = 0$

26. $x^2 - 2x - 5 = 0$

27. $3x^2 - x - 14 = 0$

28. $5x^2 - 13x - 6 = 0$

29. $6x^2 + 9x = 2$

30. $3x^2 - 9x = 8$

31. $7p^2 + 2 = 8p$

32. $11p^2 + 2 = 10p$

33. $a^2 - 6a + 2 = 0$

34. $a^2 - 10a + 19 = 0$

35. $2x^2 - 6x + 3 = 0$

36. $5x^2 - 8x + 2 = 0$

37. $3x^2 = 1 - 2x$

38. $5y^2 = 4 - y$

39. $20y^2 = 3 - 11y$

40. $2z^2 = z + 3$

41. $x^2 + x + 1 = 0$

42. $k^2 + 2k + 5 = 0$

43. $4y^2 = 6y + 1$

44. $6z^2 + 3z + 2 = 0$

Use the quadratic formula to solve each quadratic equation. See Example 5.

45. $3p^2 - \dfrac{2}{3}p + 1 = 0$

46. $\dfrac{5}{2}p^2 - p + \dfrac{1}{2} = 0$

47. $\dfrac{m^2}{2} = m + \dfrac{1}{2}$

48. $\dfrac{m^2}{2} = 3m - 1$

49. $4p^2 + \dfrac{3}{2} = -5p$

50. $4p^2 + \dfrac{3}{2} = 5p$

51. $5x^2 = \dfrac{7}{2}x + 1$

52. $2x^2 = \dfrac{5}{2}x + \dfrac{7}{2}$

53. $28x^2 + 5x + \dfrac{11}{4} = 0$

54. $\dfrac{2}{3}x^2 - 2x - \dfrac{2}{3} = 0$

55. $5z^2 - 2z = \dfrac{1}{5}$

56. $9z^2 + 12z = -1$

57. $x^2 + 3\sqrt{2}x - 5 = 0$

58. $y^2 - 2\sqrt{5}y - 1 = 0$

MIXED PRACTICE

Use the quadratic formula to solve each quadratic equation. Find the exact solutions; then approximate these solutions to the nearest tenth. See Examples 1 through 6.

59. $3x^2 = 21$

60. $2x^2 = 26$

61. $x^2 + 6x + 1 = 0$

62. $x^2 + 4x + 2 = 0$

63. $x^2 = 9x + 4$

64. $x^2 = 7x + 5$

65. $3x^2 - 2x - 2 = 0$

66. $5x^2 - 3x - 1 = 0$

Use the discriminant to determine the number of solutions of each quadratic equation. See Examples 7 and 8.

67. $x^2 + 3x - 1 = 0$

68. $x^2 - 5x - 3 = 0$

69. $3x^2 + x + 5 = 0$

70. $2x^2 + x + 4 = 0$

71. $4x^2 + 4x = -1$

72. $7x^2 - x = 0$

73. $9x^2 + 2x = 0$

74. $x^2 + 10x = -25$

75. $5x^2 + 1 = 0$

76. $4x^2 + 9 = 12x$

77. $x^2 + 36 = -12x$

78. $10x^2 + 2 = 0$

REVIEW AND PREVIEW

Simplify each radical. See Section 9.2.

79. $\sqrt{48}$

80. $\sqrt{104}$

81. $\sqrt{50}$

82. $\sqrt{80}$

Solve the following. See Section 2.6.

△ **83.** The height of a triangle is 4 times the length of the base. The area of the triangle is 18 square feet. Find the height and base of the triangle.

△ **84.** The length of a rectangle is 6 inches more than its width. The area of the rectangle is 391 square inches. Find the dimensions of the rectangle.

x

$x + 6$

CONCEPT EXTENSIONS

Multiple Choice. *Solve. See the Concept Check in this section.*
For the quadratic equation $5x^2 + 2 = x$, *if* $a = 5$,

85. What is the value of b?

  a. $\dfrac{1}{5}$ **b.** 0 **c.** -1 **d.** 1

86. What is the value of c?

  a. 5 **b.** x **c.** -2 **d.** 2

Multiple Choice. *For the quadratic equation* $7y^2 = 3y$, *if* $b = 3$,

87. What is the value of a?

  a. 7 **b.** -7 **c.** 0 **d.** 1

88. What is the value of c?

  a. 7 **b.** 3 **c.** 0 **d.** 1

△ **89.** The largest chocolate bar was a 5026-lb scaled-up model of a Novi chocolate bar, made by the Elah-Dufour United Food Company in 2000. The bar had a base area of 50.8 square feet and its length was 0.5 feet longer than twice its width. Find the length and the width of the bar, rounded to one decimal place. (*Source: Guinness Book of World Records*)

△ **90.** The area of a rectangular conference room table is 95 square feet. If its length is six feet longer than its width, find the dimensions of the table. Round each dimension to the nearest tenth.

x $x + 6$

🖩 **91.** $1.2x^2 - 5.2x - 3.9 = 0$

🖩 **92.** $7.3z^2 + 5.4z - 1.1 = 0$

A rocket is launched from the top of an 80-foot cliff with an initial velocity of 120 feet per second. The height, h, of the rocket after t seconds is given by the equation $h = -16t^2 + 120t + 80$. *Use this for Exercises 93 and 94.*

80 feet

93. How long after the rocket is launched will it be 30 feet from the ground? Round to the nearest tenth of a second.

94. How long after the rocket is launched will it strike the ground? Round to the nearest tenth of a second. (*Hint:* The rocket will strike the ground when its height $h = 0$.)

95. Explain how the quadratic formula is developed and why it is useful.

96. The gross profit y (in millions of dollars) of eBay from 2004 through 2006 is given by the equation $y = -50x^2 + 1128x + 2656$, where $x = 0$ represents 2004. Assume that this trend continues and predict the first year in which eBay's gross profit will be $6368 million. (*Source: Based on data from eBay*)

97. The number of yearly kidney transplants from 1996 to 2005 can be modeled by the equation $y = 3.6x^2 + 578x + 13{,}538$, where $x = 0$ represents the year 2000. Assume that this trend continues and predict the year in which 23,018 kidney transplants will be performed.

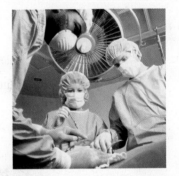

98. The number of patients on the kidney waiting list from 1996 to 2005 can be modeled by the equation $y = -181.5x^2 + 2202.2x + 40{,}000$, where $x = 0$ represents the year 2000. Assume that this trend continues and predict the year in which 43,872 patients will be on the waiting list.

99. The average annual salary y for Microsoft information technology (IT) professionals for the years 2003 through 2006 is given by the equation $y = -1100x^2 + 11{,}800x + 46{,}769$, where $x = 0$ represents 2003. Assume that this trend continues and predict the year in which the average Microsoft IT professional salary will be $78,269. (*Source: Microsoft Corporation*)

100. The number of Target stores y operating in the United States from 2003 through 2006 is given by the equation $y = 6x^2 + 75x + 1225$, where x is the number of years after 2003. Assume that this trend continues and predict the year after 2003 in which the number of Target stores will be 1891. (*Source: Target Corporation*)

INTEGRATED REVIEW SUMMARY ON SOLVING QUADRATIC EQUATIONS

An important skill in mathematics is learning when to use one technique in favor of another. We now practice this by deciding which method to use when solving quadratic equations. Although both the quadratic formula and completing the square can be used to solve any quadratic equation, the quadratic formula is usually less tedious and thus preferred. The following steps may be used to solve a quadratic equation.

> **To Solve a Quadratic Equation**
>
> **STEP 1.** If the equation is in the form $ax^2 = c$ or $(ax + b)^2 = c$, use the square root property and solve. If not, go to Step 2.
>
> **STEP 2.** Write the equation in standard form: $ax^2 + bx + c = 0$.
>
> **STEP 3.** Try to solve the equation by the factoring method. If not possible, go to Step 4.
>
> **STEP 4.** Solve the equation by the quadratic formula.

Study the examples below to help you review these steps.

EXAMPLE 1 Solve $m^2 - 2m - 7 = 0$.

Solution The equation is in standard form, but the quadratic expression $m^2 - 2m - 7$ is not factorable, so use the quadratic formula with $a = 1$, $b = -2$, and $c = -7$.

$$m^2 - 2m - 7 = 0$$

$$m = \frac{-(-2) \pm \sqrt{(-2)^2 - 4 \cdot 1 \cdot (-7)}}{2 \cdot 1} = \frac{2 \pm \sqrt{32}}{2}$$

$$m = \frac{2 \pm 4\sqrt{2}}{2} = \frac{2(1 \pm 2\sqrt{2})}{2} = 1 \pm 2\sqrt{2}$$

The solutions are $1 - 2\sqrt{2}$ and $1 + 2\sqrt{2}$.

PRACTICE
1 Solve $y^2 - 3y - 4 = 0$.

EXAMPLE 2 Solve $(3x + 1)^2 = 20$.

Solution This equation is in a form that makes the square root property easy to apply.

$$(3x + 1)^2 = 20$$

$$3x + 1 = \pm\sqrt{20} \qquad \text{Apply the square root property.}$$

$$3x + 1 = \pm2\sqrt{5} \qquad \text{Simplify } \sqrt{20}.$$

$$3x = -1 \pm 2\sqrt{5}$$

$$x = \frac{-1 \pm 2\sqrt{5}}{3}$$

The solutions are $\dfrac{-1 - 2\sqrt{5}}{3}$ and $\dfrac{-1 + 2\sqrt{5}}{3}$.

PRACTICE
2 Solve $(2x + 5)^2 = 45$.

EXAMPLE 3 Solve $x^2 - \dfrac{11}{2}x = -\dfrac{5}{2}$.

Solution   The fractions make factoring more difficult and also complicate the calculations for using the quadratic formula. Clear the equation of fractions by multiplying both sides of the equation by the LCD 2.

$$x^2 - \frac{11}{2}x = -\frac{5}{2}$$

$$x^2 - \frac{11}{2}x + \frac{5}{2} = 0 \qquad \text{Write in standard form.}$$

$$2x^2 - 11x + 5 = 0 \qquad \text{Multiply both sides by 2.}$$

$$(2x - 1)(x - 5) = 0 \qquad \text{Factor.}$$

$$2x - 1 = 0 \quad \text{or} \quad x - 5 = 0 \qquad \text{Apply the zero factor theorem.}$$

$$2x = 1 \qquad\qquad x = 5$$

$$x = \frac{1}{2} \qquad\qquad x = 5$$

The solutions are $\dfrac{1}{2}$ and 5.

PRACTICE
3   Solve $x^2 - \dfrac{5}{2}x = -\dfrac{3}{2}$.

INTEGRATED REVIEW   EXERCISE SET

Choose and use a method to solve each equation.

1. $5x^2 - 11x + 2 = 0$

2. $5x^2 + 13x - 6 = 0$

3. $x^2 - 1 = 2x$

4. $x^2 + 7 = 6x$

5. $a^2 = 20$

6. $a^2 = 72$

7. $x^2 - x + 4 = 0$

8. $x^2 - 2x + 7 = 0$

9. $3x^2 - 12x + 12 = 0$

10. $5x^2 - 30x + 45 = 0$

11. $9 - 6p + p^2 = 0$

12. $49 - 28p + 4p^2 = 0$

13. $4y^2 - 16 = 0$

14. $3y^2 - 27 = 0$

15. $x^4 - 3x^3 + 2x^2 = 0$

16. $x^3 + 7x^2 + 12x = 0$

17. $(2z + 5)^2 = 25$

18. $(3z - 4)^2 = 16$

19. $30x = 25x^2 + 2$

20. $12x = 4x^2 + 4$

21. $\dfrac{2}{3}m^2 - \dfrac{1}{3}m - 1 = 0$

22. $\dfrac{5}{8}m^2 + m - \dfrac{1}{2} = 0$

23. $x^2 - \dfrac{1}{2}x - \dfrac{1}{5} = 0$

24. $x^2 + \dfrac{1}{2}x - \dfrac{1}{8} = 0$

25. $4x^2 - 27x + 35 = 0$

26. $9x^2 - 16x + 7 = 0$

27. $(7 - 5x)^2 = 18$

28. $(5 - 4x)^2 = 75$

29. $3z^2 - 7z = 12$

30. $6z^2 + 7z = 6$

31. $x = x^2 - 110$

32. $x = 56 - x^2$

33. $\dfrac{3}{4}x^2 - \dfrac{5}{2}x - 2 = 0$

34. $x^2 - \dfrac{6}{5}x - \dfrac{8}{5} = 0$

35. $x^2 - 0.6x + 0.05 = 0$

36. $x^2 - 0.1x - 0.06 = 0$

37. $10x^2 - 11x + 2 = 0$

38. $20x^2 - 11x + 1 = 0$

39. $\dfrac{1}{2}z^2 - 2z + \dfrac{3}{4} = 0$

40. $\dfrac{1}{5}z^2 - \dfrac{1}{2}z - 2 = 0$

41. Explain how you will decide what method to use when solving quadratic equations.

10.4 GRAPHING QUADRATIC EQUATIONS

OBJECTIVE 1 ▶ Graphing $y = ax^2$. Recall from Section 3.2 that the graph of a linear equation in two variables $Ax + By = C$ is a straight line. Also recall from Section 7.6 that the graph of a quadratic equation in two variables $y = ax^2 + bx + c$ is a parabola. In this section, we further investigate the graph of a quadratic equation.

To graph the quadratic equation $y = x^2$, select a few values for x and find the corresponding y-values. Make a table of values to keep track. Then plot the points corresponding to these solutions.

If $x = -3$, then $y = (-3)^2$, or 9.

If $x = -2$, then $y = (-2)^2$, or 4.

If $x = -1$, then $y = (-1)^2$, or 1.

If $x = 0$, then $y = 0^2$, or 0.

If $x = 1$, then $y = 1^2$, or 1.

If $x = 2$, then $y = 2^2$, or 4.

If $x = 3$, then $y = 3^2$, or 9.

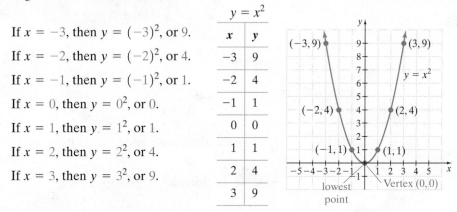

$y = x^2$	
x	y
-3	9
-2	4
-1	1
0	0
1	1
2	4
3	9

Clearly, these points are not on one straight line. As we saw in Chapter 7, the graph of $y = x^2$ is a smooth curve through the plotted points. This curve is called a **parabola.** The lowest point on a parabola opening upward is called the **vertex.** The vertex is $(0, 0)$ for the parabola $y = x^2$. If we fold the graph paper along the y-axis, the two pieces of the parabola match perfectly. For this reason, we say the graph is **symmetric about the y-axis,** and we call the y-axis the **axis of symmetry.**

Notice that the parabola that corresponds to the equation $y = x^2$ opens upward. This happens when the coefficient of x^2 is positive. In the equation $y = x^2$, the coefficient of x^2 is 1. Example 1 shows the graph of a quadratic equation whose coefficient of x^2 is negative.

EXAMPLE 1 Graph $y = -2x^2$.

Solution Select x-values and calculate the corresponding y-values. Plot the ordered pairs found. Then draw a smooth curve through those points. When the coefficient of x^2 is negative, the corresponding parabola opens downward. When a parabola opens downward, the vertex is the highest point of the parabola. The vertex of this parabola is $(0, 0)$ and the axis of symmetry is again the y-axis.

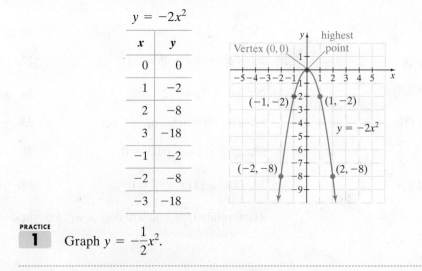

$y = -2x^2$	
x	y
0	0
1	-2
2	-8
3	-18
-1	-2
-2	-8
-3	-18

PRACTICE

1 Graph $y = -\dfrac{1}{2}x^2$.

OBJECTIVE 2 ▶ **Graphing** $y = ax^2 + bx + c$. Just as for linear equations, we can use x- and y-intercepts to help graph quadratic equations. Recall from Chapter 3 that an x-intercept is the point where the graph intersects the x-axis. A y-intercept is the point where the graph intersects the y-axis. We find intercepts just as we did in Chapter 3.

> ▶ **Helpful Hint**
> Recall that:
> To find x-intercepts, let $y = 0$ and solve for x.
> To find y-intercepts, let $x = 0$ and solve for y.

EXAMPLE 2   Graph $y = x^2 - 4$.

Solution   First, find intercepts. To find the y-intercept, let $x = 0$. Then

$$y = 0^2 - 4 = -4$$

To find x-intercepts, we let $y = 0$.

$$0 = x^2 - 4$$
$$0 = (x - 2)(x + 2)$$
$$x - 2 = 0 \quad \text{or} \quad x + 2 = 0$$
$$x = 2 \qquad\qquad x = -2$$

Thus far, we have the y-intercept $(0, -4)$ and the x-intercepts $(2, 0)$ and $(-2, 0)$. Now we can select additional x-values, find the corresponding y-values, plot the points, and draw a smooth curve through the points.

$y = x^2 - 4$

x	y
0	−4
1	−3
2	0
3	5
−1	−3
−2	0
−3	5

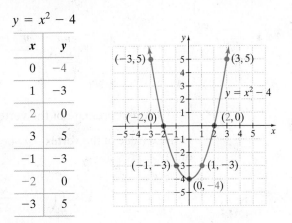

Notice that the vertex of this parabola is $(0, -4)$.

PRACTICE
2   Graph $y = x^2 + 1$.

Concept Check ☑
Tell whether the graph of each equation opens upward or downward.
a. $y = 2x^2$ **b.** $y = 3x^2 + 4x - 5$ **c.** $y = -5x^2 + 2$

> ▶ **Helpful Hint**
> For the graph of $y = ax^2 + bx + c$,
> If a is positive, the parabola opens upward.
> If a is negative, the parabola opens downward.

Answer to Concept Check: **a.** upward
b. upward   **c.** downward

Concept Check ☑

For which of the following graphs of $y = ax^2 + bx + c$ would the value of a be negative?

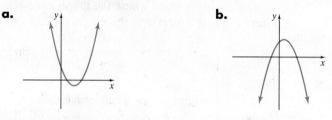

a.

b.

OBJECTIVE 3 ▶ Using the vertex formula. Thus far, we have accidentally stumbled upon the vertex of each parabola that we have graphed. However, our choice of values for x may not yield an ordered pair for the vertex of the parabola. It would be helpful if we could first find the vertex of a parabola, next determine whether the parabola opens upward or downward, and finally calculate additional points such as x- and y-intercepts as needed. In fact, there is a formula that may be used to find the vertex of a parabola.

One way to develop this formula is to notice that the x-value of the vertex of the parabolas that we are considering lies halfway between its x-intercepts. We can use this fact to find a formula for the vertex.

Recall that the x-intercepts of a parabola may be found by solving $0 = ax^2 + bx + c$. These solutions, by the quadratic formula, are

$$x = \frac{-b - \sqrt{b^2 - 4ac}}{2a}, \quad x = \frac{-b + \sqrt{b^2 - 4ac}}{2a}$$

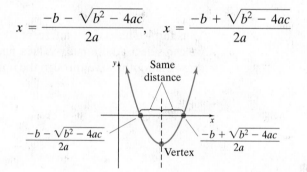

The x-coordinate of the vertex of a parabola is halfway between its x-intercepts, so the x-value of the vertex may be found by computing the average, or $\frac{1}{2}$ of the sum of the intercepts.

$$x = \frac{1}{2}\left(\frac{-b - \sqrt{b^2 - 4ac}}{2a} + \frac{-b + \sqrt{b^2 - 4ac}}{2a}\right)$$

$$= \frac{1}{2}\left(\frac{-b - \sqrt{b^2 - 4ac} - b + \sqrt{b^2 - 4ac}}{2a}\right)$$

$$= \frac{1}{2}\left(\frac{-2b}{2a}\right)$$

$$= \frac{-b}{2a}$$

Vertex Formula

The vertex of the parabola $y = ax^2 + bx + c$ has x-coordinate

$$\frac{-b}{2a}$$

The corresponding y-coordinate of the vertex is found by substituting the x-coordinate into the equation and evaluating y.

EXAMPLE 3   Graph $y = x^2 - 6x + 8$.

Solution   In the equation $y = x^2 - 6x + 8$, $a = 1$ and $b = -6$. The x-coordinate of the vertex is

$$x = \frac{-b}{2a} = \frac{-(-6)}{2 \cdot 1} = 3 \quad \text{Use the vertex formula, } x = \frac{-b}{2a}.$$

To find the corresponding y-coordinate, we let $x = 3$ in the original equation.

$$y = x^2 - 6x + 8 = 3^2 - 6 \cdot 3 + 8 = -1$$

The vertex is $(3, -1)$ and the parabola opens upward since a is positive. We now find and plot the intercepts.

To find the x-intercepts, we let $y = 0$.

$$0 = x^2 - 6x + 8$$

We factor the expression $x^2 - 6x + 8$ to find $(x - 4)(x - 2) = 0$. The x-intercepts are $(4, 0)$ and $(2, 0)$.

If we let $x = 0$ in the original equation, then $y = 8$ and the y-intercept is $(0, 8)$. Now we plot the vertex $(3, -1)$ and the intercepts $(4, 0)$, $(2, 0)$, and $(0, 8)$. Then we can sketch the parabola. These and two additional points are shown in the table.

$y = x^2 - 6x + 8$

x	y
3	-1
4	0
2	0
0	8
1	3
5	3
6	8

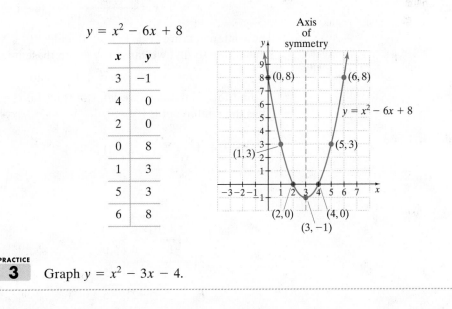

PRACTICE
3   Graph $y = x^2 - 3x - 4$.

Study Example 3 and let's use it to write down a general procedure for graphing quadratic equations.

> **Graphing Parabolas Defined by $y = ax^2 + bx + c$**
>
> 1. **Find the vertex by using the formula $x = -\dfrac{b}{2a}$.** Don't forget to find the y-value of the vertex.
> 2. **Find the intercepts.**
>   - Let $x = 0$ and solve for y to find the y-intercept. There will be only one.
>   - Let $y = 0$ and solve for x to find any x-intercepts. There may be 0, 1, or 2.
> 3. **Plot the vertex and the intercepts.**
> 4. **Find and plot additional points on the graph.** Then draw a smooth curve through the plotted points. Keep in mind if $a > 0$, the parabola opens up and if $a < 0$, the parabola opens down.

EXAMPLE 4   Graph $y = x^2 + 2x - 5$.

Solution   In the equation $y = x^2 + 2x - 5$, $a = 1$ and $b = 2$. Using the vertex formula, we find that the x-coordinate of the vertex is

$$x = \frac{-b}{2a} = \frac{-2}{2 \cdot 1} = -1$$

The y-coordinate of the vertex is

$$y = (-1)^2 + 2(-1) - 5 = -6$$

Thus the vertex is $(-1, -6)$.

To find the x-intercepts, we let $y = 0$.

$$0 = x^2 + 2x - 5$$

This cannot be solved by factoring, so we use the quadratic formula.

$$x = \frac{-2 \pm \sqrt{2^2 - 4(1)(-5)}}{2 \cdot 1}$$ Let $a = 1$, $b = 2$, and $c = -5$.

$$x = \frac{-2 \pm \sqrt{24}}{2}$$

$$x = \frac{-2 \pm 2\sqrt{6}}{2}$$ Simplify the radical.

$$x = \frac{2\left(-1 \pm \sqrt{6}\right)}{2} = -1 \pm \sqrt{6}$$

The x-intercepts are $\left(-1 + \sqrt{6}, 0\right)$ and $\left(-1 - \sqrt{6}, 0\right)$. We use a calculator to approximate these so that we can easily graph these intercepts.

$$-1 + \sqrt{6} \approx 1.4 \qquad \text{and} \qquad -1 - \sqrt{6} \approx -3.4$$

To find the y-intercept, we let $x = 0$ in the original equation and find that $y = -5$. Thus the y-intercept is $(0, -5)$.

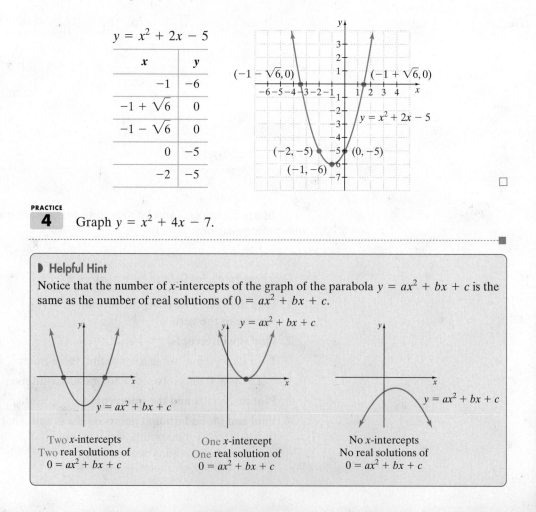

$y = x^2 + 2x - 5$

x	y
-1	-6
$-1 + \sqrt{6}$	0
$-1 - \sqrt{6}$	0
0	-5
-2	-5

PRACTICE
4   Graph $y = x^2 + 4x - 7$.

▶ **Helpful Hint**

Notice that the number of x-intercepts of the graph of the parabola $y = ax^2 + bx + c$ is the same as the number of real solutions of $0 = ax^2 + bx + c$.

Two x-intercepts
Two real solutions of
$0 = ax^2 + bx + c$

One x-intercept
One real solution of
$0 = ax^2 + bx + c$

No x-intercepts
No real solutions of
$0 = ax^2 + bx + c$

Graphing Calculator Explorations

Recall that a graphing calculator may be used to solve quadratic equations. The x-intercepts of the graph of $y = ax^2 + bx + c$ are solutions of $0 = ax^2 + bx + c$. To solve $x^2 - 7x - 3 = 0$, for example, graph $y_1 = x^2 - 7x - 3$. The x-intercepts of the graph are the solutions of the equation.

Use a graphing calculator to solve each quadratic equation. Round solutions to two decimal places.

1. $x^2 - 7x - 3 = 0$ **2.** $2x^2 - 11x - 1 = 0$

3. $-1.7x^2 + 5.6x - 3.7 = 0$ **4.** $-5.8x^2 + 2.3x - 3.9 = 0$

5. $5.8x^2 - 2.6x - 1.9 = 0$ **6.** $7.5x^2 - 3.7x - 1.1 = 0$

10.4 EXERCISE SET

Graph each quadratic equation by finding and plotting ordered pair solutions. See Example 1.

1. $y = 2x^2$ **2.** $y = 3x^2$

3. $y = -x^2$ **4.** $y = -4x^2$

Sketch the graph of each equation. Label the vertex and the intercepts. See Examples 2 through 4.

5. $y = x^2 - 1$ **6.** $y = x^2 - 16$

7. $y = x^2 + 4$ **8.** $y = x^2 + 9$

9. $y = -x^2 + 4x - 4$ **10.** $y = -x^2 - 2x - 1$

11. $y = x^2 + 5x + 4$ **12.** $y = x^2 + 7x + 10$

13. $y = x^2 - 4x + 5$ **14.** $y = x^2 - 6x + 10$

15. $y = 2 - x^2$ **16.** $y = 3 - x^2$

MIXED PRACTICE

Sketch the graph of each equation. Label the vertex and the intercepts. See Examples 1 through 4.

17. $y = \dfrac{1}{3}x^2$ **18.** $y = \dfrac{1}{2}x^2$

19. $y = x^2 + 6x$ **20.** $y = x^2 - 4x$

21. $y = x^2 + 2x - 8$ **22.** $y = x^2 - 2x - 3$

23. $y = -\dfrac{1}{2}x^2$ **24.** $y = -\dfrac{1}{3}x^2$

25. $y = 2x^2 - 11x + 5$ **26.** $y = 2x^2 + x - 3$

27. $y = -x^2 + 4x - 3$ **28.** $y = -x^2 + 6x - 8$

29. $y = x^2 + 2x - 2$ **30.** $y = x^2 - 4x - 3$

31. $y = x^2 - 3x + 1$ **32.** $y = x^2 - 2x - 5$

REVIEW AND PREVIEW

Graph the following linear equations in two variables. See Section 3.2.

33. $y = -3$ **34.** $x = 4$

35. $y = 3x - 2$ **36.** $y = 2x + 3$

The line graph shows the percent of U.S. households with computers. Use this graph for Exercises 37 through 40. See Section 3.5.

37. Estimate the percent of households with computers in 2000.

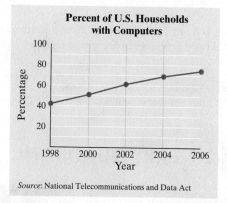

Percent of U.S. Households with Computers

Source: National Telecommunications and Data Act

38. The percent growth of computers in households was almost linear from 1998 to 2006. Approximate this growth with a linear equation. To do so, find an equation of the line through the ordered pairs $(0, 42)$ and $(8, 74.4)$, where x is the number of years since 1998 and y is the percent of households that have computers. Write the equation in slope-intercept form.

Use the equation found in Exercise 38 to find the percent of U.S. households with computers in the given years.

39. 2008.

40. 2014; explain the problem with your answer.

CONCEPT EXTENSIONS

The graph of a quadratic equation that takes the form $y = ax^2 + bx + c$ is the graph of a function. Write the domain and the range of each of the functions graphed.

41.

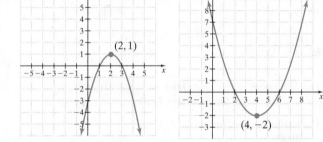

42.

(−3, −4)

43.

(2, 1)

44.

(4, −2)

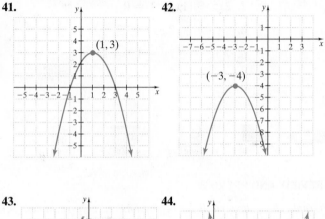

45. The height h of a fireball launched from a Roman candle with an initial velocity of 128 feet per second is given by the equation

$$h = -16t^2 + 128t$$

where t is time in seconds after launch.
Use the graph of this function to answer the questions.

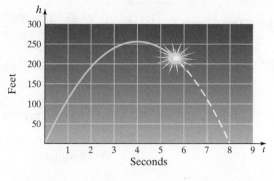

a. Estimate the maximum height of the fireball.

b. Estimate the time when the fireball is at its maximum height.

c. Estimate the time when the fireball returns to the ground.

46. Determine the maximum number and the minimum number of x-intercepts for a parabola. Explain your answer.

Matching. *Match the values given with the correct graph of each quadratic equation of the form $y = a(x - h)^2 + k$.*

47. $a > 0, h > 0, k > 0$ **48.** $a < 0, h > 0, k > 0$

49. $a > 0, h > 0, k < 0$ **50.** $a < 0, h > 0, k < 0$

A   B

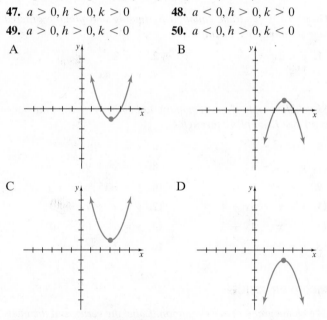

C   D

10.5 LINEAR, QUADRATIC, AND EXPONENTIAL MODELS

OBJECTIVES

1 Use exponential and linear models.

2 Use quadratic models.

3 Determine an appropriate function for modeling data.

Is there a relationship between literacy and child mortality? As the percent of adult females who are literate increases, does the mortality of children under five decrease? The graph below, based on data from the United Nations, indicates that this is, indeed, the case. Each point in the figure represents one country.

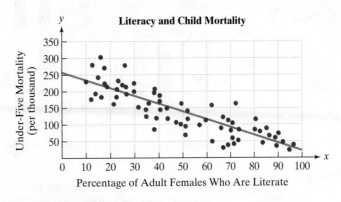

Literacy and Child Mortality

Source: United Nations

Recall that data presented in a visual form as a set of points is called a **scatter plot.** Also shown in the graph above is a line that passes through or near the points. The line that best fits the data points in a scatter plot is called a **regression line.** We can use the line's slope and *y*-intercept to obtain a linear model for under-five mortality, *y*, per thousand, as a function of the percentage of literate adult females, *x*:

$$y = -2.3x + 255.$$

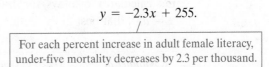

For each percent increase in adult female literacy, under-five mortality decreases by 2.3 per thousand.

Using this model, we can make predictions about child mortality based on the percent of literate adult females in a country.

In the graph above, the data fall on or near a line. Thus, we have the linear model, $y = -2.3x + 255$. However, scatter plots are often curved in a way that indicates that the data do not fall near a line. In this section, we will use functions that are not linear functions to model such data and make predictions.

OBJECTIVE 1 ▶ Modeling with exponential and linear functions. The scatter plot in the margin has a shape that indicates the data are increasing more and more rapidly. *Exponential functions* can be used to model this explosive growth, typically associated with populations, epidemics, and interest-bearing bank accounts.

Recall from Section 6.6 the definition of an exponential function.

Definition of the Exponential Function

The **exponential function** f with base b is defined by

$$y = b^x \quad \text{or} \quad f(x) = b^x,$$

where b is a positive constant other than 1 ($b > 0$ and $b \neq 1$) and x is any real number.

Recall that all exponential functions of the form $y = b^x$, or $f(x) = b^x$, where b is a number greater than 1, have the shape of the graph shown (the graph of $f(x) = 2^x$). The graph approaches, but never touches, the negative portion of the *x*-axis.

The bar graph that follows shows world population for seven selected years from 1950 through 2006. A scatter plot of this data is shown on the next page on the right.

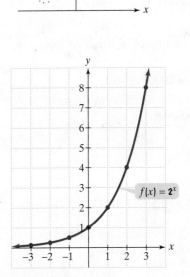

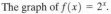

The graph of $f(x) = 2^x$.

World Population, 1950–2006

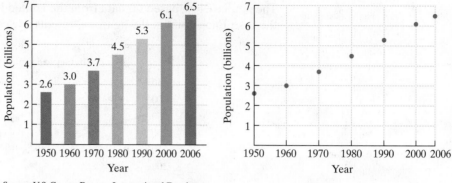

Source: U.S. Census Bureau, International Database

Because the data in the scatter plot appear to increase more and more rapidly, the shape suggests that an exponential function might be a good choice for modeling the data. Furthermore, we can probably draw a line that passes through or near the seven points. Thus, a linear function might also be a good choice for a model.

EXAMPLE 1 Comparing Linear and Exponential Models

The data for world population is shown in the table. After entering the data, a graphing calculator displays the linear model, $y = ax + b$, and the exponential model, $y = ab^x$, that best fit the data, shown below to the right.

x, Number of Years after 1949	y, World Population (billions)
1 (1950)	2.6
11 (1960)	3.0
21 (1970)	3.7
31 (1980)	4.5
41 (1990)	5.3
51 (2000)	6.1
57 (2006)	6.5

A linear model and an exponential model for the data in the table.

a. Use the graphing calculator displays to express each model in function notation, with numbers rounded to three decimal places.

b. How well do the functions model world population in 2000?

c. By one projection, world population is expected to reach 8 billion in the year 2026. Which function serves as a better model for this prediction?

Solution

a. Rounding to three decimal places, the functions

$$f(x) = 0.073x + 2.316 \quad \text{and} \quad g(x) = 2.569(1.017)^x$$

model world population, in billions, x years after 1949. We named the linear function f and the exponential function g, although any letters can be used.

b. The table shows that world population in 2000 was 6.1 billion. The year 2000 is 51 years after 1949. Thus, we substitute 51 for x in each function's equation and then evaluate the resulting expressions with a calculator to see how well the functions describe world population in 2000.

> ### ▶ Helpful Hint
> Exponential functions of the form $y = ab^x$, $b > 1$, model growth in which quantities increase at a rate proportional to their size. Populations that are growing exponentially grow extremely rapidly as they get larger because there are more adults to have offspring.

$$f(x) = 0.073x + 2.316 \qquad \text{This is the linear model.}$$

$$f(51) = 0.073(51) + 2.316 \qquad \text{Substitute 51 for } x.$$

$$\approx 6.0 \qquad \text{Use a calculator:}$$
$$\boxed{.073} \times \boxed{51} + \boxed{2.316} = .$$

$$g(x) = 2.569(1.017)^x \qquad \text{This is the exponential model.}$$

$$g(51) = 2.569(1.017)^{51} \qquad \text{Substitute 51 for } x.$$

$$\approx 6.1 \qquad \text{Use a calculator:}$$
$$2.569 \times 1.017 \boxed{y^x} \ 51 = .$$

Because 6.1 billion was the actual world population in 2000, both functions model world population in 2000 extremely well.

c. Let's see which model comes closest to projecting a world population of 8 billion in the year 2026. Because 2026 is 77 years after 1949 ($2026 - 1949 = 77$), we substitute 77 for x in each function's equation.

$$f(x) = 0.073x + 2.316 \qquad \text{This is the linear model.}$$

$$f(77) = 0.073(77) + 2.316 \qquad \text{Substitute 77 for } x.$$

$$\approx 7.9 \qquad \text{Use a calculator:}$$
$$\boxed{.073} \times \boxed{77} + \boxed{2.316} = .$$

$$g(x) = 2.569(1.017)^x \qquad \text{This is the exponential model.}$$

$$g(77) = 2.569(1.017)^{77} \qquad \text{Substitute 77 for } x.$$

$$\approx 9.4 \qquad \text{Use a calculator:}$$
$$2.569 \times 1.017 \boxed{y^x} \ 77 = .$$

The linear function $f(x) = 0.073x + 2.316$ serves as a better model for a projected world population of 8 billion by 2026. ☐

PRACTICE

1   Use the models in Example 2(a) to solve this problem.

a. World population in 1970 was 3.7 billion. Which function serves as a better model for this year?

b. By one projection, world population is expected to reach 7 billion by 2012. How well do the functions model this projection?

The Role of e in Applied Exponential Functions An irrational number, symbolized by the letter e, appears as the base in many applied exponential functions. This irrational number is approximately equal to 2.72. More accurately,

$$e \approx 2.71828\ldots.$$

The number e is called the **natural base**. The function $f(x) = e^x$ is called the **natural exponential function**.

Use a scientific or graphing calculator with an $\boxed{e^x}$ key to evaluate e to various powers. For example, to find e^2, press the following keys on most calculators:

Scientific calculator: 2 $\boxed{e^x}$

Graphing calculator: $\boxed{e^x}$ 2 $\boxed{\text{ENTER}}$.

The display should be approximately 7.389.

$$e^2 \approx 7.389$$

The number e lies between 2 and 3. Because $2^2 = 4$ and $3^2 = 9$, it makes sense that e^2, approximately 7.389, lies between 4 and 9.

Because $2 < e < 3$, the graph of $y = e^x$ lies between the graphs of $y = 2^x$ and $y = 3^x$, shown in the margin.

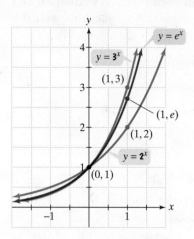

Graphs of three exponential functions

EXAMPLE 2   Alcohol and Risk of a Car Accident

Medical research indicates that the risk of having a car accident increases exponentially as the concentration of alcohol in the blood increases. The risk is modeled by

$$R = 6e^{12.77x},$$

where x is the blood alcohol concentration and R, given as a percent, is the risk of having a car accident. In many states, it is illegal to drive with a blood alcohol concentration of 0.08 or greater. What is the risk of a car accident with a blood alcohol concentration of 0.08?

Solution   For a blood alcohol concentration of 0.08, we substitute 0.08 for x in the exponential model's equation. Then we use a calculator to evaluate the resulting expression.

$$R = 6e^{12.77x}$$

$$R = 6e^{12.77(0.08)}$$

Perform this computation on your calculator.

Scientific calculator: 6 $\boxed{\times}$ $\boxed{(}$ 12.77 $\boxed{\times}$ .08 $\boxed{)}$ $\boxed{e^x}$ $\boxed{=}$

Graphing calculator: 6 $\boxed{\times}$ $\boxed{e^x}$ $\boxed{(}$ 12.77 $\boxed{\times}$ .08 $\boxed{)}$ $\boxed{\text{ENTER}}$

The display should be approximately 16.665813. Rounding to one decimal place, the risk of a car accident is approximately 16.7% with a blood alcohol concentration of 0.08.   □

PRACTICE
2   Use the model in Example 2 to solve this problem. In many states, it is illegal for drivers under 21 years old to drive with a blood alcohol concentration of 0.01 or greater. What is the risk of a car accident with a blood alcohol concentration of 0.01? Round to one decimal place.

OBJECTIVE 2 ▶ Modeling with quadratic functions. The scatter plot in the margin on the next page has a shape that indicates the data are first decreasing and then increasing. This type of behavior can be modeled by *quadratic functions*.

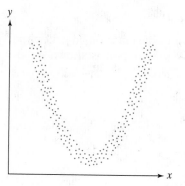

Definition of the Quadratic Function

A **quadratic function** is any function of the form

$$y = ax^2 + bx + c \quad \text{or} \quad f(x) = ax^2 + bx + c,$$

where a, b, and c are real numbers, with $a \neq 0$.

Recall that the graph of any quadratic function is called a **parabola**. If the coefficient of x^2 (the value of a in $ax^2 + bx + c$) is positive, the parabola opens upward. If the coefficient of x^2 is negative, the graph opens downward. The **vertex** (or turning point) of the parabola is the lowest point on the graph when it opens upward and the highest point on the graph when it opens downward.

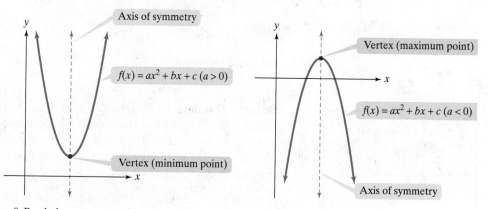

$a > 0$: Parabola opens upward. $\qquad$ $a < 0$: Parabola opens downward.

Characteristics of graphs of quadratic functions

Look at the unusual image of the word "mirror" shown to the right. The artist, Scott Kim, has created the image so that the two halves of the whole are mirror images of each other. A parabola shares this kind of symmetry, in which a line through the vertex divides the figure in half. Parabolas are symmetric with respect to this line, called  the **axis of symmetry**. This means that if a parabola is folded along its axis of symmetry, the two halves match exactly.

When using quadratic functions as models, it is frequently helpful to determine where the vertex, or turning point, occurs. Recall the vertex formula below.

The Vertex of a Parabola

The vertex of a parabola whose equation is $y = ax^2 + bx + c$ occurs when

$$x = \frac{-b}{2a}.$$

EXAMPLE 3 Modeling Wine Consumption

The bar graph on the left shows per capita U.S. adult wine consumption, in gallons per person, for selected years from 1980 through 2003. A scatter plot is shown on the right.

Wine Consumption per U.S. Adult

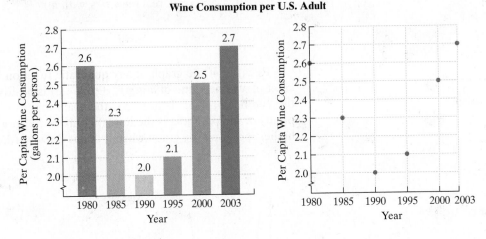

Source: Adams Business Media

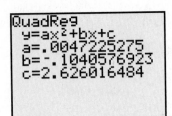

Data (0, 2.6), (5, 2.3), (10, 2.0), (15, 2.1), (20, 2.5), (23, 2.7)

Because the data in the scatter plot first decrease and then increase, the shape suggests that a quadratic function is a good choice for a model. We let x represent the number of years after 1980 and y represent U.S. wine consumption, in gallons per person. After entering the data, a graphing calculator displays the quadratic function, $y = ax^2 + bx + c$, shown in the margin.

a. Express the model in function notation, with numbers rounded to three decimal places.

b. According to the function in part (a), in which year was wine consumption at a minimum? Round to the nearest year. What does the function give for per capita consumption, to the nearest tenth of a gallon, for that year? How well does this model the data shown in the bar graph?

Solution

a. Rounding to three decimal places, the function

$$f(x) = 0.005x^2 - 0.104x + 2.626$$

models U.S. wine consumption, $f(x)$, in gallons per person, x years after 1980.

b. We can use the quadratic model to determine in which year wine consumption was at a minimum.

$$f(x) = 0.005x^2 - 0.104x + 2.626$$

$a = 0.005$ $b = -0.104$

Because the coefficient of x^2, 0.005, is positive, the parabola opens upward and the vertex is the lowest point on the graph. The x-coordinate of the vertex tells us when wine consumption was at a minimum.

$$x = \frac{-b}{2a} = \frac{-(-0.104)}{2(0.005)} = \frac{0.104}{0.01} \approx 10$$

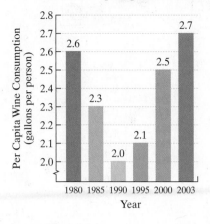

Wine Consumption per U.S. Adult

(repeated)

The quadratic model indicates that wine consumption was at a minimum 10 years after 1980, in the year 1990. Let's see what the function gives for per capita consumption for that year.

$$f(x) = 0.005x^2 - 0.104x + 2.626 \qquad \text{This is the quadratic model.}$$
$$f(10) = 0.005(10)^2 - 0.104(10) + 2.626 \qquad \text{Substitute 10 for } x.$$
$$\approx 2.1 \qquad \text{Use a calculator.}$$

The vertex, approximately $(10, 2.1)$, shows that minimum U.S. wine consumption of 2.1 gallons per adult occurred 10 years after 1980, or in 1990. Because this is close to the 2.0 gallons shown in the bar graph for 1990, the model's vertex describes the data fairly well.   □

PRACTICE

3   The quadratic function $f(x) = 0.4x^2 - 36x + 1000$ models the number of car accidents, $f(x)$, per 50 million miles driven, as a function of a driver's age, x, in years, where $16 \le x \le 74$. According to this model, drivers at which age have the least number of car accidents? How many accidents does this age group have per 50 million miles driven?

OBJECTIVE 3 ▶ Determining an appropriate function for modeling data. The table below contains a description of the scatter plots we have encountered in this section, as well as the type of function that might serve as an appropriate model for each description.

Modeling Data

Description of Data Points in a Scatter Plot	Model
Lie on or near a line	Linear Function: $y = mx + b$ or $f(x) = mx + b$
Increasing more and more rapidly	Exponential Function: $y = b^x$ or $f(x) = b^x, b > 1$
Decreasing and then increasing	Quadratic Function: $y = ax^2 + bx + c$ or $f(x) = ax^2 + bx + c, a > 0$ The vertex, $\left(\dfrac{-b}{2a}, f\left(\dfrac{-b}{2a}\right)\right)$, is a minimum point on the parabola.
Increasing and then decreasing	Quadratic Function: $y = ax^2 + bx + c$ or $f(x) = ax^2 + bx + c, a < 0$ The vertex, $\left(\dfrac{-b}{2a}, f\left(\dfrac{-b}{2a}\right)\right)$, is a maximum point on the parabola.

Once the type of model has been determined, the data can be entered into a graphing calculator. The calculator's regression feature will display the specific function of the type requested that best fits the data.

10.5 | EXERCISE SET

MathXL
PRACTICE | WATCH | DOWNLOAD | READ | REVIEW

In Exercises 1–6,

a. Create a scatter plot for the data in each table.

b. Use the shape of the scatter plot to determine if the data are best modeled by a linear function, an exponential function, or a quadratic function.

1.

x	y
0	−3
1	2
2	7
3	12
4	17

2.

x	y
0	5
1	3
2	1
3	−1
4	−3

3.

x	y
0	4
1	1
2	0
3	1
4	4

4.

x	y
0	−4
1	−1
2	0
3	−1
4	−4

5.

x	y
0	−3
1	−2
2	0
3	4
4	12

6.

x	y
0	4
1	5
2	7
3	11
4	19

7.

x	y
1	5
3	2
6	1
8	4
10	7

8.

x	y
2	8
4	5
6	3
9	4
10	5

9.

x	y
0	−6
2	−5
4	−2
5	1
7	10

10.

x	y
−4	1
0	2
2	3
4	5
6	9

11.

x	y
0	0
9	0.6
16	1.1
19	1.3
25	1.8
30	2.1

12.

x	y
0	0.4
8	0.9
15	1.2
18	1.3
24	1.6
30	1.8

APPLICATION EXERCISES

The bar graph shows the percentage of miscarriages for women at six selected ages. The graphing calculator screen displays an exponential function that models the data, where y represents the percentage of miscarriages at age x. Use this information to solve Exercises 13–14.

```
ExpReg
y=a*b^x
a=1.402292302
b=1.078382445
```

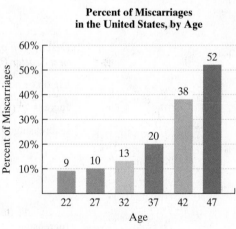

Percent of Miscarriages in the United States, by Age

Source: Time

13. a. Explain why an exponential function was used to model the data displayed in the bar graph.

b. Use the graphing calculator screen to express the model in function notation, with numbers rounded to three decimal places.

c. According to the model, what is the percent of miscarriages at age 37? Use a calculator with a y^x key or a $\wedge$ key, and round to one decimal place. How well does this describe the actual data?

14. Repeat parts (a) and (b) of Exercise 13. For part (c), apply the model to the percent of miscarriages at age 27 and follow the directions in Exercise 13(c).

Use a calculator with an $\boxed{e^x}$ key to solve Exercises 15–16. The graph shows the number of words, in millions, in the U.S. federal tax code for selected years from 1955 through 2000. The data can be modeled by

$$f(x) = 0.16x + 1.43 \quad \text{and} \quad g(x) = 1.8e^{0.04x},$$

in which $f(x)$ and $g(x)$ represent the number of words, in millions, in the federal tax code x years after 1955. Use these functions to solve Exercises 15–16.

Number of Words, in Millions, in the Federal Tax Code

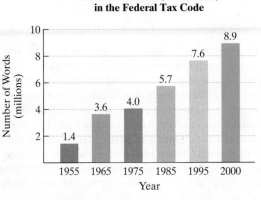

Source: The Tax Foundation

15. Which function, the linear or the exponential, is a better model for the data in 2000?

16. Which function, the linear or the exponential, is a better model for the data in 1985?

Despite high-profile legislation and lawsuits, the bar graph shows that spam has flourished.

Spam Slam: Percent of Inbound email in the U.S. Considered Spam

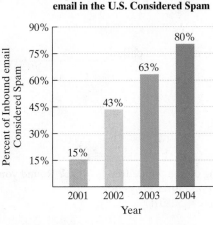

Source: Meta Group

The function $f(x) = 13.4 + 46.3 \ln x$ models the percent of inbound email in the United States considered spam, $f(x)$, x years after 2000. Use this information to solve Exercises 17–18.

17. According to the model, what percentage of email was considered spam in 2003? Use a calculator with an $\boxed{\text{LN}}$ key and round to the nearest percent. How well does this describe the actual data?

18. According to the model, what percentage of email was considered spam in 2002? Use a calculator with an $\boxed{\text{LN}}$ key and round to the nearest percent. How well does this describe the actual data?

19. The bar graph shows the number of U.S. households, in millions, participating in the Food Stamp Program from 1999 through 2004. The graphing calculator screen displays a quadratic function that models the data, where y is the number of households, in millions, receiving food stamps x years after 1999.

Data:
(0, 7.7), (1, 7.4), (2, 7.5),
(3, 8.2), (4, 9.2), (5, 10.6)

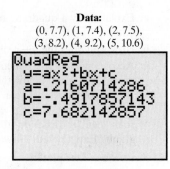

U.S. Households on Food Stamps

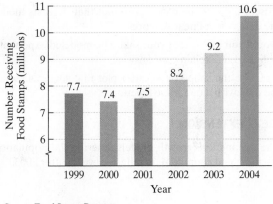

Source: Food Stamp Program

a. Explain why a quadratic function was used to model the data.

b. Use the graphing calculator screen to express the model in function notation, with numbers rounded to two decimal places.

c. According to the function in part (b), in which year was the number of households receiving food stamps at a minimum? Round to the nearest year. Use the model to find the number of households, in millions, for that year. How well does this model the data in the bar graph?

20. The bar graph shows the percent of people in the United States living below the poverty level for selected years from 1990 through 2004. The quadratic function

$$f(x) = 0.04x^2 - 0.61x + 13.5$$

models the percent below the poverty level, $f(x)$, x years after 1990.

Percent of People in the U.S. Living Below the Poverty Level

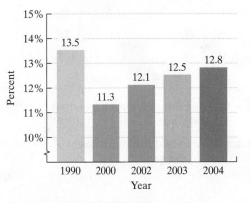

Source: Department of Health and Human Services

a. Explain why a quadratic function was used to model the data.

b. How well does the function model the data for 2004?

c. According to the function, in which year was the percentage living below the poverty level at a minimum? Round to the nearest year. What percentage of Americans lived below the poverty level in that year? Do these results seem consistent with the data displayed in the bar graph? Explain your answer.

21. What is a scatter plot?

22. What is an exponential function?

23. Describe the shape of a scatter plot that suggests modeling the data with an exponential function.

24. Describe the shape of a scatter plot that suggests modeling the data with a linear function.

25. Would you prefer that your salary be modeled exponentially or linearly? Explain your answer.

26. Describe the shape of a scatter plot that suggests modeling the data with a quadratic function.

CONCEPT EXTENSION

27. The exponential growth models describe the population of the indicated country, A, in millions, t years after 2003.

$$\boxed{\text{Canada}} \quad A = 32.2e^{0.003t}$$
$$\boxed{\text{Uganda}} \quad A = 25.6e^{0.03t}$$

According to these models, which one of the following is true?

a. In 2003, Uganda's population was ten times that of Canada's.

b. In 2003, Canada's population exceeded Uganda's by 660,000.

c. In 2012, Uganda's population will exceed Canada's.

d. None of these statements is true.

GROUP EXERCISE

28. Each group member should consult an almanac, newspaper, magazine, or the Internet to find data that can be modeled by linear, exponential, or quadratic functions. Group members should select the two sets of data that are most interesting and relevant. Then consult a person who is familiar with graphing calculators to show you how to obtain a function that best fits each set of data. Once you have these functions, each group member should make one prediction based on one of the models, and then discuss a consequence of this prediction. What factors might change the accuracy of the prediction?

CHAPTER 10 VOCABULARY CHECK

Fill in each blank with one of the words listed below.

square root   completing the square   quadratic   vertex

1. If $x^2 = a$, then $x = \sqrt{a}$ or $x = -\sqrt{a}$. This property is called the _____ property.

2. The formula $\dfrac{-b}{2a}$ where $y = ax^2 + bx + c$ is called the _____ formula.

3. The process of solving a quadratic equation by writing it in the form $(x + a)^2 = c$ is called _____.

4. The formula $x = \dfrac{-b \pm \sqrt{b^2 - 4ac}}{2a}$ is called the _____ formula.

CHAPTER 10 REVIEW

(10.1) Use the square root property to solve each quadratic equation.

1. $x^2 = 36$

2. $x^2 = 81$

3. $k^2 = 50$

4. $k^2 = 45$

5. $(x - 11)^2 = 49$

6. $(x + 3)^2 = 100$

7. $(4p + 5)^2 = 41$

8. $(3p + 7)^2 = 37$

Solve. For Exercises 9 and 10, use the formula $h = 16t^2$, where h is the height in feet at time t seconds.

9. If Kara Washington dives from a height of 100 feet, how long before she hits the water?

10. How long does a 5-mile free-fall take? Round your result to the nearest tenth of a second.
(*Hint:* $1\,\text{mi} = 5280\,\text{ft}$)

(10.2) Complete the square for the following expressions and then factor the resulting perfect square trinomial.

11. $a^2 + 4a$

12. $a^2 - 12a$

13. $m^2 - 3m$

14. $m^2 + 5m$

Solve each quadratic equation by completing the square.

15. $x^2 - 9x = -8$ **16.** $x^2 + 8x = 20$

17. $x^2 + 4x = 1$ **18.** $x^2 - 8x = 3$

19. $x^2 - 6x + 7 = 0$ **20.** $x^2 + 6x + 7 = 0$

21. $2y^2 + y - 1 = 0$ **22.** $y^2 + 3y - 1 = 0$

(10.3) Use the quadratic formula to solve each quadratic equation.

23. $9x^2 + 30x + 25 = 0$ **24.** $16x^2 - 72x + 81 = 0$

25. $7x^2 = 35$ **26.** $11x^2 = 33$

27. $x^2 - 10x + 7 = 0$ **28.** $x^2 + 4x - 7 = 0$

29. $3x^2 + x - 1 = 0$ **30.** $x^2 + 3x - 1 = 0$

31. $2x^2 + x + 5 = 0$ **32.** $7x^2 - 3x + 1 = 0$

For the Exercise numbers given, approximate the exact solutions to the nearest tenth.

33. Exercise 29   **34.** Exercise 30

Use the discriminant to determine the number of solutions of each quadratic equation.

35. $x^2 - 7x - 1 = 0$

36. $x^2 + x + 5 = 0$

37. $9x^2 + 1 = 6x$

38. $x^2 + 6x = 5$

39. $5x^2 + 4 = 0$

40. $x^2 + 25 = 10x$

41. The average price of gold (in dollars per troy ounce) from 2001 to 2005 is given by the equation $y = -x^2 + 51x + 218$. In this equation, x is the number of years since 2000. Assume that this trend continues and find the first year after 2000 in which the price of gold will be $658 per troy ounce. (A troy ounce is a little over 15 grams.) (*Source:* National Mining Association)

42. The number of combined kidney-liver transplants is increasing. From 2000 to 2005, the number of these transplants is modeled by the equation $y = 2.1x^2 + 31x + 125$, where x is the number of years since 2000. Assume that this trend continues and predict the year that the number of kidney-liver transplants will be 645.

(10.4) Graph each quadratic equation and find and plot any intercept points.

43. $y = 5x^2$ **44.** $y = -\frac{1}{2}x^2$

Graph each quadratic equation. Label the vertex and the intercept points with their coordinates.

45. $y = x^2 - 25$ **46.** $y = x^2 - 36$

47. $y = x^2 + 3$ **48.** $y = x^2 + 8$

49. $y = -4x^2 + 8$ **50.** $y = -3x^2 + 9$

51. $y = x^2 + 3x - 10$ **52.** $y = x^2 + 3x - 4$

53. $y = -x^2 - 5x - 6$ **54.** $y = 3x^2 - x - 2$

55. $y = 2x^2 - 11x - 6$ **56.** $y = -x^2 + 4x + 8$

Match each quadratic equation with its graph.

57. $y = 2x^2$ **58.** $y = -x^2$

59. $y = x^2 + 4x + 4$ **60.** $y = x^2 + 5x + 4$

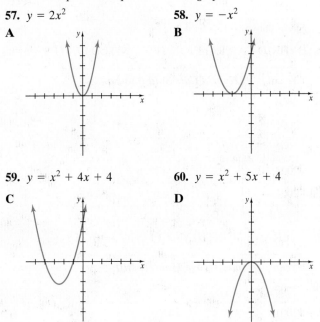

Quadratic equations in the form $y = ax^2 + bx + c$ are graphed below. Determine the number of real solutions for the related equation $0 = ax^2 + bx + c$ from each graph.

61.   **62.**

63.   **64.**

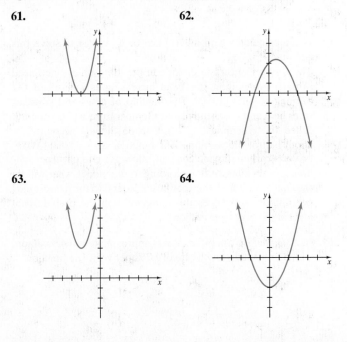

In Exercises 65–67,

  a. *Create a scatter plot for the data in each table.*

  b. *Use the shape of the scatter plot to determine if the data are best modeled by a linear function, an exponential function, a logarithmic function, or a quadratic function.*

65. PERCENTAGE OF U.S. HIGH SCHOOL SENIORS TAKING STEROIDS

Year	Percent
2000	2.5%
2001	3.8%
2002	4.1%
2003	3.5%

Source: University of Michigan

66. HYBRID CAR SALES IN THE UNITED STATES

Year	Hybrid Cars Sold (thousands)
2000	8
2001	20
2002	36
2003	47
2004	83

Source: R. L. Polk and Co.

67. AVERAGE MONTHLY CELLPHONE BILLS

Year	Average Monthly Bill
2000	$45
2001	$47
2002	$48
2003	$50
2004	$51

Source: U.S. Census Bureau

68. Use a calculator with an y^x key or a $\wedge$ key to solve this exercise.

The amount of carbon dioxide in the atmosphere, measured in parts per million, has been increasing as a result of the burning of oil and coal. The buildup of gases and particles traps heat and raises the planet's temperature, a phenomenon called the greenhouse effect. Carbon dioxide accounts for about half of the warming. The function $f(x) = 364(1.005)^x$ projects carbon dioxide concentration, $f(x)$, in parts per million, x years after 2000. According to the model, what will be the concentration in the year 2086? Round to the nearest part per million. How does this compare with the preindustrial level of 280 parts per million?

69. In 2003, Mexico's population was approximately 104.9 million, with a projected growth rate of 1.7% per year. The function

$$f(x) = 104.9e^{0.017x}$$

models Mexico's projected population, $f(x)$, in millions, x years after 2003. According to this model, what will Mexico's population be in 2044? Use a calculator with an e^x key and round to one decimal place. How does this compare with the 2003 population of 104.9 million?

70. The bar graph shows the percent of U.S. companies that performed drug tests on employees or job applicants in five selected years from 1998 through 2003. The data can be modeled by

$$f(x) = -1.7x + 74.5 \text{ and } g(x) = 0.6x^2 - 5.6x + 79$$

in which $f(x)$ and $g(x)$, model the percent of such companies x years after 1997.

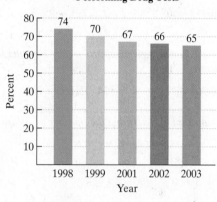

Percent of U.S. Companies Performing Drug Tests

Source: American Management Association

  a. What is the slope of the linear model? What does this mean in terms of the change in the percent of companies that performed drug tests?

  b. Which function, the linear or the quadratic, is a better model for the data in 2002?

MIXED REVIEW

Use the square root property to solve each quadratic equation.

71. $x^2 = 49$ **72.** $y^2 = 75$ **73.** $(x - 7)^2 = 64$

Solve each quadratic equation by completing the square.

74. $x^2 + 4x = 6$ **75.** $3x^2 + x = 2$ **76.** $4x^2 - x - 2 = 0$

Use the quadratic formula to solve each quadratic equation.

77. $4x^2 - 3x - 2 = 0$ **78.** $5x^2 + x - 2 = 0$

79. $4x^2 + 12x + 9 = 0$ **80.** $2x^2 + x + 4 = 0$

Graph each quadratic equation. Label the vertex and the intercept points with their coordinates.

81. $y = 4 - x^2$ **82.** $y = x^2 + 4$

83. $y = x^2 + 6x + 8$ **84.** $y = x^2 - 2x - 4$

CHAPTER 10 TEST

TEST PREP VIDEO The fully worked-out solutions to any exercises you want to review are available in MyMathLab.

Solve using the square root property.

1. $5k^2 = 80$

2. $(3m - 5)^2 = 8$

Solve by completing the square.

3. $x^2 - 26x + 160 = 0$

4. $3x^2 + 12x - 4 = 0$

Solve using the quadratic formula.

5. $x^2 - 3x - 10 = 0$

6. $p^2 - \dfrac{5}{3}p - \dfrac{1}{3} = 0$

Solve by the most appropriate method.

7. $(3x - 5)(x + 2) = -6$

8. $(3x - 1)^2 = 16$

9. $3x^2 - 7x - 2 = 0$

10. $x^2 - 4x + 5 = 0$

11. $3x^2 - 7x + 2 = 0$

12. $2x^2 - 6x + 1 = 0$

13. $9x^2 = 1$

Graph each quadratic equation. Label the vertex and the intercept points with their coordinates.

14. $y = -5x^2$

15. $y = x^2 - 4$

16. $y = x^2 - 7x + 10$

17. $y = 2x^2 + 4x - 1$

Solve.

△ 18. The height of a triangle is 4 times the length of the base. The area of the triangle is 18 square feet. Find the height and base of the triangle.

△ 19. The number of diagonals d that a polygon with n sides has is given by the formula

$$d = \dfrac{n^2 - 3n}{2}$$

Find the number of sides of a polygon if it has 9 diagonals.

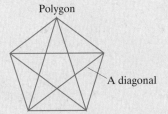

Polygon

A diagonal

Solve.

20. The highest dive from a diving board by a woman was made by Lucy Wardle of the United States. She dove from a height of 120.75 feet at Ocean Park, Hong Kong, in 1985. To the nearest tenth of a second, how long did the dive take? Use the formula $h = 16t^2$.

In Exercises 21–23, determine whether the values in each table belong to an exponential function, a linear function, or a quadratic function.

21.	x	y	22.	x	y	23.	x	y
	0	3		0	1		0	12
	1	1		1	5		1	3
	2	-1		2	25		2	0
	3	-3		3	125		3	3
	4	-5		4	625		4	12

24. The bar graph shows the number, in millions, of cellphone subscribers in the United States from 2000 through 2004. The data can be modeled by the exponential function

$$f(x) = 110.5(1.13)^x,$$

in which $f(x)$ represents the number of cellphone subscribers, in millions, x years after 2000.

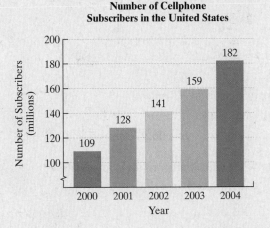

Number of Cellphone Subscribers in the United States

Source: CTIA

a. How well does the function model the data for 2003? Use a calculator and round to the nearest whole number.

b. Use the model to project the number of cellphone subscribers, in millions, in 2010.

25. The bar graph on the next page shows the number, in millions, of Internet users in the United States from 2000 through 2003. The data can be modeled by

$$f(x) = 15.3x + 106.7 \text{ and } g(x) = -5.4x^2 + 42.1x + 80$$

in which $f(x)$ and $g(x)$ represent the number of Internet users, in millions, x years after 1999.

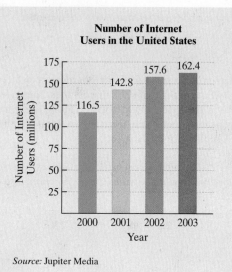

Number of Internet Users in the United States

Source: Jupiter Media

a. What is the slope of the linear model? What does this mean in terms of the change in the number of Internet users?

b. Based on the shape of the graph, which function, the linear or the quadratic, is a better model for the data?

c. Use each function to find the number of Internet users, in millions, in 2001. Which function serves as the better model for 2001? Is this consistent with your answer in part (b)?

CHAPTER 10 STANDARDIZED TEST

Multiple Choice. *Choose the one alternative that best completes the statement or answers the question.*

Solve using the square root property.

1. $3k^2 = 192$

    a. ±32 **b.** $\pm\dfrac{8\sqrt{3}}{3}$ **c.** ±8 **d.** 4096

2. $(5m - 3)^2 = 20$

    a. $\dfrac{2\sqrt{5} \pm 3}{5}$ **b.** $\dfrac{3 \pm 2\sqrt{5}}{5}$

    c. $\dfrac{3 \pm 4\sqrt{5}}{5}$ **d.** $\dfrac{3 \pm 2\sqrt{5}}{5}$

Solve by completing the square.

3. $x^2 + 4x - 45 = 0$

    a. $-36, -9$ **b.** $-36, 9$ **c.** $-5, 9$ **d.** $-9, 5$

Solve by the most appropriate method.

4. $5x^2 + 20x - 16 = 0$

    a. $\dfrac{-10 \pm 6\sqrt{5}}{5}$ **b.** $\dfrac{6\sqrt{5} \pm 10}{5}$

    c. $\dfrac{-2 \pm 6\sqrt{5}}{5}$ **d.** $\dfrac{10 \pm \sqrt{5}}{5}$

Solve using the quadratic formula.

5. $x^2 - 6x + 5 = 0$

    a. $-5, -1$ **b.** $-5, 1$ **c.** $5, 1$ **d.** $5, 0$

6. $x^2 + \dfrac{3}{2}x - \dfrac{1}{2} = 0$

    a. $\dfrac{-3 \pm \sqrt{13}}{4}$ **b.** $\dfrac{\sqrt{13} \pm 3}{4}$

    c. $\dfrac{3 \pm \sqrt{17}}{4}$ **d.** $\dfrac{-3 \pm \sqrt{17}}{4}$

Solve by the most appropriate method.

7. $(2x - 1)(x + 5) = 21$

    a. $-5, \dfrac{1}{2}$ **b.** $-2, \dfrac{13}{2}$

    c. $-5, 2$ **d.** $-\dfrac{13}{2}, 2$

8. $(2x - 3)^2 = 121$

    a. $7, -4$ **b.** $8, -14$

    c. $14, -8$ **d.** $4, -7$

9. $7x^2 + 7x - 4 = 0$

    a. $\dfrac{-7 \pm \sqrt{161}}{14}$ **b.** $\dfrac{7 \pm \sqrt{161}}{14}$

    c. $\dfrac{-7 \pm \sqrt{105}}{28}$ **d.** $\dfrac{-7 \pm \sqrt{161}}{7}$

10. $2x^2 - 5x - 7 = 0$

    a. $\dfrac{7}{2}, 1$ **b.** $\dfrac{2}{7}, -1$

    c. $\dfrac{7}{2}, -1$ **d.** $\dfrac{2}{7}, 0$

11. $7x^2 + 12x + 3 = 0$

    a. $\dfrac{-6 \pm \sqrt{57}}{7}$ **b.** $\dfrac{-12 \pm \sqrt{15}}{7}$

    c. $\dfrac{-6 \pm \sqrt{15}}{7}$ **d.** $\dfrac{-6 \pm \sqrt{15}}{14}$

12. $16x^3 = x$

    a. $0, \pm4$ **b.** $0, \pm\dfrac{1}{4}$

    c. $0, \dfrac{1}{16}$ **d.** $\pm\dfrac{1}{4}$

Graph the quadratic equation. Identify the vertex and the intercept points with their coordinates.

13. $y = -4x^2$

a. vertex: $(0, -4)$
   x-intercepts: none
   y-intercepts: none

b. vertex: $(0, 0)$
   x-intercepts: none
   y-intercepts: none

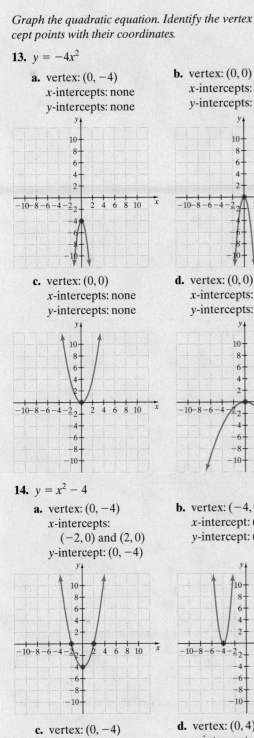

c. vertex: $(0, 0)$
   x-intercepts: none
   y-intercepts: none

d. vertex: $(0, 0)$
   x-intercepts: none
   y-intercepts: none

14. $y = x^2 - 4$

a. vertex: $(0, -4)$
   x-intercepts:
   $(-2, 0)$ and $(2, 0)$
   y-intercept: $(0, -4)$

b. vertex: $(-4, 0)$
   x-intercept: $(-4, 0)$
   y-intercept: $(0, 16)$

c. vertex: $(0, -4)$
   x-intercepts: none
   y-intercept: $(0, -4)$

d. vertex: $(0, 4)$
   x-intercepts: none
   y-intercept: $(0, 4)$

15. $y = x^2 + 2x - 3$

a. vertex: $(-1, -4)$;
   x-intercepts: $(-1, 0)$
   and $(3, 0)$;
   y-intercepts: $(0, -3)$

b. vertex: $(1, -4)$;
   x-intercepts: $(-1, 0)$
   and $(3, 0)$;
   y-intercepts: $(0, -3)$

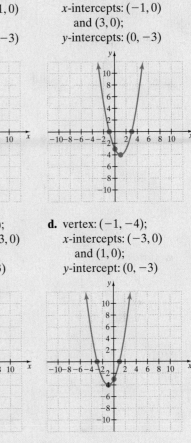

c. vertex: $(-1, -4)$;
   x-intercepts: $(-3, 0)$
   and $(1, 0)$;
   y-intercept: $(0, 3)$

d. vertex: $(-1, -4)$;
   x-intercepts: $(-3, 0)$
   and $(1, 0)$;
   y-intercept: $(0, -3)$

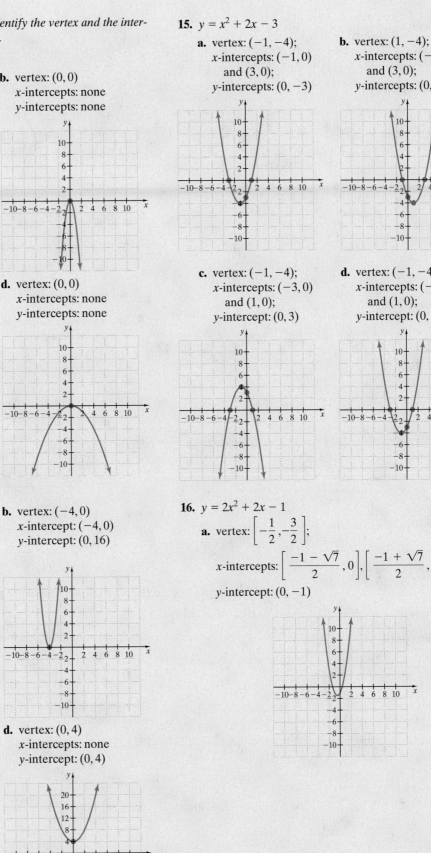

16. $y = 2x^2 + 2x - 1$

a. vertex: $\left[-\dfrac{1}{2}, -\dfrac{3}{2} \right]$;
   x-intercepts: $\left[\dfrac{-1 - \sqrt{7}}{2}, 0 \right], \left[\dfrac{-1 + \sqrt{7}}{2}, 0 \right]$;
   y-intercept: $(0, -1)$

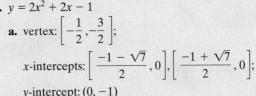

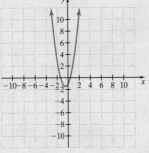

b. vertex: $\left[-\dfrac{1}{2}, -\dfrac{3}{2}\right]$;

x-intercepts: $\left[\dfrac{-1-\sqrt{3}}{2}, 0\right], \left[\dfrac{-1+\sqrt{3}}{2}, 0\right]$;

y-intercept: $(0, -1)$

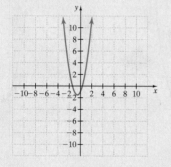

c. vertex: $\left[\dfrac{1}{2}, -\dfrac{3}{2}\right]$;

x-intercepts: $\left[\dfrac{1-\sqrt{3}}{2}, 0\right], \left[\dfrac{1+\sqrt{3}}{2}, 0\right]$;

y-intercept: $(0, -1)$

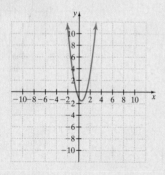

d. vertex: $\left[\dfrac{1}{2}, -\dfrac{3}{2}\right]$;

x-intercepts: $\left[\dfrac{1-\sqrt{7}}{2}, 0\right], \left[\dfrac{1+\sqrt{7}}{2}, 0\right]$;

y-intercept: $(0, -1)$

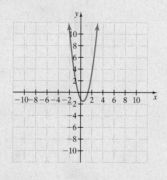

Solve.

17. The height of a triangle is 4 times the length of the base. The area of the triangle is 50 square meters. Find the height and base of the triangle.

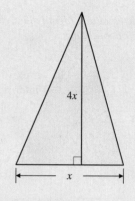

a. base $= \dfrac{5\sqrt{2}}{2}$ m, height $= 10\sqrt{2}$ m

b. base $= 5$ m, height $= 20$ m

c. base $= 5$ m, height $= 40$ m

d. base $= \dfrac{5}{2}$ m, height $= 40$ m

18. The number of diagonals d that a polygon with n sides has is given by the formula

$$d = \dfrac{n^2 - 3n}{2}$$

Find the number of sides of a polygon if it has 20 diagonals.

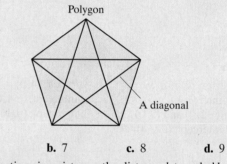

a. 5   **b.** 7   **c.** 8   **d.** 9

19. Neglecting air resistance, the distance h traveled by a free-falling object in time t is given by the formula $h = 16t^2$. Use this formula to find the time of free fall for a parachutist who falls 2938 feet before opening her parachute. Round your answer to the nearest tenth of a second.

a. 3.4 sec   **b.** 91.8 sec   **c.** 13.6 sec   **d.** 216.8 sec

Determine whether the values in each table belong to an exponential function, a linear function, or a quadratic function.

20.

x	y
0	-10
1	-8
2	-4
3	2
4	10

a. linear   **b.** quadratic

c. exponential   **d.** none of these

21.

x	y
0	−4
1	−1
2	2
3	5
4	8

a. linear **b.** quadratic
c. exponential **d.** none of these

22.

x	y
0	1
1	6
2	36
3	216
4	1296

a. linear **b.** quadratic
c. exponential **d.** none of these

Appendix A

Venn Diagrams

OBJECTIVES

1 Understand the basic ideas of a Venn diagram.

2 Determine sets involving set operations from a Venn diagram.

3 Use Venn diagrams with three sets.

▶ **Helpful Hint**

The size of the circle representing a set in a Venn diagram has nothing to do with the number of elements in the set.

OBJECTIVE 1 ▶ **Understand the basic ideas of a Venn diagram.** In discussing sets, it is convenient to refer to a general set that contains all elements under discussion. This general set is called the *universal set*. A **universal set**, symbolized by U, is a set that contains all the elements being considered in a given discussion or problem.

We can obtain an understanding of sets and their relationship to a universal set by considering diagrams that allow visual analysis. **Venn diagrams,** named for the British logician John Venn (1834–1923), are used to show the visual relationship among sets.

Figure A.1 is a Venn diagram. The universal set is represented by a region inside a rectangle. Subsets within the universal set are depicted by circles, or sometimes by ovals or other shapes. In this Venn diagram, set A is represented by the light blue region inside the circle.

The dark blue region in Figure A.1 represents the set of elements in the universal set U that are not in set A. By combining the regions shown by the light blue shading and the dark blue shading, we obtain the universal set, U.

FIGURE A.1

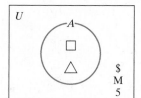

FIGURE A.2

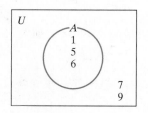

FIGURE A.3

EXAMPLE 1   **Determining Sets from a Venn Diagram**

Use the Venn diagram in Figure A.2 to determine each of the following sets:

a. U **b.** A **c.** the set of elements in U that are not in A.

Solution

a. Set U, the universal set, consists of all the elements within the rectangle. Thus, $U = \{\square, \Delta, \$, M, 5\}$.

b. Set A consists of all the elements within the circle. Thus, $A = \{\square, \Delta\}$.

c. The set of elements in U that are not in A, shown by the set of all the elements outside the circle, is $\{\$, M, 5\}$.   □

PRACTICE

1   Use the Venn diagram in Figure A.3 to determine each of the following sets:

a. U **b.** A **c.** the set of elements in U that are not in A.

There are a number of different ways to represent two subsets of a universal set in a Venn diagram. To help understand these representations, let's take a look at the following scenario.

You need to determine whether there is sufficient support on campus to have a blood drive. You take a survey to obtain information, asking students

     Would you be willing to donate blood?

     Would you be willing to help serve a free breakfast to blood donors?

Set *A* represents the set of students willing to donate blood. Set *B* represents the set of students willing to help serve breakfast to donors. Possible survey results include the following:

- No students willing to donate blood are willing to serve breakfast, and vice versa.
- All students willing to donate blood are willing to serve breakfast.
- The same students who are willing to donate blood are willing to serve breakfast.
- Some of the students willing to donate blood are willing to serve breakfast.

We begin by using Venn diagrams to visualize these results. To do so, we consider four basic relationships and their visualizations.

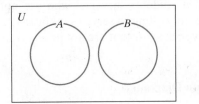

FIGURE A.4

Relationship 1: Disjoint Sets Two sets that have no elements in common are called **disjoint sets.** Two disjoint sets, *A* and *B*, are shown in the Venn diagram in Figure A.4. Disjoint sets are represented as circles that do not overlap. No elements of set *A* are elements of set *B*, and vice versa.

If set *A* represents the set of students willing to donate blood and set *B* represents the set of students willing to serve breakfast to donors, the set diagram illustrates

> No students willing to donate blood are willing to serve breakfast, and vice versa.

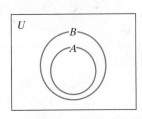

FIGURE A.5

Relationship 2: Proper Subsets If set *A* is a proper subset of set *B* ($A \subset B$), the relationship is shown in the Venn diagram in Figure A.5. All elements of set *A* are elements of set *B*. If an *x* representing an element is placed inside circle *A*, it automatically falls inside circle *B*.

If set *A* represents the set of students willing to donate blood and set *B* represents the set of students willing to serve breakfast to donors, the set diagram illustrates

> All students willing to donate blood are willing to serve breakfast.

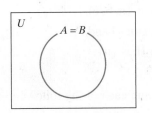

FIGURE A.6

Relationship 3: Equal Sets If $A = B$, then set *A* contains exactly the same elements as set *B*. This relationship is shown in the Venn diagram in Figure A.6. Because all elements in set *A* are in set *B*, and vice versa, this diagram illustrates that when $A = B$, then $A \subseteq B$ and $B \subseteq A$.

If set *A* represents the set of students willing to donate blood and set *B* represents the set of students willing to serve breakfast to donors, the set diagram illustrates

> The same students who are willing to donate blood are willing to serve breakfast.

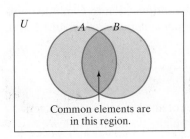

FIGURE A.7

Relationship 4: Sets with Some Common Elements In mathematics, the word *some* means *there exists at least one*. If set *A* and set *B* have at least one element in common, then the circles representing the sets must overlap. This is illustrated in the Venn diagram in Figure A.7.

If set *A* represents the set of students willing to donate blood and set *B* represents the set of students willing to serve breakfast to donors, the presence of at least one student in the dark blue region in Figure A.7 illustrates

> Some students willing to donate blood are willing to serve breakfast.

In Figure A.8 on the next page, we've numbered each of the regions in the Venn diagram in Figure A.7. Let's make sure we understand what these regions represent in terms of the campus blood drive scenario. Remember that *A* is the set of blood donors and *B* is the set of breakfast servers.

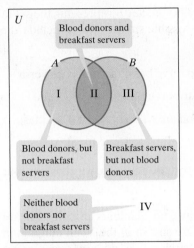

A: Set of blood donors
B: Set of breakfast servers

FIGURE A.8

In Figure A.8, we'll start with the innermost region, region II, and work outward to region IV.

Region II	This region represents the set of students willing to donate blood and serve breakfast. The elements that belong to both set A and set B are in this region.
Region I	This region represents the set of students willing to donate blood, but not serve breakfast. The elements that belong to set A but not to set B are in this region.
Region III	This region represents the set of students willing to serve breakfast, but not donate blood. The elements that belong to set B but not to set A are in this region.
Region IV	This region represents the set of students surveyed who are not willing to donate blood and are not willing to serve breakfast. The elements that belong to the universal set U that are not in sets A or B are in this region.

EXAMPLE 2 **Determining Sets from a Venn Diagram**

Use the Venn diagram in Figure A.9 to determine each of the following sets:

a. U **b.** B

c. the set of elements in A but not B

d. the set of elements in U that are not in B

e. the set of elements in both A and B.

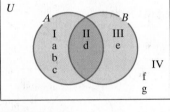

FIGURE A.9

Solution

a. Set U, the universal set, consists of all elements within the rectangle. Taking the elements in regions I, II, III, and IV, we obtain $U = \{a, b, c, d, e, f, g\}$.

b. Set B consists of the elements in regions II and III. Thus, $B = \{d, e\}$.

c. The set of elements in A but not B, found in region I, is $\{a, b, c\}$.

d. The set of elements in U that are not in B, found in regions I and IV, is $\{a, b, c, f, g\}$.

e. The set of elements in both A and B, found in region II, is $\{d\}$.   □

PRACTICE

2   Use the Venn diagram in Figure A.9 to determine each of the following sets:
a. A; **b.** the set of elements in B but not A; **c.** the set of elements in U that are not in A;
d. the set of elements in U that are not in A or B.

The Complement of a Set

In arithmetic, we use operations such as addition and multiplication to combine numbers. We now turn to three set operations, called *complement*, *intersection*, and *union*. We begin by defining a set's complement.

Definition of the Complement of a Set

The **complement** of set A, symbolized by A', is the set of all elements in the universal set that are *not* in A. This idea can be expressed in set-builder notation as follows:

$$A' = \{x \mid x \in U \text{ and } x \notin A\}.$$

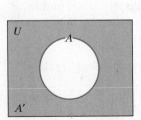

FIGURE A.10

The shaded region in Figure A.10 represents the complement of set A, or A'. This region lies outside circle A, but within the rectangular universal set.

In order to find A', a universal set U must be given. A fast way to find A' is to cross out the elements in U that are given to be in set A. A' is the set that remains.

EXAMPLE 3   **Finding a Set's Complement**

Let $U = \{1, 2, 3, 4, 5, 6, 7, 8, 9\}$ and $A = \{1, 3, 4, 7\}$. Find A'.

Solution   Set A' contains all the elements of set U that are not in set A. Because set A contains the elements 1, 3, 4, and 7, these elements cannot be members of set A':

$$\{\cancel{1}, 2, \cancel{3}, \cancel{4}, 5, 6, \cancel{7}, 8, 9\}.$$

Thus, set A' contains 2, 5, 6, 8, and 9:

$$A' = \{2, 5, 6, 8, 9\}.$$

A Venn diagram illustrating A and A' is shown in Figure A.11.

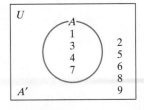

FIGURE A.11

PRACTICE

3   Let $U = \{a, b, c, d, e\}$ and $A = \{a, d\}$. Find A'.

The Intersection of Sets

If A and B are sets, we can form a new set consisting of all elements that are in both A and B. This set is called the _intersection_ of the two sets.

> **Definition of the Intersection of Sets**
> The **intersection** of sets A and B, written $A \cap B$, is the set of elements common to both set A and set B. This definition can be expressed in set-builder notation as follows:
> $$A \cap B = \{x \,|\, x \in A \quad \text{and} \quad x \in B\}.$$

In Example 4, we are asked to find the intersection of two sets. This is done by listing the common elements of both sets. Because the intersection of two sets is also a set, we enclose these elements with braces.

EXAMPLE 4   **Finding the Intersection of Two Sets**

Find each of the following intersections:

a. $\{7, 8, 9, 10, 11\} \cap \{6, 8, 10, 12\}$
b. $\{1, 3, 5, 7, 9\} \cap \{2, 4, 6, 8\}$
c. $\{1, 3, 5, 7, 9\} \cap \varnothing$.

Solution

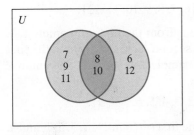

FIGURE A.12 The numbers 8 and 10 belong to both sets.

a. The elements common to $\{7, 8, 9, 10, 11\}$ and $\{6, 8, 10, 12\}$ are 8 and 10. Thus,
$$\{7, 8, 9, 10, 11\} \cap \{6, 8, 10, 12\} = \{8, 10\}.$$
The Venn diagram in Figure A.12 illustrates this situation.

b. The sets $\{1, 3, 5, 7, 9\}$ and $\{2, 4, 6, 8\}$ have no elements in common. Thus,
$$\{1, 3, 5, 7, 9\} \cap \{2, 4, 6, 8\} = \varnothing.$$
The Venn diagram in Figure A.13 illustrates this situation. The sets are disjoint.

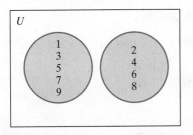

FIGURE A.13 These disjoint sets have no common elements.

c. There are no elements in $\varnothing$, the empty set. This means that there can be no elements belonging to both $\{1, 3, 5, 7, 9\}$ and $\varnothing$. Therefore,
$$\{1, 3, 5, 7, 9\} \cap \varnothing = \varnothing.$$

PRACTICE
4   Find each of the following intersections:

a. $\{1, 3, 5, 7, 10\} \cap \{6, 7, 10, 11\}$

b. $\{1, 2, 3\} \cap \{4, 5, 6, 7\}$

c. $\{1, 2, 3\} \cap \varnothing$.

The Union of Sets

Another set that we can form from sets A and B consists of elements that are in A or B or in both sets. This set is called the *union* of the two sets.

> **Definition of the Union of Sets**
>
> The **union** of sets A and B, written $A \cup B$, is the set of elements that are members of set A or of set B or of both sets. This definition can be expressed in set-builder notation as follows:
>
> $$A \cup B = \{x | x \in A \quad \text{or} \quad x \in B\}.$$

We can find the union of set A and set B by listing the elements of set A. Then, we include any elements of set B that have not already been listed. Enclose all elements that are listed with braces. This shows that the union of two sets is also a set.

EXAMPLE 5   Finding the Union of two Sets

Find each of the following unions:

a. $\{7, 8, 9, 10, 11\} \cup \{6, 8, 10, 12\}$

b. $\{1, 3, 5, 7, 9\} \cup \{2, 4, 6, 8\}$

c. $\{1, 3, 5, 7, 9\} \cup \varnothing$.

▶ **Helpful Hint**

When finding the union of two sets, some elements may appear in both sets. List these common elements only once, *not twice*, in the union of the sets.

Solution   This example uses the same sets as in Example 4. However, this time we are finding the unions of the sets, rather than their intersections.

a. To find $\{7, 8, 9, 10, 11\} \cup \{6, 8, 10, 12\}$, start by listing all the elements from the first set, namely 7, 8, 9, 10, and 11. Now list all the elements from the second set that are not in the first set, namely 6 and 12. The union is the set consisting of all these elements. Thus,

$$\{7, 8, 9, 10, 11\} \cup \{6, 8, 10, 12\} = \{6, 7, 8, 9, 10, 11, 12\}.$$

b. To find $\{1, 3, 5, 7, 9\} \cup \{2, 4, 6, 8\}$, list the elements from the first set, namely 1, 3, 5, 7, and 9. Now add to the list the elements in the second set that are not in the first set. This includes every element in the second set, namely 2, 4, 6, and 8. The union is the set consisting of all these elements, so

$$\{1, 3, 5, 7, 9\} \cup \{2, 4, 6, 8\} = \{1, 2, 3, 4, 5, 6, 7, 8, 9\}.$$

c. To find $\{1, 3, 5, 7, 9\} \cup \varnothing$, list the elements from the first set, namely 1, 3, 5, 7, and 9. Because there are no elements in $\varnothing$, the empty set, there are no additional elements to add to the list. Thus,

$$\{1, 3, 5, 7, 9\} \cup \varnothing = \{1, 3, 5, 7, 9\}. \qquad \square$$

Examples 4 and 5 illustrate the role that the empty set plays in intersection and union.

> **The Empty Set in Intersection and Union**
>
> For any set A,
>
> **1.** $A \cap \varnothing = \varnothing$
>
> **2.** $A \cup \varnothing = A$.

5 Find each of the following unions:

a. $\{1, 3, 5, 7, 10\} \cup \{6, 7, 10, 11\}$

b. $\{1, 2, 3\} \cup \{4, 5, 6, 7\}$

c. $\{1, 2, 3\} \cup \emptyset.$

OBJECTIVE 2 ▶ Determine sets involving set operations from a Venn diagram.

EXAMPLE 6   Determining Sets from a Venn Diagram

The Venn diagram in Figure A.14 percolates with interesting numbers. Use the diagram to determine each of the following sets:

a. $A \cup B$ **b.** $(A \cup B)'$ **c.** $A \cap B$

d. $(A \cap B)'$ **e.** $A' \cap B$ **f.** $A \cup B'.$

FIGURE A.14

Solution

Set to Determine	Description of Set	Regions in Venn Diagram	Set in Roster Form
a. $A \cup B$	set of elements in A or B or both	I, II, III	$\{\pi, e, \sqrt{2}, \sqrt{-1}, e^{\pi i}, 10^{100}, 2^{\aleph_0}\}$
b. $(A \cup B)'$	set of elements in U that are not in $A \cup B$	IV	$\{666\}$
c. $A \cap B$	set of elements in both A and B	II	$\{\sqrt{2}, \sqrt{-1}\}$
d. $(A \cap B)'$	set of elements in U that are not in $A \cap B$	I, III, IV	$\{\pi, e, e^{\pi i}, 10^{100}, 2^{\aleph_0}, 666\}$
e. $A' \cap B$	set of elements that are not in A and are in B	III	$\{e^{\pi i}, 10^{100}, 2^{\aleph_0}\}$
f. $A \cup B'$	set of elements that are in A or not in B or both	I, II, IV	$\{\pi, e, \sqrt{2}, \sqrt{-1}, 666\}$

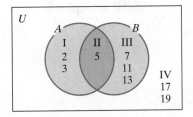

FIGURE A.15

6 Use the Venn diagram in Figure A.15 to determine each of the following sets:

a. $A \cap B$ **b.** $(A \cap B)'$ **c.** $A \cup B$

d. $(A \cup B)'$ **e.** $A' \cup B$ **f.** $A \cap B'.$

OBJECTIVE 3 ▶ Venn diagrams with three sets. Venn diagrams can contain three or more sets, such as the diagram in Figure A.16. The three sets in the figure separate the universal set, U, into eight regions. The numbering of these regions is arbitrary—that is, we can number any region as I, any region as II, and so on. Here is a description of each region, starting with the innermost region, region V, and working outward to region VIII.

The Region Shown in Dark Blue

Region V   This region represents elements that are common to sets A, B, and C: $A \cap B \cap C$.

The Regions Shown in Light Blue

Region II   This region represents elements in both sets A and B that are not in set C: $(A \cap B) \cap C'$.

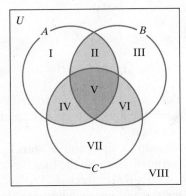

FIGURE A.16 Three intersecting sets separate the universal set into eight regions.

| Region IV | This region represents elements in both sets A and C that are not in set B: $(A \cap C) \cap B'$. |
| Region VI | This region represents elements in both sets B and C that are not in set A: $(B \cap C) \cap A'$. |

The Regions Shown in White

Region I	This region represents elements in set A that are in neither sets B nor C: $A \cap (B' \cap C')$.
Region III	This region represents elements in set B that are in neither sets A nor C: $B \cap (A' \cap C')$.
Region VII	This region represents elements in set C that are in neither sets A nor B: $C \cap (A' \cap B')$.
Region VIII	This region represents elements in the universal set U that are not in sets A, B, or C: $A' \cap B' \cap C'$.

EXAMPLE 7 Determining Sets from a Venn Diagram with Three Intersecting Sets

Use the Venn diagram in Figure A.17 to determine each of the following sets:

a. A **b.** $A \cup B$ **c.** $B \cap C$

d. C' **e.** $A \cap B \cap C$.

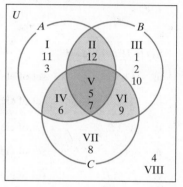

FIGURE A.17

Solution

Set to Determine	Description of Set	Regions in Venn Diagram	Set in Roster Form
a. A	set of elements in A	I, II, IV, V	$\{11, 3, 12, 6, 5, 7\}$
b. $A \cup B$	set of elements in A or B or both	I, II, III, IV, V, VI	$\{11, 3, 12, 1, 2, 10, 6, 5, 7, 9\}$
c. $B \cap C$	set of elements in both B and C	V, VI	$\{5, 7, 9\}$
d. C'	set of elements in U that are not in C	I, II, III, VIII	$\{11, 3, 12, 1, 2, 10, 4\}$
e. $A \cap B \cap C$	set of elements in A and B and C	V	$\{5, 7\}$

□

PRACTICE

7 Use the Venn diagram in Figure A.17 to determine each of the following sets:

a. C **b.** $B \cup C$ **c.** $A \cap C$

d. B' **e.** $A \cup B \cup C$.

In Example 7, we used a Venn diagram showing elements in the regions to determine various sets. Now we are going to reverse directions. We'll use sets A, B, C, and U to determine the elements in each region of a Venn diagram.

To construct a Venn diagram illustrating the elements in A, B, C, and U, **start by placing elements into the innermost region and work outward**. Because the four inner regions represent various intersections, find $A \cap B$, $A \cap C$, $B \cap C$, and $A \cap B \cap C$. Then use these intersections, and the given sets to place the various elements into regions. This procedure is illustrated in Example 8.

EXAMPLE 8   **Determining a Venn Diagram from Sets**

Construct a Venn diagram illustrating the following sets:

$$A = \{a, d, e, g, h, i, j\}$$
$$B = \{b, e, g, h, l\}$$
$$C = \{a, c, e, h\}$$
$$U = \{a, b, c, d, e, f, g, h, i, j, k, l\}.$$

Solution   We begin by finding four intersections. In each case, common elements are shown in red.

- $A \cap B = \{a, d, e, g, h, i, j\} \cap \{b, e, g, h, l\} = \{e, g, h\}$
- $A \cap C = \{a, d, e, g, h, i, j\} \cap \{a, c, e, h\} = \{a, e, h\}$
- $B \cap C = \{b, e, g, h, l\} \cap \{a, c, e, h\} = \{e, h\}$
- $A \cap B \cap C = \{e, g, h\} \cap \{a, c, e, h\} = \{e, h\}$

> This is $A \cap B$ from above.

Now we can place elements into regions, starting with the innermost region, region V, and working outward.

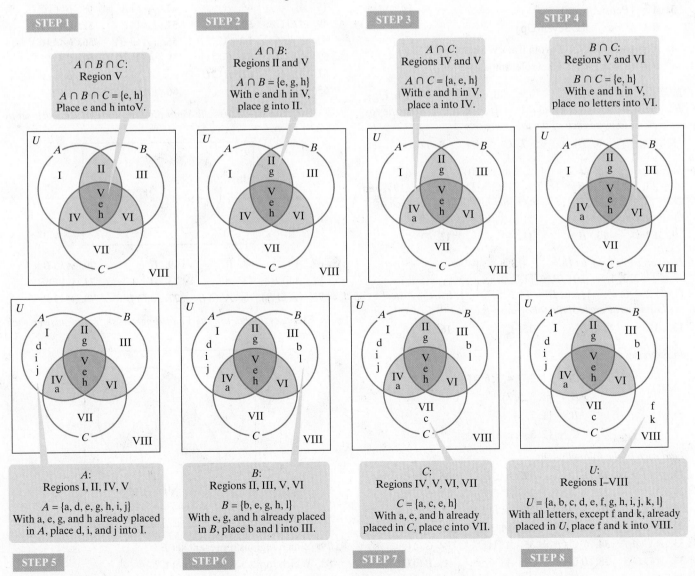

STEP 1

$A \cap B \cap C$:
Region V

$A \cap B \cap C = \{e, h\}$
Place e and h into V.

STEP 2

$A \cap B$:
Regions II and V

$A \cap B = \{e, g, h\}$
With e and h in V,
place g into II.

STEP 3

$A \cap C$:
Regions IV and V

$A \cap C = \{a, e, h\}$
With e and h in V,
place a into IV.

STEP 4

$B \cap C$:
Regions V and VI

$B \cap C = \{e, h\}$
With e and h in V,
place no letters into VI.

STEP 5

A:
Regions I, II, IV, V

$A = \{a, d, e, g, h, i, j\}$
With a, e, g, and h already placed
in A, place d, i, and j into I.

STEP 6

B:
Regions II, III, V, VI

$B = \{b, e, g, h, l\}$
With e, g, and h already placed
in B, place b and l into III.

STEP 7

C:
Regions IV, V, VI, VII

$C = \{a, c, e, h\}$
With a, e, and h already
placed in C, place c into VII.

STEP 8

U:
Regions I–VIII

$U = \{a, b, c, d, e, f, g, h, i, j, k, l\}$
With all letters, except f and k, already
placed in U, place f and k into VIII.

The completed Venn diagram in step 8 illustrates the given sets.

PRACTICE 8 Construct a Venn diagram illustrating the following sets:

$$A = \{1, 3, 6, 10\}$$
$$B = \{4, 7, 9, 10\}$$
$$C = \{3, 4, 5, 8, 9, 10\}$$
$$U = \{1, 2, 3, 4, 5, 6, 7, 8, 9, 10\}.$$

APPENDIX A | EXERCISE SET

MyMathLab® *Powered by CourseCompass™ and MathXL®*

Math XL PRACTICE | WATCH | DOWNLOAD | READ | REVIEW

PRACTICE EXERCISES

In Exercises 1–4, describe a universal set U that includes all elements in the given sets. Answers may vary.

1. A = {Bach, Mozart, Beethoven}
B = {Brahms, Schubert}

2. A = {William Shakespeare, Charles Dickens}
B = {Mark Twain, Robert Louis Stevenson}

3. A = {Pepsi, Sprite}
B = {Coca Cola, Seven-Up}

4. A = {Acura RSX, Toyota Camry, Mitsubishi Lancer}
B = {Dodge Ram, Chevrolet Impala}

In Exercises 5–8, let U = {a, b, c, d, e, f, g}, A = {a, b, f, g}, B = {c, d, e}, C = {a, g}, *and* D = {a, b, c, d, e, f}. *Use the roster method to write each of the following sets.*

5. A' **6.** B' **7.** C' **8.** D'

In Exercises 9–12, let U = {1, 2, 3, 4, ..., 20}, A = {1, 2, 3, 4, 5}, B = {6, 7, 8, 9}, C = {1, 3, 5, 7, ..., 19}, *and* D = {2, 4, 6, 8, ..., 20}. *Use the roster method to write each of the following sets.*

9. A' **10.** B' **11.** C' **12.** D'

In Exercises 13–16, let U = {1, 2, 3, 4, ...}, A = {1, 2, 3, 4, ..., 20}, B = {1, 2, 3, 4, ..., 50}, C = {2, 4, 6, 8, ...}, *and* D = {1, 3, 5, 7, ...}. *Use the roster method to write each of the following sets.*

13. A' **14.** B' **15.** C' **16.** D'

In Exercises 17–40, let

$$U = \{1, 2, 3, 4, 5, 6, 7\}$$
$$A = \{1, 3, 5, 7\}$$
$$B = \{1, 2, 3\}$$
$$C = \{2, 3, 4, 5, 6\}.$$

Find each of the following sets.

17. $A \cap B$ **18.** $B \cap C$ **19.** $A \cup B$ **20.** $B \cup C$
21. A' **22.** B' **23.** $A' \cap B'$ **24.** $B' \cap C$
25. $A \cup C'$ **26.** $B \cup C'$ **27.** $(A \cap C)'$ **28.** $(A \cap B)'$
29. $A' \cup C'$ **30.** $A' \cup B'$ **31.** $(A \cup B)'$ **32.** $(A \cup C)'$
33. $A \cup \varnothing$ **34.** $C \cup \varnothing$ **35.** $A \cap \varnothing$ **36.** $C \cap \varnothing$
37. $A \cup U$ **38.** $B \cup U$ **39.** $A \cap U$ **40.** $B \cap U$

In Exercises 41–66, let

$$U = \{a, b, c, d, e, f, g, h\}$$
$$A = \{a, g, h\}$$
$$B = \{b, g, h\}$$
$$C = \{b, c, d, e, f\}.$$

Find each of the following sets.

41. $A \cap B$ **42.** $B \cap C$ **43.** $A \cup B$ **44.** $B \cup C$
45. A' **46.** B' **47.** $A' \cap B'$ **48.** $B' \cap C$
49. $A \cup C'$ **50.** $B \cup C'$ **51.** $(A \cap C)'$ **52.** $(A \cap B)'$
53. $A' \cup C'$ **54.** $A' \cup B'$ **55.** $(A \cup B)'$ **56.** $(A \cup C)'$
57. $A \cup \varnothing$ **58.** $C \cup \varnothing$ **59.** $A \cap \varnothing$ **60.** $C \cap \varnothing$
61. $A \cup U$ **62.** $B \cup U$ **63.** $A \cap U$ **64.** $B \cap U$
65. $(A \cap B) \cup B'$ **66.** $(A \cup B) \cap B'$

In Exercises 67–78, use the Venn diagram to represent each set in roster form.

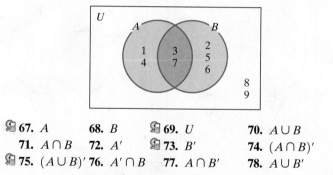

67. A **68.** B **69.** U **70.** $A \cup B$
71. $A \cap B$ **72.** A' **73.** B' **74.** $(A \cap B)'$
75. $(A \cup B)'$ **76.** $A' \cap B'$ **77.** $A \cap B'$ **78.** $A \cup B'$

In Exercises 79–86, use the Venn diagram shown to answer each question.

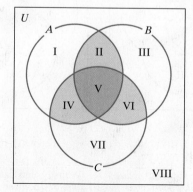

79. Which regions represent set B?
80. Which regions represent set C?

🔊 **81.** Which regions represent $A \cup C$?

82. Which regions represent $B \cup C$?

🔊 **83.** Which regions represent $A \cap B$?

84. Which regions represent $A \cap C$?

🔊 **85.** Which regions represent B'?

86. Which regions represent C'?

In Exercises 87–98, use the Venn diagram to represent each set in roster form.

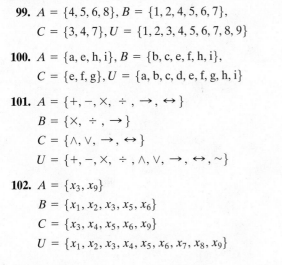

87. A	**88.** B	**89.** $A \cup B$
90. $B \cup C$	**91.** $(A \cup B)'$	**92.** $(B \cup C)'$
93. $A \cap B$	**94.** $A \cap C$	**95.** $A \cap B \cap C$
96. $A \cup B \cup C$	**97.** $(A \cap B \cap C)'$	**98.** $(A \cup B \cup C)'$

In Exercises 99–102, construct a Venn diagram illustrating the given sets.

99. $A = \{4, 5, 6, 8\}, B = \{1, 2, 4, 5, 6, 7\}$,
$C = \{3, 4, 7\}, U = \{1, 2, 3, 4, 5, 6, 7, 8, 9\}$

100. $A = \{a, e, h, i\}, B = \{b, c, e, f, h, i\}$,
$C = \{e, f, g\}, U = \{a, b, c, d, e, f, g, h, i\}$

101. $A = \{+, -, \times, \div, \rightarrow, \leftrightarrow\}$
$B = \{\times, \div, \rightarrow\}$
$C = \{\wedge, \vee, \rightarrow, \leftrightarrow\}$
$U = \{+, -, \times, \div, \wedge, \vee, \rightarrow, \leftrightarrow, \sim\}$

102. $A = \{x_3, x_9\}$
$B = \{x_1, x_2, x_3, x_5, x_6\}$
$C = \{x_3, x_4, x_5, x_6, x_9\}$
$U = \{x_1, x_2, x_3, x_4, x_5, x_6, x_7, x_8, x_9\}$

Use the Venn diagram shown to solve Exercises 103–106.

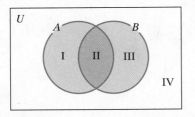

103. a. Which region is represented by $A \cap B$?

   b. Which region is represented by $B \cap A$?

   c. Based on parts (a) and (b), what can you conclude?

104. a. Which regions are represented by $A \cup B$?

   b. Which regions are represented by $B \cup A$?

   c. Based on parts (a) and (b), what can you conclude?

105. a. Which region(s) is/are represented by $(A \cap B)'$?

   b. Which region(s) is/are represented by $A' \cap B'$?

   c. Based on parts (a) and (b), are $(A \cap B)'$ and $A' \cap B'$ equal for all sets A and B? Explain your answer.

106. a. Which region(s) is/are represented by $(A \cup B)'$?

   b. Which region(s) is/are represented by $A' \cup B'$?

   c. Based on parts (a) and (b), are $(A \cup B)'$ and $A' \cup B'$ equal for all sets A and B? Explain your answer.

In Exercises 107–114, use the symbols $A, B, C, \cap, \cup,$ and $',$ as necessary, to describe each shaded region. More than one correct symbolic description may be possible.

107.
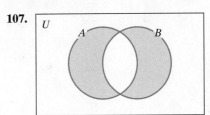

108.
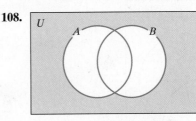

109.
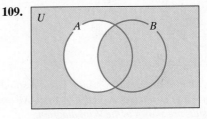

110.
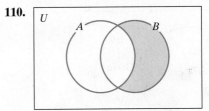

111.
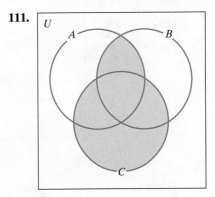

112.

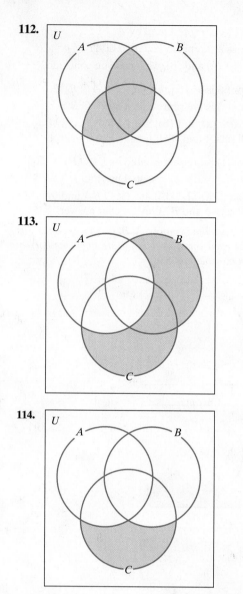

113.

114.

A math tutor working with a small study group has classified students in the group by whether or not they scored 90% or above on each of three tests. The results are shown in the Venn diagram.

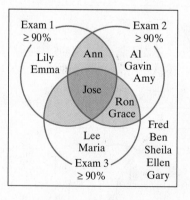

In Exercises 115–128, use the Venn diagram to represent each set in roster form.

115. The set of students who scored 90% or above on exam 2

116. The set of students who scored 90% or above on exam 3

117. The set of students who scored 90% or above on exam 1 and exam 3

118. The set of students who scored 90% or above on exam 1 and exam 2

119. The set of students who scored 90% or above on exam 1 and not on exam 2

120. The set of students who scored 90% or above on exam 3 and not on exam 1

121. The set of students who scored 90% or above on exam 1 or not on exam 2

122. The set of students who scored 90% or above on exam 3 or not on exam 1

123. The set of students who scored 90% or above on *exactly one* test

124. The set of students who scored 90% or above on *at least two* tests

125. The set of students who scored 90% or above on exam 2 and not on exam 1 and exam 3

126. The set of students who scored 90% or above on exam 1 and not on exam 2 and exam 3

127. The set of students that is the empty set

128. The set {Fred, Ben, Sheila, Ellen, Gary}

Appendix B

Survey Problems

In this section, we will see how sets and Venn diagrams are used to tabulate information collected in a survey. In survey problems, it is helpful to remember that **and** means **intersection, or** means **union,** and **not** means **complement.** Furthermore, *but* means the same thing as *and*. Thus, **but** means **intersection.**

OBJECTIVE 1 ▶ Visualizing the results of a survey. We will use the notation $n(A)$, to mean the number of elements in set A, or the cardinal number of set A.

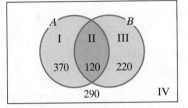

A: Set of students willing to donate blood
B: Set of students willing to serve breakfast to donors

FIGURE B.1 Results of a survey

> **EXAMPLE 1**   Using a Venn Diagram to Visualize the Results of a Survey

We return to the campus survey in which students were asked two questions:

> Would you be willing to donate blood?
> Would you be willing to help serve a free breakfast to blood donors?

Set A represents the set of students willing to donate blood. Set B represents the set of students willing to help serve breakfast to donors. The survey results are summarized in Figure B.1. Use the diagram to answer the following questions:

   a. How many students are willing to donate blood?
   b. How many students are willing to help serve a free breakfast to blood donors?
   c. How many students are willing to donate blood and serve breakfast?
   d. How many students are willing to donate blood or serve breakfast?
   e. How many students are willing to donate blood but not serve breakfast?
   f. How many students are willing to serve breakfast but not donate blood?
   g. How many students are neither willing to donate blood nor serve breakfast?
   h. How many students were surveyed?

Solution

   a. The number of students willing to donate blood can be determined by adding the numbers in regions I and II. Thus, $n(A) = 370 + 120 = 490$. There are 490 students willing to donate blood.

   b. The number of students willing to help serve a free breakfast to blood donors can be determined by adding the numbers in regions II and III. Thus, $n(B) = 120 + 220 = 340$. There are 340 students willing to help serve breakfast.

   c. The number of students willing to donate blood and serve breakfast appears in region II, the region representing the intersection of the two sets. Thus, $n(A \cap B) = 120$. There are 120 students willing to donate blood and serve breakfast.

   d. The number of students willing to donate blood or serve breakfast is found by adding the numbers in regions I, II, and III, representing the union of the two sets. We see that $n(A \cup B) = 370 + 120 + 220 = 710$. Therefore, 710 students in the survey are willing to donate blood or serve breakfast.

   e. The region representing students who are willing to donate blood but not serve breakfast, $A \cap B'$, is region I. We see that 370 of the students surveyed are willing to donate blood but not serve breakfast.

f. Region III represents students willing to serve breakfast but not donate blood: $B \cap A'$. We see that 220 students surveyed are willing to help serve breakfast but not donate blood.

g. Students who are neither willing to donate blood nor serve breakfast, $A' \cap B'$, fall within the universal set, but outside circles A and B. These students fall in region IV, where the Venn diagram indicates that there are 290 elements. There are 290 students in the survey who are neither willing to donate blood nor serve breakfast.

h. We can find the number of students surveyed by adding the numbers in regions I, II, III, and IV. Thus, $n(U) = 370 + 120 + 220 + 290 = 1000$. There were 1000 students surveyed. □

PRACTICE

1 In a survey on musical tastes, respondents were asked: Do you listen to classical music? Do you listen to jazz? The survey results are summarized in Figure B.2. Use the diagram to answer the following questions.

a. How many respondents listened to classical music?

b. How many respondents listened to jazz?

c. How many respondents listened to both classical music and jazz?

d. How many respondents listened to classical music or jazz?

e. How many respondents listened to classical music but not jazz?

f. How many respondents listened to jazz but not classical music?

g. How many respondents listened to neither classical music nor jazz?

h. How many people were surveyed?

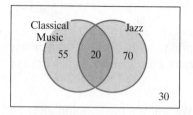

FIGURE B.2

OBJECTIVE 2 ▶ **Solving survey problems.** Venn diagrams are used to solve problems involving surveys. Here are the steps needed to solve survey problems.

Solving Survey Problems

1. Use the survey's description to define sets and draw a Venn diagram.
2. Use the survey's results to determine the cardinality for each region in the Venn diagram. **Start with the intersection of the sets, the innermost region, and work outward.**
3. Use the completed Venn diagram to answer the problem's questions.

EXAMPLE 2 **Surveying People's Attitudes**

A survey is taken that asks 2000 randomly selected U.S. and Mexican adults the following question:

Do you agree or disagree that the primary cause of poverty is societal injustice?

The results of the survey showed that

1060 people agreed with the statement.

400 Americans agreed with the statement.

Source: World Values Surveys

If half the adults surveyed were Americans,

a. How many Mexicans agreed with the statement?

b. How many Mexicans disagreed with the statement?

Solution

Step 1 **Define sets and draw a Venn diagram.** The Venn diagram in Figure B.3 shows two sets. Set *U.S.* is the set of Americans surveyed. Set *A* (labeled "Agree") is the set of people surveyed who agreed with the statement. By representing the Americans

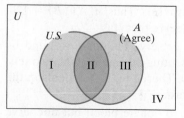

FIGURE B.3

surveyed with circle *U.S.*, we do not need a separate circle for the Mexicans. The group of people outside circle *U.S.* must be the set of Mexicans. Similarly, by visualizing the set of people who agreed with the statement as circle *A*, we do not need a separate circle for those who disagreed. The group of people outside the *A* (Agree) circle must be the set of people disagreeing with the statement.

Step 2   Determine the cardinality for each region in the Venn diagram, starting with the innermost region and working outward. We are given the following cardinalities:

There were 2000 people surveyed: $n(U) = 2000$.

Half the people surveyed were Americans: $n(U.S.) = 1000$.

The number of people who agreed with the statement was 1060: $n(A) = 1060$.

There were 400 Americans who agreed with the statement: $n(U.S. \cap A) = 400$.

Now let's use these numbers to determine the cardinality of each region, starting with region II, moving outward to regions I and III, and ending with region IV.

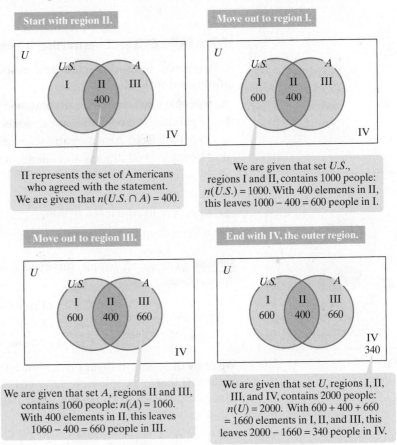

Step 3   Use the completed Venn diagram to answer the problem's questions. The completed Venn diagram that illustrates the survey's results is shown in Figure B.4.

a. The Mexicans who agreed with the statement are those members of the set of people who agreed who are not Americans, shown in region III. This means that 660 Mexicans agreed that societal injustice is the primary cause of poverty.

b. The Mexicans who disagreed with the statement can be found outside the circles of people who agreed and people who are Americans. This corresponds to region IV, whose cardinality is 340. Thus, 340 Mexicans disagreed that societal injustice is the primary cause of poverty.   □

Is the Primary Cause of Poverty Societal Injustice?

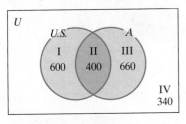

FIGURE B.4

PRACTICE

2   In a Gallup poll, 2000 U.S. adults were selected at random and asked to agree or disagree with the following statement:

Job opportunities for women are not equal to those for men.

The results of the survey showed that

1190 people agreed with the statement.

700 women agreed with the statement.

Source: The People's Almanac

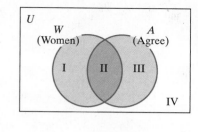

If half the people surveyed were women,

a. How many men agreed with the statement?

b. How many men disagreed with the statement?

When tabulating survey results, more than two circles within a Venn diagram are often needed.

In the next example, we create a Venn diagram with three intersecting sets to illustrate a survey's results. In our final example, we use this Venn diagram to answer questions about the survey.

EXAMPLE 3   Constructing a Venn Diagram for a Survey

Sixty people were contacted and responded to a movie survey. The following information was obtained:

a. 6 people liked comedies, dramas, and science fiction.

b. 13 people liked comedies and dramas.

c. 10 people liked comedies and science fiction.

d. 11 people liked dramas and science fiction.

e. 26 people liked comedies.

f. 21 people liked dramas.

g. 25 people liked science fiction.

Use a Venn diagram to illustrate the survey's results.

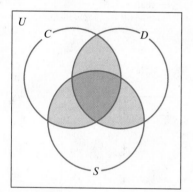

FIGURE B.5

Solution   The set of people surveyed is a universal set with 60 elements containing three subsets:

$$C = \text{the set of those who like comedies}$$
$$D = \text{the set of those who like dramas}$$
$$S = \text{the set of those who like science fiction.}$$

We draw these sets in Figure B.5. Now let's use the numbers in (a) through (g), as well as the fact that 60 people were surveyed, which we call condition (h), to determine the cardinality of each region in the Venn diagram.

(a) 6 people liked comedies, drama, and science fiction: $n(C \cap D \cap S) = 6$.

(b) 13 people liked comedies and drama: $n(C \cap D) = 13$. With 6 counted, there are $13 - 6 = 7$ people in this region.

(c) 10 people liked comedies and science fiction: $n(C \cap S) = 10$. With 6 counted, there are $10 - 6 = 4$ people in this region.

(d) 11 people liked drama and science fiction: $n(D \cap S) = 11$. With 6 counted, there are $11 - 6 = 5$ people in this region.

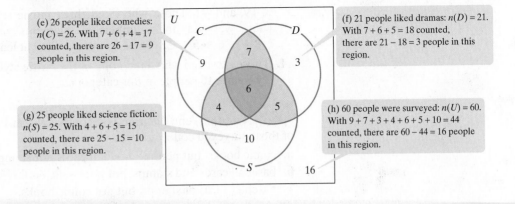

(e) 26 people liked comedies: $n(C) = 26$. With $7 + 6 + 4 = 17$ counted, there are $26 - 17 = 9$ people in this region.

(f) 21 people liked dramas: $n(D) = 21$. With $7 + 6 + 5 = 18$ counted, there are $21 - 18 = 3$ people in this region.

(g) 25 people liked science fiction: $n(S) = 25$. With $4 + 6 + 5 = 15$ counted, there are $25 - 15 = 10$ people in this region.

(h) 60 people were surveyed: $n(U) = 60$. With $9 + 7 + 3 + 4 + 6 + 5 + 10 = 44$ counted, there are $60 - 44 = 16$ people in this region.

With a cardinality in each region, we have completed the Venn diagram that illustrates the survey's results. □

PRACTICE 3   A survey of 250 memorabilia collectors showed the following results: 108 collected baseball cards. 92 collected comic books. 62 collected stamps. 29 collected baseball cards and comic books. 5 collected baseball cards and stamps. 2 collected comic books and stamps. 2 collected all three types of memorabilia. Use a Venn diagram to illustrate the survey's results.

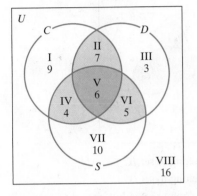

FIGURE B.6

EXAMPLE 4   **Using a Survey's Venn Diagram**

The Venn diagram in Figure B.6 shows the results of the movie survey in Example 3. How many of those surveyed liked

   a. comedies, but neither dramas nor science fiction?
   b. dramas and science fiction, but not comedies?
   c. dramas or science fiction, but not comedies?
   d. exactly one movie style?
   e. at least two movie styles?
   f. none of the movie styles?

Solution

a. Those surveyed who liked comedies, but neither dramas nor science fiction, are represented in region I. There are 9 people in this category.

$C \cap (D' \cap S')$

b. Those surveyed who liked dramas and science fiction, but not comedies, are represented in region VI. There are 5 people in this category.

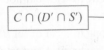
$(D \cap S) \cap C'$

c. We are interested in those surveyed who liked dramas or science fiction, but not comedies:

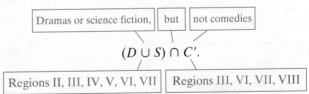

The intersection of the regions in the voice balloons consists of the common regions shown in red, III, VI, and VII. There are $3 + 5 + 10 = 18$ elements in these regions. There are 18 people who liked dramas or science fiction, but not comedies.

d. Those surveyed who liked exactly one movie style are represented in regions I, III, and VII. There are $9 + 3 + 10 = 22$ elements in these regions. Thus, 22 people liked exactly one movie style.

e. Those surveyed who liked at least two movie styles are people who liked two or more types of movies. People who liked two movie styles are represented in regions

II, IV, and VI. Those who liked three movie styles are represented in region V. Thus, we add the number of elements in regions II, IV, V, and VI: $7 + 4 + 6 + 5 = 22$. Thus, 22 people liked at least two movie styles.

f. Those surveyed who liked none of the movie styles are represented in region VIII. There are 16 people in this category. □

PRACTICE
4 Use the Venn diagram you constructed in Practice 3 to determine how many of those surveyed collected

a. comic books, but neither baseball cards nor stamps.
b. baseball cards and stamps, but not comic books.
c. baseball cards or stamps, but not comic books.
d. exactly two types of memorabilia.
e. at least one type of memorabilia.
f. none of the types of memorabilia.

APPENDIX B | EXERCISE SET

MyMathLab *Powered by CourseCompass™ and MathXL®*

MathXL PRACTICE · WATCH · DOWNLOAD · READ · REVIEW

PRACTICE EXERCISES

Use the accompanying Venn diagram, which shows the number of elements in regions I through IV, to answer the questions in Exercises 1–8.

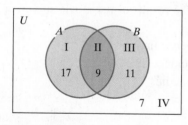

1. How many elements belong to set A?
2. How many elements belong to set B?
3. How many elements belong to set A but not set B?
4. How many elements belong to set B but not set A?
5. How many elements belong to set A or set B?
6. How many elements belong to set A and set B?
7. How many elements belong to neither set A nor set B?
8. How many elements are there in the universal set?

Use the accompanying Venn diagram, which shows the number of elements in region II, to answer Exercises 9–10.

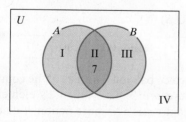

9. If $n(A) = 21$, $n(B) = 29$, and $n(U) = 48$, find the number of elements in each of regions I, III, and IV.
10. If $n(A) = 23$, $n(B) = 27$, and $n(U) = 53$, find the number of elements in each of regions I, III, and IV.

Use the accompanying Venn diagram, which shows the cardinality of each region, to answer Exercises 11–26.

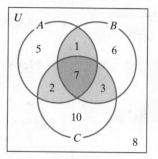

11. How many elements belong to set B?
12. How many elements belong to set A?
13. How many elements belong to set A but not set C?
14. How many elements belong to set B but not set A?
15. How many elements belong to set A or set C?
16. How many elements belong to set A or set B?
17. How many elements belong to set A and set C?
18. How many elements belong to set A and set B?
19. How many elements belong to set B and set C, but not to set A?
20. How many elements belong to set A and set C, but not to set B?
21. How many elements belong to set B or set C, but not to set A?
22. How many elements belong to set A or set C, but not to set B?
23. Considering sets A, B, and C, how many elements belong to exactly one of these sets?
24. Considering sets A, B, and C, how many elements belong to exactly two of these sets?
25. Considering sets A, B, and C, how many elements belong to at least one of these sets?
26. Considering sets A, B, and C, how many elements belong to at least two of these sets?

The accompanying Venn diagram shows the number of elements in region V. In Exercises 27–28, use the given cardinalities to determine the number of elements in each of the other seven regions.

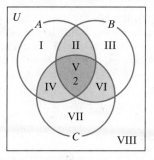

27. $n(U) = 30, n(A) = 11, n(B) = 8, n(C) = 14,$
$n(A \cap B) = 3, n(A \cap C) = 5, n(B \cap C) = 3$

28. $n(U) = 32, n(A) = 21, n(B) = 15, n(C) = 14,$
$n(A \cap B) = 6, n(A \cap C) = 7, n(B \cap C) = 8$

PRACTICE PLUS

In Exercises 29–32, use the Venn diagram and the given conditions to determine the number of elements in each region, or explain why the conditions are impossible to meet.

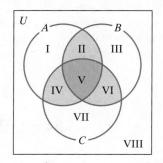

29. $n(U) = 38, n(A) = 26, n(B) = 21, n(C) = 18,$
$n(A \cap B) = 17, n(A \cap C) = 11, n(B \cap C) = 8,$
$n(A \cap B \cap C) = 7$

30. $n(U) = 42, n(A) = 26, n(B) = 22, n(C) = 25,$
$n(A \cap B) = 17, n(A \cap C) = 11, n(B \cap C) = 9,$
$n(A \cap B \cap C) = 5$

31. $n(U) = 40, n(A) = 10, n(B) = 11, n(C) = 12,$
$n(A \cap B) = 6, n(A \cap C) = 9, n(B \cap C) = 7,$
$n(A \cap B \cap C) = 2$

32. $n(U) = 25, n(A) = 8, n(B) = 9, n(C) = 10,$
$n(A \cap B) = 6, n(A \cap C) = 9, n(B \cap C) = 8,$
$n(A \cap B \cap C) = 5$

APPLICATION EXERCISES

In Exercises 33–36, construct a Venn diagram and determine the cardinality for each region. Use the completed Venn diagram to answer the questions.

33. A survey of 75 college students was taken to determine where they got the news about what's going on in the world. Of those surveyed, 29 students got the news from newspapers, 43 from

television, and 7 from both newspapers and television. Of those surveyed,

  a. How many got the news from only newspapers?

  b. How many got the news from only television?

  c. How many got the news from newspapers or television?

  d. How many did not get the news from either newspapers or television?

34. A survey of 120 college students was taken at registration. Of those surveyed, 75 students registered for a math course, 65 for an English course, and 40 for both math and English. Of those surveyed,

  a. How many registered only for a math course?

  b. How many registered only for an English course?

  c. How many registered for a math course or an English course?

  d. How many did not register for either a math course or an English course?

35. A survey of 80 college students was taken to determine the musical styles they listened to. Forty-two students listened to rock, 34 to classical, and 27 to jazz. Twelve students listened to rock and jazz, 14 to rock and classical, and 10 to classical and jazz. Seven students listened to all three musical styles. Of those surveyed,

  a. How many listened to only rock music?

  b. How many listened to classical and jazz, but not rock?

  c. How many listened to classical or jazz, but not rock?

  d. How many listened to music in exactly one of the musical styles?

  e. How many listened to music in at least two of the musical styles?

  f. How many did not listen to any of the musical styles?

36. A survey of 180 college men was taken to determine participation in various campus activities. Forty-three students were in fraternities, 52 participated in campus sports, and 35 participated in various campus tutorial programs. Thirteen students participated in fraternities and sports, 14 in sports and tutorial programs, and 12 in fraternities and tutorial programs. Five students participated in all three activities. Of those surveyed,

  a. How many participated in only campus sports?

  b. How many participated in fraternities and sports, but not tutorial programs?

  c. How many participated in fraternities or sports, but not tutorial programs?

  d. How many participated in exactly one of these activities?

  e. How many participated in at least two of these activities?

  f. How many did not participate in any of the three activities?

WRITING IN MATHEMATICS

37. Suppose that you are drawing a Venn diagram to sort and tabulate the results of a survey. If results are being tabulated along gender lines, explain why only a circle representing women is needed, rather than two separate circles representing the women surveyed and the men surveyed.

38. Suppose that you decide to use two sets, M and W, to sort and tabulate the responses for men and women in a survey.

Describe the set of people represented by regions II and IV in the Venn diagram shown. What conclusion can you draw?

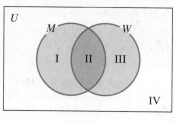

CRITICAL THINKING EXERCISES

39. Which one of the following is true?

a. In a survey, 110 students were taking mathematics, 90 were taking psychology, and 20 were taking neither. Thus, 220 students were surveyed.

b. If $A \cap B = \emptyset$, then $n(A \cup B) = n(A) + n(B)$.

c. When filling in cardinalities for regions in a two-set Venn diagram, the innermost region, the intersection of the two sets, should be the last region to be filled in.

d. $n(A')$ cannot be obtained by subtracting $n(A)$ from $n(U)$.

40. In a survey of 150 students, 90 were taking mathematics and 30 were taking psychology.

a. What is the least number of students who could have been taking both courses?

b. What is the greatest number of students who could have been taking both courses?

c. What is the greatest number of students who could have been taking neither course?

41. A person applying for the position of college registrar submitted the following report to the college president on 90 students: 31 take math; 28 take chemistry; 42 take psychology; 9 take math and chemistry; 10 take chemistry and psychology; 6 take math and psychology; 4 take all three subjects; and 20 take none of these courses. The applicant was not hired. Explain why.

GROUP EXERCISE

42. This group activity is intended to provide practice in the use of Venn diagrams to sort responses to a survey. The group will determine the topic of the survey. Although you will not actually conduct the survey, it might be helpful to imagine carrying out the survey using the students on your campus.

a. In your group, decide on a topic for the survey.

b. Devise three questions that the pollster will ask to the people who are interviewed.

c. Construct a Venn diagram that will assist the pollster in sorting the answers to the three questions. The Venn diagram should contain three intersecting circles within a universal set and eight regions.

d. Describe what each of the regions in the Venn diagram represents in terms of the questions in your poll.

Appendix C

The Fundamental Counting Principle

OBJECTIVE

1 Use the Fundamental Counting Principle to determine the number of possible outcomes in a given situation.

OBJECTIVE 1 ▶ Use the Fundamental Counting Principle. Let's suppose this morning you are selecting the clothes you will wear today. You have two pairs of jeans to choose from (one blue, one black) and three T-shirts to choose from (one beige, one yellow, and one blue). Your morning decision is illustrated in the figure below.

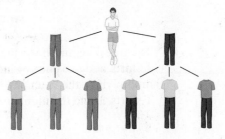

FIGURE C.1 Selecting a wardrobe

The **tree diagram,** so named because of its branches, shows that you can form six different outfits from your two pairs of jeans and three T-shirts. Each pair of jeans can be combined with one of three T-shirts. Notice that the total number of outfits can be obtained by multiplying the number of choices for the jeans, 2, by the number of choices for the T-shirts, 3:

$$2 \cdot 3 = 6.$$

We can generalize this idea to any two groups of items—not just jeans and T-shirts—with the **Fundamental Counting Principle.**

> **The Fundamental Counting Principle**
>
> If you can choose one item from a group of M items and a second item from a group of N items, then the total number of two-item choices is $M \cdot N$.

EXAMPLE 1   **Applying the Fundamental Counting Principle**

A restaurant offers 6 appetizers and 14 main courses. In how many ways can a person order a two-course meal?

Solution   Choosing from one of 6 appetizers and one of 14 main courses, the total number of two-course meals is

$$6 \cdot 14 = 84.$$

A person can order a two-course meal in 84 different ways.   □

PRACTICE

1   Another restaurant offers 10 appetizers and 15 main courses. In how many ways can you order a two-course meal?

The Fundamental Counting Principle with More Than Two Groups of Items
Let's continue our earlier clothing decision by now including a decision of shoes. You have two pairs of sneakers to choose from—one black and one red. Your possible outfits, including sneakers, are shown below.

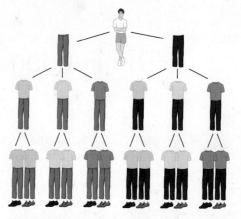

FIGURE C.2   Increasing wardrobe selections

The tree diagram shows that you can form 12 outfits from your two pairs of jeans, three T-shirts, and two pairs of sneakers. Notice that the number of outfits can be obtained by multiplying the number of choices for jeans, 2, the number of choices for T-shirts, 3, and the number of choices for sneakers, 2:

$$2 \cdot 3 \cdot 2 = 12.$$

Unlike your earlier decision, you are now dealing with *three* groups of items. The Fundamental Counting Principle can be extended to determine the number of possible outcomes in situations in which there are three or more groups of items.

> **The Fundamental Counting Principle**
> The number of ways in which a series of successive things can occur is found by multiplying the number of ways in which each thing can occur.

For example, if you own 30 pairs of jeans, 20 T-shirts, and 12 pairs of sneakers, you have

$$30 \cdot 20 \cdot 12 = 7200$$

choices for your wardrobe.

EXAMPLE 2   Options in Planning a Course Schedule

Next year you are planning to take three courses in college—math, English, and humanities. Based on time blocks and highly recommended professors, there are 8 sections of math, 5 of English, and 4 of humanities that you find suitable. Assuming no scheduling conflicts, how many different three-course schedules are possible?

Solution   This situation involves making choices with three groups of items.

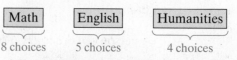

We use the Fundamental Counting Principle to find the number of three-course schedules. Multiply the number of choices for each of the three groups.

$$8 \cdot 5 \cdot 4 = 160$$

Thus, there are 160 different three-course schedules.   ☐

PRACTICE

2 A pizza can be ordered with two choices of size (medium or large), three choices of crust (thin, thick, or regular), and five choices of toppings (ground beef, sausage, pepperoni, bacon, or mushrooms). How many different one-topping pizzas can be ordered?

EXAMPLE 3   **Car of the Future**

Car manufacturers are now experimenting with lightweight three-wheel cars, designed for one person, and considered ideal for city driving. Intrigued? Suppose you could order such a car with a choice of 9 possible colors, with or without air conditioning, electric or gas powered, and with or without an onboard computer. In how many ways can this car be ordered with regard to these options?

Solution   This situation involves making choices with four groups of items.

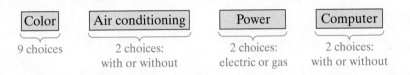

We use the Fundamental Counting Principle to find the number of ordering options. Multiply the number of choices for each of the four groups.

$$9 \cdot 2 \cdot 2 \cdot 2 = 72$$

Thus, the car can be ordered in 72 different ways.   □

PRACTICE

3 The car in Example 3 is now available in 10 possible colors. The options involving air conditioning, power, and an onboard computer still apply. Furthermore, the car is available with or without a global positioning system (for pinpointing your location at every moment). In how many ways can this car be ordered in terms of these options?

EXAMPLE 4   **A Multiple-Choice Test**

You are taking a multiple-choice test that has ten questions. Each of the questions has four answer choices, with one correct answer per question. If you select one of these four choices for each question and leave nothing blank, in how many ways can you answer the questions?

Solution   This situation involves making choices with ten questions.

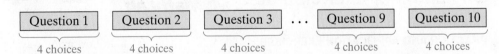

We use the Fundamental Counting Principle to determine the number of ways that you can answer the questions on the test. Multiply the number of choices, 4, for each of the ten questions.

$$4 \cdot 4 \cdot 4 \cdot 4 \cdot 4 \cdot 4 \cdot 4 \cdot 4 \cdot 4 \cdot 4 = 4^{10} = 1{,}048{,}576 \quad \text{Use a calculator: } 4 \boxed{y^x} 10 \boxed{=}.$$

Thus, you can answer the questions in 1,048,576 different ways.   □

Are you surprised that there are over one million ways of answering a ten-question multiple-choice test? Of course, there is only one way to answer the test and receive a perfect score. The probability of guessing your way into a perfect score involves calculating the chance of getting a perfect score, just one way, from all 1,048,576 possible outcomes. In short, prepare for the test and do not rely on guessing!

PRACTICE

4 You are taking a multiple-choice test that has six questions. Each of the questions has three answer choices, with one correct answer per question. If you select one of these three choices for each question and leave nothing blank, in how many ways can you answer the questions?

EXAMPLE 5 Telephone Numbers in the United States

Telephone numbers in the United States begin with three-digit area codes followed by seven-digit local telephone numbers. Area codes and local telephone numbers cannot begin with 0 or 1. How many different telephone numbers are possible?

Solution This situation involves making choices with ten groups of items.

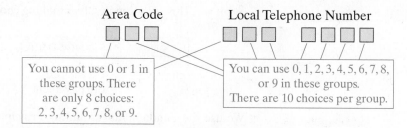

Area Code   Local Telephone Number

You cannot use 0 or 1 in these groups. There are only 8 choices: 2, 3, 4, 5, 6, 7, 8, or 9.

You can use 0, 1, 2, 3, 4, 5, 6, 7, 8, or 9 in these groups. There are 10 choices per group.

Here are the choices for each of the ten groups of items:

Area Code   **Local Telephone Number**

8 10 10   8 10 10   10 10 10 10 .

We use the Fundamental Counting Principle to determine the number of different telephone numbers that are possible. The total number of telephone numbers possible is

$$8 \cdot 10 \cdot 10 \cdot 8 \cdot 10 \cdot 10 \cdot 10 \cdot 10 \cdot 10 \cdot 10 = 6{,}400{,}000{,}000.$$

There are six billion four hundred million different telephone numbers that are possible. □

PRACTICE

5 An electronic gate can be opened by entering five digits on a keypad containing the digits 0, 1, 2, 3, ..., 8, 9. How many different keypad sequences are possible if the digit 0 cannot be used as the first digit?

APPENDIX C | EXERCISE SET   MyMathLab®

PRACTICE WATCH DOWNLOAD READ REVIEW

PRACTICE AND APPLICATION EXERCISES

Solve Exercises 1–6 using the Fundamental Counting Principle with two groups of items.

1. A restaurant offers 8 appetizers and 10 main courses. In how many ways can a person order a two-course meal?

2. The model of the car you are thinking of buying is available in nine different colors and three different styles (hatchback, sedan, or station wagon). In how many ways can you order the car?

3. A popular brand of pen is available in three colors (red, green, or blue) and four writing tips (bold, medium, fine, or micro). How many different choices of pens do you have with this brand?

4. In how many ways can a casting director choose a female lead and a male lead from five female actors and six male actors?

5. A student is planning a two-part trip. The first leg of the trip is from San Francisco to New York, and the second leg is from New York to Paris. From San Francisco to New York, travel options include airplane, train, or bus. From New York to Paris, the options are limited to airplane or ship. In how many ways can the two-part trip be made?

6. For a temporary job between semesters, you are painting the parking spaces for a new shopping mall with a letter of the alphabet and a single digit from 1 to 9. The first parking space is A1 and the last parking space is Z9. How many parking spaces can you paint with distinct labels?

Solve Exercises 7–22 using the Fundamental Counting Principle with three or more groups of items.

7. An ice cream store sells two drinks (sodas or milk shakes), in four sizes (small, medium, large, or jumbo), and five flavors (vanilla, strawberry, chocolate, coffee, or pistachio). In how many ways can a customer order a drink?

8. A pizza can be ordered with three choices of size (small, medium, or large), four choices of crust (thin, thick, crispy, or regular), and six choices of toppings (ground beef, sausage, pepperoni, bacon, mushrooms, or onions). How many one-topping pizzas can be ordered?

9. A restaurant offers the following limited lunch menu.

Main Course	Vegetables	Beverages	Desserts
Ham	Potatoes	Coffee	Cake
Chicken	Peas	Tea	Pie
Fish	Green beans	Milk	Ice cream
Beef		Soda	

If one item is selected from each of the four groups, in how many ways can a meal be ordered? Describe two such orders.

10. An apartment complex offers apartments with four different options, designated by A through D.

A	B	C	D
one bedroom	one bathroom	first floor	lake view
two bedrooms	two bathrooms	second floor	golf course view
three bedrooms			no special view

How many apartment options are available? Describe two such options.

11. Shoppers in a large shopping mall are categorized as male or female, over 30 or 30 and under, and cash or credit card shoppers. In how many ways can the shoppers be categorized?

12. There are three highways from city A to city B, two highways from city B to city C, and four highways from city C to city D. How many different highway routes are there from city A to city D?

13. A person can order a new car with a choice of six possible colors, with or without air conditioning, with or without automatic transmission, with or without power windows, and with or without a CD player. In how many different ways can a new car be ordered with regard to these options?

14. A car model comes in nine colors, with or without air conditioning, with or without a sun roof, with or without automatic transmission, and with or without antilock brakes. In how many ways can the car be ordered with regard to these options?

15. You are taking a multiple-choice test that has five questions. Each of the questions has three answer choices, with one correct answer per question. If you select one of these three choices for each question and leave nothing blank, in how many ways can you answer the questions?

16. You are taking a multiple-choice test that has eight questions. Each of the questions has three answer choices, with one correct answer per question. If you select one of these three choices for each question and leave nothing blank, in how many ways can you answer the questions?

17. In the original plan for area codes in 1945, the first digit could be any number from 2 through 9, the second digit was either 0 or 1, and the third digit could be any number except 0. With this plan, how many different area codes are possible?

18. The local seven-digit telephone numbers in Inverness, California, have 669 as the first three digits. How many different telephone numbers are possible in Inverness?

19. License plates in a particular state display two letters followed by three numbers, such as AT-887 or BB-013. How many different license plates can be manufactured for this state?

20. How many different four-letter radio station call letters can be formed if the first letter must be W or K?

21. A stock can go up, go down, or stay unchanged. How many possibilities are there if you own seven stocks?

22. A social security number contains nine digits, such as 074-66-7795. How many different social security numbers can be formed?

WRITING IN MATHEMATICS

23. Explain the Fundamental Counting Principle.

24. Figure C.2 shows that a tree diagram can be used to find the total number of outfits. Describe one advantage of using the Fundamental Counting Principle rather than a tree diagram.

25. Write an original problem that can be solved using the Fundamental Counting Principle. Then solve the problem.

CRITICAL THINKING EXERCISES

26. How many four-digit odd numbers are there? Assume that the digit on the left cannot be 0.

27. In order to develop a more appealing hamburger, a franchise used taste tests with 12 different buns, 30 sauces, 4 types of lettuce, and 3 types of tomatoes. If the taste test was done at one restaurant by one tester who took 10 minutes to eat each hamburger, approximately how long would it take the tester to eat all possible hamburgers?

GROUP EXERCISE

28. The group should select real-world situations where the Fundamental Counting Principle can be applied. These can involve the number of possible student ID numbers on your campus, the number of possible phone numbers in your community, the number of meal options at a local restaurant, and the number of ways a person in the group can select outfits for class. Once situations have been selected, group members should determine in how many ways each part of the task can be done. Group members will need to obtain menus, find out about telephone-digit requirements in the community, count shirts, pants, shoes in closets, and so on. Once the group reassembles, apply the Fundamental Counting Principle to determine the number of available options in each situation. Because these numbers may be quite large, use a calculator.

Appendix D

Permutations

OBJECTIVE 1 ▶ Use the Fundamental Counting Principle to count permutations.
Suppose you are in charge of scheduling the order of 4 musical groups playing in a concert. You can choose any of the four groups as the first performer. Once you've chosen the first group, you'll have three groups left to choose from for the second performer. You'll then have two groups left to choose from for the third performance. After the first three performers are determined, you'll have only one group left for the final appearance in the concert. This situation can be shown as follows:

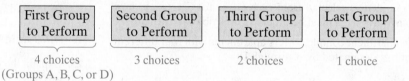

We use the Fundamental Counting Principle to find the number of ways you can put together the concert. Multiply the choices:

$$4 \cdot 3 \cdot 2 \cdot 1 = 24.$$

Thus, there are 24 different ways to arrange the concert. Such an ordered arrangement is called a *permutation* of the four groups.

A **permutation** is an ordered arrangement of items that occurs when

- No item is used more than once. (Each group performs exactly once.)
- The order of arrangement makes a difference. (It will make a difference in terms of how the concert is received if a musical group is the first or the last to perform.)

EXAMPLE 1   **Counting Permutations**

Based on their long-standing contribution to music, you decide that musical Group B should be the last group to perform at the four-group concert. Given this decision, in how many ways can you put together the concert?

Solution   You can now choose any one of the three groups, A, C, or D as the opening act. Once you've chosen the first group, you'll have two groups left to choose from for the second performance. You'll then have just one group left to choose for the third performance. There is also just one choice for the closing act—musical group B. This situation can be shown as follows:

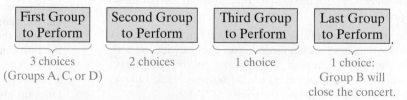

We use the Fundamental Counting Principle to find the number of ways you can put together the concert. Multiply the choices:

$$3 \cdot 2 \cdot 1 \cdot 1 = 6.$$

Thus, there are six different ways to arrange the concert if Group B is the final group to perform.   □

PRACTICE
1   For the concert in Example 1, suppose that Group C is to be the opening act and that Group B is to be the last group to perform. In how many ways can you put together the concert?

EXAMPLE 2   Counting Permutations

You need to arrange seven of your favorite books along a small shelf. How many different ways can you arrange the books, assuming that the order of the books makes a difference to you?

Solution   You may choose any of the seven books for the first position on the shelf. This leaves six choices for second position. After the first two positions are filled, there are five books to choose from for third position, four choices left for the fourth position, three choices left for the fifth position, then two choices for the sixth position, and only one choice for the last position. This situation can be shown as follows:

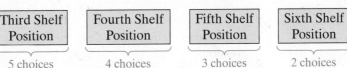

First Shelf Position	Second Shelf Position	Third Shelf Position	Fourth Shelf Position	Fifth Shelf Position	Sixth Shelf Position	Seventh Shelf Position
7 choices	6 choices	5 choices	4 choices	3 choices	2 choices	1 choice

We use the Fundamental Counting Principle to find the number of ways you can arrange the seven books along the shelf. Multiply the choices:

$$7 \cdot 6 \cdot 5 \cdot 4 \cdot 3 \cdot 2 \cdot 1 = 5040.$$

Thus, you can arrange the books in 5040 ways. There are 5040 different possible permutations.   □

PRACTICE
2   In how many ways can you arrange five books along a shelf, assuming that the order of the books makes a difference?

OBJECTIVE 2 ▶ Factorial notation. A product such as

$$7 \cdot 6 \cdot 5 \cdot 4 \cdot 3 \cdot 2 \cdot 1$$

is given a special name and symbol. It is called 7 **factorial,** and written 7!. Thus,

$$7! = 7 \cdot 6 \cdot 5 \cdot 4 \cdot 3 \cdot 2 \cdot 1.$$

To review, if n is a positive integer, then $n!$ (*n factorial*) is the product of all positive integers from n down through 1. For example,

$$1! = 1$$
$$2! = 2 \cdot 1 = 2$$
$$3! = 3 \cdot 2 \cdot 1 = 6$$
$$4! = 4 \cdot 3 \cdot 2 \cdot 1 = 24$$
$$5! = 5 \cdot 4 \cdot 3 \cdot 2 \cdot 1 = 120$$
$$6! = 6 \cdot 5 \cdot 4 \cdot 3 \cdot 2 \cdot 1 = 720.$$

Factorials From 0 Through 20

0!	1
1!	1
2!	2
3!	6
4!	24
5!	120
6!	720
7!	5040
8!	40,320
9!	362,880
10!	3,628,800
11!	39,916,800
12!	479,001,600
13!	6,227,020,800
14!	87,178,291,200
15!	1,307,674,368,000
16!	20,922,789,888,000
17!	355,687,428,096,000
18!	6,402,373,705,728,000
19!	121,645,100,408,832,000
20!	2,432,902,008,176,640,000

As n increases, $n!$ grows very rapidly. Factorial growth is more explosive than exponential growth discussed in Chapter 10.

Factorial Notation

If n is a positive integer, the notation $n!$ (read "n factorial") is the product of all positive integers from n down through 1.

$$n! = n(n - 1)(n - 2)\cdots(3)(2)(1)$$

0! (zero factorial), by definition, is 1.

$$0! = 1$$

EXAMPLE 3   Using Factorial Notation

Evaluate the following factorial expressions without using the factorial key on your calculator:

a. $\dfrac{8!}{5!}$ **b.** $\dfrac{26!}{21!}$ **c.** $\dfrac{500!}{499!}$.

Solution

a. We can evaluate the numerator and the denominator of $\frac{8!}{5!}$. However, it is easier to use the following simplification:

$$\frac{8!}{5!} = \frac{8 \cdot 7 \cdot 6 \cdot \boxed{5 \cdot 4 \cdot 3 \cdot 2 \cdot 1}}{\boxed{5 \cdot 4 \cdot 3 \cdot 2 \cdot 1}} = \frac{8 \cdot 7 \cdot 6 \cdot \boxed{5!}}{\boxed{5!}} = \frac{8 \cdot 7 \cdot 6 \cdot \cancel{5!}}{\cancel{5!}} = 8 \cdot 7 \cdot 6 = 336.$$

b. Rather than write out 26!, the numerator of $\frac{26!}{21!}$, as the product of all integers from 26 down to 1, we can express 26! as

$$26! = 26 \cdot 25 \cdot 24 \cdot 23 \cdot 22 \cdot 21!.$$

In this way, we can cancel 21! in the numerator and the denominator of the given expression.

$$\frac{26!}{21!} = \frac{26 \cdot 25 \cdot 24 \cdot 23 \cdot 22 \cdot 21!}{21!} = \frac{26 \cdot 25 \cdot 24 \cdot 23 \cdot 22 \cdot \cancel{21!}}{\cancel{21!}}$$
$$= 26 \cdot 25 \cdot 24 \cdot 23 \cdot 22 = 7,893,600$$

c. In order to cancel identical factorials in the numerator and the denominator of $\frac{500!}{499!}$, we can express 500! as $500 \cdot 499!$.

$$\frac{500!}{499!} = \frac{500 \cdot 499!}{499!} = \frac{500 \cdot \cancel{499!}}{\cancel{499!}} = 500 \qquad \square$$

PRACTICE
3   Evaluate without using a calculator's factorial key:

a. $\dfrac{9!}{6!}$ **b.** $\dfrac{16!}{11!}$ **c.** $\dfrac{100!}{99!}$.

OBJECTIVE 3 ▶ A formula for permutations. You are the coach of a little league baseball team. There are 13 players on the team. You need to choose a batting order having 9 players. The order makes a difference, because, for instance, if bases are loaded and your best hitter is fourth or fifth at bat, his possible home run will drive in three additional runs. How many batting orders can you form?

You can choose any of 13 players for the first person at bat. Then you will have 12 players from which to choose the second batter, then 11 from which to choose the third batter, and so on. The situation can be shown as follows:

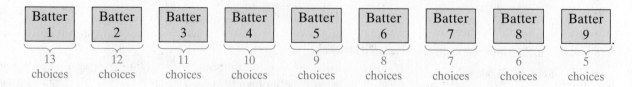

The total number of batting orders is

$$13 \cdot 12 \cdot 11 \cdot 10 \cdot 9 \cdot 8 \cdot 7 \cdot 6 \cdot 5 = 259,459,200.$$

Nearly 260 million batting orders are possible for your 13-player little league team. Each batting order is a permutation because the order of the batters makes a difference. The number of permutations of 13 players taken 9 at a time is 259,459,200.

We can obtain a formula for finding the number of permutations by rewriting our computation:

$$13 \cdot 12 \cdot 11 \cdot 10 \cdot 9 \cdot 8 \cdot 7 \cdot 6 \cdot 5$$

$$= \frac{13 \cdot 12 \cdot 11 \cdot 10 \cdot 9 \cdot 8 \cdot 7 \cdot 6 \cdot 5 \cdot \boxed{4 \cdot 3 \cdot 2 \cdot 1}}{\boxed{4 \cdot 3 \cdot 2 \cdot 1}} = \frac{13!}{4!} = \frac{13!}{(13 - 9)!}.$$

Thus, the number of permutations of 13 things taken 9 at a time is $\frac{13!}{(13 - 9)!}$. The special notation $_{13}P_9$ is used to replace the phrase "the number of permutations of 13 things taken 9 at a time." Using this new notation, we can write

$$_{13}P_9 = \frac{13!}{(13 - 9)!}.$$

The numerator of this expression is the factorial of the number of items, 13 team members: 13!. The denominator is also a factorial. It is the factorial of the difference between the number of items, 13, and the number of items in each permutation, 9 batters: $(13 - 9)!$.

The notation $_nP_r$ means the **number of permutations of *n* things taken *r* at a time**. We can generalize from the situation in which 9 batters were taken from 13 players. By generalizing, we obtain the following formula for the number of permutations if *r* items are taken from *n* items:

> **Permutations of *n* Things Taken *r* at a Time**
>
> The number of possible permutations if *r* items are taken from *n* items is
>
> $$_nP_r = \frac{n!}{(n - r)!}.$$

▶ **Helpful Hint**

Because all permutation problems are also Fundamental Counting problems, they can be solved using the formula for $_nP_r$ or using the Fundamental Counting Principle.

EXAMPLE 4   **Using the Formula for Permutations**

You and 19 of your friends have decided to form an Internet marketing consulting firm. The group needs to choose three officers—a CEO, an operating manager, and a treasurer. In how many ways can those offices be filled?

Solution   Your group is choosing $r = 3$ officers from a group of $n = 20$ people (you and 19 friends). The order in which the officers are chosen matters because the CEO, the operating manager, and the treasurer each have different responsibilities. Thus, we are looking for the number of permutations of 20 things taken 3 at a time. We use the formula

$$_nP_r = \frac{n!}{(n - r)!}$$

with $n = 20$ and $r = 3$.

$$_{20}P_3 = \frac{20!}{(20 - 3)!} = \frac{20!}{17!} = \frac{20 \cdot 19 \cdot 18 \cdot 17!}{17!} = \frac{20 \cdot 19 \cdot 18 \cdot \cancel{17!}}{\cancel{17!}} = 20 \cdot 19 \cdot 18 = 6840$$

Thus, there are 6840 different ways of filling the three offices.   □

TECHNOLOGY NOTE

Graphing calculators have a menu item for calculating permutations, usually labeled $\boxed{_nP_r}$. For example, to find $_{20}P_3$, the keystrokes are

20 $\boxed{_nP_r}$ 3 $\boxed{\text{ENTER}}$.

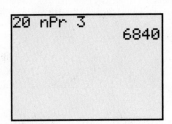

If you are using a scientific calculator, check your manual for the location of the menu item for calculating permutations and the required keystrokes.

PRACTICE
4   A corporation has seven members on its board of directors. In how many different ways can it elect a president, vice-president, secretary, and treasurer?

EXAMPLE 5   **Using the Formula for Permutations**

You are working for The Sitcom Television Network. Your assignment is to help set up the television schedule for Monday evenings between 7 and 10 P.M. You need to schedule a show in each of six 30-minute time blocks, beginning with 7 to 7:30 and ending with 9:30 to 10:00. You can select from among the following situation comedies: *Home Improvement, Seinfeld, Mad About You, Cheers, Friends, Frasier, All in the Family, I Love Lucy, M*A*S*H, The Larry Sanders Show, The Jeffersons, Married with Children,* and *Happy Days.* How many different programming schedules can be arranged?

Solution   You are choosing $r = 6$ situation comedies from a collection of $n = 13$ classic sitcoms. The order in which the programs are aired matters. Family-oriented comedies have higher ratings when aired in earlier time blocks, such as 7 to 7:30. By contrast, comedies with adult themes do better in later time blocks. In short, we are looking for the number of permutations of 13 things taken 6 at a time. We use the formula

$$_nP_r = \frac{n!}{(n-r)!}$$

with $n = 13$ and $r = 6$.

$$_{13}P_6 = \frac{13!}{(13-6)!} = \frac{13!}{7!} = \frac{13 \cdot 12 \cdot 11 \cdot 10 \cdot 9 \cdot 8 \cdot \cancel{7!}}{\cancel{7!}} = 13 \cdot 12 \cdot 11 \cdot 10 \cdot 9 \cdot 8 = 1,235,520$$

There are 1,235,520 different programming schedules that can be arranged.   □

PRACTICE
5   How many different programming schedules can be arranged by choosing 5 situation comedies from a collection of 9 classic sitcoms?

OBJECTIVE 4 ▶ Permutations of duplicate items. The number of permutations of the letters in the word SET is 3!, or 6. The six permutations are

SET,   STE,   EST,   ETS,   TES,   TSE.

Are there also six permutations of the letters in the name ANA? The answer is no. Unlike SET, with three distinct letters, ANA contains three letters, of which the two As are duplicates. If we rearrange the letters just as we did with SET, we obtain

ANA,   AAN,   NAA,   NAA,   ANA,   AAN.

Without the use of color to distinguish between the two As, there are only three distinct permutations: ANA, AAN, NAA.

There is a formula for finding the number of distinct permutations when duplicate items exist:

> **Permutations of Duplicate Items**
>
> The number of permutations of n items, where p items are identical, q items are identical, r items are identical, and so on, is given by
>
> $$\frac{n!}{p! \, q! \, r! \dots}.$$

For example, ANA contains three letters ($n = 3$), where two of the letters are identical ($p = 2$). The number of distinct permutations is

$$\frac{n!}{p!} = \frac{3!}{2!} = \frac{3 \cdot \cancel{2!}}{\cancel{2!}} = 3.$$

We saw that the three distinct permutations are ANA, AAN, and NAA.

EXAMPLE 6   Using the Formula for Permutations of Duplicate Items

In how many distinct ways can the letters of the word MISSISSIPPI be arranged?

Solution   The word contains 11 letters ($n = 11$), where four Is are identical ($p = 4$), four Ss are identical ($q = 4$), and 2 Ps are identical ($r = 2$). The number of distinct permutations is

$$\frac{n!}{p!\,q!\,r!} = \frac{11!}{4!\,4!\,2!} = \frac{11\cdot10\cdot9\cdot8\cdot7\cdot6\cdot5\cdot4!}{4!\,4\cdot3\cdot2\cdot1\cdot2\cdot1} = 34{,}650$$

There are 34,650 distinct ways the letters in the word MISSISSIPPI can be arranged. □

PRACTICE

6   In how many ways can the letters of the word OSMOSIS be arranged?

APPENDIX D | EXERCISE SET

MyMathLab   Math XL   PRACTICE   WATCH   DOWNLOAD   READ   REVIEW

PRACTICE AND APPLICATION EXERCISES

Use the Fundamental Counting Principle to solve Exercises 1–12.

1. Six performers are to present their comedy acts on a weekend evening at a comedy club. How many different ways are there to schedule their appearances?

2. Five singers are to perform on a weekend evening at a night club. How many different ways are there to schedule their appearances?

3. In the *Cambridge Encyclopedia of Language* (Cambridge University Press, 1987), author David Crystal presents five sentences that make a reasonable paragraph regardless of their order. The sentences are as follows:

   Mark had told him about the foxes.
   John looked out of the window.
   Could it be a fox?
   However, nobody had seen one for months.
   He thought he saw a shape in the bushes.

   In how many different orders can the five sentences be arranged?

4. In how many different ways can a police department arrange eight suspects in a police lineup if each lineup contains all eight people?

5. As in Exercise 1, six performers are to present their comedy acts on a weekend evening at a comedy club. One of the performers insists on being the last stand-up comic of the evening. If this performer's request is granted, how many different ways are there to schedule the appearances?

6. As in Exercise 2, five singers are to perform at a night club. One of the singers insists on being the last performer of the evening. If this singer's request is granted, how many different ways are there to schedule the appearances?

7. You need to arrange nine of your favorite books along a small shelf. How many different ways can you arrange the books, assuming that the order of the books makes a difference to you?

8. You need to arrange ten of your favorite photographs on the mantel above a fireplace. How many ways can you arrange the photographs, assuming that the order of the pictures makes a difference to you?

In Exercises 9–10, use the five sentences that are given in Exercise 3.

9. How many different five-sentence paragraphs can be formed if the paragraph begins with "He thought he saw a shape in the bushes" and ends with "John looked out of the window"?

10. How many different five-sentence paragraphs can be formed if the paragraph begins with "He thought he saw a shape in the bushes" followed by "Mark had told him about the foxes"?

11. A television programmer is arranging the order that five movies will be seen between the hours of 6 P.M. and 4 A.M. Two of the movies have a G rating, and they are to be shown in the first two time blocks. One of the movies is rated NC-17, and it is to be shown in the last of the time blocks, from 2 A.M. until 4 A.M. Given these restrictions, in how many ways can the five movies be arranged during the indicated time blocks?

12. A camp counselor and six campers are to be seated along a picnic bench. In how many ways can this be done if the counselor must be seated in the middle and a camper who has a tendency to engage in food fights must sit to the counselor's immediate left?

In Exercises 13–32, evaluate each factorial expression.

13. $\dfrac{9!}{6!}$

14. $\dfrac{12!}{10!}$

15. $\dfrac{29!}{25!}$

16. $\dfrac{31!}{28!}$

17. $\dfrac{19!}{11!}$

18. $\dfrac{17!}{9!}$

19. $\dfrac{600!}{599!}$

20. $\dfrac{700!}{699!}$

21. $\dfrac{104!}{102!}$

22. $\dfrac{106!}{104!}$

23. $7! - 3!$

24. $6! - 3!$

25. $(7 - 3)!$

26. $(6 - 3)!$

27. $\left(\dfrac{12}{4}\right)!$

28. $\left(\dfrac{45}{9}\right)!$

29. $\dfrac{7!}{(7 - 2)!}$

30. $\dfrac{8!}{(8 - 5)!}$

31. $\dfrac{13!}{(13 - 3)!}$

32. $\dfrac{17!}{(17 - 3)!}$

In Exercises 33–40, use the formula for $_nP_r$ to evaluate each expression.

33. $_9P_4$ **34.** $_7P_3$ **35.** $_8P_5$

36. $_{10}P_4$ **37.** $_6P_6$ **38.** $_9P_9$

39. $_8P_0$ **40.** $_6P_0$

Use the formula for $_nP_r$ to solve Exercises 41–48.

41. A club with ten members is to choose three officers—president, vice-president, and secretary-treasurer. If each office is to be held by one person and no person can hold more than one office, in how many ways can those offices be filled?

42. A corporation has seven members on its board of directors. In how many different ways can it elect a president, vice-president, secretary, and treasurer?

43. For a segment of a radio show, a disc jockey can play 7 records. If there are 13 records to select from, in how many ways can the program for this segment be arranged?

44. Suppose you are asked to list, in order of preference, the three best movies you have seen this year. If you saw 20 movies during the year, in how many ways can the three best be chosen and ranked?

45. In a race in which six automobiles are entered and there are no ties, in how many ways can the first three finishers come in?

46. In a production of *West Side Story*, eight actors are considered for the male roles of Tony, Riff, and Bernardo. In how many ways can the director cast the male roles?

47. Nine bands have volunteered to perform at a benefit concert, but there is only enough time for five of the bands to play. How many lineups are possible?

48. How many arrangements can be made using four of the letters of the word COMBINE if no letter is to be used more than once?

Use the formula for the number of permutations of duplicate items to solve Exercises 49–56.

49. In how many distinct ways can the letters of the word DALLAS be arranged?

50. In how many distinct ways can the letters of the word SCIENCE be arranged?

51. How many distinct permutations can be formed using the letters of the word TALLAHASSEE?

52. How many distinct permutations can be formed using the letters of the word TENNESSEE?

53. In how many ways can the digits in the number 5,446,666 be arranged?

54. In how many ways can the digits in the number 5,432,435 be arranged?

In Exercises 55–56, a signal can be formed by running different colored flags up a pole, one above the other.

55. Find the number of different signals consisting of eight flags that can be made using three white flags, four red flags, and one blue flag.

56. Find the number of different signals consisting of nine flags that can be made using three white flags, five red flags, and one blue flag.

WRITING IN MATHEMATICS

57. What is a permutation?

58. Explain how to find $n!$, where n is a positive integer.

59. Explain the best way to evaluate $\frac{900!}{899!}$ without a calculator.

60. Describe what $_nP_r$ represents.

61. Write a word problem that can be solved by evaluating $5!$.

62. Write a word problem that can be solved by evaluating $_7P_3$.

63. If 24 permutations can be formed using the letters in the word BAKE, why can't 24 permutations also be formed using the letters in the word BABE? How is the number of permutations in BABE determined?

CRITICAL THINKING EXERCISES

64. Ten people board an airplane that has 12 aisle seats. In how many ways can they be seated if they all select aisle seats?

65. Six horses are entered in a race. If two horses are tied for first place, and there are no ties among the other four horses, in how many ways can the six horses cross the finish line?

66. Performing at a concert are eight rock bands and eight jazz groups. How many ways can the program be arranged if the first, third, and eighth performers are jazz groups?

67. Five men and five women line up at a checkout counter in a store. In how many ways can they line up if the first person in line is a woman, and the people in line alternate woman, man, woman, man, and so on?

68. How many four-digit odd numbers less than 6000 can be formed using the digits 2, 4, 6, 7, 8, and 9?

69. Express $_nP_{n-2}$ without using factorials.

Appendix E

Combinations

Suppose you survey your friends and ask each the same question: "Of these five colors—red, blue, yellow, green, purple—which three are your favorite?"

OBJECTIVE 1 ▶ Distinguish between permutation and combination problems. One friend answers, "yellow, blue, and purple." Another responds, "purple, blue, and yellow." These two people have the same colors in their group of selections, even if they are named in a different order. We are interested *in which colors are named, not the order in which they are named.* Because the colors are taken without regard to order, this is not a permutation problem. No ranking of any sort is involved.

Later on, you ask your roommate which three colors she would select for your survey. She names red, green, and purple. Her selection is different from those of your two other friends because different colors are cited.

Mathematicians describe the group of colors given by your roommate as a *combination.* A **combination** of items occurs when

- The items are selected from the same group (the five colors).
- No item is used more than once. (You may adore red, but your three selections cannot be red, red, and red.)
- The order of items makes no difference. (Yellow, blue, and purple is the same group as purple, blue, and yellow.)

Do you see the difference between a permutation and a combination? A permutation is an ordered arrangement of a given group of items. A combination is a group of items taken without regard to their order. **Permutation** problems involve situations in which **order matters. Combination** problems involve situations in which the **order** of items **makes no difference.**

EXAMPLE 1 **Distinguishing between Permutations and Combinations**

For each of the following problems, determine whether the problem is one involving permutations or combinations. (It is not necessary to solve the problem.)

a. Six students are running for student government president, vice-president, and treasurer. The student with the greatest number of votes becomes the president, the second highest vote-getter becomes vice-president, and the student who gets the third largest number of votes will be treasurer. How many different outcomes are possible for these three positions?

b. Six people are on the board of supervisors for your neighborhood park. A three-person committee is needed to study the possibility of expanding the park. How many different committees could be formed from the six people?

c. Baskin-Robbins offers 31 different flavors of ice cream. One of their items is a bowl consisting of three scoops of ice cream, each a different flavor. How many such bowls are possible?

Solution

a. Students are choosing three student government officers from six candidates. The order in which the officers are chosen makes a difference because each of the offices (president, vice-president, treasurer) is different. Order matters. This is a problem involving permutations.

b. A three-person committee is to be formed from the six-person board of supervisors. The order in which the three people are selected does not matter because they are not filling different roles on the committee. Because order makes no difference, this is a problem involving combinations.

c. A three-scoop bowl of three different flavors is to be formed from Baskin-Robbin's 31 flavors. The order in which the three scoops of ice cream are put into the bowl is irrelevant. A bowl with chocolate, vanilla, and strawberry is exactly the same as a bowl with vanilla, strawberry, and chocolate. Different orderings do not change things, and so this is a problem involving combinations. ☐

PRACTICE

1 For each of the following problems, determine whether the problem is one involving permutations or combinations. (It is not necessary to solve the problem.)

a. How many ways can you select 6 free DVDs from a list of 200 DVDs?

b. In a race in which there are 50 runners and no ties, in how many ways can the first three finishers come in?

OBJECTIVE 2 ▶ A formula for combinations. We have seen that the notation $_nP_r$ means the number of permutations of n things taken r at a time. Similarly, the notation $_nC_r$ **means the number of combinations of n things taken r at a time.**

We can develop a formula for $_nC_r$ by comparing permutations and combinations. Consider the letters A, B, C, and D. The number of permutations of these four letters taken three at a time is

$$_4P_3 = \frac{4!}{(4-3)!} = \frac{4!}{1!} = \frac{4 \cdot 3 \cdot 2 \cdot 1}{1} = 24.$$

Here are the 24 permutations:

ABC,	ABD,	ACD,	BCD,
ACB,	ADB,	ADC,	BDC,
BAC,	BAD,	CAD,	CBD,
BCA,	BDA,	CDA,	CDB,
CAB,	DAB,	DAC,	DBC,
CBA,	DBA,	DCA,	DCB.

This column contains only one combination, ABC.	This column contains only one combination, ABD.	This column contains only one combination, ACD.	This column contains only one combination, BCD.

Because the order of items makes no difference in determining combinations, each column of six permutations represents one combination. There are a total of four combinations:

$$\text{ABC,} \quad \text{ABD,} \quad \text{ACD,} \quad \text{BCD.}$$

Thus, $_4C_3 = 4$: The number of combinations of 4 things taken 3 at a time is 4. With 24 permutations and only four combinations, there are 6, or 3!, times as many permutations as there are combinations.

In general, there are $r!$ times as many permutations of n things taken r at a time as there are combinations of n things taken r at a time. Thus, we find the number of combinations of n things taken r at a time by dividing the number of permutations of n things taken r at a time by $r!$.

$$_nC_r = \frac{_nP_r}{r!} = \frac{\dfrac{n!}{(n-r)!}}{r!} = \frac{n!}{(n-r)!r!}$$

Combinations of *n* Things Taken *r* at a Time

The number of possible combinations if *r* items are taken from *n* items is

$$_nC_r = \frac{n!}{(n-r)!\,r!}.$$

EXAMPLE 2   Using the Formula for Combinations

A three-person committee is needed to study ways of improving public transportation. How many committees could be formed from the eight people on the board of supervisors?

Solution   The order in which the three people are selected does not matter. This is a problem of selecting $r = 3$ people from a group of $n = 8$ people. We are looking for the number of combinations of eight things taken three at a time. We use the formula

$$_nC_r = \frac{n!}{(n-r)!\,r!}$$

with $n = 8$ and $r = 3$.

$$_8C_3 = \frac{8!}{(8-3)!\,3!} = \frac{8!}{5!\,3!} = \frac{8\cdot7\cdot6\cdot5!}{5!\cdot3\cdot2\cdot1} = \frac{8\cdot7\cdot6\cdot5!}{5!\cdot3\cdot2\cdot1} = 56$$

Thus, 56 committees of three people each can be formed from the eight people on the board of supervisors. □

PRACTICE
2   You volunteer to pet-sit for your friend who has seven different animals. How many different pet combinations are possible if you take three of the seven pets?

EXAMPLE 3   Using the Formula for Combinations

In poker, a person is dealt 5 cards from a standard 52-card deck. The order in which you are dealt the 5 cards does not matter. How many different 5-card poker hands are possible?

Solution   Because the order in which the 5 cards are dealt does not matter, this is a problem involving combinations. We are looking for the number of combinations of $n = 52$ cards drawn $r = 5$ at a time. We use the formula

$$_nC_r = \frac{n!}{(n-r)!\,r!}$$

with $n = 52$ and $r = 5$.

$$_{52}C_5 = \frac{52!}{(52-5)!\,5!} = \frac{52!}{47!\,5!} = \frac{52\cdot51\cdot50\cdot49\cdot48\cdot47!}{47!\cdot5\cdot4\cdot3\cdot2\cdot1} = 2{,}598{,}960$$

Thus, there are 2,598,960 different 5-card poker hands possible. It surprises many people that more than 2.5 million 5-card hands can be dealt from a mere 52 cards.

If you are a card player, it does not get any better than to be dealt the 5-card poker hand shown in Figure E.1. This hand is called a *royal flush*. It consists of an ace, king, queen, jack, and 10, all of the same suit: all hearts, all diamonds, all clubs, or all spades. The probability of being dealt a royal flush involves calculating the number of ways of being dealt such a hand: just 4 of all 2,598,960 possible hands. In the next section, we move from counting possibilities to computing probabilities. □

FIGURE E.1   A royal flush

PRACTICE
3   How many different 4-card hands can be dealt from a deck that has 16 different cards?

There are situations in which both the formula for combinations and the Fundamental Counting Principle are used together. Let's say that the U.S. Senate, with 100 members, consists of 54 Republicans and 46 Democrats. We want to form a committee of 3 Republicans and 2 Democrats.

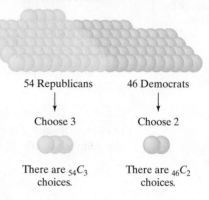

100 Senate Members

54 Republicans   46 Democrats
↓   ↓
Choose 3   Choose 2

There are $_{54}C_3$ There are $_{46}C_2$
choices.   choices.

By the Fundamental Counting Principle, the number of ways of choosing 3 Republicans and 2 Democrats is given by

$$_{54}C_3 \cdot {}_{46}C_2.$$

In Example 4, we develop these ideas in more detail.

EXAMPLE 4   **Using the Formula for Combinations and the Fundamental Counting Principle**

The U.S. Senate of the 104th Congress consisted of 54 Republicans and 46 Democrats. How many committees can be formed if each committee must have 3 Republicans and 2 Democrats?

Solution   The order in which the members are selected does not matter. Thus, this is a problem involving combinations.

We begin with the number of ways of selecting 3 Republicans out of 54 Republicans without regard to order. We are looking for the number of combinations of $n = 54$ people taken $r = 3$ people at a time. We use the formula

$$_nC_r = \frac{n!}{(n-r)!\, r!}$$

with $n = 54$ and $r = 3$.

$$_{54}C_3 = \frac{54!}{(54-3)!\, 3!} = \frac{54!}{51!\, 3!} = \frac{54 \cdot 53 \cdot 52 \cdot \cancel{51!}}{\cancel{51!} \cdot 3 \cdot 2 \cdot 1} = \frac{54 \cdot 53 \cdot 52}{3 \cdot 2 \cdot 1} = 24{,}804$$

There are 24,804 choices for forming 3-member Republican committees.

Next, we find the number of ways of selecting 2 Democrats out of 46 Democrats without regard to order. We are looking for the number of combinations of $n = 46$ people taken $r = 2$ people at a time. Once again, we use the formula

$$_nC_r = \frac{n!}{(n-r)!\, r!}.$$

This time, $n = 46$ and $r = 2$.

$$_{46}C_2 = \frac{46!}{(46-2)!\, 2!} = \frac{46!}{44!\, 2!} = \frac{46 \cdot 45 \cdot \cancel{44!}}{\cancel{44!} \cdot 2 \cdot 1} = 1035$$

There are 1035 choices for forming 2-member Democratic committees.

We use the Fundamental Counting Principle to find the number of committees that can be formed:

$$_{54}C_3 \cdot {}_{46}C_2 = 24{,}804 \cdot 1035 = 25{,}672{,}140.$$

Thus, 25,672,140 committees can be formed. □

PRACTICE

4 The U.S. Senate of the 107th Congress consisted of 50 Democrats, 49 Republicans, and one Independent. How many committees can be formed if each committee must have 3 Democrats and 2 Republicans?

APPENDIX E | EXERCISE SET

MyMathLab Powered by CourseCompass™ and MathXL® | Math XP PRACTICE | WATCH | DOWNLOAD | READ | REVIEW

PRACTICE EXERCISES

In Exercises 1–4, does the problem involve permutations or combinations? Explain your answer. (It is not necessary to solve the problem.)

1. A medical researcher needs 6 people to test the effectiveness of an experimental drug. If 13 people have volunteered for the test, in how many ways can 6 people be selected?

2. Fifty people purchase raffle tickets. Three winning tickets are selected at random. If first prize is $1000, second prize is $500, and third prize is $100, in how many different ways can the prizes be awarded?

3. How many different four-letter passwords can be formed from the letters A, B, C, D, E, F, and G if no repetition of letters is allowed?

4. Fifty people purchase raffle tickets. Three winning tickets are selected at random. If each prize is $500, in how many different ways can the prizes be awarded?

In Exercises 5–20, use the formula for $_nC_r$ to evaluate each expression.

5. $_6C_5$ 6. $_8C_7$ 7. $_9C_5$ 8. $_{10}C_6$

9. $_{11}C_4$ 10. $_{12}C_5$ 11. $_8C_1$ 12. $_7C_1$

13. $_7C_7$ 14. $_4C_4$ 15. $_{30}C_3$ 16. $_{25}C_4$

17. $_5C_0$ 18. $_6C_0$ 19. $\dfrac{_7C_3}{_5C_4}$ 20. $\dfrac{_{10}C_3}{_6C_4}$

PRACTICE PLUS

In Exercises 21–28, evaluate each expression.

21. $\dfrac{_7P_3}{3!} - {}_7C_3$ 22. $\dfrac{_{20}P_2}{2!} - {}_{20}C_2$ 23. $1 - \dfrac{_3P_2}{_4P_3}$

24. $1 - \dfrac{_5P_3}{_{10}P_4}$ 25. $\dfrac{_7C_3}{_5C_4} - \dfrac{98!}{96!}$ 26. $\dfrac{_{10}C_3}{_6C_4} - \dfrac{46!}{44!}$

27. $\dfrac{_4C_2 \cdot {}_6C_1}{_{18}C_3}$ 28. $\dfrac{_5C_1 \cdot {}_7C_2}{_{12}C_3}$

APPLICATION EXERCISES

Use the formula for $_nC_r$ to solve Exercises 29–36.

29. An election ballot asks voters to select three city commissioners from a group of six candidates. In how many ways can this be done?

30. A four-person committee is to be elected from an organization's membership of 11 people. How many different committees are possible?

31. Of 12 possible books, you plan to take 4 with you on vacation. How many different collections of 4 books can you take?

32. There are 14 standbys who hope to get seats on a flight, but only 6 seats are available on the plane. How many different ways can the 6 people be selected?

33. You volunteer to help drive children at a charity event to the zoo, but you can fit only 8 of the 17 children present in your van. How many different groups of 8 children can you drive?

34. Of the 100 people in the U.S. Senate, 18 serve on the Foreign Relations Committee. How many ways are there to select Senate members for this committee (assuming party affiliation is not a factor in the selection)?

35. To win at LOTTO in the state of Florida, one must correctly select 6 numbers from a collection of 53 numbers (1 through 53). The order in which the selection is made does not matter. How many different selections are possible?

36. To win in the New York State lottery, one must correctly select 6 numbers from 59 numbers. The order in which the selection is made does not matter. How many different selections are possible?

In Exercises 37–46, solve by the method of your choice.

37. In a race in which six automobiles are entered and there are no ties, in how many ways can the first four finishers come in?

38. A book club offers a choice of 8 books from a list of 40. In how many ways can a member make a selection?

39. A medical researcher needs 6 people to test the effectiveness of an experimental drug. If 13 people have volunteered for the test, in how many ways can 6 people be selected?

40. Fifty people purchase raffle tickets. Three winning tickets are selected at random. If first prize is $1000, second prize is $500, and third prize is $100, in how many different ways can the prizes be awarded?

41. From a club of 20 people, in how many ways can a group of three members be selected to attend a conference?

42. Fifty people purchase raffle tickets. Three winning tickets are selected at random. If each prize is $500, in how many different ways can the prizes be awarded?

43. How many different four-letter passwords can be formed from the letters A, B, C, D, E, F, and G if no repetition of letters is allowed?

44. Nine comedy acts will perform over two evenings. Five of the acts will perform on the first evening. How many ways can the schedule for the first evening be made?

45. Using 15 flavors of ice cream, how many cones with three different flavors can you create if it is important to you which flavor goes on the top, middle, and bottom?

46. Baskin-Robbins offers 31 different flavors of ice cream. One of its items is a bowl consisting of three scoops of ice cream, each a different flavor. How many such bowls are possible?

Use the formula for $_nC_r$ and the Fundamental Counting Principle to solve Exercises 47–50.

47. In how many ways can a committee of four men and five women be formed from a group of seven men and seven women?

48. How many different committees can be formed from 5 professors and 15 students if each committee is made up of 2 professors and 10 students?

49. The U.S. Senate of the 109th Congress consisted of 55 Republicans, 44 Democrats, and 1 Independent. How many committees can be formed if each committee must have 4 Republicans and 3 Democrats?

50. A mathematics exam consists of 10 multiple-choice questions and 5 open-ended problems in which all work must be shown. If an examinee must answer 8 of the multiple-choice questions and 3 of the open-ended problems, in how many ways can the questions and problems be chosen?

WRITING IN MATHEMATICS

51. What is a combination?

52. Explain how to distinguish between permutation and combination problems.

53. Write a word problem that can be solved by evaluating $_7C_3$.

CRITICAL THINKING EXERCISES

54. Write a word problem that can be solved by evaluating $_{10}C_3 \cdot {_7}C_2$.

55. A 6/53 lottery involves choosing 6 of the numbers from 1 through 53 and a 5/36 lottery involves choosing 5 of the numbers from 1 through 36. The order in which the numbers are chosen does not matter. Which lottery is easier to win? Explain your answer.

56. If the number of permutations of n objects taken r at a time is six times the number of combinations of n objects taken r at a time, determine the value of r. Is there enough information to determine the value of n? Why or why not?

57. In a group of 20 people, how long will it take each person to shake hands with each of the other persons in the group, assuming that it takes three seconds for each shake and only 2 people can shake hands at a time? What if the group is increased to 40 people?

58. A sample of 4 telephones is selected from a shipment of 20 phones. There are 5 defective telephones in the shipment. How many of the samples of 4 phones do not include any of the defective ones?

Appendix F

Arithmetic and Geometric Sequences

OBJECTIVE 1 ▶ Identifying arithmetic sequences. Find the first four terms of the sequence whose general term is $a_n = 5 + (n - 1)3$.

$$a_1 = 5 + (1 - 1)3 = 5 \qquad \text{Replace } n \text{ with 1.}$$
$$a_2 = 5 + (2 - 1)3 = 8 \qquad \text{Replace } n \text{ with 2.}$$
$$a_3 = 5 + (3 - 1)3 = 11 \qquad \text{Replace } n \text{ with 3.}$$
$$a_4 = 5 + (4 - 1)3 = 14 \qquad \text{Replace } n \text{ with 4.}$$

The first four terms are $5, 8, 11,$ and 14. Notice that the difference of any two successive terms is 3.

$$8 - 5 = 3$$
$$11 - 8 = 3$$
$$14 - 11 = 3$$
$$\vdots$$
$$a_n - a_{n-1} = 3$$

nth term   previous term

Because the difference of any two successive terms is a constant, we call the sequence an **arithmetic sequence,** or an **arithmetic progression.** The constant difference d in successive terms is called the **common difference.** In this example, d is 3.

> **Arithmetic Sequence and Common Difference**
>
> An **arithmetic sequence** is a sequence in which each term (after the first) differs from the preceding term by a constant amount d. The constant d is called the **common difference** of the sequence.

The sequence $2, 6, 10, 14, 18, \ldots$ is an arithmetic sequence. Its common difference is 4. Given the first term a_1 and the common difference d of an arithmetic sequence, we can find any term of the sequence.

EXAMPLE 1 Write the first five terms of the arithmetic sequence whose first term is 7 and whose common difference is 2.

Solution

$$a_1 = 7$$
$$a_2 = 7 + 2 = 9$$
$$a_3 = 9 + 2 = 11$$
$$a_4 = 11 + 2 = 13$$
$$a_5 = 13 + 2 = 15$$

The first five terms are $7, 9, 11, 13, 15$. ☐

PRACTICE
1 Write the first five terms of the arithmetic sequence whose first term is 4 and whose common difference is 5.

Notice the general pattern of the terms in Example 1.

$$a_1 = 7$$
$$a_2 = 7 + 2 = 9 \quad \text{or} \quad a_2 = a_1 + d$$
$$a_3 = 9 + 2 = 11 \quad \text{or} \quad a_3 = a_2 + d = (a_1 + d) + d = a_1 + 2d$$
$$a_4 = 11 + 2 = 13 \quad \text{or} \quad a_4 = a_3 + d = (a_1 + 2d) + d = a_1 + 3d$$
$$a_5 = 13 + 2 = 15 \quad \text{or} \quad a_5 = a_4 + d = (a_1 + 3d) + d = a_1 + 4d$$

(subscript $- 1$) is multiplier

The pattern on the right suggests that the general term a_n of an arithmetic sequence is given by

$$a_n = a_1 + (n - 1)d$$

> **General Term of an Arithmetic Sequence**
> The general term a_n of an arithmetic sequence is given by
> $$a_n = a_1 + (n - 1)d$$
> where a_1 is the first term and d is the common difference.

EXAMPLE 2 Consider the arithmetic sequence whose first term is 3 and common difference is -5.

a. Write an expression for the general term a_n.
b. Find the twentieth term of this sequence.

Solution

a. Since this is an arithmetic sequence, the general term a_n is given by $a_n = a_1 + (n - 1)d$. Here, $a_1 = 3$ and $d = -5$, so

$$a_n = 3 + (n - 1)(-5) \quad \text{Let } a_1 = 3 \text{ and } d = -5.$$
$$= 3 - 5n + 5 \quad \text{Multiply.}$$
$$= 8 - 5n \quad \text{Simplify.}$$

b. $a_n = 8 - 5n$
$$a_{20} = 8 - 5 \cdot 20 \quad \text{Let } n = 20.$$
$$= 8 - 100 = -92$$

PRACTICE
2 Consider the arithmetic sequence whose first term is 2 and whose common difference is -3.

a. Write an expression for the general term a_n.
b. Find the twelfth term of the sequence.

EXAMPLE 3 Find the eleventh term of the arithmetic sequence whose first three terms are 2, 9, and 16.

Solution Since the sequence is arithmetic, the eleventh term is

$$a_{11} = a_1 + (11 - 1)d = a_1 + 10d$$

We know a_1 is the first term of the sequence, so $a_1 = 2$. Also, d is the constant difference of terms, so $d = a_2 - a_1 = 9 - 2 = 7$. Thus,

$$a_{11} = a_1 + 10d$$
$$= 2 + 10 \cdot 7 \quad \text{Let } a_1 = 2 \text{ and } d = 7.$$
$$= 72 \qquad\qquad\qquad\qquad \square$$

PRACTICE

3 Find the ninth term of the arithmetic sequence whose first three terms are 3, 9, and 15.

EXAMPLE 4 If the third term of an arithmetic sequence is 12 and the eighth term is 27, find the fifth term.

Solution We need to find a_1 and d to write the general term, which then enables us to find a_5, the fifth term. The given facts about terms a_3 and a_8 lead to a system of linear equations.

$$\begin{cases} a_3 = a_1 + (3-1)d \\ a_8 = a_1 + (8-1)d \end{cases} \text{or} \begin{cases} 12 = a_1 + 2d \\ 27 = a_1 + 7d \end{cases}$$

Next, we solve the system $\begin{cases} 12 = a_1 + 2d \\ 27 = a_1 + 7d \end{cases}$ by elimination. Multiply both sides of the second equation by -1 so that

$$\begin{cases} 12 = a_1 + 2d \\ -1(27) = -1(a_1 + 7d) \end{cases} \begin{array}{c} \text{simplifies} \\ \text{to} \end{array} \begin{cases} 12 = a_1 + 2d \\ \underline{-27 = -a_1 - 7d} \\ -15 = -5d \quad \text{Add the equations.} \\ 3 = d \quad \text{Divide both sides by } -5. \end{cases}$$

To find a_1, let $d = 3$ in $12 = a_1 + 2d$. Then

$$12 = a_1 + 2(3)$$
$$12 = a_1 + 6$$
$$6 = a_1$$

Thus, $a_1 = 6$ and $d = 3$, so

$$a_n = 6 + (n-1)(3)$$
$$= 6 + 3n - 3$$
$$= 3 + 3n$$

and

$$a_5 = 3 + 3 \cdot 5 = 18 \qquad\qquad \square$$

PRACTICE

4 If the third term of an arithmetic sequence is 23 and the eighth term is 63, find the sixth term.

EXAMPLE 5 **Finding Salary**

Donna Theime has an offer for a job starting at $40,000 per year and guaranteeing her a raise of $1600 per year for the next 5 years. Write the general term for the arithmetic sequence that models Donna's potential annual salaries, and find her salary for the fourth year.

Solution The first term, a_1, is 40,000, and d is 1600. So

$$a_n = 40,000 + (n-1)(1600) = 38,400 + 1600n$$
$$a_4 = 38,400 + 1600 \cdot 4 = 44,800$$

Her salary for the fourth year will be $44,800. $\qquad\qquad \square$

5 A starting salary for a consulting company is $57,000 per year, with guaranteed annual increases of $2200 for the next 4 years. Write the general term for the arithmetic sequence that models the potential annual salaries, and find the salary for the third year.

OBJECTIVE 2 ▶ Identifying geometric sequences. We now investigate a **geometric sequence,** also called a **geometric progression.** In the sequence $5, 15, 45, 135, \ldots$, each term after the first is the *product* of 3 and the preceding term. This pattern of multiplying by a constant to get the next term defines a geometric sequence. The constant is called the **common ratio** because it is the ratio of any term (after the first) to its preceding term.

$$\frac{15}{5} = 3$$

$$\frac{45}{15} = 3$$

$$\frac{135}{45} = 3$$

$$\vdots$$

$$n\text{th term} \longrightarrow \frac{a_n}{a_{n-1}} = 3$$
$$\text{previous term} \longrightarrow$$

> **Geometric Sequence and Common Ratio**
>
> A **geometric sequence** is a sequence in which each term (after the first) is obtained by multiplying the preceding term by a constant r. The constant r is called the **common ratio** of the sequence.

The sequence $12, 6, 3, \frac{3}{2}, \ldots$ is geometric since each term after the first is the product of the previous term and $\frac{1}{2}$.

EXAMPLE 6 Write the first five terms of a geometric sequence whose first term is 7 and whose common ratio is 2.

Solution

$$a_1 = 7$$
$$a_2 = 7(2) = 14$$
$$a_3 = 14(2) = 28$$
$$a_4 = 28(2) = 56$$
$$a_5 = 56(2) = 112$$

The first five terms are $7, 14, 28, 56,$ and 112. □

6 Write the first four terms of a geometric sequence whose first term is 8 and whose common ratio is -3.

Notice the general pattern of the terms in Example 6.

$$a_1 = 7$$
$$a_2 = 7(2) = 14 \quad \text{or} \quad a_2 = a_1(r)$$
$$a_3 = 14(2) = 28 \quad \text{or} \quad a_3 = a_2(r) = (a_1 \cdot r) \cdot r = a_1 r^2$$
$$a_4 = 28(2) = 56 \quad \text{or} \quad a_4 = a_3(r) = (a_1 \cdot r^2) \cdot r = a_1 r^3$$
$$a_5 = 56(2) = 112 \quad \text{or} \quad a_5 = a_4(r) = (a_1 \cdot r^3) \cdot r = a_1 r^4$$
$$\longrightarrow \text{(subscript } -1) \text{ is power}$$

The pattern on the right above suggests that the general term of a geometric sequence is given by $a_n = a_1 r^{n-1}$.

> **General Term of a Geometric Sequence**
> The general term a_n of a geometric sequence is given by
> $$a_n = a_1 r^{n-1}$$
> where a_1 is the first term and r is the common ratio.

EXAMPLE 7 Find the eighth term of the geometric sequence whose first term is 12 and whose common ratio is $\frac{1}{2}$.

Solution Since this is a geometric sequence, the general term a_n is given by
$$a_n = a_1 r^{n-1}$$
Here $a_1 = 12$ and $r = \frac{1}{2}$, so $a_n = 12\left(\frac{1}{2}\right)^{n-1}$. Evaluate a_n for $n = 8$.
$$a_8 = 12\left(\frac{1}{2}\right)^{8-1} = 12\left(\frac{1}{2}\right)^7 = 12\left(\frac{1}{128}\right) = \frac{3}{32} \qquad \square$$

PRACTICE
7 Find the seventh term of the geometric sequence whose first term is 64 and whose common ratio is $\frac{1}{4}$.

- ∎

EXAMPLE 8 Find the fifth term of the geometric sequence whose first three terms are 2, −6, and 18.

Solution Since the sequence is geometric and $a_1 = 2$, the fifth term must be $a_1 r^{5-1}$, or $2r^4$. We know that r is the common ratio of terms, so r must be $\frac{-6}{2}$, or −3. Thus,
$$a_5 = 2r^4$$
$$a_5 = 2(-3)^4 = 162 \qquad \square$$

PRACTICE
8 Find the seventh term of the geometric sequence whose first three terms are −3, 6, and −12.

- ∎

EXAMPLE 9 If the second term of a geometric sequence is $\frac{5}{4}$ and the third term is $\frac{5}{16}$, find the first term and the common ratio.

Solution Notice that $\frac{5}{16} \div \frac{5}{4} = \frac{1}{4}$, so $r = \frac{1}{4}$. Then
$$a_2 = a_1\left(\frac{1}{4}\right)^{2-1}$$
$$\frac{5}{4} = a_1\left(\frac{1}{4}\right)^1, \quad \text{or} \quad a_1 = 5 \quad \text{Replace } a_2 \text{ with } \frac{5}{4}.$$

The first term is 5. $\qquad \square$

PRACTICE
9 If the second term of a geometric sequence is $\frac{9}{2}$ and the third term is $\frac{27}{4}$, find the first term and the common ratio.

- ∎

EXAMPLE 10 **Predicting Population of a Bacterial Culture**

The population size of a bacterial culture growing under controlled conditions is doubling each day. Predict how large the culture will be at the beginning of day 7 if it measures 10 units at the beginning of day 1.

Solution Since the culture doubles in size each day, the population sizes are modeled by a geometric sequence. Here $a_1 = 10$ and $r = 2$. Thus,

$$a_n = a_1 r^{n-1} = 10(2)^{n-1} \quad \text{and} \quad a_7 = 10(2)^{7-1} = 640$$

The bacterial culture should measure 640 units at the beginning of day 7. $\quad\square$

PRACTICE
10 After applying a test antibiotic, the population of a bacterial culture is reduced by one-half every day. Predict how large the culture will be at the start of day 7 if it measures 4800 units at the beginning of day 1.

VOCABULARY & READINESS CHECK

Word Bank. *Use the choices below to fill in each blank. Some choices may be used more than once and some not at all.*

first   arithmetic   difference
last   geometric   ratio

1. A(n) _____ sequence is one in which each term (after the first) is obtained by multiplying the preceding term by a constant r. The constant r is called the common _____.

2. A(n) _____ sequence is one in which each term (after the first) differs from the preceding term by a constant amount d. The constant d is called the common _____.

3. The general term of an arithmetic sequence is $a_n = a_1 + (n-1)d$ where a_1 is the _____ term and d is the common _____.

4. The general term of a geometric sequence is $a_n = a_1 r^{n-1}$ where a_1 is the _____ term and r is the common _____.

APPENDIX F | EXERCISE SET

Write the first five terms of the arithmetic or geometric sequence whose first term, a_1, and common difference, d, or common ratio, r, are given. See Examples 1 and 6.

1. $a_1 = 4; d = 2$

2. $a_1 = 3; d = 10$

3. $a_1 = 6; d = -2$

4. $a_1 = -20; d = 3$

5. $a_1 = 1; r = 3$

6. $a_1 = -2; r = 2$

7. $a_1 = 48; r = \dfrac{1}{2}$

8. $a_1 = 1; r = \dfrac{1}{3}$

Find the indicated term of each sequence. See Examples 2 and 7.

9. The eighth term of the arithmetic sequence whose first term is 12 and whose common difference is 3

10. The twelfth term of the arithmetic sequence whose first term is 32 and whose common difference is -4

11. The fourth term of the geometric sequence whose first term is 7 and whose common ratio is -5

12. The fifth term of the geometric sequence whose first term is 3 and whose common ratio is 3

13. The fifteenth term of the arithmetic sequence whose first term is -4 and whose common difference is -4

14. The sixth term of the geometric sequence whose first term is 5 and whose common ratio is -4

Find the indicated term of each sequence. See Examples 3 and 8.

15. The ninth term of the arithmetic sequence $0, 12, 24, \ldots$

16. The thirteenth term of the arithmetic sequence $-3, 0, 3, \ldots$

17. The twenty-fifth term of the arithmetic sequence $20, 18, 16, \ldots$

18. The ninth term of the geometric sequence $5, 10, 20, \ldots$

19. The fifth term of the geometric sequence $2, -10, 50, \ldots$

20. The sixth term of the geometric sequence $\dfrac{1}{2}, \dfrac{3}{2}, \dfrac{9}{2}, \ldots$

Find the indicated term of each sequence. See Examples 4 and 9.

21. The eighth term of the arithmetic sequence whose fourth term is 19 and whose fifteenth term is 52

22. If the second term of an arithmetic sequence is 6 and the tenth term is 30, find the twenty-fifth term.

23. If the second term of an arithmetic progression is -1 and the fourth term is 5, find the ninth term.

24. If the second term of a geometric progression is 15 and the third term is 3, find a_1 and r.

25. If the second term of a geometric progression is $-\dfrac{4}{3}$ and the third term is $\dfrac{8}{3}$, find a_1 and r.

26. If the third term of a geometric sequence is 4 and the fourth term is -12, find a_1 and r.

27. Explain why 14, 10, and 6 may be the first three terms of an arithmetic sequence when it appears we are subtracting instead of adding to get the next term.

28. Explain why 80, 20, and 5 may be the first three terms of a geometric sequence when it appears we are dividing instead of multiplying to get the next term.

MIXED PRACTICE

Decision Making. *Given are the first three terms of a sequence that is either arithmetic or geometric. If the sequence is arithmetic, find a_1 and d. If a sequence is geometric, find a_1 and r.*

29. $2, 4, 6$

30. $8, 16, 24$

31. $5, 10, 20$

32. $2, 6, 18$

33. $\dfrac{1}{2}, \dfrac{1}{10}, \dfrac{1}{50}$

34. $\dfrac{2}{3}, \dfrac{4}{3}, 2$

35. $x, 5x, 25x$

36. $y, -3y, 9y$

37. $p, p + 4, p + 8$

38. $t, t - 1, t - 2$

Find the indicated term of each sequence.

39. The twenty-first term of the arithmetic sequence whose first term is 14 and whose common difference is $\dfrac{1}{4}$

40. The fifth term of the geometric sequence whose first term is 8 and whose common ratio is -3

41. The fourth term of the geometric sequence whose first term is 3 and whose common ratio is $-\dfrac{2}{3}$

42. The fourth term of the arithmetic sequence whose first term is 9 and whose common difference is 5

43. The fifteenth term of the arithmetic sequence $\dfrac{3}{2}, 2, \dfrac{5}{2}, \ldots$

44. The eleventh term of the arithmetic sequence $2, \dfrac{5}{3}, \dfrac{4}{3}, \ldots$

45. The sixth term of the geometric sequence $24, 8, \dfrac{8}{3}, \ldots$

46. The eighteenth term of the arithmetic sequence $5, 2, -1, \ldots$

47. If the third term of an arithmetic sequence is 2 and the seventeenth term is -40, find the tenth term.

48. If the third term of a geometric sequence is -28 and the fourth term is -56, find a_1 and r.

Solve. See Examples 5 and 10.

49. An auditorium has 54 seats in the first row, 58 seats in the second row, 62 seats in the third row, and so on. Find the general term of this arithmetic sequence and the number of seats in the twentieth row.

50. A triangular display of cans in a grocery store has 20 cans in the first row, 17 cans in the next row, and so on, in an arithmetic sequence. Find the general term and the number of cans in the fifth row. Find how many rows there are in the display and how many cans are in the top row.

51. The initial size of a virus culture is 6 units, and it triples its size every day. Find the general term of the geometric sequence that models the culture's size.

52. A real estate investment broker predicts that a certain property will increase in value 15% each year. Thus, the yearly property values can be modeled by a geometric sequence whose common ratio r is 1.15. If the initial property value was $500,000, write the first four terms of the sequence and predict the value at the end of the third year.

53. A rubber ball is dropped from a height of 486 feet, and it continues to bounce one-third the height from which it last fell. Write out the first five terms of this geometric sequence and find the general term. Find how many bounces it takes for the ball to rebound less than 1 foot.

54. On the first swing, the length of the arc through which a pendulum swings is 50 inches. The length of each successive swing is 80% of the preceding swing. Determine whether this sequence is arithmetic or geometric. Find the length of the fourth swing.

55. Jose takes a job that offers a monthly starting salary of $4000 and guarantees him a monthly raise of $125 during his first year of training. Find the general term of this arithmetic sequence and his monthly salary at the end of his training.

56. At the beginning of Claudia Schaffer's exercise program, she rides 15 minutes on the Lifecycle. Each week she increases her riding time by 5 minutes. Write the general term of this arithmetic sequence, and find her riding time after 7 weeks. Find how many weeks it takes her to reach a riding time of 1 hour.

57. If a radioactive element has a half-life of 3 hours, then x grams of the element dwindles to $\dfrac{x}{2}$ grams after 3 hours. If a nuclear reactor has 400 grams of that radioactive element, find the amount of radioactive material after 12 hours.

Appendix G

Practice Final Exam

Preparing for your Final Exam? Take this Practice Final and watch the full video solutions to any of the exercises you want to review. You will find the Practice Final video in the Video Lecture Series.

Evaluate.

1. -3^4

2. 4^{-3}

3. $6[5 + 2(3 - 8) - 3]$

Perform the indicated operations and simplify if possible.

4. $(5x^3 + x^2 + 5x - 2) - (8x^3 - 4x^2 + x - 7)$

5. $(4x - 2)^2$

6. $(3x + 7)(x^2 + 5x + 2)$

Factor.

7. $y^2 - 8y - 48$

8. $9x^3 + 39x^2 + 12x$

9. $180 - 5x^2$

10. $3a^2 + 3ab - 7a - 7b$

11. $8y^3 - 64$

Simplify. Write answers with positive exponents only.

12. $\left(\dfrac{x^2 y^3}{x^3 y^{-4}} \right)^2$

Use long division to find the following.

13. $(x^2 + 7x + 10) \div (x + 5)$

Perform the indicated operations and simplify if possible.

14. $\dfrac{x^2 - 9}{x^2 - 3x} \div \dfrac{xy + 5x + 3y + 15}{2x + 10}$

15. $\dfrac{5a}{a^2 - a - 6} - \dfrac{2}{a - 3}$

16. If $B = \begin{bmatrix} 1 & -1 \\ 2 & 1 \end{bmatrix}$ and $C = \begin{bmatrix} 1 & 2 \\ -1 & 3 \end{bmatrix}$, find $C - B$.

Solve each equation or inequality.

17. $4(n - 5) = -(4 - 2n)$

18. $x(x + 6) = 7$

19. $3x - 5 \geq 7x + 3$

20. $2x^2 - 6x + 1 = 0$

21. $\dfrac{4}{y} - \dfrac{5}{3} = -\dfrac{1}{5}$

22. $\dfrac{5}{y + 1} = \dfrac{4}{y + 2}$

23. $\dfrac{a}{a - 3} = \dfrac{3}{a - 3} - \dfrac{3}{2}$

24. $\sqrt{2x - 2} = x - 5$

25. $|6x - 5| - 3 = -2$

26. $|2x - 3| = |4x + 5|$

27. $|3x + 1| > 5$

28. $-1 \leq \dfrac{2x - 5}{3} < 2$

Graph the following.

29. $5x - 7y = 10$

30. $x - 3 = 0$

31. $y > -4x$

32. $f(x) = \dfrac{2}{3}x + 2$

33. $f(x) = \begin{cases} -\dfrac{1}{2}x & \text{if } x \leq 0 \\ 2x - 3 & \text{if } x > 0 \end{cases}$

34. $g(x) = -|x + 2| - 1$

35. $f(x) = \dfrac{1}{(x + 3)^2}$

36. $y = x^2 - 4$

Find the slope of each line.

37. through $(6, -5)$ and $(-1, 2)$

38. $-3x + y = 5$

Write equations of the following lines. Write each equation in standard form.

39. through $(2, -5)$ and $(1, 3)$

40. through $(-5, -1)$ and parallel to $x = 7$

41. Find the distance between $(-3, 6)$ and $(-2, 8)$.

Solve each system of equations.

42. $\begin{cases} 3x - 2y = -14 \\ \qquad\; y = x + 5 \end{cases}$

43. $\begin{cases} \;\; 4x - 6y = 7 \\ -2x + 3y = 0 \end{cases}$

Answer the questions about functions.

44. If $h(x) = x^3 - x$, find

    a. $h(-1)$ **b.** $h(0)$ **c.** $h(4)$

45. Find the domain and range of the function graphed.

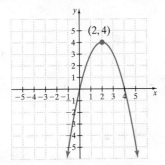

Use the frequency distribution shown to solve Exercises 46–48.

Score x	Frequency f
1	3
2	5
3	2
4	2

46. Find the mean.

47. Find the median.

48. Find the mode.

Simplify.

49. $\sqrt{54}$

50. $\sqrt{9x^9}$

Perform the indicated operations and simplify if possible.

51. $\sqrt{12} - 2\sqrt{75}$

52. $\dfrac{\sqrt{40x^4}}{\sqrt{2x}}$

53. $\sqrt{2}\left(\sqrt{6} - \sqrt{5}\right)$

Rationalize each denominator.

54. $\sqrt{\dfrac{5}{12x^2}}$

55. $\dfrac{2\sqrt{3}}{\sqrt{3} - 3}$

Solve each application.

56. One number plus five times its reciprocal is equal to six. Find the number.

57. Some states have a single area code for the entire state. Two such states have area codes where one is double the other. If the sum of these integers is 1203, find the two area codes.

58. Part of the proceeds from a hospital fund raiser was $3750 in $10 and $20 bills. If there were 30 more $20 bills than $10 bills, find the number of each denomination.

59. Suppose two trains leave a city at the same time, traveling in opposite directions. One train travels 6 mph faster than the other. In 3 hours, the trains are 282 miles apart. Find the speed of each train.

60. The wolf population in one geographic area is increasing at a rate of 12% per year. If the estimated population in this area is now 60 wolves, predict the number of wolves present in this area in 10 years.

61. Find $\sin A$, $\cos A$, and $\tan A$.

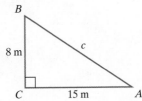

Answers to Selected Exercises

CHAPTER 1 REVIEW OF REAL NUMBERS

Section 1.2
Practice Exercises
1. a. < **b.** > **c.** < **2. a.** True **b.** False **c.** True **d.** True **3. a.** $3 < 8$ **b.** $15 \geq 9$ **c.** $6 \neq 7$ **4.** -52 **5. a.** 25 **b.** 25
c. $25, -15, -99$ **d.** $25, \frac{7}{3}, -15, -\frac{3}{4}, -3.7, 8.8, -99$ **e.** $\sqrt{5}$ **f.** $25, \frac{7}{3}, -15, -\frac{3}{4}, \sqrt{5}, -3.7, 8.8, -99$ **6. a.** < **b.** > **c.** = **7. a.** 8
b. 9 **c.** 2.5 **d.** $\frac{5}{11}$ **e.** $\sqrt{3}$ **8. a.** = **b.** > **c.** < **d.** > **e.** < **9. a.** True **b.** False. Counter example: 0 is a whole number that is
not a natural number.

Vocabulary and Readiness Check 1.2
1. whole **3.** inequality **5.** real **7.** irrational **9.** counter example

Exercise Set 1.2
1. > **3.** = **5.** < **7.** < **9.** $32 < 212$ **11.** $2631 > 2456$ **13.** true **15.** false **17.** false **19.** true **21.** $30 \leq 45$ **23.** $8 < 12$
25. $5 \geq 4$ **27.** $15 \neq -2$ **29.** $535; -8$ **31.** $-21,350$ **33.** $350; -126$ **35.** $1998, 1999$ **37.** $1998, 1999, 2000$ **39.** 279 million > 273 million
41. whole, integers, rational, real **43.** integers, rational, real **45.** natural, whole, integers, rational, real **47.** rational, real **49.** irrational, real
51. false; $\frac{1}{2}$ is a rational number but not an integer **53.** true **55.** false; $|3| < |-7|$ **57.** true **59.** false; $|-4| = 4$ **61.** > **63.** >
65. < **67.** < **69.** > **71.** = **73.** < **75.** < **77.** $-0.04 > -26.7$ **79.** sun **81.** sun **83.** c **85.** d **87.** answers may vary

Section 1.3
Practice Exercises
1. a. $2 \cdot 2 \cdot 3 \cdot 3$ **b.** $3 \cdot 5 \cdot 5$ **2. a.** $\frac{7}{8}$ **b.** $\frac{16}{3}$ **c.** $\frac{7}{25}$ **3.** $\frac{7}{24}$ **4. a.** $\frac{27}{16}$ **b.** $\frac{1}{36}$ **c.** $\frac{5}{2}$ **5. a.** 1 **b.** $\frac{6}{5}$ **c.** $\frac{4}{5}$ **d.** $\frac{1}{2}$ **6.** $\frac{14}{21}$
7. a. $\frac{46}{77}$ **b.** $3\frac{15}{26}$ **c.** $\frac{1}{2}$

Vocabulary and Readiness Check 1.3
1. fraction **3.** product **5.** factors, product **7.** equivalent **9.** $\frac{1}{4}$ **11.** $\frac{2}{5}$

Exercise Set 1.3
1. $3 \cdot 11$ **3.** $2 \cdot 7 \cdot 7$ **5.** $2 \cdot 2 \cdot 5$ **7.** $3 \cdot 5 \cdot 5$ **9.** $3 \cdot 3 \cdot 5$ **11.** $\frac{1}{2}$ **13.** $\frac{2}{3}$ **15.** $\frac{3}{7}$ **17.** $\frac{3}{5}$ **19.** $\frac{3}{8}$ **21.** $\frac{1}{2}$ **23.** $\frac{6}{7}$ **25.** 15 **27.** $\frac{1}{6}$
29. $\frac{25}{27}$ **31.** $\frac{11}{20}$ sq mi **33.** $\frac{3}{5}$ **35.** 1 **37.** $\frac{1}{3}$ **39.** $\frac{9}{35}$ **41.** $\frac{21}{30}$ **43.** $\frac{4}{18}$ **45.** $\frac{16}{20}$ **47.** $\frac{23}{21}$ **49.** $1\frac{2}{3}$ **51.** $\frac{5}{66}$ **53.** $\frac{7}{5}$ **55.** $\frac{1}{5}$
57. $\frac{3}{8}$ **59.** $\frac{1}{9}$ **61.** $\frac{5}{7}$ **63.** $\frac{65}{21}$ **65.** $\frac{2}{5}$ **67.** $\frac{9}{7}$ **69.** $\frac{3}{4}$ **71.** $\frac{17}{3}$ **73.** $\frac{7}{26}$ **75.** 1 **77.** $\frac{1}{5}$ **79.** $5\frac{1}{6}$ **81.** $\frac{17}{18}$ **83.** $55\frac{1}{4}$ ft
85. $6\frac{7}{50}$ m **87.** answers may vary **89.** $3\frac{3}{8}$ mi **91.** $\frac{7}{50}$ **93.** $\frac{1}{4}$ **95.** c **97.** $\frac{7}{36}$ sq ft

Section 1.4
Practice Exercises
1. a. 1 **b.** 25 **c.** $\frac{1}{100}$ **d.** 9 **e.** $\frac{8}{125}$ **2. a.** 33 **b.** 11 **c.** $\frac{32}{9}$ or $3\frac{5}{9}$ **d.** 36 **e.** $\frac{3}{16}$ **3.** $\frac{31}{11}$ **4.** 4 **5.** $\frac{9}{22}$ **6. a.** 9 **b.** $\frac{8}{15}$
c. $\frac{19}{10}$ **d.** 33 **7.** No **8. a.** $6x$ **b.** $x - 8$ **c.** $x \cdot 9$ or $9x$ **d.** $2x + 3$ **e.** $7 + x$ **9. a.** $x + 7 = 13$ **b.** $x - 2 = 11$ **c.** $2x + 9 \neq 25$
d. $5(11) \geq x$

Calculator Explorations 1.4
1. 625 **3.** 59,049 **5.** 30 **7.** 9857 **9.** 2376

Vocabulary and Readiness Check 1.4
1. base, exponent **3.** variable **5.** equation **7.** solving **9.** add **11.** divide

Exercise Set 1.4

1. 243 **3.** 27 **5.** 1 **7.** 5 **9.** $\frac{1}{125}$ **11.** $\frac{16}{81}$ **13.** 49 **15.** 16 **17.** 1.44 **19.** 17 **21.** 20 **23.** 10 **25.** 21 **27.** 45 **29.** 0

31. $\frac{2}{7}$ **33.** 30 **35.** 2 **37.** $\frac{7}{18}$ **39.** $\frac{27}{10}$ **41.** $\frac{7}{5}$ **43.** no **45. a.** 64 **b.** 43 **c.** 19 **d.** 22 **47.** 9 **49.** 1 **51.** 1 **53.** 11

55. 45 **57.** 27 **59.** 132 **61.** $\frac{37}{18}$ **63.** 16, 64, 144, 256 **65.** yes **67.** no **69.** no **71.** yes **73.** no **75.** $x + 15$ **77.** $x - 5$

79. $3x + 22$ **81.** $1 + 2 = 9 \div 3$ **83.** $3 \neq 4 \div 2$ **85.** $5 + x = 20$ **87.** $13 - 3x = 13$ **89.** $\frac{12}{x} = \frac{1}{2}$ **91.** answers may vary

93. $(20 - 4) \cdot 4 \div 2$ **95.** 28 m **97.** a **99.** 12,000 sq ft **101.** 6.5%

Section 1.5
Practice Exercises

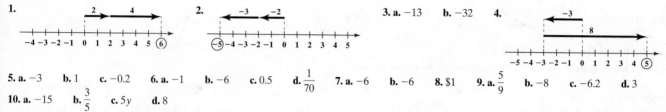

1. **2.** **3. a.** -13 **b.** -32 **4.**

5. a. -3 **b.** 1 **c.** -0.2 **6. a.** -1 **b.** -6 **c.** 0.5 **d.** $\frac{1}{70}$ **7. a.** -6 **b.** -6 **8.** \$1 **9. a.** $\frac{5}{9}$ **b.** -8 **c.** -6.2 **d.** 3

10. a. -15 **b.** $\frac{3}{5}$ **c.** $5y$ **d.** 8

Vocabulary and Readiness Check 1.5
1. opposites **3.** n **5.** positive number **7.** negative number **9.** 0

Exercise Set 1.5

1. 9 **3.** -14 **5.** 1 **7.** -12 **9.** -5 **11.** -12 **13.** -4 **15.** 7 **17.** -2 **19.** 0 **21.** -19 **23.** 31 **25.** -47 **27.** -2.1

29. -8 **31.** 38 **33.** -13.1 **35.** $\frac{2}{8} = \frac{1}{4}$ **37.** $-\frac{3}{16}$ **39.** $-\frac{13}{10}$ **41.** -8 **43.** -59 **45.** -9 **47.** 5 **49.** 11 **51.** -18 **53.** 19

55. -0.7 **57.** $-6°$ **59.** $-16,427$ ft **61.** $-\$9250$ million **63.** -9 **65.** -6 **67.** 2 **69.** 0 **71.** -6 **73.** answers may vary **75.** -2

77. 0 **79.** $-\frac{2}{3}$ **81.** answers may vary **83.** yes **85.** no **87.** July **89.** October **91.** 4.7°F **93.** negative **95.** positive

Section 1.6
Practice Exercises

1. a. -13 **b.** -7 **c.** 12 **d.** -2 **2. a.** 10.9 **b.** $-\frac{1}{2}$ **c.** $-\frac{19}{20}$ **3.** -7 **4. a.** -6 **b.** 6.1 **5. a.** -20 **b.** 13 **6. a.** 2 **b.** 13

7. \$357 **8. a.** 28° **b.** 137°

Vocabulary and Readiness Check 1.6
1. $7 - x$ **3.** $x - 7$ **5.** $7 - x$

Exercise Set 1.6

1. -10 **3.** -5 **5.** 19 **7.** $\frac{1}{6}$ **9.** 2 **11.** -11 **13.** 11 **15.** 5 **17.** 37 **19.** -6.4 **21.** -71 **23.** 0 **25.** 4.1 **27.** $\frac{2}{11}$

29. $-\frac{11}{12}$ **31.** 8.92 **33.** 13 **35.** -5 **37.** -1 **39.** -23 **41.** answers may vary **43.** -26 **45.** -24 **47.** 3 **49.** -45 **51.** -4

53. 13 **55.** 6 **57.** 9 **59.** -9 **61.** -7 **63.** $\frac{7}{5}$ **65.** 21 **67.** $\frac{1}{4}$ **69.** 100° **71.** -23 yd or 23 yd loss **73.** -569 or 569 B.C.

75. -308 ft **77.** 19,852 ft **79.** 130° **81.** 30° **83.** no **85.** no **87.** yes **89.** $-4.4°; 2.6°; 12°; 23.5°; 15.3°; 3.9°; -0.3°; -6.3°; -18.2°;$
$-15.7°; -10.3°$ **91.** October **93.** negative, -2.6466 **95.** true **97.** false; $|2| - |-10|$ is a negative number

Integrated Review—Operations on Real Numbers

1. negative **2.** negative **3.** positive **4.** 0 **5.** positive **6.** 0 **7.** positive **8.** positive **9.** $-\frac{1}{7}; \frac{1}{7}$ **10.** $\frac{12}{5}; \frac{12}{5}$ **11.** 3; 3

12. $-\frac{9}{11}; \frac{9}{11}$ **13.** -42 **14.** 10 **15.** 2 **16.** -18 **17.** -7 **18.** -39 **19.** -2 **20.** -9 **21.** -3.4 **22.** -9.8 **23.** $-\frac{25}{28}$ **24.** $-\frac{5}{24}$

25. -4 **26.** -24 **27.** 6 **28.** 20 **29.** 6 **30.** 61 **31.** -6 **32.** -16 **33.** -19 **34.** -13 **35.** -4 **36.** -1 **37.** $\frac{13}{20}$ **38.** $-\frac{29}{40}$

39. 4 **40.** 9 **41.** -1 **42.** -3 **43.** 8 **44.** 10 **45.** 47 **46.** $\frac{2}{3}$

Section 1.7
Practice Exercises
1. a. 3×2 **b.** $a_{12} = -2; a_{31} = 1$ **2. a.** $\begin{bmatrix} 2 & 0 \\ 9 & -10 \end{bmatrix}$ **b.** $\begin{bmatrix} 9 & -4 \\ -9 & 7 \\ 5 & -2 \end{bmatrix}$

Exercise Set 1.7
1. a. 2×3 **b.** a_{32} does not exist; $a_{23} = -1$ **3. a.** 3×4 **b.** $a_{32} = \dfrac{1}{2}; a_{23} = -6$ **5.** $x = 6; y = 4$ **7.** $x = 4; y = 6; z = 3$

9. a. $\begin{bmatrix} 9 & 10 \\ 3 & 9 \end{bmatrix}$ **b.** $\begin{bmatrix} -1 & -8 \\ 3 & -5 \end{bmatrix}$ **11. a.** $\begin{bmatrix} 3 & 2 \\ 6 & 2 \\ 5 & 7 \end{bmatrix}$ **b.** $\begin{bmatrix} -1 & 4 \\ 0 & 6 \\ 5 & 5 \end{bmatrix}$ **13. a.** $\begin{bmatrix} -3 \\ -1 \\ 0 \end{bmatrix}$ **b.** $\begin{bmatrix} 7 \\ -7 \\ 2 \end{bmatrix}$ **15. a.** $\begin{bmatrix} 8 & 0 & -4 \\ 14 & 0 & 6 \\ -1 & 0 & 0 \end{bmatrix}$ **b.** $\begin{bmatrix} -4 & -20 & 0 \\ 14 & 24 & 14 \\ 9 & -4 & 4 \end{bmatrix}$

17. a. $M = \begin{bmatrix} 2400 & 2700 & 3000 \\ 2200 & 2500 & 2900 \\ 2000 & 2300 & 2600 \end{bmatrix}$ **b.** $W = \begin{bmatrix} 2000 & 2100 & 2400 \\ 1800 & 2000 & 2200 \\ 1600 & 1800 & 2100 \end{bmatrix}$ **c.** $M - W = \begin{bmatrix} 400 & 600 & 600 \\ 400 & 500 & 700 \\ 400 & 500 & 500 \end{bmatrix}$
The differences between the basic caloric needs of men and women by age and activity level

19. 9 **21, 23, 25.** answers may vary

Section 1.8
Practice Exercises
1. a. -40 **b.** 12 **c.** -54 **2. a.** -30 **b.** 24 **c.** 0 **d.** 26 **3. a.** -0.046 **b.** $-\dfrac{4}{15}$ **c.** 14 **4. a.** 36 **b.** -36 **c.** -64 **d.** -64

5. a. $\dfrac{3}{8}$ **b.** $\dfrac{1}{15}$ **c.** $-\dfrac{7}{2}$ **d.** $-\dfrac{1}{5}$ **6. a.** -8 **b.** -4 **c.** 5 **7. a.** 3 **b.** -16 **c.** $-\dfrac{6}{5}$ **d.** $-\dfrac{1}{18}$ **8. a.** 0 **b.** undefined

c. undefined **9. a.** $\dfrac{-84}{5}$ **b.** 11 **10. a.** -9 **b.** 33 **c.** $\dfrac{5}{3}$

Calculator Explorations 1.8
1. 38 **3.** -441 **5.** $163.\overline{3}$ **7.** 54,499 **9.** 15,625

Vocabulary and Readiness Check 1.8
1. 0, 0 **3.** positive **5.** negative **7.** positive

Exercise Set 1.8
1. -24 **3.** -2 **5.** 50 **7.** -12 **9.** 0 **11.** -18 **13.** $\dfrac{3}{10}$ **15.** $\dfrac{2}{3}$ **17.** -7 **19.** 0.14 **21.** -800 **23.** -28 **25.** 25 **27.** $-\dfrac{8}{27}$

29. -121 **31.** $-\dfrac{1}{4}$ **33.** -30 **35.** 23 **37.** -7 **39.** true **41.** false **43.** 16 **45.** -1 **47.** 25 **49.** -49 **51.** $\dfrac{1}{9}$ **53.** $\dfrac{3}{2}$

55. $-\dfrac{1}{14}$ **57.** $-\dfrac{11}{3}$ **59.** $\dfrac{1}{0.2}$ **61.** -6.3 **63.** -9 **65.** 4 **67.** -4 **69.** 0 **71.** -5 **73.** undefined **75.** 3 **77.** -15 **79.** $-\dfrac{18}{7}$

81. $\dfrac{20}{27}$ **83.** -1 **85.** $-\dfrac{9}{2}$ **87.** -4 **89.** 16 **91.** -3 **93.** $-\dfrac{16}{7}$ **95.** 2 **97.** $\dfrac{6}{5}$ **99.** -5 **101.** $\dfrac{3}{2}$ **103.** -21 **105.** 41

107. -134 **109.** 3 **111.** 0 **113.** $-\$24{,}812$ million **115.** yes **117.** no **119.** yes **121.** answers may vary **123.** $+$ **125.** ?

127. $+$ **129.** $-$ **131.** $+$ **133.** $1, -1$ **135.** $-2 + \dfrac{-15}{3}; -7$ **137.** $2[-5 + (-3)]; -16$ **139.** $\begin{bmatrix} -12 & -9 \\ 3 & -18 \end{bmatrix}$ **141.** $\begin{bmatrix} 22 & 9 \\ -1 & 12 \end{bmatrix}$

Section 1.9
Practice Exercises
1. a. $8 \cdot x$ **b.** $17 + x$ **2. a.** $2 + (9 + 7)$ **b.** $(-4 \cdot 2) \cdot 7$ **3. a.** $x + 14$ **b.** $-30x$ **4. a.** $5x - 5y$ **b.** $-24 - 12t$ **c.** $6x - 8y - 2z$
d. $-3 + y$ **e.** $-x + 7 - 2s$ **f.** $14x + 14$ **5. a.** $5(w + 3)$ **b.** $9(w + z)$ **6. a.** commutative property of multiplication **b.** associative property of addition **c.** identity element for addition **d.** multiplicative inverse property **e.** commutative property of addition **f.** additive inverse property **g.** commutative and associative properties of multiplication

Vocabulary and Readiness Check 1.9
1. commutative property of addition **3.** distributive property **5.** associative property of addition **7.** opposites or additive inverses

Exercise Set 1.9
1. $16 + x$ **3.** $y \cdot (-4)$ **5.** yx **7.** $13 + 2x$ **9.** $x \cdot (yz)$ **11.** $(2 + a) + b$ **13.** $(4a) \cdot b$ **15.** $a + (b + c)$ **17.** $17 + b$ **19.** $24y$
21. y **23.** $26 + a$ **25.** $-72x$ **27.** s **29.** answers may vary **31.** $4x + 4y$ **33.** $9x - 54$ **35.** $6x + 10$ **37.** $28x - 21$ **39.** $18 + 3x$
41. $-2y + 2z$ **43.** $-21y - 35$ **45.** $5x + 20m + 10$ **47.** $-4 + 8m - 4n$ **49.** $-5x - 2$ **51.** $-r + 3 + 7p$ **53.** $3x + 4$ **55.** $-x + 3y$

57. $6r + 8$ **59.** $-36x - 70$ **61.** $-16x - 25$ **63.** $4(1 + y)$ **65.** $11(x + y)$ **67.** $-1(5 + x)$ **69.** $30(a + b)$ **71.** commutative property of multiplication **73.** associative property of addition **75.** distributive property **77.** associative property of multiplication **79.** identity element of addition **81.** distributive property **83.** commutative and associative properties of multiplication **85.** $-8; \dfrac{1}{8}$ **87.** $-x; \dfrac{1}{x}$ **89.** $2x; -2x$ **91.** no **93.** yes **95.** answers may vary

Chapter 1 Extension
Practice Exercises

1. a. $\dfrac{1}{6}$ **b.** $\dfrac{1}{2}$ **c.** 0 **d.** 1 **2. a.** $\dfrac{1}{13}$ **b.** $\dfrac{1}{2}$ **c.** $\dfrac{1}{26}$ **3. a.** 2:50 or 1:25 **b.** 50:2 or 25:1 **4.** 199:1 **5.** 1:15; $\dfrac{1}{16}$

Chapter 1 Extension Exercise Set

1. $\dfrac{1}{6}$ **3.** $\dfrac{1}{2}$ **5.** $\dfrac{1}{3}$ **7.** 1 **9.** 0 **11.** $\dfrac{1}{13}$ **13.** $\dfrac{1}{4}$ **15.** $\dfrac{3}{13}$ **17.** $\dfrac{1}{52}$ **19.** 0 **21.** $\dfrac{1}{4}$ **23.** $\dfrac{1}{2}$ **25.** $\dfrac{1}{2}$ **27.** $\dfrac{1}{4}$ **29.** $\dfrac{1}{9}$ **31.** 0 **33.** $\dfrac{3}{10}$ **35.** $\dfrac{1}{5}$ **37.** $\dfrac{1}{2}$ **39.** 0 **41.** $\dfrac{8}{11}$ **43.** $\dfrac{108}{187}$ **45.** $\dfrac{122}{187}$ **47.** 3:8; 8:3 **49.** $\dfrac{93}{143}$ **51.** $\dfrac{127}{143}$ **53.** $\dfrac{5}{13}$ **55.** 38:105; 105:38 **57.** 1:142; 142:1 **59.** 11:2; 2:11 **61.** 2:1 **63.** 1:2 **65. a.** 9:91 **b.** 91:9 **67.** $\dfrac{3}{10}$ **69, 71.** answers may vary

Chapter 1 Vocabulary Check

1. inequality symbols **2.** equation **3.** absolute value **4.** variable **5.** opposites **6.** numerator **7.** solution **8.** reciprocals **9.** base; exponent **10.** denominator **11.** grouping symbols **12.** set **13.** counterexample **14.** matrix

Chapter 1 Review

1. $<$ **3.** $>$ **5.** $<$ **7.** $=$ **9.** $>$ **11.** $4 \geq -3$ **13.** $0.03 < 0.3$ **15. a.** $1, 3$ **b.** $0, 1, 3$ **c.** $-6, 0, 1, 3$ **d.** $-6, 0, 1, 1\dfrac{1}{2}, 3, 9.62$ **e.** π **f.** $-6, 0, 1, 1\dfrac{1}{2}, 3, \pi, 9.62$ **17.** Friday **19.** $2 \cdot 2 \cdot 3 \cdot 3$ **21.** $\dfrac{12}{25}$ **23.** $\dfrac{13}{10}$ **25.** $9\dfrac{3}{8}$ **27.** 15 **29.** $\dfrac{7}{12}$ **31.** $A = \dfrac{34}{121}$ sq in.; $P = 2\dfrac{4}{11}$ in. **33.** $2\dfrac{15}{16}$ lb **35.** $11\dfrac{5}{16}$ lb **37.** Odera **39.** $3\dfrac{7}{8}$ lb **41.** 16 **43.** $\dfrac{4}{49}$ **45.** 70 **47.** 37 **49.** $\dfrac{18}{7}$ **51.** $20 - 12 = 2 \cdot 4$ **53.** 18 **55.** 5 **57.** $63°$ **59.** no **61.** $-\dfrac{2}{3}$ **63.** 7 **65.** -17 **67.** -5 **69.** 3.9 **71.** -14 **73.** 5 **75.** -19 **77.** 15 **79.** $x = -5, y = 6, z = 6$ **81.** $\begin{bmatrix} -4 & 4 & -1 \\ -2 & -5 & 5 \end{bmatrix}$ **83.** $-\dfrac{1}{6}$ **85.** -48 **87.** 3 **89.** undefined **91.** undefined **93.** -12 **95.** 9 **97.** -5 **99.** $\begin{bmatrix} 0 & -4 \\ 6 & 4 \\ 2 & -10 \end{bmatrix}$ **101.** commutative property of addition **103.** distributive property **105.** associative property of addition **107.** distributive property **109.** multiplicative inverse **111.** $5y - 10$ **113.** $-7 + x - 4z$ **115.** $-12x - 27$ **117.** $<$ **119.** -15.3 **121.** -80 **123.** $-\dfrac{1}{4}$ **125.** 16 **127.** -5 **129.** $-\dfrac{5}{6}$

Chapter 1 Test

1. $|-7| > 5$ **2.** $9 + 5 \geq 4$ **3.** -5 **4.** -11 **5.** -3 **6.** -39 **7.** 12 **8.** -2 **9.** undefined **10.** -8 **11.** $-\dfrac{1}{3}$ **12.** $4\dfrac{5}{8}$ **13.** $-\dfrac{5}{2}$ or $-2\dfrac{1}{2}$ **14.** -32 **15.** -48 **16.** 3 **17.** 0 **18.** $>$ **19.** $>$ **20.** $<$ **21.** $=$ **22.** $2221 < 10{,}993$ or $10{,}993 > 2221$ **23. a.** $1, 7$ **b.** $0, 1, 7$ **c.** $-5, -1, 0, 1, 7$ **d.** $-5, -1, 0, \dfrac{1}{4}, 1, 7, 11.6$ **e.** $\sqrt{7}, 3\pi$ **f.** $-5, -1, 0, \dfrac{1}{4}, 1, 7, 11.6, \sqrt{7}, 3\pi$ **24.** 40 **25.** 12 **26.** 22 **27.** -1 **28.** associative property of addition **29.** commutative property of multiplication **30.** distributive property **31.** multiplicative inverse property **32.** 9 **33.** -3 **34.** second down **35.** yes **36.** $17°$ **37.** \$650 million **38.** \$420 **39.** $\begin{bmatrix} 2 & 1 \\ 1 & 4 \end{bmatrix}$ **40.** $\begin{bmatrix} 0 & 3 \\ -3 & 2 \end{bmatrix}$

Chapter 1 Standardized Test

1. a **2.** d **3.** a **4.** a **5.** a **6.** c **7.** c **8.** c **9.** d **10.** b **11.** c **12.** a **13.** c **14.** b **15.** d **16.** c
17. b **18.** c **19.** b **20.** a **21.** d **22.** d **23.** c **24.** b **25.** a **26.** d **27.** a **28.** c **29.** c **30.** d **31.** a **32.** a
33. a **34.** a **35.** b **36.** c **37.** b **38.** c **39.** c **40.** c

CHAPTER 2 SOLVING EQUATIONS AND PROBLEM SOLVING

Section 2.1
Practice Exercises
1. a. 1 **b.** -7 **c.** $-\dfrac{1}{5}$ **d.** 43 **e.** -1 **2. a.** like terms **b.** unlike terms **c.** like terms **d.** like terms **3. a.** $7x^2$ **b.** $-2y$

c. $5x + 5x^2$ **4. a.** $11y - 5$ **b.** $5x - 6$ **c.** $-\dfrac{1}{4}t$ **d.** $12.2y + 13$ **e.** $5z - 3z^4$ **5. a.** $6x - 21$ **b.** $-15x + 20z + 25$

c. $-2x + y - z + 2$ **6. a.** $36x + 10$ **b.** $-11x + 1$ **c.** $-30x - 17$ **7.** $-5x + 4$ **8. a.** $3 + 2x$ **b.** $x - 1$ **c.** $2x + 10$ **d.** $\dfrac{13}{2}x$

Vocabulary and Readiness Check 2.1
1. expression; term **3.** numerical coefficient **5.** numerical coefficient **7.** -7 **9.** 1 **11.** $-\dfrac{5}{3}$ **13.** like **15.** unlike

Exercise Set 2.1
1. $15y$ **3.** $13w$ **5.** $-7b - 9$ **7.** $-m - 6$ **9.** -8 **11.** $7.2x - 5.2$ **13.** $4x - 3$ **15.** $5x^2$ **17.** $1.3x + 3.5$ **19.** answers may vary
21. $5y - 20$ **23.** $-2x - 4$ **25.** $7d - 11$ **27.** $-10x + 15y - 30$ **29.** $-3x + 2y - 1$ **31.** $2x + 14$ **33.** $10x - 3$ **35.** $-4x - 9$

37. $-4m - 3$ **39.** $k - 6$ **41.** $-15x + 18$ **43.** 16 **45.** $x + 5$ **47.** $x + 2$ **49.** $2k + 10$ **51.** $-3x + 5$ **53.** -11 **55.** $3y + \dfrac{5}{6}$

57. $-22 + 24x$ **59.** $0.9m + 1$ **61.** $10 - 6x - 9y$ **63.** $-x - 38$ **65.** $5x - 7$ **67.** $2x - 4$ **69.** $2x + 7$ **71.** $\dfrac{3}{4}x + 12$

73. $-2 + 12x$ **75.** $8(x + 6)$ or $8x + 48$ **77.** $x - 10$ **79.** $\dfrac{7x}{6}$ **81.** $7x - 7$ **83.** B; C; A; B **85.** -23 **87.** -25 **89.** $(18x - 2)$ ft

91. balanced **93.** balanced **95.** answers may vary **97.** $(15x + 23)$ in. **99.** $5b^2c^3 + b^3c^2$ **101.** $5x^2 + 9x$ **103.** $-7x^2y$

Section 2.2
Practice Exercises
1. -8 **2.** -1.8 **3.** $\dfrac{1}{10}$ **4.** 10 **5.** -10 **6.** 18 **7.** -8 **8. a.** 7 **b.** $9 - x$ **c.** $(9 - x)$ ft **9.** $(s - 3.8)$ mph

Vocabulary and Readiness Check 2.2
1. equation; expression **3.** solution **5.** addition

Exercise Set 2.2
1. 3 **3.** -2 **5.** 3 **7.** 0.5 **9.** $\dfrac{5}{12}$ **11.** -0.7 **13.** 3 **15.** answers may vary **17.** -3 **19.** -9 **21.** -10 **23.** 2 **25.** -7

27. -1 **29.** -9 **31.** -12 **33.** $-\dfrac{1}{2}$ **35.** 11 **37.** 21 **39.** 25 **41.** -14 **43.** $\dfrac{1}{4}$ **45.** 11 **47.** 13 **49.** -30 **51.** -0.4

53. -7 **55.** $-\dfrac{1}{3}$ **57.** -17.9 **59.** $-\dfrac{3}{4}$ **61.** 0 **63.** 1.83 **65.** $20 - p$ **67.** $(10 - x)$ ft **69.** $(180 - x)°$ **71.** $\left(m + 1\dfrac{1}{2}\right)$ ft

73. $7x$ sq mi **75.** A **77.** B **79.** G **81.** C **83.** $\dfrac{8}{5}$ **85.** $\dfrac{1}{2}$ **87.** -9 **89.** x **91.** y **93.** x **95.** $(173 - 3x)°$

97. answers may vary **99.** 4 **101.** answers may vary **103.** 250 ml **105.** answers may vary **107.** solution **109.** not a solution

Section 2.3
Practice Exercises
1. 20 **2.** -12 **3.** 65 **4.** 1.5 **5.** $-\dfrac{12}{35}$ **6.** 11 **7.** -3 **8.** 6 **9.** $\dfrac{11}{12}$ **10.** $3x + 6$

Vocabulary and Readiness Check 2.3
1. multiplication **3.** false **5.** 9 **7.** 2

Exercise Set 2.3
1. 4 **3.** 0 **5.** 12 **7.** -12 **9.** 3 **11.** 2 **13.** 0 **15.** 6.3 **17.** 10 **19.** -20 **21.** 0 **23.** -9 **25.** -3 **27.** -30 **29.** 3 **31.** $\dfrac{10}{9}$

33. -1 **35.** -4 **37.** $-\dfrac{1}{2}$ **39.** 0 **41.** 4 **43.** $-\dfrac{1}{14}$ **45.** 0.21 **47.** 5 **49.** 6 **51.** -5.5 **53.** -5 **55.** 0 **57.** -3 **59.** $-\dfrac{9}{28}$

61. $\dfrac{14}{3}$ **63.** -9 **65.** -2 **67.** $\dfrac{11}{2}$ **69.** $-\dfrac{1}{4}$ **71.** $\dfrac{9}{10}$ **73.** $-\dfrac{17}{20}$ **75.** -16 **77.** $2x + 2$ **79.** $2x + 2$ **81.** $5x + 20$ **83.** C; F; I; G

85. 1 **87.** $>$ **89.** $=$ **91.** $<$ **93.** -48 **95.** answers may vary **97.** answers may vary **99.** $\dfrac{700}{3}$ mg **101.** -2.95 **103.** 0.02

Section 2.4
Practice Exercises
1. 3 **2.** $\dfrac{21}{13}$ **3.** -15 **4.** 3 **5.** 0 **6.** no solution **7.** all real numbers

Calculator Explorations 2.4

1. solution **3.** not a solution **5.** solution

Vocabulary and Readiness Check 2.4

1. equation **3.** expression **5.** expression **7.** equation

Exercise Set 2.4

1. -6 **3.** 3 **5.** 1 **7.** $\frac{3}{2}$ **9.** 0 **11.** -1 **13.** 4 **15.** -4 **17.** -3 **19.** 2 **21.** 50 **23.** 1 **25.** $\frac{7}{3}$ **27.** 0.2

29. all real numbers **31.** no solution **33.** no solution **35.** all real numbers **37.** 18 **39.** $\frac{19}{9}$ **41.** $\frac{14}{3}$ **43.** 13 **45.** 4

47. all real numbers **49.** $-\frac{3}{5}$ **51.** -5 **53.** 10 **55.** no solution **57.** 3 **59.** -17 **61.** -4 **63.** 3 **65.** all real numbers **67.** A

69. C **71.** H **73.** C **75.** I **77.** $-3 + 2x$ **79.** $9(x + 20)$ **81.** $(6x - 8)$ m **83. a.** all real numbers **b.** answers may vary

c. answers may vary **85.** a **87.** b **89.** c **91.** answers may vary **93. a.** $x + x + x + 2x + 2x = 28$ **b.** $x = 4$

c. $x = 4$ cm; $2x = 8$ cm **95.** answers may vary **97.** 15.3 **99.** -0.2 **101.** $-\frac{7}{8}$ **103.** no solution

Integrated Review

1. 6 **2.** -17 **3.** 12 **4.** -26 **5.** -3 **6.** -1 **7.** $\frac{27}{2}$ **8.** $\frac{25}{2}$ **9.** 8 **10.** -64 **11.** 2 **12.** -3 **13.** no solution

14. no solution **15.** -2 **16.** -2 **17.** $-\frac{5}{6}$ **18.** $\frac{1}{6}$ **19.** 1 **20.** 6 **21.** 4 **22.** 1 **23.** $\frac{9}{5}$ **24.** $-\frac{6}{5}$ **25.** all real numbers

26. all real numbers **27.** 0 **28.** -1.6 **29.** $\frac{4}{19}$ **30.** $-\frac{5}{19}$ **31.** $\frac{7}{2}$ **32.** $-\frac{1}{4}$ **33.** no solution **34.** no solution **35.** $\frac{7}{6}$ **36.** $\frac{1}{15}$

Section 2.5
Practice Exercises

1. 9 **2.** 2 **3.** 9 in. and 36 in. **4.** 22 Republican and 28 Democratic Governors **5.** $25°, 75°, 80°$ **6.** 46, 48, 50

Vocabulary and Readiness Check 2.5

1. $2x; 2x - 31$ **3.** $x + 5; 2(x + 5)$ **5.** $20 - y; \frac{20 - y}{3}$ or $(20 - y) \div 3$

Exercise Set 2.5

1. $2x + 7 = x + 6; -1$ **3.** $3x - 6 = 2x + 8; 14$ **5.** $2(x - 8) = 3(x + 3); -25$ **7.** $4(-2 + x) = 5x + \frac{1}{2}; -\frac{17}{2}$ **9.** 5 ft, 12 ft

11. Armanty: 22 tons; Hoba West: 66 tons **13.** China: 42,400; U.S.: 36,594 **15.** 1st angle: $37.5°$; 2nd angle: $37.5°$; 3rd angle: $105°$
17. $3x + 3$ **19.** $x + 2, x + 4, 2x + 4$ **21.** $x + 1; x + 2; x + 3; 4x + 6$ **23.** $x + 2; x + 4; 2x + 6$ **25.** 234, 235

27. Belgium: 32; France: 33; Spain: 34 **29.** 3 in.; 6 in.; 16 in. **31.** $\frac{5}{4}$ **33.** Botswana: 32,000,000 carats; Angola: 8,000,000 carats **35.** $58°, 60°, 62°$

37. Russia: 22; Austria: 23; Canada: 24; United States: 25 **39.** -16 **41.** Weller: 108, 375; Pavich: 88, 179 **43.** $43°, 137°$ **45.** 1

47. 1st angle: $65°$; 2nd angle: $115°$ **49.** Maglev: 361 mph; TGV: 357.2 mph **51.** $\frac{5}{2}$ **53.** California: 58; Montana: 56 **55.** Colts: 29; Bears: 17

57. $34.5°, 34.5°, 111°$ **59.** 1st piece: 5 in.; 2nd piece: 10 in.; 3rd piece: 25 in. **61.** Hawaii **63.** Texas: \$31.1 million; Florida: \$29.4 million
65. answers may vary **67.** 34 **69.** 225π **71.** answers may vary

Section 2.6
Practice Exercises

1. 116 sec or 1 min 56 sec **2.** width: 9 ft **3.** $46.4°F$ **4.** length: 28 in.; width: 5 in. **5.** $r = \frac{I}{Pt}$ **6.** $s = \frac{H - 10a}{5a}$ **7.** $d = \frac{N - F}{n - 1}$
8. $B = \frac{2A - ab}{a}$

Exercise Set 2.6

1. $h = 3$ **3.** $h = 3$ **5.** $h = 20$ **7.** $c = 12$ **9.** $r \approx 2.5$ **11.** $T = 3$ **13.** $h \approx 15$ **15.** $h = \frac{f}{5g}$ **17.** $w = \frac{V}{lh}$ **19.** $y = 7 - 3x$

21. $R = \frac{A - P}{PT}$ **23.** $A = \frac{3V}{h}$ **25.** $a = P - b - c$ **27.** $h = \frac{S - 2\pi r^2}{2\pi r}$ **29. a.** area: 103.5 sq ft; perimeter: 41 ft
b. baseboard: perimeter; carpet: area **31. a.** area: 480 sq in.; perimeter: 120 in. **b.** frame: perimeter; glass: area **33.** 70 ft **35.** $-10°C$
37. 6.25 hr **39.** length: 78 ft; width: 52 ft **41.** 18 ft, 36 ft, 48 ft **43.** 55.2 mph **45.** 96 piranhas **47.** 2 bags **49.** one 16-in. pizza

51. $x = 6$ m, $2.5x = 15$ m   **53.** 0.2 hr or 12 min   **55.** 13 in.   **57.** 2.25 hr   **59.** 12,090 ft   **61.** 50°C   **63.** 515,509.5 cu in.   **65.** 449 cu in.
67. 332.6°F   **69.** $\dfrac{9}{x + 5}$ **71.** $3(x + 4)$ **73.** $3(x - 12)$ **75.**   **77.** −109.3°F   **79.** 500 sec or $8\dfrac{1}{3}$ min
81. 608.33 ft   **83.** 565.5 cu in.   **85.** It multiplies the area by 4.

Section 2.7
Practice Exercises
1. 62.5%   **2.** 360   **3. a.** 4%   **b.** 87%   **c.** 13 people   **4.** discount: $408; new price: $72   **5.** 50.7%   **6.** 520 new films

Vocabulary and Readiness Check 2.7
1. no   **3.** yes

Exercise Set 2.7
1. 11.2   **3.** 55%   **5.** 180   **7.** 69%   **9.** 1896.3 million bushels or 1,896,300,000 bushels   **11.** discount: $1480; new price: $17,020
13. $46.58   **15.** 35%   **17.** 30%   **19.** $104   **21.** $42,500   **23.** 4.6   **25.** 50   **27.** 30%   **29.** 71%   **31.** 178,778
33. 46%; 28%; 9%; 6%; total: 100%   **35.** decrease: $64; sale price: $192   **37.** 115% increase   **39.** 230 million
41. markup: $18.90; adult ticket price: $45.90   **43.** 300%   **45.** 120 employees   **47.** 4.6%   **49.** 335 decisions   **51.** 854 thousand Scoville units
53. 361 college students   **55.** >   **57.** =   **59.** >   **61.** answers may vary   **63.** 9.6%   **65.** 26.9%; yes   **67.** 17.1%

Section 2.8
Practice Problems
1. 2 liters of the 20% solution; 4 liters of the 50% solution   **2.** 106 $5 bills; 59 $20 bills   **3.** 2.2 hours   **4.** eastbound : 62 mph; west bound : 52 mph

Exercise Set 2.8
1. 2 gal   **3.** 7 lb   **5.** 0.10y   **7.** 0.05 $(x + 7)$ **9.** 20 $(4y)$ or 80y   **11.** 50 $(35 - x)$ **13.** 12 $10 bills; 32 $5 bills   **15.** 400 oz   **17.** 400 oz
19. 2 hr   **21.** 36 mph; 46 mph   **23.** 4 hr   **25.** $2\dfrac{1}{2}$ hr   **27.** $666\dfrac{2}{3}$ mi   **29.** 55 mph   **31.** 2 hr $37\dfrac{1}{2}$ min   **33.** 2.2 mph; 3.3 mph   **35.** 27.5 mi
37. − 4   **39.** $\dfrac{9}{16}$ **41.** − 4   **43.** 25 $100 bills; 71 $50 bills; 175 $20 bills   **45.** 25 skateboards   **47.** 800 books   **49.** answers may vary.

Chapter 2 Extension
Practice Exercises
1. a. Each number in the list is obtained by adding 6 to the previous number.; 33   **b.** Each number in the list is obtained by multiplying the previous number by 5.; 1250   **c.** To get the second number, multiply the previous number by 2. Then multiply by 3 and then by 4. Then multiply by 2, then by 3, and then by 4, repeatedly.; 3456   **d.** To get the second number, add 8 to the previous number. Then add 8 and then subtract 14. Then add 8, then add 8, and then subtract 14, repeatedly.; 7   **2. a.** Starting with the third number, each number is the sum of the previous two numbers.; 76   **b.** Starting with the second number, each number is one less than twice the previous number.; 257
3. The figures alternate between rectangles and triangles, and the number of appendages follows the pattern: one, two, three, one, two, three, etc.;
4. a. The result of the process is two times the original number selected.
   b. Representing the original number as n, we have
      Select a number: n
      Multiply the number by 4: $4n$
      Add 6 to the product: $4n + 6$
      Divide this sum by 2: $\dfrac{4n + 6}{2} = 2n + 3$
      Subtract 3 from the quotient: $2n + 3 - 3 = 2n.$

Chapter 2 Extension Exercise Set
1. Each number in the list is obtained by adding 4 to the previous number.; 28
3. Each number in the list is obtained by subtracting 5 from the previous number.; 12
5. Each number in the list is obtained by multiplying the previous number by 3.; 729
7. Each number in the list is obtained by multiplying the previous number by 2.; 32
9. The numbers in the list alternate between 1 and numbers obtained by multiplying the number prior to the previous number by 2.; 32
11. Each number in the list is obtained by subtracting 2 from the previous number.; −6
13. Each number in the list is obtained by adding 4 to the denominator of the previous fraction.; $\dfrac{1}{22}$
15. Each number in the list is obtained by multiplying the previous number by $\dfrac{1}{3}$.; $\dfrac{1}{81}$

17. The second number is obtained by adding 4 to the first number. The third number is obtained by adding 5 to the second number. The number being added to the previous number increases by 1 each time.; 42

19. The second number is obtained by adding 3 to the first number. The third number is obtained by adding 5 to the second number. The number being added to the previous number increases by 2 each time.; 51

21. Starting with the third number, each number is the sum of the previous two numbers.; 71   **23.** To get the second number, add 5 to the previous number. Then add 5 and then subtract 7. Then add 5, then add 5, and then subtract 7, repeatedly.; 18

25. The second number is obtained by multiplying the first number by 2. The third number is obtained by subtracting 1 from the second number. Then multiply by 2 and then subtract 1, repeatedly.; 33

27. Each number in the list is obtained by multiplying the previous number by $-\dfrac{1}{4}$; $\dfrac{1}{4}$

29. For each pair in the list, the second number is obtained by subtracting 4 from the first number.; -1

31. The pattern is: square, triangle, circle, square, triangle, circle, etc.;

33. Each figure contains the letter of the alphabet following the letter in the previous figure with one more occurrence than in the previous figure.;

d	d	d
d	d	

35. a. The result of the process is two times the original number selected.
b. Representing the original number as n, we have
Select a number: n
Multiply the number by 4: $4n$
Add 8 to the product: $4n + 8$
Divide this sum by 2: $\dfrac{4n + 8}{2} = 2n + 4$
Subtract 4 from the quotient: $2n + 4 - 4 = 2n$.

37. a. The result of the process is 3.
b. Representing the original number as n, we have
Select a number: n
Add 5: $n + 5$
Double the result: $2(n + 5) = 2n + 10$
Subtract 4: $2n + 10 - 4 = 2n + 6$
Divide by 2: $\dfrac{2n + 6}{2} = n + 3$
Subtract n: $n + 3 - n = 3$.

39. $1 + 2 + 3 + 4 + 5 + 6 = \dfrac{6 \times 7}{2}$; $21 = 21$ **41.** $1 + 3 + 5 + 7 + 9 + 11 = 6 \times 6$; $36 = 36$ **43.** $98,765 \times 9 + 3 = 888,888$; correct

45. $165 \times 3367 = 555,555$; correct   **47.** b   **49.** c   **51.** deductive reasoning; Answers will vary.

53. a. 28, 36, 45, 55, 66   **b.** 36, 49, 64, 81, 100   **c.** 35, 51, 70, 92, 117   **d.** square   **55, 57** answers may vary   **59.** 360 square units

61. a. The result is a three- or four-digit number in which the thousands and hundreds places represent the month of the birthday and the tens and ones places represent the day of the birthday.   **b.** $5[4(5M + 6) + 9] + D - 165 = 100M + D$ **63. a.** 10,101; 20,202; 30,303; 40,404
b. In the multiplications, the first factor is always 3367, and the second factors are consecutive multiples of 3, beginning with $3 \times 1 = 3$.; The second and fourth digits of the products are always 0; the first, third, and last digits are the same within each product; this digit is 1 in the first product and increases by 1 in each subsequent product.   **c.** $3367 \times 15 = 50,505$; $3367 \times 18 = 60,606$ **d.** inductive reasoning; Answers will vary.

Chapter 2 Vocabulary Check

1. like terms   **2.** linear equation in one variable   **3.** equivalent equations   **4.** formula   **5.** numerical coefficient

Chapter 2 Review

1. $6x$ **3.** $4x - 2$ **5.** $3n - 18$ **7.** $-6x + 7$ **9.** $3x - 7$ **11.** 4   **13.** 6   **15.** 0   **17.** -23 **19.** 5; 5   **21.** b   **23.** b   **25.** -12

27. 0   **29.** 0.75   **31.** -6 **33.** -1 **35.** $-\dfrac{1}{5}$ **37.** $3x + 3$ **39.** -4 **41.** 2   **43.** no solution   **45.** $\dfrac{3}{4}$ **47.** 20   **49.** $\dfrac{23}{7}$ **51.** 102

53. 6665.5 in.   **55.** Kellogg: 35 plants; Keebler: 18 plants   **57.** 3   **59.** $w = 9$ **61.** $m = \dfrac{y - b}{x}$ **63.** $x = \dfrac{2y - 7}{5}$ **65.** $\pi = \dfrac{C}{D}$ **67.** 15 m

69. 1 hr 20 min   **71.** 20%   **73.** 110   **75.** mark-up: $209; new price: $2109   **77.** 18%   **79.** 966 customers

81. 40% solution: 10 gal; 10% solution: 20 gal   **83.** 483 dimes; 161 nickels   **85.** $1\dfrac{1}{2}$ hr   **87.** 3 hr   **89.** $x = 4$ **91.** $a = -\dfrac{3}{2}$

93. all real numbers   **95.** -13 **97.** $h = \dfrac{3V}{A}$ **99.** 160

Chapter 2 Test

1. $y - 10$ **2.** $5.9x + 1.2$ **3.** $-2x + 10$ **4.** $10y + 1$ **5.** -5 **6.** 8   **7.** $\dfrac{7}{10}$ **8.** 0   **9.** 27   **10.** 3   **11.** 0.25   **12.** $\dfrac{25}{7}$

13. no solution   **14.** 21   **15.** 7 gal   **16.** 401, 802   **17.** New York: 1077; Indiana: 427   **18.** 105 $10 bills; 135 $20 bills   **19.** $1\dfrac{1}{4}$ hr

20. 44 mph; 50 mph   **21.** $x = 6$ **22.** $h = \dfrac{V}{\pi r^2}$ **23.** $y = \dfrac{3x - 10}{4}$

Chapter 2 Standardized Test

1. d   **2.** a   **3.** b   **4.** b   **5.** a   **6.** d   **7.** b   **8.** b   **9.** c   **10.** c   **11.** a   **12.** c   **13.** d   **14.** a   **15.** b   **16.** a   **17.** d   **18.** d
19. a   **20.** d   **21.** d   **20.** b

CHAPTER 3 GRAPHS AND FUNCTIONS

Section 3.1

Practice Exercises

1. a. Germany, 45 million Internet users   **b.** approximately 5 million Internet users   **2. a.** 70 beats per minute   **b.** 60 beats per minute

c. 5 minutes after lighting   **3.**

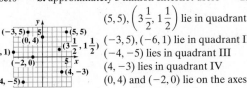

$(5,5), \left(3\frac{1}{2}, 1\frac{1}{2}\right)$ lie in quadrant I   **4. a.** $(2000, 92), (2001, 84), (2002, 73), (2003, 64),$
$(2004, 65), (2005, 67), (2006, 96)$

$(-3, 5), (-6, 1)$ lie in quadrant II
$(-4, -5)$ lies in quadrant III
$(4, -3)$ lies in quadrant IV
$(0, 4)$ and $(-2, 0)$ lie on the axes

b.

Wildfires

5. a. true   **b.** true   **c.** false   **6. a.** $(0, -8)$ **b.** $(6, 4)$ **c.** $(-3, -14)$

7.

	x	y
a.	-2	8
b.	3	-12
c.	0	0

8.

	x	y
a.	-10	-4
b.	0	-2
c.	10	0

9.

x	0	1	2	3	4
y	12,000	10,200	8400	6600	4800

Vocabulary and Readiness Check 3.1

1. x-axis   **3.** origin   **5.** x-coordinate; y-coordinate   **7.** solution

Exercise Set 3.1

1. France   **3.** France, U.S., Spain, and China   **5.** 30 million   **7.** 72,600   **9.** 2007; 104,000   **11.** 15.9   **13.** from 1996 to 1998   **15.** 2002

17.

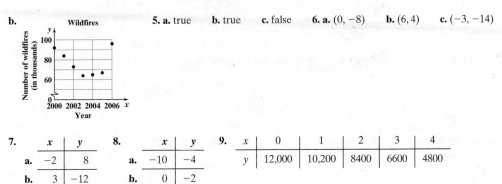

$(1, 5)$ and $(3.7, 2.2)$ are in quadrant I, $\left(-1, 4\frac{1}{2}\right)$ is in quadrant II, $(-5, -2)$ is in quadrant III, $(2, -4)$ and $\left(\frac{1}{2}, -3\right)$
are in quadrant IV, $(-3, 0)$ lies on the x-axis, $(0, -1)$ lies on the y-axis   **19.** $(0, 0)$ **21.** $(3, 2)$ **23.** $(-2, -2)$

25. $(2, -1)$ **27.** $(0, -3)$ **29.** $(1, 3)$ **31.** $(-3, -1)$ **33. a.** $(2002, 12), (2003, 14), (2004, 14), (2005, 11), (2006, 12)$

b.

**Regular Season Games
Won by Super Bowl Winner**

35. a. $(2001, 1770), (2003, 2800), (2005, 3904), (2007, 7500), (2009, 10,800)$ **b.**

**Ethanol Fuel Production
in the U.S.**

c. The ethanol production is increasing as the years increase.   **37. a.** $(2313, 2), (2085, 1), (2711, 21), (2869, 39), (2920, 42), (4038, 99), (1783, 0), (2493, 9)$

b.

**Average Annual Snowfall
for Selected U.S. Cities**

c. The farther from the equator, the more snowfall.   **39.** yes; no; yes   **41.** yes; yes   **43.** no; yes; yes

45. $(-4, -2), (4, 0)$ **47.** $(-8, -5), (16, 1)$ **49.** $0; 7; -\frac{2}{7}$ **51.** 2; 2; 5   **53.** $0; -3; 2$ **55.** 2; 6; 3

57. $-12; 5; -6$ **59.** $\frac{5}{7}; \frac{5}{2}; -1$ **61.** $0; -5; -2$ **63.** 2; 1; -6

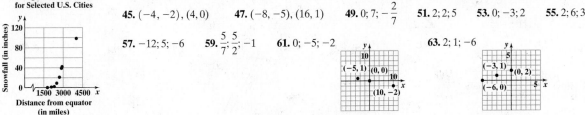

65. a. 13,000; 21,000; 29,000 **b.** 45 desks **67. a.** 53.57; 48.87; 44.17 **b.** year 4: 2005 **69.** In 2004, there were 1308 Target stores.

71. year 1: 75 stores; year 2: 100 stores; year 3: 75 stores **73.** $a = b$ **75.** (a) **77.** (f) **79.** (b) **81.** $y = 5 - x$ **83.** $y = -\dfrac{1}{2}x + \dfrac{5}{4}$

85. $y = -2x$ **87.** $y = \dfrac{1}{3}x - 2$ **89.** false **91.** true **93.** negative; negative **95.** positive; negative **97.** 0; 0 **99.** y

101. no; answers may vary **103.** answers may vary **105.** $(4, -7)$ **107. a.** $(-2, 6)$ **b.** 28 units **c.** 45 sq units

Section 3.2

Practice Exercises

1. a. yes **b.** no **c.** yes **d.** yes **2.** **3.** **4.** **5.**

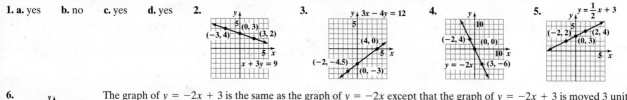

6.

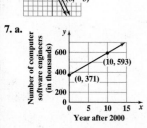

The graph of $y = -2x + 3$ is the same as the graph of $y = -2x$ except that the graph of $y = -2x + 3$ is moved 3 units upward.

7. a.

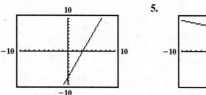

b. We predict 700 thousand computer software application engineers in the year 2015.

Calculator Explorations 3.2

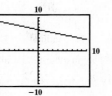

Exercise Set 3.2

1. yes **3.** yes **5.** no **7.** yes

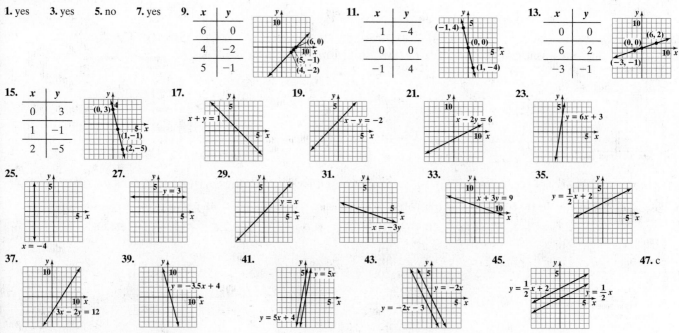

47. c

49. d   **51. a.** $(8, 7)$ **b.** In 2005, there were 7 million snowboarders.   **c.** 10.5 million snowboarders   **53.** The expected minimum salary after 5 years experience is $545 thousand.   **55.** $(4, -1)$ **57.** -5 **59.** $-\dfrac{1}{10}$ **61.** $y = x + 5$ **63.** $2x + 3y = 6$

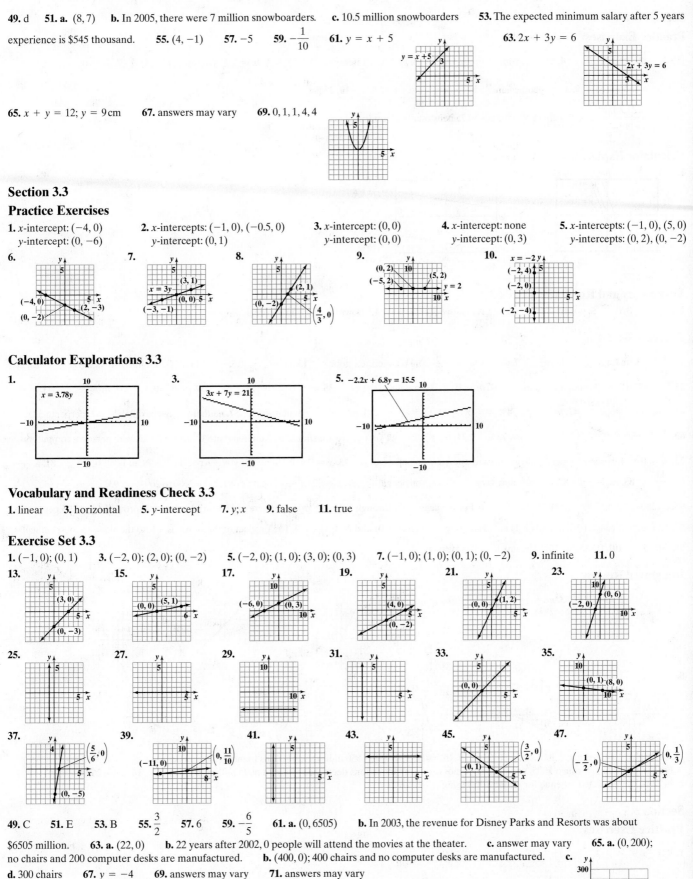

65. $x + y = 12$; $y = 9$ cm   **67.** answers may vary   **69.** $0, 1, 1, 4, 4$

Section 3.3

Practice Exercises

1. x-intercept: $(-4, 0)$ **2.** x-intercepts: $(-1, 0), (-0.5, 0)$ **3.** x-intercept: $(0, 0)$ **4.** x-intercept: none   **5.** x-intercepts: $(-1, 0), (5, 0)$
y-intercept: $(0, -6)$ y-intercept: $(0, 1)$ y-intercept: $(0, 0)$ y-intercept: $(0, 3)$ y-intercepts: $(0, 2), (0, -2)$

6.   **7.**   **8.**   **9.**   **10.**

Calculator Explorations 3.3

1.   **3.**   **5.** $-2.2x + 6.8y = 15.5$

Vocabulary and Readiness Check 3.3

1. linear   **3.** horizontal   **5.** y-intercept   **7.** y; x **9.** false   **11.** true

Exercise Set 3.3

1. $(-1, 0)$; $(0, 1)$ **3.** $(-2, 0)$; $(2, 0)$; $(0, -2)$ **5.** $(-2, 0)$; $(1, 0)$; $(3, 0)$; $(0, 3)$ **7.** $(-1, 0)$; $(1, 0)$; $(0, 1)$; $(0, -2)$ **9.** infinite   **11.** 0

13.   **15.**   **17.**   **19.**   **21.**   **23.**

25.   **27.**   **29.**   **31.**   **33.**   **35.**

37.   **39.**   **41.**   **43.**   **45.**   **47.**

49. C   **51.** E   **53.** B   **55.** $\dfrac{3}{2}$ **57.** 6   **59.** $-\dfrac{6}{5}$ **61. a.** $(0, 6505)$ **b.** In 2003, the revenue for Disney Parks and Resorts was about $6505 million.   **63. a.** $(22, 0)$ **b.** 22 years after 2002, 0 people will attend the movies at the theater.   **c.** answer may vary   **65. a.** $(0, 200)$; no chairs and 200 computer desks are manufactured.   **b.** $(400, 0)$; 400 chairs and no computer desks are manufactured.   **c.**   **d.** 300 chairs   **67.** $y = -4$ **69.** answers may vary   **71.** answers may vary

Section 3.4
Practice Exercises

1. -1 **2.** $\frac{1}{3}$ **3.** -7 **4.** $m = \frac{2}{3}$; y-intercept: $(0, -2)$ **5.** $m = 6$; y-intercept: $(0, -5)$ **6.** $m = -\frac{5}{2}$; y-intercept: $(0, 4)$ **7.** $m = 0$

8. slope is undefined **9. a.** perpendicular **b.** neither **c.** parallel **10.** 25%

11. $m = \frac{0.75 \text{ dollar}}{1 \text{ pound}}$; The Wash-n-Fold charges $0.75 per pound of laundry.

Calculator Explorations 3.4

1. 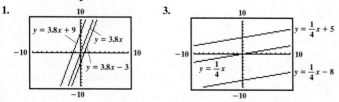 **3.**

Vocabulary and Readiness Check 3.4

1. slope **3.** 0 **5.** positive **7.** y; x **9.** positive **11.** 0 **13.** downward **15.** vertical

Exercise Set 3.4

1. -1 **3.** undefined **5.** $-\frac{2}{3}$ **7.** 0 **9.** $m = -\frac{4}{3}$ **11.** undefined slope **13.** $m = \frac{5}{2}$ **15.** $\frac{2}{3}$ **17.** 2 **19.** line 1 **21.** line 2 **23.** D

25. B **27.** E **29.** undefined slope **31.** $m = 0$ **33.** undefined slope **35.** $m = 0$ **37.** $m = 5$ **39.** $m = -0.3$ **41.** $m = -2$ **43.** $m = \frac{2}{3}$

45. undefined slope **47.** $m = \frac{1}{2}$ **49.** $m = 0$ **51.** $m = -\frac{3}{4}$ **53.** $m = 4$ **55.** neither **57.** neither **59.** parallel **61.** perpendicular

63. $\frac{3}{5}$ **65.** 12.5% **67.** 40% **69.** 79% **71.** $m = 3$; Every 1 year, there are/should be 3 million more U.S. households with personal computers.

73. $m = 0.42$; It costs $0.42 per 1 mile to own and operate a compact car. **75.** $y = 2x - 14$ **77.** $y = -6x - 11$ **79. a.** 1 **b.** -1 **81. a.** $\frac{9}{11}$ **b.** $-\frac{11}{9}$ **83.** $m = \frac{1}{2}$ **85.** answers may vary **87.** 28.5 mi per gal **89.** 2000; 28.1 mi per gal **91.** from 2000 to 2001 **93.** $x = 6$

95. a. $(2001, 1132), (2006, 1657)$ **b.** 105 **c.** For the years 2001 through 2006, the price per acre of U.S. farmland rose approximately $105 per year.

97. The slope through $(-3, 0)$ and $(1, 1)$ is $\frac{1}{4}$. The slope through $(-3, 0)$ and $(-4, 4)$ is -4. The product of the slopes is -1, so the sides are perpendicular.

99. -0.25 **101.** 0.875 **103.** The line becomes steeper.

Integrated Review

1. $m = 2$ **2.** $m = 0$ **3.** $m = -\frac{2}{3}$ **4.** undefined slope **5.** **6.** $x + y = 3$ **7.**

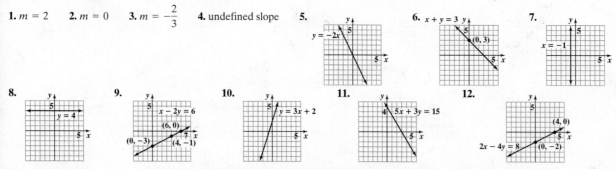

8. **9.** **10.** **11.** **12.**

13. parallel **14.** neither **15. a.** $(0, 1650)$ **b.** In 2002, there were 1650 million admissions to movie theaters in the U.S. **c.** -75
d. For the years 2002 through 2005, the number of movie theater admissions decreased at a rate of 75 million per year. **16. a.** $(9, 26.6)$
b. In 2009, the predicted revenue for online advertising is $26.6 billion.

Section 3.5
Practice Exercises

1. $y = \frac{1}{2}x + 7$ **2.** **3.** **4.** $4x - y = 5$ **5.** $5x + 4y = 19$ **6.** $x = 3$ **7.** $y = 3$

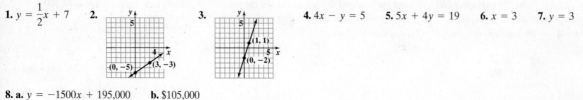

8. a. $y = -1500x + 195,000$ **b.** $105,000

Calculator Explorations 3.5

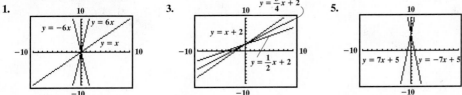

Vocabulary and Readiness Check 3.5

1. slope-intercept; m; b　　**3.** point-slope　　**5.** horizontal　　**7.** slope-intercept

Exercise Set 3.5

1. $y = 5x + 3$　　**3.** $y = -4x - \dfrac{1}{6}$　　**5.** $y = \dfrac{2}{3}x$　　**7.** $y = -8$　　**9.** $y = -\dfrac{1}{5}x + \dfrac{1}{9}$　　**11.**　　**13.**

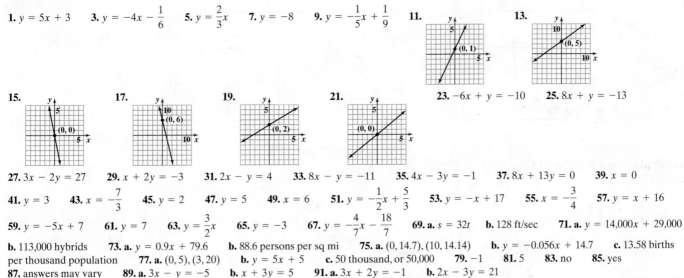

23. $-6x + y = -10$　　**25.** $8x + y = -13$

27. $3x - 2y = 27$　　**29.** $x + 2y = -3$　　**31.** $2x - y = 4$　　**33.** $8x - y = -11$　　**35.** $4x - 3y = -1$　　**37.** $8x + 13y = 0$　　**39.** $x = 0$

41. $y = 3$　　**43.** $x = -\dfrac{7}{3}$　　**45.** $y = 2$　　**47.** $y = 5$　　**49.** $x = 6$　　**51.** $y = -\dfrac{1}{2}x + \dfrac{5}{3}$　　**53.** $y = -x + 17$　　**55.** $x = -\dfrac{3}{4}$　　**57.** $y = x + 16$

59. $y = -5x + 7$　　**61.** $y = 7$　　**63.** $y = \dfrac{3}{2}x$　　**65.** $y = -3$　　**67.** $y = -\dfrac{4}{7}x - \dfrac{18}{7}$　　**69. a.** $s = 32t$　　**b.** 128 ft/sec　　**71. a.** $y = 14{,}000x + 29{,}000$

b. 113,000 hybrids　　**73. a.** $y = 0.9x + 79.6$　　**b.** 88.6 persons per sq mi　　**75. a.** $(0, 14.7), (10, 14.14)$　　**b.** $y = -0.056x + 14.7$　　**c.** 13.58 births
per thousand population　　**77. a.** $(0, 5), (3, 20)$　　**b.** $y = 5x + 5$　　**c.** 50 thousand, or 50,000　　**79.** -1　　**81.** 5　　**83.** no　　**85.** yes
87. answers may vary　　**89. a.** $3x - y = -5$　　**b.** $x + 3y = 5$　　**91. a.** $3x + 2y = -1$　　**b.** $2x - 3y = 21$

Section 3.6
Practice Exercises

1. Domain: $\{0, 1, 5\}$; Range: $\{-2, 0, 3, 4\}$　　**2. a.** function　　**b.** not a function　　**3. a.** not a function　　**b.** function　　**4. a.** function
b. function　　**c.** function　　**d.** not a function　　**5. a.** function　　**b.** function　　**c.** function　　**d.** not a function　　**6. a.** 69°F　　**b.** November
c. yes　　**7. a.** $h(2) = 9; (2, 9)$　　**b.** $h(-5) = 30; (-5, 30)$　　**c.** $h(0) = 5; (0, 5)$　　**8. a.** domain: all real numbers
b. domain: all real numbers except 0　　**9. a.** domain: $-4 \le x \le 6$; range: $-2 \le y \le 3$　　**b.** domain: all real numbers; range: $y \le 3$

Vocabulary and Readiness Check 3.6

1. relation　　**3.** range　　**5.** vertical　　**7.** $(3, 7)$　　**9.** y; x

Exercise Set 3.6

1. $\{-7, 0, 2, 10\}; \{-7, 0, 4, 10\}$　　**3.** $\{0, 1, 5\}; \{-2\}$　　**5.** yes　　**7.** no　　**9.** no　　**11.** yes　　**13.** yes　　**15.** no　　**17.** a　　**19.** yes　　**21.** yes
23. no　　**25.** no　　**27.** 9:30 p.m.　　**29.** January 1 and December 1　　**31.** yes; it passes the vertical line test　　**33.** $4.25 per hour　　**35.** 2009
37. yes; answers may vary　　**39.** $-9, -5, 1$　　**41.** $6, 2, 11$　　**43.** $-6, 0, 9$　　**45.** $2, 0, 3$　　**47.** $5, 0, -20$　　**49.** $5, 3, 35$　　**51.** $(3, 6)$
53. $\left(0, -\dfrac{1}{2}\right)$　　**55.** $(-2, 9)$　　**57.** all real numbers　　**59.** all real number except -5　　**61.** all real numbers　　**63.** domain: all real numbers;
range: $y \ge -4$　　**65.** domain: all real numbers; range: all real numbers　　**67.** domain: all real numbers; range: $\{2\}$　　**69.** $(-2, 1)$　　**71.** $(-3, -1)$
73. $f(-5) = 12$　　**75.** $(3, -4)$　　**77.** $f(5) = 0$　　**79. a.** 166.38 cm　　**b.** 148.25 cm　　**81.** answers may vary　　**83.** $f(x) = x + 7$
85. a. $-3s + 12$　　**b.** $-3r + 12$　　**87. a.** 132　　**b.** $a^2 - 12$

Section 3.7
Practice Exercises

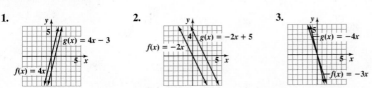

4. a. $10; \dfrac{5}{2}$ or $2\dfrac{1}{2}; 25; 5; 35$ **b.**   **c.** yes   **d.** $f(x) = 5x$

Graphing Calculator Explorations 3.7

1. $y = \dfrac{x}{3.5}$

3. $y = -\dfrac{5.78}{2.31}x + \dfrac{10.98}{2.31}$

5. $y = |x| + 3.78$

7. $y = 5.6x^2 + 7.7x + 1.5$

Vocabulary and Readiness Check 3.7

1. linear   **3.** vertical; $(c, 0)$ **5.** $y; f(x); x$

Exercise Set 3.7

1.   **3.**   **5.**   **7.**   **9.** C   **11.** D   **13.** D   **15.** C

17. $f(x) = x - 3$ **19.** $f(x) = \dfrac{x}{5}$ **21.** $f(x) = \dfrac{x + 6}{2}$ **23.** $f(x) = \dfrac{x - 4}{2}$ **25.** answers may vary

27.   **29.**   **31.**   **33.**   **35.**   **37.**

39. a. 18; 42; 3; 60; 30   **b.**   **c.** yes, a linear function   **41. a.** 1; 9; 16; 49; $\dfrac{1}{4}$ **b.**   **c.** no, not a linear function

43. a. 2.20; 2.60; 6.20; 32.20; 26.20   **b.**   **c.** yes, a linear function   **d.** $f(x) = 0.40x + 2.20$

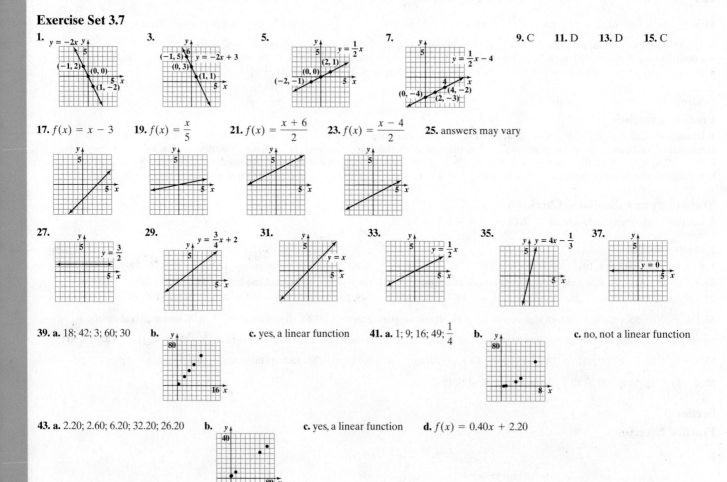
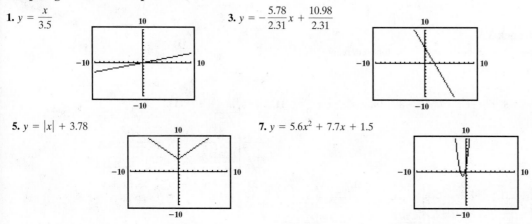

45. $\frac{3}{2}$ **47.** 6   **49.** $-\frac{6}{5}$

51. a. $(0, 500)$; if no tables are produced, 500 chairs can be produced   **b.** $(750, 0)$; if no chairs are produced, 750 tables can be produced   **c.** 466 chairs

53. a. \$64   **b.**   **c.** The line moves upward from left to right.   **55. a.** \$2855.12   **b.** 2012   **c.** answers may vary

57.   **59.**

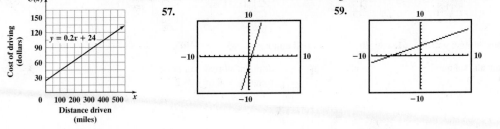

61. a. a line parallel to $y = -4x$ but with y-intercept $(0, 2)$ **b.** a line parallel to $y = -4x$ but with y-intercept $(0, -5)$ **63.** b   **65.** a

Section 3.8
Practice Exercises
1. $f(4) = 5$; $f(-2) = 6$; $f(0) = -2$ **2.**   **3.**   **4.**   **5.**

6.   **7.**

Vocabulary and Readiness Check 3.8
1. C   **3.** D

Exercise Set 3.8

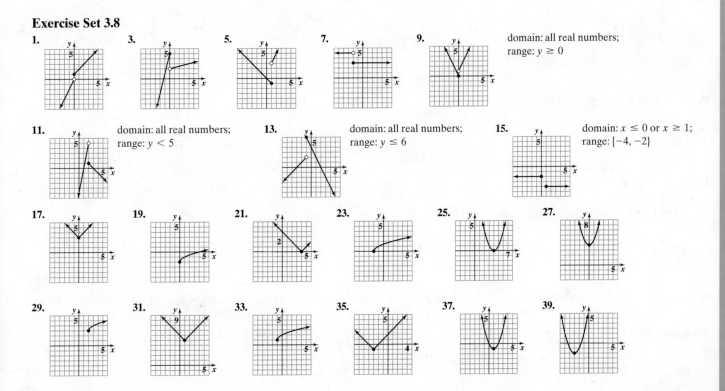

1.   **3.**   **5.**   **7.**   **9.** domain: all real numbers; range: $y \geq 0$

11. domain: all real numbers; range: $y < 5$ **13.** domain: all real numbers; range: $y \leq 6$ **15.** domain: $x \leq 0$ or $x \geq 1$; range: $\{-4, -2\}$

17.   **19.**   **21.**   **23.**   **25.**   **27.**

29.   **31.**   **33.**   **35.**   **37.**   **39.**

41. 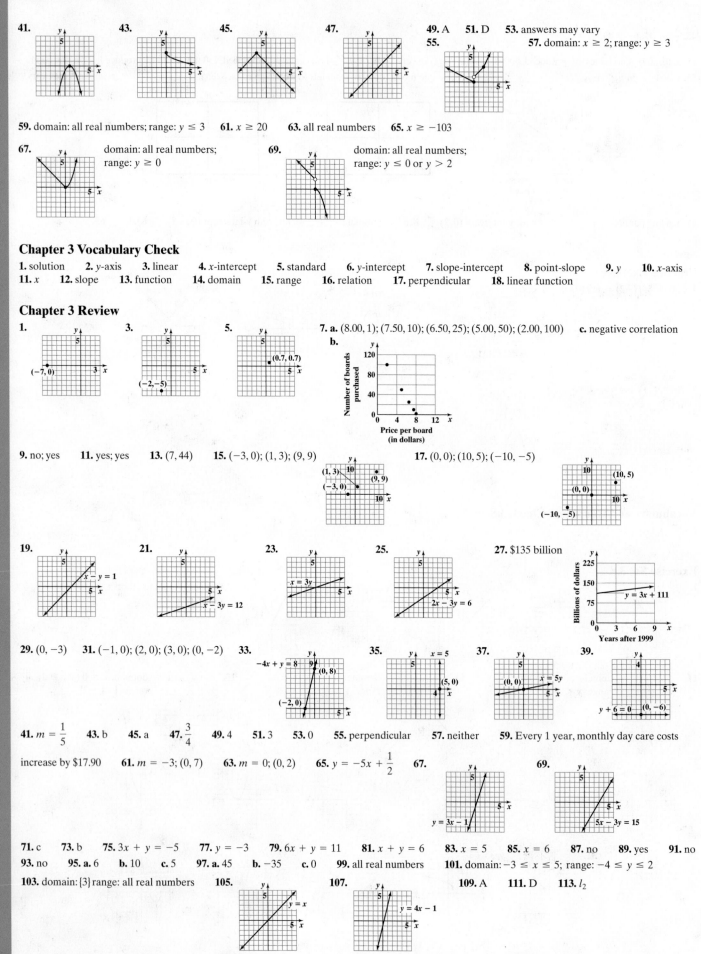 **43.** **45.** **47.** **49.** A **51.** D **53.** answers may vary

55. **57.** domain: $x \geq 2$; range: $y \geq 3$

59. domain: all real numbers; range: $y \leq 3$ **61.** $x \geq 20$ **63.** all real numbers **65.** $x \geq -103$

67. domain: all real numbers; range: $y \geq 0$ **69.** domain: all real numbers; range: $y \leq 0$ or $y > 2$

Chapter 3 Vocabulary Check

1. solution **2.** y-axis **3.** linear **4.** x-intercept **5.** standard **6.** y-intercept **7.** slope-intercept **8.** point-slope **9.** y **10.** x-axis
11. x **12.** slope **13.** function **14.** domain **15.** range **16.** relation **17.** perpendicular **18.** linear function

Chapter 3 Review

1. **3.** **5.** **7. a.** $(8.00, 1)$; $(7.50, 10)$; $(6.50, 25)$; $(5.00, 50)$; $(2.00, 100)$ **c.** negative correlation
$(-7, 0)$ $(-2, -5)$ $(0.7, 0.7)$ **b.**

9. no; yes **11.** yes; yes **13.** $(7, 44)$ **15.** $(-3, 0)$; $(1, 3)$; $(9, 9)$ **17.** $(0, 0)$; $(10, 5)$; $(-10, -5)$

19. **21.** **23.** **25.** **27.** $135 billion
$x - y = 1$ $x - 3y = 12$ $x = 3y$ $2x - 3y = 6$ $y = 3x + 111$

29. $(0, -3)$ **31.** $(-1, 0)$; $(2, 0)$; $(3, 0)$; $(0, -2)$ **33.** **35.** **37.** **39.**
$-4x + y = 8$ $(0, 8)$ $(-2, 0)$ $x = 5$ $(5, 0)$ $(0, 0)$ $x = 5y$ $y + 6 = 0$ $(0, -6)$

41. $m = \dfrac{1}{5}$ **43.** b **45.** a **47.** $\dfrac{3}{4}$ **49.** 4 **51.** 3 **53.** 0 **55.** perpendicular **57.** neither **59.** Every 1 year, monthly day care costs

increase by $17.90 **61.** $m = -3$; $(0, 7)$ **63.** $m = 0$; $(0, 2)$ **65.** $y = -5x + \dfrac{1}{2}$ **67.** **69.**
$y = 3x - 1$ $5x - 3y = 15$

71. c **73.** b **75.** $3x + y = -5$ **77.** $y = -3$ **79.** $6x + y = 11$ **81.** $x + y = 6$ **83.** $x = 5$ **85.** $x = 6$ **87.** no **89.** yes **91.** no
93. no **95. a.** 6 **b.** 10 **c.** 5 **97. a.** 45 **b.** -35 **c.** 0 **99.** all real numbers **101.** domain: $-3 \leq x \leq 5$; range: $-4 \leq y \leq 2$
103. domain: {3} range: all real numbers **105.** **107.** **109.** A **111.** D **113.** l_2
$y = x$ $y = 4x - 1$

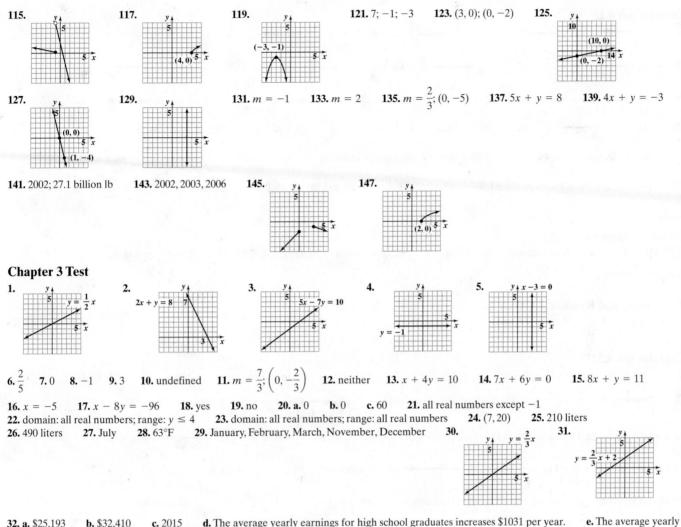

115. **117.** **119.** **121.** 7; −1; −3 **123.** (3, 0); (0, −2) **125.**

127. **129.** **131.** $m = -1$ **133.** $m = 2$ **135.** $m = \frac{2}{3}$; (0, −5) **137.** $5x + y = 8$ **139.** $4x + y = -3$

141. 2002; 27.1 billion lb **143.** 2002, 2003, 2006 **145.** **147.**

Chapter 3 Test

1. **2.** **3.** **4.** **5.**

6. $\frac{2}{5}$ **7.** 0 **8.** −1 **9.** 3 **10.** undefined **11.** $m = \frac{7}{3}$; $\left(0, -\frac{2}{3}\right)$ **12.** neither **13.** $x + 4y = 10$ **14.** $7x + 6y = 0$ **15.** $8x + y = 11$

16. $x = -5$ **17.** $x - 8y = -96$ **18.** yes **19.** no **20. a.** 0 **b.** 0 **c.** 60 **21.** all real numbers except −1
22. domain: all real numbers; range: $y \le 4$ **23.** domain: all real numbers; range: all real numbers **24.** (7, 20) **25.** 210 liters
26. 490 liters **27.** July **28.** 63°F **29.** January, February, March, November, December **30.** **31.**

32. a. \$25,193 **b.** \$32,410 **c.** 2015 **d.** The average yearly earnings for high school graduates increases \$1031 per year. **e.** The average yearly earnings for a high school graduate in 2000 was \$25,193.

33. domain: all real numbers; range: $y > -3$ **34.** **35.** domain: all real numbers; range: $y \le -1$ **36.**

Chapter 3 Standardized Test

1. d **2.** d **3.** a **4.** c **5.** b **6.** b **7.** a **8.** d **9.** d **10.** a **11.** b **12.** c **13.** c **14.** c **15.** d **16.** a **17.** a **18.** a
19. b **20.** a **21.** a **22.** b **23.** c **24.** c **25.** c **26.** c **27.** c **28.** b **29.** c **30.** d **31.** a

CHAPTER 4 SOLVING INEQUALITIES AND ABSOLUTE VALUE EQUATIONS AND INEQUALITIES

Section 4.1
Practice Exercises

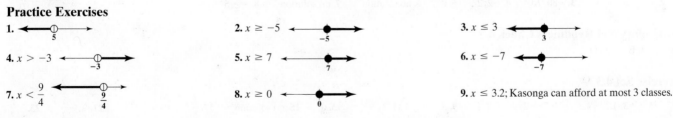

1. **2.** $x \ge -5$ **3.** $x \le 3$

4. $x > -3$ **5.** $x \ge 7$ **6.** $x \le -7$

7. $x < \frac{9}{4}$ **8.** $x \ge 0$ **9.** $x \le 3.2$; Kasonga can afford at most 3 classes.

Vocabulary and Readiness Check 4.1
1. expression **3.** inequality **5.** equation **7.** −5 **9.** 4.1

Exercise Set 4.1

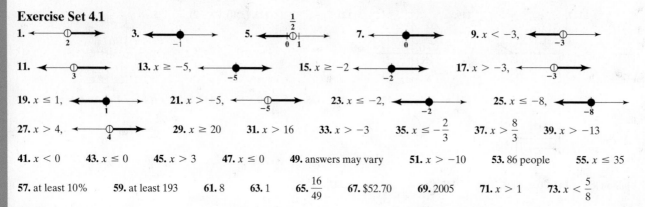

1. **3.** **5.** **7.** **9.** $x < -3$,

11. **13.** $x \geq -5$, **15.** $x \geq -2$ **17.** $x > -3$,

19. $x \leq 1$, **21.** $x > -5$, **23.** $x \leq -2$, **25.** $x \leq -8$,

27. $x > 4$, **29.** $x \geq 20$ **31.** $x > 16$ **33.** $x > -3$ **35.** $x \leq -\dfrac{2}{3}$ **37.** $x > \dfrac{8}{3}$ **39.** $x > -13$

41. $x < 0$ **43.** $x \leq 0$ **45.** $x > 3$ **47.** $x \leq 0$ **49.** answers may vary **51.** $x > -10$ **53.** 86 people **55.** $x \leq 35$

57. at least 10% **59.** at least 193 **61.** 8 **63.** 1 **65.** $\dfrac{16}{49}$ **67.** $52.70 **69.** 2005 **71.** $x > 1$ **73.** $x < \dfrac{5}{8}$

Section 4.2
Practice Exercises

1. $\{1, 3\}$ **2.** $x < 2$ **3.** no solution **4.** $-4 < x < 2$ **5.** $-6 \leq x \leq 8$ **6.** $\{1, 2, 3, 4, 5, 6, 7, 9\}$ **7.** $x \leq \dfrac{3}{8}$ or $x \geq 3$

8. all real numbers

Vocabulary and Readiness Check 4.2

1. compound **3.** or **5.** $\cup$ **7.** and

Exercise Set 4.2

1. $\{2, 3, 4, 5, 6, 7\}$ **3.** $\{4, 6\}$ **5.** $\{\ldots, -2, -1, 0, 1, \ldots\}$ **7.** $\{5, 7\}$ **9.** $\{x \mid x$ is an odd integer or $x = 2$ or $x = 4\}$ **11.** $\{2, 4\}$

13. $-3 < x < 1$ **15.** no solution **17.** $x < -1$ **19.** $x \geq 6$ **21.** $x \leq -3$

23. $4 < x < 10$ **25.** $11 < x < 17$ **27.** $1 \leq x \leq 4$ **29.** $-3 \leq x \leq \dfrac{3}{2}$ **31.** $-\dfrac{7}{3} \leq x \leq 7$ **33.** $x < 5$

35. $x \leq -4$ or $x \geq 1$ **37.** all real numbers **39.** $x \geq 2$ **41.** $x < -4$ or $x > -2$

43. all real numbers **45.** $-\dfrac{1}{2} < x < \dfrac{2}{3}$ **47.** all real numbers **49.** $\dfrac{3}{2} \leq x \leq 6$ **51.** $\dfrac{5}{4} < x < \dfrac{11}{4}$ **53.** no solution

55. $x < -\dfrac{56}{5}$ or $x > \dfrac{5}{3}$ **57.** $-5 < x < \dfrac{5}{2}$ **59.** $0 < x \leq \dfrac{14}{3}$ **61.** $x \leq -3$ **63.** $x \leq 1$ or $x > \dfrac{29}{7}$ **65.** no solution

67. $-\dfrac{1}{2} \leq x < \dfrac{3}{2}$ **69.** $-\dfrac{4}{3} < x < \dfrac{7}{3}$ **71.** $6 < x < 12$ **73.** -12 **75.** -4 **77.** $-7, 7$ **79.** 0 **81.** 2003, 2004, 2005

83. $-20.2° \leq F \leq 95°$ **85.** $67 \leq$ final score ≤ 94 **87.** $x > 6$ **89.** $3 \leq x \leq 7$ **91.** $x < -1$

Integrated Review

1. $x > -5$ **2.** $x > \dfrac{8}{3}$ **3.** $x \geq -1$ **4.** $x \geq -\dfrac{1}{10}$ **5.** $x \leq -\dfrac{1}{6}$ **6.** $x \geq -\dfrac{3}{5}$ **7.** $x < -16$ **8.** $x > 38$ **9.** all real numbers

10. $3 \leq x < 5$ **11.** $x < -9$ or $x > -5$ **12.** $-4 < x \leq -2$ **13.** all real numbers **14.** $x > 4$

Section 4.3
Practice Exercises

1. $-7, 7$ **2.** $-1, 4$ **3.** $-80, 70$ **4.** $-2, 2$ **5.** 0 **6.** no solution **7.** no solution **8.** $-\dfrac{3}{5}, 5$ **9.** 5

Vocabulary and Readiness Check 4.3

1. C **3.** B **5.** D

Exercise Set 4.3

1. $7, -7$ **3.** $4.2, -4.2$ **5.** $7, -2$ **7.** $8, 4$ **9.** $5, -5$ **11.** $3, -3$ **13.** 0 **15.** no solution **17.** $\dfrac{1}{5}$ **19.** $|x| = 5$ **21.** $9, -\dfrac{1}{2}$ **23.** $-\dfrac{5}{2}$

25. answers may vary **27.** $4, -4$ **29.** 0 **31.** no solution **33.** $0, \dfrac{14}{3}$ **35.** $2, -2$ **37.** no solution **39.** $7, -1$ **41.** no solution

43. no solution **45.** $-\dfrac{1}{8}$ **47.** $\dfrac{1}{2}, -\dfrac{5}{6}$ **49.** $2, -\dfrac{12}{5}$ **51.** $3, -2$ **53.** $-8, \dfrac{2}{3}$ **55.** no solution **57.** 4 **59.** $13, -8$ **61.** $3, -3$

63. $8, -7$ **65.** $2, 3$ **67.** $2, -\dfrac{10}{3}$ **69.** $\dfrac{3}{2}$ **71.** no solution **73.** answers may vary **75.** 34% **77.** 39.6 lb **79.** answers may vary

81. no solution **83.** $|x - 7| = 2$ **85.** $|2x - 1| = 4$ **87. a.** $c = 0$ **b.** c is a negative number **c.** c is a positive number

Section 4.4
Practice Exercises

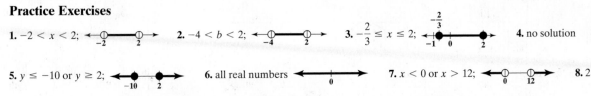

1. $-2 < x < 2$; **2.** $-4 < b < 2$; **3.** $-\dfrac{2}{3} \le x \le 2$; **4.** no solution

5. $y \le -10$ or $y \ge 2$; **6.** all real numbers **7.** $x < 0$ or $x > 12$; **8.** 2

Vocabulary and Readiness Check 4.4
1. D **3.** C **5.** A

Exercise Set 4.4

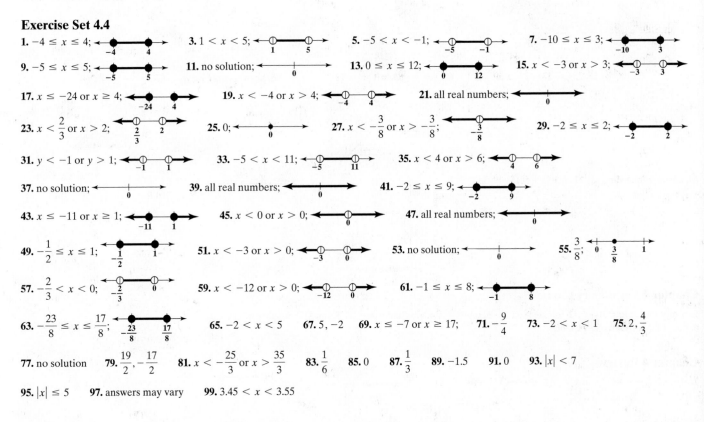

1. $-4 \le x \le 4$; **3.** $1 < x < 5$; **5.** $-5 < x < -1$; **7.** $-10 \le x \le 3$;

9. $-5 \le x \le 5$; **11.** no solution; **13.** $0 \le x \le 12$; **15.** $x < -3$ or $x > 3$;

17. $x \le -24$ or $x \ge 4$; **19.** $x < -4$ or $x > 4$; **21.** all real numbers;

23. $x < \dfrac{2}{3}$ or $x > 2$; **25.** 0; **27.** $x < -\dfrac{3}{8}$ or $x > -\dfrac{3}{8}$; **29.** $-2 \le x \le 2$;

31. $y < -1$ or $y > 1$; **33.** $-5 < x < 11$; **35.** $x < 4$ or $x > 6$;

37. no solution; **39.** all real numbers; **41.** $-2 \le x \le 9$;

43. $x \le -11$ or $x \ge 1$; **45.** $x < 0$ or $x > 0$; **47.** all real numbers;

49. $-\dfrac{1}{2} \le x \le 1$; **51.** $x < -3$ or $x > 0$; **53.** no solution; **55.** $\dfrac{3}{8}$;

57. $-\dfrac{2}{3} < x < 0$; **59.** $x < -12$ or $x > 0$; **61.** $-1 \le x \le 8$;

63. $-\dfrac{23}{8} \le x \le \dfrac{17}{8}$; **65.** $-2 < x < 5$ **67.** $5, -2$ **69.** $x \le -7$ or $x \ge 17$; **71.** $-\dfrac{9}{4}$ **73.** $-2 < x < 1$ **75.** $2, \dfrac{4}{3}$

77. no solution **79.** $\dfrac{19}{2}, -\dfrac{17}{2}$ **81.** $x < -\dfrac{25}{3}$ or $x > \dfrac{35}{3}$ **83.** $\dfrac{1}{6}$ **85.** 0 **87.** $\dfrac{1}{3}$ **89.** -1.5 **91.** 0 **93.** $|x| < 7$

95. $|x| \le 5$ **97.** answers may vary **99.** $3.45 < x < 3.55$

Section 4.5
Practice Exercises

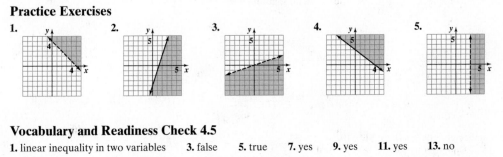

1. **2.** **3.** **4.** **5.**

Vocabulary and Readiness Check 4.5
1. linear inequality in two variables **3.** false **5.** true **7.** yes **9.** yes **11.** yes **13.** no

Exercise Set 4.5

1. no; yes   **3.** no; no   **5.** no; yes   **7.**   **9.**   **11.**   **13.**

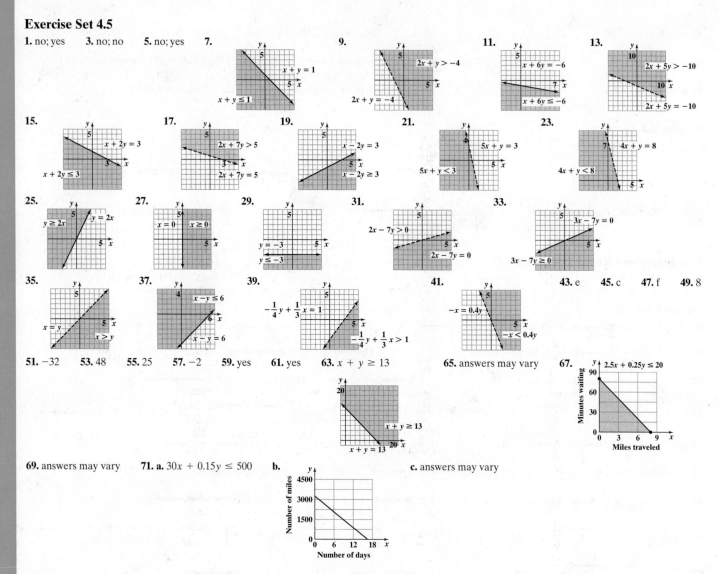

43. e   **45.** c   **47.** f   **49.** 8

51. -32 **53.** 48   **55.** 25   **57.** -2 **59.** yes   **61.** yes   **63.** $x + y \geq 13$ **65.** answers may vary   **67.**

69. answers may vary   **71. a.** $30x + 0.15y \leq 500$ **b.**   **c.** answers may vary

Chapter 4 Vocabulary Check

1. compound inequality   **2.** intersection   **3.** union   **4.** absolute value   **5.** linear inequality in one variable
6. linear equation in one variable

Chapter 4 Review

1.   **3.** $x < -4$ **5.** $x \leq 4$ **7.** $x \leq \dfrac{19}{3}$ **9.** \$2500   **11.** $2 \leq x \leq \dfrac{5}{2}$

13. $\dfrac{1}{8} < x < 2$ **15.** $\dfrac{7}{8} < x \leq \dfrac{27}{20}$ **17.** $x > \dfrac{11}{3}$ **19.** 5, 11   **21.** $-1, \dfrac{11}{3}$ **23.** $-\dfrac{1}{6}$ **25.** no solution   **27.** $5, -\dfrac{1}{3}$

29. $-\dfrac{8}{5} < x < 2;$ **31.** $x < -3$ or $x > 3;$ **33.** no solution;

35. $x < -27$ or $x > -9;$ **37.**   **39.**   **41.**   **43.** $x > 9;$

45. $x \leq 0;$ **47.** all real numbers   **49.** $-3, 3$ **51.** $-10, -\dfrac{4}{3}$ **53.** $-\dfrac{1}{2} < x < 2$ **55.**

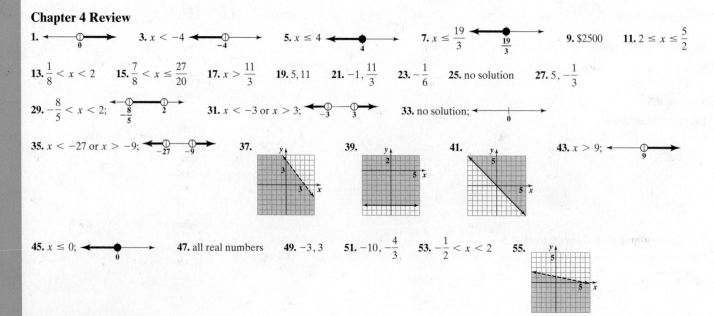

Chapter 4 Test

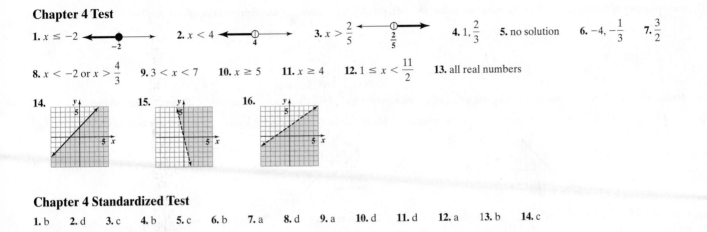

1. $x \le -2$ **2.** $x < 4$ **3.** $x > \frac{2}{5}$ **4.** $1, \frac{2}{3}$ **5.** no solution   **6.** $-4, -\frac{1}{3}$ **7.** $\frac{3}{2}$

8. $x < -2$ or $x > \frac{4}{3}$ **9.** $3 < x < 7$ **10.** $x \ge 5$ **11.** $x \ge 4$ **12.** $1 \le x < \frac{11}{2}$ **13.** all real numbers

14. **15.** **16.**

Chapter 4 Standardized Test

1. b   **2.** d   **3.** c   **4.** b   **5.** c   **6.** b   **7.** a   **8.** d   **9.** a   **10.** d   **11.** d   **12.** a   **13.** b   **14.** c

CHAPTER 5 SOLVING SYSTEMS OF LINEAR EQUATIONS AND INEQUALITIES

Section 5.1

Practice Exercises

1. no   **2.** yes   **3.** $(8, 5)$ **4.** $(-3, -5)$ **5.** no solution; inconsistent, independent

6. infinite number of solutions; consistent, dependent   **7.** one solution   **8.** no solution

Calculator Explorations 5.1

1. $(0.37, 0.23)$ **3.** $(0.03, -1.89)$

Vocabulary and Readiness Check 5.1

1. dependent   **3.** consistent   **5.** inconsistent   **7.** one solution, $(-1, 3)$ **9.** infinite number of solutions

Exercise Set 5.1

1. a. no   **b.** yes   **3. a.** yes   **b.** no   **5. a.** yes   **b.** yes   **7. a.** no   **b.** no   **9.**   **11.**   **13.**

15. **17.** **19.** **21.** no solution **23.** **25.**

27. no solution **29.** infinite number of solutions **31.** **33.** **35.**

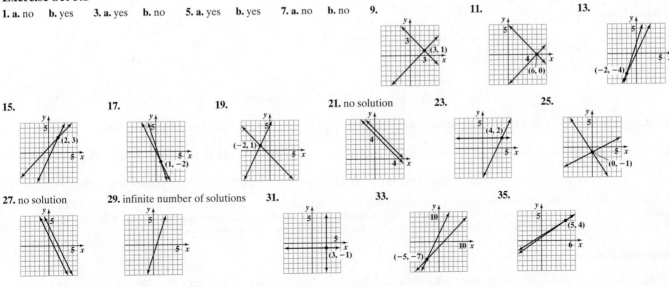

37. infinite number of solutions   **39.** intersecting, one solution   **41.** parallel, no solution   **43.** identical lines, infinite number of solutions

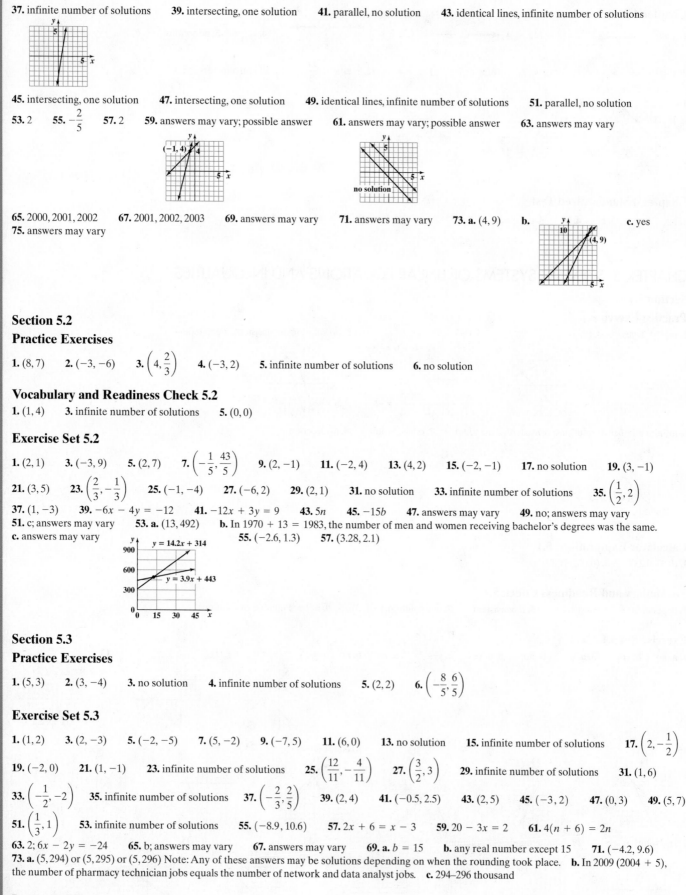

45. intersecting, one solution   **47.** intersecting, one solution   **49.** identical lines, infinite number of solutions   **51.** parallel, no solution

53. 2   **55.** $-\dfrac{2}{5}$ **57.** 2   **59.** answers may vary; possible answer   **61.** answers may vary; possible answer   **63.** answers may vary

65. 2000, 2001, 2002   **67.** 2001, 2002, 2003   **69.** answers may vary   **71.** answers may vary   **73. a.** (4, 9)   **b.**   **c.** yes

75. answers may vary

Section 5.2
Practice Exercises

1. (8, 7)   **2.** (−3, −6)   **3.** $\left(4, \dfrac{2}{3}\right)$ **4.** (−3, 2)   **5.** infinite number of solutions   **6.** no solution

Vocabulary and Readiness Check 5.2

1. (1, 4)   **3.** infinite number of solutions   **5.** (0, 0)

Exercise Set 5.2

1. (2, 1)   **3.** (−3, 9)   **5.** (2, 7)   **7.** $\left(-\dfrac{1}{5}, \dfrac{43}{5}\right)$ **9.** (2, −1)   **11.** (−2, 4)   **13.** (4, 2)   **15.** (−2, −1)   **17.** no solution   **19.** (3, −1)
21. (3, 5)   **23.** $\left(\dfrac{2}{3}, -\dfrac{1}{3}\right)$ **25.** (−1, −4)   **27.** (−6, 2)   **29.** (2, 1)   **31.** no solution   **33.** infinite number of solutions   **35.** $\left(\dfrac{1}{2}, 2\right)$
37. (1, −3)   **39.** $-6x - 4y = -12$ **41.** $-12x + 3y = 9$ **43.** $5n$ **45.** $-15b$ **47.** answers may vary   **49.** no; answers may vary
51. c; answers may vary   **53. a.** (13, 492)   **b.** In 1970 + 13 = 1983, the number of men and women receiving bachelor's degrees was the same.
c. answers may vary   **55.** (−2.6, 1.3)   **57.** (3.28, 2.1)

Section 5.3
Practice Exercises

1. (5, 3)   **2.** (3, −4)   **3.** no solution   **4.** infinite number of solutions   **5.** (2, 2)   **6.** $\left(-\dfrac{8}{5}, \dfrac{6}{5}\right)$

Exercise Set 5.3

1. (1, 2)   **3.** (2, −3)   **5.** (−2, −5)   **7.** (5, −2)   **9.** (−7, 5)   **11.** (6, 0)   **13.** no solution   **15.** infinite number of solutions   **17.** $\left(2, -\dfrac{1}{2}\right)$
19. (−2, 0)   **21.** (1, −1)   **23.** infinite number of solutions   **25.** $\left(\dfrac{12}{11}, -\dfrac{4}{11}\right)$ **27.** $\left(\dfrac{3}{2}, 3\right)$ **29.** infinite number of solutions   **31.** (1, 6)
33. $\left(-\dfrac{1}{2}, -2\right)$ **35.** infinite number of solutions   **37.** $\left(-\dfrac{2}{3}, \dfrac{2}{5}\right)$ **39.** (2, 4)   **41.** (−0.5, 2.5)   **43.** (2, 5)   **45.** (−3, 2)   **47.** (0, 3)   **49.** (5, 7)
51. $\left(\dfrac{1}{3}, 1\right)$ **53.** infinite number of solutions   **55.** (−8.9, 10.6)   **57.** $2x + 6 = x - 3$ **59.** $20 - 3x = 2$ **61.** $4(n + 6) = 2n$
63. 2; $6x - 2y = -24$ **65.** b; answers may vary   **67.** answers may vary   **69. a.** $b = 15$ **b.** any real number except 15   **71.** (−4.2, 9.6)
73. a. (5, 294) or (5, 295) or (5, 296) Note: Any of these answers may be solutions depending on when the rounding took place.   **b.** In 2009 (2004 + 5),
the number of pharmacy technician jobs equals the number of network and data analyst jobs.   **c.** 294–296 thousand

Integrated Review

1. (2, 5)   **2.** (4, 2)   **3.** (5, −2)   **4.** (6, −14)   **5.** (−3, 2)   **6.** (−4, 3)   **7.** (0, 3)   **8.** (−2, 4)   **9.** (5, 7)   **10.** (−3, −23)   **11.** $\left(\dfrac{1}{3}, 1\right)$

12. $\left(-\frac{1}{4}, 2\right)$ **13.** no solution   **14.** infinite number of solutions   **15.** $(0.5, 3.5)$ **16.** $(-0.75, 1.25)$ **17.** infinite number of solutions
18. no solution   **19.** $(7, -3)$ **20.** $(-1, -3)$ **21.** answers may vary   **22.** answers may vary

Section 5.4
Practice Exercises
1. 18, 12   **2. a.** Adult: $19   **b.** Child: $6   **c.** No, the regular rates are less than the group rate.   **3.** 1.75 mph and 3.75 mph
4. 15 pounds of Kona and 5 pounds of Blue Mountain

Exercise Set 5.4

1. c   **3.** b   **5.** a   **7.** $\begin{cases} x + y = 15 \\ x - y = 7 \end{cases}$ **9.** $\begin{cases} x + y = 6500 \\ x = y + 800 \end{cases}$ **11.** 33 and 50   **13.** 14 and -3 **15.** Taurasi: 860 points; Augustus: 744 points
17. child's ticket: $18; adult's ticket: $29   **19.** quarters: 53; nickels: 27   **21.** Apple: $87.97; Microsoft: $27.29   **23.** daily fee: $32; mileage
charge: $0.25 per mi   **25.** distance downstream = distance upstream = 18 mi; time downstream: 2 hr; time upstream: $4\frac{1}{2}$ hr; still water: 6.5 mph;
current: 2.5 mph   **27.** still air: 455 mph; wind: 65 mph   **29.** $4\frac{1}{2}$ hr   **31.** 12% solution: $7\frac{1}{2}$ oz; 4% solution: $4\frac{1}{2}$ oz   **33.** $4.95 beans: 113 lb;
$2.65 beans: 87 lb   **35.** $60°, 30°$ **37.** $20°, 70°$ **39.** number sold at $9.50: 23; number sold at $7.50: 67   **41.** $2\frac{1}{4}$ mph and $2\frac{3}{4}$ mph
43. 30%: 50 gal; 60%: 100 gal   **45.** length: 42 in.; width: 30 in.   **47.** $x > 3$ **49.** $x \geq \frac{1}{2}$ **51.** a   **53.** width: 9 ft; length: 15 ft
55. a. $(27.1, 39.5)$ **b.** For viewers 27.1 years over 18 (or 45.1 years old) the percent who watch cable news and network news is the same, or 39.5%.
c. answers may vary

Section 5.5
Practice Exercises
1.   **2.**   **3.**   **4.** Point $B = (60, 20)$; Using $T = 60$ and $P = 20$, each of the three inequalities for grasslands is true: $60 \geq 35$, true; $5(60) - 7(20) \geq 70$, true; $3(60) - 35(20) \leq -140$, true.

Exercise Set 5.5

1.   **3.**   **5.**   **7.**   **9.**

11.   **13.**   **15.**   **17.**   **19.**   **21.**

23.   **25.** 16   **27.** $36x^2$ **29.** $100y^6$ **31. a.** $A = (20, 150)$; A 20-year-old with a heart rate of 150 beats per minute is within the target range.   **b.** $10 \leq 20 \leq 70$, true; $150 \geq 0.7(220 - 20)$, true; $150 \leq 0.8(220 - 20)$, true

33. quadrant III   **35.** C   **37.** D   **39. a.** $y \geq 0$; $x + y \geq 5$; $x \geq 1$; $200x + 100y \leq 700$
b.   **c.** 2 nights   **41.** answers may vary
43.

Section 5.6
Practice Exercises

1.

Grade	Frequency
A	3
B	5
C	9
D	2
F	1
	20

2.

Class	Frequency
40–49	1
50–59	5
60–69	4
70–79	15
80–89	5
90–99	7
	37

3.

Stem	Leaves
4	1
5	8 2 8 0 7
6	8 2 9 9
7	3 5 9 9 7 5 5 3 3 6 7 1 7 1 5
8	7 3 9 9 1
9	4 6 9 7 5 8 0

Exercise Set 5.6

1. 7; 31 **3.** 151 **5.**

Time Spent on Homework (in hours)	Number of Students
15	4
16	5
17	6
18	5
19	4
20	2
21	2
22	0
23	0
24	2
	30

7. 0, 5, 10, . . . , 40, 45 **9.** 5 **11.** 13 **13.** the 5–9 class

15.

Age at Inauguration	Number of Presidents
41–45	2
46–50	8
51–55	15
56–60	9
61–65	7
66–70	2
	43

17. a.

b.

19.

21. b

23.

Stem	Leaves
2	8 8 9 5
3	8 7 0 1 2 7 6 4 0 5
4	8 2 2 1 4 5 4 6 2 0 8 2 7 9
5	9 4 1 9 1 0
6	3 2 3 6 6 3

The greatest number of college professors are in their 40s.

25. Time intervals on the horizontal axis do not represent equal amounts of time.

27, 29, 31. answers may vary **33.** Sample answers:

Length (miles)	Number of Rivers
501–1000	12
1001–1500	8
1501–2000	3
2001–2500	1
2501–3000	1
	25

Section 5.7
Practice Exercises

1. 33 **2.** median: 39.5; mode: 45

Exercise Set 5.7

1. mean: 29, median: 28, no mode   **3.** mean: 8.1, median: 8.2, mode: 8.2   **5.** mean: 0.6, median: 0.6, mode: 0.2 and 0.6

7. mean: 370.9, median: 313.5, no mode   **9.** 1214.8 ft   **11.** 1117 ft   **13.** 6.8   **15.** 6.9   **17.** 85.5   **19.** 73   **21.** 70 and 71

23. 9   **25.** 21, 21, 24

Chapter 5 Extension

Practice Exercises

1. a. $Q_2 = 11, Q_1 = 5, Q_3 = 14.5$ **b.**
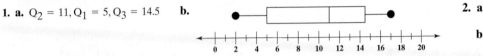
2. a. At least 1 person surveyed worked 0 hours a day, or does not work.
b. 4–8.5 hours

Chapter 5 Extension Exercise Set

1. $Q_2 = 6, Q_1 = 2.5, Q_3 = 9.5$ **3.** $Q_2 = 7.4, Q_1 = 4.6, Q_3 = 11.9$ **5.**

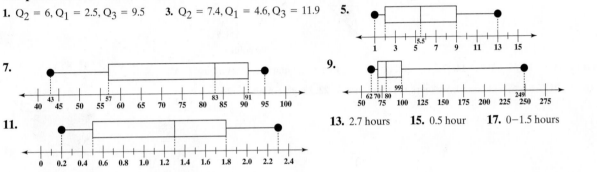

7.

9.

13. 2.7 hours   **15.** 0.5 hour   **17.** 0–1.5 hours

11.

Chapter 5 Vocabulary Check

1. dependent   **2.** system of linear equations   **3.** consistent   **4.** solution   **5.** addition; substitution   **6.** inconsistent   **7.** independent
8. system of linear inequalities

Chapter 5 Review

1. a. no   **b.** yes   **c.** no   **3. a.** no   **b.** no   **c.** yes   **5.**   **7.**   **9.**

11. no solution   **13.** $(-1, 4)$ **15.** $(3, -2)$ **17.** infinite number of solutions   **19.** no solution   **21.** $(-6, 2)$ **23.** $(3, 7)$

25. infinite number of solutions   **27.** $(8, -6)$ **29.** -6 and 22 **31.** current of river: 3.2 mph; speed in still water: 21.1 mph

33. egg: $0.40; strip of bacon: $0.65   **35.** $y \geq 2x - 3$ $y \leq -2x + 1$ **37.** $-3x + 2y > -1$ $y < -2$

39. Time Spent on Homework

Time Spent on Homework (in hours)	Number of Students
6	1
7	3
8	3
9	2
10	1
	10

41.

43.

Stem	Leaves
1	8 4 3 3 7 1
2	4 6 9 9 2 7
3	4 9 6 1 5 1 1
4	4 7 9 1 2 2 0 5
5	4 7 9 0 6 1
6	3 7 0 8 3 9
7	2 5 4 0 3
8	1 7 6
9	1 0 5

45. mean: 26.2
median: 28
mode: 28

47.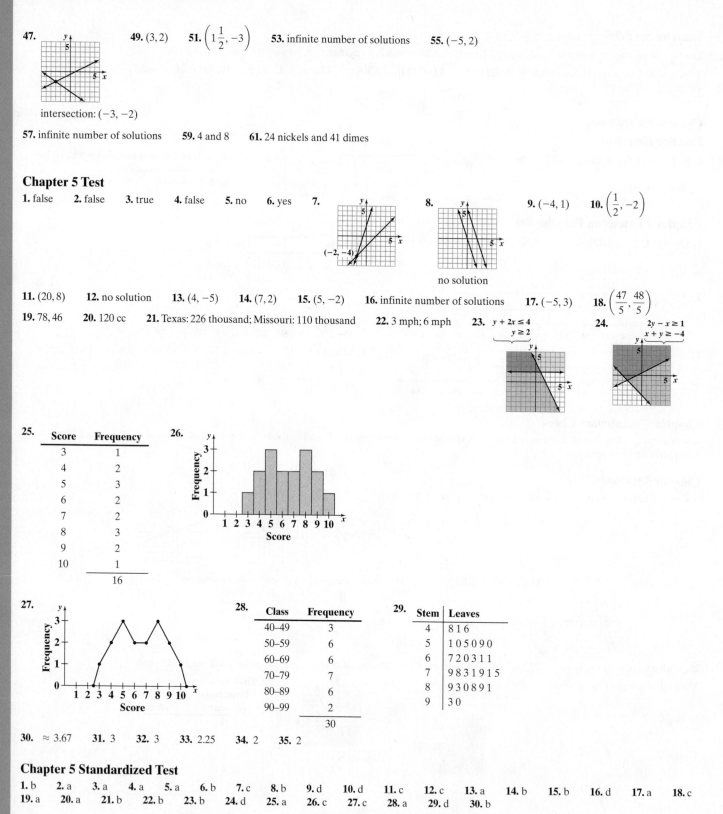

intersection: $(-3, -2)$

49. $(3, 2)$ **51.** $\left(1\frac{1}{2}, -3\right)$ **53.** infinite number of solutions   **55.** $(-5, 2)$

57. infinite number of solutions   **59.** 4 and 8   **61.** 24 nickels and 41 dimes

Chapter 5 Test

1. false   **2.** false   **3.** true   **4.** false   **5.** no   **6.** yes   **7.**   **8.**   **9.** $(-4, 1)$ **10.** $\left(\frac{1}{2}, -2\right)$

$(-2, -4)$

no solution

11. $(20, 8)$ **12.** no solution   **13.** $(4, -5)$ **14.** $(7, 2)$ **15.** $(5, -2)$ **16.** infinite number of solutions   **17.** $(-5, 3)$ **18.** $\left(\frac{47}{5}, \frac{48}{5}\right)$

19. 78, 46   **20.** 120 cc   **21.** Texas: 226 thousand; Missouri: 110 thousand   **22.** 3 mph; 6 mph   **23.** $y + 2x \le 4$; $y \ge 2$ **24.** $2y - x \ge 1$; $x + y \ge -4$

25.

Score	Frequency
3	1
4	2
5	3
6	2
7	2
8	3
9	2
10	1
	16

26.

27.

28.

Class	Frequency
40–49	3
50–59	6
60–69	6
70–79	7
80–89	6
90–99	2
	30

29.

Stem	Leaves
4	8 1 6
5	1 0 5 0 9 0
6	7 2 0 3 1 1
7	9 8 3 1 9 1 5
8	9 3 0 8 9 1
9	3 0

30. ≈ 3.67 **31.** 3   **32.** 3   **33.** 2.25   **34.** 2   **35.** 2

Chapter 5 Standardized Test

1. b   **2.** a   **3.** a   **4.** a   **5.** a   **6.** b   **7.** c   **8.** b   **9.** d   **10.** d   **11.** c   **12.** c   **13.** a   **14.** b   **15.** b   **16.** d   **17.** a   **18.** c
19. a   **20.** a   **21.** b   **22.** b   **23.** b   **24.** d   **25.** a   **26.** c   **27.** c   **28.** a   **29.** d   **30.** b

CHAPTER 6 EXPONENTS AND POLYNOMIALS

Section 6.1

Practice Exercises

1. a. 27　**b.** 4　**c.** 64　**d.** -64　**e.** $\dfrac{27}{64}$　**f.** 0.0081　**g.** 75　**2. a.** 243　**b.** $\dfrac{3}{8}$　**3. a.** 3^{10}　**b.** y^5　**c.** z^5　**d.** x^{11}　**e.** $(-2)^8$　**f.** $b^3 \cdot t^5$

4. $15y^7$　**5. a.** $y^{12}z^4$　**b.** $-7m^5n^{14}$　**6. a.** x^{12}　**b.** z^{21}　**c.** $(-2)^{15}$　**7. a.** p^5r^5　**b.** $36b^2$　**c.** $\dfrac{1}{64}x^6y^3$　**d.** $81a^{12}b^{16}c^4$　**8. a.** $\dfrac{x^5}{y^{10}}$　**b.** $\dfrac{32a^{20}}{b^{15}}$

9. a. z^4　**b.** 25　**c.** 64　**d.** $\dfrac{q^5}{t^2}$　**e.** $6x^2y^2$　**10. a.** -1　**b.** 1　**c.** 1　**d.** 1　**e.** 1　**11. a.** $\dfrac{125}{x^3z^3}$　**b.** $16z^{32}x^{20}$　**c.** $\dfrac{-27x^9}{y^{12}}$

Vocabulary and Readiness Check 6.1

1. exponent　**3.** add　**5.** 1　**7.** base: 3; exponent: 2　**9.** base: 4; exponent: 2　**11.** base: 5; exponent: 1; base: x; exponent: 2

Exercise Set 6.1

1. 49　**3.** -5　**5.** -16　**7.** 16　**9.** 0.00001　**11.** $\dfrac{1}{81}$　**13.** 224　**15.** -250　**17.** answers may vary　**19.** 4　**21.** 135　**23.** 150

25. $\dfrac{32}{5}$　**27.** x^7　**29.** $(-3)^{12}$　**31.** $15y^5$　**33.** $x^{19}y^6$　**35.** $-72m^3n^8$　**37.** $-24z^{20}$　**39.** $20x^5$ sq ft　**41.** x^{36}　**43.** p^8q^8　**45.** $8a^{15}$

47. $x^{10}y^{15}$　**49.** $49a^4b^{10}c^2$　**51.** $\dfrac{r^9}{s^9}$　**53.** $\dfrac{m^5p^5}{n^5}$　**55.** $\dfrac{4x^2z^2}{y^{10}}$　**57.** $64z^{10}$ sq dm　**59.** $27y^{12}$ cu ft　**61.** x^2　**63.** -64　**65.** p^6q^5　**67.** $\dfrac{y^3}{2}$

69. 1　**71.** 1　**73.** -7　**75.** 2　**77.** -81　**79.** $\dfrac{1}{64}$　**81.** $\dfrac{81}{q^2r^2}$　**83.** a^6　**85.** $-16x^7$　**87.** $a^{11}b^{20}$　**89.** $26m^9n^7$　**91.** z^{40}　**93.** $36x^2y^2z^6$

95. $3x$　**97.** $81x^2y^2$　**99.** 33　**101.** $\dfrac{y^{15}}{8x^{12}}$　**103.** $2x^2y$　**105.** $2y - 10$　**107.** $-x - 4$　**109.** $-x + 5$　**111.** c　**113.** e

115. answers may vary　**117.** answers may vary　**119.** 343 cu m　**121.** volume　**123.** answers may vary　**125.** x^{9a}　**127.** a^{5b}
129. x^{5a}　**131.** \$1045.85

Section 6.2

Practice Exercises

1. a. degree 3　**b.** degree 8　**c.** degree 0　**2. a.** trinomial, degree 2　**b.** binomial, degree 1　**c.** none of these, degree 3

3.

Term	Numerical Coefficient	Degree of Term
$-3x^3y^2$	-3	5
$4xy^2$	4	3
$-y^2$	-1	2
$3x$	3	1
-2	-2	0

4. 36　**5.** 114 ft; 66 ft　**6. a.** $-2y$　**b.** $z + 5z^3$　**c.** $4a^2 - 12$
d. $\dfrac{1}{3}x^4 + \dfrac{11}{24}x^3 - x^2$　**7.** $-3x^2 + 5xy + 5y^2$　**8.** $4x^2 + 7x + 4$
9. $-x^2 - 6x + 9$　**10.** $-3x^3 + 10x^2 - 6x - 4$　**11.** $5z^3 + 8z^2 + 8z$
12. $5x - 1$　**13.** $2x^3 - 4x^2 + 4x - 6$　**14.** $-8z^2 - 11z + 12$　**15.** $7x - 11$
16. a. $-5a^2 - ab + 6b^2$　**b.** $3x^2y^2 - 10xy - 4xy^2 - 6y^2 + 5$

Vocabulary and Readiness Check 6.2

1. binomial　**3.** trinomial　**5.** constant　**7.** $-14y$　**9.** $7x$　**11.** $5m^2 + 2m$

Exercise Set 6.2

1. 1; binomial　**3.** 3; none of these　**5.** 6; trinomial　**7.** 2; binomial　**9.** 3　**11.** 2　**13. a.** 6　**b.** 5　**15. a.** -2　**b.** 4

17. a. -15　**b.** -16　**19.** 1134 ft　**21.** 1006 ft　**23.** $23x^2$　**25.** $12x^2 - y$　**27.** $7s$　**29.** $-1.1y^2 + 4.8$　**31.** $-\dfrac{7}{12}x^3 + \dfrac{7}{5}x^2 + 6$

33. $5a^2 - 9ab + 16b^2$　**35.** $12x + 12$　**37.** $-3x^2 + 10$　**39.** $-x^2 + 14$　**41.** $-2x + 9$　**43.** $2x^2 + 7x - 16$　**45.** $8t^2 - 4$
47. $-2z^2 - 16z + 6$　**49.** $2x^3 - 2x^2 + 7x + 2$　**51.** $62x^2 + 5$　**53.** $12x + 2$　**55.** $-y^2 - 3y - 1$　**57.** $2x^2 + 11x$　**59.** $-16x^4 + 8x + 9$
61. $7x^2 + 14x + 18$　**63.** $3x - 3$　**65.** $7x^2 - 2x + 2$　**67.** $4y^2 + 12y + 19$　**69.** $6x^2 - 5x + 21$　**71.** $4x^2 + 7x + x^2 + 5x$; $5x^2 + 12x$
73. $18x + 44$　**75.** $(x^2 + 7x + 4)$ ft　**77.** $(3y^2 + 4y + 11)$ m　**79.** $-2a - b + 1$　**81.** $3x^2 + 5$　**83.** $6x^2 - 2xy + 19y^2$
85. $8r^2s + 16rs - 8 + 7r^2s^2$　**87.** $-5.42x^2 + 7.75x - 19.61$　**89.** $3.7y^4 - 0.7y^3 + 2.2y - 4$　**91.** $6x^2$　**93.** $-12x^8$　**95.** $200x^3y^2$
97., 99. answers may vary　**101.** b　**103.** e　**105. a.** $4z$　**b.** $3z^2$　**c.** $-4z$　**d.** $3z^2$; answers may vary　**107.** answers may vary
109. $2x^2 + 4xy$　**111.** \$8169　**113.** $10.84x^2 + 20.43x + 3285$

Section 6.3
Practice Exercises

1. $10y^2$ **2.** $-2z^8$ **3.** $\frac{7}{72}b^9$ **4. a.** $15x^6 + 15x$ **b.** $-10x^5 + 45x^4 - 10x^3$ **5.** $10x^2 + 11x - 6$ **6.** $25x^2 - 30xy + 9y^2$
7. $2y^3 + 5y^2 - 7y + 20$ **8.** $s^3 + 6s^2t + 12st^2 + 8t^3$ **9.** $5x^3 - 23x^2 + 17x - 20$ **10.** $x^5 - 2x^4 + 2x^3 - 3x^2 + 2$
11. $5x^4 - 3x^3 + 11x^2 + 8x - 6$

Vocabulary and Readiness Check 6.3
1. distributive   **3.** $(5y - 1)(5y - 1)$ **5.** x^8 **7.** cannot simplify   **9.** x^{14} **11.** $2x^7$

Exercise Set 6.3
1. $-28n^{10}$ **3.** $-12.4x^{12}$ **5.** $-\frac{2}{15}y^3$ **7.** $-24x^8$ **9.** $6x^2 + 15x$ **11.** $-2a^2 - 8a$ **13.** $6x^3 - 9x^2 + 12x$ **15.** $-6a^4 + 4a^3 - 6a^2$

17. $-4x^3y + 7x^2y^2 - xy^3 - 3y^4$ **19.** $4x^4 - 3x^3 + \frac{1}{2}x^2$ **21.** $x^2 + 7x + 12$ **23.** $a^2 + 5a - 14$ **25.** $x^2 + \frac{1}{3}x - \frac{2}{9}$ **27.** $12x^4 + 25x^2 + 7$

29. $4y^2 - 16y + 16$ **31.** $12x^2 - 29x + 15$ **33.** $9x^4 + 6x^2 + 1$ **35. a.** $6x + 12$ **b.** $9x^2 + 36x + 35$ **c.** answers may vary
37. $x^3 - 5x^2 + 13x - 14$ **39.** $x^4 + 5x^3 - 3x^2 - 11x + 20$ **41.** $10a^3 - 27a^2 + 26a - 12$ **43.** $x^3 + 6x^2 + 12x + 8$
45. $8y^3 - 36y^2 + 54y - 27$ **47.** $12x^2 - 64x - 11$ **49.** $10x^3 + 22x^2 - x - 1$ **51.** $2x^4 + 3x^3 - 58x^2 + 4x + 63$ **53.** $8.4y^7$

55. $-3x^3 - 6x^2 + 24x$ **57.** $2x^2 + 39x + 19$ **59.** $x^2 - \frac{2}{7}x - \frac{3}{49}$ **61.** $9y^2 + 30y + 25$ **63.** $a^3 - 2a^2 - 18a + 24$

65. $8x^3 - 60x^2 + 150x - 125$ **67.** $32x^3 + 48x^2 - 6x - 20$ **69.** $6x^4 - 8x^3 - 7x^2 + 22x - 12$ **71.** $(4x^2 - 25)$ sq yd
73. $(6x^2 - 4x)$ sq in.   **75.** $25x^2$ **77.** $9y^6$ **79.** $x^2 + 3x$ **81.** $x^2 + 5x + 6$ **83.** $11a$ **85.** $25x^2 + 4y^2$ **87.** $13x - 7$
89. $30x^2 - 28x + 6$ **91.** $-7x + 5$ **93. a.** $a^2 - b^2$ **b.** $4x^2 - 9y^2$ **c.** $16x^2 - 49$ **d.** answers may vary   **95.** $(x^2 + 6x + 5)$ sq units

Section 6.4
Practice Exercises

1. $x^2 - 3x - 10$ **2.** $4x^2 - 13x + 9$ **3.** $9x^2 + 42x - 15$ **4.** $16x^2 - 8x + 1$ **5. a.** $b^2 + 6b + 9$ **b.** $x^2 - 2xy + y^2$ **c.** $9y^2 + 12y + 4$

d. $a^4 - 10a^2b + 25b^2$ **6. a.** $3x^2 - 75$ **b.** $16b^2 - 9$ **c.** $x^2 - \frac{4}{9}$ **d.** $25s^2 - t^2$ **e.** $4y^2 - 9z^4$ **7. a.** $4x^2 - 21x - 18$ **b.** $49b^2 - 28b + 4$

c. $x^2 - 0.16$ **d.** $3x^6 - 9x^4 + 2x^2 - 6$ **e.** $x^3 + 6x^2 + 3x - 2$

Vocabulary and Readiness Check 6.4
1. false   **3.** false

Exercise Set 6.4
1. $x^2 + 7x + 12$ **3.** $x^2 + 5x - 50$ **5.** $5x^2 + 4x - 12$ **7.** $4y^2 - 25y + 6$ **9.** $6x^2 + 13x - 5$ **11.** $x^2 - 4x + 4$ **13.** $4x^2 - 4x + 1$

15. $9a^2 - 30a + 25$ **17.** $25x^2 + 90x + 81$ **19.** answers may vary   **21.** $a^2 - 49$ **23.** $9x^2 - 1$ **25.** $9x^2 - \frac{1}{4}$ **27.** $81x^2 - y^2$

29. $4x^2 - 0.01$ **31.** $a^2 + 9a + 20$ **33.** $a^2 + 14a + 49$ **35.** $12a^2 - a - 1$ **37.** $x^2 - 4$ **39.** $9a^2 + 6a + 1$ **41.** $4x^3 - x^2y^4 + 4xy - y^5$

43. $x^3 - 3x^2 - 17x + 3$ **45.** $4a^2 - 12a + 9$ **47.** $25x^2 - 36z^2$ **49.** $x^{10} - 8x^5 + 15$ **51.** $x^2 - \frac{1}{9}$ **53.** $a^7 - 3a^3 + 11a^4 - 33$

55. $3x^2 - 12x + 12$ **57.** $6b^2 - b - 35$ **59.** $49p^2 - 64$ **61.** $\frac{1}{9}a^4 - 49$ **63.** $15x^4 - 5x^3 + 10x^2$ **65.** $4r^2 - 9s^2$ **67.** $9x^2 - 42xy + 49y^2$

69. $16x^2 - 25$ **71.** $64x^2 + 64x + 16$ **73.** $a^2 - \frac{1}{4}y^2$ **75.** $\frac{1}{25}x^2 - y^2$ **77.** $3a^3 + 2a^2 + 1$ **79.** $(2x + 1)(2x + 1)$ sq ft or $(4x^2 + 4x + 1)$ sq ft
81. $\frac{5b^5}{7}$ **83.** $-2a^{10}b^5$ **85.** $\frac{2y^8}{3}$ **87.** $\frac{1}{3}$ **89.** 1   **91.** c   **93.** d   **95.** 2   **97.** $\left(\frac{25}{2}a^2 - \frac{1}{2}b^2\right)$ sq units   **99.** $(24x^2 - 32x + 8)$ sq m
101. $(x^2 + 10x + 25)$ sq units   **103.** answers may vary   **105.** $x^2 + 2xy + y^2 - 9$ **107.** $a^2 - 6a + 9 - b^2$

Integrated Review
1. $35x^5$ **2.** $32y^9$ **3.** -16 **4.** 16   **5.** $2x^2 - 9x - 5$ **6.** $3x^2 + 13x - 10$ **7.** $3x - 4$ **8.** $4x + 3$ **9.** $7x^6y^2$ **10.** $\frac{10b^6}{7}$
11. $144m^{14}n^{12}$ **12.** $64y^{27}z^{30}$ **13.** $48y^2 - 27$ **14.** $98x^2 - 2$ **15.** $x^{63}y^{45}$ **16.** $27x^{27}$ **17.** $2x^2 - 2x - 6$ **18.** $6x^2 + 13x - 11$
19. $2.5y^2 - 6y - 0.2$ **20.** $8.4x^2 - 6.8x - 5.7$ **21.** $x^2 + 8xy + 16y^2$ **22.** $y^2 - 18yz + 81z^2$ **23.** $2x + 8y$ **24.** $2y - 18z$
25. $7x^2 - 10xy + 4y^2$ **26.** $-a^2 - 3ab + 6b^2$ **27.** $x^3 + 2x^2 - 16x + 3$ **28.** $x^3 - 2x^2 - 5x - 2$ **29.** $6x^5 + 20x^3 - 21x^2 - 70$
30. $20x^7 + 25x^3 - 4x^4 - 5$ **31.** $2x^3 - 19x^2 + 44x - 7$ **32.** $5x^3 + 9x^2 - 17x + 3$ **33.** cannot simplify   **34.** $25x^3y^3$ **35.** $125x^9$
36. $\frac{x^3}{y^3}$ **37.** $2x$ **38.** x^2

Section 6.5
Practice Exercises

1. a. $\dfrac{1}{125}$ **b.** $\dfrac{3}{y^4}$ **c.** $\dfrac{5}{6}$ **d.** $\dfrac{1}{25}$ **e.** x^5 **f.** 64 **2. a.** s^5 **b.** 8 **c.** $\dfrac{y^5}{x^7}$ **d.** $\dfrac{9}{64}$ **3. a.** $\dfrac{1}{x^5}$ **b.** $5y^7$ **c.** z^5 **4. a.** $\dfrac{16}{9}$ **b.** x^{10}

c. $\dfrac{q^2}{25p^{16}}$ **d.** $\dfrac{6y^2}{x^7}$ **e.** $\dfrac{b^{15}}{a^{20}}$ **f.** $-27x^6y^9$ **5. a.** 7×10^{-6} **b.** 2.07×10^7 **c.** 4.3×10^{-3} **d.** 8.12×10^8 **6. a.** 0.000367 **b.** 8,954,000

c. 0.00002009 **d.** 4054 **7. a.** 4000 **b.** 20,000,000,000

Calculator Explorations 6.5
1. 5.31 EE 3 **3.** 6.6 EE −9 **5.** 1.5×10^{13} **7.** 8.15×10^{19}

Vocabulary and Readiness Check 6.5

1. $\dfrac{1}{x^3}$ **3.** scientific notation **5.** $\dfrac{5}{x^2}$ **7.** y^6 **9.** $4y^3$

Exercise Set 6.5

1. $\dfrac{1}{64}$ **3.** $\dfrac{1}{16}$ **5.** $\dfrac{7}{x^3}$ **7.** 32 **9.** −64 **11.** $\dfrac{5}{6}$ **13.** p^3 **15.** $\dfrac{q^4}{p^5}$ **17.** $\dfrac{1}{x^3}$ **19.** z^3 **21.** $\dfrac{4}{9}$ **23.** $-p^4$ **25.** −2 **27.** x^4 **29.** p^4

31. m^{11} **33.** r^6 **35.** $\dfrac{1}{x^{15}y^9}$ **37.** $\dfrac{1}{x^4}$ **39.** $\dfrac{1}{a^2}$ **41.** $4k^3$ **43.** $3m$ **45.** $-\dfrac{4a^5}{b}$ **47.** $-\dfrac{6x^2}{y^3}$ **49.** $\dfrac{a^{30}}{b^{12}}$ **51.** $\dfrac{1}{x^{10}y^6}$ **53.** $\dfrac{z^2}{4}$ **55.** $\dfrac{1}{32x^5}$

57. $\dfrac{49a^4}{b^6}$ **59.** $a^{24}b^8$ **61.** x^9y^{19} **63.** $-\dfrac{y^8}{8x^2}$ **65.** $-\dfrac{6x}{7y^2}$ **67.** $\dfrac{25b^{33}}{a^{16}}$ **69.** 7.8×10^4 **71.** 1.67×10^{-6} **73.** 6.35×10^{-3} **75.** 1.16×10^6

77. 2×10^9 **79.** 1.212×10^9 **81.** 0.0000000008673 **83.** 0.033 **85.** 20,320 **87.** 700,000,000 **89.** 9,460,000,000,000
91. Yahoo! sites, 130,000,000, 1.3×10^8 **93.** 1×10^9 **95.** 57,000,000 **97.** 0.000036 **99.** 0.0000000000000000028 **101.** 0.0000005

103. 200,000 **105.** $\dfrac{5x^3}{3}$ **107.** $\dfrac{5z^3y^2}{7}$ **109.** $5y - 6 + \dfrac{5}{y}$ **111.** $\dfrac{27}{x^6z^3}$ cu in. **113.** $9a^{13}$ **115.** −5 **117.** answers may vary

119. a. 1.3×10^1 **b.** 4.4×10^7 **c.** 6.1×10^{-2} **121. a.** false **b.** true **c.** false **123.** $\dfrac{1}{x^{9s}}$ **125.** a^{4m+5} **127.** 31,753,800 **129.** 500 sec

Section 6.6
Practice Exercises

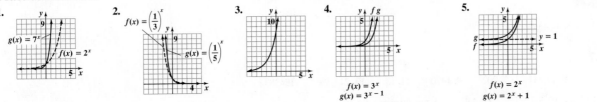

1.   **2.** $f(x) = \left(\dfrac{1}{3}\right)^x$, $g(x) = \left(\dfrac{1}{5}\right)^x$ **3.**   **4.** $f(x) = 3^x$, $g(x) = 3^{x-1}$ **5.** $f(x) = 2^x$, $g(x) = 2^x + 1$ **6.** \$3950.43

For **1.**: $g(x) = 7^x$, $f(x) = 2^x$

Vocabulary and Readiness Check 6.6
1. exponential **3.** yes; $(0, 1)$ **5.** $y > 0$

Exercise Set 6.6

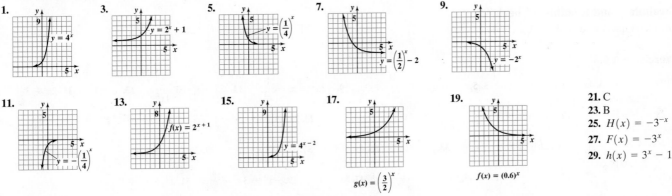

1. $y = 4^x$ **3.** $y = 2^x + 1$ **5.** $y = \left(\dfrac{1}{4}\right)^x$ **7.** $y = \left(\dfrac{1}{2}\right)^x - 2$ **9.** $y = -2^x$

11. $y = -\left(\dfrac{1}{4}\right)^x$ **13.** $f(x) = 2^{x+1}$ **15.** $y = 4^{x-2}$, $g(x) = \left(\dfrac{3}{2}\right)^x$ **17.**   **19.** $f(x) = (0.6)^x$

21. C
23. B
25. $H(x) = -3^{-x}$
27. $F(x) = -3^x$
29. $h(x) = 3^x - 1$

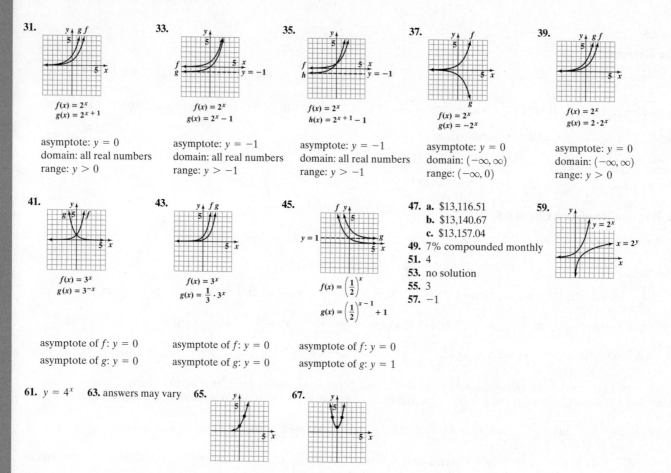

31.
$f(x) = 2^x$
$g(x) = 2^x + 1$
asymptote: $y = 0$
domain: all real numbers
range: $y > 0$

33.
$f(x) = 2^x$
$g(x) = 2^x - 1$
asymptote: $y = -1$
domain: all real numbers
range: $y > -1$

35.
$f(x) = 2^x$
$h(x) = 2^{x+1} - 1$
asymptote: $y = -1$
domain: all real numbers
range: $y > -1$

37.
$f(x) = 2^x$
$g(x) = -2^x$
asymptote: $y = 0$
domain: $(-\infty, \infty)$
range: $(-\infty, 0)$

39.
$f(x) = 2^x$
$g(x) = 2 \cdot 2^x$
asymptote: $y = 0$
domain: $(-\infty, \infty)$
range: $y > 0$

41.
$f(x) = 3^x$
$g(x) = 3^{-x}$
asymptote of f: $y = 0$
asymptote of g: $y = 0$

43.
$f(x) = 3^x$
$g(x) = \dfrac{1}{3} \cdot 3^x$
asymptote of f: $y = 0$
asymptote of g: $y = 0$

45.
$f(x) = \left(\dfrac{1}{2}\right)^x$
$g(x) = \left(\dfrac{1}{2}\right)^{x-1} + 1$
asymptote of f: $y = 0$
asymptote of g: $y = 1$

47. a. $13,116.51
  b. $13,140.67
  c. $13,157.04
49. 7% compounded monthly
51. 4
53. no solution
55. 3
57. -1

59.

61. $y = 4^x$ **63.** answers may vary   **65.**   **67.**

Section 6.7
Practice Exercises

1. 136,839   **2.** 23   **3.** 47.4 grams

Exercise Set 6.7

1. 451   **3.** 144,301   **5.** 21,231   **7.** 202   **9.** 1470   **11.** 13   **13.** 712,880   **15.** 383

17a. 10   **b.** 1.6; 13.2   **19.** 3.3; 2.1   **21.** 4.9   **23.** no; answers may vary

Section 6.8
Practice Exercises

1. $2t + 1$ **2.** $4x^4 + 5x - \dfrac{3}{x}$ **3.** $3x^3y^3 - 2 + \dfrac{1}{5x}$ **4.** $x + 3$ **5.** $2x + 3 + \dfrac{-10}{2x + 1}$ **6.** $3x^2 - 2x + 5 + \dfrac{-13}{3x + 2}$ **7.** $3x^2 - 2x - 9 + \dfrac{5x + 22}{x^2 + 2}$

Vocabulary and Readiness Check 6.8

1. dividend, quotient, divisor   **3.** a^2 **5.** y

Exercise Set 6.8

1. $12x^3 + 3x$ **3.** $4x^3 - 6x^2 + x + 1$ **5.** $5p^2 + 6p$ **7.** $-\dfrac{3}{2x} + 3$ **9.** $-3x^2 + x - \dfrac{4}{x^3}$ **11.** $-1 + \dfrac{3}{2x} - \dfrac{7}{4x^4}$ **13.** $x + 1$ **15.** $2x + 3$

17. $2x + 1 + \dfrac{7}{x - 4}$ **19.** $3a^2 - 3a + 1 + \dfrac{2}{3a + 2}$ **21.** $4x + 3 - \dfrac{2}{2x + 1}$ **23.** $2x^2 + 6x - 5 - \dfrac{2}{x - 2}$ **25.** $x + 6$ **27.** $x^2 + 3x + 9$

29. $-3x + 6 - \dfrac{11}{x + 2}$ **31.** $2b - 1 - \dfrac{6}{2b - 1}$ **33.** $ab - b^2$ **35.** $4x + 9$ **37.** $x + 4xy - \dfrac{y}{2}$ **39.** $2b^2 + b + 2 - \dfrac{12}{b + 4}$

41. $5x - 2 + \dfrac{2}{x + 6}$ **43.** $x^2 - \dfrac{12x}{5} - 1$ **45.** $6x - 1 - \dfrac{1}{x + 3}$ **47.** $6x - 1$ **49.** $-x^3 + 3x^2 - \dfrac{4}{x}$ **51.** $x^2 + 3x + 9$

53. $y^2 + 5y + 10 + \dfrac{24}{y - 2}$ **55.** $-6x - 12 - \dfrac{19}{x - 2}$ **57.** $x^3 - x^2 + x$ **59.** $2a^3 + 2a$ **61.** $2x^3 + 14x^2 - 10x$ **63.** $-3x^2y^3 - 21x^3y^2 - 24xy$

65. $9a^2b^3c + 36ab^2c - 72ab$ **67.** The Rolling Stones (2005)   **69.** \$139 million   **71.** $(3x^3 + x - 4)$ ft   **73.** c   **75.** answers may vary
77. $(7x - 10)$ in.   **79.** $5y^{10b} + y^{5b} - 4y^{2b} + 20$

Chapter 6 Vocabulary Check

1. term   **2.** FOIL   **3.** trinomial   **4.** degree of a polynomial   **5.** binomial   **6.** coefficient   **7.** degree of a term   **8.** monomial
9. polynomials   **10.** exponential   **11.** half-life

Chapter 6 Review

1. base: 7; exponent: 9   **3.** base: 5; exponent: 4   **5.** 512   **7.** -36 **9.** 1   **11.** y^9 **13.** $-6x^{11}$ **15.** x^8 **17.** $81y^{24}$ **19.** x^5 **21.** a^4b^3
23. $\dfrac{4}{x^3y^4}$ **25.** $40a^{19}$ **27.** 3   **29.** b   **31.** 7   **33.** 8   **35.** 5   **37.** 5   **39. a.** $1, 4; 5, 2; -7, 2; 11, 2; -1, 0$ **b.** 4   **41.** $2a^2$
43. $15a^2 + 4a$ **45.** $-6a^2b - 3b^2 - q^2$ **47.** $8x^2 + 3x + 6$ **49.** $-7y^2 - 1$ **51.** $-5x^2 + 5x + 1$ **53.** $-2x^2 - x + 20$ **55.** $8a + 28$
57. $-7x^3 - 35x$ **59.** $-6a^4 + 8a^2 - 2a$ **61.** $2x^2 - 12x - 14$ **63.** $x^2 - 18x + 81$ **65.** $4a^2 + 27a - 7$ **67.** $25x^2 + 20x + 4$
69. $x^4 + 7x^3 + 4x^2 + 23x - 35$ **71.** $x^4 + 4x^3 + 4x^2 - 16$ **73.** $x^3 + 21x^2 + 147x + 343$ **75.** $x^2 + 14x + 49$ **77.** $9x^2 - 42x + 49$
79. $25x^2 - 90x + 81$ **81.** $49x^2 - 16$ **83.** $4x^2 - 36$ **85.** $(9x^2 - 6x + 1)$ sq m   **87.** $\dfrac{1}{49}$ **89.** $\dfrac{2}{x^4}$ **91.** 125   **93.** $\dfrac{17}{16}$ **95.** x^8 **97.** r
99. c^4 **101.** $\dfrac{1}{x^6y^{13}}$ **103.** a^{11m} **105.** $27x^3y^{6z}$ **107.** 2.7×10^{-4} **109.** 8.08×10^7 **111.** 9.1×10^7 **113.** 867,000   **115.** 0.00086
117. 1,431,280,000,000,000   **119.** 0.016   **121.** $g(x) = 4^{-x}$ **123.** $r(x) = -4^{-x} + 3$

125.

$f(x) = 2^x$
$g(x) = 2^x - 1$

asymptote of f: $y = 0$
asymptote of g: $y = 0$
domain of f = domain of g = all real numbers
range of f = range of g = $y > 0$

127.

$f(x) = 3^x$
$g(x) = -3^x$

asymptote of f: $y = 0$
asymptote of g: $y = 0$
domain of f = domain of g = all real numbers
range of f = $y > 0$; range of g = $y < 0$

129. 5.5% compounded semiannually
131. 457,393
133. 8

135. $\dfrac{1}{7} + \dfrac{3}{x} + \dfrac{7}{x^2}$ **137.** $a + 1 + \dfrac{6}{a - 2}$ **139.** $a^2 + 3a + 8 + \dfrac{22}{a - 2}$ **141.** $2x^3 - x^2 + 2 - \dfrac{1}{2x - 1}$ **143.** $\left(5x - 1 + \dfrac{20}{x^2}\right)$ ft   **145.** $-\dfrac{1}{8}$
147. $\dfrac{2x^6}{3}$ **149.** $\dfrac{x^{16}}{16y^{12}}$ **151.** $11x - 5$ **153.** $5y^2 - 3y - 1$ **155.** $28x^3 + 12x$ **157.** $x^3 + x^2 - 18x + 18$ **159.** $25x^2 + 40x + 16$
161. $4a - 1 + \dfrac{2}{a^2} - \dfrac{5}{2a^3}$ **163.** $2x^2 + 7x + 5 + \dfrac{19}{2x - 3}$

Chapter 6 Test

1. 32   **2.** 81   **3.** -81 **4.** $\dfrac{1}{64}$ **5.** $-15x^{11}$ **6.** y^5 **7.** $\dfrac{1}{r^5}$ **8.** $\dfrac{y^{14}}{x^2}$ **9.** $\dfrac{1}{6xy^8}$ **10.** 5.63×10^5 **11.** 8.63×10^{-5} **12.** 0.0015
13. 62,300   **14.** 0.036   **15. a.** $4, 3; 7, 3; 1, 4; -2, 0$ **b.** 4   **16.** $-2x^2 + 12xy + 11$ **17.** $16x^3 + 7x^2 - 3x - 13$ **18.** $-3x^3 + 5x^2 + 4x + 5$
19. $x^3 + 8x^2 + 3x - 5$ **20.** $3x^3 + 22x^2 + 41x + 14$ **21.** $6x^4 - 9x^3 + 21x^2$ **22.** $3x^2 + 16x - 35$ **23.** $9x^2 - \dfrac{1}{25}$
24. $16x^2 - 16x + 4$ **25.** $64x^2 + 48x + 9$ **26.** $x^4 - 81b^2$ **27.** 1001 ft; 985 ft; 857 ft; 601 ft   **28.** $(4x^2 - 9)$ sq in.   **29.** $\dfrac{x}{2y} + 3 - \dfrac{7}{8y}$
30. $x + 2$ **31.** $9x^2 - 6x + 4 - \dfrac{16}{3x + 2}$

32.

$f(x) = 2^x$
$g(x) = 2^x + 1$

33. 6.5% compounded semiannually; \$230 more   **34.** 100,141   **35.** 186

Chapter 6 Standardized Test

1. b   **2.** c   **3.** a   **4.** d   **5.** c   **6.** d   **7.** b   **8.** a   **9.** d   **10.** c   **11.** c   **12.** a   **13.** c   **14.** c   **15.** d   **16.** a   **17.** b   **18.** d
19. b   **20.** c   **21.** d   **22.** a   **23.** a   **24.** b   **25.** a   **26.** b   **27.** a   **28.** b   **29.** c   **30.** d   **31.** d   **32.** b   **33.** b   **34.** b   **35.** d

CHAPTER 7 FACTORING POLYNOMIALS

Section 7.1

Practice Exercises

1. a. 6 **b.** 1 **c.** 4 **2. a.** y^4 **b.** x **3. a.** $5y^2$ **b.** x^2 **c.** a^2b^2 **4. a.** $4(t + 3)$ **b.** $y^4(y^4 + 1)$
5. $8b^2(-b^4 + 2b^2 - 1)$ or $-8b^2(b^4 - 2b^2 + 1)$ **6.** $5x(x^3 - 4)$ **7.** $\frac{1}{9}z^3(5z^2 + z - 2)$ **8.** $4ab^3(2ab - 5a^2 + 3)$ **9.** $(y - 2)(8 + x)$
10. $(p + q)(7xy^3 - 1)$ **11.** $(x + 3)(y + 4)$ **12.** $(2x + 3y)(y - 1)$ **13.** $(7a + 5)(a^2 + 1)$ **14.** $(y - 3)(4x - 5)$
15. cannot be factored by grouping **16.** $3(x - a)(y - 2a)$

Vocabulary and Readiness Check 7.1

1. factors **3.** least **5.** false **7.** $2 \cdot 7$ **9.** 3 **11.** 5

Exercise Set 7.1

1. 4 **3.** 6 **5.** 1 **7.** y^2 **9.** z^7 **11.** xy^2 **13.** 7 **15.** $4y^3$ **17.** $5x^2$ **19.** $3x^3$ **21.** $9x^2y$ **23.** $10a^6b$ **25.** $3(a + 2)$ **27.** $15(2x - 1)$
29. $x^2(x + 5)$ **31.** $2y^3(3y + 1)$ **33.** $4(x - 2y + 1)$ **35.** $3x(2x^2 - 3x + 4)$ **37.** $a^2b^2(a^5b^4 - a + b^3 - 1)$ **39.** $4(2x^5 + 4x^4 - 5x^3 + 3)$
41. $\frac{1}{3}x(x^3 + 2x^2 - 4x^4 + 1)$ **43.** $(x^2 + 2)(y + 3)$ **45.** $(y + 4)(z - 3)$ **47.** $(z^2 - 6)(r + 1)$ **49.** $-2(x + 7)$ **51.** $-x^5(2 - x^2)$
53. $-3a^2(2a^2 - 3a + 1)$ **55.** $(x + 2)(x^2 + 5)$ **57.** $(x + 3)(5 + y)$ **59.** $(3x - 2)(2x^2 + 5)$ **61.** $(5m^2 + 6n)(m + 1)$ **63.** $(y - 4)(2 + x)$
65. $(2x - 1)(x^2 + 4)$ **67.** $(x - 2y)(4x - 3)$ **69.** $(5q - 4p)(q - 1)$ **71.** $x(x^2 + 1)(2x + 5)$ **73.** $2(2y - 7)(3x^2 - 1)$ **75.** $2x(16y - 9x)$
77. $(x + 2)(y - 3)$ **79.** $7xy(2x^2 + x - 1)$ **81.** $(4x - 1)(7x^2 + 3)$ **83.** $-8x^8y^5(5y + 2x)$ **85.** $3(2a + 3b^2)(a + b)$ **87.** $x^2 + 7x + 10$
89. $b^2 - 3b - 4$ **91.** 2, 6 **93.** $-1, -8$ **95.** $-2, 5$ **97.** b **99.** factored **101.** not factored **103.** answers may vary
105. answers may vary **107. a.** 3088 thousand or 3,088,000 **b.** 3092 thousand or 3,092,000 **c.** $-2(4x^2 - 25x - 1510)$ **109.** $4x^2 - \pi x^2$; $x^2(4 - \pi)$
111. $(x^3 - 1)$ units **113.** $(x^n + 6)(x^n + 10)$ **115.** $(2x^n - 5)(6x^n - 5)$

Section 7.2

Practice Exercises

1. $(x + 2)(x + 3)$ **2.** $(x - 10)(x - 7)$ **3.** $(x + 7)(x - 2)$ **4.** $(p - 9)(p + 7)$ **5.** prime polynomial **6.** $(x + 3y)(x + 4y)$
7. $(x^2 + 12)(x^2 + 1)$ **8.** $(x - 6)(x - 8)$ **9.** $4(x - 3)(x - 3)$ **10.** $3y^2(y - 7)(y + 1)$

Vocabulary and Readiness Check 7.2

1. true **3.** false **5.** $+5$ **7.** -3 **9.** $+2$

Exercise Set 7.2

1. $(x + 6)(x + 1)$ **3.** $(y - 9)(y - 1)$ **5.** $(x - 3)(x - 3)$ or $(x - 3)^2$ **7.** $(x - 6)(x + 3)$ **9.** $(x + 10)(x - 7)$ **11.** prime
13. $(x + 5y)(x + 3y)$ **15.** $(a^2 - 5)(a^2 + 3)$ **17.** $(m + 13)(m + 1)$ **19.** $(t - 2)(t + 12)$ **21.** $(a - 2b)(a - 8b)$ **23.** $2(z + 8)(z + 2)$
25. $2x(x - 5)(x - 4)$ **27.** $(x - 4y)(x + y)$ **29.** $(x + 12)(x + 3)$ **31.** $(x - 2)(x + 1)$ **33.** $(r - 12)(r - 4)$ **35.** $(x + 2y)(x - y)$
37. $3(x + 5)(x - 2)$ **39.** $3(x - 18)(x - 2)$ **41.** $(x - 24)(x + 6)$ **43.** prime **45.** $(x - 5)(x - 3)$ **47.** $6x(x + 4)(x + 5)$
49. $4y(x^2 + x - 3)$ **51.** $(x - 7)(x + 3)$ **53.** $(x + 5y)(x + 2y)$ **55.** $2(t + 8)(t + 4)$ **57.** $x(x - 6)(x + 4)$ **59.** $2t^3(t - 4)(t - 3)$
61. $5xy(x - 8y)(x + 3y)$ **63.** $3(m - 9)(m - 6)$ **65.** $-1(x - 11)(x - 1)$ **67.** $\frac{1}{2}(y - 11)(y + 2)$ **69.** $x(xy - 4)(xy + 5)$
71. $2x^2 + 11x + 5$ **73.** $15y^2 - 17y + 4$ **75.** $9a^2 + 23ab - 12b^2$ **77.** $x^2 + 5x - 24$ **79.** answers may vary
81. $2x^2 + 28x + 66$; $2(x + 3)(x + 11)$ **83.** $-16(t - 5)(t + 1)$ **85.** $\left(x + \frac{1}{4}\right)\left(x + \frac{1}{4}\right)$ or $\left(x + \frac{1}{4}\right)^2$ **87.** $(x + 1)(z - 10)(z + 7)$
89. $(x^n + 10)(x^n - 2)$ **91.** 7; 12; 15; 16 **93.** 15; 28; 39; 48; 55; 60; 63; 64 **95.** 9; 12; 21 **97.** 5; 13

Section 7.3

Practice Exercises

1. $(2x + 5)(x + 3)$ **2.** $(5x - 4)(3x - 2)$ **3.** $(4x - 1)(x + 3)$ **4.** $(7x - y)(3x + 2y)$ **5.** $(2x^2 - 7)(x^2 + 1)$ **6.** $x(3x + 2)(x + 5)$
7. $-1(4x - 3)(2x + 1)$ **8.** $(x + 7)^2$ **9.** $(2x + 9y)(2x + y)$ **10.** $(6n^2 - 1)^2$ **11.** $3x(2x - 7)^2$

Vocabulary and Readiness Check 7.3

1. perfect square trinomial **3.** perfect square trinomial **5.** no **7.** 8^2 **9.** $(11a)^2$ **11.** $(6p^2)^2$

Exercise Set 7.3

1. $x + 4$ **3.** $10x - 1$ **5.** $5x - 2$ **7.** $(2x + 3)(x + 5)$ **9.** $(y - 1)(8y - 9)$ **11.** $(2x + 1)(x - 5)$ **13.** $(4r - 1)(5r + 8)$
15. $(10x + 1)(x + 3)$ **17.** prime **19.** $(3x - 5y)(2x - y)$ **21.** $(3m - 5)(5m + 3)$ **23.** $x(3x + 2)(4x + 1)$ **25.** $3(7b + 5)(b - 3)$
27. $(3z + 4)(4z - 3)$ **29.** $2y^2(3x - 10)(x + 3)$ **31.** $(2x - 7)(2x + 3)$ **33.** $-1(x - 6)(x + 4)$ **35.** $x(4x + 3)(x - 3)$ **37.** $(4x - 9)(6x - 1)$
39. $(x + 11)^2$ **41.** $(x - 8)^2$ **43.** $(4a - 3)^2$ **45.** $(x^2 + 2)^2$ **47.** $2(n - 7)^2$ **49.** $(4y + 5)^2$ **51.** $(2x + 11)(x - 9)$ **53.** $(8x + 3)(3x + 4)$
55. $(3a + b)(a + 3b)$ **57.** $(x - 4)(x - 5)$ **59.** $(p + 6q)^2$ **61.** $(xy - 5)^2$ **63.** $b(8a - 3)(5a + 3)$ **65.** $2x(3x + 2)(5x + 3)$
67. $2y(3y + 5)(y - 3)$ **69.** $5x^2(2x - y)(x + 3y)$ **71.** $-1(2x - 5)(7x - 2)$ **73.** $p^2(4p - 5)(4p - 5)$ or $p^2(4p - 5)^2$ **75.** $(3x - 2)(x + 1)$
77. $(4x + 9y)(2x - 3y)$ **79.** prime **81.** $(3x - 4y)^2$ **83.** $(6x - 7)(3x + 2)$ **85.** $(7t + 1)(t - 4)$ **87.** $(7p + 1)(7p - 2)$ **89.** $m(m + 9)^2$

91. prime   **93.** $a(6a^2 + b^2)(a^2 + 6b^2)$ **95.** $x^2 - 4$ **97.** $a^3 + 27$ **99.** \$75,000 and above   **101.** answers may vary   **103.** no

105. answers may vary   **107.** $4x^2 + 21x + 5; (4x + 1)(x + 5)$ **109.** $\left(2x + \dfrac{1}{2}\right)\left(2x + \dfrac{1}{2}\right)$ or $\left(2x + \dfrac{1}{2}\right)^2$ **111.** $(y - 1)^2(4x^2 + 10x + 25)$ **113.** 8

115. $a^2 + 2ab + b^2$ **117.** 2; 14   **119.** 2   **121.** $-3xy^2(4x - 5)(x + 1)$ **123.** $(y - 1)^2(2x + 5)^2$ **125.** $(3x^n + 2)(x^n + 5)$ **127.** answers may vary

Section 7.4
Practice Exercises
1. $(5x + 1)(x + 12)$ **2.** $(4x - 5)(3x - 1)$ **3.** $2(5x + 1)(3x - 2)$ **4.** $5m^2(8m - 7)(m + 1)$ **5.** $(4x + 3)^2$

Exercise Set 7.4
1. $(x + 3)(x + 2)$ **3.** $(y + 8)(y - 2)$ **5.** $(8x - 5)(x - 3)$ **7.** $(5x^2 - 3)(x^2 + 5)$ **9. a.** 9, 2   **b.** $9x + 2x$ **c.** $(2x + 3)(3x + 1)$
11. a. $-20, -3$ **b.** $-20x - 3x$ **c.** $(3x - 4)(5x - 1)$ **13.** $(3y + 2)(7y + 1)$ **15.** $(7x - 11)(x + 1)$ **17.** $(5x - 2)(2x - 1)$
19. $(2x - 5)(x - 1)$ **21.** $(2x + 3)(2x + 3)$ or $(2x + 3)^2$ **23.** $(2x + 3)(2x - 7)$ **25.** $(5x - 4)(2x - 3)$ **27.** $x(2x + 3)(x + 5)$
29. $2(8y - 9)(y - 1)$ **31.** $(2x - 3)(3x - 2)$ **33.** $3(3a + 2)(6a - 5)$ **35.** $a(4a + 1)(5a + 8)$ **37.** $3x(4x + 3)(x - 3)$ **39.** $y(3x + y)(x + y)$
41. prime   **43.** $5(x + 5y)^2$ **45.** $6(a + b)(4a - 5b)$ **47.** $p^2(15p + q)(p + 2q)$ **49.** $2(9a^2 - 2)^2$ **51.** $(7 + x)(5 + x)$ or $(x + 7)(x + 5)$
53. $(6 - 5x)(1 - x)$ or $(5x - 6)(x - 1)$ **55.** $x^2 - 4$ **57.** $y^2 + 8y + 16$ **59.** $81z^2 - 25$ **61.** $x^3 - 27$
63. $10x^2 + 45x + 45; 5(2x + 3)(x + 3)$ **65.** $(x^n + 2)(x^n + 3)$ **67.** $(3x^n - 5)(x^n + 7)$ **69.** answers may vary

Section 7.5
Practice Exercises
1. $(x + 9)(x - 9)$ **2. a.** $(3x - 1)(3x + 1)$ **b.** $(6a - 7b)(6a + 7b)$ **c.** $\left(p + \dfrac{5}{6}\right)\left(p - \dfrac{5}{6}\right)$ **3.** $(p^2 - q^5)(p^2 + q^5)$

4. a. $(z^2 + 9)(z + 3)(z - 3)$ **b.** prime polynomial   **5.** $y(6y + 5)(6y - 5)$ **6.** $5(4y^2 + 1)(2y + 1)(2y - 1)$
7. $-1(3x + 10)(3x - 10)$ or $(10 + 3x)(10 - 3x)$ **8.** $(x + 4)(x^2 - 4x + 16)$ **9.** $(x - 5)(x^2 + 5x + 25)$ **10.** $(3y + 1)(9y^2 - 3y + 1)$
11. $4(2x - 5y)(4x^2 + 10xy + 25y^2)$

Calculator Explorations 7.5

	$x^2 - 2x + 1$	$x^2 - 2x - 1$	$(x - 1)^2$
$x = 5$	16	14	16
$x = -3$	16	14	16
$x = 2.7$	2.89	0.89	2.89
$x = -12.1$	171.61	169.61	171.61
$x = 0$	1	-1	1

Vocabulary and Readiness Check 7.5
1. difference of two cubes   **3.** sum of two cubes   **5.** 8^2 **7.** $(7x)^2$ **9.** 4^3 **11.** $(2y)^3$

Exercise Set 7.5
1. $(x + 2)(x - 2)$ **3.** $(9p + 1)(9p - 1)$ **5.** $(5y - 3)(5y + 3)$ **7.** $(11m + 10n)(11m - 10n)$ **9.** $(xy - 1)(xy + 1)$ **11.** $\left(x - \dfrac{1}{2}\right)\left(x + \dfrac{1}{2}\right)$
13. $-1(2r + 1)(2r - 1)$ **15.** prime   **17.** $(-6 + x)(6 + x)$ or $-1(6 + x)(6 - x)$ **19.** $(m^2 + 1)(m + 1)(m - 1)$ **21.** $(m^2 + n^9)(m^2 - n^9)$
23. $(x + 5)(x^2 - 5x + 25)$ **25.** $(2a - 1)(4a^2 + 2a + 1)$ **27.** $(m + 3n)(m^2 - 3mn + 9n^2)$ **29.** $5(k + 2)(k^2 - 2k + 4)$
31. $(xy - 4)(x^2y^2 + 4xy + 16)$ **33.** $2(5r - 4t)(25r^2 + 20rt + 16t^2)$ **35.** $(r + 8)(r - 8)$ **37.** $(x + 13y)(x - 13y)$ **39.** $(3 - t)(9 + 3t + t^2)$
41. $2(3r + 2)(3r - 2)$ **43.** $x(3y + 2)(3y - 2)$ **45.** $8(m + 2)(m^2 - 2m + 4)$ **47.** $xy(y - 3z)(y + 3z)$ **49.** $4(3x - 4y)(3x + 4y)$
51. $9(4 - 3x)(4 + 3x)$ **53.** $(xy - z^2)(x^2y^2 + xyz^2 + z^4)$ **55.** $\left(7 - \dfrac{3}{5}m\right)\left(7 + \dfrac{3}{5}m\right)$ **57.** $(t + 7)(t^2 - 7t + 49)$ **59.** $n(n^2 + 49)$
61. $x^2(x^2 + 9)(x + 3)(x - 3)$ **63.** $pq(8p + 9q)(8p - 9q)$ **65.** $xy^2(27xy + 1)$ **67.** $a(5a - 4b)(25a^2 + 20ab + 16b^2)$ **69.** $16x^2(x + 2)(x - 2)$
71. 6   **73.** -2 **75.** $\dfrac{1}{5}$ **77.** 81.2%   **79.** $-4(0.3x^2 - x - 20)$ **81.** $(x + 2 + y)(x + 2 - y)$ **83.** $(a + 4)(a - 4)(b - 4)$
85. $(x + 3 + 2y)(x + 3 - 2y)$ **87.** $(x^n + 10)(x^n - 10)$ **89.** $(x + 6)$ **91.** answers may vary   **93. a.** 777 ft   **b.** 441 ft   **c.** 7 sec
d. $(29 + 4t)(29 - 4t)$ **95. a.** 1456 ft   **b.** 816 ft   **c.** 10 sec   **d.** $16(10 + t)(10 - t)$

Integrated Review
Practice Exercises
1. $(3x - 1)(2x - 3)$ **2.** $(3x + 1)(x - 2)(x + 2)$ **3.** $3(3x - y)(3x + y)$ **4.** $(2a + b)(4a^2 - 2ab + b^2)$ **5.** $6xy^2(5x + 2)(2x - 3)$

Integrated Review Exercise Set

1. $(x + y)^2$ **2.** $(x - y)^2$ **3.** $(a + 12)(a - 1)$ **4.** $(a - 10)(a - 1)$ **5.** $(a + 2)(a - 3)$ **6.** $(a - 1)^2$ **7.** $(x + 1)^2$ **8.** $(x + 2)(x - 1)$
9. $(x + 1)(x + 3)$ **10.** $(x + 3)(x - 2)$ **11.** $(x + 3)(x + 4)$ **12.** $(x + 4)(x - 3)$ **13.** $(x + 4)(x - 1)$ **14.** $(x - 5)(x - 2)$
15. $(x + 5)(x - 3)$ **16.** $(x + 6)(x + 5)$ **17.** $(x - 6)(x + 5)$ **18.** $(x + 8)(x + 3)$ **19.** $2(x + 7)(x - 7)$ **20.** $3(x + 5)(x - 5)$
21. $(x + 3)(x + y)$ **22.** $(y - 7)(3 + x)$ **23.** $(x + 8)(x - 2)$ **24.** $(x - 7)(x + 4)$ **25.** $4x(x + 7)(x - 2)$ **26.** $6x(x - 5)(x + 4)$
27. $2(3x + 4)(2x + 3)$ **28.** $(2a - b)(4a + 5b)$ **29.** $(2a + b)(2a - b)$ **30.** $(4 - 3x)(7 + 2x)$ **31.** $(5 - 2x)(4 + x)$ **32.** prime **33.** prime
34. $(3y + 5)(2y - 3)$ **35.** $(4x - 5)(x + 1)$ **36.** $y(x + y)(x - y)$ **37.** $4(t^2 + 9)$ **38.** $(x + 1)(x + y)$ **39.** $(x + 1)(a + 2)$
40. $9x(2x^2 - 7x + 1)$ **41.** $4a(3a^2 - 6a + 1)$ **42.** $(x + 16)(x - 2)$ **43.** prime **44.** $(4a - 7b)^2$ **45.** $(5p - 7q)^2$ **46.** $(7x + 3y)(x + 3y)$
47. $(5 - 2y)(25 + 10y + 4y^2)$ **48.** $(4x + 3)(16x^2 - 12x + 9)$ **49.** $-(x - 5)(x + 6)$ **50.** $-(x - 2)(x - 4)$ **51.** $(7 - x)(2 + x)$
52. $(3 + x)(1 - x)$ **53.** $3x^2y(x + 6)(x - 4)$ **54.** $2xy(x + 5y)(x - y)$ **55.** $5xy^2(x - 7y)(x - y)$ **56.** $4x^2y(x - 5)(x + 3)$
57. $3xy(4x^2 + 81)$ **58.** $2xy^2(3x^2 + 4)$ **59.** $(2 + x)(2 - x)$ **60.** $(3 + y)(3 - y)$ **61.** $(s + 4)(3r - 1)$ **62.** $(x - 2)(x^2 + 3)$
63. $(4x - 3)(x - 2y)$ **64.** $(2x - y)(2x + 7z)$ **65.** $6(x + 2y)(x + y)$ **66.** $2(x + 4y)(6x - y)$ **67.** $(x + 3)(y + 2)(y - 2)$
68. $(y + 3)(y - 3)(x^2 + 3)$ **69.** $(5 + x)(x + y)$ **70.** $(x - y)(7 + y)$ **71.** $(7t - 1)(2t - 1)$ **72.** prime **73.** $(3x + 5)(x - 1)$
74. $(7x - 2)(x + 3)$ **75.** $(x + 12y)(x - 3y)$ **76.** $(3x - 2y)(x + 4y)$ **77.** $(1 - 10ab)(1 + 2ab)$ **78.** $(1 + 5ab)(1 - 12ab)$
79. $(3 + x)(3 - x)(1 + x)(1 - x)$ **80.** $(3 + x)(3 - x)(2 + x)(2 - x)$ **81.** $(x + 4)(x - 4)(x^2 + 2)$ **82.** $(x + 5)(x - 5)(x^2 + 3)$
83. $(x - 15)(x - 8)$ **84.** $(y + 16)(y + 6)$ **85.** $2x(3x - 2)(x - 4)$ **86.** $2y(3y + 5)(y - 3)$ **87.** $(3x - 5)(9x^2 + 15xy + 25y^2)$
88. $(6y - z)(36y^2 + 6yz + z^2)$ **89.** $(xy + 2z)(x^2y^2 - 2xyz + 4z^2)$ **90.** $(3ab + 2)(9a^2b^2 - 6ab + 4)$ **91.** $2xy(1 + 6x)(1 - 6x)$
92. $2x(x + 3)(x - 3)$ **93.** $(x + 2)(x - 2)(x + 6)$ **94.** $(x - 2)(x + 6)(x - 6)$ **95.** $2a^2(3a + 5)$ **96.** $2n(2n - 3)$ **97.** $(a^2 + 2)(a + 2)$
98. $(a - b)(1 + x)$ **99.** $(x + 2)(x - 2)(x + 7)$ **100.** $(a + 3)(a - 3)(a + 5)$ **101.** $(x - y + z)(x - y - z)$
102. $(x + 2y + 3)(x + 2y - 3)$ **103.** $(9 + 5x + 1)(9 - 5x - 1)$ **104.** $(b + 4a + c)(b - 4a - c)$ **105.** answers may vary
106. yes; $9(x^2 + 9y^2)$ **107.** a, c

Section 7.6

Practice Exercises

1. $-4, 5$ **2.** $0, \dfrac{6}{7}$ **3.** $-4, 12$ **4.** $\dfrac{4}{3}$ **5.** $-3, \dfrac{2}{3}$ **6.** $-6, 4$ **7.** $-3, 0, 3$ **8.** $\dfrac{2}{3}, \dfrac{3}{2}, 5$ **9.** $-3, 0, 2$ **10.** The x-intercepts are $(2, 0)$ and $(4, 0)$.

Calculator Explorations 7.6

1. $-0.9, 2.2$ **3.** no real solution **5.** $-1.8, 2.8$

Vocabulary and Readiness Check 7.6

1. quadratic **3.** $3, -5$ **5.** $3, 7$ **7.** $-8, -6$ **9.** $-1, 3$

Exercise Set 7.6

1. $2, -1$ **3.** $-9, -17$ **5.** $0, -6$ **7.** $0, 8$ **9.** $-\dfrac{3}{2}, \dfrac{5}{4}$ **11.** $\dfrac{7}{2}, -\dfrac{2}{7}$ **13.** $\dfrac{1}{2}, -\dfrac{1}{3}$ **15.** $-0.2, -1.5$

17. answers may vary; for example, $(x - 6)(x + 1) = 0$ **19.** $9, 4$ **21.** $-4, 2$ **23.** $0, 7$ **25.** $8, -4$ **27.** $4, -4$ **29.** $-3, 12$ **31.** $\dfrac{7}{3}, -2$

33. $-5, 5$ **35.** $-2, \dfrac{1}{6}$ **37.** $0, 4, 8$ **39.** $\dfrac{3}{4}$ **41.** $-\dfrac{1}{2}, 0, \dfrac{1}{2}$ **43.** $-\dfrac{3}{8}, 0, \dfrac{1}{2}$ **45.** $-3, 2$ **47.** $-20, 0$ **49.** $\dfrac{17}{2}$ **51.** $-\dfrac{1}{2}, \dfrac{1}{2}$

53. $-\dfrac{3}{2}, -\dfrac{1}{2}, 3$ **55.** $-5, 3$ **57.** $-\dfrac{5}{6}, \dfrac{6}{5}$ **59.** $2, -\dfrac{4}{5}$ **61.** $-\dfrac{4}{3}, 5$ **63.** $-4, 3$ **65.** $\dfrac{8}{3}, -9, 0$ **67.** -7 **69.** $0, \dfrac{3}{2}$ **71.** $0, 1, -1$

73. $-6, \dfrac{4}{3}$ **75.** $\dfrac{6}{7}, 1$ **77.** $\left(-\dfrac{4}{3}, 0\right), (1, 0)$ **79.** $(-2, 0), (5, 0)$ **81.** $(-6, 0), \left(\dfrac{1}{2}, 0\right)$ **83.** e **85.** b **87.** c **89. a.** $(x - 2)(x + 2)$

b. $2, -2$ **c.** $(2, 0), (-2, 0)$ **91. a.** $(x + 5)(2x - 1)$ **b.** $-5, \dfrac{1}{2}$ **c.** $(-5, 0), \left(\dfrac{1}{2}, 0\right)$ **93.** $\dfrac{47}{45}$ **95.** $\dfrac{17}{60}$ **97.** $\dfrac{15}{8}$

99. $\dfrac{7}{10}$ **101.** didn't write equation in standard form; should be $x = 4$ or $x = -2$ **103.** answers may vary; for example, $x^2 - 12x + 35 = 0$

105. a. $300; 304; 276; 216; 124; 0; -156$ **b.** 5 sec **c.** 304 ft **d.**

$y = -16x^2 + 20x + 300$

107. $0, \dfrac{1}{2}$

109. $0, -15$

Section 7.7

Practice Exercises

1. 2 sec **2.** There are 2 numbers. They are -4 and 12. **3.** base: 35 ft; height: 12 ft **4.** 7 and 8 or -6 and -5
5. leg: 8 units; leg: 15 units; hypotenuse: 17 units

Exercise Set 7.7

1. width $= x$; length $= x + 4$ **3.** x and $x + 2$ if x is an odd integer **5.** base $= x$; height $= 4x + 1$ **7.** 11 units
9. 15 cm, 13 cm, 70 cm, 22 cm **11.** base $= 16$ mi; height $= 6$ mi **13.** 5 sec **15.** length $= 5$ cm; width $= 6$ cm **17.** 54 diagonals
19. 10 sides **21.** -12 or 11 **23.** 14, 15 **25.** 13 feet **27.** 5 in. **29.** 12 mm, 16 mm, 20 mm **31.** 10 km **33.** 36 ft **35.** 9.5 sec

37. 20% **39.** length: 15 mi; width: 8 mi **41.** 105 units **43.** 175 acres **45.** 6.25 million **47.** 1966 **49.** answers may vary **51.** $\dfrac{3}{4}$

53. $\dfrac{5}{9}$ **55.** $\dfrac{9}{10}$ **57.** 8 m **59.** 10 and 15 **61.** width: 29 m; length: 35 m **63.** answers may vary

Chapter 7 Vocabulary Check

1. quadratic equation **2.** factoring **3.** greatest common factor **4.** perfect square trinomial **5.** difference of two squares
6. difference of two cubes **7.** sum of two cubes **8.** 0 **9.** root **10.** k

Chapter 7 Review

1. $2x - 5$ **3.** $4x(5x + 3)$ **5.** $-2x^2y(4x - 3y)$ **7.** $(x + 1)(5x - 1)$ **9.** $(2x - 1)(3x + 5)$ **11.** $(x + 4)(x + 2)$ **13.** prime
15. $(x + 4)(x - 2)$ **17.** $(x + 5y)(x + 3y)$ **19.** $2(3 - x)(12 + x)$ **21.** $(2x - 1)(x + 6)$ **23.** $(2x + 3)(2x - 1)$ **25.** $(6x - y)(x - 4y)$
27. $(2x + 3y)(x - 13y)$ **29.** $(6x + 5y)(3x - 4y)$ **31.** $(2x + 3)(2x - 3)$ **33.** prime **35.** $(2x + 3)(4x^2 - 6x + 9)$

37. $2(3 - xy)(9 + 3xy + x^2y^2)$ **39.** $(4x^2 + 1)(2x + 1)(2x - 1)$ **41.** $-6, 2$ **43.** $-\dfrac{1}{5}, -3$ **45.** $-4, 6$ **47.** $2, 8$ **49.** $-\dfrac{2}{7}, \dfrac{3}{8}$ **51.** $-\dfrac{2}{5}$

53. 3 **55.** $0, -\dfrac{7}{4}, 3$ **57.** c **59.** 9 units **61.** width: 20 in.; length: 25 in. **63.** 19 and 20 **65.** 6.25 sec **67.** $7(x - 9)$

69. $\left(m + \dfrac{2}{5}\right)\left(m - \dfrac{2}{5}\right)$ **71.** $(y + 2)(x - 1)$ **73.** $3x(x - 9)(x - 1)$ **75.** $2(x + 3)(x - 3)$ **77.** $5(x + 2)^2$ **79.** $2xy(2x - 3y)$

81. $(5x + 3)(25x^2 - 15x + 9)$ **83.** $(x + 7 + y)(x + 7 - y)$ **85.** $2b(3a - 1)(9a^2 + 3a + 1)$ **87.** factor out the GCF, 3
89. $16x^2 - 28x + 6$; $2(4x - 1)(2x - 3)$ **91.** $-3, 5$ **93.** $3, 2$ **95.** 19 in., 8 in., 21 in. **97.** 6.75 sec **99. a.** $(x + 2)(x - 7)$ **b.** $-2, 7$
c. $(-2, 0), (7, 0)$

Chapter 7 Test

1. $(x + 7)(x + 4)$ **2.** $(7 - m)(7 + m)$ **3.** $(y + 11)^2$ **4.** $(a + 3)(4 - y)$ **5.** prime **6.** $(y - 12)(y + 4)$ **7.** prime
8. $3x(3x + 1)(x + 4)$ **9.** $(3a - 7)(a + b)$ **10.** $(3x - 2)(x - 1)$ **11.** $(x + 12y)(x + 2y)$ **12.** $5(6 + x)(6 - x)$ **13.** $(6t + 5)(t - 1)$
14. $(y + 2)(y - 2)(x - 7)$ **15.** $x(1 + x^2)(1 + x)(1 - x)$ **16.** $-xy(y^2 + x^2)$ **17.** $(4x - 1)(16x^2 + 4x + 1)$ **18.** $8(y - 2)(y^2 + 2y + 4)$

19. $-9, 3$ **20.** $-7, 2$ **21.** $-7, 1$ **22.** $0, \dfrac{3}{2}, -\dfrac{4}{3}$ **23.** $0, 3, -3$ **24.** $-3, 5$ **25.** $0, \dfrac{5}{2}$ **26.** 17 ft **27.** 8 and 9 **28.** 7 sec

29. hypotenuse: 25 cm; legs: 15 cm, 20 cm **30. a.** $(x - 7)(3x - 1)$ **b.** $7, \dfrac{1}{3}$ **c.** $(7, 0), \left(\dfrac{1}{3}, 0\right)$

Chapter 7 Standardized Test

1. c **2.** b **3.** c **4.** a **5.** a **6.** c **7.** d **8.** c **9.** b **10.** a **11.** d **12.** b **13.** b **14.** c **15.** c **16.** a **17.** c **18.** d
19. a **20.** b **21.** a **22.** d **23.** b **24.** a **25.** d **26.** c **27.** b **28.** b **29.** b **30.** b

CHAPTER 8 RATIONAL EXPRESSIONS

Section 8.1

Practice Exercises

1. a. $\dfrac{9}{7}$ **b.** $-\dfrac{3}{11}$ **2. a.** $x = -6$ **b.** none **c.** $x = -2$ or $x = -4$ **d.** none **3.** $\dfrac{x^5}{6}$ **4.** $\dfrac{x + 1}{x - 2}$ **5.** $\dfrac{x^2}{x + 9}$ **6.** $\dfrac{1}{x + 7}$ **7. a.** -1 **b.** 1

8. $-\dfrac{2x + 3}{x + 4}$ or $\dfrac{-2x - 3}{x + 4}$ **9.** $\dfrac{-(x + 3)}{6x - 11}$; $\dfrac{-x - 3}{6x - 11}$; $\dfrac{x + 3}{-(6x - 11)}$; $\dfrac{x + 3}{-6x + 11}$; $\dfrac{x + 3}{11 - 6x}$

Vocabulary and Readiness Check 8.1

1. rational expression **3.** -1 **5.** 2 **7.** $\dfrac{-a}{b}, \dfrac{a}{-b}$ **9.** yes **11.** no

Exercise Set 8.1

1. $\dfrac{7}{4}$ **3.** 3 **5.** $-\dfrac{8}{3}$ **7.** $-\dfrac{11}{2}$ **9.** $x = 0$ **11.** $x = -2$ **13.** $x = \dfrac{5}{2}$ **15.** none **17.** $x = 6, x = -1$ **19.** none **21.** $x = -2, x = -\dfrac{7}{3}$

23. $\dfrac{-(x - 10)}{x + 8}$; $\dfrac{-x + 10}{x + 8}$; $\dfrac{x - 10}{-(x + 8)}$; $\dfrac{x - 10}{-x - 8}$ **25.** $\dfrac{-(5y - 3)}{y - 12}$; $\dfrac{-5y + 3}{y - 12}$; $\dfrac{5y - 3}{-(y - 12)}$; $\dfrac{5y - 3}{-y + 12}$ **27.** 1 **29.** -1 **31.** $\dfrac{1}{4(x + 2)}$ **33.** $\dfrac{1}{x + 2}$

35. can't simplify **37.** -5 **39.** $\dfrac{7}{x}$ **41.** $\dfrac{1}{x-9}$ **43.** $5x+1$ **45.** $\dfrac{x^2}{x-2}$ **47.** $7x$ **49.** $\dfrac{x+5}{x-5}$ **51.** $\dfrac{x+2}{x+4}$ **53.** $\dfrac{x+2}{2}$

55. $-(x+2)$ or $-x-2$ **57.** $\dfrac{x+1}{x-1}$ **59.** $\dfrac{m-3}{m+2}$ **61.** $\dfrac{11x}{6}$ **63.** $x+y$ **65.** $\dfrac{5-y}{2}$ **67.** x^2-2x+4 **69.** $-x^2-x-1$ **71.** $\dfrac{2y+5}{3y+4}$

73. correct **75.** correct **77.** $\dfrac{3}{11}$ **79.** $\dfrac{4}{3}$ **81.** $\dfrac{117}{40}$ **83.** correct **85.** incorrect; $\dfrac{1+2}{1+3}=\dfrac{3}{4}$ **87.** answers may vary **89.** answers may vary

91. a. \$37.5 million **b.** $\approx$\$85.7 million **c.** $\approx$\$48.2 million **93.** 400 mg **95.** $C=78.125$; medium **97.** 101.0 **99.** 25.0%

101.

103.

Section 8.2
Practice Exercises

1. a. $\dfrac{12a}{5b^2}$ **b.** $-\dfrac{2q}{3}$ **2.** $\dfrac{3}{x+1}$ **3.** $-\dfrac{3x-5}{2x(x+2)}$ **4.** $\dfrac{b^2}{8a^2}$ **5.** $\dfrac{3(3x+1)}{4}$ **6.** $\dfrac{2}{x(x-3)}$ **7.** 1 **8. a.** $\dfrac{(y+9)^2}{16x^2}$ **b.** $\dfrac{1}{4x}$ **c.** $-\dfrac{7(x-2)}{x+4}$

Vocabulary and Readiness Check 8.2

1. reciprocals **3.** $\dfrac{a\cdot d}{b\cdot c}$ or $\dfrac{ad}{bc}$ **5.** $\dfrac{6}{7}$

Exercise Set 8.2

1. $\dfrac{21}{4y}$ **3.** x^4 **5.** $-\dfrac{b^2}{6}$ **7.** $\dfrac{x^2}{10}$ **9.** $\dfrac{1}{3}$ **11.** $\dfrac{m+n}{m-n}$ **13.** $\dfrac{x+5}{x}$ **15.** $\dfrac{(x+2)(x-3)}{(x-4)(x+4)}$ **17.** $\dfrac{2x^4}{3}$ **19.** $\dfrac{12}{y^6}$ **21.** $x(x+4)$ **23.** $\dfrac{3(x+1)}{x^3(x-1)}$

25. m^2-n^2 **27.** $-\dfrac{x+2}{x-3}$ **29.** $\dfrac{x+2}{x-3}$ **31.** $\dfrac{5}{6}$ **33.** $\dfrac{3x}{8}$ **35.** $\dfrac{3}{2}$ **37.** $\dfrac{3x+4y}{2(x+2y)}$ **39.** $\dfrac{2(x+2)}{x-2}$ **41.** $-\dfrac{y(x+2)}{4}$ **43.** $\dfrac{(a+5)(a+3)}{(a+2)(a+1)}$

45. $\dfrac{5}{x}$ **47.** $\dfrac{2(n-8)}{3n-1}$ **49.** $4x^3(x-3)$ **51.** $\dfrac{(a+b)^2}{a-b}$ **53.** $\dfrac{3x+5}{x^2+4}$ **55.** $\dfrac{4}{x-2}$ **57.** $\dfrac{a-b}{6(a^2+ab+b^2)}$ **59.** 1 **61.** $-\dfrac{10}{9}$ **63.** $-\dfrac{1}{5}$

65.

67. true **69.** false; $\dfrac{x^2+3x}{20}$ **71.** $\dfrac{2}{9(x-5)}$ sq ft **73.** $\dfrac{x}{2}$ **75.** $\dfrac{5a(2a+b)(3a-2b)}{b^2(a-b)(a+2b)}$ **77.** answers may vary

Section 8.3
Practice Exercises

1. $\dfrac{2a}{b}$ **2.** 1 **3.** $4x-5$ **4. a.** 42 **b.** $45y^3$ **5. a.** $(y-5)(y-4)$ **b.** $a(a+2)$ **6.** $3(2x-1)^2$ **7.** $(x+4)(x-4)(x+1)$

8. $(3-x)$ or $(x-3)$ **9. a.** $\dfrac{21x^2y}{35xy^2}$ **b.** $\dfrac{18x}{8x+14}$ **10.** $\dfrac{3x-6}{(x-2)(x+3)(x-5)}$

Vocabulary and Readiness Check 8.3

1. $\dfrac{9}{11}$ **3.** $\dfrac{a+c}{b}$ **5.** $\dfrac{5-(6+x)}{x}$

Exercise Set 8.3

1. $\dfrac{a+9}{13}$ **3.** $\dfrac{3m}{n}$ **5.** 4 **7.** $\dfrac{y+10}{3+y}$ **9.** $5x+3$ **11.** $\dfrac{4}{a+5}$ **13.** $\dfrac{1}{x-6}$ **15.** $\dfrac{5x+7}{x-3}$ **17.** $x+5$ **19.** 3 **21.** $4x^3$

23. $8x(x+2)$ **25.** $(x+3)(x-2)$ **27.** $3(x+6)$ **29.** $5(x-6)^2$ **31.** $6(x+1)^2$ **33.** $x-8$ or $8-x$ **35.** $(x-1)(x+4)(x+3)$

37. $(3x+1)(x+1)(x-1)(2x+1)$ **39.** $2x^2(x+4)(x-4)$ **41.** $\dfrac{6x}{4x^2}$ **43.** $\dfrac{24b^2}{12ab^2}$ **45.** $\dfrac{9y}{2y(x+3)}$ **47.** $\dfrac{9ab+2b}{5b(a+2)}$

49. $\dfrac{x^2+x}{x(x+4)(x+2)(x+1)}$ **51.** $\dfrac{18y-2}{30x^2-60}$ **53.** $2x$ **55.** $\dfrac{x+3}{2x-1}$ **57.** $x+1$ **59.** $\dfrac{1}{x^2-8}$ **61.** $\dfrac{6(4x+1)}{x(2x+1)}$ **63.** $\dfrac{29}{21}$ **65.** $-\dfrac{5}{12}$

67. $\dfrac{7}{30}$ **69.** d **71.** c **73.** b **75.** $-\dfrac{5}{x-2}$ **77.** $\dfrac{7+x}{x-2}$ **79.** $\dfrac{20}{x-2}$ m **81.** answers may vary **83.** 95,304 Earth days
85. answers may vary **87.** answers may vary

Section 8.4
Practice Exercises

1. a. 0 **b.** $\dfrac{21a + 10}{24a^2}$ **2.** $\dfrac{6}{x - 5}$ **3.** $\dfrac{13y + 3}{5y(y + 1)}$ **4.** $\dfrac{13}{x - 5}$ **5.** $\dfrac{3b + 6}{b + 3}$ or $\dfrac{3(b + 2)}{b + 3}$ **6.** $\dfrac{10 - 3x^2}{2x(2x + 3)}$ **7.** $\dfrac{x(5x + 6)}{(x + 4)(x + 3)(x - 3)}$

Vocabulary and Readiness Check 8.4

1. d   **3.** a

Exercise Set 8.4

1. $\dfrac{5}{x}$ **3.** $\dfrac{75a - 6b^2}{5b}$ **5.** $\dfrac{6x + 5}{2x^2}$ **7.** $\dfrac{11}{x + 1}$ **9.** $\dfrac{x - 6}{(x - 2)(x + 2)}$ **11.** $\dfrac{35x - 6}{4x(x - 2)}$ **13.** $-\dfrac{2}{x - 3}$ **15.** 0 **17.** $-\dfrac{1}{x^2 - 1}$ **19.** $\dfrac{5 + 2x}{x}$

21. $\dfrac{6x - 7}{x - 2}$ **23.** $-\dfrac{y + 4}{y + 3}$ **25.** $\dfrac{-5x + 14}{4x}$ or $-\dfrac{5x - 14}{4x}$ **27.** 2 **29.** $\dfrac{9x^4 - 4x^2}{21}$ **31.** $\dfrac{x + 2}{(x + 3)^2}$ **33.** $\dfrac{9b - 4}{5b(b - 1)}$ **35.** $\dfrac{2 + m}{m}$

37. $\dfrac{x^2 + 3x}{(x - 7)(x - 2)}$ or $\dfrac{x(x + 3)}{(x - 7)(x - 2)}$ **39.** $\dfrac{10}{1 - 2x}$ **41.** $\dfrac{15x - 1}{(x + 1)^2(x - 1)}$ **43.** $\dfrac{x^2 - 3x - 2}{(x - 1)^2(x + 1)}$ **45.** $\dfrac{a + 2}{2(a + 3)}$ **47.** $\dfrac{y(2y + 1)}{(2y + 3)^2}$

49. $\dfrac{x - 10}{2(x - 2)}$ **51.** $\dfrac{2x + 21}{(x + 3)^2}$ **53.** $\dfrac{-5x + 23}{(x - 2)(x - 3)}$ **55.** $\dfrac{7}{2(m - 10)}$ **57.** $\dfrac{2x^2 - 2x - 46}{(x + 1)(x - 6)(x - 5)}$ or $\dfrac{2(x^2 - x - 23)}{(x + 1)(x - 6)(x - 5)}$

59. $\dfrac{n + 4}{4n(n - 1)(n - 2)}$ **61.** 10 **63.** 2 **65.** $\dfrac{25a}{9(a - 2)}$ **67.** $\dfrac{x + 4}{(x - 2)(x - 1)}$ **69.** $x = \dfrac{2}{3}$ **71.** $x = -\dfrac{1}{2}, x = 1$ **73.** $x = -\dfrac{15}{2}$

75. $\dfrac{6x^2 - 5x - 3}{x(x + 1)(x - 1)}$ **77.** $\dfrac{4x^2 - 15x + 6}{(x - 2)^2(x + 2)(x - 3)}$ **79.** $\dfrac{-2x^2 + 14x + 55}{(x + 2)(x + 7)(x + 3)}$ **81.** $\dfrac{2x - 16}{(x + 4)(x - 4)}$ in.   **83.** $\dfrac{P - G}{P}$ **85.** answers may vary

87. $\left(\dfrac{90x - 40}{x}\right)^{\circ}$ **89.** answers may vary

Section 8.5
Practice Exercises

1. -2 **2.** 13 **3.** $-1, 7$ **4.** $-\dfrac{19}{2}$ **5.** 3 **6.** -8 **7.** $b = \dfrac{ax}{a - x}$

Graphing Calculator Explorations 8.5

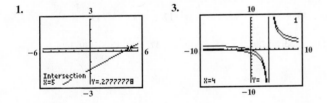

1.

3.

Exercise Set 8.5

1. 30 **3.** 0 **5.** -2 **7.** $-5, 2$ **9.** 5 **11.** 3 **13.** 1 **15.** 5 **17.** no solution   **19.** 4 **21.** -8 **23.** $6, -4$ **25.** 1 **27.** $3, -4$

29. -3 **31.** 0 **33.** -2 **35.** $8, -2$ **37.** no solution   **39.** 3 **41.** $-11, 1$ **43.** $I = \dfrac{E}{R}$ **45.** $B = \dfrac{2U - TE}{T}$ **47.** $w = \dfrac{Bh^2}{705}$

49. $G = \dfrac{V}{N - R}$ **51.** $r = \dfrac{C}{2\pi}$ **53.** $x = \dfrac{3y}{3 + y}$ **55.** $\dfrac{1}{x}$ **57.** $\dfrac{1}{x} + \dfrac{1}{2}$ **59.** $\dfrac{1}{3}$ **61.** $(2, 0), (0, -2)$ **63.** $(-4, 0), (-2, 0), (3, 0), (0, 4)$

65. answers may vary   **67.** $\dfrac{5x + 9}{9x}$ **69.** no solution   **71.** $100°, 80°$ **73.** $22.5°, 67.5°$ **75.** $\dfrac{17}{4}$

Integrated Review

1. expression; $\dfrac{3 + 2x}{3x}$ **2.** expression; $\dfrac{18 + 5a}{6a}$ **3.** equation; 3 **4.** equation; 18 **5.** expression; $\dfrac{x + 1}{x(x - 1)}$ **6.** expression; $\dfrac{3(x + 1)}{x(x - 3)}$

7. equation; no solution   **8.** equation; 1 **9.** expression; 10 **10.** expression; $\dfrac{z}{3(9z - 5)}$ **11.** expression; $\dfrac{5x + 7}{x - 3}$ **12.** expression; $\dfrac{7p + 5}{2p + 7}$

13. equation; 23 **14.** equation; 5 **15.** expression; $\dfrac{25a}{9(a - 2)}$ **16.** expression; $\dfrac{4x + 5}{(x + 1)(x - 1)}$ **17.** expression; $\dfrac{3x^2 + 5x + 3}{(3x - 1)^2}$

18. expression; $\dfrac{2x^2 - 3x - 1}{(2x - 5)^2}$ **19.** expression; $\dfrac{4x - 37}{5x}$ **20.** equation; $-\dfrac{7}{3}$ **21.** equation; $\dfrac{8}{5}$ **22.** expression; $\dfrac{29x - 23}{3x}$

Section 8.6
Practice Exercises

1. 99 **2.** $\dfrac{13}{3}$ **3.** \$9.03 **4.** 6 **5.** 15 **6.** $1\dfrac{5}{7}$ hr **7.** bus: 45 mph; car: 60 mph

Vocabulary and Readiness Check 8.6
1. c

Exercise Set 8.6

1. 4 **3.** $\dfrac{50}{9}$ **5.** -3 **7.** $\dfrac{14}{9}$ **9.** 123 lb **11.** 165 cal **13.** $y = 21.25$ **15.** $y = 5\dfrac{5}{7}$ ft **17.** 2 **19.** -3 **21.** $2\dfrac{2}{9}$ hr **23.** $1\dfrac{1}{2}$ min

25. trip to park rate: r; to park time: $\dfrac{12}{r}$; return trip rate: r; return time: $\dfrac{18}{r} = \dfrac{12}{r} + 1$; $r = 6$ mph **27.** 1st portion: 10 mph; cooldown: 8 mph

29. 360 sq ft **31.** 2 **33.** \$108.00 **35.** 20 mph **37.** $y = 37\dfrac{1}{2}$ ft **39.** 337 yd/game **41.** 5 **43.** 217 mph **45.** 9 gal **47.** 8 mph

49. 35 mph; 75 mph **51.** 3 hr **53.** $26\dfrac{2}{3}$ ft **55.** 216 nuts **57.** 510 mph **59.** 20 hr **61.** car: 70 mph; motorcycle: 60 mph **63.** $5\dfrac{1}{4}$ hr

65. first pump: 28 min; second pump: 84 min **67.** $x = 5$ **69.** $x = 13.5$ **71.** $-\dfrac{4}{3}$; downward **73.** $\dfrac{11}{4}$; upward **75.** undefined slope; vertical

77. 2000 megawatts **79.** 8,190,000 people **81.** answers may vary **83.** none; answers may vary **85.** 84 yr **87.** 30 yr **89.** 3.75 min

Section 8.7
Practice Exercises

1. $y = 5x$ **2.** $y = \dfrac{1}{4}x$; when x is 20, $y = 5$. **3.** $k = \dfrac{3}{4}$; $y = \dfrac{3}{4}x$ **4.** $y = \dfrac{8}{x}$ **5.** $k = 2.1$; $y = \dfrac{2.1}{x}$; when x is 70, $y = 0.03$. **6.** 6.48 sq units
7. 25 ml

Vocabulary and Readiness Check 8.7
1. inverse **3.** direct **5.** inverse **7.** inverse **9.** direct

Exercise Set 8.7

1. $y = \dfrac{1}{2}x$ **3.** $y = 6x$ **5.** $y = 3x$ **7.** $y = \dfrac{2}{3}x$ **9.** $y = \dfrac{7}{x}$ **11.** $y = \dfrac{0.5}{x}$ **13.** $y = kx$ **15.** $h = \dfrac{k}{t}$ **17.** $z = kx^2$ **19.** $y = \dfrac{k}{z^3}$

21. $x = \dfrac{k}{\sqrt{y}}$ **23.** $y = 40$ **25.** $y = 3$ **27.** $z = 54$ **29.** $a = \dfrac{4}{9}$ **31.** \$62.50 **33.** \$6 each **35.** $5\dfrac{1}{3}$ in. **37.** 179.1 lb **39.** 1600 ft

41. $\dfrac{1}{2}$ **43.** $\dfrac{3}{7}$ **45.** multiplied by 3 **47.** it is doubled

Section 8.8
Practice Exercises

1. a. all real numbers except 5 **b.** all real numbers except -5 and 5 **c.** all real numbers

2.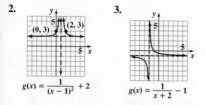

$g(x) = \dfrac{1}{(x-1)^2} + 2$

3.

$g(x) = \dfrac{1}{x+2} - 1$

Exercise Set 8.8

1. all real numbers except 4 **3.** all real numbers except -4 and 5 **5.** all real numbers except -7 and 7 **7.** all real numbers

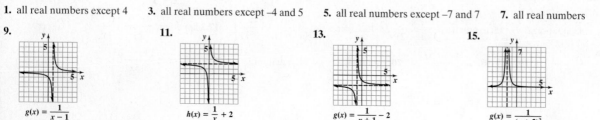

9. $g(x) = \dfrac{1}{x-1}$ **11.** $h(x) = \dfrac{1}{x} + 2$ **13.** $g(x) = \dfrac{1}{x+1} - 2$ **15.** $g(x) = \dfrac{1}{(x+2)^2}$

17.

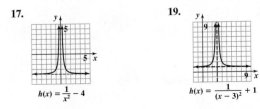

$h(x) = \dfrac{1}{x^2} - 4$

19.

$h(x) = \dfrac{1}{(x-3)^2} + 1$

21. answers may vary

23.

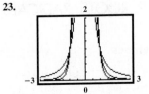

The graph approaches the horizontal asymptote faster and the vertical asymptote slower as n increases.

25. $-3, \dfrac{5}{2}$ **27.** $-2, -1, 2$

Chapter 8 Vocabulary Check

1. ratio   **2.** proportion   **3.** cross products   **4.** rational expression   **5.** polynomial   **6.** inverse variation   **7.** direct variation

Chapter 8 Review

1. $x = 2, x = -2$ **3.** $\dfrac{4}{3}$ **5.** $\dfrac{2}{x}$ **7.** $\dfrac{1}{x-5}$ **9.** $\dfrac{x(x-2)}{x+1}$ **11.** $\dfrac{x-3}{x-5}$ **13.** $\dfrac{x+a}{x-c}$ **15.** $-\dfrac{1}{x^2+4x+16}$ **17.** $\dfrac{3x^2}{y}$ **19.** $\dfrac{x-3}{x+2}$

21. $\dfrac{x+3}{x-4}$ **23.** $(x-6)(x-3)$ **25.** $\dfrac{1}{2}$ **27.** $-\dfrac{2(2x+3)}{y-2}$ **29.** $\dfrac{1}{x+2}$ **31.** $\dfrac{2x-10}{3x^2}$ **33.** $14x$ **35.** $\dfrac{10x^2y}{14x^3y}$ **37.** $\dfrac{x^2-3x-10}{(x+2)(x-5)(x+9)}$

39. $\dfrac{4y-30x^2}{5x^2y}$ **41.** $\dfrac{-2x-2}{x+3}$ **43.** $\dfrac{x-4}{3x}$ **45.** $\dfrac{x^2+2x+4}{4x}; \dfrac{x+2}{32}$ **47.** 30 **49.** no solution   **51.** $\dfrac{9}{7}$ **53.** $b = \dfrac{4A}{5x^2}$ **55.** $x = 6$

57. $x = 9$ **59.** 675 parts   **61.** 3 **63.** fast car speed: 30 mph; slow car speed: 20 mph   **65.** $17\dfrac{1}{2}$ hr   **67.** $x = 15$ **69.** $y = 110$ **71.** $y = \dfrac{100}{27}$

73. $\$3960$ **75.**

$g(x) = \dfrac{1}{(x+2)^2} - 1$

77.

$h(x) = \dfrac{1}{x-1} + 3$

79. $\dfrac{1}{2x}$ **81.** $\dfrac{x-4}{x+4}$ **83.** $\dfrac{1}{x-6}$ **85.** $\dfrac{2}{(x+3)(x-2)}$ **87.** $\dfrac{1}{2}$ **89.** 1 **91.** $x = 6$

Chapter 8 Test

1. $x = -1, x = -3$ **2. a.** $\$115$ **b.** $\$103$ **3.** $\dfrac{3}{5}$ **4.** $\dfrac{1}{x+6}$ **5.** $\dfrac{1}{x^2-3x+9}$ **6.** $\dfrac{2m(m+2)}{m-2}$ **7.** $\dfrac{a+2}{a+5}$ **8.** $-\dfrac{1}{x+y}$ **9.** 15

10. $\dfrac{y-2}{4}$ **11.** $\dfrac{19x-6}{2x+5}$ **12.** $\dfrac{3a-4}{(a-3)(a+2)}$ **13.** $\dfrac{3}{x-1}$ **14.** $\dfrac{2(x+5)}{x(y+5)}$ **15.** $\dfrac{x^2+2x+35}{(x+9)(x+2)(x-5)}$ **16.** $\dfrac{30}{11}$ **17.** -6

18. no solution   **19.** $-2, 5$ **20.** no solution   **21.** all real numbers except -3 **22.** all real numbers except 1   **23.** 28 **24.** $\dfrac{8}{9}$

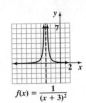

$f(x) = \dfrac{1}{(x+3)^2}$

$f(x) = \dfrac{1}{x-1} + 2$

25. 18 bulbs   **26.** 5 or 1   **27.** 30 mph   **28.** $6\dfrac{2}{3}$ hr   **29.** $x = 12$

Chapter 8 Standardized Test

1. a   **2.** a   **3.** b   **4.** c   **5.** c   **6.** d   **7.** a   **8.** a   **9.** a   **10.** a   **11.** b   **12.** c   **13.** c   **14.** c   **15.** c   **16.** c
17. b   **18.** c   **19.** d   **20.** c   **21.** d   **22.** d   **23.** c   **24.** d   **25.** d   **26.** a   **27.** a   **28.** d   **29.** c

CHAPTER 9 ROOTS, RADICALS, AND TRIGONOMETRIC RATIOS

Section 9.1
Practice Exercises

1. a. $\frac{2}{9}$ **b.** -5 **c.** 12 **d.** 0.7 **e.** -1 **2. a.** 0 **b.** -4 **c.** $\frac{1}{2}$ **3. a.** 3 **b.** 10 **c.** not a real number **d.** -5 **4.** 4.123

5. a. x^5 **b.** y^7 **c.** $5z^3$ **d.** $7x$ **e.** $\frac{z^2}{6}$ **f.** $-2a^2b^4$ **6. a.** 4 **b.** 2 **c.** 2 **d.** -2 **7.** **8.**

Calculator Explorations 9.1

1. 2.646; yes **3.** 3.317; yes **5.** 9.055; yes **7.** 3.420; yes **9.** 2.115; yes **11.** 1.783; yes

Vocabulary and Readiness Check 9.1

1. index, radicand, radical sign **3.** false **5.** true **7.** true **9.** $x \geq 0$ **11.** $(16, 4)$

Exercise Set 9.1

1. 4 **3.** $\frac{1}{5}$ **5.** -10 **7.** not a real number **9.** -11 **11.** $\frac{3}{5}$ **13.** 30 **15.** 12 **17.** $\frac{1}{10}$ **19.** 0.5 **21.** 5 **23.** -4 **25.** -2

27. $\frac{1}{2}$ **29.** -5 **31.** 2 **33.** 9 **35.** not a real number **37.** $-\frac{3}{4}$ **39.** -5 **41.** 1 **43.** 2.646 **45.** 6.083 **47.** 11.662

49. $\sqrt{2} \approx 1.41$; 126.90 ft **51.** x^2 **53.** $3x^4$ **55.** $9x$ **57.** $\frac{x^3}{6}$ **59.** $\frac{5y}{3}$ **61.** $4a^3b^2$ **63.** a^2b^6 **65.** $-2xy^9$ **67.** $\sqrt{3}$ **69.** -1

71. -3 **73.** $\sqrt{7}$ **75.** $x \geq 0$; **77.** $x \geq 3$; 0, 1, 2, 3 **79.** all real numbers; **81.** all real numbers. $0, 1, -1, 2, -2$

83. $25 \cdot 2$ **85.** $16 \cdot 2$ or $4 \cdot 8$ **87.** $4 \cdot 7$ **89.** $9 \cdot 3$ **91.** a, b **93.** 7 mi **95.** 3.01 in. **97.** 3 **99.** 10 **101.** $T = 6.1$ seconds

103. answers may vary **105.** $|x|$ **107.** $|x + 2|$

Section 9.2
Practice Exercises

1. a. $2\sqrt{6}$ **b.** $2\sqrt{15}$ **c.** $\sqrt{42}$ **d.** $10\sqrt{3}$ **2.** $10\sqrt{10}$ **3. a.** $\frac{\sqrt{5}}{7}$ **b.** $\frac{3}{10}$ **c.** $\frac{3\sqrt{2}}{5}$ **4. a.** $x^3\sqrt{x}$ **b.** $2a^2\sqrt{3}$ **c.** $\frac{7\sqrt{2}}{z^4}$

d. $\frac{y^4\sqrt{11y}}{7}$ **5. a.** $2\sqrt[3]{3}$ **b.** $\sqrt[3]{38}$ **c.** $\frac{\sqrt[3]{5}}{3}$ **d.** $\frac{\sqrt[3]{15}}{4}$ **6. a.** $2\sqrt[4]{2}$ **b.** $\frac{\sqrt[4]{5}}{3}$ **c.** $2\sqrt[5]{3}$

Vocabulary and Readiness Check 9.2

1. $\sqrt{a} \cdot \sqrt{b}$ **3.** 16; 25; 4; 5; 20

Exercise Set 9.2

1. $2\sqrt{5}$ **3.** $5\sqrt{2}$ **5.** $\sqrt{33}$ **7.** $7\sqrt{2}$ **9.** $2\sqrt{15}$ **11.** $6\sqrt{5}$ **13.** $2\sqrt{13}$ **15.** 15 **17.** $21\sqrt{7}$ **19.** $-15\sqrt{3}$ **21.** $\frac{2\sqrt{2}}{5}$

23. $\frac{3\sqrt{3}}{11}$ **25.** $\frac{3}{2}$ **27.** $\frac{5\sqrt{5}}{3}$ **29.** $\frac{\sqrt{11}}{6}$ **31.** $-\frac{\sqrt{3}}{4}$ **33.** $x^3\sqrt{x}$ **35.** $x^6\sqrt{x}$ **37.** $6a\sqrt{a}$ **39.** $4x^2\sqrt{6}$ **41.** $\frac{2\sqrt{3}}{m}$ **43.** $\frac{3\sqrt{x}}{y^5}$

45. $\frac{2\sqrt{22}}{x^6}$ **47.** 16 **49.** $\frac{6}{11}$ **51.** $5\sqrt{7}$ **53.** $\frac{2\sqrt{5}}{3}$ **55.** $2m^3\sqrt{6m}$ **57.** $\frac{y\sqrt{23y}}{2x^3}$ **59.** $2\sqrt[3]{3}$ **61.** $5\sqrt[3]{2}$ **63.** $\frac{\sqrt[3]{5}}{4}$ **65.** $\frac{\sqrt[3]{23}}{2}$

67. $\frac{\sqrt[3]{15}}{4}$ **69.** $2\sqrt[3]{10}$ **71.** $2\sqrt[4]{3}$ **73.** $\frac{\sqrt[4]{8}}{3}$ **75.** $2\sqrt[5]{3}$ **77.** $\frac{\sqrt[5]{5}}{2}$ **79.** $2\sqrt[3]{10}$ **81.** $14x$ **83.** $2x^2 - 7x - 15$ **85.** 0 **87.** $x^3y\sqrt{y}$

89. $7x^2y^2\sqrt{2x}$ **91.** $-2x^2$ **93.** answers may vary **95.** $2\sqrt{5}$ in. **97.** 2.25 in. **99.** $1700 **101.** 1.7 sq m

Section 9.3
Practice Exercises
1. a. $8\sqrt{2}$ **b.** $-7\sqrt{6}$ **c.** $4\sqrt[4]{5} + 11\sqrt[4]{7}$ **d.** $4\sqrt{13} - 5\sqrt[3]{13}$ **2. a.** $5\sqrt{5}$ **b.** $6 - 2\sqrt{10} + \sqrt{6}$ **c.** $-3\sqrt{2}$ **3.** $-7x\sqrt{x} + 3x$ **4.** $10x^2\sqrt[3]{3}$

Vocabulary and Readiness Check 9.3
1. like radicals **3.** $17\sqrt{2}$ **5.** $2\sqrt{5}$

Exercise Set 9.3
1. $-4\sqrt{3}$ **3.** $9\sqrt{6} - 5$ **5.** $2\sqrt{11} + 11$ **7.** $\sqrt{5} + \sqrt{2}$ **9.** $-2\sqrt[3]{15}$ **11.** $7\sqrt[3]{3} - \sqrt{3}$ **13.** $-5\sqrt[3]{2} - 6$ **15.** $5\sqrt{3}$ **17.** $9\sqrt{5}$
19. $4\sqrt{6} + \sqrt{5}$ **21.** $x + \sqrt{x}$ **23.** 0 **25.** $4\sqrt{x} - x\sqrt{x}$ **27.** $7\sqrt{5}$ **29.** $\sqrt{5} + \sqrt[3]{5}$ **31.** $-5 + 8\sqrt{2}$ **33.** $8 - 6\sqrt{2}$ **35.** $14\sqrt{2}$
37. $5\sqrt{2} + 12$ **39.** $\dfrac{4\sqrt{5}}{9}$ **41.** $\dfrac{3\sqrt{3}}{8}$ **43.** $2\sqrt{5}$ **45.** $-\sqrt{35}$ **47.** $12\sqrt{2x}$ **49.** 0 **51.** $x\sqrt{3x} + 3x\sqrt{x}$ **53.** $5\sqrt[3]{3}$ **55.** $\sqrt[3]{9}$
57. $4 + 4\sqrt[3]{2}$ **59.** $-3 + 3\sqrt[3]{2}$ **61.** $4x\sqrt{2} + 2\sqrt[3]{4} + 2x$ **63.** $\sqrt[3]{5}$ **65.** $x^2 + 12x + 36$ **67.** $4x^2 - 4x + 1$ **69.** $(4, 2)$
71. answers may vary **73.** $8\sqrt{5}$ in. **75.** $\left(48 + \dfrac{9\sqrt{3}}{2}\right)$ sq ft **77.** $\dfrac{83x\sqrt{x}}{20}$

Section 9.4
Practice Exercises
1. a. $\sqrt{77}$ **b.** $72\sqrt{30}$ **c.** $5\sqrt{2}$ **d.** 17 **e.** $5y^2\sqrt{3}$ **2.** 28 **3.** $5\sqrt[3]{4}$ **4. a.** $3 - \sqrt{15}$ **b.** $z\sqrt{2} + 14\sqrt{z}$ **c.** $x + \sqrt{2x} - \sqrt{7x} - \sqrt{14}$
5. a. -9 **b.** $3x - 10\sqrt{3x} + 25$ **6. a.** $\sqrt{3}$ **b.** $2\sqrt{2}$ **c.** $3y^2$ **7.** 5 **8. a.** $\dfrac{4\sqrt{5}}{5}$ **b.** $\dfrac{\sqrt{6}}{6}$ **c.** $\dfrac{\sqrt{42x}}{14x}$ **9. a.** $\dfrac{3\sqrt[3]{5}}{5}$ **b.** $\dfrac{\sqrt[3]{150}}{5}$
10. a. $-1 + \sqrt{5}$ **b.** $\dfrac{5 + 3\sqrt{3}}{2}$ **c.** $\dfrac{8(5 + \sqrt{x})}{25 - x}$ **11.** $\dfrac{7 - \sqrt{7}}{3}$

Vocabulary and Readiness Check 9.4
1. $\sqrt{21}$ **3.** $\sqrt{\dfrac{15}{3}}$ or $\sqrt{5}$ **5.** $2 - \sqrt{3}$

Exercise Set 9.4
1. 4 **3.** $5\sqrt{2}$ **5.** 6 **7.** $2x$ **9.** 20 **11.** $36x$ **13.** $3x^3\sqrt{2}$ **15.** $4xy\sqrt{y}$ **17.** $\sqrt{30} + \sqrt{42}$ **19.** $2\sqrt{5} + 5\sqrt{2}$ **21.** $y\sqrt{7} - 14\sqrt{y}$
23. -33 **25.** $\sqrt{6} - \sqrt{15} + \sqrt{10} - 5$ **27.** $16 - 11\sqrt{11}$ **29.** $x - 36$ **31.** $x - 14\sqrt{x} + 49$ **33.** $6y + 2\sqrt{6y} + 1$ **35.** 4 **37.** $\sqrt{7}$
39. $3\sqrt{2}$ **41.** $5y^2$ **43.** $5\sqrt{3}$ **45.** $2y\sqrt{6}$ **47.** $2xy\sqrt{3y}$ **49.** $\dfrac{\sqrt{15}}{5}$ **51.** $\dfrac{7\sqrt{2}}{2}$ **53.** $\dfrac{\sqrt{6y}}{6y}$ **55.** $\dfrac{\sqrt{3x}}{x}$ **57.** $\dfrac{\sqrt{2}}{4}$ **59.** $\dfrac{\sqrt{30}}{15}$
61. $\dfrac{8y\sqrt{5}}{5}$ **63.** $\dfrac{\sqrt{3xy}}{6x}$ **65.** $3\sqrt{2} - 3$ **67.** $5 + \sqrt{30} + \sqrt{6} + \sqrt{5}$ **69.** $\dfrac{3\sqrt{x} + 12}{x - 16}$ **71.** $\dfrac{\sqrt{15}}{10}$ **73.** $-8 - 4\sqrt{5}$ **75.** $\dfrac{3\sqrt{2x}}{2}$
77. $\dfrac{10 - 5\sqrt{x}}{4 - x}$ **79.** $3 + \sqrt{3}$ **81.** $3 - 2\sqrt{5}$ **83.** $3\sqrt{3} + 1$ **85.** $2\sqrt[3]{6}$ **87.** $12\sqrt[3]{10}$ **89.** $5\sqrt[3]{3}$ **91.** 3 **93.** $2\sqrt[3]{3}$ **95.** $\dfrac{\sqrt[3]{10}}{2}$
97. $3\sqrt[3]{4}$ **99.** $\dfrac{\sqrt[3]{3}}{3}$ **101.** $\dfrac{\sqrt[3]{6}}{3}$ **103.** 44 **105.** 2 **107.** 3 **109.** $130\sqrt{3}$ sq m **111.** $\dfrac{\sqrt{A\pi}}{\pi}$ **113.** true **115.** false **117.** false
119. answer may vary **121.** answer may vary **123.** $\dfrac{2}{\sqrt{6} - \sqrt{2} - \sqrt{3} + 1}$

Integrated Review
1. 6 **2.** $4\sqrt{3}$ **3.** x^2 **4.** $y^3\sqrt{y}$ **5.** $4x$ **6.** $3x^5\sqrt{2x}$ **7.** 2 **8.** 3 **9.** -3 **10.** not a real number **11.** $\dfrac{\sqrt{11}}{3}$ **12.** $\dfrac{\sqrt[3]{7}}{4}$ **13.** -4
14. -5 **15.** $\dfrac{3}{7}$ **16.** $\dfrac{1}{8}$ **17.** a^4b **18.** x^5y^{10} **19.** $5m^3$ **20.** $3n^8$ **21.** $6\sqrt{7}$ **22.** $3\sqrt{2}$ **23.** cannot be simplified **24.** $\sqrt{x} + 3x$
25. $\sqrt{30}$ **26.** 3 **27.** 28 **28.** 45 **29.** $\sqrt{33} + \sqrt{3}$ **30.** $3\sqrt{2} - 2\sqrt{6}$ **31.** $4y$ **32.** $3x^2\sqrt{5}$ **33.** $x - 3\sqrt{x} - 10$ **34.** $11 + 6\sqrt{2}$
35. 2 **36.** $\sqrt{3}$ **37.** $2x^2\sqrt{3}$ **38.** $ab^2\sqrt{15a}$ **39.** $\dfrac{\sqrt{6}}{6}$ **40.** $\dfrac{x\sqrt{5}}{10}$ **41.** $\dfrac{4\sqrt{6} - 4}{5}$ **42.** $\dfrac{\sqrt{2x} + 5\sqrt{2} + \sqrt{x} + 5}{x - 25}$

Section 9.5
Practice Exercises
1. 9 **2.** no solution **3.** $\dfrac{2}{3}$ **4.** 7 **5.** 10 **6.** 16

Exercise Set 9.5

1. 81 **3.** -1 **5.** 49 **7.** no solution **9.** 4 **11.** 2 **13.** 2 **15.** 9 **17.** -3 **19.** $-1, -2$ **21.** no solution **23.** $0, -3$ **25.** 16

27. 25 **29.** 1 **31.** 5 **33.** -2 **35.** no solution **37.** 2 **39.** 36 **41.** no solution **43.** $\dfrac{3}{2}$ **45.** 16 **47.** 3 **49.** 12 **51.** 3, 1 **53.** -1

55. $3x - 8 = 19; x = 9$ **57.** $2(2x + x) = 24;$ length $= 8$ in. **59.** 4, 7 **61.** answers may vary **63. a.** 3.2, 10, 31.6 **b.** no **65.** 7.30 **67.** 0.76

Section 9.6
Practice Exercises

1. 13 in. **2.** $2\sqrt{10}$ m ≈ 6.32 m **3.** $\sqrt{5425} \approx 74$ ft **4. a.** no **b.** yes **5.** $2\sqrt{37}$ units **6.** $(6.5, -4)$ **7.** $16\sqrt{3}$ ft/sec ≈ 27.71 ft/sec

Vocabulary and Readiness Check 9.6

1. midpoint; point **3.** midpoint

Exercise Set 9.6

1. $\sqrt{13}$ **3.** $3\sqrt{3}$ **5.** 25 **7.** $\sqrt{22}$ **9.** $3\sqrt{17}$ **11.** $\sqrt{41}$ **13.** $4\sqrt{2}$ **15.** $3\sqrt{10}$ **17.** 51.2 ft **19.** 20.6 ft **21.** 11.7 ft **23.** yes

25. no **27.** yes **29.** $\sqrt{29}$ **31.** $\sqrt{73}$ **33.** $2\sqrt{10}$ **35.** $\dfrac{3\sqrt{5}}{2}$ **37.** $\sqrt{85}$ **39.** $(4, -2)$ **41.** $\left(-5, \dfrac{5}{2}\right)$ **43.** $(3, 0)$ **45.** $\left(-\dfrac{1}{2}, \dfrac{1}{2}\right)$

47. $(6.2, -6.65)$ **49.** 24 cu ft **51.** 54 mph **53.** 27 mph **55.** 61.2 km **57.** 32 **59.** $\dfrac{1}{25}$ **61.** x^5 **63.** y^4

65. $y = 2\sqrt{10}, x = 2\sqrt{10} - 4$ **67.** 201 mi **69.** answers may vary

Section 9.7
Practice Exercises

1. $\sin A = \dfrac{3}{5}; \cos A = \dfrac{4}{5}; \tan A = \dfrac{3}{4}$ **2.** 263 cm **3.** 298 cm **4.** 994 ft **5.** 54°

Exercise Set 9.7

1. $\sin A = \dfrac{3}{5}; \cos A = \dfrac{4}{5}; \tan A = \dfrac{3}{4}$ **3.** $\sin A = \dfrac{20}{29}; \cos A = \dfrac{21}{29}; \tan A = \dfrac{20}{21}$ **5.** $\sin A = \dfrac{5}{13}; \cos A = \dfrac{12}{13}; \tan A = \dfrac{5}{12}$

7. $\sin A = \dfrac{4}{5}; \cos A = \dfrac{3}{5}; \tan A = \dfrac{4}{3}$ **9.** 188 cm **11.** 182 in. **13.** 7 m **15.** 22 yd **17.** 40 m **19.** $m \angle B = 50°, a = 18$ yd, $c = 29$ yd

21. $m \angle B = 38°, a = 43$ cm, $b = 33$ cm **23.** 37° **25.** 28° **27.** 653 units **29.** 39 units **31.** 298 units **33.** 257 units **35.** 529 yd

37. 2879 ft **39.** 2059 ft **41.** 695 ft **43.** 36° **45.** 1376 ft **47.** 15.1° **49, 51, 53, 55** answers may vary **57. a.** 357 ft **b.** 394 ft

Chapter 9 Vocabulary Check

1. like radicals **2.** index, radicand, radical **3.** conjugate **4.** principal square root **5.** rationalizing the denominator

6. trigonometry **7.** hypotenuse **8.** $\sqrt{(x_2 - x_1)^2 + (y_2 - y_1)^2}$ **9.** $\left(\dfrac{x_1 + x_2}{2}, \dfrac{y_1 + y_2}{2}\right)$ **10.** $a^2 + b^2 = c^2$

Chapter 9 Review

1. 9 **3.** 3 **5.** $\dfrac{2}{3}$ **7.** c **9.** x^6 **11.** $3x^3$ **13.** $\dfrac{4}{y^5}$ **15.** all real numbers; $-2, -1, 0, 1, 2$ **17.** $3\sqrt{6}$ **19.** $5x\sqrt{6x}$ **21.** $3\sqrt[3]{2}$

23. $2\sqrt[4]{3}$ **25.** $\dfrac{3\sqrt{2}}{5}$ **27.** $\dfrac{3y\sqrt{5}}{2x^2}$ **29.** $\dfrac{\sqrt[4]{9}}{2}$ **31.** $\dfrac{\sqrt[3]{3}}{2}$

33. $2\sqrt[3]{3} - \sqrt[3]{2}$ **35.** $6\sqrt{6} - 2\sqrt[3]{6}$ **37.** $5\sqrt{7x} + 2\sqrt[3]{7}$

39. $\dfrac{\sqrt{5}}{6}$ **41.** 0 **43.** $30\sqrt{2}$ **45.** $6\sqrt{2} - 18$ **47.** $3\sqrt{2} - 5\sqrt{3} + 2\sqrt{6} - 10$ **49.** $x - 4\sqrt{x} + 4$ **51.** 3 **53.** $2\sqrt{5}$ **55.** $x\sqrt{15x}$

57. $\dfrac{\sqrt{22}}{11}$ **59.** $\dfrac{\sqrt{30}}{6}$ **61.** $\dfrac{\sqrt{5x}}{5x}$ **63.** $\dfrac{\sqrt{3x}}{x}$ **65.** $3\sqrt{5} + 6$ **67.** $\dfrac{\sqrt{6} + \sqrt{2} + \sqrt{3} + 1}{2}$ **69.** $\dfrac{10\sqrt{x} - 50}{x - 25}$ **71.** $\dfrac{\sqrt[3]{21}}{3}$ **73.** $\dfrac{\sqrt[3]{12}}{2}$

75. 18 **77.** 25 **79.** 12 **81.** 1 **83.** $3\sqrt{13}; 10.82$ **85.** $4\sqrt{34}$ ft; 23.32 ft **87.** $\sqrt{130}; (1.5, 1.5)$ **89.** 2.4 in.

91. $\sin A = \dfrac{3}{5}; \cos A = \dfrac{4}{5}; \tan A = \dfrac{3}{4}$ **93.** 23 cm **95.** 58° **97.** 31 m **99.** 12 **101.** $4x^8$ **103.** $3x^3\sqrt{2x}$ **105.** $\dfrac{y^2}{9}$ **107.** $7\sqrt{3}$

109. $-\dfrac{\sqrt{3}}{4}$ **111.** $7\sqrt{2}$ **113.** $\sqrt{10} - \sqrt{2} + 4\sqrt{5} - 4$ **115.** $2\sqrt{6}$ **117.** $\dfrac{\sqrt{14}}{7}$ **119.** $\dfrac{3\sqrt{x} + 18}{x - 36}$ **121.** 1 **123.** 14

125. $\sqrt{58}$; 7.62 **127.** 32 ft

Chapter 9 Test

1. $\dfrac{3}{5}$ **2.** -5 **3.** not a real number **4.** $x \geq -2$; ; $0, 1, 2, 3$ **5.** $3\sqrt{6}$ **6.** $2\sqrt{23}$ **7.** $x^3\sqrt{3}$ **8.** $2x^2 y^3\sqrt{2y}$

$y = \sqrt{x + 2}$

9. $3x^4\sqrt{x}$ **10.** 2 **11.** $2\sqrt[3]{5}$ **12.** x^5 **13.** $y^3\sqrt{y}$ **14.** $\dfrac{\sqrt{5}}{4}$ **15.** $\dfrac{y\sqrt{y}}{5}$ **16.** $\dfrac{\sqrt[3]{2}}{3}$ **17.** $6\sqrt{2x}$ **18.** $-2\sqrt{13}$ **19.** $-8\sqrt{3}$

20. $3\sqrt[3]{2} - 2x\sqrt{2}$ **21.** $\dfrac{7\sqrt{3}}{10}$ **22.** $7\sqrt{2}$ **23.** $2\sqrt{3} - \sqrt{10}$ **24.** $x - \sqrt{x} - 6$ **25.** $\sqrt{5}$ **26.** $2x\sqrt{5x}$ **27.** $\dfrac{\sqrt{6}}{3}$ **28.** $\dfrac{\sqrt[3]{15}}{3}$

29. $\dfrac{\sqrt{15}}{6x}$ **30.** $-1 - \sqrt{3}$ **31.** 9 **32.** 5 **33.** 9 **34.** $4\sqrt{5}$ in. **35.** $\sqrt{5}$ **36.** $\left(-\dfrac{1}{2}, \dfrac{3}{10}\right)$ **37.** yes

38. $\sin A = \dfrac{8}{17}$; $\cos A = \dfrac{15}{17}$; $\tan A = \dfrac{8}{15}$ **39.** 70 ft

Chapter 9 Standardized Test

1. c **2.** c **3.** b **4.** d **5.** a **6.** c **7.** a **8.** a **9.** b **10.** b **11.** d **12.** c **13.** d **14.** b **15.** d **16.** a **17.** d
18. b **19.** b **20.** c **21.** a **22.** d **23.** c **24.** d **25.** b **26.** a **27.** d **28.** c **29.** c **30.** a **31.** c **32.** c **33.** d
34. a **35.** b **36.** c **37.** b **38.** b

CHAPTER 10 QUADRATIC EQUATIONS

Section 10.1
Practice Exercises

1. $-4, 4$ **2.** $\dfrac{-\sqrt{65}}{5}, \dfrac{\sqrt{65}}{5}$ **3.** $-1, 11$ **4.** $-2 \pm 2\sqrt{3}$ **5.** no real solution **6.** $\dfrac{5 \pm \sqrt{17}}{3}$ **7.** 72.8 sec

Exercise Set 10.1

1. ± 8 **3.** $\pm\sqrt{21}$ **5.** $\pm\dfrac{1}{5}$ **7.** no real solution **9.** $\pm\dfrac{\sqrt{39}}{3}$ **11.** $\pm\dfrac{2\sqrt{7}}{7}$ **13.** $\pm\sqrt{2}$ **15.** $\pm\sqrt{5}$ **17.** answers may vary

19. $12, -2$ **21.** $-2 \pm \sqrt{7}$ **23.** $1, 0$ **25.** $-2 \pm \sqrt{10}$ **27.** $\dfrac{8}{3}, -4$ **29.** no real solution **31.** $\dfrac{11 \pm 5\sqrt{2}}{2}$ **33.** $\dfrac{7 \pm 4\sqrt{2}}{3}$

35. $8, -3$ **37.** $\pm\sqrt{2}$ **39.** $-6 \pm 2\sqrt{6}$ **41.** $\pm\sqrt{10}$ **43.** $\dfrac{1 \pm \sqrt{5}}{4}$ **45.** $\pm 2\sqrt{3}$ **47.** $\dfrac{-8 \pm 3\sqrt{5}}{-3}$ or $\dfrac{8 \pm 3\sqrt{5}}{3}$ **49.** $2\sqrt{5}$ in. ≈ 4.47 in.

51. 177 m **53.** 5 sec **55.** 2.7 sec **57.** 15.8 sec **59.** 6 in. **61.** $(x + 3)^2$ **63.** $(x - 2)^2$ **65.** $2, -6$ **67.** $-7 \pm \sqrt{31}$

69. ± 1.33 **71.** 2008 **73.** 2007

Section 10.2
Practice Exercises

1. a. $z^2 + 8z + 16 = (z + 4)^2$ **b.** $x^2 - 12x + 36 = (x - 6)^2$ **c.** $b^2 + 5b + \dfrac{25}{4} = \left(b + \dfrac{5}{2}\right)^2$ **2.** $-1 \pm \sqrt{6}$ **3.** $4 \pm 2\sqrt{2}$

4. $\dfrac{13}{3}, \dfrac{-1}{3}$ **5.** no real solution **6.** $\dfrac{3 \pm \sqrt{3}}{2}$

Vocabulary and Readiness Check 10.2

1. zero **3.** quadratic equation **5.** 9 **7.** 16 **9.** 100 **11.** 49

Exercise Set 10.2

1. $x^2 + 4x + 4 = (x + 2)^2$ **3.** $k^2 - 12k + 36 = (k - 6)^2$ **5.** $x^2 - 3x + \dfrac{9}{4} = \left(x - \dfrac{3}{2}\right)^2$ **7.** $m^2 - m + \dfrac{1}{4} = \left(m - \dfrac{1}{2}\right)^2$ **9.** $-6, -2$

11. $-1 \pm 2\sqrt{2}$ **13.** $0, 6$ **15.** $\dfrac{-5 \pm \sqrt{53}}{2}$ **17.** $1 \pm \sqrt{2}$ **19.** $-1, -4$ **21.** $-2, 4$ **23.** no real solution   **25.** $\dfrac{3 \pm \sqrt{19}}{2}$

27. $-2 \pm \dfrac{\sqrt{6}}{2}$ **29.** $-3 \pm \sqrt{34}$ **31.** $\dfrac{3 \pm \sqrt{21}}{2}$ **33.** $\dfrac{1}{2}, 1$ **35.** $-6, 3$ **37.** no real solution   **39.** $2, -6$ **41.** $-\dfrac{1}{2}$ **43.** -1

45. $3 + 2\sqrt{5}$ **47.** $\dfrac{1 - 3\sqrt{2}}{2}$ **49.** answers may vary   **51. a.** $-3 \pm \sqrt{11}$ **b.** answers may vary   **53.** $k = 8$ or $k = -8$ **55.** 4 years, or 2007

57. $-6, -2$ **59.** $\approx -0.68, 3.68$

Section 10.3

Practice Exercises

1. $\dfrac{-1 \pm \sqrt{41}}{10}$ **2.** $\dfrac{4}{3}, -2$ **3.** $\dfrac{\pm\sqrt{15}}{3}$ **4.** no real solution   **5.** $\dfrac{5 \pm 3\sqrt{5}}{2}$ **6.** $\dfrac{-1 + \sqrt{41}}{10} \approx 0.5; \dfrac{-1 - \sqrt{41}}{10} \approx -0.7$
7. two distinct real solutions   **8. a.** no real solutions   **b.** two distinct real solutions

Vocabulary and Readiness Check 10.3

1. $x = \dfrac{-b \pm \sqrt{b^2 - 4ac}}{2a}$ **3.** $1, 3, -7$ **5.** $1, 1, -1$

Exercise Set 10.3

1. $-2, 1$ **3.** $\dfrac{-5 \pm \sqrt{17}}{2}$ **5.** $\dfrac{2 \pm \sqrt{2}}{2}$ **7.** $1, 2$ **9.** $\dfrac{-7 \pm \sqrt{37}}{6}$ **11.** $\pm\dfrac{2}{7}$ **13.** no real solution   **15.** $-3, 10$ **17.** $\pm\sqrt{5}$

19. $-3, 4$ **21.** $-2 \pm \sqrt{7}$ **23.** $\dfrac{1}{2}, 3$ **25.** $\dfrac{5 \pm \sqrt{33}}{2}$ **27.** $-2, \dfrac{7}{3}$ **29.** $\dfrac{-9 \pm \sqrt{129}}{12}$ **31.** $\dfrac{4 \pm \sqrt{2}}{7}$ **33.** $3 \pm \sqrt{7}$ **35.** $\dfrac{3 \pm \sqrt{3}}{2}$

37. $-1, \dfrac{1}{3}$ **39.** $-\dfrac{3}{4}, \dfrac{1}{5}$ **41.** no real solution   **43.** $\dfrac{3 \pm \sqrt{13}}{4}$ **45.** no real solution   **47.** $1 \pm \sqrt{2}$ **49.** $-\dfrac{3}{4}, -\dfrac{1}{2}$ **51.** $\dfrac{7 \pm \sqrt{129}}{20}$

53. no real solution   **55.** $\dfrac{1 \pm \sqrt{2}}{5}$ **57.** $\dfrac{-3\sqrt{2} \pm \sqrt{38}}{2}$ **59.** $\pm\sqrt{7}; -2.6, 2.6$ **61.** $-3 \pm 2\sqrt{2}; -5.8, -0.2$ **63.** $\dfrac{9 \pm \sqrt{97}}{2}; 9.4, -0.4$

65. $\dfrac{1 \pm \sqrt{7}}{3}; 1.2, -0.5$ **67.** 2 real solutions   **69.** no real solution   **71.** 1 real solution   **73.** 2 real solutions   **75.** no real solution

77. 1 real solution   **79.** $4\sqrt{3}$ **81.** $5\sqrt{2}$ **83.** base: 3 ft; height: 12 ft   **85.** c   **87.** b   **89.** 10.3 ft by 4.9 ft   **91.** $-0.7, 5.0$
93. 7.9 sec   **95.** answers may vary   **97.** 2015   **99.** 2008

Integrated Review 10.1–10.3

Practice Exercises

1. $-1, 4$ **2.** $\dfrac{-5 \pm 3\sqrt{5}}{2}$ **3.** $\dfrac{3}{2}, 1$

Integrated Review Exercises

1. $2, \dfrac{1}{5}$ **2.** $\dfrac{2}{5}, -3$ **3.** $1 \pm \sqrt{2}$ **4.** $3 \pm \sqrt{2}$ **5.** $\pm 2\sqrt{5}$ **6.** $\pm 6\sqrt{2}$ **7.** no real solution   **8.** no real solution   **9.** 2   **10.** 3   **11.** 3

12. $\dfrac{7}{2}$ **13.** ± 2 **14.** ± 3 **15.** $0, 1, 2$ **16.** $0, -3, -4$ **17.** $0, -5$ **18.** $\dfrac{8}{3}, 0$ **19.** $\dfrac{3 \pm \sqrt{7}}{5}$ **20.** $\dfrac{3 \pm \sqrt{5}}{2}$ **21.** $\dfrac{3}{2}, -1$ **22.** $\dfrac{2}{5}, -2$

23. $\dfrac{5 \pm \sqrt{105}}{20}$ **24.** $\dfrac{-1 \pm \sqrt{3}}{4}$ **25.** $5, \dfrac{7}{4}$ **26.** $1, \dfrac{7}{9}$ **27.** $\dfrac{7 \pm 3\sqrt{2}}{5}$ **28.** $\dfrac{5 \pm 5\sqrt{3}}{4}$ **29.** $\dfrac{7 \pm \sqrt{193}}{6}$ **30.** $\dfrac{-7 \pm \sqrt{193}}{12}$ **31.** $11, -10$

32. $7, -8$ **33.** $4, -\dfrac{2}{3}$ **34.** $2, -\dfrac{4}{5}$ **35.** $0.5, 0.1$ **36.** $0.3, -0.2$ **37.** $\dfrac{11 \pm \sqrt{41}}{20}$ **38.** $\dfrac{11 \pm \sqrt{41}}{40}$ **39.** $\dfrac{4 \pm \sqrt{10}}{2}$ **40.** $\dfrac{5 \pm \sqrt{185}}{4}$
41. answers may vary

Section 10.4
Practice Exercises

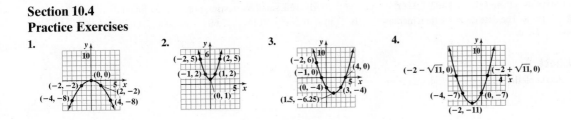

Calculator Explorations 10.4

1. $x = -0.41, 7.41$ **3.** $x = 0.91, 2.38$ **5.** $x = -0.39, 0.84$

Exercise Set 10.4

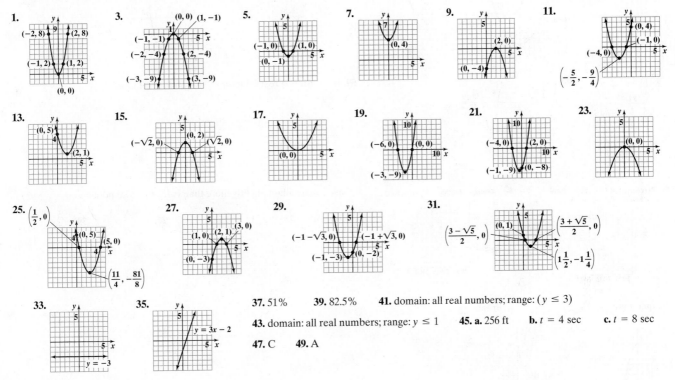

37. 51%   **39.** 82.5%   **41.** domain: all real numbers; range: $(y \leq 3)$

43. domain: all real numbers; range: $y \leq 1$ **45. a.** 256 ft   **b.** $t = 4$ sec   **c.** $t = 8$ sec

47. C   **49.** A

Section 10.5
Practice Exercises

1. a. the exponential function g **b.** f: fairly well; g: not very well   **2.** 6.8%   **3.** 45 years old; 190 accidents per 50 million miles driven

Exercise Set 10.5

1. a.
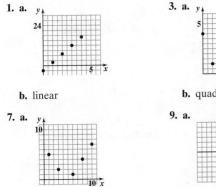
b. linear

3. a.
b. quadratic

5. a.
b. exponential

7. a.
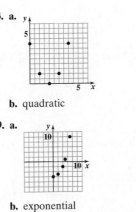
b. quadratic

9. a.
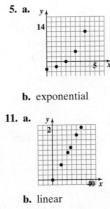
b. exponential

11. a.
b. linear

13. a. increasing more and more rapidly   **b.** $f(x) = 1.402(1.078)^x$ **c.** 22.6%; fairly well, small overestimation   **15.** linear
17. 64%; slight overestimation   **19. a.** The data decrease then increase.   **b.** $f(x) = 0.22x^2 - 0.49x + 7.68$ **c.** 2000; 7.4 million; extremely well
21, 23, 25.   answers may vary   **27.** c

Chapter 10 Vocabulary Check

1. square root   **2.** vertex   **3.** completing the square   **4.** quadratic

Chapter 10 Review

1. ± 6 **3.** $\pm 5\sqrt{2}$ **5.** 4, 18   **7.** $\dfrac{-5 \pm \sqrt{41}}{4}$ **9.** 2.5 sec   **11.** $a^2 + 4a + 4 = (a + 2)^2$ **13.** $m^2 - 3m + \dfrac{9}{4} = \left(m - \dfrac{3}{2}\right)^2$ **15.** 1, 8

17. $-2 \pm \sqrt{5}$ **19.** $3 \pm \sqrt{2}$ **21.** $\dfrac{1}{2}, -1$ **23.** $-\dfrac{5}{3}$ **25.** $\pm\sqrt{5}$ **27.** $5 \pm 3\sqrt{2}$ **29.** $\dfrac{-1 \pm \sqrt{13}}{6}$ **31.** no real solution

33. $0.4, -0.8$ **35.** 2 real solutions   **37.** 1 real solution   **39.** no real solution   **41.** 2011

43.   **45.**   **47.**   **49.**   **51.**

53. $\left(-\dfrac{5}{2}, \dfrac{1}{4}\right)$ **55.** $\left(-\dfrac{1}{2}, 0\right)$ **57.** A   **59.** B   **61.** one real solution   **63.** no real solution

65. a.   **67. a.**   **69.** 210.6 million; slightly more than twice the 2003 population

71. ± 7 **73.** $15, -1$ **75.** $\dfrac{2}{3}, -1$ **77.** $\dfrac{3 \pm \sqrt{41}}{8}$ **79.** $-\dfrac{3}{2}$

     b. quadratic   **b.** linear

81.   **83.**

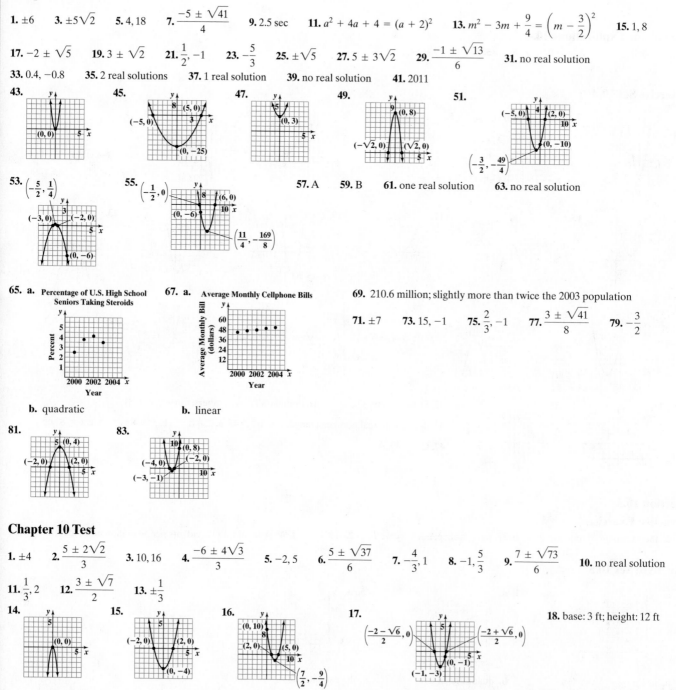

Chapter 10 Test

1. ± 4 **2.** $\dfrac{5 \pm 2\sqrt{2}}{3}$ **3.** 10, 16   **4.** $\dfrac{-6 \pm 4\sqrt{3}}{3}$ **5.** $-2, 5$ **6.** $\dfrac{5 \pm \sqrt{37}}{6}$ **7.** $-\dfrac{4}{3}, 1$ **8.** $-1, \dfrac{5}{3}$ **9.** $\dfrac{7 \pm \sqrt{73}}{6}$ **10.** no real solution

11. $\dfrac{1}{3}, 2$ **12.** $\dfrac{3 \pm \sqrt{7}}{2}$ **13.** $\pm\dfrac{1}{3}$

14.   **15.**   **16.**   **17.**   **18.** base: 3 ft; height: 12 ft

19. 6 sides   **20.** 2.7 sec   **21.** linear   **22.** exponential   **23.** quadratic   **24. a.** 159 million; extremely well.   **b.** 375 million
25. a. 15.3; The number of Internet users is increasing by 15.3 million each year.   **b.** quadratic model   **c.** f: 137.3 million; g: 141.6 million; quadratic model; yes

Chapter 10 Standardized Test

1. c   **2.** b   **3.** d   **4.** a   **5.** c   **6.** d   **7.** d   **8.** a   **9.** a   **10.** c   **11.** c   **12.** b   **13.** b   **14.** a   **15.** d   **16.** b   **17.** b
18. c   **19.** c   **20.** b   **21.** a   **22.** c

APPENDIX A VENN DIAGRAMS

Practice Exercises

1. a. {1, 5, 6, 7, 9}   **b.** {1, 5, 6}   **c.** {7, 9}   **2. a.** {a, b, c, d}   **b.** {e}   **c.** {e, f, g}   **d.** {f, g}   **3.** {b, c, e}   **4. a.** {7, 10}
b. ∅   **c.** ∅   **5. a.** {1, 3, 5, 6, 7, 10, 11}   **b.** {1, 2, 3, 4, 5, 6, 7}   **c.** {1, 2, 3}   **6. a.** {5}   **b.** {2, 3, 7, 11, 13, 17, 19}
c. {2, 3, 5, 7, 11, 13}   **d.** {17, 19}   **e.** {5, 7, 11, 13, 17, 19}   **f.** {2, 3}   **7. a.** {5, 6, 7, 8, 9}   **b.** {1, 2, 5, 6, 7, 8, 9, 10, 12}
c. {5, 6, 7}   **d.** {3, 4, 6, 8, 11}   **e.** {1, 2, 3, 5, 6, 7, 8, 9, 10, 11, 12}

8.

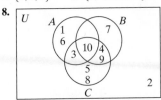

Exercise Set A

1. the set of all composers   **3.** the set of all brands of soft drinks   **5.** {c, d, e}   **7.** {b, c, d, e, f}   **9.** {6, 7, 8, 9, ..., 20}
11. {2, 4, 6, 8, ..., 20}   **13.** {21, 22, 23, 24, ...}   **15.** {1, 3, 5, 7, ...}   **17.** {1, 3}   **19.** {1, 2, 3, 5, 7}   **21.** {2, 4, 6}   **23.** {4, 6}
25. {1, 3, 5, 7} or A   **27.** {1, 2, 4, 6, 7}   **29.** {1, 2, 4, 6, 7}   **31.** {4, 6}   **33.** {1, 3, 5, 7} or A   **35.** ∅   **37.** {1, 2, 3, 4, 5, 6, 7} or U
39. {1, 3, 5, 7} or A   **41.** {g, h}   **43.** {a, b, g, h}   **45.** {b, c, d, e, f} or C   **47.** {c, d, e, f}   **49.** {a, g, h} or A
51. {a, b, c, d, e, f, g, h} or U   **53.** {a, b, c, d, e, f, g, h} or U   **55.** {c, d, e, f}   **57.** {a, g, h} or A   **59.** ∅   **61.** {a, b, c, d, e, f, g, h} or U
63. {a, g, h} or A   **65.** {a, c, d, e, f, g, h}   **67.** {1, 3, 4, 7}   **69.** {1, 2, 3, 4, 5, 6, 7, 8, 9}   **71.** {3, 7}   **73.** {1, 4, 8, 9}   **75.** {8, 9}
77. {1, 4}   **79.** II, III, V, and VI   **81.** I, II, IV, V, VI, and VII   **83.** II and V   **85.** I, IV, VII, and VIII   **87.** {1, 2, 3, 4, 5, 6, 7, 8}
89. {1, 2, 3, 4, 5, 6, 7, 8, 9, 10, 11}   **91.** {12, 13}   **93.** {4, 5, 6}   **95.** {6}   **97.** {1, 2, 3, 4, 5, 7, 8, 9, 10, 11, 12, 13}

99.   **101.**

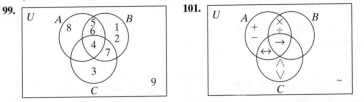

103. a. II   **b.** II   **c.** A ∩ B = B ∩ A   **105. a.** I, III, and IV   **b.** IV   **c.** no; Answers will vary.   **107.** (A ∩ B)' ∩ (A ∪ B)
109. A' ∪ B   **111.** (A ∩ B) ∪ C   **113.** A' ∩ (B ∪ C)   **115.** {Ann, Jose, Al, Gavin, Amy, Ron, Grace}   **117.** {Jose}   **119.** {Lily, Emma}
121. {Lily, Emma, Ann, Jose, Lee, Maria, Fred, Ben, Sheila, Ellen, Gary}   **123.** {Lily, Emma, Al, Gavin, Amy, Lee, Maria}   **125.** {Al, Gavin, Amy}
127. The set of students who scored 90% or above on exam 1 and exam 3 but not on exam 2

APPENDIX B SURVEY PROBLEMS

Practice Exercises

1. a. 75   **b.** 90   **c.** 20   **d.** 145   **e.** 55   **f.** 70   **g.** 30   **h.** 175   **2. a.** 490 men   **b.** 510 men
3.   **4. a.** 63   **b.** 3   **c.** 136   **d.** 30   **e.** 228   **f.** 22

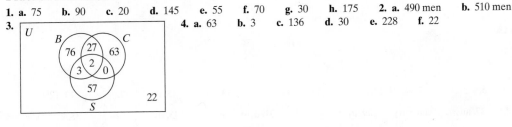

Exercise Set B

1. 26   **3.** 17   **5.** 37   **7.** 7   **9.** I: 14; III: 22; IV: 5   **11.** 17   **13.** 6   **15.** 28   **17.** 9   **19.** 3   **21.** 19   **23.** 21   **25.** 34
27. I: 5; II: 1; III: 4; IV: 3; VI: 1; VII: 8; VIII: 6   **29.** I: 5; II: 10; III: 3; IV: 4; V: 7; VI: 1; VII: 6; VIII: 2   **31.** impossible; There are only 10 elements
in set A but there are 13 elements in set A that are also in sets B or C. A similar problem exists for set C.

33.   **35.**   **37.** answers may vary

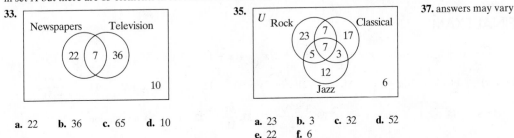

a. 22   **b.** 36   **c.** 65   **d.** 10   **a.** 23   **b.** 3   **c.** 32   **d.** 52
e. 22   **f.** 6

39. b   **41.** Under the conditions given concerning enrollment in math, chemistry, and psychology courses, the total number of students is 100, not 90.

APPENDIX C THE FUNDAMENTAL COUNTING PRINCIPLE

Practice Exercises

1. 150   **2.** 30   **3.** 160   **4.** 729   **5.** 90,000

Exercise Set C

1. 80   **3.** 12   **5.** 6   **7.** 40   **9.** 144; Answers will vary.   **11.** 8   **13.** 96   **15.** 243   **17.** 144   **19.** 676,000   **21.** 2187   **23, 25.** answers may vary   **27.** 720 hr

APPENDIX D PERMUTATIONS

Practice Exercises

1. 2   **2.** 120   **3. a.** 504   **b.** 524,160   **c.** 100   **4.** 840   **5.** 15,120   **6.** 420

Exercise Set D

1. 720   **3.** 120   **5.** 120   **7.** 362,880   **9.** 6   **11.** 4   **13.** 504   **15.** 570,024   **17.** 3,047,466,240   **19.** 600   **21.** 10,712   **23.** 5034   **25.** 24   **27.** 6   **29.** 42   **31.** 1716   **33.** 3024   **35.** 6720   **37.** 720   **39.** 1   **41.** 720   **43.** 8,648,640   **45.** 120   **47.** 15,120   **49.** 180   **51.** 831,600   **53.** 105   **55.** 280   **57, 59, 61, 63.** answers may vary   **65.** 360   **67.** 14,400   **69.** $\dfrac{n(n-1)\cdots 3\cdot 2\cdot 1}{2} = n(n-1)\cdots 3$

APPENDIX E COMBINATIONS

Practice Exercises

1. a. combinations   **b.** permutations   **2.** 35   **3.** 1820   **4.** 23,049,600

Exercise Set E

1. combinations   **3.** permutations   **5.** 6   **7.** 126   **9.** 330   **11.** 8   **13.** 1   **15.** 4060   **17.** 1   **19.** 7   **21.** 0   **23.** $\dfrac{3}{4}$ **25.** −9499   **27.** $\dfrac{3}{68}$ **29.** 20   **31.** 495   **33.** 24,310   **35.** 22,957,480   **37.** 360 ways   **39.** 1716 ways   **41.** 1140 ways   **43.** 840 passwords   **45.** 2730 cones   **47.** 735   **49.** 4,516,932,420   **51, 53.** answers may vary   **55.** The 5/36 lottery is easier to win. Answers will vary.   **57.** 570 sec or 9.5 min; 2340 sec or 39 min

APPENDIX F ARITHMETIC AND GEOMETRIC SEQUENCES

Practice Exercises

1. 4, 9, 14, 19, 24   **2. a.** $a_n = 5 - 3n$ **b.** −31   **3.** 51   **4.** 47   **5.** $a_n = 54{,}800 + 2200n$; $61,400   **6.** 8, −24, 72, −216   **7.** $\dfrac{1}{64}$ **8.** −192   **9.** $a_1 = 3; r = \dfrac{3}{2}$ **10.** 75 units

Vocabulary and Readiness Check

1. geometric; ratio   **3.** first; difference

Exercise Set F

1. 4, 6, 8, 10, 12   **3.** 6, 4, 2, 0, −2   **5.** 1, 3, 9, 27, 81   **7.** 48, 24, 12, 6, 3   **9.** 33   **11.** −875   **13.** −60   **15.** 96   **17.** −28   **19.** 1250   **21.** 31   **23.** 20   **25.** $a_1 = \dfrac{2}{3}; r = -2$ **27.** answers may vary   **29.** $a_1 = 2; d = 2$ **31.** $a_1 = 5; r = 2$ **33.** $a_1 = \dfrac{1}{2}; r = \dfrac{1}{5}$ **35.** $a_1 = x; r = 5$ **37.** $a_1 = p; d = 4$ **39.** 19   **41.** $-\dfrac{8}{9}$ **43.** $\dfrac{17}{2}$ **45.** $\dfrac{8}{81}$ **47.** −19   **49.** $a_n = 4n + 50$; 130 seats   **51.** $a_n = 6(3)^{n-1}$ **53.** 486, 162, 54, 18, 6; $a_n = \dfrac{486}{3^{n-1}}$; 6 bounces   **55.** $a_n = 4000 + 125(n-1)$ or $a_n = 3875 + 125n$; $5375   **57.** 25 g

APPENDIX G PRACTICE FINAL EXAM

1. −81   **2.** $\dfrac{1}{64}$ **3.** −48   **4.** $-3x^3 + 5x^2 + 4x + 5$ **5.** $16x^2 - 16x + 4$ **6.** $3x^3 + 22x^2 + 41x + 14$ **7.** $(y - 12)(y + 4)$ **8.** $3x(3x + 1)(x + 4)$ **9.** $5(6 + x)(6 - x)$ **10.** $(3a - 7)(a + b)$ **11.** $8(y - 2)(y^2 + 2y + 4)$ **12.** $\dfrac{y^{14}}{x^2}$ **13.** $x + 2$ **14.** $\dfrac{2(x + 5)}{x(y + 5)}$ **15.** $\dfrac{3a - 4}{(a - 3)(a + 2)}$ **16.** $\begin{bmatrix} 0 & 3 \\ -3 & 2 \end{bmatrix}$ **17.** 8   **18.** −7, 1   **19.** $x \le -2$ **20.** $\dfrac{3 \pm \sqrt{7}}{2}$ **21.** $\dfrac{30}{11}$ **22.** −6   **23.** no solution   **24.** 9   **25.** 1, $\dfrac{2}{3}$ **26.** −4, $-\dfrac{1}{3}$ **27.** $x < -2$ or $x > \dfrac{4}{3}$ **28.** $1 \le x < \dfrac{11}{2}$

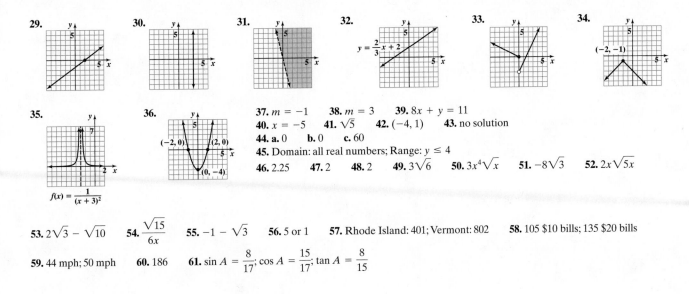

29.   **30.**   **31.**   **32.** $y = \frac{2}{3}x + 2$ **33.**   **34.** $(-2, -1)$

35. $f(x) = \dfrac{1}{(x+3)^2}$ **36.** $(-2, 0)$ $(2, 0)$ $(0, -4)$

37. $m = -1$ **38.** $m = 3$ **39.** $8x + y = 11$
40. $x = -5$ **41.** $\sqrt{5}$ **42.** $(-4, 1)$ **43.** no solution
44. a. 0   **b.** 0   **c.** 60
45. Domain: all real numbers; Range: $y \le 4$
46. 2.25   **47.** 2   **48.** 2   **49.** $3\sqrt{6}$ **50.** $3x^4\sqrt{x}$ **51.** $-8\sqrt{3}$ **52.** $2x\sqrt{5x}$

53. $2\sqrt{3} - \sqrt{10}$ **54.** $\dfrac{\sqrt{15}}{6x}$ **55.** $-1 - \sqrt{3}$ **56.** 5 or 1   **57.** Rhode Island: 401; Vermont: 802   **58.** 105 $10 bills; 135 $20 bills

59. 44 mph; 50 mph   **60.** 186   **61.** $\sin A = \dfrac{8}{17}$; $\cos A = \dfrac{15}{17}$; $\tan A = \dfrac{8}{15}$

Index

Photo Credits